HORRIBLE SCIENCE

SOUNDS DREADFUL

NICK ARNOLD

illustrated by
TONY DE SAULLES

■SCHOLASTIC

www.horrible-science.co.uk

www.nickarnold-website.com
www.tonydesaulles.co.uk

Scholastic Children's Books,
Euston House, 24 Eversholt Street,
London, NW1 1DB, UK

A division of Scholastic Ltd
London ~ New York ~ Toronto ~ Sydney ~ Auckland
Mexico City ~ New Delhi ~ Hong Kong

First published in the UK by Scholastic Ltd, 1998
This edition published 2008

Text copyright © Nick Arnold, 1998
Illustrations © Tony De Saulles, 1998, 2008

All rights reserved

ISBN 978 1407 10610 6

Printed and bound by CPI Group (UK) Ltd, Croydon, CR0 4YY

19 20

The right of Nick Arnold and Tony De Saulles to be identified as the author and
illustrator of this work respectively has been asserted by them in accordance with
the Copyright, Designs and Patents Act, 1988.

Papers used by Scholastic Children's Books are made from woods grown in
sustainable forests.

CONTENTS

YO! A SCIENCE BOOK!
SOUNDS DREADFUL?
SOUNDS COOL TO ME, MAN!

Nick Arnold has been writing stories and books since he was a youngster, but never dreamt he'd find fame writing about dreadful sound. His research involved singing in the bath, shouting at the top of his voice and trying to decipher the lyrics to pop songs and he enjoyed every minute of it.

When he's not delving into Horrible Science, he spends his spare time eating pizza, riding his bike and thinking up corny jokes (though not all at the same time).

Tony De Saulles picked up his crayons when he was still in nappies and has been doodling ever since. He takes Horrible Science very seriously and even agreed to investigate if snakes have ears. Fortunately, his injuries weren't too serious.

When he's not out with his sketchpad, Tony likes to write poetry and play squash, though he hasn't written any poetry about squash yet.

INTRODUCTION

Listen to this…
The younger you are, the LOUDER you are. Babies love making noise...

RATTLE! WAAAGH! WAAAGH! ??? RATTLE! RATTLE! WAAAGH! WAAAGH!

And so do kids...

I CAN YELL LOUDER THAN YOU

BET YOU CAN'T!

And teenagers think really loud music is **brilliant!**

BLAST BOOM

TURN THAT THING OFF!

But as people grow older they change. They settle down

and quieten down. Your parents no longer think LOUD is good. They think that anything LOUD sounds dreadful. Especially loud sounds made by YOU!

So you'd better read this book *q-u-i-e-t-l-y*.
And guess what? Teachers are *even* worse.

In fact, the only sound teachers seem to enjoy is the sound of their own voices. Sounding off about boring things. Like science, for example. And just to put you off the idea of making noise – teachers teach you about sound in science.

Sounds dreadful, doesn't it? But it doesn't have to be…

Listen to a few more exciting sound facts and see if they make your ears prick up:

• A single note can shatter glass.

• Sound makes your eyeballs shiver in their sockets.

• Sound stuns and even kills people.

And that's not all. This book is full of facts about a world of dreadful sounds – from bells that can burst your blood vessels, to sinister sound guns that can make you dash for the toilet. Read all about it and afterwards you can sound off in science class to your heart's content. You're bound to get a good hearing.

And who knows? You could become a big noise in science. One thing's for sure – the world will never sound the same to you again. So now that you're all ears, just turn the page…

SOUNDING OFF

What do the following have in common?
a) Your pet mouse.
b) Your science teacher.
c) A 60-piece orchestra.
Give up? No, the answer *isn't* that they all eat cheese. The correct answer is they all use *sound* to grab your attention. The orchestra needs sound to play a symphony, the mouse needs sound to squeak and your science teacher … well, just imagine there was no such thing as sound. You couldn't listen to a boring science lesson. And she'd never get to tell you off. That would be tragic!

For animals sound is equally vital because, just like us, animals use sound to pass on vital messages. Just imagine what would happen if your dog couldn't whimper when it was time to go out for "walkies". You might forget to take him out…

SPEAK LIKE A SCIENTIST
Scientists have their very own language which only they understand. Now's your chance to learn a few key words.

And afterwards you can sound off and amaze your friends and silence your teacher with your word-power.

Enormous AMPLITUDE (am-plee-tude)
This means how loud a sound is. Stronger sound waves mean louder sounds, or greater amplitude. The word amplitude comes from "ample" which also means BIG.

Fantastic FREQUENCY
Frequency means the number of vibrations a second that make up a sound (a vibration is the scientific name for a wobble). These can be ear-bogglingly fast – for example bats can squeak at over 100,000 vibrations a second. Higher frequency means that the sound is higher, which is why bats squeak rather than growl. By the way, frequency is measured in hertz, (pronounced hurts and written Hz). So higher frequency makes more hertz.

Tuneful TONES
No, this has nothing to do with keeping in tone by physical exercise. A tone is a sound with just one frequency (just to confuse you, most sounds have lots all

mixed up). You can make a tone by hitting a special tool called a tuning fork on a smooth surface.

Rumbling RESONANCE (rez-o-nance)

This is when vibrations hit an object at a certain frequency. These make the object wobble too. The vibrations get stronger and stronger and the sound gets louder and louder. Until it can sound really deafening. (See page 28 for more details.)

Happenin' HARMONICS

Imagine plucking a guitar string. The string vibrates in several ways to make one main tone and several lesser ones. Harmonics are the lesser tones that help to make your playing sound tuneful. And if it isn't, your music teacher is going to get a hammering headache.

Got all that? That'll give you something to shout about in your next science lesson. But here's something you can make an even bigger noise about. Just imagine what it would be like if YOU became a real-life pop star…

Now's your chance…

COULD YOU BE A POP STAR?

You don't need too many qualifications to be a pop star. Although talent helps, it doesn't seem too vital. Just so long as you actually enjoy music and dancing YOU could be the latest hottest biggest new pop sensation. But you'll need to be ready to record your first hit single. To find out how, read on.

To show us the technical side of the business we've hired (at great expense) top DJ and record producer Jez Liznin. And to help explain the vital background facts about sound that any budding pop star needs to know we've recruited scientist, Wanda Wye.

STEP ONE: SOUND SYSTEMS
Silent soundproofing

When you record a hit record you don't want to pick up the sound of next door's TV. Jez's sound studio is lined with a thick hi-tech sound insulator to keep out unwanted noises.

OK, it's only cardboard egg boxes behind plasterboard.

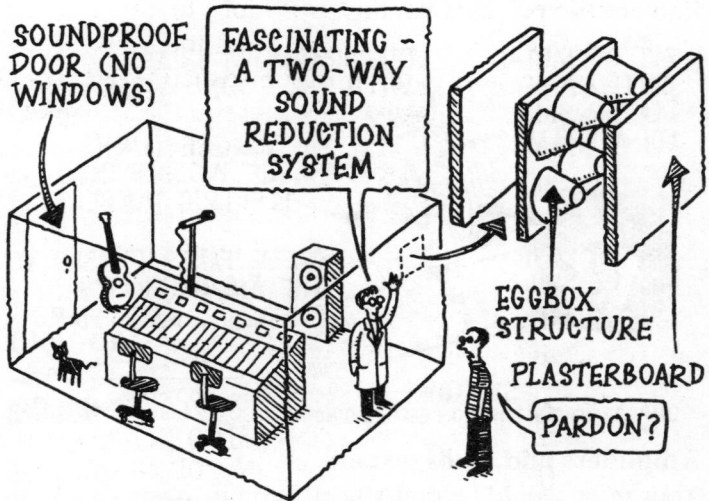

The soft cardboard soaks up the vibes like a nice comfy pillow. And they get lost in there, which is why it's so quiet in the studio. Except when Jez opens his big mouth.

Mighty microphone
This is what you'll need to sing or play instruments into. You'll need to get quite close to it, so you can call it mike for short.

What Wanda means is that the microphone turns sound into electric pulses. Like this...

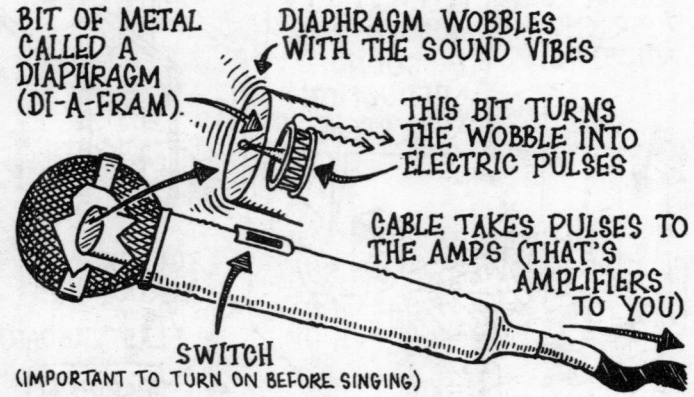

BIT OF METAL CALLED A DIAPHRAGM (DI-A-FRAM).

DIAPHRAGM WOBBLES WITH THE SOUND VIBES

THIS BIT TURNS THE WOBBLE INTO ELECTRIC PULSES

CABLE TAKES PULSES TO THE AMPS (THAT'S AMPLIFIERS TO YOU)

SWITCH (IMPORTANT TO TURN ON BEFORE SINGING)

Amplifiers and loudspeakers

Your mike would be pretty useless on its own. Thanks to the mike, the sound of your fabulous singing is now in the form of electrical pulses. And you can't listen to pulses, can you? Well, you could but it would be about as thrilling as listening to a hair dryer. So you need a loudspeaker to turn the pulses back into your own groovy tune. And an amplifier makes your tune loud enough to hear – sometimes a bit too loud.

YEAH, THEY'RE GIVING ME GREAT VIBES

AND THEY'RE GIVING ME A HEADACHE

LOUDSPEAKER

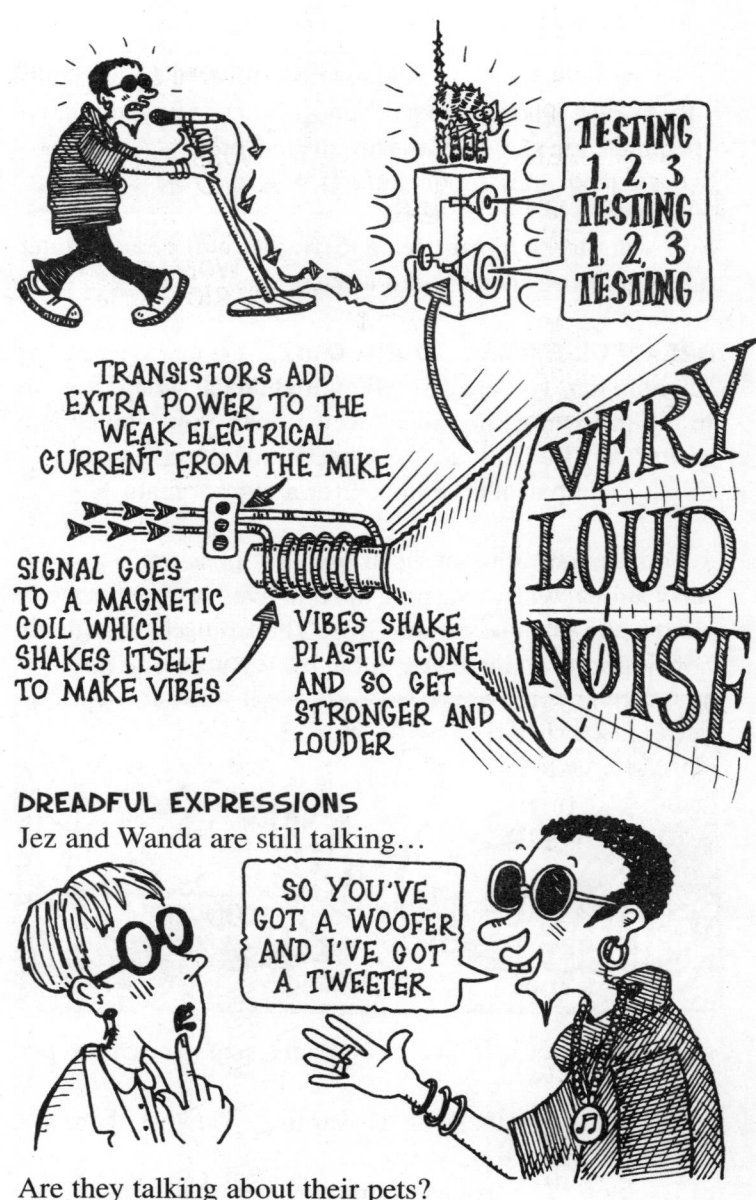

TESTING
1, 2, 3
TESTING
1, 2, 3
TESTING

TRANSISTORS ADD EXTRA POWER TO THE WEAK ELECTRICAL CURRENT FROM THE MIKE

SIGNAL GOES TO A MAGNETIC COIL WHICH SHAKES ITSELF TO MAKE VIBES

VIBES SHAKE PLASTIC CONE AND SO GET STRONGER AND LOUDER

VERY LOUD NOISE

DREADFUL EXPRESSIONS

Jez and Wanda are still talking...

SO YOU'VE GOT A WOOFER AND I'VE GOT A TWEETER

Are they talking about their pets?

Still want to be a star? Jez and Wanda will be back later on to give you more sound advice.

DREADFUL ANIMAL SOUND QUIZ

Imagine that you are a small animal. What would you do in the following situations? Remember, your choice is a matter of life and death. Choose incorrectly and you might end up as a tasty snack for a larger creature.

1 You are a South American possum (poss-um – a small furry animal with a grasping tail that lives in trees) and you meet a Brazilian screaming frog. The frog screams (that's how it got its name, oddly enough). What do you do?

a) Eat the frog. It'll take more than a scary scream to put you off.
b) Run away – the frog is warning you that there's a dangerous animal nearby.
c) Back off. The frog is telling you it's poisonous to eat.

16

2 You're a North American ground squirrel. There's a rattlesnake in your burrow and it's after your babies. You can't see the snake but you can hear its sinister rattle. It sounds surprisingly high-pitched and slow. What do you do?

a) Run for it. The rattle warns you that the snake is big and poisonous. Yikes! The babies can fend for themselves.

b) The slow rattle means the snake is moving slowly. So you've got time to dig an escape tunnel for yourself and your babies.

c) Attack the snake. The rattle proves the snake is smaller than average and rather tired. So you might just win the fight.

3 You're a lapwing (a bird) living in a swamp. You hear a loud three-note call from a redshank (that's another type of bird). What do you do?

a) Go looking for fish. The cry tells you there's food nearby.

b) The call is a warning. There's a gang of crows in the way and they'd like to eat your babies (and the red shank's). You join a posse of other lapwings to fight the invaders off.

c) Nothing. The cry tells you rain's on the way and being a swamp bird you're not scared of a drop of water.

Bet you never knew!
Human beings also use sounds to communicate – so you knew that already? Well, bet you never knew that human voices can make more different sounds than any other mammal. That's because you can move your tongue and lips in many different ways to form lots of weird and wonderful sounds. Try making a few now...

Dare you discover ... sounds all around you?

You will need:

Yourself

One pair of ears (If you're lucky you may already have these. You should find them attached to the sides of your head.)

What you do:

1 Nothing

DELIGHTED TEACHER

ABSOLUTE SILENCE

I SHOULD TRY THIS MORE OFTEN

2 Sit very still and listen.

What did you notice?

a) Nothing. And it gets really boring after the first half hour.

b) I started hearing all kinds of sounds I hadn't noticed before.

c) I heard strange sounds from inside my body.

Answer: b) and possibly **c)**. Sounds are all around us. There are loads of everyday sounds that we don't take any notice of. Sounds like the neighbour's cat throwing up fur balls, your gran sucking a wine gum, or a sparrow with a bad cough. If there aren't any sounds going on, you can always listen to your own breathing. (If you're not breathing it might be a good idea to see a doctor.)

19

Sounds dreadful fact file

NAME: Sound **THE BASIC FACTS:** What we call "sound" is actually tiny changes in air pressure (that's the force of the air squashing on your body). These changes are caused by sound waves (see page 40) and you can detect them with the aid of your incredible ear drums.

THE HORRIBLE DETAILS: A loud noise like a scream can set off avalanches as the force of the sound dislodges a huge mass of snow. In the winter of 1950–51, avalanches in Switzerland buried over 240 people alive.

COME ON! IT'S THE WRONG TIME OF YEAR FOR AVALANCHES... WHOOPS, SORRY!

COME OVER 'EAR AND WE'LL READ THE NEXT CHAPTER

DREADFUL HEARING

Bats, humans and grasshoppers all have something in common. Ears. Most of the time you don't notice them. Well, not unless there's something dreadfully odd about them...

WHAT'RE YOU STARING AT?

But you'd soon notice if your own ears weren't working too well, and you'd certainly notice if you couldn't hear because behind your ears lies an amazing bit of natural engineering. Listen up.

DREADFUL EXPRESSIONS

Two doctors are at the theatre. But can they hear the play?

WELL, MY AUDITORY OSSICLES ARE AGITATING MY OVAL WINDOWS

AAAAARGH!!

Is this painful?

Answer: Not usually. She means the bones in her ear have vibrated and passed on their motion to the "oval window" covering the entrance to her inner ear. So her answer could have been, "Yes". Confused yet? Just lend an ear to this.

21

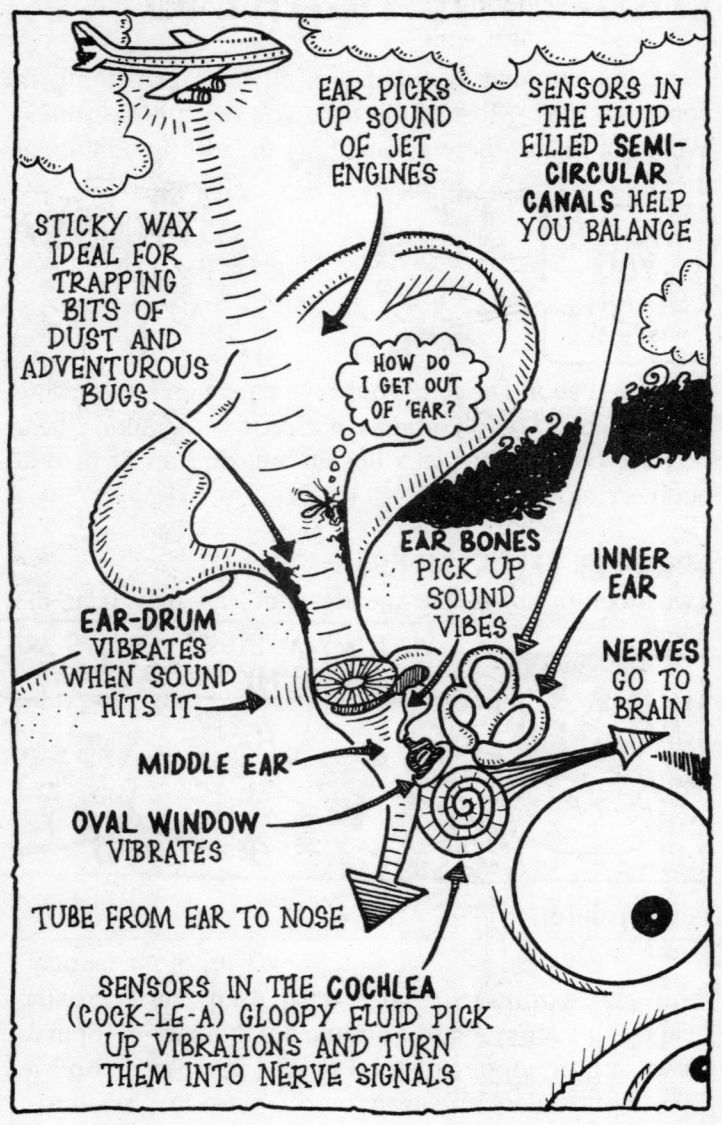

AND HERE'S THE EAR IN ACTION...

Imagine a wandering ugly bug, say a fly, sneaked into the ear. Here's what it would see.

1 The external ear canal (that's ear 'ole to you)

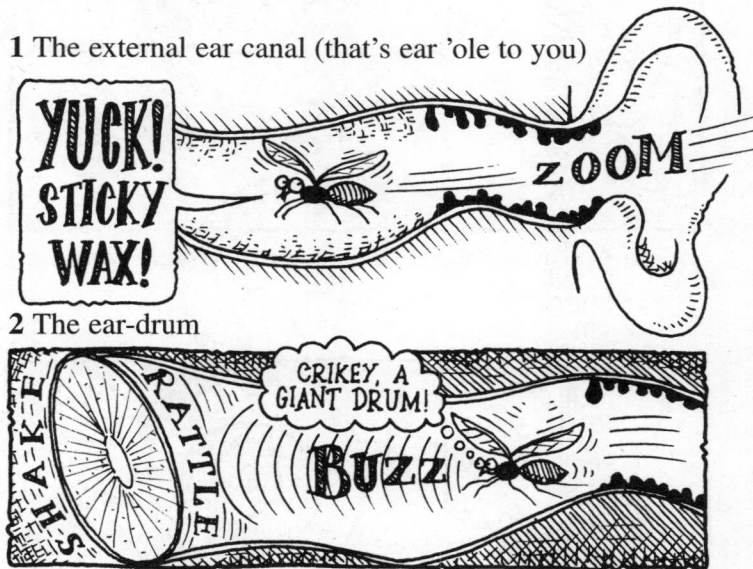

2 The ear-drum

3 Meanwhile, in the middle ear the ear bones are doing their castanets impression by passing on the fly's irritating buzz.

Can you see where the names came from?

4 The semi-circular canals

Scientists use the word "canal" to mean any long thin space in the body.

5 Cochlea

That fly's a genius. That's where the name comes from.

6 And the nerves are buzzing with sound messages for the brain.

COULD YOU BE A SCIENTIST?

Would you make a good sound scientist? Try to predict the results of these sound experiments. If you get them right you'll certainly have something to shout about.

1 Scientists have discovered that our hearing is sharpest for sounds of a certain frequency. Which sounds do we hear most clearly?

a) Loud music

b) A coin dropping on the floor

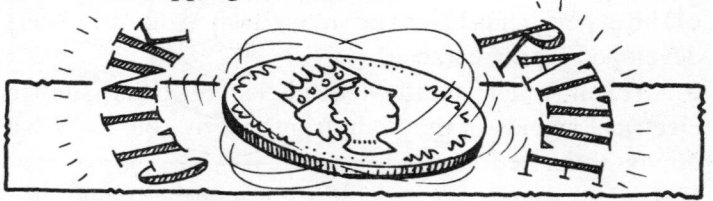

c) A teacher talking

2 Every musical instrument sounds a bit different even when they play the same note. Some make a smooth tinkling noise and some make more of a rattle or a blare. This is because of the unique pattern of sound vibrations or timbre (tim-bruh) made by each instrument. Scientist Steve McAdams wanted to discover if people could spot these differences. What did he find?

a) People are useless at spotting sound differences. They said all the instruments sounded the same to them.

EASY! BUT THEN I USED TO PLAY THE RECORDER MYSELF

PARP

b) People are brilliant at this. They could tell the difference between the instruments even when Steve used a computer to take out almost all the timbre differences.

c)The experiments had to be stopped when the volunteers developed raging earache.

3 A scientist at Harvard Medical School, USA, studied electrical signals in the brain triggered by sounds. What do you think he found?

a) Tuneful sounds trigger wild signals in the brain.

b) All sounds trigger regular patterns of signals.

c) Tuneful sounds trigger regular patterns and dreadful clashing noises trigger wild signals.

AND THIS IS ME SINGING TUNEFULLY IN THE BATH...

Bet you never knew!
Diana Deutsch, Professor of Psychology at the University of California, USA, studied the way our ears hear different notes. She played different notes in each ear of a volunteer.

   Amazingly, even when she played a high note in the left ear the volunteer said they heard the sound in their right *ear. The experiment showed that your right ear "wants" to hear higher notes than the left ear. Sounds weird, doesn't it?*

HORRIBLY HARD OF HEARING

But, of course, these sound experiments depend on one vital factor. Hearing. The volunteer had to hear the sounds in the first place, and some people can't.

Sounds dreadful fact file

NAME: Deafness

THE BASIC FACTS: About 16 per cent of people in Britain have less than perfect hearing. About one in twenty people have some difficulty in hearing conversation.

THE DREADFUL DETAILS:

1 Deafness can be caused by listening to loud music. This can destroy the nerve endings that join on to the cochlea. Better shout that to your noisy teenage brother or sister.

2 Disease can destroy hearing. Temporary deafness can occur when the middle ear gets infected and fills up with pus. Yuck!

3 As people get older the sensors in the cochlea die off. That's why you may have to shout in your gran's ear hole.

THANKS FOR THE NEW PYJAMAS, GRAN!

GO TO THE BAHAMAS? LOVELY, I'LL GO AND PACK!

HELPFUL HEARING AIDS

Nowadays deafness can be helped by hearing-aids or cochlea implants. A hearing-aid is a miniature microphone linked to an amplifier that makes sounds louder. A cochlea implant is a tiny radio receiver fitted under the skin that receives radio signals from an earpiece behind the ear. The implant then converts the signals to electrical pulses that trigger signals along the nerves to the brain. Brilliant, eh?

Bet you never knew!

In the USA, a man named Henry Koch complained of hearing music in his head. Tests showed that a tiny lump of carborundum (car-bor-run-dum), a hard black chemical from a dentist's drill, had stuck in his tooth. The crystals in the chemical were picking up and boosting the power of radio waves from a nearby transmitter. This triggered vibrations which the poor man heard as music.

But before the invention of modern hearing aids, in about 1900, people had to make do with this...

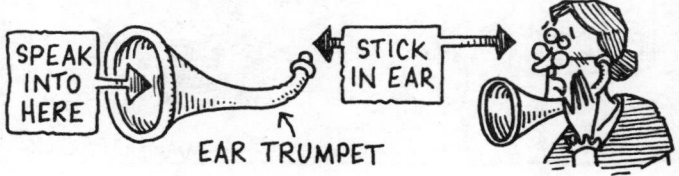

You shout into the ear trumpet. The vibrations can't escape from the trumpet except by passing into granny's lug hole. So your voice sounds louder.

But how would deafness affect a composer of music? A person for whom hearing is more important than anything else in the world. Someone like German composer Ludwig van Beethoven (1770–1827) for example.

HEARING IS BELIEVING

Some people called him a genius. Others called him crazy and sometimes even ruder things. His music was inspired by listening to country sounds, murmuring streams, storms and bird calls. He composed thrilling, dramatic melodies that mirrored his passionate feelings about life and art. Hearing had made him what he was.

But in 1800 Beethoven noticed a ringing in his ears and over the next twenty years his hearing failed. He was forced to try a weird variety of different-shaped ear trumpets. The deafness might have been caused by a disease of the bones in Beethoven's middle ear.

The treatments he took were useless:

• Cold baths in smelly river water.

• Pouring almond oil into his ear holes.

• Wearing strips of bark over his ears.

• Wearing painful plasters on his arms until he got blisters.

Beethoven couldn't hear people talking. Instead, he wrote his friends little notes and they wrote back to him.

He gave his nephew Karl piano lessons and boasted the boy was brilliant. (He must be, thought Beethoven, because he had the best teacher in the world.) It was lucky Beethoven couldn't hear the young boy's dreadful playing. Beethoven's deafness made him really miserable. He also began to pong because he rarely bothered to wash or change his clothes. He never brushed his hair. (Don't get any ideas from this – missing a bath doesn't make you a genius.)

Beethoven could no longer hear well enough to conduct his own music. Several concerts were dreadful flops because he conducted the orchestra too slowly.

But amazingly enough, deafness didn't harm Beethoven's work as a composer. Some experts think he even got better. He used to imagine how the music would sound. And he had a special trick that helped him "listen" to a piano.

Dare you discover ... how to "hear" like Beethoven?

You will need:
One 0.5 cm wide rubber band
One pair of teeth – preferably your own

What you do:
1 Stretch the rubber band between your fingers and twang it. Note how loud the sound is.
2 Put one end of the band between your teeth. Stretch the band. (Don't let go!) Twang it again.

What did you notice?
a) The twang sounded louder the first time.
b) The twang sounded louder the second time.
c) The twang sounded a higher note the second time.

Answer: b) The twang sounds louder because the sound vibrations pass directly to your inner ear via the bones in your skull. These are very good at passing on sound vibrations. Beethoven used a drumstick held in his teeth to feel sound vibrations from a piano in the same way.

33

But for some people life is even harder. Try to imagine what it's like to be completely blind and deaf. The world would be dark and silent. And if you were a baby how would you ever learn a thing? This was the challenge for Helen Keller (1880–1968) who was deaf and blind and didn't know how to talk. Here's how her teacher, Annie O'Sullivan might have told her story…

A TOUCH OF MAGIC

Boston, USA Spring 1927

The young reporter was in a hurry. He had a deadline to meet and the editor back at *The Daily Globe* office was getting impatient for his story.

"So, Annie, may I call you that? You were Helen's teacher for many years. But what was she really like?"

The old woman smiled weakly. "Well, she was very naughty when she was a young girl. She smashed her mum's plates and stuck her fingers in her dad's food. Then she'd pinch her grandma and chase her from the room."

The reporter raised an eyebrow and stopped scribbling in his notebook.

"So, the famous Helen Keller was a bit of a wild child? Our readers will be shocked."

"Helen couldn't hear or see after an illness that she'd had as a baby. She knew people talked using their lips and she wanted to join in. But she couldn't because she'd never learnt how to talk. So Helen got cross instead. She drove her parents crazy. Her uncle said she ought to be locked up somewhere."

The old woman took a sip of tea.

"So I bet Helen's parents were pleased when you turned up. You being a teacher of deaf children."

"Yes, they were! They'd written to my boss at the charity in desperation asking him to send someone and I got the job. But Helen was less impressed. I remember our first meeting like it was yesterday. I tried to give her a hug and she struggled like a wild cat."

The reporter tucked his pencil behind his ear.

"So the famous Helen Keller was like a wild cat," he smirked, "Bet you gave her a smack to keep her in line." The old lady looked shocked. Her saucer rattled as she replaced her cup.

"Oh no, that was never my way. I wanted Helen to be my friend as well as my pupil. Of course, I had to be firm sometimes..."

"Yeah, yeah," broke in the reporter, "but what our readers really want to know is how you taught her. I mean, it's not like she could hear or see anything."

"That was the big problem. All day long I tried to get Helen to understand me by tapping her hand. It was a special code – each letter of the alphabet was a certain number of taps. But Helen didn't understand. It was *so* frustrating."

"Don't suppose it meant anything to her seeing as she didn't know how to read or even what an alphabet was."

"Well, yes I know, but at the time I thought Helen would guess someone was trying to make contact. She'd already made up a few signs herself. Like when she wanted ice cream she'd pretend to shiver."

The reporter was drumming his fingers and fidgeting. "OK, Annie. So you had a problem. How did you get through to Helen in the end?"

"Don't be so fast, young man, I was coming to that. One day we were out for a walk and came across a woman pumping water. Well, I had a brainwave. I put Helen's hand under the stream, and I spelt out W-A-T-E-R by tapping on her hand. Helen twigged at once and then I knew what to do. I got Helen to feel or taste or smell things. For example, she learnt about the sea by paddling in the waves. Then I told her what they were by tapping. Yes, just like you're doing with your fingers."

The reporter stopped tapping as Annie continued...

"For Helen it was incredible, unbelievable. Just imagine it! You're locked in a totally dark and silent world for seven years, and then suddenly one day you realize that someone is actually trying to make contact with you. Helen changed as if by magic. She stopped being naughty and worked really hard."

The journalist checked his watch. Time was running short. He needed to spice up the story. A new angle.

"But Helen can talk now. What our readers want to know is how you managed to teach her."

"Helen knew things vibrate to make a sound. She could feel my throat move when I talked." Annie put her worn old fingers up to her thin neck. "We brought in a speech expert, Miss Fuller. By touching the teacher's throat and tongue and lips Helen found how they moved. Then she had a go herself.

"The first words Helen ever said were, 'I feel warm'. Well, she needed ten lessons just to get that far. But Helen stuck at it. And then..."

"You two went all over the world," interrupted the reporter as he buttoned his coat, "and Helen made grand speeches about the needs of people who can't see and hear." "Yes," the old lady agreed, "and we still live together. Thank goodness for our housekeeper Polly, she looks after Helen most of the time now as I'm getting on a bit. Matter of fact, they're both out in town shopping at the moment."

The reporter stifled a yawn as the old lady continued.

"Mind you, Helen is very capable – despite everything. As I'm sure you've heard, Helen went to university and got a degree. It was all her own work, you know."

The reporter chewed his pencil impatiently. Then he gave a nasty little smile. He scented the new angle.

"It's an amazing story, Annie. But our readers have heard it all before. Devoted teacher helps little girl to discover the world. But maybe there's another side. What do you say to people who claim Helen wasn't that smart and you did the work for her?"

The old lady looked at the young man blankly, then her face filled with anger.

"Well, that's where you're wrong!" she declared fiercely. "It was Helen who did the learning. Yes, Helen is clever – but that's not the point! You see, I'm blind now myself. Never could see much, in fact. But I've come to realize that even if they can't see or hear, quite ordinary people can still do amazing things. Helen Keller taught me that."

The reporter felt stunned, but his mind was still fixed on the story. "Ordinary people can do amazing things…" *Hmm, I like that*, he thought as he closed his notebook. It would make a great opening line.

So that's hearing for you – tiny little air vibrations that rattle your ear bones. Sound waves seem pretty harmless, don't they? Well no, actually sound waves can be dreadful. They can smash windows and buildings and shake an entire aeroplane into little pieces. Now we're in for a bumpy ride, so fasten your seat belts and prepare for a bit of TURBULENCE.

SPEEDY SOUND WAVES

Let's have a nice big round of applause for this chapter. Notice anything? When you clap your hands, the noise you hear is a sound wave. Sound waves are happening all around you all the time.

They zoom outwards like the ripples on a pond when you chuck a rock into the middle. But not all sound waves are the same…

Sounds dreadful fact file

NAME: Sound waves

THE BASIC FACTS: A sound wave happens when clumps of atoms (scientists call them molecules) get shoved together and bump apart again. As they leap apart some molecules bump into others further away. So you get a wave of bumping molecules spreading out like a ripple on a pond.

THE DREADFUL DETAILS: It's not safe to stand next to a big bell when it rings. Powerful sound waves from the huge bell at Notre Dame Cathedral in Paris can burst blood vessels in your nose. Some visitors get nasty nose bleeds.

Scientists use an amazing machine called an oscilloscope (o-sill-oscope) to measure sound waves. The sound waves make a beam of electrons (tiny high energy bits) jump about on a screen.

Here's what a sound wave looks like...

ISN'T THAT JUST BEAUTIFUL

A sound wave shows up as a curve or zigzag. The bigger the peak the greater the amplitude (loudness).

SUPER!

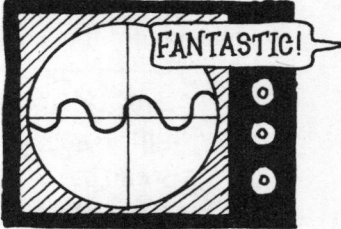

FANTASTIC!

faster vibrations =
closer together peaks =
higher frequency =
higher pitch of sound

slower vibrations =
peaks further apart =
lower frequency =
lower pitch of sound

41

FANTASTIC FREQUENCY

Frequency is measured in Hertz (Hz) – that's vibrations per second, remember (see page 9). Your amazingly alert ears can pick up low-frequency sounds from about 25 vibrations per second, and they hear up to an ear-smacking 20,000 vibrations every second!

High-frequency sounds include…
• A mouse squeaking.

• A human squeaking after seeing the mouse.

• A bike chain in need of a drop of oil.

Low-frequency sounds include...
• A bear growling.

• Your dad growling in the morning.

• Your stomach growling before lunch.

Bet you never knew!
Small things vibrate faster. That's why they make higher-frequency sounds than big things. So that's why your voice sounds higher than your dad's, and a violin sounds more squeaky than a double bass.

As you grow up, the vocal chords in your throat that make sounds get bigger. So your voice gets deeper.

Dare you discover ... how to see sound waves?

You will need:
A torch
A large piece of cling film
A cake tin without a base
A large elastic band
Sellotape
A piece of kitchen foil

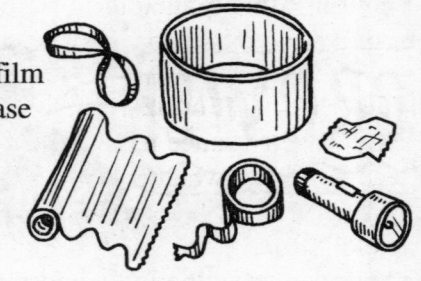

What you do:
1 Stretch the clingfilm tightly over one end of the cake tin. Secure the clingfilm using the elastic band as shown.
2 Use the sellotape to stick the piece of foil off-centre on the clingfilm as shown.

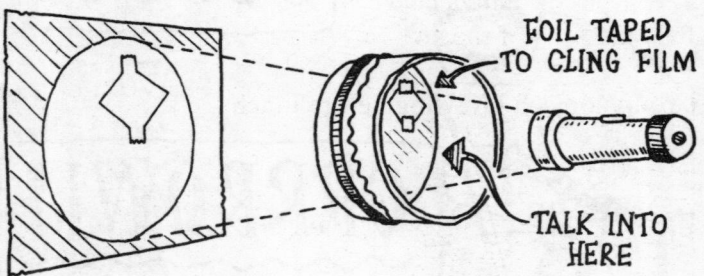

FOIL TAPED
TO CLING FILM

TALK INTO
HERE

3 Darken the room.
4 Place the torch on a table and angle it so the light reflects from the piece of foil on to the wall.
5 Talk into the open end of the cake tin.

What do you notice about the reflection?
a) It jumps around.
b) It stays rock steady.
c) The reflection gets brighter or dimmer depending on how loud your voice is.

TEST YOUR TEACHER

Here's your chance to sound your teacher out. Ask your teacher to say whether they think each answer is TRUE or FALSE, and here comes the tricky bit – ask them to explain *why*.

Important note: there are two marks for each correct answer. But your teacher is only allowed one mark if they only get the TRUE/FALSE bit right.

1 You can listen to a concert underwater even if you're at the other end of the swimming pool. TRUE/FALSE

2 You can use sound to count the number of times a fly flaps its wings in a second. TRUE/FALSE
3 You can hear sounds more quickly on a hot day. TRUE/FALSE
4 If you lived in a lead box you wouldn't be able to hear any sounds from the outside. TRUE/FALSE

Answers: 1 TRUE. Sound travels easily through water. That's why you can hear a rubber band twang even when you hold it underwater. Sound waves pass through water molecules in the same way as air molecules. But the concert would sound muffled because the water would press into your ears and stop your eardrums vibrating normally. (You could make this a trick question and say FALSE because no one can hold their breath that long.) **2 TRUE.** Scientists know the number of vibrations per second for each musical note. All they have to do is to find a note that sounds the same as the beating of a fly's wing. The wing will beat at the same speed. Using this technique scientists have found that a housefly's wings can beat over 200 times a second. **3 TRUE.** When air is warmer the molecules have more energy and move faster. But sound only travels about 3 per cent faster so you probably won't notice the difference. **4 FALSE.** Sound passes easily through solid metal. But it does pass more slowly through lead compared with steel – 4,319 km per hour (2,684 mph), compared to 18,111 km per hour (11,254 mph). But you can still hear the sound clearly.

WHAT YOUR TEACHER'S SCORE MEANS...

Score 7–8 points. This means EITHER

a) Your teacher is a genius. He/she is wasted as a teacher. We're dealing with Nobel Prize winning material here. OR

b) (More likely) they've read this book. In which case disqualify them for cheating.

Score 5–6 points. Fair but could do better. About average for a teacher.

Score 1–4 points. Your teacher may sound knowledgeable but they need to do **a lot more homework**.

COULD YOU BE A SCIENTIST?

One of the most amazing sound effects was discovered by an Austrian scientist called Christian Doppler (1803–1853). But in 1835 young Christian was desperate, dejected and departing. He couldn't find a job. So he sold all his belongings and got ready to set off for America.

At the last minute, a letter arrived offering him a job as Professor of Mathematics at Prague University (now in the Czech Republic). This was a stroke of luck because it was here that Doppler discovered what became known as the Doppler effect.

Doppler reckoned that when a moving sound passes it always changes pitch in the same way – that's the Doppler effect. As the sound waves come towards you they're squashed together. So you hear them in quick succession at a higher frequency. As the sound moves away you hear it at a lower frequency because the sound waves are more widely spaced.

To test Doppler's weird idea a Dutch scientist called Christoph Buys Ballot (1817–1890) filled a train carriage with buglers and listened as they whizzed past him. What do you think he heard?

Clue: the test proved Doppler was right.

a) As the buglers came closer the sound grew higher. As they moved away the sound got lower.

b) As the buglers came closer the sound grew lower. As they moved away the sound got higher.

c) The buglers were out of tune and the roar of the train almost drowned them out.

SUPERSONIC SOUND SCIENTISTS

Have you ever watched a distant firework display? Ever wondered why you see the lovely coloured sparks but don't hear the bangs until a moment or two later?

It proves light travels faster than sound. But how fast does sound travel? A French priest called Marin Mersenne (1588–1648) had a brilliant plan to check it out.

He got a friend to fire a cannon. Marin stood a distance away and timed the gap between the flash when the gun was fired and the bang when the sound waves reached him.

But he didn't have an accurate clock so he counted his heartbeats instead.

In fact, he didn't do too badly. After scientists measured the speed of sound accurately they realized Marin's figure, 450 metres per second was a bit fast. But maybe Marin got excited and his heart speeded up.

One cold day in 1788, two French scientists fired two cannon 18 km apart. The second cannon provided a double check on the first and the distance between the two was about as far as each scientist could see with a telescope. They counted the time between the flashes and the bangs.

But what scientists really needed was a bit of posh equipment to make a more accurate measurement. And that's why French scientist Henri Regnault (1810–1878) built this ingenious sound machine. But would it work – or was it just a long shot?

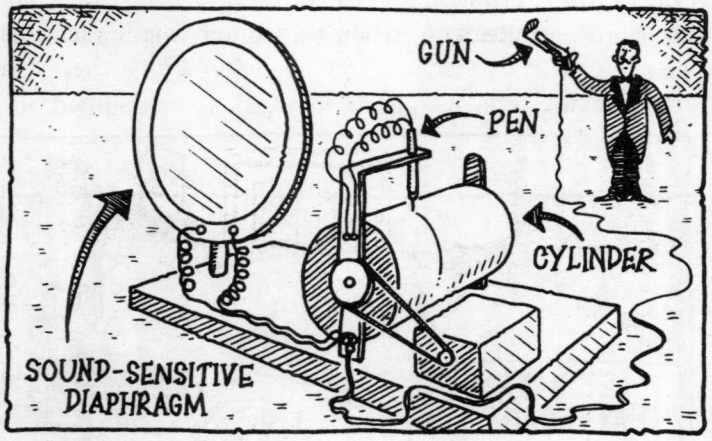

GUN

PEN

CYLINDER

SOUND-SENSITIVE DIAPHRAGM

HERE'S WHAT HAPPENED...

1 The cylinder went round at a regular speed and the pen made a line.

2 The pen was controlled by two electric circuits.

3 When the gun fired the circuit was broken and the pen-line jumped to a new position. I suppose that's what you call "jumping the gun". Ha, ha!

4 When the diaphragm picked up the sound, the circuit was restored and the pen flicked back to its original position.

Regnault knew how fast the cylinder was turning. So he measured the marks made by the pen and this told him how quickly the test had happened. His measurements proved sound travels at 1,220 km/h (760 mph).

But despite Regnault's hard work the measure for the speed of sound is named after a completely different scientist.

Hall of fame: Ernst Mach (1835–1916)
Nationality: Austrian

Ernst was ten years old when he decided that his lessons were boring. His teachers told his parents that their son was "stupid".

WOODLICE HAVE BIGGER BRAINS

"So a teacher called him stupid – what's new?" I hear you say. Well, instead of giving young Ernst a hard time his mum and dad took him away from school and he grew up to be a scientific genius. It might be worth trying this story on your parents – but I doubt it will work.

Ernst's dad bred silkworm caterpillars to make silk and was also very keen on science. His mum loved art and poetry, and between them they taught young Ernst at home. The boy learnt his lessons in the morning and in the afternoon he helped with the silkworms.

At 15 Ernst went back to school where science became his favourite subject. He went on to teach science at university, but he was so poor that he decided to study the science of hearing for which he wouldn't need to buy expensive equipment. His own ears would do fine.

In 1887 Ernst was studying missiles that flew faster than sound waves. He found that at supersonic speeds (that means faster than sound) the wave of air pushed out in front of the missile changes direction.

This allowed the missile to travel smoothly at a supersonic speed.

By 1929 some scientists were dreaming of aeroplanes that could fly faster than sound. So they decided to honour Ernst's discovery by measuring speed in Mach numbers (Mach 1 was the speed of sound). But the scientists faced a dreadful problem. It seemed no human could ever travel that fast ... and live.

THE CONE OF DEATH

Although, as Mach showed, a missile could fly at speeds faster than sound, there was a lot of bumpiness on the way. As a flying object nears the speed of sound the air forming the sound waves can't escape fast enough. The air piles up around the plane in a massive invisible cone. A cone of death. The shaking and buffeting of the air cone was enough to tear an ordinary plane to pieces.

By 1947 every pilot who had flown near the speed of sound had been killed. Pilots called it "the sound barrier".

But in a secret airfield in California, USA, one young man dreamed of breaking through the barrier in a specially strengthened plane that was designed for high-speed flight. Would tragedy strike again? If one of the project's engineers had kept a secret diary it might have read something like this:

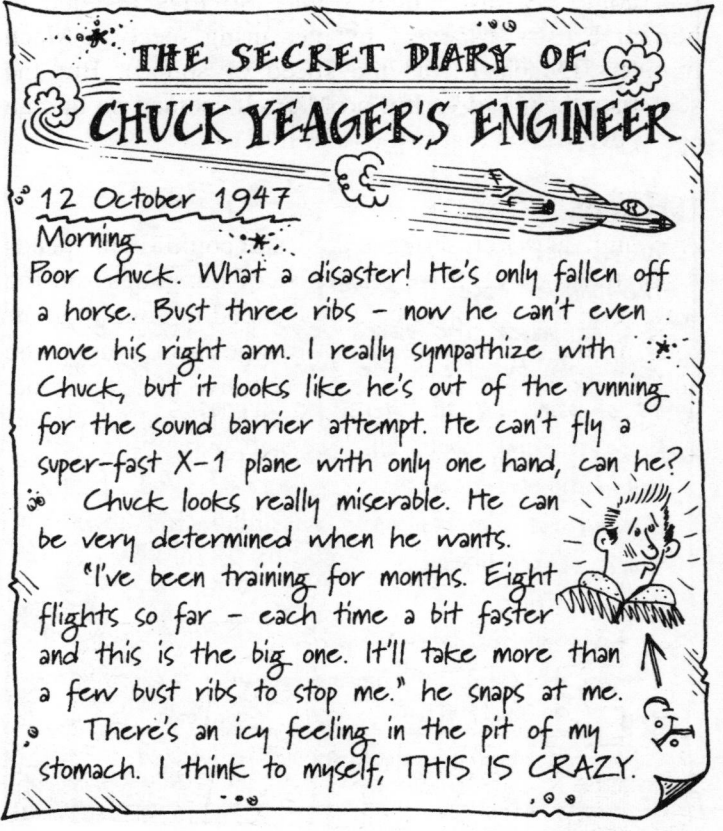

THE SECRET DIARY OF CHUCK YEAGER'S ENGINEER

12 October 1947

Morning

Poor Chuck. What a disaster! He's only fallen off a horse. Bust three ribs - now he can't even move his right arm. I really sympathize with Chuck, but it looks like he's out of the running for the sound barrier attempt. He can't fly a super-fast X-1 plane with only one hand, can he? Chuck looks really miserable. He can be very determined when he wants.

"I've been training for months. Eight flights so far - each time a bit faster and this is the big one. It'll take more than a few bust ribs to stop me." he snaps at me.

There's an icy feeling in the pit of my stomach. I think to myself, THIS IS CRAZY.

But I know he'll try it anyway, so I figure I'd
better help.

Afternoon

The main trouble with Chuck's injuries is that
he can't reach far enough to close the X-1's
door with his left hand. I poke around in the
hanger and find a broomstick. I cut it to size
and Chuck manages to close the door
using the stick. Don't know how it'll
work at 20,000 feet though.

14 October
8.00 am

We're just taking off from
the bomber base. The X-1

LIKE
THIS

is slung under the plane we're in. Chuck seems
very calm but I can see from his face he's in a
lot of pain. "I'm all right," he grimaces. "But I
keep thinking about all the pilots who have been
killed trying to break the barrier." Well, if that
doesn't put him off what will? I wish I could
think of something.

R.I.P.

A few minutes later. . . .
This is it. Chuck's climbing down a ladder into
the X-1. Now that I've said "Goodbye" to
Chuck, I can't help wondering if I'll get a

chance to say "Hi, Chuck" again. My fingers are crossed.

Then I hear the click as the X-1's door locks smoothly. Three cheers for the broomstick handle! But if anything happens to Chuck . . . it'll be down to that piece of wood, and me. I helped him after all.

We can hear Chuck over the radio link with the X-1.

"Brrr, it's cold," he complains.

IT'S COLD!

Well, I'm not surprised, I think. There's hundreds of gallons of liquid oxygen fuel on that plane. It has to be stored at −188°C (−307°F). That's cold enough to frost over the windshield from the inside. Lucky we hit on the shampoo idea. That was a neat trick!

SHAMPOO

Squirt a layer of shampoo on the glass and it stops the frost from forming.

10.50 am

"This is it," says the pilot of our plane nervously. He starts the countdown, "Five . . . four . . . three . . . two . . . one . . . "

My heart's in my mouth. Can Chuck really fly the X-1 with just one hand? Should I have stopped him?

WHOOSH

"DROP!"

Too late now he's on his way.

55

Chuck's got seconds to flick the ignition switch and start the X-1's engines. But if there's a spark near the fuel, the X-1 will be blown to bits. But the engine's firing perfectly. There she goes! Phew!

"I'm beginning to run," yells Chuck.

But we can't cheer yet.

He's hitting turbulence. Here comes the sound barrier – the next few moments are critical. Will the X-1 fall to pieces like the other planes? The seconds tick away... We hear only silence.

There's a sudden rumble. Is it thunder? No – it's the boom made as Chuck flies faster than sound. He's done it! The X-1's flying smoothly at Mach 1.05! HE'S BROKEN THE SOUND BARRIER! YES, YES, YES!!!

BOOM

WHOOPEE!

2.00 pm

Glad to be back on solid ground. I'm shattered. Chuck has a huge grin all over his face. He looks on top of the world so I ask him how he's feeling.

"Not so bad!" he laughs.

Not so bad. Not so bad for a guy with three busted ribs!

BOOMING MARVELLOUS SONIC BOOMS

Chuck Yeager had proved people can travel smoothly and safely at speeds faster than sound. And today military jet planes regularly break the sound barrier.

If this happens near you you'll hear all about it. Remember the sound like thunder made by Chuck's plane as it smashed through the sound barrier? You'll hear something similar. It'll rattle your windows, shake your chimney pots and possibly give your hamster a nervous breakdown. And the cause of this deadly force? Er – air. All those trillions of air molecules squashed together in front of the plane and fanning out behind it. When they hit the ground you hear this extraordinary sound. It's called a sonic boom.

Dare you discover … how to hear a sonic boom?

Here's your chance to check out your very own sonic boom – otherwise known as a peal of thunder. Lightning is a searing hot spark caused by a build up of electricity in a storm cloud. This heats the surrounding air and makes a giant vibration that whizzes faster than sound. This makes the sonic boom we call thunder. Are you brave enough to probe its secrets?

RAIN, RAIN, RAIN, RAIN! WE NEED SOMETHING TO BRIGHTEN THINGS UP . . .

ARGH! FIRE! WE NEED MORE RAIN!

HORRIBLE HEALTH WARNING!

During this experiment try to avoid...

a) getting struck by lightning

b) getting soaked to the skin

c) giving your family a nasty fright

In fact, you can do it perfectly well at home. Just make sure all nervous parents, small brothers/sisters and family pets are safely indoors.

You will need:
A thunderstorm
Yourself
A watch with a second hand

What you do:
Watch the thunder and lightning.

1 *What do you notice?*
a) Thunder always comes before lightning.
b) Lightning always comes before thunder.
c) Thunder and lightning always happen at the same time.

Count the seconds between the lightning and the thunder.

2 *What do you notice?*
a) There's always the same time gap between the two.
b) The harder it rains the longer the gap becomes.
c) The time gap seems to get shorter or longer each time.

But if you think thunder's loud, there are noises in the next chapter that make thunder sound like a gnat burping! Get out your ear plugs (make sure they're clean, first!) and prepare to be SHATTERED!

SHATTERING SOUNDS

What's the loudest sound you've ever heard? Your little brother/sister bawling? Your grandad snoring? Or maybe you've heard something REALLY NOISY. Like a pop concert or a high speed train in a hurry. Here's a chart to compare the loudness of sounds.

TYPE OF NOISE (((((?)))))	DECIBELS	EFFECT ON YOU →
You accidentally drop a sweet wrapper during a science lesson. WHOOPS!	10dB	So quiet no one notices. Phew! (Pick it up later)
You whisper to your friend during the lesson.	20-30dB	Sssh! People can hear you.
You start chatting to your friend. NATTER CHATTER!	60dB	Your teacher can hear you now. This could be painful.
The whole class starts chatting.	75dB	Ooh-er! Take cover!

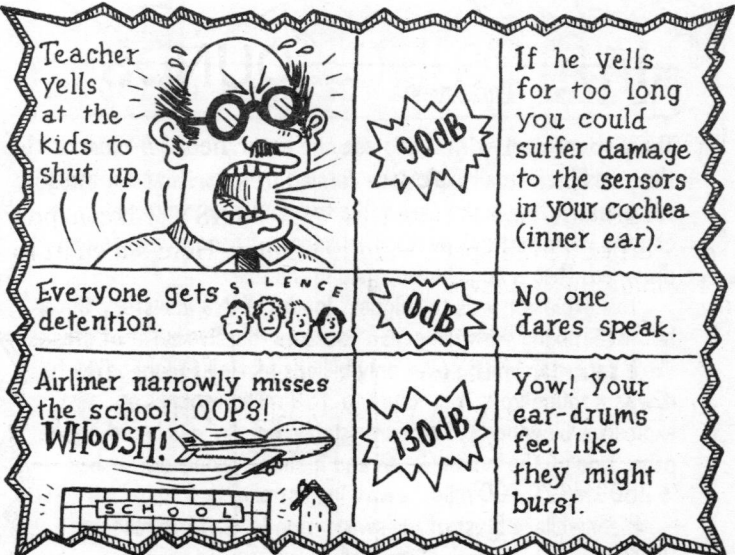

Teacher yells at the kids to shut up. **90dB** If he yells for too long you could suffer damage to the sensors in your cochlea (inner ear).

Everyone gets detention. SILENCE **0dB** No one dares speak.

Airliner narrowly misses the school. OOPS! WHOOSH! **130dB** Yow! Your ear-drums feel like they might burst.

Scientists measure the amplitude (loudness) of sound in bels and decibels (10 decibels = 10 dB – 1 bel). They're named after British-American inventor Alexander Graham Bell (1847–1922) (see page 105). By the way, just to confuse you, every time you go up three dB the sound gets about twice as loud. Got that? So 4 dB is roughly twice as loud as 1 dB.

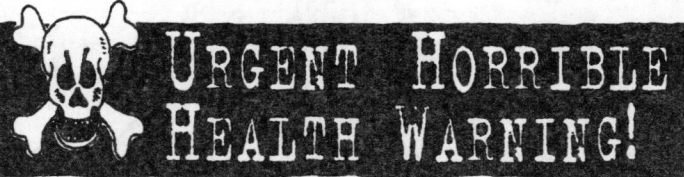

URGENT HORRIBLE HEALTH WARNING!

We interrupt this chapter to bring you a really loud noise warning. Yes, it's even louder than the plane. It's just about to happen on the next page. GET DOWN! ARGHHHHHHHHHHHHHH!!!!!!!

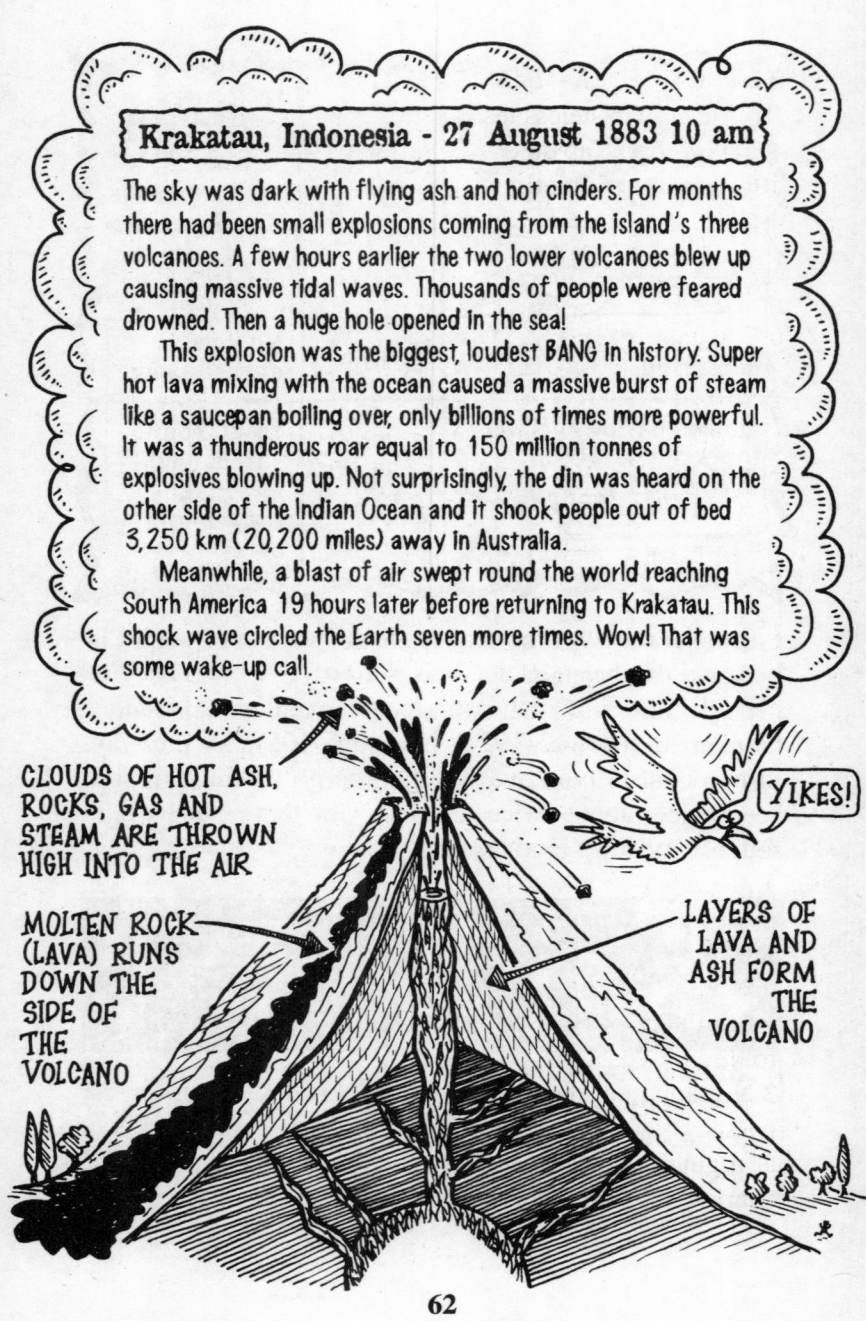

Krakatau, Indonesia - 27 August 1883 10 am

The sky was dark with flying ash and hot cinders. For months there had been small explosions coming from the island's three volcanoes. A few hours earlier the two lower volcanoes blew up causing massive tidal waves. Thousands of people were feared drowned. Then a huge hole opened in the sea!

This explosion was the biggest, loudest BANG in history. Super hot lava mixing with the ocean caused a massive burst of steam like a saucepan boiling over, only billions of times more powerful. It was a thunderous roar equal to 150 million tonnes of explosives blowing up. Not surprisingly, the din was heard on the other side of the Indian Ocean and it shook people out of bed 3,250 km (20,200 miles) away in Australia.

Meanwhile, a blast of air swept round the world reaching South America 19 hours later before returning to Krakatau. This shock wave circled the Earth seven more times. Wow! That was some wake-up call.

CLOUDS OF HOT ASH, ROCKS, GAS AND STEAM ARE THROWN HIGH INTO THE AIR

YIKES!

MOLTEN ROCK (LAVA) RUNS DOWN THE SIDE OF THE VOLCANO

LAYERS OF LAVA AND ASH FORM THE VOLCANO

TEACHER'S TEA-TIME TEASER

This terribly tasteless teatime teaser will set your teacher's teeth on edge. Tap quietly on the staff room door and when it groans open quietly ask:

I WAS JUST WONDERING WHY IT MAKES SUCH A HORRIBLE SCREECHING SOUND WHEN YOU SCRATCH YOUR FINGERNAILS DOWN THE BLACKBOARD?

GROAN!

Answer: Brr – it's enough to give you the shivers. In the mid-1980s scientists in Northwestern University, USA, played the sound to volunteers to find out why it was so bad. The fingernail rapidly touches tiny bumps on the board and sets off a mix of uneven high-frequency vibrations that sound dreadful. And maybe that's why it sets your teeth on edge.

NOISE NUISANCE

1 Are you being kept awake by noise? Maybe you've got noisy neighbours or a bawling baby brother or an anti-social parrot. Or maybe there's thundering traffic nearby? Cheer up, research shows you can sleep even when there's 40–60 dB of noise going on. If you're used to the noise, that is.

2 Nothing new about this. In ancient Rome, Julius Caesar passed a law to stop people driving noisy chariots about at night. They were keeping the citizens awake. But the chariot drivers didn't take any notice.

3 But louder noises are more of a headache – literally. Back in the 1930s, scientists found that factory workers worked harder when they wore ear-muffs to drown out noise. And people who worked in noisy places often felt bad-tempered after a hard day. (That's their excuse, anyway.)

4 Deafening noises can seriously damage your health. Scientists exposed to DREADFULLY LOUD sounds of 130 dB look a bit like this.

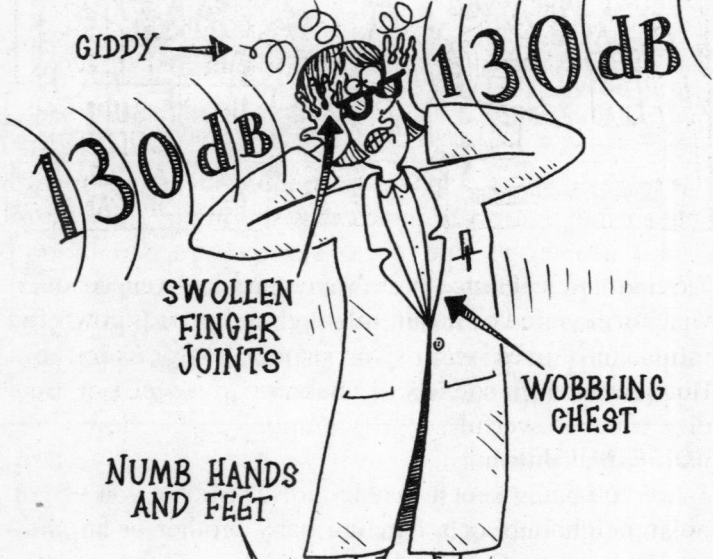

GIDDY →

130 dB   130 dB

SWOLLEN FINGER JOINTS

WOBBLING CHEST

NUMB HANDS AND FEET

5 In the 1970s, NASA scientists in the USA built a machine that made a racket registering 210 dB. (Fancy living next door to that?) The sound waves from this din were so powerful they could knock holes in solid objects.

6 In 1997 it was reported that US military bases in Britain were to be defended by powerful sound guns. Sound waves from these machines would make any intruder's intestines vibrate so much they'd need to find a toilet in a hurry. (Sounds dreadful!)

DON'T SUPPOSE YOU COULD LEND ME A CLEAN PAIR OF PANTS?

7 Scientists in France have developed an even deadlier weapon powered by an aircraft engine. It makes powerful infrasound waves – that's sounds too low for us to hear. But this sinister sound can make people feel sick and dizzy. The powerful sound vibrations shake the body's vital organs causing fatal damage. It can actually kill a person if they're less than 7 km away!

Hopefully such a horrific machine will never be fired – but ordinary sound has already been used as…

A SOUND WEAPON

In 1989 US forces invaded Panama, in Central America in a bid to arrest the suspected drugs dealer General Manuel Noriega. But the wily General, (nick-named "old pineapple face") had fled his luxury villa for the Vatican embassy. The Americans were stumped. They couldn't gatecrash the embassy to grab the General. It was against international law. So "old pineapple face" was safe. Or was he?

Someone had a seriously sound idea. Why not blast the General out with sound? Here's what their notes to the General might have looked like (if they'd sent any)...

Dear Pineapple face

You see those giant amplifiers outside your window? In 30 seconds we're going to start playing really loud music. We'll be blasting the embassy round the clock until you turn yourself in. Happy listening!

Love, the US forces
PS Any requests?

Dear Yankee loud-mouths

Ha, ha. You don't scare me. I love music - the louder the better...

Love, General Noriega XXXX
PS Got any opera?

Dear Pineapple face

OK, you've had your classical music. Now for some really heavy rock! Yeah – it's time for something seriously LOUD by sixties guitar legend Jimi Hendrix.

Hope you like it!

Love, the US forces
PS Got the message yet?
PPS Come out with your hands up!
And this one's for you, General.

Dear No-good Yankees

Ow, my head hurts!
I can't stand it anymore.
I can't sleep, I can't think,
I can't eat. I'm going
crazy – I just can't take
it. OK, OK, you win. I surrender. Just
turn that dreadful noise down. Please!

Love, General Noriega
PS Got any headache pills?

67

Bet you never knew!

The General would have loved a bit more sound-proofing. Maybe something like those cardboard egg boxes from Chapter One. Soft sound-proofing materials such as carpets and curtains soak up sound waves and take away their energy so they get weaker and quieter. The energy of the sound waves heats these materials slightly. But no, that doesn't mean you can turn up your stereo every time you feel chilly.

Oh, so you like a bit of noise then? Really wild noise? Well, you'll lurve the next chapter. It's wild all right. Wild, woolly and hungry with huge bloodthirsty fangs. Are you wild enough to read on...? Howwwwwwwwl!

NOISY NATURE

Some people think that nature is quiet. Peaceful, tranquil, serene. But animals are never quiet. Their world is full of appalling growling, yowling, howling cries, and what's more they don't care if they keep you awake. Here's your chance to hear from some dreadfully loud wildlife.

The first ever

ANIMAL CONCERT

Live from the Heart of the Jungle

(Sponsored by Bert's Pet Shop)

THE CHOIR

The fantastic FROG male voice choir

CROAK! CROAK! CROAK!*

Delightful loud croaks made louder thanks to vibrating air-filled pouches in their throats. They'll be performing their romantic love song, *"Come here you lady frogs we'd lurve to meet you!"

The rowdy RATS

Famous for their squeaky songs. Some of them perform in ultrasound – that's notes too high-pitched for us to hear. They will be performing their traditional song of welcome to visiting rats,

SQUEAK! SQUEAK! SQUEAK! *

DON'T LIKE THE SOUND OF THIS MUCH

*"Clear off you dirty rats or we'll kill you!"
(The ultrasound version is a bit wasted on humans.)

QUACK! CUCKOO! TWITTER! CHIRRUP! CHIRP! OH DEAR!

The sensational SONG BIRDS

Hear them warble away with their amazing singing syrinxes (see-rinx-es) – that's the skin stretched over their windpipes. (It's the vibrations that make a whistling sound.)

(APOLOGY. The different types of birds are refusing to sing one song and insisting on singing their own tunes all at the same time. This may prove confusing.)

The high-flying HOWLER MONKEYS

Performing their hit single, *"Get lost you other monkeys – this is our patch!"* WARNING. These monkeys can be heard 15 km (9 miles) away. Members of the audience are respectfully advised to stick their fingers in their ears.

The charming cheeky CHIMPS

Will be performing their exciting new song, "Pant hoo, pant hoo, pant hoo." Roughly translated this means, *"Come over here, there's some scrumptious fruit on this tree."*

THE ORCHESTRA
(PERCUSSION SECTION)

The wild and wonderful WOODPECKERS

PECK! PECK! PECK! PECK!*

Beat time with those wacky woodpeckers as they bash their toughened beaks twenty times a second on a tree to gouge out the delicious squirming maggots underneath. Also the males will be performing one of their famous drum solos, *"Come over to my place girls, I'm a real headbanger."

The crazy clicking male CICADAS (chick-ard-ers)

They'll be playing the vibrating skin inside their abdomens, "TSH—ee—EEEE-e-ou." Roughly translated this means, "Here I am, come and get me, you lovely lady cicadas!"

♪ TSH-ee-EEEE-e-ou

(WARNING. These cicadas are very loud – more than 112 dB. Members of the audience are advised to take cover under their chairs.)

SPECIAL ANNOUNCEMENT

We apologize to readers who were looking forward to the first ever animal concert. It's been cancelled. Unfortunately some of the choir have been eating one another, and some members of the orchestra have escaped.

72

Bet you never knew!

It's said that a nineteenth-century musician, Mr Curtis invented an instrument that looked like a piano with 48 cats inside. When Mr C pressed a key a cat yowled as its tail was pulled. He appeared in a concert in Cincinnati, USA...

YEOWWW!

But Mr C's cruel plan was far from purrfect. His playing of "Old Lang Syne" was ruined when the cats all yowled at once. The stage collapsed in a cloud of dust and an old lady shouted, "FIRE!" A passing fire engine sprayed the building and everyone got soaked. The cats, of course, escaped by a whisker.

HOP IT!

Have you ever heard a grasshopper stridulate (strid-u-late)? If you answered, "I often stride when late," then read on. Stridulating is the sound grasshoppers make by rubbing their hairy little legs together. (No, your pet gerbil can't do this – I don't care if he has got hairy little legs.) Male grasshoppers stridulate to serenade fanciable female grasshoppers.

But even when grasshoppers make a racket it's really hard to tell exactly where they're hiding. Scientists have found that the frequency of the noise is about 4,000 Hz, and it so happens that humans aren't very good at judging the direction of these sounds. Higher-pitched sounds can be found using one ear, but for lower-pitched sounds we use both ears. That's because longer sound waves bend around our heads. But with sounds in between we're a bit stuck. Well, we can't listen with one and a half ears can we?

Animals are a lot better at this hearing lark. They have to be. They've got to keep their ears open for smaller animals to scoff and for the heavy footfalls of hungry beasts out to scrunch them. Now 'ere's your chance to guess how good they are.

EAR, EAR

1 African elephants (the ones with big floppy ears) can hear better than Indian elephants (the ones with small floppy ears). TRUE/FALSE

2 Some moths have ears on their wings. TRUE/FALSE

3 Crickets have ears on their legs. TRUE/FALSE

4 Snakes have ears hidden under their scales. TRUE/FALSE

5 Frogs have ears ... er, somewhere. TRUE/FALSE

6 An owl's face picks up sound like a large ear. TRUE/FALSE

7 Aardvarks have incredible hearing. They can hear termites scuttling about underground. TRUE/FALSE
8 Indian false vampire bats (I kid you not – that's what they're called) can hear tiptoeing mice. TRUE/FALSE

Answers: 1 FALSE. Larger ears don't help African elephants hear better but they do help keep them cool. Their big ears allow more blood to flow to just under the skin and so lose body heat into the outside air. **2 TRUE.** Lacewing moths have ears on their wings. All insect ears are thin flaps of skin that vibrate in response to sound just like your ear drums. The vibes trigger nerves to send messages to the insect's tiny little brain. **3 TRUE.** And that's why you'll never see a cricket wearing spectacles. By the way, like grasshoppers, male crickets make sounds to attract females of the same species (type of insect) and so I guess they need their ears for a sound reason (groan!) **4 FALSE.** Snakes don't have ears. They can't hear noises but they can sense the vibrations made by anything walking on the ground. Snakes pick up these signals through their jaw bones. **5 FALSE.** Frogs don't have ears but they have ear drums on each side of their heads. Scientists have played different sounds to frogs. They found that frogs are best at picking up low frequency sounds – like croaks! **6 TRUE.** An owl's face is shaped a bit like a satellite dish. It's brilliant at picking up sounds and bouncing them towards the owl's ear holes at the edge of the "dish". **7 TRUE.** Then the aardvarks dig the termites up with their paws and lick them up with a long, sticky tongue. Tasteee! **8 TRUE.** The bats swoop down and grab the mice. But the mice do have a chance – they can hear the bat's high-pitched calls.

CHATTING CETACEANS

Cetaceans (see-tay-shuns) is the posh word for whales and dolphins. Use it in a science lesson and you're bound to make a big splash.

Some of the most amazing animal calls are made by dolphins and whales. They moo like cows, trill like birds, and whistle like ... er, whistles. They can even creak like a rusty old door hinge. All these sounds are made in rapid pulses of little more than a few milliseconds. But blue and fin whale calls can measure 188 dB. That's loud enough to damage your ears and be heard by other whales 850 km away.

We don't know what these sounds mean. They could be a way for the animals to keep in touch or chat to their friends. But some boring scientists have pointed out that cetaceans can make the sounds as soon as they're born. So they obviously don't learn a language like we do. They must learn something in a school of whales, though – ha ha!

TEACHER'S TEA-TIME TEASER

Tap gently on the staff room door and when it squeaks open smile sweetly and ask:

" 'SCUSE ME, I WAS JUST WONDERING HOW DOLPHINS AND WHALES SING UNDER WATER WITHOUT GETTING A MOUTHFUL OF OCEAN?"

SPLUTTER!

Answer: Your teacher can't sing with a mouthful of tea – I expect that's why she's spluttering instead. But whales and dolphins even manage to sing whilst chomping their breakfasts (you can't so don't try it). The sounds start in their throats and they force the air into bag-like structures linked to their nasal passages.

Dolphins and killer whales also make other, even stranger sounds. They make weird ultrasound clicks. In the 1950s American scientists found that dolphins could find food at the bottom of a murky pool on a dark night. Tests showed the animals were making the clicks and then picking up the echoes from an object to find food.

Amazing things, echoes. Unearthly, ghostly sounds – scary voices without bodies, and by some eerie coincidence the next chapter's all about them.

LET'S GO!

EERIE ECHOES

Here's a treat if you like the sound of your own voice. Stand about 30 metres from a wall. Shout really loudly. Listen. Can you hear your own voice echoing from the wall? Sounds kind of eerie, doesn't it?

EERIE ECHO FACTS

1 An echo is made by sound waves bouncing off a surface in the same way as light bounces off a mirror.

2 So where's the best place to hear echoes? Well, why not try an eerie old castle? There's one near Milan, Italy, where you can hear your voice echoing over forty times. The old walls trap the sound waves so they continue bouncing backwards and forwards.

3 The domes of St Paul's Cathedral, London, and the Capitol building in Washington, USA, both feature eerie whispering galleries. You can whisper something against the walls and someone across the dome can hear your whispers. The curve of the walls directs the echoes to a single point on the other side. So if you want to whisper a joke about your teacher make sure they are safely out of the building.

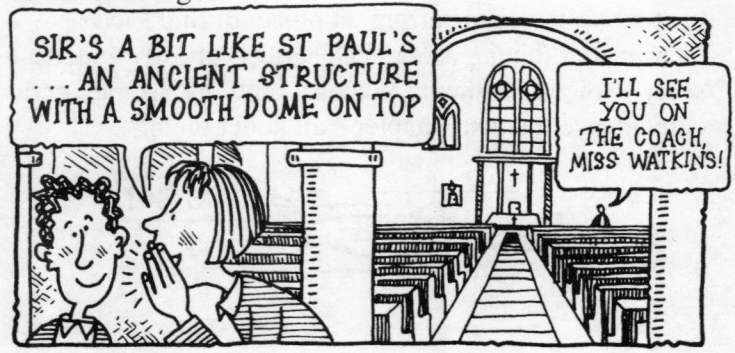

SIR'S A BIT LIKE ST PAUL'S ...AN ANCIENT STRUCTURE WITH A SMOOTH DOME ON TOP

I'LL SEE YOU ON THE COACH, MISS WATKINS!

4 Alpine horns, the incredibly long horns that people play in Switzerland, use echoes to boost their range by several kilometres. The eerie echoes rumble around the mountains, and they can be used to send simple messages.

5 Fog horn echoes also have an eerie message. The low-pitched notes of the fog horn carry a long distance and any echoes will bounce off cliffs and rocks, warning of deadly danger ahead.

6 There's nothing more eerie than the booming rumble of thunder. Much of this sound is made by echoes rebounding off clouds from the original peal of thunder.

7 But there's more to echoes than noise. Music also requires echoes to come eerily alive...

DESIGN YOUR OWN CONCERT HALL

Well CONGRATULATIONS, your school has just been awarded a special grant to build a new concert hall, and you've been asked to lend a hand with the design. Got any ideas? It's important to plan the inside carefully so people can hear music clearly. This is known as acoustics. Fortunately, we've got Jez Liznin to advise us.

1 The first thing we need is a big tank of water. You can make a ripple and watch it bounce from the walls of the tank.

A TANK HELPS TO PLAN THE WAY THAT SOUND WILL BOUNCE OFF THE WALLS OF THE HALL

2 Now let's look at the walls. Let's go for a curved wall around the back of the stage.

3 Avoid flat, smooth walls in your design. You'll get loads of echoes bouncing around in the wrong places – it'll be like being stuck in a tunnel.

4 Avoid comfy chairs and carpets and curtains. They'll soak up the sound and make the music sound rather dead. Hard chairs are better for the acoustics even if they do give you a sore bum.

5 Yes, that's right. You've got to build it. Didn't we tell you? Don't work too hard! Byeee!

DREADFUL EXPRESSIONS

Should you call the police?

COULD YOU BE A SCIENTIST?

Scientists have been keen on bats for years. So is it true all scientists are seriously batty? In 1794, for example, Swiss scientist Charles Jurinne found that bats couldn't find their way around obstacles when they had their ears blocked.

But it wasn't until the 1930s that US scientist Donald R Griffin recorded a bat's ultrasound squeaks and proved they found their way around in the dark by listening to the echoes. Can you imagine flying dolphins?

One of many batty experiments carried out by batty scientists involved trying to confuse bats by playing noise. What do you think happened?

a) The bats stopped flying and slumped to the ground.

b) The bats flew more slowly and made more noise themselves.

c) The bats beat the scientists with their leathery wings.

Answer: b) It takes more than a bit of noise to bother a bat. But the bats were put off a bit because they did fly more carefully than usual.

Bet you never knew!
Different types of bat squeak on different frequencies and amplitudes. For example, the little brown bat has a call as loud as a smoke detector. (No, don't get any ideas – it's cruel to use bats as safety equipment.) But the whispering bat has a call that's only as loud as … believe it or not … a whisper. But whatever they call it, any bat could mean dreadful danger – if you happen to be a moth.

THE TIGER MOTH SURVIVAL MANUAL

by Squadron Leader
Irma Tiger-Moth

OK, AIR CREW, PAY ATTENTION TO THIS BRIEFING. IT COULD MEAN THE DIFFERENCE BETWEEN LIFE AND DEATH.

Here's your main enemy – a bat. Take a good look. Ugly looking blighter isn't he? Could be the last thing you see. So remember – Biting Bats Scoff Moths. They open their mouths wide and scrunch us with their sharp little fangs. What a terrible way to go! No wonder we moths are miffed.

a bat

MAKE SURE YOU LEARN THE FOLLOWING PROCEDURES BY HEART

1 Listen hard for bat squeaks. They mean there's a bat about, and it's flying your way! Luckily, you can hear the bats before they detect you so RUN FOR IT – er, I mean FLY FOR IT!

SQUEAK

YIKES!

EH?

POP!

POP!

2 If the bat gets too close activate your vesicles. These are those tiny ridge plates on each side of your body, in case you didn't know. Squeeze 'em hard and the ridges make a loud pop noise. This'll confuse the bat. Ha, ha – serves 'em right.

3 While the bat's working out what's going on – you make your escape. It's best to drop to the ground. The cowardly bat will be too scared of crashing to follow you. Also, their echo sounders can't spot you on the ground. That's because they get so many echoes from the ground they can't make out which echoes are bouncing off you.

PHEW!

I GIVE UP!

Eventually, millions of years after bats and dolphins had the idea – humans decided to use echoes to find things. Or at least one brainy French scientist did.

Hall of fame: Paul Langevin (1872–1946)
Nationality: French

Young Paul was one of those kids who's always top of the class. He never came second in anything. Makes you sick, doesn't it? So I won't even tell you about how he taught himself Latin. Yuck! When Paul grew up he studied science at Cambridge University, England.

In 1912, a giant liner, the *Titanic*, sank after smashing into an iceberg, and over one thousand people drowned. After that catastrophe Langevin became interested in the idea of using sound waves to find a hidden object. He reckoned that sound waves could have been used to spot the iceberg. So in 1915, Langevin developed his idea into the invention later known as SONAR (which stands for SOund NAvigation and Ranging).

A machine called a transducer makes a kind of PING noise (too high for human ears to make out) and the sound waves from this bounce off underwater objects like shipwrecks, shoals of fish, whales, submarines and scuba diving elephants.

SOUND WAVES HIT OBJECT AND BOUNCE BACK

SONAR SENDS SOUND WAVES DOWNWARDS

The echoes are picked up by the transducer and turned into electrical impulses.

A receiver then measures the strength of the echoes and the time they took to reach the ship. The stronger the echo, the more solid the underwater object and the longer it takes to return, the more distant the object. Got all that? You can see the position of the object on a screen and find out how it's moving. Sound idea!

But sadly instead of helping to save lives, Langevin's invention helped to kill people. During the Second World War, SONAR was used to track down enemy submarines so that they could be destroyed with underwater bombs called depth charges.

Then in 1940, the Germans invaded France and Langevin found himself up to his ears in danger. His son-in-law opposed the take-over but he was executed. Then Langevin and his daughter were arrested. Surely, it was only a matter of time before the scientist faced the death penalty. Scientists around the world sent messages of support for Langevin and the Germans decided to lock him up in his own home. But he was still in danger and, helped by some brave friends, he escaped to Switzerland.

Today SONAR is still used to find underwater objects and in 1987 it faced its greatest test. Could SONAR locate the legendary monster in Loch Ness, Scotland? Mention the Loch Ness monster to most scientists and they sigh rather sadly and say, 'Oh, not that old chestnut!'

If there is a monster, say the scientists, how come there's no scientific proof like a dead monster's body? But just imagine there *was* a monster. And just imagine if this super-intelligent, super-sensitive creature could tell its own story? Here's what it might say…

"TROUBLED WATERS"

by Nessie 9-10 October 1987

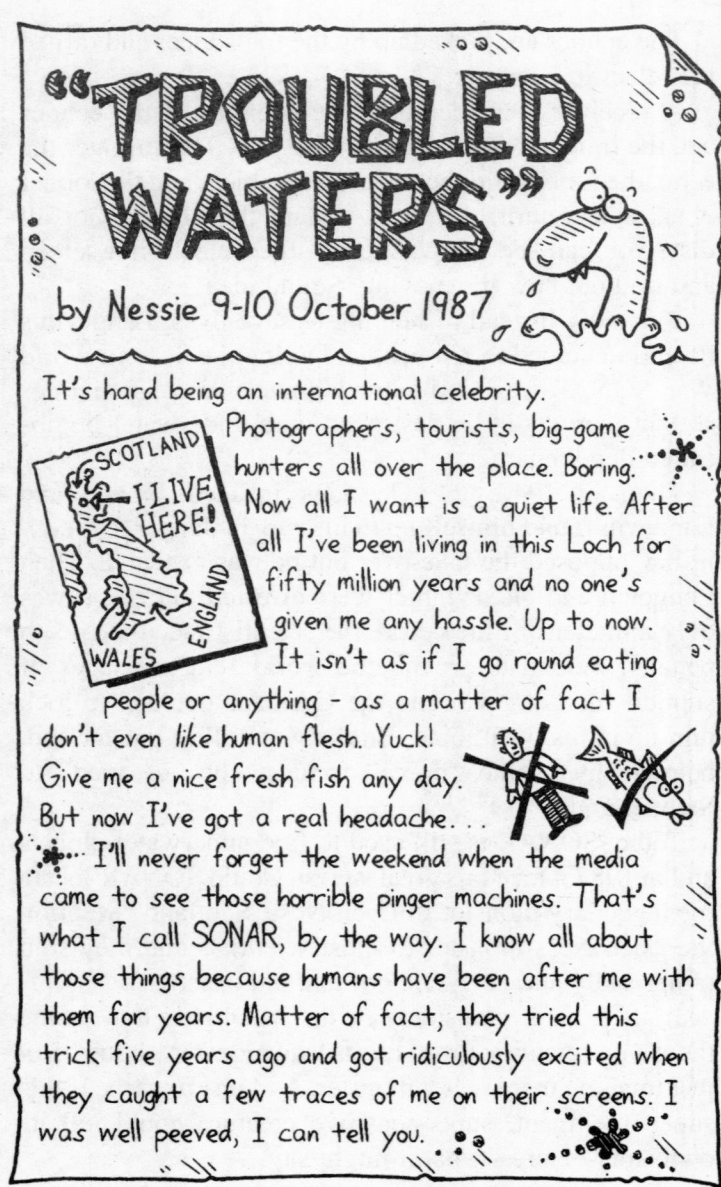

It's hard being an international celebrity. Photographers, tourists, big-game hunters all over the place. Boring. Now all I want is a quiet life. After all I've been living in this Loch for fifty million years and no one's given me any hassle. Up to now.

It isn't as if I go round eating people or anything - as a matter of fact I don't even like human flesh. Yuck! Give me a nice fresh fish any day. But now I've got a real headache...

I'll never forget the weekend when the media came to see those horrible pinger machines. That's what I call SONAR, by the way. I know all about those things because humans have been after me with them for years. Matter of fact, they tried this trick five years ago and got ridiculously excited when they caught a few traces of me on their screens. I was well peeved, I can tell you.

Of course, I never dreamt they'd try again. I was having a quiet little swim - as you do. I mean, the Loch might be deep and dark and freezing cold and gloomy but it's home to me. Anyway, I poked my head up above water for a quick nose about and that's when I saw them. Hundreds of journalists, dozens of boats, helicopters, TV cameras - the works. You could have knocked me down with a dead haddock. Luckily, they were all listening to a big guy with a bushy beard. Otherwise I'd have been spotted.

Matter of fact, I know the big guy. Adrian Shine is his name. He's a scientist and he's been trying to spot me for years. (Ha, ha, you should be so lucky, Ade.) Anyway, he was telling the pilots of the boats to, "Form a line across the loch and keep on going at a steady speed." Blimey - he even had flags on either bank to keep the boats in line - and those blinkin' pingers. Every boat had one. Noise? Huh, all that pinging all day long - I got a MONSTER headache!

flags

line of boats with SONAR

I know they spotted me a couple of times. I was hiding about 150 metres down. *That should be enough*, I thought. But I should have realized, this stupid SONAR noise goes down hundreds of metres. Anyway, I heard a ping really close and up above they were all shouting:

"It's a monster - he's down there!"

He? Blooming cheek - I'm a SHE!

So I beat a hasty retreat. But that night I surfaced and heard people talking - it was a press conference. A couple of American SONAR experts were sounding very puzzled about the signals. One said they don't look as if they've been made by fish.

Fish? Grrr, I'm not a FISH - but what did he know?

Anyway, they managed to ping me next day too, but then I made myself really scarce. Didn't want to get myself caught on SONAR again, did I?

I mean, just imagine if they got some real proof that I existed. The autograph hunters, TV wildlife documentaries, royal visits. It's not going to happen. I'm going to skulk in my cosy underwater cave until they've gone home. Yeah, push off humans, can't you see I want to be alone?

LOCH NESS - THE DREADFUL TRUTH

The SONAR sweep of Loch Ness covered two-thirds of the vast loch. It had been thorough and well-planned. But the dreadful truth was that it failed to prove Nessie existed. All the scientists had to show for their hard work was a few marks on a sonar chart. The charts were computer print-outs from a sonar screen and the marks showed moving solid objects. Could these be traces of an unknown creature? A large creature bigger than any known type of fish. The file on the Loch Ness monster remains open.

So what would you do if you managed to spot a huge monster unknown to science. Would you…

a) shout for joy
b) say hello
c) scream for your Mummy?

Chances are you'd want to make some kind of sound. Wanna know how? Better clear your throat and read the next chapter.

DREADFUL BODY SOUNDS

It's great being you, isn't it? You can make so many smashing noises. Some are musical, some aren't and some are just plain rude. After you make a rude noise have you noticed that that's when your friends make noises, too? Those strange shuddering, tinkling, squeaking, braying sounds we call "laughter".

DREADFUL BURPS, FARTS AND RASPBERRIES

Here's how to make some entertaining body noises, but **don't** make them...

a) In a science lesson

b) In school assemblies or dinner times

c) When the posh relatives come for lunch

Otherwise you'll never hear the end of it.

Farting

Made by vibrating skin around your bottom as air rushes out. You can make similar noises by putting your mouth over your arm and blowing hard.

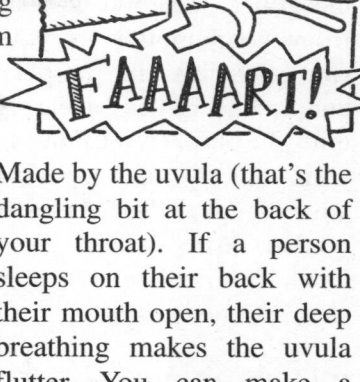

Snoring

UVULA

Made by the uvula (that's the dangling bit at the back of your throat). If a person sleeps on their back with their mouth open, their deep breathing makes the uvula flutter. You can make a disgusting snoring sound by lying in this position and breathing in.

Bet you never knew!
So you think your dad/uncle/grandad/pet pot-bellied pig snores like a pneumatic drill? Huh – that's nothing! In 1993, Kare Walkert of Sweden was recorded snoring at 93 dB. That's louder than a really noisy disco. By the way, the best thing to do with someone who snores isn't to hit them over the head. No, all you do is gently close their mouths and turn them on their sides. Ahh, peace, perfect peace!

Burping

The air comes up not from your lungs but from your stomach. The vibrations from the gullet (the food passage from your mouth to your stomach) gives the burp its unique and rather endearing tone. To burp, try pushing in your tummy and opening your mouth wide. It helps if you've just scoffed your lunch in five seconds then slurped a fizzy drink.

Whistles and humming

These aren't exactly rude, but I suppose it depends where you do them. For example, it wouldn't be a good idea to whistle the tune to "The Sound of Music" when you were at church.

Humming is caused partly by a particular set of vibrations in the skin inside the nostrils. Try pinching your nose as you hum and you'll hear how important this is.

Whistles are caused by air whistling though the round hole made by your lips forming little whirlwinds in your mouth that make its inside vibrate.

Talking about vibrating insides, there's lots of fascinating sounds going on inside your body…

SOUNDS UNHEALTHY

One day in 1751, Austrian doctor Leopold Auenbrugg (1727–1809) happened to notice a wine merchant tapping a barrel. The merchant explained that the sound told him how full the barrel was. *Hmm*, thought the doctor, *I wonder if you could do this for the human body?*

After a lot of thought Leopold wrote a book. He'd figured out a new way to discover if the body was unhealthy. Here's your chance to try it, too.

Dare you discover … how to hear your own chest?

You will need:

Two tupperware boxes with lids (these represent your chest)

Your hands

What you do:

1 Half fill one box with water.

2 Place the middle finger of your left hand so it's lying flat on the lid of the empty box.

95

3 Tap the middle portion of this finger with the middle finger of your right hand. The tap should be a smart downwards flick of the wrist.

4 Try to remember the sound.

5 Now repeat steps 1–3 on the lid of the box half full of water.

What do you notice?

a) The two sounds are exactly the same.

b) The empty box makes a dull empty sound and the box with water makes a higher sound.

c) The empty box sounds more hollow, the box with water sounds duller.

Answer: c) Doctors can still use this method to check out what's going on inside your chest. If the chest sounds hollow like a drum it means there is air in the space around the lungs (there should be fluid there).

DREADFUL EXPRESSIONS

A doctor tells you...

I'LL HAVE TO DO SOME AUSCULATION

Should you scream and ask for a painkiller?

96

THE STUNNING STETHOSCOPE

For hundreds of years doctors had a simple way to listen to their patients' breathing and heartbeat.

But one day shy French doctor René Laënnec (1781–1826) found himself in an embarrassing situation.

In desperation Laënnec remembered seeing two boys playing with a hollow log. One boy tapped the log and the other listened to the sound at the other end.

97

So Laënnec figured that a tube might be a good way to hear sounds louder. He rolled up a newspaper.

Success! Laënnec heard the young lady's heartbeat loud and clear. He wrote a book about his new technique and became rich and famous.

Sadly, though, Laënnec fell ill. And the man who had done so much to help doctors treat chest diseases eventually died ... of a chest disease.

Bet you never knew!
By listening through a stethoscope you can find out if a person has a whole range of dreadful diseases. For example, when someone with the lung disease bronchitis (bron-ki-tis), breathes they make a kind of bubbling, crackling noise. Some heartless doctors describe this dreadful sound as "bubble and squeak".

Sounds dreadful fact file

NAME: Your voice

THE BASIC FACTS: The sound waves of a voice are affected by the shape of its owner's skull and mouth, etc. So every voice is different.

THE DREADFUL DETAILS: People who have had their vocal chords removed can still talk. But their voices come out as a whisper.

Here's where your voice comes from...

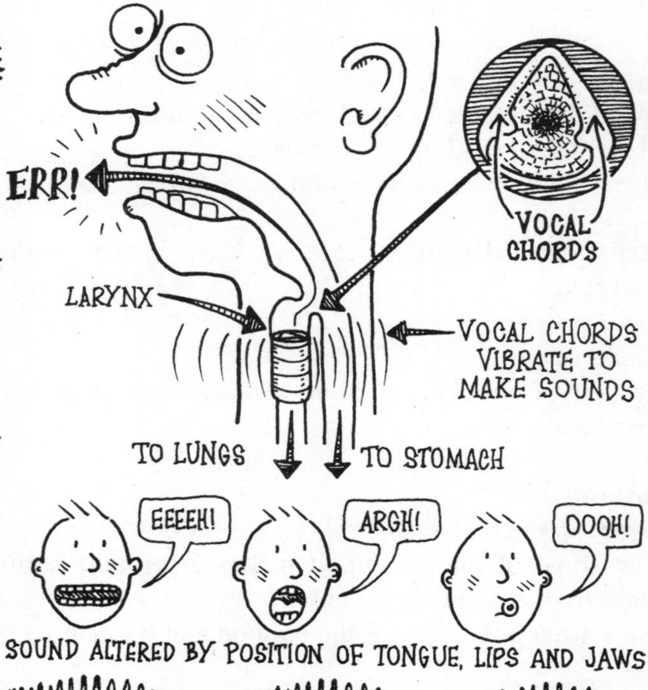

ERR!

VOCAL CHORDS

LARYNX

VOCAL CHORDS VIBRATE TO MAKE SOUNDS

TO LUNGS   TO STOMACH

EEEEH!   ARGH!   OOOH!

SOUND ALTERED BY POSITION OF TONGUE, LIPS AND JAWS

Do you like talking? Sorry, silly question. I mean do ducks like water, do elephants like buns? Here's your chance to find out how you do this amazing thing – a chin-wag.

Dare you discover 1 ... how you talk?

You will need:
A voice (preferably your own)
A pair of hands (preferably your own)

What you do:
1 Put your thumb and second finger lightly on your throat so they are touching but not pressing on it.
2 Now start humming.

What do you notice?
a) My throat seems to swell up when I hum.
b) I can feel a tingling in my fingers.
c) I can't hum when I'm touching my throat.

Dare you discover 2 ... how your voice changes?

You will need:
A balloon
One pair of hands (you could use the same pair as in experiment one)

What you do:
1 Blow up the balloon.
2 Let some of the air out. It makes a brilliant farting sound. (No, not during assembly).
3 Now stretch the neck of the balloon and try again.

What do you notice?
a) No sound comes out.
b) The sound gets higher.
c) The sound gets louder.

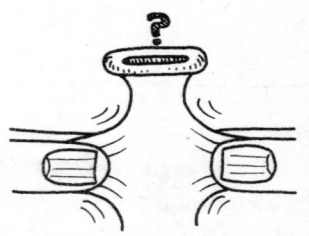

LEARN HOW TO TALK

OK, so you probably know how to do this anyway.

1 Try saying the letters A, E, I, O, U. Notice anything? The sounds are all made by complex air vibrations in your mouth.

2 Now say S, B, P. Notice what happens to your lips and tongue. Can you feel them moving? Can you say these letters without moving your tongue? Thought not.

3 Say N and M. Notice how part of the sound seems to come out of your nose. Try pinching your nose and notice what happens to the sound.

Keep going. With more practice you might do as well as these people...

The Horrible Science Vocal Awards

RUNNER-UP: In 1990, Steve Woodmore of Orpington, England, spoke 595 words in 56.01 seconds. That's roughly all the words from here to page 106. Could you do this?

SECOND PRIZE: In 1988 Analisa Wragg of Belfast, Northern Ireland shouted at 121.7 dB – that's louder than a whole noisy factory. Bet she was cross about something.

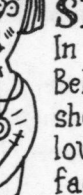

CHAMPION: In 1983 Briton Roy Lomas whistled at 122.5 dB. That's louder than a small aircraft engine.

SOMETHING TO SHOUT ABOUT

Have you ever really shouted at someone really loud? I mean at the top of your voice – just as loud as you can. Of course you have. Maybe at the same time you spread your hands on either side of your mouth. Have you noticed how this makes your voice sound louder? A megaphone is only a cone with a hole in one end, but what a difference it makes. Here's how it works.

SOUND NORMALLY SPREADS OUT FROM YOUR MOUTH IN ALL DIRECTIONS

MEGAPHONE CHANNELS SOUND IN ONE DIRECTION SO IT SOUNDS LOUDER

MEGA-MOUTH MORLAND

The megaphone was the brainchild of wacky British inventor Samuel Morland (1625–1695). Sam had an amazing life – it was certainly something to sound off about. As a young man Morland worked for the government. It was a time when Britain was ruled by Oliver Cromwell and King Charles II was in lonely exile in France.

One night Morland overheard his boss and Oliver Cromwell hatching a plot to kill the king. Morland was scared and pretended to be asleep at his desk. Cromwell saw Morland and decided to kill him before he gave away the plot.

But Sam's boss persuaded Cromwell that the young man had been asleep. In 1660 Charles returned to power and Sam convinced the King he'd been on his side all along.

Sam became interested in science and built a powerful pump. He showed it off by squirting water and red wine over the top of Windsor Castle.

And he also invented the megaphone. One day the inventor got in a boat and shouted to the king from a distance of 0.8 km. History doesn't record what he said – it might have been something like this...

For hundreds of years the megaphone was the only way to make the human voice carry over large distances. And then someone made a re-sound-ing discovery.

Hall of fame: Alexander Graham Bell (1847–1922) Nationality: British-American

Young Alexander Graham was bound to be fascinated by sound – it ran in the family. His dad was a Scottish professor who taught people with hearing difficulties to speak. This was handy because Alexander's mum also had hearing difficulties.

The young boy had a mind of his own. Aged only 11 he changed his name to Alexander Graham Bell in honour of a family friend. Unfortunately, having a mind of your own wasn't a good idea if you wanted to get on at school. Alexander hated the strict boring lessons. (Does this ring a bell with you?)

Alexander left school without any qualifications and thought about running away to sea. But then he had second thoughts and chose a life involving REAL hardship and deprivation. That's right – he became a teacher. This was quite surprising when you consider he was only 16 at the time – that's younger than some of his pupils. (But he looked older.)

In 1870 Alexander moved with his family to America and got a job teaching deaf children how to speak. Unlike some teachers Alexander was always kind and gentle and he NEVER lost his temper – sounds amazing!

But at nights he worked secretly on another interest. He began to dream of a new machine. A machine that could carry the human voice for hundreds of kilometres. A machine that would change the world for ever.

COULD YOU BE A SCIENTIST?

As a teenager, Alexander Graham Bell had a sound interest in science. Here are two of his favourite experiments. Can you predict the results?

1 Alexander and his brother built a talking machine. It was made of wood, cotton, rubber, a tin tube for the throat and a real human skull.

Alexander's brother blew air up the model's throat to supply puff to get the voice going. Alexander moved the model lips and tongue to make the noises that we call speech. But would the machine work? What do you think?

a) The model never said a word – just a quiet hissing sound.

b) The model said, "Hi, dad!" in a clear voice. Alexander's dad saw the talking skull and fainted.

c) The model spoke in a Donald Duck-style voice.

2 Alexander decided to help his pet dog talk by moving its jaw and throat. How did he get on?

a) Terrible. The dog refused to say a word.

b) Smashing. Alexander was the first human to have an intelligent conversation with a dog.

c) The dog learnt how to ask, "How are you, grandmama?"

Answers: 1 c) It could say, "Mama". The neighbours heard the voice and wanted to know whose baby it was. **2 c)** Actually the dog said, "Ow ah oo ga ma ma." But Alexander claimed the experiment was a success. And it was these experiments that paved the way to his greatest discovery.

THAT RINGS A BELL

It's actually true that five hundred and ninety-nine people said they invented the telephone before Bell. Five hundred and ninety-eight of them were liars keen to cash in on the phone's success. But one of them, American born Elisha Gray, just happened to be telling the truth.

Elisha Gray was a professional inventor with his own firm part-owned by the Western Union Telegraph Company. He'd been thinking of ways to send sounds along electrical wires and had already made a few successful experiments.

One day in 1875, Gray saw two boys playing with a toy. It was two tin cans linked by a string. One boy would speak into a tin can and the string carried the sound waves to the other can which the other boy held to his ear. A light bulb flashed in the inventor's brain. He came up with an idea for transmitting not just sounds but actual voices along a wire. It was identical to Bell's design even though the two inventors had never met.

Gray managed to sketch out his idea on 11 February – that's a month before Bell put his thoughts on paper. So Gray was now on track to win fame and fortune. But meanwhile Bell and his assistant Thomas Watson were working flat out to build their machine. Their telephone was the result of two years' hard work. Its improvements were based on trial and error. It was made up of…

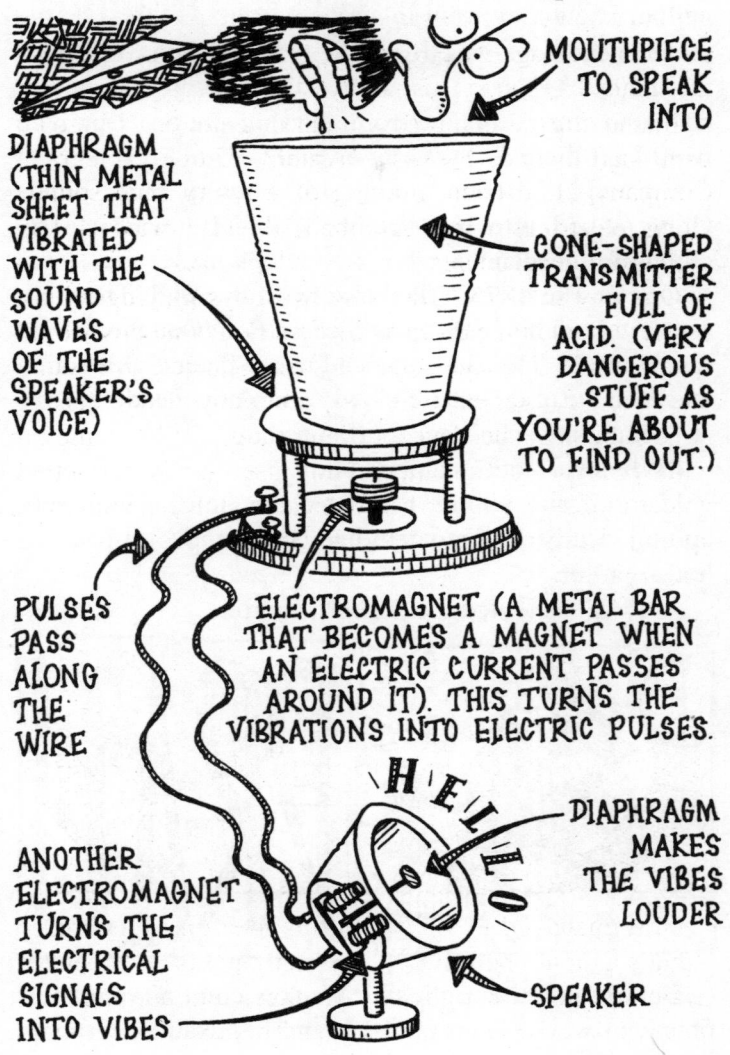

MOUTHPIECE TO SPEAK INTO

DIAPHRAGM (THIN METAL SHEET THAT VIBRATED WITH THE SOUND WAVES OF THE SPEAKER'S VOICE)

CONE-SHAPED TRANSMITTER FULL OF ACID. (VERY DANGEROUS STUFF AS YOU'RE ABOUT TO FIND OUT.)

PULSES PASS ALONG THE WIRE

ELECTROMAGNET (A METAL BAR THAT BECOMES A MAGNET WHEN AN ELECTRIC CURRENT PASSES AROUND IT). THIS TURNS THE VIBRATIONS INTO ELECTRIC PULSES.

HELLO

DIAPHRAGM MAKES THE VIBES LOUDER

ANOTHER ELECTROMAGNET TURNS THE ELECTRICAL SIGNALS INTO VIBES

SPEAKER

The race was on to grab the glory and win the huge cash prizes that would follow from the new technology. But neither inventor knew about the other, remember. So neither knew they were in a race.

The next stage was to file the plans of the invention at the Patent Office. This allows the inventor exclusive rights to make money from their invention. But who would get there first – Gray or Bell?

On a cold Valentine's Day, 14 February 1876, Elisha Gray rushed into the Patent Office. He was eagerly clutching the plans for his new telephone. It was 2 pm precisely. The clock ticked loudly on the wall. The clerk sat writing in his high-backed chair. Gray coughed to get his attention. The clerk glanced at the patent application and then put it down. He slowly shook his head.

"Sorry, sir, I can't accept this patent."

"Why ever not?" snapped Gray.

"I'm afraid you're too late," announced the clerk apologetically. Bell's patent had been handed in just two hours earlier.

"DRAT!" shouted the foiled inventor.

But meanwhile Bell and Watson couldn't get their phone to work. Then on 10 March, Alexander Graham

Bell slopped some acid from the phone speakers on his clothes and made the world's first telephone call by accident.

"Mr Watson, come here I want you!" he yelled, perhaps adding under his breath, "and this acid's eating my trousers."

Thomas Watson ran to the aid of his boss whose faint and crackling voice he heard through the strange machine.

This was the call that launched a million chat lines. A defining moment in modern history. But when Bell rang Watson he hadn't rehearsed the words that would change the world, and he hadn't planned to dissolve his pants either.

(Some boring historians point out that Watson didn't get round to telling this story until 50 years later. So was it true? Perhaps. Maybe Watson kept it quiet until then to avoid making his good friend Bell look like a dumb-Bell.)

So Watson got a bell from A Bell and Elisha Gray was beaten to the bell. In 1877, Gray and the Western Union Telegraph Company took legal action against Bell and his backers claiming that Gray had got to the telephone first. Who would win? Would Bell get his just desserts or would Gray's story ring true with the judge?

What do you think?
a) The judge agreed with Gray. Bell's claim was phone-y and he had to give all his profits to Gray's company, leaving Bell penniless.
b) Gray and Bell agreed to split the money fifty-fifty. It was a fair dial – er, sorry deal.
c) Gray lost and had to call it a day. He didn't get a bean.

111

Answer: c) Bell won because he got his patent in first. The judge gave Bell and his friends a ringing endorsement and poor Gray was left wringing his hands. Gray hadn't seen the potential of the new invention. He thought the phone was just a toy. Meanwhile, Bell and Watson had worked night and day to realize their dream. But Gray was still convinced that he'd been robbed.

DREADFULLY SUCCESSFUL

The telephone was an instant smash-hit. By 1887 there were 150,000 telephones in the USA alone. For its inventors it was a chance to ring in the profits. But for Alexander Graham Bell personally it was a nightmare come to life. He once said:

Financial dealings are distasteful to me and not at all in my line.

The point was, Bell was happier just being a scientist. So at the ripe old age of 33 he retired to devote the rest of his life to scientific research. And he came up with plenty more inventions including:
• A probe to find bullets stuck in the body.
• An idea for making water from fog.
• A super-fast hydrofoil boat.

Bell loved machines and gadgets but one gadget in particular got on his nerves: he never allowed a phone near his lab. It was, he said, a distraction from his work.

Bet you never knew!
In the early days of telephones there were attempts to use them to broadcast music. In 1889, a company in Paris used phone lines to broadcast concerts to loudspeakers in hotels. The audience had to put money in the machines to get to the end of the piece. Sounds dreadful.

But it's not as bad as some of the dreadful musical moments you'll find in the next chapter. Can you stand crazy concerts, mad musicians and hideous clashing discords? If not, stuff a big wad of cotton wool in your ears and read on anyway.

DREADFUL MUSICAL MAYHEM

It's official! 99.9 per cent of us reckon music is smashing. Yes, great music can make our hearts jump for joy. It makes the world dance and sing, and laugh or even cry with its beauty. And bad music? Well, that's just a pain between the ears.

COULD YOU BE A SCIENTIST?

A scientist at the University of California, USA, used a computer to show patterns of nerves firing in the brain. His colleague suggested making the computer play the pattern in the form of sounds. And amazingly, these sounded just like classical music. So the scientists wondered whether listening to classical music could actually make the nerves work more effectively. Could the brain work better?

The scientists decided to test the idea by giving three groups of students some tricky questions.

Group 1 had ten minutes of silence before they started.

Group 2 listened to a voice tape designed to make them more relaxed.

Group 3 listened to ten minutes of classical music by Mozart.

Which group did best in the tests?

a) Group 1. Any sound puts the brain off. That's why people need peace and quiet to work.

b) Group 2. The brain is best stimulated by the sound of a human voice.

c) Group 3. The theory was correct!

Answer: c) These students scored 8-9 points above the others. Could this help you in a science test? In 1997 scientists in London found that children aged nine to 11 learn more easily when there's soothing music in the background. So why don't teachers use it to liven up science lessons?

Research shows that listening to music can boost mental performance owing to a similarity between sound waves and nerve signal patterns.

A DISGUSTING DIN?

Despite the possible brain-boosting powers of music, every musician has had to put up with lots of unkind people who hated their work. It just goes to show that good music like good food is really a matter of taste.

Here's just one example – German composer Richard Wagner (1813–1883). Wagner composed grand and often incredibly loud music for huge orchestras. He had many fans but some people thought Wagner's music was worse than toothache. "Wagner has beautiful moments but awful quarter hours," commented GA Rossini (1792–1868). Other comments on the subject of Wagner's music were:

"I love Wagner, but the music I prefer is that of a cat . . . outside a window and trying to stick to the panes of glass with its claws."

Charles Baudelaire (1821–1867)

Mark Twain (1835–1910) thought Wagner's music sounded dreadful:

". . . at times the pain was so exquisite I could hardly keep the tears back. At those times, as the howlings and wailings and shriekings of the singers and the ragings and roarings and explosions of the vast orchestra rose higher and higher . . . I could have cried."

I expect your music teacher feels the same during school orchestra and school choir practice. And talking about great musicians, are you still itching to become a pop star? Brilliant, 'cos it's time to re-join Jez and Wanda in the sound studio to tackle the next stage of your training – learning to sing. (Admittedly some pop stars don't bother with this bit, but it can help!)

COULD YOU BE A POP STAR? STEP 2: SINGING

Wanda's just explaining the science of singing:

It's actually harder than you might think to become an expert singer, but these few tips should help:

1 First choose a song to practise. It helps if you know the tune and at least some of the words.

HORRIBLE HEALTH WARNING!

Loud singing can seriously damage your family life, your pets and other defenceless creatures such as teachers. So before you start . . .

▶ check there's no human life within earshot – that's at least 180 metres.

▶ put earmuffs on any family pets.

▶ avoid singing when parents are watching their favourite TV programme or first thing in the morning.

2 Stand with your head back and your shoulders back. Breathe in deeply to the pit of your tummy. Easy, innit?

3 Now it gets a bit trickier. Start singing. Carry on with the deep breathing as you sing. Try to open your mouth more widely than you usually do when you speak.

4 You'll find it's easier to produce higher and clearer notes if you smile whilst you sing. Try it and see.

5 OK, that's enough singing. I SAID THAT'S ENOUGH! Now here's the hard bit: singing in tune (some people never get this far). Try singing the same note as a key on the piano or a note on a recorder. Can you get it right? On a piano the keys are arranged in order of pitch. You may know them as...

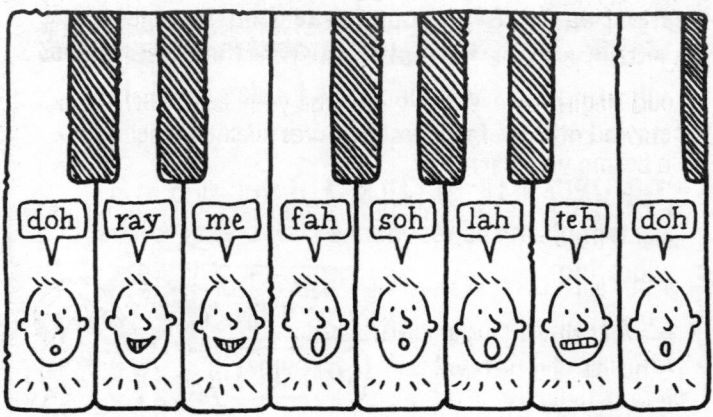

But the most amazing musical secret is in the vibes. Yep, we're talking about resonance again ... but *beware* this info could really SHAKE you up.

Sounds dreadful fact file

NAME: Resonance

THE BASIC FACTS: Everything has a natural frequency. That's the speed at which it vibrates most easily. When sound waves hit an object with the same natural frequency the object starts vibrating. So the sound gets louder. This is how most musical instruments work (see page 122).

THE DREADFUL DETAILS: 1 If you sing at a certain pitch the resonance starts your eyeballs vibrating.

2 A trained singer can sing at the natural frequency of a glass and make it vibrate. Some singers can even smash the glass if they sing loudly enough.

WHAT DO YOU THINK?

SMASHING!

LAAH!

Dare you discover ... how to make sounds resonate?

You will need:
A sea shell shaped like this...

What you do:
Put it to your ear and listen.
What is causing those eerie sound effects?

a) The ghostly echoes of the sea.

b) It's the sounds around you resonating in the shell.

c) These are faint sounds stored by chemical structures in the shell and released by the heat of your body.

CHECK FIRST THAT NOTHING'S LIVING IN THE SHELL – SORRY, SHOULD HAVE MENTIONED THAT EARLIER

Answer: b) Scientists say the boring everyday sounds sound louder because they resonate. That's why you get a similar effect using a cup or even your hand. And it's also why if you put a shell to your ear in a soundproof room you can't hear anything. By the way putting your hands over your ears cuts out distracting sounds and that's why pop stars put their hands over their earphones when they're singing. It helps them to concentrate on the music coming through their earphones. That's right, it's nothing to do with their terrible singing.

COULD YOU BE A POP STAR? STEP 3: MUSICAL INSTRUMENTS

To be a real star it might help to do more than just sing. In fact, why not learn a few instruments so you can really impress your fans? In the sound studio Jez and Wanda are comparing notes on musical instruments.

STRINGS AND THINGS

A stringed instrument is made up of strings stretched tight over an empty case.

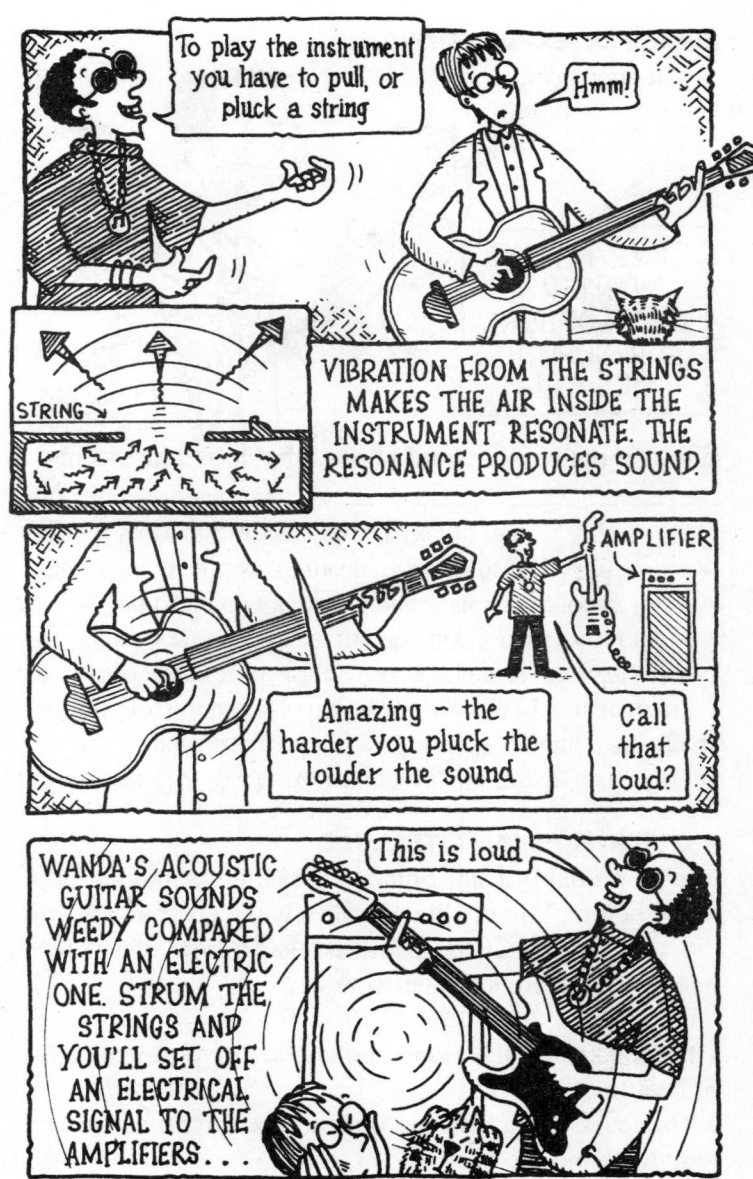

123

DREADFUL EXPRESSIONS

A scientist says...

I'VE ALWAYS WANTED A CHORDOPHONE (KOR-DO-FONE) LIKE THIS

Can you really buy chord phones that look like violins?

Answer: No. A chordophone is the posh term for a stringed instrument like the violin. It means "stringed sound" in Greek. By the way, woodwind instruments are aerophones (air-ro-fones) (not aeroplanes – dimwit), brass instruments and drums are membranophones (mem-brain-o-fones) and percussion instruments are idiophones (i-deo-fones). No, that doesn't mean that they're played by idiots – even if these instruments seem easier to play.

A QUICK MUSICAL INTERLUDE

You've probably seen someone "tickling the ivories" of a piano before. You might even have had a go yourself. But did you know that the piano is also a type of stringed instrument? Here's how it works...

1 Press a key on the piano and you set in motion a series of levers.
2 The levers lift a hammer that strikes a tightly stretched wire to sound the note.

But things can go wrong. For example, damp air can make the felt between the piano keys take in moisture and swell up. The keys stick together and the pianist plays two notes instead of one. Then you get dreadful scenes of mayhem. This is what really happened at the Erawan Hotel in Bangkok, Thailand...

CONTINUED

You'll be pleased to know that Mr Kropp was stopped from totally wrecking the piano by the Hotel Manager, two security guards and a passing police officer. If you're having piano lessons I hope this doesn't give you any ideas.

WARBLING WIND INSTRUMENTS

To make a really mellow sound you'll probably need more than just stringed instruments. How about adding a few woodwind instruments to your line up? A funky saxophone, a cool clarinet or a soulful flute.

Note: Woodwind instruments were once made from wood – that's how they get their name. Now they're often made from metal or other materials.

Wanda has volunteered to show us how to play a few wind instruments. Ever tried to play a milk bottle? That's a bit like blowing into a flute. You need to blow across the top:

Well, in theory the air inside the flute vibrates to make the sound. In a saxophone or clarinet a reed in the mouthpiece vibrates when you blow to get the same effect.

A deeper sound comes out. Larger things make a lower sound when they vibrate, remember.

BRILLIANT BRASS

A fanfare of trumpets would really add some oomph to your hit. Brilliant brass instruments include…

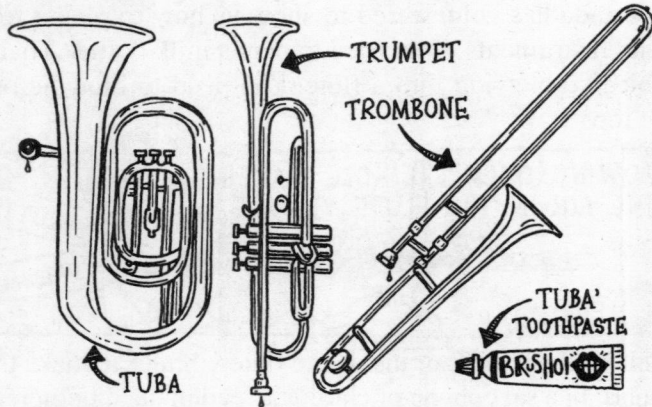

TRUMPET

TROMBONE

TUBA' TOOTHPASTE

BRUSHO!

TUBA

Like woodwind instruments you get the sound from air vibrating inside the instrument. But the vibes come from the special way you move your lips. By blowing a raspberry – here's Wanda's attempt.

SPIT!

RASP!

You make higher sounds by pressing your lips tighter during the raspberry. Lengthening the pipe makes a deeper sound. You do this by pushing out the sliding part of the trombone or pressing the valve buttons on the trumpet and tuba.

TEACHER'S TEA-TIME TEASER

Are you feeling brave? Now's your chance to sound your teacher out on a vital scientific question. Hammer boldly on the staff room door and when it grinds open smile sweetly and say:

I WAS JUST WONDERING WHY YOUR KETTLE HISSES WHEN IT'S JUST ABOUT TO BOIL AND STOPS WHEN THE WATER IS BOILING?

GROAN!

Answer: Bubbles form in hot water at the base of the kettle. They rise and collapse in cooler water. Like a wind instrument, air in the kettle vibrates and you hear a hiss. Hotter water means more bubbles and a louder hiss. But when the water boils it's not cool (yes really!) The bubbles don't collapse and the hissing stops. I bet there'll be steam hissing from your teacher's ears when they can't answer your question!

PECULIAR PERCUSSION

Percussion instruments include anything that you can bash together to make sounds. Like...

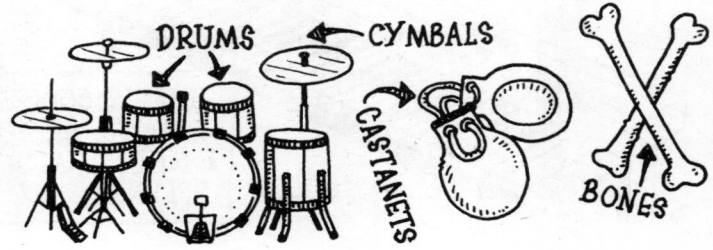

DRUMS ← CYMBALS

CASTANETS

BONES

Now how about a serious drumbeat? It'll give a great rhythm to your track. It's easy to make a sound on the drums – you just hit them with drumsticks. (No, not chicken drumsticks.)

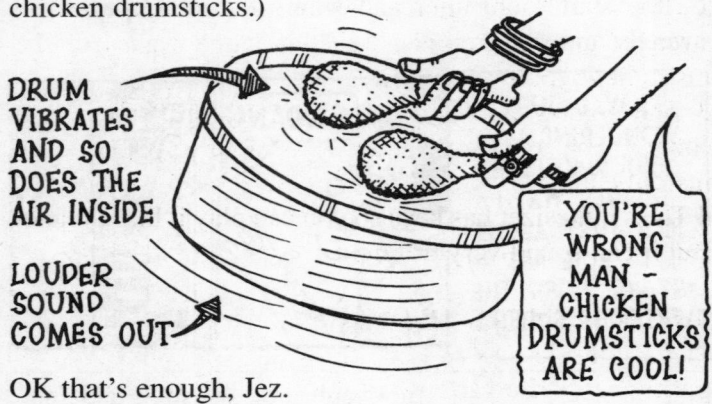

DRUM VIBRATES AND SO DOES THE AIR INSIDE

LOUDER SOUND COMES OUT

YOU'RE WRONG MAN – CHICKEN DRUMSTICKS ARE COOL!

OK that's enough, Jez.

Bet you never knew!
Can't decide which instrument to play? Just imagine an awesome machine that can make the sound of any instrument in the world. Impossible? No it's really true – it's called a synthesizer.

This is what it looks like:

WHAT D'YOU THINK WANDA?

THAT'S COOL, MAN – ER, I MEAN THAT'S SPLENDID, JEZ

Here's how to use it:

1 It's amazing, you just set the controls for the type of instrument you want to play.

2 The synthesizer makes electronic signals that get stronger and weaker just like the sound waves of the instrument you want to copy.

3 The signals go to an amplifier and are turned into sounds. The sounds are strangely similar to your chosen instrument.

4 The synthesizer has keys so you can play it like a piano. But it can sound very different.

SUPER SAMPLERS AND MIXING

Playing music was fun but here's the tricky bit. You've got to record the various instruments and mix the tracks together. Jez can do this with the help of a fantastic brain-boggling machine. Or more accurately *two* fantastic mind-boggling machines in one.

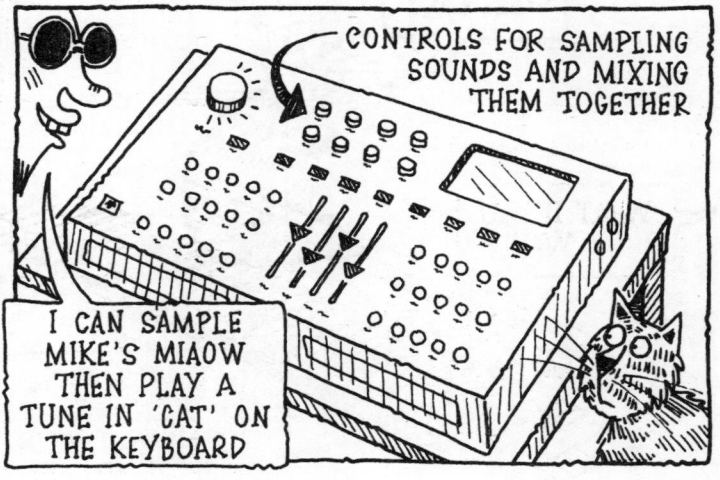

CONTROLS FOR SAMPLING SOUNDS AND MIXING THEM TOGETHER

I CAN SAMPLE MIKE'S MIAOW THEN PLAY A TUNE IN 'CAT' ON THE KEYBOARD

The mixer allows Jez to record, or dub, the sound of your voice over the sound of the instruments.

The sampler part of the machine can take ANY sound – an annoying yowling cat for example – and play it back at a different speed. The sampler makes a sound more echoey; it can even play sound backwards. With a sampler your singing will sound even more brilliant.

So how do you feel? Are you bursting to make a big noise? Or in need of a nice cup of tea and a couple of headache pills? Jez and Wanda will be back with some even more serious sound machines later. But for now, keep your earplugs firmly in place. 'Cos the next chapter is LOUD and it really does sound *dreadful*.

ANNOYING YOWLING CAT? CHEEK!

DREADFUL SOUND EFFECTS

Here's what you've been waiting for – the chance to blow your own trumpet … and everything else too. You don't need posh and expensive instruments to make your own music. The good news is you can make interesting and rather horrible sound effects using everyday objects.

ODD ORCHESTRA QUIZ

Musicians have used some really strange things and some really dreadful things to make "musical" instruments. Which of these "instruments" has never been played in a public performance? TRUE/FALSE

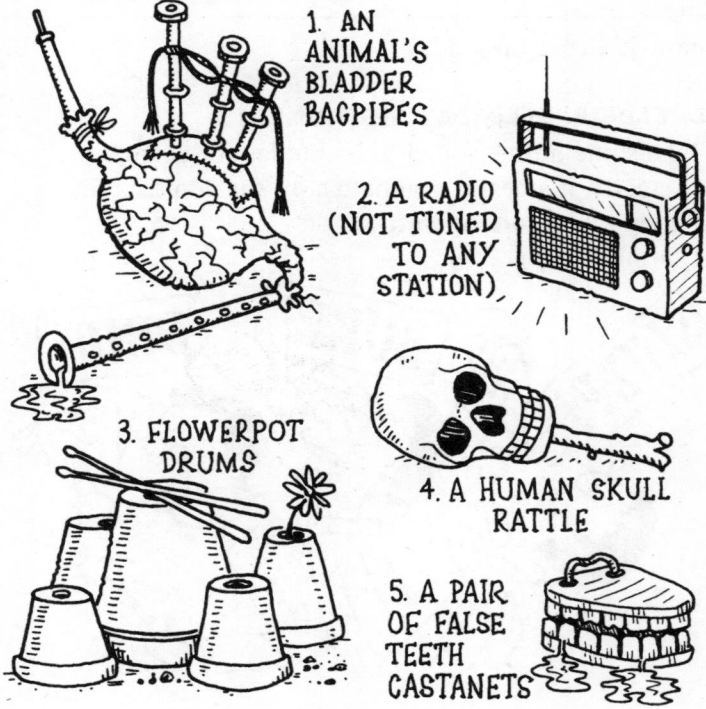

1. AN ANIMAL'S BLADDER BAGPIPES

2. A RADIO (NOT TUNED TO ANY STATION)

3. FLOWERPOT DRUMS

4. A HUMAN SKULL RATTLE

5. A PAIR OF FALSE TEETH CASTANETS

Now it's your turn...

DREADFUL EVERYDAY INSTRUMENTS

Take some milk or other glass bottles for example...
(Actually, it's best if you polish off the contents first.)

Playing a lemonade bottle

1 Drink (slurp)

Dare you discover … how to play bottles?

You will need:
Three identical bottles
Some water
A spoon

What you do:
1 Fill a bottle with 2.5 cm of water.
2 Puff a short breath across its rim. The sound you hear is the air inside vibrating up and down.
3 Half-fill another bottle with water.
4 Puff across its rim as before.

What do you notice?
a) The sound is higher from the nearly empty bottle.
b) The sound is lower from the nearly empty bottle.
c) The sound is much louder in the half empty bottle.

Now try this…
What you do:
1 Fill the third bottle three-quarters full with water.
2 Line the bottles up in a row.
3 Tap each one with a spoon.

What do you notice?
a) The sound is higher from the nearly empty bottle.
b) The sound is lower in the nearly empty bottle.
c) When you tap the bottles water splashes everywhere.

KRAZY KAZOOS

Kazoos make an interesting if slightly weird sound.
Here's how to make your own.

You will need:
A piece of greaseproof paper
A comb

What you do:
1 Fold the greaseproof paper round the comb as shown.
2 Press your lips to the side of the kazoo as shown.
3 Here's the tricky bit. Put your lips together so they're
only just open and try humming a tune. The air should be
blowing out of your mouth and making the paper
vibrate.
4 The wacky sound effects are made by the vibrating
paper.

WARNING – Your kazoo is guaranteed to drive any adult within earshot crackers in around three seconds. Playing your kazoo while they're watching television, after bedtime, in the car or any public place can seriously damage your pocket money.

Bet you never knew!
In the 1970s one of the largest kazoos in the history of the universe was created in a factory in New York State. It was roughly the size of a door and needed five people to play it. (It's definitely a VERY SILLY idea to make your kazoo this big.)

RULER RACKETS
You will need:
One 30 cm ruler (either wood or plastic)
A table

What you do:
1 Place the ruler half on and half off the table. Hold it in place with one hand on the table.
2 Flick the free end of the ruler with your other hand.

3 You can experiment with different lengths of ruler off the table to make different notes. You'll find that you hear deeper notes when more of the ruler is off the table. Yep, you got it, it's all to do with that larger area vibrating more slowly and making a lower sound.

HORRIBLE HEALTH WARNING!

Don't be tempted to play your ruler during a science lesson. Otherwise your teacher might be tempted to play the ruler, too – using you as a sounding board!

Sonic spoons

Spoons can make some brilliant sounds. The easiest way to do this is to bash two spoons together. This is best done in the privacy of your own home and not in the school canteen. Please note: I did say knock spoons together and not to knock the spoon on...

a) Any nearby priceless ornaments. This could have an effect you'll live to regret.

b) Your teacher's head. The effects of this on you would be too painful to mention.

SUPER SPOON STEREO SYSTEMS

If you want to experience vibrant spoon sounds in stupendous stereo try this high-tech method. Go on, it's dreadfully awesome.

What you need:
Some string
A metal spoon

— LIKE THIS!

What you do:
1 Tie some string round the metal spoon as shown.
2 Press the ends of the strings to the opening of your ear holes. Allow the spoon to bang against a tabletop. (No, I don't mean the objects in **a)** and **b)** above.) Incredible sound effect – isn't it? Solid objects like the string are very good at carrying sound waves, remember? That's why you can hear the various sounds made by the vibrating spoon amazingly well.
3 Try holding the spoon by one string whilst tapping it gently with a metal spoon. You could even try playing a tune.
4 Try experimenting with different sized spoons and metal objects such as metal colanders, egg tongs, etc.

DREADFUL SOUND EFFECTS

Of course, there's much more to sounds than making noise. How about making scary sound effects too? You could try recording them on tape to see how effective they are. Then see if your friends can guess what each one is.

A HIDEOUS SQUEAK

Rub a piece of polystyrene on a window. The squeaks you hear are actually sound waves caused as tiny lumps on the polystyrene rub quickly over bumps on the glass. Remember – don't make these noises at the wrong moment or you'll hear some hideous squeaks from your family too!

A HORRIBLE GIANT FLY

What you need:

An old cereal bag (that's the waxy bag inside a cereal packet)

A glass

A fly

What you do:

1 Catch a fly by putting a plastic glass over it. Be gentle – remember flies have feelings too.

2 Quickly put the cereal bag under the glass and gently shake the fly into it.

3 Hold the bag to your ear. The fly's footsteps and buzzing resonates in the bag and it sounds seriously dreadful.

4 After you've finished let the fly go outside. After all this is no ordinary hairy little fly – it's a hairy little sound-effect superstar.

A PHANTOM TWEET

What you need:
Half a used matchstick
40 cm of thin string
A small cottage cheese carton and lid
A pair of scissors
Sellotape

What you do:
1 Cut a 1-cm-wide hole in the side of the carton.
2 Ask for help to make a small hole in the bottom of the carton – just wide enough for the string to go through.
3 Tie one end of the string to the matchstick. Place the matchstick inside the carton and thread the string through the hole in its bottom.
4 Tape the lid in place on the carton.
5 Swing the carton on the string around your head to make a ghostly tweeting sound.

HORRIBLE HEALTH WARNING!

Don't be a tweet – er, twit. Never swing your tweeter anywhere near people or priceless ornaments. Otherwise you can expect dreadful tweetment from your parents.

STRIKING SOUND EFFECTS

The incredible thing about the human brain is, not only can we hear sounds but we instantly know what they are. We can remember them from the first time we heard them. So you can recognize the curious choking spluttering noise made by a teacher who is just about to lose their temper and dive for cover.

If you listen to a play on the radio you will hear sound effects for things going on in the play. So how sound is your judgement? Can you match the sound effect to the way it's produced? You won't be disqualified for trying the sound effects out. Try recording them on tape and then play them back with the volume turned up.

1 A GALLOPING HORSE

2 A SLAP ROUND THE CHOPS

3 RAIN BEATING ON A ROOF

4 FOOTSTEPS ON A GRAVEL DRIVE

5 A COLLAPSING HOUSE

a) CRUSHING A WOODEN MATCHBOX

b) SCRUNCHING A BALL OF STIFF PAPER

c) SHAKING DRIED PEAS IN A BOX

d) SMACKING A HOT WATER BOTTLE

e) BEATING TWO YOGHURT POTS TOGETHER

Answers: 1 e), 2 d), 3 c), 4 b), 5 a)

If you had a go at recording those sounds, you probably won't be surprised to hear that these sound effects have all been recorded for use in radio plays. And if you want to find out more about the weird world of recorded sound, just press the button and tune in to the next chapter.

READ ON AND BE AMAZED!

ROTTEN RECORDINGS

No sound lasts for ever – it dies away as the vibrations lose energy. This is good news if the sound happens to be dreadful. No matter how rotten your school concert solo, once it's over – it's over. But thanks to the incredible invention of recorded sound your family can listen to the entire school performance full of embarrassing hiccups, raspberries and screeches over and over and over again. ARRGGGGGGHHH! So who's to blame?

Hall of fame: Thomas Edison (1847–1931)
Nationality: American
Young Thomas or Al as he was called (from Alva, his middle name) was useless at school. (Now where have we heard that before?) Al's teacher told him…

And told his mum…

Actually, what no one seemed to realize was young Al couldn't hear too well. So he couldn't hear his teachers clearly. Lucky for him, considering the cruel things they said. But it was even luckier that Al's parents were kind and understanding. They took their son away from school and taught him at home. "Luck!" I hear you say. "Sounds more like a miracle to me!"

Al loved it. He turned his dad's wood yard into a chemistry lab and burnt it down when an explosive experiment went wrong. At the age of ten he set up another chemistry lab in the basement. This was the scene for loads of dreadfully fascinating experiments that generally resulted in horrible smells, burnt clothes and wrecked furniture.

Then, at the age of 12, Al decided to get a job and started work selling newspapers and drinks on local trains. This gave him lots of time to convert the baggage carriage into a mobile chemistry lab resulting in ... you guessed it ... horrible smells, burnt clothes and wrecked furniture.

Young Al wasn't cut out to be a newspaper seller. (His destiny lay as an inventor and a scientist.) His next job was working as a telegraph clerk on his own each night.

But he found the job really tedious so he invented a machine that sent a special telegraph signal every hour to show his bosses he was still awake – while he slept. The machine worked perfectly until one night an incoming signal came in while Al was in the land of Nod. He'd hit the sack and as a result he got it – the sack that is.

For a while Al drifted from job to job. He wore scruffy clothes and rarely washed and didn't care what he ate. (Know anyone like that?) He often worked at night so he could spend the day doing scientific experiments. His big break came in New York.

He was snoozing in a friend's office because he had nowhere else to stay when the stock ticker broke. This was a kind of telegraph used to send financial information. Of course, Al was a telegraph wizard, and he fixed the machine and made it work better than before. The company bosses were so impressed that they offered Al a job.

In fact, the Western Union Telegraph Company also took an interest in the bright young man and offered him a huge contract to invent an improved telegraph. Could you achieve this kind of success? How would you measure up against the great Edison?

THOMAS EDISON QUIZ

Imagine you are Thomas A Edison. All you need to do is decide how you would act in each situation.

1 You have a technical problem with an urgent order for stock tickers. How do you solve it?

a) You lock the lab and send everyone on holiday until the problem is solved. (People have good ideas on holiday.)

b) You lock your entire staff in the lab until the problem is solved.

I'VE GOT A TECHNICAL PROBLEM WITH MY TICKER, SIR. CAN I GO HOME?

c) You lock yourself in the lab for 60 hours without food until the problem is solved.

2 You have a serious scientific problem to tackle. What do you do?

a) Call a meeting of your scientific staff and argue the question over. Make sure everyone has their say.

b) Shut yourself in a cupboard and stay there until you think of an answer.

c) Make your staff undertake dangerous experiments to prove your theories.

3 In 1871 you marry a young lady called Mary Sitwell. How do you spend your wedding day?

a) You take the week off work.

b) You go to the wedding but spend the rest of the day at the lab working on science problems.

c) You spend the whole day at the lab and ask your best man to stand in for you at the wedding.

4 You decide to improve the telephone. The acid-filled speaker invented by Alexander Graham Bell wasn't that good at picking up sounds. You look around for an alternative and discover that carbon granules are ideal for passing on the sound waves. How many substances do you test first?

a) 200 **b)** 2,000 **c)** 20,000

During the 1870s Edison made a series of brilliant inventions. After working on the telephone he became interested in the idea of storing and passing on sound waves, and in 1877 he made an unheard-of discovery.

Sounds Amazing

DOH, RAY, ME, ARGHH!

THIS WAS HIS LAST RECORDING JUST BEFORE THE ACCIDENT

TRUMPET
SOUND CYLINDER
DIAPHRAGM
NEEDLE

Flabbergast your friends with a phonograph – the latest amazing invention from Thomas A. Edison. It's really true, you *can* record and enjoy music in your own home. And guess what? Long after the singer is dead and gone, you'll still be able to hear their voice on the stunning sound cylinder!

THE SMALL PRINT
1 It's not our fault if the sound's a bit faint and scratchy.
2 Beware - the cylinder might fall apart at any moment. (That's not our fault either, OK?)

1 HOW TO RECORD YOUR OWN VOICE

SPEAK HERE
SOUND MAKES DIAPHRAGM VIBRATE
DIAPHRAGM MAKES NEEDLE VIBRATE - NEEDLE CUTS WAVY GROOVE IN CYLINDER
TURN CYLINDER

2 HOW TO LISTEN TO YOUR VOICE

SOUND WAVES FROM DIAPHRAGM PASS OUT THROUGH TRUMPET
GROOVES MAKE NEEDLE VIBRATE
TURN CYLINDER
NEEDLE MAKES DIAPHRAGM VIBRATE

The phonograph, as it was called, was a massive success. When one of Edison's workers took a machine to show the French Academy of Science, the scientists were so thrilled that they wanted to spend the rest of the evening playing with it.

Bet you never knew!
Amongst the weird and wacky inventions inspired by the phonograph was a talking watch made by a Mr Sivan of Geneva, Switzerland. The watch contained a tiny phonograph that called out, "WAKE UP, GET UP!" first thing in the morning. Edison himself invented a talking doll containing a phonograph that said, "Mama" or "Papa" and told stories.

Trouble was, those fragile foil cylinders really did fall apart after a couple of plays. Other inventors developed phonographs that used wax cylinders instead of foil, and then, after 1888, discs on a flat turntable. The gramophone was born.

HORRIBLE HEALTH WARNING!

Whatever you do never, never, never tamper with one of your mum's or dad's classic vinyl LPs. Grown-ups can be very strange about these dusty relics which remind them of their distant youth. A gramophone stylus needle can press down with a force of 13,608 kg per 6.5 square cm. Ignore this warning and you can expect to feel the same pressure on your head.

Of course, the march of technology has moved on dramatically since those far off prehistoric days when your parents were rather less crinkly than they are today. When you hit the big time you'll have some brilliant machines to play your latest sounds. Want to find out more?

COULD YOU BE A POP STAR? STEP 4: SERIOUS SOUND MACHINES

Once you've recorded your first single you're sure to want to listen to it again and again. And get your friends to listen to it too and even their mums and dads, pet gerbils, etc. So what sort of sound system will show you in the best possible light? Jez and Wanda are back again to help you decide.

CLASSIC CASSETTE PLAYER

Jez is fiddling with this cassette recorder. This machine turns sound into magnetic signals and back again. Sounds incredible, doesn't it?

SOUND CAUSES THE RECORDING HEAD TO MAKE A MAGNETIC SIGNAL

WOOF!

MIKE PICKS UP SOUND WAVES

THE SIGNAL MAKES A PATTERN OF MAGNETIC BITS ON THE TAPE

And now Wanda's going to demonstrate what happens when you play a tape.

MAGNETIC BITS ON THE TAPE HEAD FIRE ELECTRICAL PULSES

WOOF!

AMPLIFIER TURNS THE PULSES INTO SOUNDS THAT MAKE UP THE DOG'S WOOF

Jez and Wanda are investigating a CD player. A CD stores sounds as tiny pits on its surface. The CD player turns these into electrical signals … here's what happens.

153

When Jez plays the CD disc it spins round mega fast…
And here's where it gets really technical…

Look inside the CD player and you'll find how to turn the pulses back into sounds.

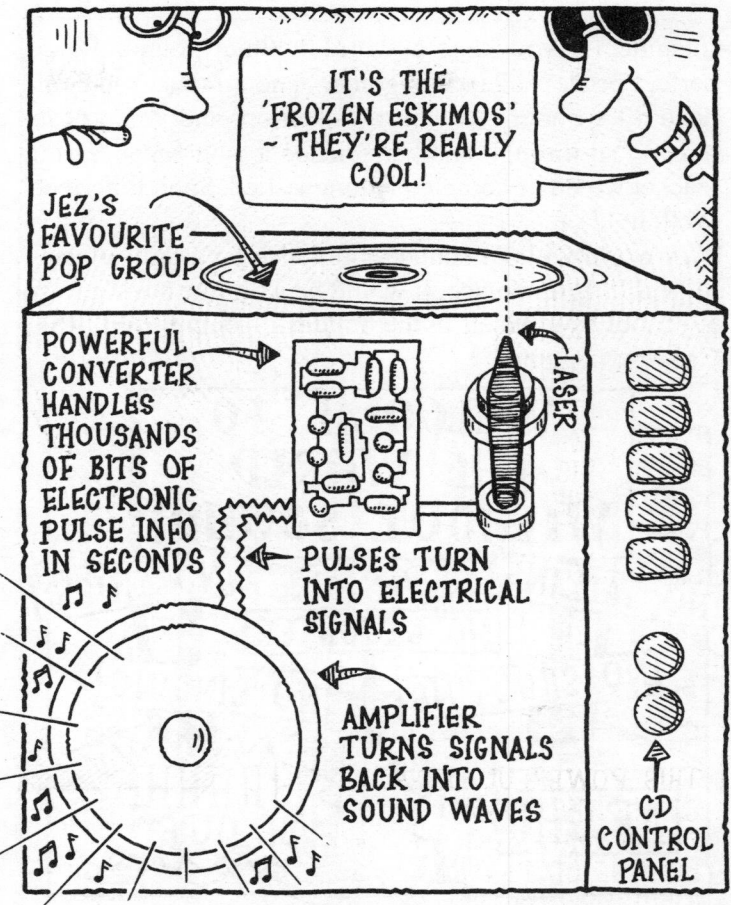

If it all works the CD player produces better sound quality than the tape. Tapes can get twisted or dirty which spoils the sound quality. But the laser beam only picks up the pits on the CD rather than any bits of grease or fluff on its surface.

SOUNDING IT OUT

Imagine (if you can) a world without sound. Peace, perfect peace – silence is golden, and all that. You could doze off without ever being woken up, and you'd never have to sit through another science lesson because your teacher would be completely tongue-tied. Sounds perfect? Well, hold on…

A world without sound would also be a dull, lifeless, joyless kind of a place. It would be a bit like having to go to school by yourself in the holidays – only far WORSE. Can you imagine it?

There'd be no games of football (can you imagine a totally quiet game?), no chatting on the phone, no one telling jokes, and definitely NO rude noises. There'd be NO FUN. Nothing but a vast horribly gloomy silence. Sounds dreadful. Could you bear it?

OK, you can turn the volume up again now, and appreciate some of the good sounds you can tune into…

And every year brings sensational sound discoveries… Time was when the most thrilling sound experience you could look forward to was listening to your grandad tinkling a dodgy old piano and singing awful old songs. Nowadays you can listen to whatever you want, whenever you want, and you can pick up a phone and natter to people on the other side of the world.

BUT SOUND SCIENCE DISCOVERIES AREN'T JUST FOR FUN…

At this very minute scientists are working on new and incredible sound discoveries. Discoveries that will make it easier for people to keep in contact and find out new information. Here are a few that we're already using…

SUPERSONIC SOUND SIGNALS

• Optical fibres send signals as pulses of light to be made into sounds by a phone. So your voice can be turned into an incredible flashing light code. It's then turned back into sound waves so the person on the other end of the phone can understand you.

• Video phones transmit not only the sound of your voice but also live pictures of you talking. (This could be embarrassing if someone called when you were on the toilet.)

• A computer can actually chat to you. Here's how...

1 Someone speaks words into a machine that turns sound into electronic pulses.

2 These pulses are stored as codes in the computer's vast memory.

3 When the computer speaks the codes are turned back into pulses.

4 And these are converted into sounds which come out of the computer's speakers.

And sounds can even make people *healthier.*

STUNNING SURGICAL SOUND SYSTEMS

• Ultrasound pulses blast kidney stones. The vibrations break up the painful stones but don't harm the wobbly flesh that surrounds them. Pow!

• Ultrasound scans can produce SONAR-style pictures of unborn babies inside their mums. The picture can be used to check that the babies are OK.

EVERYTHING'S FINE, SHE'S GIVING US THE THUMBS UP!

Sometimes science seems boring, and at times the boring bits can sound really dreadful. But outside the classroom there's a great big world bursting with sound. A huge exciting vibrant world alive with loud, shocking, shrieking, spectacular noises, and thanks to science it's getting more amazing all the time.

The future sounds dreadfully exciting, doesn't it?

SOUNDS DREADFUL

DREADFUL

QUIZ

Now find out if you're a
Sounds Dreadful expert!

So – reckon you've understood ears and sussed out sound? Take these quick quizzes and find out whether you've really been listening carefully or whether these words have fallen on deaf ears...

Horrible human sounds

Humans are among the nastiest, noisiest creatures in the animal kingdom. We might not be able to hear as well as other animals, but we can distinguish between thousands of different sounds – and, boy, can we make a racket...

1 In which part of the ear are the ear bones found?
a) Middle ear
b) Inner ear
c) Ear drum

2 Which of the following can cause deafness?
a) Listening to birdsong.
b) Listening to loud music.
c) Listening to your science teacher droning on.

3 What hideous human sound is made by air escaping from the stomach?

a) A fart

b) A burp

c) A whistle

4 What is the fluid in your ears' semi-circular canals for?

a) It helps you balance.

b) It makes you sneeze.

c) It picks up sound vibrations.

5 What is a cochlea implant?

a) An ear trumpet made of brass to help the hard of hearing.

b) A flap of skin added to the ear lobe to help the hard of hearing.

c) A tiny radio receiver placed under the skin to help the hard of hearing.

6 What is the more common name for cerumen?
a) Ear lobe
b) Ear wax
c) Snot

7 What would a conversation be like in space?
a) Slower – it takes sound waves longer to pass through a vacuum.
b) Faster – sound waves travel more quickly through a vacuum.
c) Nothing – sound waves can't travel through a vacuum.

8 What horrible body noise is made by a vibrating uvula?
a) A snore
b) A humming in your head
c) A fart

Answers:
1a; 2b; 3b; 4a; 5c; 6b; 7c; 8a

Super sound waves

Sound is a bit like the sea – OK, it's not wet and full of fish but it does come in waves. So are you wired up to making sense of those weird waves of sound?

1 Which part of the ear vibrates when sound waves hit it? (Clue: Your teacher might *beat* it out of you!)

2 What unit is used for measuring sound? (Clue: 1 bel = ten of them)

3 What sound is heard when sound waves hit a solid surface? (Clue: What sound is heard when sound waves hit a solid surface?)

4 Where do the vibrations that cause humming originate? (Clue: Come on – you *nose*...)

5 What noise do you hear when you break the sound barrier? (Clue: sounds like Chronic Doom)

6 What carries sound signals to the brain? (Clue: You might be shaking with these)

7 What sound technology was used to try and find the Loch Ness Monster? (Clue: … and yet *so far*)

8 What amazing machine did Alexander Graham Bell invent to carry sound waves thousands of kilometres? (Clue: It was a good call)

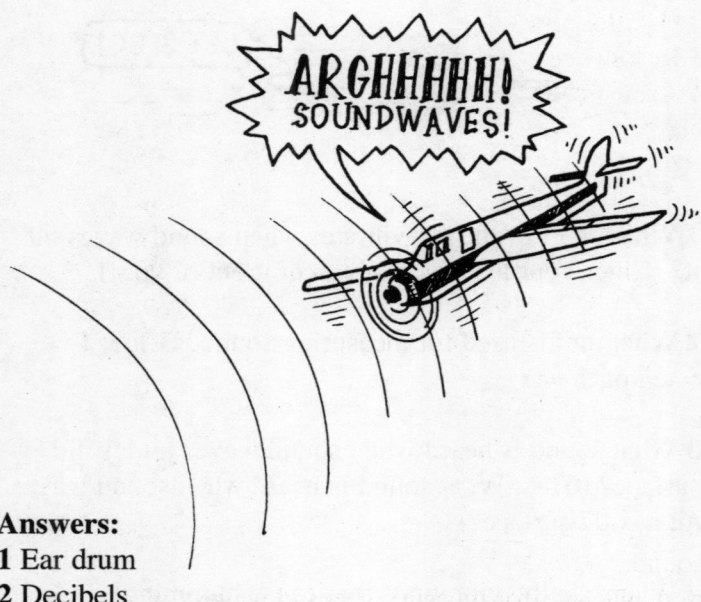

Answers:
1 Ear drum
2 Decibels
3 Echo
4 Nostrils
5 Sonic boom
6 Nerves
7 SONAR
8 Telephone

Strange sound sayings

The science of sound is filled with strange vocabulary. Have you been listening carefully enough to match the following weird words with their deafening definitions?

1 Frequency

2 Oscilloscope

3 Resonance

4 Acoustics

5 Amplitude

6 Ultrasound

7 Tone

8 Harmonics

a) A group of different tones.

b) A sound with just one frequency.

c) Sound above the range of human hearing.

d) The number of vibrations a second that make up a sound.

e) A machine for measuring sound waves.

f) Sound vibrations at a certain frequency.

g) The science of sound production, transmission and effects.

h) How loud a sound is.

Answers:
1d; 2e; 3f; 4g; 5h; 6c; 7b; 8a

Strange sound facts

Scientists have made many amazing discoveries about sound and how it works. Some are almost unbelievable. And some perhaps shouldn't be believed... Can you tell the fact from the fiction among these strange sound facts?

1 Sound travels much more quickly through air than it does through metal.
2 Sound waves can knock holes in solid objects.
3 The variety of sounds a human can make is fewer than those of other mammals.
4 The sound you hear when you crack your knuckles is just a load of old gas.
5 Each of your ears hears sounds of slightly different pitches.
6 If you put a seashell to your ear the sound you hear is the sound of your own blood moving through your body.
7 Snores can be as loud as a pneumatic drill.
8 A whip makes a cracking sound because its tip moves faster than the speed of sound.

Answers:

1 FALSE. Sound travels 15 times faster through steel than it does through air!

2 TRUE. A machine built by NASA could make 210 decibels of sound – and could damage more than just ear drums…

3 FALSE. Humans can make many more different sounds than other animals because their tongues and lips can move in so many different ways.

4 TRUE. It's the sound of nitrogen gas bubbles bursting.

5 TRUE. The right ear often hears higher noises than the left.

6 FALSE. Sorry, it's just the boring old sounds around you resonating in the shell. It works just as well with your granny's tea cup – just make sure it's empty first.

7 TRUE. Snores have been known to reach over 90 decibels – as loud as a drill and loud enough to cause damage to your ears!

8 TRUE. It's a *striking* sonic boom!

Amazing animal noises

You might know what it means when your cat purrs or your dog barks, but animals have many amazingly complicated ways of saying different things. Can you recognize these cunning creatures just by the sound of their voices?

1 My voice sounds like a series of curious clicks, but I don't use vocal chords – I just pass air through air sacs in my head!

2 I stand a much better chance of romancing a lady because vibrating air-filled pouches in my croaking throat make my song of luurrve even louder.

3 I make a s-s-special s-s-sound by vibrating pieces of bone in my tail to warn that I'm in a bad mood.

4 I just rub my legs together, and hey presto, a cacophony of sound shimmers through the quiet evening as I chat with my friends.

5 My eyesight is poor so I emit tiny squeaks – too high for you humans to hear – to find my way around.

6 My moods aren't hard to spot – I will purr, grunt, moan, growl and snarl. But my scariest sound can carry for kilometres across the savannah…

7 I can get a message to a mate more than 800 km away. My strange song starts in my throat and moves to a bag linked to my nose!

8 My ears have a wide range of motion, so I can hear sounds up to 16 km away – and I'll react to them by throwing back my head and making my own distinctive sound in the moonlight…

a) Whale
b) Bat
c) Dolphin
d) Grasshopper
e) Rattlesnake
f) Wolf
g) Frog
h) Lion

Answers:
1c; 2g; 3e; 4d; 5b; 6h; 7a; 8f

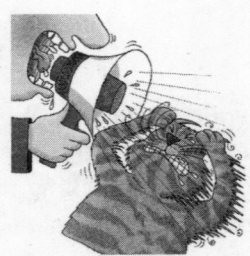

HORRIBLE INDEX

172

175

HORRIBLE SCIENCE

PAINFUL POISON

NICK ARNOLD   illustrated by **TONY DE SAULLES**

■SCHOLASTIC

www.horrible-science.co.uk

www.nickarnold-website.com
www.tonydesaulles.co.uk

Scholastic Children's Books,
Euston House, 24 Eversholt Street,
London NW1 1DB, UK

A division of Scholastic Ltd
London ~ New York ~ Toronto ~ Sydney ~ Auckland
Mexico City ~ New Delhi ~ Hong Kong

First published in the UK by Scholastic Ltd, 2004
This edition published 2009

Text copyright © Nick Arnold, 2004
Illustrations copyright © Tony De Saulles, 2004

ISBN 978 1407 10957 2

Page layout services provided by Quadrum Solutions Ltd, Mumbai, India
Printed and bound by CPI Group (UK) Ltd, Croydon, CR0 4YY

19

The rights of Nick Arnold and Tony De Saulles to be identified as the author and
illustrator of this work respectively has been asserted by them in accordance
with the Copyright, Designs and Patents Act, 1988.

CONTENTS

Nick Arnold has been writing stories and books since he was a youngster, but never dreamt he'd find fame writing about poison. His research involved turning a teacher into a zombie and testing the vomit goblet and he enjoyed every minute of it.

When he's not delving into Horrible Science, he spends his spare time eating pizza, running and thinking up corny jokes (though not all at the same time).

Tony De Saulles picked up his crayons when he was still in nappies and has been doodling ever since. He takes Horrible Science very seriously and even agreed to make friends with a black widow spider. Fortunately, he has made a full recovery.

When he's not out with his sketchpad, Tony likes to write poetry and eat liquorice, though he hasn't written any poetry about liquorice yet.

Introduction

BEWARE! I'm worried that this horrible book could be too scary for you!

But this book's about poison and lots of people think poison is a scary subject. Especially if they drink poison by mistake – now that would be DEAD SCARY!

OK – but I have to warn you that this book is more scary than a chemistry class and more terrifying than a terrible test. In fact when we tried to measure the fear factor in this book by wiring it to a fright-detector, the machine blew up!

So it's sure to send shivers down your spine. Won't that put you off?

Yes, but this book is about the sick secrets of killer chemicals and the painful effects of drinking them. And it tells you which poisons turn people pink or blue or yellow and all about poisonous plants, snakes, spiders and other cruel creatures…

And then there's the *seriously* sickening stuff like how to turn your sister into a mummy … while she's still alive!

But I really shouldn't be telling you all this…
Maybe I should take this book away?

Oh well, read on if you think you're brave enough. BUT DON'T HAVE NIGHTMARES!

KILLER CHEMICALS

Let's start with a *seriously* scary fact. The whole world is oozing and dripping and squelching with poisons…

• There are poisonous gases.

• And poisonous plants.

• And poisonous animals.

MR STINKS THE CHEMISTRY TEACHER

But what is a poison? Well, read on – you're about to find out!

SO WHAT IS A POISON?

A poison is a substance that upsets the chemical workings of your body. To show you what I mean let's

7

turn Mr Stinks into a giant test tube and check out what's going on inside him... Like any other human body, Mr Stinks' test-tube body is fizzing with billions of chemical changes (or "reactions" as scientists call them).

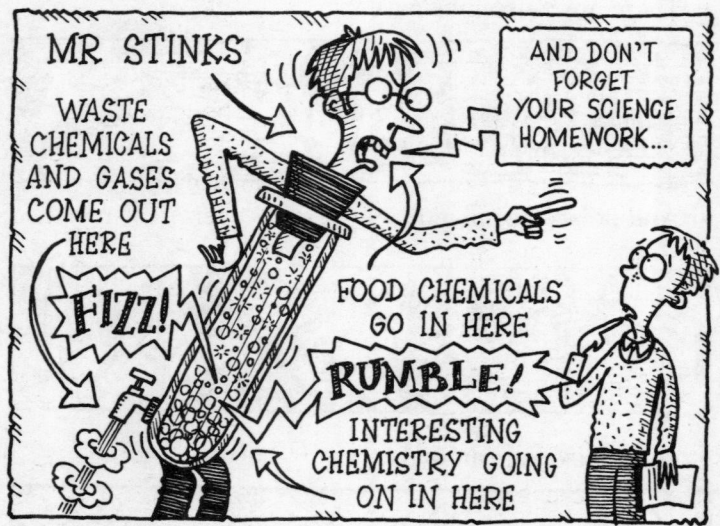

MR STINKS

WASTE CHEMICALS AND GASES COME OUT HERE

AND DON'T FORGET YOUR SCIENCE HOMEWORK...

FIZZ!

FOOD CHEMICALS GO IN HERE

RUMBLE!

INTERESTING CHEMISTRY GOING ON IN HERE

But poisons mess up these crucial chemical changes. You can imagine a chemical reaction as kids playing a playground game. It might look like chaos, but the game has rules and everyone has a part to play. A poison is like a gang of bullies rampaging through the playground. The bullies chase away the other kids and take over the game and play it to rules that they make up themselves.

In other words, pesky poisons ruin reactions!

SO WHY IS A POISON DEADLY?

Without chemical reactions the poor old body can't stay alive. Let's just take another peek at Mr Stinks. He needs chemical reactions every time...

• His brain sends signals to his muscles.

• His muscles move when and where he wants them to.
• His guts digest his food.
• His body makes energy using sugar from his food and oxygen from the air. (The body needs energy to stay alive and power more chemical reactions.)

But if these chemical reactions get messed up by a poison, they may not happen. And Mr Stinks' body might not work properly or even grind to a halt … forever.

THE LETHAL LOW-DOWN ON TYPES OF POISON

Now, as I said, the world's full of poisons – here are some of the main types…
• Poisonous gases such as carbon monoxide and chlorine – pages 47 and 52 will leave you breathless.
• Poisonous metals such as lead and mercury. You can dig them up on pages 61 and 65 – but don't take a *shine* to them!
• Poisonous substances called metalloids – these include arsenic and antimony. They're on pages 72 and 69, but don't forget your sick bag!

• Poisons made by plants such as deadly nightshade. You can gasp at the gruesome greens in your garden on page 81.

• Poisons made by bugs and animals – including the black widow spider and the green mamba snake. Page 94 will have you howling with horror.

• Acids like nitric acid (see below) and alkaline chemicals such as drain cleaner. These are so strong they can actually dissolve you. Page 128 is fizzing with facts.

Of course, some poisons have even more horrible effects than others...

HORRIBLE FAMILY WARNING!

POO, BLAH BLAH, SICK...

Do NOT read this next bit aloud at family meal-times. Failure to obey this warning will result in your supper being fed to the cat...

BUT I'M NOT FEELING TOO HUNGRY!

• Phosphorus (page 68) makes poo and sick glow in the dark.

• Nitric acid causes white frothy snot, burning pain and other effects too revolting for a respectable book like this. Victorian doctors used watered-down nitric acid as an anti-itching lotion – but that was a gloopy loopy lotion notion!

• Sodium nitrite stops the blood from taking up oxygen. Oxygen gives the blood its cheerful red colour and without it the body turns bright blue.

But before we go any further there are some people you must meet. They're our very own poison experts, Count Orlando Vomito and his assistant Donna Venoma...

So what's your favourite poison, Count?

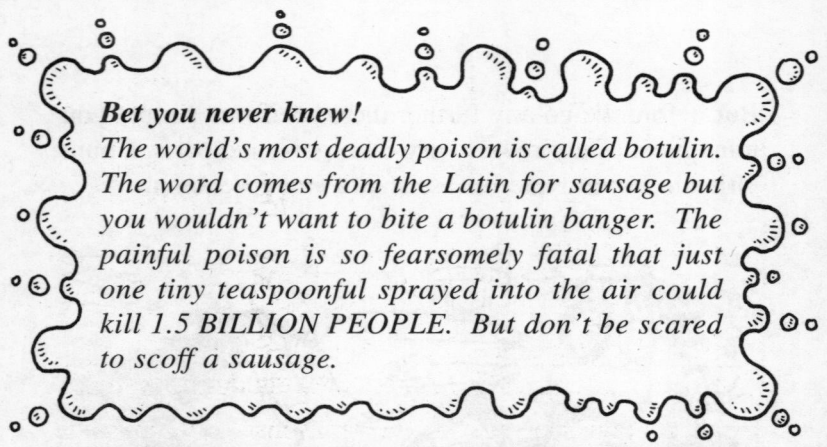

A SURPRISING AND SCARY FACT ABOUT POISONS

Don't panic! Are you sitting calmly? Good – I don't want to worry you but you probably eat and drink poisons regularly! In fact, I'm sure you had some today! I said, DON'T PANIC! Your lunch didn't kill you, did it? These chemicals are only poisonous if you have too much of them at once...

SCHOOL DINNER – REVOLTING BUT NOT POISONOUS

1 Water is a poison! If you drink too much of it you upset the chemistry of your nerve signals. You feel confused and tired and can't stay awake. Death can follow. But don't worry – feeling like this on a Monday morning is nothing to do with the glass of water you drank on

12

Sunday night! Water is only poisonous if you slurp huge amounts in a few hours.

2 Salt contains not one but *two* poisons – sodium and chlorine. The poisons are bound together in the salt like two tied-up bullies.

But if you ate too much salt (and we're talking about quite a few tablespoonsful) it could upset the working of your nerves, with fatal results.

3 Sugar is a poison! It draws water from your body bits into your blood. And when your poor old body tries to get rid of the sugar by weeing, it dries out even more. Sugar can dry out a microbe and shrivel its slimy little body. But DON'T PANIC – since you're a lot bigger than a microbe, you'd need to scoff LOADS of sickly sugary sweets before you suffer this fate…

To find out how much sugar is poisonous let's spoil a teacher's day armed only with a sticky bun and a sickly smile…

TEACHER'S TEA-BREAK TEASER

You will need:

A sticky bun

A sickly smile

Knock politely on the staffroom door. Smile sweetly and offer your teacher the sticky bun. (Make sure you haven't taken a bite out of it first.) When your teacher bites the bun, you say...

THAT BUN CONTAINS POISON!

Take a few moments to enjoy the sight of your teacher turning green and clutching their throat ... and then explain that the bun contains sugar which can poison you.

And if you're feeling kind you can go on to explain that you need to eat an awful lot of sugar before it kills you. I mean your teacher would have to scoff about 100 sticky buns before they suffered the full fatal effects. And NO, you can't add 200 tablespoonfuls of sugar to your teacher's tea (or any other substance, including salt or anti-constipation pills). And if you do, you'll probably get extra science homework for life ... in prison!

HORRIBLE HEALTH WARNING!

NEVER try poisons or give them to anyone else — ever! Poisons can kill people and people who mess with poisons are dead stupid ... and sometimes end up stupidly dead.

HOW NOT TO GET POISONED!

Poisons are only deadly if they get into your body – and that means you're safe as long as you DON'T…

Eat or drink a poison. GULP!

Breathe or sniff it in. SNIFF!

SQUIRT!

Inject it into your blood.

DIP!

Touch it (some poisons can soak through the skin).

Bet you never knew!

In Denmark in 2000 a gang of girls sneaked into a toilet to sniff butane gas. These girls had the brain power of an absent-minded woodlouse. Butane is a poisonous gas used for cooking, so it burns easily. Guess what happened when one of the girls lit a cigarette?

KABOOM!

Well, what do you expect? Smoking is BAD for you! And the girls were smoking non-stop after they caught fire. As I said, taking poison is stupid and those girls were playing with fire.

BUT NO MATTER HOW SENSIBLE YOU ARE, ACCIDENTS CAN HAPPEN

And if they do I bet you'll be glad you read this next bit about what to do if someone gets poisoned. But before you start, I'd like to say a BIG thank you to our guests, New York private eye MI Gutzache and his faithful dog, Watson.

MI Gutzache has agreed to act the part of a poisoned person. Don't worry, Watson, he's just pretending!

IF THE PERSON ISN'T AWAKE...

1 Can you see what they've taken? Look for poison bottles, half-eaten food, etc. Are there any stains on their skin or clothes?

2 Dial 999 FAST and tell the experts what's happening. Take their advice.

3 Check the person's mouth for bits of food or false teeth or anything that might make them choke.

HEY, I AIN'T GOT NO FALSE TEETH!

4 Put them in the recovery position ... like this.

5 Make sure they're warm and comfortable.

OK, MR GUTZACHE, YOU CAN GET UP NOW. MR GUTZACHE?!

ZZZZZZ

Hmm – looks like we've made him a bit *too* warm and comfortable!

IF THE PERSON IS AWAKE...

1 Ask them what they've taken and how much.

2 Dial 999 FAST and tell the experts what's happening. Take their advice.

3 The poisoned person should see a doctor as soon as possible...

NURSE-GET THE STOMACH PUMP!

YIKES!

The doctor treating Gutzache is our medical expert for this book – Dr Grimgrave. Just don't try to make Dr G laugh – he hasn't got a sense of humour!

Doctors often give poisoned patients a substance called activated charcoal to soak up poisons in the stomach. But Dr G is using a stomach pump to suck up poisoned sick … DON'T TRY THIS AT HOME – and definitely not at mealtimes!

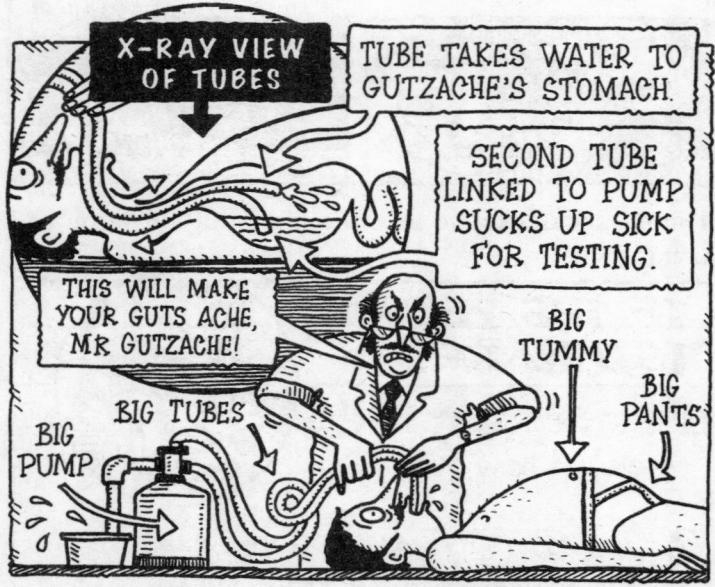

Having your stomach pumped out sounds like a painful experience, but I promise you it's NOTHING compared to being poisoned! And I know what that's like because I've been peeping at the next chapter. You'll need real GUTS to read on!

PAINFUL POISON PANGS

Count Vomito is keen to show us the effects of some of his rather large collection of poisons. And that's handy because this chapter is all about what poisons do to the body. All we need is a volunteer to test them on…

HEY, WHY IS EVERYONE LOOKING AT ME?

And now it's time for some sickeningly scary secrets about how poisons work…

HOW DO DIFFERENT TYPES OF POISON WORK?

WARNING!
SCIENTIFIC WORDS COMING UP!

You'd best close your eyes if you don't want to get blinded by science! Sorry, readers, in order to answer this question, we need to check out a few scientific words. (Mind you, with word-power like this you can sound off like a brainy boffin.)

The PROTEIN MOLECULES and ENZYMES in my CELLS contain millions of ATOMS!

YOU'RE TOO BRAINY FOR THIS SCHOOL, SIMPKINS!

NEARLY ALL THE SCIENCE WORDS YOU NEED TO MAKE SENSE OF THIS BOOK

ATOMS – Tiny blobs of matter that make up everything, including you.

MOLECULE – A group of atoms that join up to make up a chemical. It's a bit like you hanging out with your mates at school.

PROTEIN (pro-teen) – A type of molecule found in living things.

ENZYME (en-zime) – A type of protein that speeds up chemical reactions in the body. Without them the body's chemical reactions would be too slow to keep you alive.

CELLS – Your body is made up of billions of microscopic cells…

AND HERE'S HOW POISONS WORK…

1 Some poisons, such as cyanide (see page 92), block key enzymes, so the body dies.

2 Nerve poisons mess up nerve messages from your brain to your muscles. So vital orders such as "KEEP BREATHING" don't get through. Evil examples include nerve gas (page 54).

3 Some poisons dissolve body bits. These poisons are either acid like sulphuric acid (found in car batteries), or alkaline such as oven cleaners (see page 129).

4 And then there's irritant (irr-rit-tant) poisons. These poisons are irritating, like a little brother (only much more so). Irritating brothers make you feel sore and drinking irritant poison can make your guts sore and your stomach vomit. One especially irritating poison is arsenic (see page 72 for the painful particulars).

5 Narcotic (nar-kot-tick) poisons such as morphine (mor-feen) knock the victim out. But some, like strychnine (strick-neen) (see page 90), also have a nasty irritant effect or poison the nerves into the bargain. So the poor poisoned person gets double the trouble!

BIG PROBLEMS FOR LITTLE ANIMALS

But the way a poison works doesn't just depend on what poison it is. The amount of poison you've taken is also vital. Or to be more exact – how much you've taken *compared to your size.*

If you wanted to poison an elephant with a poisoned bun, you might need a bun the size of a football. But you can murder a mouse with a bun no bigger than a sugar lump. And to prove this point, the Count has set up an evil experiment involving MI Gutzache, an over-friendly fly and a container of fly spray...

I HAVE RIGGED THE FLY SPRAY SO IT SPRAYS BACKWARDS...

HEE HEE!

BUZZ

PSSSS!

ERK!

FORTUNATELY, GUTZACHE ISN'T KILLED. ALTHOUGH HE'S HIT BY ENOUGH FLY SPRAY TO KILL A FLY, HE WEIGHS 100,000 TIMES MORE THAN A FLY SO IT WOULD TAKE 100,000 TIMES MORE POISON TO FINISH HIM OFF

THE BODY STRIKES BACK

All this talk about how poisons poison people sounds seriously sickening but you'll be pleased to read that you're not completely defenceless. Your battling body has a few secret plans up its sleeve although they're a bit sickening too…

TOP-SECRET **BODY DEFENCE PLANS!**

(Don't let a poisoner see this on pain of death!) Message from the brain to all body bits... °°°○✲☽°

IT'S DEATH IF WE CAN'T GET RID OF POISON, SO MAKE SURE YOU KNOW OUR PLANS OF ACTION!

IMPORTANT WARNING!
These plans only work with small amounts of not totally deadly poisons such as antimony or arsenic. If there's lots of poison our defences will be overwhelmed. And if the poison's deadly enough to kill in minutes there won't be time to go through all our plans! Go straight to PLAN F!

PLAN A °°○ ✲ ○
The body eats or drinks some poison. The stomach and guts try to clear the poison by vomiting and diarrhoea. If the poison gets from the guts into the blood, try...

SPLURB!

BLURRRRGH!

22

PLAN B

We can get rid of some poisons straight away by weeing. And it might be worth giving Plan C a go...

PLAN C

Sweat the poison out through the skin. This plan is especially useful for poisons injected into the blood by snakes or spiders. Trouble is if we sweat and wee too much we'll be drying out and dying out! Hmm – looks like we could use some help and luckily there's still Plan D.

PLAN D

The liver to the rescue! Yes, the liver can get rid of poisons if anything can! Well, let's hope so because...

PLAN E
Er – there isn't one.

PLAN F
PANIC!!!!!!!

Now I bet you'd love to read how your life-saving liver can rescue you from a painful poisoning peril. Well, here's your chance...

Painful poison fact file

NAME: The life-saving liver

THE BASIC FACTS: **1** Your liver weighs as much as a bag and a half of sugar (about 1.5 kg) and snuggles under your ribs on the right side of your body.

2 The liver is like a sieve filtering your blood. In just five minutes it can filter all the blood in your body. In a year it filters enough blood to fill 23 milk tankers.

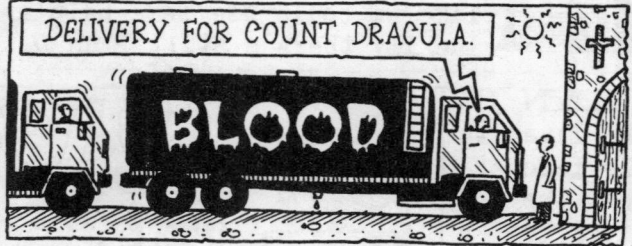

DELIVERY FOR COUNT DRACULA.

BLOOD

3 What the liver's after is vital chemicals you need to stay alive – such as vitamins. But it also filters out harmful poisons and treats them chemically to make them safer.

4 Some poisons are sent to the kidneys in the blood and got rid of in wee. Other poisons are chucked out in a digestive juice called bile. They end up in poo.

SO MAKE SURE YOU WASH YOUR HANDS PLOPERLY!

THE PAINFUL DETAILS: **1** At any time, the liver can only deal with small amounts of a poison. Too much poison can be too much for the liver. Poisons that are especially dangerous for the liver include phosphorus and some mushroom poisons.

2 If the liver is damaged it can't do its job. Waste chemicals that should go out in the bile turn the skin and eyeballs bright yellow.
As Dr Grimgrave says:

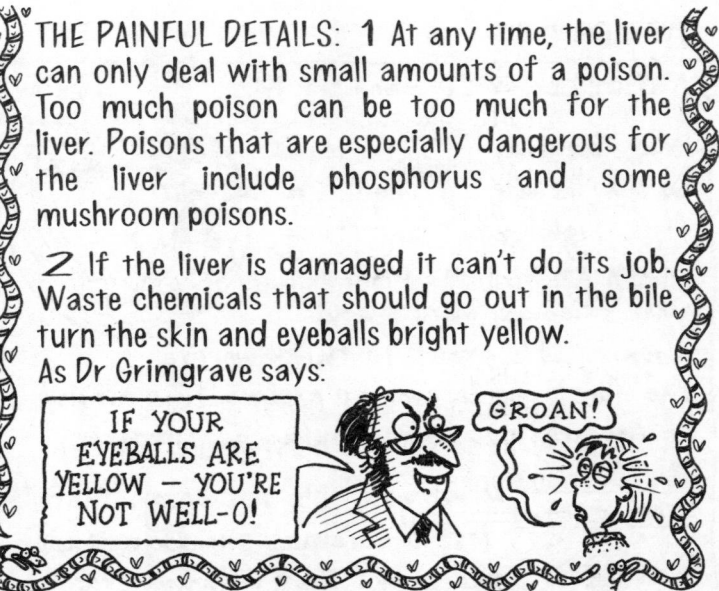

Remember how those lovely useful substances like water and sugar can be poisons if you take too much? Another too-much-of-a-good-thing chemical is vitamin A. You can find vitamin A in fish, eggs, butter, milk and carrots. And since it's stored in the liver – guess where else you can find it!

That's right, in *liver!* Without the vital vitamin you suffer from skin problems and poor eyesight in the dark. But if you have too much, it can *kill.* Australian explorer Douglas Mawson found this out the hard way. Here are the letters he might have written to his girlfriend...

LIVER OR DIE!

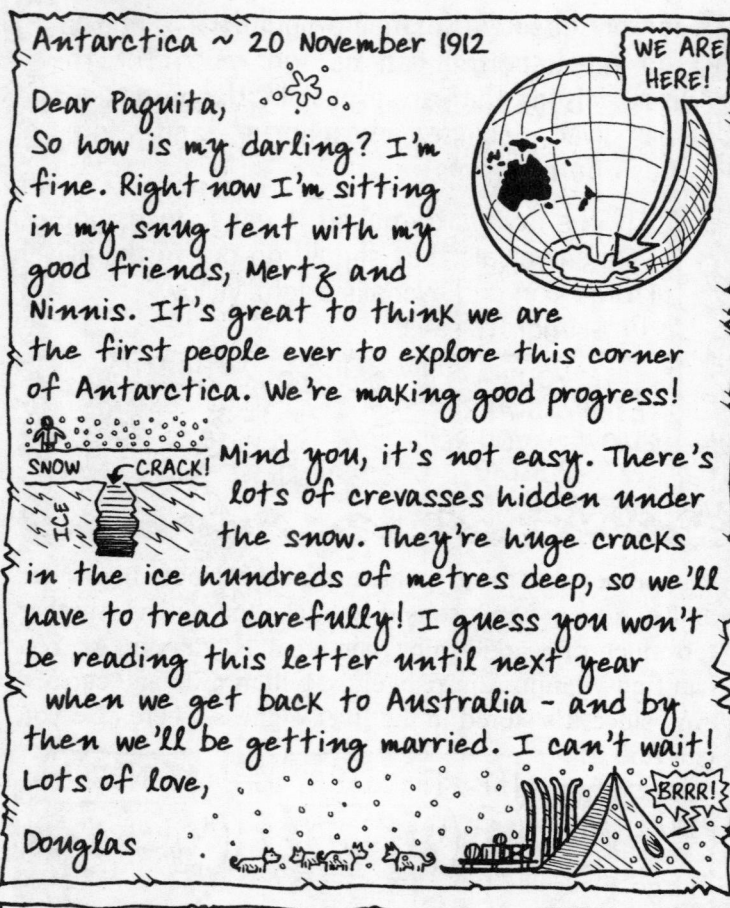

Antarctica ~ 20 November 1912

WE ARE HERE!

Dear Paquita,
So how is my darling? I'm fine. Right now I'm sitting in my snug tent with my good friends, Mertz and Ninnis. It's great to think we are the first people ever to explore this corner of Antarctica. We're making good progress!

SNOW CRACK! ICE

Mind you, it's not easy. There's lots of crevasses hidden under the snow. They're huge cracks in the ice hundreds of metres deep, so we'll have to tread carefully! I guess you won't be reading this letter until next year when we get back to Australia - and by then we'll be getting married. I can't wait! Lots of love,

BRRR!

Douglas

Antarctica ~ 13 December 1912

ARGH!

Dear Paquita,
Terrible news! Ninnis has fallen into one of those dreadful crevasses.

With Ninnis went the sledge carrying most of our food and equipment and the dogs that were pulling the sledge.

We spent the whole day calling into the crevasse, listening for a faint cry for help. But we heard nothing — Ninnis must be dead. At least we've still got one sledge and its dogs. If we ration our remaining food, eat the dogs one by one and feed the rest of the dogs on the bones, we might make it back to camp ...just. Here's hoping!

Love,
Douglas

PS Mertz says, "Glad you're not here!"

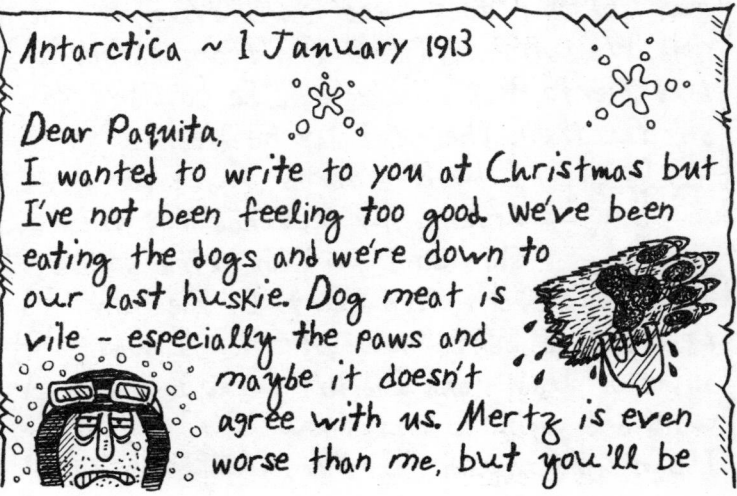

Antarctica ~ 1 January 1913

Dear Paquita,
I wanted to write to you at Christmas but I've not been feeling too good. We've been eating the dogs and we're down to our last huskie. Dog meat is vile — especially the paws and maybe it doesn't agree with us. Mertz is even worse than me, but you'll be

pleased to hear I'm giving him the
best meat - the liver.
Lots of love,

Douglas YUM YUM!

I don't care where I am any more
15 January 1913

SKIN NOT SNOW!

Dear Paquita,
Perhaps this letter will
be found on my frozen
body. By 6 January
Mertz felt worse. We
both had gut pains.
Our skin peeled, our hair was dropping
out and our toes were numb from the
cold. We were still 160 km from safety,
but Mertz had a fever and he couldn't go
any further. The next day he died.

I built a tomb of ice for my
friend. My feet had lost their
skin so I put on extra socks.
Every step hurt. In the next
few days I didn't know whether I was
alive or dead - and I didn't care. I
walk and walk. I don't know if
I can walk much further."

GASP!

Will we ever meet again?
Love you for ever!
Douglas

Antarctica
8 February 1913

SHIVER!

Dear Paquita,
You'll never guess what
happened! Somehow I found
my way to an ice cave
where I knew some food was
stored. Outside a storm raged.
I couldn't leave the cave even though the
camp was just 8 km away! At last the storm
cleared and I set off. I stumbled over a
rise and saw the camp ... and the ship
sailing away. I stared
after it in horror. They've
given up waiting, I
thought. If they don't
come back I'm a dead man...
I staggered into the empty camp. I gazed
about me in despair and that's when I saw
the men who had stayed behind to wait. I
looked so bad they didn't know who I was!
When I looked in the mirror I didn't know

29

who I was either. I look like a scruffy, skinny, smelly scarecrow. Worse, I'm as bald as an egg!

See you soon!
Love,
Douglas

♥ YOU!

PS If you don't want to marry me any more, I'll understand!

THE HERO'S RETURN

You'll be delighted to know that Douglas Mawson and the other men were able to call the ship back by radio. He returned to Australia a hero and Paquita still wanted to marry him…

But what was the mystery illness that killed Mertz and almost destroyed Mawson? Although no one knew it at the time, they'd been poisoned … by liver. The dogs were Arctic huskies. Like most Arctic animals they store huge amounts of vitamin A in their livers. Enough to cause gut pain, sickness, skin and hair loss if you ate it. Easily enough to kill a man.

Douglas Mawson was the lucky one – he lived because he didn't eat too much liver. And at least his story had a happy ending. Unlike the terrible tales in the next chapter…

THE GORY STORY OF POISON

If there's one thing more scary than poison, it's a horrible human armed with a poison. Here are some painful tales of how people have used poison.

Thousands of years ago, and no one knows quite when, humans learnt to use poisons for weapons. Native peoples as far apart as Japan, South Africa and South America used poisoned weapons for hunting.

The ancient Greeks knew about poisoned arrows and how poison can get through the skin. In one of the legends about Hercules, the Greek superhero and strong man gets killed by a poisoned vest. The Roman poet Ovid put it a bit more bloodily…

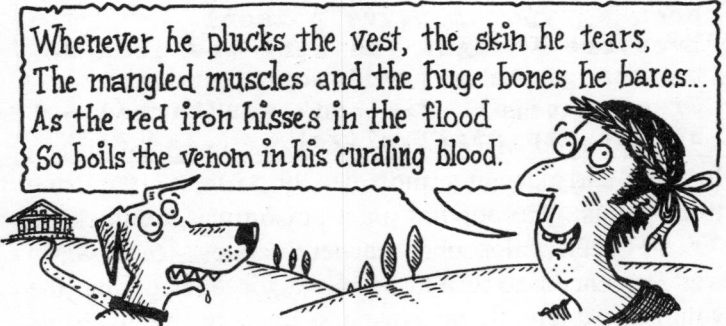

Whenever he plucks the vest, the skin he tears,
The mangled muscles and the huge bones he bares…
As the red iron hisses in the flood
So boils the venom in his curdling blood.

What a great poem! Why not read it in an English class and watch your teacher run out of the room with her hand over her mouth! (By the way, venom is a poison made by an animal.)

Understandably Hercules decided the only way to stop the pain was to burn himself alive – which he did with the aid of a friend. But all wasn't lost, because the gods let him into heaven where he married a goddess. So that's all right then...

Although the story of Hercules is just a story, the ancient Greeks and Romans knew lots about how to poison people. Here's just one case from thousands...

POISON MURDER CASE FILE

VICTIM'S NAME: Agathocles
JOB: King of Syracuse
DATE: 289 BC
PLACE: Sicily
POISONED BY: His grandson
HOW POISONED: He was using the pointy tip of a feather to clean bits of food from between his teeth. But the king's wicked grandson had dipped the feather in poison. The poison stopped the king from moving (it might have been a type of nerve poison).
Everyone thought the king was dead so he was given a traditional ancient Greek funeral. His body was burned — but he was *still alive!*

In those early days the most deadly poisons often came from plants. One popular plant poison was hemlock. In 399 BC Greek philosopher-teacher Socrates (469–399 BC) was sentenced to drink hemlock for "corrupting the youth of Athens". The poison seemed to creep up his body, as his pupil Plato recalled...

The teacher lay down. The man with the poison squeezed his foot. Socrates said he felt nothing. He said that when the poison reached his heart he would be gone.

But all the time he was awake and his thoughts remained clear. Perhaps that's the cruellest thing about hemlock poisoning.

Bet you never knew!
There's no point in daydreaming that your teacher will drink poison. No, it's already happened! In 1928, Hungarian teacher Leo Bruck was teaching his pupils about the death of Socrates. To show what happened he drank some poison ... and died. While we all like teachers who liven up lessons, this could be going a bit too far!

Poisons were often used to bump off important people. In 16th century Italy poisoning was so common that some people killed people for a living!

POISON MURDER CASE FILE

VICTIM'S NAME: Bianca Capello
JOB: Poisoner
DATE: Sixteenth century
PLACE: Florence, Italy
POISONED BY: Herself
HOW POISONED: She was trying to poison Cardinal Ferdinand with a rather tempting poisoned tart. But the clever cardinal switched the sweets and Bianca bumped herself off by mistake.

By Bianca's time, poisons had even become fashion items... We'll be back after the commercial break. Don't go away!

COUNT VOMITO'S POISON PRODUCTS

proudly present...

The Fatal Fashion Poison Jewellery Catalogue

Why not order the latest in our range of delightfully deadly designer jewellery? You can poison your enemies whilst looking really glitzy! IT'S FASHION TO DIE FOR! Everything the well-dressed poisoner needs, including...

POISON RINGS

Store the poison in your ring and put a few drops in your enemy's drink. It's guaranteed to break the ice at parties!

POISON NECKLACES

Supplied complete with a little locket and some poison to put in it. All poison is guaranteed 100% deadly and if you get caught you can always try it on yourself. Satisfaction guaranteed or your money back (if you're still alive, that is!).

34

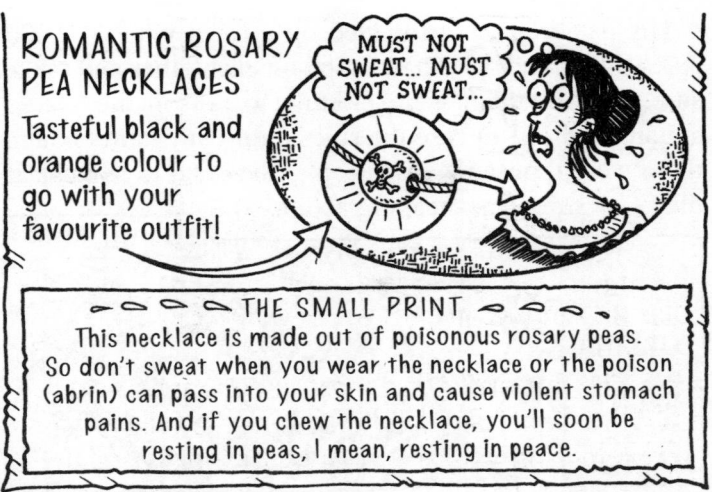

ROMANTIC ROSARY PEA NECKLACES

Tasteful black and orange colour to go with your favourite outfit!

MUST NOT SWEAT... MUST NOT SWEAT...

~~~~ THE SMALL PRINT ~~~~
This necklace is made out of poisonous rosary peas.
So don't sweat when you wear the necklace or the poison
(abrin) can pass into your skin and cause violent stomach
pains. And if you chew the necklace, you'll soon be
resting in peas, I mean, resting in peace.

With so many pesky poisoners about, powerful rulers
were dead scared of poison and some were mad scared of
it... Sultan Abdul Hamid of Turkey (1842–1918) was
especially nervous:

- He only drank water from a secret spring.
- His cow had its own bodyguard to protect its milk.

COWARD

COW

THIS IS **UDDERLY** RIDICULOUS!

- He would only touch food if it had been tested on his
food taster AND a cat or a dog.
- He would only put on clothes if they had been tried on
by a slave to make sure there was no poison on them.

• His palace was surrounded by a town where 20,000 spies lived. The spies had to spy on each other and make sure none of them were plotting to poison the scared sultan. And just in case the spies didn't spy hard enough there were thousands of parrots – they had to squawk if they saw strangers sneaking about.

You might like to know that awful Abdul was eventually kicked out by the Turkish people when they got tired of his weird ways – but at least he wasn't poisoned!

What these rattled rulers really required was some remedy for poison. But what?

PAINFUL EXPRESSIONS

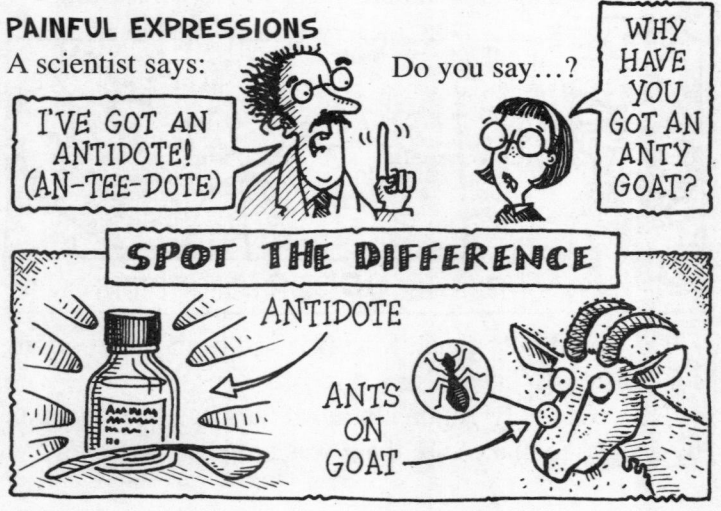

That's right – he said DOTE, not *goat*! An antidote is a substance that stops a poison. Mind you, goats did feature in early antidotes, as you're about to find out…

AMAZING ANTIDOTES

The antidote molecules stick to the poison molecules and stop them doing any harm in the body. Just imagine the poison as a nasty gang of kids looking for trouble. The antidote is a group of nice kids who stick close to the nasty kids to stop them getting into mischief.

In their desperate search for antidotes, important people tried all kinds of weird and wonderful stuff. Do you think either of these would actually work?

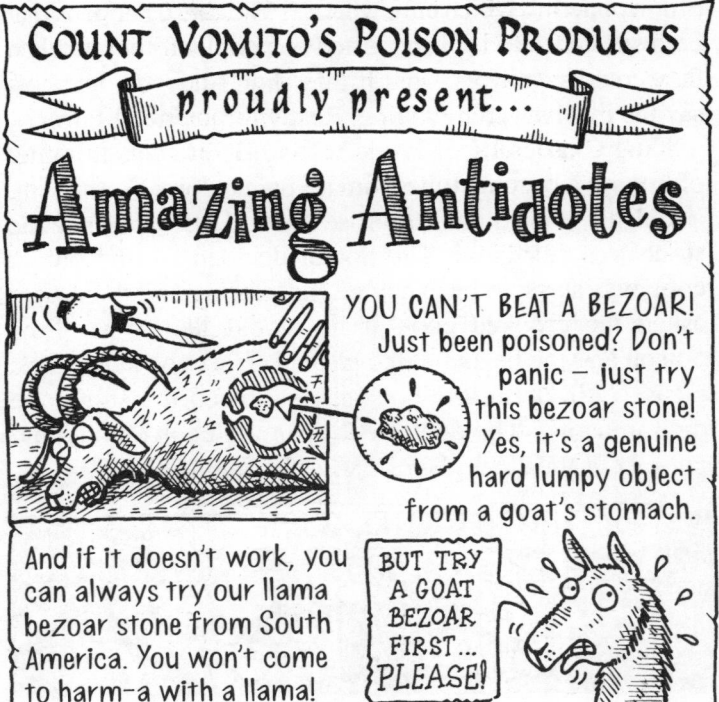

COUNT VOMITO'S POISON PRODUCTS
proudly present...
Amazing Antidotes

YOU CAN'T BEAT A BEZOAR! Just been poisoned? Don't panic – just try this bezoar stone! Yes, it's a genuine hard lumpy object from a goat's stomach.

And if it doesn't work, you can always try our llama bezoar stone from South America. You won't come to harm-a with a llama!

BUT TRY A GOAT BEZOAR FIRST... PLEASE!

THIS PRODUCT COULD MAKE YOUR CLAY!

If you've been poisoned, why not try tasty Terra Sigillata – OK, so it's not that tasty! It's clay from the Greek island of Lemnos mixed with goat's blood for that extra-special flavour. Take one with every meal, just in case there's something nasty in it!

WE REALLY DIG THIS CLAY, MAN!

LEMNOS

Still wondering which cure worked? Well, it so happens that both substances have been tested on people. If they worked they could save lives – but if they didn't … well, let's just say the results were revolting. Ready for a taste of terror?

King Charles IX of France (1550–1574) was thinking of buying a bezoar stone from a Spanish lord. So the king asked his top doctor Ambrose Paré (1510–1590) if the stone was any good. The doctor decided to find out. A cook was about to be executed for stealing and the doctor asked the crooked cook if he would like to swallow poison and the bezoar stone instead. The cook said, "Yes, please." He drank the poison, swallowed the stone and died in agony. The doctor cut open the cook's body and pulled out the stone. Here's what he said to the King…

DO YOU WANT IT?

NO, BURN IT!

Meanwhile in Germany, the curious clay was put to the ultimate test and once again a human life was at stake. I've made up some details, but the basic story is TRUE!

A TESTING TALE

Baden, Germany, 1581

I must die and I know it. I'm a thief – there's no point in denying it now. I've broken the law and I must be hung by the neck until I am dead. And yet ... and yet I'm too young to die! I know about medicine. Maybe I'll make a great discovery one day ... if I live!

"Mercy!" I beg the judge. "Spare my life – I'll never steal again."

But the old judge shakes his head. "It is the law," he says sternly. "You will die tomorrow."

My heart races and my mouth dries. The guards grab my arms to drag me back to my prison cell. Just then, an idea flashes into my head. It's so strange and so terrible that it seems mad – even to me. But like a drowning boy, I'm clutching at straws...

"Please, please," I beg. "Grant me one."

"Well?" said the judge. "Make it quick – I haven't got all day."

"Let me take poison. I'll take anything you like..."

"*Poison?*" The judge frowns. "But that will be far more painful than being hung. It will take longer, too. You're not making this easy for yourself, young man!"

"Exactly, but let me also take a little clay. It will be an experiment – and if I die, well, I've saved you the cost of a rope."

The judge whispers to his usher and the public executioner.

Finally, slowly, he nods his head. "Very well," he says. "Have it your own way. You may take mercuric chloride – although I must say_you are choosing a worse death for yourself."

Late that night...

I am alone in my cold cell. As I stare at the slimy stone walls I can't get the judge's words out of my head. Tomorrow I must stand in the town square. I will open my lips and drink a tiny spoonful of poison. But that's enough to kill six men – nastily.

I gulp – I try to swallow, but all the muscles of my throat have locked together. I know what the poison can do. I will dribble and throw up and roll around in agony and mess my pants. It could take hours, but I know I'll die in terrible pain.

My only hope is a lump of earth. It's said to help – but no one's ever tested it like this... I don't want to sleep but somehow I doze off in the cold, dark hour before dawn.

The next morning...

It's time. I haven't eaten. Somehow I don't feel like food. Not with my whole body filled with the terror of dying... I am not listening to the court usher's speech... All I see is the small table with a glass of wine, a spoon, a bottle of poison and a small piece of clay. The usher ends his speech with a warning...

"If he lives he will be set free. But if he dies he will not be a pretty sight. You may want to leave now..."

I wish I could leave too.

I gaze blankly at the crowd. They are whispering and shuffling their feet. But no one is leaving.

I stare at the poison in the spoon. It might as well be a sword. The executioner puts the spoon to my lips. I open my mouth and take the poison. I can taste the metal, it burns. I swallow.

The crowd gasps.

I stare at the clay. It's only the size of my thumbnail and it has a goat stamped on it. The executioner drops the clay in the wine and hands me the cup. The pain is worse now. I must swallow the wine fast. Maybe it'll stop the burning…

NO – IT'S NOT WORKING! The poison is racking me, burning me up inside. I close my eyes. I can't … … stand it … … any more! And then … … somehow the pain is easing. Am I dying? I open my

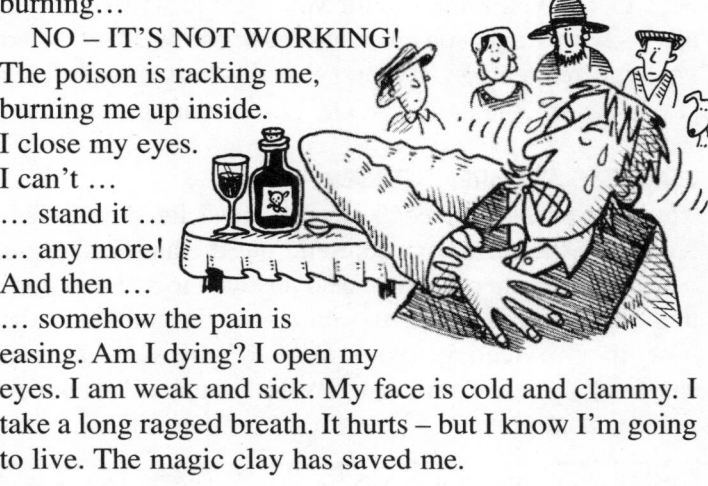

eyes. I am weak and sick. My face is cold and clammy. I take a long ragged breath. It hurts – but I know I'm going to live. The magic clay has saved me.

The clay works like activated charcoal. It soaks up some poisons so that they can't get into the blood. (Actually, charcoal works better than clay.) But there are some poisons for which clay and charcoal are as useless as a bat that's scared of the dark. I'm talking about the grisly, gasping, ghastly poisons in the next chapter…

GHASTLY GASES

SAFETY WARNING

If you smell something nasty, DO NOT PANIC! The whiff is wafting from your dog or your little brother and NOT this book. If the smell is very bad you may need this item of safety equipment.

IT'S NO CHOKE!

There's something especially scary about poison gas, isn't there? You think the air you breathe will keep you alive – but with poison gas it has the opposite effect. Mind you, you're breathing poison gas at this very moment! *Oh yes, you are!*

TEACHER'S TEA-BREAK TEASER

You'll need a large handkerchief and a lot of courage. Knock on the staffroom door and put the hankie to your nose. Your teacher may not be overjoyed to see you after the sticky-bun incident, so smile sweetly and ask them how they're feeling. Your teacher will stare at you suspiciously before muttering, "OK, I suppose." At which point you can say…

BUT YOU'RE BREATHING POISON GAS!

EH?

Take two seconds to enjoy the look of panic in your teacher's eyes before...

a) Running off at high speed chased by a maddened teacher.

b) Explaining that air contains oxygen – and oxygen is a poison!

Painful poison fact file

NAME: Deadly oxygen

THE BASIC FACTS: **1** Oxygen makes up 21% of the air you breathe. It has no colour, no taste and no smell – but it's there. And you need it to stay alive.

2 Oxygen is breathed in by your lungs and taken on a tour of your body in your blood. It's needed to help your cells make energy.

3 The oxygen you breathe is usually in the form of a molecule made up of two oxygen atoms. To understand how they affect the body, just imagine terrible twins muscling in on playground games and spoiling them.

4 OK, so you'd put up with one set of twins – but not billions of them. Too much oxygen means loads of murderous molecules messing up the vital chemical reactions that keep you going. × BILLIONS =

5 That's why your body puffs out most of the oxygen it breathes in without using it. The oxygen your body does need is locked in red blood cells until it gets to your cells.

I'M ABOUT TO USE THIS ANIMAL AS A GUINEA PIG FOR MY EXPERIMENT.

I AM A GUINEA PIG, YOU IDIOT!

THE PAINFUL DETAILS:
1 The first scientist to find out that oxygen was poisonous was French chemist Antoine Lavoisier (1743–1794). He put a guinea pig in 100% oxygen … and you can guess the rest.

2 In 1951 doctors gave tiny newborn babies lots of extra oxygen to help them breathe. But Australian doctor Kate Campbell warned that this was harmful. She was right – the oxygen damaged blood vessels in the babies' eyes and thousands of them lost their sight.

So that's oxygen for you. You can't live without it and you can't live with too much of it! But those naughty oxygen twins also get into the wrong kind of company and make different poison gases. And here are the painful results…

THE GRUESOME GUIDE TO POISON - PART 1
GASPING GASES

Name: CARBON DIOXIDE

Alias: CO_2 (this is the chemical symbol of the gas)

Description: The terrible oxygen twins plus a new pal - a carbon atom. Together they make a colourless gas that you can't see or smell.

Horrible habits: The count says that breathing in too much carbon dioxide can suffocate the body. He says he's got some spare gas if we want to find out what it's like. Thanks, but no thanks, Count.

Known haunts: Bonfires and coal fires. 0.03% of air is carbon dioxide. When your cells make energy, carbon dioxide is a waste product, which you breathe out.

Redeeming features: Plants love it. They take carbon dioxide from the air and use the carbon atoms to make food. And that means all the fruit and vegetables you eat - including the slimy broccoli you were force-fed for lunch - contain chemicals from a poisonous gas.

BUT I'M GOOD FOR YOU!

Name: SULPHUR DIOXIDE

Alias: SO_2

Description: A smelly gas. Contains the terrible oxygen twins plus one sulphur atom.

Horrible habits: Turns water acid. In the atmosphere it can make rainwater into poisonous "acid rain". When the gas mixes with moisture in the lungs it can make acid lungs too.

Known haunts: Coal smoke, traffic fumes.

Redeeming features: Dissolves boring historic buildings that children get dragged round on school trips. But you like old buildings? Well, cheer up, kids, the gas kills germs too.

DISSOLVE!

BLAST IT! WE'LL HAVE TO TAKE THEM TO *FUN-RIDE PARK*, MISS SIMKINS.

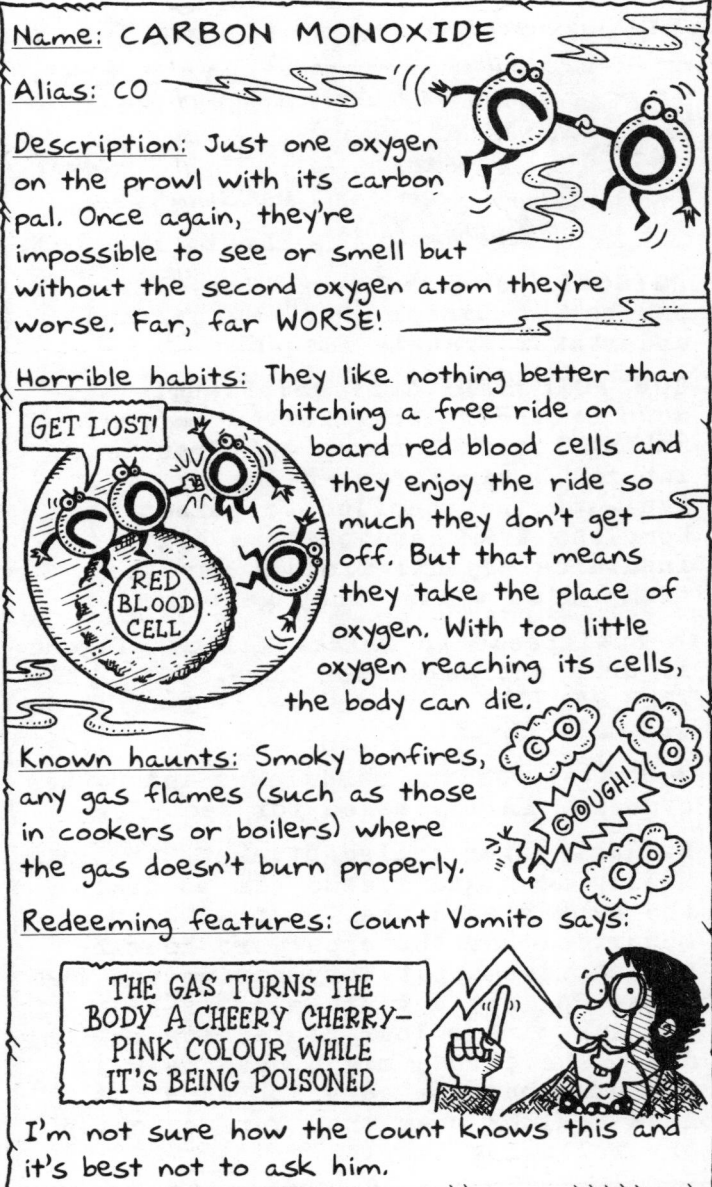

Name: CARBON MONOXIDE

Alias: CO

Description: Just one oxygen on the prowl with its carbon pal. Once again, they're impossible to see or smell but without the second oxygen atom they're worse. Far, far WORSE!

Horrible habits: They like nothing better than hitching a free ride on board red blood cells and they enjoy the ride so much they don't get off. But that means they take the place of oxygen. With too little oxygen reaching its cells, the body can die.

GET LOST!

RED BLOOD CELL

Known haunts: Smoky bonfires, any gas flames (such as those in cookers or boilers) where the gas doesn't burn properly.

COUGH!

Redeeming features: Count Vomito says:

THE GAS TURNS THE BODY A CHEERY CHERRY-PINK COLOUR WHILE IT'S BEING POISONED.

I'm not sure how the Count knows this and it's best not to ask him.

POISON MURDER CASE FILE

VICTIM'S NAME:
Michael Malloy

JOB: Tramp

DATE: 1933

PLACE: New York

POISONED BY: Bar owner Tony Marino, his barman Daniel "Red" Murphy and undertaker Frankie Pasqua.

HOW POISONED: Tony and Frankie were down on their luck. Tony's bar wasn't making too much money and Frankie's funeral business was dying on its feet. So they decided to poison the homeless tramp and claim a big insurance payout. Trouble was the tramp didn't die. They gave him...

● Antifreeze to drink. Malloy glugged it down and asked for more. DON'T TRY THIS AT HOME! Antifreeze is deadly even in small doses.

● Rotten sardine sandwiches and rotten oysters. Malloy asked for seconds.

At last, after failed attempts to run Malloy down and freeze him to death, the gang gassed the tramp with carbon monoxide. But the cops were hearing bad stories about Tony Marino and the boys. So they dug up Malloy's body and its pink colour proved how he'd died. The corpse might have been in the pink but the gang looked a lot less healthy when they were executed the following year.

48

Carbon monoxide is a real danger, so if you have gas heating or a gas cooker, it's a good idea to pester your parents to get a carbon-monoxide detector. It's a serious matter – but at least poison gases have their funny side. It's true! There's one type that makes you laugh and act rather silly – the Gruesome Guide has the full funny facts…

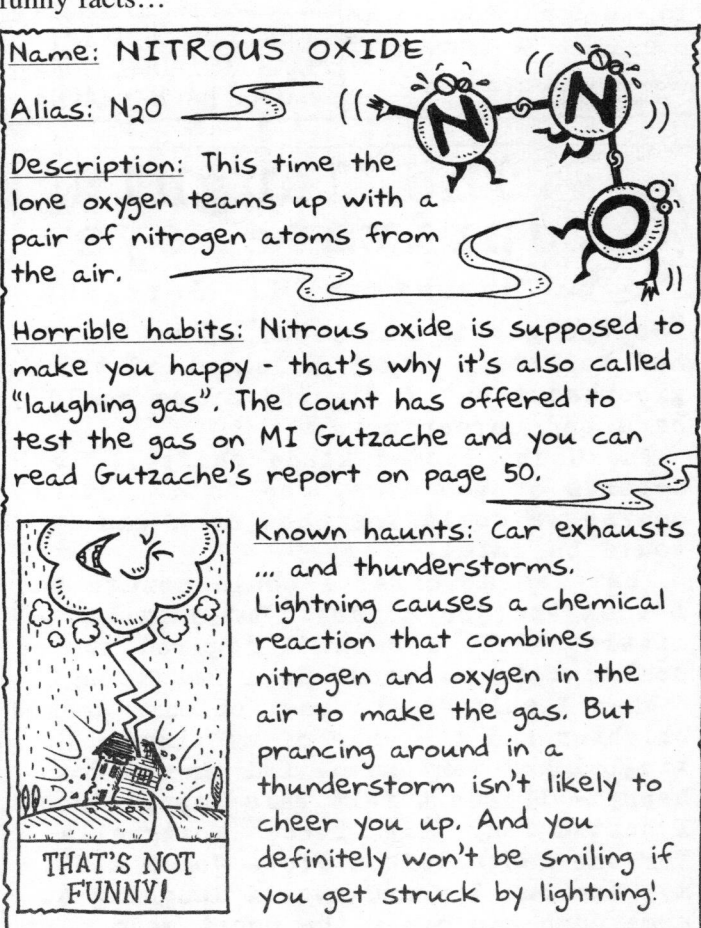

Name: NITROUS OXIDE

Alias: N_2O

Description: This time the lone oxygen teams up with a pair of nitrogen atoms from the air.

Horrible habits: Nitrous oxide is supposed to make you happy - that's why it's also called "laughing gas". The Count has offered to test the gas on MI Gutzache and you can read Gutzache's report on page 50.

THAT'S NOT FUNNY!

Known haunts: Car exhausts … and thunderstorms. Lightning causes a chemical reaction that combines nitrogen and oxygen in the air to make the gas. But prancing around in a thunderstorm isn't likely to cheer you up. And you definitely won't be smiling if you get struck by lightning!

Redeeming features: A bit of nitrous oxide relaxes the muscles and lowers the blood pressure. The gas can be mixed with oxygen to numb pain during an operation or when a woman gives birth.

YOU'VE HAD SEXTUPLETS, MRS BROWN!

HA! HA! OOH, DON'T MAKE ME LAUGH, NURSE! HA! HA! HA! HA! HA! HA!

The laughing private eye

REPORT BY MI GUTZACHE

"So the gas is harmless?" I asked. I had to know - I may be short of the greenbacks but I figured dying could be a bad career move.

The Count looked kinda shifty. "It depends on the dose," he said. "Of course we could test how much gas would be fatal."

That was an offer I could refuse but I took the job anyhow. "But just a little sniff," I said. I figured it couldn't do no harm. So I was wrong.

When I sniffed the gas, colours seemed brighter and the ends of my fingers tingled and went numb. And then I got happy - I hadn't felt this happy since I busted Tony "Big Cheese" Mozzarella for the Pasta Poison Plot. Jokes ain't my game but I found myself laughing at some dumb wisecrack the Count made...

WHAT IS DONNA'S JOB? HUH?

SHE'S MY **POISON-AL** ASSISTANT!

HA HA HA HA HA!

GET A LIFE!

I was laughing so hard I banged my head. But I didn't feel no pain!

IMPORTANT ANNOUNCEMENT

We would like to deny rumours that Horrible Science books have been sprayed with laughing gas in a pathetic attempt (ho ho!) to make you laugh at the painfully corny jokes (giggle, snort). This is a laughable, HA HA HEE HEE! lie. And anyway, someone's already tried it...

Bet you never knew!
In 1996 an Italian club owner was found guilty of pumping laughing gas into his club. Maybe he was trying to make people laugh at his jokes, but the judge didn't see the funny side. The crazy club owner was fined. What's that? You fancy playing a trick like that too? OK, go ahead, just so long as you don't mind losing all your pocket money for the next 2,000 years.

GRUESOME POISON-GAS WEAPONS

One of the best things you can say about nitrous oxide is that it can block pain and save lives. But some scientists have been working to make poison gases that have the opposite effects – poison-gas weapons...

To get an idea how scary poison-gas weapons are, let's join a group of French soldiers. In 1985 they were training to deal with poison gas on the island of Corsica. The soldiers were told a plane would let off steam to give the impression of gas. Sure enough the plane flew over, but the spray was RED – it looked like *real* poison gas! The soldiers fell down and rolled about in agony. But there was no poison and no gas. Someone had simply added red dye to the steam.

These men were big tough soldiers. If they could be terrified by poison gas, what about the rest of us?

FIVE PAINFUL POISON GASES (IN ORDER OF NASTINESS)
5 Chlorine gas
This gruesome yellowish-green gas cloud irritates the lungs. The lungs fill with fluid, and victims drown on dry land. It was first used by the Germans against the French in 1915 during the First World War. Later on in the war, the British used it against the Germans.

Vicious verdict:

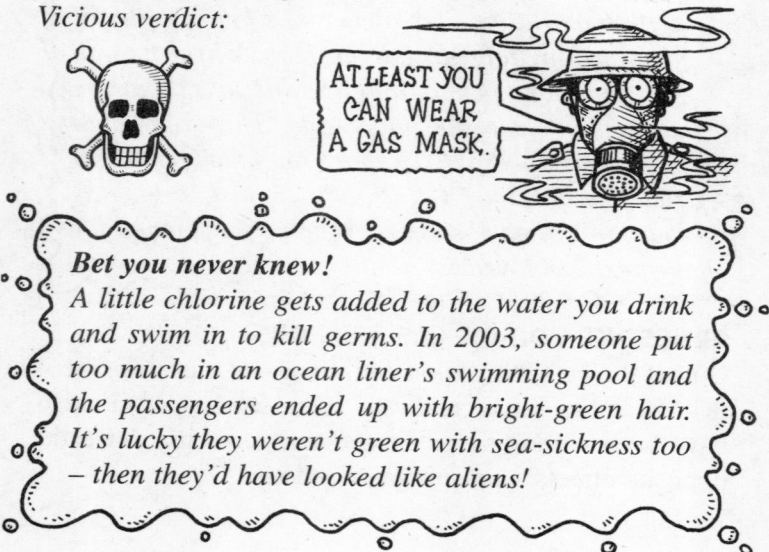

AT LEAST YOU CAN WEAR A GAS MASK.

Bet you never knew!
A little chlorine gets added to the water you drink and swim in to kill germs. In 2003, someone put too much in an ocean liner's swimming pool and the passengers ended up with bright-green hair. It's lucky they weren't green with sea-sickness too – then they'd have looked like aliens!

4 Mustard gas

Used by both sides in the First World War. Causes skin blisters that can rot. Victims can go blind for a short while and suffer damage to their stomach and lungs that can last for years.

Vicious verdict:

Very, *very* nasty. You *must* wear a gas mask, and you can't let the gas touch your skin either. It stays dangerous for weeks, too. On Friday, 13 July 1917, a group of soldiers had mustard gas fired at them for eight hours. The next day their captain said...

Everyone was round the shell holes vomiting ... breathing was very difficult ... as we got going the road seemed to fade away ... (we were) stone blind! I think the worst part was when they opened your eyes to put droplets in them – it was just like boiling water dropping in!

3 Hydrogen cyanide gas

More deadly than chlorine or mustard gas. You feel faint and weak and throw up. Then you can't breathe, and die. It only takes a few minutes. It's said to smell of bitter almonds, although most people can't make out the smell. By the way, the Count is offering free sniffing sessions if anyone wants to try… (Don't all rush at once.)

Vicious verdict:

A killer. Although a gas mask will protect you, you have to keep changing the filter. Luckily the gas blows away quickly.

2 BZ

An especially revolting weapon. It causes confusion, diarrhoea and drying of the guts and mouth resulting in disgusting bad breath. After about 12 hours victims see things that aren't there and start talking to trees.

Vicious verdict:

A real stinker in more ways than one.

1 Nerve gases

Remember those nasty nerve poisons from page 20? Nerve gases are the ultimate horror. They're so deadly that even a few drops on the skin will kill. Victims suffer headaches and throw up and have to go to the toilet in a hurry. They can't stop dribbling and they can't breathe. They die.

Vicious verdict:

What can you say about a gas that makes you need to wear a nappy? The only protection is a hot, clumsy suit that's horrible to wear. But it's less horrible than nerve gas.

Bet you never knew!
The actual use of chemical weapons in war has been banned since 1925 and today many world leaders and scientists would like to get rid of these terrible weapons altogether.

Of course, war always brings out the worst in people, but some people don't need a war to show their worst side. No, I'm not talking about unkind teachers, bullies and the sort of people who complain about children chatting in libraries. I'm talking about people who use poison to kill their enemies, their friends ... and even their pets!

LET'S GET OUTTA HERE!

METALS, MURDER AND MADNESS

QUESTION: What's shiny and cold and passes on electric shocks?

If you said "my dog's nose" then **a)** you really do need to read on and **b)** unplug your puppy from the fairy lights – AT ONCE! The answer is actually – METAL.

Now, you probably know that your home is full of metal things and if you're lucky your pockets are jingling with metal items in the shape of coins. But I bet you never knew there are over 60 types of atom (or elements as a chemist would call them) that happen to be metals. And some are amazingly odd – like caesium (see-zee-um), a metal that burns in air.

But some metals should carry a special health warning…

They can do scarily painful things to the poor human body. And if there's one thing more scary than the metals themselves – it's the fact that some inhuman humans like nothing better than putting them in a cup of coffee.

And here's what makes these murderous metals so dreadfully deadly…

Painful poison fact file

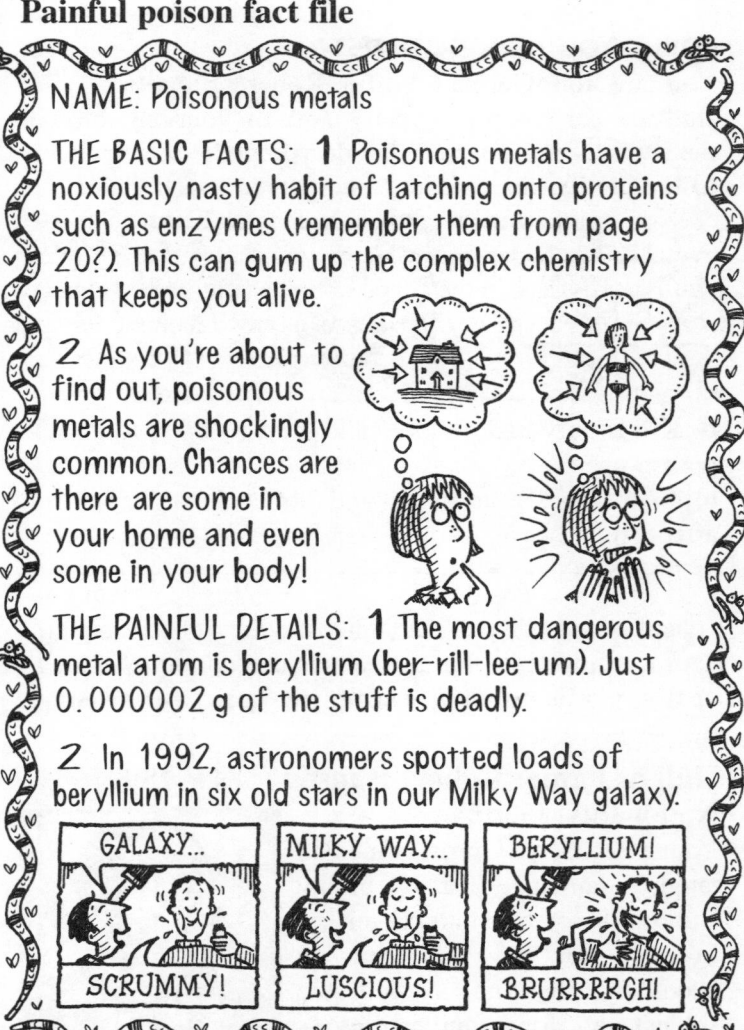

NAME: Poisonous metals

THE BASIC FACTS: **1** Poisonous metals have a noxiously nasty habit of latching onto proteins such as enzymes (remember them from page 20?). This can gum up the complex chemistry that keeps you alive.

2 As you're about to find out, poisonous metals are shockingly common. Chances are there are some in your home and even some in your body!

THE PAINFUL DETAILS: **1** The most dangerous metal atom is beryllium (ber-rill-lee-um). Just 0.000002 g of the stuff is deadly.

2 In 1992, astronomers spotted loads of beryllium in six old stars in our Milky Way galaxy.

GALAXY…
SCRUMMY!

MILKY WAY…
LUSCIOUS!

BERYLLIUM!
BRURRRRGH!

And now you've picked up a couple of nasty nuggets of knowledge about beryllium – can you solve this poison puzzle?

COULD YOU BE A SCIENTIST?

You are top German boffin Robert Bunsen. You're studying beryllium when a fly lands on your only blob of the stuff … and eats it. What do you do?

a) Eat the fly in a nice ham and mustard sandwich.

BUT I HATE MUSTARD.

ME TOO, BZZZZ!

b) Kill the fly and dissolve and burn its body to get the poison back.

c) Keep the fly as a pet and notice how the poison affects it.

Answer: b) The fly ate the beryllium because it tasted sweet. Although Bunsen wasn't daft enough to eat the fly, he was a really crazy chemist and deserves a place in our…

Hall of Fame: Robert Bunsen (1811–1899)
Nationality: German

Young Robert's professor dad taught languages but brainy Bunsen junior was into chemistry. In fact he was so keen on chemistry that he studied the subject at four universities –

58

Göttingen, Paris, Berlin and Vienna. He became most interested in cacodyl (ca-co-di-al), an evil-stinking mixture that includes arsenic. The awful arsenic almost bumped off Bunsen and the killer cacodyl blew up, blasting Bunsen with bits of test tube. The scientist went blind in one eye. (And you thought your chemistry lessons were tough!)

Now most sane people would have given up chemistry and taken up something a bit less dangerous, like bungee jumping into volcanoes. But not reckless Robert...

He went on to discover two new elements – the metals caesium and rubidium. And, thank you for asking, he DIDN'T discover the Bunsen burner. It was actually developed by his assistant Peter Desaga in 1855. But Bunsen deserves some credit because he let other scientists copy the idea for free.

Like most crazy chemists Bunsen kept forgetting things (I blame all those poisons). He always forgot the dates of dinner parties and would turn up one day late and expect to be fed. In the end his friends got into the habit of organizing special one-day-late parties just for him. And this may have been a good idea because he was very smelly from all the chemicals he used. The wife of his friend Emil Fischer said:

First I would like to wash Bunsen, then I would like to kiss him because he is such a charming man.

By the way, turning up for school one day late and smelling oddly won't necessarily make you a great scientist. Bunsen was a genuine genius, so he got away with some barmy behaviour!

And now let's get to grips with some more murderous metals ... er, maybe you'd better put some gloves on first...

THE GRUESOME GUIDE TO POISON – PART 2
MURDERING METALS

Name: COPPER

Alias: Cu

Description: A pretty, orangey-pinky, shiny metal (in fact you could even say it's copper-coloured!). Like all metals, copper warms up quickly when you heat it and electricity can run through it easily.

Horrible habits: Too much copper is poisonous.

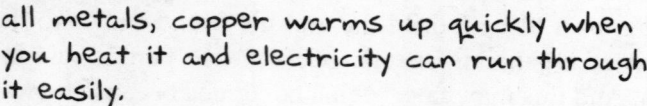

Known haunts: Copper water pipes, electrical cables and saucepans in posh kitchens.

Redeeming features: Copper atoms help make up some proteins and enzymes – so SHOCK, HORROR! a tiny amount of copper is GOOD for you!

The really seriously sickening stuff isn't actually pure copper, it's copper sulphate. It can be mixed with water to make the sinister blue liquid much loved by science teachers. But don't add copper sulphate to your teacher's tea. The poison causes cramps and a dose of just one gram can kill - and then you'll get collared by the coppers. Mind you, the ancient Egyptians used copper sulphate as an ointment for sore eyes.

I LOVE IT!

SINISTER SCIENCE TEACHER

Name: LEAD

Alias: Pb

Pb CLONK! ERK!

Description: A heavy, soft, grey metal. You'd know if you dropped it on your foot, but at least you could take out your rage by bending it into interesting shapes.

Horrible habits: Very poisonous. It can get into the body through the lungs, skin, food and drink. Although the body chucks some of it out in poo, lead can build up in the bones and teeth and other body bits (where it sticks to proteins).

URRRRGH! **K-SPLOSH!**

CENSORED
SOMEBODY WITH LEAD POISONING, GETTING RID OF SOME HEAVY POO...

CRACK!

Victims of lead poisoning have...

MADNESS

GROAN, GIBBER!

BELLY ACHE

BLUE GUMS

MUSCLE PAINS AND WEAKNESS

Known haunts: Batteries, soldering (soft metals melted to glue other metals together), hair dye for greying hair (yes, your ageing teachers could have a head full of lead). Lead also lurks in old paint, and in the flashing on the roofs of houses (the metal between the roof and the brickwork). And it was once added to petrol to stop the engine making knocking sounds, but that's now banned in many countries. The one place you WON'T find lead is in pencil "lead". As any clued-up chemist knows that stuff is graphite - so it's all right, you can suck your pencil in a science test and live to tell the tale...

CLEANER FUMES

RATTLE! KNOCK!

DRIBBLE

Redeeming features: Lead has loads of uses, and these days it's kept away from food and drink ... unlike the good old days when your teacher wore short, baggy trousers and got whipped for not doing their science homework. See you after the commercial break...

COUNT VOMITO'S POISON PRODUCTS
proudly present...

The Lethal Lead Experience

Complete with free hospital treatment!

LIVE IN THE PAST WITH THESE GENUINE IMITATION ANTIQUES!

1. Victorian lead pipes for your home – guaranteed to gurgle loudly in the middle of the night!

2. Roman lead boiling pot – for sweet wine with a kick!

SUCK! 3. Lead dummies for babies flavoured with real-tasting lead paint.

IMPORTANT ANNOUNCEMENT
Er, sorry, readers – the Count's just confessed that one of these items is a fake. Which one?

63

TEACHER'S TEA-BREAK TEASER

You will need:

A pair of running shoes for a speedy getaway

An elderly teacher

Hammer loudly on the staffroom door (elderly teachers can be a little hard of hearing). When your teacher appears, ask them…

DO YOU HAVE ANY LEAD IN YOUR BODY?

If they say "no", you could say…

a) "But there's lead in your hair dye."

b) "What about the wine you drank in Roman times?"

But even lethal lead poisoning isn't as bad as our next murderous metal…

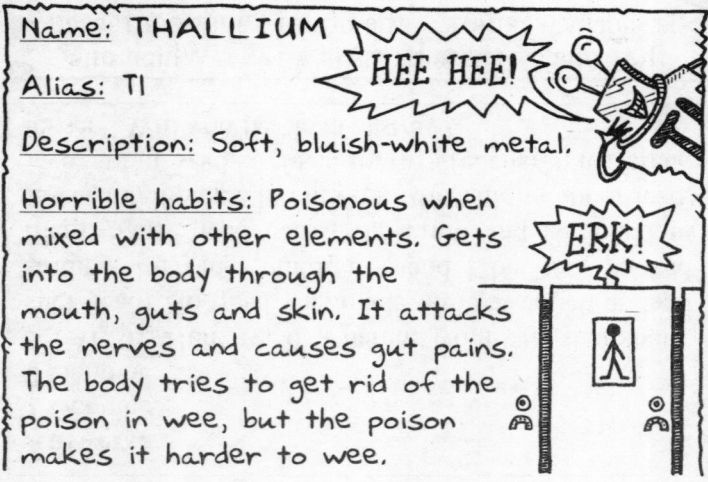

<u>Name:</u> THALLIUM

HEE HEE!

<u>Alias:</u> Tl

<u>Description:</u> Soft, bluish-white metal.

ERK!

<u>Horrible habits:</u> Poisonous when mixed with other elements. Gets into the body through the mouth, guts and skin. It attacks the nerves and causes gut pains. The body tries to get rid of the poison in wee, but the poison makes it harder to wee.

The skin becomes so sensitive it can't be touched and the victim can't smile or change the expression on their face. They lose control of their eyeballs and their hair drops out.

Known haunts: Used in industry.

Redeeming features: It's useful for getting rid of rats.

AND PEOPLE TOO! READ ON...

Bet you never knew!
In 1971, mad poisoner Graham Young tried to poison his work-mates with thallium. He killed two people but gave himself away when some scientists came to investigate the poisonings. Graham seemed to know a lot about poisons and actually asked the scientists if they suspected thallium. As they say, a little learning is a dangerous thing – but that shouldn't put you off reading this book!

Name: MERCURY

Alias: Hg

COOL!

Description: A silvery-grey metal that's runny at room temperature. Like most substances, mercury takes up more space as it warms up, and that's why mercury in a thermometer goes up when it's hot and down when it's cold. And when it's frozen you'd best go to bed and snuggle up with this book.

<u>Horrible habits:</u> Builds up in the body. Damages the brain and kidneys. Bad poisoning results in madness and stops you from weeing. And you end up with yellow skin, black gums and teeth falling out.

> BY GUM, I'M FEELING A BIT "DOWN IN THE MOUTH".

<u>Known haunts:</u> Thermometers and industrial chemicals.

<u>Redeeming features:</u> If you can't wee, you won't feel the urge to visit the loo halfway through a long film.

Mind you, the horror movie in this poster sounds scary enough to make anyone dash for the toilet.

So take my advice – make sure you go *before* you start reading the next page!

INVASION OF THE METALLOIDS

"Metalloids" – they sound like aliens that do terrible things to people involving lots of gagging noises and gory goo. And that's more or less what they do. Fancy finding out a few painful facts…?

Painful poison fact file

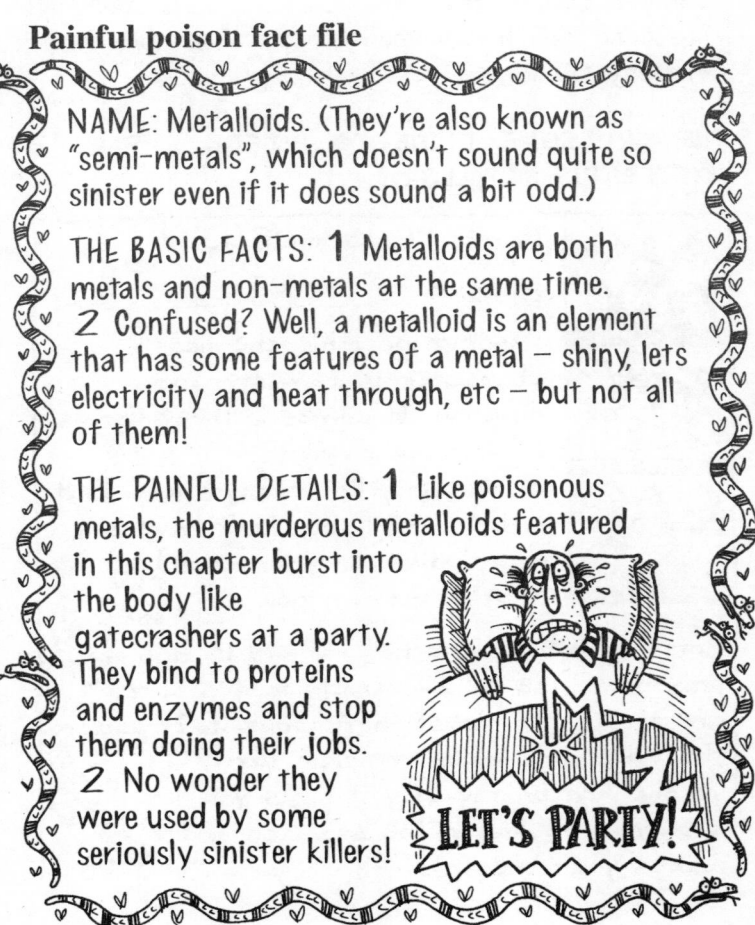

NAME: Metalloids. (They're also known as "semi-metals", which doesn't sound quite so sinister even if it does sound a bit odd.)

THE BASIC FACTS: **1** Metalloids are both metals and non-metals at the same time. **2** Confused? Well, a metalloid is an element that has some features of a metal – shiny, lets electricity and heat through, etc – but not all of them!

THE PAINFUL DETAILS: **1** Like poisonous metals, the murderous metalloids featured in this chapter burst into the body like gatecrashers at a party. They bind to proteins and enzymes and stop them doing their jobs. **2** No wonder they were used by some seriously sinister killers!

LET'S PARTY!

The Count has kindly offered to show us the effects of metalloids by testing them on MI Gutzache...

YOU CAN COUNT ME OUT, COUNT!

On second thoughts, maybe it's better if we stick to the Gruesome Guide...

THE GRUESOME GUIDE TO POISON – PART 3
MYSTERIOUS METALLOIDS

Name: PHOSPHORUS

Alias: P

Description: This chemical character is a master of disguise. It comes in three forms...
a) A black powder.
b) Whitish-yellow waxy stuff. (But CALM DOWN! You don't have any waxy poison in your ears!)
c) A red-brown powder.

Horrible habits: The red variety is less poisonous. The yellow variety tastes horrible - and that's the nicest thing about it. It poisons the liver and makes the skin turn yellow. And on the way it gives you a burning feeling in the stomach and makes your breath smell of garlic.

Known haunts: Fertilizer. Once used
for match heads, and rat poison.

Redeeming features: You need
phosphorus to stay healthy.
Linked up with other chemicals
it does no harm in your body.
In fact it's used (amongst other
things) to build your bones. Mind
you, don't eat the pure poison
or you'll end up with just bones and no body.

NOT AGAIN!
WHY NOT
GERBIL OR
HAMSTER
POISON?

Name: ANTIMONY

Alias: Sb

Description: Nice shiny look.
But no, it's NOT silver, so don't
try putting it in your pockets.
It breaks easily and it's a poison!

Horrible habits: Antimony
can build up in the body until
one day you wake up dead. The Count says
that victims feel sick, throw up and make
lots of extra snot. It's like having bad flu
and food poisoning all rolled into one.
Oh yes, and you get diarrhoea thrown in
for good measure.

69

<u>Known haunts:</u> Used in industry and also some types of enamels and paints.

<u>Redeeming features:</u> If you got poisoned at least you wouldn't have to go to school - maybe not ever!

WORRY!

ER — I THINK WE'D RATHER GO TO SCHOOL!

We'll be back with the most murderous metalloid of all after the commercial break – bye for now!

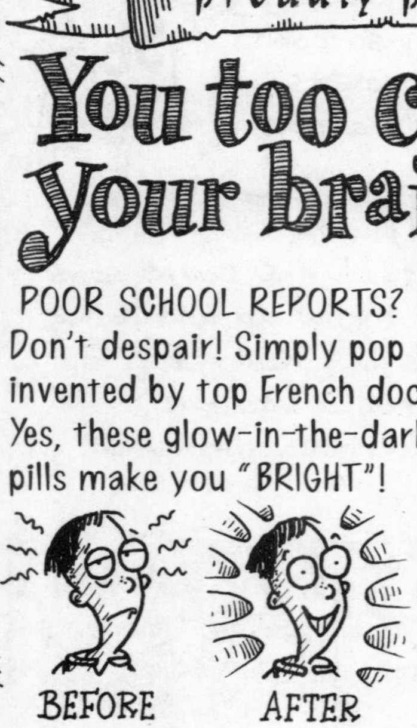

70

GET THIS, GIRLS! New glow-in-the-dark funky phosphorus skin cream! As worn by Victorian ladies in the 1870s – it gives you a healthy glow when you're "glowing" out clubbing!

VICTORIAN HANDBAGS

THE SMALL PRINT – And it's smelly and damages the skin.

FANCY A BIT MORE ICE CREAM? FEELING A BIT TOO FULL UP?

TOO RIGHT!

Make room for it by drinking from the...

VOMIT GOBLET

One sip and you'll be chucking up all over the carpet! (Made from genuine antimony.)

As used by the Romans so they could eat even more in their giant greedy banquets...

ATE TWO, BRUTUS?

NO, 20, CAESAR... BLEURRRRRGH!

And now, it's time to get a flavour of the most murderous metalloid. Well, maybe getting a "flavour" isn't the best way to put it. And no, Count Vomito, I DON'T want to sample it!

71

Name: ARSENIC Alias: As

Description: Grey-white and easy to crunch if you chew it, but that's a bit silly.

Horrible habits: Some good news: on its own, arsenic would happily pass through the guts on a one-way trip to the toilet. Some bad news: it's never on its own. For example, it combines with oxygen from the air. And it can get into the body through the mouth or skin, or by being breathed in as a gas.

Known haunts: YIKES! It's EVERYWHERE! There's arsenic in soil, the sea, and not to mention a teeny bit in your body. In tiny doses it's not too bad, but in large doses it's deadly.

Redeeming features: If it wasn't for arsenic, you couldn't play your favourite computer game. Yes, there's arsenic in the semiconductors - vital electrical bits - of a computer.

The effects of arsenic are complicated and painful, so we've asked Dr Grimgrave for an expert medical opinion. Beware – he's in a grumpy mood. Er – come to think of it, he's *always* in a grumpy mood…

THE EFFECTS OF ARSENIC
by Dr H Grimgrave

Arsenic is a fascinating poison because it can affect the body in so many interesting ways.

Sadly I don't see too many of these cases — but if anyone's got any spare poisoned body bits I could do with some for my private medical collection!

A small dose

Arsenic widens blood vessels in the skin and gives it a "glow", as ill-educated persons say. Can you believe some idiots in Victorian times took the poison as a tonic and their idiot doctors encouraged them?! As the poison builds up in the body, the hair and nails fall out and the skin turns yellow from liver damage.

AH YES, YOU'RE LOOKING MUCH BETTER! HAVE ANOTHER BOTTLE!

IDIOT DOCTOR   IDIOT PATIENT

Other problems are weakness, vomiting, diarrhoea, a puffy face, dizziness, sore eyes, nose and mouth. In fact there are enough ailments to keep an overworked doctor like me busy for hours!

A large dose

Patients who have taken a lot of arsenic suffer terrible vomiting and diarrhoea, violent gut pains and death in an hour. I usually see these patients first. Of course one has to make hard choices at times. One idiot who wasn't poisoned at all said he would die in 50 seconds so I told him "Sit down and I'll see you *in a minute*, ha ha!" But I can't sit here blathering all day — I've got some more idiots to see!

Now I bet you'd rather share your home with a bad-tempered hippo with bottom problems than a lorry-load of arsenic – but in Victorian times people didn't understand the full dangers of this poison. Let's go and spend Christmas with this typical Victorian family … and their amazing collection of arsenic items!

1. Arsenic paint on wall 2. Arsenic rat poison
3. Arsenic-coated playing cards 4. Arsenic paper
to kill flies 5. Arsenic in dye on curtains
6. Arsenic in dye on carpet 7. Arsenic Christmas
tree decorations 8. Arsenic wrapping paper
9. Arsenic cloth on card table

Feeling unwell yet? If you're worried about all that nasty arsenic on your fingers, don't try licking it off! NO, why not wash it off with the Victorian family's de-luxe arsenic soap?

AWFUL ARSENIC MURDERS

Arsenic has no taste and no smell and since it was easy to buy in shops, the poison was first choice for cruel Victorian killers. Most arsenic murder stories go like this...

Someone dies. The poisoner inherits their money, plus a large insurance payout. Someone else gets suspicious. The body is dug up and arsenic is found. The poisoner gets caught, put on trial and executed. End of story.

But there's one true arsenic murder story that's different. Firstly, it might not have been a murder at all and secondly, the accuser was a ghost! This scary tale from Count Vomito's private poison library is sure to chill your blood...

St John's Church, London, 1850

Mr Graves blew the dust off a coffin lid and squinted at the brass plate. "I fink we've found her, Mr Archer," he called to the young artist.

Archer was perched on a nearby coffin, sketching the ancient crypt with its stone walls and huge dusty cobwebs. Next to him sat Mr Graves's young son, Joe.

"Is your drawing for a book, Mr Archer?" asked Joe. The boy shivered. The winter's night was cold as the grave.

"Yes, Joe. A drawing of Fanny Kent for a book of strange stories."

75

"It's a strange story, right enough," remarked Mr Graves as he rubbed some warmth back into his hands.

"I heard you knew about her," said Archer, without looking up.

"Ho yes, sir, I know everything!" replied Graves. "And if you likes, I can tell you and Joe the 'ole story."

Archer nodded his agreement and Graves sat down heavily. Then he began his tale...

"It happened about 50 years afore I was born. William Kent and his wife, Fanny, came to lodge with Richard Parsons. And that's when it all started. The ghostly knocking and scratching. All night long it went on – a-knocking and a-scratching on the wall."

"It must have been frightening," said Archer.

"I should say so! No one slept a wink. And poor Fanny said it was a sign that she must die..."

"Why did she fink that, Dad?" asked Joe.

"I dunno, son. Maybe she felt unwell or somefink..."

"So who was this ghost?" asked Archer.

"Well, sir. That's the mystery. Some said it was Fanny's sister come to warn Fanny that her husband was poisoning her. He stood to gain £100 in Fanny's will. And there were some what even saw the ghost. They said it was a woman shining so bright you could see your watch by the light! Soon after, the Kents moved out and Fanny died. Mr Kent said it was smallpox wot carried her off, but the ghost told Parsons it was *arsenic*."

"How did it say that? I thought it just made noises," said Archer with a frown.

"Parsons invented a code. One knock for 'yes' and two for 'no'. By now it was the talk of the town. Lords and ladies came to listen to the ghost. And the Lord Mayor asked a group of experts to find out the truth."

"And did they?" asked Archer.

"They found out the ghost didn't knock unless Parson's little girl was around. And it didn't knock when the girl was watched closely. Some days before the experts arrived, the ghost had said it would knock on Fanny's coffin. So the experts came to this very spot and called out, 'ARE YOU THERE, FANNY KENT?' ... but nuffink happened."

All at once something bumped in the shadows. Joe nearly jumped out of his skin.

"Don't worry son, it's only a rat," said Graves sounding rather rattled. "There's always a few of 'em in these old churches!"

Archer let out a cloud of foggy breath. "So the girl made the ghost sounds?" he asked.

"No one could prove nuffink."

"And the arsenic story – was that made up too?"

"Kent said so, but then he would."

Far above their heads the church clock struck midnight.

"It's getting late," said Archer.

Graves cleared his throat. "Begging your pardon, sir," he said "Are you sure you want to draw her? She's been dead a long while and I wouldn't fink your readers would like to see her if she's a bit … worm-eaten."

"We had better find out," said Archer grimly.

"Very good, sir," said Graves, standing up. "It's too perishing cold to sit much longer."

He fished in the pocket of his grubby apron and pulled out his screwdriver. Slowly and with much scraping, he undid the rusty fastenings and lifted the heavy wooden coffin lid. He reached into the coffin and gently pulled the cold dusty sheet from the dead woman's face.

Joe gulped and closed his eyes. He felt scared of ghosts. And what horrors they might find in the coffin.

"Well … I never!" gasped Graves.

Archer sucked in his breath. Slowly, Joe opened his eyes.

Fanny lay in her coffin with a peaceful expression on her beautiful face. Her eyes were closed and there were no smallpox scars on her cheeks.

"It looks like she's asleep," whispered Joe.

"I've never seen nuffink like this," muttered Graves. "Not once in 30 years."

Archer stared at the woman's face, taking in every detail.

"There's only thing that could have preserved her like this…" he said.

"It's arsenic, innit, sir?" said Graves quietly.

So maybe the ghost was telling the truth, thought Joe. He shuddered. But this time it wasn't the cold.

TWO ROTTEN ARSENIC RUMOURS

1 Arsenic is said to preserve bodies by killing the germs that make the body decay. But some experts think that dry conditions may be more important in keeping germs at bay.

2 Arsenic may have been used by Japanese monks to turn their bodies into mummies … WHILE THEY WERE STILL ALIVE! What's that? You'd like to do this to your brother or sister (purely in the interests of science)? Well, don't let me stop you…

THE DIY JAPANESE MUMMY KIT

HERE'S WHAT YOU DO...

PUFF, PANT!

DAY 1 TO 1,000 — Live off nothing but nuts and seeds and enjoy happy healthy runs up mountains. This should get rid of all the fat on your body. (Fat makes the body rot quicker.)

CHOMP!

DAY 1,001 TO 2,000 — Eat only pine tree bark and pine needles. And don't forget to munch a bit of arsenic — it makes a tasty change from eating trees!

GLUG!

DAY 2,001 — Drink some more poison to kill the maggots after you die.

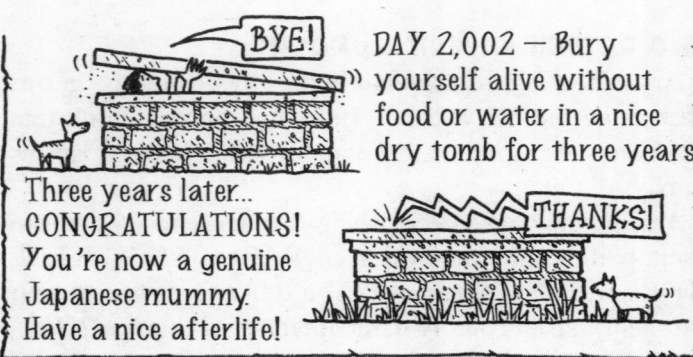

DAY 2,002 – Bury yourself alive without food or water in a nice dry tomb for three years.

BYE!

Three years later... CONGRATULATIONS! You're now a genuine Japanese mummy. Have a nice afterlife!

THANKS!

IMPORTANT ANNOUNCEMENT

We would like to apologize to readers who have ordered DIY mummy kits. They've been confiscated by the police. It's been against the law in Japan to make anyone into a mummy since 1895. And it's considered a very grave matter.

WHAT A SWIZ!

Well, I don't know about you – but all that talk about eating is making me hungry. And *not* for arsenic and pine needles! No, I fancy a nice big crunchy salad!

Ooh-er! I've peeped at the next chapter and I've changed my mind...

PAINFULLY POISONOUS PLANTS

How often have you heard this?

> ## EAT YOUR GREENS!

> WHY?

> ## BECAUSE THEY'RE GOOD FOR YOU!

But the plants in this chapter are so VERY BAD for you that if you ate them you wouldn't just have green fingers – you'd probably be green all over. Time for a word of warning…

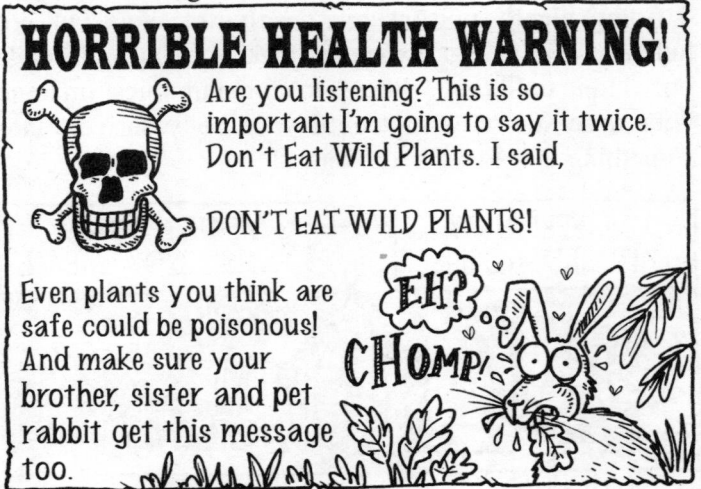

HORRIBLE HEALTH WARNING!

Are you listening? This is so important I'm going to say it twice. Don't Eat Wild Plants. I said,

DON'T EAT WILD PLANTS!

Even plants you think are safe could be poisonous! And make sure your brother, sister and pet rabbit get this message too.

EH?

CHOMP!

And now for everything you ever wanted to know about poisonous plants in ten seconds – but only if you read this next bit *really* F-A-S-T!

DANGER! POISONOUS PLANTS FACT ATTACK

1 There are hundreds of poisonous plants – including many plants you eat!

2 They're poisonous because they want to stop bugs and animals from eating them as side salads.

ERK! YUCK! UGH! MUNCH! NIBBLE! CHOMP!

SPOT THE POISONOUS PLANT!

3 The reason we're still alive is because we cook them first to destroy the poisons, or only eat the non-poisonous bits.

4 Some plants' poisons are deadly for bugs but not humans. Garlic, for example, makes slugs and snails ooze slime until they wither into slug mummies. Imagine your nose squirting snot until your body shrivels into something that lives in a pyramid!

I'M FEELING A BIT SLUGGISH... YEAH, I KNOW WHAT YOU MEAN.

5 Some poisonous plants are useful. In 1640, plant expert John Parkinson found out that mice won't eat books printed with ink containing poisonous wormwood juice. By the way, it's not very likely that this book is printed with poisonous ink, but don't let the dog chew it to find out.

6 Some plant poisons can be used as medicines...

• Digitalis (didge-it-ah-lis) is a drug that speeds up the heartbeat. It was first found as a poison in foxgloves.

• Curare (cu-rah-ray) comes from South American strychnos (strick-nos) vines. It's a nerve poison that stops signals getting to the muscles. The muscles can't move, so they relax – and that's handy for surgeons who need to operate on nice relaxed bodies.

• Atropine (at-rop-peen) comes from deadly nightshade. Like curare, atropine blocks nerve messages and relaxes muscles.

7 Some plants are irritating rather than deadly. Touch them and they'll make you sore – now that would be a little rash! Eat them and you'll get a sore mouth, but that would be even more stupid.

Bet you never knew!
The dumb cane of South and Central America gets its name because if you eat it you can't say a word. The poison in the leaves makes your mouth so sore you can't talk for hours. Mind you, you'd have to be pretty dumb to sample this unspeakable poison.

HOW CAN I HELP THIS IDIOT IF HE WON'T TELL ME WHAT HE'S EATEN?

CHOKE!

AN IRRITATING IRRITATING-PLANTS QUIZ

Which of these plants are irritating and which aren't?

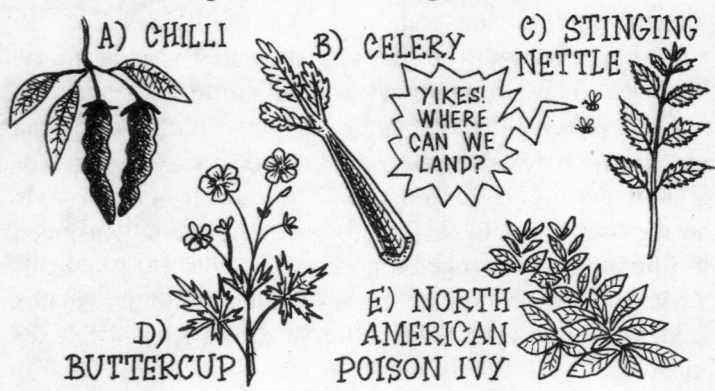

A) CHILLI

B) CELERY

YIKES! WHERE CAN WE LAND?

C) STINGING NETTLE

D) BUTTERCUP

E) NORTH AMERICAN POISON IVY

Answers:

Sorry, readers, it's a trick quiz – they're ALL irritating! Now isn't that an *irritating* result? Oh well, you can always try it on your teacher!

a) Hot chillies irritate the mouth. Eat a few of them and your face turns red and your eyes turn bloodshot. But that doesn't stop strange people in Wisconsin, USA, holding chilli-eating contests.

HERE'S MI GUTZACHE AND WATSON AT A RECENT CHILLI-EATING CONTEST...

SCOFF!

SWEAT!

CHOMP!

HOT DOG

CHILLI

NOT CHILLY

b) Celery-stem juice can sting your skin in sunlight.

c) Stinging nettles. Well, that was an easy one! Did you know that the nettles in the centre of a clump are said to sting less? These plants are older and their poison isn't as strong – but don't go bounding into clumps of nettles to find out!

d) Sorry, but pretty yellow buttercups are more like *bitter*-cups. Their juice can sting the skin.

e) Another DEAD giveaway. The sticky oily poison sticks to the skin. You can pick up the poison from clothes and it can even be carried in smoke on specks of ash. It's said that you can get a rash even by touching a dog that's been in contact with poison ivy. The Count has offered to test this idea using Gutzache and Watson...

Hmm – Gutzache doesn't seem *up to scratch*. Oh well, at least Watson's coat protected *him* from the poison.

So irritating plants can be a sore subject, but at least they don't kill people. Unlike the pizzas Donna Venoma cooks up...

THE DEATH-CAP
SURPRISE PIZZA
(The surprise is how deadly
it is – it's guaranteed to cause
vomiting and liver failure!)

TOMATO
(MAKE SURE
YOU PUT
IN A FEW
POISONOUS
BITS*)

DEATH-CAP
TOADSTOOLS

GREEN OLIVES
(TO MATCH THE
COLOUR OF THE
DEATH CAPS)

FRESHLY
CHOPPED
HEMLOCK
LEAVES

EESH!

(OTHER INGREDIENTS AS BEFORE)

THE DESTROYING ANGEL
SUPREME PIZZA
(Just as deadly as death cap)

DESTROYING ANGEL
TOADSTOOLS (THEY
LOOK LIKE ORDINARY
MUSHROOMS BUT THEY'RE
MUCH MORE FUN)

A FEW RED-
HOT CHILLIES
TO SPICE IT UP

UGH!

* see page 88.

87

Hopefully the pizzas served in your school canteen aren't quite as deadly as these poison pizzas – but the canteen is a great place to torture a teacher (all in the interests of education, naturally!).

TEACHER'S LUNCHTIME TEASER

Your teacher is relaxing with a healthy school-dinner salad and a baked potato. Smile sweetly and say...

LOOKS LIKE YOU'RE EATING POISONOUS PLANTS!

HUH?

At this point your teacher might turn a colour of a ripe tomato (this is probably rage and not a sign of poisoning). If you're very brave you could point out...

IT'S TRUE, THE SPROUTING AND GREEN BITS OF THE POTATO ARE POISONOUS. SO ARE THE LEAVES. AND GUESS WHAT? TOMATO LEAVES AND STEMS ARE POISONOUS TOO! EATING THE WRONG BITS OF THESE PLANTS CAUSES DIARRHOEA AND BREATHING PROBLEMS!

RED FOR DANGER?

In 1820 many Americans believed that red tomatoes were as poisonous as the rest of the plant. But – so the story goes – Colonel Robert Johnson had other ideas...

| TOMATOES ARE GOOD FOR YOU. | SO PROVE IT! | VERY WELL, IN BOSTON, ON 26 SEPTEMBER, I WILL EAT A WHOLE BASKET OF TOMATOES! | BUT THAT'S A DEADLY DOSE! |

EVERYONE THOUGHT THAT ROBERT WOULD DIE AND THOUSANDS TURNED UP TO WATCH...

IS HE EATING THEM WITH DRESSING?

YES, HE'S KEEPING HIS CLOTHES ON.

THE GREAT TOMAT[...]

ROBERT ATE A TOMATO.

MMMM

ROBERT ATE 20 TOMATOES ... AND LIVED!

NOW HE'S SHOWING OFF.

SLURP!

MUNCH!

DO TOMATOES MAKE YOU RETCH UP?

CHOMP! CHEW!

GREAT TOMATO EATING DIS[...]

NO, THEY MAKE YOU KETCHUP.

89

So there we are. The garden is gruesome, mushrooms are murderous and salads are sinister. But the very worst plant poisons are coming up right now. And when I say worst, I mean the really WORST!

SEVEN SINISTER PLANT PRODUCTS THAT YOU WOULDN'T WANT TO SAMPLE IN A SALAD

1 Castor-oil seeds. Eat the seeds and they'll probably pop straight through your guts and ... you know the rest. But the actual poison – RICIN – is twice as deadly as a cobra's bite. It causes a burning mouth and blisters, bleeding guts and kidney failure.

2 Strychnos seeds. The same vicious vine that makes curare also brings you – STRYCHNINE. This painful poison attacks the nerves and stops them switching off after a signal passes along them. The muscles go mad. Victims end up arched over with a giant grin on their faces. And no, it's not because they're happy – it's all a result of the mad muscle twitches.

3 Henbane and deadly nightshade contain HYOSCINE. It's another nasty nerve poison, but this time the nerve signals get blocked at junctions between nerves and muscles. It's a bit like a traffic jam when the traffic lights break down. And the body breaks down too.

4 There's hyoscine in mandrake. This human-shaped root was supposed to scream when it was pulled up. The scream was said to kill all who heard it, so the Romans trained dogs to dig up the root.

DON'T WORRY, YOU'LL BE FINE!

PARDON?

5 Rhubarb contains OXALIC (ox-al-lick) ACID. It's used in dyeing (sorry, that's not a dire joke) and it also gets rid of unwanted stains and rust. But don't let that put you off rhubarb – the poison's only in the leaves.

6 Apricot kernel (seed). Apricots are fine but their kernels contain the deadly nerve poison CYANIDE ... and you can find out some more about cyanide.

7 Aconite. Otherwise known as wolf's bane, it's a pretty white flower, but the effects of the poison are far from pretty. They include tingling and burning skin, followed by heart failure.

Bet you never knew!
In 1881, police suspected aconite had been used to murder a man but there was no scientific test to prove it. So scientist Dr Stevenson had to take fluid from the guts of the body and touch it with his tongue. Sure enough, the scientist felt tingling and pain for four hours. Oh well, at least he had the problem licked.

Painful poison fact file

NAME: Cyanide

THE BASIC FACTS: **1** Remember that ghastly hydrogen cyanide gas from page 54? Cyanide is a carbon and a nitrogen atom that get together to cause trouble.

2 They latch on to many types of atom, including sodium, hydrogen and potassium, to make poisons.

3 If cyanide gets in the body, it sticks to enzymes. Especially the enzyme needed to use oxygen to make energy.

4 So the effect of cyanide is the same as if the body can't breathe. The body weakens, the face turns blue and the heart stops.

THE PAINFUL DETAILS: **1** Now I really don't want you to panic about this — OK? Not only is there cyanide in apricot seeds, it's in apple and plum pips too!

EEK! OOER! YIKES!

2 I said, DON'T PANIC! You can eat a fruit salad safely! Even if you swallow a pip by mistake it will pass through your guts without harm. But eating an apricot seed can cause vomiting and breathing problems.

Millions of people in Africa eat cassava, a type of root that contains cyanide. The root came from Brazil, where native people made it safe by spitting on the root and leaving it to rot. Germs in the spit make enzymes that stop the poison working. But that's not an excuse to spit on your school dinner…

In Africa, people get rid of the poison by letting cassava rot in ponds. And although eating veg that's been mouldering in a smelly green pond doesn't sound like fun, it's much more jolly than a dose of cyanide.

But humans aren't the only animals that can eat some poisonous plants safely. Some creatures actually *enjoy* picnicking off poison! Goats happily dine off deadly nightshade and colorado beetles eat it all the time – even though it's heaving with horrible hyoscine. And some creatures eat poisons and store them in their body which makes them become poisonous too. Monarch butterfly caterpillars chomp their way through poisonous milkweed. The poison makes the caterpillars poisonous and they turn into poisonous butterflies. Other animals won't touch them.

Scientists aren't too sure how some creatures can eat poisons and live. But one thing is certain, monarch butterflies aren't the only lethal life forms around. The next chapter is *alive* with them…

APPALLINGLY POISONOUS ANIMALS

Say the word "animal" to your little sister and she'll probably say...

AHHHH!

She'll be thinking of cute kittens and playful puppies, of course. But if she saw the animals in this chapter she'd probably say...

ARRRRRRGH!!

There are hundreds of poisonous creatures. Like plants, they use poison to defend themselves from being eaten – but some, like spiders and snakes, use poison to catch animals to eat. And now let's pay a visit to Count Vomito's private zoo. He says visitors are always dying to see the animals – or is it dying *after* they've seen them?

THIS IS A BIG JOB!

AND WHEN YOU'VE FINISHED, THERE'S A PILE OF VISITORS THAT NEEDS CLEARING UP.

QUEASY POISON QUIZ

Here's a selection of creatures – which of them
ARE poisonous and which of them AREN'T?

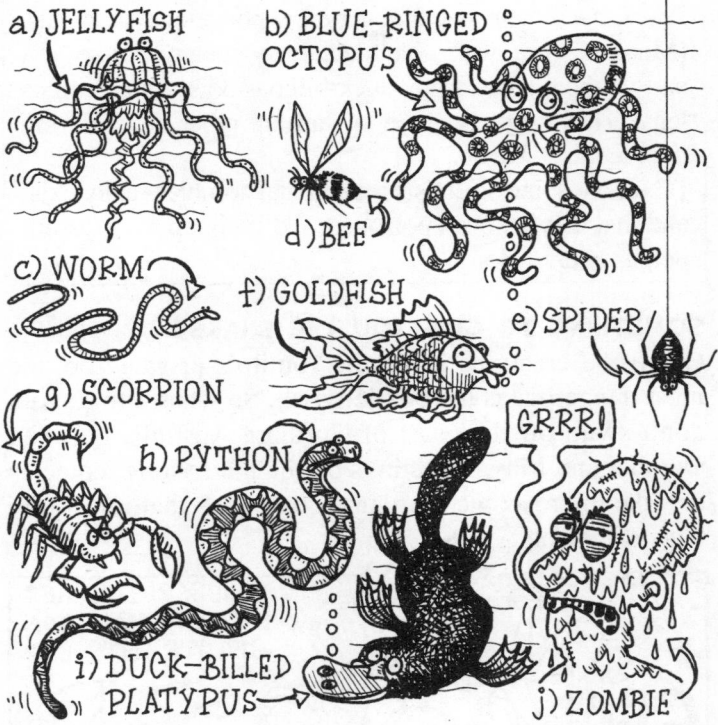

a) JELLYFISH

b) BLUE-RINGED OCTOPUS

d) BEE

c) WORM

f) GOLDFISH

e) SPIDER

g) SCORPION

h) PYTHON

GRRR!

i) DUCK-BILLED PLATYPUS

j) ZOMBIE

Answers:

a) Yes (see page 96).

b) Yes (see page 101).

c) No – so good news! You can eat as much worm spaghetti as you like!

d) Yes (see page 103).

e) Yes (see page 107).

f) No, which is why the Count's cat is taking a close interest in Bubbles the goldfish.

g) Yes (see page 107).

h) No, the python squeezes its victims to death – fancy a hug?

i) Yes, the male is one of a very few poisonous mammals. (Mammals are warm-blooded, furry creatures like you and your cat.) The dippy duck-bill has poison spurs on its legs. They might be there to warn off other males during the breeding season.

j) No, but some scientists reckon that zombies really exist and that they've been poisoned. We'll dig up the dreadful details later…

SOMETHING TO GIVE YOU THE SHAKES

Of all the creatures in Count Vomito's private zoo, the most dangerous is the box jellyfish. So whatever you do, don't swim off the coast of Northern Australia between October and May. The stings on the metre-long tentacles are like microscopic murderous harpoons that inject tiny bags of poison.

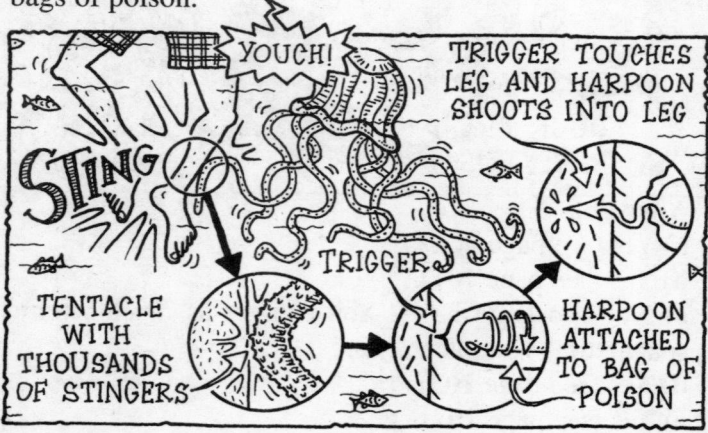

The painful poison can kill a man in just 120 SECONDS – it's enough to turn your legs into quivering jelly!

One victim, John Carrier, was stung in 1990. He said it felt like he'd walked into a "bush of flame". The pain is so violent many people drown because they forget to swim. Passer-by Peter Miller heard John's cry of pain and said it was...

> A horrible blood-curdling scream that went right through my body. It made my skin crawl.

But John was lucky! He hadn't been stung badly enough to die in seconds and an ambulance crew saved his life with a substance that stops the stings – vinegar.

And now for a rather painful question. What's even more painful than being stung by a jellyfish? Answer – being stung by a jellyfish *and* a fish. To find out more, let's take a look at the Count's fish tank. There are things in there that would give Bubbles the goldfish a heart attack...

NO TANKS!

FEARSOME FISH FACTS

There are about 28,000 types of fish and at least 1,200 could be poisonous. Count Vomito is especially fond of his stonefish. They have poison spines to stop other fish eating them. It's nothing personal but they'll also stab anyone who treads on them by mistake. And it's easily done, because guess what? They look just like stones! (By the way, if you do tread on a stonefish the pain makes you froth at the mouth and roll around and bite anyone who comes near. The poison makes your leg swell up like an elephant's leg and your toes turn black and drop off. So tread carefully!)

COULD YOU BE A SCIENTIST?

You are working in a British oceanarium in 2001 and you've got a poison problem. Dottie the dicefish is feeling tense and squirting poison. How do you calm her down?

a) Play her a selection of relaxing music.

b) Give her a big toy dice to make friends with.

c) Stun her with an electric shock – BEWARE, you could be DICE-ing with death!

Answer: If you said c) be warned – it's extremely dangerous. And putting electrodes in your goldfish's bowl is a criminal offence! The answer is **b)**! Dottie was given a dice and, true to her name, daft Dottie decided the dice was her dad (or mum). Soon Dottie and her dice were deeply devoted. Would you make a mistake like this?

SPOT THE DIFFERENCE COMPETITION

a) DICE   b) DOTTIE   c) DOTTIE'S DAD

THE PERILS OF PUFFERFISH

Pufferfish don't have poison spines, but parts of the pufferfish *are* poisonous – and they're 275 times more deadly than cyanide. The first sign of poisoning is tingling. Then you go numb and can't move and can't breathe. And there's NO antidote. But that doesn't stop people in Japan *eating* the non-poisonous bits. They're popular with people who enjoy dangerous dinners (so why don't they just eat school dinners – they're *really* risky!).

We needed someone to go undercover to sample the perilous pufferfish. But who was up to this scary job?

HEY I LOVE FISH – IT'S EASY MONEY!

The possibly poisonous pufferfish

Report by MI Gutzache

So I took the job...
Sure there was a danger of poison but the risk ain't too bad. The chefs are trained for three years to cut out the bad bits so I figured my life was in good hands. I was more worried about eating the fish raw – it's how they eat it in Japan. I'd rather eat a hot dog than cold cat food any day!

DELICIOUS!

99

So I sat in the restaurant and waited for the fish. I started thinking and I wished I hadn't. I'd done my homework and I knew that just 10 g of poisonous pufferfish can kill. Then the fish arrived. I was finally face-to-face with the fish. Could it be a fatal fish? Watson sniffed it and he kinda turned up his nose. Mind you, he ain't too keen on seafood.

I took a very small bite. It was enough, I figured. The fish tasted fishy. I began to sweat – would I die? I felt sick. It was the poison – I knew it! I cursed my luck. To think I'd survived organized crime to get puffed out by a pufferfish.

I wanted out so I headed for the door. As luck would have it there was a large hole in the street so I was able to test an ancient Japanese remedy. Burial up to the neck in cold earth. It didn't help.

Then the waiter came out. He was hollering. He said he was mighty sorry – they'd given me sardines by mistake. And the cat wanted them back!

MORE SERIOUSLY SCARY SEA-LIFE

If you're swimming off an Australian beach you've got more than killer jellyfish and fearsome fish to be scared of…

OK, so it may look cute but the blue-ringed octopus bites!

And its bite is deadly poisonous. Which means that if you're silly enough to take it home as a pet you'll regret it for the rest of your life ... but that won't be very long!

In fact, a bite from a blue-ringed octopus doesn't feel too bad. At first the bite doesn't hurt. But the octopus' spit contains a nasty nerve poison that makes you blind, throw up and lose control of your muscles. Death can follow in three hours.

And now for another creature that will put you off your seafood salad...

COULD YOU BE A SCIENTIST?

In the 1950s the CIA (the US secret service) had an embarrassing problem. They'd absent-mindedly lost enough poison to kill 110,000 people...

1 But the amazing thing is that this poison came from a rather tasty shellfish. Which one?

a) Scampi.

b) Starfish.

c) Clams.

2 Where did the poison turn up?

a) In a seafood soup served in the canteen.

b) A toilet.

c) A freezer.

3 What happened to the poison?

a) It was poured into an enemy leader's tea.

b) It was fed to 110,000 very unlucky hamsters.

c) It was given away free to scientists.

OOER!

Answers:

1 c) Yes, clams. A man working for the CIA had collected hundreds of clams. The poison is found in just one part of the clam, so you need an awful lot of clams to make it.

2 c) In the 1970s it turned up in a US Navy freezer in a US Navy Office... I bet it was cold and "clammy" by then! Of course the poison was a secret and the Navy "clammed-up" about it...

3 c) The poison was sent back to the man who made it, and he gave it away. What an un-shellfish thing to do!

By the way, the scientists used it for peaceful experiments and DIDN'T put it in each other's tea.

Hmm – maybe we're safer on dry land... Or maybe not!

102

BULLY BEES AND WICKED WASPS

Each year brutal bees and wicked wasps kill more than 40,000 people all over the world. Their stings aren't usually deadly but lots of people get stung and some victims are allergic (dangerously sensitive) to poison. They suffer heart attacks as a result of the shock.

Unlike wasps, bees die when they sting. Their stings have barbs like tiny harpoons and the bee can't yank them out of your skin. So the bee flies off leaving half its insides behind...

You'd think that would be enough to make bees think twice about stinging. And they do – but not all of them. African honeybees sting first and ask questions later. (Correction – they're too dead later to ask questions so they just sting.)

THE BUZZ ABOUT BEES

1 I bet you'd rather not know – but in 1964 a young Zimbabwean boy was stung 2,243 times by bees. He tried to hide from them in a river but the brutal bees stung him until his head turned black with stings and swelled up like a football. Amazingly he lived.

2 A scientist tried to find out how dangerous African honeybees really are. He juggled a ball in front of their hive to see how many times the ball got stung. But the bad-tempered bees attacked the stupid scientist instead. He was stung 92 times in a few seconds and ran 800 metres to get away. Sadly nobody clocked his time – it could have been a new world record.

3 In 1957, a South American scientist had a smart idea. Why not breed bad-tempered African bees with the friendly buzzy European bee? You'll get a well-behaved bee that does well in hot countries – well, that was the idea. But what they got was … KILLER BEES! The bees escaped in Brazil and reached the USA by 1990.

Killer bees attack anything that goes near their hive and they like nothing better than nesting in people's houses. In fact, they'd like to move in with YOU!

EEK! OUCH! **BEEHIVE** YOURSELVES! YEOW! ARGH! OOF! ERK!

Bet you never knew!
One insect has poison that's even more painful than bee stings. I'm talking about the Spanish fly. It's a bit of a misleading name because this bug isn't a fly and it isn't always Spanish – it's a green beetle that also lives in France! The beetle's juice makes blisters on the skin and burns your insides if you swallow it. One victim threw up multi-coloured sick. (And no, it wasn't a new art form.)

Fancy making friends with a few more cruel creepy-crawlies? Well, tough, because they don't want to make friends with you!

REALLY REVOLTING CREEPY-CRAWLIES

It turns out that Count Vomito has a passion for centipedes, scorpions and spiders. He's got a special corner of his zoo where they live and he calls them his "willing little helpers", but I wouldn't like to think what they're helping him with. Anyway, he's promised to let us have a peek in his top-secret book of poisons…

Count Vomito's Book of Poisons

NAME: Centipede

DESCRIPTION: 30-46 legs, body divided into segments. At least 28,000 different types.

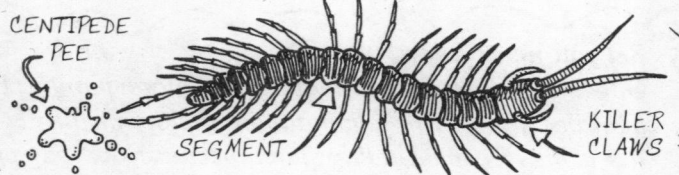

CENTIPEDE PEE

SEGMENT

KILLER CLAWS

WHERE FOUND: Damp, sheltered places all over the world.

HOW THEY POISON: Poison claws at front.

EFFECTS ON VICTIM: Kills millipedes, but only some types hurt humans. One variety that lives in the Philippine Islands can cause pain for three weeks — how fascinating!

POISONING POSSIBILITIES: Centipedes can live for a few hours in the human stomach. The poison causes sickness and breathing problems. Hmm — I wonder if anyone would like to try a cheese and centipede sandwich?

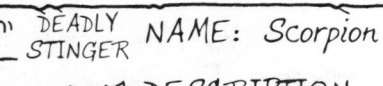

NAME: *Scorpion*

DESCRIPTION: Powerful pincers and and eight legs. Over 2,000 types.

WHERE FOUND: Hot countries.

HOW THEY POISON: *Sting on end of tail.*

EFFECTS ON VICTIM: Kills small animals. Sadly, most scorpions aren't dangerous to humans although a bad sting feels like a nail hammered into your thumb. Fatal stingers include Deathstalker and Androctonus (the name means "man-killer") scorpions from North Africa and the Middle East. HEE HEE!

POISONING POSSIBILITIES: Scorpions hide in shoes and beds. I must put a few in the guest bedroom!

NAME: *Spider*

ABDOMEN

HEAD/CHEST

EYES

DESCRIPTION: Eight legs, body divided into a head/chest and abdomen, eight eyes. At least 40,000 different types — but probably thousands more await discovery. (Oh good! I hope they're deadly!) Their bodies measure between 0.5 mm and 9 cm long. They make good pets, too!

WHERE FOUND: All over the world including my bathroom, I'm pleased to say.

HOW THEY POISON: Poison fangs.

EFFECTS ON VICTIM: Stops victim escaping so it can be eaten at leisure. Only a few spiders are deadly to humans — the black widow of the USA, the wandering spider of Brazil and the funnel-web of Australia are examples. Unfortunately, most spiders can't bite through human skin and those that can, such as tarantulas, don't have a powerful enough poison to kill. It's all very frustrating!

@#!!!

POISONING POSSIBILITIES: Black widow spiders hide under toilet seats and wandering spiders wander about the house. I think I feel an evil plot coming on!

BOG-STANDARD BLACK WIDOW

So would you volunteer to be bitten by a black widow spider? If you think that sounds like a hairy situation you may be shocked to learn that in 1933 a Canadian scientist named Allan Blair actually let himself be bitten as an experiment!

But let's hear the spider's side of the story...

The Spider Magazine
1933

In this week's issue:
- THE GOOD WEB GUIDE — FLY CUISINE
- I BIT A SCIENTIST ... AND LIVED

I BIT A SCIENTIST ... AND LIVED!

A black widow's heart-warming human-interest story. As told to Airey Legges  HI!

For years we spiders have lived in terror of humans trapping us in their baths and breaking our webs for fun. But now a brave black widow spider is biting back.

 BZZZ!

I sure am. It all started with a scientist starving me for two weeks to make me bad-tempered...

So you were pretty mad?

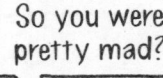 BZZZ!

Not as mad as he was to let me bite his little finger!

So what happened to him?

ERK!

Well, the finger turned blue and red and then swelled up like a giant purple sausage. It was all very colourful. (And the things he was saying sounded even more colourful. But I'm a spider and I don't understand that kind of language!)

I heard the scientist went to hospital.

BZZZ!

Is it true the scientist was planning to let you bite him again?

BZZZ!

Yes, he was a bit wimpy if you ask me. All that stuff about sweating and vomiting and going mad with pain! He should be grateful he wasn't a fly!

Well, that was the idea – but he changed his mind for some reason. Never mind, sounds like there's something else for me to get my fangs into...

GULP!

STAYING FOR DINNER, AIREY?

Bet you never knew!

1 The so-called tarantulas that live in southern USA aren't proper tarantulas – they're Aphonopelma (A-fon-o-pel-ma) spiders.

2 People once thought their bite was deadly and the cure was drinking lots of whisky. Scientists find this idea hard to swallow (unlike the whisky drinkers who found it very easy to swallow).

3 In fact the spider's bite is painful rather than deadly, so you don't have to worry about them. But of course some people do worry about them – rather a lot...

And here to prove it is a scary bedtime story from *Poison Pen Tales*. It's sure to scare your little brother or sister's pants off, especially if you tell the story by torchlight and keep a toy spider hidden up your sleeve until the vital moment...

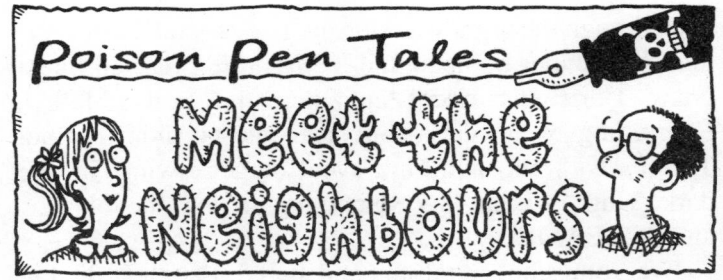
Meet Elbert and Wilma, a typical all-American couple who worked hard and saved up to achieve their ultimate dream: to build their very own home in sunny Arizona.

After years of saving, Elbert and Wilma had enough money. So they built their dream house and made ready to move in.

"Say, Elbert," said Wilma. "I figure there's one thing missing from our lovely new home."

"So what's that, my little patootie?" asked Elbert.

"Why, big huggy-bear, I'm talking about one of them big saguaro cactus things. I've always wanted one. And I figure it will look just fine in our living room!"

"Well, honey bunch," replied Elbert, "what are we waiting for? Let's get ourselves down to the garden centre and purchase one."

And so they did. And Wilma was right – the cactus did look good in the new living room.

Three weeks later Wilma and Elbert threw a house-warming party. All their friends and neighbours came, even though the night was stormy. The rain fell in torrents and the thunder boomed and the lightning flashed like a crazy Christmas tree. And then the power failed. Everything went dark, but the guests didn't mind. The party went with an even bigger swing in the dark. Until Wilma saw something in the shadows ... and SCREAMED!

Everyone stopped talking and stared. Laughter died in their throats. Their drinks dropped on to the new carpet.

Was it just the flickering lightning – or had the cactus come to life? Yes – there was no doubt. The giant plant was wiggling and wriggling as if it were dancing!

With trembling hands Elbert switched on his torch and pointed the light at it. And everyone began to scream at the tops of their voices. What they saw emptied the house in just 30 seconds.

The cactus was alive all right! It was alive ... with *spiders*. Deadly, poisonous, biting baby tarantulas. Their mother had laid them as eggs in the cactus and now they had hatched. And the babies were hungry!

Hundreds of tarantulas were creeping and crawling over the carpet and climbing the curtains. They were scuttling over shoes, hiding in handbags and tiptoeing up trouser legs. They would bite anything that moved and their poison was four times more deadly than a big tarantula's.

(And that's when you quietly place the toy spider on your brother or sister and shout, WHAT'S THAT IN YOUR HAIR?!)

112

So how do you feel now? A bit green perhaps? Oh good, you'll be just the right colour to make friends with the Count's next group of poisonous pets...

FRIGHTENING FROGS AND TOADS

1 Frogs and toads have poison in their skin.

2 Some frogs go a little over the top in this area. The poison-arrow frog of Columbia, South America, is so dreadfully deadly that just 0.0001 g of its poison can kill.

3 And that means that (help ... where's my calculator?) a yoghurt pot full of poison (weighing 28.3 g) could kill 2.5 million people! That's some frog.

4 In the 1970s scientists discovered the South American terrible frog. The poison from this frog is so deadly that the scientists had to wear rubber gloves to touch it. When a chicken and a dog touched the gloves they died.

5 If frogs are frightening, toads can be terrifying. A dog that chews a toad will throw up and foam at the mouth. It could die.

WHAT'S HAPPENED TO REX?

HE ATE A TOAD AND CROAKED.

But there's one creature that makes even the most poisonous frog or toad look like a harmless happy hopper. On a scale of one to ten, this scaly beast is right off the scale…

SCARY POISONOUS SNAKES

So how would you like your very own poisonous snake pet? Of all the creatures in his private poison zoo, Count Vomito's favourite is his pet rattlesnake…

RATTLE!

SNAKES WILL ONLY ATTACK PEOPLE IF THEY'RE UPSET. I'M TRYING TO TRAIN SLIPPY, BUT HE'S EASILY RATTLED!

And now for some slippery snake secrets…

Painful poison fact file

NAME: Poisonous snakes

THE BASIC FACTS: 1 There are 2,300 types of snake, but only 300 are poisonous to people.

2 As Count Vomito says, no poisonous snake makes a habit of harming humans for no reason. They much prefer biting a juicy mouse or a tender baby bird. But we have an

unfortunate habit of treading on them. And the snakes have an even more unfortunate habit of giving us free poison in return.

3 Snakes inject poison through hollow fangs or along grooves in their fangs. The poison is made in special glands on the sides of the head.

JAB!

X-RAY VIEW OF POISON IN A FANG

SQUIRT!

X-RAY VIEW OF SNAKE'S SKULL

THE PAINFUL DETAILS: You've got similar glands on the side of your head, but they just make spit. (And luckily human spit isn't poisonous, or teachers who spray spit when they talk would kill off half their classes.)

THE SPITTING COBRA – AN ESPECIALLY POISONOUS SPECIES!

Different snakes produce different poisons and some are more deadly than others. You can imagine them as different "flavours" and Count Vomito has just made two of them into milkshakes...

Extra-strong strawberry and nerve-poison flavour from real green mambas — stops you moving for ever!

Blackcurrant and blood-dripping flavour from rattlesnakes — makes the blood leak from your blood vessels, so your cells can't get enough oxygen... and die.

But if snakes can be sinister, humans can be even more horrible. In the southern states of the USA, there are festivals called "rattlesnake round-ups". Thousands of innocent snakes are killed during these cheery celebrations. The story goes that one rattlesnake rounder-upper used to grab rattlesnakes by their tails and crack them like whips until their heads flew off. One day a head flew off ... and bit him. He died.

HE WAS SO DARN PROUD OF THAT TRICK!

YEP! I GUESS IT WENT TO HIS HEAD

Bet you never knew!

OK, so being bitten by a poisonous snake isn't a barrel of laughs – but snake poison isn't all bad news. Honest!

• *Brazilian pit-viper poison narrows the blood vessels and raises the blood pressure, so it makes a useful drug for people with low blood pressure.*

• *Russell's viper poison helps the blood to clot. Some people have a condition which means that their blood doesn't clot easily and the poison is made into a medicine to help them.*

The Count asked MI Gutzache if he'd like to try a snakebite and tell us what it's like. But after thinking about it for half a second, Gutzache made up his mind…

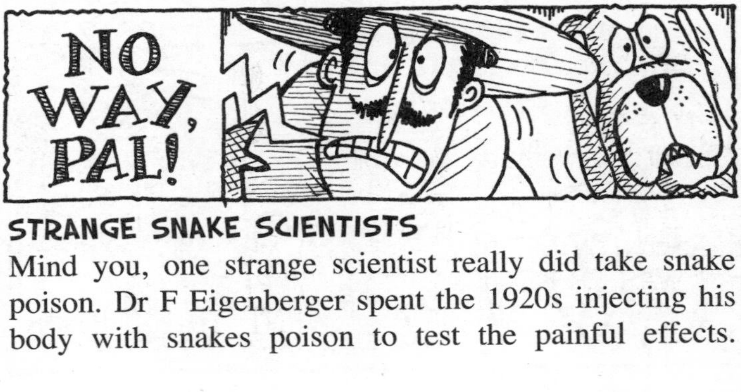

STRANGE SNAKE SCIENTISTS

Mind you, one strange scientist really did take snake poison. Dr F Eigenberger spent the 1920s injecting his body with snakes poison to test the painful effects.

And he was determined to find out the truth … even if it killed him. Here's what his notebook might have looked like…

Wednesday
Today I injected myself with green-mamba poison.

GREEN MAMBA

OOOOCH! My skin is itching and I've got a burning pain. Eh? Everything sounds strange. My neighbour's car sounds like it's got a flat tyre. I feel drunk - and that's odd, because I haven't touched a drop! Oh yuck! I feel sick. My eyes are sore and my face is numb. I can't feel my fingers and toes - have they dropped off?! Phew! No, they're still there, but now I can hardly breathe. Er - maybe it was a bad idea to take that poison!

Six hours later
I'm in agony. I'm dying, this is a most interesting scientific experience. Oh well, goodbye, cruel world!

Next day
Well, fancy that - I'm still alive! I'm sitting up in bed. I'm still a bit groggy but I'm over the worst. Great, I can try another experiment. Now where did I put that cobra poison?

Hmm, it sounds like the dodgy doc was one test tube short of a rack. But the most shocking thing about the test is that he weakened the poison *ten times* before he used it! If he'd tried it at full strength, it would have been exit Eigenberger.

Others weren't so lucky. In 1921, snake-show entertainer Tom Wanless was bitten by a green mamba. The next morning Tom looked really rough and was coughing up blood. He dragged himself over to the mirror and remarked...

THE GREEN MAMBA WINS!

Then he dropped down dead.

What Tom Wanless and Dr Eigenberger needed was a substance that could stop the snake poison working. In other words, an antidote – or anti-venom as it's known. And you'll be delighted to hear that snakebite antidotes actually exist...

Painful poison fact file

NAME: Anti-venom

THE BASIC FACTS: 1 Snake poisons are proteins. When the body detects the poison, it tries to fight it by making its own proteins called antibodies.

ANTI-VENOM

2 The job of the antibodies is to latch on to the poison proteins and clump them together so they can't do any harm.

3 Trouble is, in a fatal bite there's too much poison and it works too fast for the body to make enough antibodies.

4 If the body survives, it keeps some antibodies. And they can be useful if the person gets bitten again.

EH?

5 Scientists make anti-venom by injecting horses or sheep with small amounts of snake poison and taking the antibodies they make.

THE POISON IS COLLECTED BY MAKING THE SNAKE BITE INTO PLASTIC FILM

THE VENOM DRIPS INTO A JAR

THE PAINFUL DETAILS: But scientists need snake poison to give to the horses or sheep. And that means catching live deadly dangerous poisonous snakes. Anyone want to have a go? Thought not.

HEE HEE!

One person who did want to have a go was Australian snake expert Kevin Budden. Back in 1950, scientists needed to get hold of a live taipan from northern Australia to make an anti-venom. So Budden set off for Cairns to find one. But things went terribly wrong…

CAIRNS CHRONICLE ☼ 1950

BITE BEATS BRAVE BUDDEN!

We're sorry to report the death of Kevin Budden. Courageous Kev, 20, found a taipan under some stones. But before the young snake expert could bag the slippery stinger, it wrapped itself around his hands.

Kev needed expert help to free himself, so he asked passing truck driver Jim Harris to take him to the home of snake expert, Mr Stephens. Said Jim, "I'd never given a lift to a killer snake before but I wasn't going to argue!" At Stephens' house Kev was again trying to bag the taipan when it bit him. He died the following day.

J. Harris

But Kevin Budden's death wasn't in vain. Scientists used the snake's poison to make the first-ever taipan anti-venom.

And now for our next painful chapter – er hold on, a reader wants to say something…

BUT YOU WERE GOING TO TELL US ABOUT ZOMBIES!

OOPS, sorry, silly me! Amazingly, some scientists think that zombies really exist and that people can become zombies by drinking poison. In 1980 a man named

Clairvius knocked on his sister's door in Haiti. Nothing odd about that except that Clairvius had been dead and buried for 18 years! He said that he'd been dug up and worked as a zombie slave by a voodoo priest.

US scientist Wade Davis heard the story and headed to Haiti in search of the truth. He paid a priest to let him in on a few trade secrets and found out how to make a zombie. Would you like to give it a go? Thought so!

THE DIY ZOMBIE KIT

NOW YOU CAN TURN YOUR BROTHER OR SISTER INTO A ZOMBIE SLAVE IN THE COMFORT OF YOUR OWN HOME!

All you need is...

A brother or sister

Our special top-secret zombie poison mix, which includes real genuine baby bones and pufferfish poison.

All you do is...

Give your brother or sister some poison (not too much now — you don't want to really kill them!)

DON'T WORRY, IT'S DELICIOUS!

With the right dose, your victim appears dead and gets buried. Then, all you have to do is dig them up and put them to work tidying your room and doing your science homework!

So there's NO WAY you'll be trying this at home? Well, I'm glad to hear that because it saves me the bother of telling you that there may be a law against poisoning members of your family and using them as slaves. And anyway most scientists aren't too sure that the zombie poison recipe was genuine.

So what do you think? Was Wade Davis told a load of voodoo-hoodoo? And would you be brave enough to find out the painful truth? If so, you could become a budding poison detective ... but you'll need to investigate the next chapter to be sure...

HOW TO BE A POISON DETECTIVE

Welcome to the Horrible Science Poison Detective Training Course! Your mission is to become a completely clued-up poison detective by the end of this chapter!

LESSON 1: FIND OUT WHERE POISONS ARE KEPT

We sent MI Gutzache (now fully recovered from his embarrassing experience in the fish restaurant) to check out this perfectly normal house…

The poison house mystery

REPORT BY MI GUTZACHE

So I got hired. It was my first bad move. I figured I knew the score – Watson could sniff out the poisons and I'd finger the greenbacks. We'd done it a thousand times but I didn't know the half of it. For one thing, I reckoned without the cat. Now don't get me wrong, cats are OK in their place – but that place is Mars. I know Watson shares my feelings...

BUT SHE'S ONLY A KITTEN!

HISS! SNARL!

After the kitty had been locked up, we continued our search. It was soon clear that the job was no cinch. The house contained more poison than Peter Popov's Poison Pepperoni Pizza Parlour – I mean the whole place was a danger zone! We came out with a box-load and we had to go back for more. Here's our haul...

① COFFIN MIXTURE
② BUGOFF
③ STICKIT
④ GOOD HAIR DAY

125

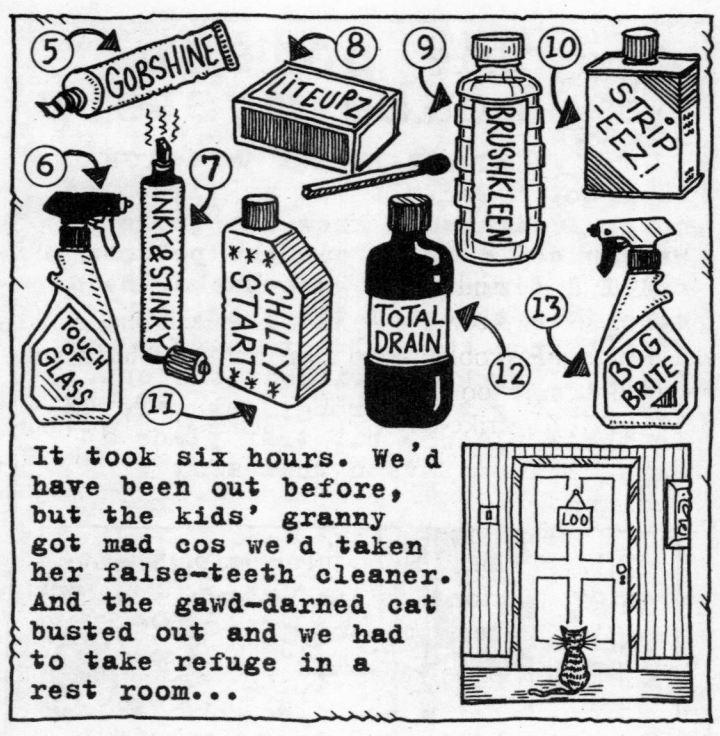

It took six hours. We'd have been out before, but the kids' granny got mad cos we'd taken her false-teeth cleaner. And the gawd-darned cat busted out and we had to take refuge in a rest room...

Let's take a closer look at what Gutzache found...

1 MEDICINES. All medicines and pills are poisonous in too-large doses. And so are denture-cleaning tablets.

2 INSECT AND WEED KILLERS are designed to kill pests and weeds. But they can also kill human pests and weedy people too.

3 The only safe GLUE is labelled safe for children. Most modelling glue or superglue could bring a person to a sticky end.

4 Things like WASHING-UP LIQUID, WASHING POWDER, SHAMPOO, SHOWER GEL and BUBBLE BATH aren't good to eat. You'd better not swallow any if you want a clean bill of health.

5 MOUTHWASH, DEODORANT and TOOTHPASTE are fine on the bits of body they're designed for, but you wouldn't want them for dinner.

6 GLASS CLEANERS and WINDOW CLEANERS may contain harmful chemicals. Breathing the mist from a spray can be *very* dangerous.

7 FELT-TIP PENS. The only safe ones are marked safe for children. Their ink is water-based. The ink in "smelly" felt-tip pens may contain harmful chemicals that could cause breathing problems and turn your skin blue if you breathed them in too much.

8 MATCHES. Strike-anywhere matches (the type that don't need to be struck on a matchbox) are poisonous if sucked. And only stupid suckers suck safety matches – they can cause an upset stomach.

9 TURPENTINE and WHITE SPIRIT are very poisonous. 200 years ago, doctors gave turps to patients with bladder stones. Some of them got tombstones instead.

10 PAINT STRIPPERS. Don't touch them or breathe their fumes. They're designed to strip paint but they're pretty good at stripping skin too.

11 ANTIFREEZE is scary stuff. Antifreeze reacts with body chemicals to make oxalic acid. So you get all the rotten results of rhubarb-leaf poisoning without eating rhubarb.

12 DRAIN CLEANERS and OVEN CLEANERS are good at dissolving those stubborn bits of burnt food. And good at dissolving stubborn people who ignore the warnings on the containers.

13 TOILET CLEANERS and BLEACH kill germs, *and* people if they try to drink them.

Well, that's the end of your first lesson, but before we start Lesson 2, you may like to know that drain, oven and toilet cleaners damage the skin because they're alkaline. And here are the painful details...

EVERYTHING YOU NEED TO KNOW ABOUT ALKALINE POISONS

1 Alkaline chemicals are dissolved in water. The more water there is, the weaker the chemical, as the Count is about to show us...

2 The atoms in an alkaline chemical pull hydrogen atoms away from any other substance they come in contact with.

3 As it loses hydrogen atoms, the other substance dissolves. And you would dissolve too if you had a bath in drain cleaner.

But now for some good news: if you're wondering how alkaline chemicals are made, we've persuaded an oven cleaner to spill the beans (and clean them up again).

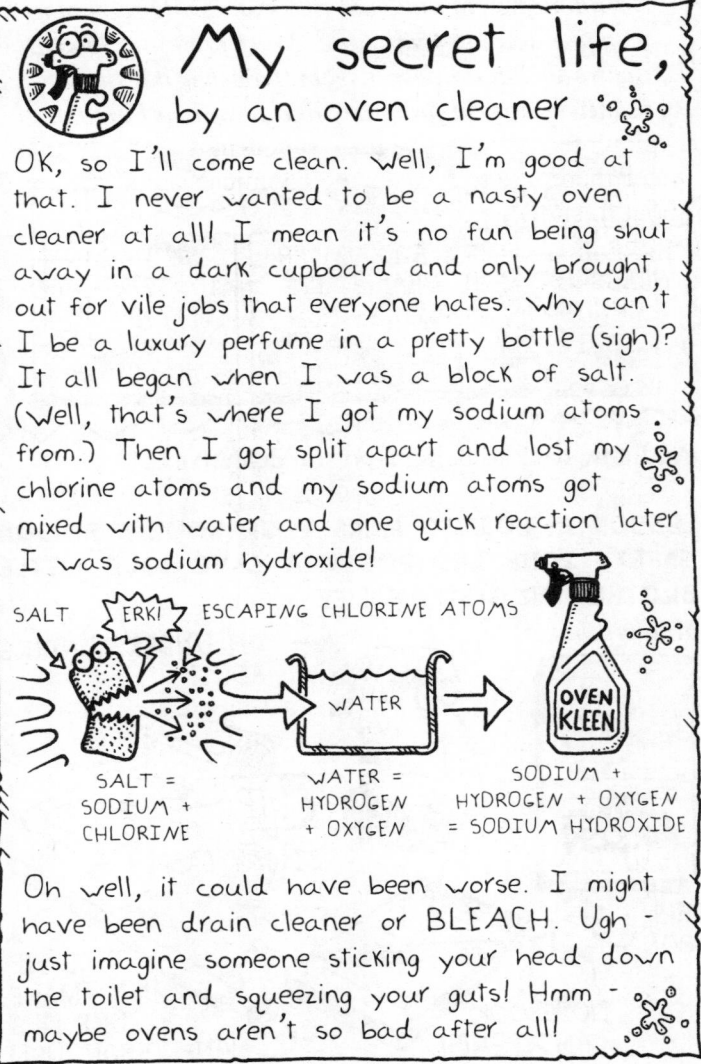

My secret life,
by an oven cleaner

OK, so I'll come clean. Well, I'm good at that. I never wanted to be a nasty oven cleaner at all! I mean it's no fun being shut away in a dark cupboard and only brought out for vile jobs that everyone hates. Why can't I be a luxury perfume in a pretty bottle (sigh)? It all began when I was a block of salt. (Well, that's where I got my sodium atoms from.) Then I got split apart and lost my chlorine atoms and my sodium atoms got mixed with water and one quick reaction later I was sodium hydroxide!

SALT   ERK! ESCAPING CHLORINE ATOMS

WATER

OVEN KLEEN

SALT = SODIUM + CHLORINE

WATER = HYDROGEN + OXYGEN

SODIUM + HYDROGEN + OXYGEN = SODIUM HYDROXIDE

Oh well, it could have been worse. I might have been drain cleaner or BLEACH. Ugh - just imagine someone sticking your head down the toilet and squeezing your guts! Hmm - maybe ovens aren't so bad after all!

Not everyone hates sodium hydroxide. There's a type of shrimp that loves it. In places such as Lake Natron in Kenya the local rocks and water combine to make sodium hydroxide. Most creatures die in the water but it doesn't seem to bother the shrimps that live in it (in fact, they find it quite a laugh!).

EEK! MY FEET ARE BURNING!

OUCH! MINE TOO!

HEE HEE!

HA HA!

And now back to being a poison detective...

LESSON 2: HOW TO MAKE YOUR HOME A POISON SAFETY ZONE AND POSSIBLY SAVE YOUR LITTLE BROTHER OR SISTER'S LIFE

You will need:

AN UNDERSTANDING ADULT

Horrible Science
PAINFUL POISON

THIS BOOK

LOTS OF STICKY LABELS

NOTEBOOK AND PENCIL

A FELT-TIP PEN (MAKE SURE IT'S NON-POISONOUS!)

What you do:

1 Ask permission for this activity and make sure your baby brother or sister and pet hamster are under lock and key first. We don't want them sampling any poisons you find.

2 Draw a skull and crossbones poison logo on your sticky labels. Here's an arty one for you to copy – thanks, Tony!

3 Tour your home putting stickers on any poisons you find – you'll be amazed by how many stickers you need!

4 Make a note of any poison dangers you discover such as…

• Poisons or medicines that have been poured into different bottles.

HORRIBLE HEALTH WARNING!

This is SHOCKING! Just imagine trying to shampoo your hair with oven cleaner or taking paint stripper for a ticklish cough. If your family put poisons in different bottles, it's best to ring up social services and book yourself into a children's home. It's safer!

- Poisons stored in low-level unlocked cupboards that hungry little brothers and sisters and hamsters might get at.
- Poisons with lids that little kids can take off easily.
- Medicines kept in low cupboards that aren't locked.
- Poisons in leaking containers.

5 Report any dangers to the adult and suggest they take action. The best place for poisons is locked away out of reach of troublesome toddlers.

IMPORTANT MESSAGE!

The next two lessons are about advanced high-level stuff and you may want to leave it until you get a job with the police.

LESSON 3: DIG UP A POISONED BODY FOR TESTS

IMPORTANT NOTE!

Make sure you ask permission before digging up bodies. You wouldn't want to be chased around a graveyard by a vicious vicar, would you? And don't go digging up departed family pets to test your skills! Let Harry the hamster rest in peace!

VICIOUS VICAR

1 Put up a canvas screen around the grave. A seaside windbreak will do just so long as it isn't covered in silly cartoon characters in bright cheery colours.

THAT'S GROSS!

YUCK!

UGH, PUTRID!

2 Check to make sure you're digging up the right grave. It might be a bit embarrassing if you dig up the wrong body by mistake!

3 Open the coffin a bit to let the smelly gases out. (Put a clothes peg over your nose first.)

4 Don't forget to collect some earth from the grave. There might already be poisons in the soil that could affect your tests.

5 Take the coffin with the body in it away for further tests. It really is that easy (NOT)!

LESSON 4: TEST THE BODY FOR POISONS

Besides the earth you collected from the grave, you're going to need samples (small amounts) of body to test. Here's a quick list...

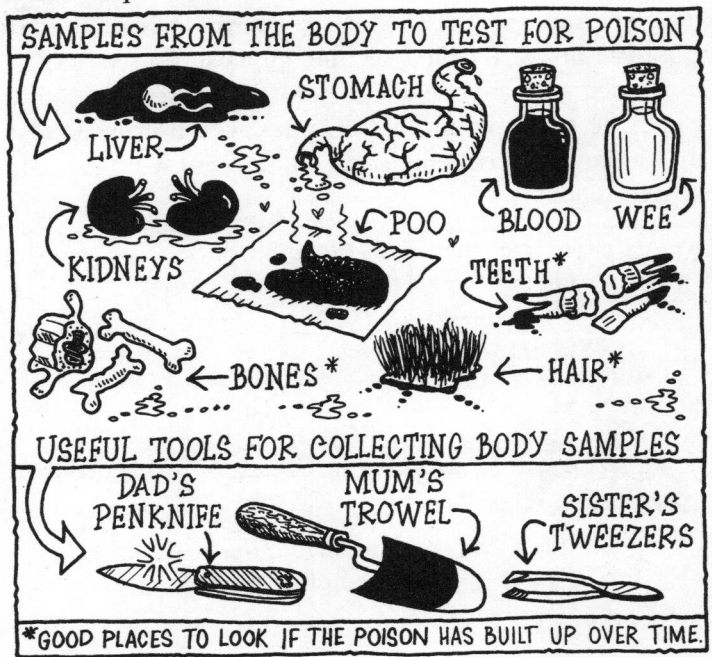

SAMPLES FROM THE BODY TO TEST FOR POISON

LIVER — STOMACH — POO — BLOOD — WEE

KIDNEYS — TEETH* — BONES* — HAIR*

USEFUL TOOLS FOR COLLECTING BODY SAMPLES

DAD'S PENKNIFE — MUM'S TROWEL — SISTER'S TWEEZERS

*GOOD PLACES TO LOOK IF THE POISON HAS BUILT UP OVER TIME.

But before we try some poison tests you might like to know who got the science of poison testing off the ground...

Hall of Fame: Mathieu Orfila (1787–1853)
Nationality: Spanish (later French)

The scientist faced a painful choice. Should he get involved in a murder enquiry?

Factory owner Charles Lafarge was dead. His wife Marie was on trial for murder and the court wanted to know if she'd used arsenic. Marie had bought arsenic rat killer but the police could find no trace of the poison in Charles' body. Orfila was the greatest poison expert in France – if anyone could find the poison he could. But if he got it wrong his enemies would crow louder than a crowd of cockerels. And an innocent woman could be executed.

MAYBE I'D BETTER THINK ABOUT IT.

IT WASN'T ME!

R.I.P. MARIE LAFARGE

Young Mathieu had studied medicine in Spain and he was such a good doctor the city of Barcelona gave him some money for more study. And that's how he came to

Paris. In 1814, Mathieu produced a brilliant book about poisons, full of painful details about what they do to the body and how to detect poisons in bodies. So he was the ideal person to solve the mystery death of Charles Lafarge.

Mathieu tried a test that had been invented just four years before, in 1836. It worked. The test proved that Lafarge had been killed by arsenic and Marie was found guilty. She was locked up for life and Orfila went on to carry out poison experiments on 4,000 unfortunate dogs. He founded a whole new science of poisons, which, if you want to sound dead scientific, is now known as toxicology (toxy-col-o-gy).

I'd like to say Mathieu Orfila lived happily ever after, but he didn't. After a revolution in 1848, the scientist didn't get on with the new government. He was no longer invited to top parties and offered top jobs. The stress made him ill and he died five years later. Today few people remember him or even know where he's buried. But at least no one's dug him up yet.

And that reminds me, we were supposed to be testing the body for poisons. Well, it helps if you have some whizzy equipment – so here are a few ideal presents for all you budding toxicologists!

COUNT VOMITO'S POISON PRODUCTS

proudly present...

Everything for the well-equipped poisons lab

ON SPECIAL OFFER THIS WEEK...

THIN-LAYER CHROMATOGRAPHY* KIT

It's easy-peasy! You dissolve your sample in a chemical and dip the paper in it. The sample soaks upwards and the poisons separate out. This test detects 90% of all known poisons!

*That's cro-ma-tog-graf-fee

DISSOLVE!

MASS SPECTROMETER

Use a powerful magnet to separate poison chemicals in a gas. It's something to gas about with your scientist friends.

I'M GETTING ONE FOR MY BIRTHDAY!

IMMUNOASSAY

Add the poison to other chemicals to make it fairly safe and inject it into an animal. The animal makes antibodies that you can test to show you what the poison was. (Animals not supplied.)

AND I'M NOT VOLUNTEERING!

What's that? You're not old enough for advanced detective work but you're itching to try some poison tests right now? Oh all right, here's a special experiment you can practise your skills on...

Dare you discover ... how to test for poisons using paper chromatography?

You will need:
Some newspaper
A ruler
A strip of kitchen towel or blotting paper 5 cm wide and 20 cm long
Some green food colouring
A small paintbrush
A large pudding basin with 2 cm of water

What you do:
1 This is a messy experiment, so put down some newspaper or the next tests might be on *your* dead body.
2 Use the paintbrush to paint a blob of food colouring 0.5 cm across and 3 cm from one end of one of your paper strip.
3 Dip the first 1 cm of the paper strip into the water and lay it over the edge of the basin.

NOW WATCH WHAT HAPPENS...

...AND BEWARE OF THIRSTY DOGS!

GREEN

You should find:

The water soaks upwards. When the water reaches the food colour, other colours begin to separate out. (It takes a few minutes to happen.) You can imagine painful poisons oozing out of a sinister sample. Why not experiment with different food colourings and water-based felt-tip pens?

CONGRATULATIONS! You've nearly finished this book! But can you remember the painful details? Well, here's your chance to find out if you're a dazzling detective or a bumbling boffin. This quiz is based on facts you've just read about. If you know the info, you can solve these murderous true mysteries!

PAINFUL POISON QUIZ

1 In 1838 a wicked wife in Germany tried to poison her husband. She made him a nice hot soup containing phosphorus. What made him suspicious?
a) The soup smelled of toilet cleaner.
b) The soup carried on bubbling even after it went cold.
c) The soup glowed in the dark.

2 In 1954 two women were poisoned by Spanish-fly juice. How did scientist Dr Lewis Nickells prove what poison was involved?
a) He heated it until it exploded.
b) It turned his pet rabbit into a zombie.

c) He put some of the victim's vomit on his arm and it made a blister.

3 Scarlet macaws are a type of parrot that live in South America. They live off seeds and fruit, including some poisonous plants. Why don't they end up as sick as parrots?
a) They eat clay afterwards.
b) They get monkeys to test the fruit first.

c) They store the poisons in their fantastic feathers.

4 In 1953 Clare Luce, the US ambassador to Italy, had it all – a top job, a palace to live in, servants to look after her and a lovely old painted ceiling to admire. Then she fell ill with a mysterious illness. She suffered from sickness and diarrhoea, her hair started to fall out, she felt dizzy and she said she saw a flying saucer. A doctor found arsenic in Mrs Luce's wee. Who was poisoning her?
a) Aliens.
b) The ceiling.
c) The doctor.

Answers:

1 c) Don't forget phosphorus glows in the dark! The only soup that does this normally is alien stew. The husband showed the soup to the police and his wife found herself glowing to jail.

2 c) The poison causes blisters, remember? (See page 105.) The scientist was very brave – the painful poison could have killed him.

3 a) The brainy birds fly off to riverbanks for a peck of clay to soak up the poison. After all, if it works for humans...

4 b) The ceiling paint contained arsenic, and it was flaking off and dropping into Clare's coffee! Mrs Luce was lucky not to lose her life. The discovery of arsenic was kept secret and no one believed Mrs Luce when she told them about the poisoning. After all, her nickname was "Arsenic".

It's frightening, isn't it? There you are sitting in your palace drinking a lovely cup of coffee … and the ceiling is plotting to kill you! It shouldn't be allowed! There's no doubt – poisons are the most painful, scary chemicals ever … or are they?

Are you ready to face the PAINFUL truth?

EPILOGUE: THE PAINFUL TRUTH

OK, so it's 100% official – poisons are painful. And if you've just read this book then you won't need reminding of how painful poisons can be ... but if you have forgotten, Count Vomito will be happy to remind you...

TAKE A SIP OF THIS AND YOU'LL NEVER FORGET ANYTHING, **EVER** AGAIN!*

As you'll be dead!

And because poisons are painful and deadly and dangerous – they're scary. So it's not too surprising that people like Sultan Abdul Hamid were terrified of poisons. And while we're on the subject, here's someone else who was scared of them...

Welcome to the TV show where we interview famous people about how they died!

THIS IS YOUR **DEATH!**

This week we talk to King Mithradates VI (died 63 BC).

I guess the story of King Mithradates VI may hold a lesson for us. It's easy to be scared of poisons – but there are even more scary things out there. Like cruel human enemies.

And if you think about it, should we really be scared of poisons? After all...

• Some poisons can be made into life-saving medicines – just think of those ever-so-valuable plant poisons and snake venoms. Thanks, guys!

*You're welcome

• Some poisons can be useful in industry. OK, so you wouldn't want to drink an arsenic and lead fizzy drink. But if it wasn't for the arsenic and lead in solder the author couldn't have typed this book on his computer.

• Some substances are poisonous if you take too much of them. But in smaller doses they're vital for life. Anyone fancy a sugar lump, a glass of water or a puff of oxygen? Well, if you don't have some soon, you'll be hungry, thirsty and gasping!

It's easy to feel scared by all those thousands of poisonous plants and animals or the poisons lurking in your kitchen cupboard. But even the most painful poison, such as cyanide, is only really scary if it's used as a weapon. If it falls into the wrong hands – the hands of people who use poison for killing and murder.

So the best way to deal with poisons isn't to be scared of them. It's to learn about poisons so you can protect yourself. You see, science is about more than making new chemicals – it's about using them safely and wisely too. Happy Horrible Science, everyone!

(DON'T WORRY – IT WAS ONLY A GLASS OF HEALTHY BRUSSELS SPROUT JUICE!)

PAINFUL POISON

QUIZ

Now find out if you're a
Painful Poison expert!

No doubt you've found all these tales of death and danger awfully interesting, but now it's time to find out how much you've picked up. Are you brave enough to have a pufferfish as a pet or will a measly mushroom make you faint with fear? Take these quizzes to prove your worth...

All clued up

The world is full of dangerous things – fast cars, volcanoes, your little brother's bottom burps – but as you've discovered, poisons are poised to strike in the most unexpected places. Use the clues to answer the spine-chilling questions below about the power of poison.

1 What muscle-freezing substance used by the rich and famous comes from the powerful poison botulin? (CLUE: Good for wrinkle removal)
2 Which evil gas was used in the First World War to blind its victims? (CLUE: You might eat it with your roast beef)
3 What menacing mixture of the poisons sodium and chlorine do you use every day? (CLUE: Just a sprinkle of seasoning)
4 Noxious nitrous oxide used to be used by surgeons to block pain. What nickname is this gruesome gas known by? (CLUE: It'll give you the giggles)
5 Which bumbling insect kills around 40,000 people a year? (CLUE: Stripy stingers)
6 What brilliant body part filters out perilous poisons? (CLUE: This could be served up in your sickening school canteen)

7 Which hazardous household product can contain the terrible toxins exylene and toluene? (CLUE: You might get STUCK on this question)
8 What everyday item can shrivel your cells so your beastly body dries out like a prune? (CLUE: It's a sweet way to die)

Answers:
1 Botox
2 Mustard gas
3 Salt
4 Laughing gas
5 Bees
6 Liver
7 Glue
8 Sugar

Murder file

Over the centuries, many mad murderers have picked poison as their weapon of choice. Here are some gruesome examples of painful poison cases. Are you a good enough detective to work out the facts of these sinister situations?

1 In sixteenth-century Italy, Bianca Capello tried to poison Cardinal Ferdinand with a toxin-riddled tart. What happened to the cardinal?

a) Nothing – Bianca accidentally ate the tart herself and died

b) Nothing – the onions in the tart eliminated the poison

c) He turned blue, vomited and died a slow and agonising death

2 Ancient philosopher Socrates was sentenced to death by poisoning. Which painful plant poison did he take?

a) Hollyhock

b) Henbane

c) Hemlock

3 What did wicked wife Agrippina feed her husband, Emperor Claudius, to bump him off in the first century AD?

a) Poisoned mushrooms

b) Poisoned peanuts

c) Poisoned grapes

4 Which famous poisoner murdered his wife with hyoscine and buried her body in the basement?

a) Dr Who

b) Dr Lamson

c) Dr Crippen

5 Cyanide poisoner Richard Kuklinski earned himself a chilling nickname because of the way he froze his victim's bodies. What was it?

a) The Snowman

b) The Iceman

c) Mr Whippy

6 In 1978, Bulgarian Georgi Markov was murdered by a stab in the thigh from which poisoned pointy object carried by a passer-by?
a) A walking stick
b) An umbrella
c) A fountain pen

7 Nannie Doss, known as the 'Giggling Granny', killed four of her husbands and other members of her family by sprinkling their prunes with which poison?
a) Arsenic
b) Cyanide
c) Magic mushrooms

8 In 1895, Robert Buchanan was executed for poisoning his wife to death with morphine. What profession did Buchanan enjoy before exiting via the electric chair?
a) Lawyer
b) Professional poisoner (no case too small)
c) Doctor

Answers:
1a Barmy Bianca looked away and the cunning cardinal switched tarts
2c Sorry Socrates swallowed hemlock and waited for the poison to stop his heart
3a Evil Agrippina is also thought to have poisoned several other unlucky Romans.

4c Careless Crippen was eventually caught trying to escape to Canada

5b Crazy Kuklinksi even stuffed one of his victims in the freezer of an ice-cream van

6b No one is quite sure who was responsible for unlucky Markov's death

7a Mad Nannie was also nicknamed 'Arsenic Annie'

8c Bad Buchanan's medical knowledge was his downfall – he knew too much about committing the perfect crime

The evil effects of poison

Different deadly poisons affect the body in different ways (and make no mistake, most of these side-effects are awesomely excruciating). See if you can identify the poison by the awful effects below.

1 Breathing in this ghastly gas will irritate your lungs. They'll fill with fluid and eventually you'll drown to death on dry land.

2 This dreadful metal will make you mad. It'll damage your brain and kidneys, stop you from peeing and turn you a strange shade of yellow. Then you'll die.

3 The effects of this metalloid poison will start with a beastly burning in your stomach. Your poo and sick will

glow in the dark and your skin will turn yellow. Then you'll die.

4 A swallow of this deadly poison, and you'll begin by feeling a bit befuddled. Soon you'll be rushing to the toilet with deadly diarrhoea as your guts dry out. When you start seeing giant rabbits, you'll know that death isn't far off...

5 A build up of this murderous metal in the bones will affect your whole body. You'll get a stomach ache, but that's just the start. Your gums will turn blue, your muscles will be mangled and your brain will go bananas. And yes, you'll probably die.

6 This gruesome gas is said to smell of almonds, but that's the only good thing about it. A few lungfuls and you'll start to feel faint, then you'll vomit until you can't breathe. And then you'll die.

7 When mixed with other elements, this evil metal will first give you a bit of a tummy ache. But don't be fooled – it'll work it's way into your nervous system, where it will make sure you lose control of your body. Your skin will be so sensitive you won't even be able to smile (not that you'd want to...). I expect you'll die.

8 Like many poisons, you'll probably just feel a bit sick at first with this one. But then you'll start leaking out of every part of your body. You'll probably poo your pants and you'll fill your hanky with bucketloads of snot. You won't have time to be embarrassed, though, because you'll be dead.

a) Phosphorus
b) Lead
c) Chlorine
d) Antimony
e) Thallium
f) Mercury

g) Hydrogen cyanide
h) BZ

Answers:
1c; 2f; 3a; 4h; 5b; 6g; 7e; 8d

Powerfully poisonous plants

Next time you're out munching an apple while picking flowers, you might want to remind yourself that poisons are lurking in leaves and secreted in the seeds of all sorts of plants. Are you clued-up enough to know where the terrible toxins below come from?

1 Cyanide
2 Oxalic acid
3 Ricin
4 Aconite
5 Hyoscine
6 Solanine
7 Amatoxin
8 Coniine

a) Wolf's bane
b) Deadly nightshade
c) Death-cap mushroom
d) Apple pips and apricot kernels
e) Hemlock
f) Castor-oil seeds
g) Potatoes
h) Rhubarb
Answers:

Angry animals

Nasty nature has provided many creatures with powerful protective poisons, but things are not always what they seem when it comes to evil animals. Can you spot which of the statements below are the terrible truth, and which are just pretend poison facts?

1 The beastly blue octopus can kill you with one sting from its toxic tentacles.

2 The ruthless rattlesnake injects a poison that bursts your blood vessels.

3 The male platypus has a stinging spur on its back foot that will make you hopping mad with pain.

4 A bite from a terrible tarantula can kill a grown man within three hours.

5 If you get poisoned by a pufferfish, you can take away the pain by peeing on the affected area.

6 The golden poison frog – the most venomous vertebrate in the world – is not poisonous at all if you keep it as a pet.

7 The green mamba snake injects a nerve poison that can

kill you in 15 minutes.

8 Spiders can control the amount of venom they inject into their victims.

Answers:

1 FALSE. The blue octopus is definitely a deadly creature – but its poison is in its spit, so it'll kill you with a single bite.

2 TRUE. Rattlesnake poison makes the blood leak from your blood vessels so your cells can't get enough oxygen and you die

3 TRUE. There aren't many poisonous mammals, but the cuddly-looking platypus is one of them…

4 FALSE. There's not a single tarantula that has a bite bad enough to kill a human.

5 FALSE. Say your prayers if you fall out with this fish – there is no known antidote for pufferfish poison.

6 TRUE. The golden poison frog is only deadly because of its diet. If you keep it in a cage and feed it fresh fruit it'll be the friendliest frog around.

7 TRUE. It'll go a bit like this: your fingers will tingle, you'll start foaming at the mouth and probably poo your pants, then you'll be paralysed, have a fit and slip into a coma. And all in the time it takes to have a cup of tea.

8 TRUE. Scary spiders don't always fill their fangs with venom – they might bite your bum if you disturb them on the toilet, but often these are defensive bites, known as 'dry bites'.

ARRRRRRGH!!

HORRIBLE INDEX

156

HORRIBLE SCIENCE

MICROSCOPIC MONSTERS

NICK ARNOLD

illustrated by
TONY DE SAULLES

SCHOLASTIC

www.horrible-science.co.uk

www.nickarnold-website.com
www.tonydesaulles.co.uk

Scholastic Children's Books,
Euston House, 24 Eversholt Street,
London, NW1 1DB, UK

A division of Scholastic Ltd
London ~ New York ~ Toronto ~ Sydney ~ Auckland
Mexico City ~ New Delhi ~ Hong Kong

First published in the UK by Scholastic Ltd, 2001
This edition published 2008

Text copyright © Nick Arnold, 2001
Illustrations © Tony De Saulles, 2001, 2008

All rights reserved

ISBN 978 1407 10613 7

Printed and bound by CPI Group (UK) Ltd, Croydon, CR0 4YY

20

CONTENTS

Nick Arnold has been writing stories and books since he was a youngster, but never dreamt he'd find fame writing about microscopic monsters. His research involved interviewing fleas and getting friendly with bacteria and he enjoyed every minute of it.

When he's not delving into Horrible Science, he spends his spare time eating pizza, riding his bike and thinking up corny jokes (though not all at the same time).

Tony De Saulles picked up his crayons when he was still in nappies and has been doodling ever since. He takes Horrible Science very seriously and even agreed to draw magnified toilet germs. Fortunately, he has made a full recovery.

When he's not out with his sketchpad, Tony likes to write poetry and play squash, though he hasn't written any poetry about squash yet.

INTRODUCTION

Which of these is the smallest?

a) Your pocket money.

MISERLY AMOUNT

b) Your teacher's brain.

PATHETICALLY PUNY

c) A mite (a bug that looks like a scaled-down spider).

TINY BUT TERRIFYING

Well, hopefully you said **c)** because at just 0.2 mm, a mite is one of the smallest objects anyone can see. Your eyes can't see smaller things because the lenses in your eyeballs can't focus on them. And that means that whatever you look at has a whole lot of detail that's too small to make out. This tiny world can be very incredible, and very beautiful (they say small is beautiful don't they?).

But it can also be very *horrible*!

WARNING!

(18) This book has an 18 certificate (that's UNSUITABLE FOR PERSONS OVER 18). This means it's too frightening for adults – if they read it their eyes could pop out on stalks!

Now, as I said, your eyes can't see tiny things, but your mind's eye can *imagine* them. And when you read this book your imagination will be working so hard there'll be steam coming out your ears! You'll be imagining a whole new world – the terribly tiny microscopic world. And as you're about to find out, it's a world of violence and sudden death.

Yes, it's a world of microscopic horrors and MONSTERS that make made-up monsters in stories appear loveable and fluffy. And make no mistake – the microscopic monsters in this book are as REAL as you are! At this very second they're strolling on your skin and snuggling into your bed and scoffing your sandwiches and splashing about in your toilet! So brace yourself for a feast of fearsomely fascinating facts. Find out…

• how millions of creatures *die* when you walk on the grass.

• what slimy animals lurk between your *teeth*.

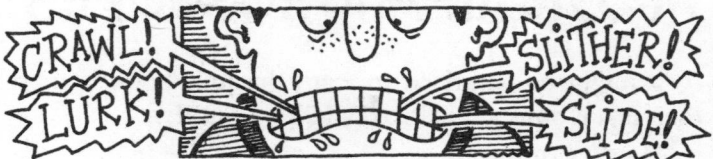

• how germs can make dead bodies *explode*.

• and WORST OF ALL, how flushing the toilet can cover you in *poo*.

ANOTHER WARNING!
These facts could turn a frog green! And don't leave this book on Granny's chair — it could make her false teeth fall out!

No, you'd best read this book right now before someone else takes it away and starts reading it for themselves!

MAGICAL MICROSCOPES

You might be surprised to learn that this book is more than just a book … IT'S A MICROSCOPE!

THE MAGIC MICROSCOPE

You're holding a *microscope* … a wonderful instrument for peering at tiny objects and seeing them like no human eye ever can. A device for making things appear hundreds of times larger than they really are…

What's that? This book doesn't look like a microscope? Oh, but I'm telling you it *is* – try putting your eye up close to this circle. Look closely…

o

Concentrate hard … very hard … see anything?

Well, look over the page and prepare to be amazed. Thanks to the power of this book … er, I mean microscope, we are now looking at the page enlarged 100 times.

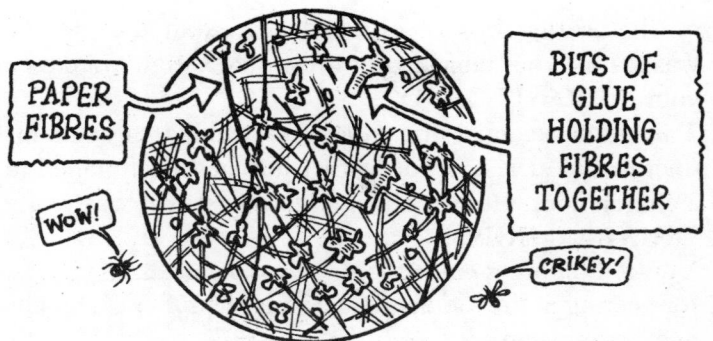

So you knew that paper is made up of little fibres that were once wood from trees? Well, here's your chance to check out what else you know…

A TINY, TINY QUIZ

This quiz is so easy that you're even told what the answers are! Trouble is, the letters in the answers are muddled up so you've got to work out what they say!

1 Whenever you ride your bike the tyres leave tiny microscopic traces of melted … REBRUB.

2 A fungus makes microscopic seeds called spores. When the sun shines they go dark just like you do when you get a … STUNNA.

3 When you go outside your hair, your clothes and the snot in your nose become coated in thousands of microscopic bits of rock half the width of a hair. They're known as … TRIG.

4 At the heart of every raindrop is a microscopic speck of dust. Some of this dust fell to Earth from … ROUTE CAPES.

5 Look at a spider's web under a microscope and you'll see tiny lumps of … GUEL.

6 All the tiny bits of dirt and dead skin that you've washed off your hair in your life would weigh more than your … HOWLE ODBY.

7 In 1848 scientist John Queckett peered through his microscope at a scrap of leather that had been nailed to a church door. He was shocked to discover it was really … UNHAM INKS.

UNHAM INKS! THAT'S DISGUSTING!

Answers:

1 No, not *rhubarb* – it's RUBBER. When your tyres touch the road a tiny surface layer 0.025 mm thick melts – so in fact your wheel slides over the ground! The tyre cools immediately as the wheel turns away from the road but microscopic traces of rubber remain stuck to the tarmac. When your tyre has lost lots of rubber it looks worn and tyred, I mean tired.

2 Are you stunned? It's a SUNTAN. Yes, fungal spores get suntans and the chemical that makes this dark colour is melanin – the same substance that makes the dark colour in human skin!

3 Yes, it's a TRIGY question. It's GRIT, made up of finely ground-up rock or sand just 0.03 mm in size that's blown on the wind. Some grit comes from deserts or erupting volcanoes on the other side of the world! If it gets in your pudding you could have a bit of desert in your dessert!

4 Every day millions of specks of dust about 0.002 mm across fall to Earth from OUTER SPACE. Inside a cloud drops of rain form around the dust and when a raindrop plops down the back of your neck you could be making contact with a 4.7 billion-year-old lump of alien rock! It's even older than your dad's favourite music – that's just ancient rock.

5 Do they serve GUEL in your school dinners? Actually, it's GLUE to stick insects to the web. Did you know that spider's silk is one of the strongest materials in the world – yet a spider's web that stretched around the world would weigh no more than an orange?

6 Don't "HOWL ODDLY" – it's WHOLE BODY! In just one year you could collect 3 kg of grotty, greasy gunk from your hair. You could fill a small bucket and butter your sandwiches with it!

7 What do you INK this stuff is? It turned out to be HUMAN SKIN cut from a dead Viking 900 years before. Well, I'm sure the Viking was really cut up about that.

So how did you get on? If you thought it was easy then maybe you fancy really getting to grips with the microscopic world.

Test your teacher...

WHO INVENTED THE MICROSCOPE?

Answer: The correct answer is "I dunno!" because no one is sure – but teachers don't like admitting they don't know things and historians don't mind guessing…

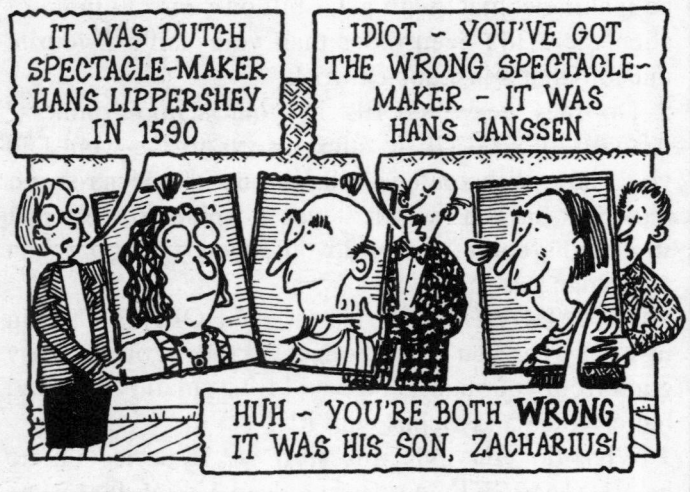

IT WAS DUTCH SPECTACLE-MAKER HANS LIPPERSHEY IN 1590

IDIOT – YOU'VE GOT THE WRONG SPECTACLE-MAKER – IT WAS HANS JANSSEN

HUH – YOU'RE BOTH **WRONG** IT WAS HIS SON, ZACHARIUS!

The truth is, ALL three *said* they invented the microscope. Well, I suppose anyone could have made the discovery. Once you've got a couple of lenses (the glass bits that make objects appear larger) it's easy enough to put them together and realize that two lenses make things appear larger than just one lens. And when your arms start aching from holding the lenses apart at the right distance to see tiny things in focus, sooner or later you'll hit on the idea of sticking the lenses at either end of a tube. And hey presto – you've invented the microscope!

But what about the lens? Well, guess what – no one's too sure who invented the lens either! We've brought some experts together to try and solve the mystery.

1 Archaeologists have found a piece of rock crystal in a cave on the island of Crete. It was carved 4,500 years ago.

IT'S SHAPED LIKE A LENS AND IT MAKES THINGS LOOK BIGGER!

2 In 1850 archaeologists found another lens-shaped crystal in what is now Iraq. It was carved by the Assyrian people in 800 BC.

YES, BUT MINE'S OLDER!

MINE'S BETTER QUALITY – IT'S CRYSTAL CLEAR!

3 Boring historians point out that there is no actual *proof* that these crystals were used as lenses at all. But there is proof in the writings of short-sighted Roman philosopher Seneca (AD 4–65) that he used a bowl of water as a lens to help him read the scrolls at his local library. So does that mean Seneca invented the lens?

IT'S TRANSPARENTLY OBVIOUS!

SOUNDS FISHY TO US!

LOVELY LENSES

Anyway, *someone* invented the lens and around 1300 someone else in Italy (yes, you guessed it, no one knows who) found out how to grind glass to make lenses. The trick was getting the right shape – wanna know how it's done? Well, why not make your own? Go on, it's easy!

Dare you discover ... how to make your own lens?

In the olden days you had to cut the glass carefully to shape and then grind it with gritty substances by hand until you had made exactly the right curve. And then you had to "polish" it to get rid of any scratches. (Basically, this meant grinding the glass some more with fine powders.) This grinding toil might take days of toil.

But you'll be pleased to know there's an easier way…

You will need:
A bottle shaped like this…
(An empty mouthwash bottle is ideal.)

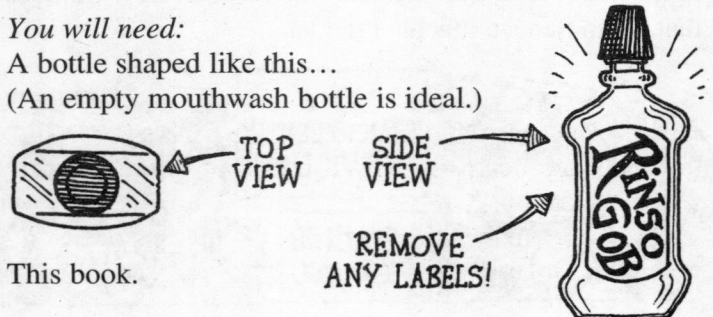

TOP VIEW

SIDE VIEW

REMOVE ANY LABELS!

This book.

What you do:

1 Completely fill the bottle with water so there are no air bubbles.

2 Place the bottle sideways on over this page, put your eye close to the bottle and look at this fascinating blood-sucking flea.

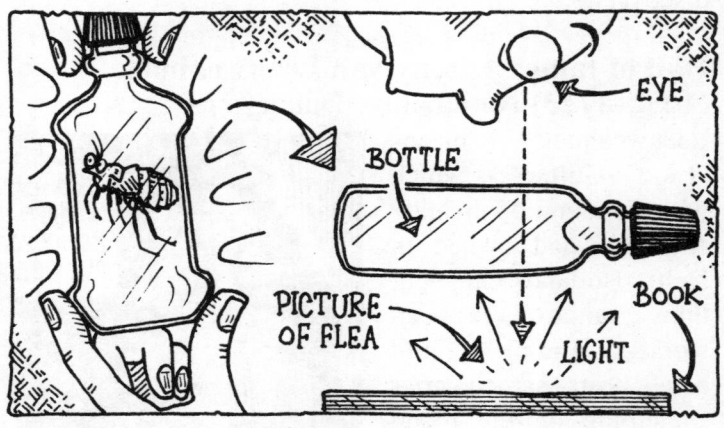

HURRY UP, I HAVEN'T GOT ALL DAY!

You should be able to see that the flea has got bigger – but how? Here's a clue: you have to imagine light bouncing off the page and bouncing into your eyeballs.

EYE

BOTTLE

PICTURE OF FLEA

BOOK

LIGHT

Which of these explanations is correct:

a) The light speeds up as it passes through water and this makes your brain think the flea is bigger than it is.

b) The water bends the light towards a point. If I put my eye at this point I can see the flea close up.

c) The water makes the light brighter and this makes my brain think that the flea is bigger.

For about 70 years after they were invented, microscopes weren't terribly powerful and few scientists had cottoned on to the potential of the new invention. But a lone genius was about to change all that. With his own hands he would make the most powerful microscopes then known and use them to make some monster discoveries…

Hall of fame: Antony van Leeuwenhoek
(1632–1723) Nationality: Dutch

Leeuwenhoek means "Lion's Corner" – which was the name of the café Antony's dad owned in Delft, Holland. Oh well, things could have been worse. Antony could have been named after something on the menu – he might have had to go through life as "Antony Supa-dupa whopper-burger"!

EGG AND CHIPS READY FOR TABLE NINE!

Antony's dad died when he was still at school. The young boy went to live with a relative and learned how to be a cloth merchant. For much of his life he was a

16

quietly hard-working, quietly prosperous shopkeeper in his home town of Delft. It sounds seriously boring but at least he had an interesting hobby…

You've guessed it! Microscopes!

Like other cloth sellers of the time, Antony used a lens to check the quality of his wares by checking the condition of the threads that made up the cloth. But unlike the others, Antony was *seriously* into lenses. He actually enjoyed grinding and polishing them laboriously by hand, and he mounted them on metal plates to make simple microscopes. Here's one now…

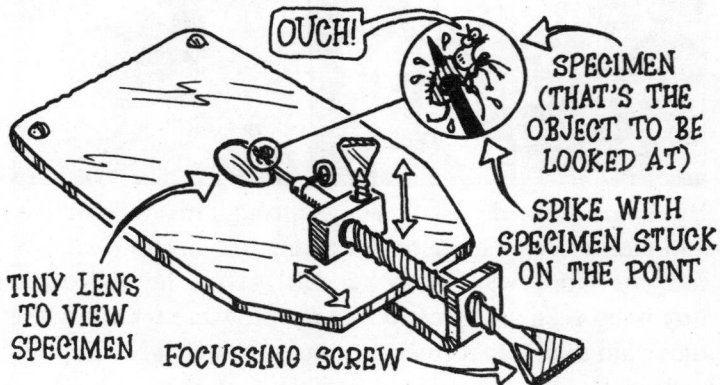

Antony was very good at his work because he had incredibly sharp eyesight which was ideal for spotting tiny details and he was a very curious man – I mean curious in the sense of wanting to find out more about the tiny world. So he decided to use his microscope to look at other tiny things. One day he looked at a raindrop and saw that it was alive with tiny slithering creatures. Encouraged, he checked his own spit, skin, tree bark, leaves and one of his rotten teeth after someone pulled it out. And everywhere he saw tiny wriggling creatures. He was the first human being to glimpse the things that we now call bacteria (for the slimy details see page 68).

Before Leeuwenhoek, people had no idea that things could happen on a scale too small for them to see. So they made up fanciful explanations for why things happen...

But Leeuwenhoek saw flea eggs through his microscope, and realized that's where fleas came from. (So it sounds like his work was up to scratch!) Then he looked at tiny baby eels, and proved that people were wrong when they said that eels formed from dew. Yes, once again he dew the right conclusion! Leeuwenhoek was so keen on his microscopes that he nearly blinded himself watching gunpowder explode at close quarters. And that nearly blew his chances of seeing anything!

18

As Antony's excitement grew he wrote letters to the Royal Society, the top scientific club in Britain, and told them about his discoveries. Here's what one letter might have said (the letter was in Dutch but we've translated it)…

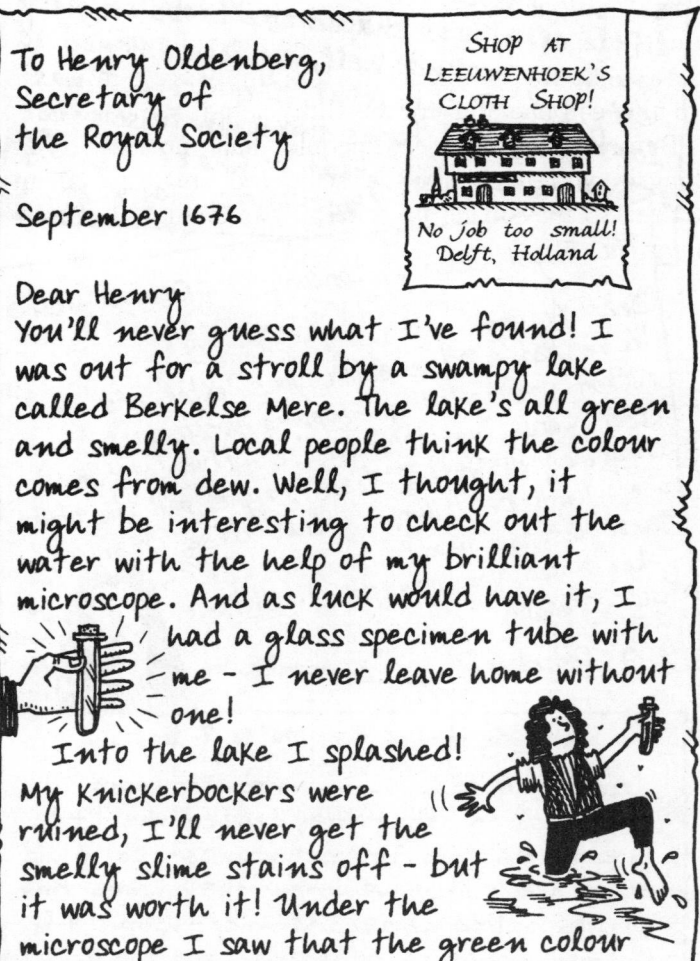

To Henry Oldenberg,
Secretary of
the Royal Society

September 1676

SHOP AT
LEEUWENHOEK'S
CLOTH SHOP!

No job too small!
Delft, Holland

Dear Henry
You'll never guess what I've found! I was out for a stroll by a swampy lake called Berkelse Mere. The lake's all green and smelly. Local people think the colour comes from dew. Well, I thought, it might be interesting to check out the water with the help of my brilliant microscope. And as luck would have it, I had a glass specimen tube with me – I never leave home without one!
  Into the lake I splashed! My knickerbockers were ruined, I'll never get the smelly slime stains off – but it was worth it! Under the microscope I saw that the green colour

was actually tiny little strands, thinner than a hair. And there were things like tiny green raspberries swimming about and little creatures shaped like blobs of jelly squishing around. Well, my legs turned to jelly too. At this point, I realized I was looking at life forms unknown to science! Is this great or what?

Yours, Tony

The Royal Society, London.

October 1676

Dear Antony

We've had a chat about your letter and we reckon you're telling whopping porkie-pies. In other words, we think you're fibbing! Little creatures in water? Yeah — right, pull the other one! You'll be telling us that these creatures cause disease next!

Let's see you prove it — OK!?

Yours crossly,

Henry Oldenberg

A QUICK NOTE...

Antony got some important people to write saying that they'd seen the little creatures too. The creatures really did exist and today we know they were tiny plants called algae and microscopic life forms known as protozoa (pro-toe-zo-a).

Leeuwenhoek published a book on his work and became famous. Soon scientific clubs were rushing to have him as a member and kings and lords flocked to his little shop and begged to look at germs. Leeuwenhoek died at the ripe old age of 90 with his eyesight still perfect, and as a parting gift he left some microscopes to his old pals at the Royal Society. Each had a tiny lump of dried blood or hair or teeth or muscle glued to the spike. Unfortunately, the glue rotted and the tiny specimens fell off.

Leeuwenhoek's microscopes really were the business – some could make out things 0.0015 mm across! But no one knew how he could grind such incredible lenses and he never shared his skills with anyone. He feared people might copy him. So could YOU follow in Leeuwenhoek's footsteps and become a great microscope scientist? To help you here's … the world's smallest ruler…

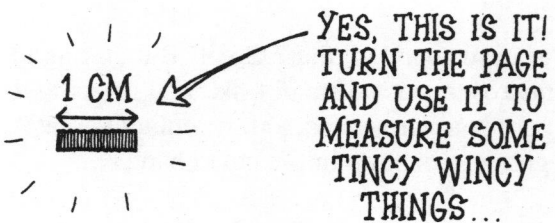

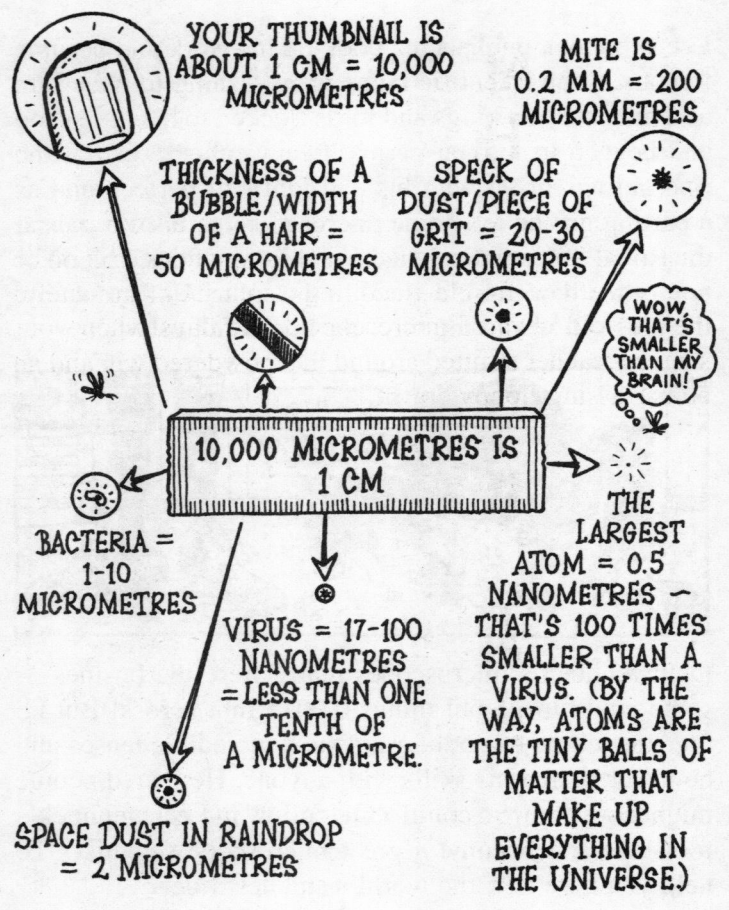

YOUR THUMBNAIL IS ABOUT 1 CM = 10,000 MICROMETRES

MITE IS 0.2 MM = 200 MICROMETRES

THICKNESS OF A BUBBLE/WIDTH OF A HAIR = 50 MICROMETRES

SPECK OF DUST/PIECE OF GRIT = 20-30 MICROMETRES

WOW THAT'S SMALLER THAN MY BRAIN!

10,000 MICROMETRES IS 1 CM

BACTERIA = 1-10 MICROMETRES

VIRUS = 17-100 NANOMETRES = LESS THAN ONE TENTH OF A MICROMETRE.

THE LARGEST ATOM = 0.5 NANOMETRES — THAT'S 100 TIMES SMALLER THAN A VIRUS. (BY THE WAY, ATOMS ARE THE TINY BALLS OF MATTER THAT MAKE UP EVERYTHING IN THE UNIVERSE.)

SPACE DUST IN RAINDROP = 2 MICROMETRES

Got your head round all that? Great! But getting to grips with a microscope is no small task. You're going to need a bit more knowhow and, oddly enough, that's what you're going to pick up in the next chapter…

CRUCIAL MICROSCOPIC KNOW-HOW

In this chapter you can practise using a microscope and even follow in Leeuwenhoek's footsteps and make your own. But first, a quick jog down memory lane to the bad old days of microscopes. The days when your science teacher strutted around in a powdered wig and an embarrassing floppy cravat.

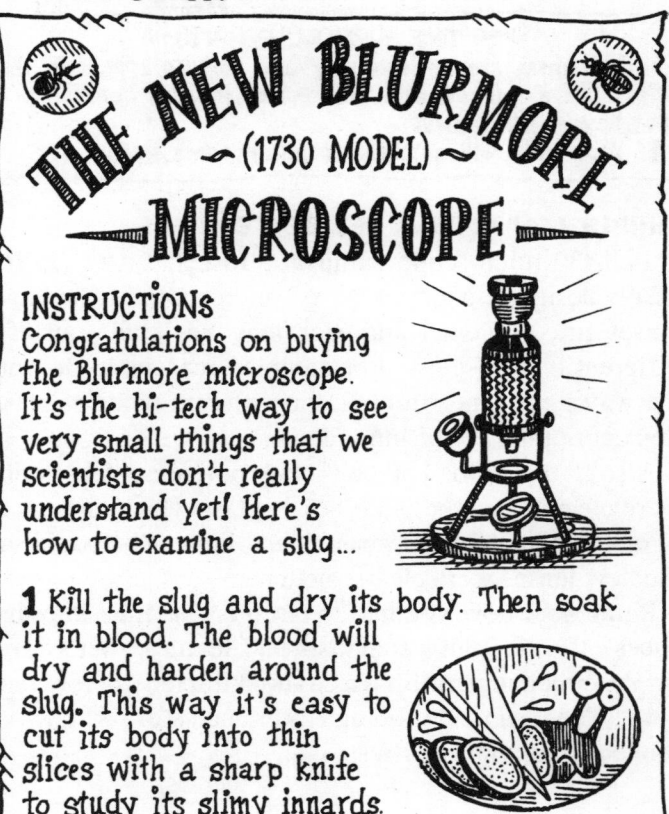

THE NEW BLURMORE
~(1730 MODEL)~
MICROSCOPE

INSTRUCTIONS
Congratulations on buying the Blurmore microscope. It's the hi-tech way to see very small things that we scientists don't really understand yet! Here's how to examine a slug...

1 Kill the slug and dry its body. Then soak it in blood. The blood will dry and harden around the slug. This way it's easy to cut its body into thin slices with a sharp knife to study its slimy innards.

2 Lay a slice of slug on a microscope slide. Add a few blobs of smelly glue made of boiled up fish-bones to hold your slug in position. If you happen to be out of fish you could try a blob of fat from a dead animal.

3 Now you are ready to look at your slide, so simply place it under the lens of your microscope and peer through the eyepiece!

GAZOOKS!

~ **THE SMALL PRINT** ~

1. Our lenses are rather blurry and colours appear in the glass like a rainbow and that makes it a bit confusing. But hey — it's pretty!

2. Your slide will quickly rot and become smelly.

THINGS COULD ONLY GET BETTER...

1 In 1830 microscope enthusiast Joseph Lister (1786–1869) designed a new type of microscope. It had two lenses fitted together and each lens was made out of a different type of glass. For complex reasons to do with the way light bends through the different types of glass, this cut out the confusing colours.

2 Also in the 1830s you could buy pure glass lenses that were clearer than the old types of glass which had traces of other chemicals that made them blurry. You could say the new lenses were clearly better!

3 Remember how you had to cut the specimen into thin slices? By the 1860s scientists had learnt how to cover the specimen in paraffin wax to hold it steady before they cut it. The idea made slicing easier and safer so I guess it proved a cut above the rest.

4 By the 1890s scientists were using a chemical called formalin to harden the specimen before the wax stage. The formalin preserved the specimen and made it easier to cut. The discovery was made by a scientist who was using formalin to kill germs on a dead mouse. But he absent-mindedly left the mouse in the formalin overnight and in the morning it was harder than a school cheese.

Today undertakers use formalin to preserve dead bodies but school cheeses are preserved using slightly less poisonous chemicals.

STILL WANT TO BE A MICROSCOPE EXPERT?

Wow, that's great! This magazine should be right up your eyepiece…

(PUBLISHED WEEKLY BY TERRIBLY ENTHUSIASTIC INC.)

MICRO-MAG

GETTING THE BEST FROM YOUR MICROSCOPE
by Howie Doitt

Hi, fellow microscope dudes! The microscope is a wonderfully wicked, cool invention! Here's a few dos and don'ts to get the very best from your machine!

25

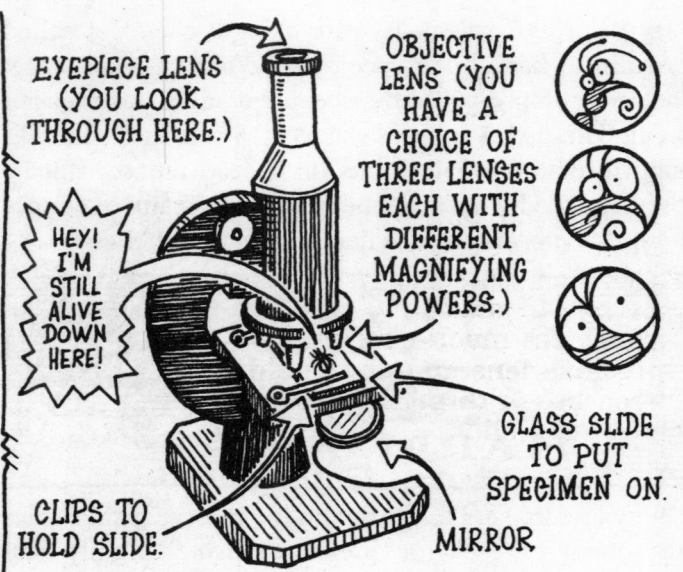

EYEPIECE LENS (YOU LOOK THROUGH HERE.)

OBJECTIVE LENS (YOU HAVE A CHOICE OF THREE LENSES EACH WITH DIFFERENT MAGNIFYING POWERS.)

HEY! I'M STILL ALIVE DOWN HERE!

GLASS SLIDE TO PUT SPECIMEN ON.

CLIPS TO HOLD SLIDE.

MIRROR

DOS AND DON'TS

DO

Shine a bright light on your microscope. The mirror will reflect light under the specimen. Of course, if the object is solid like the head of a dead insect you could try lighting the object from above otherwise it'll appear as a dark blob and you blobably won't see much.

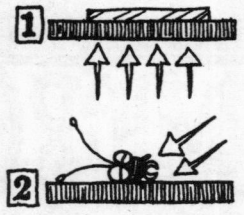

DO

Use a very soft cloth or air brush to remove dust from your microscope lenses. (Oh, by the way, an air brush is an air bulb with a brush attached. You

ERK!

squeeze the bulb and puff air to blow away that nasty dust and the brush gets rid of any sticky bits.) TLC for lenses – that's what I say!

DON'T
Lower your objective whilst looking through the eyepiece. The mere thought of this is enough to make me cry! You might get muck over your precious lens and you could even break through your glass specimen slide – BOO HOO!

DON'T
Forget to replace the dust cap on your eyepiece and cover your microscope when it's not in use. Once again, dust might get on the lenses. And then all your observations could bite the dust...

MIND YOU, DUST CAN BE FASCINATING – JUST TURN TO PAGE 84 IF YOU DON'T BELIEVE ME!

MICROSCOPIC EXPRESSIONS
Two microscope scientists are talking…

WAS THE DEPTH OF FIELD OK FOR THE BODY TUBE?

YES – BUT I LACKED THE RESOLUTION!

Do you say…?

HELP! THEY'VE MURDERED SOMEONE AND PUT THE BODY IN A TUBE AND THEN BURIED IT IN A FIELD AND ONE OF THEM IS FEELING SCARED!

Answer: Poppycock, codswallop, humbug! The body tube is the main part of a microscope that contains the lenses. Depth of field means the amount that you can move the body tube up and down and still get a clear image and resolution means the amount of detail you can see. D'you see?

Bet you never knew!
How scientists make slides of specimens…
1 They stain the specimen so it shows up really clearly under the microscope. A stain is a special dye that colours certain chemicals and shows up certain parts of the tiny object the scientist is looking at. A commonly used stain is cochineal – made from ground up beetles!

GULP!

NEXT!

2 Cut a thin slice of the object. That's so that the light can shine through it from below and you can see it clearly under the microscope. How thin? Well about one thousandth of a millimetre (one micrometre) will do. Scientists use a tool called a microtome to do the cutting – and I expect very mean scientists use it to cut cake.

SPECIMEN

THE BLADE IS MADE FROM VERY SHARP GLASS (ITS CUTTING EDGE IS SHARPER THAN METAL)

HANDLE

RIGHT, THAT'S ONE MICROMETRE FOR YOU AND THE REST FOR ME!

3 They place the specimen on a glass with a drop of water to stop it drying out and a thin piece of glass called a cover slip to protect it. Or if they want to store the specimen they might cover it in glycerine and gelatine and seal the edges of the cover slip with gum arabic to stop it from drying or rotting.

☠ HORRIBLE HEALTH WARNING!

Don't you try cutting *your* specimens! You might end up examining an interesting slice of fingertip!

Now as I said, this book is a *microscope*. And you don't need another microscope to read this book. (Unless you're *really* short-sighted!) But if you'd like another microscope, here's how to make one so powerful that everyone in your class will be jealous including your teacher! Think about it … your very own ELECTRON MICROSCOPE!

Microscopic monsters fact file

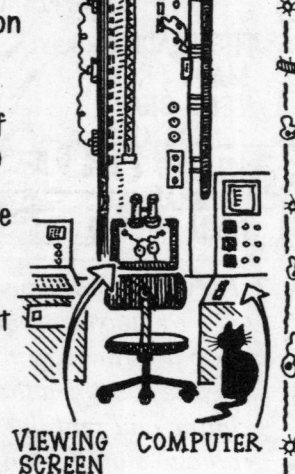

VIEWING SCREEN   COMPUTER

NAME: Electron microscope

THE BASIC FACTS: **1** An electron microscope fires electrons at the object you're looking at. (Electrons are the tiny blips of energy that surround atoms.)

2 Like electrons, light is made of tiny blips of energy but they zig-zag very fast to form light waves. If the object is smaller than a light wave (0.5 micrometres) then your eyes won't be able to see it *with an ordinary microscope.*

3 The beam of electrons is far smaller than a light wave. So you can actually study objects 200,000 times smaller than with an ordinary microscope.

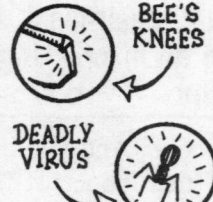

BEE'S KNEES

DEADLY VIRUS

MONSTROUS DETAILS: An electron microscope is fab for looking at really horrible tiny objects. Things like the viruses that cause deadly diseases such as rabies.

HOW TO BUILD YOUR OWN SCANNING ELECTRON MICROSCOPE
Wanna get closer to the action? Well, if your answer is "Not 'arf" then you've come to the right place!

WARNING!

Please read these directions before you get started. But beware: some of them might not be very sensible!

First assemble your materials…

A large metal pipe. (A sewer pipe will do – better give it a good scrub!)

A fluorescent screen and electron gun from a TV set. (No, don't take your TV set to pieces, I'm sure you can borrow one from school.)

Some *very* powerful magnets.

A computer. (It needs software suitable for presenting pictures from an electron microscope. Perhaps a friendly computer programmer could knock you up some?)

A powerful air pump to suck air out of the microscope and form an airless space called a vacuum.

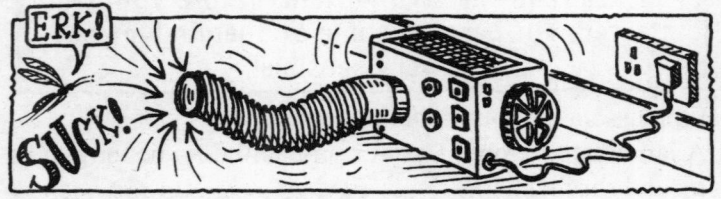

A wire and plug linked up to the electron gun.

Here's what you do...

1 Fix the electrode gun in the metal pipe so that it fires a beam of high energy electrons downwards and sweeps from side to side.

2 Below this, fix magnets on either side of the pipe. The magnetic forces direct the electrons into a narrow beam. Make sure the electron beam hits the place where the specimen is to be fixed and bounces on to the fluorescent screen. The screen should light up where it's hit by electrons.

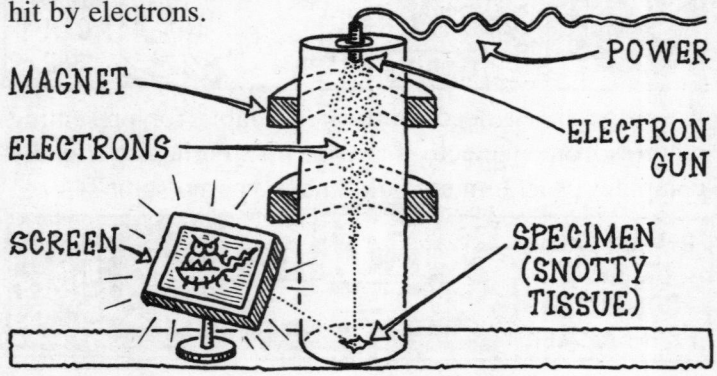

3 Link the screen up to a computer that can interpret the hits on the screen as a picture of the specimen you'll be studying.

4 Use the pump to pump out the air from the tube. Atoms of air get in the way of the electrons and distort the picture.

5 Whoops! Silly me! Don't forget to place your specimen inside the machine. Actually this should be step **4** because if you put your hand in the airless tube your fingers could be wrenched out of their sockets!

6 Plug in and switch on! NO, DON'T!!!!!!

An important announcement...

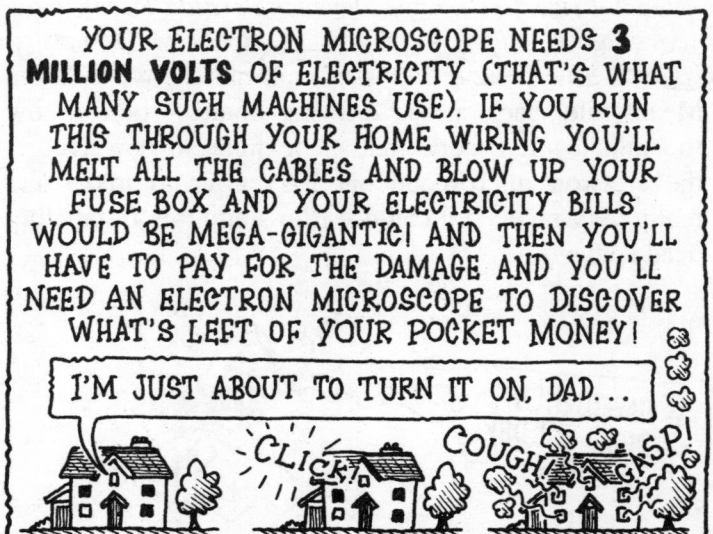

YOUR ELECTRON MICROSCOPE NEEDS **3 MILLION VOLTS** OF ELECTRICITY (THAT'S WHAT MANY SUCH MACHINES USE). IF YOU RUN THIS THROUGH YOUR HOME WIRING YOU'LL MELT ALL THE CABLES AND BLOW UP YOUR FUSE BOX AND YOUR ELECTRICITY BILLS WOULD BE MEGA-GIGANTIC! AND THEN YOU'LL HAVE TO PAY FOR THE DAMAGE AND YOU'LL NEED AN ELECTRON MICROSCOPE TO DISCOVER WHAT'S LEFT OF YOUR POCKET MONEY!

I'M JUST ABOUT TO TURN IT ON, DAD...

CLICK!

COUGH! GASP!

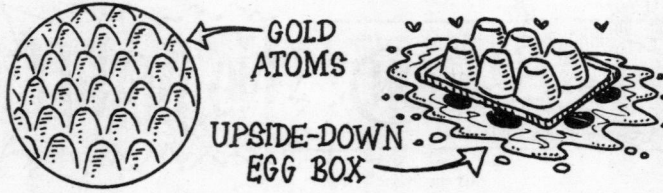
Meanwhile, back at the drawing board – here's how to build a microscope that's not quite so powerful as the electron microscope but it's easier to make and really very nice. You can use it to study this fascinating dead spider...

FASCINATING DEAD SPIDER

Dare you discover ... how to build your own microscope?

You will need:

A piece of card 2.5 cm wide by 5 cm long
A piece of cellophane (try using the clear wrapping from a greetings card)
Scissors
Sticky tape
Pencil or hole punch
A cardboard tube from a kitchen roll

What you do:

1 Use the hole punch or pencil point to make a hole 5 mm across in the centre of the card.

2 Cover the hole with cellophane and secure with sticky tape.

3 Cut a length of tube 5 cm long and then cut into it two slots 3 cm long and 2.5 cm apart coming down from one end. Lift up the cardboard between them to make a little window. Place the tube on top of the spider and place the card on top of the tube.

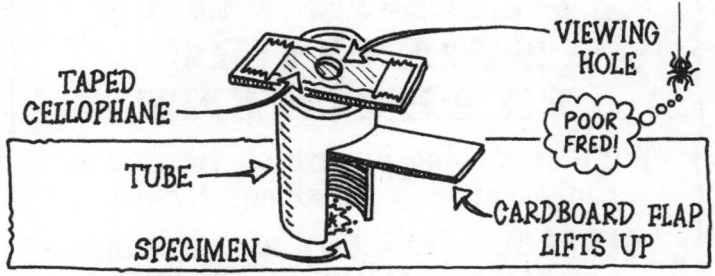

TAPED CELLOPHANE

VIEWING HOLE

POOR FRED!

TUBE

SPECIMEN

CARDBOARD FLAP LIFTS UP

4 Pick up a drop of water on the tip of the pencil and let it fall over the cellophane covering the hole. Make sure the drop covers the hole.

5 Hold your eye very close to the drop and look through it. You should see the spider's eight eyes and fangs in fascinating close up detail. Just don't let it give you nightmares afterwards...

Now just imagine you could use your microscope to spot a tiny human being. That's right an actual human being shrunk to a microscopic size. Impossible? Wait till you read this story...

IT'S A SMALL WORLD!

WANTED
PERSON FOR SCIENTIFIC EXPERIMENT
You'll be testing diminution technology equipment — a shrinking machine.
GENEROUS PAYMENT and a chance to **HELP THE CAUSE OF SCIENCE!**
Phone Professor N Large
(01924) 849382

No one knew what to expect from the professor's new shrinking machine, but one thing was clear. The person who agreed to test it had to be ever so brave … or ever so stupid. Only fearless private eye MI Gutzache had the experience for the job – and a very bad experience it was. And *no way* was he falling for that "all for the cause of science" cockamamie clap-trap!

But then a couple of words caught his eye…

I'm afraid none of my scientific colleagues wanted to volunteer for the test - they all muttered something about "unacceptable risk factors". I explained to Gutzache that the new machine was capable of shrinking a human to the size of a microbe!

SO YOU WON'T BE NEEDING THAT!

I heard the Prof but I didn't like what I was hearing. I wanted out but the Prof suggested a small test. "No risk," he said. But he was wrong and I was the fall guy. I stood under the machine as he switched it on. Just one tiny little test...

I placed a pin upright under the microscope but outside the shrinking ray for Gutzache to inspect and report on. It would be a fascinating opportunity to compare Gutzache's view with that of the microscope.

Gutzache felt the gentle warmth of the rays falling on him like summer sunshine. It didn't feel too bad until he noticed that he was shrinking. The pin beside him was getting bigger and bigger until it looked like a giant column. There were ridges and furrows running down its sides and its top was no longer sharp and pointed but rounded like an enormous Christmas pudding.

The big, wide world was getting bigger and wider by the second. Too big. A good private eye plays a hunch and mine said "get out!" – but it was too late. The pin wasn't a pin – it looked like the Washington Monument. And that wasn't all. There were things squirming and oozing in the wrinkles that appeared in the metal. Living things – like squelching blobs of jelly. The pin didn't look too lucky and I was hollering for the Prof to make me bigger.

WASHINGTON
MONUMENT

39

Amazing! Gutzache is describing microscopic dents and bacteria on the pin. At this point I observed Gutzache under the microscope. I could see him waving even if I couldn't hear his tiny voice. He seemed happy so I decided to press on. But just then I had ... ahem, an unfortunate accident...
Well, I sneezed...

It was like something blew up somewhere close. It blew me off my feet and sent me flying. I saw blobs all around, I figured they were snot. Getting in the way of a sneeze is bad for you - it sure was bad for me. Didn't the Prof know about handkerchiefs?

The floor looked hundreds of miles away and the only way was down. One thing I knew for sure - thanks to a sneeze ... I was gonna be crowbait.

Will Gutzache make a tiny little mess on the carpet? You can find out later! But first we'll stick with the detective theme and find out how microscopes solve small but messy mysteries ... including the sinister case of the treacherous toilet thief!

MICROSCOPIC DETECTIVE MYSTERIES

There's a whole branch of police work called forensic science that uses microscopes to search for clues to crimes. Here are some forensic clues that we've borrowed from a police museum.

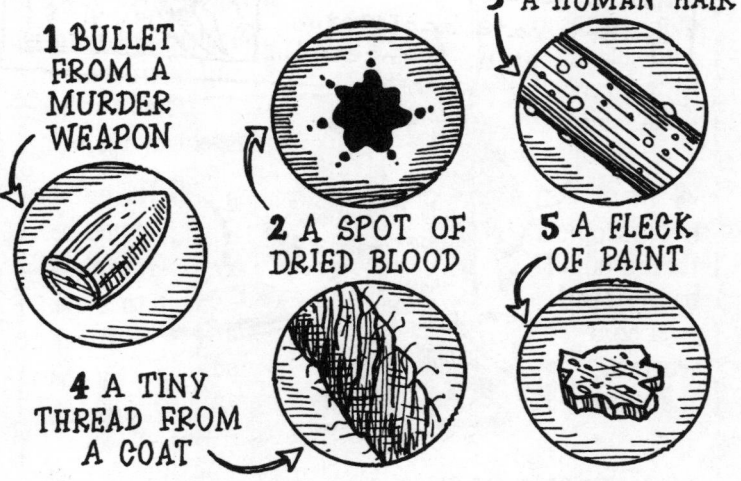

1 BULLET FROM A MURDER WEAPON

3 A HUMAN HAIR

2 A SPOT OF DRIED BLOOD

5 A FLECK OF PAINT

4 A TINY THREAD FROM A COAT

And here's how these clues can catch a villain…

Microscopic monsters fact file

NAME: Forensic science

THE BASIC FACTS: Forensic scientists check the scene of a crime for tiny clues.

THE VICTIM SEEMS TO HAVE BEEN HOLDING A BOWL OF, ER, TOMATO SOUP AT THE TIME OF THE SHOOTING…

1 Scratches on the side of the bullet might match grooves in the barrel of the suspect's gun – who said science isn't groovy?

2 Blood can be tested for DNA. This substance – known as deoxyribonucleic acid (de-oxy-ri-bo new-clay-ick acid) – forms a unique chemical code in all of us. If DNA from the victim is found on the murder suspect then chances are they did it.

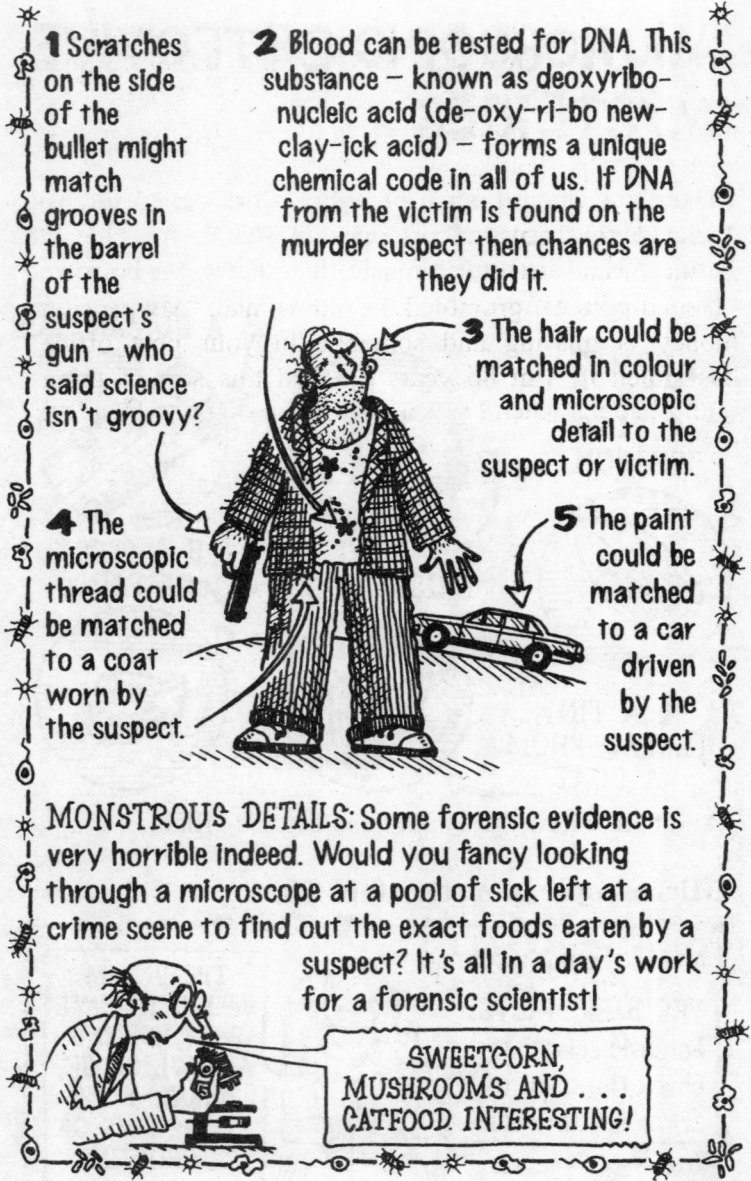

3 The hair could be matched in colour and microscopic detail to the suspect or victim.

4 The microscopic thread could be matched to a coat worn by the suspect.

5 The paint could be matched to a car driven by the suspect.

MONSTROUS DETAILS: Some forensic evidence is very horrible indeed. Would you fancy looking through a microscope at a pool of sick left at a crime scene to find out the exact foods eaten by a suspect? It's all in a day's work for a forensic scientist!

SWEETCORN, MUSHROOMS AND . . . CATFOOD. INTERESTING!

So how would you measure up as a forensic scientist? Don't worry, there won't be any pools of sick to peer into. Just a true crime story of how the microscope helped to catch a ruthless thief … with his trousers down. Can you help trap the suspect?

THE TREACHEROUS TOILET THIEF

Lyons, France 1922

"It's a disgrace!" grumbled the old woman. "My pension money is missing and someone in your post office has stolen it! I'm 86 years old and this sort of thing didn't happen when I was a girl! There ought to be a law against it!"

The postmaster looked harassed.

"There *is* a law, madam, and rest assured I will make it my business to catch the thief and return the money."

The old woman shuffled out still wagging her skinny finger and muttering complaints. When she had gone the postmaster took a deep breath and summoned his two most trusted staff. They were very different. Jean was small and wiry and Jacques was built like an extra-large pillar box. The postmaster looked sternly at the pair.

"That's the third complaint today. I am ordering you to catch the thief before he gets us into any more trouble. I have devised a cunning plan but I am afraid it is rather unpleasant."

Jacques was so proud of winning his chief's confidence that he didn't notice the words "rather unpleasant". He beamed self-importantly.

"That's all right boss, you can count on us for anything!"

"Very well," said the postmaster. "I believe that the thief is opening the letters and stealing the money in the toilet." And with that he outlined his plan.

By the time the two postmen left they were looking rather less happy.

Jean prodded his friend's bulging tummy. "You fat fool! Why did you tell him he could count on us? Now look what you've done!"

Jacques looked as if he was going to cry. "It wasn't my fault!" he moaned. "How was I to know we'd be spying on the toilets?"

"It's a terrible inconvenience!" continued Jean.

Jacques nodded gloomily. "I know it's terrible in them conveniences, but we could always wear clothes pegs on our noses."

"Oh, shut up!" snapped Jean.

By 11 the next morning the two postmen were very uncomfortable. They were cramped and doubled up in the roof space of the toilets. And they were sickened by the revolting sights they'd been subjected to as they spied through the eyeholes that had been drilled in the ceilings of the cubicles.

"How many have you seen?" whispered Jean.

"Oh, I haven't been counting – ten, maybe 12."

"Anyone do anything bad?"

Jacques giggled. "All of them. The last one in my cubicle must have eaten lots of beans – he was a real stinker! This investigation is getting up my nose."

But Jean put his finger to his lips.

"Shut up, Jacques, there's someone in the toilet!"

"Where's he going – yours or mine?"

"Mine. Ssh, Jacques – I think it's the thief!"

There was a ripping sound as envelopes were opened and a rustling as their contents were rifled and a crackle as postal orders and bank notes were hurriedly stuffed into the thief's pockets.

"I want a look!" cried Jacques shoving aside his friend. But his huge knee banged the floor sending a fine drizzle of plaster into the cubicle. The thief hastily unlocked the door and fled the toilet.

"Now look what you've done!" hissed Jean.

"It wasn't my fault!" said Jacques miserably. "How can I help it if the floor got in the way?!"

Back in the postmaster's office the boss was drumming his fingers on the table.

"Well, what did he look like?" he asked the two postmen.

"He wore a cap," said Jacques.

The postmaster gave him a dirty look. "You fool, all postmen wear a cap – it's one of our regulations. Is that it? So all we've got is a damaged toilet roof and nothing to go on!"

Jacques whispered, "Does he mean that no one can go on the toilet?" and Jean gave him a kick.

"What was that?" said the postmaster sharply.

"Jacques said the thief might still have the envelopes on him." said Jean.

"You fool!" snapped the postmaster. "The thief is not stupid. The first thing he'll have done is to throw them away. Are you sure you didn't see anything else – any tiny clues. You'd better think of something or I'll have you watching the toilets for the next six months!"

Jean shuffled his feet unhappily. "Chief, it's not our fault! I mean – we don't have microscopes for eyes!" he said.

Suddenly the postmaster thumped his desk, making the two postmen jump.

"Microscopes!" he cried excitedly. "Of course – that's it!"

Police scientist Edmond Locard was middle-aged and neatly dressed and looked like a mild-mannered bank manager. As he listened to the postmaster's story he polished his glasses and placed the tips of his fingers together – showing off his clean, neatly trimmed fingernails.

"Hmm," he said. "A fascinating case. We'll need all the postmen's coats for microscopic laboratory analysis."

A few days later Locard was staring down the eyepiece of his microscope at the crucial evidence. His face betrayed no excitement as he adjusted the focus knob. Then he made a few neatly scripted notes in his tiny handwriting.

After examining the evid... make a very interesting discovery. Sometimes it is a mistake by an innocent party that leads to the solution of the crime. A thorough investigation was carried out. Every worker at the Post Office ... notes have been taken with

What vital clue had Locard spotted?
a) Germs that the thief picked up in the toilet.
b) Threads on the thief's coat that matched threads found in the toilet.
c) Tiny bits of plaster from the ceiling.
d) Tiny fibres of paper from the envelopes.

Answer: c) The thief had brushed his coat but there were microscopic specks of plaster still on it. If there were germs from the toilet these could have been picked up by any of the postmen, and since all the postmen wore the same type of coat the threads would not have identified the thief. Paper fibres might have proved that the thief handled the envelopes but not that he had stolen the money.

47

COULD YOU BE A FORENSIC DETECTIVE?

Don't worry! You *don't* have to spy on the school toilets!
Here's an easy experiment to do instead…

Dare you discover … how to collect fibres?

You will need:
A piece of sticky tape.

What you do:
Press the sticky tape firmly on the carpet and then lift
it up.

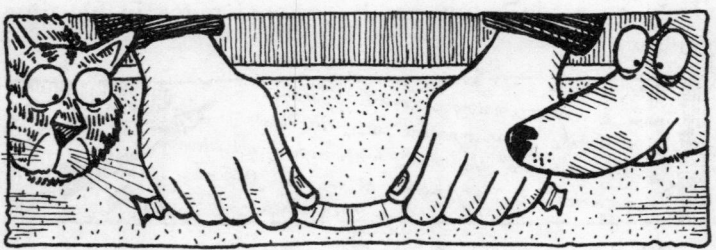

What do you notice?

Answer:
The tape is covered with carpet fibres which you can
examine with your microscope. If you're lucky, you'll
find a few human hairs or hairs from the dog or cat.
This technique is used by forensic scientists to collect
fibres from a crime scene. If they're found on the
clothes of a suspect then this could link the suspect
with the crime.

THE MAGIC MICROSCOPE

Here are samples of polyester and cotton cut from two
pairs of underpants…

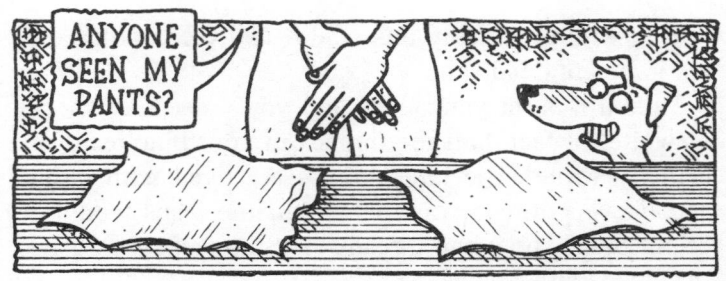

Look identical, don't they? Well, let's look closer through the magic microscope...

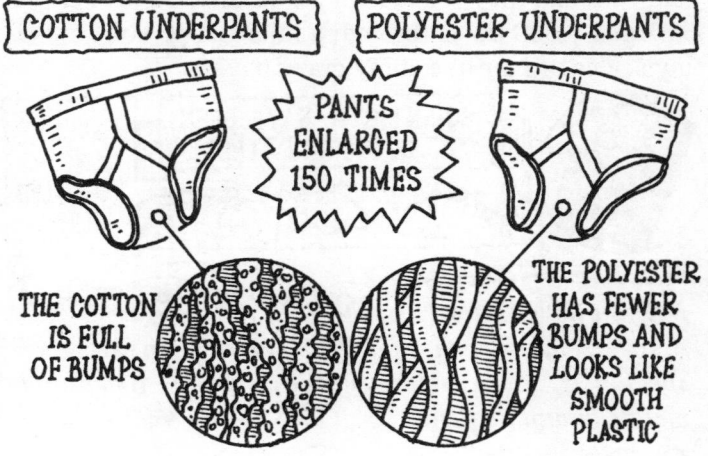

COTTON UNDERPANTS   POLYESTER UNDERPANTS

PANTS ENLARGED 150 TIMES

THE COTTON IS FULL OF BUMPS

THE POLYESTER HAS FEWER BUMPS AND LOOKS LIKE SMOOTH PLASTIC

Foul fibre facts

1 Cotton fibres come from the outer layer of seed cases on the cotton plant and they're never perfectly smooth. Polyester fibres begin life as a plastic substance that's squeezed through a tube so they're smooth and regular.

2 We've been looking at clean underwear. Seen through the microscope, dirty underwear hides all kinds of horrors. The fibres look like tangled spaghetti with lumps of brown stuff and cornflakes in it. The brown stuff is ... no, you're wrong, it's tiny bits of dirt and the "cornflakes" are lumps of dead skin.

3 Take a look at your jeans and you'll see tiny specks of white. In fact, half the threads in your blue jeans are actually white! The blue threads are dyed with indigo and if every thread was this colour the jeans would be bright blue. The white threads give the jeans a "washed 'n' faded" appearance.

4 Wool comes from sheep. Oh, so you knew that? Well, stop bleating – the fibres in wool are sheep hair and like your own hair they're made of a substance called keratin. Enlarged 1,000 times through a microscope you can see tiny scales of hair like shiny crazy paving.

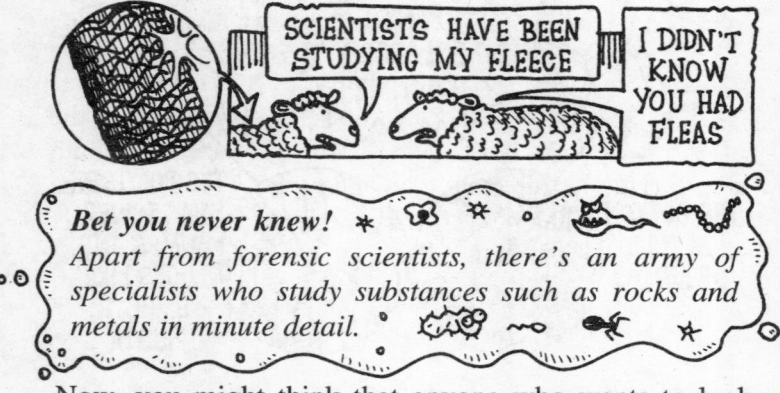

Bet you never knew!
Apart from forensic scientists, there's an army of specialists who study substances such as rocks and metals in minute detail.

Now, you might think that anyone who wants to look closely at boring things like rocks and metals is the sort of person who is called Norman and wears an anorak and very thick glasses. And of course, you'd be right.

Here's Norman to explain his hobby...

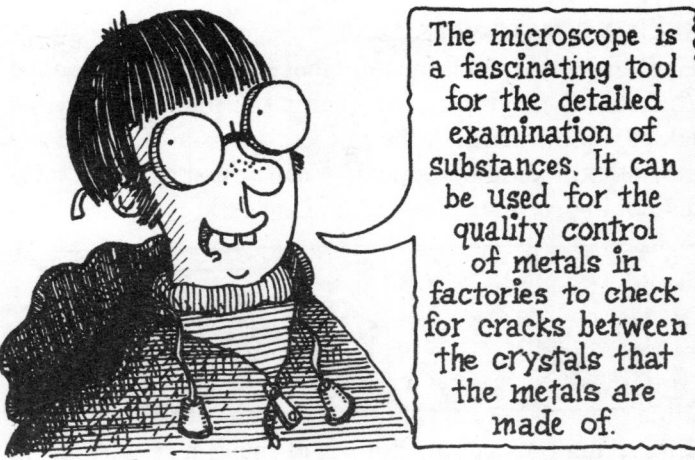

The microscope is a fascinating tool for the detailed examination of substances. It can be used for the quality control of metals in factories to check for cracks between the crystals that the metals are made of.

The first scientist to study crystals in metals using a microscope was Henry Sorby (1826–1908). He sounds a bit like Norman – after all, his idea of a fun holiday was to sail his yacht up and down the coast studying how the tides move lumps of sewage that have been flushed into rivers. (He did this for a British Government Committee on the River Thames.) But he must have been a clever person because he taught himself science, and he once said his aim was...

...not to pass an examination but to qualify myself for a course for original investigation

Are you brave enough to quote this to your teacher?

In fact, microscopic investigation of materials can be very exciting – as you're about to find out...

EXCITING MATERIALS QUIZ

Here are some exciting jobs that require a microscope. And just to make the quiz even more interesting, we've added a job for which the microscope is as sensible as a pair of exploding underpants – can you spot it?

1 Looking for the causes of a plane crash.

2 Studying rocks at the bottom of the sea.

3 Checking the quality of diamonds.

4 Looking at gold to make sure that it's 100 per cent gold and not mixed with some cheaper metal.

But come to think of it, there are even more scientists who use microscopes. A microscope is pretty essential for scientists who study miniature lifeforms like putrid little plants and extra small (but still revolting) bugs. They might be small, but they make up for it in the horrible habits department.

Are you ready to uncover their slimy little secrets?

TINY TERRORS

Somebody had to be the first person to make an in-depth microscopic study of plants and bugs and that somebody happened to be an ugly hunch-backed dwarf. Well, that's how his friends described him ... his enemies were a little more unkind.

Hall of fame: Robert Hooke (1635–1703)
Nationality: British
Robert looked like an ugly dwarf and his hobby was spreading ugly rumours about people he didn't like such as mega-star scientist Isaac
Newton (1642–1727).

NEWTON? PAH! THE MAN'S A BUFFOON. YOU'D NEED ONE OF MY MICROSCOPES TO CHECK IF HE'S GOT A BRAIN AT ALL! AND THAT RIDICULOUS FALLING APPLE THEORY, BLAH, BLAH, DRONE, WITTER, ETC. ETC.

But Hooke was also a brilliant scientist who built his own microscope and published a book called *Micrographia* full of stomach-turning pictures of his discoveries. As you might expect our old pal, Leeuwenhoek was a big fan of this book and although he couldn't read the English words he enjoyed looking at the pictures. And now for a remarkable *Horrible Science* exclusive. Here is Robert Hooke in person! He's been dug up and brought back from the dead to tell us all about his discoveries...

DEAD BRAINY: ROBERT HOOKE

Is that the time? How long have I been dead?

Ah! here is my pride and joy — my microscope. Yes, you are allowed to gasp at my skill and cunning workmanship — it's all my own work you know!

OH GET ON WITH IT!

Sorry readers, RH was an extremely conceited and self-important person.

The light is provided by this oil lamp and this glass ball brightens the light and focuses it on the viewing platform on which I have placed the specimen.

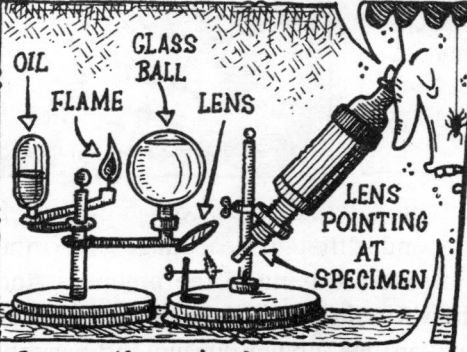

OIL

FLAME

GLASS BALL

LENS

LENS POINTING AT SPECIMEN

Actually the lenses Hooke used were not as good as Leeuwenhoek's and he missed out on some of the things the Dutch scientist spotted.

I peer through the eyepiece of the microscope like so.

Using my microscope I looked at fungi (that's more than one fungus) and snowflakes. Those snowflakes were hard to see because they kept melting so I had to sit out in the cold with my microscope. It was snow joke, I can tell you!

SNOWFLAKE

FUNGI

One day I was looking at cork. Cork is a type of wood and I saw little boxes. Well, I called them "cells". It was a corker of a discovery — if I say so myself!

I was especially interested in plants. I looked at a stinging nettle and saw it had tiny hairs on its leaves. 'Hair's a mystery!' I thought — what are they for?

I touched a hair under the microscope and saw the end stick in my skin and poison run into my finger. I was stung into action I can tell you! Let's try it again...

OUCH — MY HAND! I WISH I WAS DEAD!

Hooke didn't actually understand what cells are for and how they worked (*you* can find out on page 101) but discovering them was still a great achievement. Later on we'll find out how Hooke studied bugs, but for the moment let's stick with those fungi and nasty little green plants. Oh yes, I'm afraid we have to...

Microscopic monsters fact file

NAME: Fungi and tiny plants

THE BASIC FACTS: We're talking about...

1 Fungi – aren't plants. They include moulds and yeasts.

2 Algae – including the green, slimy stuff that you find in ponds.

3 Lichens – actually a partnership between fungi and algae. Often found in tough places like Antarctica – fancy going there for a summer holiday?

MONSTROUS DETAILS: Algae thrive in water filled with sewage. And this is one of their nicer habits...

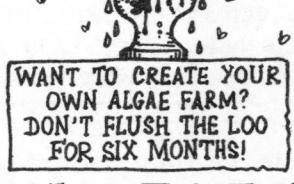

WANT TO CREATE YOUR OWN ALGAE FARM? DON'T FLUSH THE LOO FOR SIX MONTHS!

CUTE LITTLE ALGAE?

Some scientists think that algae have their charms, especially the microscopic algae that look like living balls of slime under a microscope. We decided to take them at their word and open up the world's first pet shop for algae...

A QUICK NOTE...

Yes, I know the word "pet" normally means a cute, furry animal but when you've got "plants" that swim around under their own steam, the distinction gets a little blurred.

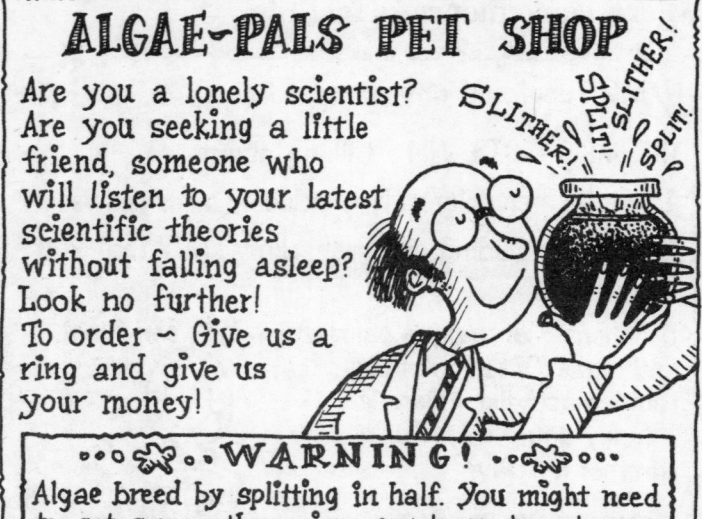

1 Cute ceratium (ser-rat-tee-um)

Description: Looks like a homemade Christmas decoration that's gone wrong.

Size: 0.5 mm

Cute features: Dagger-like spikes for protection from other microscopic creatures.

Feeding: Don't worry about feeding them – they use sunlight and carbon dioxide gas in the air to make sugar for food – a process called photosynthesis (as if you didn't know!).

Note: you can use your pet as a thermometer. The warmer the water, the more they stick their spikes out. This can be useful for working out if your bath is the right temperature!

2 Delightful diatoms
Description: Indescribable – pretty aren't they?

Size: 0.2 mm
Delightful features: They shine in the light because they have see-through bodies and hard boxlike outer bodies that contain silica, which also makes up sand and glass.
Feeding: Photosynthesis.

To stop your pets multiplying too much, why not use an animal that looks like a plant? It's wild and wacky...

3 Hungry hydra
Description: A green rubber glove.

Size: 1.25 cm
Cute features: Stinging threads in its "fingers" kill anything that comes near. Er, that's not too cute, is it?
Feeding: "Fingers" grab the prey and bring it into the creature's mouth.

FOUL FUNGAL FEEDING

So you're anti-algae? Oh well, perhaps you'll be fungi-friendly? Enlarged over 500 times through a microscope, fungi look like trendy worms with Afro haircuts. But their eating habits are less pretty – as you're about to find out...

THE FUNGI GUIDE TO ETIQUETTE
by Madame Mould

IF YOU DESIRE TO BE ACCEPTED IN THE BEST HOUSES THEN ETIQUETTE IS ESSENTIAL – SO MIND YOUR MANNERS, MOULDS!

TABLE MANNERS
Eating is very important for fungi – so make sure you eat as much as you can whenever you can. (It's acceptable to burp gas afterwards.)

MUNCH! NIBBLE! SCOFF! CHEW! BURP!

BURP!

Four things not to do
NEVER...
● Ask permission before eating.
● Say "please" or "thank you".
● Ask for a second helping – just help yourself anyway.
● Leave the table (before you've eaten it).

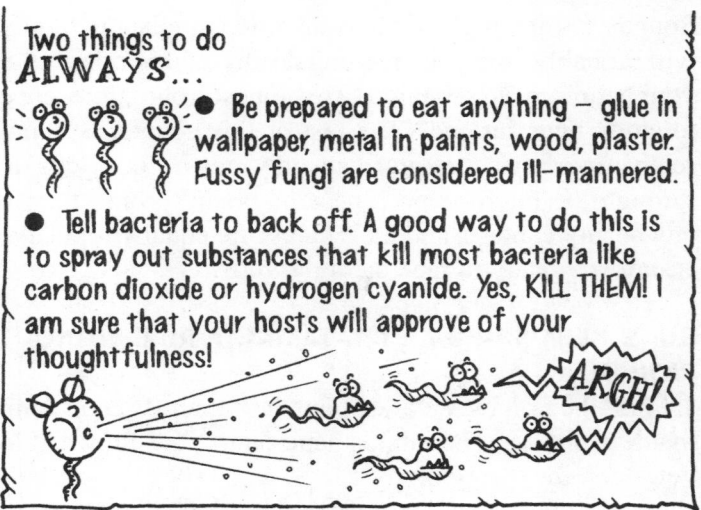

Two things to do
ALWAYS...

● Be prepared to eat anything – glue in wallpaper, metal in paints, wood, plaster. Fussy fungi are considered ill-mannered.

● Tell bacteria to back off. A good way to do this is to spray out substances that kill most bacteria like carbon dioxide or hydrogen cyanide. Yes, KILL THEM! I am sure that your hosts will approve of your thoughtfulness!

ARGH!

FOUL FUNGUS FACTS

1 Dry rot fungus will eat all the wooden bits in your house. It starts by growing in damp areas and extends its feeding tubes into dry areas of walls and floors! The only way to stop it is to cut out huge chunks of your home.

2 A fungus will push anything aside. Its feeding tubes are armoured with chitin, the tough stuff that protects insect bodies and makes beetles so hard to squash.

A TOUGH MATERIAL STOPS US GETTING SQUASHED...

IT'S CHITIN!

WHAT D'YOU MEAN, CHEATING? IT'S NOT A FLAMIN' GAME!!

3 Fungi only make small amounts of poisons and they don't harm humans – usually. But before the 1920s the deadly poison arsenic was often added to paints. Fungi ate the paints and sprayed out arsenic gas that smelt of garlic, and some people died.

Sounds fascinating? Well, your rotten spoilsport family will probably stop you breeding deadly fungi or dry rot in your bedroom. Never mind, why not use your microscope to study bugs instead? The rest of this chapter is about really tiny bugs that you can only get a good look at through the microscope. These bugs ain't going to win any beauty contests and their habits are equally repulsive ... are *you* ready to face the ugly truth?

BUGS BEHAVING BADLY 1: TAKING A RIDE WITHOUT PAYING

1 Many bugs have smaller bugs less than 0.2 mm long that live on them. Bee mites hang on to ... well, what do you think they hang on to...?

They don't do any harm, so I guess they just think it's a nice place to bee and it gives them a buzz.

2 Feather mites live on birds. There's a type of Mexican parrot that has 30 varieties of feather mite. The mites eat bits of worn feather and dead skin, and if they overeat they probably feel sick as a parrot.

3 A pseudoscorpion hitches lifts on a fly's hairs. If it gets bored of the high life, it brings the fly down to earth with a nasty nip of its poison claws and eats its body!

So you're not afraid to see a pseudoscorpion up close? Well, here's something for you to get your claws into... Who said science wasn't down to earth?

THE MAGIC MICROSCOPE: SOIL CREATURES

Soil is alive with bugs and here are two of the most common.

You know what to do … look very hard…

Can you see it? It's just coming into focus now. Wow, this microscope is magical! You can really see these bugs…

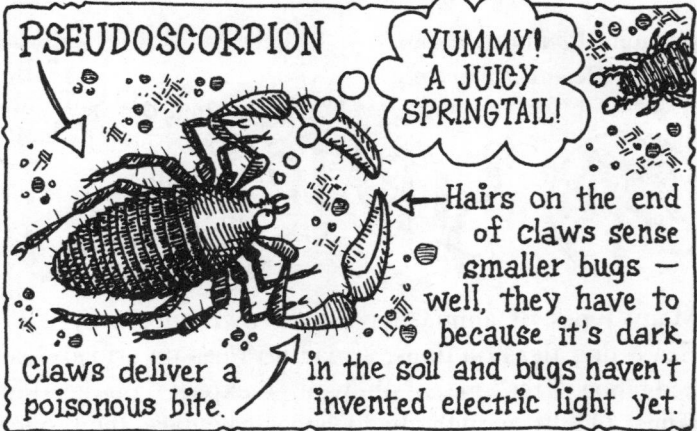

PSEUDOSCORPION

YUMMY! A JUICY SPRINGTAIL!

←Hairs on the end of claws sense smaller bugs — well, they have to because it's dark in the soil and bugs haven't invented electric light yet.

Claws deliver a poisonous bite.

The pseudoscorpions eat springtails. (Yes, they really do have springs in their tails and if they were bigger they'd win the world pogo-jumping contest!)

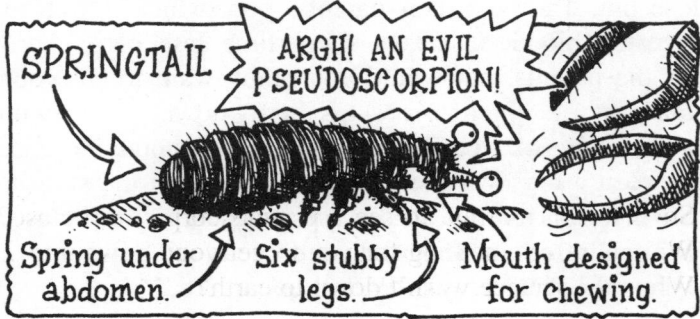

SPRINGTAIL

ARGH! AN EVIL PSEUDOSCORPION!

Spring under abdomen.

Six stubby legs.

Mouth designed for chewing.

So what do you think of the chapter so far? Are you appalled and shocked by the ugliness and the brutality of the bugs featured? You will be. Now here's a never-to-be-repeated opportunity to get the microscopic details on brutal blood-sucking bugs.

BUGS BEHAVING BADLY 2: SUCKING BLOOD

Forget vampires – some bugs make Count Dracula look like a vegetarian – as you can find out by studying them through the microscope.

1 Take fleas for example…

YEAH, TAKE THEM!

Many types of animal have their own special type of flea – dog fleas on dogs, armadillo fleas on armadillos, hedgehog fleas on … oh well, I expect you get the point. Oddly enough, hedgehog fleas have their own passengers. Tiny mites hide under their scales. I expect they enjoy life at the sharp end.

2 Flea babies are too small to suck blood but they don't lose out. They eat their parents' poo, which is rich in digested blood. It makes suppertime less of a chore for the parents, but would you really want to eat your dad's poop?

3 One type of flea is called a jigger. It lays its eggs between a person's toes. As it digs a pit in the skin in which to lays its eggs, the female sucks the victim's blood and can introduce germs which cause blood poisoning. I expect the victim says, "Well, I be jiggered!"

1 Three hundred years ago, people wore special flea traps round their necks. Each trap was a container with holes for the fleas to creep into and a little sticky rod to ensure they didn't creep out again. Queen Kristina of Sweden (1626–1689) invented an alternative method – she blasted the fleas with a tiny 10-cm cannon.

THANK YOU MA'AM!

2 Wacky Victorian scientist Frank Buckland actually liked fleas. He spent 20 years learning how to train them to do tricks and even made a model ship for them to pull. He used to feed his pets each night with a refreshing drop of his own blood.

A LOUSY EXPERIMENT

Our long dead pal Robert Hooke did another revolting experiment with another blood-sucking bug – a louse. Through his microscope he watched a louse sucking blood from his hand into its see-through body. He said:

SUCK!

I could plainly see a small current of blood which came from its snout and poured directly into its belly.

I expect the louse was wondering why this funny man was staring at him over lunch.

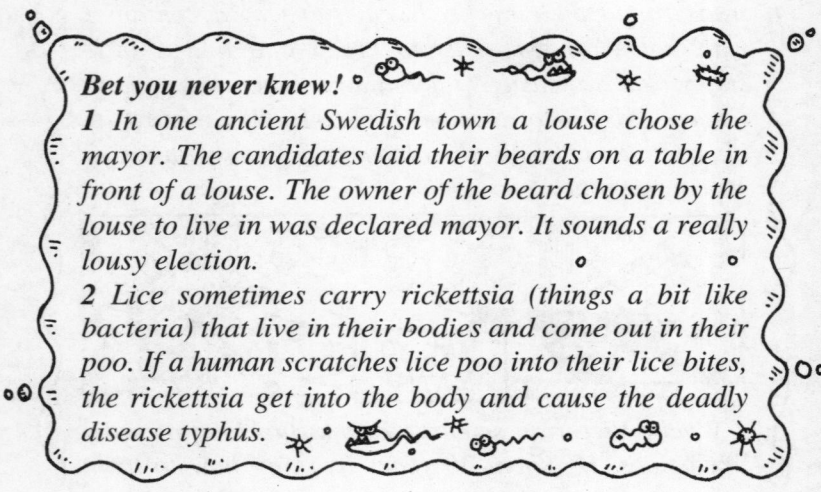

Bet you never knew!

1 In one ancient Swedish town a louse chose the mayor. The candidates laid their beards on a table in front of a louse. The owner of the beard chosen by the louse to live in was declared mayor. It sounds a really lousy election.

2 Lice sometimes carry rickettsia (things a bit like bacteria) that live in their bodies and come out in their poo. If a human scratches lice poo into their lice bites, the rickettsia get into the body and cause the deadly disease typhus.

And by some revolting coincidence we're going to be meeting some murderous microbes in the next chapter. Did I say "coincidence"? Oh well, it's a small world...

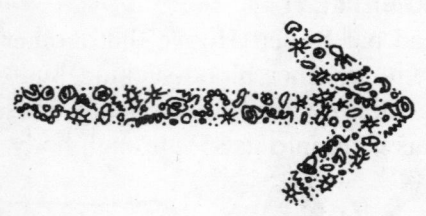

MURDEROUS MICROBES

Imagine everything became invisible and the microbes currently invisible began to glow. Everything – trees, houses, people, school dinner and dogs' poo would disappear. But you could still see where they were because the outlines of these objects and almost everything else would be picked out in ghostly glowing microbes. Yes, I'm afraid everything is CRAWLING with the little monsters!

Microscopic monsters fact file

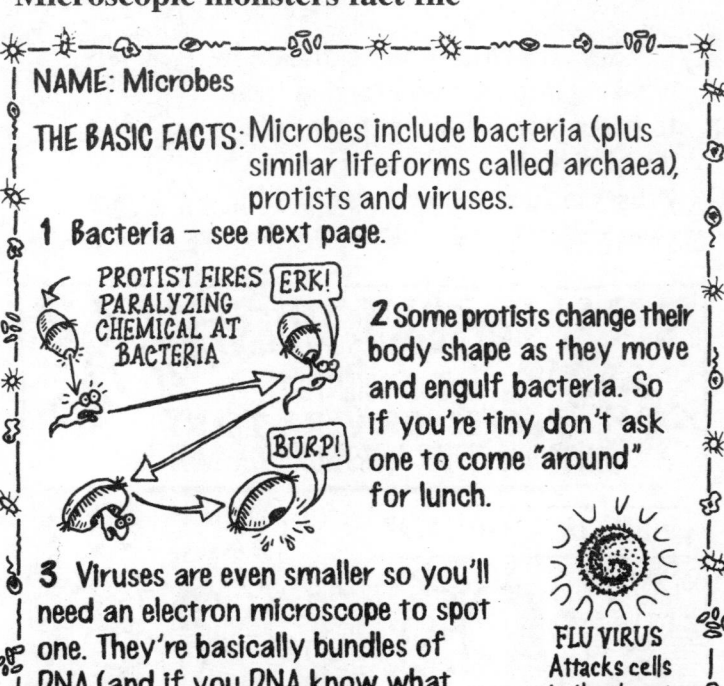

NAME: Microbes

THE BASIC FACTS: Microbes include bacteria (plus similar lifeforms called archaea), protists and viruses.

1 Bacteria – see next page.

PROTIST FIRES PARALYZING CHEMICAL AT BACTERIA

ERK!

BURP!

2 Some protists change their body shape as they move and engulf bacteria. So if you're tiny don't ask one to come "around" for lunch.

3 Viruses are even smaller so you'll need an electron microscope to spot one. They're basically bundles of DNA (and if you DNA know what I'm talking about turn back to page 42 to refresh your memory).

FLU VIRUS
Attacks cells in the throat (can be a pain in the neck).

MONSTROUS DETAILS: All three can cause deadly diseases.

1 Bacteria cause diseases such as the plague and the lung disease TB.

COUGH!

SWEAT!

2 Protists cause malaria — a killer disease which is spread by mosquitoes.

3 Viruses cause disease by breaking into cells and forcing them to make new viruses until the cells die of exhaustion. Diseases caused by viruses include yellow fever and flu.

YELLOW!

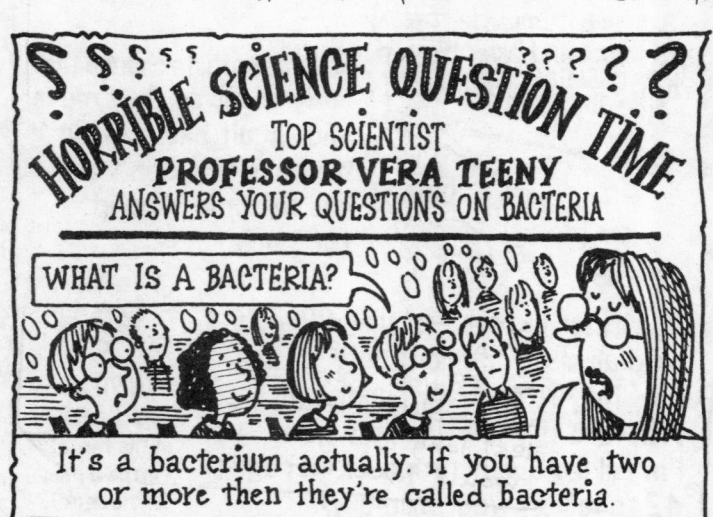

HORRIBLE SCIENCE QUESTION TIME

TOP SCIENTIST
PROFESSOR VERA TEENY
ANSWERS YOUR QUESTIONS ON BACTERIA

WHAT IS A BACTERIA?

It's a bacterium actually. If you have two or more then they're called bacteria.

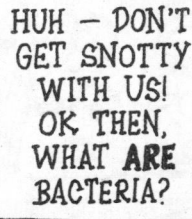

HUH — DON'T GET SNOTTY WITH US! OK THEN, WHAT **ARE** BACTERIA?

Any one of thousands of types of tiny living things. They have roughly the same features.

THREE OUTER LAYERS OF SLIME TO PROTECT BODY FROM DRYING OUT.

NUCLEUS AREA CONTAINS DNA.

To get around, bacteria wriggle through the water in which they like to live. Some beat a whip-like tail called a flagellum (fla-gell-lum) and others have tiny beating hairs called cilia (silly-a).

WRIGGLE!

BEAT!

Bacteria come in all shapes and sizes - though, to be honest, they're all pretty tiny. They can be round, and thin, and lemon-shaped, and pear-shaped, and corkscrew-shaped, and square, and comma-shaped and ... oh well ... you get the picture. And you can fit millions in a match box. If you were this small the kitchen table would appear to be 640 km (400 miles) long and getting to school would take for ever!

SO HOW MANY TYPES OF BACTERIA ARE THERE?

Lots

CAN YOU BE MORE EXACT?

No

Scientists from the University of Southern California found 61 types of bacteria living in a hot spring in Yellowstone National Park. 57 were unknown to science. Some scientists think that every pinch of soil could contain 10,000 different types of bacteria but they haven't got round to counting them all yet.

Any volunteers to count them?

Although, we're talking awfully big numbers. An average-sized lawn holds countless billions of individual bacteria — about 4.5 kg by weight.

And they're eaten by an army of tiny creatures such as protists and slimy nematode worms with no eyes and six rubbery lips

WHERE ELSE DO BACTERIA LIVE?

Where don't they live! Most bacteria live in "cities" of slime in massive piles like tower blocks 200 micrometres high (that's BIG by their standards). Favourite places for slime cities are — are you ready for this? — sewage pipes, false teeth, contact lenses, the guts and just about anywhere else you can imagine...

SO WHAT DO BACTERIA DO ALL DAY?

Well, they eat and divide to make new bacteria and they eat and divide and when they're bored of that they divide and eat. Well, I suppose they could play football under the microscope but then they might be caught off-slide! Ha, ha — sorry, just my little joke.

MUNCH! SPLIT!

MUNCH! MUNCH!

SPLIT! SPLIT!

A NOTE TO THE READER...
Some people are scared of bacteria. After reading this book you might feel scared too. DON'T. Most do us no harm and some are actually good for us: the bacteria that live in your gut help to make Vitamin K, a substance that helps your blood to clot. Bacteria have been around for thousands of millions of years and they'll still be there at the end of the world. And anyway, they're scientifically fascinating!

Bacteria might be tiny – but they're TOUGH. Their secret is to form spores. These are thick capsules that protect their bodies and they can live for years. You might be surprised to learn that bacteria have really boastful personalities and love bragging about their survival feats. OK, I just made that bit up but just imagine they *were* like this…

BOASTFUL BACTERIA

Of course, we had it tough when I were a lad. I was stuck for 300 years in a grain of soil stuck to a dried plant…

That's nothing. I remember when I was living on the bottom of a ship and all I had to eat was … the ship.

I'd have killed for a bit of ship to eat. I spent years living in a car park and all I had to eat was tarmac.

Well, of course when I was younger I spent 3,000 years living at the bottom of the sea in the freezing cold with enough water pressing down from above to crush a human flat.

Huh — you had it soft lad! Before I was in the soil I had to live in central heating pipes and eat them!

ALL these boasts are TRUE!

1 Scientists have revived bacteria on plant specimens this old.

2 Bacteria that live in polluted sea water can eat ships! What happens is bacteria in the water eat the sulphur and turn it into sulphide. This joins to iron atoms on the ship to make a black smelly chemical called iron sulphide. Other bacteria happily guzzle this foul mixture – and eat the ship.

3 It's true – some bacteria eat tarmac. Mind you, it takes them hundreds of years to do it – it's a bit like you trying to eat a pile of hamburgers the size of Mount Everest!

4 Bacteria live at the bottom of the sea. But they're so used to the pressure of the water that when they are brought up to the surface where there's less water crushing down on them, their little bodies go pop.

5 Some bacteria like it hot and they're quite happy in your hot copper pipes. They eat the chemical sulphur in the water and poo out a chemical called sulphide which joins with copper atoms in the pipes to make a chemical called copper sulphide that makes the water in your hot taps smell of rotten eggs.

6 Disinfectant contains a chemical called phenol that kills most bacteria – but some bacteria think it's a treat and happily guzzle it!

> ### Bet you never knew!
>
> **1** When bacteria feed inside a dead body, the methane gas they give off makes the body swell up to three times its size. There have even been cases of dead bodies blowing up. A state funeral in 1927 of British King George V's brother-in-law was interrupted by an embarrassing bang as the corpse exploded.
>
> **2** Methane is also made inside cows by bacteria that live in the cow's stomach and digest the tough cell walls of grass. The cow can then digest the grass more easily. Cows get rid of the methane in huge burps or farts. The cows don't mean to be rude but there's no udder choice.

MICROSCOPIC EXPRESSIONS

A scientist says:

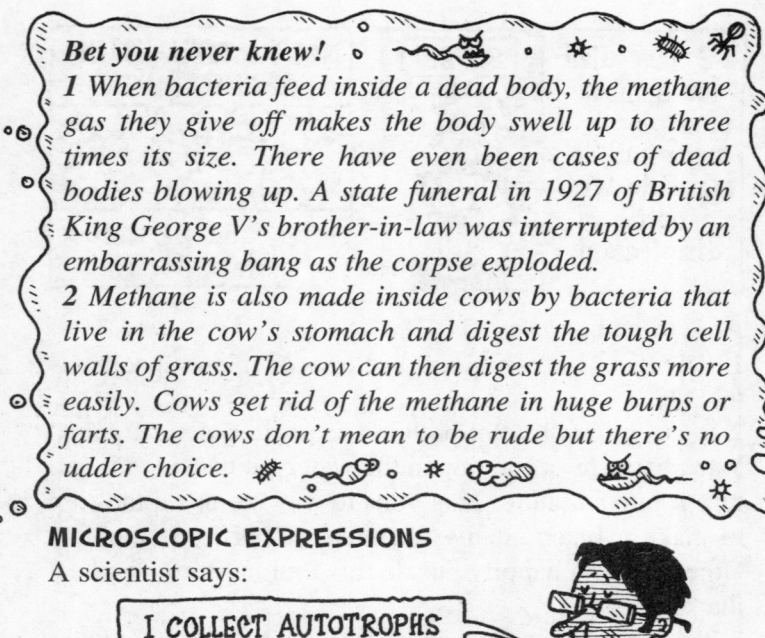

I COLLECT AUTOTROPHS

Do you say…?

COOL! I COLLECT AUTOGRAPHS TOO!

Answer: No. He said *autotrophs* – and if you don't know what they are, keep reading! It's a posh term for being able to make food from simple chemicals – and no, we're not talking cookery lessons here. Autotrophs include plants and certain bacteria that make their food using photosynthesis. (Remember that word? It's on page 58.) Other autotrophic bacteria feed off chemicals such as sulphur, as you've just found out…

74

BACTERIA BREAKFAST QUIZ

Which of these "foods" would bacteria NOT fancy for breakfast...?

a) Your mum's bottle of vitamin C pills.
b) A bucket of sulphuric acid.
c) An old pair of Wellie boots.
d) An ancient temple.

COULD YOU BE A SCIENTIST?

The landlord of a bar in the Yukon, Canada offered his guests a disgusting cocktail. It was champagne ... with a human toe in it complete with toenail. (The toe had been found in a log cabin – no one knew what it was doing there but I expect it was trying to find its feet.) Anyway, the landlord challenged his customers to drink the concoction saying:

You can drink it fast, you can drink it slow — but the lips have got to touch the toe!

ARGH!

But why didn't bacteria eat the toe and make it rot?
a) It was too revolting even for bacteria.
b) It was so cold in the Yukon that the bacteria froze.
c) The toe had been pickled in alcohol and few bacteria can live in these conditions.

Answer: c) You'll be interested to know that 725 people actually drank the disgusting drink but in 1980 someone accidentally swallowed the toe. I guess that was just toe bad.

TEACHER'S TEA-BREAK TEASER

Arm yourself with this treacherously tricky teaser and a pencil and terrorize your teacher's tea-break. Beat out a little tune on the staffroom door. When it opens smile an angelic smile and ask:

I WAS WONDERING IF BACTERIA WOULD EAT THIS PENCIL?

I WISH THEY'D EAT YOU!

STA

THE MAGIC MICROSCOPE

An old pair of leather shoes.
Not much to look at perhaps
but they hide a fascinating
range of tiny life forms.
Looks like another case for
the magic microscope…

Go on – don't be shy take a peek! Oh – that is GROSS!
Doesn't that mouldy leather look like crazy paving?
Well, it's crazy all right…

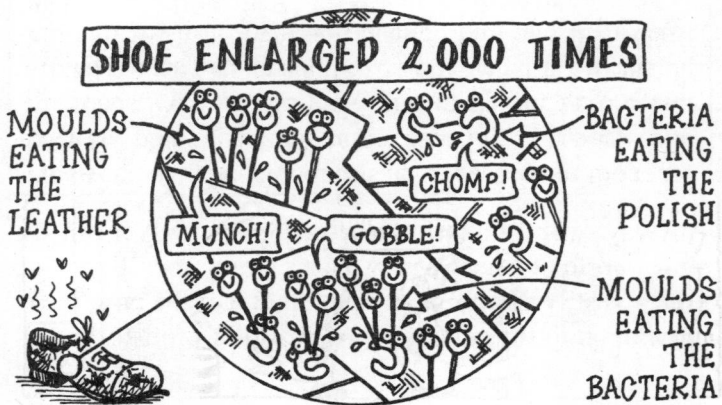

SHOE ENLARGED 2,000 TIMES

MOULDS EATING THE LEATHER

CHOMP!

MUNCH!

GOBBLE!

BACTERIA EATING THE POLISH

MOULDS EATING THE BACTERIA

Dare you discover … how to provide a snug, cosy home for bacteria?

You will need:
A jar filled with water
Some grass and a pair of scissors
Adult to handle the scissors
Cling film and a pin.

What you do:
1 Order the adult to cut the grass into pieces and add it to the water.
2 Cover with cling film and use the pin to make tiny holes in the top.
3 Leave the jar in a warm place for a week.

What do you notice?
a) The liquid has gone cloudy.
b) The liquid has gone green.
c) The liquid has gone frothy and orange and is escaping from the jar and eating everything in sight.

Answer: a) The cloudiness is made by millions of bacteria plus algae and fungi guzzling the grass. The microbes were on the grass and in the air before you sealed the jar. Get an adult to empty the jar in an outside bin and wash it down an outside drain and then wash their hands. If c) GREAT – it's a new form of bacteria… NOW GET OUT FAST!

Anyway, we're going to tear ourselves away from the slimy world of bacteria now. Don't worry, they'll plop up pretty nastily in the next chapter. But right now we're moving on to the equally slimy world of protists.

PROWLING PROTISTS

The first person to spot protists under the microscope (they're too small to see any other way) was our old pal Leeuwenhoek. Wanna know what he saw? Here's what a protist looks like. Fancy finding that on your cornflakes?

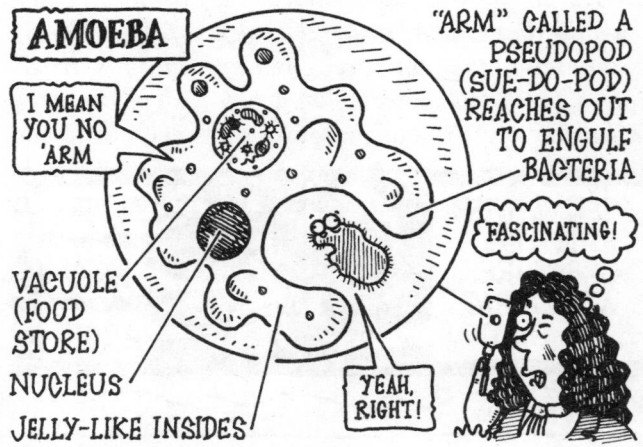

AMOEBA

I MEAN YOU NO 'ARM

"ARM" CALLED A PSEUDOPOD (SUE-DO-POD) REACHES OUT TO ENGULF BACTERIA

FASCINATING!

VACUOLE (FOOD STORE)

NUCLEUS

JELLY-LIKE INSIDES

YEAH, RIGHT!

Dare you discover … how to make an amoeba?

You will need:

A paper hankie (not a snotty one).

What you do:

1 Make two tears 4 cm long in each side of the hankie. (This will help to make an amoeba-like shape in the water.)

2 Screw the hankie up tightly.

3 Twist any sticking out points of hankie into points to make an amoeba shape.

4 Put it in water. If you stir the water around your amoeba will appear to move. BEWARE, it might engulf your finger! And if you find that hard to swallow read this…

Protists can breed very fast. For example, a paramecium (pa-ra-me-see-um) divides every 22 hours. If one started splitting on New Year's Day, by 7 March it would have formed a huge slimy ball 1.6 km across. Little more than a month later it would have grown to the size of the Earth! Fortunately, other tiny creatures are public-spirited enough to eat the paramecium before it takes over the world!

WELL, I WISH THE TINY CREATURES WOULD EAT A BIT FASTER!

OOER!

ERK!

ARGH!

AN URGENT NOTE TO THE READER...

Do you walk on the grass? Well, don't. IF YOU WALK ON THE GRASS MILLIONS OF INNOCENT TINY CREATURES WILL DIE!!!! Your feet squash the soil and push moisture out of it and this causes the slime moulds to appear!

"So what's a slime mould?" I hear you ask nervously. Well, don't feel too anxious – slime moulds are harmless to humans and you probably didn't eat one in your school dinner the other day. But if you're still curious, this slime mould's autobiography should answer all your questions…

MY LIFE AS A SLIME MOULD

By A Meeba
Published by Slimy & Creep

I don't remember when I was born because I was very young at the time. But I was certainly an amoeba - I only became part of a slime mould later on. I loved playing in the dark, murky soil - well, it's where my roots are! And although I didn't have too many friends there were always bacteria to keep me company - until I gobbled them up!

One day a kid walked over the lawn. I felt a huge rumble and a crash and a shaking and the soil became so dry that the bacteria stopped dividing. Soon my vacuole was rumbling. Then I saw another amoeba. This amoeba made a chemical signal and I felt drawn to follow it. And soon there was another amoeba following me and before I knew it I was part of a long line of amoebas. "Oh goodie!" I thought. "Let's go line dancing!"

Soon we were flowing together (still under the ground, of course). So I just went with the flow until we oozed into a slug shape. "Wow!" I thought. "I've always wanted to be a gastropod!"

Editor's note: This formation is actually called a "slug" and it's a form of slime-mould.

Editor's note: That's the posh name for a slug.

We crept onwards. Behind us was a glistening trail of

81

slime made out of the jelly-like insides of amoebas that had been trampled in the rush and ripped to bits on sharp grains of earth. What an heroic sacrifice - those amoebas really had guts! Well, I could see them!

On the way I chatted to the other amoebas and they said the world was ending. So I asked the others where we were heading but no one knew. Then one old amoeba mumbled something about heading to the light and heat - or did she say we were going for a light eat? I'd have happily murdered a few bacteria for breakfast! When we got to the surface I was gob-smacked - I'd never seen anything like it in my entire life. (Oh, all right, I hadn't seen much at all in my life!) It was a slimy tower made of living, squishing, squirming amoebas! It was vast, it was huge, IT WAS GIGANTIC! It must have been - hmm, let me think - all of one-tenth of a millimetre high!

Thousands of millions of amoebas were piling together higher and higher. Groaning noises came from deep inside the pile and wild rumours flew amongst us that millions of amoebas were making a hard chemical that turned their bodies stiff and killing themselves just to make sure our lovely tower didn't topple over!

I started climbing. Higher and higher I crawled, past the groaning amoebas who were turning themselves into hard lumps, past the amoebas who were holding up countless others. Call me ambitious but I just had to get to the top! As I climbed I noticed that I too was changing. My body was becoming hard and tough. "OOPS!" I thought, "It's tough at the top." But no, I was growing a capsule. A space capsule to protect my body. Then I was on top of the tower and I felt the wind. A breath of air blew me away and all I remember was a buffeting on my capsule - but I'd escaped the end of the world! I was shaking like a bag of jelly! (Well, maybe that's because I am a bag of jelly?)

Eventually I landed in this nice damp bit of earth with plenty of bacteria. But I was lucky - 99.9 per cent of the amoebas didn't make it. I might be a humble amoeba but I'm a survivor and that makes me a bit special, in my own small way...

THE END

SCIENTIFIC NOTE...
And all this happens because YOU walked on the grass! Scientists aren't too sure of the details but amoebas form slime moulds in dry conditions. The process is controlled by chemicals that amoebas make themselves.

Had enough of microbes yet? Well, tough – they haven't had enough of you! At this very second there are several million crawling over your face and exploring your nostrils. And if you wanna know what else they're up to you'd better read on!

Because from now on it's gonna get personal...

MEDICAL MICROSCOPES

Where would modern medical science be without the microscope? Up a blind alley, that's where! Without microscopes scientists couldn't spot the more interesting little details of the body that really make it tick – like flakes of skin, for example. Chances are you've already seen a few of these disgusting details...

Imagine a summer's morning. A speck of dust dances in the sunlight like a gilded gnat. It's a perfect moment *... until you realize what dust is actually made of...*

Dare you discover ... what dust is made of?

You will need:
A shaft of sunlight. (Draw some dark curtains allowing only a gap of 15 cm.) Alternatively, wait until night and use a small bright torch.

What you do:
1 Face the light.
2 Brush your hands through your hair, brush your hands over your arms, then lift your shirt and give it a shake.

What do you notice?
a) A cloud of black dots comes off me.
b) A cloud of shiny dots comes off me.
c) Huge chunks of skin fall off my body.

Bet you never knew!
Specks of dust are some of the smallest things you
can see. They're just 20 micrometres across and not
much larger than bacteria. They're floating around all
the time but you can't see them unless the light glints
on them.

So, how well do you know your body? Just take a really
close look at your hair, your eyes, your skin colour, the
shape of your nose, the location of any moles or freckles.
Spotted anything new? Well, in actual fact there's a lot
you've never seen … the tiny bits.

COULD YOU BE A SCIENTIST?

Scientists estimate that you lose 50,000 bits of skin every
minute. But the most incredible thing is that they've
found that skin flakes from a man have about five times
as many germs as skin flakes from a woman. Why? Is
it because…

a) Male sweat has more food in it so more germs can live
on male skin?
b) Men are dirtier than women?
c) Germs are killed by perfume on a woman's skin?

Would you like to explore the human body in grisly detail? Well, if you're a bacterium you'd be doing this all the time and loving it! For bacteria, every day's a holiday…

THE INCREDIBLE BODY TOUR…

HORRIBLE SCIENCE and Bacteria Breakaways present…

The get away from it all (but not very far) tour
It's the ultimate mini-break on

THE HUMAN SKIN & HAIR!

"I had a rotten time and enjoyed every minute of it." A. Bacterium

ITINERARY

DAY ONE

Morning: First stop is the mouth for a quick tour of the tongue. Marvel at the sight of 9,000 tastebuds in clusters, some with round tops like mushrooms

86

and others pointed and ideal for moving food around. Enjoy the sight of the playful local bacteria frolicking amongst the tastebuds!

Afternoon: Sign up for the fascinating microbe safari. Watch the different bacteria in between the teeth. But beware – amoebas lurk in this area and they might try to eat you!

NOTES

1 Chinese leader Mao Tse-tung (1893-1976) never brushed his teeth and they eventually turned green. Eek by gum, I bet Mao just had to green and bear it.

2 The amoebas eat bacteria and are harmless to humans. One place to get a free amoeba is a dog's mouth. When a friendly dog gives you a big slobbery kiss you get an amoeba thrown in too.

DAY TWO

Morning: Enjoy a relaxing walking tour of the skin! Carefully does it – in some teenagers the skin pumps out half a bucket of oil a day so the going might get a bit slippery! Feel free to snack on the delicious oil and any dead bits of skin you might find.

Afternoon: Admire the volcanoes on the face plain. Well, they're not really volcanoes, they're pimples – so watch out when they erupt pus!

Evening: Slake your thirst at the sweat gland cocktail bar. The local tipple (sweat) is a great tonic for us bacteria. It's full of delicious salts and sugars and minerals to keep us healthy!

~ **NOTE** ~

With more than two million sweat bars you're spoilt for choice but beware – women make nice easy-to-drink little sweat droplets, but men can make giant globules that splash onto the floor!

DAY THREE

Morning: Explore the enchanting hair forest. There's always something new to see – like exciting split ends that look like splintered wood or the cute new hairs that look like pink worms emerging from the soil. Let's hope it's not a bad hair day!

SPOOKY!

GUZZLE!

Lunch: Dine on delicious fresh dandruff washed down with fatty oil from the hair.

Afternoon: Admire the fine collection of dust and pollen sticking to the oil on the hair tree trunks. (It's the oil that gives unwashed hair that lovely greasy shine.) If we're particularly lucky we might see some nits (louse eggs) or that shy retiring creature, the human head louse, with its hairy body, jointed legs and feelers and crab-like shell. Unforgettable!

LOOK, OVER THERE!

Evening: That's the end of the tour. Time to hop off the skin and take an air tour of the house before landing on the cat.

More tours

1 THE EYEBALL CELLS EXPERIENCE

Feast your eyes on the cornea with its patchwork of cells like a tiled roof. Seeing is believing as you'll see with the see-through cells of the lens arranged in lines like a venetian blind. (If they weren't see-through the human would be blind instead!)

2 THE BONE BREAKAWAY

Tour the eerie world inside the bones. The spongy bone inside the hard outer layer is like an immense cave system full of inter-connecting tunnels. You'd be a bone-head to miss it!

3 THE LONG LUNG WEEKEND

Visit the lungs for a breath of fresh air! Explore the tiny tubes into which air flows and admire the alveoli. These are the bags 0.01 cm across surrounded with blood vessels where oxygen goes into the blood and carbon dioxide flows out! Bags of fun for all the family!

WARNING: The walls of the tubes are lined with snot and you risk being stuck and then coughed up!

But if you didn't fancy taking a bacterial break then there's another way to see the human body. You could shrink down to the size of MI Gutzache. Let's check out where he's got to... Can you remember where we left him?

IT'S A SMALL WORLD! (CONTINUED)

The story so far. A shrinking experiment has gone horribly wrong and intrepid private eye Gutzache is floating in a cloud of snot...

Gutzache could see where he was going and he didn't relish it one bit. Tiny movements in the air puffed him towards the massive furry form of the Professor's cat, Tiddles. Gutzache drifted through a forest of tree trunks – at least, that's how it appeared to him. In fact, it was the fur on the cat's back.

Cats. Don't ask why but they're not my favourite animals. If things had worked out different I'd have taken my chances with organized crime. But I was on the cat and at least it was warm. Then she started licking herself. I felt rough but her tongue looked rougher – in fact, it was more like a giant rubbery sheet covered in cat dribble with spikes as long as my fingers.

So Gutzache was on Tiddles? How clever of her to rescue him! The cat's rough tongue acts like a comb separating the hairs and making glands in her skin produce oils that keep the fur in good condition. The spit dries (or evaporates as we scientists say) off the hairs, taking away heat and cooling her down.

Huh - the cat was cooling down but the heat was on me. That giant tongue got closer and closer. I smelt the hot fishy breath and I knew I was in for a licking...

But just when all seemed lost Gutzache was rescued by a rather unlikely helper. Well, it wasn't so much of a helper as something that just came along and Gutzache grabbed hold of it and held on tight. It had a huge shield-shaped body about three times larger than Gutzache, covered in armoured plates. It had a dagger-like feeding tube and inside its see-through body Gutzache glimpsed a mass of freshly swallowed blood. Suddenly, the creature sprang high into the air – to Gutzache it seemed higher than a skyscraper. He had hitched a ride on a flea!

My whole life flashed before my eyes - it didn't make for pretty viewing. Then my stomach lurched as the flea touched down on another part of the cat's back. "Life's full of ups and downs," I thought, hastily jumping free and fleeing the flea.

I had no idea where Gutzache was and I was looking everywhere! I had divided the room into squares and I was searching each one using the strongest magnifying glass I could find. Where had he got to?

Nearer than you thought, Prof. Remember you were down on the floor and the cat came up? Maybe you remember stroking her and saying the words: "Naughty Tiddles, don't walk here - you might tread on Gutzache!" You didn't look too hard at your fingers afterwards - did you?

ER, NO!

Well, I was on one of them! You picked me up from the cat's back. You stood up - I was hollering like crazy, something like, "Listen up you stupid scientist I'm on your finger!" But you didn't hear me!

The Professor's skin was full of cracks like dried mud.
Here and there tiny pits bubbled oily beads of moisture.
Meanwhile Gutzache was sweating too.

It was an ugly situation and the Prof wasn't too pretty neither. The hand was going up. I clung to a hair on the back of a finger. I knew it was going to be bad - I just didn't know how bad. But then I saw where we were headed and I knew. The giant mouth opened and a blast of hot air hit me. My stomach heaved - it smelt of sour milk, strong cheese, onions, garlic and old cow pats. Round globs of spit and slimy bacteria flew towards me. The Prof could sure use some mouthwash.

YUK!

Honestly, this is too bad, I DO NOT HAVE BAD BREATH! It is nonetheless a fascinating fact that every human breath contains hundreds of bacteria from the mouth. Of course, I still had no idea that Gutzache was on my finger...

ERK!

The Prof's nails didn't look in too good a shape. They were rough as tree bark and the ends were jagged. Bite marks I thought. I was right.

Helpless with horror, Gutzache watched as the Professor's finger was inserted into his giant mouth. The teeth looked like huge yellow cliffs and here and there slimy bacteria nestled in their folds and ridges. The teeth began to work backwards and forwards and the nail buckled and bent under the chewing action.

The job had become a gross-out. At that moment I longed to be anywhere but where I was. Well, maybe not anywhere - I'd give the Prof's guts a miss. Meantime, the Prof was making a meal of them fingernails. °⚓°...

Actually, nails are made of keratin. Seen through an electron microscope keratin looks like a rope with smaller chemicals wound around it. This makes it very hard to tear and that's why my nail was buckling and not breaking.

Meanwhile Gutzache was right under the Professor's nose – literally. The finger didn't seem too safe so he decided to climb up a thick rope. It turned out to be one of the Professor's nostril hairs and it was encrusted with dried snot. Feeling faint Gutzache swung himself into the hot, windy nostril and then clambered higher up the cheek.

The Prof and me were face to face but he still couldn't see me. He had some cheek! But the worst of all, his skin was crawling. It was oozing with slimy balls of bacteria that hid in tiny cracks. I figured I'd crack too if I stuck around. So I thought about it plenty but I couldn't figure how to escape...

I had no idea all this time that Gutzache was on my face. Interestingly, over two million bacteria live on the cheeks and nose - and 72 million live in the grease on the forehead. Well, not that I've counted them ... but perhaps Gutzache could be persuaded to make a small survey...

Hey, I'd rather bungee jump off Brooklyn Bridge! The Prof still hadn't spotted me but something else had. It had a body like an armoured car and eight legs and a face that would sink a battleship. It wasn't too fast but for a minute I thought I was chicken-feed. But the bug wasn't too bothered - it was eating the squirming things off the Prof's skin. I said, "You're welcome pal!"

This is incredible! Gutzache is describing a demodex mite. These creatures, no more than 50 micrometres long, mostly live on human eyelashes and eyebrows. They do no harm and spread between people sharing towels so that every family has its very own special demodex family.

But things were about to get even worse for Gutzache. The Professor frowned as he wondered what to do next. He decided to resume his search of the floor, but the damage had been done. His skin rumpled and crinkled as if moved by an earthquake and tiny chunks dislodged themselves and slipped into the air – a perfectly normal event caused by frowning. Once more, Gutzache felt himself falling helplessly – this time gripping on for dear life to what looked like a giant cornflake but was actually a flake of skin...

I was flying again and this time I figured I'd be ketchup. The room was spinning but my luck was in...

Gutzache landed on the very microscope slide that he had been sneezed off at the start of his adventure. And a minute or two later a familiar face peered down at him through the microscope...

I had found an interesting cat flea egg on the floor and I decided to take a closer look. Imagine my surprise to find Gutzache waiting for me. But he didn't look too happy...

IT'S A LONG STORY...

WHERE HAVE YOU BEEN?

The Prof enlarged me. He was talking about me taking a dip in a drop of pond water. Two seconds later I gave him my considered reply – "I don't swim," I snapped. And with that I quit. After what happened today it was small wonder ... a very, very small wonder.

FORGET IT!

If YOU don't fancy shrinking as small as Gutzache in order to check out some body bits, you could always look at them through a microscope. Surgeons use microscopes all the time for what's called microsurgery. This can involve re-attaching bits and pieces of the body that have been chopped off by accident. Hey – d'you fancy a bash at microsurgery? This quiz will have you in stitches!

COULD YOU BE A MICROSURGEON?

Unfortunately, your teacher has cut off his little finger. It happened whilst he was showing your class how to use a microtome. Even more unfortunately you're the only person who can help – but you've got to answer these questions correctly...

WHO ME?

1 You hastily prepare an operating theatre. Why do you need a video camera and monitor linked up to a microscope?
a) So you can make a souvenir video to show your friends.

b) So you can see what you're doing without having to peer through the microscope all the time.
c) So other doctors can watch your progress and give you advice.

2 How do you protect your teacher's finger from bacteria?
a) Cook the finger. It smells bad but kills the germs.
b) Put it in the fridge but DON'T feed it to the cat.
c) Waggle the finger until the bacteria drop off.

3 OK, you're ready for the op but how are you going to re-attach the finger?
a) Superglue.
b) Sew it back on using a tiny needle.

c) Put it in a special bandage to hold it in place and wait two weeks for the finger to grow back on to the hand.

4 How do you join up the smaller blood vessels?

a) They're too small to bother about.
b) Melt the ends and weld them together.
c) Use a tiny staplegun.

5 After the op your teacher's finger needs a blood supply or it will die and rot and drop off. Keeping your teacher warm and giving him fluids helps. How do you deal with blockages in the finger's small veins?
a) Suspend your teacher upside down with his finger pointing downwards.

b) Get a huge hungry slimy leech to suck the blood from the little finger so that more rushes in.
c) Rub the finger so that the blood rushes into it.

Answers:
All the answers are **b)**.
1 Sometimes surgeons use special microscopes with several eyepieces so that they can all see what's going on without shoving each other out of the way and taking turns.

2 Cold slows bacteria down. The finger should be kept moist in a germ-free bag floating in iced-water.

3 The trick is to use a tiny needle the size of this dash – with thread 0.2 mm wide to sew together all the nerves and blood vessels and bits of flesh that have been cut. Got all that? Good, well get going then. And no, you can't practise first.

4 Electrical probes are used for this delicate job.

5 It's true – leeches are often used after microsurgery because their spit contains a substance that stops blood clotting and keeps it on the move.

WHAT YOUR SCORE MEANS...

0–1 You're a public menace who should not be allowed within 50 km of an operating theatre. Your poor teacher may need another operation to repair the damage...

2–3 OK, but I'm still a bit worried you might sew your teacher's finger on the wrong hand.

4 Go for it!

☠ HORRIBLE HEALTH WARNING!

You're not going to practise microsurgery on your little brother or sister, are you? Put that scalpel down at once!

Even whilst the surgeons are battling to save your teacher's finger another group of scientists are glued to their microscopes as they take a closer look at the human body. Who are they and what are they up to? Well, I'd like to tell you now but I can't because ... the answer's in the next chapter!

PSST, IT'S A SECRET!

SECRET CELLS

The amazing thing about the body is that the closer you look, the more you see. Seen close the body is an amazing landscape of hills and forests – oh all right, they're goosebumps and hairs – but seen closer still, it's an even more incredible assembly of ... cells.

You remember cells? Robert Hooke was discovering them on page 56. Well, now it's time to look at animal and especially human cells. Here's the vital facts you need to get started...

Microscopic monsters fact file

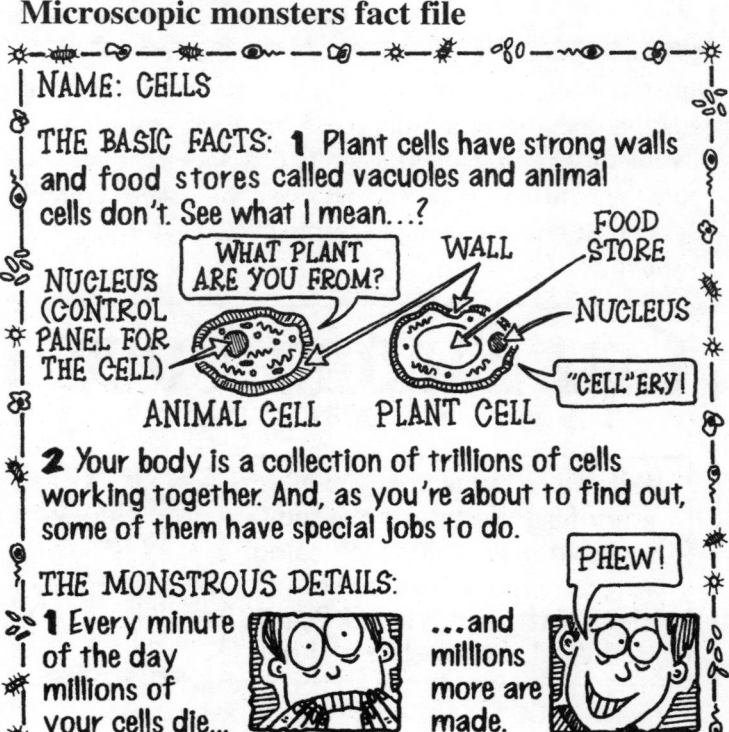

NAME: CELLS

THE BASIC FACTS: **1** Plant cells have strong walls and food stores called vacuoles and animal cells don't. See what I mean...?

NUCLEUS (CONTROL PANEL FOR THE CELL)

WHAT PLANT ARE YOU FROM?

ANIMAL CELL

WALL

FOOD STORE

NUCLEUS

"CELL"ERY!

PLANT CELL

2 Your body is a collection of trillions of cells working together. And, as you're about to find out, some of them have special jobs to do.

THE MONSTROUS DETAILS:

1 Every minute of the day millions of your cells die...

...and millions more are made.

PHEW!

2 Your mouth cells only last a few days and then they flake off into your spit and get swallowed and eaten – so you actually eat tiny bits of your own body. Eat too many and you'd be much too full of yourself! Other cells stick around longer. Liver cells, for example, liver longer – up to five years.

WHAT ARE YOU EATING, JENKINS?

MYSELF, MISS!

But it's when you get down to the real nitty-gritty of cells that they become truly amazing. Each cell is like a tiny factory – in fact, it's so like a factory that you could imagine it is a factory. We've asked factory boss and Supreme Chief Executive Dick Taytor to guide us round...

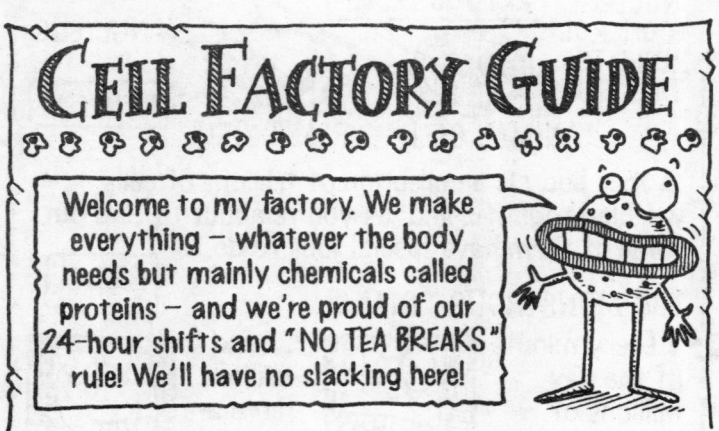

CELL FACTORY GUIDE

Welcome to my factory. We make everything – whatever the body needs but mainly chemicals called proteins – and we're proud of our 24-hour shifts and "NO TEA BREAKS" rule! We'll have no slacking here!

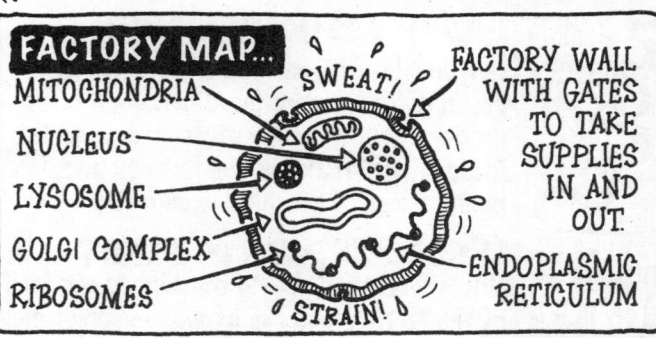

FACTORY MAP...

- MITOCHONDRIA
- NUCLEUS
- LYSOSOME
- GOLGI COMPLEX
- RIBOSOMES

SWEAT!

STRAIN!

FACTORY WALL WITH GATES TO TAKE SUPPLIES IN AND OUT.

ENDOPLASMIC RETICULUM

First stop, my office — known as **"THE NUCLEUS"**. Here are the DNA computers that send the orders to those lazy workers on the shopfloor.

DO THIS!

DO THAT!

MITOCHONDRIA POWER STATIONS

GENERATE!

Here in the cell factory we generate our own power. Don't ask me how we do it — I'm only the boss! It's all done with glucose and oxygen and the end-product is ATP* (That's a little energy brick chemical that can be broken to release power whenever it's needed in the cell.)

KEEP OUT!

GOLGI COMPLEX
That's our storeroom for proteins.

RIBOSOMES

"TOIL!"

"WORK!"

This is where the real work is done. The workers put together protein that the cell needs to grow. Nice work guys and no, you can't have a pay rise!

> ***SCIENTIFIC NOTE...**
> ATP is adenosine triphosphate (ad-deeno-sin tri-foss-fate). Say this in a science lesson and the shock could make your teacher's wig fall off!

ENDOPLASMIC RETICULUM

CHOO CHOO!

(En-do-plas-mic ret-tick-u-lum) We're proud of this underground railway. It boosts productivity by taking proteins around the factory with maximum efficiency and minimal loss of productive capacity.

LYSOSOME WASTE PLANT

YOU'RE RUBBISH

CHEERS!

This is where we get rid of clapped out bits of the factory and I'm afraid we sometimes have to get rid of workers here too. But don't worry, they're dissolved in acid and it's quite painless really.

BUSINESS STRATEGY

When the factory gets too big we divide it down the middle into two separate enterprises. It's a big job because we have to copy everything in the factory including the nucleus and DNA computers but it's worth it to double production output.

STAGES OF DIVISION → CELL   CELL IN FIGURE OF 8   TWO CELLS

Bet you never knew!

If a nucleus from a cell on the end of your nose was the size of your local park, the atoms that make up water will still be smaller than a postage stamp but your head would be the size of planet Earth! Know anyone that big-headed?

So you don't fancy working in the cell factory? Well, if you're looking for something to do, Dick Taytor has recommended some interesting openings for body cells...

THE BODY NEWS

~WANTED!~

Are you an outgoing adventurous cell?
Come and work in the lungs as a...
MACROPHAGE
Your duties will involve catching and
eating bacteria. Free lunches on the job!
And you get to travel ... up to the nose
on the awesome giant-snot travelator!

HELP!

Are you a lazy slob? Do you enjoy hanging around?
Then be a FAT CELL!
Hold a globule of oily fat until the body
needs it for energy. That's it. And you
have a choice of living quarters – the
sloppy stomach or the bulging bum!
Plus all the free food you can eat!

WOBBLE!

Are you bone idle?
Well DON'T apply for this job!
We're after hard-working
OSTEOBLAST cells to build
up bones using the chemical calcium.
It's skilled work and the bone tips are great!

IT'S A BLAST!

SCIENTIFIC CELL-SPOTTERS

It took ages for scientists to realize how important
cells were to living things. One of the first to make
the connection was German scientist Theodor Schwann

105

(1810–1882). Young Theo was a revoltingly good little child who was brilliant at school and kind to everyone he knew. YUCK! When he grew up he became a scientist and discovered that yeasts make alcoholic drinks by feeding on sugars and making alcohol. He also studied lots of bits of animals and found out that they were all made of cells. Unfortunately Schwann's views on yeasts were attacked by jealous rival scientists and he got so upset he gave up much of his work.

Gradually, with improved stains and microscopes scientists discovered many different types of cells in the body. But they lost their nerve with one type of cell … the nerve cells. Nerves are your body's telephone wires that take messages to and from the brain – but they were hard to make sense of under the microscope.

That was before…

Hall of fame: Santiago Ramon y Cajal (1852–1934) Nationality: Spanish

Young Santiago was a sensitive artistic lad who wanted to be an artist. His dad was less sensitive and less artistic and wanted his son to be a doctor like him. But the boy rebelled and played truant from school. Don't try this – you might not get away with it.

Santiago didn't. He was punished by being sent to work for a shoemaker. (It must have given him a terrible sense of de-feet.) Santiago decided that medicine wasn't so bad after all, and so the boy and his dad studied medicine together. But they had a problem – there was a shortage of skeletons to use to study bones and the family were too poor to buy them.

What did they do?

a) Made shoes and sold them to buy bones.

THESE'LL GET US TWO HIP BONES AND A SET OF RIBS!

b) Killed people and studied their bones.
c) Dug up bones in the local churchyard.

PRAY! PRAY!

HURRY UP, THEY'LL BE COMING OUT IN A MINUTE!

> **Answer:**
> c) This was a grave crime and they had to do it at *dead* of night – geddit? If the local priest had found out he'd have had a bone to pick with the pair of them!

After boning up on his medical knowledge Santiago's dad became a professor and after a spell in the army medical service Santiago studied at his dad's university. By the 1880s Santiago was really into microscopes, but he had a problem. Here's what his diary might have looked like…

JANUARY 1888

These nerves are getting on my nerves. I'm trying to study them but they're all tangled up and I can't see where one begins and one ends. Scientists reckon they're long fibres like bits of string but its hard to be sure and I'm getting in a real tangle! I'm a bag of nerves!

FEBRUARY 1888

I've heard about a new discovery by Italian scientist, Camille Golgi.* He was mixing up chemicals in a hospital kitchen and cooked up this stain to show nerves clearly. It's based on silver nitrate. Hmm, I thought, that was the chemical used to develop photos. It could be an exciting development, but all the other scientists think it's useless.

MARCH 1888

mumble!

mutter, moan!

WOW AND WOW AGAIN! It was tough to get the stain to work - it's hard to mix and get the right quantity. But I've done it - and guess what! I can see the nerves clearly! I was really nervous that it wouldn't work but now I can see that the nerves are a network of cells. I can't wait to tell everyone!

APRIL 1888

I don't believe it - I've sent my account of the discovery to a science magazine and they haven't

published it! What happens if someone makes the same discovery and grabs the glory first?

MAY 1888 | NERVOUS TREMBLE! |→

I know what I'll do. I'll publish my own magazine! It'll be full of fascinating articles about me, | EXCELLENT! | saying how clever I am and everything, and I can also publish the account of my discovery! It's going to cost a lot but I'm sure my wife and children can go without food for a bit...

* Yes, he *was* something to do with the Golgi complex – he discovered it!

The magazine was in Spanish, a language most foreign scientists didn't understand, but eventually the news of the discovery got around. Santiago became famous, and in 1906 he and Golgi were awarded the Nobel Prize. But they were still arguing about nerves because Golgi still reckoned they were fibres.

Mind you, looking at dead nerve cells isn't half as scary as peering at the creatures in the next chapter. They're the most disgustingly ugly microscopic monsters of them all! Unfortunately these little monsters share your home and no, I'm NOT talking about your little brother or sister here!

Will your nerve hold for the next chapter?

HIDDEN HORRORS IN YOUR HOME

This is a chapter about the microscopic monsters that haunt your home and skulk in your supper. So, is your home as safe as houses? Better read on and find out!

Well, one thing's certain: things are better than they used to be. Almost 400 years ago a guest was shocked at the condition of his guest's house. The famous writer Erasmus looked down and saw:

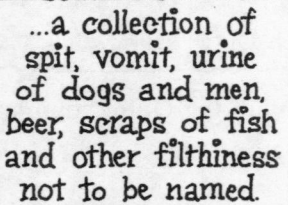

...a collection of spit, vomit, urine of dogs and men, beer, scraps of fish and other filthiness not to be named.

In those days every house was this dirty and every house must have been a microbe's paradise. (Hopefully your house is a bit cleaner.) But even today, no matter how clean a house appears, there are horrible microscopic surprises in store.

Like these.

FIVE HIDDEN HORRORS IN YOUR HOME

1 For every 0.03 cubic metres of air in your home there are 300,000 tiny floating lumps of grit, dead skin, ash and rubber. You breathe this lot in all the time but luckily most of it gets stuck in your wonderful snotty throat.

2 Have you got a cat? If so, when it licks itself tiny

globules of spit will be released in invisible clouds. In a few hours of grooming your cat will have produced several billion balls of spit that float gracefully through the air and splatter every surface in the house with kitty drool.

3 If you've got a dog your house may be littered with dog hairs. You'll get more of them in the spring when the dog moults and you might see there are two different types: ordinary hairs and longer hairs that help protect the others and help them trap warm air next to the dog's skin. Oh, nearly forgot – attached to the hairs you'll find clumps of rotting doggie dandruff.

4 And that's not all. If you're really unlucky your dog might have dog lice. There'll be tiny eggs on the hairs and lots of little 1.5-mm-long flea-like creatures keen to explore your home and make new friends.

5 Under your carpet you might find "woolly bears". No, these aren't large grizzly teddies that roam the forests of North America – they're grisly little carpet-beetle grubs that happily chomp their way through your carpets. They relish a nice dollop of cat fluff or dog hair or even human hair – well, carpets for breakfast, lunch and supper must get a bit boring. Mind you, if your parents find them they'll be chewing the carpet too.

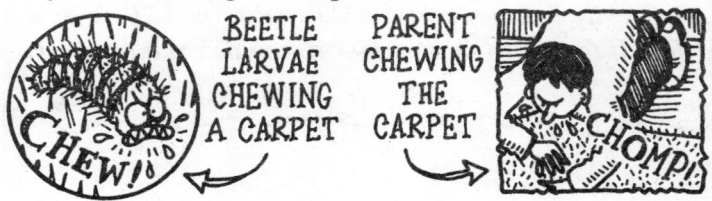

But that's nothing. *Nothing* compared to what else lurks in your carpets...

THE MAGIC MICROSCOPE

It's time to switch on the magic microscope and take a look at this pinch of dust from a vacuum cleaner bag. Take a look in the circle. Go on, you know you want to...

OH THAT IS SO YUCK!

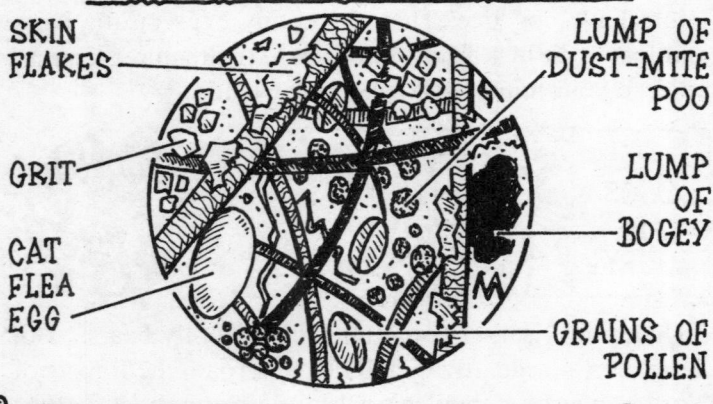

DUST ENLARGED 7,000 TIMES

SKIN FLAKES

GRIT

CAT FLEA EGG

LUMP OF DUST-MITE POO

LUMP OF BOGEY

GRAINS OF POLLEN

Bet you never knew!
Your home is swarming with tiny creatures – called dust mites. These bugs don't do any harm but we can breathe in their poo and this can trigger asthma attacks in some people that make breathing hard. And the really bad news is that dust mites poo 20 times a day (If they used toilet paper it would cost a fortune!)

COULD YOU BE A SCIENTIST?

In 1973 physician Dr Robert Haddock found a fishy mystery on the island of Guam. Cases of food poisoning by salmonella bacteria were soaring but why? The islanders were eating the same food as usual – it was mostly brought to the island in tins and free of bacteria. So how were bacteria getting into the food? Eventually the doctor discovered the truth.

But what was it?

a) People weren't washing their hands after visiting the toilet and the germs were on their hands when they cooked the food.

b) Cats were spreading the germs by leaping on to the dinner table and dribbling over the food.

c) Vacuum cleaners were sucking up the germs and spraying them everywhere.

Answer:

c) Yes – I'm sorry to say that when you vacuum the floor tiny things like germs get sucked in the cleaner and because they're very small they get through the bag and the filter and out the exhaust pipe and spray all over you. Actually, it's even *worse* than that because along with the germs emerges a huge cloud of mite poo from the mites in the carpet! Meantime any sucked-up baby mites stay in the cleaner bag and happily dine on the vast collection of scrumptious dead skin they find there!

 # HORRIBLE HEALTH WARNING!

What are you saying "yuck" for? You've helped with the hoovering haven't you? It didn't kill you – did it? Well, your body can fight off the germs and the mite poo mostly gets stuck in the snot of your nose and throat so it's not an excuse to refuse to help with the cleaning.

Bet you never knew!
Hold on to this book, sit down and take a deep breath. Ready now? I've got a bit of bad news ... you know those revolting mite things in the carpet? Well, they're not just in the carpet. There's some in your bed and in your pillow and there's even worse news to come ... you'd best read on!

A quick note to the reader…

Remember what I said about bacteria? Don't panic! Mites have been living with humans since the day when people lived in caves and the Internet was just a smart way to catch mammoths. And they've never done us any harm! (That's the mites not the mammoths.)

Let's imagine a dust mite wrote letters to her friend on the carpet. OK, I know this is a mite silly – after all I expect dust mites use mobile phones these days…

To Cara Petmite,
The carpet.

The Pillow.

Dear Cara,
Greetings from Pillowtown! It's comfy here and everything's fine. Trouble is a giant human insists on getting into bed with us every night and he snores! Mind you, the night life's great - there's 40,000 of us and I've got loads of mites. How's things with you?
Your mite,
Pilla Mite

HI!

← SOME OF MY MITES

Dear Cara,
As I was saying it's great - I've got the whole family with me including grandma and great grandma. Great-great-grandma's dead now but I see her mouldering body every time I go for a poo. And there's loads of food!

CHOMP!

Actually that's all down to the human I mentioned. The human lays on dead skin and grease and tasty dried dribble for us to eat. Is that generous or what? And the human even keeps us warm - so mustn't grumble!

Write soon!

DEAD SKIN

Pilla

115

Dear Cara,

A terrible day! And it started **DRIBBLE!** so well – the cat slept on the pillow and left delicious globs of dried spit for our breakfast! The interesting fishy flavour makes a change from all that dead skin! Anyway, I puffed out a bit of gas **PUFF** from my bum (no it wasn't a fart, silly, it was a chemical signal to the family to come and eat) and I saw the huge jaws...

A cheyletus. I don't have to tell you what these bugs do to us dust mites! It was after me but I got away. It grabbed my little sister and gobbled her up! I always used to argue with my sister but she went down a treat with the monster. Well, if I can't be safe in my own bed where can I be safe? I've crawled into the human's clothes and when the human gets into them I'm off to seek my fortune. See you on the carpet.

Your mite,   Pilla   **BYE!**

☠ HORRIBLE HEALTH WARNING!

Pillow mites don't do any harm and if you make a fuss about going to bed you'll probably be given a block of wood for a pillow. Oh well, you'll sleep like a log!

Mind you, there are more mites in your home than you mite think. There's a *mitey* BIG number … and there are lots of other bugs too!

117

And that's not all... Not surprisingly, your house is *bulging* with bacteria. They're oozing over the furniture and slurping into the wallpaper and in the kitchen they're slobbering and squelching in your food. Dinner anyone?

THE MICROBE GOOD FOOD GUIDE...
By Mike Robe

Hi micro-munchers! There's nothing that we bacteria like better than a little nibble of nosh but we all suffer little dinner-time disasters. I'll never forget the day I tried to eat disinfectant! Anyway, here's our guide to the smartest and cheapest places to eat out as sampled by our team of inspectors — the slime squad!

A word about safety...

Safety is very important. Every year billions of bacteria suffer fatal accidents which could have been prevented by a little safety awareness. Things to beware of when eating out...

1 BLEACH Run a mile – and if you can't manage a mile, you'd better squirm a few millimetres. **BLEACH WILL KILL YOU INSTANTLY!**

2 SALT Don't eat too much of this. You'll find that your body will suck in water to dilute the salt and you'll explode!

THE KITCHEN BIN BISTRO

The classic eatery! A must for all gourmet bacteria. Easily the most wide-ranging menu, plus old favourites such as "cat food and cold mashed potato cottage pie" and "dad's cooking's gone wrong again" and that all-time favourite "last night's leftover curry". For pudding why not try slimy yoghurt scum? Recommended!

A cheap and cheerful watering hole with a smelly atmosphere all of its own. Here you can relax in the moist surroundings and dine on a delightful range of dishes including mouldy breadcrumb surprise and greasy fat soup.

THE DISHCLOTH DINER

THE COLD STEW CAFÉ

Delicious boiled meat and vegetables proved easy to digest with just a sprinkling of salt (but thankfully not enough to spoil the taste). There were delicious and tempting extras on offer such as "fresh fungi and mite-poo pudding". No wonder the restaurant was packed with bacteria! Recommended!

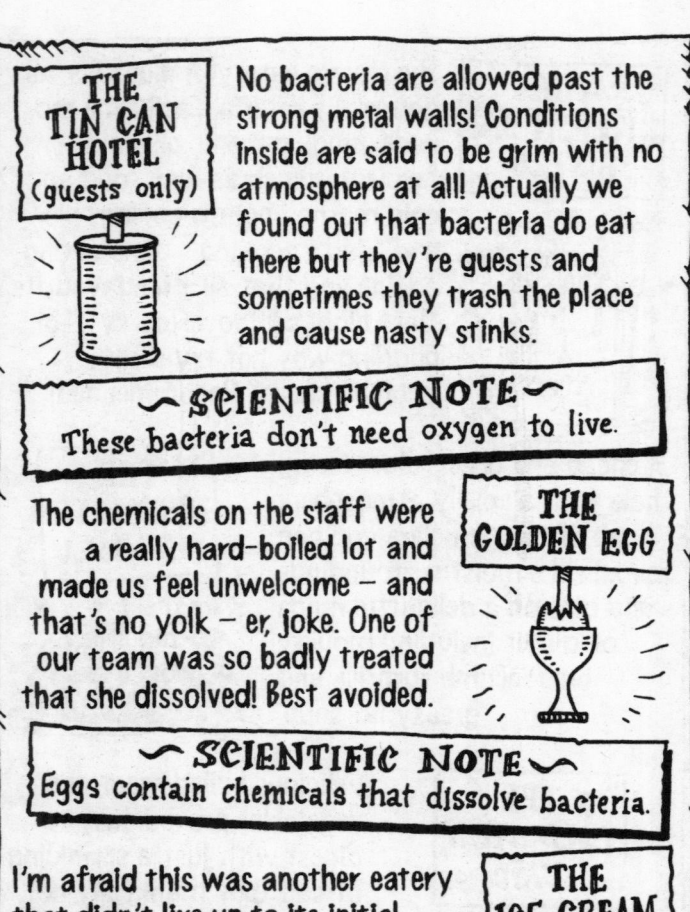

THE TIN CAN HOTEL (guests only)

No bacteria are allowed past the strong metal walls! Conditions inside are said to be grim with no atmosphere at all! Actually we found out that bacteria do eat there but they're guests and sometimes they trash the place and cause nasty stinks.

~ SCIENTIFIC NOTE ~
These bacteria don't need oxygen to live.

THE GOLDEN EGG

The chemicals on the staff were a really hard-boiled lot and made us feel unwelcome – and that's no yolk – er, joke. One of our team was so badly treated that she dissolved! Best avoided.

~ SCIENTIFIC NOTE ~
Eggs contain chemicals that dissolve bacteria.

THE ICE-CREAM PARLOUR

I'm afraid this was another eatery that didn't live up to its initial promise. Although there was delicious fat on the menu the service was rather cold and eventually we felt we were being frozen out.

Now you've had your meal, how about ruining your teacher's lunch?

This may not be very wise. If you get expelled for doing this you don't know me, OK?

The HORRIBLE SCIENCE guide to

PUTTING TEACHERS OFF THEIR LUNCH

Step one – Make sure you sit at the same table as your teacher. Bellowing these facts across the canteen could get you into even worse trouble.

Step two – During the meal it's important to make sure that your table manners are perfect.

Things not to do...**DO NOT** pick your nose. **DO NOT** eat with your mouth open or smack your lips. **DO NOT** burp and wipe your greasy mouth on your sleeve...good luck!

Rotten taste? Did you know that the taste of that chicken is mostly due to the bacteria that are crawling over the dead meat?

The mashed potato should be OK.

Dud spud, you mean. Under a microscope you can see how boiling the potato has broken open its box-like cells. This makes it easier for bacteria to feed on the food inside. Chances are it's crawling with germs!

I need a glass of water!

Has this glass been washed properly? If not it might contain a tiny amoeba that dribbled out of the mouth of the last person to drink from it. If you drink from the glass the amoeba will slop into your mouth and make itself at home.

Where's the bathroom?

Bet you never knew!
If you looked at milk under a powerful microscope it wouldn't be white! The white colour comes from blobs of a chemical called casein that contains proteins. The casein reflects the light to give a white colour. But the rest of the liquid is clear water with blobs of yellow fat and smaller chemicals and minerals bobbing about in the milk. Hope you've got enough bottle to drink it!

TEACHER'S TEA-BREAK TEASER

Try this one and you'll be as welcome as a woodworm in a wooden leg factory … so don't forget to SMILE.

Pound your fists on the staffroom door. When it opens your teacher will be desperately clutching a well-earned cup of tea. Ask them:

Answer:
When you boil a kettle there are bound to be bacteria in the water. They may have got into the kettle from the air or they may have been in the water. As the water heats up the bacteria will start to feel warm and comfy. But the growing heat will burn their tiny hairs and melt their slimy bodies. This is a very cruel fate even for bacteria. How can your teacher stomach drinking tea flavoured with murdered melted germs?

Mind you, if this talk of slimy bacteria has you dashing to the toilet I've got bad news. The bacteria have got there first and you're about to encounter THE ULTIMATE HORROR!

Dare you face…

THE TERROR IN YOUR TOILET!

TERROR IN THE TOILET

If bacteria are getting under your skin or on your skin or up your nose or anywhere else, what should you do?

a) Pick your nose and spots.

b) Get someone else to pick your nose and spots.

c) Wash the bacteria off.

Microscopic monsters fact file

NAME: Washing and germs

1 Most people think that soap kills germs, but in fact most people are wrong. Soap doesn't usually kill germs, but it does send them on a one-way trip to the sewer. Here's how...

ARGH!

2 Washing your hands in water won't get rid of germs because they cling to the greasy surface of the skin. The water and grease don't mix so nothing happens.

CLING!

GERMS

3 Tiny bits of soap (scientists call them molecules) consist of a "head" containing sodium and a "tail" made of chemicals called hydrocarbons (hi-dro-car-bons).

GREASE

This allows the water to wash grease, soap and germs down the plug hole!

SOAP MOLECULE ← HEAD ← TAIL

HEAD REMAINS IN THE WATER

TAIL STICKS IN THE GREASE

GREASE

MONSTROUS DETAILS: Soap can also contain...

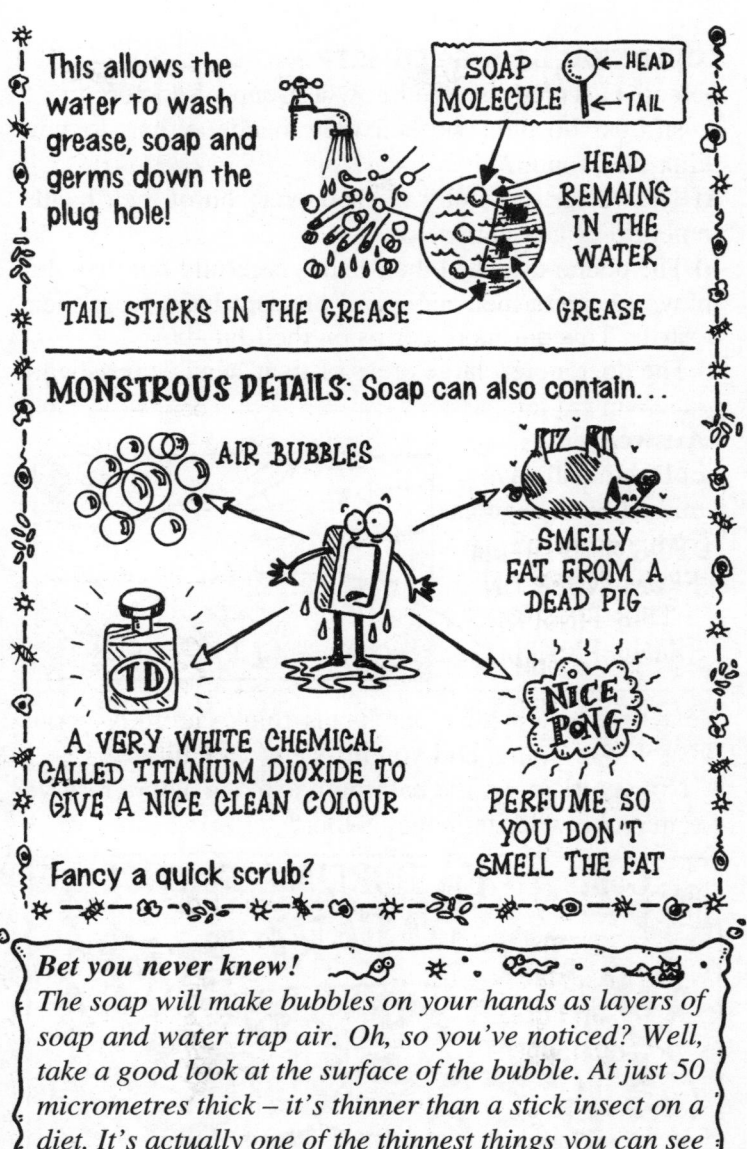

AIR BUBBLES

SMELLY FAT FROM A DEAD PIG

TD

A VERY WHITE CHEMICAL CALLED TITANIUM DIOXIDE TO GIVE A NICE CLEAN COLOUR

NICE PONG

PERFUME SO YOU DON'T SMELL THE FAT

Fancy a quick scrub?

Bet you never knew!
The soap will make bubbles on your hands as layers of soap and water trap air. Oh, so you've noticed? Well, take a good look at the surface of the bubble. At just 50 micrometres thick – it's thinner than a stick insect on a diet. It's actually one of the thinnest things you can see without a microscope.

COULD YOU BE A SCIENTIST?

Scientists secretly studied how a group of doctors in an Australian hospital washed their hands. What do you think they found?

a) The doctors carefully washed every bit of their hands to get rid of any germs.

b) The doctors washed their hands carefully but then did things like bite their nails and plucked hairs from their nostrils. This put more germs on their hands.

c) The doctors left large areas of their hands unwashed.

Answer:
c) Doctors always missed these regions:

LOADS OF BACTERIA FROM NOSE ON THIS FINGER (HAND-PICKED!)

Next time you wash your hands think carefully about what you're doing. Did you miss any vital bits?

Not surprisingly, the bathroom is like a nature reserve for microbe wildlife. Fancy a tour?

Lots of fun for all the family... in fact it's so much fun you won't be able to get them out of the bathroom even when you want to go to the toilet!

❶ EXPLORE THE EXCITING BLACK MOULD FOREST!

The black spots you can see are actually the structures that make spores to make more black moulds whilst the little feeding tubes underneath eat your bathroom!

❷ GO SCUBA DIVING

in the romantic sink overflow – it's the place in the bathroom which has more germs than any other!

❸ CLIMB THE TOOTHBRUSH!

It's crawling with germs – if you're lucky you'll spot a mouth-amoeba eating the bacteria!

❹ EXPLORE THE TOWELS for

stray dust mites and demodex creatures.

❺ THE DOOR KNOB is a

wonderful place to spot germs especially after someone's had a poo and not washed their hands properly. (One in five toilet door knobs have tiny lumps of poo on.)

6 FEEDING TIME AT THE SOAP BAR. If it's wet you should see lots of germs happily eating the soap!

7 Round off your visit with a trip to the taps to be entertained by the amazing TAP-DANCING BACTERIA!

8 Grand Finale: Marvel at the TOILET FLUSH-FOUNTAIN as it showers you with tiny droplets of water and pee and germs and lumps of poo...

PLOP!

FLUSH!

Smellie School
Greater Whiffing
Dear Sir,
I would like to complain about your book where it says that toilets spray germs and other unmentionable matter. As a result of your book no one's dared to flush the toilets in our school for six weeks and the situation is getting desperate. Excuse me as I adjust my clothes-peg on my nose. This time you've really gone too far! It's not even true ... is it?
Yours crossly,
Mrs Head (Head)

128

Well Mrs Head, I'M AFRAID IT'S TRUE...

Admittedly the droplets are too small to see – a few micrometres across. But just for you, Mrs Head, here's an experiment designed to make them visible. We've recruited fearless private eye MI Gutzache to flush this toilet.

The water has been stained with a brown dye and when you turn the lights off the dye glows in the dark. Mind you, the toilet hasn't been cleaned for a few months so we hope that brown stuff in the water is just the dye. We've also rigged up a high-speed camera with special high-speed film capable of photographing microscopic droplets flying about in the dark...

Oh well, now for the moment of truth!

THE DEADLY EXPLODING TOILET EXPERIMENT

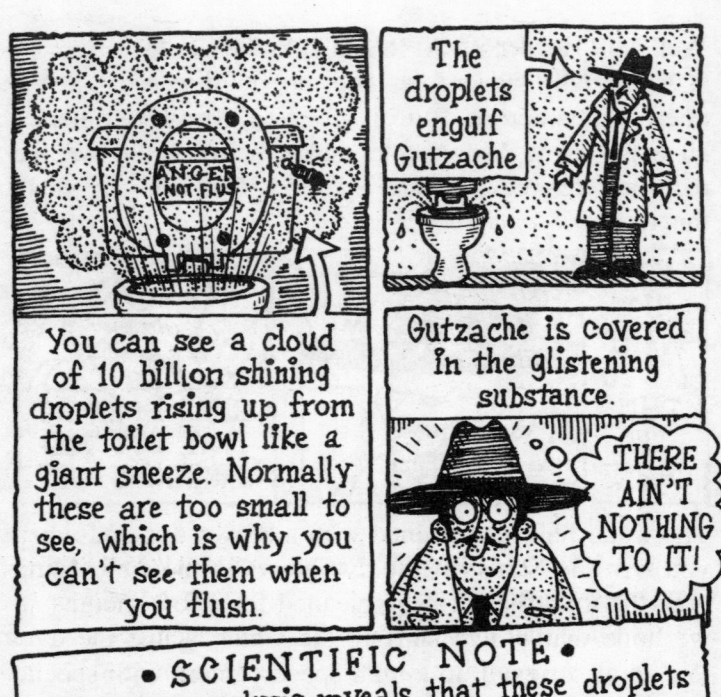

You can see a cloud of 10 billion shining droplets rising up from the toilet bowl like a giant sneeze. Normally these are too small to see, which is why you can't see them when you flush.

The droplets engulf Gutzache

Gutzache is covered in the glistening substance.

THERE AIN'T NOTHING TO IT!

• SCIENTIFIC NOTE •
Laboratory analysis reveals that these droplets contain bacteria, viruses, poo and pee. Let's hope Gutzache doesn't read this bit!

A quick note to the reader...
Scared yet?
1 DON'T try flushing the chain with the lid down. Apparently this makes the cloud of droplets and germs worse because it squirts out under the lid with greater force.
2 DO flush the chain yourself – no, don't bribe your little brother/sister to do it or leave you-know-whats bobbing about in the loo. And don't be scared! Your body fights off the germs.

And whilst we're on the toilet – I mean on the *subject* of the toilet – here are some facts that you definitely shouldn't read aloud at mealtimes…

EIGHT MICROSCOPIC FACTS THAT YOU ALWAYS WANTED TO KNOW ABOUT TOILETS AND NEVER DARED ASK...

- Public toilet urinals (the things that men pee in) often spray back microscopic drops of pee on to shoes and trousers. This can be a wee bit embarrassing.
- The nasty sharp smell in dirty public toilets is probably ammonia. This is a chemical produced by bacteria which they make by eating another chemical found in pee called urea. You might be interested to know that ammonia is great for growing plants but when babies get it on their skin it causes nappy rash.
- In Roman times the ammonia from pee was used to make mouthwash and toothpaste. Fancy a gargle?

WE RAN OUT OF PEE SO I MADE THIS BATCH FROM POO

- In some places in the USA toilet seats are covered in disposable paper to protect your bum from germs. Actually there aren't that many germs on toilet seats. Maybe they get squashed when people with large bottoms sit on them.

- Are you keen on saving paper? One of the cleanest toilets in the world is a Japanese invention that sprays your bum with water and dries it with hot air so you don't need any toilet paper. It even sprays scent on your bum to give it a nice fresh smell.

- Alternatively, if you really want to look after the environment why not buy a compost loo? There's lots of versions available. On one Dutch invention you can rock back and forward whilst you sit on the toilet. (You might as well take a radio in and listen to rock and roll music while you're at it.) The rocking motion mixes the poo with soil inside the toilet. Within a few weeks germs rot the poo into lovely fertilizer for the garden!

WHAT A BEAUTIFUL GARDEN. YOU MUST HAVE GREEN FINGERS!

THEY'RE BROWN, ACTUALLY!

- Much of the nasty smell in farts is from chemicals made by germs that live in the gut. Oh, so you knew that? Well, did you know that farting *killed* one man? Simon Tup was a Victorian entertainer – well, it's entertainment if you like that kind of thing. His act was called "the farting blacksmith" and he used to fart in time to music. Sadly, one night Simon's version of "Blow high and blow low" proved too much. He burst a blood vessel and died for his fart … er, I mean art.

- One night in 1856 Matthew Gladman went to the toilet in his home town of Lewes, England. Unfortunately the floor of the toilet had been removed prior to cleaning the pit underneath. Down Matthew fell into a deep pit of doo-doo… Gladman wasn't a glad man! He died of suffocation by methane gas from the germs as they fed on the rotting poo.

Of course, things have improved since those days. Nowadays your school toilets are not placed above a deep pit full of poo (and children are no longer thrown in when they're naughty). Chances are they're connected up to a sewage works. And when it comes to getting rid of big jobs the tiny microbes have a BIG JOB!

Bet you never knew!

At sewage works sewage is rotted down by a range of bacteria that eat the poo and paper. OK, so you knew that? Well, did you know that scientists have found that bacteria in sewage are very good at making vitamin B12, a chemical that helps build healthy nerve cells. In fact, if you take a vitamin supplement the B12 may have been made by these bacteria!

133

Actually, this is just one of many discoveries made as scientists learn more about the microscopic world. But what are these discoveries and where are they taking us? Is small really going to be beautiful or are we heading for a GINORMOUS monster disaster?

Time to leave this chapter and start the next page...

WASH YOUR HANDS FIRST!

EPILOGUE: IT'S A SMALL, SMALL, SMALL, SMALL WORLD

Some people think BIG. Big plans, big ideas, big money and they often have big heads to match. Other people think small and amongst them are many scientists who believe that microscopic technology holds the tiny little key to our future… But will these plans work out…?

Well, the only way to be sure is to go and see and that means time travel into the future. As luck would have it, Professor N Large has been working on a time machine and the obvious person to test it is fearless investigator MI Gutzache…

Oh all right, maybe we'll have to experiment on an animal. Perhaps Tiddles can be coaxed into trying it…

I am keen to discover the future direction of micro-research. I've written a letter to future scientists to introduce Tiddles and fitted her with a video camera to record her experiences in the year 2050.

Dear Future Colleague,
This is to introduce my cat Tiddles who I have sent into the future to test my time-machine and return with a record of micro-technology in your time. Please help her with the video controls and send her back in one piece.
Thanks a lot,
Prof N Large

Dear Prof N Large
Thanks for your letter. We couldn't work out how to work that funny old-fashioned video camera. Anyway, we sorted it out in the end.
Prof I B Smalle

And here's the video Tiddles brought back...

Hi Prof. Things are great in 2050! Thanks to micro-technology, we've solved the world food problem! Everyone now eats chlorella algae — you can grow it much faster than any other food. It tastes like spinach but hey — you get used to it!

Anyway, you can genetically engineer it to look and taste like anything — even cat food!

SCIENTIFIC NOTE...

Genetic engineering involves adding new bits to the DNA of bacteria. The new DNA programs the microbes to make any protein chemical you like. One example is human growth-hormone. (Oddly enough, that's the substance that makes people grow.) In the past people who couldn't make enough were treated with injections of the stuff taken from dead bodies. Now back to the future...

And now, thanks to genetic engineering, we grow elastin — as you know that's the stretchy substance in your body found around joints and elsewhere. Anyway, its great for making bandages and new blood vessels!

STRETCH! STRETCH! STRETCH!

And right now genetically engineered bacteria are being produced for space travel! They eat astronauts' poo and pee and turn it into delicious snack bars which they can eat again! Yum yum!

GOAL!

And micro-technology is BIG BUSINESS NOW. My favourite game is nanofootball. You use a nanomanipulator — a super-powerful virtual reality electron-microscope with 3D graphics that makes you feel you're kicking atoms about! It's cool!

Mind you, these nanomanipulators aren't toys. We use them all the time to make tiny nanomachines! When I'm out and about, I use the computer embedded in my fingernail. I wouldn't leave home without it and it's stopped me biting my nails!

There are nanomachines in my clothes that make them change colour whenever I feel like it!

See!

SORRY READERS, YOU'LL HAVE TO IMAGINE THE COLOURS.

And there are nanomachines inside my body at the moment killing germs! Oh well, your cat doesn't like microbe cat food so I'm sending her back! Bye for now!

139

SO YOU DON'T BELIEVE A WORD OF ALL THIS?

Well … it's based on FACT *because the future is already happening*!

1 Scientists have already suggested chlorella algae as a future food source.

2 Biotechnology was developed in the 1980s and 1990s. In 1996 scientists made bacteria that made elastin-type substances.

3 It's possible to make the bacteria that recycle human waste into food using genetic engineering.

4 Nanomanipulators really exist! They were developed in American university labs in the later 1990s.

5 As for the nanomachines, they don't exist … yet. But they've made a small beginning! Here's some simple stuff that's been around long enough to reach the shops…

140

LITTLE TIME TO SPARE?

You need the world's smallest watch. Each gear is thinner than a hair!

WATCH!

I AM WATCHING BUT I STILL CAN'T SEE IT!

The very small print: Your watch can only count seconds. Anyway, if it had hands you wouldn't be able to see them.

FANCY A LITTLE MUSIC?

I GIVE UP!

PLUCK!

You will with this cool six-string guitar made at Cornell University in 1996. Made out of silicon atoms, it's the size of a human cell. All your concerts will be cell-outs!

The very small print: You may have trouble playing your guitar because it's millions of times smaller than your fingers and the strings don't twang.

NEED A LITTLE MATHS HELP?

Solve maths problems with an atom abacus! You move the atoms along tiny grooves and it helps you do sums. Get every answer right without your teacher even realizing it's there!

WHAT ARE YOU UP TO, JENKINS?

The very small print: Hopefully, your teacher won't notice you're using a giant electron microscope to operate your abacus.

OK, these inventions could do with a tiny bit of improvement. So is the future really full of BIG POSSIBILITIES or are scientists just being small-minded? Well, come what may – tomorrow's bound to hold a few little surprises. But at least you can be sure of one thing: this book has been about the horrible world of the really, really tiny – the world that you can see through a microscope. But once you've peered down that eyepiece and glimpsed this strange place the outside world that you see every day will never seem the same again…

Oh well, that's Horrible Science for you!

THE END

MICROSCOPIC MONSTERS

QUIZ

Now find out if you're a
Microscopic Monsters expert!

Magical microscopes

Let's begin with a quick quiz to see how much you know about microscopes and the strange scientists who used them to find out all about the weird world of microscopic monsters.

1 What are the mega-important glass bits in a microscope called?

2 What type of extra-special, very expensive microscope can make pictures of atoms?

3 What type of microscope do you need to spot minuscule monsters like viruses?

4 What is the name given to the objects people look at under microscopes?

5 What jelly-like microbes did crazy scientist Antony van Leeuwenhoek discover when he started splashing about in his local pond?

6 What chemical do scientists use to harden the bodies of the curious creatures they study under their microscopes?

7 What amazingly important body bit did Robert Hooke discover under his microscope?

8 What type of science uses microscopes to solve crimes?

Answers:
1 Lenses
2 A scanning-tunnelling microscope
3 An electron microscope
4 Specimens
5 Amoebas
6 Formalin
7 Cells
8 Forensic science

Beastly bugs and malicious mites

Many microscopic monsters are tiny enough to fit inside one of your body cells. But there are also bigger (but still really small) bugs and mites that can lurk everywhere – from your bed to your head. Peep at them down a microscope and you'll be gasping at their gruesome appearance.

1 Which bloodsucking bugs cause the deadly disease malaria?
a) Mosquitoes
b) Lice
c) Assassin bugs

2 Where will you find demodex mites?
a) At the bottom of the sea
b) In the yoghurt pot in your lunchbox
c) In your eyebrows

3 Which of these beastly bugs can give you blood poisoning by burrowing between your toes?
a) The fungal verruca
b) The bloody burrower
c) The jigger flea

4 What is the name given to a bug that has to live on or inside another creature (like you!) in order to survive?
a) A protist
b) A parasite
c) A parachute

5 Which murderous mite can chew its way through a whole fly after killing it with its poisonous claws?
a) The springtail
b) The pseudoscorpion
c) The less-spotted lunch-muncher

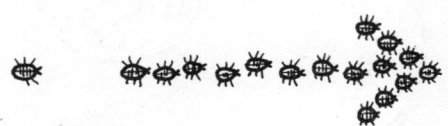

147

6 What do flea babies eat to get their fill of blood when they're too small to bite through your skin?
a) Their parents' poo
b) Their own poo
c) Your poo

7 What horrible bug fluid do doctors use in microsurgery to stop blood from clotting?
a) Mosquito blood
b) Flea pee
c) Leech spit

8 What do you get when long lines of slimy amoebas join together?
a) A bogey
b) A slug
c) An algae

Answers:
1a; 2c; 3c; 4b; 5b; 6a; 7c; 8b

Murderous microbes

*From foul fungi to peculiar parasites,
microscopic monsters have been shocking
Horrible scientists ever since microscopes were
invented. Can you figure out which of the freakish
facts below are true and which are just microbe
moonshine?*

1 It only takes a dozen or so cold viruses to give you the
sniffles.

2 Slime mould is a type of bacteria that makes you
vomit.

3 Some bacteria that live in the deathly depths of the
ocean actually glow in the dark.

4 Viruses are so vile that they can even infect other
microbes like bacteria.

5 Some bacteria are so sturdy that they could survive a blast of radiation a thousand times greater than would kill a human.

6 Microbes are responsible for puffing out about half the carbon dioxide in the air.

7 Beastly bacteria are smaller than vicious viruses.

8 You can treat a virus using antibiotics, which are amazingly made from mould!

Answers:
1 TRUE. Just a few putrid particles are all that is needed to catch a common cold.
2 FALSE. Slime moulds are FUNGI that grow in your garden. They don't make you vomit, but they do look a bit like sick!

3 TRUE. The black angler fish is one of the few creatures that can live in the inky depths. It lures prey into its mouth by the light of the glowing bacteria that lurk on its lips!

4 TRUE. There are viruses called bacteriophages, whose name actually means "bacteria eaters".

5 TRUE. So it'd be good to be a bacteria if there was a nuclear explosion!

6 FALSE. Microbes actually create about half of the OXYGEN that you need to breathe. In fact, if it wasn't for microbes you wouldn't even exist!

7 FALSE. Viruses are very, very tiny – so tiny that you need an electron microscope to see them. You can see some bacteria through an ordinary microscope.

8 FALSE. You can't treat viruses with antibiotics – they only work on infections caused by bacteria.

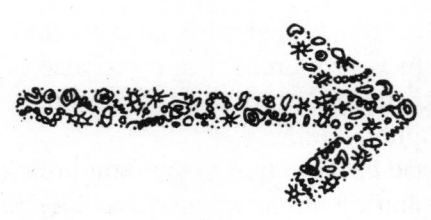

Microscopic Monsters identity parade

The problem with microscopic monsters is that you can't see most of them with the naked eye (and how can you run away from them if you don't even know they're there?). Here are some dreadful descriptions of the best and most murderous microscopic microbes. Can you work out which is which?

1 This is the evil type of microbe that causes disease. It likes to lounge about in your guts and make your stomach ache.

2 One squirt of this microbe's horrible hydrogen cyanide and any bacteria it hits are dead as a dodo. That doesn't stop humans putting some types on their pizza though!

3 This is the good guy – the microbe that lives in your guts and fights off the bad bacteria that make you sick.

4 All this algae needs to survive is sunlight and carbon dioxide, so you can find it in lots of places! Don't worry, though – it won't make you sick, but other measly microbes had better watch out for its dagger-like spikes…

5 It's OK to eat this fungal microbe – it's used to make bread and is full of vitamins. But it can also cause foul infections like athlete's foot!

6 These beastly bacteria live in the mouth, lurking in plaque and loitering on the tongue, and they can cause horrible halitosis (that's bad breath to you!)

7 These badly behaved bacteria happily hang about in raw dairy products and eggs. Once you've swallowed them, they'll wriggle their way into your intestines. And then they'll work their malicious magic to give you a nasty case of diarrhoea and make you so sick you'll think your eyes are going to pop out!

8 This is one fast-breeding type of microbe. Equipped with a special arm, it can fire chemicals that paralyze and destroy bacteria. Don't be fooled though – they're not on your side, in fact they can cause diseases like malaria.

a) Salmonella
b) Yeast
c) Fungi
d) Protist
e) Pathogen
f) Anaerobic bacteria
g) Probiotic
h) Ceratium

Answers:
1e; 2c; 3g; 4h; 5b; 6f; 7a; 8d

Microscopic body bits

If you could look at your insides under a microscope you'd see an amazing world of activity. All your tiny body bits work together to ... well ... make you work. Match the words with the phrases below to show which microscopic body bit does what to keep you working.

1 Macrophages...
2 Osteoblasts...
3 Ribosomes...
4 Mitochondria...
5 Lysosomes...
6 Golgo complex...
7 DNA...
8 Endoplasmic reticulum...

a) ...make the all-important proteins that cells need to grow.
b) ...digest food and break down cells when they die.
c) ...takes proteins around the cell to boost productivity.
d) ...sends orders to other parts of the cell.
e) ...work in the lungs to catch and eat bacteria.
f) ...create energy by breaking down nutrients.
g) ...help build up bones using calcium.
h) ...stores proteins and makes lysosomes.

WASH YOUR HANDS FIRST!

Answers:
1e; 2g; 3a; 4f; 5b; 6h; 7d; 8c

HORRIBLE INDEX

HORRIBLE SCIENCE

THE FIGHT for FLIGHT

NICK ARNOLD

illustrated by
TONY DE SAULLES

■SCHOLASTIC

www.horrible-science.co.uk

www.nickarnold-website.com
www.tonydesaulles.co.uk

Scholastic Children's Books,
Euston House, 24 Eversholt Street,
London NW1 1DB, UK

A division of Scholastic Ltd
London ~ New York ~ Toronto ~ Sydney ~ Auckland
Mexico City ~ New Delhi ~ Hong Kong

First published in the UK by Scholastic Ltd, 2004
This edition published 2009

Text copyright © Nick Arnold, 2004
Illustrations copyright © Tony De Saulles, 2004

ISBN 978 1407 11027 1

Page layout services provided by Quadrum Solutions Ltd, Mumbai, India
Printed and bound by CPI Group (UK) Ltd, Croydon, CR0 4YY

17

CONTENTS

WHAAAAAAAAA!

Nick Arnold has been writing stories and books since he was a youngster, but never dreamt he'd find fame writing about flight. His research included humming at humming birds and doing jumbo jet impressions and he enjoyed every minute of it.

When he's not delving into Horrible Science, he spends his spare time eating pizza, riding his bike and thinking up corny jokes (though not all at the same time).

Tony De Saulles picked up his crayons when he was still in nappies and has been doodling ever since. He takes Horrible Science very seriously and even agreed to test a Flying Flea plane. Fortunately, he has made a full recovery.

When he's not out with his sketchpad, Tony likes to write poetry and play squash, though he hasn't written any poetry about squash yet.

INTRODUCTION

Humans aren't designed to fly. But it's a fact with us humans that no sooner do we find out that something's impossible than we try to do it. And that's why this silly man thinks he can fly with a dodgy home-made pair of wings...

Well, he found out the hard way and this book's full of guys like him. It's called *The Fight for Flight* because it tells the stomach-turning story of how people struggled for the skies and you'll be finding out how hundreds of people came to messy ends along the way.

Ready to read on? Great – let's imagine we're going on a plane journey. Please make sure you're comfortable and I'll tell you about our route. We'll be taking off with a bird's eye view of how flight works and cruising past the flapping foolishness of barmy birdmen and brainless balloonists reach the heights of plane-crazy aircraft and horrible helicopters. Then we'll come down to earth with the fateful future of flight and afterwards you might find yourself thinking more about flight and even whether air travel is a good thing.

We'll be getting underway very shortly but first please listen to some vital safety announcements from your Horrible Airline Stewardess...

THIS BOOK INCLUDES GRISLY GRUESOME BITS. YOU MAY WANT TO KEEP YOUR SICK BAG HANDY!

VoM-SAK

ANOTHER SAFETY WARNING...

This book is designed for reading only and should not be used as...

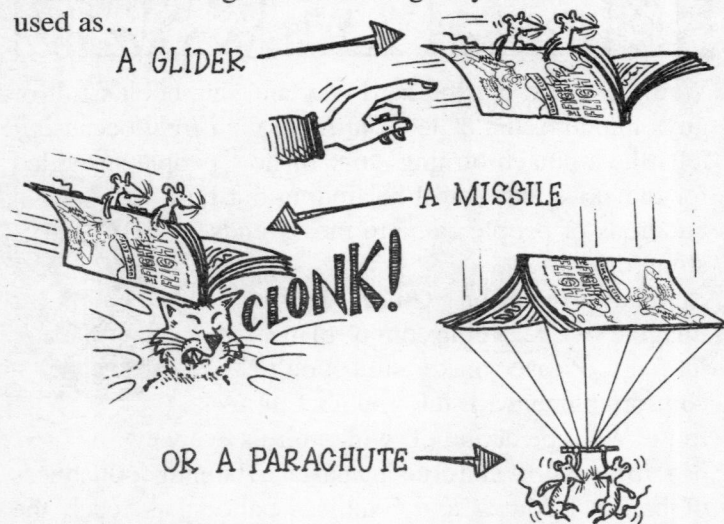

A GLIDER

A MISSILE

CLONK!

OR A PARACHUTE

There is some science in this book, but it's been cushioned with lots of jokes to stop it damaging your brain too much.

YET ANOTHER SAFETY WARNING...

We'd like to warn readers that it's a very BAD idea to try to copy the crazy people and stupid stunts in this book. Yes, only airheads prance around on aircraft wings 1,000 metres in the air. And as for leaping off tall buildings armed with a pair of feather dusters ... that's only suitable for bird-brains.

Provided you follow these warnings, this book is perfectly safe to read. You may feel an urge to giggle – but this is perfectly normal. In fact, the jokes have been tested on teachers and, although rather old, they're very reliable (and that goes for the jokes too!).

Well, thank you for listening... We are now cleared to fly. So, if you'll kindly fasten your safety belt and turn the page, we can take to the air...

Have a HORRIBLE flight!

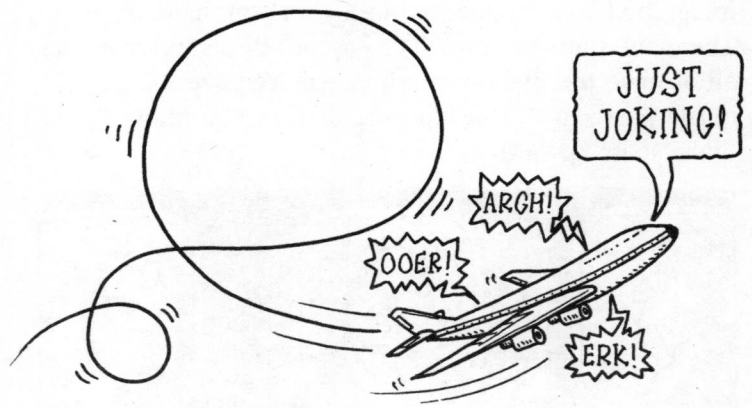

DEATH-DEFYING FLYING FACTS

This chapter is all about why planes fly and don't flop out of the sky like soggy pancakes. But before we get to grips with their soaraway secrets, let's check out how it feels to fly.

The date: TODAY
The time: EVENING
The place: ANY AIRPORT IN THE WORLD
You're about to fly. Your plane waits on the runway like a high jumper ready for their run-up.

How do you feel? Tense? Nervous? Just a teeny-weeny bit scared? Will the plane *really* fly? you worry. Or will it plummet from the sky with a crash, a bang and a splat? And how can anything as heavy as a plane fly anyway?

All is silent except for the whining engines. Then they moan louder and louder until they set your teeth on edge. The plane starts to move. The engines throb and roar, and all at once the plane races forward. You see the airfield hurtle past – it's all a blur and, before you know it, the plane soars upwards.

Your ears pop as the ground drops away and the plane climbs towards the rolling clouds. Then, all at once, you're as high as the clouds and the ground is a map seen from above. Up in the dark evening sky, a lone star gleams...

Yes – flying is magic! I mean when you fly you get to see loads of things that you don't normally see. Stuff like...

• The tops of the clouds.

• The sun shining *above* the clouds.

And if you're really lucky you could get to see...

• The sunset for the SECOND time in a day. (If you take off after sunset, the sun reappears as you fly higher.)

• The shadow of the Earth. (You can see the curving shadow to the east on the tops of clouds after sunset.)

But the most amazing sensation is to have nothing under your feet. Nothing except for the plane floor and 7,000 metres of empty air.

9

A QUICK NOTE ABOUT HEIGHTS...

I hope you're not scared of heights, because there are lots of hair-raising heights and dizzying drops in this book. Here are a few to get you worried...

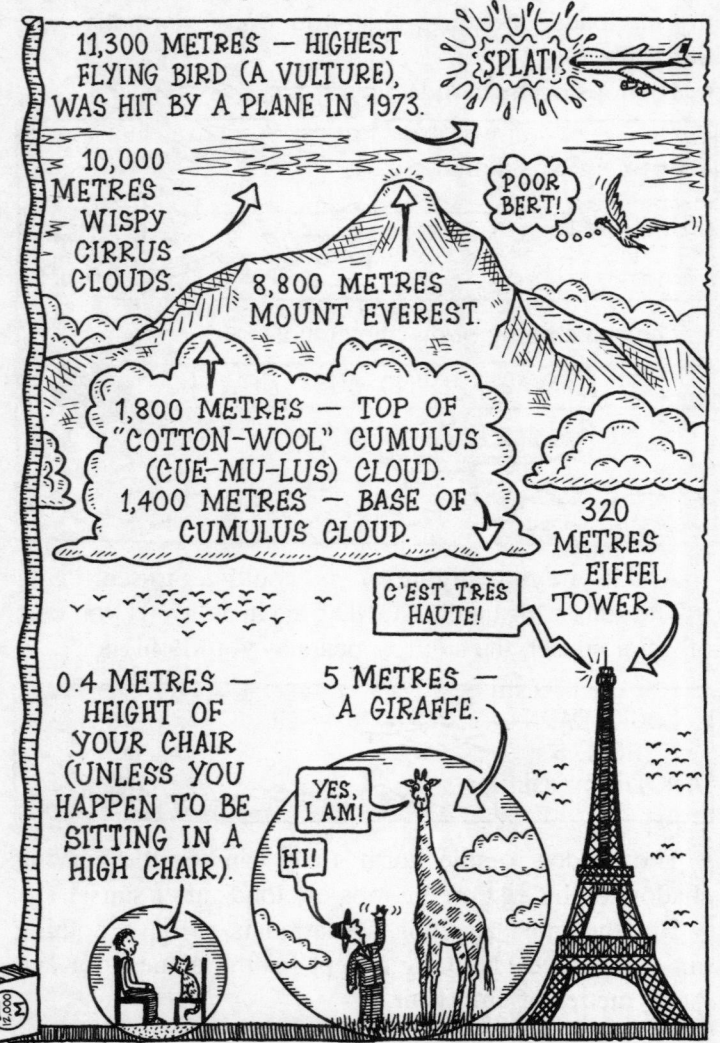

11,300 METRES — HIGHEST FLYING BIRD (A VULTURE), WAS HIT BY A PLANE IN 1973.

SPLAT!

10,000 METRES — WISPY CIRRUS CLOUDS.

POOR BERT!

8,800 METRES — MOUNT EVEREST.

1,800 METRES — TOP OF "COTTON-WOOL" CUMULUS (CUE-MU-LUS) CLOUD.
1,400 METRES — BASE OF CUMULUS CLOUD.

320 METRES — EIFFEL TOWER.

C'EST TRÈS HAUTE!

0.4 METRES — HEIGHT OF YOUR CHAIR (UNLESS YOU HAPPEN TO BE SITTING IN A HIGH CHAIR).

5 METRES — A GIRAFFE.

YES, I AM!

HI!

10,000 M

It feels scary but thrilling to fly so high. And to get this thrill, people have lost their lives and broken their legs and done terrible things to puppies and kittens. But before we get to grips with these fearsome facts, we need to find out exactly how planes fly…

A CRASH COURSE IN HOW PLANES FLY

We've asked brainy boffins Professor N Large and Wanda Wye to build us a plane…

And now all we need is a fearless pilot to show us how it flies… Any volunteers? Well, we've just heard of a hard-up, hard-boiled, New York private eye who'll do anything for cash…

As luck would have it, MI Gutzache used to be a pilot but he quit for some reason. Anyway, he's agreed to find out how planes fly…

AND SO…

I WONDER WHY I QUIT…

OH YEAH — I GET AIRSICK!

BLEURGH!

GROSS!

Er, sorry about Mr Gutzache's sickening problem. Here are the forces involved in flying…

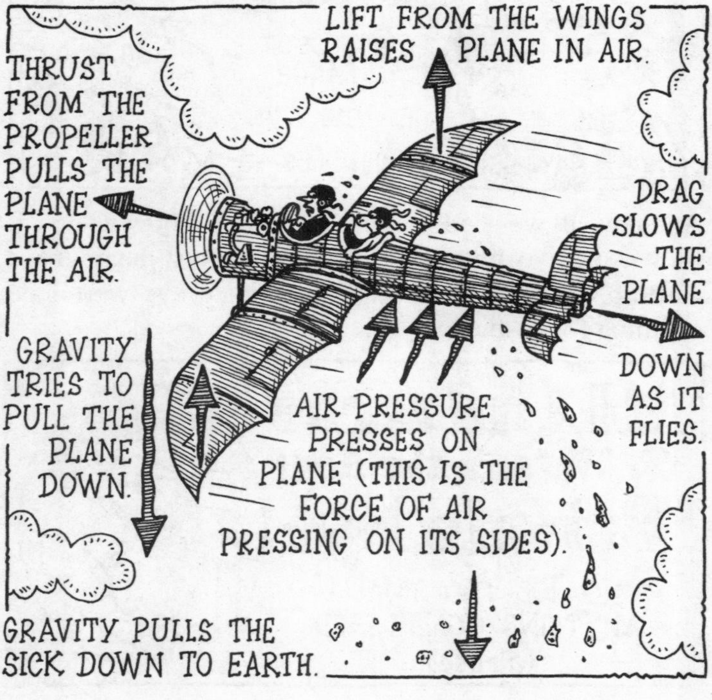

LIFT FROM THE WINGS RAISES PLANE IN AIR.

THRUST FROM THE PROPELLER PULLS THE PLANE THROUGH THE AIR.

DRAG SLOWS THE PLANE DOWN AS IT FLIES.

GRAVITY TRIES TO PULL THE PLANE DOWN.

AIR PRESSURE PRESSES ON PLANE (THIS IS THE FORCE OF AIR PRESSING ON ITS SIDES).

GRAVITY PULLS THE SICK DOWN TO EARTH.

FEARSOME EXPRESSIONS

A scientist says…

I STUDY THE SCIENCE OF DRAG

Do you say…?

MY SCIENCE LESSONS ARE A DRAG TOO!

Answer:
Say that and the scientist might "drag" you around his lab! Drag is the force made by air hitting something flying through the air. It affects planes and birds and an enormous pair of purple underpants blowing off your teacher's washing line. And the faster the object flies, the harder drag tries to slow it down.

But what is this mysterious "lift" that raises the plane in the air? Well, in order to make sense of lift we need to know that air is made of countless tiny clumps of atoms called molecules (moll-eck-ules). They spend their time zooming about.

YE-HAR!

WHAY-HEY!

WHEEE!

WHAT MOLECULES DO ALL DAY

And now we can take a look at lift in action. Let's see what those air molecules are up to around the wings of Gutzache's plane…

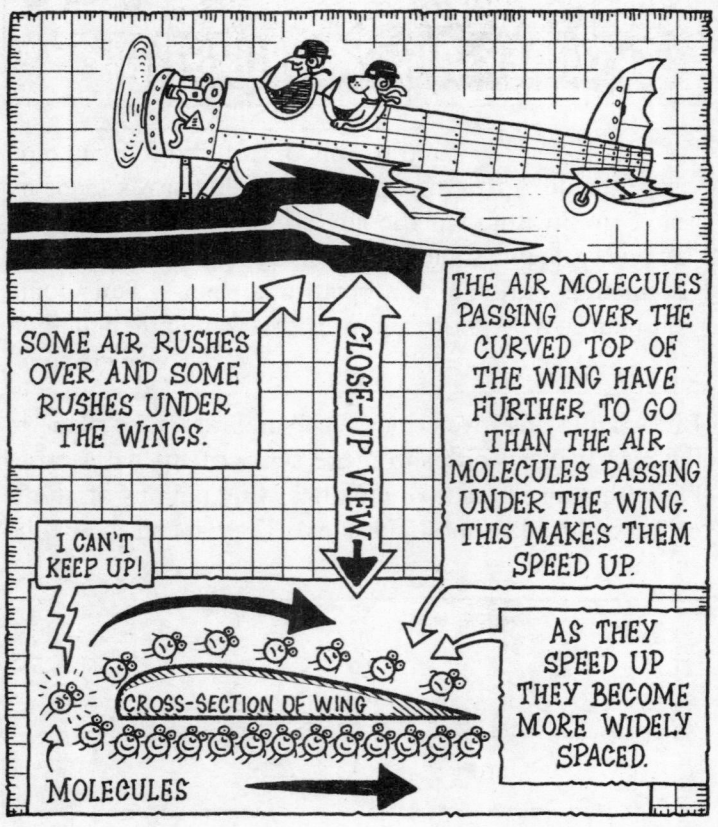

The force of air pressure becomes weaker above the wing than under it. And BINGO – the air pressure under the wing lifts the wing (and the plane) higher! Yes, every plane in the world stays up with the help of tiny air molecules!

Phew – did you get all that? Oh well, it's easy to remember. You get a lift in a plane and the plane gets a lift from its wings. And now for a quick quiz to "lift" your spirits...

The wing shape, curved on top and flatter underneath, is called an aerofoil. Which TWO of the following has an aerofoil shape?

a) A ski-jumper's body

b) A flying custard pie
c) A boomerang

Answer:

a) YES. Ski jumpers lean forward as they fly to make an aerofoil shape. This keeps them in the air for longer.

b) NO … and don't go chucking one at your little sister to find out.

c) YES, the aerofoil shape of the boomerang makes it glide through the air at 160 km per hour.

Bet you never knew!
Native Australians used boomerangs for hunting animals. The thin edge of the boomerang came in handy for cutting open the skins of dead animals in order to get at the tasty heart, kidneys and liver.

But of course a plane can only get lift to fly if it has wings. So can you guess what would happen if the wings fell off while the plane was flying? Well, it's just happened to MI Gutzache and Watson…

Without wings, the plane loses lift and Gutzache and Watson have to leap for their lives. Only drag slows them down as they fall – but luckily they're wearing parachutes. The parachutes open and trap billions of air molecules, massively increasing the force of drag and slowing their fall. So they have a nice soft landing…

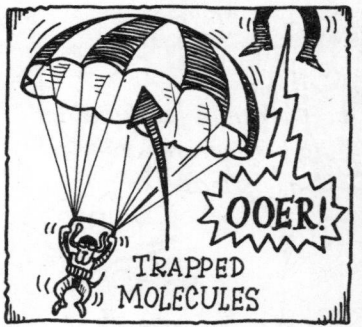

Well, that was scientifically interesting – by the way, I wonder where Gutzache's sick landed?

Now I bet you can't wait to build a plane that'll fly better than the Professor and Wanda Wye's effort – and you can on page 109. But first you'll need a bit more technical know-how, so let's start with two simple experiments…

Dare you discover … how life can be a drag?
You will need:
Two pieces of paper (but *don't* use your science homework and DEFINITELY don't tear pages from this book). The pieces of paper should be the same size.

1 Screw up one of the pieces of paper. (I warned you *not* to use your science homework!)

2 Hold one piece of paper in each hand. Hold them as high as you can…

3 And drop them a few times…

You should find:

The screwed-up paper ALWAYS hits the ground first. The flat sheet may see-saw or glide through the air. It falls more slowly because it has a larger surface area for billions of air molecules to push against.

Dare you discover … how to make a flying saucer?

You will need:

A polystyrene party or picnic plate (better make sure there isn't a custard pie on it before you throw it!)

Eight 1p coins (It might be worth asking for £1 coins. They're not useful for the experiment, but they are useful for spending!)

Sticky tape

Scissors (plus a helpful adult to help with cutting)

What you do:

1 Use the sticky tape to stick the coins to the rim of the plate as shown.

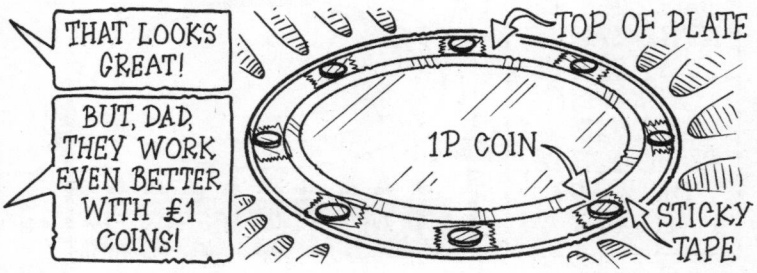

2 Practise throwing the plate upside down. (That's holding the plate upside down, NOT standing on your head!) By the way, you only need a gentle waft of your wrist to throw the plate. It doesn't work if you chuck it.

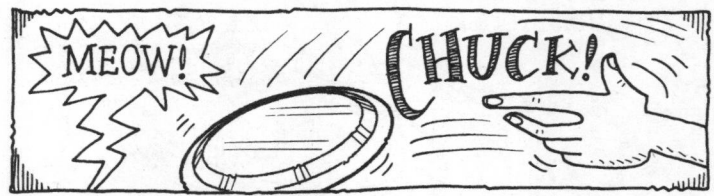

3 Throw the plate the right way up.

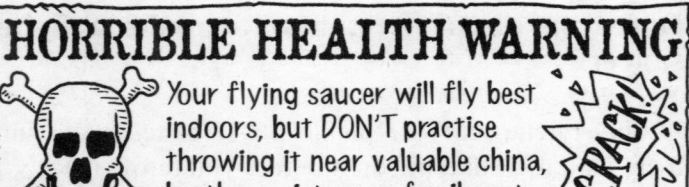

You should find:

1 When you throw it upside down, the plate should glide smoothly through the air. If it doesn't, flick it more gently. Upside down, it forms an aerofoil shape and flies like the well-known toy called a frisbee.

THE AEROFOIL SHAPE LIFTS THE FLYING SAUCER JUST LIKE THE WINGS ON GUTZACHE'S PLANE (BEFORE THE WINGS FELL OFF!)

WEAKER AIR PRESSURE

STRONGER AIR PRESSURE

2 When it's the right way up, the plate doesn't have an aerofoil shape and so it crashes.

THIS IS GETTING RIDICULOUS!

FLOP!

But frisbees aren't the only things that glide – birds such as seagulls glide, too (as you'll find out on page 71). Birds glide and fly so well because their wings are aerofoil shaped. And now here's a pigeon to explain how they compare to planes…

21

1 According to legend, in 1500 BC King Kai Kaoos of Persia was flown to China by eagles tied to his throne. The eagles were flapping after some goat's meat stuck on spears just out of reach. Sadly, when they got to China the birds guzzled the meat and the miserable monarch was stuck in the desert.

2 But that didn't stop an inventor in Baltimore, USA. In 1865 he dreamt up an eagle-powered flying machine. The eagles could be steered using cords but they might not have worked if the eagles had spotted a tasty rabbit far below…

Psst – I'll let you into a secret! These machines were as useless as a hamster in a body-building contest. In fact, all attempts to fly like a bird with flapping wings risked a messy death. Which is a bit scary, because a little bird tells me the next chapter is full of them. Oh well, at least it's got parachutes in it too!

BIG-BRAINED BIRD MEN AND PLUNGING PARACHUTES

Have you ever had a secret urge to be a bird?

Me neither – I mean, I don't even like budgie seed! But that's probably how the story of human flight began – people looking at birds and longing to soar into the sky as free as a … er, bird. And they told stories about people who could fly. Let's look at these dusty old legends…

Hmm, maybe they're a bit *too* dusty.

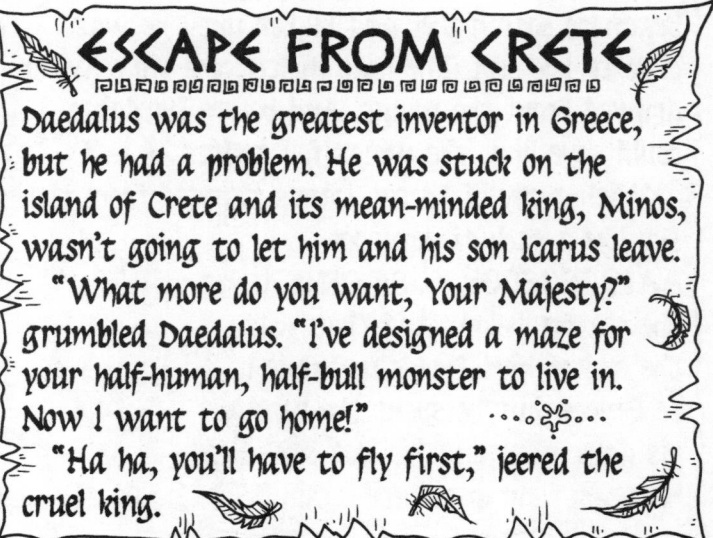

ESCAPE FROM CRETE

Daedalus was the greatest inventor in Greece, but he had a problem. He was stuck on the island of Crete and its mean-minded king, Minos, wasn't going to let him and his son Icarus leave.

"What more do you want, Your Majesty?" grumbled Daedalus. "I've designed a maze for your half-human, half-bull monster to live in. Now I want to go home!"

"Ha ha, you'll have to fly first," jeered the cruel king.

That gave Daedalus an idea, and secretly he built two pairs of wings from feathers and wax — one for Icarus and one for himself.

"Now, son," said Daedalus. "These wings are our ticket out of here. They've only got one problem — the wax melts easily, so don't you go flying too close to the sun."

"I won't!" promised Icarus.

One morning, before King Minos's men could stop them, the brave pair launched themselves from a cliff and flew over the sea.

"Whee! This is COOL!" laughed Icarus as he whizzed over the waves like a seagull. On and on they flew, but Icarus forgot his promise and began to soar higher and higher until he was close to the sun. The heat melted the wax, which dripped from the wings. And before Daedalus could save him, the wings fell to bits.

With a cry of horror, Icarus plunged from the sky like a sack of potatoes. AARRGGGGGGH — SPLOSH! He hit the sea far below. And that was the end of him. Daedalus made it to Greece, but he spent the rest of his days mourning his lost son. And he never flew anywhere again...

THE HAPPY HAT TRICK

Young Shun had a problem. His dad didn't like him BIG TIME and had him locked up. Shun escaped disguised as a bird, but his dreaded dad caught him. The boy escaped a second time, this time disguised as a dragon... Now, if you ask me, the guards must have been a bit dozy. I mean, wouldn't you notice if a giant goose hopped past your nose? And wouldn't you look twice if a huge scaly dragon slithered over your shoes? Anyway, Shun's dad wasn't too impressed by his son's acting ability and decided to do him in.

So he locked poor Shun in a high tower and set it on fire. Surely, thought the dastardly dad, this time I'll cook Shun's goose (and his dragon too). But Shun had one more card to play...

Seizing two big reed hats, the boy leapt fearlessly from the tower and floated harmlessly to the ground. And after that you won't be too surprised to know that Shun became Emperor of China and his dad... well, the legend doesn't say, but I hope he suffered a fearsome fate.

The reed hats were probably too small to act like parachutes and slow the boy's fall. But supposing they were extra-large hats – it's just possible that the parachute was invented in ancient China!

As for the Daedalus story, that couldn't possibly be true. But don't take my word for it – here's our pigeon pal to tell us why humans can't fly like birds…

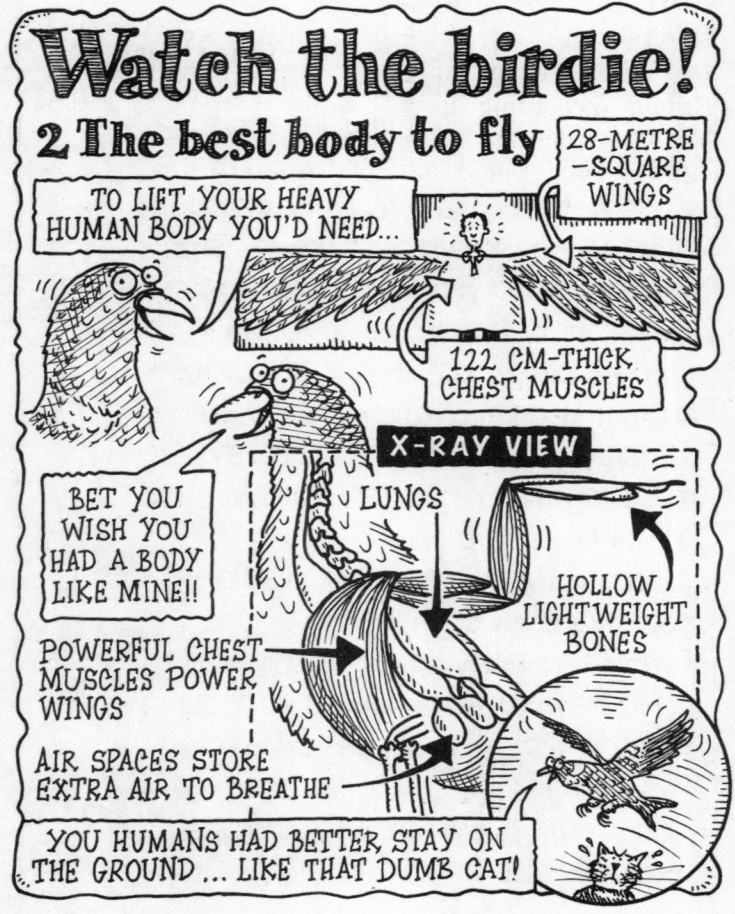

Watch the birdie!

2 The best body to fly

28-METRE-SQUARE WINGS

TO LIFT YOUR HEAVY HUMAN BODY YOU'D NEED…

122 CM-THICK CHEST MUSCLES

X-RAY VIEW

LUNGS

BET YOU WISH YOU HAD A BODY LIKE MINE!!

HOLLOW LIGHTWEIGHT BONES

POWERFUL CHEST MUSCLES POWER WINGS

AIR SPACES STORE EXTRA AIR TO BREATHE

YOU HUMANS HAD BETTER STAY ON THE GROUND … LIKE THAT DUMB CAT!

Of course, if there'd been Horrible Science books 1,000 years ago, the people you're just about to meet might have read that last bit and decided to throw away their wings. But come to think of it, they were foolish enough to jump anyway…

FOUR FOOLISH FALL GUYS

1 Bladud
Date: 863 BC
Day job: King of Britain (according to legend). Educated in Athens and founder of the first English college. (If he invented schools, he sure had it coming.)

Flying machine: Feathered wings
Deadly downfall: Off the top of a temple.
Rotten result: SPLAT! Bloody for Blad.

2 Oliver of Malmesbury
Date: 1029
Day job: English monk
Flying machine: Feathered wings
Deadly downfall: Off the tower of Malmesbury Abbey.
Rotten result: Two broken legs. Oddball Ollie blamed his dangerous dive on not sticking a feathered tail on his battered bum.

3 Giovanni Battista Danti
Date: 1503
Day job:
Italian mathematician
Flying machine: Feathered wings
Deadly downfall: His first glide over a lake left him unhurt, so he celebrated by jumping off Perugia Cathedral.
Rotten result: Serious injury.

4 Marquis de Bacqueville
Date: 1742
Day job: French nobleman
Flying machine: Wings on his arms and legs
Deadly downfall: Tried to fly across the River Seine in Paris.

Rotten result: Crashed into a washerwoman's dirty old barge and broke both his legs.

The stick-insect-brained nobleman was described as…

And you might say that about the rest of them too – and the dozens of other tower jumpers I haven't got time to tell you about. "So what's the answer?" I hear you cry. Well, they could have tied themselves to a giant kite...

Fearsome flight fact file

NAME: How a kite works

THE BASIC FACTS: 1 As a kite leans into the wind, the air molecules hit the underside of the kite and slide down it.

FORCE OF THE WIND (AIR MOLECULES)

BUT WHAT ARE THEY FOR?

NO IDEA!

WEIGHT OF THE TAIL KEEPS THE KITE STEADY

TIGHT STRING

WHOA!

2 The kite can't blow away because you're holding the string tight (so don't let go!).

3 The force of the wind keeps the kite in the air.

THE FEARSOME details: 1 The kite was invented in China around 200 BC when General Han Hsen was lifted up at night to scare an enemy army. The man-carrying kites were used to spy on enemy armies.

2 According to Italian traveller Marco Polo (1254–1324), stupid or drunken men were picked for this perilous job. And some men were tied to kites as a punishment. Let's hope your ancient teacher doesn't think of this torture!

WHAAAAA!

I THINK SHE'S SORRY, SIR!

But for the half-witted, human-powered flight fans in this chapter, a kite was out of the question. It wasn't powered by humans and it was far too sensible. Some of them were dreaming of quite complicated machines – and they were even more silly...

THE GRAND ALL-COMERS SILLY HUMAN-POWERED FLYING MACHINE COMPETITION

Grand prize for the silliest flying machine – free medical care (one way or another, you're going to need it!).

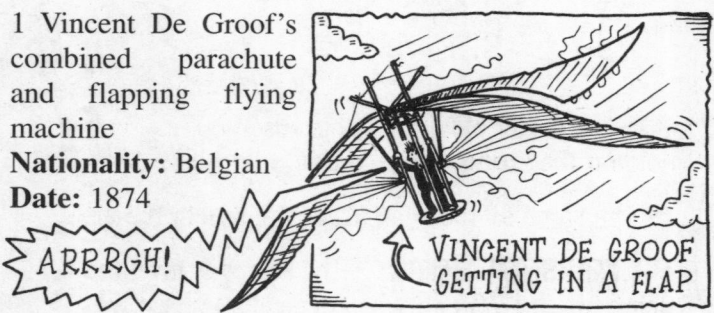

1 Vincent De Groof's combined parachute and flapping flying machine
Nationality: Belgian
Date: 1874

ARRRGH!

VINCENT DE GROOF GETTING IN A FLAP

Advantages: It worked the first time in Belgium as a parachute. Pity the flapping wings were useless.

Disadvantages: It didn't work in a later test over London. The frame broke and the machine was a dead loss. Sadly, De Groof was an even deader loss.

Judge's verdict: The machine isn't strong enough to fly. I'd rather bounce up and down on an exploding whoopee cushion than go up in that thing.

2 Leonardo da Vinci's flapping machine
Nationality: Italian
Date: About 1500

YES! YES! YES! YES! YES! ... NNNNNO!

THE GROUND

Advantages: It looked kind of arty in Leo's sketch book – but then he was a great artist.

Disadvantages: If anyone had built it and flown it, they would have found they didn't have enough muscle power to flap the wings.

Judge's verdict: It would make a good exercise machine.

3 Jacob Degen's flapping flying machine and balloon
Nationality: Swiss
Date: 1809

IGNORE THIS BIT!

HE THINKS THAT ADDING WINGS WILL HELP HIM WING – I MEAN, WIN

Advantages: The machine hangs from a balloon, so it flies even if the wings don't work.

Disadvantages: The wings DON'T work.

Judge's verdict: Grr! This machine is a disgrace – using a balloon to fly is cheating! Degen is DISQUALIFIED and he's been suspended – er, hold on, he's already suspended from the balloon.

Bet you never knew!

In 1809 a crowd in Paris was so cross that Degen's invention wasn't a proper flying machine that they chased dodgy Degen out of town.

AND DON'T COME BACK!

4 Dr WO Ayre's pedal-powered propeller thingie
Nationality: USA
Date: 1885

RATTLE!

SHAKE!

CARDBOARD CLOUDS FOR ADDED EFFECT

Advantages: It would make a great kiddie's climbing frame or even a bedstead. You had to pedal very hard to pump the tubes full of air that in turn powered the propellers – so it kept you fit.

Disadvantages: Everyone laughed at you.

Judge's verdict: The propellers would never get enough power to lift anything heavier than a hamster. But it's a worthy RUNNER-UP in our competition. It's almost silly enough to win … but not quite!

5 Jean Pierre Blanchard's sail- and pedal-powered flapping machine
Nationality: French
Date: 1781

PREPARE FOR TAKEOFF!

Advantages: Included a musician to play soothing music so you wouldn't get scared. Guaranteed 100 per cent safe. (It's too heavy to leave the ground!)
Disadvantages: See advantages. Especially the bit about not flying.
Judge's verdict: THE WINNER! Easily the most freaky flying machine ever – and it's even got in-flight entertainment!

GOLDEN BRICK AWARD

ZANK YOU!

Human-powered flight sounds a fatal flop, doesn't it? And so it was … until the 1970s when scientists built a human-powered flying machine that flew. But a lot of things happened in the story of flight before then, so you'll have to hang on until page 139 to find out what happened. And no peeping!

In the meantime, the tower jumpers continued their deadly dives and the machine makers continued to create crazy contraptions. And the only reason more weren't killed was because their wings sometimes worked like Shun's hats – as parachutes. Pity they didn't work for poor de Groof.

Obviously the parachute is a vital bit of kit for every fearless flier – but who invented it? Well, experts argue about it until they're blue in the face and the question is a bit of a hot potato…

THE FEARSOME FIGHT TO PARACHUTE

1485 Leonardo da Vinci designs a parachute but doesn't test it – any volunteers?

1779 Joseph Montgolfier makes a parachute and tests it by dropping a sheep from a tower. The sheep lands safely – now that's what I call a woolly jumper.

1785 Our pal Jean Pierre Blanchard experiments by tying a puppy to a parachute and dropping it from a balloon. (Don't try this at home.) The pup was fine, but as you'll find out on page 51, Blanchard was DOG-ged by misfortune.

1808 The parachute saves its first life when Polish balloonist Jordaki Kuparento makes a hasty exit when his balloon catches fire.

But early parachutes weren't all they were cracked up to be – and sometimes they did crack up. And my deeply dodgy mate, Honest Bob, wants to sell you some. Er, you'd best be warned – you may want to take what he tells you with a pinch of salt … or even a few tonnes of salt.

HONEST BOB'S PLANE PRODUCTS PRESENTS...

"You can trust Bob to look after your money – and he'll even spend it for you!" Bob's mum

LOVELY CHOICE OF PARACHUTES

(and they come in pretty colours, too)

1 André Garnerin's perfect parachute (1797)
This chute's a beaut! You stand in the basket and get a good view of the ground (before you hit it).

YOURS IS STEADIER!

2 Robert Cocking's parachute (1837)
It's a real classy mover! Guaranteed not to swing from side to side, and you can even use it as an umbrella.

YIKES... AND FASTER!

A COUPLE OF FACTS THAT HONEST BOB LEFT OUT...

1 Garnerin's parachute swayed a lot in the wind. Each time he tried it he swayed until he was sick – but at least he lived, unlike…

2 Robert Cocking. "I never felt more comfortable," declared the 61-year-old artist just before falling to his death when the parachute broke.

What's that? You feel your teacher or puppy or brother or sister would enjoy a parachute jump? You haven't asked them, but you feel sure they'd like the idea once they were plunging through the air…? Well, I think it's a good idea to find out how they might get on…

Dare you discover … how to make your teacher try a parachute jump?

You will need:

Ruler

Biro and paper

Scissors (and the same helpful adult who helped with the cutting in the previous experiment – hopefully they weren't injured too badly)

Paper napkin (about 32 x 32 cm)

Blu tack

Thread

Sticky tape

Paperclip

What you do:

1 Cut a piece of paper 4.5 cm long and 2 cm wide. Fold it as shown and draw your teacher on both sides.

2 Cut an 80 cm length of thread. Fold it in half lengthways and cut again to make two 40 cm lengths.

3 Thread one length of thread through the paperclip. Stick the ends of the threads to the napkin as shown.

4 Repeat step three with the second length of thread.

5 Make sure the paperclip is halfway along the lengths of thread and use a tiny blob of Blu tack to stick the threads to the paperclip.

6 Place the napkin on the table so that the paperclip is underneath. Cut 7-cm corners off the napkin as shown.

7 Add the sticky tape as shown. Tuck the ends of the tape under the edges of the napkin.

8 Gently use the point of a biro to make a hole 0.5 cm across at the centre of the sticky-tape cross.

9 Slide the paper with your teacher's picture into the paperclip.

10 Now for the fun bit. Drop your teacher from a height! No, I didn't mean your real teacher!

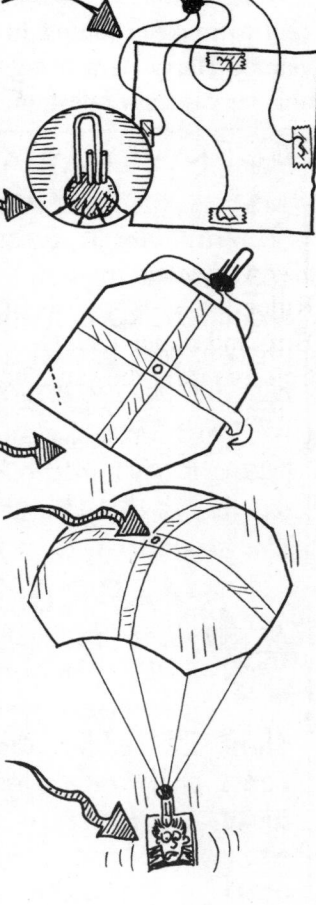

You should find:

The parachute swings from side to side just like Garnerin's bucket chute. This happens because air trapped under the parachute tries to escape, pushing it from side to side. The hole lets air escape and stops the parachute from swaying too much – and that's why modern parachutes have holes in their tops...

OK, so that's how a parachute works – but how does it *feel* to make a jump? In 1935, a US Air Corps scientist named Harry Armstrong made a jump and asked himself this very queasy question. Here's my version of his notes…

MY PARACHUTE JUMP
by Harry Armstrong

So here I am in the plane. I feel a mixture of fear and excitement - well, fear mostly. I really should have gone to the toilet when I had the chance. Oddly enough, I'm so scared that I can't hear the plane's engine. It is still working, isn't it? I'm trembling with nerves - please forgive the shaky writing. OK, this is it - I'm at 670 metres. I'm about to jump ... wish me luck!

TREMBLE!

ARRRGGGGGGGGGGGGH! I'm tumbling head over heels at 190 km per hour (please forgive the even more shaky handwriting). I think I'd better close my eyes. Oh — that feels oddly relaxing — I think I'll keep them closed ... Hmm — but what if I hit the ground before I open my eyes? YIKES! I could even wake up to find myself dead! Hmm, I'd best open my eyes. I'm at 579 metres and the ground is coming up to meet me. Er, hello, ground! Now where's my parachute rip cord? Oh no, that's my shoelace...

TUG!

And you'll be cheering out loud to hear that Harry landed safely. But the girl in our next story didn't look set for a happy landing. I've got three excuses to tell this terrible true tale…

a) It's exciting.

b) It was the first time anyone used a parachute to rescue another person.

c) It features a flying machine that you can find out about in the next crazy chapter.

The Daily News
——— 1908 ———

DARING DOLLY SAVES MAY'S DAY!
~

Daring parachute stunt jumper Dolly Shepherd and her friend Louie May faced certain death yesterday. As the girls dangled from an unmanned balloon 7,000 metres in the air, luckless Louie couldn't free her chute.

Daring Dolly (whose previous jobs include being a waitress and a target for a blindfolded sharp-shooter) bravely battled to free her friend.

When Louie was freed, the two girls jumped using Dolly's parachute. But they fell too fast and Dolly hurt her back. Said Dolly from her bed, "It gave me a nasty jolt — especially the landing. Ouch! My poor back! Where's me vapour rub?"

Dolly Shepherd

39

But you'll be jumping with joy to read that, four years later, Dolly realized that too many scary stunts would kill her, so she gave up parachuting. And she lived to the ripe old age of 97.

So, did you spot the flying machine we'll be talking about next? No? Huh! Well, here are a few more clues: it's big and round and filled with hot air or gas (which sometimes leaks). It can be dangerous…

NO! It's a balloon – so read on. The next chapter will take you to new heights…

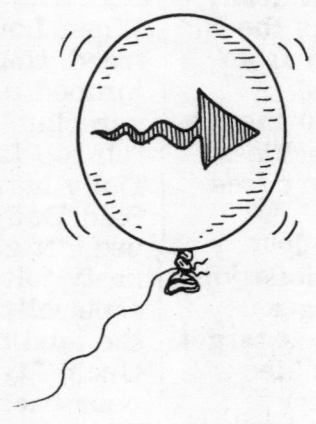

BARMY BALLOONS

Balloons are a pretty sight as they sail silently through the skies – but the fight to fly them was far from pretty. We're about to take to the air with a curious crew of brilliantly barmy balloonists and be swept away on a gale of fearsome facts... Er, do you think this chapter's actually *safe*?

THE FEARSOME FIGHT FOR BALLOON FLIGHT

1670 Italian priest Francesco de Lana hits on a nifty plan. Get some really light air from high up in the sky and fill hollow copper balls with it to lift a flying machine. So how do you get this air (that no one is sure exists)? Er, build a flying machine. And how do you do that when you haven't got the air yet...?

THAT'S WHERE MY PLAN FALLS DOWN...

1709 Brazilian priest Laurenço de Gusmão shows the King of Portugal a model hot-air balloon complete with fire. The fire spreads to the royal palace. The fire is put out, but oddly enough His Majesty isn't put out, despite nearly ending up as a roasted royal.

1755 French priest Joseph Galien (and by the way, why is it that priests were barmy about balloons?) suggested a de Lana-style flying machine 1 km long. His bosses tell him to take a nice long holiday. Now that's a holy order I could live with...

Meanwhile, a pair of brothers who weren't actually priests were about to make a brilliant, if barmy, breakthrough…

A PUFF OF SMOKE

We last saw Joseph Montgolfier (1740–1810) chucking an unfortunate sheep from the top of a tower. But that was just a harmless hobby – the real business of Joe and brother Jacques (1745–1799) was making paper. I expect they were quite rich … on paper. One day in 1782, Joseph watched sparks floating up his chimney – well, there wasn't too much on telly as it hadn't been invented yet.

Joe saw that hot gases from the fire were lifting the sparks, so he decided to fill a paper bag with hot air to test whether that would rise. His landlady suggested a silk bag as it would be less likely to burn, and they watched as the bag sailed up to the ceiling. (By the way, don't go lighting fires in your house to make bags rise up – this is not a sensible thing to do, unless you'd enjoy eating prison food until you're no longer a menace to society.)

Anyway, Joe's experiments led to models that got bigger and flew higher until...

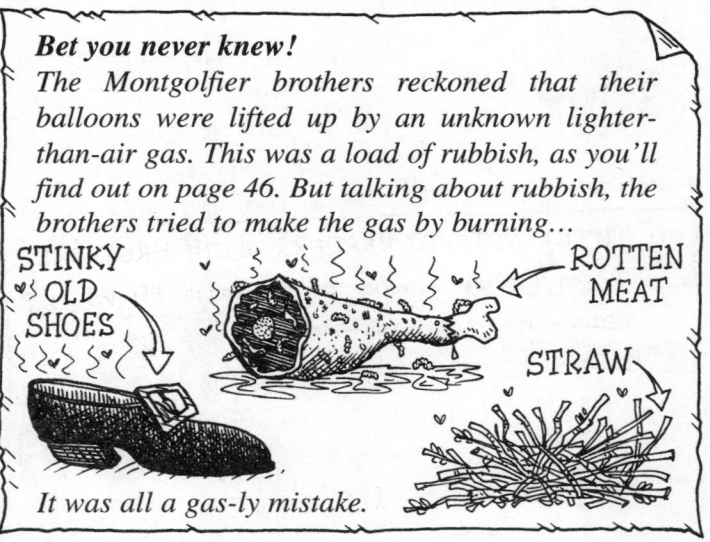

Bet you never knew!
The Montgolfier brothers reckoned that their balloons were lifted up by an unknown lighter-than-air gas. This was a load of rubbish, as you'll find out on page 46. But talking about rubbish, the brothers tried to make the gas by burning...

STINKY OLD SHOES

ROTTEN MEAT

STRAW

It was all a gas-ly mistake.

But the Montgolfiers were scenting success (and lots of other smelly things). And at last they were able to launch the first flight with an air crew in the history of the world.

AND WE'RE THE COCK-A-DOODLE-CREW!

Yes, the first living beings to fly in a flying machine were farmyard animals! And now, in a Horrible Science World Exclusive, the animals quack, bleat and crow for themselves, with a little help from King Louis XVI of France...

The King

14 September 1783 was a great day at my royal palace of Versailles. The balloon was a huge ball of blue and gold with a cage slung beneath it. I wanted to take a close look at the fire but le pong was too stinky. Pfwoar! What were they burning? Anyway, we all cheered as the balloon rose high in the sky.

The cockerel

Yes, it was a great day for us fowls - the first time we've flown without wings! Yes, it certainly was a booster for this rooster! Pity the woolly-minded sheep had to kick me as we landed in a forest 3.2 km away.

The sheep

Baah! That stupid rooster kept pecking at my legs the whole time. I'm not one to bleat, but I reckon he was scared chicken!

The duck

I'm just a duck - so what do I know? But personally I think they're all quackers. I mean, if they want to fly, why don't they just flap their wings? It works for me!

44

BARMY BALLOON QUICKIE QUIZ

1 How were the Montgolfier brothers rewarded by the King?

a) They were given a cake in the shape of a balloon.

b) They were given a gold medal.

c) They were locked up in prison and forced to sniff stinky socks for making nasty whiffs in the palace.

2 How was the sheep rewarded?

a) It was made into a rather tasty mutton stew.

b) Its wool was made into an itchy pair of royal underpants.

c) It was given a home in the royal zoo.

Answers:
1 b)
2 c) And that was a good deal nicer than King Louis' fate. He had his head chopped off in 1793.

> *Bet you never knew!*
> Scientist Jean-François Pilâtre de Rozier (1757–1785) and the Marquis d'Arlandes volunteered to fly in the Montgolfiers' balloon. The flight was a soaraway success, although they did set the balloon on fire and had to put it out using wet sponges. And they spent the flight arguing because the Marquis was too busy admiring the view to put straw on the smelly fire.

Meanwhile, French scientists were feeling mightily miffed because the balloon breakthrough had been made by a pair of papermakers and not a superb scientist. So the French Academy of Sciences asked Jacques Charles

(1746–1823) to invent a scientific flying machine. And he did – the hydrogen balloon. So what happened next? Did Charles's balloon rise to the occasion or did he go down like a lead – er – balloon?

Well, before we find out, let's look into how balloons work – it's sure to be a gas but it's nothing to sniff at! It's all to do with density…

FEARSOME EXPRESSIONS

A scientist says…

YOU'RE TOO DENSE TO FLY…

Do you say…?

I'M QUITE BRAINY, ACTUALLY.

Answer:
Say that and the scientist really will think you're dense stupid. The scientist means your body weighs more than an equal volume of air – so it's too heavy to fly.

BUT HERE'S A REALLY COOL THOUGHT…

Just imagine that your body was *less* dense than air. If your body weighed less than 5 grams, the weight of a sugar lump, you could actually float in the air! Instead of swimming pools there'd be air pools, and instead of high dives there'd be sky dives! You'd feel light-hearted as you walked on air … unless you sat on a pin and you went pop, or the gas escaped from you like a balloon with its neck open and you whizzed around making rude noises.

Anyway, when a balloon is full of hydrogen gas or hot air, it's less dense than the surrounding air. And that means it rises up like a bottom burp bubble in a bath…

HERE'S A MODERN HOT-AIR BALLOON…

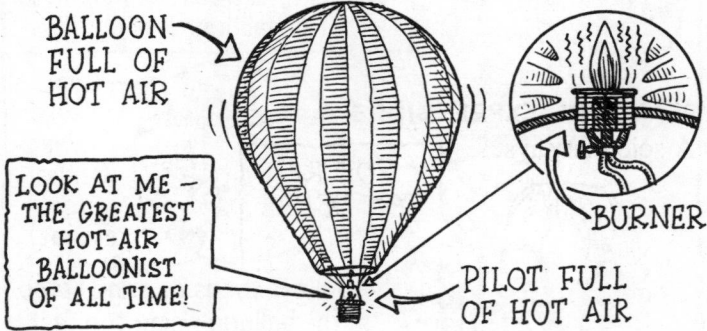

BALLOON FULL OF HOT AIR

LOOK AT ME — THE GREATEST HOT-AIR BALLOONIST OF ALL TIME!

BURNER

PILOT FULL OF HOT AIR

Air is heated by the burner. Heat gives the air molecules more energy so they travel faster and further. They push against the sides of the balloon, filling them out.

IT'S GREAT TO BE WARM!

YEAH, LET'S RUSH AROUND!

To bring the balloon down, you simply switch off the burner. The air cools and takes up less room. More cool air can enter the base of the balloon and as it becomes heavier it dips down. Simple, innit?

AND NOW FOR THE HYDROGEN BALLOON…

The hydrogen balloon is a bit more complicated but, as luck would have it, we're about to see one in action.

After the embarrassing near-fatal failure of their plane, Professor N Large and Wanda Wye have built a balloon. And MI Gutzache's been paid loads of money to fly it…

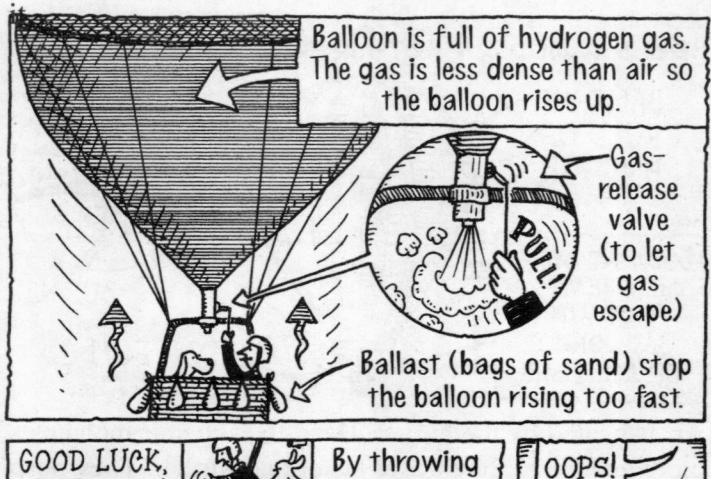

Balloon is full of hydrogen gas. The gas is less dense than air so the balloon rises up.

Gas-release valve (to let gas escape)

Ballast (bags of sand) stop the balloon rising too fast.

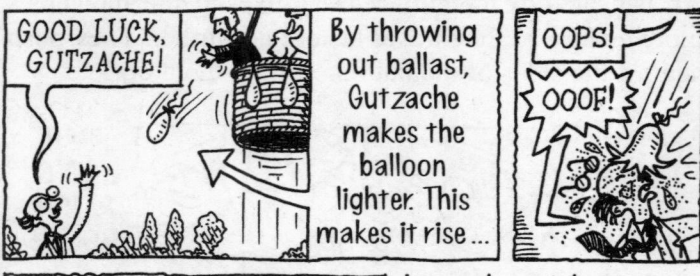

GOOD LUCK, GUTZACHE!

By throwing out ballast, Gutzache makes the balloon lighter. This makes it rise…

OOPS!

OOOF!

By opening the valve, Gutzache reduces the balloon's lifting power, so it should come down…

TUG!

GRR — THE VALVE'S STUCK!

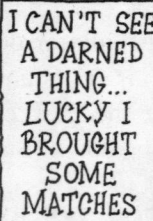

Later that night…

I CAN'T SEE A DARNED THING… LUCKY I BROUGHT SOME MATCHES

No, Gutzache! Hydrogen burns easily when mixed with air…

Oh dear. Is our hero a grilled Gutzache? Is Watson a hot dog? All will be revealed on page 102. But now back to Jacques Charles, who is still busily inventing the hydrogen balloon...

> ***Bet you never knew!***
> *A number of scientists hit on the idea of using hydrogen in a balloon before Charles, but they couldn't think of anything to put the gas in. Scottish scientist Joseph Black planned to fill a body bit from a dead calf with the gas, but he never got round to it. Maybe he was a bit of a cow-ed.*

In fact, Charles's hydrogen balloon hid a silky secret...

TOP-SECRET PLAN
by Jacques Charles
Not to be read by anyone —
especially not those
bungling, jumped-up
Montgolfier brothers...

My plan is to use lightweight silk lined with rubber made by the Robert brothers* of Paris. The rubber stops the hydrogen gas from escaping.

* Yes, more brothers!

Thousands of people turned up to see the balloon launch and the scientist put his invention under armed guard to keep the crowds away. Sadly, the guards weren't around when the unmanned balloon landed near a village and a gang of scared peasants and their dog ripped it to bits. It must have been an un-peasant surprise for the annoyed inventor.

On 12 December Charles and his friend Noel Robert took off from Paris in another balloon. An even bigger crowd came to wave them off. Overcome with emotion, Charles exclaimed...

HOW HAPPY WE ARE! THE SKY BELONGS TO US.

SEE YOU LATER...

PROBABLY...

Which was true – the trouble was the sky was also rather cold. After a flight of 43 km, Robert got out. The lightened balloon rose 2,743 metres and chilly Charles nearly froze to death. But he did get to be the first man ever to see the sun set twice in one day...

I SAW IT SET TW-TW-TWICE. THE VIEW WAS N-N-N-NICE!

SHIVER!

SHAKE!

By now, all Europe was balloon barmy and what better challenge for fledgling fliers than to fly the English

Channel between France and Britain? The race was on, and by June 1784 Englishman James Sadler and Frenchman Pilâtre de Rozier were planning to make the trip. But first to start was Jean Pierre Blanchard... Now I know they didn't have radio in those days, but if they had, I bet the flight would have been broadcast live and it might have sounded like this... (Why not get a friend to read this bit aloud? You can close your eyes and imagine you were there!)

LIFE IS FULL OF UPS AND DOWNS

Hello and welcome to Dover... My name's Mike Commentator... As I speak, brave balloonist Jean Pierre Blanchard and his passenger Dr John Jeffries are about to fly the Channel. But all is not well. We've heard that the two fliers had a row after Blanchard was caught wearing a weight-belt. The sneaky sky-sailor planned to pretend the balloon was too heavy for Jeffries – and grab all the glory for himself!

But now they've taken off! They're rising slowly – the balloon is laden with food and scientific equipment, as well as animal bladders to help it float if it lands in the sea. They've even got the world's first airmail letter...

OH NO! Blanchard's let too much gas out of the balloon. They're coming down in the sea. They're throwing things out to lighten the balloon. Out goes food, drink and scientific equipment. And now Blanchard's chucked out the useless oars and propeller he brought to control the balloon. Will the balloonists escape a ducking?

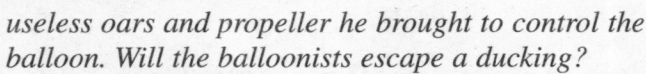

YES! They're going up – but will they make it? NO, they're coming down again! And now it looks like they're arguing! Oh my goodness, they're taking off their clothes! Yes, Blanchard's just dropped his trousers. They're down to their underwear and things are looking desperate – they've even thrown away their bottle of brandy. But they're still coming down. They're just about to hit the sea and Blanchard and Jeffries are trying to throw each other over the side! Is it all over? NO! They're rising up again. THIS IS INCREDIBLE – they're going to make it! What a goal! Now that's what I call an up-and-under

CHUCK!

FLING!

GET OUT!

GRRR!

HOORAY!

YIPPEE!

– or is it an up-and-down-and-over? Oh no, they're coming down in a forest – they could hit the trees! Don't look at this disgusting sight – they're weeing in the bladders and dropping them over the sides to lighen the balloon. Let's hope they don't plop on any passing peasants!

SPLURB!

SPLOOSH!

Well, that was a relief – they've just missed the forest. And they've landed! The crowd are going potty and the balloonists are parading about in their pants! It looks like a potty pants party! And now back to the studio!

And so the world's first airmail letter got through to Paris. But you'll be heartbroken to hear that Blanchard died of a heart attack in his balloon in 1809.

BARMY BALLOONISTS

There's something about ballooning that brings out the barmy side of the most sensible person. And as for silly people, well, they can turn barkingly barmy. The quiz you're about to tackle is based on a very barmy balloonist...

THE ADVENTURES OF LOOPY LUNARDI

The characters:

GEORGE BIGGIN
— A LARGE
GENTLEMAN, IN FACT
A BIT OF A BIG 'UN

VINCENT'S PETS

VINCENT LUNARDI — AN
ITALIAN BALLOONIST

1 Lunardi had promised to give Biggin a ride in his balloon. But the big man was too heavy. Lunardi preferred to carry his pet cat, dog and pigeon … and what else?

a) Lots of food and wine.

b) His collection of garden gnomes.

2 During the flight everyone wanted to watch Lunardi – what was the result?

a) He killed a woman and saved a criminal's life.

b) 22,000 people visited the doctor's with stiff necks.

LET US IN, DOC – DON'T BE A PAIN IN THE NECK!

3 During the flight Lunardi's cat got cold. What did he do to help it?

a) He fed the pigeon to the cat.

b) He landed the cat in a field … and flew off.

WELL, I WOULDN'T TECHNICALLY DESCRIBE IT AS A LANDING...

MEEEOW!

Bet you never knew!

The next year George Biggin and his even bigger friend Letitia Sage forced Lunardi to let them fly. Mrs Sage started scoffing Lunardi's lunch and squashed his scientific equipment with a jangling crash. A few hours later they landed in a bean field. Local children thought it was a great excuse to skip lessons, but everyone got chased by a furious farmer for trampling his beans.

GRRRR!

OOER!

ERK!

YIKES!

And if you think that sounds barmy, you ain't read nothing yet. French balloonists started doing really barmy publicity stunts. For example, in 1817 a Monsieur Mergot flew over Paris in a balloon … while sitting on the back of a white stag named Coco.

But balloons had a darker side – these things were DANGEROUS with a capital "D"!

GRUESOME GAS BAGS – 1
Even after Blanchard beat him to it, Pilâtre de Rozier still wanted to fly the Channel. Trouble is, he wanted to do it in a combined hot-air and hydrogen balloon – and remember what happens when you mix fire and hydrogen? When the balloon burst into flames, the scientist and his co-pilot were the first people to die in an air crash. And in honour of the event the bloody scene was painted for some rather sick souvenirs. Sick bags, anyone?

GRUESOME GAS BAGS – 2
Meanwhile, other scientists were dreaming of taking a balloon as high as they could to find out how the air changed with height. But this turned out to be *incredibly* dangerous. Read on, this next bit's a "height" for sore eyes…

Fearsome flight fact file

NAME: How air changes with height

THE BASIC FACTS: **1** The higher you go, the more spaced-out the air molecules are. The air is said to be "thin".

MOLECULES

2 The air is too thin to provide lift for a bird's wing. In 1862 scientist James Glaisher (1809–1903) dropped a pigeon from a balloon at a great height. The poor pigeon plummeted like a stone.

3 The temperature can be well below freezing.

THE FEARSOME DETAILS:
1 Pioneer balloonists suffered from frostbite and their hands turned black. The air was too thin to breathe easily and they often blacked out.

I DIDN'T KNOW YOU'D BROUGHT GLOVES...

NEITHER DID I!

LACK OF HAIR

GASP!

LACK OF AIR

2 In 1875 top French balloonist Gaston Tissandier and two scientists blacked out at 8,600 metres. By the time Tissandier woke up, the two scientists had died from lack of air.

Another danger with taking a hydrogen balloon to a great height is that the balloon can explode. Because the air is thinner, the air pressure is weaker on the sides of the balloon. This allows the hydrogen inside to push out with greater force and burst the balloon. And that's what happened to this fearless flier...

FAMOUS FEARLESS FLIER FILES

Name: John Wise (1808–1879)

Nationality: American

Got into flying by: Trying lots of horrible flight experiments. For example:

- He tied a kitten to a kite and flew it.
- He dropped a cat tied to a parachute from a window.

The animals lived but John's neighbours banned him from trying any more cruel experiments, so he decided to make a hot-air balloon. But it crashed on his neighbour's roof and set it on fire.

High point: Invented the rip panel. You pull it to let the gas out of your balloon if the wind is blowing it along the ground.

Low point: In 1859 he was flying with some friends when he went to sleep under a leaky gas valve. He nearly died from breathing hydrogen gas, but luckily his friends woke him because he was snoring.

58

Most dangerous moment: In 1838 his balloon burst at 4,000 metres. Luckily Wise had wisely packed a parachute.

Deadly death details: In 1879 Wise made his 463rd balloon flight. The balloon was flimsy and Wise thought it might be dangerous. He was prepared to risk his own neck, but he asked the young man who was about fly with him to stay behind. The man didn't listen. The balloon crashed into Lake Michigan and both men died.

YOU SHOULDN'T HAVE COME...

NO, IT WASN'T WISE, WISE!

Got the message? Balloons are horribly hard to fly and easy to crash, and even today they're only safe in the hands of experts. But in the 1850s, flight fans thought they'd invented a superb solution...

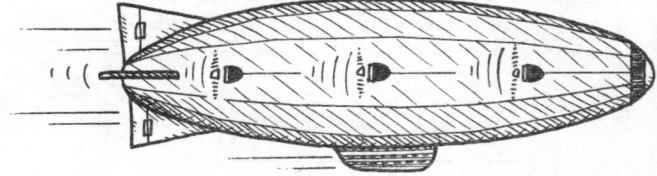

ARRGGGGH! Am I seeing things or did a huge cigar-shaped balloon just drift across the page? Oh well, you'd best read on. Reading is believing...

AWESOME AIRSHIPS

WOW, that really *was* an airship! An airship is a giant balloon that you can steer – so let's steer our way through this crazy chapter and check out their stunning secrets...

Fearsome flight fact file

NAME: Airships

THE BASIC FACTS: 1 An airship is made from several gas bags inside a tough wooden or metal skeleton. The outside of the ship is protected by a fabric or metal skin.

2 The craft is powered by engines and propellers, and steered by rudders.

3 The pointy shape of the airship enables it to move with less drag than a balloon.

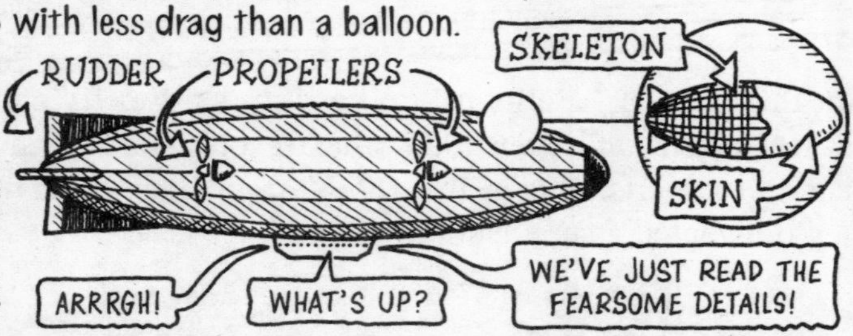

RUDDER — PROPELLERS

SKELETON

SKIN

ARRRGH!

WHAT'S UP?

WE'VE JUST READ THE FEARSOME DETAILS!

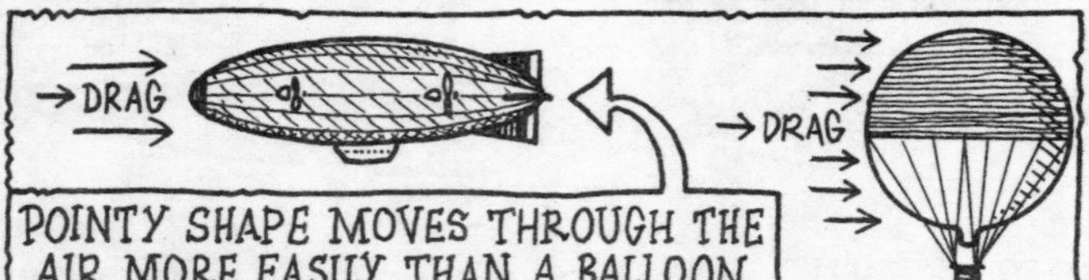

→ DRAG

→ DRAG

POINTY SHAPE MOVES THROUGH THE AIR MORE EASILY THAN A BALLOON

THE FEARSOME DETAILS: Until the 1930s, airships were filled with hydrogen gas, which, as you know, burns rather easily. So guess what happened in awesome airship crashes?

THE FEARSOME FIGHT FOR AIRSHIP FLIGHT

1852 Frenchman Henri Gifford (1825–1882) adds a small engine to a cigar-shaped balloon. The engine is too weak to power the balloon and the craft gets blown backwards.

1883 Gaston Tissandier (remember him from page 57?) and his brother Albert experiment with a 4.8 km per hour motor. The airship flies as fast as a granny shuffles to the shops. Well, almost.

1898 Brazilian genius Albert Santos-Dumont builds his first airship and learns how to fly it. Awesome Albert is so immensely interesting that you can read all about him on page 62.

1900 Retired General Ferdinand von Zeppelin (1838–1917) builds his first airship or zeppelin. (I wonder where the name came from?)

1915 Zeppelins bomb Britain in the First World War. The Brits panic until they realize the big slow zeppelins are easy to shoot down. And then the Germans' panic and stop zeppelin raids.

1924 A zeppelin flies the Atlantic. In the 1930s zeppelins are the poshest way to travel the world.

1930 The British airship R101 crashes, killing 48 people. The Brits give up on airships.

1937 The *Hindenburg*, the biggest zeppelin ever built, crashes in the USA. Suddenly the balloon bubble bursts for airships.

So airships were as dangerous as a dinner date with a dinosaur, and one man who knew this more than most was Albert Santos-Dumont. Let's go and meet him right now…

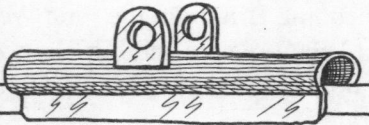

FAMOUS FEARLESS FLIER FILES

Name: Albert Santos-Dumont (1873–1932)

Nationality: Brazilian

Got into flying by: Having an incredibly rich coffee-maker for a dad. That meant he was wealthy enough to build and fly airships for fun.

And when he wasn't flying he was racing cars. He once tested an airship engine by putting it on a tricycle and entering a car race and beating the leaders!

High point: In October 1901 Santos-Dumont tried to win a 100,000-franc prize for flying from St Cloud on the outskirts of Paris, rounding the Eiffel Tower and returning to St Cloud in half an hour. He did it with seconds to spare.

"Have I won the prize?" Santos-Dumont called.

YES! YES! YES!

roared the crazy, cheering crowd.

"No", muttered a grumpy judge from the Paris Aero Club. The fearless flier hadn't lowered his guide rope in time. At this point the rich businessman who had offered the prize said that he had won – it was either that or face a riot. Albert gave the money away to the poor.

Low point: Following his triumph, Santos-Dumont toured Britain and the USA, but his airships were damaged by vandals.

Most dangerous moment: In his bid to win the prize, Santos-Dumont suffered many hair-raising crashes. For example his first airship folded over in mid-air. He said later...

FOR A MOMENT I WAS IN THE PRESENCE OF DEATH

But just as the craft crashed downwards, he saw two boys flying a kite. The falling flier shouted to them to grab his airship guide rope and run with it against the wind. The ship gained some lift from the wind and made a soft landing.

Deadly death details: Oddly enough Santos-Dumont wasn't killed in a crash – but be warned, it's NOT a happy ending! Make sure you've got a box of paper hankies handy...

AWESOME ALBERT'S DOWNFALL

In the 1900s Albert Santos-Dumont was the most famous flier in the world. Well, come to think of it, he was the ONLY flier in the world.

In fact he even helped the first-ever child to fly in a powered flying machine. One day in 1903 the brave Brazilian landed in a children's fair. All the kids begged for a ride and all their spoil-sport parents said…

But seven-year-old Clarkson Potter pestered his parents so hard they gave in. In the end, though, he only went up a few metres.

But after planes became popular Albert didn't do so well. Although he was the first person to fly a powered plane in Europe, his planes always seemed to crash. As he grew older many people thought he was mad. He spent time in mental hospitals and dreamt of making a pair of wings and flying from a window. Quite unfairly, he blamed himself for the way planes had been used to kill people in war. One day Santos-Dumont was staying in a hotel in Sao Paolo, Brazil. Civil war was raging and the ageing flier spotted a plane dropping bombs.

"What have I done?" he muttered.

He went up to his room and took his own life.

64

ZERO HOUR FOR THE ZEPPELINS

By the time Santos-Dumont died, a lot had changed in the floating world of airships. Zeppelins were the world's number-one airships but things were about to go fearsomely wrong…

HORRIBLE HOLIDAYS PRESENT

Come fly on the Hindenburg!

It's got everything you've ever wanted and a lot of things you don't.

● Your very own cabin.
● Hot and cold water.
● Air conditioning.
● Library, lounge (complete with piano) and bar.
● On-board pastry chef bakes fresh buns every day!
● Guaranteed smooth flight so you can munch your buns and enjoy the view with none of that nasty air sickness.

It's a gas!

THE SMALL PRINT
The hydrogen gas and chemicals used to stiffen the fabric sides of the craft have turned the Hindenburg into a flying bomb. Have you written your will yet?

OOER!

On 6 May 1937 the *Hindenburg* was just coming into dock at Lakehurst, New Jersey... Suddenly a flame appeared that rapidly swallowed up the ship. The great airship crashed to the ground amid the screams of its unlucky passengers. Forty people died, the *Hindenburg* was destroyed ... and it all took just 34 seconds.

That was bad enough. But a cine-camera recorded the explosive event and a local radio reporter recorded it. The world got the message – airships were awesomely unsafe.

But were they? Even in 1937 it was possible to use the safer gas helium instead of hydrogen. Airships needn't burn. What killed off the airship in the end wasn't safety fears – it was the success of a nippy little rival with two wings and a whizzy propeller. And in the next chapter we'll find out how it got off the ground... Get ready to spin that propeller!

THE WRIGHT WAY TO INVENT THE PLANE

So how does anyone invent the plane? Well there's a bit more to it than sitting on the toilet and getting inspired and shouting "Eureka!" In fact, inventing is HARDER than chewing a concrete toffee. In this cruel chapter we'll find out why the Wright brothers got it Wright and why nearly everyone else ended up grumpy, wet ... or dead.

FEARSOME FLYING FLOPS

Back in Victorian times lots of inventors dreamt of making a flying machine. Trouble is, most of them had little idea of the forces that affect flight, and their planes were as useless as a giraffe with a sore throat. But that won't stop Honest Bob trying to sell you one. YOU HAVE BEEN WARNED!

HONEST BOB'S PLANE PRODUCTS PRESENTS...

"My Bob's really musical. When he was little he was always on the fiddle." Bob's mum

I Fancy a trip to Beijing? Henson and Stringfellow's steam-powered plane will get you there! Finest 1840s technology!

Only £99,999.05p – but I'll knock off the 5p for cash.

HERE ARE SOME CLASSIC PLANES YOU'LL BE FLYING TO DIE, I MEAN, DYING TO FLY...

ARE WE REALLY FLYING?

NO, IT'S JUST AN ADVERT!

2 You'll be batty not to buy this bat–winged plane (1890) by Clement Ader. People say it's an objet d'art – although it looks more like a paper dart to me.

Only £150,000 plus a few hidden extras.

HE'S WAVING GOODBYE, MUM!

DON'T GET TOO EXCITED

3 Get fired up to the MAX–im with Hiram Maxim's monster plane (1894). Yeah, this plane's the business – I mean, old Maxim invented the machine gun and a mousetrap, so I bet he knew all about planes. Look, I'll even throw in a free Maxim mousetrap and cheese if you buy it.

PREPARE TO TAKE OFF...

... ALL THE HEAVY STUFF THAT'S STOPPING THIS CONTRAPTION FROM FLYING!

Price £299,999.99.
Buy now or regret it later!

4 You'll be Venetian blind not to buy it! (Well, it looks like a Venetian blind!) Horatio Phillips's multi-wingy thingie (1904). I mean, talk about character – this plane's got it in spades. If it doesn't take off, you can always put it in your window and it'll keep the sun out.

Price £199,999. Unless I'm in a good mood – then it's £299,999.

STILL ON THE GROUND

OH WELL, I'LL USE IT AS A CAR!

A FEW FACTS THAT BOB WAS GOING TO TELL YOU SOME DAY...

1 The designers thought plane 1 would fly to China, but it was too heavy to fly at all.

2 Plane 2 hopped in 1890, but that was all.

3 Plane 3 hopped slightly in the air and broke the rail it was running on.

4 According to its inventor, plane 4 hopped 152 metres – yeah, right. Mind you, old Horatio was one of the first people to realize the importance of aerofoil wings. He just made rather too many of them...

These inventors had their heads in the clouds, but other flight fans had their feet firmly on the ground. They wanted to understand about flight before trying to build a plane, so they studied birds, and built and flew gliders and learnt to fly them. Let's glide over a few facts and pay them a flying visit...

Fearsome flight fact file

NAME: Gliders

THE BASIC FACTS: 1 Gliders are towed into the air and their wings produce enough lift to fly. Gliders have long wings to pick up as much lift as they can.

THAT'S HIGH ENOUGH – PASS ME THE SCISSORS!

2 Gliders gradually glide down to earth but they can stay up longer if they find a rising column of hot air called a thermal. Thermals rise from hot rocks or tarmac.

HOW'S IT GOING?

THERMALS

I'M GETTING THE HANG OF IT!

3 A hang-glider is a one-person glider with an A-shaped wing.

THE FEARSOME DETAILS: Two leading glider pioneers – Otto Lilienthal and Percy Pilcher – met fearsome fates. Crash on to pages 76 and 78 if you want to read the deadly details.

Watch the birdie!

3 Gliding, soaring birds

WE VULTURES HAVE WIDE WINGS FOR PICKING UP THERMALS...

...SO WE CAN SOAR HIGH TO SPOT DEAD ANIMALS

OH-ER, I HATE HEIGHTS!

← LONG, THIN WINGS

HIYA, I'M A SEAGULL! MY WINGS ARE LIKE A GLIDER. I CAN GLIDE OVER THE WAVES...

... WITHOUT GETTING PUFFED OUT!

WAIT FOR ME!

Not surprisingly, the cleverest bloke in this book was keen to study how birds flew. And that's how he came to build the world's first glider…

Hall of fame: Sir George Cayley (1771–1857) Nationality: British

Young George was just 12 years old when he heard about the Montgolfier brothers' amazing balloon, and he

71

became flight-mad. He started making his own hot-air balloons powered by candles (very dangerous, so don't try it). And then he experimented with model helicopters made of feathers. As he liked to boast…

I HAVE IDEAS, LOTS OF IDEAS THAT MAY BE MADE TO WORK.

And so he had! In a lifetime of spare-time study (he was a busy landowner and politician), Cayley worked out…
• The ideal shape for a plane.
• The ideal shape for a wing.
• The importance of the forces of lift and thrust.
• The sort of controls a plane would need.

Here's an experiment which shows clever Cayley at his best. Eager to find out the angle of a wing that gives the most lift, he made a model wing based on the wing of a dead crow. He spun the model on a whirling arm powered by a weight that he dropped downstairs and found that an angle of 45° was best. Now that's what I call a stair-lift. By the way, cunning Cayley had to weight, er wait, for his wife to be away as she didn't approve of him experimenting in the house.

AND HERE'S HOW CAYLEY BUILT HIS GLIDER…
Cayley built his first model glider in 1799 and flew it as a kite – but he didn't get round to building a full-sized glider for ten years, and he didn't test one with a human on board for another *thirty* years! As I said, George was *very* busy.

In 1849 Cayley finally tested his glider with a person on board. That person was a ten-year-old boy and he flew a few metres. The boy was the first person to have flown in a glider and you might think the lucky lad became incredibly famous and sold his story to the newspapers for pots of money. But no – science is horribly unfair and no one even noted the boy's name!

Four years later, Cayley built a machine that could carry an adult. Once again there are few records of this world-shattering event, but Cayley's ten-year-old granddaughter saw the whole thing and here's how she might have described it…

How John Appleby flew
Homework by Dora

Yesterday Grandpa took me to Brompton Dale to see his flying machine.

"It's a very special day," said Grandpa. "We're going to test it out and John Appleby's to be the pilot."

"Not your coachman!" I gasped. "Why, he's so old, he'll probably have a heart attack!"

"He's younger than me, and he's in the pink of health," chuckled Grandpa.

JOHN APPLEBY

When I saw the glider, my eyes nearly popped out of my head. Of course, I'd seen Grandpa going into his workshop with Mr Vick the mechanic and I'd heard lots of hammering and sawing, and one or two rude words when they hammered their fingers. But I'd never dreamt of anything like this...

downhill

Proudly Grandpa showed off his creation. He pointed out the rudder at the rear to help Mr Appleby steer the craft and the elevators on the wings to help it go higher.

"All my own inventions," Grandpa beamed.

By now a crowd of villagers had gathered to watch the takeoff and some of the men offered to pull the rope on the front of the craft to get it going.

John Appleby was sitting in the craft, wearing his warmest coat – but I noticed he didn't look quite as jolly and red-faced as usual.

"You'll be fine, Appleby," smiled Grandpa, cheerfully slapping his coachman on the back.

John Appleby gulped and nodded. I bet he was thinking what would happen if the glider crashed and he broke all his bones and his brains came out of his ears.

SPLURB!

With a signal from Grandpa, the men started pulling on the ropes. Harder and harder they pulled. The glider slid over the grass and bounced downhill and then...

Everyone gasped as it took off. It flew like a paper dart over the stream and across the valley and... OH NO! It bashed into the other side of the valley in a big cloud of dust. I felt disappointed - I thought Grandpa's glider would fly much further. Everyone rushed over to see if John Appleby was all right. Was he dead?

No. Mr Appleby was coughing and spluttering and spitting out dust. He leapt from the glider as if it was a boiling-hot bath. His chins were wobbling, his face was the colour of cold porridge and his whiskers were sticking up like a wire brush.

"SIR GEORGE," he yelled, "I WISH TO GIVE NOTICE. I WAS HIRED TO DRIVE AND NOT FLY!"

"Don't worry, Grandpa!" I cried. "I'll fly the glider if John Appleby won't."

"Oh no, you don't!" snapped Grandpa. "It's far too dangerous for girls!"

"Oh well," I hear you remark, "at least John Appleby became world-famous..." But he didn't. In fact, the newspapers didn't even report the story. Most people thought that making a plane was impossible and they couldn't see the point of Sir George's experiments. You see, no one had invented an engine that was light and powerful enough to get a plane in the air.

> **Bet you never knew!**
> **1** The steam-powered engines of Cayley's day were very heavy and needed boilers to make steam. Not to mention a supply of water to boil and coal to burn.
> **2** Cayley realized this made it impossible for a plane to fly and planned to build a gunpowder-powered engine … before he realized it was too dangerous.

MAYBE NOT!

So, for now, the future of flight depended on building better gliders and that's exactly what flying freaks tried to do. The most famous of them all was a German genius who didn't mind making the odd sacrifice…

FAMOUS FEARLESS FLIER FILES

Name: Otto Lilienthal (1849–1896)

Nationality: German

Got into flying by: Watching storks fly as a child. He became an engineer but he retired to build gliders.

High point: Gliding several hundred metres at heights of 30 metres. Lilienthal was the first human in history to glide like a bird and he made 2,000 glides – some from a specially built hill. Today the modern sport of hang-gliding is inspired by his work.

WEEEEEE!

Low point: Trying to build a flying machine with flapping wings. Experts say it wouldn't have got off the ground.

Most dangerous moment: Just about every moment he was in the air. Lilienthal's gliders were built out of wood and fabric, and they were hard to control in windy weather. To change course, he had to swing his body from side to side.

Deadly death details: Luckless Lil was trying to turn in a wind. He fell and broke his back and his final words were, "Sacrifices must be made." In other words, he was dying for flying.

Oddly enough, Lilienthal's famous fate did nothing to put people off gliding. It even seemed to encourage them!

Bet you never knew!
The US champion gliding geek was another ex-engineer named Octave Chanute (1832–1910). Chanute was a little too old to fly so he asked a man named Augustus Herring to test his gliders. (When the glider didn't work too well, I bet he lost his temper and turned into a red Herring.)

In Britain, Lilienthal's lead was taken up by Percy Pilcher (1867–1899). Percy had worked for Hiram Maxim (remember him from page 68?), but he became a fan of Lilienthal and even flew with his hero. And, like Lilienthal, he was to die in a glider crash.

FLYING NEWS

— 1899 —

PERCY PILCHER PERISHES!

Flying freak Percy Pilcher perished after a gliding glitch caused a cruel crash. Penniless Percy invited some bigwigs to watch the takeoff of his new powered plane. But bad weather and engine trouble caused his hopes to take a nosedive. Plucky

Percy decided to show off his glider even though it was soaked by the rain. The glider fell to bits and Percy's fall proved fully fatal.

Bet you never knew!
Experts think that, with a couple of tweaks, Percy's plane might have flown. So thanks to a spot of engine bother and rotten weather, Percy missed out on flying the world's first powered plane. Sadly, instead of tasting the high life he ended up biting the dust.

And talking about powered planes, it's time for some very exciting news for anyone who gets excited by engines…

EXCITING ENGINE NEWS

The reason why Percy could build a powered plane was that a new kind of engine had been developed. Let's face the facts – this new engine was vital for the fearsome future of flight…

Fearsome flight fact file

Name: The very vital petrol engine

THE BASIC FACTS:
1 The petrol engine was invented in 1883 by German Gottlieb Daimler (1835–1900).

2 It was vital for planes because it was powerful enough to power plane propellers and provide the thrust they need to fly but was light enough not to weigh the plane down.

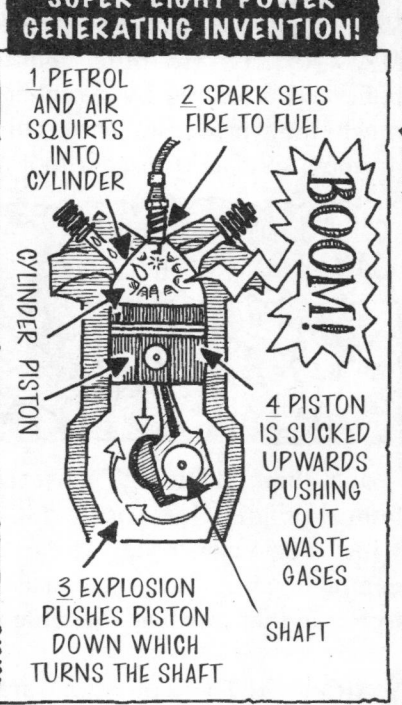

SUPER-LIGHT POWER GENERATING INVENTION!

1 PETROL AND AIR SQUIRTS INTO CYLINDER

2 SPARK SETS FIRE TO FUEL

BOOM!

CYLINDER   PISTON

4 PISTON IS SUCKED UPWARDS PUSHING OUT WASTE GASES

3 EXPLOSION PUSHES PISTON DOWN WHICH TURNS THE SHAFT

SHAFT

THE FEARSOME DETAILS: The only problem was that petrol burns easily – with fiery results in plane crashes.

And it was thanks to the petrol engine that a pair of bicycle mechanics from Ohio, USA, were able to make the world's first powered flight. Back in 1899 no one had ever heard of them (except maybe their mum), but armed with a few bike spares, cloth and some bits of wood they would change the history of the world...

EVERYTHING YOU EVER WANTED TO KNOW ABOUT THE WRIGHT BROTHERS

When Orville Wright (1871–1948) and his brother Wilbur (1867–1912) were little, their dad gave them a toy helicopter powered by a rubber band. They loved it so much they broke it. They built a new one but their grumpy, spoilsport teacher took it away.

Just think about it! That teacher set back the tide of human progress by years and it's worth sharing this idea with your teacher next time they seize your pocket computer game. And you can always get your revenge by torturing them with this terrible test...

WARNING! These questions are rated really hard, if not impossible. They are only suitable for teachers and NOT friends. If you are feeling kind, you can give your teacher the right to ask the class to vote on the answer to ONE question.

1 Who was the unsung star who helped the Wrights with their work and never got any glory?
a) Their sister.
b) Their pet fly Francis.
c) Their teacher.

2 What did Wilbur and Orville do as a hobby?
a) They printed a newspaper.
b) They entered custard-pie throwing competitions.
c) They gave lessons to local children.

3 What did Wilbur do when a boy sat on his best hat?
a) He made the boy test a dangerous glider.
b) Nothing at all.
c) He gave the boy loads of horribly hard homework.

4 The Wrights tried to fly at Kill Devil Sandhill near Kitty Hawk, North Carolina. Why?
a) The sand gave them a nice soft landing when they crashed.
b) The wind blows all the time.
c) Their old teacher lived there.

5 Where did a bit of the Wrights' plane end up?
a) Holding up their mum's washing line.
b) The moon.
c) On display at their old school.

Answers:

1 a) So let's hear three cheers for Katharine Wright, who ran the bike business when the boys were off inventing the plane. She gave them the cash they needed to get off the ground.

2 a) But the really interesting thing is that the inventive brothers actually built their own printing press from an old tombstone and the top of a pram (plus other bits 'n' pieces).

3 b) This story shows how patient Wilbur was. You could try to explain that patience with children is a sign of genius – but would your teacher be patient enough to listen?

4 Ha ha – trick question. The answer is **a)** AND **b)** and your teacher can't have a point unless they said both. In fact the wind wasn't as constant as the brothers hoped, and millions of mosquitoes sucked their blood. But at least there was no one around to spy on them and pinch their ideas. (The Wrights were keen to keep their invention a secret until they could make money from it.)

5 b) When the Apollo 11 astronauts landed on the moon in 1969 there was a bit of the Wrights' plane in their spacecraft. Well, you didn't think it flew there on its own, did you?

WHAT YOUR TEACHER'S SCORE MEANS…

5 CHEAT! Clearly this person is unfit to be a teacher!

3–4 Good. Make sure the questions are harder next time.

0–2 Poor. Make your teacher write out 1,000 times "I really ought to know more about the Wright brothers" while you take the day off.

By the way, the c) answers were to do with school, so if your teacher's answers were all c) they are clearly overworked and deserve a long holiday. And you'll have to take one too!

THE WRIGHTS GET BUSY...

From 1899 onwards the Wright brothers spent all their spare time building and testing gliders and planes until they had built a plane that could fly. And that's not all...
• They invented a lighter and more powerful petrol engine.
• Plus a new, more powerful propeller.
• They built a wind tunnel (that's a machine in which air is blown through a box) to work out which aerofoil wing shape gave the most lift.
• But, best of all, they realized that it wasn't enough to build a plane. They had to be able to control it in the air. And so they invented wing-warping, which means flexing the wings to alter the amount of lift they provide. By doing this the Wrights could tilt and turn the plane in mid-air.

And they did all this by trial and error – testing, testing and testing their designs until they worked. In all, they tested...
• Hundreds of aerofoil shapes in their wind tunnel.
• Their third glider nearly 1,000 times.

Although they didn't know it at the time, the Wrights were in a race to invent the plane. And their rival was scenting success. His name was Samuel P Langley (1834–1906) and he was an astronomer who got hooked on flying after going to a scientific talk. Now I could tell you more about Langley, but it so happens he's coming back from the dead to tell you himself. He's on the TV show that digs the dirt to unearth its guests...

Welcome to Dead Brainy — the programme where we give dead scientists the time of their lives, er, deaths.

Tonight's guest is Samuel Langley.

GOOD EVENING.

You're looking grave, Sam.

WELL, THAT'S WHERE I'VE BEEN SINCE 1906.

So tell us about your plane...

IT COST THOUSANDS OF DOLLARS AND IT WAS LAUNCHED FROM A GIANT CATAPULT ON TOP OF A BOAT.

So is it true everyone you worked with had to dress smartly and wasn't allowed to swear?

WHY AREN'T YOU WEARING A TIE?

And what's more, we're getting ahead of our story. After all, back in 1903, when Langley's plane flopped in the river, the Wrights' plane, the *Flyer*, wasn't a flyer. It hadn't even got off the ground.

And to tell the story of what happened, let's peek at Orville Wright's secret diary. Er, I bought it from Honest Bob, so it *might* be a forgery.

Orville Wright's Secret Diary

December 16 1903, Kitty Hawk, North Carolina. It's all my brother's fault. Two days ago he tried to take off but the controls were set wrong and he crashed. Ever since, we have been repairing the damage and waiting for the wind to drop so we can risk trying to fly again. Time is running out and we've got to be home for Christmas or Pa will never forgive us!

GRR, WHERE ARE THEY?

December 17 1903
We decided to fly this morning. To be honest, there's been times when I've doubted we'd do it. It's taken four years of hard work. Would it all be worth it? I wondered. I asked a local named John Daniels to take a photo if the plane flew – but John hadn't used a camera and he didn't know which end was which. Slowly, we pushed the plane from its shed. John and his friends helped.

CAN I GO FIRST, BRUV?

NO WAY!

I lay on the lower wing (that's where the pilot has to go – we really ought to invent a comfy seat!). As Wilbur swung the propeller to start the engine, the others pushed the plane along our home-made rails. The engine coughed and spluttered into life... WHOOSH! My heart jumped into my mouth. I was up in the air. I WAS FLYING! At last the plane came down but I'd done it. The flight was awesome, it was MASSIVE, it was all of 40 metres – and I must have been in the air for a WHOLE 12 SECONDS. WOW!

I CAN DO BETTER THAN THAT!

And it just got better. John Daniels did manage to take my photo – pity I wasn't smiling at the time! And after coffee Wilbur flew 52 metres – huh, trust my brother to try to beat me! So I showed him – I flew 61 metres, although I did go up and down a bit. But just when I felt like crowing, my big-headed brother flew 100 metres, although he did crash. Luckily he's fine – what's with him always crashing? Then it was my go and I beat his record, but then he flew for nearly a minute and got 260 metres. Show-off!

We sent a telegram to Pa telling him we'd be home for Christmas. Now that's what I call a GOOD day's work!

ANYBODY WANT A WING?

And so, after years of trying, humans were flying powered planes. But many people thought it was no big deal. After all, the Wrights had flown for less than a minute and the only papers that reported the event got it all wrong and said Wilbur ran around shouting "Eureka!"

But one thing was clear. From now on the fight wasn't simply to fly. It was to fly *better*! And the race was on to build better planes…

PLANE-CRAZY PLANES

This is a chapter about machines. Flying machines and not-so-flying machines. It's got the sort of machines that you wouldn't send your worst teacher up in, and it's even got helicopters too. So, if you're all aboard, let's take to the air…

Now I bet you're itching to find out what happened to the Wright brothers, who were last seen celebrating their success with a slap-up Christmas dinner. The Wrights knew they had to improve their plane before they could think of selling it and making money. So they built not one but two planes, *Flyers* 2 and 3. And they tested the planes until they could…

- Fly 66 km.
- Reach the dizzy height of 110 metres.

At last, in 1908, the brothers set out to wow the world and sell planes. Orville went to Washington to wow the US army. And Wilbur went to Paris to wow European flying fans.

At first the French didn't think much of Wilbur. They didn't like his greasy old clothes and the way he slept in a plane shed and ate from tins and burped in public. But once they saw what his plane could do, they changed their tune…

After all, the best the Europeans could manage was a giant box-kite, which our old pal Santos-Dumont managed to hop 4.5 metres off the ground: not even as far as Wilbur's best 1903 effort.

So when the Europeans saw Wilbur flying happily across country and changing course in mid-air, they were gobsmacked. They rushed to their own garden sheds and started knocking up all kinds of crazy craft based on the Wrights' planes. But tragedy was just around the corner…

The Wrights' planes were FEARSOMELY dangerous fliers:
• They had NO brakes.
• No undercarriage wheels.
• No safely belt.
• The only way women could fly in them was with their legs tied together so their dresses wouldn't blow over their heads.

In 1908 Orville was flying over a cemetery in Washington when he lost control. He was badly hurt and his passenger Thomas Selfridge was killed. The aeroplane had claimed its first victim...

> ***Bet you never knew!***
> *1 Despite the safety problems, the Wrights made plane-loads of money from selling their planes. But they hated other pilots stealing their ideas and they spent years in the courts fighting their rivals. Wilbur ruined his health with worry. In 1912 he died of a grisly gut disease.*
> *2 The Europeans didn't copy everything from the Wrights. They began to use wing flaps called ailerons (a-ler-rons) instead of wing warping. Ailerons proved ideal for tilting wings to turn a plane in mid-air (see page 104 for the full flap facts).*

But talking about dangerous machines ... here's Honest Bob with a collection of perilous planes. Yes, they're more dangerous than a tiger with toothache, so which one would you fancy for your death-day, er, birthday?

91

1 The Christmas Bullet (1918) This ye olde antique plane was designed by Dr William Christmas, so it makes an ideal Christmas present. Dr C was a medical doc and I bet that came in handy when his plane crashed. It goes like a bullet and it's twice as deadly. (Oops, I'm getting a bit too honest!) Price – it's only £999,999.99.

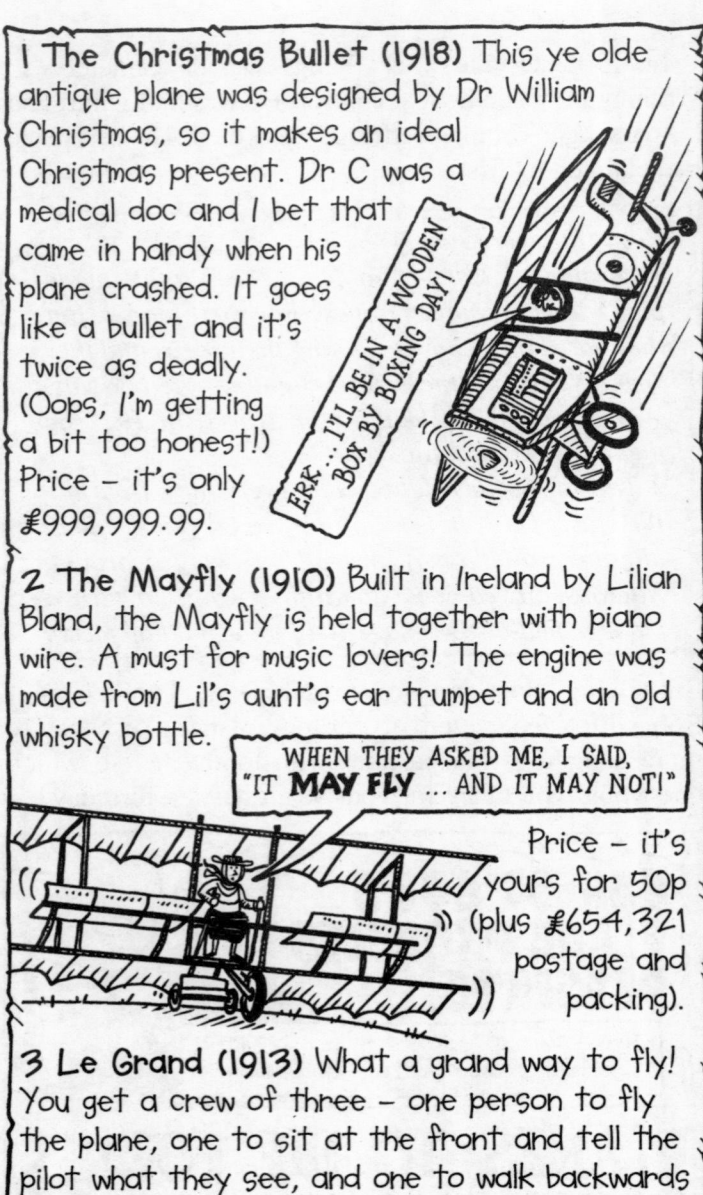

ERK... I'LL BE IN A WOODEN BOX BY BOXING DAY!

2 The Mayfly (1910) Built in Ireland by Lilian Bland, the Mayfly is held together with piano wire. A must for music lovers! The engine was made from Lil's aunt's ear trumpet and an old whisky bottle.

WHEN THEY ASKED ME, I SAID, "IT **MAY FLY** ... AND IT MAY NOT!"

Price – it's yours for 50p (plus £654,321 postage and packing).

3 Le Grand (1913) What a grand way to fly! You get a crew of three – one person to fly the plane, one to sit at the front and tell the pilot what they see, and one to walk backwards and forwards to balance the plane. Relax on the supplied-as-standard comfy four armchairs and sofa! Price – you can't put a price on this kind of luxury but I'll try – it's £2,222,222.22.

A BIT TOO COMFY!

ZZZZZ ZZZZZ ZZZZ

ZZZZZ ZZZZ

4 Count Gianni Caprioni di Taliedo's seaplane* (1921) You can count on this superb seaplane (probably). I mean, it's got nine wings and eight engines so it doesn't matter if a few drop off! Price – if you give me £10,000,000, I'll tell you!

WELL, IT FLOATS!

BUT DOES IT FLY?

* A seaplane is a plane that's designed to take off and land on water. For this reason seaplanes have skis rather than wheels underneath. Yes, they're water-skiing planes!

5 The Granville Gee Bee (GB Sportster) (1930s) OK, so it's a bit dangerous and it might just give you the heebie-jeebies – but it flies at 470 km per hour and it adds spice to your death, er, life. This plane makes a real deep hole when it crashes – so it saves

getting buried! Price –
name your price, and I'll
just add £456,789!

...BETTER
HEAD FOR
THAT
GRAVEYARD

6 The Flying Flea
(Pou de Ciel) (1930s)

Supplied as a kit – you build this plane
yourself in your shed. Yeah, it's ideal for DIE
fans, er, I mean DIY fans. It's cheap and
cheerful, and it even flies
upside down. Well, it does
that most of the time.
Price – just 50p.
Glue: £89,000.
Come to think of it,
you can just fly it
away – if you dare!

YIKES!
I'VE BEEN
ITCHING
TO FLY
ONE BUT
IT'S NOT
UP TO
SCRATCH!

SIX THINGS HONEST BOB FORGOT TO TELL YOU ABOUT THESE PLANES

1 The Christmas Bullet was a killer craft. On its first flight, its wings fell off and its pilot was killed. On the third test flight, another pilot died. Dr C was a flying fibber who stole many of his inventions from other companies.

2 Lilian's Mayfly didn't fly – it hopped. Her uncle was so scared that he offered her a car if she never flew again.

3 In 1913 Le Grand was the biggest plane in the world and the first with a cabin. Despite, or because of, all its pilots, the plane designed by Russian genius Igor Sikorsky (1889–1972) actually flew!

4 The good news – this plane took off from Lake Maggiore. The bad news – the middle wings fell off and it crashed, killing both its unlucky pilots. Perhaps they should have used it as a boat.

5 The Gee Bee was built for racing and actually set a speed record. It also had a nasty habit of killing its pilots. Two Gee Bees crashed and killed their pilots. So the makers put bits of the two downed planes together to make a third Gee Bee – which crashed and killed its pilot. For some reason this put people off flying it.

6 In the 1930s there was a craze in France, Britain and the USA for these home-built planes designed by Henri Mignet. Mad Mignet had been plane-crazy since he built a glider that landed on his little sister. He said:

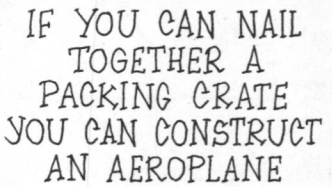 

IF YOU CAN NAIL TOGETHER A PACKING CRATE YOU CAN CONSTRUCT AN AEROPLANE

Trouble was, when the Flea flopped upside down, you couldn't get it the right way up until you crashed and died (probably).

AN IMPORTANT ANNOUNCEMENT BY THE AUTHOR…

So far, all the planes in this chapter have been dismal embarrassing flops, but there *were* good planes in the 1920s and 1930s… Between 1919 and 1931 the Schneider Trophy seaplane races encouraged designers in the USA, Germany, Italy, Britain and France to build faster planes. The designs inspired fighter planes, like the British Spitfire and the Italian Maachi C200.

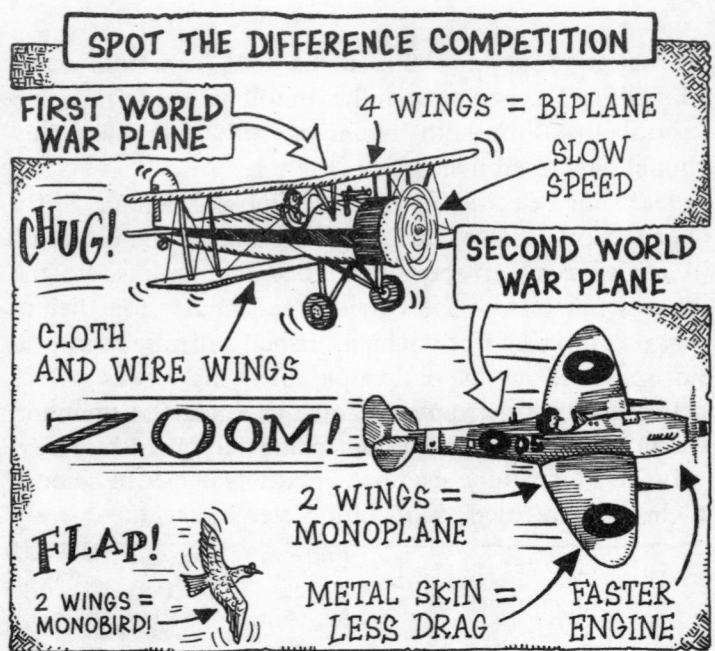

SPOT THE DIFFERENCE COMPETITION

FIRST WORLD WAR PLANE

4 WINGS = BIPLANE

SLOW SPEED

CHUG!

SECOND WORLD WAR PLANE

CLOTH AND WIRE WINGS

ZOOM!

FLAP!
2 WINGS = MONOBIRD!

2 WINGS = MONOPLANE

METAL SKIN = LESS DRAG

FASTER ENGINE

HORRIBLE HELICOPTERS

And that wasn't all. In the 1930s designers were working on a totally new type of flying machine. A machine that took off and hovered without bother. Or at least it was supposed to…

FIVE FACTS THAT YOUR TEACHER PROBABLY DOESN'T KNOW ABOUT HELICOPTERS

1 The helicopter was invented in ancient China. Or at least a toy helicopter that whizzed up in the air when you pulled a string was invented there. It reached Europe in the Middle Ages.

2 Before 1900 loads of people tried to invent the helicopter, including Leonardo da Vinci. But, as with planes, there were no powerful engines that could make them fly. In 1877, for example, French inventor Emmanuel Dieuaid tried to solve the problem by putting a steam boiler on the ground to feed a steam engine on a helicopter. But the craft couldn't fly higher than the steam pipe. So I guess it was all a pipe dream.

3 In the 1880s US inventor Thomas Edison (1847–1931) tried to solve the problem with a helicopter engine powered by explosive gun cotton. But then his lab blew up. Edison was a bright spark but he didn't need that sort of spark.

4 In the 1900s inventors began to get off the ground in their helicopters – but not more than a few metres.

5 The first really useful helicopters were inspired by Spanish inventor Juan de la Cieva, who invented the idea of a spinning rotor on top of a flying craft. By the end of the 1930s German inventor Heinrich Focke and Igor Sikorsky (yes, the guy who brought us Le Grand) had built their own helicopters.

Bet you never knew!
Helicopter pilots have silly slang terms for their machines. It's worth learning them so you can impress your friends by pretending to be a helicopter pilot...

But if you really want to be a helicopter pilot, you need to know how they work – or even how to build one yourself...

Fearsome flight fact file

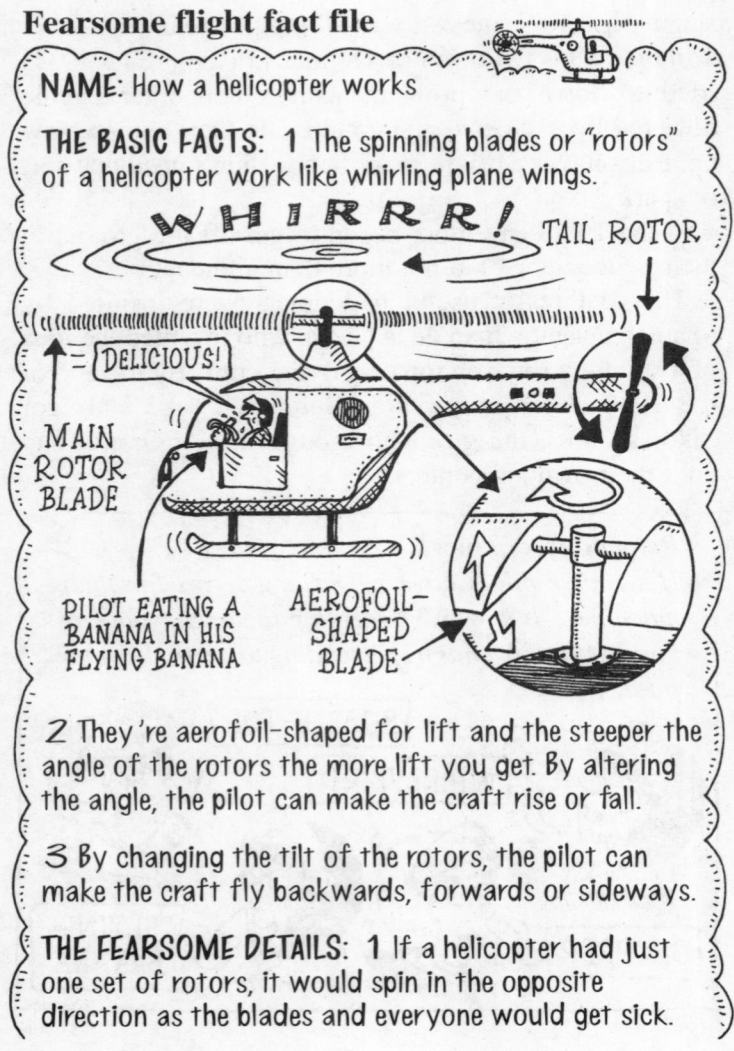

NAME: How a helicopter works

THE BASIC FACTS: **1** The spinning blades or "rotors" of a helicopter work like whirling plane wings.

WHIRRR!

TAIL ROTOR

DELICIOUS!

MAIN ROTOR BLADE

PILOT EATING A BANANA IN HIS FLYING BANANA

AEROFOIL-SHAPED BLADE

2 They're aerofoil-shaped for lift and the steeper the angle of the rotors the more lift you get. By altering the angle, the pilot can make the craft rise or fall.

3 By changing the tilt of the rotors, the pilot can make the craft fly backwards, forwards or sideways.

THE FEARSOME DETAILS: **1** If a helicopter had just one set of rotors, it would spin in the opposite direction as the blades and everyone would get sick.

2 Helicopters often have tail rotors that push the tail in the same direction as the main rotors. This stops the craft spinning and saves on the sick bags.

WITH TAIL ROTOR

BLEURGH!

WITHOUT TAIL ROTOR

Watch the birdie!

4 Hummingbirds and helicopters

WE HUMMINGBIRDS CAN HOVER...

UNLIKE ROTORS, OUR WINGS BEAT BACKWARDS AND FORWARDS IN A FIGURE OF EIGHT... UP TO 70 TIMES A SECOND!

OUR LONG BEAK IS HANDY FOR DRINKING NECTAR FROM FLOWERS.

I NEED A STRAW!

Hmm – I expect the burgers would be chargrilled and, all in all, I guess it's safer to build a helicopter than to try to be one…

Dare you discover … how to build a helicopter?

A QUICK NOTE TO OVER-EXCITED YOUNGER READERS NO, it's not a real helicopter and you shouldn't try flying in it. You'll have to carry on pestering your parents if you want a real chopper for your birthday.

You will need:
Piece of paper 21 cm by 9 cm
Ruler
Scissors (and that ever-helpful adult helper)
Paperclip
Pencil

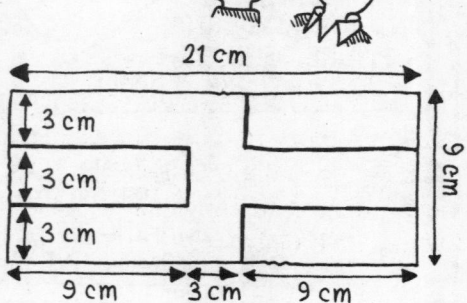

HERE WE GO AGAIN

What you do:
1 Draw the solid lines on the paper as shown.

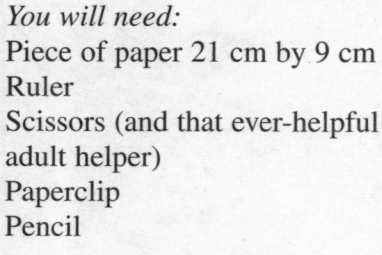

21 cm

3 cm

3 cm

3 cm

9 cm

9 cm

3 cm

9 cm

2 Cut the paper along the solid lines.

3 Fold the paper along the dotted lines as shown. These folded bits are your rotors.

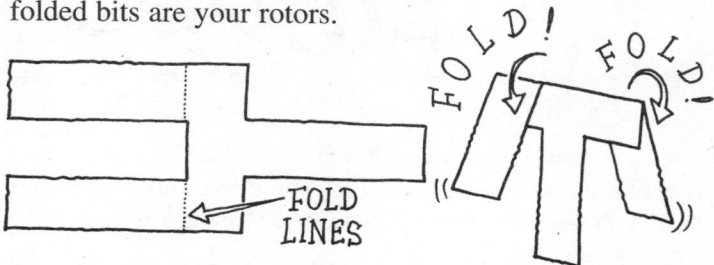

4 Now open up your rotors and slide the paperclip over the bottom end of your helicopter.

5 Ready for your first flight? Simply drop it from a height!

You should find:
The rotors spin – just like the blades of a real helicopter.

AN IMPORTANT ANNOUNCEMENT...

Talking about building flying machines, I've just heard that our scientist buddies have built another plane. Once again they need someone to put it through its paces. So where's MI Gutzache? Oh, silly me – I forgot, he was last seen getting blown up.

KABOOM!

As luck would have it, Gutzache and Watson escaped by parachute and were only a bit singed. But no sooner has Gutzache recovered than Wanda Wye is pestering him to teach her to fly. Is this a disaster in the making? You better read on and find out!

MI GUTZACHE'S FLYING SCHOOL LOG-BOOK

Flying lessons, they said. Nice and simple - no balloons, no blasts. "Yeah, right," I said - that's what I always say and, as always, I was right. But the balloon had blown up my wallet and I needed the cash. I played a hunch and I took the job. Would I be the fall guy again? I wondered. Time would tell - but just then time wasn't letting on.

LESSON I WEAR THE RIGHT CLOTHES

It's cold up there, I wear...

FLYING HELMET

GOGGLES

RIDICULOUS MOUSTACHE

SCARF TO STOP ME GETTING STIFF NECK

GOOD LUCK, WANDA!

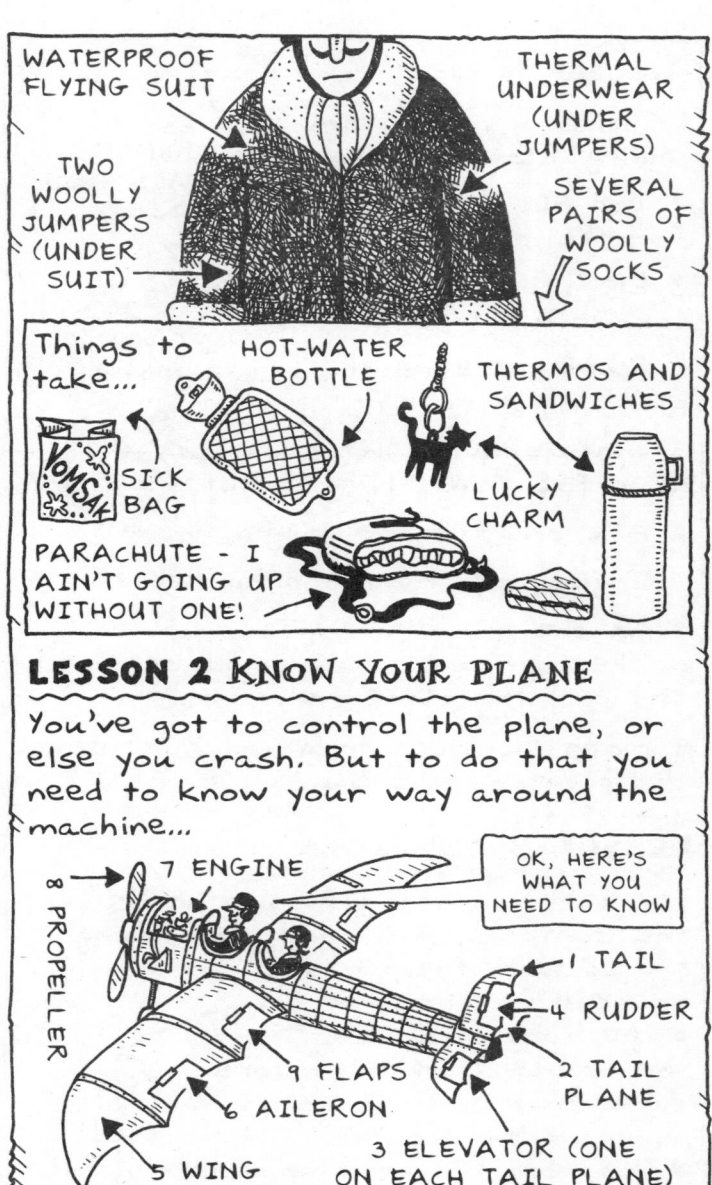

WATERPROOF FLYING SUIT

THERMAL UNDERWEAR (UNDER JUMPERS)

TWO WOOLLY JUMPERS (UNDER SUIT)

SEVERAL PAIRS OF WOOLLY SOCKS

Things to take...

HOT-WATER BOTTLE

THERMOS AND SANDWICHES

VOMSAK SICK BAG

LUCKY CHARM

PARACHUTE - I AIN'T GOING UP WITHOUT ONE!

LESSON 2 KNOW YOUR PLANE

You've got to control the plane, or else you crash. But to do that you need to know your way around the machine...

8 PROPELLER

7 ENGINE

OK, HERE'S WHAT YOU NEED TO KNOW

1 TAIL

4 RUDDER

9 FLAPS

6 AILERON

2 TAIL PLANE

3 ELEVATOR (ONE ON EACH TAIL PLANE)

5 WING

103

And here's what they do...

1 Tail stops the plane sliding from side to side.

I'LL NEVER REMEMBER ALL THIS!

2 Tail plane provides lift for the tail.

3 Elevators are used to take off, climb and dive.

4 Rudder steers the plane right or left.

5 Wings provide lift and keep the plane flying level.

6 Ailerons tilt the wings.

7 Engine powers the propeller.

8 As the propeller speeds up, it pushes air past it to produce thrust and pull the plane forwards.

9 Flaps increase drag and slow down the plane for landing.

LESSON 3 CONTROLS

It feels good to get your hands on the controls, but don't do nothing stupid with them in the air or we'll be kitty meat.

● The control column moves the ailerons and elevators.

● The brakes slow the plane down on the ground.

● The pedals move the rudder.

KITTY SNAX

104

- The compass shows your direction.
- The throttle controls the engine speed.
- The speedometer shows your speed.
- The altimeter shows your height.

CONTROL COLUMN

PILOT SEAT

THROTTLE

PEDALS

LESSON 4 TAKEOFF AND LANDING

Before you take off it's a smart idea to check out your plane. Make sure the wings are stuck on, etc. Then check your instruments and make sure they work. Now have I forgotten anything? Nope!

Switch on the engine. Get a good buddy to swing your prop - that's what we pilots call turning the propeller to get it started. Taxi along the runway, open up the throttle to power up the engine - hey cat, get your mangy butt out the way of the plane!

CHEERS, PROF!

When you're going fast enough, pull up the control column to raise the elevators. This boosts the lift over the tail - so it rises up.

WE'RE FLYING!

MEOW!

RUN FOR IT, TIDDLES!

To land, slow the engine and push the control column forward to lower the elevators and reduce lift. Don't forget to brake your wheels after you land!

LESSON 5 STEERING THE PLANE

You can steer the plane using the rudder pedals: left for left and right - well, you get the picture. But if you do just this, the plane skids about in the sky...

So it makes sense to bank the plane. "Bank"... I love that word - it reminds me of wads of cash. Up here it means tilting the wings and steering the rudder at the same time. So to bank right, it's control column right and right rudder pedal down...

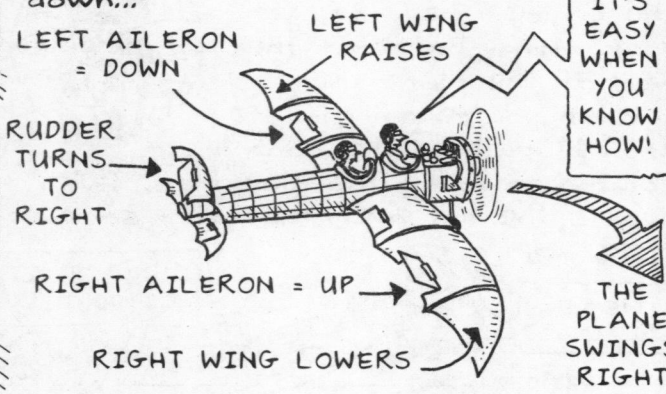

LEFT AILERON = DOWN

LEFT WING RAISES

IT'S EASY WHEN YOU KNOW HOW!

RUDDER TURNS TO RIGHT

RIGHT AILERON = UP

RIGHT WING LOWERS

THE PLANE SWINGS RIGHT

I showed Wanda Wye the move again, but I banked too far and that's when I found out I'd forgotten to fasten my seat belt in Lesson 4. As luck would have it, Wanda had belted up without me telling her to...

WHAAAAA!

HANG ON, GUTZACHE!

Somehow Wanda righted the aircraft - I guess she didn't do too badly for a girl.

HUH, CHEEK!

AND TIDDLES ISN'T TOO HAPPY ABOUT WHAT HAPPENED!

CHOMP!

HEESH! HEESH!

So you'd like to learn to fly, too? Well, don't let me stop you!

Dare you discover ... how to bank a plane?

You will need:

Yourself

That's it. (No, you don't need a plane – I bet you're not old enough to fly one anyway, are you?)

What you do:

1 Place your arms out straight like wings. Make sure your hands are facing down and your wings are pointing slightly upwards and well away from your granny's glass goblet collection or your dad's chin.

2 Your hands are your ailerons. Practise using them...

a) Tilt your right hand so your little finger is higher than your thumb.
b) Tilt your left hand so your thumb is higher than your little finger.

3 Now you've raised your right aileron, your right wing (arm) should lower. And because you've lowered your left aileron, your left wing (arm) should raise. This means you can bank to the right.

4 Now try banking left.

NEEEEEEEEEEE EEEEOOOOWW WWWWWW!

You should find:

You get the hang of the controls quite quickly. Now try running around as you practise banking complete with sound effects. Just don't try it at family mealtimes ... or in posh china shops.

Oh, so now you want your very own plane to practise flying in? Well, here's one that's safer than a Flying Flea and less grisly than a Gee Bee...

Dare you discover … how to build a world-beating plane?

> This plane was inspired by Ralph Barnaby's winning entry in the 1967 Great International Paper Airplane competition.

You will need:
An A4 piece of paper

HORRIBLE HEALTH WARNING
Do NOT use family photos or your little brother's homework for this job. Soggy toilet paper is also STRICTLY banned.

A table (it helps to do the folding on a hard surface).
Scissors (ask your local friendly adult to do the cutting).

What you do:
1 Fold the paper lengthways. Make sure the fold is nice and sharp.
2 Draw this shape and cut it out.
3 Now draw this line using a ruler. Use the ruler to make sure the line joins up with the bottom left corner.
4 Fold along the dotted line as shown.

5 Fold the front edge of the plane up as shown and then fold it twice more, as if you were rolling up a carpet.
6 Fold up the ends of the wings as shown.

7 Throw the plane *gently*. But don't absent-mindedly throw it at your brother or sister, overhead power line, priceless family heirlooms or the dog.

8 Now cut an aileron on each wing, like so...
9 And an elevator on each half of the tail, like so...
10 Try throwing your plane with the controls set in different ways.

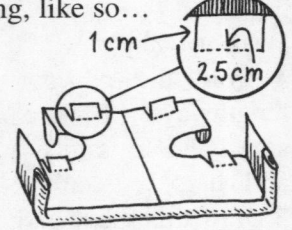

You should find:
The ailerons and elevators work just like the plane Gutzache was flying on page 106. Well, a bit better actually.
Mind you, it doesn't matter how well your plane flies – it's not going anywhere without someone to fly it. Someone brave and fearless who doesn't mind risking their neck. In the early days of flight, pilots had to be barmy or brave to fly at all ... but are you brave enough to read about them?

110

POTTY PIONEER PILOTS

OK, so it was a bad idea to throw a pioneer pilots' party. The wacko wing-nuts are showing off and swinging from the light fittings and doing handstands on the windowsills. But then I guess if you risk your life to fly it helps if you're a little loopy…

> **Bet you never knew!**
> In 1922, star US pilot Jimmy Doolittle did handstands on a windowsill at a party in Chile. He fell, breaking both his ankles – but that didn't stop him putting on an awesome air display a few days later.

Anyway, we've got to make our excuses and dash off for France in 1909, where a pair of fearless fliers are about to race for glory … or death.

TIME FOR A CHANNEL CHASE (AGAIN!)
Inspired by the sight of Wilbur Wright flying with ease, the European flying freaks began to build better planes and set their sights on a new goal. Just as in the early days of ballooning, the race was on to fly the English Channel and win £10,000 from a British newspaper. Here are the front runners – who do you fancy to win?

DATE	Name: LOUIS BLÉRIOT 	Name: HERBERT LATHAM 
1906	I'm a rich car headlamp maker.	I'm a rich thrill-seeker.
1908	I've spent all my money building planes that crash.	I've got a deadly lung disease. I don't mind if I die!
1909	If I don't win the prize, I'll be ruined!	I'm going to fly the Channel - or die!
19 JULY	Wait! I'm not ready yet!	Grr - I tried to fly but I crashed into the sea! 
23 JULY	I've burnt my foot! I can't sleep!	Wake me up at 3.30 am to fly!
24 JULY 3.30 am	Time to go!	ZZZZZZZZ.
4.50 am	OH NO, I'm lost and my engine's overheating! Phew! It's raining. That'll cool it down	Grr - why didn't you wake me up? Now it's too late to catch Blériot!

5.10 am

HURRAH – I've won! I've arrived in England!

Good morning!

GRRRR – I'VE LOST!

Bet you never knew!

1 Blériot was cheered by a crowd as he landed. And then he was questioned by a miserable customs official, who thought he was a smuggler.

2 The future held very different fortunes for our two fearless fliers. Blériot made another fortune as a plane maker – everyone wanted to buy his channel-flying plane, the Blériot XI. *Latham went big-game hunting and got gored to death by a charging buffalo.*

THIS IS ONE CHARGE I CAN'T AFFORD!

The race across the Channel wasn't the only risky race around. In 1911 a US newspaper boss offered $50,000 to the first pilot to fly across the USA in 30 days. Pilot Calbraith Rodgers tried to win the prize, but on the way he suffered...

- 16 crashes.
- Including five really BIG crashes.
- And used enough spare parts to build *four* planes.

His worst crash was just 19 km from the sea. He wrecked his plane, spent weeks in hospital with a broken leg and didn't win the prize. The next year he went back to the area and crashed after smacking into a seagull. Rodgers died and the seagull probably hopped the twig too.

But even without the perils of racing, pilots were crashing and dying in fearsome numbers. In just one year, 1910, 37 pilots were killed in crashes. And that was a fair proportion of all the people who could fly at the time!

FOUR WAYS TO NEARLY KILL YOURSELF IF YOU'RE AN EARLY FLIER

1 The death dive

The Wrights' *Flyer* had a fatal fault, shared with most planes. If you tried to fly upwards with the wings not quite straight, one wing would stall whilst the other wing rose. That meant that one wing was producing more drag and the other had more lift and this difference made the plane roll. The wings couldn't produce lift and the plane plunged from the sky in an uncontrollable spin. Pilots

FAST AIR
CROSS-SECTION OF WING
LIFT
SLOWER AIR
REMINDER OF AEROFOIL DIAGRAM FROM PAGE 15

called it the "death dive".

By 1914 nearly every pilot caught in the death dive had been killed. Then top test pilot Harry Hawker (1889–1921) hit on a plan. If he steepened the dive as the plane fell, he could get the air flowing over the wings in the right way to produce lift and pull out of the killer dive. But the only way Hawker could test his hunch was to try it. He was right. Had he been wrong, it would have been less of a hunch and more of a CRUNCH!

2 Stunt flying

Stunt flying attracts the real winged wackos – folk like Lincoln Beachey, nicknamed "the Flying Fool". His tricks included:

• Flying *under* bridges.
• Flying along a street over the heads of passers-by.
• When a group of people climbed a tree to see one of his shows for free, Lincoln buzzed the tree so they fell out.

All of this was deeply dangerous and luckless Lincoln lost his life in 1915 in front of 50,000 people.

> *Bet you never knew!*
> *In 1910 the Wright brothers set up a flying team to show off their planes, but all but one of the team were killed. The survivor's name was Frank Coffyn.*

3 Wing walking

But there's one sport that makes stunt flying sound as sensible as a pair of boring old lace-up shoes. It was started by potty US pilot Ormer Locklear and to do it you had to walk on the wings of your plane – *while it was in the air*! Or hang from the wheels by your teeth. Or leap to another plane.

Now that's plane crazy, but after the First World War, scores of out-of-work pilots tried it for a living – or dying. And Ormer ended up crashing into a pool of sludgy oil – so he came to a sticky end.

Sorry, readers, you'll have to read this next bit standing on your head. Or you could try flying your plane upside down!

4 Flying upside down
This was pioneered by Russian pilot Petr Nesterov, the first man to loop the loop. The loopy army pilot was rewarded with ten days in prison for risking government property. By the 1930s, upside-down flying was a curious craze and Italian pilot Tito Falconi even flew 420 km from St Louis to Chicago the wrong way up.

Clearly, life for the first pilots was a bit of a gamble and they weren't exactly good risks for life insurance. But at least it was peaceful... In time of war, a pilot's life became even more dangerous...

THE DEADLY DEMANDS OF WAR

What is it with humans? No sooner do they invent something than they want to use it to kill each other. In 1917 Orville Wright said that when he and his brother built the world's first plane...

We thought we were introducing into the world an invention that would make future wars practically impossible...

HOW WRONG THEY WERE! Just look at this...

THE FEARSOME FIGHT FOR FIGHTING FLIGHT

1914–1918 First World War. British, French and American pilots battle with German pilots in the air. The Germans lose because they have fewer planes and pilots.

1939 War breaks out again. The German Air Force rules the skies.

1940 Britain's RAF saves the country from German invasion by shooting down more German planes than it loses.

1940–1942 The Germans bomb British cities instead.

1942–1945 The British and Americans bomb German cities to get back at them.

1942–1945 American and Japanese planes take off from aircraft carriers to fight vast battles across the Pacific. The Americans win.

In the First World War the life of a fighter pilot was exciting and glorious ... and short. In 1915 a British pilot in France could expect to live just 11 days and pilots were sent into battle with just five hours of flying experience. The British, French or American pilots weren't even allowed parachutes because they might try to escape from their plane rather than fight.

Here's a song by the American squadron in France that you might like to sing at school dinners (adding "boy" or "girl" instead of "man").

> So stand by your glasses steady
> The world is a web of lies
> Here's a toast for the dead already
> Hurrah for the next man who dies!

Nearly one in three of the brave American pilots were killed – but hopefully your mouldy mashed potato and cabbage aren't quite so dangerous.

But the story of flight in the twentieth century wasn't all doom and destruction. In the 1920s, trail-blazing pilots opened new air routes. These pilots included famous female fliers such as…

• American Amelia Earhart (1898–1937), the first woman to fly the Atlantic in 1928. She was actually a passenger but she amused herself by trying to drop oranges on the head of the captain of a passing ship.

She missed. Four years later she made the trip on her own.

• Briton Amy Johnson (1903–1941), the first woman to fly on her own from Britain to Australia. She also flew the length of Africa and across Asia and lots of other places.

So would you want to sign up for these pioneering flights? Well, they might prove a hair-raising holiday…

HONEST BOB'S HOLIDAYS PRESENTS...

FABULOUS FLIGHTS TO FARAWAY PLACES...
YOU'LL BE THE FIRST ONE TO DO IT!
HEY, IT'S AN ADVENTURE AND
YOU'LL REMEMBER IT FOR THE
REST OF YOUR LIFE (AND THAT
MAY NOT BE VERY LONG –
OOPS, PRETEND I NEVER SAID THAT!)

FREE CRASH COURSE IN FLYING WITH EVERY HOLIDAY SOLD!

I NEWFOUNDLAND TO IRELAND (1919)

As flown by John Alcock (1892-1919) and Arthur Whitten Brown (1886-1948)

HOPE YOU CAN READ MAPS

HOPE YOU CAN SWIM

● First World War bomber with open cockpit. Lots of lovely fresh freezing air and a hard wooden bench to sit on (it's good for your bum!).

● Experience the first non-stop flight ac ross the Atlantic Ocean. Relive the drama as your radio aerial falls off, so you can't call for help if things go wrong!

- Enjoy lots of exercise as you climb onto the wings to remove ice.
- Free sandwiches.
- All this, plus a thrilling crash landing in an Irish bog!

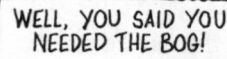

WELL, YOU SAID YOU NEEDED THE BOG!

PLOOP!

2 THE CHUBBIE MILLER AND BILL LANCASTER WORLD TOUR – Britain to Australia (1928)

It's a thrill a minute as you...

- Find a poisonous snake in your plane in Rangoon.
- Crash in Muntok. (Don't worry if you get a couple of black eyes and a smashed plane – hey, it's all part of the fun!)
- Get your very own de–luxe runway built by prisoners so you can take off from a jail at Attambre.
- Nearly crash into the Timor Sea and get eaten by sharks. You can write a farewell letter at this point (free stamp).

I'M CHUBBIE

AND I'M QUITE THIN

THE SMALL PRINT – When you get to Australia no one takes much notice of you because another flyer's already made the trip. And you're not allowed to leave your plane until you've been checked for tropical diseases.

3 THE LINDBERGH SPECIAL
– New York to Paris (1927)

Need a little peace and quiet? Well, here's the flight for you! It's only 33 hours but you do it all on your own!

• Lovely break in Paris when you get there – if you get there.

• Your plane has no radio so you don't have to talk to anyone – even if you want to call for help! (Some pilots end up chatting to themselves.)

FANCY A SANDWICH? THANKS, DON'T MIND IF I DO! WHAT'S IN THEM? FISHPASTE. LOVELY!

THE SMALL PRINT

Just make sure you don't fall asleep – or you'll crash and die. By 1927 five pilots had died trying to make this flight.

Lindbergh kept himself awake by slapping his face, bouncing in his seat and sticking his hands out of the window. And by the time he landed in Paris, he probably needed a good night's snooze. He woke up to find himself a world mega-star. He was so incredibly famous...

• The US Government sent a warship to pick him up.
• He got a gold medal from the US Congress.
• He met Orville Wright.

But Charles was so modest and polite that everyone thought he was the best thing since apple pie AND custard

Lindbergh's famous flight had made flying fab and fashionable like nothing else could. People queued to train as pilots, and passengers queued to fly to the remote parts of the world opened up by pioneer pilots. But what really made passenger flight take off (geddit?) was a new engine that could carry people faster than ever before. Today this engine powers most of the world's passenger planes and we're about to jet off to find out more about it.

Hmm – it's rather noisy. Maybe you'd better put on a pair of these before you read on...

JUMPING JETS

If you've ever flown, the chances are you've flown in a jet plane. This chapter is about how the jet engine was invented and how it changed flying for ever. But first let's check out the basics about this marvellous machine…

Fearsome flight fact file

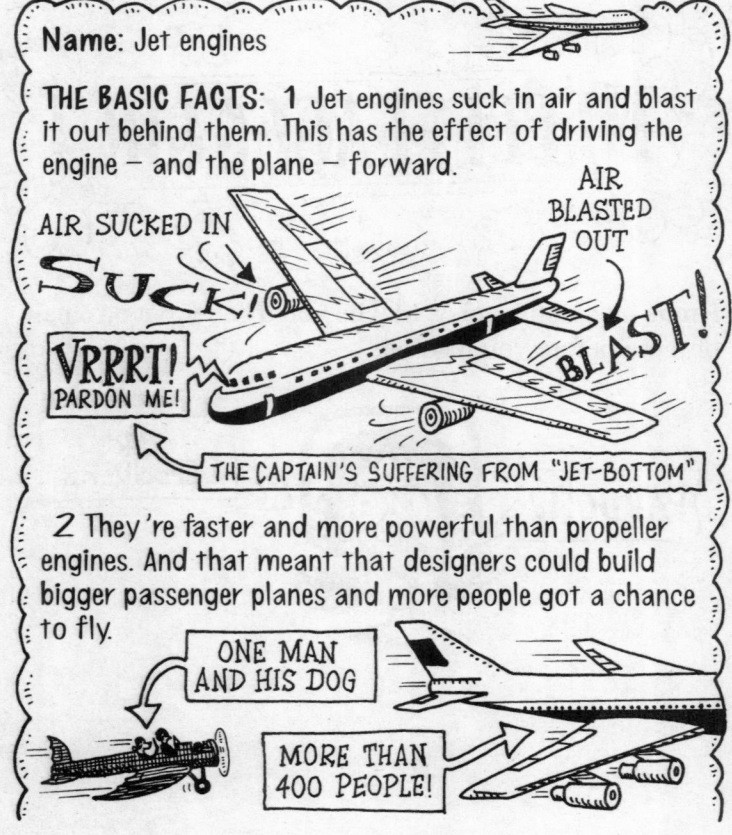

Name: Jet engines

THE BASIC FACTS: 1 Jet engines suck in air and blast it out behind them. This has the effect of driving the engine – and the plane – forward.

AIR SUCKED IN

SUCK!

AIR BLASTED OUT

VRRRT! PARDON ME!

BLAST!

THE CAPTAIN'S SUFFERING FROM "JET-BOTTOM"

2 They're faster and more powerful than propeller engines. And that meant that designers could build bigger passenger planes and more people got a chance to fly.

ONE MAN AND HIS DOG

MORE THAN 400 PEOPLE!

BOOM!

THERE'S GOTTA BE A BETTER WAY...

JET ENGINE

Now, I bet you're wondering who actually came up with the whizzy, wonderful jet engine. Well, as ever in horrible science, the answer is confusingly complicated.

It really is a question to stupefy a scientist...

WHO INVENTED THE JET ENGINE?

TONGUE-TIED SILENCE →

You see, crowds of inventors had the idea and some of them even designed jet engines that *nearly* worked. I bet if they all met up there'd be a fearsome punch-up over who got the glory...

IT WAS ME!

NEVER!

NO WAY!

IT WAS MY IDEA!

RUBBISH!

TOSH!

THE FEARSOME FIGHT FOR JET ENGINES

1st century AD Hero, a Greek scientist from Alexandria in Egypt, invents a device that whizzes round, powered by jets of steam. It's not a jet engine but it works in the same way.

1783 Joseph Montgolfier thinks about letting the air out of a balloon so it will whizz off with a rude sound, like a toy balloon. There wasn't enough air pressure in the balloon for this – worse luck!

1791 Inventor John Barber cooks up an engine powered by burning gas. But it's not powerful enough to be much use and anyway he wants to use it in ships.

1837 Sir George Cayley dreams of an air-powered engine – but he never builds it. Too busy as usual, no doubt.

All these inventors missed out on the jumping jet engine, so let's jet our time machine forward to the 1930s, when two incredible inventors were about to grab a bigger slice of the action…

Bet you never knew!
British inventor Frank Whittle (1907–1996) had the idea for the jet engine while studying at flying college in 1929, but his teacher didn't take his brainwave seriously. So, in 1936, Whittle set up his own company to make the new engine, but the British government didn't take him seriously either. Until the Second World War broke out and a fast jet fighter plane suddenly seemed like a good idea…

The incredible thing was that German inventor Hans von Ohain (1911–1998) was also working on the jet engine. The two inventors knew nothing of each other, so we've let them tell their stories separately.

Frank Whittle's story

DATE

1939 — At last, my government has ordered one plane with my jet engine!

1941 — My plane flies perfectly.

1944 — Hurrah! My jets are fighting the enemy and they're winning.

HOORAY!!

Hans von Ohain's story

At last, my government has ordered two planes with my jet engine!

My two planes fly perfectly.

Grr - my jets are fighting the enemy, but they're dangerous to fly.

ERK!

THE SECRET LIFE OF THE JUMPING JET ENGINE

And now to find out the innermost secrets of how jet engines work – and a vital new word…

FEARSOME EXPRESSIONS

A scientist says…

I'M KEEN ON TURBINES

Do you say…?

YUCK – I HATE THEM IN SOUP!

Answer:
NO, they're turbines not TURNIPS! A turbine is a sort of spinning fan with angled blades. Turbines produce electricity and power boats and they're vital for jet engines.

It so happens that Professor N Large and Wanda Wye have added a couple of jet engines to their plane. And that's handy because it means we'll be able to see the engines in action. Er, we'd better hurry – Gutzache is just taking off…

WHAAAAAA!

ZEOW!

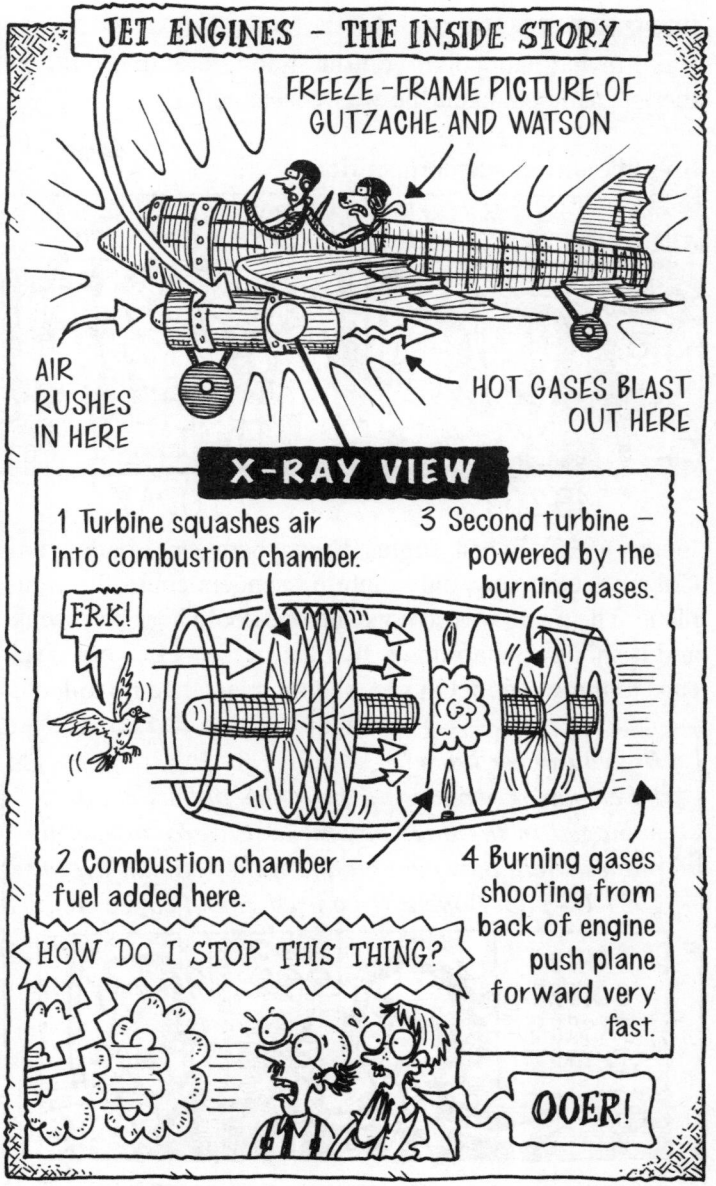

JET ENGINES - THE INSIDE STORY

FREEZE-FRAME PICTURE OF GUTZACHE AND WATSON

AIR RUSHES IN HERE

HOT GASES BLAST OUT HERE

X-RAY VIEW

1 Turbine squashes air into combustion chamber.

ERK!

3 Second turbine – powered by the burning gases.

2 Combustion chamber – fuel added here.

4 Burning gases shooting from back of engine push plane forward very fast.

HOW DO I STOP THIS THING?

OOER!

HORRIBLE HOLIDAYS

Well, if that hadn't put you off flying, let's find out how the jet plane changed the way passengers fly…

Spot the difference competition…

1920s   TODAY

In the 1920s, when flights began between London and Cologne, Germany, only eight passengers could fit on the plane. The plane was so noisy no one could hear you speak, and it shook so alarmingly that the passengers were given cans to throw up in. Oh yes, and the plane had no toilet…

Bet you never knew!
I bet you're wondering how the old-style pilots managed in the days before there were toilets on planes. Well, they held on and if they couldn't… In 1931 US pilot Bobbie Trout used an old coffee can.

By the 1950s, passengers could relax on large jet planes (with toilets) and the jet engine provided a smoother flight. But flying could still be a fearsome experience. You had to be *really brave* to fly in some early jets…

COULD YOU BE A SCIENTIST?

In 1954, Britain's new Comet jets had an annoying habit of falling to bits in the air and crashing.

1 How did scientists find the cause of the crashes?

a) They built a new plane and flew in it.

b) They put the plane in a giant pool and pumped it full of water.

c) They let a bad-tempered elephant wreck the plane and inspected the damage very carefully.

2 What proved to be the problem?

a) The wings were only glued on.

b) The plane was rusty.

c) The square windows had cracked at the corners.

Answers:

1 b) The sides of the plane were too thin. Jet planes fly fastest at heights where the air is thin and causes less drag. But that means air has to be pumped into the cabin so the passengers won't gasp and black out for lack of air to breathe.

… BUT DON'T PUMP TOO MUCH!

THE PASSENGERS ARE COMPLAINING THAT THERE'S TOO MUCH ROOM, CAPTAIN

The changes in air pressure weakened the plane and the scientists found this out by increasing the pressure of the water on the plane.

2 c) And the weakest point was the corner of the windows.

> *Bet you never knew!*
> *Modern jets are far stronger. For example, the sides of a jumbo jet are 19 cm thick and the windows are toughened glass as thick as your fist.*

TEACHER'S TEA-BREAK TEASER

Tap lightly on the staffroom door. When your teacher appears, smile sweetly and ask them…

WHAT'S THE DIFFERENCE BETWEEN A BOEING 747 AND A JUMBO JET?

HUH?

Your teacher will crossly inform you that a Boeing 747 *is* a jumbo jet. This is true – jumbo jet is a nickname for the plane – but you can say…

ONE IS A PLANE AND THE OTHER IS WHAT HAPPENS WHEN YOU GET SQUIRTED BY AN ELEPHANT!

SPLOOSH!

By the 1970s flying was an everyday event – in 1977 nearly two-thirds of Americans had flown … in the previous year! And air travel has continued to grow. Today, jets fly millions of passengers all over the world. And there's even a choice of jet engines…

• Ordinary plain old turbo-jet engines, like the ones on Gutzache's plane.

• Turbo-fan engines, used in large jets. A fan draws air into the engine and wafts some air round the combustion chamber to keep it cool.

• Turbo-prop or prop-fan engines, which combine turbines with propellers.

Bet you never knew!

Some jet engines can be turned downwards to make a plane hover in mid-air! They're used on the Harrier jump-jet fighter. When the engines were tested in the 1950s, engineers built a thingie known

as the "flying bedstead" that hovered in mid-air. In 1957 it killed a test pilot. Fancy a snooze on a flying bedstead?

IT SOUNDS MORE LIKE A NIGHTMARE!

And by the 1970s there was another type of plane to fly in. A plane that travelled faster than your VOICE and made the jumbo jet look like a slug with a wooden leg. Yes, this next bit is sure to take the words out of your mouth…

Fearsome flight fact file

NAME: Supersonic jets

THE BASIC FACTS: 1 Imagine your teacher telling you to go home early. The sound of her voice actually reaches your ears at 1,235 km per hour. And that's only slightly slower than the class leaving the classroom.

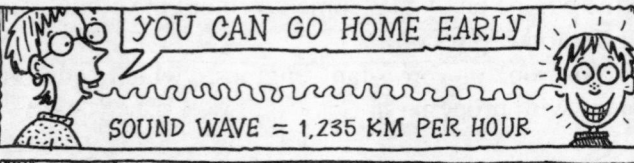

YOU CAN GO HOME EARLY

SOUND WAVE = 1,235 KM PER HOUR

DESK   WHOOSH!   DOOR

CLASS LEAVING = 1,236 KM PER HOUR

2 Jets that fly faster than sound travel faster than the air can get out of the way. The air builds up in front of the plane like a wall – it's called the sound barrier. Once through this wall, the flight is smoother.

STAND BY FOR A BIG BANG...

YOU MEAN, THE SONIC BOOM AS WE BREAK THE SOUND BARRIER?

NO, THE LOUD BOOM WHEN WE HIT THAT MOUNTAIN

3 Supersonic planes are streamlined to reduce drag. They have swept-back, "delta-shaped" wings so the wing hits the sound barrier at an angle rather than straight on. This makes the ride less bumpy.

THE FEARSOME DETAILS: In 1946 British pilot Geoffrey de Havilland Jr died trying to break the sound barrier. Sadly it broke his plane to bits. The first pilot to do the feat was US pilot Chuck Yeager in 1947.

G de Havilland

Chuck Yeager

Watch the birdie!
5 Birds that fly fast

WE HAWKS HAVE WINGS SHAPED LIKE A JET.

ITS SHAPE GIVES ME LIFT WITHOUT TOO MUCH DRAG...

LIKE SOME JETS, I CAN FOLD MY WINGS BACK FOR A MORE STREAMLINED SHAPE.

SWEPT-BACK WING

POINTED SHAPE

THEN I DIVE AT 180 KM PER HOUR. OK, SO IT'S NOT AS FAST AS A JET...

ERK! BUT IT'S FAST ENOUGH TO CATCH ME!

But you could interest your parents in a vintage classic plane from the 1970s. Concorde was a supersonic passenger jet developed in Britain and France, and it so happens that Honest Bob's got one for sale...

HONEST BOB'S PLANE PRODUCTS PRESENTS...

CONCORDE They don't make Concordes like they used to. Well, they don't make them at all! But just look what you get for your £50,999,999 (bring the money in a suitcase and don't ask awkward questions).
Top speed = 2,333 km per hour.
Gold-plated windows cut down on harmful rays from the sun.

PARACHUTE TO SLOW IT DOWN FOR LANDING

NOSE DROOPS ON TAKEOFF AND LANDING SO THE PILOTS CAN SEE WHERE THEY'RE GOING

MY NOSE ISN'T DROOPY!

NO TAIL PLANE

ELEVONS = COMBINED AILERONS AND ELEVATORS

THE VITAL FACTS THAT SOMEHOW SLIPPED BOB'S MIND

1 Concorde was so noisy that it was banned from flying over many countries.

2 In a bid to make the plane quieter, it flew at 800 km per hour over land. But then it used fuel eight times more quickly than a normal jet plane.

A FANTASTIC FUTURE IN THE AIR?

So what do the next 50 years hold for the future of flight? Er, well, I'd love to give you the lowdown on tomorrow's high-flyers, but sadly I can't. My crystal ball is cracked and my tea leaves have dribbled down the sink… And anyway, the fight for flight is full of obscure inventors who suddenly pop up with machines that no one believed possible.

But we can take a look at some cutting-edge, state-of-the-art aircraft that might just become more common in years to come. They're built from new materials called composites (com-po-sits). These substances are made up of two different materials such as carbon and kevlar, and they're very light and strong. So they're a plane-designer's dream…

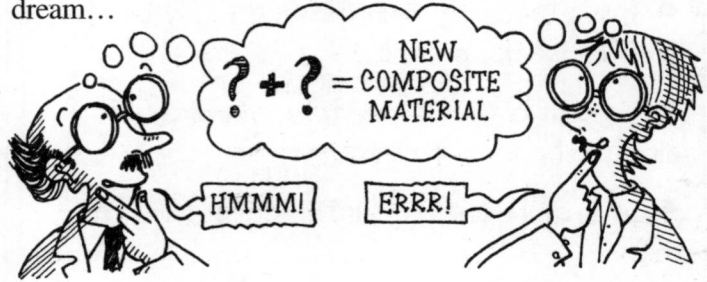

Honest Bob is selling the planes, but he's just bumped his head and now he's a changed man… He's actually become honest!

137

EVEN-MORE HONEST BOB'S PLANE PRODUCTS PRESENTS...

"Bob telling the truth? It ain't natural!" Bob's mum

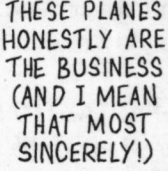

THESE PLANES HONESTLY ARE THE BUSINESS (AND I MEAN THAT MOST SINCERELY!)

1 THE HELIOS SOLAR-POWERED PLANE

GULP! WHAT HAPPENS WHEN THE SUN GOES IN?

- Stays up on its own, powered only by the sun for weeks on end.

- It's got lots of solar cells to make electricity from sunlight.

- Lots of engines – just in case some fall off.

- 76–metre wingspan for maximum lift.

Price: To be honest, I think it's a bit more than you can afford.

138

2 THE GLOBAL HAWK

If you're into radio planes, this is the machine for you!

TEATIME!

HANG ON, MUM. I'M FLYING OVER RUSSIA

- You can fly it from your computer on the other side of the world.
- Super-sensitive spy cameras can spot your teacher's underpants on the washing line from 74 km away. It's your very own spy in the sky!
- As used by the US military.
- It's even got a self-destruct programme.

Price: I'll do you the cheapest price I can — but it's still a bit steep!

3 THE GOSSAMER ALBATROSS PEDAL-POWERED PLANE

CHOMP! MUNCH! HMM, NICE CHOC!

- Lovely pedal-powered plane made of plastic and piano wire.

HE'S FILLING HIS ENGINE WITH FUEL

- 30-metre wing span for maximum lift.
- Three-metre propeller powered by your pedals.
- Guaranteed not to fly more than a few metres in the air, so you won't get hurt if it crashes.

Price: Unlike the plane ... it's too high!

Yes, at last humans had achieved the ultimate dream of muscle-powered flight. But hold on ... a human flying from Crete? Isn't that how the fateful fight for flight began?

THANKS FOR REMINDING ME!

EPILOGUE: FATEFUL FLIGHT

As Jacques Charles lifted off in his hydrogen balloon in 1785, wise old American scientist Benjamin Franklin (1706–1790) was among the crowd. A man next to him asked, "What's the use of it?"
Franklin replied…

No, silly! Franklin didn't mean that flying would only be good for eating, dribbling, crying and other unmentionable baby behaviour. He meant that, like a baby, flight was the start of something new and exciting. Something that would grow and grow. And boy was he right!

Flying has proved to be the biggest success story in the history of the world. It's changed the lives of countless millions of people in an incredibly short time…

• The first engine-powered plane flight happened in 1903. Just 44 years later, humans were flying faster than sound. It all happened inside a human lifetime.

• Just five people saw the *Flyer's* first flight. There was no airfield except a pair of rails that cost $5.

• Today there are airports all over the planet and the biggest ones, such as King Khalid Airport in Saudi Arabia, are larger than small countries. (It's four times bigger than the entire island of Bermuda.)

• The *Flyer* flew no higher than a budgie and no faster than a racing bicycle.

• Today's fastest planes can zoom 16 km in the air at the speed of a rifle bullet. In 2004 US scientists tested a robot plane than could fly at *seven times* the speed of sound.

• The Flyer weighed no more than 338 kg including its pilot. By 2009 a fully-laden A320 European airbus could carry 1,900 times more weight including 900 passengers.

• In 1903 most letters were carried on carts pulled by wheezy old horses. Today a letter can sent anywhere on Earth and arrive in days by air. And where letters go, so can people.

PLANES ... THE GOOD NEWS

1 Flying has helped millions of people visit new parts of the world and make new friends in other countries.

2 Flying has brought food and medicines to hungry and sick people in disaster areas.

3 Scientists have gained the chance to study pollution and rocks and mountains and wild animals from the air. In terms of what flying can do, the sky really is the limit and yet … and yet.

PLANES … THE FEARSOME NEWS

1 As more and more people fly, airports are getting overcrowded.

2 There's more noise and more pollution and more danger of planes bashing into each other as they wait to land.

3 Planes have killed thousands of people by bombing.

4 People have paid a fearsome price for flight and I'm not talking about the sizeable sums your parents cough up for air tickets. Experts reckon that even before the *Flyer's* first flight, 200 people were killed trying to fly with wacko wings, barmy balloons and grisly gliders.

So was the fight for flight worthwhile? Was it worth all the tears and terror? What do you think? One thing's for sure – it had to happen. After all, it's in our nature to follow our dreams and reach for the skies. Happy horrible flying everyone!

THE FIGHT for FLIGHT

QUIZ

Now find out if you're a
Fight for Flight expert!

YIPPEE, I'M FLYING!

OK – it's time to put that sick bag down. You've no doubt marvelled at those marvellous men in their flying machines and groaned at the hapless no-hopers who've plummeted straight out of the skies. But when it comes to the facts, are you cruising through the clouds or heading for a crash? It's test time!

Death-defying flying facts

As many pea-brained souls have discovered, there's a lot more to keeping a craft in the air than strapping a couple of huge engines to it and throwing it off the nearest cliff. Have a bash at these brain-busting questions to see if you've grasped the basics...

1 In 1973, a plane splatted into a bird soaring at over 11,300 metres. What sort of feathered friend was it? (CLUE: They're usually found on the ground, feasting on dead animals)

2 You'll remember Mr Gutzache – he chucked up his lunch while looping the loop. But what's the name of the force that sent his sick hurtling towards the ground? (CLUE: It's the same grave glue that keeps you stuck to the ground)

3 Every plane in the world stays up thanks to 1,000s of tiny, invisible clumps of atoms in the air. What are they called? (CLUE: Think of moles that are cool and you're nearly there!)

4 What's the fantastic force that slows a plane down as it flies? (CLUE: Dragons aren't affected by it)

5 Boomerangs fly through the air with ease – but what else did native Australians use them for? (CLUE: Their sharp edges came in handy)

6 How did the crafty King Kai Kaoos of Persia rig up his throne to fly? (CLUE: Eagle-eyed readers will get this one right!)

7 Frisbees glide thanks to a difference in what kind of force? (CLUE: No pressure – take as long as you like!)

8 What enormous entity weighs over five million billion billion tonnes? (CLUE: You can't even see it)

Answers:
1 A vulture
2 Gravity
3 Molecules
4 Drag
5 Cutting up animals
6 He tethered eagles to each corner
7 Air pressure
8 All the air covering the planet

YIPPEE, I'M FLYING!

Big-brained bird men and plunging parachutes

How would you fare if you tried to fly with the birds by building a human-powered flying machine? Would you reach their lofty heights? Or would you come down to earth with a bum-numbing bump?

IT'S MR SNODGRASS, THE SCIENCE TEACHER!

1 Oliver of Malmesbury broke his legs in 1029 when he threw himself off the top of Malmesbury Abbey. Why did he think his bird suit had failed?

a) It was lacking a feathered tail.

b) It was made of cheese.

c) He'd neglected to strap it on properly.

2 How did Giovanni Battista Danti celebrate gliding over a lake unhurt in 1503?

a) He tried, unsuccessfully, to fly into space.

b) He jumped off Perugia Cathedral – and crashed at the bottom.

c) He went to live with monkeys, and became King of the Apes.

3 In 1742, the Marquis de Bacqueville tried unsuccessfully to soar across the River Seine in Paris, but what did he crash into?

a) A washerwoman's dirty old barge.

b) A passing penguin on his holidays.

c) The Eiffel Tower.

4 How does the tail on a kite aid flight?

a) It gives the kite more lift.

b) It helps the person flying it concentrate.

c) It keeps the kite steady.

5 The crafty Chinese army invented man-carrying kites over 2,000 years ago. What did they use them for?

a) To drop stink bombs on their enemies.

b) To spy on their enemies.

c) To see what the weather was going to be like.

6 Which of the following artists was involved in the invention of the parachute?

a) Jackson Pollock.

b) Horrible Science super-scribbler Tony de Saulles.

c) Leonardo da Vinci.

7 In 1781, Jean Pierre Blanchard invented a rather peculiar flying machine. What special feature made it unique?

a) It had an on-board musician to play soothing music.

b) Every passenger was given a dog to keep their feet warm.

c) A bungee jump.

8 Joseph Montgolfier tested an early version of the parachute by lobbing a creature from a tower. What was it?

a) A frightened ferret.

b) A petrified porcupine.

c) A seriously-scared sheep.

Potty pioneers

Don't ask how we did it, but we've managed to grab hold of the ghosts of a few famous inventors to ask them to talk about the fabulous flying machines that they dreamed up. That was the hard bit. The easy bit is to put a name to their creations – and that's where you come in!

1 It was the hot sparks rising up my chimney that first gave me the idea of harnessing the lifting power of hot gases. My silk creation worked like a dream and King Louis XVI of France gave me the funds to develop it still further.

2 During my lifetime (1825–82), I was lucky enough to have the wondrous notion of adding a small engine to a cigar-shaped balloon. It didn't work – the engine was way too weak and it blew my craft backwards. Ah well!

3 Good day. My name is Otto Lilienthal and, together with my chum Percy Pilcher, I managed to construct a plane-shaped craft without an engine. How did it fly? It glided on rising columns of hot air called thermals.

4 I am Wilbur Wright, and my brother Orville and I went one step further than those who just glided through the ether. Our historic plan was to add an engine to the craft – the result changed the world!

5 I, Count Gianni Caprioni de Taliedo, took the Wright brothers' magnificent machine and stuck skis underneath it in 1921. By doing that, my nine-winged craft could take off and land on water.

6 People may say that Leonardo da Vinci, the ancient Chinese, or even Thomas Edison invented my aircraft, but I was the first to add a spinning rotor to the top that actually worked – clever old me!

7 Don't let anyone tell you different – it was me, Frank Whittle, who first had the idea of building a super-swift plane powered by an engine that sucks in air at the front, squeezes it, burns it with fuel and forces it out the back very fast indeed.

8 I am one of a team of French engineers who, together with our English friends, created what they say is the most beautiful plane in flight history. Slick, sleek and supersonic, it even had a nose that would droop on takeoff and landing.

Answers:
1 Hot air balloon
2 Airship

3 Glider
4 First powered aeroplane
5 Seaplane
6 Helicopter
7 Jet plane
8 Concorde

Plain crazy planes

Below are the notes taken by air ace Baron Von Lipquiver during his first flying lessons. But some of the words are obscured – can you fill in the gaps?

If I'm to prevent myself from hurtling to the ground and ending up as dog meat, there are a few basic controls I need to master – quickly! The 1)_____, located on the back of the plane, steers it from left to right and is controlled by the 2)_____ pedals.

My height – not my height, the height of the plane – is shown on the 3)_____ and the 4)_____ shows my speed, which I control with the 5)_____. The 6)_____ column, however, moves the airlerons and elevators – though I'm not quite sure what they do yet!

When I'm coming into land, 7)_____ on the wings will slow me right down and I mustn't forget to use my 8)_____ to bring me to a final, shuddering stop!

a) Altimeter
b) Throttle
c) Brakes
d) Rudder
e) Flaps
f) Speedometer
g) Control
h) Foot

I'M NOT REPEATING THE **BLOOMER** I MADE ON MY LAST FLIGHT!

BLOOMERS

Answers:
1d; 2h; 3a; 4f; 5b; 6g; 7e; 8c

Jumping jets fact or fiction

Jet planes have been screaming across our skies since the 1950s, taking us to far-flung destinations in double-quick time (and making many of us throw up in the process). But which of the following facts are true of these goliaths of the air, and which are jet-powered lies?

1 Jet engines are tested by firing dead birds into them with a special cannon.
2 Back in the 1920s, the planes were so unsafe that passengers had to put on parachutes before taking to the skies.
3 Some jet engines can be fixed to aircraft to make them hover in mid-air, like helicopters.

4 The sonic boom is the sound made by flushing toilets on jet planes.

5 Concorde was so fast that it was fitted with a parachute to slow it down.

6 The glass in the windows of modern jumbo jets is as thick as your fist.

7 The world's biggest jumbo jet can carry over 1,000 passengers.

8 Jet planes have to be pumped full of air to prevent the passengers from suffocating.

Answers:

1 TRUE. Birds can cause awful accidents by flying into jet engines.

2 FALSE. The flights were so shaky that passengers were given cans to vomit in, though.

3 TRUE. A military plane called a harrier jump jet does just that.

4 FALSE. The sonic boom is the noise created when the plane crosses the sound barrier.

5 TRUE.

6 TRUE. It's a good idea not to try and an open one of those windows though.

7 FALSE. Not quite – an A380 can carry upwards of 500 passengers.

8 TRUE. The air is too thin to breathe at the dizzy heights these jumbos reach.

HORRIBLE INDEX

HORRIBLE SCIENCE

EVOLVE OR DIE

PHIL GATES

illustrated by
TONY DE SAULLES

SCHOLASTIC

Visit Tony De Saulles at
www.tonydesaulles.co.uk

Scholastic Children's Books,
Euston House, 24 Eversholt Street,
London, NW1 1DB, UK

A division of Scholastic Ltd
London ~ New York ~ Toronto ~ Sydney ~ Auckland
Mexico City ~ New Delhi ~ Hong Kong

First published in the UK by Scholastic Ltd, 1999
This edition published 2008

Text copyright © Phil Gates, 1999
Illustrations copyright © Tony De Saulles, 1999

ISBN 978 1407 10535 2

Printed and bound by CPI Group (UK) Ltd, Croydon, CR0 4YY

25

The right of Phil Gates and Tony De Saulles to be identified as the author and
illustrator of this work respectively has been asserted by them in accordance
with the Copyright, Designs and Patents Act, 1988.

CONTENTS

HAVEN'T SEEN YOU FOR AGES. WHAT HAVE YOU BEEN UP TO?

NOT MUCH REALLY... JUST EVOLVING

Phil Gates is an extraordinary man. Not only is he a successful writer and respected scientist, he has won several awards for his sculptures made from wet tissues. His hobbies include standing in rock pools in the freezing cold and playing snooker. He hopes to win a game before his next birthday.

Other books written by Phil include *Interview with a Dinosaur, Molluscs! Are they really boring?* and *A Mosquito called Fred.*

Tony De Saulles picked up his crayons when he was still in nappies and has been doodling ever since. He takes Horrible Science very seriously and even agreed to sketch *Megachasma pelagious* – the sixth largest shark in the world. Fortunately, he has made a full recovery.

When he's not out with his sketchpad, Tony likes to write poetry and play squash, though he hasn't written any poetry about squash yet.

INTRODUCTION

Biology lessons can be totally mind-boggling. So many amazing creatures to consider. So many tongue-twisting names to remember. It's utterly unfair of teachers to expect us to learn all the jaw-breaking scientific jargon that they insist on using to describe the simplest things.

But there's a much better way to learn about biology, if teachers would only use it. All they need to do is to stop ranting about so many sickening scientific facts, and turn it all into a story. So instead of beginning a lesson by saying "Today we're going to learn about the chemical reactions in chloroplasts" – which sends any self-respecting class into a deep sleep almost instantly – they ought to start with the words, "Once upon a time..." That would work wonders for turning their pupils into better biologists. Everyone likes a good story, so the whole class would hang on to their every word.

The thing that biology teachers need to remember is that life is a story. Life had an incredible beginning when the first creatures crept around on the ocean floor, 3,500 million years ago. Since then it's been through some terrible times. Sometimes it's been almost wiped out completely by awesome accidents. Sometimes it's tried out unbelievable experiments, producing crazy creatures like Hallucigenia (see page 98).

There's a name for the story of life on Earth. It's called evolution. It's a story that's been going on now for 3,500 million years, and no one has any idea when it will end.

Evolution is an epic adventure, on a scale that even Hollywood film directors could never contemplate. It's got disasters, surprises, villains, heroes, horror – and even sometimes a happy ending or two along the way.

Evolution is simply amazing. It's incredible. So here's the full story. Read it, and biology lessons will never be quite the same again.

A HIGH-SPEED HISTORY OF LIFE ON EARTH

Earth can be a horribly hostile habitat sometimes. Since life first appeared here, our planet's weather has often been appalling. It's been sizzling hot and dry as dust, teeth-chatteringly cold and covered in ice, or dismally wet and waterlogged – sometimes for millions of years at a time. And at one time or another our planet has been surrounded by poisonous gases, bombarded by asteroids from outer space and showered with invisible (but deadly) ultraviolet rays.

But somehow life has struggled through. It's done it by evolving – by constantly changing, a little bit at a time. Lucky life forms, that just happened to be born with the best body bits for living in horribly hostile environments, thrived, bred and produced descendants that are well adapted for survival too. The unluckier life forms, that weren't so well equipped, died out.

This is what scientists call evolution. It's a bit like fashion. You've got to move with the times, or – as scientists say – you've got to evolve.

But fashion changes every few months. Evolution is horribly slow. It can take millions of years for something interesting – like an extra set of legs, or a pair of wings – to evolve.

Evolutionary time is even longer than an average school lesson, so let's speed it up a bit. Here's a lightning-fast history of life on Earth. Hold tight – over the next few pages we'll be whizzing along at over 150 million years per second.

Millions of years ago

4,500
Earth formed from the remains of exploding star. Everything horribly hot. Volcanoes everywhere. No water. No air. No life.

4,000
Planet cooling down. Water forms. It rains. That makes a change!

3,500
Atmosphere smells like a gigantic fart – it's full of sulphurous gases. An evil-smelling chemical cocktail in the oceans reacts to build an amazing molecule called deoxyribonucleic acid (dee-oxy-ry-bow-nuk-lay-ik acid) – but you can call it DNA.[1]

1 Molecules, by the way, are made when simple chemicals combine to make more complicated ones. The DNA molecule is inside all living things and can make copies of itself (see page 52).

3,000

Conditions on the planet keep changing, so DNA molecules must keep evolving to survive in hostile habitats. Some devious DNA slips into a tough survival suit and becomes the first nasty bacterium. These bugs breed until they cover every surface in a layer of slime. They feed on sulphur, so the atmosphere soon smells like the inside of a pair of your old trainers on a hot day.

DNA MOLECULE

2,000

All this activity needs energy. Some bacteria turn green, because they're crammed full of a chemical called chlorophyll, which can trap energy from the sun. Instead of developing a suntan, these bacteria use the sun's rays to turn water and carbon dioxide into sugars for their food. This means that they give off oxygen, which poisons most of the other sulphur-feeding bacteria. They retreat into deep oceans and down into stinking muds, where they still survive today.

1,000

At last! After 3,500 million years of evolution, something that looks like an animal. Primitive worms crawl around under water.

570

Suddenly evolution goes mad. Hordes of weird wildlife evolve. Then some of it dies out again. That's evolution for you: two steps forward, one step back. Luckily some life survives, so evolution doesn't have to start again from the very beginning.

500

 Make way for the terrible trilobites, which look like underwater woodlice but grow up to 50 times larger.

440

Plants invade the land, which slowly goes green. Seas full of savage, three-metre-long sea scorpions called Eurypterids (you-rip-ter-rids). The first fish with jaws evolve (until now, all they could do was give you a nasty suck). Some fish evolve legs and begin to crawl on to land.

410

The sea is seething with an amazing variety of fish species – an angler's paradise. Life on land gets noisy, because croaking amphibians (distant relatives of frogs and newts) are everywhere. Not a good time to go collecting tadpoles, though – some of the amphibians are as big as crocodiles. Life takes off when the first flying insects evolve.

365

Atmosphere like a steamy bathroom. Plants just love this warmth and wetness. Swampy forests of giant ferns, hiding demon dragonflies (as big as birds), monstrous millipedes and the first reptiles.

290

Phew, wot a scorcher! It's getting hotter and drier now. Revolting reptiles begin to take over from artful amphibians. After 210 million years of trundling around on the seabed, the trilobites' luck runs out – it's extinction for them, because sea levels drop and the edges of their ocean habitat dry out.

230

Those cute little reptiles that first put in an appearance 135 million years ago are bigger and fiercer now. Yes, that's right – they've evolved into dinosaurs. Evolution invents dinosaurs for every purpose. Giant herbivores like Brachiosaurus, that could eat a whole tree for breakfast; vicious Velociraptors that hunted in packs; terrible Tyrannosaurus Rex, the largest predator of them all. Rapacious reptiles also ruled most in the air and sea. Pterosaurs soared overhead, while Ichthyosaurs and giant turtles cruised the oceans. No, this wasn't a good time to be small and edible.

210

Flowers flourish. All sorts of insects evolve, in horrible hordes. Small furry animals called mammals appear. They're smart and nimble. They need to be, or they'll be trampled by dinosaurs.

140

Birds evolve from small running dinosaurs. Oceans full of awesome ammonites, which look like octopuses wrapped up in a flat curly shell.

65

Whoops! Dinosaurs become extinct. Once the dinosaurs have gone, the smarter furry mammals turn nasty – now they're Planet Earth's most deadly predators.

2

Horrible humans evolve. Regular Ice Ages make their teeth chatter. Mammoths become very hairy to keep warm, but they still die out. Did human hunters turn them all into fur coats and mammoth burgers?

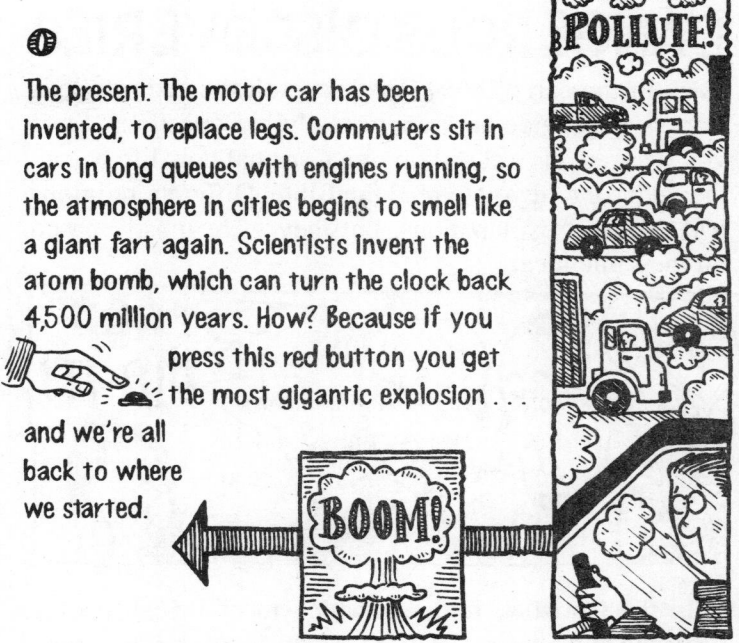

The present. The motor car has been invented, to replace legs. Commuters sit in cars in long queues with engines running, so the atmosphere in cities begins to smell like a giant fart again. Scientists invent the atom bomb, which can turn the clock back 4,500 million years. How? Because if you press this red button you get the most gigantic explosion . . . and we're all back to where we started.

BOOM!

POLLUTE!

Still with me? Good. Keep up.

So here we are today. Human beings: masters of Planet Earth.

How did we get here?

Where did we come from?

What happened over the last 4,500 million years to turn a lifeless, fiery planet into a green and watery home for millions of animal and plant species?

Big questions.

Scientists can answer some of them, but it takes quite a while. So stock up on some crisps, sweets and fizzy drinks to give yourself stamina, make yourself comfortable and get ready for the answers to some horribly hard scientific questions.

DANGEROUS DISCOVERIES

Back in the early 1800s most people expected religious leaders to provide answers to really big questions. So if you'd asked an Archbishop or a Cardinal how life began, they'd have told you to read the Bible. Different religions had different explanations, but they were mostly based on the same idea:

In the Christian religion, which most British people followed at the time, God created Heaven and Earth, then filled Earth with all the living things. It's all there in the Bible, in Genesis Chapter One.

You should read it – it's a horribly good story. If you do, you'll see that people were a bit of an afterthought, made on the sixth and last day of Creation.

That must have been a busy week. One clergyman even went to the trouble of working out exactly when it happened…

Bet you never knew!

In 1620, Archbishop Ussher worked out when the world began. He did it by carefully reading through the Bible and adding up the ages of all the characters in its pages. Right back to the first humans – Adam and Eve – in Genesis Chapter One. He calculated that God created Adam and Eve at 9 am on Sunday 23 October 4004 BC.

Today, modern scientific tests prove that our planet was created after the explosion of a star, about 4,500 million years ago. The Earth is nearly a million times older than Bishop Ussher's estimate. And a lot can happen in 4,500 million years!

NEW IDEAS COME FLOODING IN…

Bishops found that geologists – scientists who study rocks – were terrible troublemakers. They'd been digging up fossils of ancient animals, buried in rock. Some were hideously different from any creature that anyone had ever seen before.

And funnily enough, amongst the fossils of these ugly beasts there wasn't a sign of a human skeleton to be found. Not even the half-chewed bits of an unfortunate human that the beasts had eaten for breakfast. It began to look as though humans were newcomers on Earth, arriving after almost everything else was already here.

Even before Darwin (see page 19) thought of the idea, there were a few scientists who had already begun to suspect that everything alive had evolved from extinct ancestors. But most were far too scared to say so. A few brave scientists did speak out, but people were usually shocked by what they had to say. And clergymen still had some explanations up their sleeve.

Then how come, when you dig down through layers of rock, you find dozens of layers of dead animals? They all became extinct at different times. Does that mean there were lots of floods and lots of Noah's Arks?

Ha-ha, no! It's God's little joke. He put them there to confuse you.

It looks like evolution to me. Newer rocks at the surface have different fossils than the older rocks lower down. Animals that were fossilized recently must have evolved from older ones.

Prove it!

If living things really did evolve, scientists would have to come up with a convincing theory to explain how they did it. Across the English Channel, one flamboyant Frenchman thought he had the answer…

Hall of fame: Jean Baptiste Pierre Antoine de Monet, Chevalier de Lamarck (1744–1829)
Nationality: French

Lamarck – as he used to call himself, in case he fell asleep before he got to the end of his name – was a distinguished soldier who decided to put down his sword, pick up a dissecting knife and become a zoologist. After exploring the innards of all sorts of animals Lamarck came up with a shocking theory of evolution, that went something like this...

If an animal has to do the same task over and over again, its body gradually changes to make the task easier. So if a deer reaches higher and higher into trees for food, day after day, its neck will gradually stretch as it gets older.

If a deer's neck grows longer during its lifetime, all its babies will be born with long necks too. In this way, long-necked giraffes could have eventually evolved from short-necked deer that had to stretch to reach food.

When you think about it, this is a daft idea. It would mean that all Olympic athletes who trained hard and ended up with strong, muscular bodies would have children that could be Olympic athletes without bothering to practise as much.

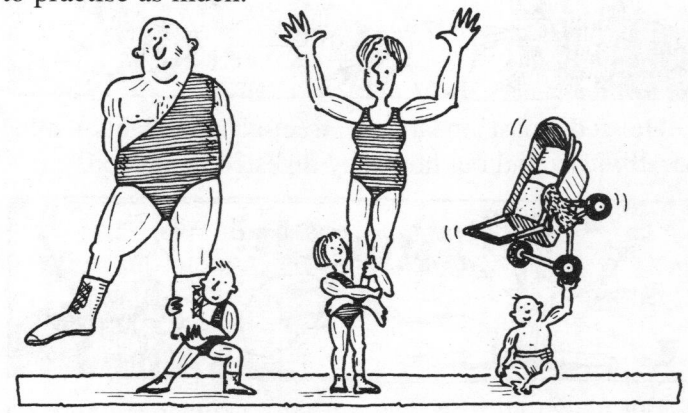

Most scientists didn't think much of Lamarck's ideas either. They laughed at him. But at least he had a theory that tried to explain the way that living things evolved, even if it was wrong. By doing that, he encouraged another great scientist to search for the right one. Enter...

Hall of fame: Charles Darwin (1809–1882)
Nationality: British

Charles Darwin was one of the greatest scientists who ever lived. He was the grandson of Josiah Wedgwood – a world-famous pottery manufacturer – and married his cousin, Emma Wedgwood.

So pottery ran in the family, and some say that Charles was a bit of a crackpot himself. His curiosity made him do strange things...

He played musical instruments to worms to see if they could hear different sounds.

He fed roast meat to insect-eating plants called sundews, to find out how they digested their food.

But above all else, Darwin is remembered today for discovering how evolution really works.

TEST YOUR TEACHER ON THESE DARWINIAN DETAILS

Ask them to guess which of these are true or false.

1 Which of these books did Darwin write?

a) *The Origin of Species*

b) *The Lost World*

c) *Evolve or Die*

2 Darwin's favourite plant was…

a) the meat-eating Venus's fly-trap

b) squirting cucumbers

c) caulifower

3 Darwin was the world's leading expert on…

a) barnacles

b) fleas

c) monkeys

4 One day, when he was out collecting beetles, he saw one that he wanted, but he already had one in each hand. Did he...

a) put them under his hat and grab it?

b) put one of the beetles in his mouth, leaving one hand free to grab it?

c) stomp on it with his welly?

5 Which of the following is named after Darwin:

a) A city in Australia?

b) A frog that keeps its babies in its mouth?

c) A sweet-scented plant that's used to make perfume?

Answers: 1 a) is true, **b)** and **c)** are false. He also wrote loads of other books, on coral reefs, climbing plants, orchids, earthworms and chickens, pigeons and other domestic animals. **2 a)** is true, **b)** and **c)** are false. He called Venus's fly-trap "the most wonderful plant in the world", because its leaves are like jaws that snap shut and catch flies that land on them. **3 a)** is true, **b)** and **c)** are false. If you needed to know anything about barnacles, Darwin was the bloke to ask. Until he took a detailed look at barnacles, people believed that they were close relatives of snails. He proved that their closest relatives were really crabs. **4 b)** is true, **a)** and **c)** are false. The beetle that he put in his mouth was a bombardier beetle, that squirted a hot liquid out of its bum and burnt his tongue, so he had to spit it out. **5** They're all named after Darwin. Baby Darwin frogs jump into their mum's mouth when there's danger about.

Charles wasn't much good at passing exams at college. He preferred to spend his time studying beetles and other creepy-crawlies. When he left university he signed up as a ship's naturalist on a five-year voyage around the world, where his knowledge of natural history might be useful.

DARWIN'S DANGEROUS IDEA

Darwin was just 22 years old when he set off on his voyage around the world to study wildlife. He wasn't much of a sailor, and spent quite a bit of time being seasick.

On their way down to South America they made plenty of stops along the way. The captain was busy making maps of the coast, which left Darwin with spare time to go ashore and add to his creepy-crawly collection.

They sailed around the treacherous Cape Horn, at the tip of South America, and through some of the worst weather that ships ever come across.

The ship, HMS *Beagle*, was only 30 metres long, but no fewer than 74 crew members lived on her for five years.

It's hard to imagine what life on the *Beagle* was like, but it might have been something like this…

The year is 1835, and HMS Beagle is pitching and rolling in the waves as it crosses the southern Pacific Ocean. Seated in the cabin are two men. One is a naval officer, resplendent in gold braid. The other, an amiable looking bloke with bushy whiskers and a balding head.

Charles Darwin belched contentedly and leaned back in his chair. He picked at a morsel of tortoise flesh that had stuck between his teeth.

"That made a tasty meal, Captain Fitzroy," he said. "But I wish we could have taken the giant tortoises home alive."

Fitzroy sighed the deep sigh of a man whose patience was running out. For four and a half years now he'd shared his cramped cabin with Darwin. Sometimes he wished he'd never let this eccentric naturalist aboard his ship. Everywhere Fitzroy looked there were dead, goggle-eyed animals peering at him from pickling jars. Bunches of parrot skins swung from a hook over his head and frequently knocked his hat askew. Piles of pressed plants slid off tables every time the ship rolled in the heavy swell. Whenever he tried to pace the deck he stubbed his toe on fossil bones of giant extinct animals that Darwin had collected.

"I'm sorry, Darwin, but there's just no room for any more live animals. Look around you. Where could we put six giant tortoises?"

Darwin eyed Fitzroy's hammock, but said nothing. His gaze shifted idly to the pile of empty tortoiseshells. Each one came from a different island in the group of Galapagos Islands that they had just left behind. Suddenly Darwin noticed something that he hadn't spotted before. Each shell had a slightly different pattern. *Why?* he wondered.

He pondered the question for some time before a thunderous thought hit him. His jaw dropped. His eyes glazed over. The jars of preserved specimens swam before his eyes.

The penny finally dropped. It was the Galapagos tortoises that set Darwin's mind racing. Could it be that a single type of tortoise had originally landed on one island, swimming across from the coast of South America? And could it be that its descendants changed a bit, every time they'd colonized a new island? Each island was a bit different, with different kinds of plants growing on it, so maybe the tortoises that lived on each island needed to be a little bit different too.

Suddenly, it all seemed to make sense. He thought back to the birds that he'd seen on the islands. There were little brown finches on every island, and each island had its own special versions of these birds. They were all basically the same, but each species on each island had a slightly different beak shape. Perhaps they'd all evolved from the same species which had arrived on one island then evolved a bit when it spread to the others.

GALAPAGOS GUIDE BOOK

The Spanish discovered these islands in 1535. They found giant tortoises there, so they called them the Galapagos Islands after *galapago*, the Spanish word for tortoise.

The islands were created by undersea volcanic eruptions, 960 km west of the coast of Ecuador in South America. Volcanoes still erupt there quite often.

The islands were once a favourite holiday destination for pirates and buccaneers, who came for a bit of rest and relaxation after raiding South American cities. The peckish pirates were particularly partial to a giant tortoise barbecue on the beach.

Evolve or die fact file

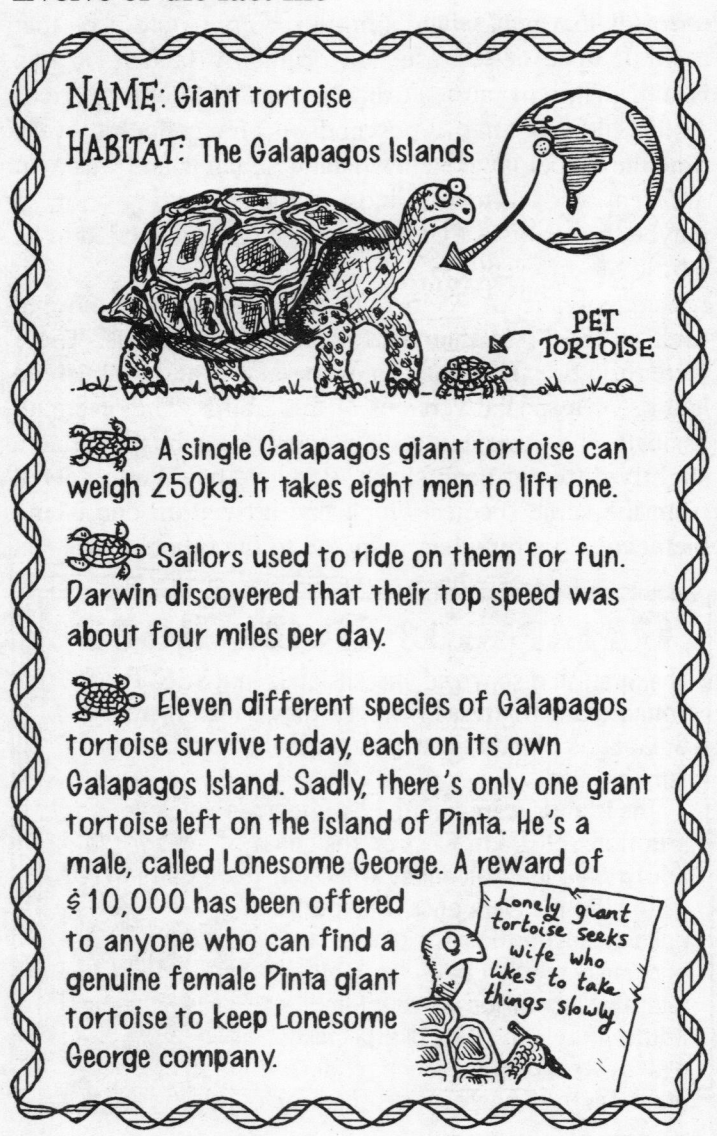

NAME: Giant tortoise

HABITAT: The Galapagos Islands

PET TORTOISE

A single Galapagos giant tortoise can weigh 250kg. It takes eight men to lift one.

Sailors used to ride on them for fun. Darwin discovered that their top speed was about four miles per day.

Eleven different species of Galapagos tortoise survive today, each on its own Galapagos Island. Sadly, there's only one giant tortoise left on the island of Pinta. He's a male, called Lonesome George. A reward of $10,000 has been offered to anyone who can find a genuine female Pinta giant tortoise to keep Lonesome George company.

Lonely giant tortoise seeks wife who likes to take things slowly

As they sailed home Darwin became certain that you could tell which island a tortoise came from by the pattern on its shell. They probably had other tell-tale features too, but unfortunately it was too late to find out. They'd loaded some live giant tortoises on board HMS *Beagle*, and he and Fitzroy had eaten them.

Still, it looked suspiciously like all the different types of tortoise had evolved from a single ancestor. Darwin began to wonder whether all kinds of living things had evolved in the same sort of way.

The differences between the tortoises were quite small, but later he began to wonder whether evolution could explain bigger differences between species too? Could fish have wriggled out of the sea, grown legs and evolved into amphibians like newts and frogs?

And what if men had evolved from the same ancestors as monkeys?

Now that *was* a dangerous theory. Darwin knew that the Church wouldn't like the idea that men and apes might be close cousins.

AN AWESOME IDEA

When Darwin returned to England he settled down to write about his trip. As he wrote, he remembered all the strange plants and animals that he'd seen. He was sure that modern life forms must have evolved from ancient ancestors.

That meant that you could trace the ancestors of all living things on Earth today back to those slimy life forms that slithered in the primaeval soup of Earth's ancient seas!

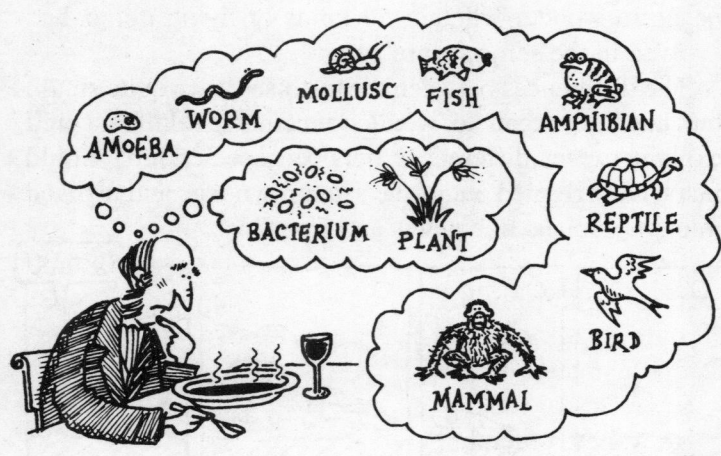

And humans and chimpanzees must have evolved from the same distant, extinct ancestor.

Men and monkeys share the same ancestors, but they've evolved different skills.

Darwin could only come to one conclusion. Living things weren't all created at once by God in 4004 BC. Today's plants and animals evolved very slowly from ancient ancestors.

It was a horribly big idea. And he knew it would get him into big trouble. So Darwin decided to wait a while before he told anyone what he thought.

He waited a week.

He waited a month.

He waited a year.

In the end it took him *twenty* years to pluck up enough courage to write his famous book on evolution. It was called *The Origin of Species*[1] and became an instant bestseller. People had heard rumours that it contained some scandalous ideas, so they rushed to the book shops to buy a copy. Every single copy was sold on the day that it appeared in 1859.

There was a reason why Darwin finally decided to publish his ideas in 1859. Someone else was about to beat him to it. Alfred Russell Wallace (1823–1913), a naturalist who made a living collecting animal specimens on Pacific Islands and selling them to museums, had also realized that living things must have evolved from one another. And he wrote to Darwin to tell him about his bright idea. Darwin wasn't too pleased – he'd thought of it first, and no scientist ever became famous by being the second person to make a discovery. So Darwin sat down and wrote his book as fast as he could.

1 Actually, it's not. Its full title is – take a deep breath – *The Origin of Species by means of Natural Selection or The Preservation of Favoured Races in the Struggle for Life. The Origin of Species* is just easier to say.

To be fair, Darwin and Wallace's ideas were announced at a gathering of some of the world's eminent scientists at the same time, but few people remember poor old Wallace. Darwin got all the glory. Science can be horribly tough.

THE GLOVES COME OFF...

Darwin's book made him famous, but he had to put up with a torrent of criticism from people who hated his ideas. His followers were called Evolutionists. His opponents became known as Creationists, because they believed every word of the story of Creation in the Bible.

They had some ding-dong rows. Darwin couldn't stand public arguments. He stayed at home most of the time and left it to his Evolutionist friends to flatten the opposition.

Their most famous fight took place at the meeting of the British Association for the Advancement of Science in the University Museum at Oxford on 30 June 1860.

The war of words between the Creationists and Evolutionists didn't always end happily. One famous supporter of Bishop "Soapy Sam" Wilberforce came to a tragic end.

He was Captain Fitzroy, who had commanded HMS *Beagle* during Darwin's voyage around the world and shared a cabin with the naturalist. Like many Victorians, he believed every word of the Creation story in the Bible. He was horrified that he'd accidentally helped Darwin to collect evidence for his vile evolutionary theory and helped to cast doubt on people's religious beliefs.

One Sunday morning on 30 April 1865 he locked himself in his study and killed himself, by cutting his own throat. You might think that's a bit much, but it just goes to show how much people hated the idea of having monkeys in the family.

Poor old Fitzroy wasn't the only one who wouldn't believe Darwin's theory. Scores of sceptical scientists pointed out that creatures had to have some way of passing on their best body bits to their babies. It was no good being brilliantly equipped for life on Earth if they couldn't pass on their finest features to their descendants before they died.

Otherwise the features that made them so successful would die out with them. Nothing would ever change: evolution wouldn't happen.

Darwin didn't come up with a convincing answer to this question.

After all, even Charles Darwin didn't have all the answers. But other scientists were able to pick up his ideas and test them out for themselves, by studying fossils (see pages 72–90) and some of the animals and insects that are still around today. Cute, cuddly animals like rabbits. Or small, vicious insects like mosquitoes. Slowly, but surely, a picture began to emerge. It wasn't always a pretty picture but, finally, scientists could see how the theory of evolution actually worked. So cover up, slap on some insect repellent and prepare yourself for an encounter with some … murderous mosquitoes!

MURDEROUS MOSQUITOES

Evolution was a big, new idea. Scientists needed to come up with some pretty impressive evidence if they wanted to convince everyone that they were right.

Luckily, scientists can prove that evolution really does happen, because they can see species change before their eyes. Big changes in evolution take millions of years, but small changes can be amazingly quick.

Evolve or die fact file

NAME: Malarial mosquito

HOME: Anywhere that's horribly hot and wet.

MOST FRIGHTENING FEATURE: Spreads a dreadful disease called malaria. The mosquitoes suck your blood, then squirt squirming parasites into your veins. These give you a fever with horribly high temperatures, and they can even attack your brain.

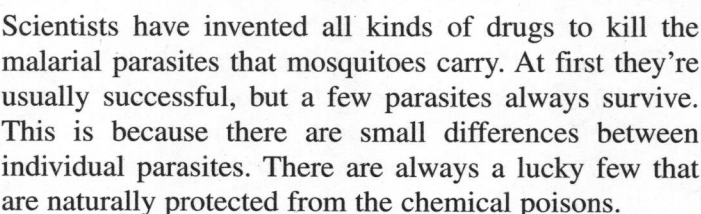

Scientists have invented all kinds of drugs to kill the malarial parasites that mosquitoes carry. At first they're usually successful, but a few parasites always survive. This is because there are small differences between individual parasites. There are always a lucky few that are naturally protected from the chemical poisons.

These vile variations survive in someone's body and are passed around when another mosquito sucks their blood and then moves on to a new victim.

So then it's back to the drawing board for the scientists, in search of another drug that will wipe out this new version of their old enemy.

If it wasn't for the fact that malarial parasites are constantly changing, we might have got rid of this disgusting disease long ago. The trouble is, the parasites keep evolving and stay one step ahead of scientists.

Bet you never knew!

- *When characteristics of individual living things change slightly, they're called mutants. The changes are called mutations.*

- *Most of the time mutations aren't much use to their owners. A cauliflower is just a mutant cabbage, with a horrible-looking head of white flower buds that never open properly. Cauliflowers only survive because people who like to eat vegetables that look like brains deliberately grow them. From a cauliflower's point of view, flowers that never open are a dead loss, so cauliflowers can't survive without human help.*

- *Sometimes mutations are useful. When animals change – when people start attacking them with chemical sprays, or when the climate gets hotter or colder, or when finding food gets tougher – then the right kind of mutation can be very useful indeed. Then a mutant with better body bits might survive. And if it survives, it'll breed – leaving lots of copies of itself – just like the mutant malaria parasites. So then a new, slightly different version of the species has evolved.*

This is exactly what happened to polar bears, when they first arrived in the Arctic. Originally the bears had brown fur, but over time some of them evolved into bears with white fur. But not all. Those bears that still had brown fur found that it was more difficult for them to sneak up on seals in the snow, so they were less able to feed themselves ... and slowly died out.

RABBITS' RECIPE FOR SUCCESS

Rabbits breed like, well, like rabbits, really. *Very* fast. Each one can produce around 50 baby bunnies each year.

The population of animals in a species tends to increase as long as there's plenty of food, water and somewhere to live. When these start to run out, life gets tough. Animals have to compete against other members of their own species in order to survive.

Suppose you were a rabbit. OK, so it's not that simple, but give it a try. Which would you rather be? A brown rabbit, a black rabbit or a white rabbit?

Choose your colour now, then see long you'd survive: Imagine...

a) You're foraging for nice juicy vegetables in a ploughed field.

b) You're out at night – are you protected from danger?

c) Humans are hunting for rabbit fur. Are you safe?

d) There's thick snow on the ground, and the stoats are sniffing around for a tasty snack.

Survival scores:

a) Two years if you are a brown rabbit – you'll blend in easily against the field. One year if you're black – you don't stand out too much. Almost no time at all if you're white – you'll stick out like a sore thumb and make easy prey for passing stoats.

b) Two years if you're brown or black. You won't be easily snapped up by passing owls. It's bad news if you're white, though. They'll see you easily, so you won't have long to live.

c) Two years if you're brown. Your fur is too dull for a fashionable fur coat. Almost no time at all for black or white rabbits, though. Your handsome fur is far too attractive.

d) Two years if you're white. You blend perfectly with the snow. But brown or black rabbits won't survive long – the stoats are on their tails in no time.

So now, if you add up your total survival scores, you can work out how long you'd live.

For a brown rabbit, it comes to a total of six years. And remember, you can produce 50 babies each year, so this is long enough to leave behind at least 300 bunnies that look exactly like you, and are just as successful.

For a black rabbit, it comes to just two years ... only long enough to leave behind 100 baby bunnies, if you're lucky, but their survival chances aren't as good as their brown cousins.

And as for white rabbits ... well, if they're lucky they can expect to live for two years too, so they'll leave behind 100 white rabbits that will be hoping that it snows more often!

So it's easy to see why black or white rabbits are rare. If you chose to be a boring old brown rabbit, you'll have survived these conditions best of all. But what if the climate changed? Suppose it got colder and snow was on the ground all year round. It'd be a different story then, your white cousin would become fittest and survive more successfully.

In any rabbit population, most animals will share similar characteristics, but there will always be a few rabbits with mutations that might come in handy. They can vary in all sorts of ways – they might have longer guts, for example, so they can digest food more easily – always useful if you spend all day chewing grass.

TEST YOUR TEACHER

Most scientific words sound horribly difficult, but actually the language scientists use is supposed to make complicated things easier to understand. Ask your teacher what coprophagous (cop-roff-a-gus) means. Is it:

1 TO EAT DUNG?   **2** TO EAT POLICEMEN?   **3** THE COFFIN THAT EGYPTIAN PHARAOHS ARE BURIED IN?

Answer: 1 Rabbits are coprophagous, because their guts aren't long enough to digest their food on its first trip through their bodies. So they send it around again by eating their own dung.

Scientists love making up weird words like coprophagous. It's the easiest way to describe this particular rabbit habit. But most people don't understand them, so they just call it "dung-eating" – but that doesn't sound half as impressive, does it?

Mutants that are slightly better at getting the things they need survive and thrive and breed. Gradually they start to take over. Evolution has happened and the species has changed a bit.

Scientists sometimes call this natural selection because in wild plants and animals the individuals that succeed are the ones that are lucky enough to inherit a winning set of characteristics from their parents.

Conditions on Earth are always changing slightly, so animals and plants with new, useful mutations do better as time passes. If mutations never happened, then plants and animals couldn't evolve to suit the changing conditions, and they would eventually become extinct. So if you want to survive, it's evolve – or die!

"AAAAAH - HE'S GOT HIS MOTHER'S NOSE"

All living things have small differences – mutations – that are passed on from their parents. You've probably noticed how certain features tend to run in families. Don't you just hate it when this happens…?

Sadly, all kids have to put up with these kinds of comparisons. Aunts, uncles and grannies just can't stop themselves. People have always marvelled at the way characteristics are passed down through families. And they have always wondered why it happens. One of the first people to come up with an answer was…

Hall of fame: Hippocrates (460–??? BC. No one is quite sure when he died.) Nationality: Greek
Hippocrates is famous for all sorts of things. He's sometimes called "the father of medicine" because he invented ways of finding out what was wrong with sick people, and tried to find cures. Even today doctors swear a Hippocratic Oath, which is a promise that they'll do their best for their patients and won't do anything to harm them.

REALLY MR CRUSHER, THIS IS BAD FOR YOUR BLOOD PRESSURE AND YOU'LL STRAIN THE MUSCLES IN YOUR HAND!

Hippocrates came up with a half-baked hypothesis to explain how parents pass on their characteristics to their children…

CHARACTERISTICS LIKE BLUE EYES, BIG NOSES, LONG LEGS AND KNOBBLY KNEES ARE PASSED ON FROM BOTH PARENTS TO THEIR CHILDREN.

EACH PART OF A MOTHER AND FATHER'S BODY PRODUCES MYSTERIOUS DROPLETS THAT BLEND TOGETHER TO PRODUCE THESE PARTS IN THEIR BABY.

Hippocrates got it horribly wrong. After all, when you mix the colours of a paint box together you always get the same muddy colour when you've finished. All the individual colours disappear into the mixture. So if characteristics from both parents were just mixed together in their children, everyone in the family would soon look more or less the same.

If a tall father and a short mother had children, they would all be medium height, and then all *their* children would be medium height, and all *their* children would be medium height. Borr-ring!

GREAT GREAT GRANDAD GREAT GRANDAD GRANDAD DAD ME

Darwin knew there was something slightly dodgy with this idea. His theory of evolution depended on individuals passing on their different features to their children. If they didn't, mutants couldn't pass on their useful body bits to their children. Evolution wouldn't happen.

Hippocrates' explanation lasted for 2,300 years. It was time for a new one, and the person who produced it was…

Hall of fame: Gregor Mendel (1822–1884)
Nationality: Austrian, (but born in the country that's now called the Czech Republic)
Mendel came from a peasant family, so getting him a decent education was pretty tough on them. His parents knew their son was a clever lad, though, and managed to

get enough money together to send him to school and then on to university. Eventually Mendel became a monk. But there was something very different about him. Mendel was a monk with a passion for plants. Peas in particular. He spent most of his time in the garden.

Just like Darwin, he set out on a voyage of discovery – but Gregor only got as far as the vegetable plot at the bottom of the garden. Every year between 1856 and 1863 he filled his garden with peas: 30,000 plants altogether. Tall ones, short ones, yellow ones, green ones, wrinkled ones, smooth ones. Then he cross-pollinated the flowers with a paintbrush, collected the seeds that they produced and sowed them again.

Dare you discover ... how flowers work?
You will need:
A small paintbrush
Some flower seeds – nasturtiums are ideal for this experiment
A flower pot
Some seed compost to sow the seeds in

What you do:

Sow the seeds, water them and wait for them to grow and flower. When the flowers open, use the paintbrush to collect some pollen grains. As you may know, these are the bits that bees collect and carry from flower to flower. Use the paintbrush to put the pollen on the flower's stigmas, where it will fertilize and make the seeds form. Then all you need to do is plant the seeds to make them germinate and grow.

Here's a picture to remind you what's what and where's where in a flower:

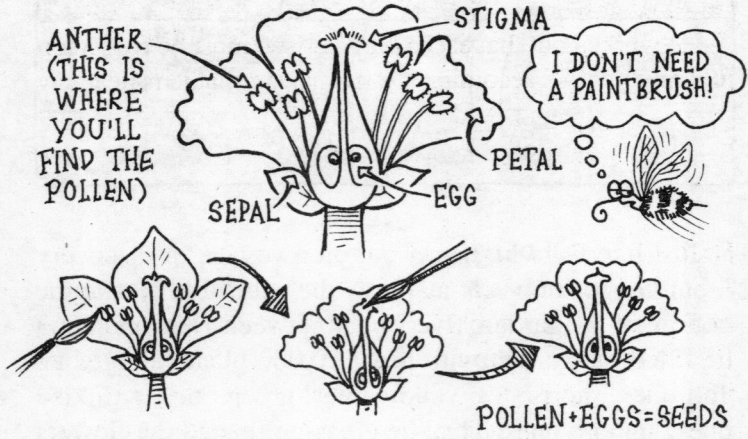

ANTHER (THIS IS WHERE YOU'LL FIND THE POLLEN)

STIGMA

I DON'T NEED A PAINTBRUSH!

PETAL

SEPAL

EGG

POLLEN+EGGS=SEEDS

Mendel took over the bees' job and carried the pollen from flower to flower, so he'd know exactly which plants were paired together.

Once the flowers turned to seeds Mendel spent all his spare time sorting them out into different types and counting them. Then he sowed the seeds again and counted all the different kinds of plants that grew from them – wrinkled seeds, smooth seeds, tall plants and short plants. Then he got out his paintbrush and cross-pollinated these plants all over again. Mendel was a monk with a mission. He'd

44

find out how living things passed on their characteristics, no matter how long it took.

One day, after years and years of tedious work, Mendel was struck by a thunderous thought (at long last!).

He worked out that each characteristic must be passed on in a tiny particle according to an amazing mathematical law that never changed. And if he wanted to know what the next generation would look like, all he had to do was to look at each parent's features and remember some simple rules.

MENDEL'S GOLDEN RULES

1 Characteristics such as the colour of a flower in plants, and nose size or knobbly knees in humans, are passed on from parents to their children through invisible particles inside their cells.

2 A different particle carries the instructions for each characteristic.

3 The particles work in pairs, and one of each pair comes from each parent.

4 Particles exist in two different forms. Particles can be dominant, which means that their effects always show up. Or they can be recessive, which means that the effects of a recessive particle can be hidden behind the effects of a dominant one. But if two recessive particles pair up, then their effects always show up in the plant or animal that carries them.

45

It works like this...

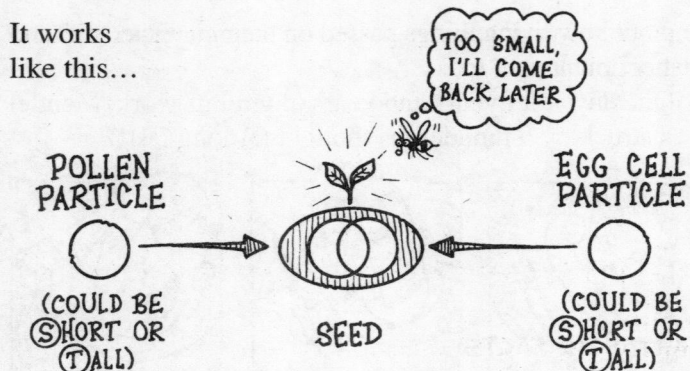

In this example, remember these rules: tall particles are dominant, short particles are recessive.

So...

A tall particle paired with a tall particle produces a tall plant.

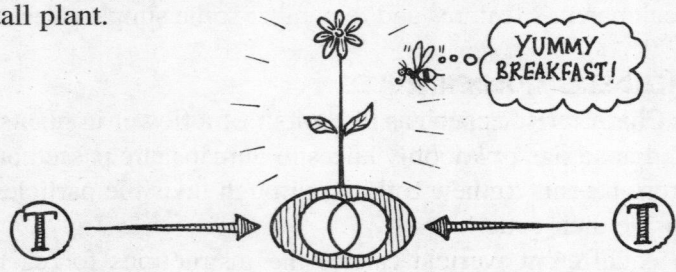

A tall particle paired with a short particle produces a tall plant (the short particle is recessive, so its effects are hidden behind the tall one).

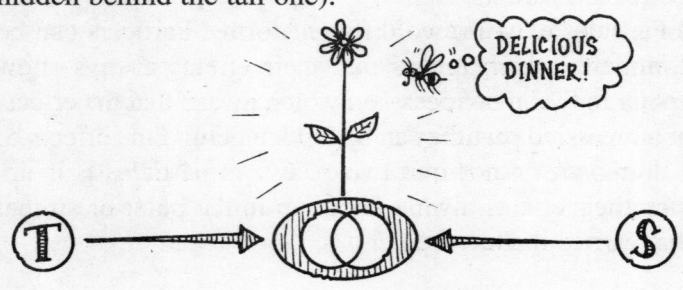

A short particle paired with a short particle produces a short plant.

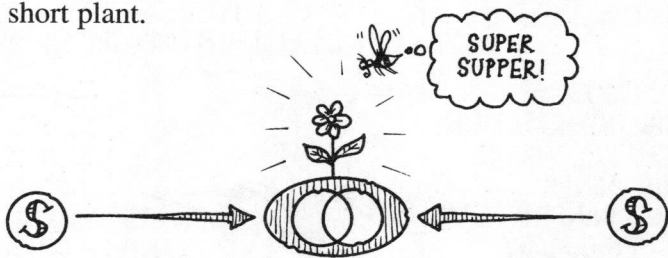

FANTASTIC FACTS

- Today we call Mendel's particles genes. All the characteristics of all living things are controlled by genes, which are passed on from parents to children. They're like a set of instructions carried inside the cells of your body.
- Even a tiny, simple organism like a bacterium is controlled by over 10,000 genes. It takes around 25,000 genes to form the complete set of instructions for making something as complicated as a human.
- Mutations happen when genes change. Mutant genes are nature's way of changing the instructions slightly and inventing new body bits.

Mendel's discovery started a whole new science, called genetics. And a whole new bunch of scientists, called geneticists.

But geneticists couldn't really study genes properly until they knew where they were. By the beginning of the twentieth century, geneticists were tearing their hair out trying to find these pesky particles. To their surprise, they soon realized that they'd been staring at them for years.

Well, that's not quite true. You can't actually see a single gene, even with a really powerful microscope. It's far too small. But you can see genes when thousands of them are collected together in one place. And the place to look is inside a cell.

CYTOPLASM = SNOT-LIKE SLIME

NUCLEUS =
THE INFORMATION
CENTRE, WHERE
THE GENES
ARE, SENDING OUT
A STREAM OF
INSTRUCTIONS
TO THE CELL

COME ON, CELL, GET A MOVE ON!

MITOCHONDRIA = POWER STATIONS THAT BREAK DOWN FOOD AND TURN IT INTO ENERGY

SEVEN SENSATIONAL FACTS ABOUT CELLS

1 Insects, plants, animals, bacteria … from ants to elephants, all living things are made up of cells.

2 Cells are usually tiny. If you lined up 40 average-sized plant cells they would only just stretch across the head of a pin.

3 If humans had the same cells as plants, we'd be green! Plant cells each have special green, shiny chloroplasts to turn sunlight, water and carbon dioxide into food.

4 Did you have a nice fried egg for breakfast this morning? Actually, you ate a fried giant cell! Birds' eggs are special, they are made up of a single cell covered in a hard shell that helps them survive outside their owner's body.

CAN I HAVE BEANS WITH MY GIANT BIRD'S CELL PLEASE, MUM?

5 Ostrich eggs weigh about one and a half kilogrammes, so they hold the record for the largest cells in the world.
6 If you took your clothes off and stood in front of a mirror, everything you'd see would be dead. All the cells on the outside of your skin have died and are falling off. But you'll be relieved to know that the cells under your skin are dividing all the time to make brand new cells. You get a nice new layer of skin about every six weeks!

NOT TONIGHT, JOE – I'M WAITING FOR MY NEW SKIN TO COME THROUGH

7 The dandruff on your teacher's collar is made up of dead cells. When the cells were alive the genes inside them contained all the information to create an exact copy of your teacher.

INCREDIBLE CHROMOSOMES
Even way back in Mendel's day, scientists had some pretty powerful microscopes. They were strong enough to reveal the nucleus of the cell. And sometimes in place of the nucleus they identified long worm-shaped things. They called the wormy bits chromosomes. *Chroma* means coloured and *soma* means body – they are slightly coloured compared with cells, which you can see through.

Chromosomes are pretty incredible:
1 Chromosomes carry all your genes, like a long string of sausages.

2 They spend most of their time hanging around in pairs. Different animals and plants have different numbers of chromosomes.

You have got 46 (23 pairs).

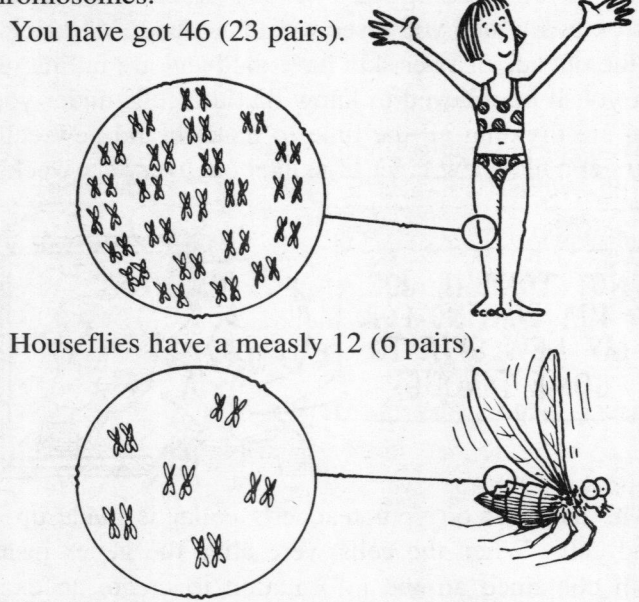

Houseflies have a measly 12 (6 pairs).

But the adder's tongue fern holds the record with an incredible 1,260 (630 pairs). No one knows why it needs so many!

3 When your skin grows, and its cells divide, weird things happen to the chromosomes inside them. The chromosomes divide too, so that each new cell carries a full set of instructions that tells it everything it needs to know about being part of you.

4 A human female egg cell and a male sperm cell carry only 23 chromosomes each. When they join together to make a baby, the two sets of chromosomes make up a full set of 46 chromosomes, but half the chromosomes come from the mother and half from the father.

5 So your genes come half from your mum and half from your dad. The sets of genes or chromosomes in egg or sperm cells are all slightly different, and no one can ever know which egg and sperm cells will join together to make a new person. So, unless you have an identical twin, there's nobody anywhere in the world who is *exactly* like you.

A POTTED HISTORY OF GENETICS

These days scientists know a lot more about genes than Mendel did. They even know what they're made of, thanks to...

Hall of fame: James Dewey Watson (1928–)
Nationality: American

Watson grew up in Chicago, USA. Even as a young lad he showed amazing brain power and entered the University of Chicago at the tender age of 15!

He was an amazing 25 years old (most scientists are really ancient) when he and his pal Francis discovered DNA.

Francis Crick (1916–2004) Nationality: British

When he was a kid, Crick's parents bought him a children's encyclopedia and reading it made him decide he wanted to be a scientist. But he was worried that by the time he grew up, everything would already have been discovered. Little did he know, that along with Watson, he would make one of the greatest discoveries ever – how DNA was structured.

Watson and Crick worked together at Cambridge University. Later James Watson spent most of his time helping to make a map of all the genes that produce the instructions for making a human. Francis Crick moved on to finding out how brains work, but they're both most famous for discovering the struture of DNA, the magic molecule of life, that first turned up in those pongy primaeval oceans, 3,500 million years ago. They won a Nobel Prize for it.

A HORRIBLE THOUGHT...

The DNA that existed inside the first bacteria 3,500 million years ago still survives inside us, in a mutated form. It's been inside slimy worms and giant sea scorpions, pterodactyls and eventually people. All the time it's been mutating, building different body bits around itself to carry it safely into the next generation. All the different animals that have lived on Earth have been built by DNA molecules. And we're just the latest creatures that have evolved to carry that ancient DNA.

That means that we're really just slaves that carry this amazing molecule. Life evolved just to make sure that genes made of DNA molecules survived.

A British scientist, Professor Richard Dawkins (1941-) had an idea about the DNA molecule. He called his idea the Selfish Gene theory.

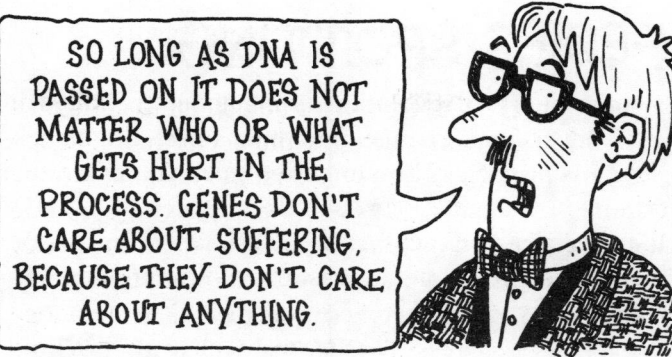

SO LONG AS DNA IS PASSED ON IT DOES NOT MATTER WHO OR WHAT GETS HURT IN THE PROCESS. GENES DON'T CARE ABOUT SUFFERING, BECAUSE THEY DON'T CARE ABOUT ANYTHING.

He suggests that all plants and animals are really just slaves to this amazing molecule. We only exist to make sure genes made of DNA molecules survive. Other scientists disagree – of course!

AHA! I SEE YOU HAVE A NEW BATCH OF DNA MOLECULES IN PRODUCTION!

ER, WELL THAT'S ONE WAY OF PUTTING IT!

Darwin's evolutionary theory really took off once scientists discovered that evolution happens because genes change, so that better body bits can be passed on from generation to generation. But it didn't come up with all the answers. If one species could evolve into a new one, that meant that scientists urgently needed to answer a new and horribly difficult question.

Where did one species finish, and a new one begin?

SPECIES SPOTTING

Darwin's theory of evolution is all about the ways in which old species change into new ones. So what – exactly – is a species? You might be sorry you asked that question.

It's a well-known fact that if you ask two scientists the same question you'll get at least three different answers. If you're lucky.

If you are unlucky they'll answer your question with another question.

It's also a well-known fact that if you ask the same scientist the same question twice, you'll probably get two different answers.

Scientists are like that. Can't make up their minds. Always looking for that final piece of evidence that will provide conclusive proof. Always changing their minds. You've got to expect this really, because they are always discovering new things.

Why do you need to know what a species is? Because the next bit of this story is horribly tricky.

The trouble is that – even today – scientists can't agree on exactly how to describe a species. This is a bit of a disadvantage if you are trying to explain how species evolve.

Confused? So are they. It's a horrible mess, but they're doing their best to sort it out.

CAN YOU SPOT A SPECIES?

Easy-peasy?

You must be joking!

You might think that you can identify most species just by looking at them closely. After all, you can tell most wild flowers apart by the shape of their leaves and the colour of their flowers.

And you can tell different snakes apart by the patterns on their bodies.

And you can identify most fish by their shapes, sizes and colours – and even by the way they behave:

This is all very convenient. The world would be a dangerous place for people who couldn't tell domestic cats from cougars, just by looking at them. If you can't, just be very careful next time you stroke a cat.

But (and you'll have guessed by now that "but" is one of scientists' favourite words) the only reliable way to be sure that two species are different is if you can be certain that they can't breed with one another. And the trouble is that a surprising number of species that look different enough to be different species can actually interbreed..

Take domestic cats and fierce Scottish wildcats, for example. They can breed with one another and their kittens have characteristics of both species – they'll bite your fingers off, then purr with pleasure.

Animals that interbreed like this are a real problem for scientists who study evolution, because you can't be sure where one species finishes and another begins. Take, for example, the ridiculous situation with the ruddy duck and its Spanish relative, the white-headed duck...

RUDDY DUCKS ON RAMPAGE

White-headed ducks hadn't seen their ruddy relatives for tens of thousands of years, so it was a happy day when Sir Peter Scott brought them back together again.

Sir Peter brought ruddy ducks from America and released them in a British bird reserve.

BREEDING BRILLIANT
The ruddy ducks settled down really quickly, and soon the pitter-patter of tiny ruddy feet

meant that they were here to stay. Some even fancied seeing the sights of Europe, and flew over to Spain, where their relatives - the white-headed ducks - live.

RED FACED

But then things started to go horribly wrong. If Sir Peter Scott were alive today, he'd certainly be red in the face when he realized the chaos his ruddy ducks have caused. Unfortunately, the ruddy duck seems to think that it belongs to the white-headed duck family. The families look quite different, but when white-headed ducks and ruddy ducks get together, they only produce ruddy babies. There's not a white head to be seen. So it may not be long before the last white-headed duck kicks the bucket!

ROTTEN LUCK FOR RUDDY DUCKS

The white-headed duck was already rare, so now bird experts are raring to get at the ruddy duck - and they've got their rifles ready. So must we bid the ruddy ducks bye bye, or will they see the hunters coming - and duck?

The ruddy duck and white-headed duck aren't really separate species, even though they look different. They're one species that's on the way to splitting into two separate species, but hasn't quite got there yet. Which just goes to prove that old Darwin was dead right – species weren't all created at once and they haven't stayed the same since the beginning of time. They're always changing, a little bit at a time. Ruddy ducks and white-headed ducks breed together to produce ducklings that grow up looking like ruddy ducks and can breed with both bewildered parents. Biologists call them hybrids.

So there you have it. You asked: "What's a species?" As any decent scientist would say, a species is either:

a) a group of creatures that look similar.

b) a group of creatures that can't interbreed with any other groups of creatures.

Two answers. What did you expect? This is science! Scientific ideas evolve too, just like life.

TEST YOUR TEACHER

See if your teacher can spot a true species by asking them which of these horrible hybrids is too ridiculous to be real?

a) Tigons have a lionness for a mother and a tiger for a father.

b) When a zebra mates with a donkey, you get a zonkey.

c) The barking pussyfish is a hybrid between a catfish and a dogfish.

> Answers: a) true b) true c) ridiculous

Hybrids create horrible problems for scientists who are trying to explain how evolution works. Species are formed when one species evolves into another, new one – but how can the new species become different if it keeps interbreeding with the old one? Somehow the old species and the new species have got to become completely separate. It's a mind-boggling problem – a problem, in fact, that has boggled many minds since Darwin's day.

Luckily, scientists have come up with an explanation for the way that one species separates into two. It's a bit like the way that English and American people have come to speak different versions of the same language.

Four hundred years ago, when the first boatload of English people sailed to America, they all spoke the same kind of English.

But since then, Americans and English people have evolved separate words for the same things.

Of course, English and American people haven't split into separate species. But imagine what it must be like for animals that have been separated for millions of years, then meet up again. They can't understand each other's squeaks, squawks and roars, so they just ignore each other and behave like separate species.

In nature, all sorts of barriers can break up a species into small groups of creatures that begin to evolve separately. They can be separated by:

- rivers, earthquakes or volcanic eruptions;

- mountain ranges;
- sinking land, which leaves animals stranded on islands above the waves;

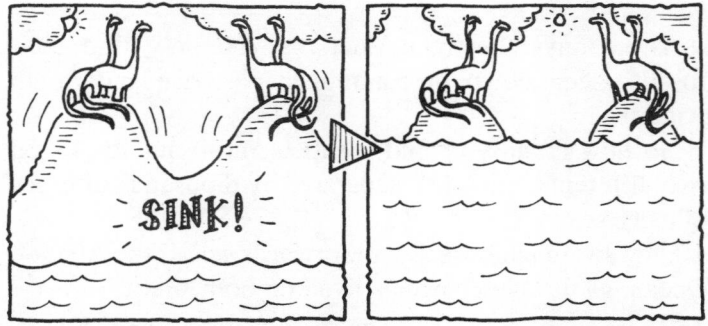

- breaking bridges. Snowy Siberia (in Asia) was once joined to Arctic Alaska (in America) by a bridge of land that sunk beneath the sea. Once a single species of bear could stroll between the continents. Now two types of bear have evolved – grizzly bears in North America, black bears in Asia – separated by the sea;

• rising land, which leaves marine animals separated.

Sometimes animals can become castaways. They can get carried out to sea and end up stranded on islands. Remember those Galapagos giant tortoises, and Darwin's finches that he found on the Galapagos Islands?

TEST YOUR TEACHER

See if your teacher can work out the answer to this primaeval problem.

Mesosaurs were reptiles that spent their time swimming and sunbathing in fresh water lagoons about 300 million years ago.

These days they're extinct, so you only find their fossils, deep down in coalmines in Africa and South America.

So how come you find identical mesosaur fossils on two different continents, separated by thousands of miles of salty sea?

1 They swam backwards and forwards across the Atlantic Ocean, so the same species lived on both sides.

2 They floated across on logs.

3 They walked across on a land bridge that's disappeared below the waves.

4 It's just a coincidence. Identical mesosaurs evolved separately, at the same time, in each continent.

5 South America and Africa were joined together 300 million years ago when mesosaurs lived. Much later, they split in two and drifted apart, carrying away some of the fossilized remains of mesosaurs on each continent.

Answers: 1 Not very likely – they hated salt water. **2** Could you cross all that ocean balanced on a log?! **3** Scientists have searched, but they can't find any sign of a bridge. **4** Too much of a coincidence. **5** This is how it happened, and the person who proved it was Alfred Lothar Wegener.

Hall of fame: Alfred Lothar Wegener (1880–1930) Nationality: German

Alfred Wegener led a colourful life. When he finished his studies at Heidelberg University, starry-eyed Alfred became an astronomer. Then he became a balloonist and made a record-breaking 52-hour balloon flight to test scientific instruments. Still looking for adventure, he became a polar explorer and trekked off into the frozen wastes of Greenland, once nearly coming to grief when the ice broke up under his expedition's feet. Alfred saw plenty of weather, one way and another – during his balloon flights, and drifting around on icebergs – so he eventually settled down to become a professor of meteorology – the posh name for the scientific study of weather.

That was when he had a brainwave. Earth's continents, he decided, were moving under our feet. Not very fast, but they were definitely moving. It was obvious, really.

When Wegener looked at the atlas, he could see that South America and Africa had once been joined together.

YOU NEED ONLY LOOK AT THE MAPS OF THE TWO CONTINENTS TO SEE THAT I'M RIGHT. THE EAST COAST OF SOUTH AMERICA FITS QUITE SNUGLY INTO THE WEST COAST OF AFRICA. THEY'VE SPLIT AND DRIFTED APART

Wegener called his theory "continental drift".

THE CENTRE OF THE EARTH IS SO HOT THAT ALL THE ROCKS HAVE MELTED INTO A WHITE-HOT LIQUID. SOMETIMES THIS MOLTEN MASS BREAKS THROUGH THE SOLID CRUST ON THE OUTSIDE – AS A VOLCANO

ALL THE CONTINENTS FLOAT ON A MOLTEN CORE AND DRIFT AROUND. SOMETIMES THEY SPLIT APART TO MAKE SEPARATE CONTINENTS. SOMETIMES THEY JOIN TOGETHER TO FORM A NEW ONE

CLAPTRAP! RUBBISH!

TWADDLE! TOSH!

In 1930 Wegener set off on another expedition, to Greenland. Sadly, he never came back and didn't live to see the day his theory was proved right. Modern-day geologists have proved beyond doubt that Earth's continents really have been slowly moving for millions of years.

Dare you discover ... how continents are like custard?

Continental drift is hard to imagine because it's so slow. Even slower than evolution. But here's an experiment to show how it works without having to wait several years for the result.

You will need:
a large bowl of warm, runny custard
two pieces of cling film
three flavours of potato crisps (cheese and onion, salt and vinegar and prawn cocktail)
a small heavy object – like a key

What you do:
1 Lay the two pieces of cling film on the custard. Then place the crisps on the cling film as shown:

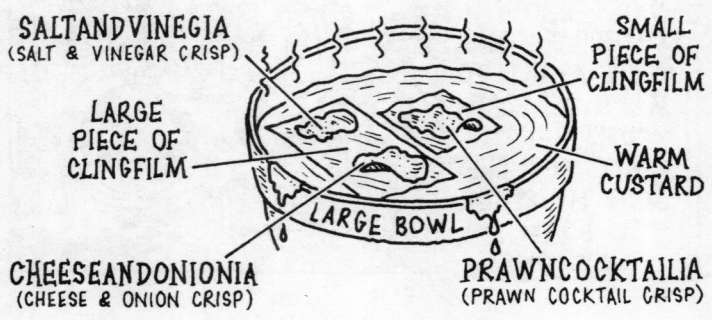

SALTANDVINEGIA
(SALT & VINEGAR CRISP)

SMALL
PIECE OF
CLINGFILM

LARGE
PIECE OF
CLINGFILM

WARM
CUSTARD

LARGE BOWL

CHEESEANDONIONIA
(CHEESE & ONION CRISP)

PRAWNCOCKTAILIA
(PRAWN COCKTAIL CRISP)

2 You have now created the weird planet of "Custard World". Here, three continents float on a sea of custard, supported by drifting plates of cling film.

3 Now choose a spot in between Saltandvinegia and Cheeseandonionia and put the key on the cling film, so that it begins to sink into the molten core of the custard.

And now:
* *Marvel!* at the way Saltandvinegia and Cheeseandonionia move closer together and their crispy surfaces collide as they're drawn together by the sinking cling film!
* *Gasp!* in amazement as you watch Cheeseandonionia and Prawncocktailia drift apart!
* *Tremble!* with excitement as you watch the lake of molten custard between Cheeseandonionia and Prawncocktailia solidify in the cold air, adding new solid skin to the edge of the cling film continent!

CONTINENTAL DRIFT

Continental drift works in similar ways on Planet Earth and on Custard World. Continents like Africa, South America and Australia are plates of rock that float on the molten core of the Earth.

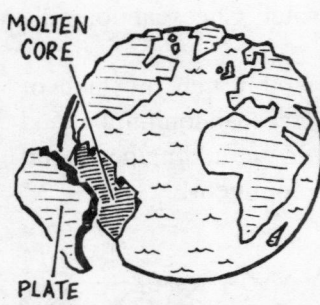

MOLTEN CORE

PLATE

Mountain ranges are the result of colliding continents. The land has nowhere to go but up as the plates of rock push against each other.

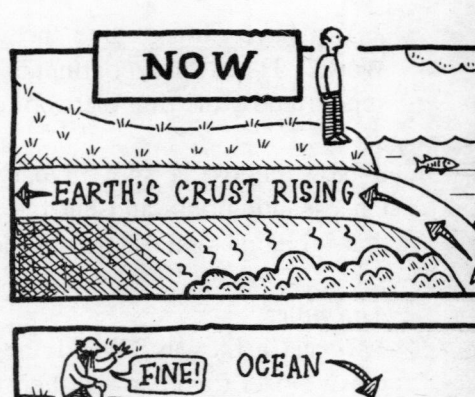

MILLIONS OF YEARS AGO INDIA COLLIDED WITH ASIA

HIMALAYAS

INDIA

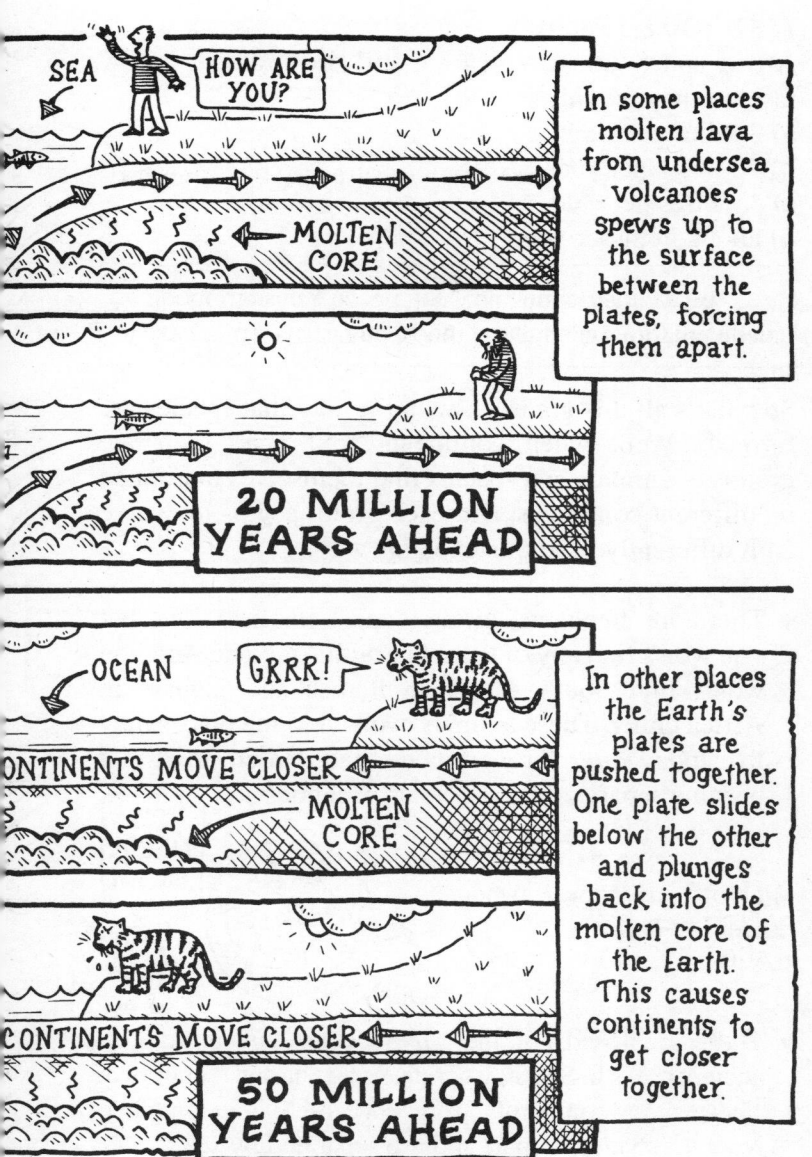

69

TEST YOUR TEACHER

Africa and South America are still drifting apart. How fast are they moving?

a) 2 miles per year

b) 20 miles per year

c) 3 metres per year

d) about 5 cm per year

> **Answer: d)** Africa and South America are moving apart at about the same speed that your fingernails grow.

So what's all this got to do with the way that species are formed? Well, when continents split apart, separate groups of animals in a species find themselves marooned on different continents, and each group begins to evolve a bit differently. And this explains why...

- There are elephants, giraffes and lions in Africa, but you won't find any of them in South America. And you won't find South American llamas and jaguars in Africa either. These animals evolved in the places they live today *after* the continents had drifted apart and became separated by the South Atlantic.

- There are fossils of the *same* plants and animals in ancient rocks in South America, Australia and Antarctica. These three continents were once all joined together. Now they've split apart and are separated by sea.

- Early explorers found fossils of sea creatures on mountain tops. The rock that the mountains are made from formed beneath the sea. Sea creatures turned into fossils in the slimy ooze on the sea floor. Then continents collided, forcing the Earth's crust to buckle like a wrinkled rug, and the sea floor was pushed up in the air, to form mountains.

MOUNTAIN RISING FISH FOSSIL

CRIKEY! FISH FOSSIL!

- Some of the fossils you find in Britain are the remains of animals like corals, that lived in warm, tropical seas. That's because millions of years ago Britain started out south of the equator, and had been slowly drifting northwards – towards the North Pole – ever since. There are no living corals like this around our coasts today – the water is far too cold – but the fossils are a reminder of the tropical seas that once surrounded our islands.

OLD FOSSIL (CORAL)

OLD FOSSIL (CAROL)

THE SEA WAS WARMER WHEN I WAS A GIRL

So that's how new species are formed. Groups of animals get separated, and they evolve into a new species.

But when new species form, the old ones often die out. And we wouldn't know that they'd ever existed, if it wasn't for the fact that some of them have turned to stone...

FASCINATING FOSSILS

Rows about evolution rage on to this day. Like all scientific ideas, Darwin's theory of evolution convinced a lot of people, but for a time that was all it was – a brilliant theory. Just like the theory of continental drift it needed more proof! And ever since Darwin died, scientists all over the world have been tracking down clues to the horrible history of life on Earth.

Scientists know all about dinosaurs and other extinct animals because their remains are buried in the earth, preserved as fossils. You've certainly heard of dinosaurs, you've probably read quite a bit about them, but did you know that all sorts of other eerie creatures crawled over our planet millions of years ago? Scientists find fossils to piece the facts together.

FANTASTIC FOSSIL FACTS

1 When ancient animals died they were often covered by layers of mud, especially if they lived in water. Their soft bits usually rotted away quickly, but their hard teeth, claws and bones often turned to stone after they were buried. They became fossils.

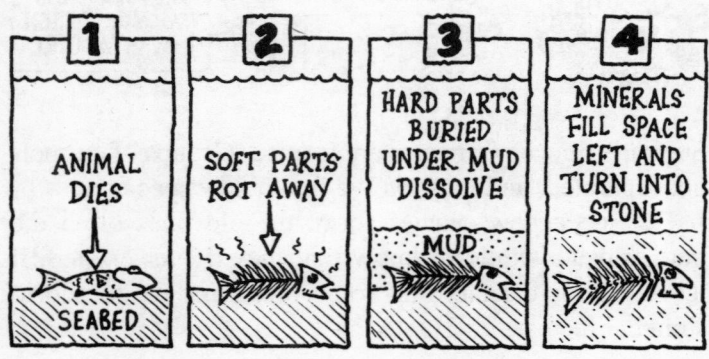

2 The word fossil has evolved from a Latin word – fossilis – which means "dug up".

3 When people first discovered fossils they weren't sure what they'd found. One theory was that these strange creatures that looked like nothing on Earth could only have come from one place – Hell! They firmly believed that fossils were bits of devils and dragons. Since then, science has shown that these bits of mythical beasts are really fossilized parts of animals that had once roamed the Earth.

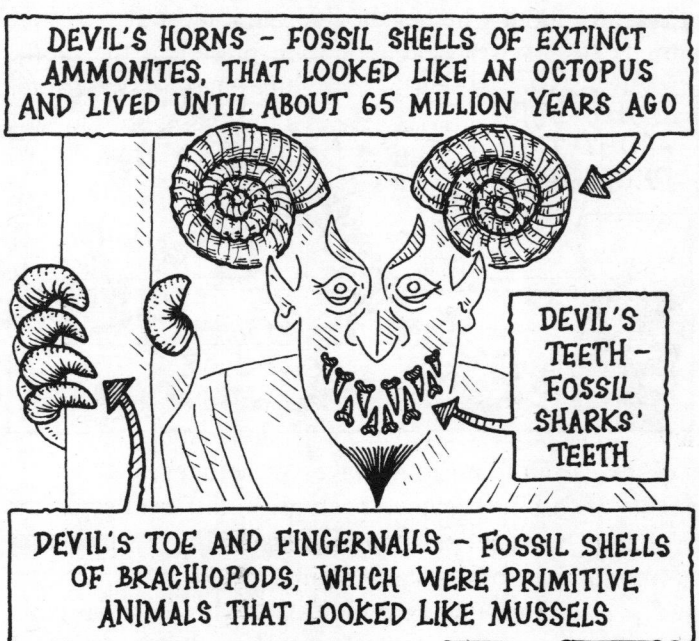

DEVIL'S HORNS – FOSSIL SHELLS OF EXTINCT AMMONITES, THAT LOOKED LIKE AN OCTOPUS AND LIVED UNTIL ABOUT 65 MILLION YEARS AGO

DEVIL'S TEETH – FOSSIL SHARKS' TEETH

DEVIL'S TOE AND FINGERNAILS – FOSSIL SHELLS OF BRACHIOPODS, WHICH WERE PRIMITIVE ANIMALS THAT LOOKED LIKE MUSSELS

4 Belemnites (bell-em-nights) are bullet-shaped fossils that we now know were once the hard parts of extinct animals that looked like squid. When they were first found, people thought that they were made by thunderbolts hurled at the earth by the gods.

5 People who study fossils are called palaeontologists (pally-on-tol-o-gists). They try to rebuild the skeletons of ancient animals from the fossil bones that they excavate. Sometimes they're lucky and find a complete skeleton, but often they only find a few scattered bones. Reconstructing a fossil skeleton is a bit like doing a giant jigsaw puzzle, and it can be horribly confusing if pieces of the puzzle are just a bag of bones. It took several attempts to put *Tyrannosaurus rex* together, and some palaeontologists still argue about whether they've got it right.

They certainly make mistakes sometimes:

- Bits of fossil trees have been given different scientific names because palaeontologists didn't realize they were all part of the same plant.
- The same mix-ups have happened with fossil animals. At first, when scientists found three kinds of weird, 500-million-year-old fossils they thought they were different species, and gave them each a name. Finally they realized that they all fitted together, to make *Anomalocaris* – a strange undersea predator that lived on the sea floor about 500 million years ago.

REVOLTING RECONSTRUCTIONS

With a bit of practice palaeontologists can become really skilled at rebuilding fossil animals, and some of these long-lost creatures have turned out to be spine-chilling predators...

Name: EURYPTERUS (you-rip-ter-us), the giant water scorpion.

Size: About as long as an alligator.

Lived: 435 million years ago.

Most frightening features: Ferocious. So paddling at the seaside when *Eurypterus* was around would have been horribly hazardous.

Name: DIATRYMA (dy-er-try-mer), the devil bird.

Size: A flightless bird, over two metres tall, that strutted around the grassy plains of Europe and North America.

Lived: 40 million years ago.

Most frightening features: Probably ate horses. It had a sharp-edged beak like a giant can-opener that could have sliced you in half!

Name: SMILODON (smile-o-don), the sabre-toothed tiger.

Size: A bit bigger than today's tigers.

Lived: 16,000 years ago

Most frightening features: Lurked in bushes and ambushed anything that came too close. Meeting smilodon was nothing to smile about.

Its name means "knife tooth" and its horrible grin would reveal two giant teeth that were as long as swords, and every bit as dangerous.

PETRIFIED POO

To a scientist who studies evolution, there's nothing so fascinating as a lump of fossil faeces (fee-sees). Faeces, by the way, is a posh scientific name for a pile of poo.

Fortunately, not many animals manage to digest all the food that they eat. Some interesting food fragments are often left in the dollops of dung that they leave behind. If this foul faeces finds itself in the right conditions – like a bog where there's no oxygen for bacteria that would normally eat it – then the poo gets preserved. It becomes a fossil.

Many a pile of steaming dinosaur poo has turned into solid rock, full of interesting plant fragments. Millions of years after an ancient animal's last meal, scientists can explore its petrified poo and find out who or what it ate.

Scientists called these lumps of fossil faeces

"coprolites". And some coprolites are unbelievably ancient. One discovery dates from the Silurian period, over 400 million years ago. It is about the size of a mouse dropping and it probably belonged to an animal like a large millipede, which was one of the first animals to crawl from the sea and live on land.

HOW SCIENTISTS DEAL WITH DINOSAUR DUNG
(in four very careful steps)
1 First, they find a coprolite. They need a beady pair of eyes for spotting millipede poo – it's a specialist job – but giant lumps of dinosaur doings are hard to miss. They sometimes turn up alongside piles of fossil dinosaur bones.

2 Now they stew the poo in hydrofluoric acid – very nasty stuff. Hydrofluoric acid eats through just about anything – stone, metal, even school dinners – everything, in fact, except the tough outer covering of plants, called cutin.
3 Then they sort through the sludge of plant bits that's left behind.

4 Finally, they peer at them down a microscope, taking a

close look at the left-overs from the dinosaur's last meal.
When scientists did this with 400-million-year-old
millipede poo they discovered that:

- prehistoric plants were completely different from
  modern ones, because the fragments of their leaves
  didn't match anything you find today!
- these ancient plants grew from minute, dust-like spores
  instead of large seeds.

Bet you never knew!

*During his round-the-world trip Charles Darwin
collected loads of plant and animal fossils. His most
spectacular discoveries were the fossil skeletons of a
giant South American ground sloth called*
Megatherium. *It looked a bit like an overgrown bear.
If* Megatherium *hadn't become extinct it would have
been able to peer through the first-floor bedroom
windows of today's houses, just by rearing up on its
hind legs. Nothing to worry about, though – it only
ate leaves.*

*Darwin was sure that today's sloths, which are only
about the size of a ten-year-old child and live in the
South American jungles, were related to these extinct
monsters from the past.*

NOT MANY
LEAVES ON
THIS TREE

MODERN
SLOTH

FANTASTIC FREE-RANGE DINO EGGS

When palaeontologists find a really good fossil they sometimes take it along to a local hospital, and borrow a CAT scanner to see what's inside. CAT stands for computerized axial tomography, and a CAT scanner is machine that lets doctors see what's going on inside their patients. It also lets palaeontologists see inside lumps of rock that may contain an important fossil.

Palaeontologists are always digging up amazing fossils. Dinosaur eggs are quite common in some parts of the world. Put them in a CAT scanner and you can sometimes even see baby dinosaur bones inside.

Recently a fossil *Oviraptor* dinosaur was actually found sitting on its nest. It turned up in 1995, in the Gobi Desert in Mongolia. People used to think that *Oviraptor* was a thief, stealing and eating eggs of other dinosaurs, because it was often found around dinosaur nest sites. Then they discovered this unlucky specimen, which must have been sitting on its own nest, protecting its eggs – just like today's ostriches do – when it was buried in a sand-storm.

Dinosaurs have a reputation for being horribly fierce but it looks like this *Oviraptor* was a bit of a heroine, buried alive while she tried to save her babies.

COULD YOU BE A PALAEONTOLOGIST?

You need...
A hammer
Goggles
Tons of patience!

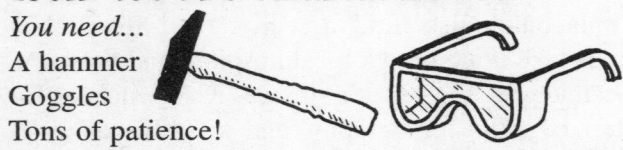

Where to look...
If you're going to be a palaeontologist you'd better learn to recognize rocks that contain fossils. Here's how:

IGNEOUS ROCKS

How formed: spewed out as molten lava by erupting volcanoes.

Fossil finds: usually none – molten lava melts fossils.

BURNT DINOSAUR PONG!

Typical type: granite

ERUPT!

SEDIMENTARY ROCKS

How formed: produced when particles of sand, mud or skeletons of tiny sea creatures cover dead plants and animals, then slowly turn everything to rock.

Fossil finds: full of fossils

Typical types: sandstone, limestone and chalk

METAMORPHIC ROCKS

How formed: from sedimentary or igneous rocks that have been cooked at horribly high temperatures by volcanic activity and turned into different kinds of rock.

Fossil finds: contain some fossils but they're usually burnt to a frazzle by the heat.

Typical types: marble, made when limestone is heated under great pressure.

So your best bet is to search in sedimentary rocks. As you chip down through layers that took millions of years to form, you should find trapped plants and animals from the past. It's a bit like taking a trip back through time, and it can be terribly tedious. It might take hours, days, months or even years to find anything interesting. But if you're really, really lucky, you might just come across a fossil bed...

Fossil beds were formed when dead animals and plants were washed into piles by currents in ancient rivers or seas. They're heaps of fossils all bundled together in a huge lump of rock. So you *could* find hundreds of fossils, all at once.

What to do:
If you *do* find a fossil, you'll need to chip away really carefully with your hammer around the edges.

HORRIBLE HEALTH WARNING!

1 Always wear a pair of safety glasses. Flying rock fragments do serious damage to eyes.

2 Never work under dangerous rocks or cliffs.

A FOSSILIZED HAND. . . AND IT'S WAVING AT US

If all this chipping gets too boring you could fake some fossils instead.

FOSSIL FAKERY

Here are some foolproof methods for fossilizing familiar objects, like your dad's slippers. Choose from the following menu of methods, depending on how much time you're prepared to wait:

For quickest results, you could:
- shut them in a deep freeze. This worked well with mammoths in Siberia, which have been deep frozen and perfectly preserved for thousands of years, since

the last Ice Age. Some are so well preserved that one Japanese scientist thinks he can use their frozen cells to recreate baby mammoths. He's busy searching for a suitable mammoth right now.

SO FAR ALL I'VE FOUND IS SLIPPERS

If you're not in such a hurry, you could:

- hang your dad's slippers under the water that drips from the roof of a limestone cave. The water will be full of dissolved lime, which will soak into the slippers and eventually set like concrete. Come back a few years later and you'll be able to give your dad fossil footwear for his birthday.

BUT THINK HOW HARD-WEARING THEY'LL BE, DAD

For the prettiest results:

- cover them with amber resin, which is formed from the tacky, golden liquid that oozes out of pine trees. When it dries it turns to a transparent yellow stone.

But don't expect rapid results – the amber resin has to fossilize first, and that can take thousands of years. Still, this has worked brilliantly in the past with fossil insects, but you'll need an awful lot of amber to fossilize a pair of slippers.

FOSSILIZED SPIDER IN AMBER, JURASSIC ERA, NEW MEXICO

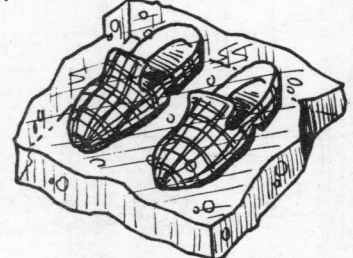

BOB ARKWRIGHT'S SLIPPERS, POST-WAR ERA, GRIMSBY

An even messier method is to:

- dunk the slippers in a pit of thick tar. You can find one of these at Rancho La Brea near Los Angeles in California, where gooey tar bubbles up from below the ground. All sorts of fossil animals have been found perfectly preserved in these pits, even though they fell in thousands of years ago. If it's good enough for sabre-toothed tigers, it's good enough for your dad's slippers.

MY MUM!

10,000 YEARS AGO

MY SLIPPERS!

LAST TUESDAY

But for something really spectacular:

- find an erupting volcano and leave the slippers at the bottom. When Mount Vesuvius in Italy erupted in AD 79 its ash buried the Roman city of Pompeii. Hundreds of people (and slippers) were buried in the ash. It slowly hardened into rock and the bodies (and slippers) rotted away, leaving holes that archaeologists could use like moulds to make plaster casts of the bodies.

And finally, the method that has worked so well for all sorts of sea creatures:

- chuck the slippers into the sea. When they sink they'll be slowly covered in silt. After a few million years, they should turn to stone – and then some poor palaeontologist in the future will have to spend hours, days, months ... even years, chipping them out again.

LIVING FOSSILS

Some fossils aren't dead. (You knew that anyway, didn't you? You only need to look at some of your teachers.)

There are plants and animals that are alive today that look exactly like their ancient relatives that were fossilized millions of years ago. Palaeontologists call them "living fossils".

They're brilliant finds because somehow they've survived natural disasters that wiped out most of the creatures and plants that once lived alongside them.

Most fossils only tell us what the tough bits of animals – like shells, bones and teeth – looked like. All the squashy bits, like blood and guts, skin and fur, rot away without becoming fossilized. But living fossils show us what these missing bits looked like, making it easier to imagine what other fossils would be like if you could put the intestines, muscles, brains and other assorted bloody bits back in their original places.

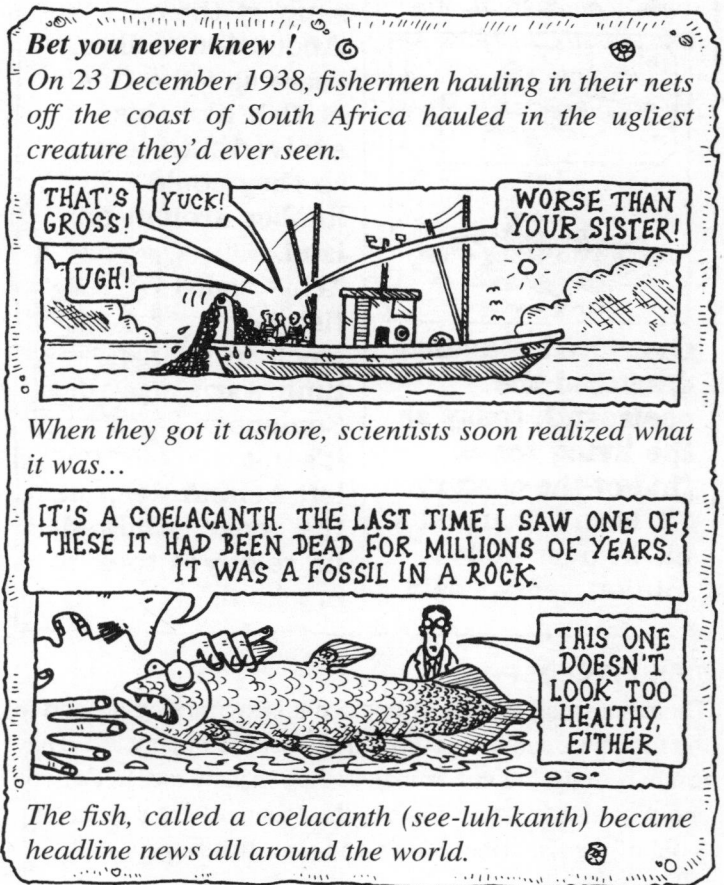

Bet you never knew !

On 23 December 1938, fishermen hauling in their nets off the coast of South Africa hauled in the ugliest creature they'd ever seen.

THAT'S GROSS!

YUCK!

UGH!

WORSE THAN YOUR SISTER!

When they got it ashore, scientists soon realized what it was...

IT'S A COELACANTH. THE LAST TIME I SAW ONE OF THESE IT HAD BEEN DEAD FOR MILLIONS OF YEARS. IT WAS A FOSSIL IN A ROCK.

THIS ONE DOESN'T LOOK TOO HEALTHY, EITHER

The fish, called a coelacanth (see-luh-kanth) became headline news all around the world.

CAPE TOWN CHRONICLE

23 December 1938

Fintastic FIND!

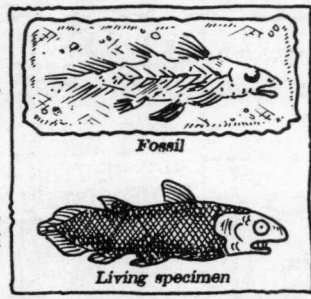
Fossil

Living specimen

Overjoyed scientists described the coelacanth today as the living fossil find-of-the-century.

"It hasn't changed a bit in over 400 million years," said one ecstatic expert, "it's got fantastic fins with bones that support them. About 400 million years ago the fins of fish like this evolved into legs, so they could lumber around on land.

"This weird fish is stuck in a time warp. Somehow it's got left behind deep in the ocean, while all its relatives took to dry land."

Dr. C. Lacanth (Fish expert)

FISH FINGERS?

There's a small colony of coelacanths swimming around in the Indian Ocean to this day, but there aren't many left. They might be ugly, but unfortunately they're tasty too. Let's hope coelacanths stay deep down in the ocean, where they belong – out of the fishermen's nets and your fish fingers.

DINOSAUR FARTS: FACTS YOUR TEACHERS ARE TOO EMBARASSED TO TELL YOU

If you think that vegetables in school dinners are hard to digest, spare a thought for vegetarian dinosaurs.

1 They used to eat plants called cycads (sigh-kads), which still survive as living fossils.

2 Cycad leaves are so tough and hard to digest that dinosaurs had to swallow pebbles, to help them grind up the leathery leaves in their gizzards.

I DON'T KNOW WHAT'S WORSE, EATING THE CYCADS OR THE STONES

SMOOTH PEBBLES

3 These gizzard stones, called gastroliths, are often found amongst fossil dinosaur skeletons, in the place where their gizzard was before it rotted away.

4 Some scientists suspect that vegetarian dinosaurs' indigestible diet explains why these animals got to be so big. Their bodies had to contain huge lengths of guts so that the fibrous fronds could slowly go soft inside them.

5 One thing's for sure – the digestion of cycad leaves produced plenty of gas, so dinosaurs would have produced some thunderous farts.

EARTHQUAKE? METEORITE? VOLCANO?

BOOM!

WORSE... DINOSAUR FART!

FANTASTIC FACTS

Living fossils are still being discovered. One of the latest finds is the Wollemi pine, a relative of the monkey puzzle tree. Specimens were first found in a hidden Australian valley in 1994. Some cheeky monkeys have dug some up and pinched a few already. Sadly living fossils, like ordinary fossils, are very popular collector's items.

There are probably loads more living fossils just waiting to be found. Who knows what strange surprises are hidden in dark and dingy corners of the planet?

Species don't last for ever. They all eventually disappear, and are replaced by new ones. You've probably noticed that there are no dinosaurs roaming around in your local nature reserve today. All that's left of them is their fossil bones. So how did they meet their horrible end?

As usual, scientists came up with a whole load of theories, but now they think they know, thanks to a neat piece of detective work.

DINO DOOMSDAY

The disappearance of the dinosaurs is one of evolution's greatest mysteries. Hundreds of species became extinct, all at once. We know this because geologists find their fossils in rocks that were formed up to 65 million years ago, but in later finds, there's not a dinosaur bone to be seen.

While they lived dinosaurs were fantastically successful, and for over 150 million years they dominated almost every habitat. The biggest meat-eating dinosaurs, like *Tyrannosaurus rex*, had no enemies. So why did the fiercest, meanest, most successful animals on Earth suddenly become extinct 65 million years ago?

TEST YOUR TEACHER

Why did the dinosaurs die? Was it because of...

1 Ultra-violent hurricanes (called ultracanes), that whisked dust into the air, blotted out the sun and plunged the planet into a winter that lasted for years, so the dinosaurs died of the cold?

2 Showers of deadly particles called neutrinos (new-tree-nose), released from the explosion of a dying star, called a supernova? The neutrinos caused fatal cancers in the dinosaurs' bodies.

3 A wayward asteroid, cruising through the solar system? The asteroid collided with Earth causing a massive tidal wave, earthquakes and fires that filled the atmosphere

with dust and smoke, hiding the sun so that dinosaurs
died of cold.

4 Volcanic eruptions in India, that made the atmosphere
hellishly hot? The dinosaurs overheated, couldn't lay
fertile eggs any more, and died out.

Understanding evolution would be a lot simpler if we
could take a trip back in time, so we could witness what
went on in the past. So just for a moment, imagine that
you and your teacher are time travellers, and that you've
been whisked back to that fateful day when the destiny
of the dinosaurs was decided...

You're in North America and the land is swarming
with dinosaurs. It's the dawn of a summer's morning and
you are standing on the edge of a forest of tough cycad
plants. It's 65 million BC!

It's been a cold night and most of the dinosaurs are still chilled and sluggish. They yawn, snore and now and then let loose a deafening fart. You're safe for now, as they won't start moving about much until the sun has warmed them up.

Watch where you put your feet, though! There's dinosaur dung all over the place. In 65 million years' time it will have turned into fossilized coprolites, but for now it's squelchy and very, *very* smelly.

This morning, the dinosaurs are unusually restless. There's a distant, pale yellow glow in the eastern sky. In a few minutes the sun will rise, but all eyes that are open are already looking south, towards a brilliant glow in the sky that has been growing brighter every day. It started as a shining speck, months ago, and grew until it looked as large as the moon.

Today it's as bright as the sun that's about to creep over the horizon – and it is rushing towards the Earth like a giant thunderbolt. It's moving towards the Earth's surface at a speed of 9 km (6 miles) per second. It's been wandering through the solar system for millions of years, until at last gravity started to pull it towards our planet.

There is a flash of light hundreds of miles south of where you're standing now. The asteroid has struck at last. All is still and silent as the rising sun begins to strike the leathery hides of the dinosaurs.

At first it seems as though nothing has happened. Then, after several minutes the sound of the distant explosion arrives, as a thunderous, ear-splitting rumble. The dinosaurs struggle to their feet and lumber around in a blind panic. Look out! Dive for cover behind a rock! They'll crush underfoot everything that gets in their way.

The ground trembles and shakes. Earthquakes tear the soil apart, creating yawning chasms big enough to swallow the largest dinosaurs. There are scenes of terrible and total destruction all over Earth. Thousands of square miles of land around the asteroid's crater are lifeless. Great fires sweep across dry grasslands and forests, fanned by howling gales.

At sea, a towering tidal wave over a kilometre high is rolling away from the crater where the asteroid landed. It will engulf islands, washing them clean of life, and then sweep inland over the coasts of continents, drowning anything in its path.

But most frightening of all, a giant mushroom cloud of smoke and dust is already rising into the stratosphere, and spreading. By the middle of the day it will have blotted out the sun, casting the world into a twilight that will last for years. Plants, starved of sunlight, wither and die – very bad news if you're a giant and very hungry plant-eating dinosaur.

You can breathe a sigh of relief now, 'cos you can leap forward in time, back into the twentieth century. Did you remember to remind your teacher to come back with you? I know it's tempting, but...

So **3** – a collision with an asteroid – is the answer that most scientists favour, but how did they work it out? The scientist who came up with the answer was...

Hall of fame: Luis Walter Alvarez (1911–1988)
Nationality: American

Luis Alvarez was a man with a lively mind. He was a physics professor who studied cosmic rays. During the Second World War he invented a kind of radar that let aeroplanes land when the ground was hidden under a blanket of fog. After that he spent his life working out what atoms are made from – and won a Nobel Prize for his discoveries. In his spare time he used X-rays to find out what was inside an Egyptian pyramid, and also found time to figure out what happened to the dinosaurs.

Alvarez and his son, Walter, believed that a giant asteroid collided with Earth 65 million years ago. The awesome asteroid collision sent out a giant tidal wave that swept over islands in the oceans and flooded the edges of the land. It filled the atmosphere with dust and choking gases that spread around the planet, blocking out the sun and plunging Earth into a winter that went on for years.

Several years of continuous winter would have been very bad news for dinosaurs. We mammals generate and store warmth in our bodies from the chemical reactions that break down our food, so our body temperature stays steady even on the coldest days. But dinosaurs were cold-blooded and needed warmth from sunshine to boost their body temperature. They probably spent most of their time lounging around in the sun all day, soaking up the rays.

So once winter set in the cold-blooded dinosaurs started to shiver, and soon died out. The asteroid wiped out three-quarters of all the living things on the planet. The era of the dinosaurs was over. The reign of the warm-blooded mammals, that had survived the catastrophe, was about to begin.

But could it really have happened like this?

FANTASTIC FACTS: CLUES TO A CALAMITOUS COLLISION

- Asteroids collide with planets all the time. The icy centre of a comet that exploded five miles above Tunguska in Siberia in 1908 flattened 1,200 square miles of forest and singed the clothes of people 60 miles away.

VИeH ЛК ТЛИGVSKA ЛЛHг ЛЛ ЬИЛOр ИOЛр eIIV ИЛЛ!*

*LIVING IN TUNGUSKA IS SO BORING – NOTHING EXCITING EVER HAPPENS

- The solar system is a bit like a 3D snooker table. Sooner or later the smaller lumps of rock that are whizzing around are bound to collide with something big. Our moon is covered with asteroid craters. We can still see them because there's no wind or water up there, to wear them away.

- Geologists have found a monster crater, made by an asteroid about 65 million years ago, in the sea off the Yucatan Peninsula in Mexico. Could this be the big one, that brought doomsday for dinosaurs?

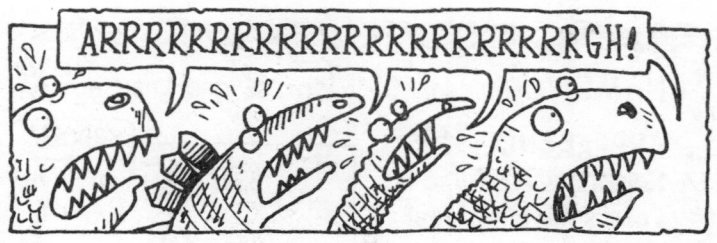

- Any asteroid that made a hole that big would have been 10,000 times more destructive than all the nuclear bombs that have ever been built.
- Asteroids carry a rare element called iridium. There is a layer of dust loaded with iridium covering rocks all over the world that was laid down 65 million years ago. The iridium particles must have settled from the dust cloud after the asteroid struck.

Bet you never knew!
The mass extinction of dinosaurs 65 million years ago is the one that everybody talks about, but it wasn't the only time when life on Earth had nearly been wiped out. About 245 million years ago nearly 96 per cent of all species became extinct. That was doomsday for the trundling trilobites and savage sea scorpions. No one is really sure why that happened. Many scientists believe the planet got hotter, so some of the seas dried up, wiping out animals that lived in shallow water. Also most of the sea creatures that died out had tiny larval stages that began life swimming in the plankton in the surface layers of the sea. So perhaps chemical changes in the sea poisoned them. We'll never know for sure.

Even earlier than this, another mysterious mass extinction wiped out these incredible creatures:

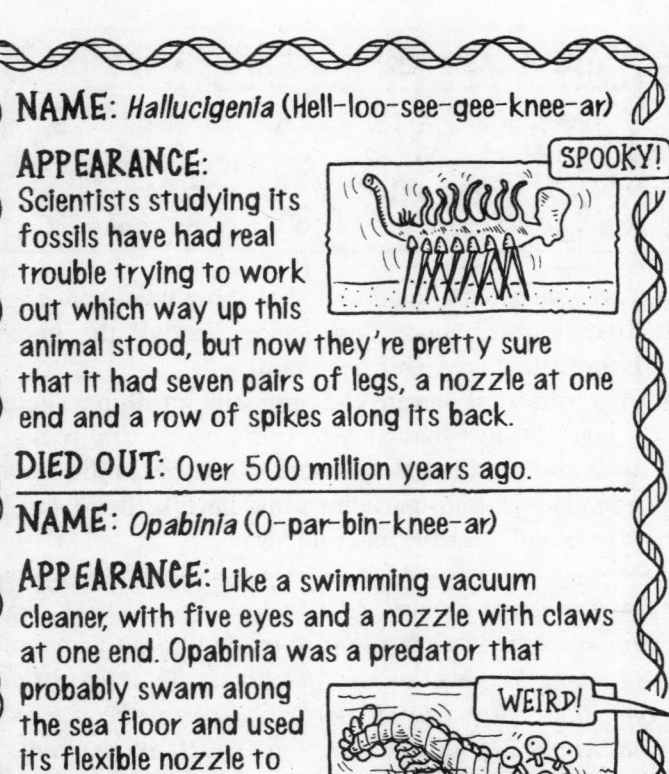

NAME: *Hallucigenia* (Hell-loo-see-gee-knee-ar)

APPEARANCE:
Scientists studying its
fossils have had real
trouble trying to work
out which way up this
animal stood, but now they're pretty sure
that it had seven pairs of legs, a nozzle at one
end and a row of spikes along its back.

SPOOKY!

DIED OUT: Over 500 million years ago.

NAME: *Opabinia* (O-par-bin-knee-ar)

APPEARANCE: Like a swimming vacuum
cleaner, with five eyes and a nozzle with claws
at one end. Opabinia was a predator that
probably swam along
the sea floor and used
its flexible nozzle to
grab anything that
came too close.

WEIRD!

DIED OUT: Over 500 million years ago.

Fortunately, evolution is very good at coming up with
new designs to equip creatures for tough conditions in
a changing world. Some life has always pulled through
after catastrophic mass extinctions. Sometimes it seems
that – if you give it enough time – evolution can invent
just about anything…

FISH WITH FEET

Evolution is very good at inventing new animals without any help from us. Nothing big happens overnight. Each small step can take millions of years. But give it enough time and evolution can come up with some amazing inventions. Take eyes, for example...

It all started with a simple chemical that was sensitive to light.

This was useful because it allowed its owner to tell whether it was:

• out in the open, where it might be eaten by its enemies.

• or under a stone, where it would be safe.

Next, the light detector chemical became concentrated inside a light sensitive patch inside a small pit in the skin, with just a tiny hole letting light in. The result was a kind of camera eye, which could form a picture. It works surprisingly well...

Dare you discover ... how to see the world through a pinhole camera?

• Find a tube. Something about 30 cm long and 8 cm wide would be ideal, but the exact size doesn't matter.

- Tape some aluminium foil over one end and prick the tiniest possible hole in the middle with a sharp pin.
- Tape a piece of tracing paper over the other end.
- Then point the pinhole at a bright window or bright light. You'll see an image upside down on the tracing paper. This is how a pinhole camera works. Some snails have got eyes like this.

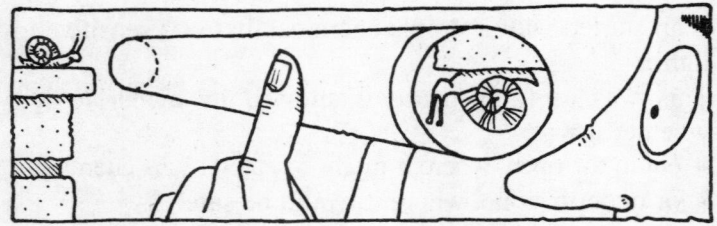

So, now you've seen the world through the eye of a snail. The picture is clear enough to tell you whether that animal lurking outside your home is a friend or an enemy – even if it's upside down.

After that, eyes just got better and better, one step at a time.

- In some animals the pit became filled with jelly that bent the light rays and focused them on to light sensitive cells. So the picture got clearer.

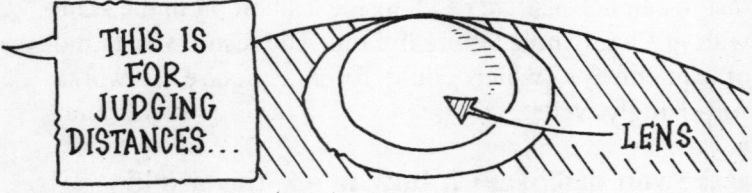

THIS IS FOR JUDGING DISTANCES...

LENS

- Then the jelly hardened into a lens which could be pulled by muscles into different shapes. This focused things that were close up or far away.

- A transparent skin evolved, that covered the delicate eye to protect it.

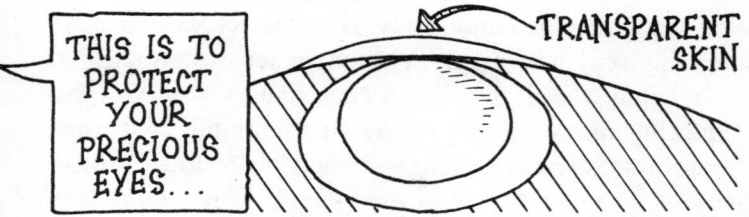

- A pupil evolved inside the eye, to open and close the hole where light entered, so that it worked in bright or dim light.

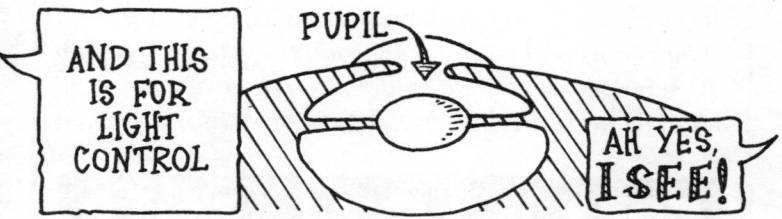

It's taken evolution the best part of 1,000 million years to come up with an eye like ours – but it managed it in the end. And what's even more amazing is that it's done it more than once, in different groups of animals. Squid, which are members of the snail family, have eyes that are almost as good as ours.

CAVE CREATURES

Deep in underground caves there are animals that biologists call troglodytes – species that live in caves all their lives and never come to the surface. Some troglodytes, like the poor old Texas blind salamander, evolved from ancestors that once lived on the surface and had eyes. When they evolved into cave dwellers their eyes gradually disappeared again, because they were useless in total darkness. It's scary living in places like this, and the salamander has to grope its way around, pursuing prey with an extra-sensitive sense of smell.

Imagine what it must have been like to be a biologist exploring one of these creepy caves for the first time. Some blind spiders have evolved a horrible hunting method, feeling for their prey with long dangly legs, before they sink their jaws into its body. You need nerves of steel if you want to explore the eyeless world of the troglodytes.

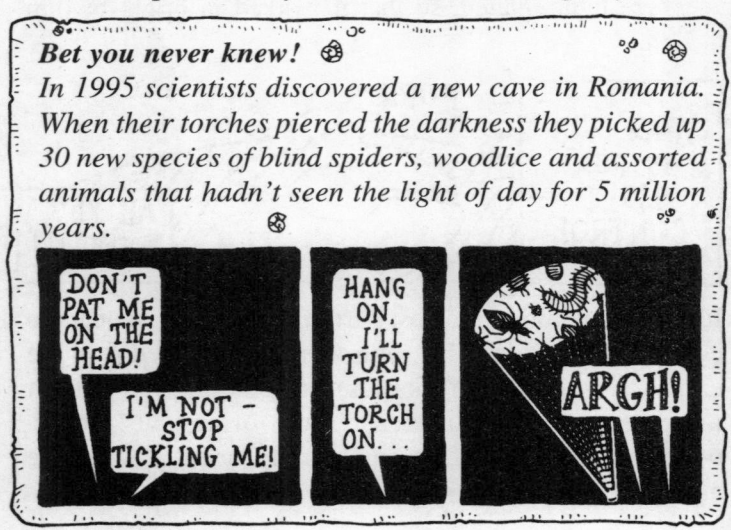

Bet you never knew!
In 1995 scientists discovered a new cave in Romania. When their torches pierced the darkness they picked up 30 new species of blind spiders, woodlice and assorted animals that hadn't seen the light of day for 5 million years.

DON'T PAT ME ON THE HEAD!

I'M NOT – STOP TICKLING ME!

HANG ON, I'LL TURN THE TORCH ON...

ARGH!

TEST YOUR TEACHER
Stygophilic (say sty-go-fill-ik) means:
1 to live in a pig sty.
2 to live in dark caves.
3 a pig that's so fat it can't fit in its sty.

Answer: 2)

PTEROSAURS TAKE OFF

Sometimes evolution creates new inventions by taking something that already exists and adapting it so that it can be used for something else.

Back in the Jurassic era, 200 million years ago, it was horribly hot during the day and uncomfortably cool at night. Some small ancestors of pterosaurs found themselves shivering at dawn, after a long cool night, and wilting by lunchtime, when the sun blazed down overhead.

But some of these ancestral pterosaurs evolved a terrific trick for preventing their body temperature from going up and down like a yo-yo. They grew sheets of thin skin full of blood vessels between their limbs and their body, to increase their surface area. This meant they could cool down faster in the day, and spread their wings to catch the first warm rays of the sun at dawn.

On really hot days they might have flapped these sheets of skin to create a cool breeze. And suddenly, they were airborne. Their cooling devices were perfectly pre-adapted to become glider wings.

ONE SMALL STEP FOR FISH...

Remember the coelacanth (see-la-kanth), the living fossil on page 87?

Similar animals crawled out of the sea millions of years ago and evolved into animals that could live in water or on land – they became amphibians, like today's frogs, toads and newts. The coelacanth's bony fins were already well on their way to becoming bony legs.

Of course, climbing out on to land was only half the battle. Fish breathe through gills that are designed to take in oxygen from water, and these aren't much use on land. Clambering out onto dry land would have been a disaster unless they'd already begun to evolve a way of breathing oxygen from air instead of from water. And luckily, they'd done just that.

Today, if you dig down into dried mud in African lake beds in the dry season, you'll find fish. Lung fish. They evolved extra loops in their guts that expanded into lungs, for breathing air. They probably first evolved these extra gut gas-exchangers for living in murky, muddy waters where there wasn't much oxygen. Today they can use them to breathe air when they're buried in a dry lake bed, waiting for the rain to come and fill up their lake again.

So when fish began to scramble out on to land they were already equipped with a primitive kind of lung that allowed them to breath oxygen from air if they gulped it into their gut extensions, which eventually evolved into proper, more efficient lungs.

A WHOLE NEW YOU?

If you look at animals closely enough, you often find that they already have the essential equipment for evolving into something new. Shrink a bit here, stretch a bit there and they can be transformed into something that looks completely different.

These days scientists can transform animals by snipping genes out of one animal and splicing them into another one, to alter the genetic instructions for making its body. It's called genetic engineering.

Who knows, maybe in the future – with a little help from genetic engineers – we'll be able to equip people with some useful new body bits, like...

INFRARED VISION

What's infrared?

Invisible light given out by warm objects.

Who can see it?

Horribly poisonous snakes called pit vipers. They use it to "see" the warm bodies of their prey in total darkness.

What could we use it for?

You'd never tread on the cat in the dark, for a start. Everyone would emit a warm, rosy glow after dark. And you could go bird-watching at night.

BUILT-IN COMPASSES

What do they do?

They allow some animals to find their way around the world (and get back home again) without using a compass. They're tiny magnetic granules in their brains, that give them a sense of direction.

Who's got them?

Honey-bees and pigeons, for certain, and maybe some other animals too. Pigeons and migrating birds use a built-in compass to find their way home over hundreds of miles of unfamiliar territory.

How would it help us?

You'd never get lost. You'd always know which direction

to walk in, wherever you were, to get home. The bad news would be that you'd never be able to say you got lost when you were late for school.

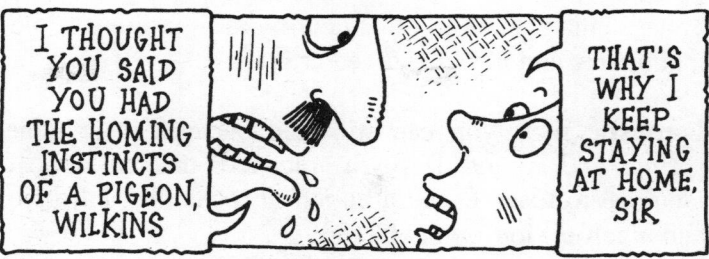

BODY ELECTRICITY
What is it?
Electric charges stored in body muscles.
Who's got it?
Electric eels. They use it to stun their prey.
How would it help us?
You'd never need batteries for your torch again. But you'd need to be very careful when you shook hands.

It's fun trying to imagine how humans could be modified in the future, either by evolution or by genetic engineers, but we're only just beginning to discover what kind of animals we evolved from in the past. Ever since Darwin came up with his theory of evolution, scientists have suspected that monkeys and men share the same ancient ancestors…

NEW KIDS ON THE BLOCK

Today our planet is inhabited by a mixture of old inhabitants and newly evolved arrivals.

Fantastic fact: you can still find bacteria in sulphur springs and around deep-sea volcanoes that are almost identical to fossil bacteria buried in rocks that are three and a half billion years old.

Bet you never knew! 🐞
Mosses – those tiny green plants that grow in cracks in pavements and are trodden underfoot without a second thought every day – are incredible survivors. They haven't changed much since they first invaded land, over 500 million years ago. Today's moss species are very similar to the ones that were trodden underfoot by the dinosaurs. They are one of evolution's success stories.

We humans are recent arrivals – the new kids on the block. Will we be as successful and survive as long as sulphur bacteria and mosses? It's too soon to tell. But we can look backwards through the human family photo album and search for clues to one of evolution's most fascinating questions … who were the first humans?

You probably think you've got a pretty good idea what

the first humans looked like, from the pictures that are often drawn in comics. You know the kind of thing…

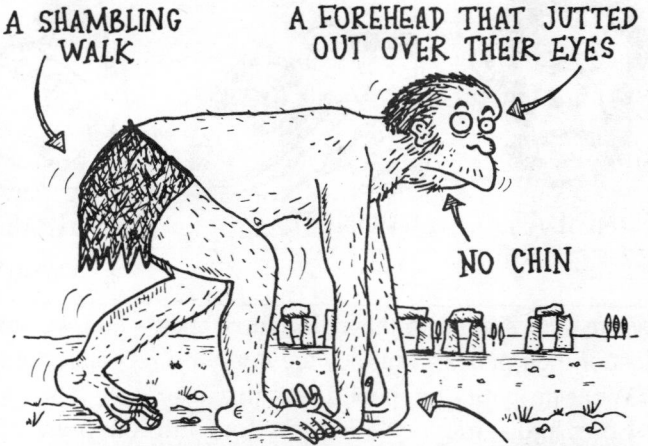

A SHAMBLING WALK

A FOREHEAD THAT JUTTED OUT OVER THEIR EYES

NO CHIN

LONG ARMS THAT DANGLED SO THAT THEIR KNUCKLES DRAGGED ALONG THE GROUND

Sounds familiar?

That's right. They looked very much like today's PE teachers.

Actually, we can't really be sure what the first humans looked like, because we've only got a few scattered bones to go on. If they were around today the first humans would probably be very upset at being drawn like this in comics (and being compared with PE teachers).

But let's get one thing straight. Whatever you might have heard, humans didn't evolve from chimpanzees, gorillas or PE teachers.

TEST YOUR TEACHER

Pongidae (pon-gid-ee) is:

1 The scientific name for the chimp family.

2 The scientific name for the bacteria in smelly trainers.

3 The breathtaking brand of aftershave used by teachers.

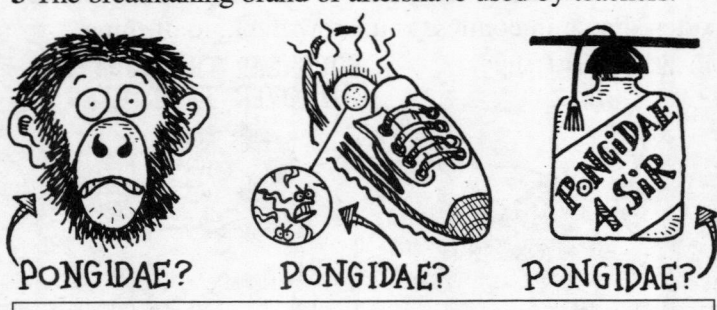

PONGIDAE? PONGIDAE? PONGIDAE?

Answer: 1

We are very similar to these fine furry apes – and we share most of their genes – but they are not our direct ancestors.

What probably happened was this.

Long ago – maybe as long as four million years – an unknown chimp-like ape lived in Africa. It was probably horribly hairy and probably walked on all four legs.

...AND **PROBABLY** LOOKED LIKE THIS

OOH, OOH, AH, AH!

Some of these ancient ancestors evolved into today's chimps. Another branch of the family took off in a different direction, and evolved into hominids – the name the scientists give to the branch of the ape family that humans belong to. Today's chimps will never evolve into humans, however many million years we wait – they're following their own evolutionary path, one that leads away from humans.

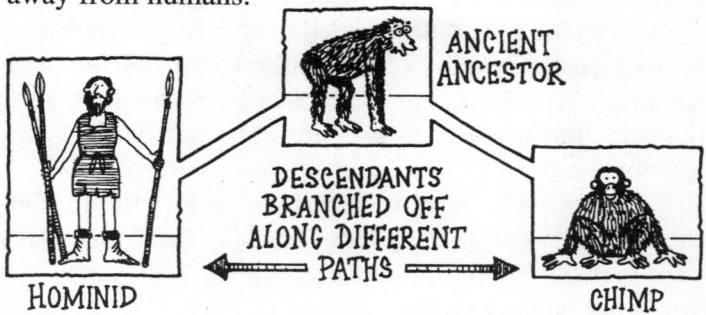

DESCENDANTS BRANCHED OFF ALONG DIFFERENT PATHS

ANCIENT ANCESTOR

HOMINID

CHIMP

For most of this century scientists have been trying to find remains of our mysterious, extinct hominid ancestors – the missing links in the evolutionary story – who left the trees and walked upright across the African Plains.

This, for example is Australopithecus (Os-tral-o-pith-e-cus), whose name means "southern ape". He lived about four million years ago.

AUSTRALOPITHECUS

NOT TO BE CONFUSED WITH MR BROWN SCIENCE TEACHER

WALK TALL

The first person to prove that our ancient ancestors walked upright like us was an anthropologist called Mary Leakey. In 1976, at a place called Laetoli in Tanzania, she discovered three trails of 3.6-million-year-old hominid footprints – rock-solid evidence that, even that long ago, our ancestors walked on two legs, and not on all fours like monkeys.

So what made humans decide to walk upright, after they'd started out padding around on all fours? Scientists have come up with different suggestions. See which one you think might be right.

1 Walking on two legs helped humans to lose heat in hot climates. Standing up straight meant they exposed less of their body to the scorching African sun and might have helped keep their heads and brains cool.

2 Or it might have been for protection. If they stood up straight, maybe they could see predators coming more easily? Life for early hominids could be horribly hazardous.

3 Frees the hands for making and using tools.

In 1924 a group of palaeontologists working in Taung, South Africa unearthed a pile of bones. They were able to work out that the bones were about 3 million years old and belonged to several small animals. Most of the bones came from rat-like creatures, but some bones looked strangely familiar. When they looked more closely, they discovered that these bones belonged to a child. But this child wouldn't have looked anything like you do. This child belonged to an early species of hominid, called *Australopithecus africanus*. He seems to have come to a horrible end. But how did it happen?

a) Was he pounced on by a pack of rats and did he die fighting them off, killing several in the struggle?

b) Was he buried alongside the family pets, after he died of natural causes?

c) Or was he killed by an eagle, that cut him up into pieces with its fearsome beak and carried him back in bite-sized chunks to its nest, to feed its chicks.

LUCY OR LUCIAN?

Scientists tend to get very wrapped up in their work. When they find a particularly interesting specimen, they can really get quite attached to it. Sometimes they might even give it a name.

This happened when a well-preserved specimen was found, piece by piece, in the 1970s in Ethiopia. It was a female member of a hominid called *Australopithecus afarensis* (which means "southern ape from the Afar region of Ethiopia"). Like us, she walked upright but when she was fully grown she was no bigger than an average 12-year-old child today – about 1.3 metres tall.

She was such a fantastic specimen that she got herself a name: Lucy, after the Beatles song, "Lucy in the Sky with Diamonds".

More recently a question has arisen about Lucy. She might not be a girl after all. After 3 million years it's

114

hard to tell. So will Lucy have to be renamed Lucian? Scientists are still arguing about that one.

LUVERLY LATIN

I bet you're wondering where all these strange, tongue-twisting scientific names come from.

Scientists give all living things a name written in Latin, the language of the ancient Romans. This is because Latin names are understood by all scientists, everywhere. If the names were written in English or Chinese or Spanish, they wouldn't mean much to people who didn't speak those languages.

Latin names come in two parts. The first part is called the genus and the second part is the species. There are often dozens of different species in a genus. For example, there are several different kinds of big cat. They're all in the genus *Panthera*, but each one has a different species name, so...

- *Panthera tigris* is the tiger
- *Panthera leo* is the lion
- *Panthera pardus* is the African leopard
- *Panthera onca* is the jaguar

If the Pink Panther had a Latin name it would be *Panthera rosea*.

115

Latin names usually tell you something about their owners. So…

GLUTINOSUS MEANS STICKY

STICK!

FOETIDUS MEANS SMELLY

DRIP!

SORDIDUS MEANS DIRTY-LOOKING

SCHOOL CUSTARD

LUBRICUS MEANS SLIPPERY

SPLOSH!

GLEBOSUS MEANS LUMPY

SLIP!

SNARL!

FEROX MEANS FIERCE

SIGH!

PUFF!

ARMATUS MEANS ARMED

MACULATUM MEANS SPOTTY

116

FOSSIL MAN'S FAMILY ALBUM

Once human evolution got into its stride, a whole series of hopeful hominids appeared on the scene. It's time to meet a few relatives you didn't know you had:

HANDYMAN

NAME: *Homo habilis* (which means "tool-making man").

AGE: Lived between one and a half and two million years ago.

LAST KNOWN ADDRESS: First found by Mary Leakey in Africa, alongside the bones of lots of our other relatives.

APPEARANCE: Hard to say, because scientists have only found a few bones. But probably very hairy, and walked upright.

BEST KNOWN FOR: Inventing stone tools. Humans were starting to get clever.

FIRE MAN

NAME: Could be another member of the species *Homo erectus* (the species lasted a long time), although some scientists have given him the more impressive name of *Homo heidelburgensis*, because suspiciously similar bones have been dug up around Heidelburg in Germany.

AGE: First appeared about one and a half million years ago.

LAST KNOWN ADDRESS: Africa, Asia and Europe.

APPEARANCE: Taller, and larger brain than *Homo habilis*.

BEST KNOWN FOR: Setting fire to things. The first hominid to use fire.

BOXGROVE MAN

NAME: *Homo heidelbergensis*. Seen by some scientists as another kind of *Homo erectus*.

AGE: Oldest known Englishman – is 450,000 years old. May have still been around 30,000 years ago in some parts of the world.

LAST KNOWN ADDRESS: Boxgrove in Sussex, England.

APPEARANCE: Hard to tell. A jaw bone was found near Heidelburg. Then archaeologists found a few teeth and a leg bone in 1995. That's not a lot to go on.

BEST KNOWN FOR: Butchery. His remains were found amongst rhinoceros bones that probably belonged to one that he skinned and ate (rhinoceros lived in Britain before Ice Ages drove them further south).

NEANDERTHAL MAN

NAME: *Homo neandertalensis* (which means "wise man, from the Neander valley in Germany").

AGE: Was still around in Europe until about 30,000 years ago.

LAST KNOWN ADDRESS: Lived in several places in Western Europe.

BEST KNOWN FOR: Living in caves. Probably far more intelligent than we gave them credit for. They had bigger brains than us, for a start.

WISE MAN

NAME: *Homo sapiens* (which means "wise man"). And that means you. You are a member of this species.

AGE: About 250,000 years.

ADDRESS: Everywhere.

BEST KNOWN FOR: Outrageous behaviour.

Until the 1950s, scientists believed there was another type of hominid roaming around on Earth about 200,000 years ago. His name was Piltdown Man, because his skull was found in Piltdown, Sussex in England. He was discovered in 1908.

Chemical tests finally proved that Piltdown Man was a complete hoax! His skull was made by glueing together broken pieces of skulls from a variety of skeletons. No one is absolutely certain to this day who made a monkey out of so many scientists, but there have been all sorts of theories.

Some say the forger was Charles Dawson, the amateur geologist who first unearthed the skull. Others point the finger at Sir Arthur Conan Doyle, the author and creator of Sherlock Holmes. Conan Doyle was a keen amateur bone hunter who lived just next door to the quarry where the skull was found, **and** *he once wrote a book called* The Lost World *where forged fossils play a part in the plot.*

ABOMINABLE BUT TRUE?

In the last century Chinese scientists made a remarkable discovery. They found strange items on sale in Chinese markets, labelled "dragon's teeth". The scientists soon proved that these teeth were actually fossilized teeth of a giant, gorilla-like animal. More teeth were discovered in caves, alongside some outsized skeletons.

The scientists were able to prove that, once upon a time, something like a million years ago, there lived a monster ape, who was almost twice as big as today's humans. Scientists called the creature *Gigantopithecus* (Jy-gan-toe-pith-ikus) – which means giant ape. Could that be how myths about giants have come about? Was the American Bigfoot, or the Abominable Snowman of the Himalayas really *Gigantopithecus*? And does it still exist?

We may never find an Abominable Snowman, but finding all the other species that exist today is a high priority for scientists. And that's turning out to be a major problem, because if you don't know a species exists, how do you know what to look for...?

WHAT ELSE IS OUT THERE?

It's surprising how easily scientists can overlook large animals. You might think that they would have found all the most spectacular creatures long ago, but new ones keep turning up.

So how on earth did scientists manage to miss...

MEGAMOUTH SHARKS

(Megachasma pelagios – which means "great yawning mouth of the open sea ")

FIRST FOUND: Caught accidentally by a research ship off Hawaii in 1976. No more seen until another one turned up off the Californian coast in 1983. Since then a few more have been seen around Australia and Japan.

QUICK! IN HERE!

FINEST FEATURES: The sixth largest shark in the world, five metres long, with a massive mouth. Seems surprisingly friendly, even though it has 400 teeth arranged in 236 rows. Luckily, they're all very small. The inside of its mouth glows in the dark and biologists believe that it cruises around in the deep ocean with its mouth open, looking like a predatory torch and inviting minute marine life to swim towards the glow.

As an added treat, scientists have also discovered a new kind of parasitic worm that lives in megamouth's guts.

FUTURE PROSPECTS: Not too bad. They're shy – always a good policy when humans are around. Mention the word "shark" and most people reach for a harpoon.

And who'd have thought that we could overlook something as large as…

THE VU QUANG OX
(Pseudoryx nghetinhensis)

I LIKE MY MEAT RARE!

FIRST FOUND: In bits, in a meat market in Vietnam, in 1992. Local people already knew what it looked like (and how to cook it). Living specimens not seen by Western scientists until 1994.

FINEST FEATURES: About as big as a goat, with extremely handsome horns.

FUTURE PROSPECTS: Succulent meat, so the Vu Quang's future might not be too bright. And those horns would make a tempting hunter's trophy . . .

And why did it take so long to find…

ASTBESTOPLUMA SPONGE

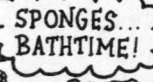

SPONGES... BATHTIME!

PRAWNS... TEATIME!

FIRST FOUND: By divers exploring underwater caves in the Mediterranean, in 1994.

FINEST FEATURES: The world's only meat-eating sponge. Seems to like eating small prawns. It catches them with hooks on tiny tentacles all over its surface – they work like Velcro, snaring anything that blunders into them.

FUTURE PROSPECTS: Murky. The Mediterranean is horribly polluted, so it may not survive.

123

And, although we've probably been eating them for years, scientists failed to spot the tiny…

SYMBION PANDORA

I'M QUITE ATTACHED TO THEM, REALLY!

FIRST FOUND: Attached to the mouths of Norwegian lobsters in 1995.

FINEST FEATURES: A small animal, only one millimetre long, but a mega discovery. *Symbion* is a Cycliophoran (Sy-klee-off-or-ran) – a completely new, major group of animals that are unlike anything else on Earth. Males spend their whole lives perched on females. Both can rebuild parts of their bodies if they get damaged.

FUTURE PROSPECTS: Depends on how well Norwegian lobsters do, really, because *Symbion* is permanently attached to their mouths. People eat Norwegian lobsters, so they've been eating *Symbion* for years, without realizing it.

Look closely, and who knows what weird and wonderful creatures might be lurking in unexplored parts of the world? Although scientists have been exploring the Earth for centuries in their search for new species, they've still only found a tiny fraction of the total number that live on the planet.

COUNTING SPECIES

We share our planet with vast numbers of other kinds of plants and animals. Have you any idea how many species exist?

Try asking your teacher first. Are there:
a) 1 million?
b) 10 million?

c) 30 million?

d) 100 million?

Answer: No one really knows. So far biologists have found and described about one and a half million, but they all agree (for once!) that there must be many more. One of the scientists who's tried harder than most to search out new species is an American beetle expert, called Terry Erwin.

Erwin carried out a devastatingly simple experiment. He covered a tree called *Luehia seemannii* in the Panamanian rain forest with smoke and collected all the dazed beetles that fell out of its branches.

He found over 160 undiscovered beetle species amongst the pile of beetles that collected around his feet. He knew that there are about 50,000 different species of tropical rain forest tree, so Terry did a few simple sums to work out how many more undiscovered beetles might be hiding in rain forests.

Terry Erwin was only looking at beetles. If there are 8 million of them, how many other insects might there be?

How many worms, snails and other creepy-crawlies, not to mention fungi, plants and bacteria, are there? Not long ago, researchers in Norway dug up 4,000 new species of bacteria in a single teaspoonful of soil.

So if your teacher guessed that 100 million species was the answer, they might be right. (Don't tell them, though. Teachers can get cocky if they think they're right all the time.)

Today, sadly, extinctions are happening faster and faster, and man is mostly to blame. Many of the best habitats are being destroyed by man through pollution or to make way for new homes, industries and farmlands. So far we humans haven't been too clever when it comes to conserving biodiversity. One way or another, we are wiping out thousands of species. So spare a thought for:

- The dodo. Once lived on the tiny island of Mauritius in the Indian Ocean. It was especially happy because it had no enemies on the island. Until, of course, man arrived and brought rats, cats and dogs. The poor old dodo had no wings, so it couldn't fly off. The last dodo was so slow, it bit the dust as long ago as 1680.
- Steller's sea cow. A tame and gentle creature. Named after George Steller, a German naturalist who discovered the sea cow when he was shipwrecked in 1742. The last sea cow was spotted in 1769, and it followed the fate of the rest of its family … to be eaten by sailors.
- The passenger pigeon. In the early 1800s the skies above the American forests were filled with passenger pigeons, as they flew in flocks up to 300 million strong.

Incredibly, by 1914 there was only one passenger pigeon left. Passenger pigeons had been hunted down for food and the forests where they nested were destroyed. Each pair of birds only laid a single egg each year, so farmers simply killed them faster than they could breed. When the last passenger pigeon popped off its perch in Cincinnati Zoo the species was finally finished.

- The Tasmanian wolf looked like a smaller, slimmer version of the European wolf, but was striped and used to carry its babies in a pouch, like a kangaroo. Sheep farmers on the island of Tasmania were furious when it took a fancy to their flocks, so they wiped it out. The last survivor died in Hobart Zoo in 1936.

- The dusky seaside sparrow. Once upon a time, the Cape Kennedy space centre was just a vast stretch of marshland. It was a sparrow's paradise. But then the rockets went up, and the bird's came down as the development of the site wiped out their food supply. Scientists couldn't save them, and this sparrow made its final flight in 1984.

EPILOGUE

Nothing can bring back extinct species, but there's still time to save tigers, Spix's macaw, the Californian condor, the Madagascan serpent eagle, the ivory-billed woodpecker, the hawksbill turtle and the giant panda, which are all sliding towards extinction...

One thing is certain. It's taken a horribly long time for them to evolve, so scientists aren't going to let them disappear without a fight.

EVOLVE OR DIE

QUIZ

Now find out if you're an Evolve or Die expert!

Prove it!

So, do you think you've got the gist of genes and understood evolution? Take these quick quizzes and find out if you are a true Homo sapiens ("wise man") or nothing more than a moronic monkey.

GRIPPING GENES

The discovery of genes opened up a whole new world of understanding the human body. It was as though strange scientists had suddenly mastered the meaning of life. But what are these peculiar particles, and just why are they so important? Take this quick quiz and find out.

1 What role do genes play in the human body?
a) They create blood cells.
b) They control inherited characteristics.
c) No one knows...

2 What happens when a dominant gene and a recessive gene combine in offspring?

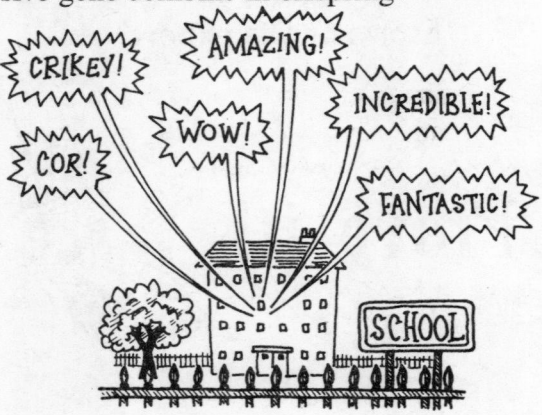

a) The characteristics of both genes combine to make a hybrid.
b) The characteristic of the recessive gene show.
c) The characteristics of the dominant gene show.

3 What is the name of the body bit that carries your genes?
a) Chromosome
b) Metronome
c) Garden gnome

4 What is the name given to the process by which genes change naturally?
a) Genetics
b) Mutation
c) Alteration

5 How long does it take for one human cell to completely copy its DNA?
a) Eight hours
b) One year
c) Your whole lifetime

6 How many pairs of chromosomes are found in each cell of the human body?
a) 23
b) 46
c) 2

7 What human cells don't have this number of chromosomes?
a) Egg and sperm cells
b) Hair cells
c) Skin cells

8 Which of the following statements is true?
a) Goldfish have the same number of chromosomes as humans.
b) Goldfish have more chromosomes than humans.
c) Goldfish have few chromosomes than humans.

Answers:
1b; 2c; 3a; 4b; 5a; 6a; 7a (Egg and sperm cells have 23 chromosomes each – not 23 pairs); **8b**

DOTTY DARWIN

Old Charles Darwin turned beliefs about the origin of living things upside down with his theory of evolution. Can you tell which of the following statements about the nutty naturalist are true and which are false?

1 Darwin originally studied medicine but dropped out to study theology (religion) instead.

2 Crazy Charles married his niece, Emma Wedgewood.

3 On the journey back from the Galapagos Islands, Darwin and others on board the Beagle ate all the giant tortoises they had collected as a tasty meal.

4 Other than tempting tortoises, Darwin was actually a very fussy eater.

5 Darwin suffered badly from seasickness throughout the whole five-year voyage of the Beagle.

6 Darwin tried to create flying tortoises by breeding them with birds.

7 When his book On the Origin of Species was published, Darwin thought that the 1,250 copies of the original print run was way too many.

8 Darwin took 20 years to publish his book.

Answers:

1 True. As it turned out, he didn't like theology much either (even though his dad hoped he'd become a clergyman).

2 False. Emma was actually his first cousin.

3 True. Having tucked into the tortoises, greedy Darwin was left with only their shells to study.

4 False. Even as a student Darwin had a passion for the unusual, and presided over "The Glutton Club", which met every week to eat "strange flesh" (like hawks and owls).

5 True. Charles chucked up A LOT.

6 False. Although legend has it he once tried to create flying monkeys by breeding them with vultures!

7 True. He was horribly wrong about that though – every copy of the book sold on the first day!

8 True. He knew that religious people would be mighty mad at his suggestions so he kept mum.

UNDERSTANDING EVOLUTION

It took strange scientists hundreds of years to understand evolution, so journey through this potted history of dramatic discovery and see how much you've grasped.

1 What do geologists study? (Clue: The answer will rock your world.)

2 What do scientists use to study the evolution of prehistoric plants and animals? (Clue: It remains to be seen.)

3 What event is believed to have killed the dinosaurs 65 million years ago? (Clue: It had a big impact.)

4 Which group of animals does the term Homo sapiens cover? (Clue: They're very wise animals.)

5 What are the names of the chromosomes in reproductive cells that that control the sex of offspring? (Clue: Not quite Z.)

6 What happens to the chromosomes inside a cell when the cell splits? (Clue: Divide and conquer.)

7 What did Watson and Crick discover in 1953?
(Clue: Do Not Answer?)

Answers:
1 Rocks (including things like fossils).
2 Fossils – the remains of ancient plants and animals.
3 An asteroid hitting the Earth.
4 Humans.
5 X and Y chromosomes. Boys have an X and a Y chromosome; girls have a pair of X chromosomes.
6 The chromosomes also divide so each new cell still has a full set of instructions.
7 The structure of DNA.

EVOLUTION INSIDE OUT

So, have you worked out evolution from the inside out? Put these beastly body bits in order of size with the smallest first, like a set of Russian dolls...

a) DNA
b) Cells
c) Chemical bases
d) Body
e) Genes
g) Chromosomes
f) Nucleus

Answers:
1 c) Chemical bases, which make up…
2 e) Genes, which are units of…
3 a) DNA, which makes up…
4 g) Chromosomes, which can be found in the…
5 f) Nucleus, which is the middle of…
6 b) Cells, which form the…
7 d) Body

GREGOR MENDEL AND HIS GIANT GENE DISCOVERY

Mad monk Mendel was the man who discovered genes (although he didn't call them that). His careful experiments started a new science called genetics – all by messing about with some plants in the monastery garden! See if you can figure out his explanation to his abbot by filling in the missing words.

Dear Abbot,

I am writing to tell you of a most interesting discovery I made while playing with my 1_____ plants. There I was, admiring all the different 2_____, when I started wondering what determined such 3 _____. I began to experiment by carefully 4_____ different types of plants to see what happened. I found that each characteristic is passed on by a tiny 5_____. And these always come in 6 _____. Some are 7_____, which means that their characteristics will always show in the offspring. Others are 8_____, which means that their characteristics can be hidden by a dominant one. I'm sure you'll agree that for a gardener I make a pretty good scientist, and for years to come people will remember how I founded a new branch of science... Do I deserve a promotion?
Yours sincerely,
Brother Mendel

a) cross-pollinating
b) Colours
c) Dominant
d) Pea
e) Particle
f) Pairs
g) Characteristics
h) Recessive

Answers:
1d; 2b; 3g; 4a; 5e; 6f; 7c; 8h

HORRIBLE INDEX

139

141

HORRIBLE SCIENCE
NASTY NATURE

I LOVE FAST FOOD!

NICK ARNOLD   illustrated by TONY DE SAULLES

ISBN 978 0439 94451 9

HORRIBLE SCIENCE
DISGUSTING DIGESTION

IT TAKES GUTS!

NICK ARNOLD   illustrated by TONY DE SAULLES

ISBN 978 0439 94445 8

HORRIBLE SCIENCE
UGLY BUGS

NOT A PRETTY SIGHT!

NICK ARNOLD   illustrated by TONY DE SAULLES

ISBN 978 0439 94452 6

HORRIBLE SCIENCE

FATAL FORCES

NICK ARNOLD

illustrated by
TONY DE SAULLES

SCHOLASTIC

Visit Nick Arnold at
www.nickarnold-website.com

www.horrible-science.co.uk

Scholastic Children's Books,
Euston House, 24 Eversholt Street,
London, NW1 1DB, UK

A division of Scholastic Ltd
London ~ New York ~ Toronto ~ Sydney ~ Auckland
Mexico City ~ New Delhi ~ Hong Kong

First published in the UK by Scholastic Ltd, 1997
This edition published 2008

Text copyright © Nick Arnold, 1997
Illustrations © Tony De Saulles, 1997

ISBN 978 0439 94448 9

Printed and bound by CPI Group (UK) Ltd, Croydon, CR0 4YY

22

CONTENTS

Nick Arnold has been writing stories and books since he was a youngster, but never dreamt he'd find fame writing about Fatal Forces. His research involved falling off buildings, lying on a bed of nails and skiing uphill and and he enjoyed every minute of it.

When he's not delving into Horrible Science, he spends his spare time teaching adults in a college. His hobbies include eating pizza, riding his bike and thinking up corny jokes (though not all at the same time).

Tony De Saulles picked up his crayons when he was still in nappies and has been doodling ever since. He takes Horrible Science very seriously and even agreed to test what happens when your parachute doesn't open. Fortunately, his injuries weren't too serious.

When he's not out with his sketchpad, Tony likes to write poetry and play squash, though he hasn't written any poetry about squash yet.

INTRODUCTION

Science has one fatal flaw. It can be **seriously** boring. Ask a simple question and you're forced to listen to a really boring, complicated answer.

And some answers have masses of mysterious mathematics

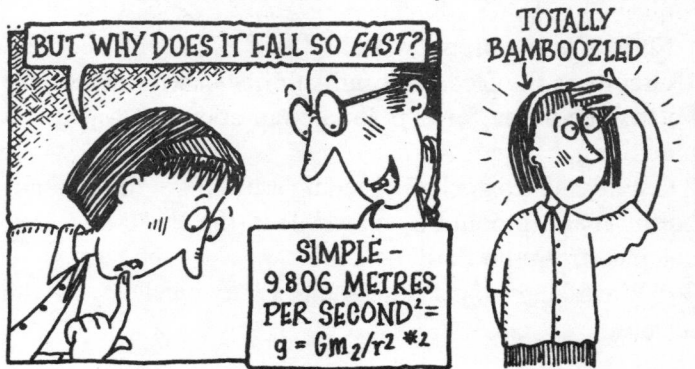

And don't try arguing with a scientist either…

Or you'll get a forceful reply…

See what I mean? It's enough to make you die of boredom. Now that *would* be fatal.

* English translations:
1 Gravity is the force that pulls things down towards the Earth. The same force pulls a smaller object towards a much larger object.
2 Gravity makes the ball speed up as it falls. This depends on the mass (amount of material) in the Earth and your distance from the Earth's centre.
3 You're asking too many questions. I'll try blinding you with science.

So what are these laws? And what happens if you break them? Do you get expelled? Or perhaps there's a *really horrible* punishment in store for you. Maybe you'll be *forced* to endure extra science lessons with megatons of homework? And who *forces* you to obey these horrible laws anyway? Teachers? No.

WELL WHAT'S FORCING ME TO FALL, THEN?

Forces force you. Because forces force things to move. And a force can be anything from you flicking a pea, to the awesome gravity of a giant star. So the effects of forces can be an inter-galactic explosion or the pea ending up in your teacher's ear-hole. (This might cause an explosion too!)

But forces can have fascinating fatal effects. Like crushing people, or making them sick, or pulling their heads off. (Getting forces wrong at school isn't usually quite as fatal – just a bit of en-forced detention from your teacher.)

CRUNCH!!

ARGHH!

THAT MUST BE ONE OF THOSE HORRIBLE FORCES YOU WERE TELLING US ABOUT, SIR

So here's the real-life story of forces. It's a story involving fatal fortunes and horrible happenings. And it's all true. And who knows? Afterwards you might feel that forces have a fatal attraction for you, too. You might even force your teacher to take your science homework seriously. If you can just force yourself to read the next page now...

NASTY NEWTON

The prisoner was sick. In the madness of his fever he imagined the courtroom candles were fiery ghosts. Again and again he heard the sentence of the judges: "Death!" Then he fainted.

He awoke in darkness. Dragging himself upright he tried to explore the pitch black cell. His feet slithered on the slimy floor. Then he stumbled, his hands grabbing at empty air. He'd collapsed on the edge of a bottomless pit. One more step and he'd have dropped like a stone. Exhausted, the prisoner fell asleep. But when he awoke he found himself strapped to a low bench. Helpless, he peered upwards and gasped in horror.

A giant statue towered over him. The grotesque figure had a huge pendulum swinging from its hands. The pendulum swung to and fro with an evil hiss. It ended in a razor-sharp blade and each slow sweep brought the blade a little lower. A little closer. Hiss ... hiss ... HISSSSSS! Scores of huge rats stared hungrily from the shadows, waiting to feast on the prisoner's butchered corpse. The deadly hissing blade skimmed his bare chest...

DON'T PANIC! It's only a story – *The Pit and the Pendulum* was written in 1849 by the American author Edgar Alan Poe. But for scientists Poe's story has a fatal fascination. The nasty forms of death – the pit and the pendulum – involve forces. Falling into the well under the influence of gravity; the pendulum's swing controlled by gravity and centripetal force (see page 106). (That's the force on the pendulum shaft that stops the swinging weight pulling away from the rest of the machine.) These forces are fatal for the prisoner.

HORRIBLE HEALTH WARNING!

Forces aren't human. You can't reason with them or persuade them. They are physical forces of nature with the power to kill. Fatal forces. Once you fall foul of fatal forces you're FINISHED!

Postscript:
Oh – by the way you'll be pleased to know the prisoner escapes. How? By getting the rats to gnaw through his straps, of course. Bet you didn't think of that! Amazingly enough these forces had already been explained by a forceful scientific mega-star, the amazing Sir Isaac Newton.

Hall of fame: Sir Isaac Newton (1642–1727)
Nationality: British

Isaac Newton was born on Christmas Day. The doctor thought baby Isaac wouldn't live because he was so weak and small.

But Isaac survived. He soon became interested in science but his teachers didn't think he was especially brainy. In fact, Isaac was too busy performing experiments at home to work hard at school. (Don't try this excuse.) When young Isaac was 16 his mum asked him to run the family farm. But he proved to be a useless farmer. He spent all his time experimenting and allowed the sheep to guzzle their way through a cornfield.

HE WAS THE BEST FARMER WE EVER HAD!

So Isaac went to Cambridge University instead. At University he read every maths book he could find. (Including the ones without pictures.) He wore scruffy clothes and was so absent-minded he often got lost on his way to supper. As far as Isaac was concerned supper was for wimps. Who needed supper when you could do lovely science calculations instead?

INCREDIBLY DIFFICULT MATHS

In 1665 a deadly plague struck London. Soon 7,000 people were dying every week and the authorities closed Cambridge University to stop the plague spreading. So Isaac went home. But instead of taking a holiday he did *extra homework*. Very strange. But what homework! He invented calculus – a mathematical system still used today to plan rocket trips, and he also discovered that light contains colours.

These vital discoveries were to influence maths and physics for 300 years. Then Isaac made a *really* incredible breakthrough. It may have happened like this...

THE APPLE AND THE MOON

Woolsthorpe, England 1666

It was getting dark, but the skinny young man ran his fingers through his shoulder-length hair and carried on reading. Isaac Newton was sitting in the orchard trying to figure out how the moon went round the Earth. Suddenly a call rang out from the old farmhouse:

"Hmm," thought Isaac, "she always calls me half an hour *before* supper. It's a trick to get me in on time."

So he did nothing. If he had left the orchard when his mother called him the entire history of science would have been different. But just then something grabbed his attention.

It had been waiting for this moment. Waiting for months, silently. At first it was no larger than a tiny green bulge. But now it was bright red and the size of a man's fist. A living bubble of water and sugars with sweet juicy flesh and bitter seeds all wrapped in a waxy skin. An apple. The most famous apple in science.

"Isaac! Your supper's on the table and it's your favourite!"

"Coming, mother!"

Isaac shivered as a cool breeze rustled the trees. Then he sighed and reluctantly closed his book. There was a silent snap. The slender stalk holding the apple to the tree gave way. Wrenched by an unseen force the apple hurtled downward. It tumbled through the rustling leaves and bounced gently on Isaac's brainy bonce.

What would you have done? Perhaps you'd have eaten your supper and forgotten the apple. But Isaac wasn't like that. He rubbed his head and looked at the moon. It shone like a bright silver coin in the evening sky.

"So why doesn't the moon fall, too?" he asked himself, as he absent-mindedly munched the famous apple.

For some strange reason Isaac remembered his school and the dreaded "bucket game". He hated the other kids for making him play. He remembered having to whirl a bucket of water around his head on a rope. It was hard work and Isaac was a thin little boy. But amazingly all the water had stayed in the bucket as if trapped by an unseen force.

"Maybe that's what keeps the moon in place," he murmured.

Then his mother shouted again: "Isaac, your supper's on the table and it's stone cold."

"I said I'm coming, mother!"

As Isaac threw the apple away he wondered what would happen if it reached the moon. The most famous apple core in science disappeared. There was a muffled meow as it splatted on the cat.

Isaac had forgotten his supper. He was calculating how strong gravity would need to be to stop the apple sailing into space. Then he thought about how fast the moon has to move to prevent it crashing down to Earth.

Later a very annoyed Mrs Newton stood in the doorway shielding her candle from the cold night air.

"Isaac!" she yelled. "I've fed your supper to the cat. And I'm going to feed your breakfast to the pigs!"

There was no answer from the orchard. But Isaac was still out there. And still thinking hard.

TEST YOUR TEACHER

How much does your teacher really know about this famous scientist?

1 As a child what was Isaac Newton's favourite toy?
a) A chemistry set.
b) A toy windmill powered by a mouse in a wheel.
c) He hated toys. He preferred tricky maths sums.

2 What did he buy on his first day at university?
a) A desk, ink and a notebook for extra homework.
b) New clothes and a ticket to the local fun fair.
c) A loaf of bread to eat.

3 How did Newton solve tricky scientific problems?
a) The answers came in a flash of inspiration when Newton was on the toilet.
b) By talking things over with scientific friends.
c) Worrying away at the problem day and night until he figured out the answer.

4 Newton became Professor of Mathematics at Cambridge but no one attended his bum-numbingly boring lectures.

So what did he do?

a) He rounded up students and *forced* them to listen.

b) Carried on talking to an empty room.

c) Tried to make his lectures interesting with a few jokes and amusing stories.

5 Newton's dog, Diamond, knocked over a candle and years of hard work went up in flames. What did he do?

a) Drew his sword and killed the dog.

b) Re-wrote his work from memory.

c) He told the dog off and went on to study something new and experimental.

Answers: 1 b) He designed it himself. **2 a), 3 c), 4 b)**

Does your teacher have this problem? **5 b)**.

What your teacher's score means.

1-2 Your teacher's guessing.

3-4 Your teacher knows a bit but doesn't know everything. (Much like any other teacher.)

5 Hard luck. Your teacher's read this book.

NEWTON'S MOVING BOOK

Newton didn't publish his discoveries for 20 years. He was too busy with his mathematical work. But then at last, fearful others might grab the glory, Newton wrote a book about his ideas. He shut himself away for 18 months and worked 20 hours a day.

Sometimes Newton's assistant reminded him that he'd missed supper.

"Have I?" Newton would murmur sleepily. Then he nibbled at the food and got back to work.

Newton's book was called *The Philosophiae Naturalis Principia Mathematica* and it was the most brilliant science book ever written. In it he explained the whole universe in a way that made sense. (Well – it would have made sense if the book hadn't been in Latin and filled with mystifying maths.) Newton described gravity and three crucial laws about forces and how things move. These laws show how squids squirt water backwards in order to move forwards. They explain what happens when distant stars blow up and why low-flying sparrow droppings splat on your head.

One way to imagine Newton's laws is to think of a really horrible morning. What d'you mean – every day's like that?

What the law says...
If left alone a motionless object
doesn't move. A moving object carries
on moving in a straight line at a
constant speed as long as another
force doesn't make it change course.

What the Law means...

You stare wearily at your breakfast. Your cornflakes are motionless and they're going to stay that way until you summon up the energy to eat them. You clumsily knock your spoon and half your breakfast goes flying. A cornflake falls on your dad's head. The cornflake would have flown in the same direction for ever but the force of gravity pulled it down.

CORNFLAKE WOULD TRAVEL IN A STRAIGHT LINE FOR EVER IF IT WASN'T FOR THE FORCE OF GRAVITY (AND THE CEILING).

OOPS! SORRY, DAD!

DOWNWARD FORCE OF THE HAND CATAPULTS THE CORNFLAKE UPWARDS

NEWTON'S SECOND LAW

what the law says...
A force changes an object's speed. The change in speed is proportional to the strength of the force. The change in speed happens in the direction of the force.

What the Law means...
The harder you kick the ball, the faster it flies in that direction. It's a rotten result for the goalie!

NEWTON'S THIRD LAW

What the law says...
When an object exerts a force on another object the second object will push back just as hard.

What the Law means …

You're late and you're jogging to school. But you're still not properly awake. You slam into a lamppost. And the lamppost wallops you back! It's true – this really does happen.

NEWTON'S NASTY NATURE

1 When Newton was three years old his mum remarried. Isaac hated his stepfather and often thought of killing him. He didn't of course, but he was pleased when the stepfather died.

21

2 At school Newton had no friends until he thumped the school bully with great force. Newton was smaller than his opponent but his courage helped win the fight. After this nasty incident Newton became popular.

3 Newton disliked women and never married. He hated his friend John Locke's attempts to introduce him to ladies. Later Newton wrote to Locke:

when (a woman) told me you were sickly and would not live, I answered 'twere better you were dead

THANKS A LOT!

But that didn't stop Newton generously allowing his niece Catherine to do his cooking and cleaning.

4 Newton was a miserable man. He had no hobbies apart from work. He rarely laughed and he called poetry:

A KIND OF INGENIOUS NONSENSE

5 In 1686 Newton fell out with scientist Robert Hooke (1635–1703). Hooke unjustly accused Newton of pinching *his* ideas on gravity. In a letter Newton called Hooke "a pretender and a grasper" and refused to talk to him.

6 After writing the *Principia* Newton had a nasty turn. He went mad for two years and did no scientific research. Some historians reckon Newton was a bit depressed but others say he was poisoned by the mercury he used for chemistry experiments.

7 When he got better Newton was appointed Warden of the Royal Mint and reformed Britain's coinage. It was said that nasty Newton enjoyed catching forgers and arranging especially nasty executions for them.

I WILL NOW DEMONSTRATE ANOTHER OF THE FATAL FORCES...

8 German Gottfried Leibniz (1646–1716) claimed he invented calculus. Newton accused Leibniz of pinching his idea. But in fact Leibniz had made the discovery independently at the same time as Newton. (And it was Leibniz who actually coined the word "calculus" – Newton called it "fluxions" – which sounds like the effects of a nasty tummy bug.)

9 Newton came to a horrible end. He moved to the country to improve his health. But a few weeks later he fell sick and died of a stone in his bladder. By then, however, he was a nasty-tempered old man of 84, but still a great genius.

NEWTON IN HIS OWN WORDS

Like many geniuses Newton was hard to understand.
Here's what he said about himself:

Note: Newton didn't mean human pyramids. The giants
he referred to were earlier scientists who inspired him.
He also said:

Note: Newton meant that he'd learnt enough to realize there was more to learn. He was right. He'd only scratched the surface. There are loads more fatally fascinating facts about forces. You'll find them in the next chapter.

FORCEFUL FACTS

Forces are *everywhere*. You can't do much without bumping into them. But hopefully not with a fatal *CRUNCH*. Oddly enough, though, before Newton, people knew very little about how forces worked.

MIXED-UP MOTION THEORIES

A scientist will tell you that a force is something that affects the movement or shape of an object or person. Sounds fairly vague. But before Newton, scientific theories were even more mixed-up. One of the first people to write about forces was a Greek genius called Aristotle.

Hall of fame: Aristotle (384–322 BC) Nationality: Greek

Aristotle was a doctor's son. His parents died when he was a child and as a young man he blew their money on wild parties. But when he was 17 years old Aristotle had a sudden change of heart and sent himself back to school.

He went to study under the brainy philosopher called Plato in the Academy at Athens. Aristotle liked it there so much that he stayed for the next 20 years as a pupil and then as a teacher.

Aristotle travelled for four years and eventually moved to Macedonia where his old mate Philip happened to be king. Phil asked Aristotle to teach his boy, Alexander. Aristotle must have done a good job because young Alexander became Alexander the Great and conquered a great chunk of Asia. By the time Aristotle died (of acute indigestion) he had written about everything from politics to how grasshoppers chirp. And he even had a few things to say about forces.

MYSTERY MOTIONS

Here's how Aristotle explained forces:

THINGS MOVE AS LONG AS THEY'RE IN CONTACT WITH WHATEVER IS MOVING THEM.

OH, YEAH? SO HOW COME ARROWS DON'T FALL TO THE GROUND AS SOON AS YOU FIRE THEM?

THAT'S BECAUSE THE AIR BEHIND THE ARROW PUSHES IT ALONG.

SMART-ASS

Wrong, wrong and wrong again. But for 2,000 years everyone thought Aristotle's wacko ideas were RIGHT. Eventually Newton used maths to prove Aristotle WRONG. So nowadays we've got forces sussed. As a scientist might say, "Learning about forces is as easy as riding a bike." Oh, yeah? Riding a bike is LOADS harder and just to prove it we've asked a scientist to try.

THE SMALL PRINT:
IT'S NOT OUR FAULT IF YOU END
UP IN HOSPITAL – OK?

LESSON 1: WOBBLY BALANCE

Remember learning to ride a bike? Tough, wasn't it? Inside the scientist's ears are fluid-filled spaces, called semi-circular canals. (Teachers have a larger air-filled space where their brains should be. Ha ha.) These canals help her balance on two wheels. As the liquid sloshes around, sensors tell her brain whether she's still upright. Her brilliant brain also notices the force of gravity, her speed, the slope and wind direction. Yep – all at the same time.

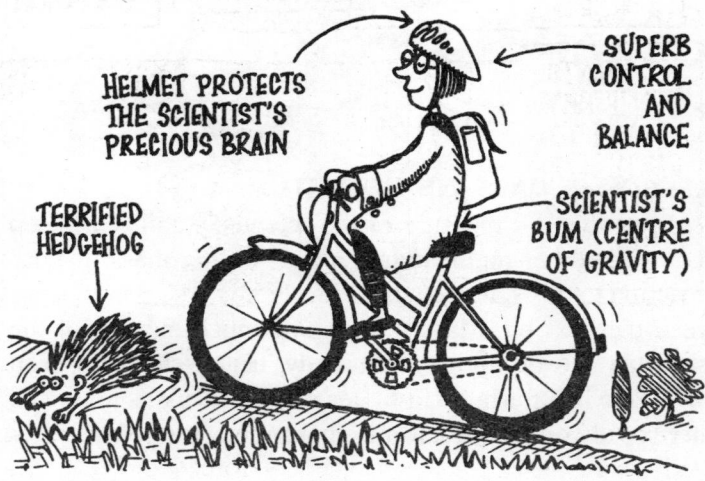

HELMET PROTECTS THE SCIENTIST'S PRECIOUS BRAIN

SUPERB CONTROL AND BALANCE

TERRIFIED HEDGEHOG

SCIENTIST'S BUM (CENTRE OF GRAVITY)

It helps her balance if her science books, sandwiches, etc. aren't draped over one handlebar. Ideally her bum is the centre of gravity – the point around which everything else is sensibly balanced.

LESSON 2: EFFORTLESS INERTIA

When she stands still inertia keeps her there. She overcomes inertia to get moving. Once she's moving, inertia keeps her going in a straight line. Mind you, she needs more pedal power to get up hills! Larger objects have more inertia. That's why it's hard to stop a charging elephant. And if you're daft enough to try you might feel a bit flat afterwards!

LESSON 3: MASS-IVE MOMENTUM

Momentum is a measure of the scientist's ability to keep going. And her momentum depends on her mass. If your reaction to this statement is to say "yer wot?", you'd better read the next bit. Mass means how much there is of the scientist – everything in her body, her clothes and even what she had for breakfast. Her mass, her bike's mass and her speed combine to produce her momentum. Wheee!

LESSON 4: MIXED-UP MOMENTUM

Oops! She knocks the school bully flying. Scientists would say she's "transferred momentum" to the bully and call this "conserving momentum". The posh scientific word for speed in one direction is "velocity". So she'd better pedal at quite a velocity in order to conserve her life!

TRANSFER OF MOMENTUM TAKES PLACE HERE

BULLY LANDS SOMEWHERE OVER HERE

BAD

Oo-er the bully's heading towards her on a skateboard. THEY'RE GOING TO CRASH! As they crash the two momentums cancel each other. So they both grind to a halt. Result = TROUBLE!!!

LESSON 5: GALLOPING GRAVITY

Velocity is greater when cycling downhill. Gravity tries to pull the scientist to the centre of the Earth. And the bottom of the slope is a bit nearer the centre of the planet than the top. This explains why, if she loses her balance, it's easier to fall off her bike than stay on. By the way, if she did make it right through to the Earth's centre, there would be no gravity and she would float around being roasted in the fiery heat. Not nice! Tired yet? Our scientist is. She's run out of kinetic energy. That's the posh scientific name for the energy she uses when moving. Oh well – we'll give her a few minutes to recover and then we'll put her back to work.

LESSON 6: AWKWARD ACCELERATION AND DRAG

For the scientist the word "acceleration" means changing speed or direction. So even when she slows down, she calls it "acceleration". But when she accelerates down a hill she feels the wind whistling up her nostrils (and everywhere else), and trying to slow her. This force is called "drag". If it's particularly windy it'll "drag" her off her bike – the result could be fatal.

WIND BLOWS AGAINST THE SCIENTIST AND CAUSES "DRAG" WHICH SLOWS HER DOWN

CROUCHING DOWN REDUCES THE DRAG AND HELPS HER TO GO FASTER!

LESSON 7: CURIOUS CORNERING

As the scientist rounds the corner, centripetal (sen-tre-pee-tal) force pulls her bike into the corner. But her inertia opposes the change in course. It tries to keep her moving in a straight line - (remember Newton's First Law?) The scientist feels as if a force is pushing her outwards. As a scientist she knows this isn't a real force – it's all in her imagination!

SCIENTIST
LEANS
THIS WAY
→

TO
COUNTER-BALANCE
HER MOMENTUM
←

LESSON 8: GRINDING GEARS

The gears on the scientist's bike help her cycle uphill. The gears allow her to pedal quicker but with less force. This means she can cycle up the slope without getting puffed out. Yep – gears are great. As a scientist would say, "They're a great way of transferring forces."

LESSON 9: FURIOUS FRICTION

The force of friction slows moving objects. It happens when a moving object touches another object. The scientist's rubber tyres grip the road and provide this force. This helps her control the bike and avoid fatal collisions. Lack of friction makes cycling on ice a slippery experience. And performing wheelies on the local skating rink is definitely out.

When she wants to slow down, or stop the rubber brakes grip her wheels. Friction stops her bike. Hopefully. If she brakes too hard, her momentum throws her forward. And she performs spectacular but possibly fatal handlebar acrobatics.

LESSON 10: VICIOUS VIBRATIONS

When the scientist rides her bike along a bumpy path she may feel a few vibrations. These are shock waves carrying the force of impact from the tyres. Her tyres and saddle springs are designed to soak up some vibrations. But that doesn't stop her body vibrating, her muscles twitching and her eyeballs bouncing slightly in their sockets.

FREAKY PHYSICISTS

Scientists who study forces are called physicists (*fizzy-sists*). They also explore motion, probe what things are made of, and try to figure out how the universe works. A typical physicist is slightly scruffy and enjoys tinkering with things. A physics lab is rather untidy and full of interesting bits and pieces that have been salvaged in order to build a freaky machine.

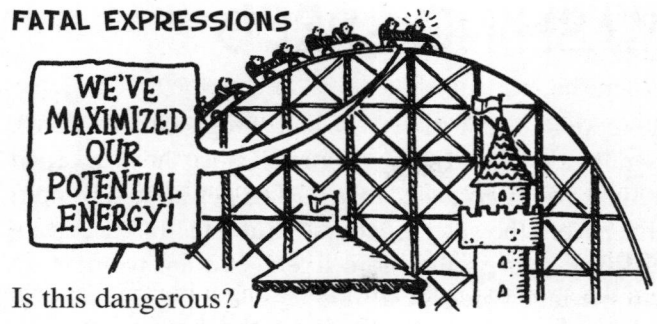

WE'VE MAXIMIZED OUR POTENTIAL ENERGY!

Is this dangerous?

Answer: Just a bit. By the time the roller-coaster gets to the top of the slope it has built up a lot of energy to make it zoom downhill really fast. HOLD ON TO YOUR LUNCH!

Bet you never knew!
Physicists use two strange words in connection with forces – "energy" and "work". Well hopefully, they don't sound too strange to you. But we're not talking about summoning up the energy to do homework or wash the dishes here. No way.

Physicists say "work" when they want to explain what happens when a force causes an object to move a distance. According to them writing your maths homework is "work" but reckoning up the answers in your head isn't. Energy is the ability to do work. Sounds sensible – after all you need energy to work. Don't you?

Just thinking about energy and work is pretty exhausting isn't it, so why don't you take a little rest? Yeah – put your feet up. Get your breath back for the next chapter. You'll need it. 'Cos it's about speed and crashes!!! Fasten your safety belt.

SMASHING SPEED

Some people think speed is smashing. Others don't. Early railways scared some people because they reckoned no human could go faster than 32 km per hour (20 mph) and live. Well, they can, of course. But one thing's certain – the faster you go the more likely you are to meet up with some fatal forces. Gulp!

TEST YOUR TEACHER

Is your teacher quick-witted? Smile sweetly and ask:

WHAT WAS THE FASTEST SPEED ATTAINED ON A BICYCLE DURING THE NINETEENTH CENTURY?

(Note the subtle wording – your teacher probably thinks you're talking about pedalling – but she'd be wrong.)
Your teacher will probably say something like, "50 km per hour" (31 mph) – hopelessly wrong. At this point you can say, "No, I think you're wrong. In 1899 Mr C M Murphy smashed the record. He tied his bike to the back of a train and travelled 1.6 km in a minute." *Don't* try this at home.

QUICK QUIZ

1 Super speedy

See if you can put these three objects in order of speed, starting with the fastest.

a) A bullet from a high-powered rifle.

b) The planet Mercury moving through space.

c) Three astronauts aboard the Apollo 10 spacecraft in 1969.

2 Fairly speedy

Which of these three objects do you think is the fastest?

a) A chameleon's tongue as it grabs a juicy fly.

b) A message sent along one of your nerves.

c) A person falling from the top of a 99.4-metre-high building.

3 Slow and sluggish

Can you put these three objects in order of speed starting with the fastest?

a) Your fingernails growing.

b) Bamboo plants growing.

c) The Atlantic Ocean getting wider.

Answers: 1 b) 172,248 km per hour (107,030 mph)
When it comes to orbiting the sun, Mercury is the
speediest planet in the solar system. **c)** 39,897 km per
hour (24,791 mph) Feeling a teensy bit space sick? **a)**
3,302 km per hour (2,052 mph). That's too fast to see.
The bullet travels faster than sound so a person could
be shot before they heard the gun firing. Doesn't sound
fair somehow.
2 b) 483 km per hour (300 mph). **c)** 141 km per hour (80
mph). This was the speed achieved by stuntman Dan
Koko in 1984 as he leapt off the Las Vegas World Hotel.
Lucky for Dan he smashed into an air cushion rather than
the pavement. **a)** 80.5 km per hour (50 mph). Then it's
bye-bye fly.
3 b) 3 cm an hour. If your fingernails grew any faster than
this, you'd have problems. **c)** 0.0006 cm an hour. The
Atlantic Ocean is getting wider due to the movements of
enormous slabs of rock deep beneath the Earth's surface.
a) 0.00028 cm an hour. Any faster than this and it could
be fatal.

Bet you never knew!
You'd move faster if your shape allowed the air to flow
round you rather than bumping into you. This kind of shape is
called "aerodynamic" and it cuts down on drag. A bullet with
its pointed head is an aerodynamic shape but a human head
isn't. If it was we'd all have pointy heads. Record-smashing
speed cyclists wear pointed helmets instead. And more speed
means more momentum. Smashing!

Fatal forces fact file

NAME: Momentum

THE BASIC FACTS: Momentum keeps you moving. That way you don't smash Newton's First Law. (That's the one about going in a straight line unless something stops you.)

THE HORRIBLE DETAILS: Momentum makes your stomach jump when you go over the top on a roller coaster.

ARGHHHH!

The momentum of your half-digested food carries on up. If it comes up too far it could be fatally embarrassing!

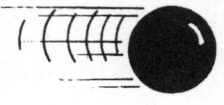

CHATTER
TREMBLE

MURDEROUS MOMENTUM FACTS

1 In 1871 showman John Holtum tried to catch a flying cannon-ball *with his bare hands*. It wasn't fired from a real cannon, of course. Holtum used a specially built gun that fired a slow-moving ball. But even so he nearly lost a finger. The stunt proved very popular and John bravely practised until he'd perfected the trick. He should have changed his name to "Halt-em".

2 In nineteenth-century America railways were rarely fenced off and brainless buffalo often blundered onto the tracks. To tackle this menace, by the 1860s trains were fitted with wedge-shaped "cow catchers". The idea was that the train's momentum would scoop the buffalo out of harm's way.

3 In Finland, elk (otherwise known as moose) cause fatal road accidents. When hit by a car, the momentum of the car flips the moose over. So the loose moose lands on the car roof. Its weight crushes both the car and its driver. Perhaps the cars should be fitted with "moose catchers".

IDLE INERTIA
Physicists use the word inertia to describe how things stay the same. Motionless things stay idle and moving things carry on until another force gets in the way. That's Newton's First Law again.

Dare you discover ... the inertia of an egg?
You will need:
A plate
A raw egg
A hard-boiled egg

What you do:

1 Gently spin the raw egg on the plate.

2 To stop the egg touch it with your finger.

3 Gently lift your finger up.

4 Now repeat steps 1–3 with the hard-boiled egg.

What do you notice?

a) When you lift your finger the hard-boiled egg continues to spin.

b) When you lift your finger the raw egg continues to spin.

c) When you lift your finger the raw egg spins and the hard-boiled egg rocks from end-to-end.

WHOOPS

DON'T PUSH
DOWN
TOO HARD

Answer: b) When you stop the raw egg, inertia keeps the egg white inside spinning. And this starts the entire egg spinning again when you lift your finger. The inside of the hard-boiled egg is hard, of course, so the white doesn't have its own inertia.

Important note: The egg should spin on the plate. Not spin through the air and smash on the floor. If this happens you'll be force-fed omelette. And talking about smashing things...

A SMASHING TEST

Car designers spend fortunes building new cars. And then they smash them up. This may sound stupid, but they need to test the car's structural design and materials under crash conditions and also find the best ways to ensure that the driver and passengers are as well protected as possible. These days most smashes happen on a computer screen. The engineers peer at a simulation of crashes at various speeds. They can even slow down the movement to one image every two milliseconds – that's far slower than a TV action replay.

But afterwards the engineers need real-life tests to check their findings. And this is when the poor old dummies get wheeled in to show the effects of the crash on real people. Of course, dummies don't have brains – that's why they're dummies. But they do have a smashing time.

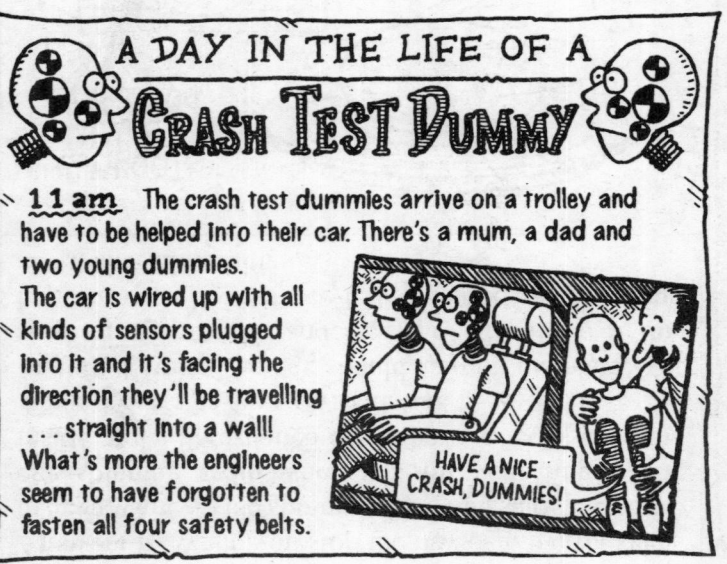

A DAY IN THE LIFE OF A CRASH TEST DUMMY

11 am The crash test dummies arrive on a trolley and have to be helped into their car. There's a mum, a dad and two young dummies.

The car is wired up with all kinds of sensors plugged into it and it's facing the direction they'll be travelling ... straight into a wall! What's more the engineers seem to have forgotten to fasten all four safety belts.

HAVE A NICE CRASH, DUMMIES!

11.02 am The engineers crouch behind steel barriers to protect themselves from the impact of the crash, and it turns out they *deliberately* forgot about the safety belts. Steel cables at the front of the car catapult it forward at speed. CRAACK! the car hits the wall. The dummies crash through the windscreen. The front of the car is completely smashed in.

12.00 noon
The dummies are cut free from the wreckage. They're a little bit battered but they've survived to crash another day. They're pretty tough dummies.

1.00pm
The engineers stop for a sandwich. The dummies aren't all that hungry.

SUIT YOURSELF!

2.00pm Telly time! The dummies have become movie stars, but they don't even know it. As the dummies are wheeled away the engineers settle themselves in front of a screen to watch an action replay of the crash on video.

You can see how Newton's First Law affects the dummies. That's the law about things continuing to move in a straight line. When the car stops, the inertia of the dummies forces

TERRIFIC!

SUPER!

them to carry on moving – straight through the windscreen. So the force of the wall hitting the car is transferred to the poor old dummies. You can see why seat belts are lifesavers. You'd be a real dummy not to wear one.

5.00pm The engineers set up tomorrow's test. This time the dummies will be trapped in a car as it rolls over in a crash. But that's just another smashing day in the life of the crash test dummies.
A dummy's life is full of hard knocks.

Safety first

As a result of this testing, engineers have come up with a few ingenious devices to help reduce the impact of a car crash on passengers:

SCIENTIST'S CAR

Collapsible steering wheel. If the air bag fails, the steering wheel collapses rather than spearing the driver in the chest.

Seat belts soak up the force that throws the body forward.

Airbags If a driver is thrown forward onto the steering wheel of most modern cars, the bag inflates for a nice soft landing.

WUMPFF!

FORCE 1

Crumple zones (found in some new cars). When the car crashes, part of the front of the car is designed to crumple up and soak up some of the shock.

Side-impact bars (found in some new cars). Strengthens the doors so they won't get smashed in if another car whacks into them.

SMASHING SOUND SPEEDS

Fatal though they often are, the forces in a car crash are nothing compared to those in really high-speed accidents like an air crash. Or the horrible effects of falling out of an aeroplane at high speed. The effects of high speeds were studied by Austrian physicist Ernst Mach (1838–1916). Mach found that it's hard to travel faster than the speed of sound – 1,220 km per hour (760 mph). (By the way, the speed of sound is the speed sounds travel through the air.)

Here's why it's so difficult. All aircraft push air in front of them. But a plane flying at the speed of sound smashes into this air before it can escape. This makes for a violently bumpy ride that can shake the plane to pieces (not to mention your insides). In the 1940s several pilots died trying to smash the sound barrier. But in 1947 American pilot Charles E Yeager broke the barrier in a rocket-powered plane. It was known to be dangerous to fly really, really fast, but at this time no one knew what hitting the air at these speeds would do to an unprotected body. Could it be fatal?

FLY FOR YOUR LIFE

26 February 1955, California, USA

At 9.30 am precisely, ace test pilot George Franklin Smith picked up his washing. He turned left out of the launderette and walked slap bang into the worst day of his life.

He should have known better. How many people volunteer to work on a Saturday? But he had nothing better to do than finish a report. And of course when he got to work someone offered him a test flight in a gleaming brand new Super-sabre jet. This was a new type of jet plane capable of flying faster than sound.

George grinned. He loved test flying the powerful planes. In his laid-back way he replied:

YEAH, SURE I'LL TAKE HER UP. WON'T TAKE MORE THAN FORTY-FIVE MINUTES OR SO.

It wasn't worth putting on a protective suit.

As George took off he noticed the controls were a bit stiff. But there seemed nothing to worry about – the pre-flight checks had been just fine. He chatted happily to a pilot friend over the intercom.

Minutes later he broke the sound barrier. Then the plane nosed down and the controls jammed. The jet was diving to destruction at supersonic speed.

As his speed increased George yelled: "Controls locked – I'm going straight down!"

His friend's voice exploded in the headphones. "Bale out, George! Get out of there!" He had seconds to escape or die.

About 2,100 metres below the blue sea glittered in the sunshine.

George wrenched the armrest and jettisoned the jet's perspex canopy. A tearing gale filled the cockpit. At this speed the violent force of the air pinned him down. He painfully stretched out his hand. His fingertips brushed the ejector seat handle. There was no time. No time to think of the danger. *Every* pilot who had baled out at supersonic speeds had been killed.

George's straining fingers clutched the handle. *KERBAAAM!* A powerful explosion tore him from the cockpit. He hit a wall of air. The world and the sky tumbled crazily. In a few seconds his shoes and socks, his watch and helmet were torn away. He was bleeding fast and very, very scared.

His falling body felt like a feather. "A falling body" he thought vaguely, "has no weight – it's ... something to do with gravity." There was a crack and a sharp jerk as the parachute opened, its canopy trapping and slowing the air as it rushed past. Then George felt himself slip into darkness. He felt no pain as his body slammed into the sea and began to sink.

"Hey, give me a hand!" shouted the fisherman to his friend as he hauled the heavy body from the water.

The other man looked doubtful. "There's no point – I think the pilot's dead."

But George Smith was still alive. Just...

The Air Force took a month to scoop up all the mangled pieces of George's plane from the sea bed 1.6 km from the shore. The wreckage filled 50 barrels and still no one knew what had caused the crash.

But scientists now had a chance to study the effect of extreme forces … on poor George's half-dead body.

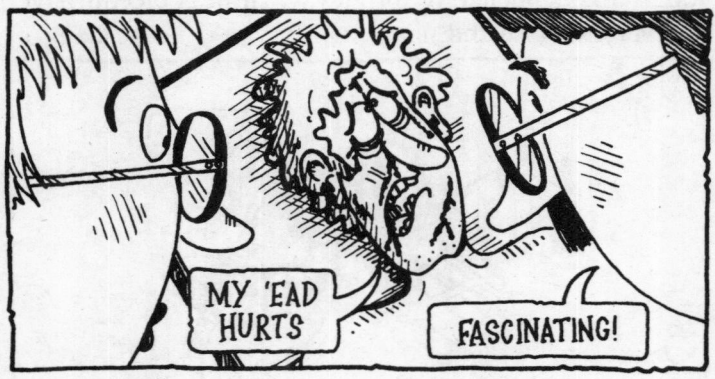

MY 'EAD HURTS

FASCINATING!

Here's what they found out:

1 As George ejected from the plane his speed boosted the effects of gravity. What we call "weight" depends on the strength of the gravity affecting our bodies. So every part of the pilot's body became 40 times heavier. You may have felt this yourself. It's that weird feeling of being stuck to your seat as you climb a roller-coaster. Only George was moving much faster so this effect was almost fatal.

2 Even his blood became heavier for a few moments. Heavy blood squirted from his heavy blood vessels. This caused a mass of bruises to appear on his body. He was so bruised that his head swelled up like a purple football.

3 George's eyelids bled after fluttering violently in the howling wind as he fell at speed.

In all George spent seven months in hospital. But he made a full recovery and went back to flying. He was the luckiest pilot in the world. Of course, every pilot's worst nightmare is to fall out of the sky. Because falling – under the influence of gravity – can be fatal. So if you want to survive the next chapter you'd better hang on tight. And DON'T FORGET YOUR PARACHUTE!

GRUESOME GRAVITY

What goes up must come down. This old saying is true as long as you're not in outer space where things float around all the time and don't "come down". Why? Because there's no gravity in space to bring you down to Earth. So what is this unearthly force? Read on for the full and gruesome details.

Fatal forces fact file

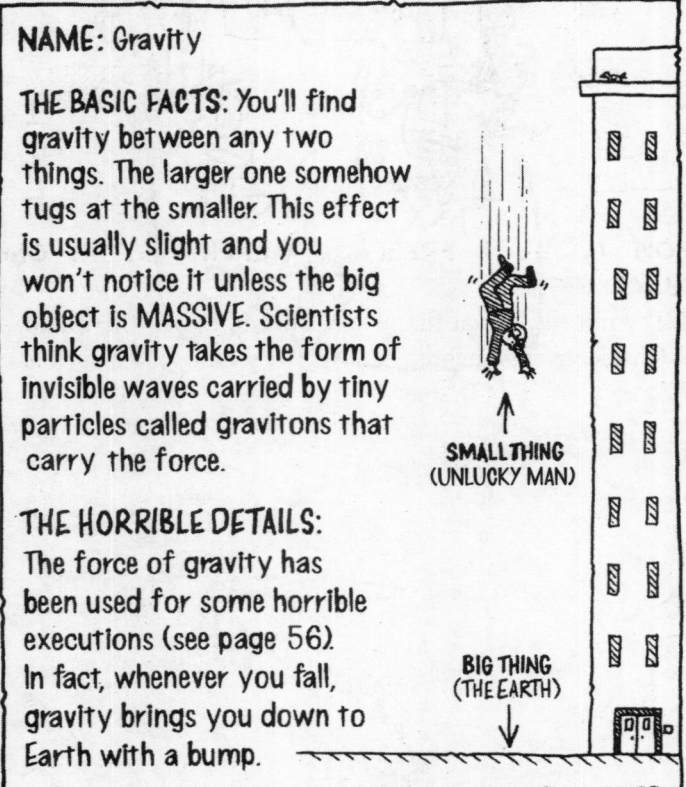

NAME: Gravity

THE BASIC FACTS: You'll find gravity between any two things. The larger one somehow tugs at the smaller. This effect is usually slight and you won't notice it unless the big object is MASSIVE. Scientists think gravity takes the form of invisible waves carried by tiny particles called gravitons that carry the force.

SMALL THING
(UNLUCKY MAN)

THE HORRIBLE DETAILS: The force of gravity has been used for some horrible executions (see page 56). In fact, whenever you fall, gravity brings you down to Earth with a bump.

BIG THING
(THE EARTH)

TERMINAL VELOCITY

How's this for a thrill? You go for a flight in a plane up to, say, 6,100 metres and then you jump out. And you don't use a parachute. Well – not until you've fallen halfway to the ground under the influence of gravity. Is this completely crazy? No, it's a popular sport called freefall parachuting. If you don't mind heights and enjoy a bit of danger you'll love this. If not, you'd better put on a blindfold before you read this next bit.

HOW TO BE A FREEFALL PARACHUTIST IN ONE QUICK LESSON

1 Try not to look at the ground. Jump out of the plane.
2 Check your parachute is strapped securely to your back. (Come to think of it, that should have been Step One.)

3 Start tumbling. That's not something you've got to do – it's something that will happen to you anyway. You'll find your sense of balance can't help you stay upright. You'll feel sick. Try not to panic at this stage.

4 For 15 seconds you fall faster and faster. Every second you fall 9.8 metres faster until you hit – 50 metres a second (100–150 mph). That's the maximum speed you can fall. It's called terminal velocity. Gulp! It's horrible feeling there's nothing under you except empty air, but some people can't get enough of it.

5 Good news. You won't fall any faster because the air slows you down – this force is known as drag.

6 Here's your chance to practise your freefall parachuting technique. Try to fall face downwards. Spread your arms and legs and stick your stomach out. You'll find your body curves forwards and your arms and legs are pushed backwards.

This makes a larger area for the drag to act upon. So you don't fall quite so fast. Flying squirrels and sky-diving cats do this in mid-air.

7 One minute later. Had fun? Good. You're going to hit the ground in 25 seconds. Better pull your parachute rip cord now or you'll really fall foul of gravity. And make a rather deep hole in the ground.

8 As you land make sure you drop down to a squatting position. Bending your knees soaks up some force as you hit the ground. Enjoyed it? Great – you'll be falling over yourself to make another jump.

Bet you never knew!
If you don't happen to have a parachute things can get a teensy bit more difficult. In 1944 Flight-Sergeant Nicholas Alkemade was in desperate danger 5,500 metres above Germany. His plane was on fire and his parachute was burnt to a cinder. He jumped and fully expected to die. But he was lucky. He fell on top of a tree and then onto a deep bank of snow and as a result much of the force of his fall was soaked up. Alkemade survived to tell his remarkable story and he didn't even break any bones!

MORE GRUESOME GRAVITY

In the past gravity was used to make executions more efficient. During a hanging the victim dropped through a trapdoor and gravity acting on the rope broke the victim's neck. If the drop was too far the force yanked their head off too. Gruesome!

Another gruesome method of execution was the guillotine. This featured a 30.4 kg weight attached to a sharp blade. The force powering the gruesome blade as it fell was gravity. In the 1790s working model guillotines were popular children's toys. Their parents must have been off their heads.

In England in the seventeenth century criminals who refused to plead guilty or not guilty at their trials were crushed to death under heavy weights. Once again it was gravity doing the damage. You may be interested to know that a louse can withstand a force of 500,000 times its own weight. Unfortunately for the criminals, humans scrunch more easily.

Now for something a bit less fatal. Hopefully. You'd think that lying on a bed of nails would turn you into a gruesome human pin cushion. Surely gravity pins you to those nasty nails? Not necessarily. You can press down with a force of 450 g on a nail without harm. (Don't try proving this at home – nails are usually crawling with disgusting germs.) So 400 nails can support a huge 182 kg man for a comfortable night's sleep. Bet that's a weight off your mind.

FATAL EXPRESSIONS

Answer: No. He's got a weight problem. Scientists say "mass" instead of weight because weight is just a measure of how strongly gravity is pulling you towards the Earth. Some Americans measure mass using a unit called the "slug". The overweight scientist weighs about ten slugs – 145 kg. Mind you, scientists use kilograms instead of slugs. The moon's gravity is weaker than Earth's, so a human only weighs $1/6$ as much there.

TEST YOUR TEACHER

Your teacher's bound to fall down on this really tricky question. Smile sweetly and say:

EXCUSE ME, IS IT TRUE THAT GRAVITY CAN HELP YOU LOSE WEIGHT?

Answer: Yes – but you'd have to be in a lift with a set of scales to prove it. If one day the lift cable snaps, quickly leap on the scales. In the few seconds you take to hurtle to the ground you're weightless! Weight is just a measure of gravity's pull. But when you fall you're not resisting gravity and you're weightless! You can blame Galileo for all this, he was the first person to discover how the force works.

Hall of fame: Galileo Galilei (1564–1642)
Nationality: Italian

Young Galileo wanted to study maths (strange boy), but his dad forced him to learn medicine instead. Doctors got more pay than mathematicians. But sneaky Galileo secretly studied sums until his dad gave up on him. When he was 25, Galileo became a maths professor at Pisa University. Then he got interested in gravity and performed amazing experiments to measure the force. Here's what his notebooks may have looked like.

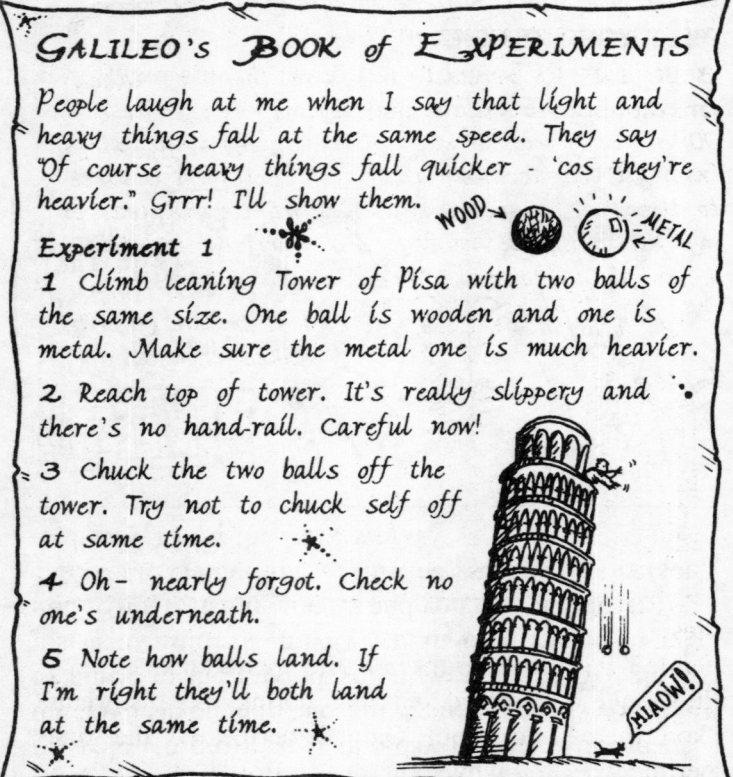

GALILEO's BOOK of EXPERIMENTS

People laugh at me when I say that light and heavy things fall at the same speed. They say "Of course heavy things fall quicker - 'cos they're heavier." Grrr! I'll show them.

WOOD → METAL

Experiment 1

1 Climb leaning Tower of Pisa with two balls of the same size. One ball is wooden and one is metal. Make sure the metal one is much heavier.

2 Reach top of tower. It's really slippery and there's no hand-rail. Careful now!

3 Chuck the two balls off the tower. Try not to chuck self off at same time.

4 Oh - nearly forgot. Check no one's underneath.

5 Note how balls land. If I'm right they'll both land at the same time.

MIAOW!

ME

People still don't believe me.
Huh - this'll teach them a lesson.

Experiment 2

1 Get a wooden board with a little wooden gully on it. Line it with some nice shiny parchment made from animal skin with the fat scraped off.

USE SKIN FROM CAT KILLED IN EXPERIMENT 1

2 Raise the gully on a slope and roll a bronze ball down it. (If you don't have a bronze ball any other metal will do.)

3 Be sure to precisely measure the time taken for the ball to roll to the bottom of the slope. OOPS - silly me, I was about to forget, no one's invented an accurate clock yet. Better use pulse to time ball's speed. Mustn't get too excited, or my pulse will be racing. Better repeat the test a few times to make sure.

3, 4, 5, 6, 7, ..

RUMBLE

RUMBLE

4 I believe gravity makes things accelerate at the same speed. If I'm right balls of different weights will roll at the same speed too.

Notes:

1 Galileo was proved right in both experiments.

2 It should be pointed out that boring old historians reckon there's no proof Galileo performed the first experiment. Huh – why spoil a good story?

GALILEO'S GENIUS

There's no doubt Galileo was a genius. He invented the thermometer, a pendulum driven clock and an amazing compass that you could use to work out the purity of metals. He even discovered that cannonballs fall in a curved path. They move forwards at a constant speed and downwards at an increasing speed under the influence of gravity. This fatal discovery helped gunners fire more accurately and kill more people.

Could you think like Galileo? Now's your chance to find out.

BURNING AMBITION QUIZ

1 You are Galileo. You look through the newly invented telescope and see planets orbiting the sun. (As Newton later proved, gravity stops them wandering off into space.) But there's one teeny little problem. Important people in the Church claim planets go round the Earth. They're all-powerful in Italy. And they don't want a smarty-pants scientist proving them wrong. You realize you'd be wise to get the backing of these people. What do you do?

a) Start a reasoned debate.

b) Get them to look through your telescope.

c) Shout at them until they admit you're right.

2 You reckon the Church's experts that you talked to are friendly. They aren't. Your enemies falsely accuse you of being anti-Church. What do you do?

a) Go into hiding.

b) Write a book making fun of your enemies.

c) Set the record straight in a public statement.

3 In 1623 you have a stroke of luck. An old pal of yours is elected Pope. You drop in for a chat. He allows you to write a book so long as it doesn't support your views. What's in the book?

a) Support for your views and amusing abuse of your enemies.

b) A balanced survey of the different opinions which doesn't come to any conclusion.

c) A cleverly written argument which seems to back the traditional view whilst actually making it look stupid.

4 Your book is a best-seller but the Pope is chewing the carpet. You're accused of heresy and put on trial before the dreaded Inquisition. Your enemies forge a letter that claims the Church had banned you from teaching your views. If you're found guilty you could be tied to a stake and burnt alive. What do you do?

a) Proudly insist you were right.

b) Quietly remind the Pope that you're his friend.

c) Crack a joke about liking your "stake" well done.

5 In a bid to scare you, the Inquisition show you the torture chamber that is used to extract confessions. You see the rack, the thumbscrews and the red hot pincers. What do you say?

a) OK, where's the confession – I'll sign anything … Oh dear, I can't sign that, it's not grovelling enough.

b) The truth is the truth. I scorn your puny instruments of torture and laugh in the face of danger.

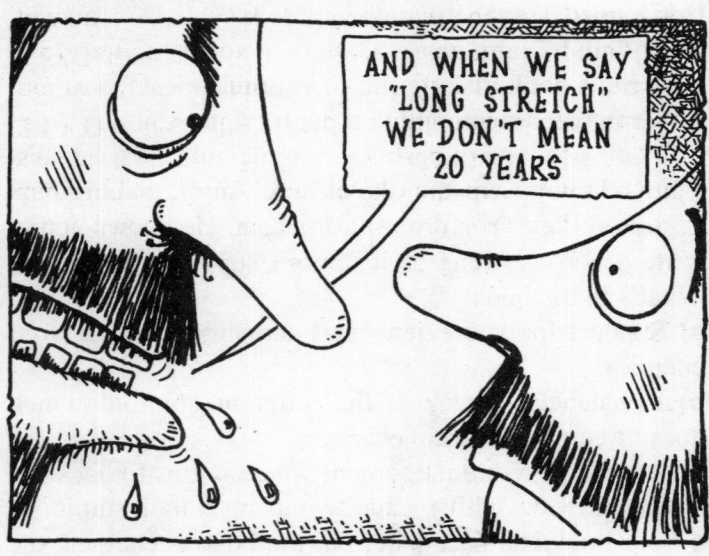

c) Can I have 20 years to think about it, please?

WOBBLY BALANCE

Everything has a centre of gravity. Imagine a tightrope walker.

Her centre of balance is the point inside her body where gravity is pulling most strongly. If this crucial point is supported underneath and the performer's weight is evenly balanced around it she's OK. If not there'll be a gloopy mess on the pavement. Yet some balancing acts seem impossible.

WOBBLY BALANCING QUIZ

See if you can guess which of these incredible balancing acts are true and which are false.

1 In 1553 a Dutch acrobat balanced on one foot on the weathervane of St Paul's Cathedral, London waving a 4.6-metre streamer. And he didn't fall off.
TRUE/FALSE

2 In 1859 French tightrope walker Jean Blondin (1824–1897) walked across the raging Niagara Falls 50 metres in the air. And he was wearing a blindfold.
TRUE/FALSE

3 In 1773 Dutch acrobat Leopold van Trump juggled ten tomatoes whilst balancing on a tightrope 30 metres in the air. If he had fallen he might have invented tomato ketchup.
TRUE/FALSE

4 In 1842 a Miss Cooke wowed London circus goers when she sat at a table and drank a glass of wine. Boring? Not really. Everything was balanced on a high wire.
TRUE/FALSE

5 In 1995 Aleksandr Bendikov of Belarus balanced a pyramid made of 880 coins. The coin pyramid was upside down and balanced on top of the edge of a single coin. Luckily, no one needed change for the bus.
TRUE/FALSE

6 In 1996 American Bryan Berg built a house of cards 100 storeys high – that's 5.85 metres.
TRUE/FALSE

7 In 1990 Brazilian Leandro Henrique Basseto cycled on one wheel of his bicycle for 100 minutes.
TRUE/FALSE

Answers:

1 TRUE. Some people will do *anything* to get attention.

2 TRUE. Blondin also went across on stilts. By then he was just showing off.

3 FALSE

4 TRUE

5 TRUE

6 TRUE He built the record house of cards in Copenhagen, Denmark. Couldn't he find anything more exciting to do?

7 FALSE. In fact he cycled for an incredible 640 minutes.

Yes, it's amazing what incredible death-defying, gravity-defying, balancing acts people can do just as long as the force of gravity is exactly balanced. But getting it right on the high-wire certainly puts you under pressure. And oddly enough, the next chapter is about pressure too. The kind of pressure that can fatally crush a human being. Ouch!

I'VE BEEN UNDER A LOT OF PRESSURE RECENTLY

UNDER PRESSURE

Air and water are common enough on Earth but they contain vital chemicals – in fact we couldn't live without them. But if they're under pressure it's hard to live with them. And they can easily prove fatal.

Fatal forces fact file

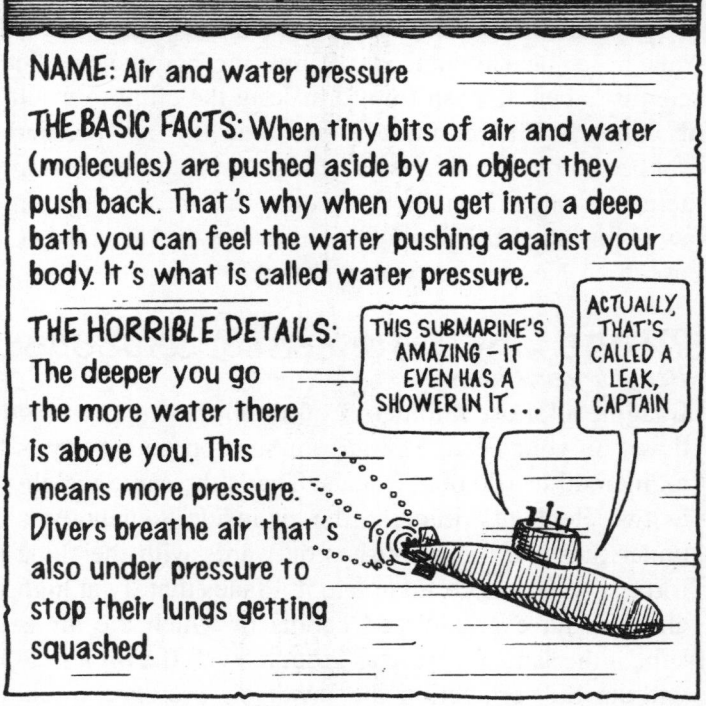

NAME: Air and water pressure

THE BASIC FACTS: When tiny bits of air and water (molecules) are pushed aside by an object they push back. That's why when you get into a deep bath you can feel the water pushing against your body. It's what is called water pressure.

THE HORRIBLE DETAILS: The deeper you go the more water there is above you. This means more pressure. Divers breathe air that's also under pressure to stop their lungs getting squashed.

THIS SUBMARINE'S AMAZING – IT EVEN HAS A SHOWER IN IT...

ACTUALLY, THAT'S CALLED A LEAK, CAPTAIN

One of the first people to study air pressure was French physicist Blaise Pascal.

Hall of fame: Blaise Pascal (1623–1662)
Nationality: French

Blaise Pascal had no sense of humour. Not surprising really, he suffered all his life from violent indigestion so he didn't have the stomach for too many jokes. But that didn't stop brainy Blaise from making some amazing discoveries. At the age of 19 he built a machine to help his tax collector dad count up the loot. And in 1646 he invented a barometer – a machine that measures air pressure. High air pressure pushes a column of mercury upwards.

To test his invention Blaise forced his brother-in-law to walk up a local mountain carrying the barometer. (The scientist's health wasn't up to making the climb himself, of course.) The climber found that the air pressure dropped as he went higher. The higher you go the less air there is pushing down on you. Today the brave brother-in-law is forgotten but pressure is measured in "Pascals". (1 Pascal = 1 Newton per square metre.)

Bet you never knew!

Imagine all those kilometres of air above you pressing down on your head. The air pressure on your body is an incredible 100,000 Pascals. That's the same weight as two elephants. Luckily, the air inside your body is under pressure too. It pushes outwards with the same force so you don't even notice it. Planes that fly at high altitudes have pressurized cabins in which the air is kept at the same pressure as ground level. If a pilot flew without this protection the lower air pressure would cause air bubbles in his or her body to get bigger. The guts and lungs would swell painfully and air bubbles trapped in fillings could make their teeth explode.

Dare you discover ... how air pressure helps you drink?

You will need:

Yourself

A bottle of your favourite drink (it's all in the interests of science) – just so long as the bottle's got a narrow neck.

What you do:

1 Try drinking from the bottle. Sit upright and tip the bottle up so it's level with your mouth. You can easily suck the liquid up.

2 Now stick the mouth of the bottle in your mouth. Wrap your lips around the neck of the bottle. Now try to drink.

What do you notice?

a) It's as easy as before.

b) You can't suck any more drink up.

c) You dribble uncontrollably into your drink.

Answer: b) Liquids flow to areas where the air pressure is less. As you try to suck your drink the air space in the bottle gets bigger. Since no more air gets into the bottle the air pressure drops below the air pressure in your mouth. This keeps the liquid in the bottle. Don't suck too hard – you might swallow the bottle. Mind you, that's not as horrible as a vacuum in your bottle. Here's why…

TERRIBLE TEACHER JOKE

UNDER PRESSURE

1 The first man-made vacuum was made by Otto von Guericke (1602–1686) Mayor of Magdeburg, Germany. In his spare time Otto was keen on scientific experiments but in 1631 Magdeburg was destroyed in war and 70,000 people were killed. Von Guericke got away and carried on researching.

2 In 1647 he tried pumping air from a beer cask. But more air got in and made a strange whistling noise.

3 So he put the beer cask in a barrel of water. Water was sucked into the cask with a strange squelching noise.

4 Next he made a hollow copper ball. But when he pumped the air out it was crushed by an unseen force.

5 In 1654 von Guericke made a hollow ball from two stronger copper cups and pumped out the air. He'd made a vacuum. The pressure of the air outside jammed the cups together. It was this pressure that had crushed the earlier ball.

6 Fifty men couldn't pull the cups apart.

7 Two teams of horses didn't stand a chance.

8 But when von Guericke pumped air into the hollow centre the cups fell apart.

SOME PRESSING FACTS

1 In the 1890s Aimée, a young circus performer, used the power of vacuums to walk upside down. Her shoes had suction caps attached to them and as she walked the air was pushed out of the caps. The pressure of the air outside the caps then glued her feet to a board hung from the ceiling. Very im-press-ive!

2 Champagne in a bottle is under pressure too. This is due to all the gas bubbles squeezed into the drink. When shaken and heated the cork fires at 12.3 metres a second – as fast as a rock blasted with dynamite. It definitely makes a party go with a bang.

3 Pressurized liquid or gases are used in hydraulic machines such as the powerful pistons that lift crane jibs. One early hydraulic machine was a nineteenth-century vacuum cleaner. Water was squirted one way and the falling pressure sucked in air and dirt behind it. But when water went the wrong way it flooded your home.

I THINK WE'LL STICK TO THE DUSTPAN AND BRUSH, POLLY

4 In 1868 American inventor George Westinghouse (1846–1914) made an air brake. It used the cushioning effect of air pressure to halt a train. Rail tycoon Cornelius Vanderbilt called it a "foolish notion". He didn't think air could stop a train. But nowadays air brakes are used on buses and lorries too.

Air pressure can do amazing things but could it also haul a train? It took a genius to see the possibilities in this "train of thought". A hard-driving ruthless workaholic genius in a black top hat.

Hall of fame: Isambard Kingdom Brunel
(1806–1859) Nationality: British

Isambard Kingdom Brunel dedicated his life to engineering. He developed some spectacular engineering projects that used the forces of nature to help make people's lives easier. He built railways, giant iron ships and tunnels on a grand scale. At times he was so wrapped up in his work that he showed little concern for others. He even sent his crippled son to a school where there were daily floggings. When the child complained bossy Brunel snapped at him:

IT IS VERY DISTRESSING, BUT ONE MUST PUT UP WITH IT

Issie loved to attempt the seemingly impossible. Sometimes he was successful but he also made many fatal mistakes. This story is about one of them … a railway powered by air pressure.

PIPE DREAMS
Devon, England 1848

Isambard Kingdom Brunel chewed on his giant-sized cigar as he strode angrily along the railway. As usual his mind was jumping with ideas. Fantastic ideas. Mighty plans. Pipe dreams. They had all seemed so easy. Once.

Four years ago Brunel and some other leading engineers visited Ireland to see the world's first "atmospheric railway". A railway where the carriages were pulled quickly and silently. Pulled along by the amazing power of air.

The idea was simple…

HOW TO BUILD YOUR OWN ATMOSPHERIC RAILWAY.

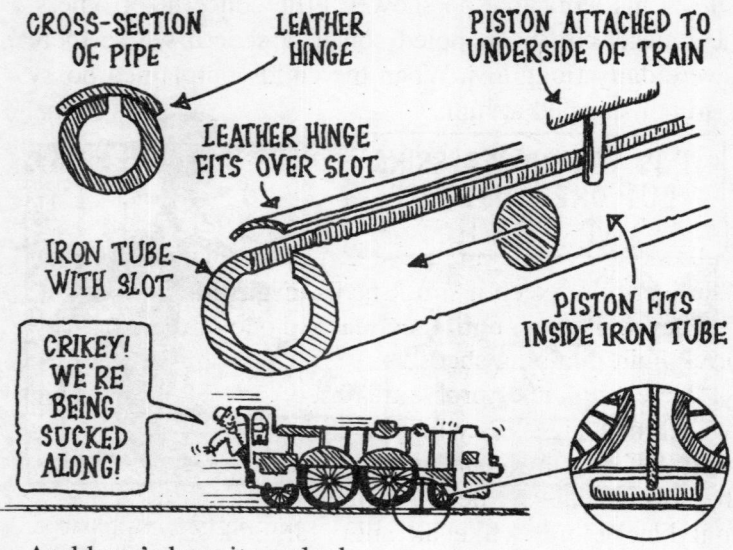

And here's how it worked.

1 Powerful steam engines pump the air from the pipe.
2 A piston travels along the pipe. It's pushed by air trying to rush back into the vacuum.
3 The piston is linked to passenger carriages and provides the moving power.

The other engineers laughed at the strangely silent railway. They thought it was impractical. But Isambard was quietly impressed. He suggested using atmospheric pressure for the South Devon Railway. But he forgot to mention to anyone that the Irish railway was always breaking down. Little old ladies rushed to sink their savings in a scheme backed by the world's greatest engineer. But the pipe dream soon turned into a pipe nightmare.

Now Brunel had come to see things for himself and young Tom the signalman's boy was showing him around.

"It's the leather hinges, Mr Brunel," said Tom slightly in awe of the great man. "They dry and crack in cold winter weather. And they rot in warm sunshine."

"So I see," said Brunel wrinkling his nose in distaste. "What's that appalling smell?"

"That'll be the fish oil. The railway pays people to walk along the line and paint the leather with soap and fish liver oil to keep it soft. Smells disgusting, it does."

They walked on until they reached one of the massive brick-built pumping sheds.

"Here's the other problem!" cried Tom. He nervously twisted his pale sweaty fingers. "It's the pipes…"

"What do you mean pipes?" bellowed Brunel above the noise of the engines. The huge steam engine snorted foul black smoke like an angry dragon. The gasping pumps sucked the air from the hollow iron pipes. And with the air came a stream of horrible things.

Oily water, rust and dead rats.

Rats. *Water.*

"How did they get there?" Brunel roared into the boy's ear. But he'd already guessed the terrible truth.

Hungry rats chewed the oily leather flaps until they were no longer air-tight. Water seeped in and rusted the pipes.

The famous engineer strode on furiously with the signalman's boy jogging to keep up. Suddenly Brunel bent down to touch the rat nibbled leather. Tom watched in fascinated horror. "No!" he shouted.

Brunel had his hand on the flap when Tom grabbed his arm.

"Stand aside boy!" ordered Brunel curtly.

"*Please* don't touch it," gasped Tom.

"Why NOT?"

Then Brunel saw the ghastly danger.

The vacuum inside the pipe wasn't 100 per cent. But it could still pluck his finger bones from their sockets. Scrunch, squelch, plop. No more fingers.

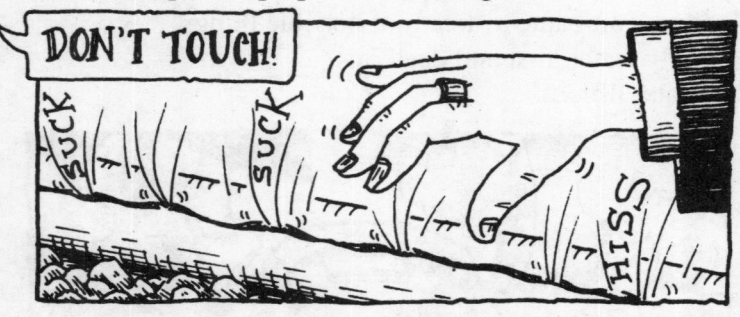

He backed off, muttering. There were some things even the great Brunel dared not do.

In February 1848 Brunel told the Company the problems were almost solved. But seven months later he advised the directors to scrap the entire project. The little old ladies had lost their savings. And they were angry.

So how did Brunel make it up to them?

a) He offered to build a new railway for nothing.

b) He said he wouldn't send his bill for engineering advice.

c) He offered them a lifetime's supply of smelly fish oil.

Answer: b) Brunel kindly offered not to send his bill. Not just yet. Bet that cheered them up. There was a lot of anger and friction. You get friction in the world of forces too. But this sort of friction can wreck machines and spark fatal fires. That's why the next chapter is *RED HOT*.

FACTS ABOUT FRICTION

Newton said that a moving object would carry on moving for ever if another force didn't slow it down. That force is called friction. People use the word friction to mean aggro, anger or annoyance. Like a really bad day at school. And in the world of fatal forces friction can also often spoil your whole day.

Fatal forces fact file

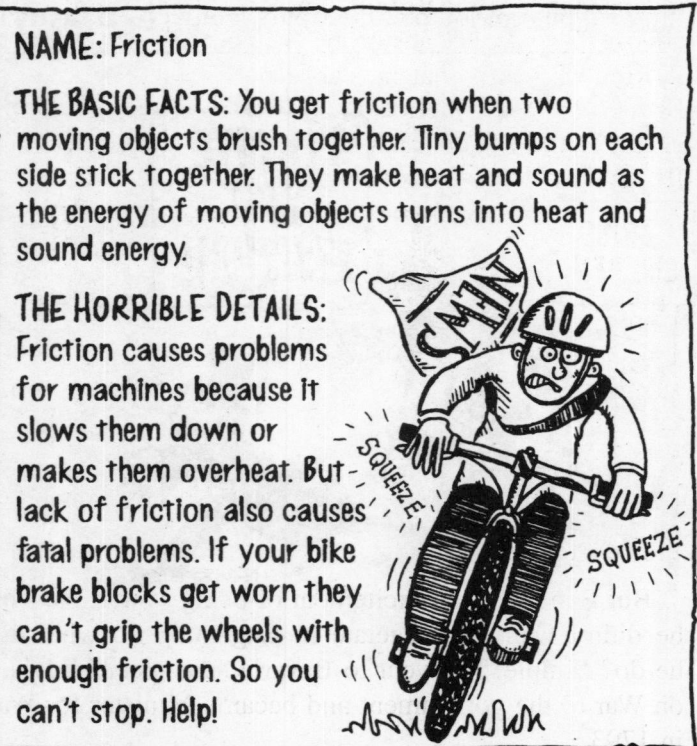

NAME: Friction

THE BASIC FACTS: You get friction when two moving objects brush together. Tiny bumps on each side stick together. They make heat and sound as the energy of moving objects turns into heat and sound energy.

THE HORRIBLE DETAILS: Friction causes problems for machines because it slows them down or makes them overheat. But lack of friction also causes fatal problems. If your bike brake blocks get worn they can't grip the wheels with enough friction. So you can't stop. Help!

Mind you, the man who discovered friction had an amazing life story. He could almost have been a character from friction – er, fiction.

Hall of fame: Benjamin Thompson (Count Rumford of Bavaria) (1753–1814) Nationality: American

Ben Thompson was a teacher who escaped from school. He was born in the United States and besides being a teacher, he was a gymnast and a medical student. Until the war. The American colonists were fighting for their independence from Britain. But which side should Ben choose? The Americans or the British?

Rumour has it that he chose both. He spied for the British *and* the Americans. He was a sort of a double-agent. But the British never knew this and King George III gave Ben a knighthood when the war was over.

But Ben liked the excitement of being at war. He said he didn't want to "vegetate in England". So what did he do? Simple! He went to Bavaria as a special adviser on War to the government and became Minister for War in 1793.

As Minister of War, Ben devised a cunning plan. The streets were full of beggars and the army was short of uniforms. Ben's idea was to force the beggars to make uniforms. But how should he feed the beggars? After much research Ben found the cheapest food was watery vegetable soup. So he "vegetated" in Bavaria instead of in England – ha, ha. Ben was so keen on his idea he even published a book of recipes. Could this be a new line in school dinners? Then he had a second brainwave.

He put soldiers to work growing potatoes to make the soup to feed the beggars who made their uniforms. Ben's plan was a great success so at least it didn't land him in the soup! Brainy Ben made many other interesting discoveries. A new chimney for houses, a new stove and a coffee percolator to put on the stove.

And then he discovered friction.

One day Ben was watching a cannon being made. The barrel of the cannon was bored by a drill. Ben could feel the heat wafting off the cannon. In those days people thought heat was an invisible liquid. But Ben found you got extra heat if you used a blunt drill. So he figured the heat was produced by the drill. Dead right. The blunt drill had tiny bumps on its surface – and this caused extra friction. And more heat.

FACT OR FRICTION?

Often, just like Benjamin Thompson, physicists draw conclusions from things they noticed. Could you do this? Here are some everyday happenings. Which ones are caused by friction?

1 Friction helps you to build a house of cards.
2 Friction explains how you can whip a table cloth off a fully-laid table without breaking anything.

3 Friction makes electrical equipment heat up.
4 The patterns on tyres causes friction with the road. This helps to control the vehicle.
5 People use friction to start fires.
6 Friction helps skiers to ski up hills.

7 Runners use friction to run without slipping.

8 Friction causes people to get burnt by snow.

Answers:

1 Fact. Tiny bumps on the surface of the cards help them to stick to the surface of the table. That's friction. It works if the cards are at a steep angle.

2 Friction. The inertia of the crockery and the force of gravity pins it to the table. If you pull the table cloth fast enough there isn't enough friction to pull the crockery off the table. However, practising this trick at home may cause fatal friction with your family.

3 Fact. As the electrical current runs through the circuits it causes friction which heats up the machine. That's why TVs can burst into flames if you cover their ventilation holes.

4 Friction. Smooth tyres provide more friction in dry weather. The treads are better in wet weather. The wheel scoops the water out of the way so the tyres can grip the road.

5 Fact. One of your ancestors hit on a hot method of lighting fires. Rub two sticks together. The heat of the friction can set fire to some dried fungus. Later on people found that partially burnt underwear caught fire again very easily. So it was ideal for getting a blaze going.

6 Fact. Traditional up-hill skis used sealskin for this purpose. Nowadays they have man-made bristles. It's kinder to seals.

7 Fact. Spiked shoes increase friction with the track.

8 Fact. Crazy skiers can suffer serious burns if they go too fast and then fall over. At high speeds, friction causes enough heat to burn the skin before the snow melts.

MESSED-UP MACHINES

Here's the bad news about friction. It slows machines down. Yes, it's a real spanner in the works for generations of freaky physicists who've tried to devise the ultimate machine. One that keeps on working without power. Perpetual motion.

Between 1617 and 1906 the British Patent Office received ideas for 600 perpetual motion machines. None worked.

Here are four more. Which one was successful?

1 A perpetual bicycle

The power for this bike comes from your bum bouncing on the saddle. This drives the rear wheel using a drive belt. So you could cycle for ever or until you get a sore bum.

2 A self-powered pump
The water-lifting pump is powered by a waterwheel that is powered by water falling from buckets tied to the wheel as it runs around.

3 A perpetual wind machine
Dreamt up by an Italian doctor in 1500. Air from the fan is funnelled down a horn linked to a propeller which in turn powers the fan.

Answer: None of them! The fatal truth is that perpetual motion is as about as likely as a vegetarian vampire bat. And here's why…

A HOT HALT

Perpetual motion, unfortunately, breaks a law of physics. The Second Law of Thermodynamics to be exact. (Thermodynamics is the branch of physics to do with heat and energy. It's a subject you can really warm to.) The Second Law of Thermodynamics says that energy is lost from a machine as sound, noise, heat and, of course, friction.

So the machine stops because it runs out of energy. By the way, the First Law of Thermodynamics says you can turn energy from motion into heat. And it's true. Try rubbing your hands and friction turns the energy of your moving hands into a nice warm sensation.

A SLIPPERY SUBJECT

Sometimes we want friction. Brakes, tyres, rubber-soled shoes, sandpaper and driving belts in machines would be useless without it.

THESE 'FRICTION' BOOTS ARE GREAT FOR WALKING UP STEEP HILLS!

But sometimes we don't want friction. We want things to go smoothly. That's why some slippery character invented lubrication. A lubricant such as oil fills out the little bumps that cause friction and allows the surfaces to slide past one another.

Most winter sports depend on lubrication. Sledges, skis and skates move easily because they melt a thin layer of ice beneath them. So they float along on this watery lubricant without too much friction. Until you slip over.

VERY LITTLE FRICTION

LOTS OF FRICTION

Lubrication also launches ships. That's why in the Middle Ages slipways were coated in revoltingly greasy animal fat. A slave got the risky job of knocking away the props under the ship. At the last minute the slave had to jump clear. If he slipped the ship would crush him – that's why they called it the slip-way. If the slave survived he was given his freedom.

I'M FREE ARGHH!

But if lubrication is lethal, friction can be fatal. That was certainly the case in Rome four centuries ago.

FATAL FRICTION
Rome, 1586

It was an ancient obelisk. For 2,000 years it had lain forgotten in the dirt, west of St Peter's Cathedral. But times had changed. The Pope decided that the stone would look great in front of St Peter's. But how could it be raised? It was quite a problem. The obelisk weighed 327 tonnes.

"They say," murmured old Roberto, "that two engineers turned down the job. Reckoned it couldn't be done."

"I can see why," replied young Marco gazing in awe at the huge stone in its protective cage.

"Well – we'd better give it a try. Gotta earn our pay," grumbled Roberto with a wheezy cough. He and Marco were amongst hundreds of sailors hired to raise the obelisk. They took up their ropes.

The square was ringed by crowds. Thousands of people were cheering and waving handkerchiefs and waiting impatiently for the big event. A smartly dressed young man leapt onto a platform.

Roberto screwed up his creased old face in a scowl. "That's Fontana – he's the engineer who claims he can do it. What a big-head!"

"People of Rome!" proclaimed the young man. "Today we'll raise this great monument from the past. When the trumpet sounds you sailors must pull the ropes. Only stop when you hear the bell. It's vital that these signals are obeyed in silence. There must be no talking on pain of death!" The young man pointed sternly to the nearby gallows.

There was a shocked silence.

The older sailor made the sign of the cross. "That's a bit over the top," he whispered.

The sailors spat on their hands. The moist spit would stop friction with the rope burning the skin off their fingers.

The trumpet blared. The harsh note echoed around the square. Silently the men took the strain. The ropes creaked. Windlasses squealed. Capstans groaned round. Slowly, painfully the great stone began to lift.

Then the bell rang. Everyone rested for a few moments. The trumpet sounded again. Once again the sailors' muscles bunched and knotted until sweat trickled down their backs. Then disaster struck.

The ropes jammed – halted by friction between the ropes and windlasses. The sailors pulled the ropes until their faces screwed up in agony. Nothing moved. The taut ropes groaned and frayed. The stone tottered. Young Marco saw the danger. He shouted instantly: "Water, give water to the ropes!" Then he realized what he'd done. And knew he must die.

"Seize him!" screamed Fontana, his voice cracking with tension and disappointment. "Seize him for breaking the silence!"

Strong arms grabbed Marco. The guards dragged the young sailor towards the scaffold and the waiting executioner. The people gasped in horror but no one dared speak.

"I'm sorry," whispered Marco. But it was too late.

The executioner tightened the harsh hemp rope around Marco's bare throat.

A thin, old priest touched the sailor's arm.

"What's your last request?" the priest mumbled.

"Please, father," croaked Marco. His heart was racing and he couldn't speak clearly. His throat was dry and the rope didn't help. "Please, tell them to pour water on the ropes."

"I don't know if that's possible, my son."

"*Please* do it!"

The steel-helmeted guards beat their drums. It was the signal for the execution to begin.

The priest hurried over to Fontana. The young engineer nodded his head impatiently. A large water pitcher was found and its contents poured over the straining ropes.

"Come on mate, let's get it over with," said the executioner cheerfully shoving Marco up the ladder of death.

Just then a trumpet blared and the ropes took the strain.

"Why were the people cheering?" thought Marco wildly. Were they pleased to see him die?

No. The ropes were moving easily. The stone was being lifted smoothly and quickly. At the foot of the ladder stood Domenico Fontana. Shamefaced.

"Release that man!" he shouted.

As a sailor Marco was used to hauling wet ropes at sea. He knew that there was less friction on wet ropes because the water acted as a lubricant. You'll be pleased to know that the brave sailor was pardoned and given his freedom. But what was his reward for saving the obelisk?

a) A golden pitcher of water.

b) Tea with the Pope.

c) His very own ship.

Well, hopefully you won't slip-up over this easy experiment.

Dare you discover … how to give things the slip?

You will need:

What you do:

1 Flick the bottle top along the first tray. Make sure the top stays on the tray and doesn't fly through the air.

2 Carefully pour a few drops of cooking oil on the first tray. Smear it over the surface with a kitchen towel until the surface is shiny and there is no extra oil on the tray.

3 Now flick the bottle top again as hard as before. Note what happens.

4 Mash up the banana and, using another kitchen towel, smear a little of the mixture over the second tray. Make sure the surface is smooth and shiny and there are no lumps of banana left.

5 *(optional)* Mash the remaining banana with a little cream and sugar. Eat it. Tell your feeble-minded folks it's all part of the experiment. Who said science was tough?

6 Now flick the bottle top again as hard as before.

What do you notice?

a) Both the oil and the banana make good lubricants. They help the top move faster.

b) The top stuck to the banana and skimmed along over the oil.

c) The top stuck in the oil but skimmed over the banana.

Answer: a) Lubricating oils are squeezed from peanuts, coconuts or bits of dead fish. In some countries bananas are used because they're slippery too. That's why you slip on a banana skin!

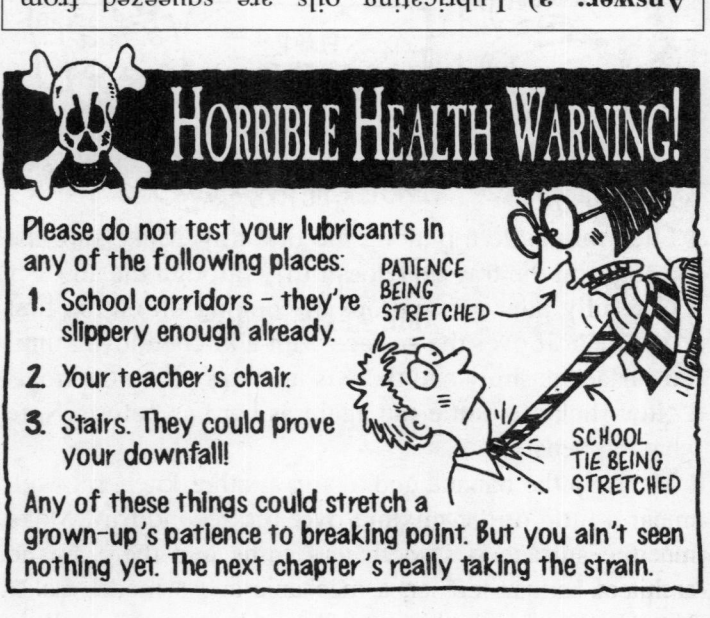

HORRIBLE HEALTH WARNING!

Please do not test your lubricants in any of the following places:

1. School corridors – they're slippery enough already.

2. Your teacher's chair.

3. Stairs. They could prove your downfall!

PATIENCE BEING STRETCHED

SCHOOL TIE BEING STRETCHED

Any of these things could stretch a grown-up's patience to breaking point. But you ain't seen nothing yet. The next chapter's really taking the strain.

STRETCHING AND STRAINING

Hold an elastic band between your fingers. Pull one end ever so carefully. The elastic band is storing the energy you put into pulling it. Let go – the released energy sends the elastic band flying. Oh dear – why does a teacher always get in the way? But just tell him that it's all part of a very technical scientific experiment – he'll understand! One of the first people to experiment with stretching was scientist Robert Hooke.

IT WAS THAT ROBERT HOOKE'S FAULT!

WELL TELL HIM TO SEE ME AFTER SCHOOL

Hall of fame: Robert Hooke (1635–1703)
Nationality: British

After his bust-ups with Newton (see page 22), Robert must have known all about tension. But this talented scientist was interested in everything from telescopes to making flying machines that didn't fly. Incredibly, he also worked as an architect, an astronomer, a mechanic and a model maker. Yes. Hooke liked working at full-stretch.

According to one story Robert wrote a strange code in his will which deciphered into Latin reads "*ut tensio sic vis*". Mean anything to you? Thought not. Further translated into English it means "as the extension so the force". And these weird words turned out to be Hooke's Law on stretching. Imagine hanging a weight on a spring – the spring stretches. Double the weight and the spring stretches twice as far. Simple, innit?

Dare you discover 1 ... what happens when something stretches?

You will need:
Yourself
A 0.5-cm-thick elastic band

What you do:
Suddenly stretch the elastic band.
Put it against your face.
What happens and why?
a) The elastic band feels strangely cold because all the energy has been stretched out of it.
b) The elastic band feels warm. This is due to the energy that you have provided by stretching it.
c) The elastic band feels warm because stretching causes friction with your hot sweaty little fingers.

Answer: b) The band briefly stores energy from the force that stretches it. The energy tries to escape as heat and that's why the band feels hot.

Dare you discover 2 ... the power of an elastic band?

Here's a machine that uses stored energy in an elastic band to get moving. Ask an adult to help with some of the cutting.

You will need:

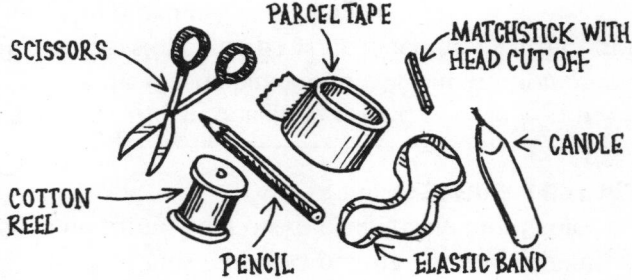

SCISSORS

PARCEL TAPE

MATCHSTICK WITH HEAD CUT OFF

CANDLE

COTTON REEL

PENCIL

ELASTIC BAND

What you do:

1 Cut 2.5 cm off the bottom of the candle.

2 Remove the wick from the wax and make its middle hole large enough for the elastic band.

3 Pass the elastic band through the centres of the candle stump and the cotton reel.

4 Pass the matchstick through the elastic band at its cotton reel end. Secure the matchstick with a strip of parcel tape.

5 Pass the pencil through the elastic band at its candle end.

6 Wind the elastic band by turning the pencil. Watch your vehicle creep along as the elastic band unwinds. Compare its performance on rough and smooth slopes.

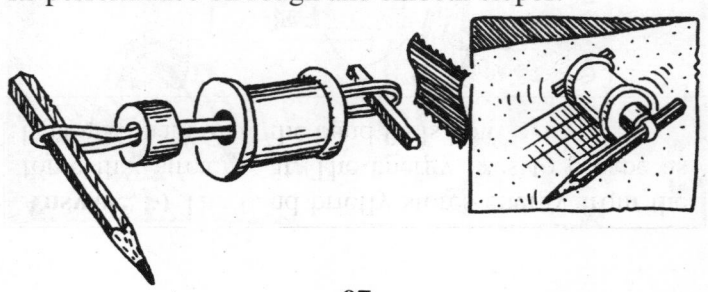

What do you notice?

a) It climbs better on smooth slopes.

b) It climbs better on rough slopes.

c) It can't climb slopes.

A STRETCHY SUBJECT

Here's some more elastic info to stretch your brain cells. A few hundred years ago you could be sent to prison in England for a long stretch. Stretched out on a timber frame with rollers at each end. This was the rack. The most anyone was ever stretched on a rack was 15 cm. After that their arm and leg joints popped out of their sockets. Rumours that racks were used in schools are just "tall stories". No – teachers just racked children's *brains*.

In the 1700s rubber thread was used in clothes and underwear. Sadly, the rubber melted in hot weather and cracked in cold.

In 1839 scientists discovered a chemical treatment that stopped this happening and rubber thread known as elastic was used in corsets and knickers from the 1930s. (Corsets are the tight-fitting garments some women wore to squeeze their bulging bodies into shape. Before elastic, corsets were reinforced with bits of whale bone.)

HORRIBLE HEALTH WARNING!

NEVER ask your mature female teachers if they still wear whalebone corsets. This could be fatal.

WHEN I CATCH YOU I'M GOING TO SQUEEZE YOUR BONY BODY **OUT OF SHAPE**

Nowadays man-made elastic is used for much more than just corsets – including the rope bungee jumpers use. Would you want to bungee jump?

If your answer to this question is "ARGGGGGH!" you wouldn't envy Gregory Riffi who in 1992 jumped 249.9 metres from a helicopter over France. With his life hanging by a thread – all right – an elastic rope.

BY THE WAY CAPTAIN, I COULDN'T FIND ANY ELASTIC SO I USED ROPE INSTEAD – OK?

By the way, bungee jumping isn't usually fatal if it's done by experts. But as the jumper falls the blood rushes to their head and this can make their eyeballs bleed a bit. Another sport that depends on stretching is archery.

BIG BAD BOWS

1 The bow was invented before 20,000 BC. The idea was that you could store energy by pulling back the string and transfer the force of the energy to fire the arrow.

2 Five seconds later the bow may have claimed its first victim. Ooops!

3 In the 900s the Turks hit upon a better bow. It was made from grisly bits of animal horn and tendons and strengthened with wood. The outward curve of the bow allowed it to be drawn with greater force.

4 Meanwhile the Europeans had invented the crossbow. This deadly weapon could fire a bolt 305 metres

5 But the crossbow string had to be cranked slowly back. And during that time ordinary archers with ordinary bows were so skilled, they could turn the crossbow soldier into a pin-cushion in no time – unless he bolted first.

6 And then a Welsh person invented the long-bow. It could fire an arrow 320 metres. And straight through chain mail. At shorter ranges, the arrows could pierce armour too.

CROSS BOWMAN

GRRRR

CROSSBOW

7 Modern bows are really high-tech.

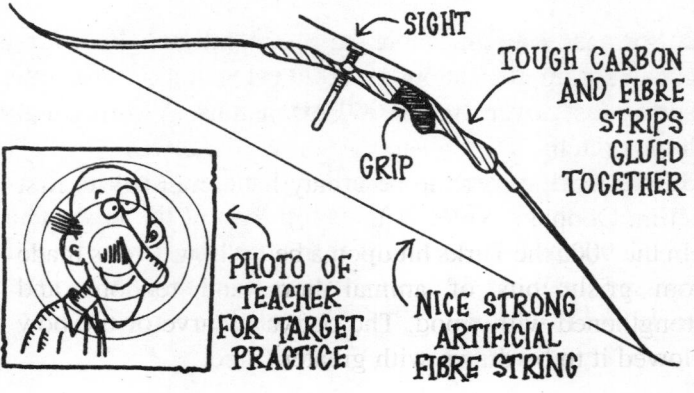

SIGHT

GRIP

TOUGH CARBON AND FIBRE STRIPS GLUED TOGETHER

PHOTO OF TEACHER FOR TARGET PRACTICE

NICE STRONG ARTIFICIAL FIBRE STRING

8 In free-style shooting the archers lie on their back, strap the bow to their feet and draw the string with both hands. Of course, it isn't only stretchy things that can store force. Springs can do this too when you push them down and then they pop up again. You'll be surprised to know that the earliest springs were used 600 years ago in mousetraps. And springs can spring real surprises on you. Here are seven more.

SEVEN SPRINGY SURPRISES

1 The first toasters sold in 1919 had powerful springs that shot toast into the air. Bet that surprised a few people.

2 Springs sometimes break. Metal fatigue does for a cheap spring after about 100,000 extensions, but a better spring lasts over 10,000,000 extensions. A surprisingly long stretch.

3 Bed springs are a surprising shape. They're cone shaped – that's wider at their top than at the base. This makes them squeeze easily at first but the harder they're pressed the more difficult they are to squash. A bed that feels comfy and springy to you feels like a rock to a big, sprawling grown-up.

4 You know the circus act where a person is fired from a cannon? You may be surprised to discover that springs rather than explosions are used to provide the necessary force. The bang is a firework let off to make it look like the cannon had really fired.

5 And did you know we've got springs in our legs too? The ligaments that hold your joints together are a bit springy and your "S" shaped backbone jogs up and down as you walk. Together they'll put a spring in your step.

6 In the 1970s two American scientists trained a pair of kangaroos to hop on a treadmill. The scientists found that kangaroos jump using their springy tendons. It's a bit like jumping on a pogo stick.

7 Springy things are important for sport. Traditional tennis rackets were very expensive and strung with springy sheep's guts. Sounds like a bit of a racket. And talking about springy sports equipment, trainers have to be springy too.

SUPER SPRINGY SHOES

HAS ANYONE SEEN MY TRAINERS?

SMELLY PONG

MIDSOLE – NICE SPRINGY BUBBLES

RUBBER LAYER – GOOD FOR PROVIDING FRICTION TO GRIP THE GROUND

Do this to your brother's trainers and you better run for it before he takes a swing at you. Funnily enough the next chapter's about swinging and spinning too. Better stand clear.

FASCINATING!

GETTING IN A SPIN

Ever wondered why cars don't have square wheels? No – me neither. Well – round wheels go round better (howls of amazement). Also the force on the outer parts of the wheel produces greater force at the axle. And this is ideal for wheel-based machines such as waterwheels and cars. And there's lots more wheel-life facts to go around (and pathetic jokes too)…

Fatal forces expressions

STOP IT! IT'S CONSERVATION OF ANGULAR MOMENTUM!

Who's to blame?

Answer: No one – his 10p is rolling away. He's describing how coins and any other spinning objects have a habit of turning until another force gets in the way. That's why wheels work so well. Best put your foot over the coin and pretend you haven't seen it.

And wheels **are** wonderful. They were invented by some bright spark who lived in the Middle East in about 3500 BC. When a wheel goes around, centripetal force tries to pull it towards its centre – remember that force from page 33? And now let's face a few more facts to get your head spinning … Oh go on – give it a whirl!

Fatal forces fact file

NAME: Centripetal force

THE BASIC FACTS:
Imagine whirling a
small ball round your
head on a bit of string.

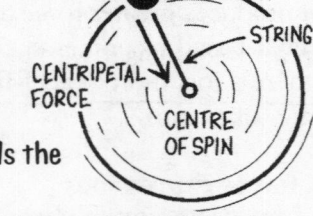

1. Centripetal force tries
to move the ball towards the
centre of its spin.

2. When you let go, the ball's momentum sends it
flying off at an angle in a straight line.

O.K – SO I NEED
TO PRACTICE A
BIT MORE...

THE HORRIBLE DETAILS: A bolas
uses centripetal force for catching
animals or people. It 's two balls
on a rope. You whirl the bolas
above your head and let go. The
rope winds around your target 's
legs. Here's how to make
your own.

HANG ON WHAT DID
YOU SAY ABOUT
CENTRIPETAL FORCE?

If centripetal force is making you dizzy, this rhyme might help you...

Centripetal's in a spin
All the time it's pulling in
Let go the string – it's worth a try
In a straight line it will fly

Dare you discover ... how a bolas works?

You will need:
Two balls of Blu tak each 2.5 cm across
A piece of strong string or twine 52 cm long

What you do:
1 Wrap a ball of Blu tak around each end of the string.
2 Squeeze the Blu tak to make sure it is holding the string securely.
3 Now you can practise throwing it. Hold the string between your thumb and fingers half-way between the two balls. Whirl the string round your head. Let go.

WHIZzzz

NOTE: READ HEALTH WARNING FIRST ON PAGE 108

HORRIBLE HEALTH WARNING!

1 Practising throwing your bolas indoors could be fatal for you if it knocks any priceless ornaments off the mantelpiece. Much better to practise outside in a wide open space.

2 Try to resist the temptation to throw your bolas at a small brother/sister/cat/dog, even if it is in the interest of science. You could use a small tree for target practice instead.

From your observations how does the bolas work?

a) Centripetal force makes the bolas fly straight. When the force stops it wraps round the tree trunk.

b) The bolas flies straight until centripetal force does the wrapping.

c) Centripetal force makes the bolas come back like a boomerang.

Answer: b) When you release the string, the momentum of the bolas makes it fly off in a straight line in the direction it was heading when you let go. When it hits the tree, centripetal force on the string wraps the bolas around the trunk.

Going round in circles

Between them centripetal force and momentum keep the show on the road and ensure that wheels are an all-round success story. They're useful for cars and trains, and buses and bikes, and tractors and windmills, and capstans that raise anchors. And thousands of other things too. Here are some amazing uses for wheels.

Weird wheels

1 The big Ferris wheels you see in funfairs were first invented in Russia in the 1600s. They were said to be inspired by the custom of giving children rides in the wheels used to scoop water from rivers. If the wheels went round too fast the children would be thrown into the river.

2 The name actually comes from American showman George Ferris who built a 75-metre wheel in 1893. Trouble is it took all of 20 minutes to go round once. Sounds as thrilling as watching porridge cool.

3 Wacky inventor Joseph Merlin gate-crashed a London party to show off the roller skates he'd just invented. The eighteenth-century boffin glided along playing his violin and feeling dead cool as he swished across the polished floor. Until he found he couldn't stop and crashed into a mirror. Merlin's problem was that his wheels spun easily on the smooth floor. And there wasn't much friction to slow them down. Bet he was really cut up about it.

PERHAPS ON REFLECTION, THEY'RE NOT SUCH A BRILLIANT INVENTION

4 By turning a wheel you can produce a force that can be used to power all kinds of machines. In the nineteenth century prisoners were put on the treadmill. They had to climb a revolting revolving wheel but they never reached the top because the wheel kept turning towards them. In the rotting prison ships the treadmills operated the pumps that stopped the ship sinking!

IT'S THE HAMSTER FOOD THAT REALLY GETS ME DOWN

Remember the imaginary force from page 33? As the scientist cycled round the corner she felt as if a force was trying to throw her outwards. Some people wrongly think this is a real force called "centrifugal force". They imagine the force making a lasso fly thorough the air in a cowboy movie. Well, sorry folks – it doesn't really exist!

TEST YOUR TEACHER

The non-existent force is caused by an object's inertia, which opposes centripetal force. So can your teacher tell the difference between this effect a) and b) centripetal force? Or will their head start spinning instead?

1 It's used in labs to separate red blood cells from the rest of the blood.

2 The reason a pendulum swings more slowly in Central Africa than in Europe. (This is true.)

3 It helps your bike go round a corner.

4 The reason that you can whizz upside down on a

roller-coaster and not fall out even if you weren't strapped in.

5 The reason why a spacecraft doesn't fall to Earth.

6 You'll find this inside a rotor. That's the theme park ride that whirls you around as the floor drops away leaving you stuck to the wall.

Answers:

1 b The machine is called a centrifuge. It consists of a wheel on which a container is secured. The wheel whirls round hundreds of times a minute and the heavier cells in the blood sink to the bottom. A centrifuge is also used to separate the lighter cream from the rest of the milk. And they don't use the same machine!

2 b There's a special bonus point if your teacher can explain how it works. As the Earth spins round, its middle – otherwise known as the equator – bulges slightly. This is why gravity is a bit weaker than at the poles. – and weaker gravity explains the pendulum puzzle. Our old pal Newton made the pendulum prediction and in 1735 French expeditions to Peru and Lapland swung pendulums and proved him right.

3 a But you remembered that from page 106 – didn't you? In fact the centripetal force is supplied by friction between your tyres and the road.

4 b But it only works as long as you keep moving. Stop and you'll fall out – which is why it's essential to be strapped in.

5 b Imagine you're flying round the Earth. The surface curves away beneath you. This increase in distance cancels out the effects of gravity as you fall. If you weren't moving so fast you would fall to Earth with fatal results!

6 b You spin so fast that you stick to the wall. And if you vomit, your sick sticks to you.

TEACHER'S TEA-BREAK TEASER

If you are feeling madly brave, knock on the staffroom door. When it groans, creaks, or scrapes open, smile sweetly at your teacher and say:

EXCUSE ME, I WAS WONDERING WHY WHEN YOU STIR YOUR TEA, THE TEA LEAVES SETTLE AT THE CENTRE OF THE BOTTOM OF YOUR TEA CUP? SURELY THE TEA LEAVES SHOULD MOVE TOWARDS THE SIDES OF THE CUP?

Answer: Incredibly two of the world's greatest scientists puzzled over this for years. That's Nobel prize winners Albert Einstein (1879–1955) and Erwin Schrödinger (1887–1961). In 1926 Mrs S asked Erwin the question but he didn't know the answer. So she asked Einstein. After many calculations Einstein worked out the answer and even wrote an article about it in 1933.

According to Einstein, momentum does move the tea leaves towards the sides of the cup. But friction between the liquid and the sides slows down the tea leaves at the sides and base of the cup. And the liquid stops turning the leaves fall towards the centre of the cup. Wow! And you thought it was just a cup of tea! Here's another amazing story to keep things swinging.

114

GETTING IN THE SWING

It was 1586 and 17-year-old Galileo (yes, him again) was in Pisa Cathedral listening to a boring sermon. He noticed a chandelier swinging in the breeze. Sometimes it swung in a long arc and sometimes in a shorter swing. But each swing seemed to take the same time.

So Galileo timed the swings using his pulse. He was right. (Could you make a similar discovery during a boring science lesson?)

Galileo used this newly discovered fact to design a new kind of clock. The grandfather clock used a swinging pendulum to keep time. What a time-ly invention.

In 1650 two priests spent a whole day counting the swings of a pendulum in a bid to prove the pendulum really did keep time. It did and they counted 87,998 swings.

But one sickly scientist had even bigger pendulum plans.

Hall of fame: Jean Bernard Léon Foucault
(1819–1868) Nationality: French

Young Jean was a sickly child. And his parents reckoned school would finish him off, so they educated him at home. Why can't all parents be so considerate? Poor Jean was never any good at his lessons. For a time he went nowhere. His bid to become a surgeon failed after he ran away from an operation. One squirt of blood and a bit of suffering and wimpy Jean burst into tears.

But Jean loved writing. So he became a science journalist instead. Then he got interested in experiments. He measured the speed of light and tried to photograph the stars. He then became fascinated by the idea that you could use a pendulum to prove the Earth turned during the day. Although everyone knew this, no one had ever tried to prove it actually happened.

In 1851 Jean devised an amazing test. He hung a huge steel ball 60 cm in diameter and weighing 30.4 kg from the dome of the Pántheon in Paris, a large building where many famous people were buried.

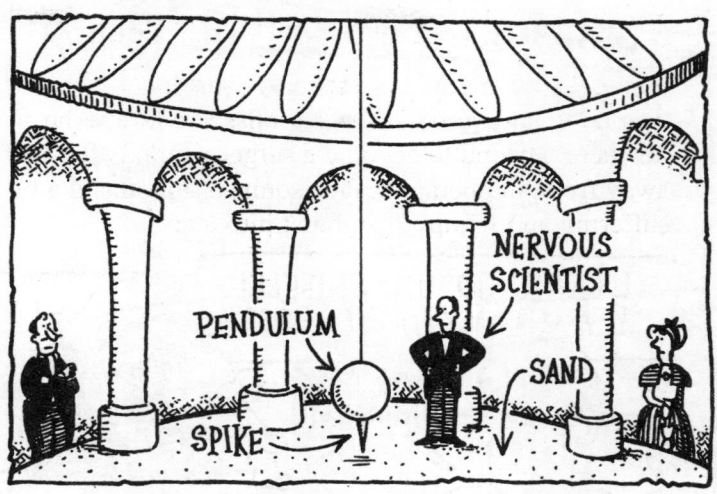

The night before...

Last minute preparations for the big day. A brave worker climbs a very high ladder to check the cable is secured to the roof. The pendulum itself is tied to the wall by a cord. At last everything is ready!

NOTES We can't have the pendulum swinging around until the experiment is ready to start.

Later that night...

nibble! chew!

I can't sleep for nerves. I've been working to set up this experiment for months. Had to get the permission from Emperor Napoleon III himself. Will everything work?

The press are going to be there too. If this experiment fails I'll be the laughing stock of all France. Gulp!

Sand

Up early – groan! Last minute preparations. Sprinkle floor with sand. Talk to reporters, say everything will be fine. Oh dear, I hope I'm right. ...Supposing the pendulum stops swinging...

Mid-morning...

Blimey! Look at all those people. All come to see my experiment. Better make a little speech. Then I'll set fire to the cord holding back the pendulum. My fingers shake. Ouch – I've burnt them. Hope it's not a bad omen.

NOTES If you simply push the pendulum it might not swing straight

NOTES This track should get wider. The pendulum's swing shouldn't alter but as the ground turns underneath, the track will seem to move to the side. That's the idea anyway.

Lunch-time...

I can't take my eyes off the pendulum. It swings quite slowly and the spike makes a track in the sand on the floor.

track

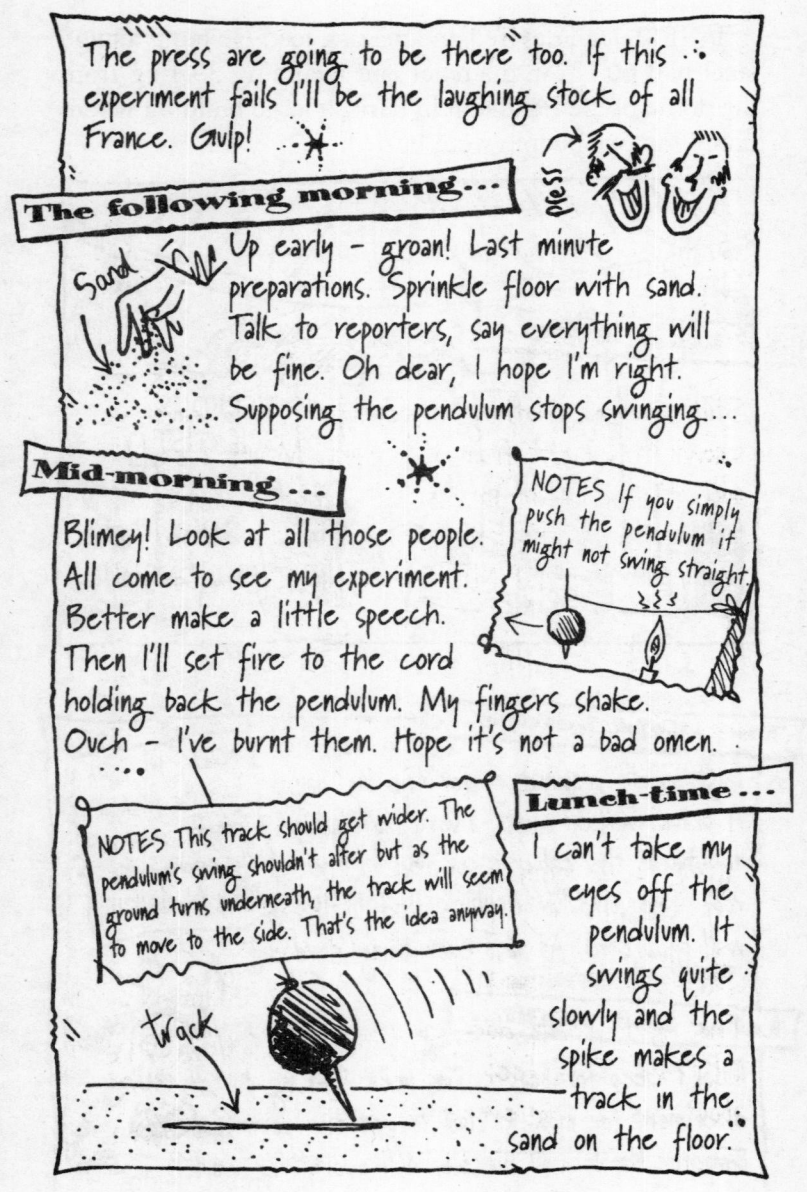

Still swinging. Time seems to drag. I count the swings. It's like counting sheep.
I'm dozing off. Yawn - should have got more sleep last night. Zzzzzzzzz.z

An hour later ...

Still swinging. Nothing happening. I should have known this right from the start. Maybe I could push the pendulum to one side when no one's looking. Help! The Emperor's glaring at me and he's really cross. I'M FINISHED. PANIC STATIONS!!!!

Nap III glaring

← Still sleeping

Just then . . .
I open my eyes. Phew! It must have been a dream. Everyone's pointing to the sand and talking. THE TRACK HAS GOT WIDER. I'M SAVED!!!

The world really does go round. YIPPEEEEE! I feel like dancing about and kissing everyone.

119

Foucault found himself a hero. He was awarded the *Légion d'Honneur* medal. He went on to invent gyroscopes ... which work on the same principle as tops as you'll see in a moment. And tops are top toys for freaky physicists.

TOP TRICKS

Physicists like nothing better than playing with their favourite toys. Well, according to them they're investigating forces. Oh, yeah:

There are loads of toys that use the forces of spinning. Toys like, yo-yos, hula-hoops, frisbees. And tops. A top was a favourite toy of Nobel prize winner Wolfgang Pauli (1900–1958) who was trying to work out the physics of inertia. Here's some crucial info to get *you* "tops" of the class.

Tops balance because angular momentum keeps them going – remember the coin running away from the scientist? Tops keep turning in the same way despite the efforts of gravity to pull them down. Bigger tops need more effort to get going but spin for longer. Tops are popular with kids the world over. Here's a traditional Inuit game you might like to play when it gets really cold.

You will need:

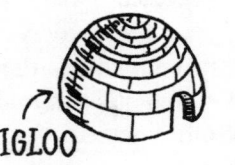

IGLOO

SPINNING TOP

What you do:
Spin the top. Run round your igloo (or house). Try to get back inside before the top falls down. (This could be fatal if you don't wrap up warm first.)

YOU ONLY HAVE TO GO ROUND ONCE!

In 1743 English inventor John Smeaton (1724–1794) invented a sort of top that would stay level even on a ship in a storm. This allowed mariners to check where the horizon should be. They could then work out the positions of the sun and stars to navigate by. But the new fangled top didn't catch on because seafarers were useless at spinning it.

But Smeaton's brainwave was the ancestor of gyroscopes found on most ships and planes today.

Foucault's invention – the gyroscope – works like a series of tops. They balance on one another and always stay upright. And this is ideal if you want to steer a steady course. Amazingly, your bike wheels work in much the same way. When they spin round the bike is much less likely tip over than when it's stationary. Scientists call this "precession". Something to think about next time you go for a precession on your bike.

Bet you never knew!
The tighter your circle of spin the faster you go. That's why ice-skaters pull in their arms to spin faster. It's the law of conservation of angular momentum again. Because the circle of spin is smaller they go round quicker. This fact also explains why water speeds up near the centre of a whirlpool. You can check this fact by watching the dregs of your washing-up gurgle down the plug hole. And if this isn't your idea of fun you'd better dive into the next chapter. You'll soon get your bounce back.

BAKED BEAN

PEA IS SPINNING FASTER THAN THE BAKED BEAN

BOUNCING BACK

What's always "around" for a game and doesn't mind a good kicking? No, not your sports teacher. It's a *ball*. And oddly enough balls do other forceful things. Like rolling and spinning and bouncing. Here are a few facts to bounce off your friends.

Fatal forces fact file

NAME: Bouncing

THE BASIC FACTS: When a rubber ball hits the floor the springy coiled rubber molecules that make up the ball are all squashed together. They soak up the energy of the impact and then bounce out again – making the ball bounce.

THE HORRIBLE DETAILS: The first chewing gum was made of chicle, a type of tree sap. American scientists tried to make the chicle into a type of rubber but it wasn't bouncy enough. So they just chewed the problem over, or rather chewed the chicle.

KEEP YOUR EYE ON THE BALL

When a ball flies through the air, strange things start to happen. Scientists have put loads of effort into working out what these mysterious effects are.

Fatal forces fact file

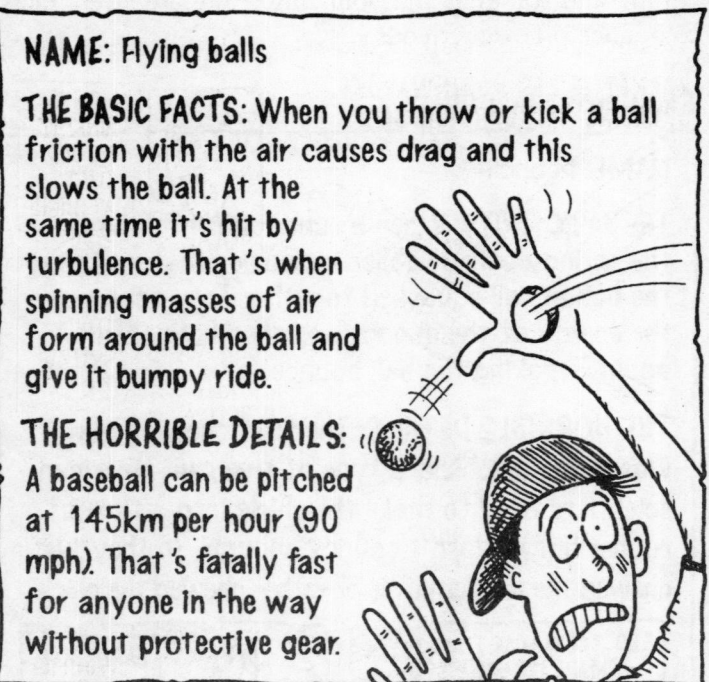

NAME: Flying balls

THE BASIC FACTS: When you throw or kick a ball friction with the air causes drag and this slows the ball. At the same time it's hit by turbulence. That's when spinning masses of air form around the ball and give it bumpy ride.

THE HORRIBLE DETAILS: A baseball can be pitched at 145km per hour (90 mph). That's fatally fast for anyone in the way without protective gear.

Any old scientist will tell you that ball games involve forces. So we invited a tame scientist along to show you how science can help you improve at sports such as tennis. According to the scientist you don't need to work up a sweat. All you need is a few brain cells and a small computer. *Oh, yeah?*

THE SCIENTIST'S GUIDE TO TENNIS

Tennis ball seams are the same on each side. This means equal amounts of air turbulence. So the ball flies straight. That's quite a velocity. Slice the racket downwards and you'll get back-spin. The ball tumbles backwards as it flies forwards. This drags air over it. As this air speeds up, the pressure above the ball drops and the greater air pressure under the ball raises it. We call this effect, lift.

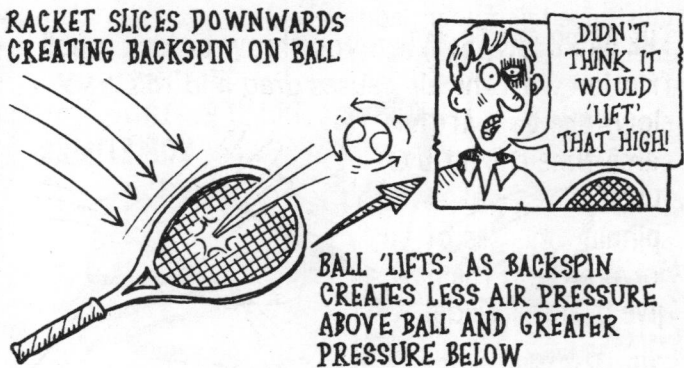

RACKET SLICES DOWNWARDS
CREATING BACKSPIN ON BALL

DIDN'T THINK IT WOULD 'LIFT' THAT HIGH!

BALL 'LIFTS' AS BACKSPIN CREATES LESS AIR PRESSURE ABOVE BALL AND GREATER PRESSURE BELOW

Top spin is the opposite. Strike the ball upwards and the ball tumbles forwards as it flies forwards. This drags air under the ball. And as it speeds up the pressure drops and the ball is pushed lower and it bounces faster.

DIDN'T THINK IT WOULD BOUNCE THAT FAST!

RACKET MOVES UPWARDS CREATING TOP SPIN.

BALL BOUNCES FASTER AS TOPSPIN CREATES MORE AIR PRESSURE ABOVE THE BALL AND LESS BELOW

If you hit the ball a glancing blow it bounces extra slowly when it hits the ground. So it's even easier to whack.

PAINLESS PADDING

If you find games a pain in the sports bag maybe you need a bit more protection. Here's a few bits and pieces of equipment designed to help you play safe.

• Cushioned shoulder padding and shin pads as worn by American footballers.

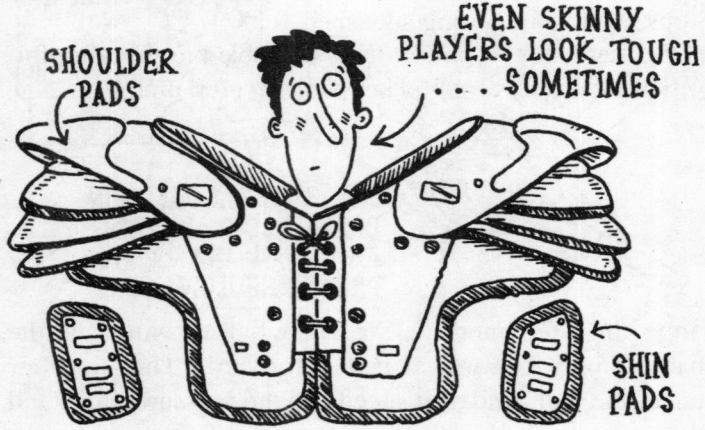

SHOULDER PADS

EVEN SKINNY PLAYERS LOOK TOUGH ... SOMETIMES

SHIN PADS

• Boxer's gum shield. Stops teeth from being knocked out of their sockets.

NO PROBLEM

• American footballer's helmet. Cage to protect face.

CAGE TO PROTECT FACE

UNBREAKABLE PLASTIC

• Dome shape spreads force of blow over whole helmet. Stops head from getting squashed.
• Cricketer's box to protect the vulnerable bits. Very useful – cricket balls travel at 160 km per hour (100 mph).

HOWZAT!

PAINFUL!

WITH → BOX

WITHOUT → BOX

Here are a few more facts to prove that science really is a ball.

HAVING A BALL

1 The first balls were made by the Romans from bits of dead animal skin stitched together and filled with air.

Later on in the Middle Ages balls were made from pigs' bladders filled with air. Yuck – who had to blow them up?

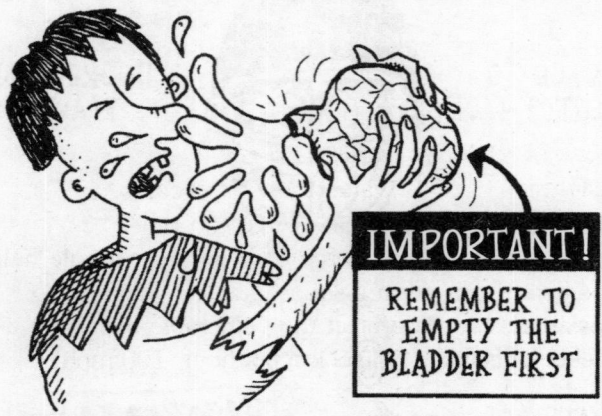

IMPORTANT!

REMEMBER TO EMPTY THE BLADDER FIRST

2 The first golf balls were leather bags packed with boiled chicken's feathers. Bet that made the feathers fly. The balls flew very well until it rained when they soon got waterlogged and split. Covering the players in grotty old feathers.

3 In the 1850s someone had the idea of making golf balls out of rubbery tree sap. But they didn't fly as straight as the old balls until they became scratched and worn. Then they flew really well.

4 So what was going on? Turned out the rough surface of the golf ball trapped tiny pockets of air. The turbulent air flowed around the trapped air and this actually gave a smoother quicker flight. And that's why modern golf balls have little dimples.

5 Cricket balls also do strange things as they fly through the air. Normally the ball just spins horizontally. But at speed, air turbulence makes the ball swerve if the edge of the ball's seam is smooth. That's why some cricketers polish the ball by rubbing it on their trousers.

6 At speeds of 100 km (62 mph) plus, the ball can swerve even more. Especially if the edge of the seam is rough. And that's why some cricketers rub dirt into the ball. But don't do this in your games lesson – it's called cheating.

FRAUDSTER'S BEEN CHEATING, SIR

WHERE'S YOUR PROOF, GRASSMAN?

7 The ball used in rugby and American football has pointed ends. If it's tumbling forward it can bounce oddly. Sometimes it bounces high, sometimes low.
8 This makes it tricky to pick up. And dangerous too unless you enjoy twenty giant people jumping on your head. The good news is that the ball is easier to throw. Pitch it with one end pointing forwards and it'll spin horizontally like an over-sized bullet. This means you can easily get rid of it before you get flattened. It's safer than just standing and juggling the ball…

Dare you discover … how to juggle?
Juggling is a great way to see how forces affect balls in the air. Tell your gullible folks you're doing your homework. Then you can have a bit of fun.

You will need:

Yourself

Something to juggle with. Three balls small enough to fit in your hands would be good. Or you could try rolled up socks

Plenty of space

A mirror

Safety note: When you are learning to juggle try to resist the urge to use your granny's priceless antiques, food (especially at meal-times), and living creatures such as hamsters, goldfish, small brothers and sisters, etc.

1 Stand in front of a mirror with your elbows tucked close to your body and your hands level with your waist. Place your legs apart with your knees slightly bent. Easy, isn't it? Are you ready?

ADOPT A CONFIDENT AND RELAXED EXPRESSION

REMAIN CALM AND STILL

2 Take a deep breath and let it out slowly. That's right – relax. Now without looking at your hands … throw the ball gently up and over your head. Notice how it falls in an arc under the influence of gravity just like the cannonballs Galileo studied – remember? Catch the ball in the palm of your other hand. Keep your eyes in the top part of the ball's flight. OK – that's the easy bit.

3 Now it gets a bit harder. Juggling with two balls takes a bit of practice. Throw one ball up as before. When the ball is just about to drop, throw your second ball up from the other hand. Ideally the second ball should pass just under the first ball.

4 OK, this takes practice. Better practise now to get it right.

5 This is where it gets *really* hard. Three balls. Sure you want to try? OK. Hold two balls in one hand and one in the other. Repeat Step 3.

6 Now here's the clever bit. When ball 2 is just about to drop throw ball 3 up and try to get it to pass under ball 2.

Meanwhile catch ball 1 and throw it up just when ball 3 is about to drop. Easy!

7 Fantastic, keep going!

And while you're doing this, here are some interesting facts to juggle with.

1 It's REALLY difficult to juggle with more than 12 balls. This feat was achieved by several people including American Bruce Sarafian in 1996.

2 Kara, a nineteenth-century German performer used to juggle with his hat, lighted cigar, gloves, newspaper, matches and a coffee cup. Don't try this at home ... or at school.

3 It's also possible to juggle with your feet. As long as their back is supported, the performer can juggle quite weighty objects including a small child. And this is something you shouldn't try either!

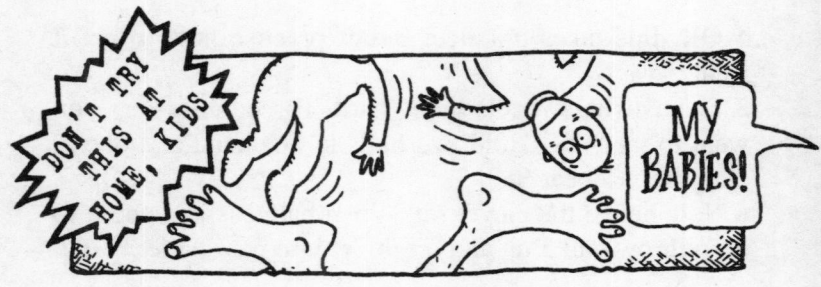

Sooner or later they'll invent a juggling machine. Then people could enjoy the fun of juggling without ever having to learn for themselves. That's typical of us humans. Always inventing machines to get out of hard work. There are loads more mighty machines that use forces to do work. Listen hard and you'll hear them grinding up their gears for the next chapter...

MIGHTY MACHINES

A machine is a way of using a force in the right place to get a job done with less effort. Good idea. So why, after 10,000 years of science and invention is there no machine for doing homework? Anyway, to make a mighty machine all you need is a collection of effort-saving levers, pulleys and gears.

FATAL EXPRESSIONS

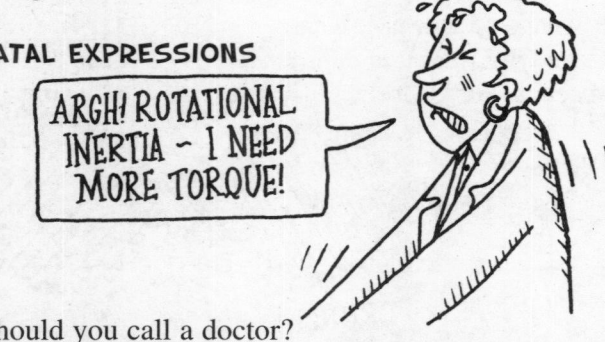

ARGH! ROTATIONAL INERTIA – I NEED MORE TORQUE!

Should you call a doctor?

Answer: No – a mechanic. The scientist can't loosen a nut. Torque is the word scientists use to describe the turning force you produce using a spanner. Rotational inertia is the resistance of the nut to being turned. And spanners are good for doing this job because they work like levers, as you'll see.

LOVELY LEVERS

A lever is a pole that you use to lever something up or push or pull something around. Either way the lever rests on a point known as the fulcrum. Levers work because the most effective turning force is at right angles to the thing you want to move. So levers help you do more work for less effort. Lovely!

Dare you discover ... how a lever works?

You will need:
Yourself
A door

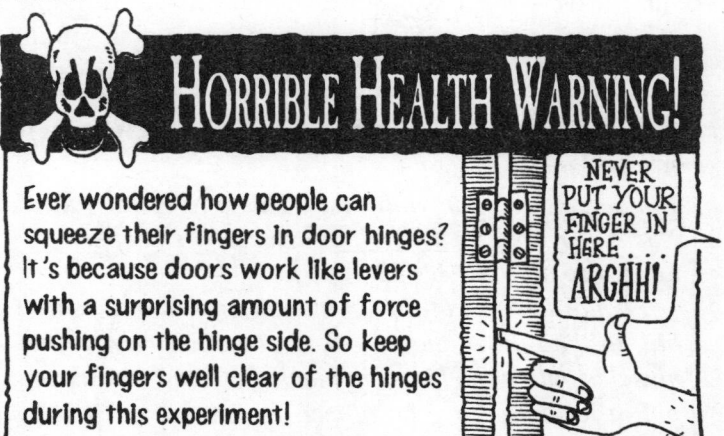

What you do:

1 Open the door slightly. Make sure no one charges through the door.

2 Stand outside the door and try to push it by pressing with one finger 2 cm from the hinges.

3 Now press with the same finger 2 cm from opposite side to the hinges.

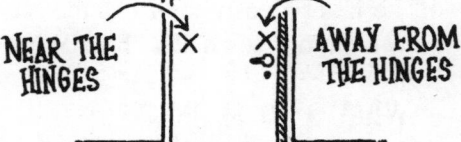

Which is easier?

a) They're both impossible and you got a sore finger.

b) It's easier to push the door near the hinges.

c) It's easier to push the door further away from the hinges.

135

Answer: c) The door works like a lever with the hinges as the fulcrum. You move the door further but at any moment you are using less force – so it feels easier. Nowadays you'll find levers everywhere – from typewriters to tin openers and from scissors to see-saws.

Bet you never knew!

You've got levers in your body. This interesting fact was discovered by the Italian artist and scientist Leonardo da Vinci (1452-1519).

Leonardo was cutting up human arms and legs in a bid to find how they worked. He discovered that muscles pulled the bones in much the same way as you pull a lever to move an object. He was so excited by this discovery that he even made a working model leg using copper wires and bits of real human bones. Then he could see it in action.

TEACHER'S TEA-BREAK TEASER

This playground puzzle spells break-time bafflement for your teacher. Two children are playing on a see-saw. If the little child jumps off she might get hurt. If the big child gets off he'll get a nasty injury as the see-saw swings up under the weight of the smaller child. What's to be done?

WHAT'S TO BE DONE?

FULCRUM

POWERFUL PULLEYS

Another method of lifting heavy weights off the ground – including large children – is the pulley. Basically it's a wheel hung off the ground with a rope passing over it. This re-directs force. So you can pull on the rope and lift something tied to the other end of the rope.

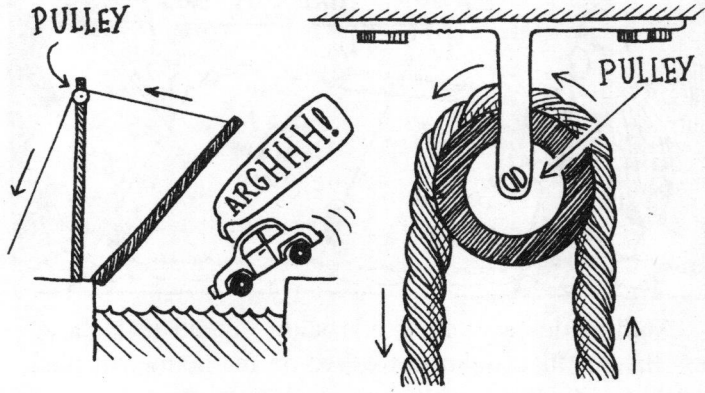

Add another wheel to the first one and it's even easier. By pulling the rope a longer distance you spread the effort so it seems easier to lift the load. Nowadays you'll find pulleys on cranes and lifts. So whom do we have to thank for this amazing invention? It was a Greek genius – Archimedes (287?–212 BC).

A LOVELY LITTLE MOVER

Archimedes had a little problem. His relative, Hieron, had asked him to pull a full-sized ship down a beach and out to sea – without help! Now most of us would tell the brother-in-law to jump in a vat of custard and go back to watching the telly. But Archimedes couldn't say that.

Unfortunately, Hieron was the local king – Hieron II of Syracuse to be exact. And you don't refuse royalty even if they are family. Besides, Archimedes was an all-round genius. He was supposed to know these things. He'd already worked out the maths of levers and boasted that with a long enough lever he could lift the world. Hieron thought his brainy relative should be taught a lesson. So he deliberately set him an impossible task.

Archimedes scratched his balding head and chewed his lip. All that night he worked on mathematical plans. And eventually he hit on a solution. An answer so stunningly original, so forceful and amazing that no one had ever thought of it before. A new machine. Meanwhile, hundreds of grim-faced guards grunted and groaned as they hauled the ship up the beach. Hieron ordered them to load the ship with cargo and told some of them to wait on board.

138

Archimedes and a few assistants spent the next few hours setting up the machine. History doesn't record what it looked like. But it must have been a series of pulleys standing on wooden frames with the rope tied securely to the ship. When all was ready Archimedes gripped the free end of the rope. He looked rather thin and weedy. Hieron couldn't resist a quiet chuckle as Archimedes rolled up his sleeves and tugged on the rope.

But then the ship slid smoothly down the beach. It moved with eerie ease as if it was sailing on a calm sea. Archimedes' machine was a lovely little mover. The watching crowds gasped in disbelief. The people on the ship looked stunned and Hieron nearly had a heart attack. If he hadn't seen it with his own eyes the king would have accused his brainy relative of pulley-ing his leg.

GRINDING GEARS

No one knows who invented gears but the Romans certainly used them. They're interlocking toothed wheels that pass on force and they have odd sounding names that wouldn't be out of place in an ancient torture chamber. Names such as "bevels", "rack and pinion", "spurs" and "worms". They all work the same way. A smaller wheel that turns quickly and a larger wheel that turns more slowly.

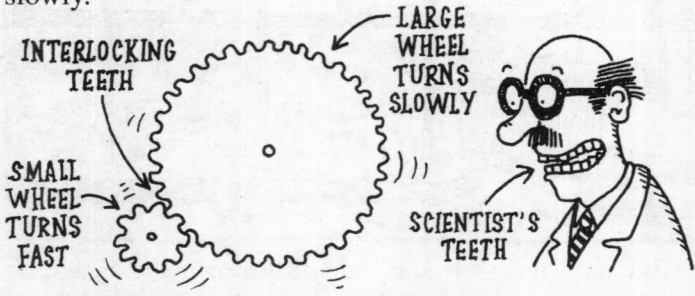

INTERLOCKING TEETH

LARGE WHEEL TURNS SLOWLY

SMALL WHEEL TURNS FAST

SCIENTIST'S TEETH

Gears control the speed and direction of the turning force you put in. Take your bicycle gears, for example. The gear wheels on your bike have fewer teeth than the chain wheel. So the gear wheels turn faster and they make your rear bike wheel turn faster than you pedal. So it does you a really good turn.

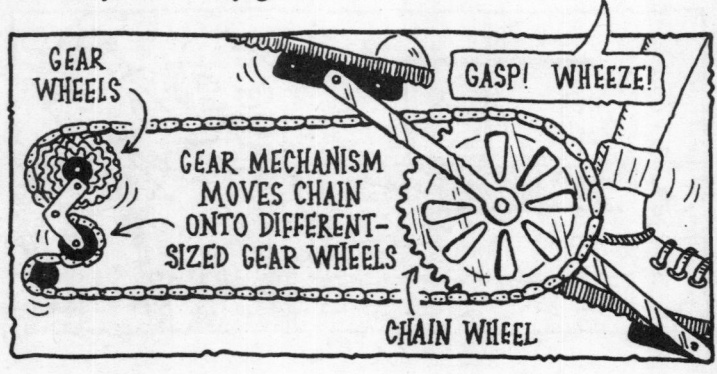

GEAR WHEELS

GASP! WHEEZE!

GEAR MECHANISM MOVES CHAIN ONTO DIFFERENT-SIZED GEAR WHEELS

CHAIN WHEEL

The bicycle was such a good idea that nineteenth-century inventors began to peddle their own pedal-powered machines. Which of these are too silly to be true?

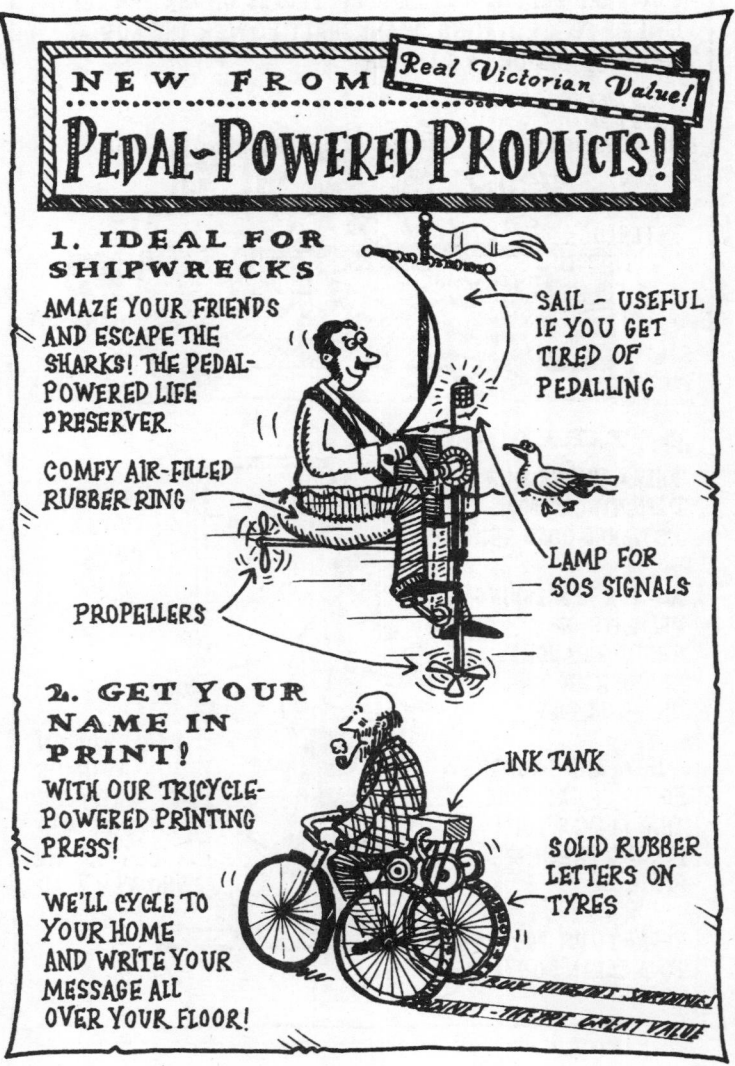

NEW FROM *Real Victorian Value!*

PEDAL-POWERED PRODUCTS!

1. IDEAL FOR SHIPWRECKS

AMAZE YOUR FRIENDS AND ESCAPE THE SHARKS! THE PEDAL-POWERED LIFE PRESERVER.

COMFY AIR-FILLED RUBBER RING

PROPELLERS

SAIL – USEFUL IF YOU GET TIRED OF PEDALLING

LAMP FOR SOS SIGNALS

2. GET YOUR NAME IN PRINT!

WITH OUR TRICYCLE-POWERED PRINTING PRESS!

WE'LL CYCLE TO YOUR HOME AND WRITE YOUR MESSAGE ALL OVER YOUR FLOOR!

INK TANK

SOLID RUBBER LETTERS ON TYRES

3. DON'T MISS OUR BUS!

NO MORE SCHOOL BUS BREAKDOWNS. TRY THE NEW PEDAL-POWERED SCHOOL BUS. SPECIAL PEDALS UNDER THE SEATS LINKED TO A ROTATING CRANKSHAFT POWER THE BUS AT 35 KM PER HOUR (22 MPH).

"GETS THE KIDS TO SCHOOL ON TIME AND KEEPS THEM FIT."
I. FLOGGEM (HEADMASTER)

4. TIRED OUT?

RELAX UNDER OUR DELIGHTFUL PEDAL-POWERED COLD SHOWER!

ALL THE REFRESHING DELIGHTS OF GETTING CAUGHT IN THE RAIN WHILE ON YOUR BIKE!

A NEW AND EXCITING FORM OF EXERCISE THAT LEAVES YOU FEELING FRESH AND FIT.

PEDAL YOUR WAY TO A CLEAN BODY!

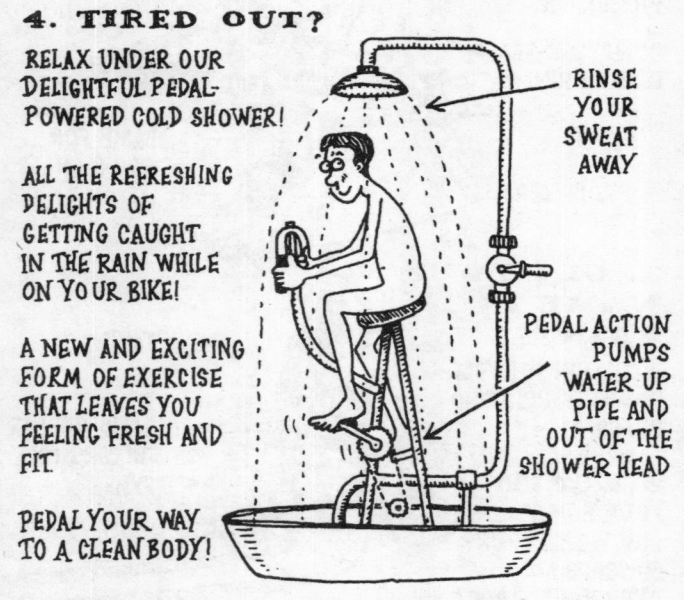

RINSE YOUR SWEAT AWAY

PEDAL ACTION PUMPS WATER UP PIPE AND OUT OF THE SHOWER HEAD

MARVELLOUS MIGHTY MACHINES

A complicated machine is simply lots of simple machines joined together. Easy. Just a load of old screws, pulleys, levers, gears, wheels, axles, chains, transmission shafts and springs that you just happen to find lying about in the garage. Throw them all together and everything should go like clockwork.

From bikes and gears it's a small step to steam engines, petrol engines, trains, buses, cars and planes. Just think. If it wasn't for forces they wouldn't be able to force you to go to school. Terrible. Still, you can relax at home, can't you? No need to worry about forces is there? Safe as houses and all that … er – well, actually, forces *can* be fatal for buildings, too. The next chapter will really shake you up.

ACTUALLY, THE GARDEN COULD DO WITH A DROP OF RAIN

BUILD OR BUST

Fallen down under the influence of gravity, blown down, blown up or just shaken about. Yep. Forces are fatal for buildings, too.

BODGE-IT BUILDINGS

Some buildings stand for hundreds of years. Others stand for hundreds of days ... or minutes.

Would you be interested in buying any of these structures?

GO UNDERCOVER!

THE KEMPER ARENA, Kansas City, USA (built 1973)

▶ Spectacular covered all-weather sports stadium. Keeps that nasty rain off your head.

▶ Winner of an architectural award in 1976.

▶ Cost $23.3 million to build.

THE SMALL PRINT
In 1979 the roof of the Kemper Arena fell in after heavy rain. Engineers believe rainwater collected on the roof making it sag until its supports couldn't take the weight any longer.

ARGHHH!

HELP!

I CAN'T SWIM!

WAT-ER GREAT BRIDGE!

LONDON BRIDGE, Spanning the River Thames in London on 20 narrow arches. (built 1176-1209)

DON'T DIG THE GRAVE THERE!

ARGHH!

▶ Waterwheels and shops.

▶ Sensational tidal surges through the narrow arches.

▶ All this and the dead body of the architect, Peter Colechurch. He's buried in the chapel on the bridge.

▶ Complete with drawbridge and spikes for traitors' rotting heads.

ROTTEN TRAITOR

THE SMALL PRINT

The arches were narrow and close together, and this forced the river to surge violently. This damaged the bridge and made life dangerous for boatmen. Up to fifty were killed each year trying to pass under the bridge. Part of the bridge fell down in 1281 and again in 1482. It was finally knocked down in 1832. Peter Colechurch should have designed his bridge with wider arches to allow the water to flow more easily. He should also have banned buildings on the bridge itself because their weight was too great for the bridge to bear.

Go With a Swing!

THE TACOMA NARROWS BRIDGE, Washington State, USA (built 1940)

▶ A graceful lightweight suspension bridge. (That's a bridge supported by cables hung from towers.)

▶ Amazing 853-metre span.

▶ Swings about in the wind for a really exciting crossing.

WIND YOUR WINDOWS UP, KIDS

THE SMALL PRINT

The Tacoma Narrows Bridge swayed so violently in the wind that it earned the nickname "Galloping Gertie". People actually felt seasick crossing it. The bridge had to be reinforced to stop the swaying spreading to the towers that held up the cables. But four months later a strong wind twisted the roadway sideways until it collapsed.

BECOME AN ARCHITECT IN SIX EASY LESSONS
LESSON 1: UNDERSTAND THE EFFECT OF FORCES ON YOUR BUILDING

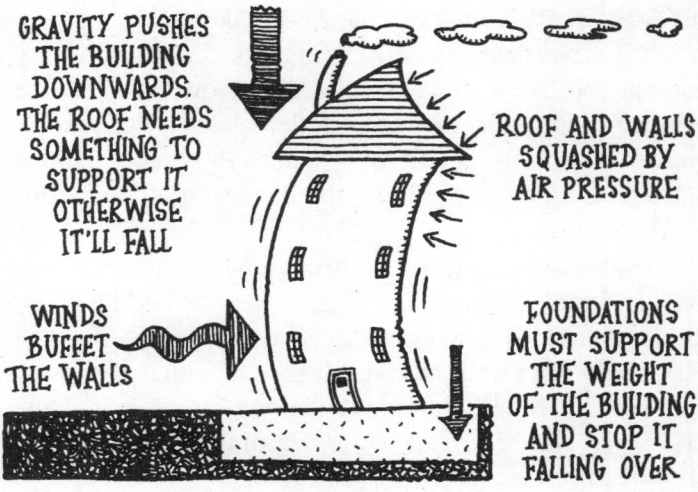

GRAVITY PUSHES THE BUILDING DOWNWARDS. THE ROOF NEEDS SOMETHING TO SUPPORT IT OTHERWISE IT'LL FALL

ROOF AND WALLS SQUASHED BY AIR PRESSURE

WINDS BUFFET THE WALLS

FOUNDATIONS MUST SUPPORT THE WEIGHT OF THE BUILDING AND STOP IT FALLING OVER

Nowadays architects make computer simulations and models of their buildings and even test the models in wind tunnels.

LESSON 2: DEVELOP AN EYE FOR FORCES

A good architect or engineer can look at a building and spot whether the building is well built enough to stand up to the forces on it. Marc Brunel (that's Isambard's dad) once looked at a bridge in Paris and said:

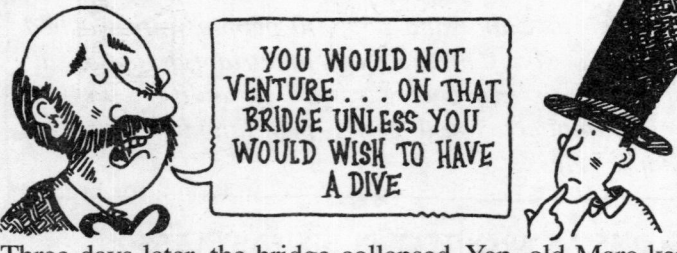

YOU WOULD NOT VENTURE ... ON THAT BRIDGE UNLESS YOU WOULD WISH TO HAVE A DIVE

Three days later, the bridge collapsed. Yep, old Marc kept dry and he certainly had a dry sense of humour too.

LESSON 3: PUT IN PROPER FOUNDATIONS

If you've ever tried to carry some tall glasses on a tray one-handed like a waiter, you'll know how tricky it is to balance them. It would help if the glasses were partly buried in a really thick tray. That's how foundations work. The taller the building the deeper the foundations you need.

Foundations stop the wind from blowing your building over and they support the weight of your building too. Remember Galileo working at Pisa University? In 1173 Pisa's bell tower was built on soft ground with foundations that weren't broad enough to support its weight. Now Pisa University's famous for its learning and the tower's famous for its leaning.

LESSON 4: ALWAYS BUILD YOUR BUILDING THE RIGHT SHAPE

Triangles are a good strong shape. That's why the Egyptian pyramids have lasted 4,700 years. The Eiffel Tower was also made up of a series of triangles and many modern skyscrapers use triangles as the basis of their metal frames.

YOU MUST BE BETTER BY NOW, MUMMY – YOU'VE HAD THE BANDAGES ON FOR 4000 YEARS

A column is a good strong shape and ideal for holding up heavy weights. Like the roof, for example. You can use arches to hold up part of the walls. Like columns, arches are great because the harder you push down on them the more they push back. Yes – it's Newton's Third Law again.

Dome shapes are also very strong. But you knew that from finding out about helmets in Chapter 3. An egg shape is also surprisingly strong and can take a weight of 22.7 kg. But don't try leaving an egg on your teacher's chair.

TEACHER WHO WEIGHS MORE THAN 22.7KG

CRUNCH!

LESSON 5: MAKE SURE YOUR WALLS DON'T FALL DOWN

If you are designing a very tall stone building you may choose to make your walls very thick like an old cathedral or castle – the walls of the Tower of London are more than 4.6 metres thick. So you want to put in larger windows but you know they will weaken your walls. No problem. Try using buttresses to hold your walls up.

Mind you, disasters do happen. In 1989 the Civic Tower in Pavia, Italy (built 1060) fell with a crash. The cement holding the stones together had slowly crumbled away. Engineers reckoned that the shock waves from years of ringing the bells at the top had brought on the destruction. If this puts you off building in stone you could use a strong steel frame for your tall building and use lighter materials for your walls. This makes them stronger but the building might sway a bit in windy weather.

LESSON 6: GET YOUR ROOF THE RIGHT SHAPE

Roofs are usually sloping because the curved shape is more difficult to bend. You can prove this by holding a piece of paper in different ways.

HOLD IT LIKE THIS AND IT'S FLOPPY

BUT HOLD THE PAPER LIKE THIS AND ITS STRAIGHT.

VICIOUS VIBES

One thing that can be very destructive is vibration. Have you ever watched a washing machine shuddering and shaking as it washes and spins the clothes. Perhaps you've bravely laid a finger on the machine and felt the shaking passing up your arms. These are vibrations. And beware. They can be vicious.

TRAPPING YOUR TIE COULD PROVE FATAL . . .

Should you dial 999? No, her car's shuddering with vibrations. Probably because it's so clapped out. Oscillatory motion is in fact what vibrations are called. Oscillations are regularly repeated movements or shaking. The only way to stop them is to "damp them down". No, this doesn't mean chucking water over the car. Still confused? Well, it means using some soft substance to absorb the vibrations and stop the shuddering.

VICIOUS VIBRATION FACTS

Vibrations are particularly vicious in their effects on buildings and bridges. In 1850, 487 soldiers were marching across a suspension bridge in Algiers in Africa. Their heavy boots thudded on the roadway. And soon the whole bridge was shaking with the vibrations. It shook so much that bits fell off it and finally the entire bridge collapsed into the river. Tragically 226 soldiers were killed.

Ever since, soldiers avoid marching in step when they cross a bridge in order not set off the deadly vibrations. That takes a bit of foresight but sometimes it pays to plan the crossing of your bridges before you come to them.

Mind you, the most vicious vibrations aren't caused by people – they're caused by the Earth itself.

Every year there are hundreds of earthquakes. Some of them are fatal for people. Movement of vast rocky areas deep under the ground trigger powerful vibrations in the form of shock waves that can destroy entire cities. The damage is done because shock waves make the walls vibrate so violently that the building falls down. Feeling a little shaky?

Dare you discover ... how much your body vibrates?

You will need:

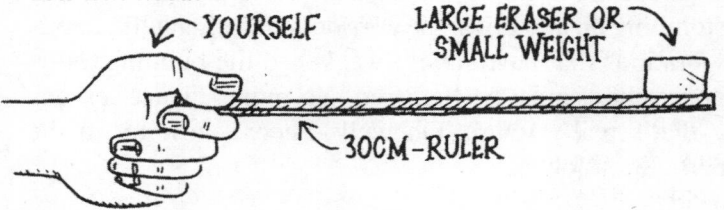

YOURSELF LARGE ERASER OR SMALL WEIGHT

30CM-RULER

What you do:

1 Place the eraser on the end of ruler.

2 Grip the opposite end of the ruler by your thumb and forefinger. Then hold the ruler as close to its end as you can.

3 Stretch out your hand balancing the eraser on the opposite end of the ruler.

What do you notice?

a) Nothing. I did the test for ten minutes and my hand was steady as a rock.

b) After a few seconds the end of the ruler began to dance around as my arm twitched.

c) I lost my balance and fell over forwards.

153

A SMASHING FINALE

Now you've learnt about how forces affect buildings,
let's practise using forces to knock one down. An old
school will do. Imagine your school has been condemned
as an unsafe building. Perhaps all those hundreds of feet
stomping up and down the corridors has triggered vicious
vibrations that have fatally weakened the building. Now
your school must be flattened. No more science lessons
– that's really tough. Oh well – here's how to do the
demolition job...

1 Make sure that the school is empty of all pupils
and there are no teachers lurking in the corners. You
wouldn't want to knock the building down on top of
them would you?

STAFFROOM

2 Start off by swinging a heavy steel ball against the
walls of your school. The ball transfers its momentum to

the wall as it crashes into it. Cement is dislodged from the bricks and the wall falls down.

3 If you don't have a steel ball you'll have to smash the walls with a sledge hammer. This has the same effect but it's far slower and much harder work.

4 Some buildings have pre-stressed concrete beams. These are concrete beams with steel wires running through them. The wires are held tight by the weight of the building's upper floors. Be careful if your school has these beams. When you knock down the upper floors the wires in the lower floor's beams aren't held tight any more. So they go *ping* and the entire building crashes down around your ears.

Alternatively you could try one of these demolition methods.

Method 1. Explosives

In a hurry? Want to knock your school down before science class on Monday? You could blow it up. Place explosive charges around the building and weaken the supporting beams so they collapse easily. Set off the explosives and wait for the dust to clear!

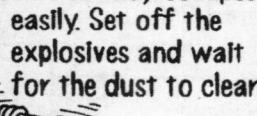

Method 2. Hands

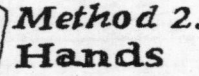

If you can't blow up your school, try using your bare hands instead. A karate blow is forceful enough to break bricks. In 1994 15 karate experts demolished a seven-room house in Saskatchewan, Canada using only their bare feet and hands.

MAY THE FORCES BE WITH YOU

Forces were around long before we got here. And although we try to use forces – in the end we can't control them. We can only forecast what forces might do to new buildings or cars. And although designers make fatal mistakes, these embarrassing slip-ups are thankfully rare.

THE DESIGN IS FINE ~ YOU'VE GOT THE PLANS UPSIDE DOWN

Meanwhile, physicists are making more brain-boggling discoveries about forces. Before Galileo and Newton, no one knew how forces worked. Today we know more about them than ever. And because forces affect so much of our world, they pop up in every area of scientific knowledge.

Take atoms, for example. Scientists are probing how forces hold an atom together. (Atoms are the tiny bits of matter that make up everything in the universe.) The trick is to smash the atoms together in awesome machines called accelerators tens of kilometres long. Then you sift the debris for clues. If you're a scientist it sometimes pays to think small, ha ha.

157

Forces also come into space travel. To plan a little trip around the solar system you need to know how a planet's gravity will pull your craft. And you need to be sure what happens when you whizz round a planet and zoom off into the depths of space. So you'll be needing an advanced computer to cope with the necessary maths.

Other physicists are looking into how gravity itself works. Are there really tiny things, even smaller than atoms, called gravitons that are somehow involved? And once scientists have found this out, could they perhaps defeat gravity and make planes that hover effortlessly in the air?

And even if we don't crack this one – there's always something new. Like a really wacky new sport. Take sky-surfing, for example. To do this you have to be seriously off your trolley. It involves jumping from an aeroplane strapped to a board. You enjoy some mid-air acrobatics before your parachute opens – assuming it does.

But one thing is certain – humans will go on pushing forces to their limits and scientists will go on studying how forces work. After all there may be limits to our knowledge, but our curiosity knows no bounds. Yep. You're forced to admit it. Forces are horribly intriguing. Fatally fascinating. But that's Horrible Science for you!

FATAL FORCES

QUIZ

Now find out if you're a
Fatal Forces expert!

To be a Horrible Scientist you need more than horrible habits. As every genuine genius knows you need brainpower too. The question is, having read this book have you got what it takes upstairs? (Don't decide until you've got to grips with this queasy quiz!)

Fun forces (these are the basic bits that even a teacher ought to know!)

Before we see if you really can be a Horrible Scientist and test your knowledge of fatal forces, let's see if you've understood the basics. Match the forces below with their mysterious meanings and effects.

1 Mass
2 Velocity
3 Acceleration
4 Friction
5 Energy
6 Momentum
7 Vibrations
8 Work
a) Changing speed or direction
b) The ability to do work
c) Keeps an object in motion
d) The amount of matter contained in an object
e) When a force causes an object to move a distance

ACTUALLY, THE GARDEN COULD DO WITH A DROP OF RAIN

f) Speed in a single direction
g) Carry force of impact away from an object
h) Slows moving objects

Answers:
1d; 2f; 3a; 4h; 5b; 6c; 7g; 8e

Fantastic forces quiz

So – reckon you've got the measure of forceful forces? Take this quick quiz and find out if you could truly be a freaky physicist...

1 Isaac Newton began investigating the force known as gravity when something fell out of a tree and hit him on the head. What was it?
a) An apple
b) A pear
c) A tomato

2 What would your terminal velocity be if you fell out of an aeroplane?
a) 9.8 metres a second
b) 50 metres a second
c) No one has been brave enough to try this experiment.

3 Why don't smooth golf balls fly as straight as pitted ones?

FASCINATING!

a) Smooth things naturally move in curves.
b) The pits create turbulence on the surface so fly better.
c) The pits trap flies rather than allowing the flies to bump the ball off-course.

4 Why would a perpetual motion machine break the Second Law of Thermodynamics?
a) All machines lose energy in the form of sound, heat and friction. The machine would run out of energy.
b) Any machine that ran for ever would over-heat and melt.
c) A perpetual motion machine would be bound to run out of spare parts sooner or later.

5 Which of the following can be defined by gravity?
a) The force of attraction between two cars
b) The force of attraction between two tennis balls
c) The force of attraction between two people in love.

6 How heavy is the Moon (to the nearest few kilograms)?
a) 73,490,000,000,000,000 million kg
b) 1.5 kg
c) 597,420, 000,000,000,000,000 million kg

7 How does living in space affect the size of an astronaut?
a) He grows several centimeters.
b) He shrinks a few centimeters.
c) He doubles in size.

8 What kind of apple did Isaac Newton get hit on the head with?
a) Flower of Kent
b) Allington Pippin
c) Golden Delicious

Answers:
1a; 2b; 3b; 4a; 5 – all of the above (every object with mass has a gravitational pull); **6a; 7a; 8a**

Force fact or fiction

There are still many misleading myths about fatal forces. Can you figure out which of these silly statements are totally true and which are forcefully false?

1 Archimedes managed to move an entire ship by himself using a pulley system.

2 The longbows used in medieval times were capable of firing an arrow further than a kilometre.

OH YES, VERY FUNNY

3 In 1996 Bryan Berg built a card tower 13.96 metres high.

4 The furthest a man has been fired out of a cannon using an explosive charge is 87.5 metres.

5 It is possible to create fire by rubbing two sticks together.

6 False. Because the Earth bulges out slightly at the Equator it is further from the centre. This makes the gravitational pull a tiny bit weaker than at the poles.

7 The pressure you would feel at the deepest point of the ocean is equivalent to two men standing on your head.

8 Water can be made to boil at 40° Celsius.

Answers:
1 True.
2 False. The arrow could only travel 320 metres – but that was still far enough to injure an enemy before he got to you!
3 False. Bryan's card tower was only 5.85 metres high. Mind you, that's quite a height if you were on top of it.
4 False. To propel a human cannon ball they don't use explosives – they use a very strong spring!
5 True. The friction creates enough heat for it to start to smoke. And where there's smoke there's fire…
6 True. Because the Earth bulges out slightly at the Equator it is further from the centre and this makes the gravitational pull a bit weaker at the poles.
7 False. It's the equivalent of an average person balancing 48 jumbo jets on their head!

8 True. If the pressure is low enough, the water will boil.

Speed, pressure and temperature

You can't escape forces on Earth – or even in space! Speed, pressure and temperature and three of the effects of forceful forces that physicists find fearfully fascinating. But how much do you know about them?

1 How much gravity is there at the centre of the Earth? (Clue: It's nothing to worry about.)

2 Why do super-speedy cyclist wear funny-shaped helmets? (Clue: Oh, what's the point?!)

3 What happens to your lungs as you diver deep under water (Clue: Take a deep breath now)

4 What would happen if you accelerated at a force of 9 g? (Clue: This one's dead easy)

5 Why did American cars have cow catchers? (Clue: think of a flying cow)

6 Where was the lowest temperature recorded on Earth? (Clue: Don't go "Russian" into this answer)

7 Is the acceleration due to gravity on the Moon more or less powerful than it is on Earth? (Clue: Floating free)

8 A person standing in high heels on a floor exerts a massive pressure on a small point. How many elephants would pressure be equivalent to? (Clue: It'd be standing on tiptoe…)

Answers:

1 None. The force of gravity doesn't exist at the Earth's centre – but you don't really want to go there to see if I'm right!

2 The pointed front on the helmet makes the air move around them rather than bumping into them and slowing them down.

3 They get squashed – more and more so as the pressure increases the deeper you go.

4 A force of 4 to 6 g managed for only a few seconds before you'd pass out (or your eyes would start to bleed). At 9 g you'd be dead!

5 They scooped buffalo out of the way of the train.

6 It was recorded in Russia – a bone-chilling -89.4°C.

7 Less. The gravitational pull on the surface of the Moon is 1.62 metres per second squared. This is only about one-sixth of that on Earth.

8 Just one – but it would be standing on one foot!

Freaky physicists

Over the years, strange scientists have conducted many evil experiments and come up with hundreds of ingenious inventions to learn about fatal forces. Can you identify the freaky physicist by what they might have said?

1 "Ow! That will leave a bump!"
2 "Can I have my balls back please?"
3 "Everyone thinks I'm full of hot air!"
4 "I've been under a lot of pressure recently."
5 "I'm in the swing of it"
6 "This invention really sucks!"
7 "Pass me that screw, will you?"
8 "You spin me right round… la la la."

a) Blaise Pascal
b) Otto von Guericke
c) Isaac Newton
d) George Ferris
e) Archimedes
f) Galileo Galilei
g) Jean Foucault
h) Isambard Kingdom Brunel

I'VE BEEN UNDER A LOT OF PRESSURE RECENTLY

Answers:

1 c) Isaac Newton discovered gravity when an apple fell on his head.

2 f) Galileo used balls to experiment with gravity.

3 a) Pascal invented the barometer – a device to measure air pressure.

4 h) Among other things, Brunel invented a train that was powered by atmospheric pressure.

5 g) Foucault did some amazing experiments with his pendulum.

6 b) Von Guericke invented the vacuum pump.

7 e) Ancient Archimedes invented the machine known as the screw or screwpump.

8 d) Ferris invented the Ferris wheel – well, what did you think he invented the mini-roundabout?

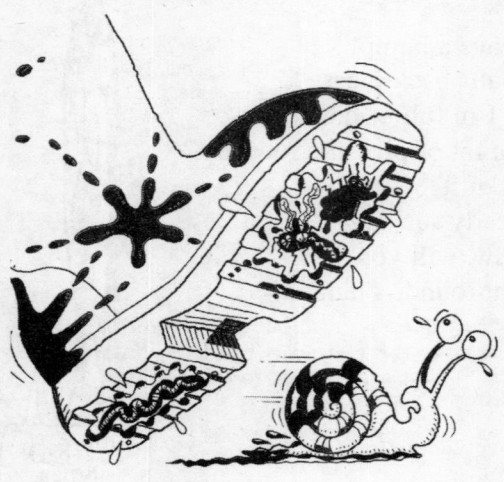

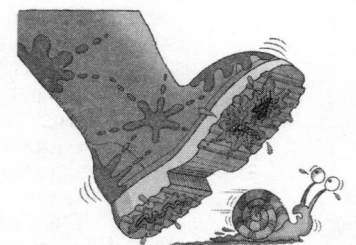

HORRIBLE INDEX

172

kinetic energy (used when moving) 31–2
knicker elastic 99

labs, untidy 34
laws 6–7, 18–21, 33, 39–40
         lousy 44, 86–7, 96, 122, 149
legs
         model 136
         springs in 103
         winding round 106
Leibniz, Gottfried (German philosopher) 23
levers, lovely 134–8, 143
lift, going up 125
light, containing colours 13
Locke, John (English philosopher) 22
lubrication, slippery 87–8, 92, 94

Mach, Ernst (Austrian physicists) 46
machines, mighty 134–43
mass 5, 30, 58–9
mathematics 5, 12–13, 16–17, 28, 35, 60, 138, 158
mechanics, amazing 134
molecules 69, 123
momentum 20, 30–1, 33, 38–40
         angular 105, 120, 122
         conservation of angular 105, 122
         momentous 106, 108, 111, 113–14
moon 13–16, 59
moose, loose 40
motion 80, 111, 113
         laws of 19–21, 39–40
         oscillatory 152
         perpetual 85–7
         theories of 26–35
mousetraps 102
moving *see* motion

nails, bed of 58
Napoleon III 117, 119

navigation (finding yourself) 121
Newton, Isaac (English scientist) 9, 11–26, 28, 33, 39–40, 44, 62, 65, 80, 95, 113, 149, 157
Newton's First Law 19, 33, 39–40, 44
Newton's Second Law 20
Newton's Third Law 20–1, 149
Newtons (units of force) 21, 70

obelisks, raising 88–92

padding, painless 126–7
parachutes 49, 51, 53–6, 158
Pascal, Blaise (French physicist) 69–70
Pascals (units of pressure) 70
Pauli, Wolfgang (Austrian-born physicist) 120
pedals 141–2
pendulums 10, 62, 111, 113, 115–20
Philip (king of Macedonia) 27
The Philosophiae Naturalis Principia Mathematica (Newton's book) 18, 23
physicists, freaky 34, 40, 46, 69, 83, 85, 120, 157–8
physics, laws of 6, 13, 34, 86, 120
pistons, powerful 74, 76
plague, deadly 13
planes 46–51, 70, 122, 143, 158
planets, moving 62, 65, 158
Plato (Greek philosopher) 26
Poe, Edgar Alan (American author) 10
potential energy 35
precession, while spinning 122
pressure, under 68–79, 125, 147
pulleys, powerful 137, 143
pyramids
         of coins 67
         strength of 148

racks, stretching on 98
railways, building 74–9
relaxing

173

HORRIBLE SCIENCE

DISGUSTING DIGESTION

NICK ARNOLD

illustrated by
TONY DE SAULLES

SCHOLASTIC

Visit Nick Arnold at
www.nickarnold-website.com

Scholastic Children's Books,
Euston House, 24 Eversholt Street,
London, NW1 1DB, UK

A division of Scholastic Ltd
London ~ New York ~ Toronto ~ Sydney ~ Auckland
Mexico City ~ New Delhi ~ Hong Kong

First published in the UK by Scholastic Ltd, 1998
This edition published 2008

Text copyright © Nick Arnold, 1998
Illustrations © Tony De Saulles, 1998

All rights reserved

ISBN 978 0439 94445 8

Printed and bound by CPI Group (UK) Ltd, Croydon, CR0 4YY

28

CONTENTS

Nick Arnold has been writing stories and books since he was a youngster, but never dreamt he'd find fame writing about Disgusting Digestion. His research involved battling with threadworms, bathing in stomach acid and eating pork pies and he enjoyed every minute of it.

When he's not delving into Horrible Science, he spends his spare time teaching adults in a college. His hobbies include eating pizza, riding his bike and thinking up corny jokes (though not all at the same time).

Tony De Saulles picked up his crayons when he was still in nappies and has been doodling ever since. He takes Horrible Science very seriously and even agreed to sample several school dinners for us. Fortunately, he has made a full recovery.

When he's not out with his sketchpad, Tony likes to write poetry and play squash, though he hasn't written any poetry about squash yet.

INTRODUCTION

Here's a disgusting science story...

It's ten minutes to the end of a particularly boring science lesson. The hands on the clock are crawling round like dozy snails. You're struggling to stay awake. It's so tedious.

So you try to think about something – anything to stop yourself from dropping off. Lunch, perhaps? Yes, that sounds like a good idea. OK – so it's only school lunch but breakfast was centuries ago. You're so hungry. Couldn't you just murder a scrumptious steaming pudding oozing with hot jam and custard?

But then your teacher asks a tricky question.

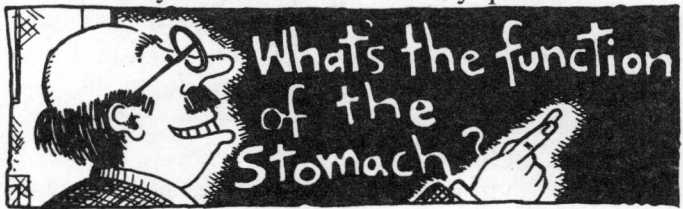

Dead silence.

No one answers. Just then your tum lets rip with a huge, hearty rumble. It sounds deafening – just like a massive rumble of thunder. The echoes bounce off the classroom walls. Everyone stares at you. What do you do?

a) Turn scarlet and mumble "Sorry".

b) Blame the smart, goody-goody kid next to you.

c) Jump up, and close all the classroom windows saying, "There must be a storm coming, wasn't that thunder?"

A scientist, of course, would know the scientific answer. Some scientists actually spend their lives delving into digestion. Digestion is when food is taken into your body to help you stay alive and grow. It sounds about as thrilling as last night's dirty dishes.

But it doesn't have to be.

Digestion is disgusting. Amazingly disgusting! And this disgustingly amazing process is going on inside your body right now. In this book there are some foul scientific secrets and disgusting discoveries served up with a hearty helping of belly-laughs. And afterwards you'll be able to Answer:your teacher's question like this…

* (Bor-bor-rig-mus) Posh medical term for a rumbling tummy. The stomach and gut walls squash the gas and liquids inside.

After all, there are plenty of laws in science but not one of them says it's got to be boring. So now there's only one question. Have you got the stomach for some really disgusting discoveries?

Better read on and find out…

DISGUSTING DISCOVERIES

The young medical student turned white. His eyeballs bulged in his head and his mouth opened in a soundless scream. He wanted to yell but nothing came out. Not even a muffled gasp. He wanted to run. Run anywhere. But his legs wouldn't budge. He wanted to wake from his nightmare but this was no dream. It wasn't a scene from a horror film either. This was real life.

There really were sparrows flapping around the room. They were pecking at bits of dead body on the floor. And that really was a huge hungry rat skulking in the corner and gnawing greedily on a lump of human bone. This was a room in a hospital … and the year was 1821.

Don't panic! Hospitals aren't like this any more. But when 18-year-old medical student Hector Berlioz (1803–1869) visited a dissecting room in Paris this is what he really saw. (A dissecting room was where dead bodies were cut up so that their different parts could be studied.) This is just one example of the disgusting conditions endured by doctors and scientists in the past as they probed the secrets of digestion.

DISGUSTING DIGESTION DATES

The ancient Egyptians were into dissecting 5,000 years ago. In fact, every time they made a mummy they got their hands on the human guts. They always removed the intestines, or guts, and other vital organs and put them into jars because they would rot easily and spoil the preserved mummy. They kept all the body bits in jars for the mummy to use in the afterlife.

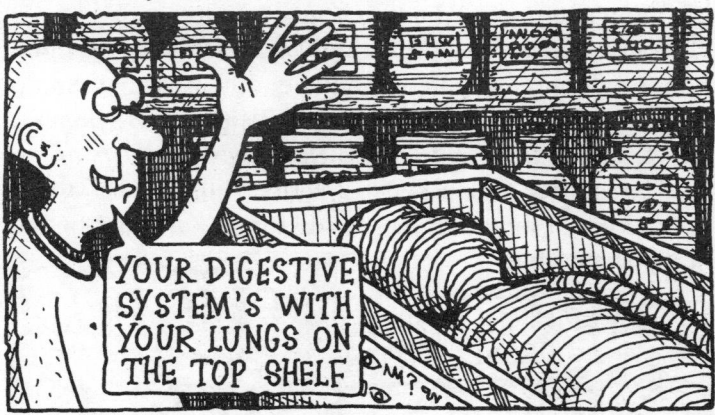

YOUR DIGESTIVE SYSTEM'S WITH YOUR LUNGS ON THE TOP SHELF

But the Egyptians weren't interested in the structure of the guts or how they worked. One of the first people to be genuinely interested in the guts was a foul-tempered Roman doctor.

Hall of fame: Claudius Galen (AD129–201)

Nationality: Roman

Galen said:

My father was amiable, just and benevolent, but my mother had a very bad temper. She used to bite the serving maids and was always shouting at my father.

Hope your mum isn't like that. Sadly Galen inherited his mum's temper and nothing much from his dad.

Young Galen was disgustingly clever. He wrote three books before he was 13 and another 500 after that. Some of them had intriguing titles like *Bones for Beginners*, *On the Black Bile*, and *On the Usefulness of Parts of the Body*. One day Galen kept 12 scribes busy as he strode up and down dictating the words for 12 different books at the same time.

DICTATE, BLAH BLAH, DRONE, WITTER

BIG-HEAD!

Galen reckoned he had the last word on medicine. He once said:

Whoever seeks fame needs only become familiar with all that I have achieved.

Modest, eh? The problem was Galen wasn't always right. In fact he was often WRONG. For example, he reckoned blood was made in the guts and went to the liver where it turned blue.

WRONG. Blood is made in the bone marrow and spleen. Just goes to show you can't believe everything you read in books. Mind you, Galen wasn't the only one – in his day many people thought that men had more teeth than women. WRONG – it's incredible they never bothered to count them!

DO YOU MEAN I'M NOT NORMAL?

Galen made silly mistakes because he got his ideas from cutting up dead animals rather than humans. But no doctors dared to argue with him. They were scared of Galen's famously foul temper. (Once Galen had even dared to shout insults at an opponent in the sacred

Temple of Peace.) And they were even more scared he might ask his pal the Roman Emperor to dispose of them in a disgusting fashion.

For about 1,500 years doctors believed Galen's theories. They could have cut up a few bodies to check for themselves. But few did. Governments often banned dissection and where it *was* allowed doctors felt they were too grand for all the messy, gory cutting up stuff and left that to their humble assistants. Then a doctor came along who was...

A CUT ABOVE THE REST

Whilst he studied in the Belgian town, Andreas Versalius (1514–1564) had a horrible habit. He stole dead bodies. And he wasn't particular either – anybody's body would do. Young, old, men or women – it didn't matter as long as the corpse wasn't too rotten. While he worked in the Belgian town of Louvain he used some disgustingly dodgy tricks to gain his revolting ends. He would:

• dig up bodies in cemeteries.

• steal the bodies of criminals left on public display.

• attend executions and sneak the body away at the end of the proceedings.

Then he would hide the bodies in his room. And late into the night by the flickering flame of a candle, he probed their grisly innards. Andreas Versalius wasn't crazy. He was a scientist and he was determined to go to any lengths to solve the mysteries of how the body worked. The appalling methods he used were the only way to get any answers. Dissection was banned, remember.

Things became easier in 1536 when Versalius became Professor of Anatomy in Padua, Italy. Here, the authorities were sympathetic to dissection. They even fixed execution dates so that the criminal's body would be nice and fresh for anatomy classes.

NOW I CAN'T MANAGE TUESDAY, WOULD WEDNESDAY BE OK?

You'll be pleased to know doctors no longer need to steal bodies to practise dissection. Some people actually agree to allow their bodies to be dissected after death to help train medical students.

Bet you never knew!
Here's how to play Andreas Versalius's favourite game.
1 Allow yourself to be blindfolded.
2 Ask your friends to hand you a selection of human bones.
3 Identify them by their shape and the way they feel.
4 You win if you get them all right.

ER, WELL, UM, I DON'T THINK IT'S A SKULL

ROTTEN READING

Versalius discovered more about the inside of the human body than anyone before him. He was the first person to describe the structure of the human guts accurately. In 1543 he published his discoveries in a book *The Fabric of the Human Body*. It was packed with tasteful pictures of bits of bodies and skeletons with lovely scenery to make the revolting subject matter nicer to look at. The book was a bestseller.

SKELETON RECLINING IN A FIELD OF DAFFODILS – NICE!

But Versalius came to a disgusting end. According to one story he was cutting up a nobleman's body when it twitched. The "corpse" was still alive! Versalius decided to make himself scarce and embarked on a long sea voyage. But poor old Versalius was shipwrecked and starved to death on a lonely island. And what's more he had no body to keep him company!

IF ONLY I HAD MY TOOLBOX I COULD GET THE SEAGULL I ATE FOR BREAKFAST OUT OF MY STOMACH AND EAT IT AGAIN FOR DINNER

Could you have made these disgusting discoveries? Here's your chance to probe those gruesome innards and their grisly secrets. Delicate readers may find this next chapter not quite to their taste. It's a little bit sick.

DISGUSTING DIGESTIVE BITS'N'PIECES

Would you want to inspect the guts in grisly close-up detail? It's a horrible job but sometimes it's vital to check on problems. The scientist in this chapter has a real problem. He was absent-mindedly sucking his pen when he swallowed the top. It got stuck somewhere in his guts.

As luck would have it he'd just invented an incredible shrinking machine.

So all he needed was a volunteer to shrink down to 2.5 cm high and venture into his guts in search of the missing top. Any takers? Unfortunately, every doctor the scientist asked seemed to have an excuse. So he hired hard-bitten Private Eye, M I Gutzache for this unpleasant job.

First Gutzache had to change into special protective clothing so he wouldn't be digested during his hazardous mission.

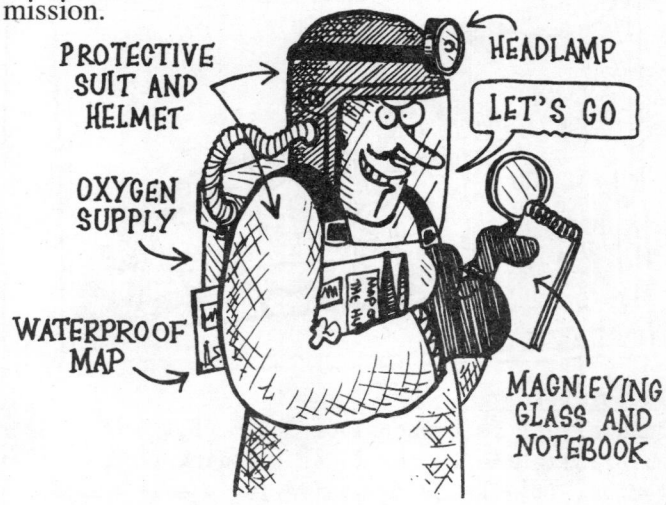

Here's Gutzache's report. Go on take a look, you know you want to – it's fascinating.

It seemed a cinch. Just a quick surveillance operation. "No problem," I said. So I took the job. That was my first big mistake. I may be a small-time private eye but under the shrinking ray I started to feel even smaller. But the worst was yet to come. I was going to be swallowed by a scientist!

Tough teeth

The teeth looked tough. There were several types. Some geared for biting, and some for chewing, gnawing or nibbling. They all looked mighty mean to me. Teeth are as hard as they come – d'you know you need a diamond to cut into them?

ARE YOU SURE YOU BRUSHED THEM THIS MORNING, DOC?

Tasteful tongue

Suddenly, I felt the floor heave. Not surprising really, as I was standing on a tongue. It's a living, quivering muscle and a real smart mover. While the scientist guy was talking, his tongue tossed a lump of carrot into a huge puddle of spit, and another piece came flying in between his teeth. It's awesome.

what that muscle can do! But if I didn't act fast I figured I'd be next for a spit dunking. I cast around for an exit.

Salivary (sal-i-very) glands

But I was too late, all of a sudden I felt wet and hot. Looking down I saw I was up to my knees in saliva (that's spit to you). It looked like trouble — but trouble is my business. I knew there were six hidden glands pumping this stuff out. I was going to have to swim for it. I dived down the gullet. It seemed the safest place to be. But I was wrong.

The scientist writes...

I was trying hard not to bite Detective Gutzache. It was actually quite lucky that he fell into my saliva — it helped me to swallow him. Spit may seem disgusting stuff, but it's full of proteins called enzymes.

1. A food molecule (molecule = group of atoms) slots into an enzyme molecule.

2. A chemical reaction takes place in which the food molecule gets broken up into smaller molecules that can pass through my gut walls. (This happens all the time in my small intestine!)

Then disaster struck. Gutzache got stuck in my gullet, or oesophagus (a-sof-fer-gus), to use the technical term. What would happen to him now?

Oesophagus

Just my luck to get wedged in his throat! The scientist guy started coughing and spluttering. My body shook as he gulped. Then I felt all this water flooding over me — I was on the move! Now, I often find myself in tight spots and I can tell you this next one was seriously tight. The sides of his gullet squeezed together forcing me down. Then I hit some half-chewed food. The gullet walls squeezed the food into a ball. I knew that I could be squashed too. I wanted out. But it was too late.

STOP SWALLOWING DOC!

The scientist adds…

My oesophagus walls squeezed together behind Mr Gutzache and pushed him down. This is called peristalsis (perry-stal-sis). It's Greek for "push around". It was lucky he didn't fall down my windpipe. That would have started me choking until I'd coughed him back into my mouth.

Stomach

I hit the stomach with a splash. It was more of a bellyflop than a dive. I found myself swimming in a lake of mush. It looked and smelled like sick. It was sick! I felt sick too. I was churned around as the stomach walls squeezed in and out. I felt like a sock in a washing machine. I figured the juice was acid because I could see it dissolving the food. I was real glad of my protective suit!

CURRY AND RICE PUDDING, YUCK!

The scientist writes…

My stomach lining makes up to 2 litres of acid juice every day to dissolve the food I eat. And there are enzymes at work too.

Small intestine

After a few hours I managed to squeeze through the exit below the stomach. I found myself in a long tube that looked like a subway. I switched on my headlamp and peered at my waterproof map. My route was clear. I should head down the duodenum (dew-o-dee-num), jejunum (gee-june-num) and ileum (ill-ee-um). Whatever they were.

21

The map said "small intestine" - but it seemed
endless. I knew I had to keep moving. The gut
walls were closing behind me and I wasn't
hanging around to get squashed again. So I
walked. My feet squashed on the soft rubbery
ground. Just then I saw something large and blue
trapped in a fold in the wall. Success! It was
the missing pen top. I gingerly pulled it out
and tucked it under my arm. Now all I had to do
was to get out without getting digested on the
way.

A squirt

Suddenly I was splattered with digestive juices.
I felt like an automobile in a car-wash, except
I wasn't getting any cleaner. I was covered in
brownish slimy bile from the liver and pale
juice from the pancreas, I didn't stop to admire
the view. I made tracks for the large intestine.

The scientist writes…

It's me again. I just wanted to explain that my bile breaks
up the remains of greasy, fatty foods. It comes from my
gall bladder, which is a little bag under the liver. My
pancreas is about 18cm long and it's draped under
my stomach. Besides enzymes, it makes vital chemicals
that control the amount of sugar in my blood.

Appendix

In the large intestine I saw a weird sight. A little tube, about 5cm long, leading to a dead end. In the end I figured it out. It was the appendix. It wasn't doing much — just hanging out, I guess.

The scientist writes...

Gutzache's got it right for once! My appendix spends its life doing nothing and I'm not even sure why it's there. My large intestine is definitely there for a reason though, it sucks up any spare water and minerals from my food.

The rectum

I was dead beat. So I sat down. Big mistake. I sank into something soft and brown and it didn't smell too good. I was in the rectum. It was the final stretch of the large intestine. And there was only one way out. I could see the toilet bowl. It seemed a long way down but there was nowhere else to go. I shoved the pen top out and it splashed into the water far below. *My turn next*, I thought.

The scientist writes…

The large intestine is where waste food is stored. Most of the spare water is sucked out of the waste and through the sides of the gut. Er . . . 'scuse me a minute. Got to dash . . .

Splash-down

It was time to check out. I never liked parachute jumps. After I crawled out of the water I quit the job. The scientist wanted me to check out his liver but I'd had enough. I needed a vacation. Fighting violent crime seemed easy after this.

DISGUSTING EXPRESSIONS

Bet you never knew!

1 Some people have worms in their guts. It's true! Roundworms, pin worms and flukes can all live in the guts and feast on half-digested food. They generally get there in infected food. And once in, they lay eggs that pass out of the body with the faeces ready to infect someone else. But don't panic! Nowadays these nasty little suckers can be beaten using drugs.

2 The gut also contains microbiological* bacteria or as you might know them – germs. Up to 500 types of bacteria happily splash around in your guts where they make nasty smells. And they make up over 1 kg of your total weight! But most of them are harmless and some even make useful K and B vitamins to keep us healthy (see pages 77–80 for more details). *Microbiological means the study of tiny life. Go on, say it. It's a brilliant word to chuck into a Friday afternoon science lesson. It means you need a microscope to see these bacteria because they're so small. You could actually find hundreds on the pointy end of a pin.

MORE BITS 'N' PIECES

In his hurry to get away, Gutzache missed out a few important digestive bits and pieces. It's time to take a closer look at…

The life-saving liver

Tiny bits of digested food molecules in the blood go to the liver to make vital substances your body needs. The liver also does hundreds of other vital jobs such as making bile (see page 22).

The vagus (vay-gus) nerve

The vagus nerve is like a long telephone wire that "vaguely" snakes round the guts carrying messages to and from the brain. These include orders to squeeze the gut wall and move the food ball on to its next destination.

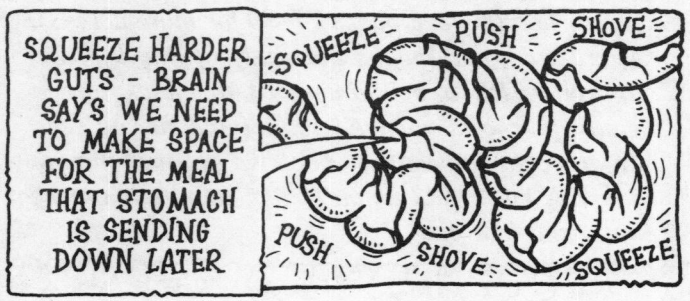

Crucial kidneys

These are the body's filters. As blood passes through them they clear out all the spare water and waste products and send them down for storage in the bladder.

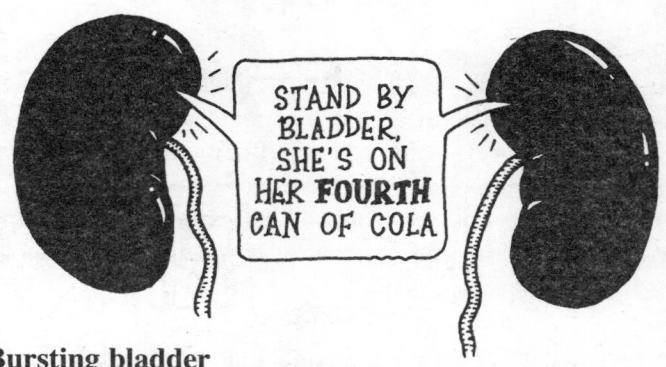

Bursting bladder

This is an incredibly wrinkled sack. It looks like a prune after a really long bath, but as it fills up, it gets bigger and it looks more like a balloon. The speed this happens depends on how much a person has had to drink. Most people need to pee about four to six times a day.

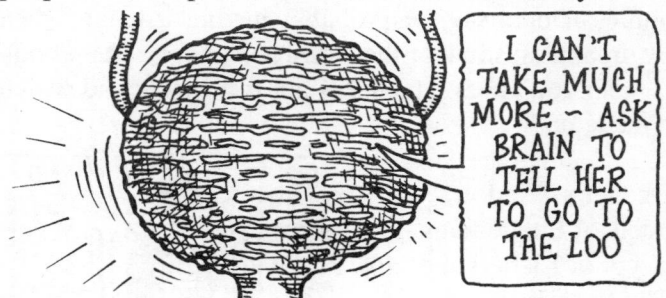

How can you tell when someone's bladder is full? Easy. They start twitching, writhing and dancing around looking for the nearest loo. If you were feeling heartless you could...

a) Join in the dancing.

THAT'S REALLY GROOVY. LET'S ALL DANCE, WEEEE!

b) Tell them not to worry – the bladder can store up to 400 ml of pee (or urine, to use the posh word for it) fairly easily.

In fact, the bladder is so strong that in an adult it can swell to 10 cm across without going pop.

DISGUSTINGLY ODD BITS 'N' PIECES QUIZ

Now you've checked out the main digestive bits, you've just got time to check out the obscure nooks and crannies. Doctors were probably having a laugh when they dreamt up some of the weird names for certain body bits. Can you guess which bits are inside you and which are made up?

1 Deaver's Windows
2 Islets of Langerhans
3 Crypt of Lieberkühn
4 The Pustule of Volvo
5 Flint's Arcade
6 Ferrein's Pyramid
7 Fibres of Mummery
8 Verheyen's Stars

IS THIS MY PUSTULE OF VOLVO, SIR?

NO, THAT'S YOUR NOSE, SMITH

CLASS 4

Answers: 1 TRUE. These are spaces in the flesh that hold the guts securely in position. The spaces are named after their discoverer, American scientist John Blair Deaver. **2 TRUE.** These are areas in the pancreas which make a hormone called insulin that controls the speed your body stores energy in the form of fats or sugars. They're named after eagle-eyed German doctor Paul Langerhans who spotted them in 1869. **3 TRUE.** And what's more they aren't crypts where dead bodies are buried. They're tiny pits in the small intestine that produce digestive juices. But you'd be a dead body without them because they're vital to digest your food. **4 FALSE.** The Volvo is a Swedish car. **5 TRUE.** These are arch-shaped blood vessels in the kidneys and nothing to do with amusement arcades. They're named after their discoverer, American professor Austin Flint. **6 TRUE.** An area of the kidney above Flint's arcade. These pyramid-shaped bits were named after a French professor of surgery called Antoine Ferrein, who wrote about them in 1746. They're nothing to do with the pyramids in Egypt and you won't find a mummy skulking inside one. **7 TRUE.** These are stringy bits inside the teeth. They're nothing to do with mummies or pyramids either. **8 TRUE.** These are star-shaped veins on the kidney named after Philipe Verheyen who described them in 1699. Verheyen was planning to be a priest but he had an accident and doctors had to chop his leg off. He was so fascinated by this horrible ordeal that he gave up the priesthood. He decided to study medicine instead and became a professor.

29

Congratulations! You've finished the chapter. Feeling peckish? Desperate enough to eat a school dinner? Better scoff some now before you read about the vile food in the next chapter. It really takes the cake ... or is it the biscuit?

FOUL FOOD FACTS

This chapter is about food. It's about what we eat and how much we eat. But don't expect a mouth-watering feast. This is Horrible Science, remember, so you'll be reading about really foul foods. Got a brown paper bag handy? Good – you might need it!

ENORMOUS EATERS

In your lifetime you'll guzzle about 30 tonnes of food – that's the weight of six elephants or 20 rhinos. In one year the average greedy grown-up can munch their way through 34 kg of potatoes, 11.8 kg of sugar, 500 apples, 150 loaves of bread and 200 eggs, and still have room for pudding.

If you only ate boring pieces of bread and butter all the time you'd still get through about 250,000 slices in a lifetime. But some people eat a lot more than that.

All-time glutton Edward "Bozo" Miller of Oakland, California used to guzzle 11 times more food than anyone else. In 1963 he scoffed 28 chickens in a single stomach-splitting feast and became a legend in his own lunchtime. Now you might think that's a lot, but compared with some animals it's just a tiny snack.

• An elephant can knock back up to half a tonne of leaves and bark every day.

• Every day a blue whale swallows four tonnes of tiny sea creatures called plankton – that's more food than a human eats in a year. Mind you, the whale is 2,000 times heavier than a human.

• Even tiny creatures can munch more for their size than humans. For example, the 2-gram Etruscan shrew scoffs up to three times its own weight every day. That's like a human eating one entire sheep, 50 chickens, 60 family-sized loaves and 150 apples every day. You'd never cram all that into your lunch box, would you? So why do the shrews stuff their little faces? Well, they have to. Shrews need the energy all this food gives them to keep active and warm in cold weather.

COULD YOU BE A SCIENTIST?

If you like food, you don't have to become a chef. You could become a scientist instead. Yes, scientists have performed some mouth-watering experiments. Can you predict the results?

1 In the 1970s a group of American scientists went to a party and watched people eating. (Don't do this at parties – it's rude.) The scientists found that overweight people ate more than thinner people. The scientists quickly grabbed the food and took it into another room. What happened next?
a) The overweight people went into the next room to get the food.
b) The overweight people couldn't be bothered to move. The thinner people went next door and helped themselves.
c) A fight broke out and the scientists were chucked out for spoiling the party.

WHO SAID SCIENCE IS HORRIBLE?
SCRUMMY! YUMMY!
You're invited to a food party - eat as much as you like, but watch out for people in white coats trying to snatch the food away from you!

2 In the 1970s scientists at Virginia University, in America asked a group of people to sample a selection of yummy ice creams after first slurping down a rich, sweet milk-shake. (And this was a science experiment?!) The aim was to see which group ate the most ice cream.

What did they find?

a) People who were trying to lose weight ate more ice cream.

b) People who were trying to lose weight ate less ice cream.

c) Everyone scoffed as much as they could because the food was free and then threw up everywhere.

Answers: 1 b) The overweight people only ate more if the food was available. If food wasn't available, the thinner people ate more because they were more willing to go and find it. **2 a)** The people trying to lose weight were upset. The scientists had told them that the milk-shake was fattening and that they'd broken their diet. So they pigged out on ice cream because they felt they might as well enjoy themselves.

ENORMOUS APPETITES

The amount you can eat depends on how big your stomach is. After all, you've got to put all that food somewhere. This is also controlled by a pea-sized lump on the underside of the brain called the hypothalamus (hi-po-thala-mus). This signals to your brain when it's time to eat and when to stop. If you don't want to stop, then chances are that you're eating something you really enjoy. And if you don't want to start eating, then you're probably sitting in front of your school dinner...

FOUL FOOD FAVOURITES

Food is vital. It does more than simply fill you up. It supplies the chemicals that your body needs to stay healthy and grow. But we all have foods we love. And we all have foods we love to hate. Here's a school dinner menu. Which dishes might tempt you?

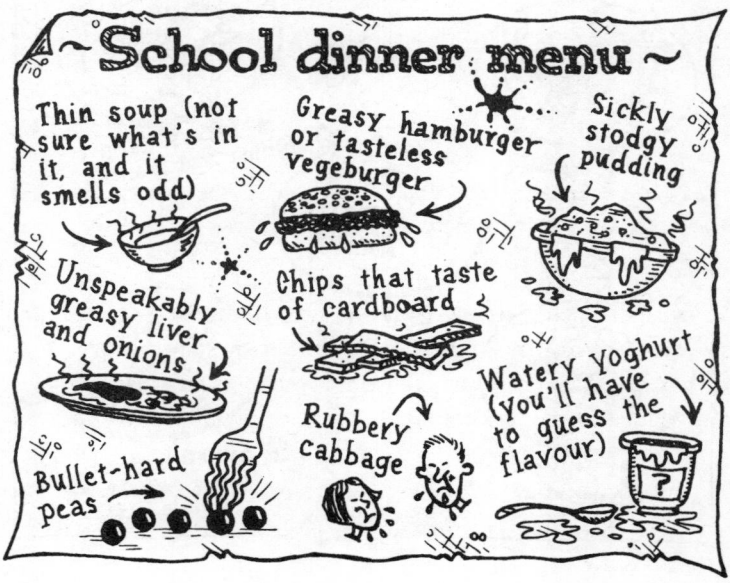

~ School dinner menu ~

Thin soup (not sure what's in it, and it smells odd)

Greasy hamburger or tasteless vegeburger

Sickly stodgy pudding

Unspeakably greasy liver and onions

Chips that taste of cardboard

Watery yoghurt (you'll have to guess the flavour)

Rubbery cabbage

Bullet-hard peas

It's really strange, but some teachers and even a few otherwise quite normal people think school dinners are the height of good taste! Because that's all a favourite food is – just a matter of taste. Like most people you probably chose your favourite foods when you were about two years old. But all over the world people enjoy different foods. Including some that might seem horrible to you. We managed to talk fearless Private Eye M I Gutzache into sampling a few of these foreign delicacies.

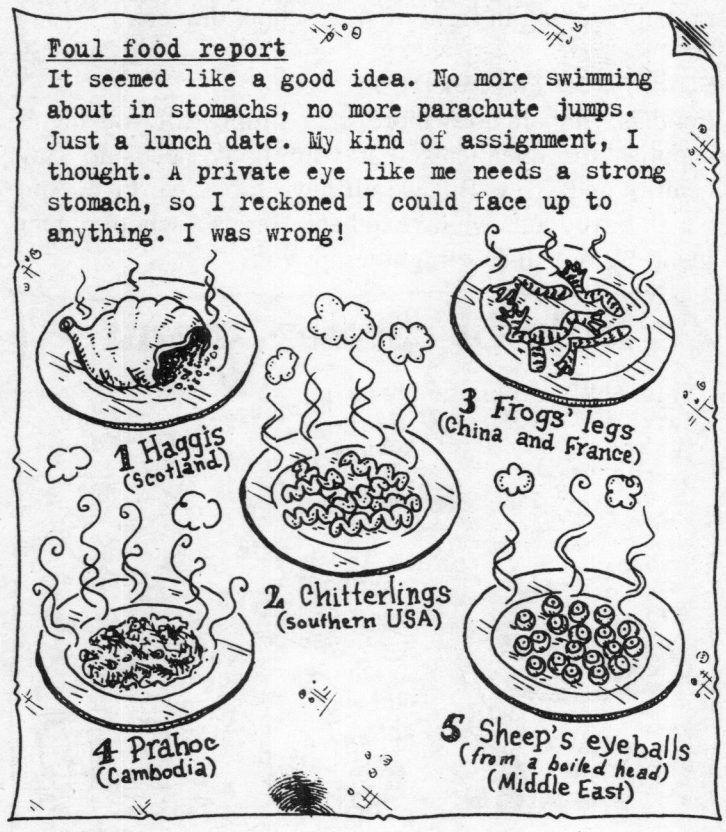

Foul food report
It seemed like a good idea. No more swimming about in stomachs, no more parachute jumps. Just a lunch date. My kind of assignment, I thought. A private eye like me needs a strong stomach, so I reckoned I could face up to anything. I was wrong!

1 Haggis (Scotland)

2 Chitterlings (southern USA)

3 Frogs' legs (China and France)

4 Prahoc (Cambodia)

5 Sheep's eyeballs (from a boiled head) (Middle East)

1. Tasted good — I like the savoury taste of onions and herbs and meat. I was just enjoying my second helping when someone mentioned that the meat was sheep's heart and lungs wrapped up in its stomach. I suddenly needed some fresh air.

2. This was really good. Nice crunchy batter. Then they told me it was chopped pigs intestines with corn meal fried in lard. I swallowed hard and went on to the next dish.

3. I could see what this dish was. I shut my eyes and took a bite. It tasted like watery chicken. I'd prefer chicken any day.

4. Tasted a bit fishy. No, I don't mean fishy suspicious - just fishy and kind of salty. But when I learned the fish had been squashed to paste and left to rot for a few days, I decided they could keep their rotten fish.

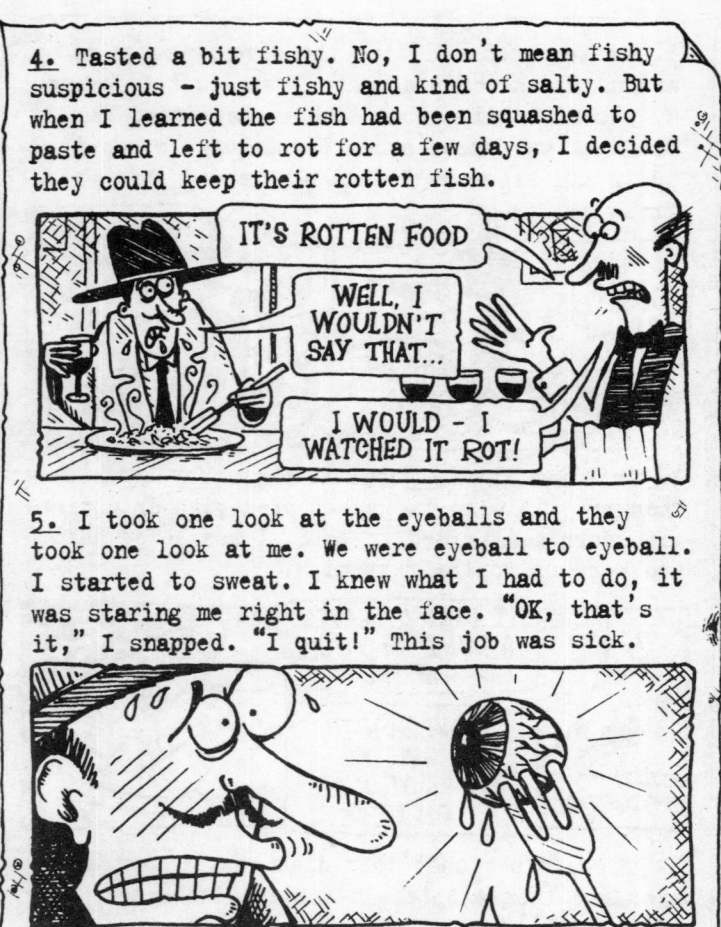

IT'S ROTTEN FOOD

WELL, I WOULDN'T SAY THAT...

I WOULD - I WATCHED IT ROT!

5. I took one look at the eyeballs and they took one look at me. We were eyeball to eyeball. I started to sweat. I knew what I had to do, it was staring me right in the face. "OK, that's it," I snapped. "I quit!" This job was sick.

Poor old Gutzache, he couldn't cope with the eyeball because he wasn't used to eating that part of an animal. But if he eats tongue, breast and neck, what difference does an eyeball make? It's all a question of what you're used to. If Gutzache had grown up in the Middle East he'd have been eating eyeballs since he was two – and loving them!

And here's something else you shouldn't try.

POISON PILLS

Some people will eat just about anything. But would you believe that some people used to eat poison? In 1733 dangerously dodgy doctor Ned Ward sold antimony pills as a cure for everything including upset tummies. But antimony is a poison once used by the ancient Egyptians to bump off flies. So not surprisingly the pills caused

39

violent stomach pains. One joker wrote a poem about Ned Ward:

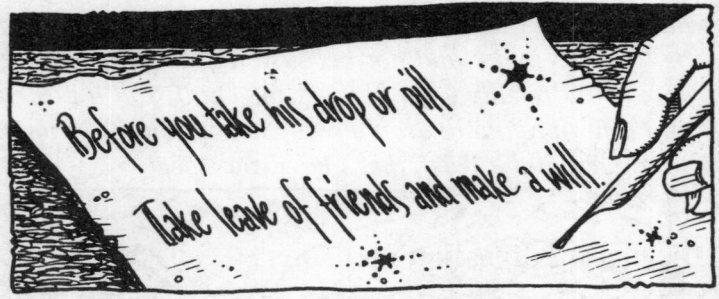

Before you take his drop or pill

Take leave of friends, and make a will.

But most people believed the adverts and thought the pain was part of the cure. The doctor made his fortune. He even gave poor sick people free samples of the wonderful pills. How kind! But oddly enough Ward never tried his own pills. This may explain why he lived to a ripe old age.

But antimony is just one of a host of disgusting poisons that turn up in food. Watch out, the next chapter could give you a nasty reaction...

FATAL FOOD POISONING

Food can be fatal. Well, not the food itself but what's lurking inside it. There may be all sorts of hidden poisons and germs lying in wait for your unsuspecting innards. So in order to protect yourself, you need to know all the disgusting details.

Disgusting digestion fact file

NAME: Poisons

THE BASIC FACTS: A poison is a chemical that gets into your body and makes you sick. Poisons include acids that dissolve the guts. Other poisons get to the brain in the bloodstream and knock the victim out.

THE HORRIBLE DETAILS: 1 Some of the deadliest poisons are called toxins. They're made by germs that get into food. Some can kill.

2 The best way for your body to get rid of a poison is to throw it back up again. That's why people spend the whole night throwing up after eating a dodgy dinner that's alive with germs.

BARF!

41

TEACHER'S TEA-BREAK TEASER

Try this teaser during a teacher's tea break. It'll be as welcome as a snail in a salad bar. Tap lightly on the staffroom door. When the door creaks open your teacher will be holding the regulation mug of sludgy mud-coloured coffee. Smile sweetly and say:

Answer: Coffee can be poisonous if you drink too much too fast. It contains a chemical called caffeine (also found in tea and cola drinks) that makes the heart beat faster. Normally it's quite harmless but scientists reckon that if someone drank 100 cups in four hours the caffeine would be strong enough to put their heart and blood vessels under fatal pressure.

SOME GOOD AND SOME BAD NEWS

Here's the good news: it's not easy to get poisoned. As long as you're sensible about what you put in your mouth, you're not going to get poisoned by man-made chemicals. If it isn't a drink don't drink it, and if it isn't food don't eat it. And food poisoning caused by germs is fairly rare, too.

Now the bad news: crowds of germs hang around in the hope of causing some really foul food poisoning. At best these awful invaders cause an upset tummy. At worst they can kill – as you'll discover in the next chapter.

So what does food poisoning do to you? We've managed to get hold of a doctor's notes on a case of food poisoning. See if you can decipher the doctor's dodgy handwriting.

THE CASE OF THE POISON PORK PIE

The patient is in great distress. He's a teacher at Gunge Street School and says he ate an ancient pork pie in the school canteen. He now has pain in the intestines and is vomiting every half-hour and he's producing diarrhoea (runny faeces). I believe that the muscles of the patient's gut are squeezing all the food and water out of each end. The patient's body is trying to get rid of infected food.

DIAGNOSIS: The patient has food poisoning

TREATMENT: The patient needs complete rest from school for a few days. For the first day or two he should drink only flat lemonade or warm water with a pinch of sugar and salt. This should stop his body drying out or dehydrating, whilst the white blood cells from his blood move into the gut and eat up the remaining germs.

PROGNOSIS: He'll live to bite another day.

Yes, germs are always ready to attack us. As you'll find out on page 48, our favourite private eye M I Gutzache is hot on the trail of the germs. But the germs are hatching their own dastardly plans...

Right lads, our enemy is the entire human race. Your mission is to get into their food and drink and raid their guts. Your orders are to make 'em sick. Make 'em throw up, and make 'em really miserable. You will start your mission as soon as the fridge door opens. Read these plans carefully and then eat them. Good luck, lads!

TOP SECRET BATTLE PLANS~
KEEP OUT OF REACH OF HUMANS

1 GO UNDER COVER IMMEDIATELY

Good hiding places: soil, dirty water. Humans won't dare look for you there. Lumps of dung or rubbish bins provide even better cover.

SOIL → DIRTY WATER ↓ ← DUNG RUBBISH

2 GET MOBILE

Your first objective: get on a human's hands and fingers and clothes and then onto their food. Human fingernails provide excellent shelter, and they'll do the job for you. You'll be inside the body in no time!

A fly can offer first-class aerial support. Aim to be picked up from a cowpat when the fly drops in to suck up moisture. The fly will then proceed to rendezvous with human food. The fly sicks its digestive juices over the food and sucks up the mixture. Now's your chance to drop onto the food.

FLY

COWPAT
HUMAN FOOD

GNASH!

MUNCH!

SUCK!

SQUIRT!

GUZZLE!

3 GET STUCK IN

Start eating. Squirt out enzymes that turn the food into slime and suck it into your body. Be sure to make plenty of waste chemicals to make the food rotten and stinking.

SAUSAGE BEFORE

SAUSAGE AFTER

4 GET NEW RECRUITS

Another simple task: pull yourself in half. Again and again. Soon you'll have hundreds, then thousands and millions of reinforcements. This will provide overwhelming numbers for the big attack on the guts.

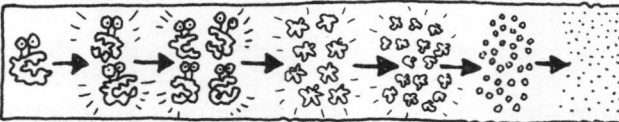

5 A FINAL WARNING

Humans will try to fight back with every weapon at their disposal. Be on your guard for antibiotics – medicines made from chemicals that us germs produce to defend ourselves against rival germs. And watch out. If a human uses enough antibiotics your entire army could be wiped out.

MESSAGE TO ALL GERMS

KEEP AWAY FROM ANTIBIOTICS

Dare you discover … how things rot?

You will need:
A freshly cut piece of orange
A large polythene bag
An adult helper

What you do:
Place the orange in the bag and seal the bag tightly so that no air can escape. Leave the bag in a warm place for six days.
What do you notice?
a) The orange stays the same.
b) The orange goes mushy and smelly.
c) The orange grows bigger.

Answer: b) Germs have been feeding on the orange and slowly digesting it and making a foul pong. The germs may be harmful, so *don't open the bag* – throw it away unopened!

HOW NOT TO HANDLE FOOD

Here are some sure-fire ways to give germs a helping hand into your food…
• Sneezing into food.

46

• Coughing into food. This shoots germs from your mouth and nose into the air. Use a handkerchief. Do not wrap your food in the handkerchief or use it as a bandage afterwards. Germs can also get into your body through unwashed wounds.

• Handling food without washing your hands. (There are usually a few germs hanging around on your hands.)
• Picking your nose or biting nails. This is a marvellous way to pick up a few million germs. It's especially anti-social if you try to do both at the same time.

• Picking bits of food from your teeth with your fingers and then eating it. Not recommended.

DISGUSTING DETECTIVE WORK

Following the sad case of the food-poisoned teacher (see page 43), we decided to investigate the school kitchen that was suspected of foul play and even fouler pork pies. It needed someone with experience, with dedication and above all … with guts. There was only one man for a case like this…

FOUL FOOD REPORT by M I Gutzache

At last, some real detective work! Something undercover. I'd heard that school kitchens were clean places that were inspected regularly by public health officers. But this one was different. It proved a real dirty business. Stomach churning, in fact, but I got the pictures in the end.

Can you spot the germ danger signs in each picture?

Answers: 1 Hair can carry germs even when it's clean, so it's a bad idea to comb it in a kitchen because germ-laden dandruff and old skin could fall into the soup. **2** Hair not tied back or covered. An ideal way to leave greasy germ-laden hairs in the jelly. **3** Blowing on food to cool it. A wonderful way for germs to get from the mouth onto the food. You might as well dribble into it. **4** Dirty hands, fingernails and clothes, and not wearing overalls. If they touch food they'll pass on loads of germs. **5** Flies should be kept out of kitchen. On pain of death – to the flies that is! **6** Fridge door left open so the food isn't being kept cold. The cold should stop the germs from breeding so fast. **7** All kinds of food mixed up in the fridge so germs can slop and spill from raw meat to cooked meat where they will breed happily. **8** Litter bins overflowing and full of rotten food are a luxury hotel for germs to breed. **9** Cockroaches love slinking about in damp, dark places. And they're happy to pass on their germs when they investigate any food that's been left out. **10** Get that cat off the table! You might like Tiddles but you won't like her germs. Do you really want germ-encrusted cat fluff in your butter?

FRESH FOOD QUIZ

If cooks manage to get rid of bacteria they can keep food fresh for longer. Which of the following methods will work?

1 Boiling food and sealing it in an air-tight container.

2 Squashing the food and germs into a plastic box.

3 Mixing the food with lots of sugar or salt.

4 Smoking the food over a really smoky fire.

5 Sucking all the air out of the food so the bacteria can't breathe.

6 Freezing the food with the bacteria in it.

7 Drying the food out so the bacteria can't drink.

8 Spinning the food around really fast. The germs get so dizzy that they die.

Answers: 1 Yes. Any thorough heating, as in cooking, will kill bacteria. Keeping food in an air-tight container such as the cans you buy in a supermarket will stop bacteria from getting back in. **2 No.** The bacteria will still live and breed, and destroy the food. **3 Yes.** The sugar draws water from the food and the bacteria can't live without water. That's why jam doesn't go rotten. **4 Yes.** The smoke covers the food with chemicals such as nitrites that kill the bacteria. This is what keeps smoked fish such as kippers fresh. **5 Yes.** This is what happens when food is vacuum packed. The food will keep in this form for months. **6 Yes.** The cold kills the bacteria. That's why food stays fresh in the freezer. **7 Yes.** The bacteria can survive as tiny seeds called spores, but drying out stops them from being active. **8 No.** Bacteria don't get dizzy.

We've painted a pretty grim picture of the germ world and maybe we're being a bit unfair. After all, they're just doing what comes naturally – for a germ that is. And we can't get rid of germs altogether. There are different germs in different countries and some will always manage to get into our bodies. Then our bodies have to fight against the disgusting, deadly digestive diseases that are lurking in the next chapter. BEWARE!

DEADLY DIGESTIVE DISEASES

If there's something even more disgusting than digestion then it's the dreadful digestive diseases that germs can cause. There's a long, horrible list of them and many are not just disgusting, they're deadly, too. We asked our Private Eye M I Gutzache to compile a dossier on the worst villains. Gunge Street School was in trouble. More teachers and some children too were going down with dangerous diseases. The kitchens needed inspection, there were various germs under suspicion. Gutzache was ready for the job.

A DEADLY GERM DOSSIER

by MI Gutzache

They're a real mean bunch of no-good low-lifes. Even I was shocked at the things these guys get up to. I shuddered to think they were hiding out in the very school kitchen I'd visited. These germs hit the young and the old hardest. That's bad news for young kids and tired old teachers. These germs must be stopped before they close down the school.

NAME: Salmonella
KNOWN HAUNTS: A real shady character - hides out in raw meat and eggs. Its favourite bolt-holes are chicken guts. I saw a chicken in the fridge at Gunge Street. It didn't look too healthy.
ALIASES: Over 1,000 varieties - just take your pick.
KNOWN CRIMES: Causes repeated vomiting and diarrhoea. Responsible for hundreds of thousands of attacks all over the world. A killer.

NAME: Listeria
KNOWN HAUNTS: Soil, dung, dirty water, cheese, chicken or salads. I've got my doubts about the cheese at Gunge Street. It smelt kind of prehistoric. The germ's known to be at home at -5°C (24°F). So putting the cheese in the fridge won't do

much good. This character is tough - it can even
live at 42°C (106°F). If a human got that hot
they'd need a doctor fast.
KNOWN CRIMES: Causes violent sickness. These
germs could spoil your whole day.

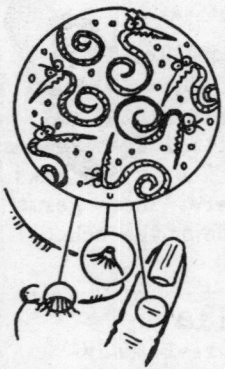

NAME: Staphylococcus
KNOWN HAUNTS: Nostrils, on
skin especially in cuts and
boils. The Gunge Street cooks
must have been crawling with
these germs. The germs hang out
on food that should be kept in
the fridge but that's been left
out too long. Like the awful-
smelling Gunge Street mince that
was left out mouldering for
three whole days.

MODE OF OPERATION: Gets on to food from un-
bandaged cuts on hands.
KNOWN CRIMES: Causes diarrhoea, vomiting and
painful cramps in the guts. These germs could spoil
your whole week.

NAME: Clostridium botulinum
CAUSES: Botulism
KNOWN HAUNTS: Soil, fish, meat
and vegetables.
MODE OF OPERATION: Thankfully no
one's seen this germ at Gunge Street.
KNOWN CRIMES: Botulism causes
double vision, weakness, difficulty
talking and . . . DEATH.
WEAPONS: The toxin produced by
this germ is deadly. Just 10mg
could poison every human on Earth.

Conclusion

These guys are bad news. They must be rounded up. But it's going to be a tough job. They're a big mob and they've got so many hideouts. There's just one weapon that'll get them beat — and that's cleanliness!

But some germs are much more deadly and hopefully we'll never come across these criminal characters in Gunge Street kitchens ...

USEFUL WEAPONS

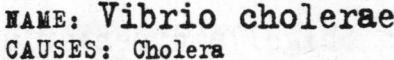

NAME: Vibrio cholerae
CAUSES: Cholera
KNOWN HAUNTS: Water mixed with faeces from another cholera sufferer.
MODE OF OPERATION: Gets into the body through eating shellfish that live in this dirty water. (Must be careful next time I eat oysters.) More usually spread by drinking the dirty water itself.

Drinking water sounded like a real dumb move. So I checked out the local water company and they said they had the problem sussed. They put chlorine in the water to blow the germs away.

KNOWN CRIMES: Causes violent vomiting, deadly diarrhoea and painful cramps. The victim's body dries out and turns blue. You could easily wake up to find yourself DEAD.

CHOLERA VICTIM

NAME: Salmonella typhi
CAUSES: Typhoid
KNOWN HAUNTS: The faeces of someone who has had the disease and survived. Typhoid is a relative of the notorious salmonella crime family.
MODE OF OPERATION: Gets around on dust or flies or dirty fingers.
KNOWN CRIMES: Causes a rash and a nasty cough. Turns the victim's faeces into a green and runny soup. If untreated it kills 20 per cent of its victims. Hey, that's nasty!

NAME: Shigella dysenteriae
CAUSES: Dysentery
KNOWN HAUNTS: The guts and faeces, dirty water and food.
KNOWN ALIASES: Can be caused by amoeba - the scientist guy says that's a microscopic blob-like animal. I'll take his word for it.
KNOWN CRIMES: Spreads from the guts to the liver and causes a deadly fever. It can even make holes in the gut.

Conclusion

I'm feeling sick. During my mission to the school kitchen I came over kind of hungry. Figured a piece of fruit wouldn't do any harm - now I've got pains in my gut and I'm feeling feverish. It's dysentry . . . I'm sure of it. ARGHH my guts! QUICK - where's the bathroom?

Over 1,000 years later one man was determined to stamp out the curse of dysentery and all the other deadly digestive diseases.

Hall of fame: Louis Pasteur (1822–1895)
Nationality: French

Louis Pasteur had embarrassing table manners. He would fiddle with his bread. He'd tear a slice into crumbs and inspect them for dust and wool and bits of cockroaches. If he found anything suspicious he would examine it at the table using a portable microscope. (Don't start getting ideas now!)

57

Next Pasteur would study the glasses. He'd wipe away tiny specks of dirt that no one else could see. And if that wasn't bad enough he'd launch into a loud and detailed account of his latest gruesome experiments with mice or bits of mashed-up body and germs. This was because Louis Pasteur was obsessed with germs. He was so desperate to keep germs off his hands that he wouldn't shake hands with anyone. But oddly enough Mrs Pasteur didn't complain about her husband's habits. She was his most devoted helper.

Louis Pasteur was the deadliest enemy the germ world ever had. He hunted germs like a determined cop hunts a master criminal. With a total and ruthless dedication he worked weekends and evenings – refusing to give up ever. But then Pasteur had every reason to hate germs. Two of his children had died of typhoid.

At school no one thought young Louis was especially clever. His teachers said he was "passable" at physics and "mediocre" at chemistry. But Louis stuck at his science studies and eventually became a Professor of Chemistry. These are just a few of his achievements:

• He proved that germs make wine and beer go sour. This work involved going to vineyards and sampling wines (all in the interests of science, of course). Pasteur discovered that if you heat liquids to 72°C (161°F) for a few seconds you can kill germs without spoiling the taste. He had invented pasteurisation – which is used today to stop your milk going off too quickly.

• He went on holiday leaving a mix of chicken cholera germs and broth. (Chickens suffer a different type of cholera to humans.) When he got back he found that many of the germs had died. He gave the mixture of weakened germs to some chickens and found they stayed healthy. The chickens' bodies had produced chemical defences against the dead germs that they could use to fight living germs. We call the dead germs a vaccine and it's what you get when you're vaccinated against a disease.

COME ON, DON'T BE A CHICKEN . . . I MEAN DON'T BE SCARED

• Pasteur went on to develop vaccines against the killer diseases anthrax and rabies. The rabies vaccine was particularly welcome because rabies *always* kills its victims. Trouble is, the rabies vaccine has to be delivered by painful injections, but at least the victim gets to live.

COULD YOU BE A SCIENTIST?

In 1860 Pasteur climbed a mountain carrying sealed flasks containing yeast extract broth and sugar. At 1,500 metres (5,000 feet) he opened the flasks and filled them with cold mountain air then re-sealed them. Pasteur believed that the broth would only go off if germs from the air could get to it. He had already filled other flasks with air from the top of one hill, then another higher hill, and a cellar. What were the results?

a) All the flasks showed the same amount of germs. This proved that germs are found at all heights.

b) The most germs were found up the mountain and on the higher hill. This is because the wind blows germs up in the air.

c) The most germs were on the lower hill. The least germs were found up the mountain and in the cellar.

Answer: c) Pasteur proved that germs spread on specks of dust. The cellar was well sealed so the dust couldn't get in easily and the mountain air had even less dust so there were fewer germs. The germs couldn't get into the sealed flasks and their contents stayed fresh. In fact, one of the flasks from 1860 is now a museum exhibit and the broth is still fresh ... anyone want to try it?

TYPHOID MARCHES ON...

Despite Pasteur's hard work he couldn't trace the deadly germ that had killed his children. The typhoid germ was eventually tracked down by Karl Joseph Eberth (1835–1926) in 1880. But the disease continued to claim lives. Edith Claypole (1870–1915), a talented American scientist, died of the disease in 1915. She was in the middle of a study of ... typhoid fever. And in 1909 doctors faced the killer disease again. Here are the facts in a story that tells how they might have happened.

TYPHOID MARY

New York, 1909

Mary Mallon was a killer and her lethal weapon was ice cream. Delicious, home-made ice cream. But could it really kill people? Guns or bombs, maybe – but ice cream?

And Mary didn't look dangerous. She was a shy woman of about 40 years of age with grey hair tied neatly in a bun. She wore small round spectacles and her plump figure seemed an excellent advertisement for her wholesome cooking. No wonder Dr George Soper felt confused as he stood in the kitchen in Park Avenue.

Surely Mary wouldn't harm a fly?

GOOD EVENING, DOCTOR SOPER

Then the doctor noticed Mary's hands. Big red raw hands that were used to hard kitchen work – hands that hadn't been washed in a week. They weren't just dirty – they were filthy. Every hollow and vein and knuckle was smeared with grime, and there was thick, black dirt under her fingernails.

"Well, sir, why did you want to see me?" she asked in her soft Irish voice. "I haven't got all day. The people here are taken badly. The daughter is dead and the servants are sick. I've lots to do."

The doctor pulled himself together. He had difficult and unpleasant things to say. "Mary Mallon, I have reason to believe you are spreading an infectious and fatal disease."

Mary didn't even blink. It was as if the doctor had said something about the weather.

"I don't know what you're talking about, sir," she said quietly.

"Let me explain," said the doctor. "Last year you worked as a cook at Oyster Bay, Long Island. Six people in that house fell sick with typhoid fever."

"So they got sick. People do – what's that to me?" asked Mary sounding a bit more annoyed.

"I talked to the family and I checked what they ate. The family all said they enjoyed eating ice cream. Your ice cream that you always make by hand."

Mary's mouth drooped crossly at the corners and she slowly pulled open a drawer under the table.

"You've had eight jobs in seven years," continued the doctor grimly. "And in seven of those eight houses there have been cases of typhoid fever."

Mary's filthy fingers groped for the meat cleaver.

"Mary," said the doctor coldly, "I think the typhoid was spread on your dirty hands."

"ARRRGGGGH!" With a banshee wail Mary threw herself on the doctor. She screamed in fury, "I'll learn ye. You meddling doctor – I'll chop ye up for sausages. I'll have ye for breakfast. I'LL KILL YE!"

Dr Soper leapt sideways just in time. The heavy cleaver hacked into the table top. He tore round the kitchen chased by Mary brandishing her weapon.

Dr Soper escaped and gasped out his story to New

York's Chief of Police. The police moved in swiftly. They raided Mary's house and found her hiding in an outside toilet. It took seven policemen to carry her shrieking and wailing to a waiting ambulance.

A few months later at the Riverside Hospital for Communicable Diseases in New York, Dr Soper sat in his office a little uneasily. The time had come for a talk with Mary. Or "Typhoid Mary" as the newspapers were now calling her.

"Typhoid is a terrible disease," began the doctor. "You get fever, spots, stomach pains, a cough and bowel movements that look like pea soup. But you'll remember all that, won't you Mary?"

"Why should I remember anything?" asked Mary grumpily. She glared up at Dr Soper's two hefty assistants who stood either side of her. Ready for the first sign of trouble.

Dr Soper sighed, "Our tests prove that you've had the disease. Although you got better, the germs are still in your gall bladder. They pass out of your body every time you visit the toilet. Some germs get on your hands and if you don't wash them they also get onto food."

"I don't understand," moaned Mary, "I'm a cook. I do me job but no one tells me nothing."

Then Dr Soper offered his reluctant patient a choice. She could give up cooking or she could stay locked up in the island hospital. For ever.

"You can't keep me here," protested Mary. "Why are you doing this to me?"

Dr Soper grimly shook his head. "Oh, but we can keep you here, Mary. We have the legal power. But you do have another choice. Allow us to cut out your gall-bladder. It's a risky operation, but you'll be free of germs after we've done it. And then we'll let you go."

"I'll kill ye!" spat Mary struggling with the two assistants. "I'll never let ye near me gall-bladder – whatever that is."

But three years later Mary had a change of heart. Not about the operation, though. She agreed to give up cooking and report to Dr Soper every three months. But after she left the hospital she promptly disappeared.

In 1915 an epidemic of typhoid fever hit New York's Sloane Hospital for Women. Two members of staff died. One morning the kitchen maid was having a laugh with a friend. "That old cook, Mrs Brown," she sniggered, "she's so grumpy and guess what? She looks just like that woman in the papers a few years ago. What's-her-name – Typhoid Mary!"

Listening at the door, the cook, who was really Mary Mallon, clenched her dirty fists in rage.

Once again Mary disappeared but this time the police were on her trail. She was arrested soon afterwards. Mary Mallon had knowingly spread typhoid and people had died. How do you think she was punished?

a) Mary Mallon was executed for murder. The judge said: "Mary, you are too dangerous to live."

b) Mary was drugged by Dr Soper and while she was unconscious he removed her gall bladder. When she was completely free of typhoid germs the doctors let her go.

c) Mary was never released. She was locked up on the island for the rest of her life.

Answer: c) Mary was never released. She was the first known carrier of typhoid fever and although she was never charged with a crime she was judged a menace to public health. In 1923 the doctors built her a cottage in the hospital grounds and gave her a job working in the hospital lab that studied germs – such as typhoid.

Today Mary Mallon is world famous as "Typhoid Mary." All she ever wanted to do was to make ice cream. But her name is linked for ever to a disease she never truly understood.

THE FIGHT GOES ON

Louis Pasteur's work showed scientists how to discover germs and how to develop new drugs and vaccines to combat them. Today doctors cure typhoid using drugs. Meanwhile, the world-wide battle against other diseases continues. For example, in the 1970s 4,000,000 children a year were dying of cholera. In 1974 World Health Organization scientists invented a drink made from clean water, minerals and sugar which can be given to cholera victims to stop them drying out. This simple drink, named ORT (oral re-hydration therapy), has saved the lives of thousands of children.

So that's the answer. If we can keep germs at bay we can all live happily ever after. Er, no. Here comes the really bad news. Eating clean food can make you ill! Some people even die from their diets! Will you be able to stomach the next chapter? Better read on and find out...

A HORRIBLY HEALTHY DIET

There's a lot more to food than meets the eye. There are loads of vital ingredients that you must have in your daily diet. To find out more we persuaded Private Eye M I Gutzache to sneak back into the school kitchens to collect samples. At first he said he couldn't face going back to that revolting place. But after a bit of bribery and gentle persuasion with a roll of banknotes he dragged himself off his sick bed.

GUTZACHE GOES INTO ... SCHOOL DINNERS

It was time for the protective suit. And I insisted on a gas mask for this dirty job. Some of the samples smelled kind of ancient. They were days old, and I figured they could be emetic. (Hey, I'm starting to talk like a scientist! An emetic is something that makes you sick as a dog.)

Sample 1 – A school potato
This rather sad potato was about to be boiled in a school dinner. But it was still a healthy specimen. This is what I found hiding inside it:
Slug*
81 per cent water
0.4 per cent protein
16 per cent carbohydrates
(in the form of a
chemical called starch)
0.1 per cent fat
0.8 per cent fibre
0.7 per cent vitamins
1 per cent minerals

Hi!

NOTES
The slug had no complaints

* The slug also contains these ingredients but in different amounts. At least this time it didn't get cooked with the potato.

Sample 2 - A glass of water

NOTES
Useful for washing taste of dinner away

STRAY PEA

GREASY FINGER PRINTS

It wasn't much to look at, but my investigation revealed that you need about two litres of this clear runny stuff every day. Half of this comes from water in your food (like the watery potato), and half from what you actually drink. You've got to top up your water supply 'cos your body is two-thirds water and bits such as your brain are 80 per cent water. So you know what'll happen if you don't drink enough of it – pea-brain!

Sample 3 - Jam pudding
This pudding is oozing with sticky sugar. It looked good enough to eat, but the news was bad.

SUGAR

NOTES
Just looking at it gave me toothache

The scientist guy says sugar gives you the energy your body needs but nothing else. He says I eat more sugar than my body needs. Seems there's enough sugar rolling around inside me to fill a jam jar. I was chewing a candy bar at the time. I put it down and decided I'd had enough sugar for one day. Only a scientist could spoil my appetite.

Sugar hangs out in loads of savoury foods, too – just a small tin of baked beans contains two to three teaspoonfuls of sugar. And you'll find it in cereals, tinned meat, soup, tinned vegetables, peanut butter and even coleslaw. Sweet foods have even more sugar – a chocolate bar has ten teaspoonfuls. Most of us probably get through 30 teaspoonfuls of sugar a day. Wow!

Sample 4 – Mashed swede

Hidden inside this strange and tasteless lump of orange vegetable I came across a strange and tasteless food chemical. It's called starch, a type of carbohydrate the same as I found in that potato. It's made out of sugar chemicals joined in a chain. The scientists say that inside your muscles enzymes can rip apart the sugar chemicals and free the energy to help your body move. Sounds good – why did it have to taste so bad?

Sample 5 – School dinner chips

The chips were cold and greasy and oozing with fat. They hang around in your stomach like a sack of cement. The fats stay down longer than most foods and at least they make you feel nice and full. But it seems spare fat turns into body fat slopping lazily around your stomach and backside. And get this - there's usually enough fat in your body at any one time to make seven bars of soap!

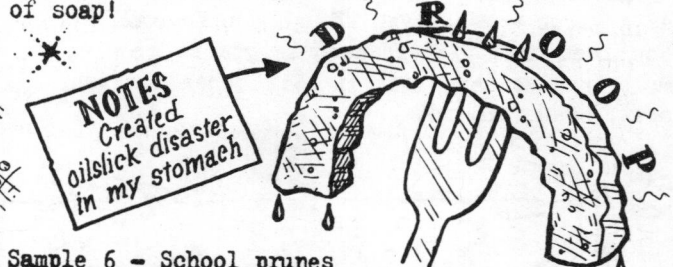

NOTES
Created oilslick disaster in my stomach

Sample 6 - School prunes

Hmm, prunes. Can't say I liked the taste, they had a weird kind of leathery texture. But my investigation showed that's 'cos they're loaded with fibre. That's the stuff that makes brown bread chewy and fruit and veg stringy. Seems your body can't digest fibre but it keeps the rest of your food moving in the gut. The gut walls can grip the fibre more easily than ordinary food. In the end this gets moving, too ... to the bathroom.

Sample 7 - Smelly cheese

NOTES
Relieved to find the smell wasn't from my socks

GHASTLY PONG

Some of the kids I interviewed had strange ideas about where the cheese came from. Well, I wasn't here to find out about its past - I was looking for the inside story and I found it. Cheese is

25 per cent protein – your body uses this substance to build muscles. Although your body is 20 per cent protein you don't need tonnes of the stuff. If you're 12 years old you need about 45 grams of protein a day. That's as much as a as a grown woman, even though you're smaller. You need more protein because you're growing. Protein also hangs out in milk, cheese, fish, meat, beans and nuts.

NOTES
I've sketched some useful sources of protein

Sample 8 – Suspect salt

All this suspect food had got to me. A cold bead of sweat trickled down my face. I tried to lick it off. Ugh – salt! Try it yourself – that's what sweat contains. We use salt for killing germs and, as I found, it comes in handy for disguising the vile taste of school dinners. There are 14,000 different uses for salt – but I've got a report to finish, so I'm not going to list them all here.

Salt is vital for many of the chemical reactions that go on in your body. Sweating is one way your body gets rid of any spare salt. But salt isn't the only mineral you've just gotta have.

MYSTERIOUS MINERALS

The school dinner samples were loaded with mysterious minerals. They're vital in tiny amounts for building your body and making useful chemicals.

You might be amazed to learn that your school dinner contains all these strange and foul-smelling chemicals. Oh – you aren't? Well, your teacher might be...

TEST YOUR TEACHER

Try testing your teacher or even your school cook (if you dare) on this fascinating topic.

1 Sulphur is a foul-tasting chemical but it makes up 0.25 per cent of your body. How much sulphur is that?
a) Enough to kill all the fleas on a dog.
b) Enough to kill all the fleas on an elephant.
c) Enough to kill all the fleas on a rat.
2 Iron is a vital mineral that your body uses to give blood it's brilliant red colour. What happens when you don't eat enough?
a) Your blood turns yellow.
b) You come out in spots and a fever.
c) You become pale and tired and don't feel like eating.

3 Your body is 0.004 per cent iron (lucky it doesn't rust!). How much iron is that?

a) Enough to make the head of a pin.

b) Enough to make a 5-cm nail.

c) Enough to make an iron lump the size of your arm bone.

4 Calcium is a vital raw material for bones. A 12-year-old child needs 700 mg of calcium a day. What's that equal to?

a) Four plates of spinach.

b) 40 plates of spinach. (Yuck!)

c) No spinach because this vegetable doesn't contain calcium.

5 What's the best source of iodine?

a) Rainwater

b) Snails

c) Seaweed

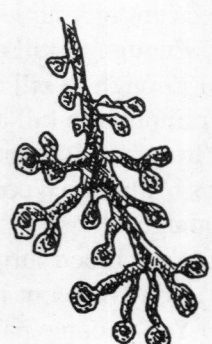

Answers: 1 a) That is if your dog has fleas, of course!
Warning: don't eat too much sulphur or it won't just be
the fleas that get bumped off. **2 c)** The red bit in blood
is a chemical that takes vital oxygen around your body.
Lack of iron causes anaemia (a-nee-me-a). If you don't
eat anything the anaemia gets worse. **3 b)** But that's no
excuse to start sucking rusty old nails. No – it's much
easier to get your iron from liver, wholemeal bread,
dried fruit or treacle. **4 a)** You'll find the same amount
of calcium in three glasses of milk, 16 large slices of
bread or 85 g of cheese. Take your pick. **5 c)** Iodine is
the most amazing mineral of the lot. Read on to find
out why...

GETTING IT IN THE NECK

You only need 0.004 grams of iodine every day. But
without it life is a pain in the neck. Here's why.

Iodine comes from the sea – that's why seaweed has so
much of it. The iodine gets blown inshore as sea spray
and collects on plants.

You eat them. A special part of your neck called the
thyroid gland uses the iodine to make a chemical called
thyroxine (thi-rox-een). Thyroxine makes your body
grow and use up food faster.

IS YOUR THYROID GLAND SWOLLEN?

NO, I'M CHOKING ON A PING PONG BALL, YOU TWIT!

75

Without enough iodine the thyroid gland swells up as it tries to filter every last drop of the mineral from your blood. It forms a hideous lump called a goitre (goy-ter).

In the 1800s part of the mid-west USA furthest from the sea was known as the "goitre belt". There was less iodine there so, of course, more people developed goitres.

You'll find lots of iodine in seafood, fish and, of course, seaweed (if you can face eating it).

COULD YOU BE A SCIENTIST?

This disgusting experiment is common in university science courses. The aim is to show how thyroxine works. Take one harmless little bull-frog tadpole. It can take up to two years to turn into a frog. Feed it one drop of thyroxine. What happens next?

a) The tadpole turns into a frog.

b) The tadpole turns into a giant tadpole.

c) The tadpole grows a goitre.

Answer: a) Within a few hours the thyroxine turns the tadpole into a tiny frog the size of your little fingernail. Sadly, when the other tadpoles become frogs they're 100 times bigger. And given half a chance they'll gobble up their tiny brother or sister.

VITAL VITAMINS

Vitamins aren't an optional extra. They're vital chemicals that keep you healthy. They're so important that you can buy lots of different pills and drinks that aim to provide extra vitamins. The adverts are everywhere:

Vit·A

Carrot-cocktail-Slurp

Do you suffer from spots? Having trouble shaking off the dandruff? Can't see in the dark? You could be missing out on vitamin A. Vit A Carrot-Cocktail-Slurp is the obvious answer.

BEFORE

AFTER

Just one slurp and you'll be spotting black cats in coal cellars! Yes that lovely vitamin A makes a chemical called visual purple at the back of the eye, so helping your eyes to see better in poor light.

THE SMALL PRINT
You CAN get too much of a good thing. Drink too much Vit A Vita-Slurp and your hair will fall out and you could die. Yes DIE. Too much vitamin A can poison you which is why people can die if they eat a vitamin A-rich polar-bear liver.

Ingredients: extract of liver, milk, butter, eggs, fish and carrots.*

*That's why people say that carrots help you see in the dark.

77

Vit B

Drink Vita-Slurp
A brand new range of vitamin drinks.
A slurp-a-day keeps the doctor away!

Get-up-and-go-Slurp

Tired and run-down? You need Vit B Get-up-and-go-Slurp! Why not try all eight mouth-watering varieties?

"B3" "B5" "B6" "B7"

"B2"   "B8"

B1   "B12"

BEFORE   **AFTER**

Just one slurp and you'll be back on your feet. Yes, these vital vitamins help your body turn food into energy. Healthy nerves and blood guaranteed.

Ingredients: extracts of wholemeal bread, yeast extract, milk, nuts and fresh vegetables.

THE SMALL PRINT
Lack of vitamin B5 makes a rat's fur go grey. But humans go grey anyway. And not even Vita-Slurp can stop it.

78

Vit D
Sunny-Slurp

▶ Do your fingernails break at awkward moments?

▶ Are you getting enough vitamin D a day?

▶ One slurp of Vit D Sunny-Slurp and you'll be D-LIGHTED!

FANTASTIC!

Your tough fingernails will be the envy of your friends and you'll be proud of your strong bones and gleaming healthy teeth. Ingredients: Extracts of oil from a cod's liver, milk and cheese.*

THE SMALL PRINT
Don't let the delicious taste of this Slurp make you drink too much. Overdose on Vit D and you'll be sick and constipated (unable to produce poo).

*The body also makes vitamin D from the sunlight that falls on the skin.

Vit E
Suppleskin-Slurp

Drink Vita-Slurp
A brand new range of vitamin drinks.
A slurp-a-day keeps the doctor away!

BEFORE

AFTER!

Do you have tired sagging skin? Are there strange brown marks, or liver spots, on your hands? You need a shot of Vit E Suppleskin-Slurp. In no time you'll be glowing with good health and your body cells and blood system will heal damage more quickly.

Ingredients: extracts of vegetable oils, nuts and cereals.

> **THE SMALL PRINT**
> Some people have baths in Vit E Suppleskin-Slurp in a bid to stay young-looking. But this is going too far – it doesn't work – sorry!

Vit K
Kwik-clot Slurp

Drink Vita-Slurp
A brand new range of vitamin drinks.
A slurp-a-day keeps the doctor away!

Are you having trouble with clots? (No, not stupid people – we mean *blood* clots.) When you cut yourself, do you just keep bleeding? Essential for those more serious wounds, Vit K Kwik-clot Slurp will help your blood to clot-a-lot, so it stays where it belongs – that's inside your body, and not all over the carpet!

Ingredients: extracts of green vegetables and liver, and germs from the human gut!

IT'S SO ANNOYING!

BUT NOT ANY MORE

OK – got the message? Missing out on vitamins makes you sick. But it took doctors many years to discover which foods were the best sources of which vitamins. Here's the story of one man's search for the truth about the most horrible sickness of all – scurvy.

THE TERROR OF THE SEA

Stinking bad breath, swollen purple gums, easy bruising, wounds not healing, bleeding eyeballs, tiredness and death. Yep. Scurvy was no picnic. A few hundred years ago you could walk round any port and spot the sickly seafarers a mile off. They were the ones with no teeth.

But why did sailors suffer from scurvy more than other people? For sailors in the 18th and early 19th centuries it wasn't just the sea that was rough, life on board ship was pretty rough, too. Conditions were really grim and scurvy used to be the terror of the sea. Sailors feared catching scurvy more than shipwrecks, pirates or shark attacks. But for years no one knew what caused this terrible disease.

But some captains thought they knew…

And, of course, the captains had their favourite cures…

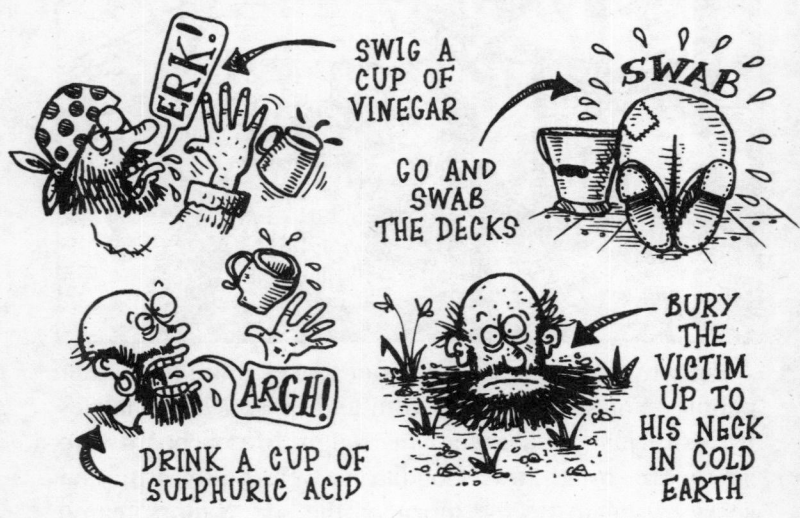

Ship's doctor James Lind (1716–1794) felt sure these cures were useless. But he had to prove it. He reckoned that the disgusting food on board ship was part of the problem. In the days before fridges and freezers it was impossible to keep food fresh at sea. So a typical meal looked like this.

1 HARD TACK AND MAGGOTS.*

2 WATER THAT STANK LIKE A BLOCKED TOILET.

3 STALE CHEESE WITH MORE MAGGOTS.

4 SALTY BACON.**

5 GREASY RANCID BUTTER

*A dried biscuit so hard that a London museum has a 200-year-old example. You had to tap your hard tack before you ate it to get the maggots out.

**It was so salty that it made you thirsty enough to drink the disgusting water.

But which of these foul foods caused scurvy? Or maybe as the food was so horrible, the seafarers were missing out on something in their diet. Perhaps they were getting the disease because of something they *weren't* eating.

HMS Salisbury, somewhere in the English Channel, 1747.

It's so frustrating. Here I am with 12 sailors sick with scurvy. I'm sure they're missing something in their diet - but what? I can't watch them die - I'm the doctor, I've got to try something. I'll have to experiment. I've always wanted to be a scientist. I'll divide the sailors into pairs and get each pair to try a cure suggested by other doctors. One of them has to work! Here goes!!

Sailors Walker Planke and Spike de Gunn will get a few drops of sulphuric acid a day. (Note: Mustn't make it too strong or it'll dissolve their guts.)

I'll give Davy Jones-Locker and Andy Cutlass two spoonfuls of vinegar a day.

I'll give Wilby Sicke and Len Ho a cup of seawater a day.

Jim Ladd and Roger Jolly will eat garlic and horseradish bound together with smelly plant glue.

84

Chivers Metimbers and Downey Hatch will get a daily quart of cider. Our two stowaway female crew members Eve Too and Raisa Anchor will each get two oranges and a lemon a day.

Fourteen days later

Eve and Raisa are cured! I'm brilliant! (Shame about the others, though.) The girls leapt out of their hammocks on the sixth day and raced each other round the ship. They said they hated all that nasty sour fruit but felt much better anyway. They've offered to help me nurse the other ten who are still sick.

1 Poor Walker and Spike are in a bad way. I feel a bit sorry for them. They've still got scurvy and now they've got raging gut ache, too. Must be all that acid.

2 Davy and Andy are in a sour mood. That'll be the vinegar. And they've still got scurvy.

85

3 Poor Wilby and Len keep throwing up. Must be all that seawater. They've still got the scurvy.

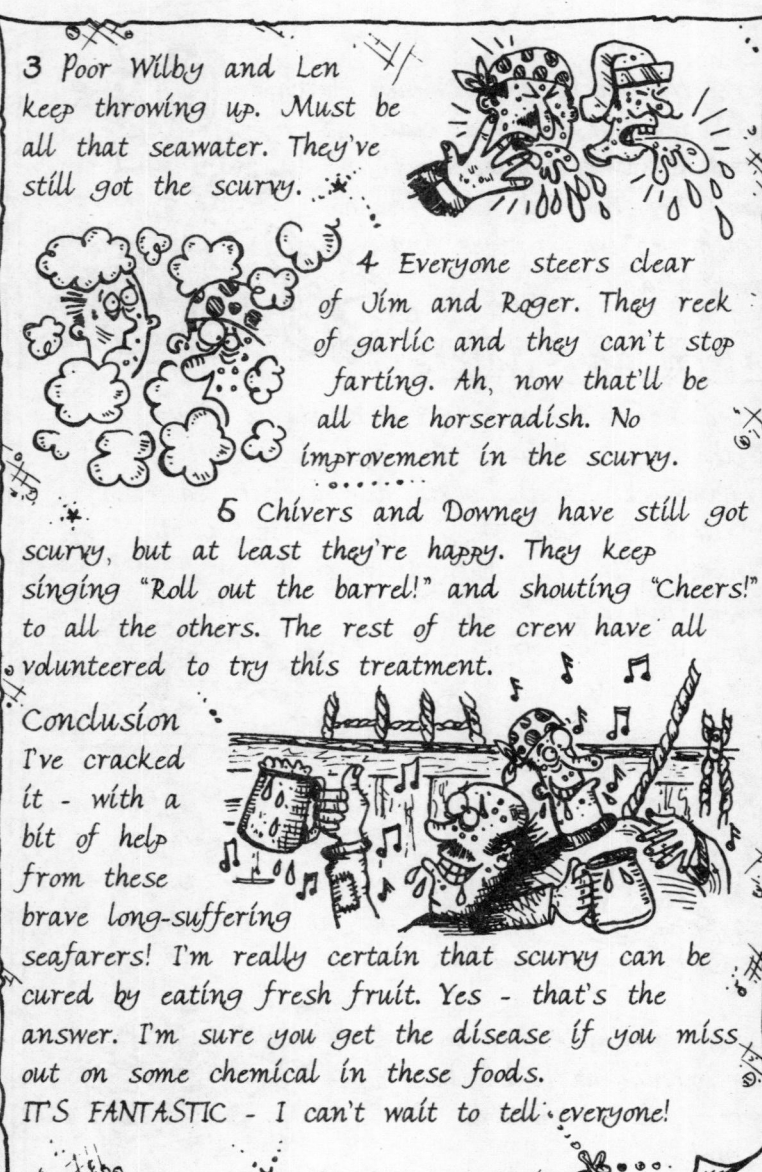

4 Everyone steers clear of Jim and Roger. They reek of garlic and they can't stop farting. Ah, now that'll be all the horseradish. No improvement in the scurvy.

5 Chivers and Downey have still got scurvy, but at least they're happy. They keep singing "Roll out the barrel!" and shouting "Cheers!" to all the others. The rest of the crew have all volunteered to try this treatment.

Conclusion

I've cracked it - with a bit of help from these brave long-suffering seafarers! I'm really certain that scurvy can be cured by eating fresh fruit. Yes - that's the answer. I'm sure you get the disease if you miss out on some chemical in these foods.

IT'S FANTASTIC - I can't wait to tell everyone!

James Lind sent his report to Admiral Lord Anson (1697–1762) who was in charge of the Royal Navy. He thought Anson would support him. After all when Anson sailed round the world in 1740–1744 most of his crew had died of scurvy. So what happened next?

a) Lord Anson was impressed. Lind was given a £20,000 reward and in future all seafarers were ordered to eat a lemon a day. No one got scurvy ever again.

b) The Navy ignored Lind's findings and it took another 40 years before they took action.

c) The Navy decided that the acid treatment was better. Lind was sacked from his job as a nuisance and a trouble-maker.

Answer: b) Disgusting but true. The Navy decided that lemons were too expensive. They actually felt it was cheaper to hire new sailors to replace the ones who died. Things only changed after the sailors mutinied and demanded lemons to beat scurvy. Although some sailors didn't like the fruit they changed their minds when lemons and limes were added to their rum ration. But it wasn't until the 1930s that scientists found the mystery chemical that prevented scurvy was ascorbic acid – better known as vitamin C.

A DISGUSTING DIET

So, eat lots of different foods and you'll get everything your body needs to stay healthy. Brilliant! But what happens if you are vegetarian and don't eat meat or fish? Or if you're vegan and don't eat meat, fish or foods made by animals such as milk and eggs? Either way it's fine as long as you get the vitamins and minerals you need.

But eat just a few things and you won't get all the vital goodies. The most disgusting diet of all is not to eat anything. Surprise! Food is good for you, hunger is bad for you. Scientists have found that children who miss breakfast find it hard to learn new things at school. Don't try this excuse. And just look what happens to a really starving body...

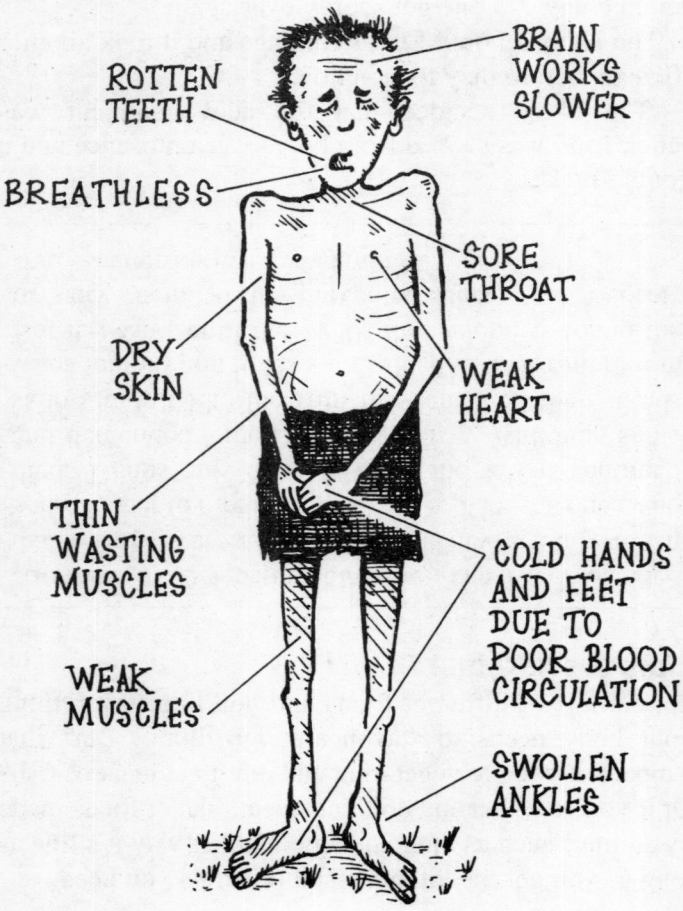

Miserable, isn't it? In the bad old days hunger was a cheap way of punishing naughty children.

Luckily, you're equipped with the perfect gear to chomp any kind of food. The next chapter will really give you something to chew over.

THE MIGHTY MOUTH

Shovel food in your gob and something disgusting happens. Your food, even the stringiest steak and crunchiest carrots, turn into a shredded gooey pulp before vanishing for ever down the black hole of your throat. So what's going on? Get your teeth into these amazing facts.

Dare you discover ... what's in your mouth?

Stand in front of mirror. Open wide. Go on – take a look – it won't bite you. What do you see? An amazing chewing machine – that's what.

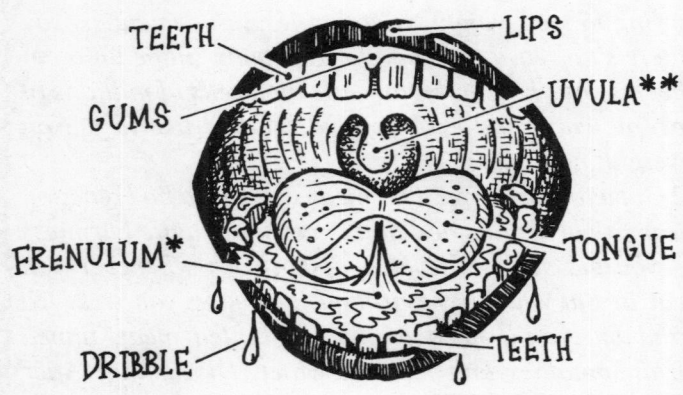

*This supplies your tongue with blood. Can you see the blood vessels? Pretty, aren't they? Well, pretty disgusting really.

**This little dangling bit hangs around in the throat and no one knows quite what it's for. It seems to help you swallow and its name means "little grape" in Latin – can you see why?

THE TALENTED TONGUE

The tongue is a lump of muscle. You can take a good look at it in the mirror, it's one part of your digestive system you can actually see, but don't go showing it to headteachers, parents, etc. Your talented tongue is amazingly agile. It moves around while you eat, talk or even eat and talk at the same time.

Disgusting digestion fact file

NAME: Taste

THE BASIC FACTS: Your tongue is covered in tiny bumps called papillae (pap-pill-ay). Can you see them? On their sides are even tinier clumps called taste buds. Your brilliant buds pick up tastes and send the info. along nerves straight to your brain.

I FEEL SICK AND DIZZY - IS IT THE MONOSODIUM GLUTAMATE IN THIS MEAL?

EITHER THAT OR THE SLUGS

THE HORRIBLE DETAILS: There's a chemical called monosodium glutamate (mon-o-so-di-um gloo-ta-mate) that boosts your sense of taste. It's found in some Chinese recipes. But it makes some people feel sick and dizzy.

SOME TASTELESS FACTS

1 In traditional Chinese medicine there were five tastes – bitter, salty, sweet, sour and spicy.

2 Modern scientists more or less agree. They say you can detect five tastes – sweet, sour, salty, bitter and umami. This is a sort of meaty, savoury sensation – just think of burgers, yum!

3 But your tongue can recognize hundreds of flavours made up of a mixture of tastes. Take crisps, for example. There are over 70 flavours including chocolate, strawberry, and hedgehog*. (It's true – manufacturers really did make crisps in these foul flavours.)

ER, WEASEL AND ONION. OR IS IT TOAD AND VINEGAR?

* Before you get on the phone to the World Wide Fund for Nature, they don't use any dead hedgehogs – this is an entirely man-made flavour.

4 Some people have sensitive taste buds. Cheese experts can sample a really smelly cheese and tell exactly where the cheese was made, whether the milk that made it was heated, and even what time the cow was milked. But if they're wrong they can get a bit cheesed off.

5 A doctor always looks at your tongue to check your state of health. For example, a thick white scum on your tongue might be caused by a disgusting infection called thrush (nothing to do with tweety-birds that eat worms).

6 In ancient China doctors peered at tongues too. They believed that the appearance of the tongue reflected the health of the rest of the body. Here are a few things they looked for...

a) Whitish tongue = lack of energy.

b) Bright red tongue = body is too hot.

c) Purple/blue tongue or purple spots = blood not moving fast enough.

d) Fur-like growth* on the tongue = death will follow within a week.

*This could really be a sign the body is unwell. The "fur" may be a type of fungus which flourishes when the body's defences, the white blood cells, are weakened by other diseases.

Here are two experiments that are in the best possible taste.

Dare you discover 1... Test your taste

You will need:
2 small cubes of uncooked potato
2 small cubes of apple

What you do:
1 Close your eyes and hold your nose. Ask someone to hand you one of the foods.
2 Put the food in your mouth and try to guess what you're eating. Now try the other food.
3 Stop holding your nose and repeat step 2. What do you notice?
a) It's easier to make out tastes when you hold your nose.

b) It's harder to make out tastes when you hold your nose.

c) Foods taste sweeter when you hold your nose.

Dare you discover 2... Can you change your sense of taste?

You will need:

Your favourite wine gums or fruit-flavoured sweets. (Tell your parents you need them for science homework – if they believe that, you might as well go for extra pocket money while you're at it.)

2 extra extra strong mints or an ice cube. Put it in a glass of water for a few seconds first.

Don't put an ice cube straight from the freezer into your mouth. The freezing cold ice cube might actually freeze the outside of your tongue and make it sore.

What you do:

1 Pop the extra strong mints OR the ice cube in your mouth. Keep it there until it melts.

2 Pop the wine gum in your mouth. What do you notice?

a) You can't taste it easily.

b) It tastes twice as fruity.

c) When you take it out of your mouth it's gone black.

94

Disgusting digestion fact file

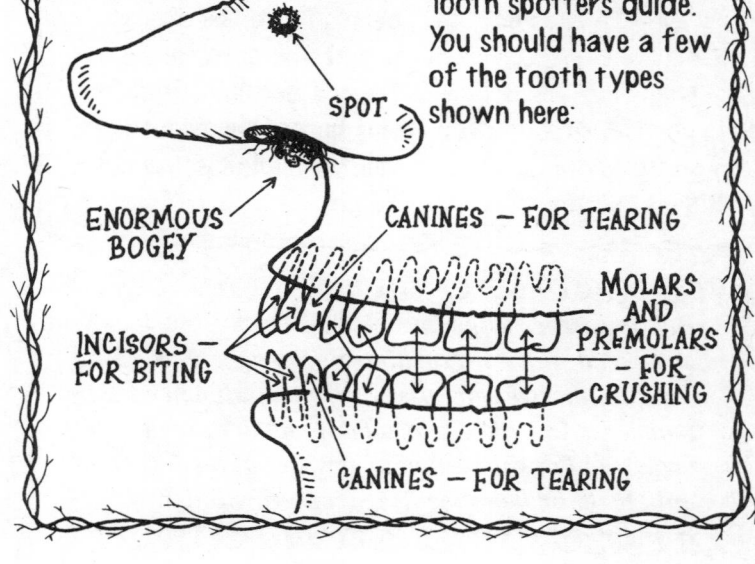

NAME: Teeth

THE BASIC FACTS: Tooth spotters guide. You should have a few of the tooth types shown here:

SPOT

ENORMOUS BOGEY

CANINES – FOR TEARING

INCISORS – FOR BITING

MOLARS AND PREMOLARS – FOR CRUSHING

CANINES – FOR TEARING

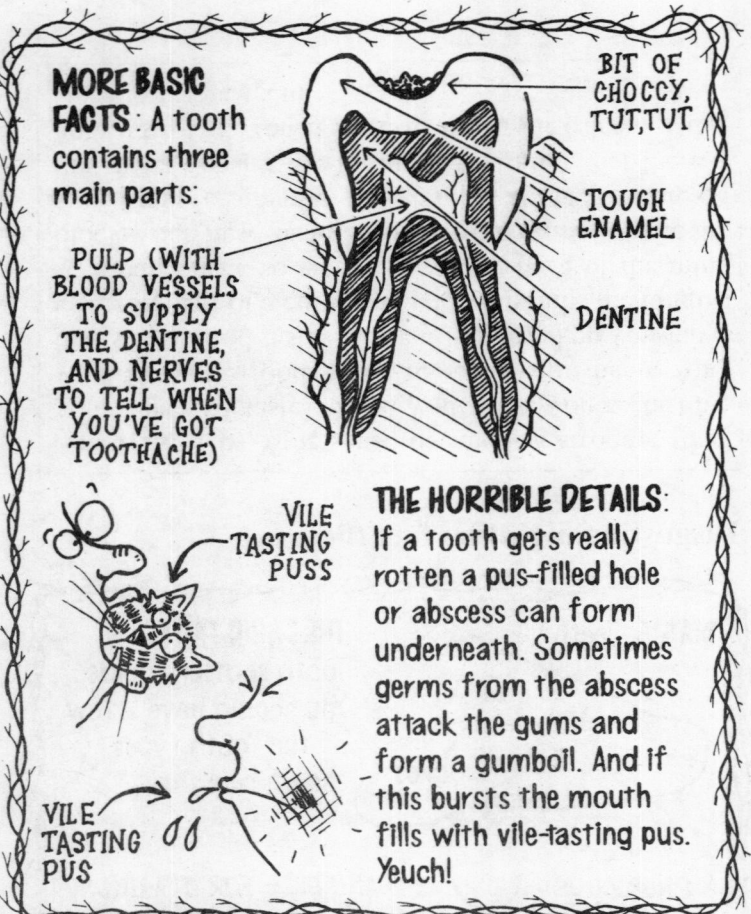

MORE BASIC FACTS: A tooth contains three main parts:

PULP (WITH BLOOD VESSELS TO SUPPLY THE DENTINE, AND NERVES TO TELL WHEN YOU'VE GOT TOOTHACHE)

BIT OF CHOCCY, TUT, TUT

TOUGH ENAMEL

DENTINE

VILE TASTING PUSS

VILE TASTING PUS

THE HORRIBLE DETAILS: If a tooth gets really rotten a pus-filled hole or abscess can form underneath. Sometimes germs from the abscess attack the gums and form a gumboil. And if this bursts the mouth fills with vile-tasting pus. Yeuch!

Bet you never knew!
Your teeth have a crushing power of about 73 kg – that's the weight of one of your slimmer male teachers! You have two sets of teeth. Your new set grows and pushes out your first set of teeth (called milk teeth or baby teeth) as you grow older.

But that's nothing…

• Elephants have 24 molar teeth and they're replaced six times. When the last set of teeth falls out the elephant starves.

POOR OLD THING! IT'LL BE PORRIDGE FROM NOW ON

• Crocodiles grow new teeth whenever they need them. This could be handy for humans, too. You could grow extra teeth to handle all those rubbery school dinners.

I'VE GROWN MINE TO HANDLE RUBBERY SCHOOL CHILDREN

• Some sharks' teeth get replaced every eight days – that's 30,000 teeth in a shark lifetime.

B-B-BUT YOU MIGHT LOSE SOME TEETH IF YOU BITE INTO MY RUBBER SUIT…

SO WHAT?

DREADFUL DENTURES

Humans only get two sets of teeth and when these fall out we're stuck. That's why millions of people have to wear false teeth or dentures. Nowadays these are made from a tough plastic but before then people had to make do with some really disgusting dentures. Here are a few examples…

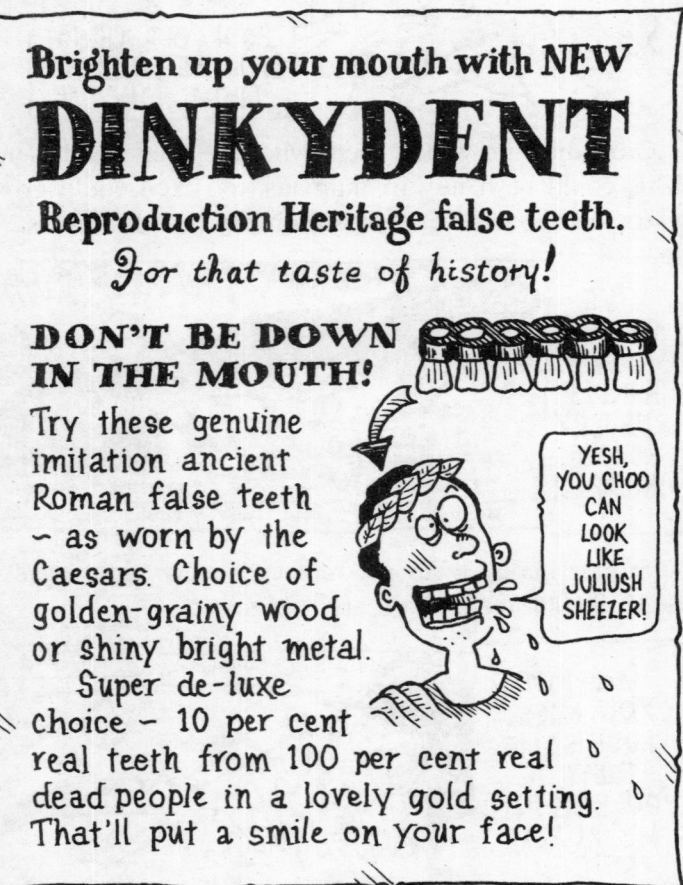

Brighten up your mouth with NEW

DINKYDENT

Reproduction Heritage false teeth.

For that taste of history!

DON'T BE DOWN IN THE MOUTH!

Try these genuine imitation ancient Roman false teeth – as worn by the Caesars. Choice of golden-grainy wood or shiny bright metal.

Super de-luxe choice – 10 per cent real teeth from 100 per cent real dead people in a lovely gold setting. That'll put a smile on your face!

YESH, YOU CHOO CAN LOOK LIKE JULIUSH SHEEZER!

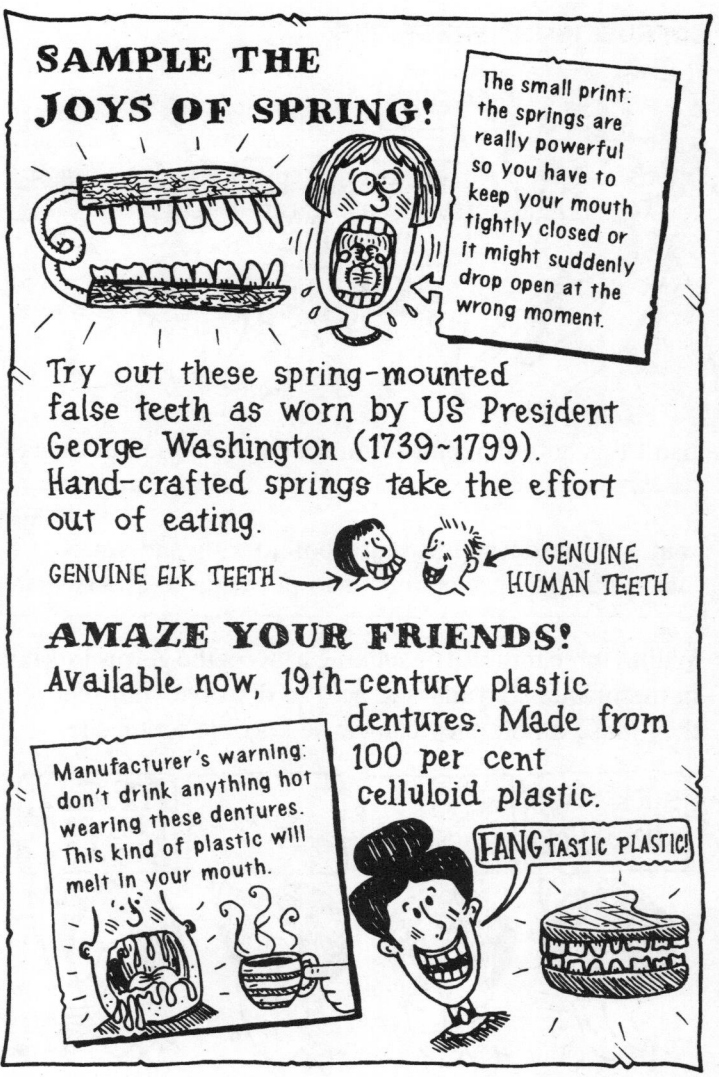

Of course, you'd probably rather not have false teeth. So it's a good idea to take care of the ones you've got.

DISGUSTING EXPRESSIONS

Isn't this an ornamental sign found in public buildings?

Answer: No, this kind of plaque is a disgusting layer of germs and bits of food that builds up around the teeth.

Within three minutes of sucking a sweet the germs lurking in the plaque start making acid to dissolve your teeth. If they make a hole they can cause horrible toothache.

Here are some disgusting ideas to help for making a clean sweep of the problem.

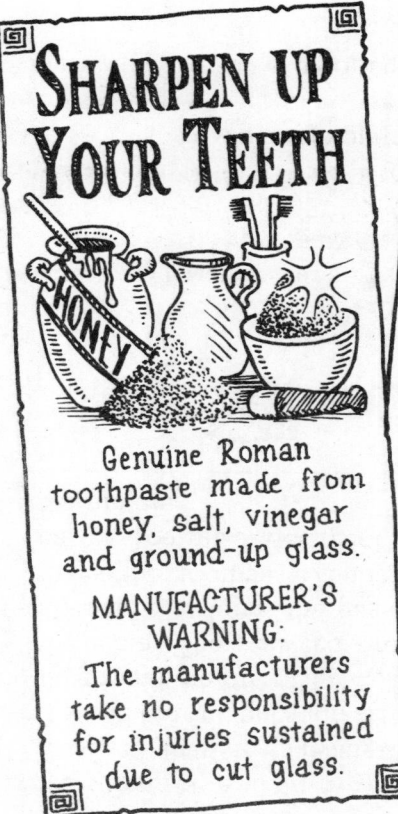

SHARPEN UP YOUR TEETH

Genuine Roman toothpaste made from honey, salt, vinegar and ground-up glass.

MANUFACTURER'S WARNING:
The manufacturers take no responsibility for injuries sustained due to cut glass.

A toothy red letter ~ day ~

Tasteful Victorian toothpaste. Original and unique recipe including ground-up coral and cuttlefish, burnt eggshells, bits of china and cochineal (made from powdered insects). Guaranteed to turn your teeth a pleasing purple colour.

And here are some more sensible ideas.
• Flossing teeth cleans out germs lurking between teeth and near gums – some of their favourite hiding places.
• Chewing a sugar-free chewing gum makes you produce spit. Spit contains chemicals that help combat the acid made by tooth germs, and so helps to keep your teeth clean.
But don't do either of these in science lessons. Instead, you could try this…

TEACHER'S TOOTH TEST

Does your teacher know the tooth – er, sorry, the truth about teeth? Find out now as you ask…

1 How many teeth does a child of ten have?

a) About 52

b) About 12

c) About 26

2 Which of the following isn't a raw material of modern toothpastes?

a) Chalk

b) Seaweed

c) Washing-up liquid

> **Answers: 1 a)** With a bit of luck your teacher will fall for this one. Although they're not all on display, a child of ten should have grown-up teeth hidden under their first set. And when you take a bite the vibration makes all these teeth twang slightly like guitar strings. **2** Another trick question. They're *all* used. The chalk is ground up to make a fine powder that cleans the teeth. The seaweed provides a chemical called alginate that binds the paste together. The detergent gives the toothpaste bubbles and makes cleaning easier. Too much detergent and you'd be foaming at the mouth.

SUPER-SLURPING SPIT

Picture your favourite food. A giant pizza with your favourite topping and hot bubbling cheese. Sizzling juicy burgers or crispy fried chicken and a giant pile of fries. Can't you smell that lovely just-cooked aroma? Are you drooling yet? You should be. Just thinking about food makes your mouth water – and the smell and sight of food helps even more. Your spit is ready and waiting to come out whenever you need it.

Spit is made by six salivary glands – two under your tongue, two under your jaw and two under your ears. When you get mumps the salivary glands under your ear get infected by a virus and swell up so your face looks fat. But cheer up face-ache – help is at hand...

Ye Olde Mumps Cure

1 Take a donkey's lead and put it around the patient's neck.

2 Lead them three times round a pig sty.

After that embarrassing experience you probably wouldn't care about having a swollen face. Every day your sensational salivary glands squirt out 1–1.5 litres of spit. All of this you swallow. Some people spit it out instead – disgusting! Don't do it. It's a waste of good spit – look what it can do for you.

Have you ever eaten really dry food, like bread, when your mouth is also dry and there's nothing to drink? Disgusting, isn't it? By making your food wet, spit makes it easier to swallow. And spit helps you taste food. You can only taste food by detecting chemicals floating around in water. When food is dry its chemicals can't flow amongst the taste-buds so it seems tasteless.

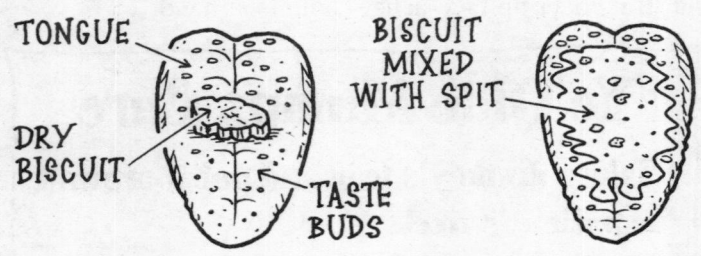

Spit has some disgusting ingredients, such as mucus – basically the same stuff that streams from your nose when you have a cold. This makes it quite slimy and stringy so you can suck it back into your mouth. There's no need to demonstrate this interesting scientific accomplishment just now.

Then there are the germs. Your spit is swarming with them. In fact, there could be 15,000,000,000 (15 billion) bacteria in your mouth at any one time. Many germs end up getting eaten when you swallow spit. Hmm, tasty! But strangely enough, spit contains chemicals that kill some germs, and dentists have found that spit helps to keep your mouth clean and free from infection.

Spit also contains a waste product called urea that your body makes from spare protein. And guess what? You'll find it in urine too – it gives urine its yellow colour. If you eat too much protein your body makes more urea and your spit also turns yellow. Either that or you've been slurping extra thick banana milkshakes. But the real magic spit ingredient is an enzyme called amylase (am-me-laze) that helps to rip carbohydrates into the sugars that make them up. (You can find out more about enzymes on page 127.)

DISGUSTING EATING HABITS
Mealtimes used to be tough for kids.

One of the worst things to do when you're eating is to eat too quickly. Like these people...

FAST FOOD FACTS

• Do you like pickled onions? If you find them disgusting you'll be horrified to hear that Pat Donahue crunched 91 in 68 seconds in Victoria, Canada in 1978.

106

• Peter Dowdeswell ate 144 prunes in 31.27 seconds in Rochester, New York, in 1986. Prunes are full of fibre and are well known for making you want to go to the toilet. So you can guess what the next world record was...

AH YES, CERTAINLY SIR. YOU'LL FIND THEM OVER BY THE...

• In the same year Peter also ate 91.44 metres of spaghetti in 12 seconds in Halesowen, Britain.
And then ... well you can guess what happened next.

DISGUSTING DIGESTION EXPRESSIONS

GLASS OF LEMONADE?

NO, THANK YOU, IT CAUSES ERUCTATION

Is this dangerous?

BIGGER, BETTER BURPS

Huge hearty great burps are just your body's way of getting rid of some of the air you swallowed with your food. The faster you eat and the more you talk as you eat the more you burp. It's easier to burp when you're standing up. So imagine a posh party where people are eating and talking, and drinking fizzy drinks (with lots of gas) and standing up, too. They all want to burp but they're far too polite.

By the way, if you ever go to lunch in Arabia it's OK to burp loudly after the meal. It's considered a sign of good manners. This is sensible because you've got to let the air out somehow.

CONGRATULATIONS! You've managed to eat your supper without hiccups, heartburn, burping or food dribbling out of your nostrils. NOW for the tricky bit. Can you keep it down?

THE STAGGERING STOMACH

You're in control. You decide what you eat, don't you? Think again. There's a part of your body that seems to have a mind of its own. It's a muscular bag just under the left part of your chest. It makes you feel sick, it makes you feel queasy and it rumbles. And it does a whole load of other tricks, too … it's staggering!

Disgusting digestion fact file

NAME: Stomach

THE BASIC FACTS: The stomach is a storage tank for your food. Its job is to mix and squash food to make it easier to digest. The stomach also makes enzymes that help to digest protein. And it does all this while you get on with your life.

THE HORRIBLE DETAILS: The stomach is staggeringly horrible. For example, there's a type of germ that lives quite happily in the stomach eating up your half-digested food.

GOOD OLD STOMACH!

RUMBLE CHURN, GURGLE, PLOP!

STAGGERING STOMACH STATISTICS

The human stomach can hold up to 1.5 litres of food.
   Mind you, that's nothing.
• It takes your speedy stomach just 60 minutes to digest a cup of tea and a jam sandwich.

• Milk, eggs and meat take a bit longer. Eat a boiled egg with a ham sandwich washed down with a milk-shake and it'll take 3–4 hours to clear your stomach.

• But if you really want your stomach to work harder try a huge three-course dinner with soup and meat, and fruit for afters. That'll take your tired-out tum 6–7 hours to process.

HURRY UP, STOMACH

I'M GOING AS FAST AS I CAN

• A wolf's stomach can hold 4.5 litres of food. Does that mean they have to "wolf" their meals?

• Cow stomachs can hold 182 litres of food – that's enough to fill a bath if the cow sicked it up again. (Cows have an advantage – they actually have four stomachs not one.) One stomach is used for storing the grass before they sick it up and re-chew it – lovely! This is known as "chewing the cud" – or rumination (roo-min-ay-shun) as the scientists call it. The other stomachs are useful for storing the re-chewed grass whilst it rots. (Rotten grass is easier to digest.) Yum-yum!

GRASS IN

GRASS OUT (COWPAT)

• The mangrove monkey eats leaves all day. It needs an extra-big tum to hold all those leaves and its stomach weighs as much as the rest of its body. If you had a stomach this big you really would be staggering.

STAGGERING STOMACH QUIZ

How well do you know your own stomach?

1 The word stomach comes from the Greek word for "throat". TRUE/FALSE

2 Butterflies in your stomach aren't anything to do with the stomach. TRUE/FALSE

3 It's possible to live without a stomach. TRUE/FALSE

4 It's possible to eat and eat until your stomach bursts. TRUE/FALSE

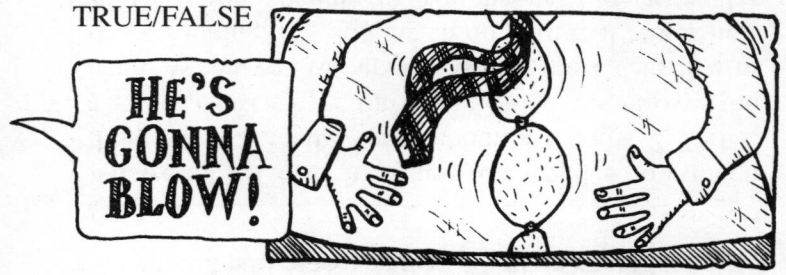

5 When you eat ice cream the cold freezes your stomach. TRUE/FALSE

6 Your stomach stops moving when you're asleep. TRUE/FALSE

7 Your stomach produces an acid strong enough to dissolve a lump of bone. TRUE/FALSE

The vital goings on in the stomach were first probed by a scientist with a taste for staggeringly sick experiments.

Hall of fame: Lazzaro Spallanzani (1729–1799)
Nationality: Italian

Brainy Laz wanted to be a lawyer until his even brainier cousin Laura Bassi (1711–1778) talked him into becoming a scientist. As luck would have it, Laura happened to be the world's first woman professor of physics and introduced Laz to her scientist pals. So Laz became interested in many areas of science including such scintillating topics as where thunder clouds and sponges come from. (That's the sea creatures, not the cake you eat for tea or the thing you use in the bath.)

Laz had a hands-on approach to science. When locals claimed that Lake Ventasso in Italy had a giant whirlpool, the brave scientist built a raft and sailed across the lake – so proving the whirlpool didn't exist. In 1788 he decided to study volcanoes so he climbed a series of Italian craters. At Mount Etna in Sicily he had to be rescued after getting knocked out by poisonous gases. Undaunted he climbed Mount Vulcano but gave up when his walking stick caught fire and his feet got burnt.

OOH! AH! EEH! OUCH! TIME TO GO HOME I THINK

Finally, by watching Mount Stromboli he discovered that gas explosions are the reason rocks fly out of volcanoes.

It took more than a few disgusting sights to stop Laz in his tracks. In 1765 he became interested in how some animals can re-grow parts of their bodies. So he cut up thousands of unfortunate worms, slugs and salamanders.

(He discovered that younger animals are best at re-growing.) He took the same fearless approach to his work on digestion. Would you want to make yourself sick? Laz did – in the interests of science – umpteen times.

Then he studied vile vomit. Amongst other disgusting discoveries he found that stomach acid could dissolve soft bone and gristle but this took longer than ordinary meat.

DISGUSTING DIGESTION EXPRESSIONS

One doctor says to another:

I MAY BE ABOUT TO REGURGITATE

Should you take cover?

Answer: YES. It's the posh word for being sick.

This can be triggered by:
a) Fear – e.g. a science test.
b) A horrible sight or smell – e.g. a revolting science experiment.
c) Disgusting food or poison or germs – e.g. a school dinner.
Oddly enough, doctors also use the term to describe leaking of the blood from a dodgy valve in the heart.

A SICKENING STORY

You're dizzy, you turn pale, you sweat and your mouth is full of spit. You're about to chuck up. Run for the bathroom! The muscles in your lower body and stomach all squeeze together until your half-digested food erupts from your gullet. Vomiting, as it's called, is controlled by a part of your brain known as the vomiting centre. It's well-known that throwing up can be triggered by fear. Scientists don't quite know how this happens. They think that your nerves produce chemicals that make your stomach heave when you're scared of something.

What your vomit looks like depends on how long it's been in your stomach. If it's only been there for a few seconds it won't look too different from when you ate it. Especially if it happens to be carrot stew. But if it's been down for a couple of hours it will be a thick soupy mess. Scientists call this disgusting substance chyme (pronounced chime). How chyming, er, sorry, charming.

COULD YOU BE A SCIENTIST?

Have you ever bent over and thought you were about to be sick? Don't try to do it now – take my word for it, it happens. The half-digested food slips out of your stomach. The acid mixture can burn the oesophagus so badly that some sufferers think they're having a heart attack. This is called heartburn. Some scientists looked at the effects of exercise on heartburn. They measured the amount of acid stomach juice there was in the oesophagus one hour after…

a) Running
b) Weightlifting
c) Cycling

Which do you think caused the most heartburn?

Answer: a) Perhaps the jogging up and down made the stomach contents slop upwards? Cycling was the least likely to cause heartburn. You can get heartburn if you go to bed straight after a big meal. If you lie down with a full stomach its contents can leak into the oesophagus. So you've got an excuse to stay up late? No such luck. You'll just have to eat earlier. No more midnight feasts, and raiding the larder is definitely out.

UNBEARABLE ULCERS

Life can be tough for the stomach, too. One of the nastiest things that can happen to a stomach is when it starts digesting itself! This is what's known as an ulcer. Ulcers can be unbearably painful and need to be treated with substances such as chalk (yes, chalk) that neutralize the acid.

Your stomach has three lines of defence.
1 A thick layer of jelly-like mucus (the same stuff as slimy, runny snot, remember). This stops the acid leaking out and causing an ulcer.
2 A wall of 800 million cells wedged together to block

any acid that does escape. The cells are being replaced and every three days you get a brand new shiny pink stomach lining!

3 If the stomach gets too acidic the cells make a chemical called bicarbonate of soda. This is actually the same chemical you find in alka-seltzer and other medicines that settle an upset tum. The chemical neutralizes the acid so it isn't so strong.

Normally, though, ulcers only happen to stressed-out grown-ups.

HOW ARE YOU GETTING ON WITH YEAR 5, MR SIMPKINS?

Scientists reckon that ulcers are caused by bacteria that stop the stomach lining from making so much lovely protective mucus. This allows the stomach's acid to make a hole in the lining – and that's the ulcer. Sounds painful.

Talking about the guts, which we were a moment ago, it's time to leave the stomach and check out the intestines. And the going is going to get seriously disgusting from now on.

POO-EY PONG

DISGUSTING GUT FEELINGS

Welcome to the intestines – the most horrible bit of your digestive system. The place where it's all happening. It's where fats, carbohydrates and proteins get broken down to smaller chemicals and sucked into the blood. And it's home to all sorts of disgusting goings-on.

Remember Gutzache's epic journey through the guts? Here's the map he used. It'll help you find your way around this chapter, too.

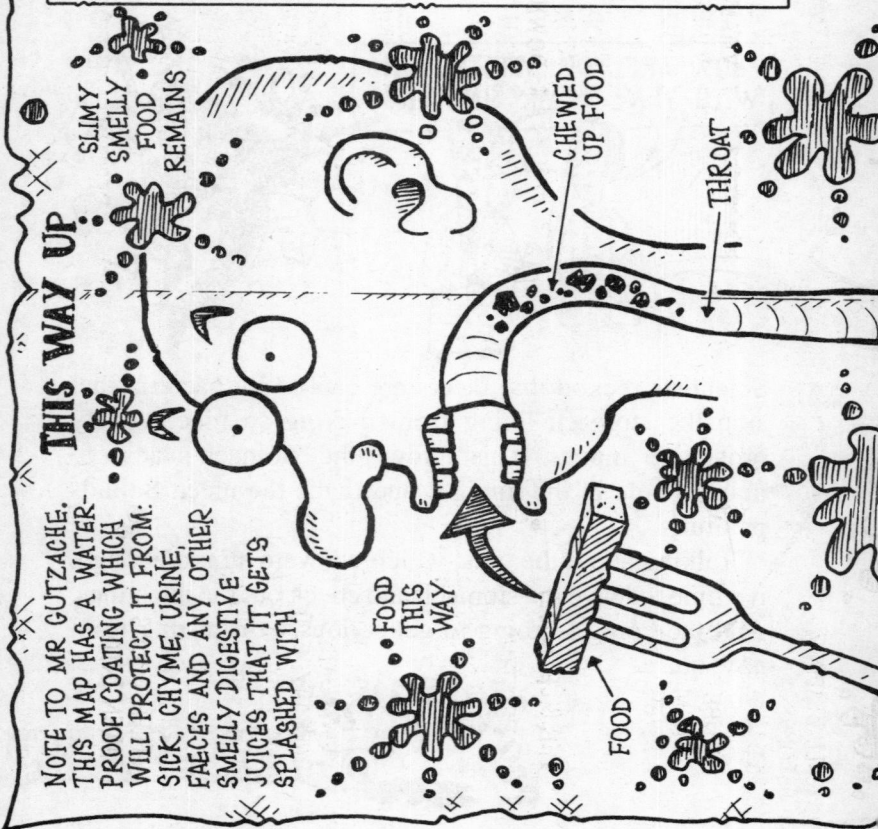

THIS WAY UP

SLIMY SMELLY FOOD REMAINS

CHEWED UP FOOD

THROAT

FOOD THIS WAY

FOOD

NOTE TO MR GUTZACHE. THIS MAP HAS A WATER-PROOF COATING WHICH WILL PROTECT IT FROM: SICK, CHYME, URINE, FAECES AND ANY OTHER SMELLY DIGESTIVE JUICES THAT IT GETS SPLASHED WITH

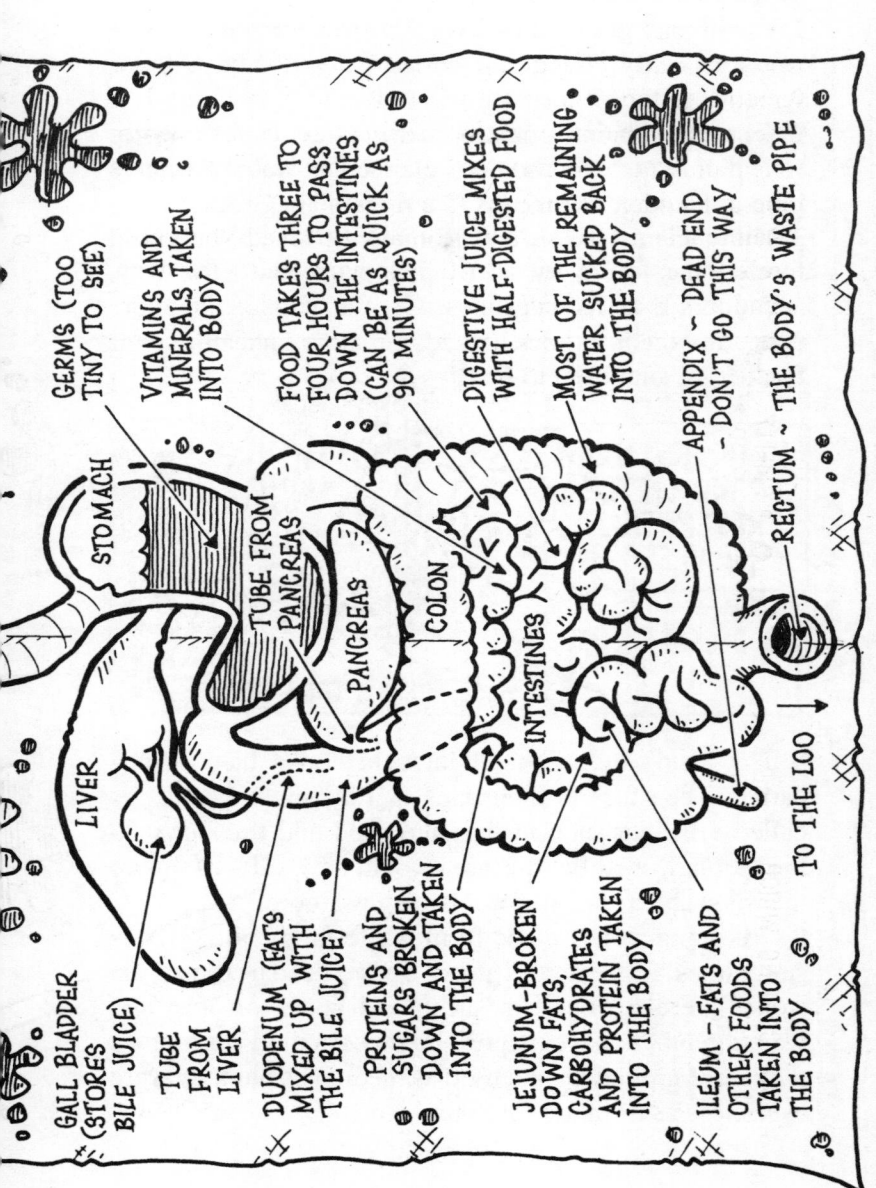

GERMS (TOO TINY TO SEE)

VITAMINS AND MINERALS TAKEN INTO BODY

FOOD TAKES THREE TO FOUR HOURS TO PASS DOWN THE INTESTINES (CAN BE AS QUICK AS 90 MINUTES)

DIGESTIVE JUICE MIXES WITH HALF-DIGESTED FOOD

MOST OF THE REMAINING WATER SUCKED BACK INTO THE BODY

APPENDIX ~ DEAD END - DON'T GO THIS WAY

RECTUM ~ THE BODY'S WASTE PIPE

STOMACH

TUBE FROM PANCREAS

PANCREAS

COLON

INTESTINES

TO THE LOO →

LIVER

GALL BLADDER (STORES BILE JUICE)

TUBE FROM LIVER

DUODENUM (FATS MIXED UP WITH THE BILE JUICE)

PROTEINS AND SUGARS BROKEN DOWN AND TAKEN INTO THE BODY

JEJUNUM-BROKEN DOWN FATS, CARBOHYDRATES AND PROTEIN TAKEN INTO THE BODY

ILEUM - FATS AND OTHER FOODS TAKEN INTO THE BODY

119

GRUESOME GUTS FACTS

1 The human guts can be over 7 metres long and if they weren't tightly coiled and curled up you'd have to be 9 metres tall to fit them all in.

2 The duodenum got its name after Greek doctor Herophilus (4th century BC) claimed it was 12 fingers long. ("Duodenum" means "12 fingers" in Greek.)

3 The ancient Greeks and Romans believed you could foretell the future by sacrificing a sheep to the gods and peering at its intestines. On the whole, the more unhealthy the intestines looked, the more unhealthy your future was supposed to be.

4 The inside of the small intestine looks like a furry carpet. The "fur" is thousands of tiny sticking out bits called villi that suck in digested food and transfer it to the blood. Ironed flat this area would cover 20–40 square metres – about the size of a large classroom.

5 Gruesome stones made from waste food and minerals sometimes form in the guts. These bezoar (be-zo-ar) stones are also found in sheep and goat stomachs and were thought to have magical powers. In the 17th century they were ground up and used as medicines but they were as useless as a square football.

6 In fifth-century India doctors were not afraid to perform operations to remove blockages in the guts. They cut open the patient and afterwards joined the sides of the cut using … ants. Yes, ants. They got a giant black ant to bite the sides of the wound then cut the ant's head off. This left the jaws in position just like a little stitch. Luckily your guts can't feel pain apart from a bit of cramp. So at least the operation didn't hurt the human patient, even if the ants were a bit cut up about it.

Dare you discover … what bile juice does to fats?

You will need:
Washing-up liquid
A bowl of warm water
Cooking oil

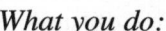

What you do:
1 Pour a little cooking oil into the water. The oil will float on the water. This is like the fat in your intestines.
2 Add a drop of the washing-up liquid representing the bile juice. Give the mixture a rapid stir.
What happens next?
a) The oil sinks to the bottom of the bowl and forms a kind of sludge.

b) The oil, washing-up liquid and water mix together in lots of little bubbles.

c) The oil, washing-up liquid and water form huge bubbles that don't burst easily.

Answer: b) The washing-up liquid (bile juice) breaks up the cooking oil (fats) so that it mixes easily with the water (liquid in your intestines). In this form it's far easier for the gut walls to take it into your bloodstream.

GRUESOME GREETINGS

You might wonder how all this activity is controlled by your body. Why doesn't the food in one part of the intestine simply stop moving so that the rest of your supper piles up behind it?

In fact, special chemicals in the blood called hormones carry messages from one part of the body to another to control this vital job. Just imagine if you could hear these messages – what would they say?

One hormone is called secretin (see-creet-in) and here's its message…

Another hormone is called cholecystokinin (kole-sis-toe-ki-nin) – we'll let it speak for itself.

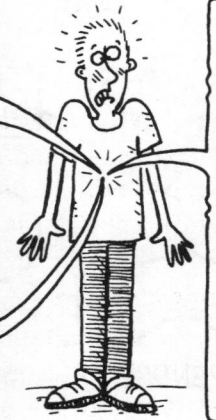

Small intestine calling pancreas: hurry up, we need some digestive enzymes down here quick!

Small intestine calling body: you're not as hungry as you think you are – lay off that cream cake!

Small intestine calling gall bladder: where's that bile juice you promised us? We need a big squirt now!

Meanwhile, the guts also keep in touch using nerves like a kind of telephone line. Let's listen in to a few more conversations

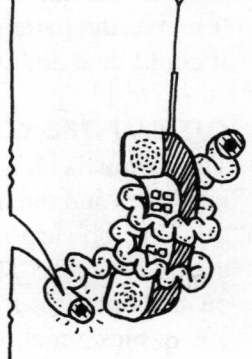

Small intestine to brain control centre: everything's under control. Things are moving nicely. No, hold on – looks like we've got a problem. It's an alien substance – could be a school dinner. Tell the vomiting centre it's action stations. Get ready to heave!

THE GRUMBLING APPENDIX

Sometimes when the appendix gets infected by germs it swells up like a disgusting pus-filled balloon. It can even explode.

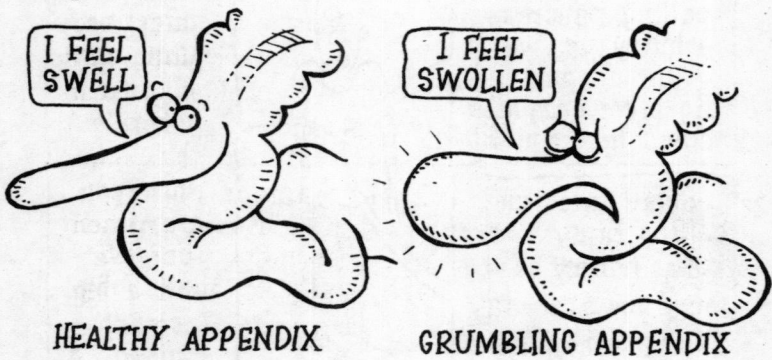

HEALTHY APPENDIX   GRUMBLING APPENDIX

This appalling ailment is called appendicitis and in serious cases the appendix has to be removed. But if the infection isn't too bad the body's white cells guzzle most of the germs and the appendix gets better. If the germs multiply again you get more pain. This delightful condition is known as a "grumbling appendix". No doubt it makes the patients grumble too. But it could be worse. It could be a dodgy colon.

CUT OUT THE COLON

The colon is 1.5 metres long. It's the last bit of the intestines and the name given to the : sign in punctuation. So don't be surprised if your teacher finds a "colon" in a library book. The colon stores your poo before it's pushed out of your body. During this time the walls of the colon suck much of the remaining water from the poo. This stops you spending your life on the toilet getting rid of watery diarrhoea.

Top surgeon Sir William Arbuthnot Lane (1856–1943) was keen on ballroom dancing and designing new types of surgical instruments. But he wasn't too keen on colons. He thought they were useless and caused disease when germs escaped from the colon to infect the body. And he claimed the victim smelt of graveyards. Willie also said people with dodgy colons had cold, bluish ears, cold noses, clammy sweaty hands and...

Well, Willie was in the know when it came to colons. His claim to fame was to discover the sudden twists and turns in the colon now known as Lane's kinks.

Worried about the appearance of his patients, Willie invented an operation in which the offending colon was removed. This was fine, so long as the victim, sorry patient, didn't mind the consequences. These involved spending the rest of their life with a hole in their guts through which their poo passed into a bag. Yuck! Fortunately, other doctors criticised Lane for performing the operation unnecessarily. And so Lane's treatment of the colon came to a : er, sorry, a full stop.

Meanwhile, back in the intestines things are really hotting up. Boiling and bubbling as mysterious chemicals get to work. Enter the energetic enzymes. Is your gut getting fizz-ical? Better find out now…

AM I TOO LATE FOR THE NEXT CHAPTER?

NO, YOU'RE JUST EN-ZYME!

ENERGETIC ENZYMES

Look inside your body and you'll see a gruesome assembly of bones, muscles and blood. But look closer and you'll see a fizzing mass of chemical reactions that would make most chemists green with envy. It's all done with enzymes. Without them digestion would be a dead loss and so would you. But with them you're fizzing with physical fitness. So what do enzymes do all day?

Disgusting digestion fact file

NAME: Enzymes

THE BASIC FACTS: 1 An enzyme is a protein that changes other chemicals. In digestion, enzymes help to break other chemicals to pieces.

2 Every cell in your body contains over 3,000 different enzymes.

THE HORRIBLE DETAILS: If you didn't have enzymes the only other way to digest your food would be to heat your body. This also breaks the food chemicals up. Unfortunately, your body would need to be 300°C (572°F) to do this. So you'd need to cook yourself to enjoy your food.

Dare you discover … how enzymes work?

You will need:

A hardboiled egg. (Ask an adult to boil the egg for six minutes.) Cool the egg and peel off the shell.

Biological washing powder

A jar and spoon

What you do:

1 Add eight tablespoonfuls of warm water to the jar.

2 Ask your adult helper to put on protective gloves and mix in one tablespoonful of washing powder. They should stir the mixture until the powder disappears.

3 Add a piece of boiled egg white (not the yellow yolk).

4 Wrap the jar in a towel and leave in a warm place such as an airing cupboard for two days.

5 Take a look at the piece of egg white. What do you notice?

a) The egg is a horrible brown colour.

b) The egg has turned into a white liquid.

c) The egg has got smaller.

Bet you never knew!
Enzymes make heat as they rip chemicals to pieces inside your guts. That's why Arctic sledge drivers give their dogs butter to eat in very cold weather. Butter is digested by enzymes and this makes enough heat to warm the dogs. And if enzymes make heat, let's visit a few hot spots.

Disgusting digestion fact file

NAME: Pancreas

THE BASIC FACTS:
The pancreas is like a chemical factory pumping out enzymes to digest carbohydrates, fat and protein. It makes 1.5 litres of digestive juice a day.

ENZYMES ← PANCREAS

HORMONES

INSULIN   GLYCOGEN

THE HORRIBLE DETAILS: The pancreas also makes two hormones – insulin and glycogen that control the sugar that gets to your muscles to provide energy. Lack of insulin causes a horrible disease called diabetes.

A WORTHY WINNER?

Scientists toil away for years until at last they make a great discovery. But who should get the glory for discoveries? Take insulin, for example. When scientists found out about insulin they were able to give extra insulin to people with diabetes. Thousands of lives were saved. In Sweden a committee met to award the 1923 Nobel Prize for Medicine... But who should get credit? These were the main contenders:

Frederick Banting (1891–1941)
A First World War hero. Like many scientists of his time, Banting was convinced there was something in the pancreas that prevented diabetes. He discovered insulin in 1922.

Charles Best (1899–1978)
Brilliant laboratory assistant who helped make Banting's work possible. He and Banting bravely injected one another with insulin to make sure it was safe.

James Collip (1892–1965)
A talented chemist. Showed Banting and Best how to make a pure kind of insulin suitable for injecting into humans.

John Macleod (1876–1935)
In charge of the lab in Canada where Banting and Best worked. Didn't think much of Banting as a scientist. Was on holiday when insulin was discovered.

Two scientists were awarded the coveted Nobel Prize in 1923 – but which two?

Answer: Macleod and Banting. Although Macleod had been on holiday at the time, he was honoured because he was in charge of the lab. Which just goes to prove that science can be disgustingly unfair. Fortunately, Macleod decided to share his prize money with Collip and Banting generously shared his prize with Best.

Disgusting digestion fact file

NAME: Liver

THE BASIC FACTS: It's brown and weighs about 1.5 kg. It has hundreds of jobs including making bile which helps to digest fats. After food has been digested, the liver stores food chemicals and vitamins.

THE HORRIBLE DETAILS : Bile is disgusting stuff, it's thick, brownish and bitter tasting. After the bile has digested fats, the salts in the bile are taken back into the blood and end up back in the liver. Then they're used to make more bile . . . this sickening cycle can continue up to 18 times.

One man played a vital role in probing the liver's secrets...

Hall of fame: Claude Bernard (1813–1878)
Nationality: French

Bernard was the son of a humble grape picker but when he died he was the first French scientist to enjoy a full state funeral. Well, maybe "enjoy" isn't the right word since he was dead at the time. Young Claude Bernard didn't want to be a scientist. He wanted to be a playwright. Fortunately (for science), his plays were so bad that Claude took up medicine instead.

He discovered that carbohydrates are broken down into sugars during digestion and fats are broken down by bile juice. Then he found that the liver can make sugar. He fed a dog on a sugar-free diet and then opened up its liver to find that sugar had mysteriously appeared there.

Mrs Bernard was just one of many who believed that Claude's experiments were cruel to dogs. No dog owner would allow Claude near their pets and the scientist soon found that his programme of research was in trouble owing to a shortage of subjects.

ARE YOU ABSOLUTELY SURE THAT'S A BABY, MY DEAR?

YES, AND I'M JUST TAKING HIM BACK TO HIS KENNEL, ER, I MEAN MOTHER.

So he took to kidnapping dogs for his research. One day one of Bernard's stolen dogs escaped from the lab and ran home to its owner. Unfortunately, the owner happened to be the Chief of Police and he came round to ask the scientist some awkward questions…

What do you think happened next?

a) Claude Bernard was sentenced to three years' hard labour for cruelty to dogs. Mrs Bernard was the chief prosecution witness.

b) The scientist was let off after paying a hefty fine and making a big donation to the local stray dogs home.

c) Bernard made a grovelling apology and was let off with a caution.

Answer: c) And you'll be pleased to know the dog lived happily ever after with his owner.

DISGUSTING LIVER DISEASES

The ancient peoples of Babylonia (modern Iraq) had a disgusting method of finding out what liver disease a person was suffering from. Let's take a look at this ancient tablet. (That's a clay tablet, not the sort of tablet you'd take for an upset tum or sore throat.)

AN ANCIENT
TABLET

How to spot liver disease
You need one sheep
1. Blow into the sheep's nostrils
2. Sacrifice the sheep to the gods and look at its liver
3. Compare the liver to a clay model. If there's anything different about the real animal liver you'll have this problem, too.

AN ANCIENT
TABLET

Stones similar to those in the guts can also appear in the liver. They often form in the gall bladder where they do no harm unless they get big enough to stop bile from reaching the guts. If there is a blockage, the bile leaks into the blood and ends up in the skin and eyeballs. Bile contains colours made from waste chemicals from the liver and these turn the skin and eyeballs a tasteful yellow. This disgusting condition is known as jaundice.

CAN YOU TELL WHICH OF THESE YELLOW OBJECTS HAS JAUNDICE?

Nowadays, it's easy for surgeons to crush the stones or in the worst cases simply whip out the gall bladder in one easy operation. Meanwhile, your body is busy using up all your hard-digested food.

JUICY JOULES

Your blood carries the juicy digested food chemicals to all parts of your body. In your muscles the chemicals are ripped apart to produce the energy that keeps you going. We measure this energy in kilojoules (ke-lo-jools) or kJ for short.

Bet you never knew!
A boy aged 9–11 needs 9,500 kJ of food per day to keep going and between the ages of 12 and 14 this goes up to 11,000 kJ. A girl of 9–11 needs only 8,500 kJ per day and at 12–14 she needs 9,000 kJ. So why do girls need less food? Some girls are smaller or less active than boys. Or maybe they're just not so greedy.

Compare that with…
• A canary needs just 46 kJ a day to avoid hopping off its perch for good.
• An elephant uses up a jumbo 385,000 kJ a day.
• A rocket needs 100,000,000 (one hundred million) kJ to get into space.
Confusing isn't it? Maybe this quiz will help you digest the facts.

ENERGY QUIZ

Can you find the food with the right amount of energy to keep you going through each challenge?

CHALLENGE	FOOD

1 Shovelling snow for an hour.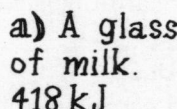

a) A glass of milk. 418 kJ

2 Cycling for ten minutes.

b) 4 apples. 840 kJ

3 Scrubbing the floor for twenty minutes.

c) A bar of chocolate. 1255 kJ

4 Swimming round the pool for four minutes without touching the sides.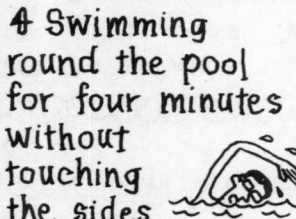

d) A slice of of buttered toast. 314 kJ

5 Dancing for ten minutes.

e) 300 grams (10.6 oz) of sausages. 3000 kJ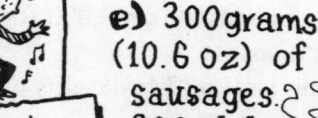

WARNING If you eat too little food you'll feel horribly hungry and weak and light-headed. You might even faint. Eat too much and you'll put on extra fat.

136

A HOT PROBLEM

Producing all that energy also generates heat. That's
why you feel really hot and sweaty after a run.
Every day we produce the same heat as burning 500g
of coal. Twelve people sitting in a room give off
as much heat as a small electric fire. Luckily, the
blood takes the heat outwards to the skin where it escapes
into the air through the pores in your skin. Phew – that's
a relief!

Sometimes the heat takes water away from your body in the form of sweat and this also cools you down. But if you've got too much water in your body there's another way to get rid of it. Any idea what that might be?

GOING ROUND THE BEND

You can't get away from the toilet. Ultimately it will command your presence with all the power of a giant magnet. Once your breakfast has worked its way through your system, your body will insist on it. It doesn't matter how busy you are – even if it's the middle of a vital science test. You've gotta do what you've gotta do.

But why? The story starts with a couple of rather crucial organs – the kidneys.

Disgusting digestion fact file

NAME: Kidneys

THE BASIC FACTS: You've got two – one on either side of your body – although you only need one to stay alive. Each one is about 11 x 6cm and its job is to filter spare water and waste chemicals from your blood.

THE HORRIBLE DETAILS: The waste stuff is urine – that's pee to you.

SUPPER'S READY. IT'S YOUR FAVOURITE – STEAK AND KIDNEY PIE

KIDNEYS? ACTUALLY I'M NOT VERY HUNGRY, DAD.

FANTASTIC FILTERS

Every day about 1,700 litres of blood flows through your kidneys. Now, as you may have noticed, you don't have that much blood. So we're talking about the same blood going through the kidneys lots of times.

Here's what happens...

Just imagine your kidneys as a pair of fantastic coffee filters. (They do filter coffee along with everything else.)

LEFT KIDNEY

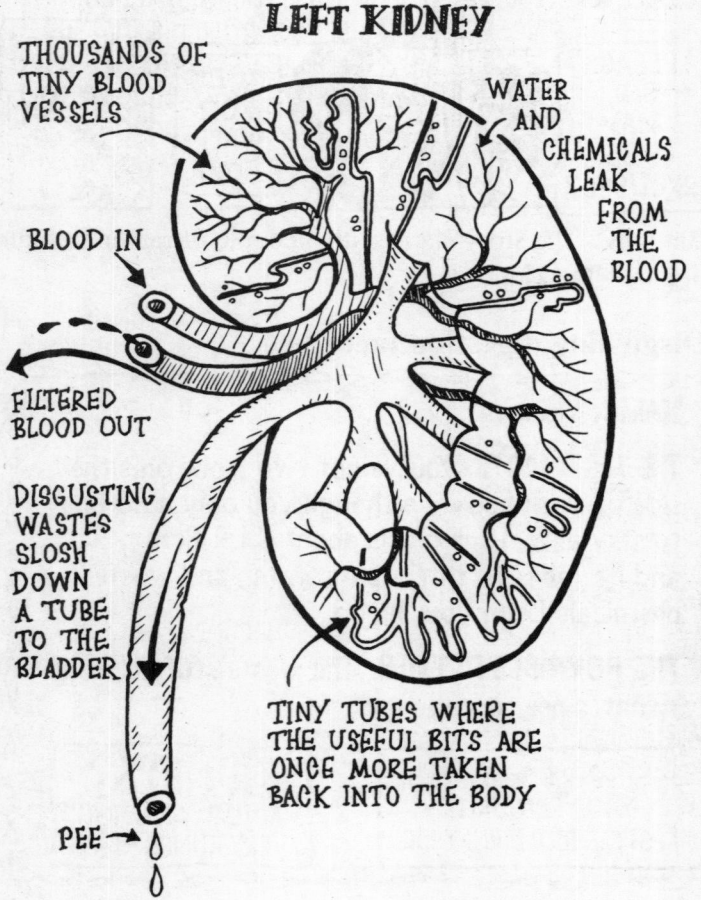

THOUSANDS OF TINY BLOOD VESSELS

WATER AND CHEMICALS LEAK FROM THE BLOOD

BLOOD IN

FILTERED BLOOD OUT

DISGUSTING WASTES SLOSH DOWN A TUBE TO THE BLADDER

TINY TUBES WHERE THE USEFUL BITS ARE ONCE MORE TAKEN BACK INTO THE BODY

PEE →

People with defective kidneys can be wired up to an artificial kidney. This is known as dialysis (di-al-is-sis). The first artificial kidney was made by US scientists in Baltimore in 1914. The blood passes out of the body and along a tube where the wastes are filtered out just like in a real kidney.

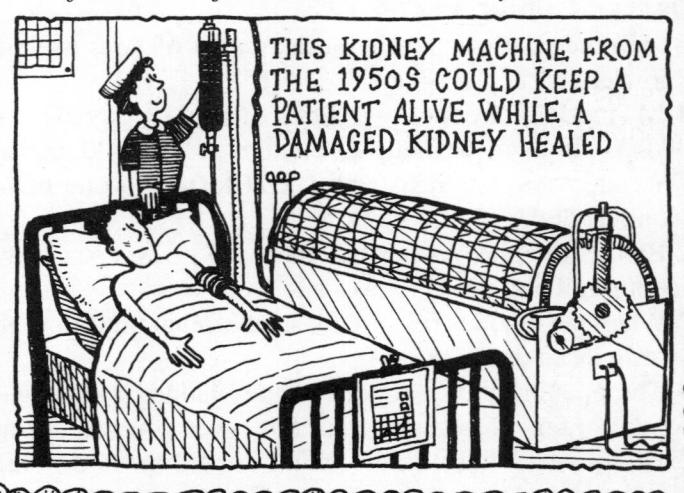

THIS KIDNEY MACHINE FROM THE 1950S COULD KEEP A PATIENT ALIVE WHILE A DAMAGED KIDNEY HEALED

DISGUSTING DIGESTION EXPRESSIONS

COFFEE?

BETTER NOT, I MIGHT HAVE MICTURITION (MICK-TUR-RISH-EON) PROBLEMS

Shouldn't she be in hospital?

USELESS URINE FACTS

Shock the whole school with the extent of your useless knowledge.

1 Most adults produce 1–2 litres of urine a day. That's 40,000 litres in a lifetime, enough to fill 500 baths. (Warning: it's extremely anti-social to pee in one bath, let alone 500.)

2 By the time the bladder has about 0.3 litres it's already feeling full and needs to take a leak.

3 When the bladder fills up, its sides stretch until they're as thin as an onion skin.

4 The opening at the bottom of the bladder is operated by the brain. That's why you don't wet yourself (or at least not very often). Babies don't know how to do this, and that's why they wear nappies. When you go to sleep, messages from your brain keep the opening locked to prevent little disasters in the night.

5 You produce pee faster if you take a deep breath. This allows your diaphragm, the muscle above your liver, to push down on your guts. This in turn squashes the bladder and forces the urine to squirt down its exit tube. Why not try this fascinating experiment for yourself?

6 Urine is about 96 per cent water. The rest is a mix of urea (remember, that's a waste chemical made by your body), and a bit of waste protein and salt. It's a bit smelly but it's usually germ-free...

142

7 That's why urine was once used to wash wounds on the battlefield. No need to try this next time you get a cut.

GO ON THEN, IF YOU REALLY THINK IT WILL HELP

8 Most of the time urine is yellow – that's the urea. But sometimes it can be a different colour – such as red, that's when you've eaten too much beetroot. And disgusting facts such as this were once incredibly useful to a breed of...

USELESS URINE DOCTORS

Sometimes your doctor will ask for a sample of your urine. This can help to detect certain diseases. But for hundreds of years doctors thought that you could identify every kind of disease by looking at the patient's urine. Some doctors even tasted it, too. Erk!

In the Middle Ages Spanish urine doctor, Arnold of Villanova, said:

If you find nothing wrong with the patient's urine, but he still insists he has a headache, tell him it is an obstruction of the liver. Continue to speak of obstruction, it is a word he won't understand, but it sounds important.

Surely doctors aren't like that nowadays. They wouldn't use long words just to confuse their patients … would they?

DISGUSTING EXPRESSIONS

ARE YOU HAVING PROBLEMS WITH YOUR DEFAECATION?

How should she answer? Clue: it's nothing to do with Christmas paper chains, they're *decorations*.

Answer: Defaecation is the posh medical term for making poo. For most people this is once a day or once every two days. But people who eat lots of fibre can defaecate *five times* per day. Bet they get through a fortune in loo rolls.

FOUL FAECES

You remember all that waste food piling up in the colon? Well, it's got to go some time. So every day some of it is shoved out of the anus – usually about 150g for a child. About three-quarters of this is water and the rest is waste food such as fibre and germs. Lovely!

Note: anus = the hole in your bum where the waste products come out. Not to be confused with Uranus which is a distant planet. Clearly you wouldn't want your anus to be that distant.

COULD YOU BE A SCIENTIST?

You are a doctor. Two patients see you. One says…

Doctor, doctor, my poo is red.

1 What do you say?

a) It's blood. You'll be dead in a week.

b) You've got a liver disease that's turned your bile red.

c) Stop eating so many tomatoes.

The other patient says...

Doctor, doctor, my poo is blue!

2 What do you say?

a) You have a rare colon disease.

b) That's impossible – you must be an alien.

c) Stop eating those blue food-colourings!

Answers: 1 c) 2 c)

CRUNCHED-UP CONSTIPATION

When you're very worried you'd think your body would help you feel better. But it doesn't. Instead the vagus nerve for some reason doesn't send the signals from the brain that make you go to the toilet. As a result the poo piles up in the colon where its moisture is sucked back into the blood. The poo becomes dry and crammed together – that's constipation. So it's painful to get rid of – and that really is a worry. And here's another worry – sometimes stress can speed up peristalsis resulting in diarrhoea and extra farts.

If this happens to you, maybe you'd like to try Sir William Arbuthnot Lane's patent constipation remedy...

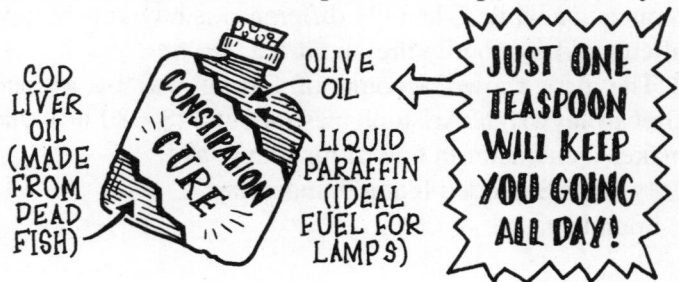

COD LIVER OIL (MADE FROM DEAD FISH)

CONSTIPATION CURE

OLIVE OIL

LIQUID PARAFFIN (IDEAL FUEL FOR LAMPS)

JUST ONE TEASPOON WILL KEEP YOU GOING ALL DAY!

145

The paraffin acts like oil in a rusty bike chain. It gets the poo moving again. No, on second thoughts better not – you wouldn't want your guts to turn into a paraffin lamp would you now? And there are enough dangerous gases down there already.

DISGUSTING DIGESTION EXPRESSIONS

YOU'VE GOT A FLATULENCE PROBLEM

Does this need surgery?

Answer: No, just a clothes peg over the nose. Flatulence is the scientific name for farting. It's nothing to do with being flat – although you might feel a bit flattened after being given this diagnosis.

TEN THINGS YOU ALWAYS WANTED TO KNOW ABOUT FARTING BUT WERE AFRAID TO ASK

1 Kings and Queens fart. Presidents fart and so do Emperors. Children fart and even teachers are said to do it once in a while. The only difference is how much, how often and how loudly they let it out.

2 The first known account of farting was by ancient Greek playwright Aristophanes (about 448–380 BC) who makes a character in one of his plays say,

"My wind exploded like a thunderclap."

Sounds nasty.

3 Farting is simply your body's way of getting rid of air that you've swallowed by eating too fast, talking while eating, or swallowing bubbly spit. Of course, you can burp some air up. The more you burp, the less you fart. Better not try explaining this important principle at family meal-times.

Or this one...

4 This air gets mixed up with poo in the gut. If there's a lot of air in poo it'll float.

5 Amazingly, a group of fearless scientists analysed the chemical ingredients of a fart. (Did they wear gas masks?) They bravely discovered that a fart is a mixture of five different gases – mainly nitrogen (59 per cent) which is a boring gas that floats about in the air without people taking too much notice of it. Except when someone farts!

6 Well, the smell comes from the chemicals indole and skatole. These are given off when germs get to work on bits of protein from your food.

7 Sometimes a gas called hydrogen sulphide forms in farts. This happens when chemicals from different foods get together in the guts. You'll know all about it because the fart smells like rotten eggs. It's bad news – and not only in the social sense. Hydrogen sulphide is poisonous and it can explode if too much of it mixes with oxygen in the air.

Crisps are full of little air bubbles. Chewing gum makes you swallow air. Like the air in crisps this may re-emerge as farts. Fizzy drinks are full of bubbles.

8 Beans, brussel sprouts, cauliflowers and bran contain a type of carbohydrate that the germs in your gut can change into gas.

Scientists reckon that meat contains many of the chemicals that cause some of the smelliest farts.

9 US astronauts are banned from eating certain foods, especially beans, before a space-flight. Well, how would you fancy being cooped up in a cramped spacecraft on a ten-day space mission with someone who had a bit of a bottom problem?

10 Mind you, flying can make you fart. As a plane flies higher the air pressure around the passengers drops. This makes the air in the guts expand and the result is . . . well, I think you can guess.

When it comes to getting rid of smells there is one invention that has proved more than a flush in the pan.

FLUSHED WITH SUCCESS

1 The world's first flush toilets were invented by people in the Indus Valley of Pakistan over 3,500 years ago. In some towns nearly every house had its very own luxury loo.

2 In the Middle Ages most people had toilets that were nothing more than seats over smelly holes in the ground.

3 In 1590, Englishman Sir John Harrington invented a loo that could be flushed with water.

4 But the loo really came into its own after 1778 when inventor Joseph Bramah devised the ball valve which automatically filled the cistern and the "U" bend.

5 Gradually toilets became more and more popular with anyone rich enough to afford them.

But there was a problem.

SOMETHING IN THE AIR

The problem had been festering for some time, growing ever more gross, ever nastier with each passing year. And with each year the truth became ever more unpalatable, ever more horrible. London, one of the greatest cities in the world, stank. It didn't just pong, whiff or smell – it STANK. By the 1850s it reeked of rotting sewage and filth and every kind of loathsome rubbish. And it stank because London's sewerage system had broken down.

The London Times
4th August 1857

A BIG JOB?

Today we bring you an exclusive interview with genuine London "tosher" - Bert Smellie.

Bert's unenviable job is to crawl into the sewers in search of valuables accidentally flushed down toilets.

On a good day Bert finds coins, bits of rag and bones. "The work's all right," he says, "it's good money but it's dangerous too!"

"What sort of dangers?" I ask him.

Bert Smellie

"Them sewers is diabolical," says Bert. "Falling to bits - they can fall on you without warning and you'd be

150

buried alive. Others have deep pools that'll suck you down in rotten slime. And the smell is bad enough to make you heave.

"And then there's the rats. Yeah. Giant rats big as cats some of them. At night they come out of the sewers into houses. They've been known to attack babies. Even some of my mates have been attacked by rats. All we ever found was their skeletons. Horrible ... and to think, it could have been me."

"Come off it Bert," I laugh. "Pull the other one!"

Then Bert holds up

one of his hands. It's covered in white scars. Rat bites.
Blimey!

The Editor writes ...

We at the *London Times* say something must be done about this disgrace. London must have new sewers. The politicians must get their act together and pay for it ... this issue STINKS and we believe there's a real whiff of corruption here.

Eventually the sewers couldn't take it any more. And so began the Great Stink. It was the most horrible smell anyone could remember. In the hot summer of 1858 the smell of the sewage-clogged River Thames was so foul that people were physically sick. Eventually people kicked up such a stink about it that the politicians were forced to act. The problem was so urgent that the Government agreed to fork out for a brand new sewerage system. At once!

SUPER SEWERS

In all, 209 km of new sewers were constructed. They mainly ran downhill to take the waste away from London. And the system is still operating today. Nowadays complex sewage systems are commonplace in large cities. But in the 19th century some of them were considered so amazing that they became tourist attractions. Can you imagine it?

For a holiday with a difference...

The Municipal Sewage Experience

GREAT VALUE - IT WON'T BE A DRAIN ON YOUR POCKET!

A unique thrilling close-up view of how our fascinating sewage system deals with waste water from washing and toilets, and rainwater from gutters.

GASP WITH AMAZEMENT

as the watery mass of sewage is filtered to remove large objects and then left to settle.

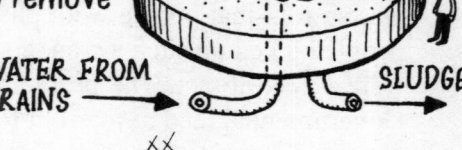

WOW!

FANTASTIC!

WATER FROM DRAINS →

→ SLUDGE

BE TOTALLY GOBSMACKED

as watery waste is left in tanks where much of it is eaten by hungry germs. Or we can use the poison chlorine to bump them off!

YES, NOTHING IS WASTED

HOLD YOUR BREATH as the

sludgy solid sewage is left for a few weeks for germs to feast on.

This pongy process gives off smelly gas that can be used to power the sewage works. And it can even be used to light gaslights in the streets. Even the smelly sludge is dried and used as fertilizer.

So sewage makes excellent plant food! Ideally suited for growing crops. Crops to make into a school lunch.

A school lunch. But that's where this book started, isn't it?

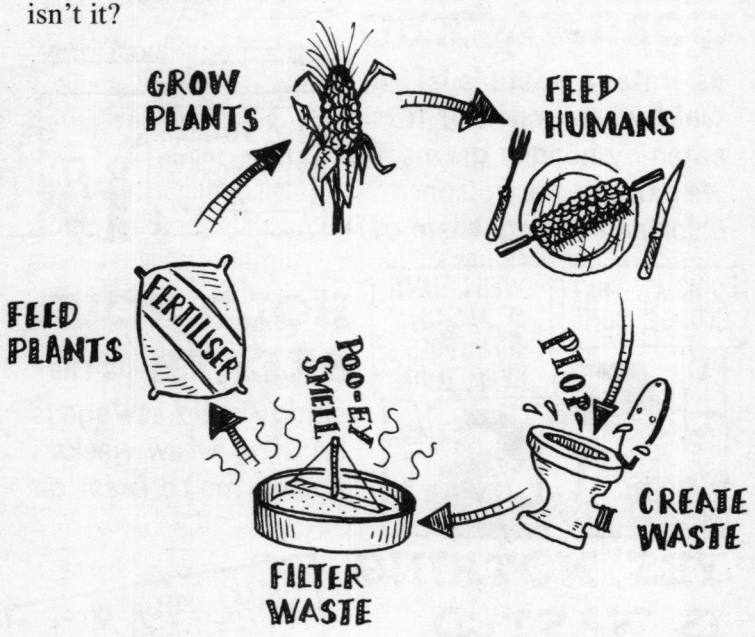

GROW PLANTS

FEED HUMANS

FEED PLANTS

FERTILISER

POO-EY SMELL

PLOP!

FILTER WASTE

CREATE WASTE

SOMETHING TO CHEW OVER (FOOD FOR THOUGHT)

Food's brilliant. We think about it, we talk about it, we even dream about it. And when it's on our plates we play with it before we eat it. But what goes inside our bodies is even more fascinating.

If your digestive system was a machine it would be the most amazing and incredible machine ever invented. Every day it systematically sorts through whatever you choose to feed it with. It sorts out the bits your body can use and chucks out the bits it can't.

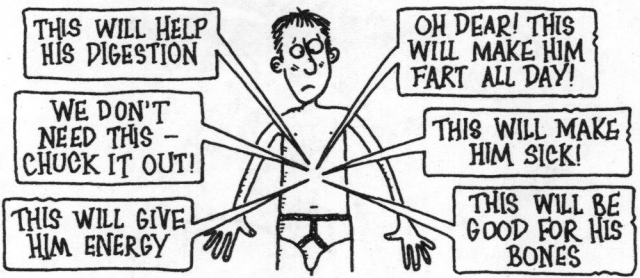

All the time you're busy watching TV, sitting in a science lesson or chatting with your friends, your guts are quietly (leaving aside the odd gurgle) getting on with this vital task. They hardly ever protest – OK, so they make you throw up from time to time, but only if they've got a good reason.

So how long has it taken you to read the first bit of this chapter? About one minute? Right, prepare to be amazed... In just one minute:

• Your stomach has churned three times.

• 500,000 new cells have been made for lining your stomach.

• The food in your guts has moved 2.5 cm.

• And your kidneys might have filtered out 1.4 ml of urine that even now could be trickling into your bladder.
• Meanwhile all the glands and organs in your digestive system are happily pumping and squirting away: salivary glands, stomach, liver pancreas. All of them producing their vital juices and enzymes.

And so it carries on 24 hours a day. Even when you're asleep. Even when you're in a science lesson and not thinking about food at all. You've got to admit, it's fascinatingly disgusting.

OH HI DOC! . . .
YOU'VE SWALLOWED
A WHAT? . . . AND
YOU'D LIKE ME TO
DO WHAT AGAIN? . . .
FORGET IT PAL!

DISGUSTING DIGESTION
QUIZ

Now find out if you're a
Disgusting Digestion expert!

Can you stomach it?

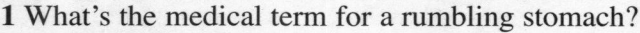

Your digestive system may gurgle like a drain and produce more wind than a Force 9 gale, but it's still a biological miracle. Try this tricky test and see if you know your enzymes from your appendix.

1 What's the medical term for a rumbling stomach?
a) Eructation
b) Borborygmus
c) Regurgitation

2 In which two areas of the body is blood made?
a) Liver
b) Stomach
c) Bone marrow
d) Guts
e) Spleen
f) Pancreas

3 Where would you find the Islets of Langerhans?
a) In the sea.
b) In your kidneys.
c) In the pancreas.

4 What does the appendix do?
a) Breaks down food.
b) Kills germs in the guts.
c) Nothing.

5 How do enzymes work?
a) They stick food molecules together so they can be digested by the guts.
b) They help to split up food molecules until they are small enough to be absorbed by the gut walls.
c) They heat up food molecules to warm up the body and provide energy.

6 How much food does a person eat in their lifetime?
a) 10 tonnes
b) 30 tonnes
c) 100 tonnes

7 How many types of taste can your tongue detect?
a) 3
b) 4
c) 5

8 Lack of vitamin C causes an illness that gives you smelly breath, bleeding eyeballs and swollen gums and can even kill you. What's it called?
a) Scurvy
b) Rickets
c) Green monkey disease

9 What are your molar and premolar teeth used for?
a) Crushing food
b) Tearing food
c) Slicing food

10 What is a pus-filled hole in a tooth called?
a) A scab
b) An abscess
c) A pimple

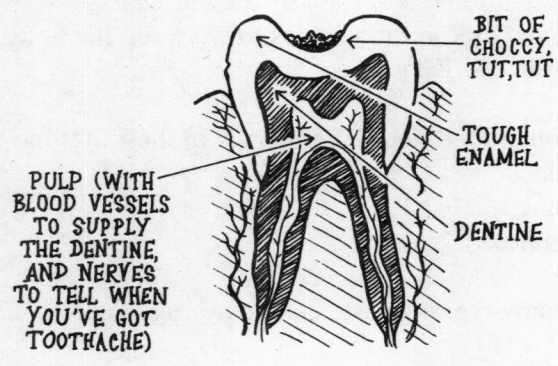

BIT OF
CHOCCY,
TUT, TUT

TOUGH
ENAMEL

DENTINE

PULP (WITH
BLOOD VESSELS
TO SUPPLY
THE DENTINE,
AND NERVES
TO TELL WHEN
YOU'VE GOT
TOOTHACHE)

Answers:
1b; 2c and **e;** The bone marrow and the spleen.
3c; 4c That's right. Nothing – not a sausage! **5b;**
6b; 7c; They are sweet, sour, salty, bitter and umami;
8a; 9a; 10b

Busting a gut

Take the strain and try these gut-wrenching, brain-teasing questions – like one of Typhoid Mary's delightful dishes, they'll keep you on the go for ages!

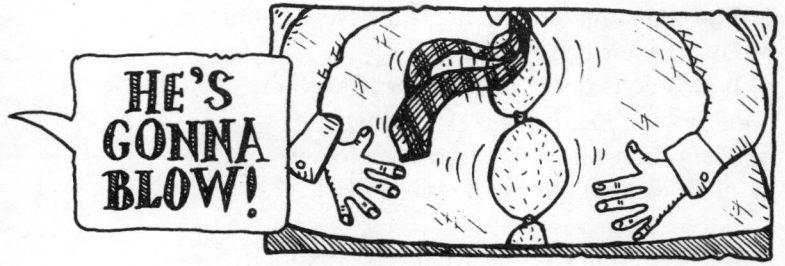

1 What was the name of Versalius's ground-breaking book, published in 1543?
a) *The Fabric of the Human Body*
b) *Guts – The Ultimate Guide*
c) *Versalius's Anatomy*

2 What delicious but deadly dessert did Typhoid Mary make that killed so many people in New York in 1909?
a) Chocolate cake
b) Ice cream
c) Jam roly poly

3 Which ancient Roman wrote over 500 books on medicine?
a) Julius Caesar
b) Claudius Galen
c) Nero

4 How did the scientist Andreas Versalius spend his spare-time?
a) Playing football
b) Dissecting animals
c) Grave-robbing

5 Why did some people in Papua New Guinea eat the brains of their dead relatives?
a) It was considered to be respectful to the dead and a good way to make yourself brainier!
b) They didn't have enough food to eat.
c) They wanted the extra vitamins.

6 In fifth-century India, what did doctors use to hold the gut walls together after an operation to remove a blockage?
a) Thread
b) Ants
c) Sticky tape

7 In ancient China, doctors believed that the appearance of a certain part of your body reflected the health of the rest of your body.
Was it:
a) Your nose
b) Your big toe
c) Your tongue

8 In which part of the world is it considered polite to burp after a meal?
a) England
b) Japan
c) Arabia

9 Which doctor sold poisonous antimony pills in 1733 as a cure for everything?
a) Ned Ford
b) Ned Ward
c) Fred Ward

10 What is the name of the gas that makes farts smell like rotten eggs?
a) Hydrogen sulphide
b) Nitrous oxide
c) Hydrogen peroxide

Answers: 1a; 2b Typhoid germs were transferred from her hands into her handmade ice cream. You wouldn't want her to be cooking your school dinners! **3b; 4c; 5a; 6b;** They used the jaws of ants to bite the sides of the wound together like a stitch. **7c; 8c; 9b; 10a**

Chew it over

Here are some toothy teasers and disgusting digestive queries – you may find some of them a little hard to swallow! What's the missing word or phrase in these foul facts?

1 Every day the tiny Etruscan shrew scoffs up to _____ times its own weight.
a) one
b) five
c) three

2 Several types of _____ can live in people's guts.
a) worm
b) spider
c) snail

3 It _____ to taste your food if you hold your nose when eating.
a) is easier
b) is harder
c) is quicker

4 _____ germs are found in the nostrils and on skin, and can cause diarrhoea, vomiting and cramps in the guts.
a) Staphylococcus
b) Listeria
c) Salmonella

5 The human intestine is _____ long.
a) 9 metres
b) 15 metres
c) 5 metres

6 In the Middle Ages doctors looked at _____ to work out cause of illnesses.
a) spit
b) blood
c) urine

7 Cows have _____ stomachs.
a) two
b) four
c) six

8 A bezoar stone is found in the guts of some animals. It forms from _____.
a) swallowed air.
b) waste food and minerals.
c) blood.

9 If you don't get enough iodine in your diet your _____ gland swells up and forms a horrible lump called a goitre.
a) pineal
b) salivary
c) thyroid

10 Your hypothalamus is a _____ lump on the underside of your brain that signals to your brain when it's time to eat and when to stop.
a) tangerine-sized
b) pea-sized
c) tennis-ball sized

Answers: 1a; 2a This includes roundworms, pin worms and flukes. **3b** It is harder as you can't smell the food – your senses of smell and taste are connected. **4a; 5a; 6c** Some doctors tasted it to test it too! **7b** One stomach stores grass before it's sicked up and the other three store grass as it rots. **8b; 9c; 10b**

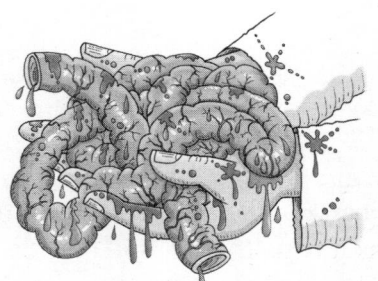

HORRIBLE INDEX

167

169

170

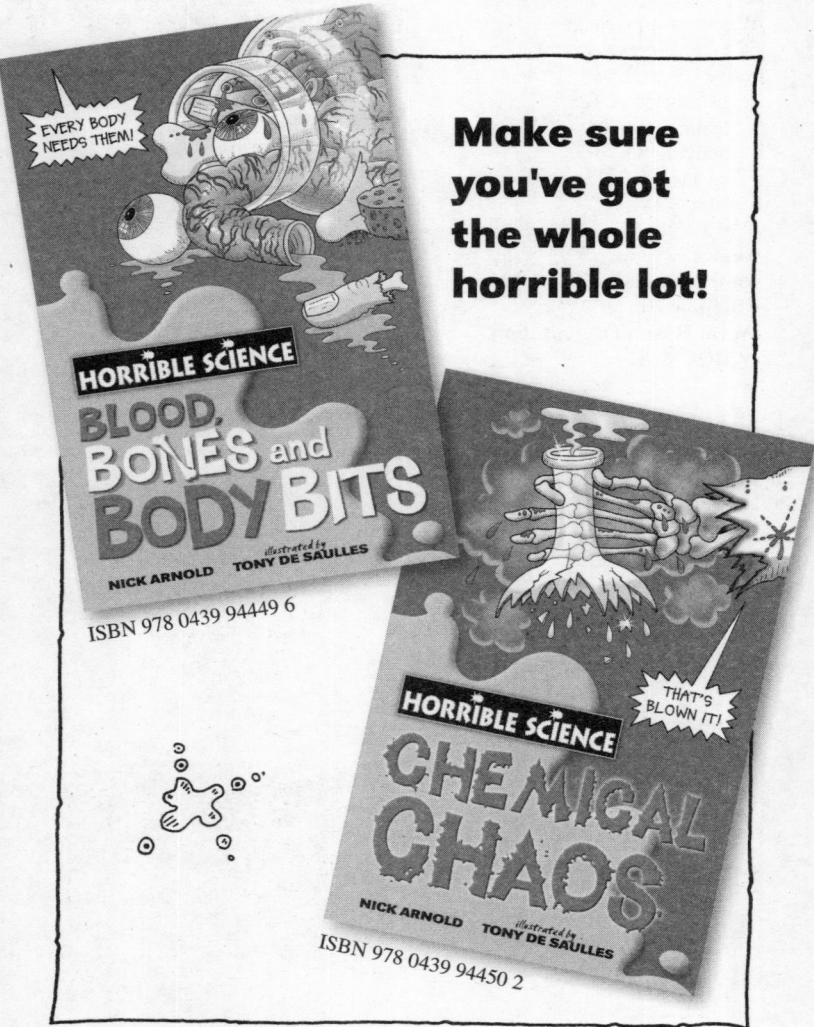

HORRIBLE SCIENCE

NASTY NATURE

I LOVE FAST FOOD!

NICK ARNOLD   *illustrated by* TONY DE SAULLES

ISBN 978 0439 94451 9

HORRIBLE SCIENCE

DEADLY DISEASES

IT'S A GRAVE SITUATION

NICK ARNOLD   *illustrated by* TONY DE SAULLES

ISBN 978 0439 94445 8

HORRIBLE SCIENCE

UGLY BUGS

NOT A PRETTY SIGHT!

NICK ARNOLD   *illustrated by* TONY DE SAULLES

ISBN 978 0439 94452 6

Science with the squishy bits left in!

Ugly Bugs • Blood, Bones and Body Bits
Nasty Nature • Chemical Chaos • Fatal Forces
Sounds Dreadful • Evolve or Die • Vicious Veg
Disgusting Digestion • Bulging Brains
Frightening Light • Shocking Electricity
Deadly Diseases • Microscopic Monsters
Killer Energy • The Body Owner's Handbook
The Terrible Truth About Time
Space, Stars and Slimy Aliens • Painful Poison
The Fearsome Fight For Flight • Angry Animals
Measly Medicine • Evil Inventions

Specials
Suffering Scientists
Explosive Experiments
The Awfully Big Quiz Book
Really Rotten Experiments

Horrible Science Handbooks
Freaky Food Experiments
Famously Foul Experiments
Beastly Body Experiments

Colour Books
The Stunning Science of Everything
Dangerous Dinosaurs Jigsaw Book

HORRIBLE SCIENCE

BULGING BRAINS

NICK ARNOLD

illustrated by
TONY DE SAULLES

Visit Nick Arnold at
www.nickarnold-website.com

Scholastic Children's Books,
Euston House, 24 Eversholt Street,
London, NW1 1DB, UK

A division of Scholastic Ltd
London ~ New York ~ Toronto ~ Sydney ~ Auckland
Mexico City ~ New Delhi ~ Hong Kong

First published in the UK by Scholastic Ltd, 1999
This edition published 2008

Text copyright © Nick Arnold, 1999
Illustrations © Tony De Saulles, 1999

ISBN 978 0439 94447 2

Printed and bound by CPI Group (UK) Ltd, Croydon, CR0 4YY

23

The right of Nick Arnold and Tony De Saulles to be identified as the author and
illustrator of this work respectively has been asserted by them in accordance with
the Copyright, Designs and Patents Act, 1988.

CONTENTS

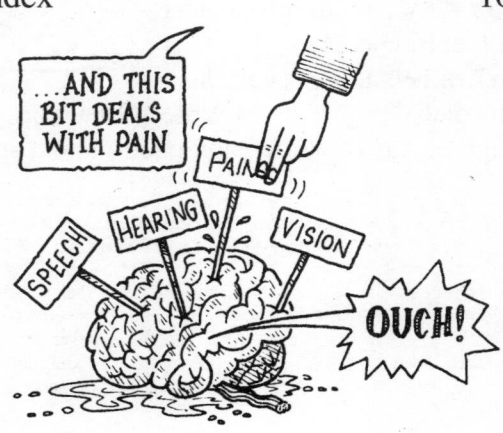

Nick Arnold has been writing stories and books since he was a youngster, but never dreamt he'd find fame writing about Bulging Brains. His research involved volunteering for brain surgery and checking his reflexes with a giant hammer and he enjoyed every minute of it.

When he's not delving into Horrible Science, he spends his spare time eating pizza, riding a bike and thinking up corny jokes (though not all at the same time).

Tony De Saulles picked up his crayons when he was still in nappies and has been doodling ever since. He takes Horrible Science very seriously and even agreed to sketch Nick's brain operation. Fortunately, it didn't make him feel too poorly.

When he's not out with his sketchpad, Tony likes to write poetry and play squash, though he hasn't written any poetry about squash yet.

INTRODUCTION

To hear some scientists talk you'd think they knew everything about science...

But don't be fooled – scientists *don't* know everything. After all, if they did there would be no need for any new experiments. Scientists could sit around all day with their feet up. But, in fact, there are lots of mysteries left to solve. Lots of things we don't know or don't understand.

For example, there's one object that's so mysterious it makes the brainiest scientists scratch their heads. It's wet and squishy and looks revolting – and oddly enough, it's found between their ears. What is it? No, it's not their disgusting, snotty nose. It's the bit *inside* their heads – their bulging brain. Scientists aren't too sure how it works...

But if scientists are puzzled by their own little grey cells what chance do the rest of us have? No wonder learning about your brain can make your head ache.

THE MEDULLA OBLONGATA IS CONNECTED TO THE PONS... BLAH... DRONE... WITTER

GROAN!

ACHE!

THROB!

Well, if science scrambles your brains, help is at hand. This book is bulging with brain facts. For example, bet you never knew that in 1998 US scientists found the part of the brain that makes you laugh. They gave an electric shock to this area of a girl's brain and she started giggling uncontrollably.

HA HA! GIGGLE! GIGGLE!

THIS IS NO LAUGHING MATTER

And that's not all. Did you know that in one brain experiment children were forced to sniff their little brother's stinky old T-shirts? (Page 52 will give you all the smelly details.) Now that really is cruelty!

So by the time you've finished reading this book your knowledge will be so vast you could easily become the brains of your class. And who knows? Your teacher might even mistake you for a scientific mega-genius. But to enjoy the full benefits you've got to ask your brain to help you read this book.

Your eyeballs scan the letters, your brain makes sense of the words, and your memory reminds you what they mean. But hold on – looks like you've already started ... oh well, don't let me stop you. Now ask your brain to send a message down thousands of nerves to tell your finger muscles to gently lift the next page.

BULGING BRAIN BASICS

Dr Funkenstain felt a rush of excitement as she gazed into the glass tank. For five years she had been planning this experiment. Now she had done it and she was looking at the result. The tank was bathed in an eerie light. And floating ghostlike in the tank's centre was a strange and horrible looking object. It was pink like a sausage and wrinkled like an old walnut. And it gave out the faintest whiff of blue cheese.

Could it be an unknown creature from the depths of the ocean? Or perhaps an alien from another world? Dr Funkenstain knew better. She was gazing at a real human brain. A very special human brain because...

IT'S ALIVE!

Dr Funkenstain whispered excitedly. Peering closer she could see the tiny wormlike blood vessels criss-crossing the brain's surface. Dr Funkenstain had done it. She was the first scientist in history to keep a brain alive outside the body.

DON'T PANIC! It's only a story. Scientists can't keep human brains in tanks – yet. But this technique might be possible in the future. Perhaps you'd like to become the first brain surgeon to keep a brain in a tank? If so beware: it's a bad idea to rush into brain surgery without getting to know a bit about your subject. Important facts like…

WHAT'S YOUR BRAIN FOR?

The brain is the part of your body that tells you what's going on around you. You can use your brain to order your body around and even to order everybody else around. But there's much more to your brain. Much, much more.

Inside your brain are your precious memories, your dreams, your hopes for the future and the knowledge of everything you love and care about. In your brain you can sense lovely smells and tastes and colours. Your brain helps you feel great and happy about life and that's the good side. But your brain also creates horrible fears and worries that can make you miserable.

Your brain makes the thoughts and feelings that make your personality. Your brain turns your body from a living object into *you* the person. Without a brain you'd be as dead as a dodo's tombstone, so it's good to know that you've got your very own bulging brain right now between your ears … hopefully.

IT MAKES YOU THINK, DOESN'T IT?

INSIDE THE BULGING BRAIN

Still want to be a brain surgeon? Excellent. Now you've found out a bit about what the bulging brain does, you're ready to check out how it works…

Bulging brains fact file

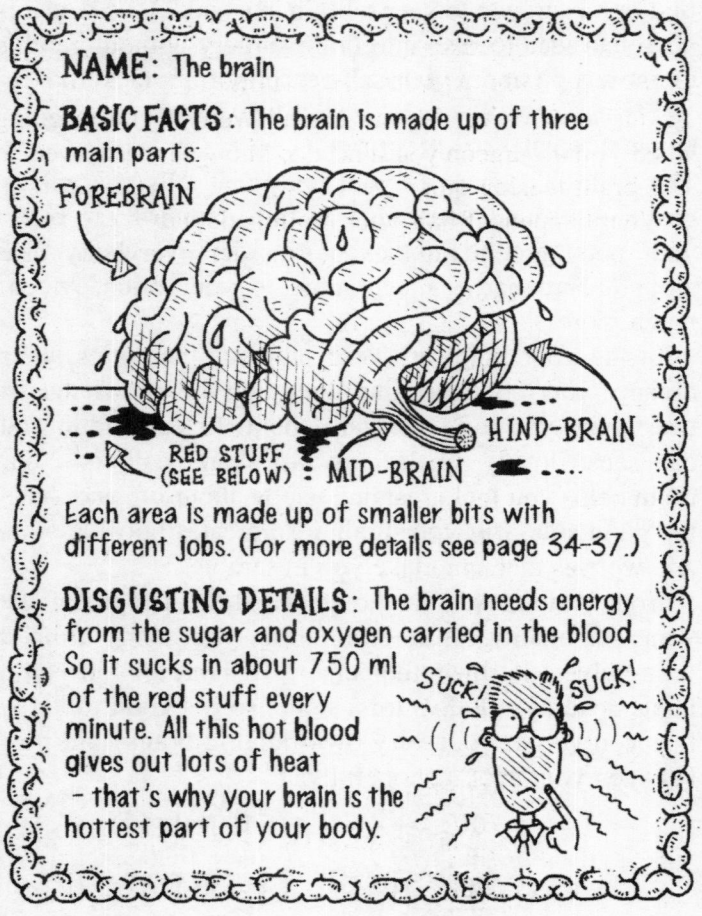

NAME: The brain

BASIC FACTS: The brain is made up of three main parts:

FOREBRAIN

HIND-BRAIN

RED STUFF (SEE BELOW) : MID-BRAIN

Each area is made up of smaller bits with different jobs. (For more details see page 34-37.)

DISGUSTING DETAILS: The brain needs energy from the sugar and oxygen carried in the blood. So it sucks in about 750 ml of the red stuff every minute. All this hot blood gives out lots of heat – that's why your brain is the hottest part of your body.

SUCK! SUCK!

HAVE YOU GOT A BULGING BRAIN?

So just how clever is your brain? Well, if you're going to be a brain surgeon you'll need to know all the answers to this brain-teasing quiz:

1 What happens if half your brain is damaged?

a) It doesn't half hurt, ha-ha. No, seriously, you can't remember anything.

SORRY, WHAT WAS THE QUESTION AGAIN?

b) You die. No one could survive such a terrible injury.

c) You can live normally although you have to re-learn vital skills such as talking.

2 What happens if someone cuts your brain in two?

a) Your brain becomes twice as clever.

b) Your brain functions normally but you may find yourself doing your science homework twice.

WHY HAVE YOU DONE IT TWICE?

I DON'T KNOW MISS... I DON'T KNOW MISS

c) Each side of your brain behaves like a separate person.

3 Imagine you were born without 97 per cent of your cortex (cor-tex) – that's the wrinkly part of your brain at the top where you do your thinking. You're left with a tiny slice of brain in this area. What would happen to you?

a) You'd be left with the brains of a half-witted stick insect.

b) You'd be as brainy as anyone else … but only for five minutes a day. The rest of the time you'd blunder around like a zombie in a horror movie.

c) Your brain would work normally and you could be as brainy as your science teacher. (Yes, teachers are said to be intelligent.)

4 What would you feel if someone stuck a finger into your brain and waggled it about?

a) Unbearable agony – the worst pain in the world.

b) You'd feel hot and cold shivers all over your body.

c) Nothing because the brain cannot feel touch.

5 How much energy does your brain use in a science test?

a) Such a small amount that it can't be measured (especially if you don't know the answers).

b) Enough to light up the classroom. No wonder the test makes you light-headed, ha-ha.

c) Just enough to power a dim light bulb.

IT'S YEAR 5 ...WE WON'T NEED OUR SUNGLASSES

6 Why do you feel tired after the test?

a) All that mental effort strains the brain.

b) During the test your brain drew extra energy in the form of sugar in your blood. After the test your body feels tired because it lacks this vital blood sugar.

c) You were so tense your muscles bunched up and used up energy. And your muscles feel tired – not your brain.

7 How much of your brain is water?

a) About 5 per cent

b) 32 per cent

c) About 80 per cent

Answers:

All the answers are **c)**, so you can check them without taxing your brain too much. And here are a few more details to get you thinking.

1 A bump on the head can injure the brain (see pages 129–139 for the grisly details). Yet the brain can survive dreadful injuries. If one half of the brain is injured, the half that's left learns how to do the work of the damaged half.

2 This operation was performed in the 1960s on patients suffering from violent fits. The operation stopped the fits from spreading through the brain. But afterwards the two sides of the brain acted like separate people. One woman tried to put on a different shirt with each hand. She ended up wearing two shirts.

3 People can live a normal life with very little cortex. This can be the result of a condition called hydrocephalus (hi-dro-cef-al-us). This results in too much fluid sloshing around the skull, so there's less room for the brain.

4 Your nerves take signals from elsewhere in your body to your brain. This means you actually experience pain, touch, taste, smell, sound and vision in your brain. But oddly enough, there are no touch sensors on the brain itself. (You'll find the low-down on senses on pages 45–64.)

5 Yes, in light bulb terms we're all rather dim. Scientist Louis Sokoloff of the US National Institute of Mental Health has found the brain uses the same amount of energy gazing dreamily at a sunset as it does in a tough science test. So what would you rather do?

6 If the questions were really easy, and you managed to relax in the science test, you wouldn't feel so whacked.

7 That's why when you become a brain surgeon and get to touch a brain it'll feel like squidgy blancmange or a soft-boiled egg. The brain needs water for vital chemical reactions such as sending nerve signals. Without water, a brain begins to overheat and starts to see things that aren't there. Ultimately it will die.

BULGING BRAIN SECRETS

Psst – wanna know a brain secret? There's more to your brain than water. For example, your brain's made up of millions of cells and each one is so small you need a microscope to see it. (No, these aren't cells that people get locked up in.) Read on, your brain might learn something...

BULGING BRAIN CELLS

1 Your brain is bulging with 100,000,000,000 – that's 100 *billion* – nerve cells or neurons. These are special cells used for sending signals inside the brain. If you don't believe it, try counting them yourself.

2 Each cell is a living blob and some are so tiny that you can fit 25 on to this fullstop. (You'll need a steady hand for this.)

3 If you laid the cells from just one brain in a line they would stretch 1,000 km – a quarter of the way across the USA.

4 Unborn babies grow about 2,000 new neurons every second, but by the time you reach 25, 12,000 of your neurons. are dying off every day (that's 4.4 million a year). DON'T PANIC – parts of your brain grow new neurons For example, new neurons grow in the part of your brain that deals with smelling – and that really is something to get sniffy about.

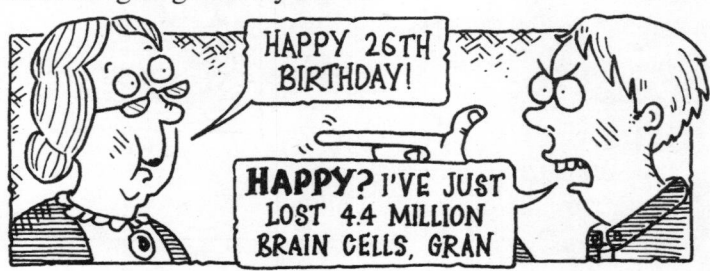

And anyway you won't run out of neurons. You can live a long life and still have 98 per cent of them left.

5 Your brain cells are desperate for oxygen. Starve a brain of blood for just seven seconds and it goes on strike and switches itself off. You might call this fainting. Scientists aren't quite sure how this fascinating process takes place.

Yep – even now scientists are baffled by the mysterious brain. But not quite as baffled as the people who first probed the brain's grisly secrets. Check out the next page and prepare to be baffled, bewildered, bemused and ... *horrified*.

BULGING BRAIN BOFFINS

The first brain surgeons had a problem. The bulging brain is mysterious because you get no clues to tell you what's going on inside it. I mean there's no helpful sign saying...

Unlike certain other parts of the body the brain doesn't do interesting things like digest food, burp or even fart. The brain just sits around all day squelching to itself.

So it's not so surprising that these early pioneers made some mind-boggling mistakes.

MIND-BOGGLING MISTAKES

The ancient Egyptians and Greeks thought that the thinking part of the body was the heart. This seemed right because your heart beats faster when you're upset or excited. Is that why your teacher (who could be as old

17

as the pyramids) makes you learn boring facts "by heart"? Well, anyway, the ancient Greeks and Egyptians were *wrong*.

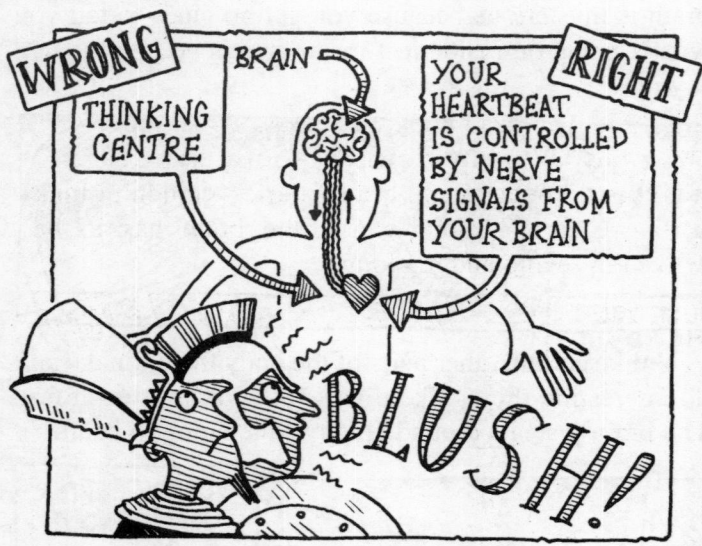

Brainy Greek philosopher Aristotle (384–322 BC) also thought the heart did the thinking. He reckoned the brain was simply a cooling system for the blood. According to Aristotle when you get a cold your cooling system overflows. (That's why snot dribbles out of your nose.)

But he was *wrong* too. Snot is made in the lining of the nose to catch germs and dust. Your nose is runny in a cold because your body is trying to flush out the germs that cause the illness.

Actually, Greek doctor Alcmaeon of Croton (6th century BC) had already figured out what the brain was up to. He cut up dead bodies and noticed that there were nerves running from the eyeballs to the brain. He also noted that patients with head injuries couldn't think clearly. "Clearly," thought Al, "the brain has to be involved in seeing and thinking."

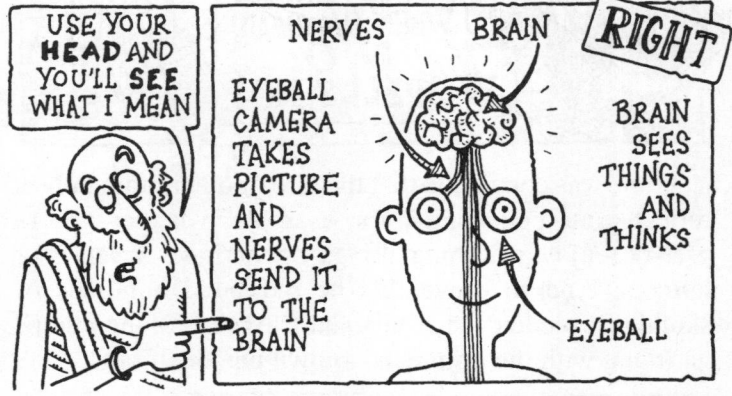

But for over 1,000 years doctors remained puzzled. They weren't sure how the brain worked or what the different bits were for. There were theories, of course. One widely held view was that you did your thinking in the fluid-filled spaces inside the brain known as ventricles (ven-trick-als). The rest of the brain was a squelchy bubble-wrap to cushion the vital holes. But by the 18th century scientists were looking at the brain in a more scientific way. And making strange and grisly discoveries...

BULGING BRAIN SECRETS: FRANZ GALL (1758-1828)

As a child Franz noticed that one of his school friends had bulging eyes. This boy was good at spelling and Franz wondered if everyone who is good at spelling has bulging eyes. After he became a doctor in Vienna he cut up dead bodies and came to the conclusion that the eyes bulged because the brain behind them was also bulging. Franz reckoned this bulging area dealt with spelling.

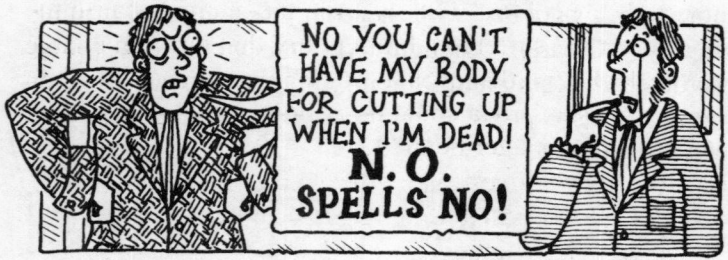

Franz was convinced that the size of other brain bulges reflect your personality, for example, whether you're greedy, enjoy smashing things up or have a sense of humour. And to prove this he measured hundreds of skulls of executed criminals and tried to link the bumps he found with the criminals' known personal traits.

Despite his many skulls, er, I mean skills, Franz was on the wrong track. There is no link between the shape of your brain and your personal qualities. But up to the 1850s many people believed Franz had found a way to measure personality. And when Franz's own brain was examined after his death it was found to be smaller than average. Now, I wonder what that could mean?

THE TALKING BRAIN: PAUL BROCA (1824-1880)

Paul was working as a surgeon in Paris when he met a patient named Tan. "Tan" was his nickname because the poor man had suffered a brain injury that left him unable to speak any word except "tan". Tan was already ill when he saw Broca. Broca could do nothing to help his patient and a few days later he died.

Tan's misfortune was a great opportunity for science. Broca cut open Tan's brain and found that the injury was in what's now imaginatively known as Broca's area (surely it ought to be called Tan's area?). Broca realized that this area of the brain helps you pronounce words properly.

This was a major discovery, but as far as speech goes it wasn't the last word – geddit? In 1874 German scientist Carl Wernicke (1848–1905) found another bit (now known – surprise, surprise – as Wernicke's area) which helps you *choose* the right words. People with brain damage in this area often talk utter drivel but with perfect grammar. (For more details see page 75.)

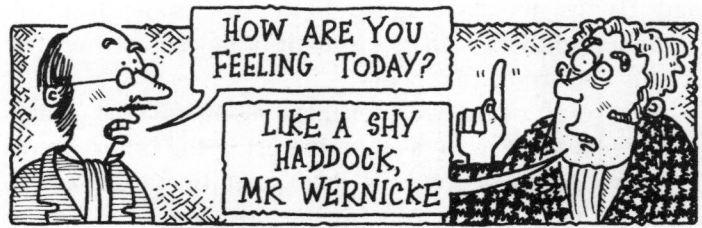

21

THE TWITCHING BRAIN: JULIUS EDUARD HITZIG (1838-1907)

If Mrs Hitzig had walked into the bedroom unexpectedly one day in 1870 she would have received a horrible shock. Her husband and his pal Gustav Fritsch were experimenting on a dog's brain using her dressing-table as a workbench.

At the time, Hitzig was working as a doctor in Switzerland but he didn't have a lab of his own. (By the way it's a bad idea to use your mum's dressing-table to practise your brain surgery. You could use the bathroom instead, but make sure you mop the floor afterwards.)

Actually, the dog was getting quite a shock too. An electric shock to the left side of its brain. Hitzig found that this made the dog's right legs twitch. This electrifying test proved that the left side of the brain controls the right side of the body and vice versa. Later in the year war broke out between Germany and France, and Hitzig got the chance to try the same tests on wounded soldiers with bits of their brains shot away. The results confirmed his theory.

As a result of the work of these pioneers, new groups of scientists began to take an interest in the brain. You'll be coming across some of them later on in this book. Here's a handy guide to help you spot them...

Spot the scientist

1. Neurophysiologist
(new-ro-fizzy-olo-gist)

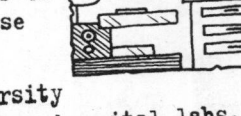

INTERESTED IN: finding out
how the brain and nerves work.

WHAT THEY DO: study bits of
chopped-up brain and analyse
chemicals from the brain.

WHERE THEY WORK: University
laboratories or large hospital labs.

2. Neurologists (new-rol-lo-gists)

INTERESTED IN: Studying
the brain and nerves, too,
but they're especially keen
on horrible but fascinating
brain and nerve diseases.

WHAT THEY DO: Treat
patients with diseases of the nerves and brain.
Some of them are also neurosurgeons which is
the posh term for brain surgeons.

WHERE THEY WORK: Hospitals.

3. Psychiatrists (si-ki-a-trists)

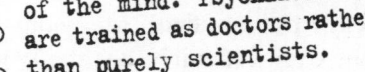

INTERESTED IN: Diseases
of the mind. Psychiatrists
are trained as doctors rather
than purely scientists.

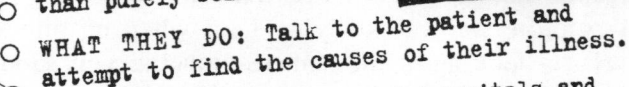

WHAT THEY DO: Talk to the patient and
attempt to find the causes of their illness.

WHERE THEY WORK: general hospitals and
psychiatric hospitals and clinics.

4. Psychologists (si-col-lo-gists)

INTERESTED IN:
Studying the brain by looking at the way it makes people behave.

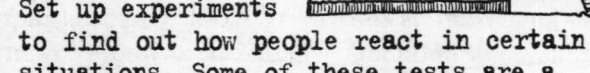

WHAT THEY DO:
Set up experiments to find out how people react in certain situations. Some of these tests are a bit wacky. Some psychologists are interested in diseases of the mind, but unlike psychiatrists they are not trained as doctors.

WHERE THEY WORK: University labs and hospitals.

PECULIAR PSYCHOLOGISTS

The psychologists take their lead from a very peculiar German scientist, and here's his story...

Hall of fame: Gustav Fechner (1801–1887)
Nationality: German

Fechner's brain was always bulging with ideas but his interest in the mind began with a horrible accident. The physics professor was studying light when he blinded himself by looking at the sun. (Something you should never do.) So you could say poor old Gus got blinded by science – geddit. He became so miserable that he went mad for two years.

But one day he was sitting in the garden and he felt a sudden impulse to tear off his bandages. Amazingly, he found he could see again! Incredible colours flooded his brain and he was so excited he imagined he could see brains inside flowers. (Yes, you did read that last bit correctly.) Gus wrote a peculiar book describing how plants have minds. (Believe this and you're a real cabbage-brain.)

Two years later Gus was enjoying a lie-in. Well, maybe "enjoying" is the wrong word. Gus was racking his brains. And not about whether he'd find a toy in his packet of breakfast cereal or how to make contact with a turnip. He was trying to think of a way to study the brain using scientific experiments rather than cutting it open on an operating table. Then he had a brainwave.

All you had to do was measure how the brain reacts to different sensations. For example, in one test Gus shone a light in a volunteer's eyes and slowly increased the brightness until they noticed the change. This allowed him to measure the brain's ability to notice changes in brightness.

ARGH! MY #!!□*!# EYES!!

INCREASED BRIGHTNESS TILL VOLUNTEER REQUESTED I HALT

Gus had launched a new branch of science called psychology – the study of human behaviour (although the name actually means "study of the mind" in Greek).

And this exciting new science owed its existence to the fact that the scientist fancied an extra snooze. (Tell your parents this story next time you want a lie-in, you never know they might even fall for it.)

Fechner's work was continued by German Wilhelm Wundt (1832–1920), who set up the world's first psychology lab. Wundt never laughed or smiled or joked and spent his entire life working.

SORRY READERS, NO JOKES ALLOWED WITH THIS PICTURE

His books totalled 53,735 pages – that's equal to writing a 500-page book every year for 100 years. He wrote so much that critics complained that it was hard to discover what Wundt actually thought. American psychologist George A Miller wrote…

The sheer bulk of his writing made Wundt almost immune to criticism. A critic would be … buried under mountains of detail.

Brilliant, eh? So if you want to baffle your teacher write a 500-page essay for your science homework. But this tactic didn't stop other psychologists disagreeing with Wundt's approach to psychology. Increasingly they were finding that the brain did a lot more than simply respond to sensations.

Another German psychologist Max Wertheimer (1880–1943) wondered if the brain plays tricks to help make sense of a film. A film is made up of thousands of pictures that you see very quickly – about 24 pictures a second. The brain can't keep up with this rapid change so it sees the pictures as a continuously moving scene. So your brain gets the whole picture – and you get the whole movie, including the exciting bits *and* the happy ending.

Max dreamt up this idea on a train in 1910. He was supposed to be on holiday but he excitedly leapt off the train (he waited for it to stop first – he wasn't that excited) and set up experiments to find out why.

Max proved the brain sees the whole scene first and then figures out how the moving objects relate to one another. And he worked out a new theory of psychology called Gestalt (ges-stal-t) based on these ideas. Gestalt actually means "whole" in German and the new theory underlined the importance of finding out how the brain makes sense of things like the film. This was a step forward from Wundt's work, which simply looked at how the brain responds to sensations.

Meanwhile American psychologists such as John B Watson (1878–1958) and, later, Burrhus Skinner (1904–1990) were changing the behaviour of rats by training their brains. (You can read more about Watson and his wacky experiments on pages 86–89.)

BULGING BRAIN EXPRESSIONS
Two brain surgeons are quarrelling...

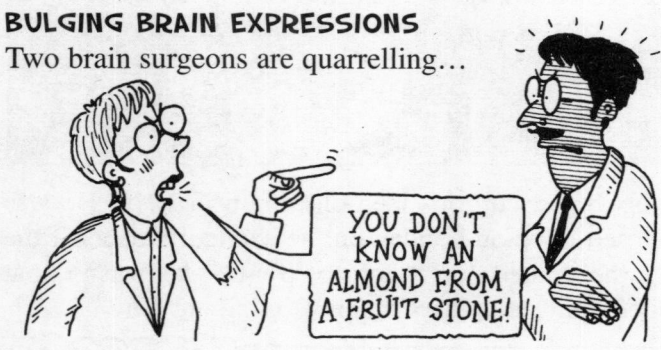

YOU DON'T KNOW AN ALMOND FROM A FRUIT STONE!

Is the quarrel about gardening?

Answer: No. The amygdala (a-mig-dal-a) and putumen (putt-you-men) – almond and fruit stone in Greek – are odd names for areas of the brain.

Confused yet? Well, there are lots more bits and pieces you'll need to know about if you're going to be a brain surgeon. Maybe things would be clearer if you could get your hands on a real dripping brain. Fancy a squidge? Hope so, if not the next chapter's so nasty, it could drive you out of your mind.

Better sharpen that scalpel...

BULGING BRAIN BITS 'N' PIECES

As a brain surgeon you need to know all about the main bits and pieces in the brain. Fortunately we've got hold of a real genuine brain from a real genuinely dead person to help you. Go on, take a peek – it won't bite you.

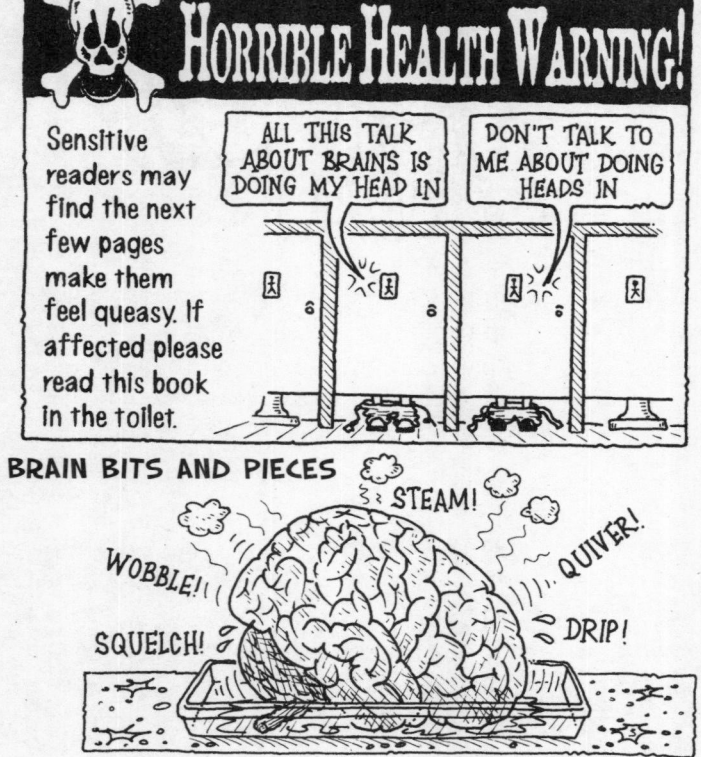

HORRIBLE HEALTH WARNING!

Sensitive readers may find the next few pages make them feel queasy. If affected please read this book in the toilet.

ALL THIS TALK ABOUT BRAINS IS DOING MY HEAD IN

DON'T TALK TO ME ABOUT DOING HEADS IN

BRAIN BITS AND PIECES

STEAM!

QUIVER!

WOBBLE!

DRIP!

SQUELCH!

The main area you can see is the cortex (that's the wrinkly, thinking bit, remember?).

Dare you discover ... why the cortex is wrinkly?

Ever wondered why brains are wrinkly? Now's your chance to discover the *real* answer...

You will need:
Two sheets of A4 paper. (Your school report might come in handy here.)

What you do:
1 Screw one sheet of paper into a tight little ball.

2 Open it up but don't flatten it.
3 Place it over the second sheet of A4 paper.

What do you notice?
a) The screwed-up paper seems to have shrunk.
b) The screwed-up paper has got bigger.
c) Both sheets of paper are the same size.

To find out more about some of the vital brain bits and pieces let's have a peek at this gory but fascinating medical textbook.

31

Brain Surgery for Beginners

Chapter 1: Brain bits and pieces

Cerebrum (ser-ree-brum)

This is the largest bit of the brain – it's so big it makes up 85 per cent of the brain. This area is REALLY important because its wrinkly surface is the cortex, where thinking takes place. The cerebrum is divided into two halves (no one knows the reason for the split). The halves are linked by a bridge at the base made of millions of nerves cells.

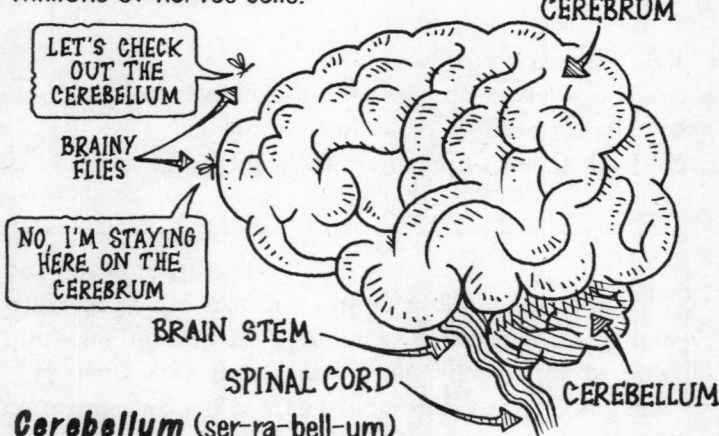

LET'S CHECK OUT THE CEREBELLUM

BRAINY FLIES

NO, I'M STAYING HERE ON THE CEREBRUM

CEREBRUM

BRAIN STEM

SPINAL CORD

CEREBELLUM

Cerebellum (ser-ra-bell-um)

The name means "little brain" in Latin – because it looks a bit like a little brain. This pear-sized blob has two halves – one for each side of the brain. Both sides help the brain balance and control its body's movements.

Bet you never knew!
When you learn a skill such as riding a bike you think about what you're doing. Well, hopefully – otherwise you'd fall off. But after a while you happily pedal around without thinking. Oh, so you knew that? Well, when you stop thinking about what you're doing your cerebellum takes over from your thinking cortex and tells your body what to do. Scientists have found that with the cerebellum in charge you can move faster and less clumsily. (For more details on what the cerebellum can do check out pages 73–75 and 100.)

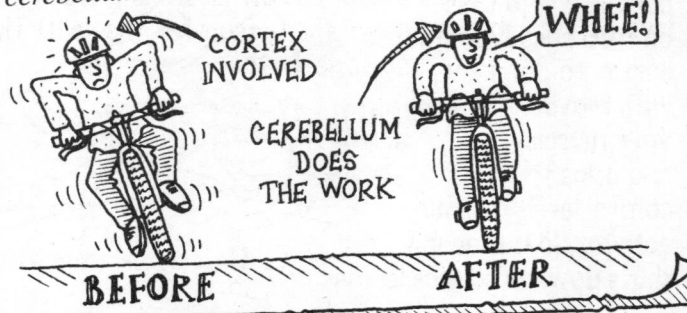

CORTEX INVOLVED

WHEE!

CEREBELLUM DOES THE WORK

BEFORE   AFTER

Spinal cord
This is a bundle of nerves about 45 cm long and as thick as a thumb. Although it's not part of the brain, as a brain surgeon you need to know what it does. It actually takes signals to and from the brain.

Brain stem
This bit links the brain with the spinal cord. It's useful for helping the brain to go to sleep. And it's also useful for waking up the brain to danger or something interesting.

As a brain surgeon you'll need to know a bit more about the even smaller but still vital bits and pieces that lurk deep within the brain. We've cut some brains in half to help you...

Thalmus

Scientists are still finding out what this bit does. You've actually got a pair of them — one for each side of your brain. Each thalamus is packed with neurons and seems to work like a switchboard, routing nerve signals from all your senses except smell to your cortex. It also passes on messages from the cortex to do with moving your muscles and helps to control levels of brain activity. So it probably shuts down in science lessons.

PINEAL GLAND   HYPOTHALAMUS

PITUITARY GLAND

half a brain (side view)

Hypothalamus (hi-po-thal-a-mus)

A bossy little blob the size of one of your knuckles. It reckons *it's* the boss of the entire body. Controls the water content in the blood, its temperature, sweating, shivering, growing, when you sleep, etc.

The pituitary gland

Vital sidekick for the hypothalamus. Follows its orders and makes the chemicals that go round in the blood. These chemicals, or hormones as scientists call them, order the body to do what the hypothalamus wants.

34

The pineal (pi-nee-al) gland

The pineal gland is linked to your eyes and is sensitive to light and dark. In the dark it makes a substance that stops children from developing into adults too early. You may also like to know there's a fish called a lamprey that has a pineal like an extra eye on top of its head. The extra eye gives it all-round vision. (Scientists have failed to prove the common belief that teachers have this eye in the back of their heads.)

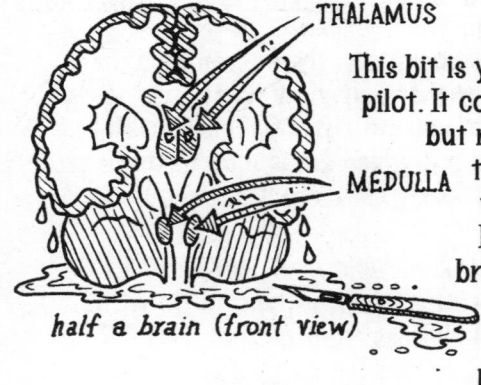

THALAMUS

MEDULLA

half a brain (front view)

Medulla

This bit is your brain's auto-pilot. It controls those vital but rather boring jobs that you need to do without thinking. I'm talking about breathing and heart rate and reflex movements (see page 60). This is all very handy and your mighty medulla also makes you vomit which isn't quite as nice. Mind you, this can be vital if you've eaten some poison or a school dinner.

Limbic (lim-bick) system

An odd mixture of bits and pieces including the amygdala (known in English as the "almond") and hypothamus deep in the brain. Shapes your feelings and also involved in memory.

WHOOPS! ER, FANCY AN ALMOND SLICE, NURSE?

35

BRAIN SURGERY FOR BEGINNERS

Chapter 2: Vital brain tests

Of course, as a brain surgeon you'll be performing operations on living patients (hopefully they'll still be alive after the operation too).

DON'T WORRY, I'VE READ A BOOK ABOUT IT!

To help you plan your operations there is an amazing collection of machines that can show what's going on inside the brain before you get cutting. This is useful because you can find out which areas may be damaged or not functioning properly. Let's check them out ...

Machine 1: a CAT

No, this is nothing to do with Tiddles, your pet cat. This CAT is a machine. CT means computerised tomography (toe-mog-graf-ee). Well, you need to spout the jargon effortlessly if you're a brain surgeon.

The machine sends weak X-rays through the brain and shows up the result on a computer screen. These days it's often used with other machines such as _

COMPUTER

X-RAY VIEW INSIDE CAT MACHINE

Machine 2: a PET

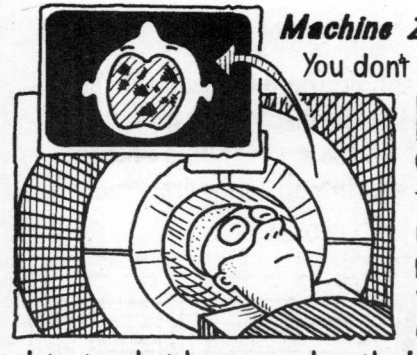

You dont need cat food for this pet — it's a Positive Emission Tomography (poz-it-tron e-miss-e-on toe-mog-graf-ee) machine. Your poor old patient has to be injected with a radioactive chemical. The scanner detects what happens when the blood takes the chemical into their brain. The blood flows to the bits of the brain that are most active. So you can see what's going on and spot any areas that don't seem to be working properly.

Machine 3: a MRI means Magnetic Resonance Imaging

This is the hight-tech gizmo you really want to get your surgical gloves on. It surrounds the brain with magnetic force and zaps the brain with radio waves. The machine detects radio waves bouncing back from hydrogen atoms in the brain (hydrogen is an ingredient of water so there are billions of hydrogen atoms in your brain). The scanner turns the signals into a cool picture of slices of brain and even shows where blood is flowing. And since a brain bit gets more blood when it's busy, it can show which brain bits are used for jobs such as talking or making a chewing gum sculpture. **37**

Machine 4: an EEG

This stands for electroencephalograph (el-leck-tro-en-cef-falo-graf) machine. The metal electrodes pick up electrical signals given off as the brain thinks and the machine displays them as a print-out showing the signals as peaks.

Important note to the reader:

Sorry to interrupt the book. Just a quick message to say that the EEG machine is an ultra-sensitive piece of equipment. This was tested by an American doctor in the mid-1970s who wired up a lime-flavoured jelly to an EEG machine. (The flavour didn't actually affect the test.) According to the machine, the jelly was alive and thinking! In fact, it was reacting to people chatting in the next room. So make sure you read this book q-u-i-e-t-l-y.

Checking the print out

Here's what your EEG print out might show.

1 An alpha rhythm.
This means the
brain's thinking in a
dreamy kind of way.

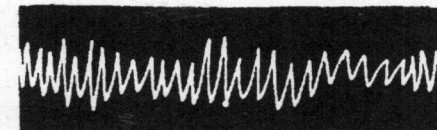

2 Beta rhythm (a
bit faster). The brain
is paying attention
to what's going on.

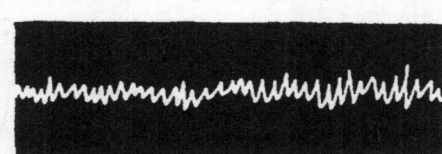

3 Theta rhythm
(a bit slower). The
brain is feeling
sleepy.

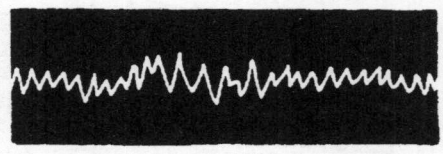

4 Delta rhythm
(very slow). The
brain has fallen into
a deep sleep. (This
has been found to be
a common condition amongst children in science
lessons.)

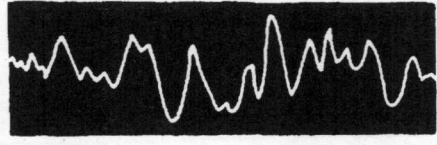

If the line is completely flat you
should check that your patient
is still alive. A flat line normally
means the patient is dead!

Bet you never knew!

The EEG was invented by German Dr Hans Berger (1873–1941) who spent five years sticking electrodes on people's heads to measure brain activity. He even tested his invention on his children. Hans reckoned he would be able to show what his children and the other patients were thinking. He couldn't do this but he spent another five years writing up his experiments. And then ... no one took any notice.

It wasn't until British Scientist Edgar Adrian (1889–1977) showed that unusual wave patterns could be a sign of brain disease that EEG machines were used in hospitals.

BRAIN SURGERY FOR BEGINNERS

Chapter 3: Surgical tools

Congratulations, you're now almost ready for your first brain operation! First, though, you need to get familiar with a few brain surgeon's tools.

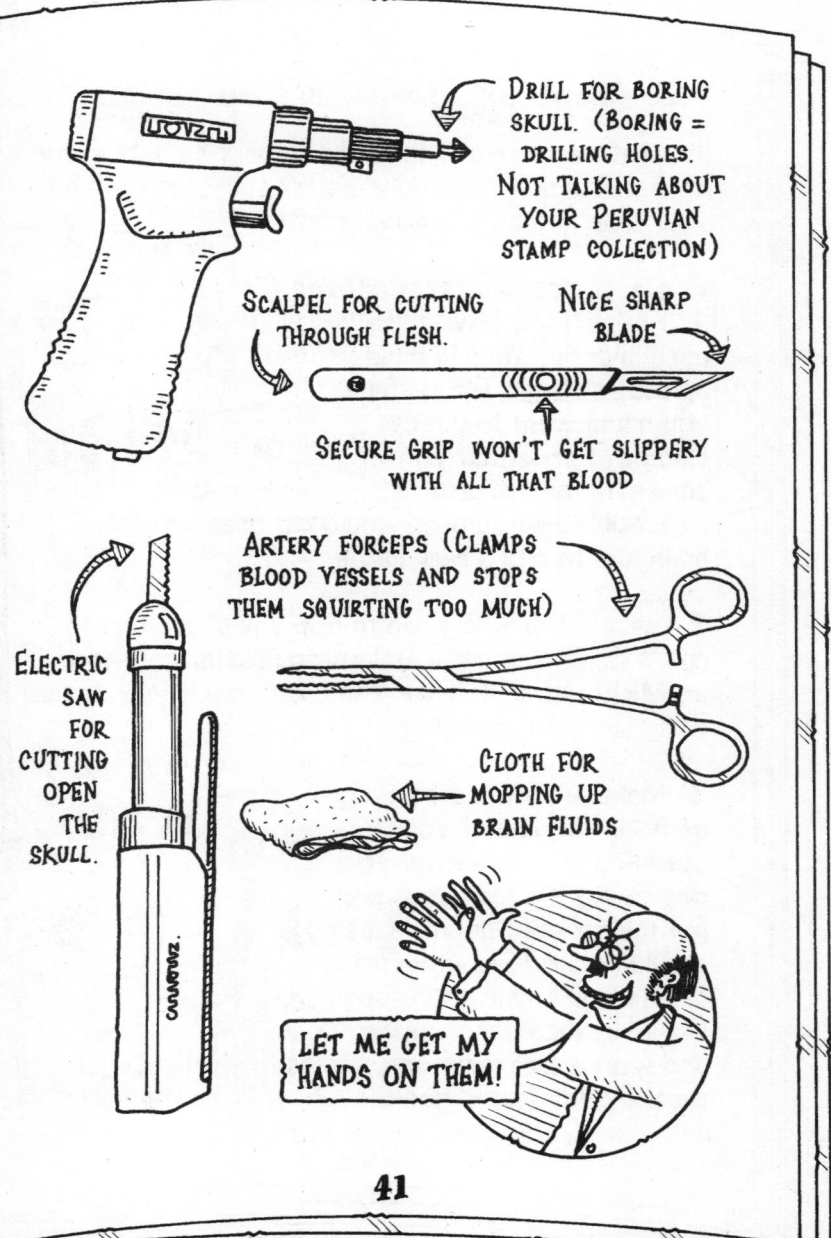

41

Chapter 4: Your first operation

Just before you move on to the surgery bit, take a look at these handy instructions. Better still, keep them by your side during the actual operation.

Brain surgery instructions

1 It helps if you have a particular operation in mind before you begin. For example you might want to remove a blood clot or a fragment of bone after an accident. No

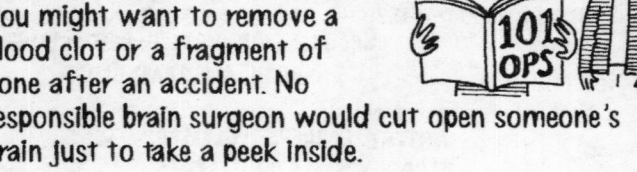

responsible brain surgeon would cut open someone's brain just to take a peek inside.

2 Use a PET or MRI scan to help you plan where to cut. In 1998, scientists at Toronto Hospital developed an MRI scanner that you can use to guide your scalpel whilst actually operating.

3 Make sure there are no germs in the area of your operation. It's not enough to clear away the tea things and put the cat out. The entire area should be scrubbed with strong disinfectant to kill germs. You should be thoroughly washed and wear a face mask and a specially disinfected gown.

4 Draw a line on the patient's head to show where you intend to cut. Oops! Nearly forgot. The patient's head should be shaven to prevent bits of hair getting mixed in with their brain.

5 To get at the brain you need to remove a bit of skull. First drill some holes in the skull. (You'll have to concentrate. One slip and you might drill through the brain.)

6 Next, saw between the holes and lift up a flap of skull and meninges (men-in-gees) – the protective layers under the skull. As you lift the meninges you may hear a *sclurping* noise as the clear fluid that surrounds the brain bubbles out.

7 If everything goes according to plan the brain should be pulsing as the blood squirts through its blood vessels.

8 Now to begin your brilliant brain operation....

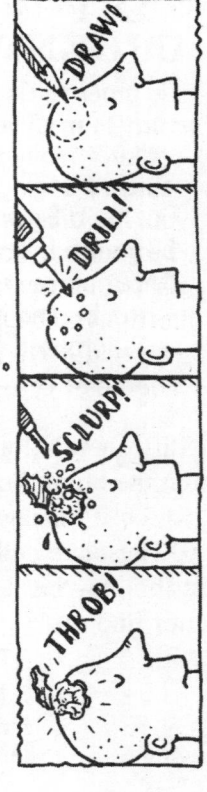

☠ HORRIBLE HEALTH WARNING!

Stop! Don't do anything until you've read the next page!

IMPORTANT AND VERY URGENT ANNOUNCEMENT:

In order to do brain surgery properly you have to study in medical school for at least seven years. You didn't really think you'd be allowed to do brain surgery at your age did you? Sorry to disappoint you. You'd better stick everything back together and be grateful. Why? Because practising brain surgery without proper training could land you in serious legal trouble and result in your pocket money being stopped for 33,000,000 years. Sorry!

Still, there's lots more fascinating things to find out about the brain. For example, there are the amazing ways in which it manages to find out what's going on around you. These are called "senses". So here's a challenge for your brain – has it got the sense to read the next chapter? Better find out!

I'VE GOT A HEADACHE – CAN WE READ IT LATER?

SURE!

STARTLING SENSES

Without senses life would be like sitting in a dark cupboard. Yep, even more boring than a science lesson. But thanks to your brain you are bombarded with startling sights and sounds and smells. It's lucky you've got strong nerves to cope with it all. After all, your senses won't work without nerves...

Bulging brains fact file

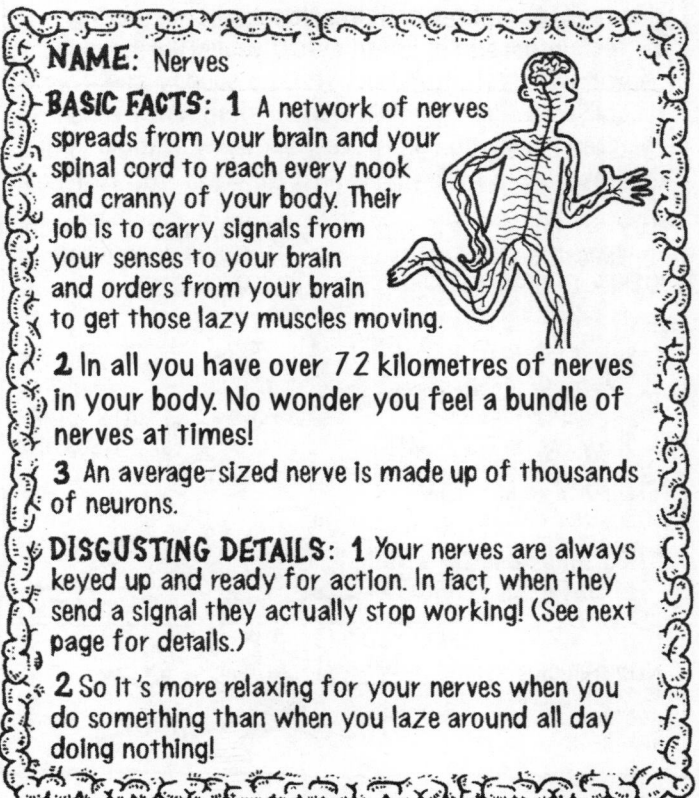

NAME: Nerves

BASIC FACTS: 1 A network of nerves spreads from your brain and your spinal cord to reach every nook and cranny of your body. Their job is to carry signals from your senses to your brain and orders from your brain to get those lazy muscles moving.

2 In all you have over 72 kilometres of nerves in your body. No wonder you feel a bundle of nerves at times!

3 An average-sized nerve is made up of thousands of neurons.

DISGUSTING DETAILS: 1 Your nerves are always keyed up and ready for action. In fact, when they send a signal they actually stop working! (See next page for details.)

2 So it's more relaxing for your nerves when you do something than when you laze around all day doing nothing!

Your nerves are a bit like an amazing telephone system that takes messages all around your body. Just imagine they were a phone system – the manual would make fascinating reading...

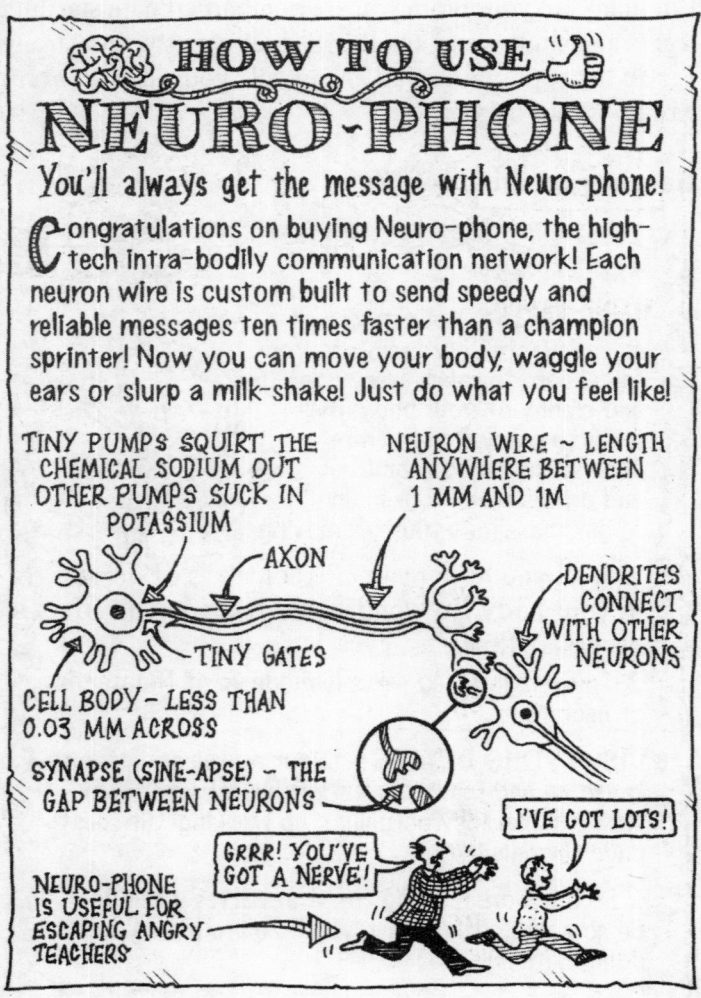

To activate your Neuro-phone system you don't need to worry about boring dialling codes or numbers. Simply ask your brain cortex to send a message anywhere you want in the body. Neuro-phone will do the rest for you. . . here's how.

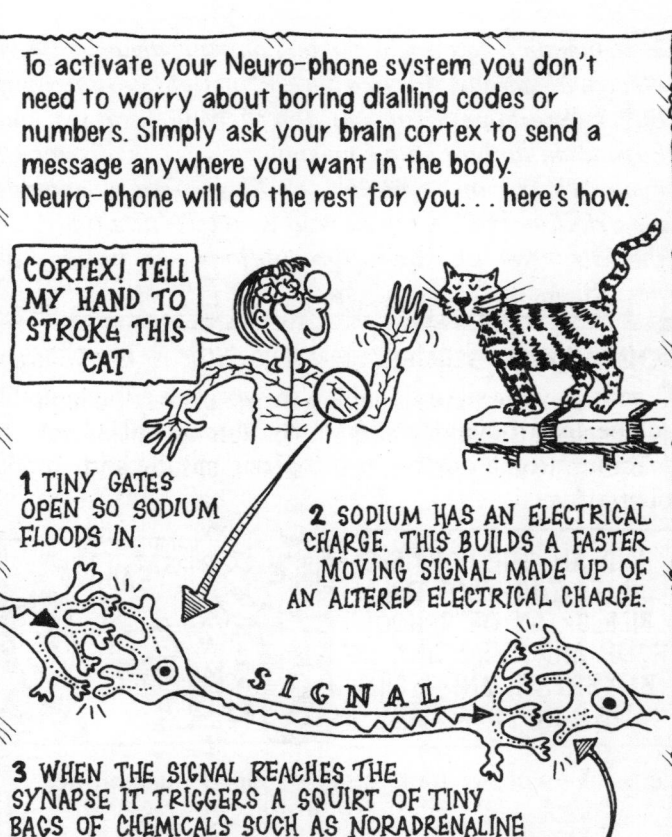

CORTEX! TELL MY HAND TO STROKE THIS CAT

1 TINY GATES OPEN SO SODIUM FLOODS IN.

2 SODIUM HAS AN ELECTRICAL CHARGE. THIS BUILDS A FASTER MOVING SIGNAL MADE UP OF AN ALTERED ELECTRICAL CHARGE.

S I G N A L

3 WHEN THE SIGNAL REACHES THE SYNAPSE IT TRIGGERS A SQUIRT OF TINY BAGS OF CHEMICALS SUCH AS NORADRENALINE (NOR-AD-REN-A-LIN) THAT FLOOD ACROSS TO THE NEXT NEURON AND TRIGGER A SIGNAL THERE.

Bet you never knew!
1 Nerve signals are F-A-S-T. Tests show a monkey can spot a banana, use its cortex to decide what to do, reach out and grab the food – all inside one second. Could you move any faster if someone offered you a choccie?

> **2** *Remember that a science test only produces enough electrical activity in your brain to light a dim light bulb? (See page 13 if you don't.) Well, what do you have to do to light up a Christmas tree? The answer is, even when you're doing nothing there's enough electrical nerve energy in your nervous little body for the job. After all you've got billions and billions of nerve cells.*

SENSATIONAL SENSES

Thanks to your sensational senses you can appreciate the true beauty of the world. A lovely blue cloudless sky, the delicious aroma of new-baked pizza and the soft smooth touch of velvet…

AND ALL THE HORRIBLE BITS TOO, LIKE THE BILE GREEN OF SCHOOL SOUP AND THE STINK OF BAD BREATH AND ITCHY NITS IN YOUR HAIR

YEAH!

Let's take a closer look at these marvellous abilities…

BULGING BRAIN EXPRESSIONS

Some psychologists are chatting over dinner…

MY ANOSMIA IS REALLY BAD

YOU'RE LUCKY IT ISN'T PAROSMIA

Are these weird types of food?

Answer: No. These are problems caused by blows on the head.

Anosmia = you can't smell anything.

Parosmia = all food tastes disgusting. Of course the scientists might have been eating a school dinner. Then their food would have tasted truly terrible!

Bet you never knew!
The sense of taste gets weaker as we grow older. At present scientists don't understand why this happens, but you can observe the effects any lunchtime. Many children can't stand the vile flavour of school dinners but elderly teachers happily relish the revolting recipes.

Dare you discover ... a touch of the ridiculous?

You will need:
Your body
Clothes (don't forget to put some on your body)

What you do:

1 Nothing. If only all science experiments were this easy!

2 Concentrate on trying to feel the clothes you are wearing against your skin. (Don't touch them with your hands.)

What do you notice?

a) I can't feel anything except my itchy socks.

b) I can feel the material against my skin. Funny I never noticed it before.

c) This experiment has given me a headache.

Answer: b) If your nerves feel a constant sensation like your clothes they get used to it and stop firing. That's why you don't feel your clothes and you may forget you're wearing any. Hopefully, you should notice if you're not wearing any.

If **c)** stop concentrating so hard and if **a)** consider the possibility that you're only wearing your socks. This could be a sight for sore eyes, and talking about vision...

SEEING IS BELIEVING

You might think that you see with your eyes. But your eyeballs simply act like cameras and pick up light patterns from the outside world. It's the brain that makes sense of this information. Sounds complicated? Well, fortunately, the Neuro-phone people have logged the neuron calls involved so you can make sense of it all.

Take a look at this...
You see through your eyeballs. An image of the scene falls on the retina and the one million neurons in your optic nerve take the image in the form of nerve pulses to your brain. Now read on...

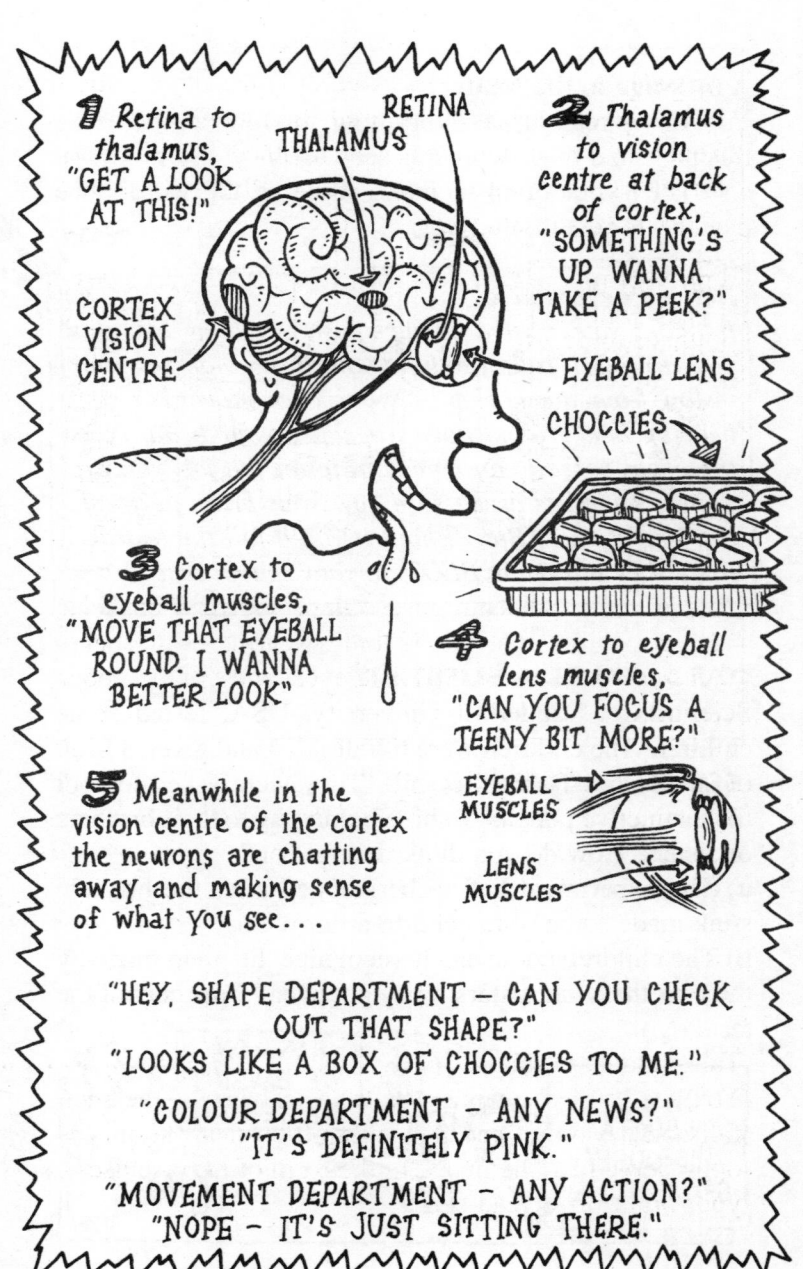

1 Retina to thalamus, "GET A LOOK AT THIS!"

RETINA

THALAMUS

2 Thalamus to vision centre at back of cortex, "SOMETHING'S UP. WANNA TAKE A PEEK?"

CORTEX VISION CENTRE

EYEBALL LENS

CHOCCIES

3 Cortex to eyeball muscles, "MOVE THAT EYEBALL ROUND. I WANNA BETTER LOOK"

4 Cortex to eyeball lens muscles, "CAN YOU FOCUS A TEENY BIT MORE?"

5 Meanwhile in the vision centre of the cortex the neurons are chatting away and making sense of what you see...

EYEBALL MUSCLES

LENS MUSCLES

"HEY, SHAPE DEPARTMENT – CAN YOU CHECK OUT THAT SHAPE?"
"LOOKS LIKE A BOX OF CHOCCIES TO ME."

"COLOUR DEPARTMENT – ANY NEWS?"
"IT'S DEFINITELY PINK."

"MOVEMENT DEPARTMENT – ANY ACTION?"
"NOPE – IT'S JUST SITTING THERE."

A message to the reader:
Yep, this is really true. Everything you look at, including this page and these words, is seen *inside* your brain. You also need your brain to make sense of the words (see page 81 for details).

> *Bet you never knew!*
> *Imagine you're in a science test. At times like this you're concentrating so hard your brain blots out your vision from the corner of your eyes. You also stop hearing background noises because your brain blots these out so you can concentrate on the job you are doing. Scientists aren't sure how your brain performs this useful trick. But without it you'd fail the test and there'd be a terrible BLOT on your school record.*

COULD YOU BE A SCIENTIST?

Scientists at Vanderbilt University, USA, tested some children. The children were blindfolded and given a heap of smelly old T-shirts to sniff. They were asked to spot the distinctive pong of T-shirts belonging to their brothers or sisters. How do you think they got on?

a) The experiment had to be stopped after the horrible stink made some of the children throw up.

b) The children could easily recognize the pong made by their brothers and sisters. They got over 75 per cent of the tests right.

c) The children found it impossible to identify the smell made by their brothers and sisters.

Answer: b) And in tests 16 out of 18 parents could identify their children by their smell. Your sense of smell is better than you may imagine. If you lie on the floor you can actually detect the cheesy pong where someone in a dirty sock walked on the floorboards.

(No need to test this remarkable skill just now.) And you can identify over 10,000 different whiffs and stinks. (Heaven nose how you do it!)

BRINGING IT ALL TOGETHER

Of course in everyday life your brain uses all your senses together to build up a picture of what's going on outside your head. Maybe you'd like to discover how it all slots together. Your mission, should you choose to accept it is to … (BIG ROLL OF DRUMS HERE) … eat a chocolate.

(Yep, but it's not as simple it sounds.) Before we start let's listen into those Neuro-phone messages and get an idea of what's involved.

53

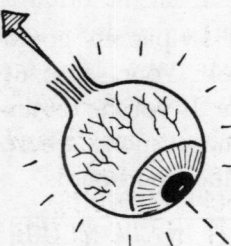

Retina to vision centre and brain stem, "I CAN'T TAKE MY EYES OFF THOSE CHOCOLATES."

Brain stem to cortex, "THERE'S SOMETHING INTERESTING AHEAD. WANNA CHECK IT OUT?"

Cortex to fingers and arms, "EXTEND FINGERS AND PICK UP A CHOCOLATE. HOW DOES IT FEEL?"

Finger-touch receptors to thalamus, "TELL THE CORTEX IT'S LOVELY AND COOL AND SMOOTH AND VELVETY."

Thalamus to sensory area of cortex, "YOU GOT ALL THAT?"

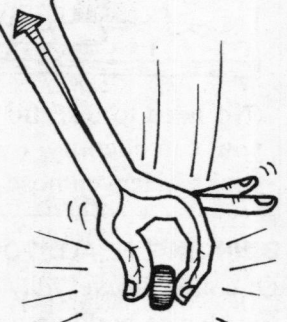

Ears to medulla, "HEY, LISTEN TO THAT LOVELY RUSTLE IN THE BOX."

Medulla to thalamus, "PSST! TELL THE CORTEX TO GET A LOAD OF THIS."

Nose to thalamus, "WOW! WHAT A LOVELY CHOCOLATEY WHIFF – TELL THE CORTEX TO GET A SNIFF OF THIS."

Tongue to cortex, "I'M READY TO SWALLOW. THERE'S LOADS OF SPIT DOWN HERE!"

A note to the reader:
Drooling spit at the sight of a choccie is a reflex (see page 60), triggered by nerves leading from the brain to your gooey saliva glands. Are you starting to drool too? If so, try not to dribble on the nice clean page.

Another note to the reader:
So do you fancy trying this mission for yourself? Chances are you've already had quite a bit of practice.

But if you feel like checking whether your brain can handle all these senses it's worth asking your parents for chocolates. You could explain that you need an extra large box in order to get this vital science experiment absolutely right. And if your parents fall for that, you might as well ask for a day out at a theme park, too.

So how did you get on…?
a) I ate the chocolate so fast I didn't have a chance to follow the instructions.
b) I got muddled up with the instructions and bit my tongue by mistake. Ouch!
c) It was great and all my senses and brain bits worked perfectly.
(If you chose **a**): oh dear, that's tough, better practise on another choccie. If **b**): you might as well go on to the next section. Because it's a bit of a PAIN too.)

PUTTING UP WITH PAIN
Pain is the worst thing you can sense. But you know all about pain already…

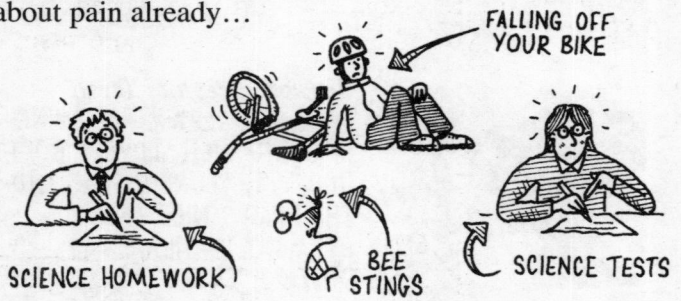

FALLING OFF YOUR BIKE

SCIENCE HOMEWORK

BEE STINGS

SCIENCE TESTS

Dare you discover … how to put up with pain?
Note to the reader:
This experiment has been banned on the grounds that it's far too cruel. Here are a few facts instead.

A FEW PAINFUL FACTS

1 Pain is a big trick played by your bulging brain on the rest of your body. Imagine you stub your toe on a stone or even the cat.

You might think you feel the resulting pain in your big toe. But you actually experience the pain in your brain because that's where the nerve signal goes.

2 Your body is crowded with countless thousands of pain receptors. Obviously any damage to the body is red-hot urgent news for the brain – there may be more damage just about to occur so the pain receptors try to let the brain know what's going on NOW.

3 So the pain receptors fire off high-speed nerve signals to blast your brain. It's hard to ignore them – isn't it?

4 The deeper the pain receptors the less sensitive they are – that's why a really bad injury can hurt less than a little scratch. Pain deep in the body often feels like a dull miserable ache.

5 Different pain signals move at different speeds. A sharp prick on your skin hits your brain at 29.9 metres a second. A longer pulse like a burning or aching pain moves through the neurons at a slightly more leisurely 1.98 metres a second.

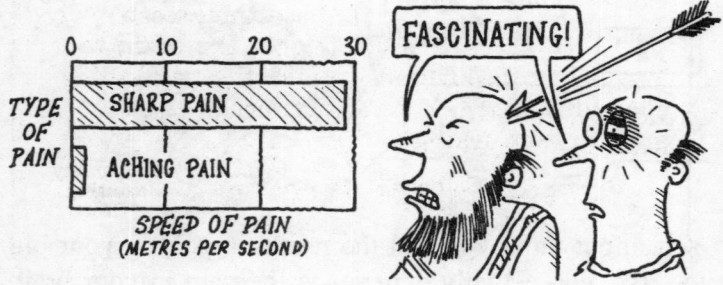

But there's much more to pain than just a horrible feeling in the brain. Here, for a change, is a bit of good news...

THE DAILY BRAIN

The paper that makes you think!   Issue 3,752 . 1975

What a relief!

Scientists at Aberdeen University, Scotland, claim brains help deaden pain. Brain researchers John Hughes and Hans Kosterlitz were following a lead from neurophysiologists in Baltimore, USA. Now they reckon they've found what they were after. Previously unknown chemicals called enkephalins (en-kefa-lins) that block pain signals. Well we at *The Daily Brain* salute this great new discovery.

If we didn't have these chemicals we're sure they'd be *sorely* missed.

Daily Brain Science Correspondent Dr Alan de Mind writes...

The newly discovered chemicals may explain why taking exercise or other distractions such as a white-knuckle ride or an exciting film takes your mind off pain. Presumably doing these things can trigger the brain to make the painkilling chemicals.

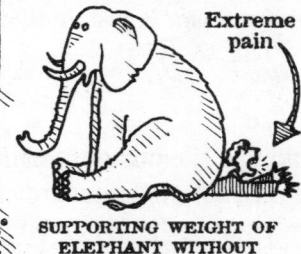

Extreme pain

SUPPORTING WEIGHT OF ELEPHANT WITHOUT ENKEPHALINS

Extremely exciting film

SUPPORTING WEIGHT OF ELEPHANT WITH ENKEPHALINS

Bet you never knew!
Another way to deaden pain is to confuse your nerves by getting them to send other signals. So if you bang your shin you could try rubbing it with your hand or a lump of ice. This gets the nerves sending more signals that swamp the pain signals.

THE PAINFUL TRUTH

Afterwards it's hard to remember exactly what pain is like. Your cruel heartless brain wants every pain you feel to seem really awful and unexpected. That way you'll do something about it. The painful truth is that pain is there so your brain can teach you a painful lesson.

You might think it would be lovely to live in a world without pain. Life would be brilliant, wouldn't it? You could wander around endlessly bumping into things, and not worrying about how much it was going to hurt. Until one day you noticed that your fingers had dropped off. Of course, if you'd felt pain in the first place you'd have got away with a nasty cut rather than no fingers on one hand.

By the way, if the thought of all that blood makes you feel like throwing up at this point feel free – being sick, or vomiting to use the technical term, is just another of your…

ACTION-PACKED REFLEXES

Do you do things without thinking? If your answer is "yeah, all the time" then you've probably been making a few reflex actions. Reflexes are actions that your body does in response to startling signals from your senses. These are things like sneezing and coughing and dribbling that you can't stop once they start. (For this reason farting or burping are not reflexes and you've got no excuse for doing them during mealtimes.)

A few more facts you ought to know about reflexes

1 Your brain isn't involved in reflexes. The signals go to your spinal cord and out again in nerves that control your muscles. This saves time and means that you can whip your hand away from the hot plate of the cooker in 0.03 seconds instead of up to 0.8 seconds if your brain was consulted.

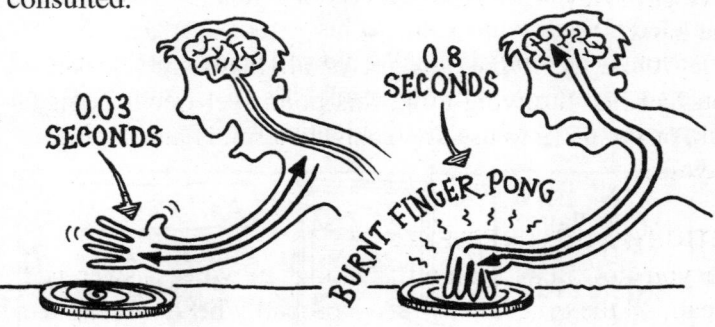

0.03 SECONDS

0.8 SECONDS

BURNT FINGER PONG

2 Some of the most important work about reflexes was carried out by Russian Ivan Pavlov (1849–1936). Pavlov was a cold unfriendly man who flew into terrible rages if anyone dared criticize him. And no, he wasn't a teacher, he was a scientist.

UNFORTUNATE REFLEX ACTION

@#a!!ΣX!!б б#!!ØXK#!!

YOU WORK TOO HARD, IVAN MY FRIEND

3 His most famous experiment was to show that you could train dogs to make reflex actions. Dogs dribble when they see food. Pavlov rang a bell every time the dogs were fed. After a while he stopped feeding the dogs but they still dribbled when he rang the bell.

4 Pavlov was so keen on scientific accuracy that he even measured the amount of spit the dogs dribbled. This added no particular value to his work but it showed how seriously he took his job. Would you want a job measuring dog's dribble? If you think it's a mouth-watering opportunity you're a born scientist.

Dare you discover ... a reflex action?

You will need:

One dog (count first to make sure it's got four legs)

What you do:

1 Rub the dog's back until the dog reacts.

2 Note what happens next.

What happens next?

a) The dog falls over.

b) The dog scratches its back with its hind legs. (It probably thinks your hand is an extra large flea.)

c) The dog wags its tail and sticks its tongue out and dribbles everywhere.

Answer: b) The dog often scratches its back without thinking in a reflex action — much like you sneezing. The nerves involved in the dog's reflex were discovered by British scientist Sir Charles Sherrington (1857–1952) who won the Nobel Prize for this breakthrough. I expect he was itching to tell his pals about it — ha-ha.

If a) your dog is probably missing a leg or two.

HORRIBLE HEALTH WARNING!

Don't try the above experiment with the neighbour's Rottweiler or you may never tie your own shoelaces again.

CONGRATULATIONS! You've successfully read this chapter. Now for the bad news. So far you've been looking at the easy-peasy stuff your brain gets up to. You might find the next chapter rather more mind-bending.

Yep – it's time to put your bulging brain to work.

Bulging Brain-work

Sometimes you need your bulging brain for something more intelligent than scoffing a choccie. Jobs like listening to music, and thinking and talking and reading. Oh, so you don't think they sound too difficult? Well, they are. But don't worry, by the time you've read this chapter you'll have boosted your bulging brainpower. Well, maybe – just a bit.

FIRST SORT YOUR LEFT FROM YOUR RIGHT

Your cortex (that's the wrinkly, thinking bit of the brain, remember) is split into two halves. To understand how you use your brain you first need to know how the two halves work together. Bear in mind that one side of the cortex is stronger than the other and takes over most of the work. But which side is that? Well, the diagram below will help you sort that out. But don't forget that the left side of the cortex looks after the right side of the body and vice versa. Got all that?

Anyway, here's the diagram...

X-RAY OF SCIENCE TEACHER'S HEAD

LEFT SIDE OF BRAIN IS IN CONTROL

PEN IN RIGHT HAND

(If the teacher was left-handed these arrangements would be reversed.)

ARE YOU AMBIDEXTROUS?

Ambidextrous means that you're able to write or draw or hold a tennis racquet or play the guitar or pluck a chicken equally well with both hands.

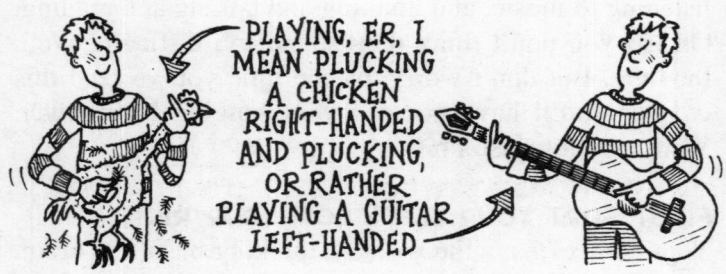

PLAYING, ER, I MEAN PLUCKING A CHICKEN RIGHT-HANDED AND PLUCKING, OR RATHER PLAYING A GUITAR LEFT-HANDED

This is because neither side of the cortex is stronger than the other. Famous ambidextrous people include English artist Sir Edwin Landseer (1802–1873) who often drew a horse with his right hand and a stag with his left hand at the same time. Try it for yourself – it's much harder than it sounds.

TEST YOUR TEACHER

Is your teacher left-handed, right-handed or ambidextrous? Well, this teacher-teasing test will certainly keep her brain fully occupied until the end of the class. By the way, if you're feeling kind you can give your teacher one clue before you start the test: all the answers are for right-handed people.

1 Are babies always...

a) Left-handed?

b) Right-handed?

c) Ambidextrous?

2 Which side of your brain do you use for working out hard maths questions?

a) The left.

b) The right.

c) Neither, I use a calculator.

3 Which side of your brain do you use for having a chat with your friends?

a) The left.

b) The right.

c) The left for chatting with friends but the right when talking to important people like the Head Teacher.

IT'S NOT GOOD ENOUGH, SMITH – I EXPECT YOU TO USE BOTH SIDES WHEN TALKING TO ME

4 Which part of your brain do you use for painting a watercolour?

a) The left.

b) The right.

c) Neither, it's the cerebellum that does the work.

I USE THE WHOLE BRAIN – IT MAKES NICE PATTERNS

5 How do Japanese people differ from the usual right–left division of work within the brain?

a) They use both sides of their brains for talking.

b) Annoying insect sounds trigger brain activity on the left side of their brains instead of the right for everyone else.

c) They can talk aloud without their brains showing unusual activity.

Answers:

1 c) In babies, both halves of the cortex are equally strong. One side doesn't take over until the child is about two.

2 a) If you're right-handed you read, write and work out sums mostly using the left part of your brain. (If you're left-handed you are more likely to use the right side of your brain for these tasks.)

3 a) The left side also deals with talking aloud. The poor old right side has to spend its life listening to the left side nattering.

4 b) At least the right side of the brain gets to deal with all the enjoyable artistic jobs like making a collage or drawing.

5 b) This finding was reported by Japanese scientist Tsunoda Tadanobu. Some Japanese words sound like insect or water sounds. So the scientist suggested Japanese people listen to these sounds with the left side of their brains that normally deals with language. (Award your teacher an extra mark if they managed to explain this theory.)

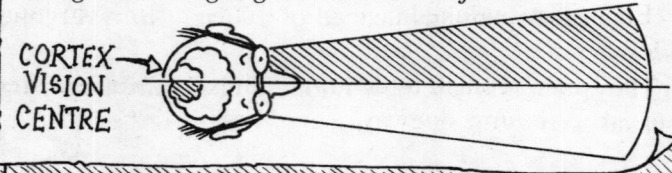

Bet you never knew!
For reasons that scientists don't quite understand...
You see things at the back of your cortex (not at the front, which is where your eyes are). You see things to the left in the right side of your brain.
Things to the right get seen in the left side.

CORTEX
VISION
CENTRE

Dare you discover ... if you're left- or right-eyed?

Your left eye is controlled by the right side of your brain and vice-versa. But which side of your brain is stronger? Here's how to find out...

You will need:
A finger (preferably one of your own)
Two eyes (these should definitely be your own)
A stationary object 1 metre away (it doesn't matter what this object is. It could be a picture, the wallpaper or even a dead wombat)
A ruler

What you do:
1 Stick your finger 12 cm in front of your nose.
2 Focus your eyes on the stationary object. The finger should appear out of focus. Note the position of the finger.
3 Now wink each of your eyes in turn.

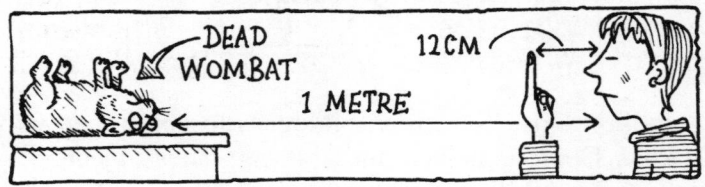

What do you notice?
a) Nothing and people started asking me whom I was winking at. It was all very embarrassing.
b) Each time I winked an eye the finger seemed to jump sideways.
c) The finger seemed to stay where it was when I winked one eye and jump sideways when I winked the other.

COULD YOU BE A SCIENTIST?

When you listen to music the following areas of your brain are involved...

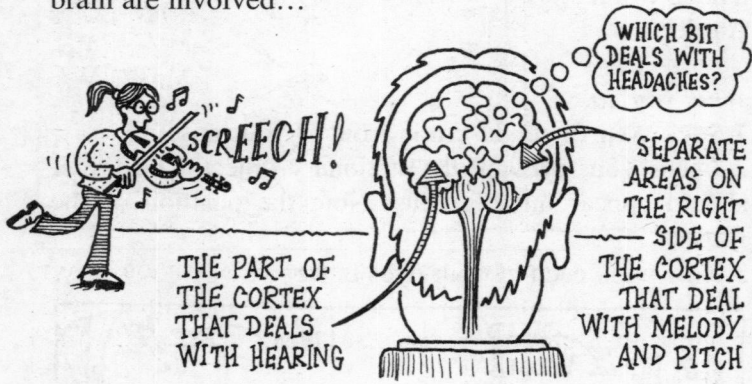

SCREECH!

WHICH BIT DEALS WITH HEADACHES?

THE PART OF THE CORTEX THAT DEALS WITH HEARING

SEPARATE AREAS ON THE RIGHT SIDE OF THE CORTEX THAT DEAL WITH MELODY AND PITCH

In the 1970s US neurophysiologists Joseph Bogen and Harold Gordon studied these areas. They injected a powerful painkiller into blood vessels that fed the right side of their patients' brains. This put the right side of the brains to sleep for a while. When the patients tried to sing using only the left sides of their brain what did they sound like?

a) They sang beautifully, like trained opera singers.

b) They could open their mouths but no sound came out.

c) They sounded like a calf bellowing.

Answer: c) Without the help of the right side of their cortex the singers couldn't produce a tune. Mind you, some people seem to have this problem with both sides of their brain in working order.

TEACHER'S TEA-BREAK TEASER
A note to the reader:
You try this teaser at your own risk, OK? Don't blame me if you get expelled. To do it all you have to do is sing loudly outside the staff room…

Answer: Words are controlled by the left side of your brain and tunes by the right. When you sing it's hard for your cortex to cope with two sets of information at the same time. I mean – just think, you have to access your memory centres to remember what the words and notes actually sound like. Very musical people actually grow extra neurons in the areas of the right cortex that deal with sound and hearing. OK, got all that? No? Why not ask your brain to chew it over…

THINK FOR YOURSELF (IT'S NOT THAT EASY)
1 Thinking is the way that your brain makes sense of the world and organizes the information it gets from your senses. Scientists believe that thinking is a wave of brain

activity that spreads as neurons fire signals at each other. Does that get you thinking?

2 The brain has different areas for different jobs like talking or sniffing things, remember. But neurons all over the cortex are involved in thinking and the active areas vary according to what you're doing. Your level of concentration or even your feelings can affect the pattern of brain activity.

3 Brain neurons fire most of the time and scientists think that this could mean your brain is vaguely mulling over past memories. The increased activity caused by thinking might be due to your brain drawing on memories to build up a particular thought.

4 When you do two different things at once (see page 73) each half of your brain has separate thoughts. Is that a good thing? Well, maybe you're in two minds about it.

Bet you never knew!

There is no limit to the number of thoughts you can have. So you don't believe me? Well, read on. Your brain has billions of nerve cells, remember that bit? If you look at a neuron magnified 10,000 times it appears like a tiny tree with over 5,000 branches.

Scientists think there are more than 100,000,000,000,000 that's ONE HUNDRED TRILLION brain synapses. (These are the gaps between neurons, remember.) And scientists believe a thought can travel through these synapses in ANY order. So there may be more possible routes for a thought than atoms in the entire universe. And that means that there's NO LIMIT to the thinking power of your brain.

WOW! That really was something to think about. But oddly enough, although your brain is unbelievably powerful it finds doing several things at once a bit of a strain…

COULD YOU BE A SCIENTIST?

Some psychologists gave two students a brain-teasing task.

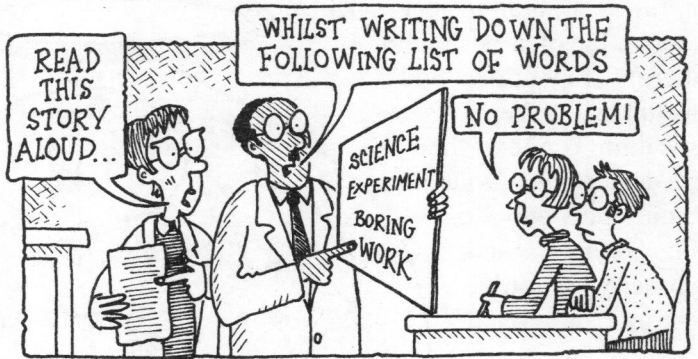

How do you think the students got on?
a) They were useless. The brain simply can't manage to read, talk, listen and write all at the same time.
b) The students found themselves writing the story and repeating out loud the lists the scientists were reading to them.
c) Although the students started off slowly and made mistakes they soon learnt how to do the tasks at the same time.

Answer: c) The brain can be trained to do different things at once. The part that helps you to do this is the cerebellum. And this explains how your hairdresser can cut your hair and chat at the same time without snipping your ears off.

And speaking of talking or talking about speaking the next bit of this chapter will really get your tongue wagging.

SPEAK FOR YOURSELF

Try listening to yourself talking and you'll realize that speech is full of hesitation – er ... (sorry, bit of a hesitation there), repetition and mistakes. Yep – speaking is one of the hardest things your brain gets up to. In order to talk properly you've got to...

Access your memory (**1**) for the correct words and your memory of how to pronounce them.

Use the Broca's area (**2**) of your cortex to pronounce the words correctly. It should send a message to the bit of the cortex that controls the movement of your vocal cords, tongue and lips to speak the words.

You will need your cerebellum (**3**) to co-ordinate all these complex movements.

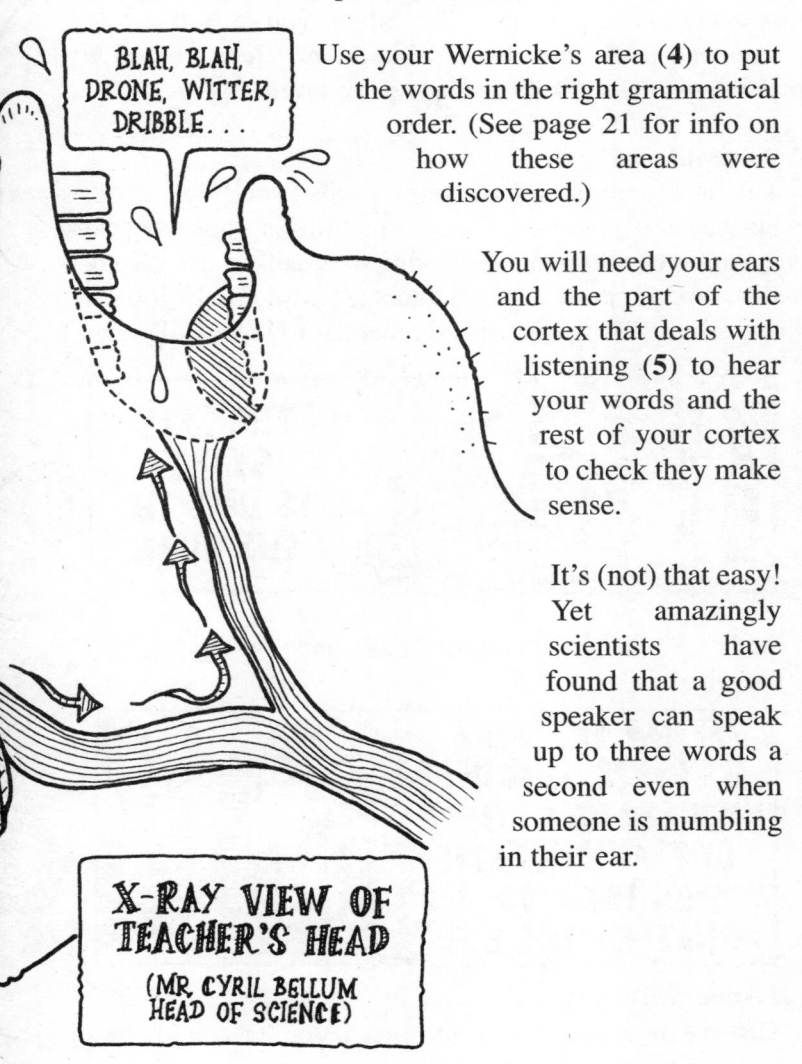

BLAH, BLAH, DRONE, WITTER, DRIBBLE...

Use your Wernicke's area (**4**) to put the words in the right grammatical order. (See page 21 for info on how these areas were discovered.)

You will need your ears and the part of the cortex that deals with listening (**5**) to hear your words and the rest of your cortex to check they make sense.

It's (not) that easy! Yet amazingly scientists have found that a good speaker can speak up to three words a second even when someone is mumbling in their ear.

X-RAY VIEW OF TEACHER'S HEAD

(MR CYRIL BELLUM HEAD OF SCIENCE)

UNSPEAKABLE SPEECH PROBLEMS

But, of course, things can still go wrong. Usually at embarrassing moments like when you're talking to someone really famous and important. Here are a few problems that may be caused by the brain…

1 Stupid sayings

This is when you say the right words in the right order but because your cortex hasn't had time to consider the meaning of what you are saying it sounds really stupid. Fast-talking sports commentators are particularly good at this. Here's British sports commentator David Coleman:

"THE LATE START IS DUE TO THE TIME"

And US baseball commentator and manager Jerry Coleman:

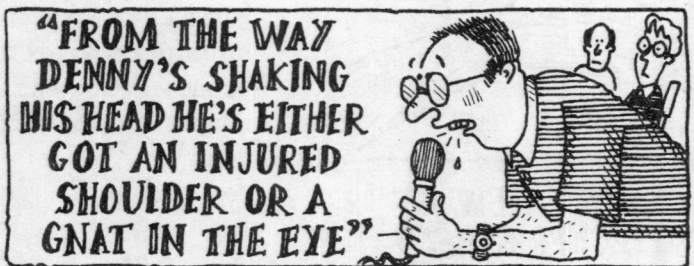

"FROM THE WAY DENNY'S SHAKING HIS HEAD HE'S EITHER GOT AN INJURED SHOULDER OR A GNAT IN THE EYE"

2 Spoonerisms

This means muddling up the first letters or sounds in a series of words. For example, instead of saying, "I have a half-formed wish in my mind," you might accidentally say,

Usually you wouldn't realize you had made a mistake. It's most likely caused by a fault in the Broca's area (that's the bit of the cortex that deals with speaking words, remember?). Spoonerisms are named after British clergyman Dean William Spooner (1844–1930) who made rather a lot of them.

Bet you never knew!
1 About one in a hundred children suffer from stammering. Stammering is jerky, hesitant speech in which the first sounds of some words are often repeated. Sufferers report that they know what they want to say but they can't say it.
2 Scientists aren't quite sure what causes stammering but it seems to affect boys more than girls and it seems

to be made worse by worry. It's probably linked to a problem in the Broca's area.

3 In the Middle Ages the problem was thought to be due to the tongue not working properly and useless cures were tried such as burning the tongue with a hot iron.

4 Nowadays stammering can be overcome by helping the sufferer to feel more relaxed when talking. Techniques used include learning to speak more slowly and to begin words with a more gentle movement of the lips and tongue.

BULGING BRAIN EXPRESSIONS

Two psychologists are chatting...

Maybe you could ask this LAD to help with your homework?

A WHOLE NEW LANGUAGE

Sometime in your school career you will have to learn a foreign language. There are about 5,000 languages in the world and they use a huge range of sounds.

For example, some languages in Southern Africa such as Xhosa and Zulu include unusual clicking sounds. Well, whatever languages you learn, once you've learnt to speak the words you then have to learn how to read them. And by some eerie coincidence that's what you're doing right now.

READ ALL ABOUT IT

OK, so how are you getting on reading this book? Finding it easy or having a bit of bother with some of the incomprehensible inapprehensible numinous words...

Go on, have a go at remembering them – they're numinous words for bamboozling science teachers.

Scientists reckon that children learn about ten new words a day at school – but that's not such a bad thing because everywhere you look there are written words.

A grown-up who reads a daily paper might get through about 100,000 words every week. This includes all the words they might read in an office job, road signs and even the back of cornflakes packets.

RIVETING READING

Reading is great. You can settle down with a good book and forget about the rest of the world. But you won't even reach the end of this sentence without the help of your brain. Here's your chance to discover what your brain is up to when you read. Simply listen in to some more of those fascinating Neuro-phone calls…

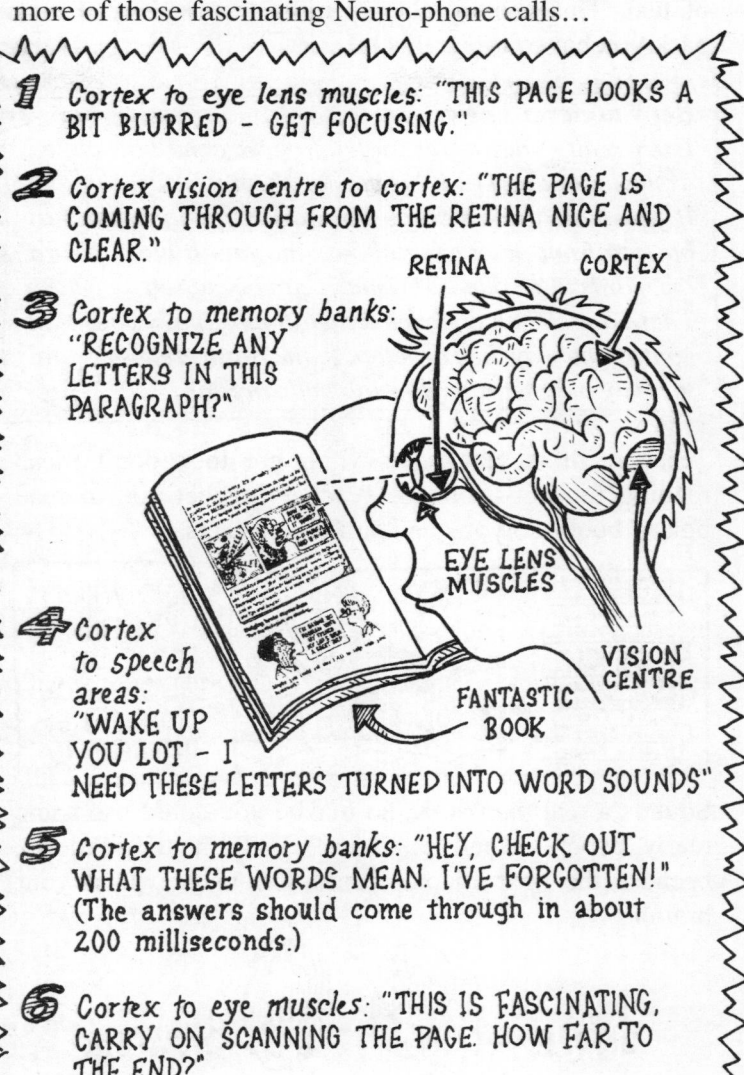

1 Cortex to eye lens muscles: "THIS PAGE LOOKS A BIT BLURRED - GET FOCUSING."

2 Cortex vision centre to cortex: "THE PAGE IS COMING THROUGH FROM THE RETINA NICE AND CLEAR."

RETINA   CORTEX

3 Cortex to memory banks: "RECOGNIZE ANY LETTERS IN THIS PARAGRAPH?"

EYE LENS MUSCLES

4 Cortex to speech areas: "WAKE UP YOU LOT - I NEED THESE LETTERS TURNED INTO WORD SOUNDS"

FANTASTIC BOOK

VISION CENTRE

5 Cortex to memory banks: "HEY, CHECK OUT WHAT THESE WORDS MEAN. I'VE FORGOTTEN!" (The answers should come through in about 200 milliseconds.)

6 Cortex to eye muscles: "THIS IS FASCINATING, CARRY ON SCANNING THE PAGE. HOW FAR TO THE END?"

A note to the reader:
Now ask your brain to move your eyes to the next chunk of text. This should take 30 milliseconds. Hey! Come back you haven't read this bit...

> *Bet you never knew!*
> *Even really smart kids suffer from a condition called dyslexia that makes it harder for them to learn to read. If you have the condition you might see the words as back to front or moving about, and find it hard to turn the words into sounds. Dyslexia can be caused by genes. These are chemical codes found in most body cells that control the way they develop. In the brain, genes control the way that neurons develop and wire up.*

Teachers think reading is vital, but they don't mean reading for fun – oh no. Teachers expect you to read boring books so you can learn lots of facts.

AND WHEN YOU'VE FINISHED THAT LOT I'LL GIVE YOU SOMETHING INTERESTING

Sounds a real pain? OK, so maybe you could use some really expert scientific advice? Well, better read on, because the next chapter could seriously expand your brainpower...

BEFORE → ← AFTER

LOATHSOME LEARNING

Do you find learning fun? Do you tumble out of bed shouting…

YIPPEE! IT'S SCHOOL TODAY. MORE LOVELY FACTS TO LEARN!

Or do you crawl out of bed thinking…

OH NO, NOT ANOTHER BORING DAY LEARNING STUPID OLD SCIENCE

Well, cheer up! Learning is one of the most vital tasks of your bulging brain and it CAN be fun – but only if you've got something interesting to learn. Like now – so read on.

Bulging brains fact file

NAME: Learning

BASIC FACTS: Here's how you learn . . .

1 Someone tells you something.

2 You remember it.

3 You use this information to help you in whatever you are doing.

DISGUSTING DETAILS: Some psychologists believe that learning gets harder over the age of 25. This could be because the memory starts to weaken. But other scientists claim that learning gets easier as you get older. So why don't they send grown-ups back to school?

A FEW FACTS TO LEARN (AND MAKE SURE YOU DO)

1 You learn things all the time – not just in school. You learn whenever you notice anything new or try out a new skill.

2 Learning can be nice or nasty:

NICE THINGS TO LEARN: CHOCOLATE ICE CREAM TASTES YUMMY.

NASTY THING TO LEARN: EAT TOO MUCH AND YOU'LL WANT TO THROW UP.

3 Most people learn by trial and error. Remember learning to ride a bike. But once you've learnt something you can do it effortlessly and without thinking. Like riding that bike.

TEACHER'S TEA-BREAK TEASER

Put a fly in your teacher's morning cuppa with this tricky teaser. And remember, if your teacher doesn't believe you – this fact is TRUE. Tap gently on the staffroom door. When it opens, smile brightly and enquire...

IS IT TRUE THAT THERE WERE ONCE PLANS TO INTRODUCE MACHINES TO DO THE JOB OF TEACHERS?

SPLUTTER!

Answer: Yes, in the 1960s US psychologist Burrhus F Skinner invented a teaching machine called a didak. The machine showed a sentence and you had to complete it. If you got the answer right you got a chance to answer harder questions. Oh goodee! THE GOOD NEWS: The machine never told you off. THE BAD NEWS: It couldn't answer your questions and didn't know how to chat.

Bet you never knew!
It doesn't matter whether they have real teachers or machines to help them – some kids have trouble learning. There are loads of possible reasons for this. Sometimes the difficulties are caused by dyslexia or an eye problem so the child can't read easily. More often the child isn't interested in the lessons. Or perhaps the lessons require skills such as speaking or writing that the child isn't good at. Oddly enough one psychologist who studied how the brain learns suffered learning difficulties as a lad...

Hall of fame: John B Watson (1878–1958)

Nationality: American

As a boy John B Watson had a problem with learning. Maybe that's why he was for ever getting into trouble, starting fights and terrorizing his home town in South Carolina, USA.

As he grew older John got mixed up in crime. But when he turned 16 he had a sudden change of heart and started to study really hard at home. He had to study really hard because he had decided to go to university and become a scientist.

But at university John continued to find learning difficult. He couldn't understand his teachers and their boring lectures (sound familiar?).

But he did become fascinated by how rats learn things. Here's what Watson's notebook may have looked like...

The Great Rat Experiment

Today's the BIG day!!! I'm planning to find out if rats can learn from a nasty experience. I've been working hard all week building a three-metre-long alley for the tests – I call it the "rat-run".

Stage 1
←RAT-RUN   ME

Now to try it out. Will the rat do the obvious and go and grab the food? YES! YES! YES!

The rat runs down the rat-run and grabs the food. Atta boy! This proves that learning happens when you give a rat something new – like the food. This changes the rat's behaviour. Now to test my idea a bit further.

NEXT DAY   Stage 2

I've blocked off the rat-run with a thick glass barrier. Will the rat still go down it? Here goes...

Yes – like a streak of lightning and bumped his little nosy on the barrier. Oh dear, poor old ratty. If I'm right the new information about the barrier will change the rat's behaviour – let me see... CRUNCH!

FOOD

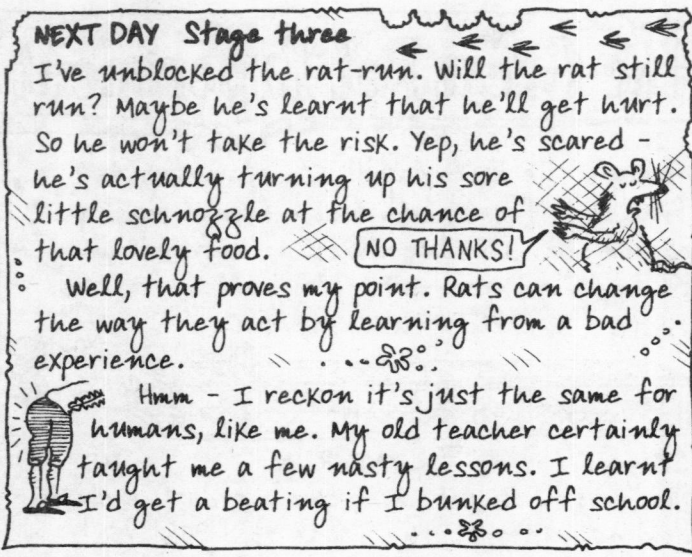

NEXT DAY **Stage three**

I've unblocked the rat-run. Will the rat still run? Maybe he's learnt that he'll get hurt. So he won't take the risk. Yep, he's scared – he's actually turning up his sore little schnozzle at the chance of that lovely food. NO THANKS!

Well, that proves my point. Rats can change the way they act by learning from a bad experience.

Hmm – I reckon it's just the same for humans, like me. My old teacher certainly taught me a few nasty lessons. I learnt I'd get a beating if I bunked off school.

Watson's experiments inspired a whole new movement of psychologists called behaviourists who believed that you could help rats – or humans – learn with rewards or punishments. But although Watson was certain that you could learn about human behaviour from studying rats there were squeaks of protest from other scientists when he compared humans to rats…

Eventually Watson resigned his university job to go into advertising. Here he put his ideas on learning into practice by selling baby powder. Watson reckoned:

1 Rats chased down the rat-run because they learnt there was food at the end. So by giving the rats a reward you could change their behaviour.

2 You could use advertising to give people the impression that by buying your brand of baby powder they would feel happier and be better parents. This feeling would be a kind of reward. So people would choose to buy your brand.

But did the plan work? What do you think?

a) Watson was sacked after featuring a rat on the advertising posters.

b) Watson's plan failed. People can't be compared to rats. We don't have to feel good when we go shopping.

c) Watson's plan worked and he became a millionaire. His ideas form the basis of modern advertising.

Answer: c) If advertising teaches you that buying a product will improve your life, then you'll probably feel like buying it.

ARE YOU INTELLIGENT?

Are you good at learning things? If so, you may be intelligent. But you might be surprised to know that psychologists don't agree what intelligence is all about. Many, though, believe that intelligence means an ability to solve new problems. Anyway, whatever you call it –

intelligence, being clever, smart or brainy – here's a quick intelligence test to put you through your paces.

True or false?

1 People with small heads aren't as intelligent as people with big heads. This is because people with big heads have bigger brains. TRUE/FALSE

2 As you learn new skills your genes help you develop new neuron connections and links in your cortex so that you can remember them. TRUE/FALSE

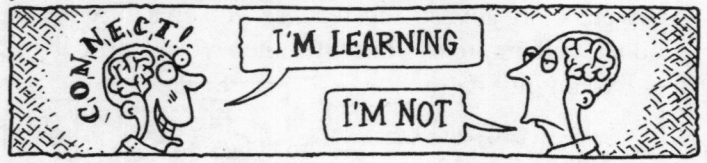

3 Playing lots of computer games can make you more intelligent. TRUE/FALSE

4 Eating fish is good for your brain. TRUE/FALSE

help your neurons repair themselves.

chemicals such as noradrenaline and fatty acids that help your neurons repair themselves.

There's iodine to speed up the way that your cells (including neurons) work, amino acids to make neuron turn you into Einstein but fish contains brain goodies. 4 TRUE – maybe. Munching fish fingers for tea won't helps them play the games faster and win more often. This cortex that controls delicate hand movements. This games develop extra connections in the area of the scientists think that children who play lots of computer brain will rewire itself for the job! 3 FALSE. But sing opera whilst juggling on a unicycle – your brilliant practice. So go ahead – learn how to read Russian and depends on what skills you choose to learn and way your neurons rewire themselves and all that 2 TRUE Your genes are constantly influencing the one fancies an elephant to win this year's Nobel Prize. brain is more than five times heavier than ours, but no with intelligence. For example at 8 kg an elephant's **Answers: 1 FALSE.** Your brain size is nothing to do

BULGING BRAIN DEVELOPMENT

Did you know that you learnt half of everything you know in your first five years?

YOU MEAN IT'S TAKEN YOU 75 YEARS TO LEARN THE OTHER HALF, GREAT-GRAN?

In some countries that's before children even start school! Oh, so you don't remember this vital learning period? Well, here's a quick reminder…

The first five years...

0 to six months

When you were born you could breath, suck, swallow and then throw up, dribble, cry, sneeze, cough and stretch. And that's about all because your brain wasn't developed.

DRIBBLE! CRY! ATCHOO! COUGH! STRETCH! THAT'S BETTER

Six months

Your brain had doubled in size. The neurons were growing and branching and forming millions of synapses. You could roll over and smile. You could also copy the expressions on grown-up faces. (Don't try this now – you'll only get told off.)

One year

You had learnt how to pick things up with your hands and you had just spoken your first word. Before then grown-ups probably spoke to you in baby talk and you tried to make the same sounds back. But you hadn't got the hang of the tongue and lip movements so it came out as baby noises. You were just beginning to learn to walk, and falling over quite a lot.

I HATE RUSKS

GOO, GOO GAGA

Two years ...

You could walk run and speak about 274 words. Two vital words you learnt were "wee" and "poo". You were able to recognize the feeling when you had to go and now you could even tell people about it. Soon afterwards you learnt how to use a potty without making an embarrassing mess. And if things went wrong you could take off your underwear without help.

Three years.

WEEEEE!

You could speak up to a 1,000 words in short sentences and feed yourself (but not at the same time). You were also learning to draw. Sometimes you were so wrapped up in your drawing or games you might poo or wee in your underwear.
(Hopefully this no longer happens.)

WELL DONE!

four years

Your brain was four times bigger than when you were born. You were asking loads of questions using about 1,500 words, and going to the toilet all by yourself.

five years

You could tell stories and hop and skip and you knew about 2,000 words. And round about this time you started school.

ARGH! SCHOOL!

THE NEXT FEW YEARS...

After you turned six, things in your brain got a bit less hectic but the neuron links in your cortex carried on forming. Some time between the ages of six and ten most children learn the following skills:

Tick here

☐ How to play ball games really well.

☐ Reading and joined-up writing.

☐ Writing and telling stories.

☐ Drawing, painting and making models.

☐ Simple cooking and cleaning and even washing up. Oh yes – this is part of growing up, I'm afraid.

☐ Loads of facts and new words at school.
So how far have you got?

Of course not all kids develop at the same speed. Some are late-developers. That doesn't make them stupid – scientific mega-genius Albert Einstein didn't learn to talk until he was four. And girls' and boys' brains develop to different time-tables anyway. For example, for reasons scientists can't quite explain, the parts of the cortex that deal with speech develop earlier in girls than boys. So girls often learn to talk earlier. And boys' and girls' brains go on developing in different ways at different times.

BOYS V GIRLS

Not surprisingly psychologists have found that boys and girls are better at different things…

Bet you never knew!
For example, girls may be better at talking than boys. Oh so you knew this already? Brain scans performed at Yale University School of Medicine, USA, show that men only use the left side of their brains to talk but women use both sides. But who comes out top overall – the battling boys or the gutsy girls?

Read on and find out in…

THE BATTLE OF THE SEXES

Scientists have found that boys and girls tend to be better at different things. Of course, you might be different and scientists always argue about the results...

1 One study showed that boys are often quicker at solving tricky maths problems in their heads. Very gifted boys use the right sides of their brains to concentrate on the problem. But girls tend to use both sides and waste time putting their thoughts into words.

2 When boys and girls are given 3-D puzzles to assemble, the boys are better at imagining what the finished puzzle will look like. Once again girls tend to waste time explaining to themselves in words how they will solve the puzzle.

3 But girls' brains are better at controlling their finger movements for delicate fiddly tasks. So the girls might well be quicker at putting the puzzle together.

4 Boys tend to have a good sense of direction. They are very good at building up a clear idea of a route in the right side of their brains.

5 But they're not so good at remembering landmarks. Girls with their better memory for words can remember the landmarks even if they're sometimes less sure about the direction.

Important note: In conclusion, every scientific study has found that boys and girls have differing abilities in some areas and use their brains in different ways. But, and here's the important bit, OVERALL, THEY ARE EQUALLY CLEVER. So shut it, OK?

And there you have it. Learning is a vital function of your bulging brain. Now, have you learnt everything in this chapter? Well, one thing's for certain – you won't have learnt anything without a memory. Luckily, the next mind-expanding chapter can help you. And you'll soon find those memories flooding back...

MIXED-UP MEMORY

Welcome to this unforgettable chapter. It's about memory. Just what is this mysterious ability? And how does it work? And will you remember anything after you've read this book? Er ... now what was I talking about?

Bulging brains fact file

NAME: Memory

BASIC FACTS: Memory works like this ...

1 You sense something.

2 You put it in your memory.

3 You can recall the memory when something reminds you of it. The reminder might be a word, an event or even a smell.

DISGUSTING DETAILS: You've got not one but *three* memories.

1 Short term memory. Useful for phone numbers, etc. You forget these memories in 30 seconds. Some kids store their science knowledge in here.

...BUT I JUST TOLD YOU ABOUT SHORT TERM MEMORY!

THAT WAS 40 SECONDS AGO, MISS

...OF COURSE CHALKY ONLY TOOK ONE SUGAR IN HIS TEA — IT WAS HARD STUFF TO GET HOLD OF SEVENTY YEARS AGO

2. Long term memory. This is stuff you remember for years. It's where Grandpa stores all those boring old yarns of life when he was a lad. These first two memory systems are based in your cortex.

3 A special memory for skills like riding a bike that you can use without being aware of having to remember them. This memory seems to be based in your cerebellum.

IT'S ALL THANKS TO YOUR CEREBELLUM

SARAH BELLUM — WHO'S SHE?

MYSTERIOUS LONG-TERM MEMORY-MAKER

Stuck in the limbic system of your brain is an interesting brain bit called the hippocampus (hippo-camp-us). According to scientists your helpful hippocampus helps to turn your short-term recollections into linked-up neurons. And they form memories that you can remember for the rest of your life. In 1953 an American who suffered from fits had his hippocampus taken out. The fits stopped but the poor man lost his ability to remember things. He still had his memories of life before the op, though.

Bet you never knew!
1 Remember that your neurons are dying off? Well, the hippocampus can actually make nice new neurons to help protect your memories. Good news – huh?
2 Sadly older people do seem to suffer from memory loss. This may be due to a shrinking hippocampus or stress. Perhaps some of your stressed-out more mature teachers are sinking into a state of foggy-brained forgetfulness?

Hopefully your memory is much better? Well, let's pick up the Neuro-phone and check out how it works...

A MEMORABLE JOKE

The brain is about to try and remember a joke...

(OK, I didn't say the joke was any good.)

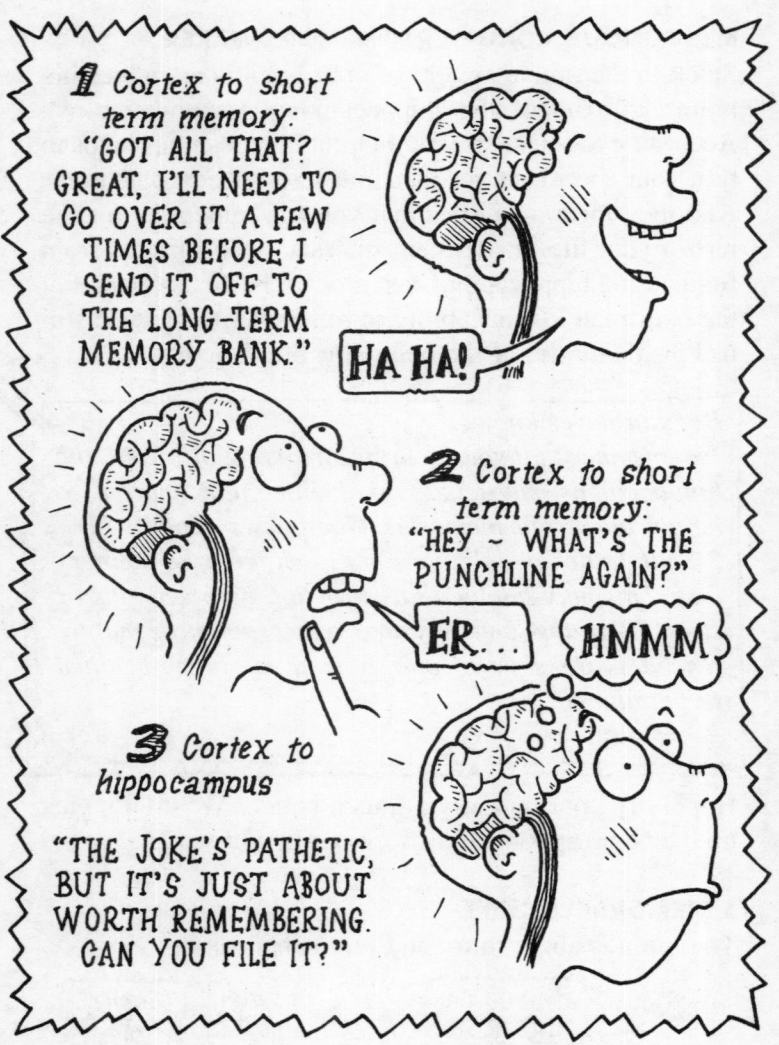

Scientific note
So how does it happen? Scientists reckon that the neurons
produce chemicals called proteins that make it easier to

send a message across certain synapses. This creates pathways through the neuron maze in your bulging brain. (It's thought that each pathway is storing a part of the memory. Some store colours and others can store shapes.) The memory of the joke should remain in your brain even if you can't recall it. People call this "sub-conscious memory".

A few weeks later...

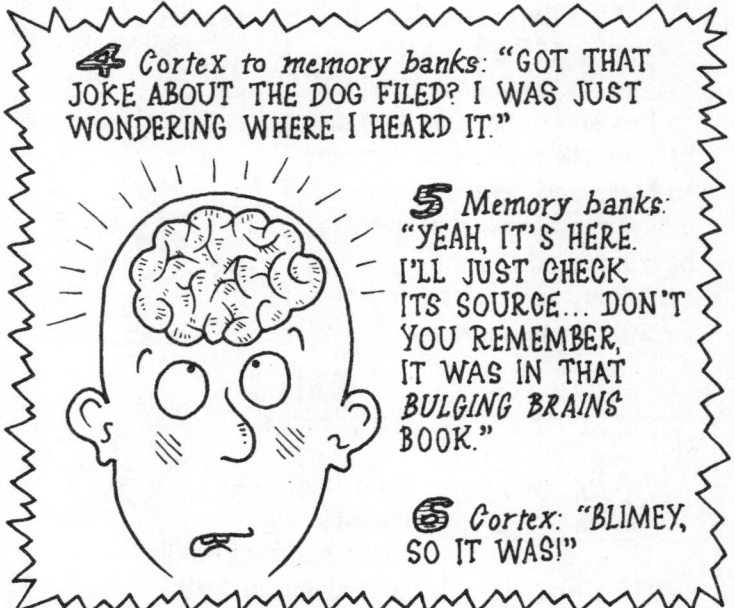

4 *Cortex to memory banks:* "GOT THAT JOKE ABOUT THE DOG FILED? I WAS JUST WONDERING WHERE I HEARD IT."

5 *Memory banks:* "YEAH, IT'S HERE. I'LL JUST CHECK ITS SOURCE... DON'T YOU REMEMBER, IT WAS IN THAT *BULGING BRAINS* BOOK."

6 *Cortex:* "BLIMEY, SO IT WAS!"

No doubt you'll be pleased to hear there's room in your memory for lots more jokes (and other stuff). Remember all those billions of neurons and synapses in your cortex? Well, scientists reckon you can squeeze facts in your memory to fill 20,000 encyclopaedias. Do that and your brain really would be bulging. You might even win a memory competition...

THE HORRIBLE SCIENCE MEMORY COMPETITION

This competition is unforgettable. All the prize winners have shown powers of recollection that will live long in our memories.

Fourth Prize

German conductor Hans von Bülow (1830–1894)

Hans was never one to forget a good tune. One day he took the train from Hamburg to Berlin and read the music of a new symphony. That evening he conducted the entire symphony without any mistakes *entirely from memory.*

ERRR – OH YES, I REMEMBER TUM-TE-TUM...

Third Prize

FLUSH!

56937 09785

You'd think that remembering boring numbers would be hard. But in 1995 **Hiroyuki Goto of Japan** recited the mathematical number pi to 42,195 places with no mistakes. The performance took over 17 hours including breaks to go to the toilet. At the end I expect he was flushed with success.

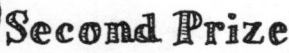

Second Prize

Devout **Mehmed Ali Halici of Turkey** recited 6,666 verses of religious text

BLAH BLAH

AND NOW FOR VERSE 3772...

in 1967. Could you do that in your school assembly? Come to think of it would you fancy an assembly that was 18 hours long?

First Prize

I WILL NOW RECITE THE ENTIRE BIBLE... IN LATIN

Goes to **Russian Solomon Veniaminoff.** Solomon wanted to be a violinist but an ear disease slightly damaged his hearing. In the 1930s he decided to become a journalist. Later he worked as a stage entertainer where he wowed the crowds with his unforgettable talent for remembering incredibly long numbers or lists of words. From time to time he also helped psychologist Alexander Luria (1902-1977) with his work on memory. Here's Solomon's story. Of course, we can't remember the exact details but this story is based on the real facts...

THE MAN WHO NEVER FORGOT
Moscow, May 1928

The slender young man was clearly on edge. "My name is Solomon," he stammered. "My editor sent me to see you because of my memory."

"What's wrong with it?" asked Alexander Luria curiously as he leaned back in his rocking-chair. Solomon nervously swept his black hair from his eyes.

"People say that I have an exceptional memory. The fact is I can remember every single thing that has happened to me since I was one year old."

"Fascinating but unlikely," smiled Luria. There was an uncomfortable silence broken only by the ticking of the large old clock on the mantelpiece. Then Luria sighed.

"Oh well, I suppose we'd better test you. I'd like you to try to remember this sequence of numbers."

The scientist quickly jotted down a series of 30 numbers and then read them out to the young man.

Solomon looked even more worried and gazed briefly into nothing. His dark, dreamy eyes seemed fixed on a distant object that Luria couldn't see.

Then he repeated the numbers perfectly.

The scientist's mouth dropped open. "But that's astounding!" he gasped.

"I could say them backwards if you like," said Solomon quietly. And he gave a shy, fleeting smile.

1958

Thirty years later Alexander Luria sat in the warm sunshine gazing vacantly at his garden. He was lost in thought and as usual he felt rather tired. In front of him lay a pile of old papers covered in his spidery handwriting. The paper was crinkled and yellow with age.

"So how do I turn all this into a book?" he mused to himself. "Where to begin, that's the first problem."

"Why not begin at the beginning?" said a voice. Luria looked up in surprise at the man sitting quietly in the corner. The visitor's hair was grey with age and his figure was stooped and thick-set.

"Oh, Solomon I'm so sorry, I quite forgot you were here. Now what were we saying?"

"We were discussing the book you were going to write about memory and our 30 years of working together. That's why you invited me here at 4.24 p.m. yesterday."

"Has it really been that long?" asked the scientist wearily.

"Well, on and off, when I wasn't working on the stage."

"I think I'll begin my book on that day in June, when was it? 1929 when you first came to see me."

"It was 1928," said Solomon firmly, "and the month was May. I remember you in your grey suit sitting in your rocking-chair. And that old-fashioned clock you had. And then those 30 numbers … what were they now? 62, 30, 19, 41…"

Luria gazed in growing shock at the first page of his yellowing notes. Yes, there in his own handwriting was the exact sequence of numbers repeated with eerie accuracy over a gap of 30 years.

"But that's astounding!" he wheezed breathlessly.

"That's what you said at the time," said Solomon with his familiar shy smile.

"But you must have remembered millions of pieces of information since then. You're a lucky man Solomon, I do admire this gift of yours."

"It's no gift!" exclaimed Solomon bitterly. "As I told you in 1929 it's a curse. I often wished I could forget things. Sometimes all these facts and numbers and lists jostle in my mind like a huge crowd – like words in poetry or sparks in a fireworks display. They drive me crazy! The greatest gift is to forget things. But that's one gift I will never possess. Forgetting is a wonderful thing."

And his eyes sparkled with tears.

SOLOMON'S SECRET

After years of patient study Luria figured out the secret of Solomon Veniaminoff's astonishing memory. It was due to the way his mind worked. Solomon suffered from a disease called synaesthesia (sin-ees-thees-ia). Incredible though it sounds this rare brain disease made Solomon experience sounds as colours. He told one psychologist…

WHAT A CRUMBLY YELLOW VOICE YOU HAVE!

By remembering the colours he saw when hearing things and by imagining numbers as people he found it easy to remember tons of information. But the only way he could ever forget something was to imagine it was written on paper and he was burning it.

BOOST YOUR MEMORY

Would you want a memory like Solomon's? Probably not – but with a more powerful memory you could get top marks in your science tests every time and even remember your dad's birthday. The good news is you don't need a special brain to develop an excellent memory.

Bet you never knew!
One painful way to improve your memory is to stick electrodes into your brain. Experiments in the 1900s by surgeon Wilder Penfield in Canada found this gives you vivid flashbacks from your past. I expect some of them proved a bit shocking.

PICTURE THIS...

But don't worry, there are many less painful methods of improving your memory. Here's one of them. Supposing tomorrow you have a science test and you need to remember to feed the goldfish and take your sandwiches to school.

1 *Try* to remember to do these things. This should store the information in your short-term memory.

2 For reasons that scientists don't quite understand you can remember pictures better than facts. It might be because you can link pictures with other memories more easily and in some way this makes them easier to recall. So make up a mental picture to help you remember. For example, you could imagine your teacher eating a goldfish in a sandwich.

3 When you get up the next morning and get ready for school, the thought of facing your teacher again will immediately make you remember the image of her eating a goldfish sandwich. So you use your teacher as a memory cue – that's a kind of clue to help you remember the goldfish, the sandwiches and the test, stupid.

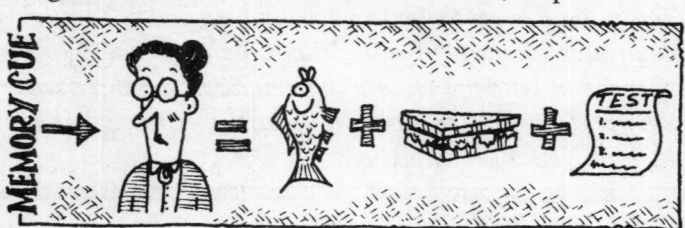

TERROR IN THE AIR

Your memory can be affected by your feelings. In the 1950s Mitchell Berkun, a scientist working for the US Army, dreamt up this horrible experiment.

Of course, the whole incident including the fire engines on the ground had been set up by Berkun. The terrible test showed that the recruits could only remember half the instructions when they were scared out of their wits.

And talking about feelings ... the next chapter's all about them – the highs, the lows, the excitement and the horror. So, do you feel like reading a bit further?

FORCEFUL FEELINGS

Are you a touchy-feely person who is always laughing or weeping? Do you pride yourself on being the strong, silent type? Well, whatever you're like on the surface, your brain is bulging with powerful feelings.

FEELING THE FORCE

Scientists claim there are six types of emotion that people feel all over the world. Huh – what do they know? When was the last time you saw an emotional scientist? Well, we've managed to find one and photograph the full range of his six emotions.

Of course, feelings can get horribly mixed up. That's why people cry when they're happy or sometimes feel a bit down after some good news.

I'VE WON THE NOBEL PRIZE!

Scientists have scarcely begun to explain why our emotions get so tangled. However, as you're about to discover, emotions can be triggered by several different chemicals. With so many of these chemicals sloshing about at the same time it wouldn't be surprising if your brain got some mixed messages.

COMPLICATED FEELINGS

Feeling emotion is actually more complicated than you might think. For one thing you need to co-ordinate three areas of your brain. And that really gets the Neuro-phone lines buzzing. Just listen to this: Your teacher is telling you off...

LIMBIC SYSTEM – THIS IS THE AREA THAT SHAPES EMOTIONS, REMEMBER

CORTEX

IF YOU DON'T DO YOUR HOMEWORK YOU'RE IN BIG TOUBLE!

BRAIN STEM

Brain stem to cortex: WAKE UP! Cortex to mid-brain: SEND ME SOME DOPAMINE!

Scientific note:

Dopamine (dope-a-mean) is a chemical that seems to make your neurons more active and fire more signals. Obviously the emotion you feel depends on what's going on. It could be terror or joy or anything in between.

Limbic system to cortex: "YIKES! THAT DOPAMINE'S GETTING ME ALL WORKED UP! I'M SCARED!"

Cortex to limbic system: "CALM DOWN, I'M TRYING TO THINK!"

BULGING BRAIN EXPRESSIONS

One neurologist says to another...

IS YOUR WORK INTERESTING?

WELL MY **RAS** IS FIRED UP!

Is that some kind of stove?

Answer: No. The reticular (ret-tick-u-lar) activating system, or RAS for short, is the area of your brain stem that makes you conscious and alert. By the way, you might be interested to know that in small kids the RAS is easily switched on and that's why they get so easily scared. As you grow up the RAS quietens down because your cortex learns when there's a real monster and when it's just a curtain blowing in a darkened room.

DIZZY DOPAMINE V SERIOUS SEROTONIN

So dopamine shakes up your limbic system and you feel emotion. But you don't always do what you feel like doing. That's because of another brain chemical called serotonin (seer-ro-tone-in). This is squirted by neurons linking the limbic system and the cortex. Serotonin tends to calm the neurons down and makes you feel more sensible. (It can also make you feel happy and relaxed.)

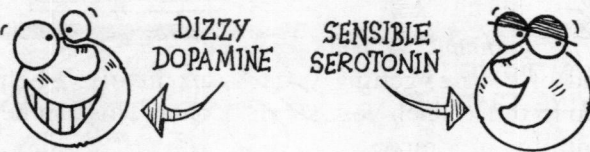

Imagine you've guzzled some lovely cream buns and you're greedily eyeing up the rest.

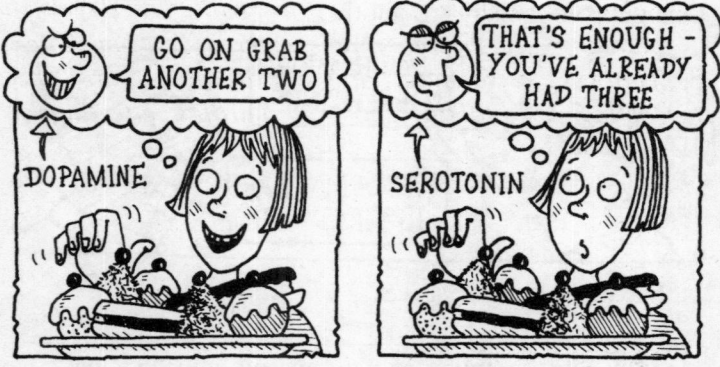

In other words serotonin tells you *not* to do things. It's like having a sensible teacher stuck between your ears. (Now that *is* a scary thought!)

By now you might be wondering why your cortex needs to get involved in feelings. After all, you feel things in the limbic system and you've got dizzy dopamine to get you all worked up and serious serotonin

116

to calm you down. Well, the cortex is there to think things over and make the ultimate decision...

And of course, getting your cortex involved helps you stop to think when you get emotional. This can help you control your temper.

Bet you never knew!
Scientists believe that people with low levels of serotonin can become bad-tempered or even violent. That's because they find it harder to control their feelings. And talking about uncontrollable feelings...

HORRIBLE SCIENCE HEALTH WARNING
There's a feeling of TERROR lurking just over the page.

FEAR AND FURY

Although feelings are controlled and felt in your brain, your body also joins in and helps you to feel emotions. Sometimes in a horrible way. Just imagine you haven't done your homework for the third time running: your teacher is seething. Never mind, here's your chance to make interesting scientific observations on the effect of anger and fear...

ADRENAL GLANDS OVER KIDNEYS SQUIRTING A
HORMONE CALLED ADRENALINE (AD-REN-A-LIN) INTO
THE BLOOD. THIS CAUSES ALL THE OTHER EFFECTS...

Did someone mention scientific observations? Well, maybe
you're not in the mood. Inside you might be feeling a bit
wobbly, petrified even. Maybe a bit like this...

A SCARED CHILD

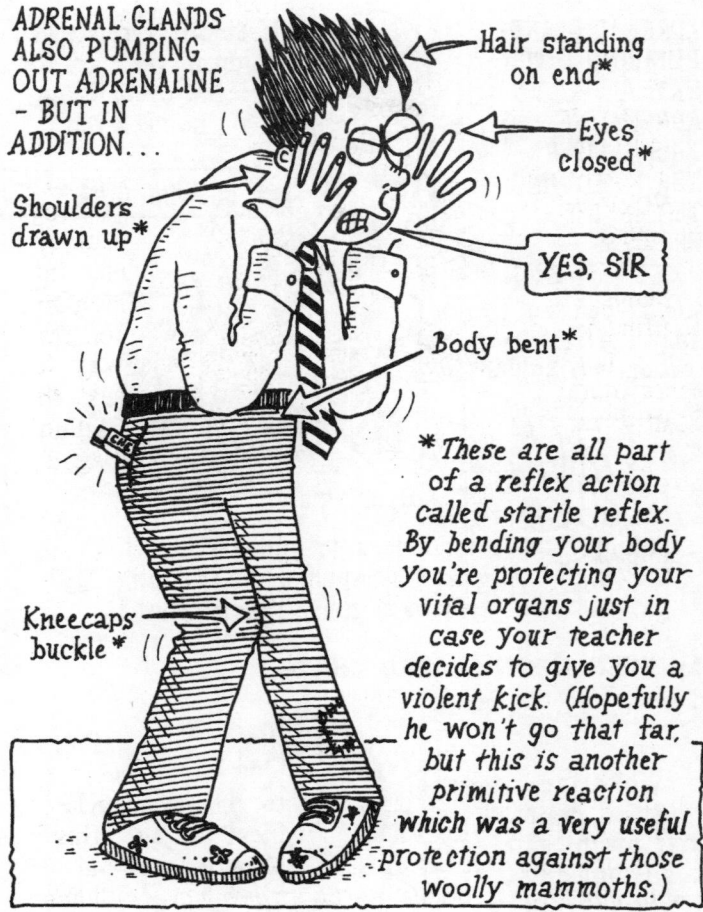

ADRENAL GLANDS ALSO PUMPING OUT ADRENALINE – BUT IN ADDITION...

Hair standing on end*

Eyes closed*

Shoulders drawn up*

YES, SIR

Body bent*

Kneecaps buckle*

*These are all part of a reflex action called startle reflex. By bending your body you're protecting your vital organs just in case your teacher decides to give you a violent kick. (Hopefully he won't go that far, but this is another primitive reaction which was a very useful protection against those woolly mammoths.)

Important note:

Oh no! Your teacher's figured out it was you who absent-mindedly left chewing gum on his chair. Oh-er, you're going to cop it now. TAKE COVER! YOUR TEACHER IS ABOUT TO GO BALLISTIC...

A TEACHER WHO IS JUST ABOUT TO EXPLODE

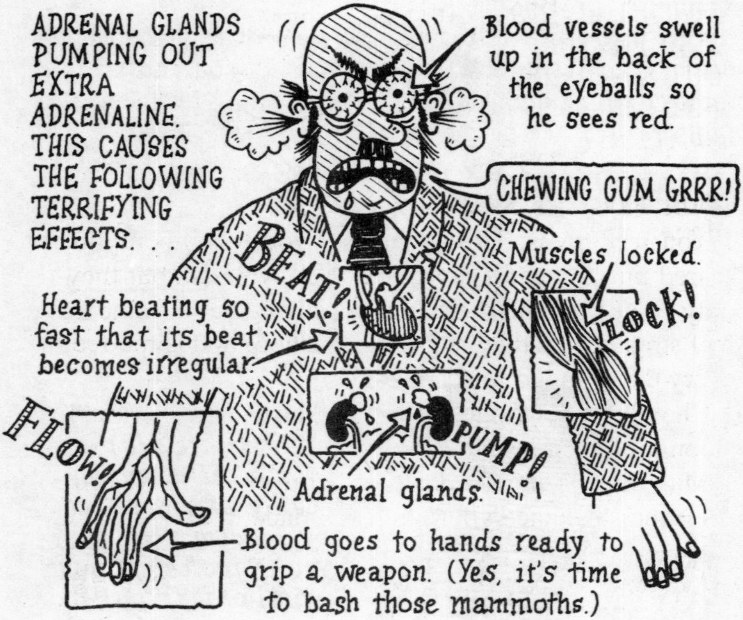

ADRENAL GLANDS PUMPING OUT EXTRA ADRENALINE. THIS CAUSES THE FOLLOWING TERRIFYING EFFECTS...

Blood vessels swell up in the back of the eyeballs so he sees red.

CHEWING GUM GRRR!

BEAT!

Muscles locked.

LOCK!

Heart beating so fast that its beat becomes irregular.

FLOW!

PUMP!

Adrenal glands.

Blood goes to hands ready to grip a weapon. (Yes, it's time to bash those mammoths.)

AN EVEN MORE SCARED CHILD

White face. (Blood drains out of the skin so that any wounds you get won't bleed too much. Another sensible Stone Age precaution.)

Spit dries up. GULP!

JIBBER TREMBLE!

THUMP! THUMP!

Heart speeds up.

THE LONG, LONG, LONG WAIT OUTSIDE THE HEAD TEACHER'S ROOM

So you've been sent for a little chat with the head teacher? Oh dear, this could prove painful. Here are a few things to think about whilst you're waiting for the axe to fall...

FOUR FEARFUL FEELINGS FACTS

1 You feel stress. This is the fear you feel when you're scared but you can't run away. Well, you can but they'll only catch you and then you'll really catch it. Some kids feel stress when they start a new school and some feel it every day they go to school.

2 Chewing your fingernails yet? Masticating keratin* is a common response to stress.

*(Mas-tic-kate-ing) = posh term for chewing. (Ker-rat-in) = the substance your nails are made of.

Scientists think that people feel more cheerful when they chew things. It's healthier to chew gum (sugar-free, of course) but that's what got you into this mess. By the way, when you're stressed-out your sense of taste stops working. So the gum would taste like someone's already chewed it.

3 Your adrenal glands are squirting a hormone called cortisone (cor-ti-zone). The aim of this chemical is to prepare your muscles for action later on. Sugar pours into your blood, your brain feels more alert because it's getting more sugar and the nerves are firing like crazy. But you feel rotten – all nervy and jittery. Yikes!

4 You'd better apologize to the head teacher – you might even be let off without a punishment. But there's one feeling that's even worse than being stressed. It's worse because it makes you feel really miserable, really sad. It can spoil your whole life…

Bet you never knew!
Depression is a brain condition that makes you so miserable you want to go to bed and cry and stay there for ever. Scientists think it may be the result of a shortage of brain chemicals such as serotonin. If you ever feel this way try taking a deep breath. Let it out slowly and relax. Yep, that's it: for some reason relaxing actually helps you feel better. Remember this rotten scary fearful miserable feeling is caused by a few chemicals in your bulging brain.

TA VERY MUCH BRAIN!

Happiness

THE SECRET OF HAPPINESS

For hundreds of years people have searched for this elusive secret and got very uptight and miserable because they couldn't find it. But it's here, here in this very book! Ahem, wait for it... This next bit is based on research by US psychologists Paul Costa and Robert McRae. In the 1970s, Costa and McRae interviewed large numbers of different people and tried to discover what it was in their personalities that made them happy or sad. Here's what they found: to be happy it helps if you enjoy meeting new people.

Don't expect too much from life. That way good things come as a pleasant surprise.

But always look for the bright side of every situation.

And if you can't find happiness by using these simple techniques then don't worry. Science has found ways of making you cheer up whether you like it or not...

Bet you never knew!

1 In the 1950s it was common to treat diseases of the mind by cutting the nerves to the front part of the cortex. This made the patient less emotional (maybe that's because it's hard to be emotional when you've got a thumping headache).

2 US surgeon Walter Freeman invented his own version of this horrible treatment. Walt stuck an ice-pick through a patient's eye-socket into the brain and cut the nerves that way. I expect he only wanted to pick their brains, ha-ha. Hardened doctors were known to swoon at this revolting spectacle. The patients also felt sick and confused afterwards.

3 In 1963 scientist RG Heath tried a new technique to control feelings. He stuck electrodes in the brain of a man with a brain disease that caused uncontrollable rages. By pressing buttons the man gave electric shocks to different areas of his brain.

But you don't have to drill holes in your skull or wield ice-picks or even suffer electric shocks to feel emotional. Try tuning into your favourite music. Yep, why not enjoy the feel-good factor with our exclusive relaxation tapes…?

The Horrible Science ♫ Feel-good Tapes ♫

Recorded by Austrian psychologist Manfried Klein…

SPONSORED BY SOOTHIE-BONCE HEADACHE TABLETS.

BEFORE   AFTER

Chill out to the brain calming tones of musical gems such as "The Brandenberg Concertos" by German composer JS Bach (1685-1750)

IMPORTANT NOTE:

Yeah, it's dead boring classical stuff by an even more dead composer. But Klein found that people all over the world go gooey when they listen to it. Yes, even people like you who think classical music is best enjoyed by zombies and elderly teachers. So get in the groove, chill out and feel mellow…

COULD YOU BE A SCIENTIST?

The situation you're in and the reactions of other people can affect the way you feel. Sounds common sense, doesn't it? But psychologists have tried to find out precisely how important these factors are. And they've dreamt up a few brain-boggling experiments…

1 In the late 1960s two psychologists from New York University, USA, played frisbee in the waiting-room of Grand Central station. They laughed and joked and got in the way. After a while they threw the frisbee to a third scientist who was pretending to be a stranger. She joined in the game. What happened next?

a) Other people joined in the game.

b) Everyone ignored the frisbee players.

c) The scientists were arrested for causing a nuisance.

2 The same team put three people in a room and gave them forms to fill in. Then they wafted smoke through vents to make it look like the room was on fire. Two of the people were actually psychologists in disguise and they ignored the smoke. What did the third person do?

a) Ran about shouting…

b) Ignored the smoke.
c) Got a fire extinguisher and squirted the scientists with foam from head to foot.

3 US psychologist Philip Zimbardo set up a tasteless experiment. A nice, friendly scientist was given the job of persuading complete strangers to eat fried grasshoppers.

Next, another scientist rudely ordered people to eat the insects. What did the results show?
a) People were more likely to eat the grasshoppers when they were asked nicely.
b) The test was scrapped when someone threw up. This is odd because grasshoppers are a delicacy in parts of Africa such as Morocco. They have a lovely crunchy texture and taste like dried shrimp.
c) People ate the grasshoppers on both occasions. But they said they felt different when they were ordered to eat them.

Mind you, there's one situation where you'd feel nothing. It's when you get knocked out cold by a bash on the head. And if you want to find out what it does to your brain take a look at the next chapter. It's a real knockout.

CLONK

FASCINATING!

BANGS 'N' BASHES

As you've probably realized by now, the brain is an intricate and delicate bit of equipment. So, not surprisingly, a bash on the head can damage the brain in all sorts of horrible and unexpected ways. Luckily, you do have a bit of natural protection.

BULGING BRAIN PROTECTION

Your bulging brain is naturally well protected. Let's take a look at this MRI scan.

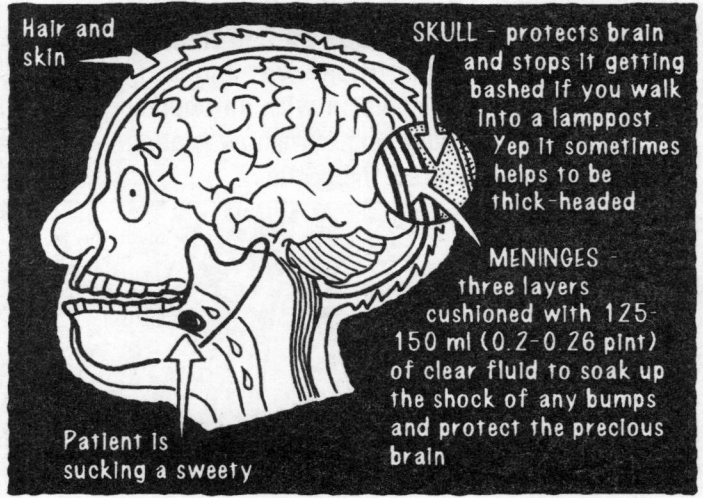

Hair and skin

SKULL – protects brain and stops it getting bashed if you walk into a lamppost. Yep it sometimes helps to be thick-headed

MENINGES – three layers cushioned with 125-150 ml (0.2-0.26 pint) of clear fluid to soak up the shock of any bumps and protect the precious brain

Patient is sucking a sweety

A nasty blow

Despite these elaborate defences a bash on the bonce can make you lose your memory – or cause amnesia to use the scientific term. In this state you can't remember what hit you, or even that you've been hit. And you may lose consciousness. And consciousness is actually the most incredible thing your bulging brain gets up to...

Bulging brains fact file

NAME: Consciousness

BASIC FACTS: It means being aware of your thoughts and feelings. Scientists aren't too sure how this happens. The whole of your cortex seems to be involved in making you aware of your thoughts and what they mean.

DISGUSTING DETAILS: It's possible to run around and perform simple actions whilst unconscious. In the 1956 FA Cup Final goalkeeper Bert Trautmann was knocked unconscious in a collision with an opposing player. But battling Bert somehow made a vital save and completed the game.

His team, Manchester City, won the cup.

BULGING BRAIN BUMPS

Here are some vital facts to bump up your knowledge.
1 When you get up in the morning your brain gets a rude awakening. As you lift your head up your brain slops forward and bangs against the front part of your skull.

Luckily your meninges and the fluid around the brain stop it getting too battered.

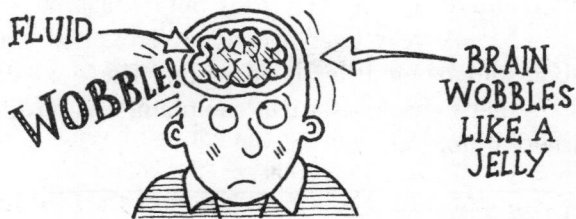

FLUID
WOBBLE!
BRAIN WOBBLES LIKE A JELLY

2 Some neurologists think the shock makes some people feel bad-tempered in the morning. (It's either that or the sour milk in their tea.)

WHAT D'YOU THINK YOU'RE STARING AT?

3 In car crashes the effect of the brain being thrown forwards is far more damaging than a blow on the head. The shock is more likely to tear blood vessels and the brain itself, leaving wounds that cannot easily be treated because they're inside the skull.

4 The effects of an injury can depend on which part of the cortex gets damaged. It can lead to problems reading, smelling or tasting, or amnesia – that's loss of memory, remember?

THANKS – WHO ARE YOU?

25th WEDDING

5 In 1997 Vicky, a ten-year-old British girl, banged her head and started writing backwards and upside down. Vicky could read her own writing but it must have baffled her teacher. A year later she got overexcited watching football and banged her head again. The next day, for reasons that neurologists can't explain, her writing had returned to normal.

Bet you never knew!

In 1998 a retired Scottish footballer said that his memory loss was due to heading the ball too much. His wife said that he often chatted to his grandchildren and then forgot whom he was talking to. Before the 1950s, footballs were made of heavy leather and when it rained they sucked in water and got heavier. If they hit you on the head they could knock you out.

HORRIBLE HEALTH WARNING!

So let that be a warning. Don't go bashing your head against hard solid objects such as brick walls, floors or teachers. It's horribly unhealthy.

BRICK WALL: HARD SOLID OBJECT

HEAD: NOT SUCH A HARD SOLID OBJECT

Bulging brains fact file

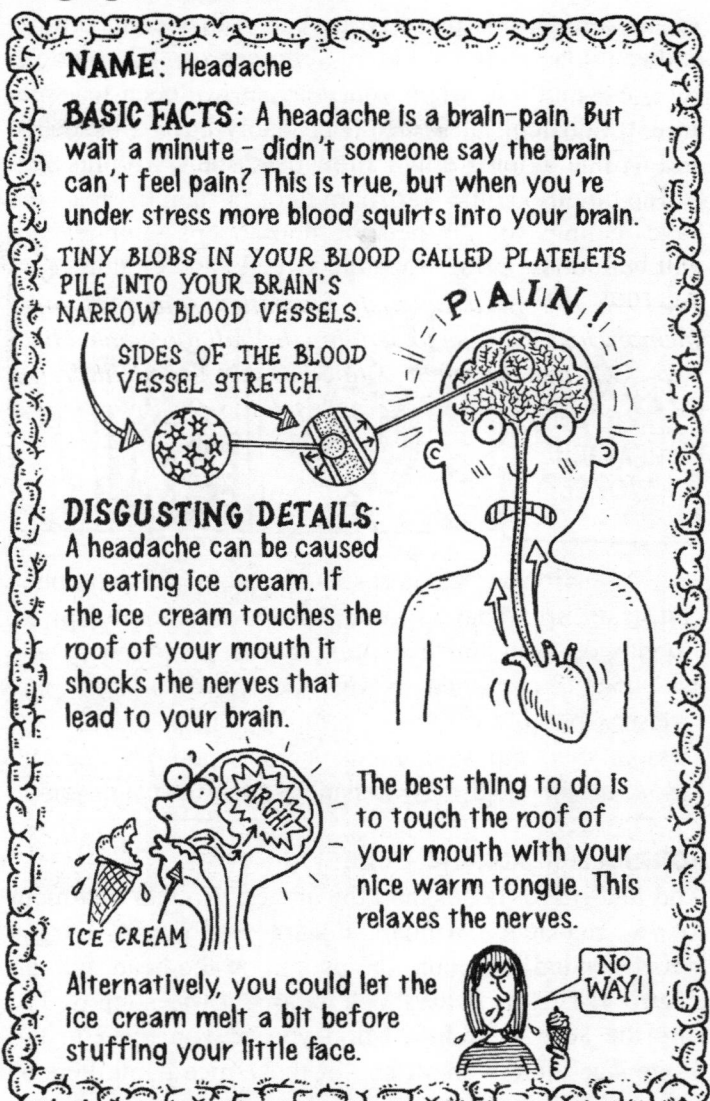

NAME: Headache

BASIC FACTS: A headache is a brain-pain. But wait a minute – didn't someone say the brain can't feel pain? This is true, but when you're under stress more blood squirts into your brain.

TINY BLOBS IN YOUR BLOOD CALLED PLATELETS PILE INTO YOUR BRAIN'S NARROW BLOOD VESSELS.

PAIN!

SIDES OF THE BLOOD VESSEL STRETCH.

DISGUSTING DETAILS: A headache can be caused by eating ice cream. If the ice cream touches the roof of your mouth it shocks the nerves that lead to your brain.

ICE CREAM

ARGH!

The best thing to do is to touch the roof of your mouth with your nice warm tongue. This relaxes the nerves.

NO WAY!

Alternatively, you could let the ice cream melt a bit before stuffing your little face.

TEACHER'S TEA-BREAK TEASER

To succeed in this teaser you need split-second timing, oodles of charm and skin like a rhinoceros. All you do is choose a morning when your teacher has been teaching an extra-difficult class. He'll probably have a headache and will be gulping down a few painkillers with his tea.

Tap quietly on the staffroom door (remember teachers have feelings too). When the door opens your teacher will be looking grim. So smile sweetly and enquire…

DOES FROWNING MAKE YOUR HEADACHE WORSE?

Answer: Frowning squishes the platelets in your teacher's blood vessels and makes the pain worse. Your teacher should smile to relax his blood vessels. Or take a painkiller. Some painkillers, such as paracetamol, stop the brain sensing pain so much, whilst others such as ibuorofen tackle the swelling and other chemical changes in the aching area.

HORRIBLE HEADACHE CURES

And that's a lot better than the ancient Roman treatment for a headache. Roman doctor Scribonius Largus recommended whacking the patient on the head with an electric fish. This fishy shock treatment was supposed to cure the ache. It didn't. Mind you, if you lived in the Stone Age there weren't any of those nice painkillers or even an electric fish around.

STONE AGE BRAIN SURGERY

1 Take a sharp bit of flint.

2 Scrape the hair and skin off the patient's head.

3 Ignore any screams from the victim, sorry patient.

4 Carry on until a hole appears in the skull.

No one is sure why this operation was carried out in the Stone Age but it was used in ancient Greece to tackle persistent headaches. Although it didn't do much good the victims often survived with their brains bulging out of the gory hole. Stone Age skulls have been found in which the skull had started to heal.

Actually this treatment – known today as trepanning – is still performed by surgeons. You'll be relieved to know they use modern instruments rather than lumps of rock. It's done in an emergency to relieve a build-up of blood pressure in the brain caused by a blood clot. And, as you now know, people can survive with a hole in the bonce. A person can even survive with a hole made by an accident.

GROANING GAGE

Everyone liked Phineas Gage of Vermont, USA. The young railway foreman was a lively and happy-go-lucky chap. Until one day in 1848...

Phin was blasting a path for a new railway. He was trying to push some dynamite down a hole using an iron bar. When disaster struck...

The dynamite blew up and the iron bar shot straight through Phin's head. The bar was found a few metres away spattered with bits of poor Phin's brains.

Phin was knocked out by the blow but quickly came

round and even managed to walk to the doctor's. The hole was big enough for the doctor to put his fingers inside Phin's skull…

Amazingly, Phin lived – although he was ill for a few weeks. But as a result of his injuries he was a changed man. He was moody, foul-mouthed, rude and often drunk.

He lost jobs frequently, but his wits remained sharp. He made money by exhibiting himself in fairs with the iron bar stuck through his head.

Scientists were eager to study Phin's battered bonce. So he sold his body to *several* medical schools for cash up front.

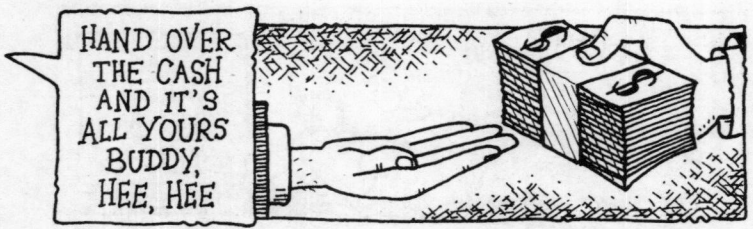

After Phin's death the medical schools argued over who owned the body and, of course, the brain. The doctors were keen to remove Phin's brain and look at the damage.

The doctors found that Phin's brain hadn't been able to repair the damage it suffered. The damaged front cortex area wasn't vital for life but it had clearly shaped Phin's personality.

The famous bar and Phin's skull ended up on display at the museum of Harvard Medical School. I hope they were given a good clean first.

But you don't need a near-fatal brain injury to lose consciousness. No, in fact you do it far less painfully every night when you curl up your tootsies and snuggle down in your nice warm bed. And if that's where you are right now why not take a peek at the next chapter? It's a real dream.

Or is it a nightmare?

NASTY NIGHTMARES

This chapter is about sleep. It's about dreams and it's about nightmares…

Warning to sensitive readers: Are you easily scared and reading this chapter in bed? Well, if you must scream, scream quietly.

But, try not to be too petrified – nightmares and dreams are fascinating effects made by your bulging brain in the middle of sleep. Here are a few more facts to sleep on…

Bulging brains fact file

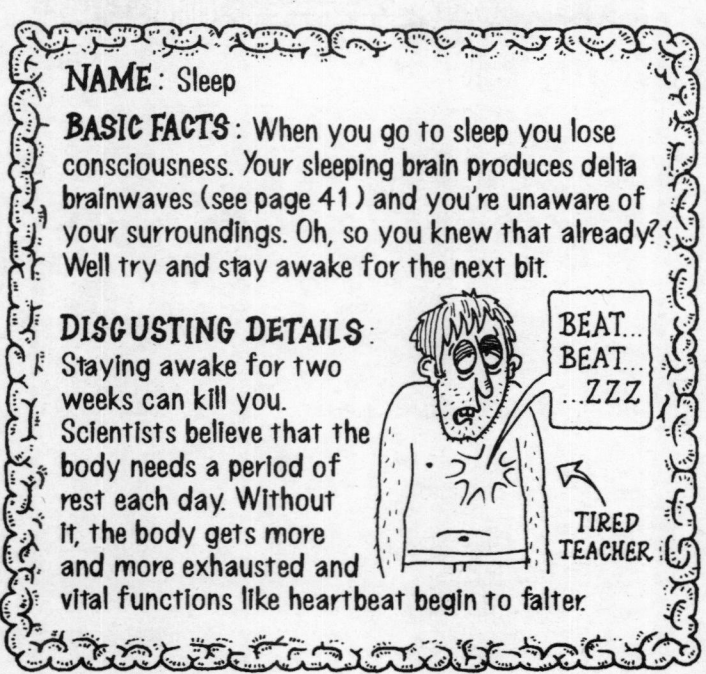

NAME: Sleep

BASIC FACTS: When you go to sleep you lose consciousness. Your sleeping brain produces delta brainwaves (see page 41) and you're unaware of your surroundings. Oh, so you knew that already? Well try and stay awake for the next bit.

DISGUSTING DETAILS: Staying awake for two weeks can kill you. Scientists believe that the body needs a period of rest each day. Without it, the body gets more and more exhausted and vital functions like heartbeat begin to falter.

BEAT...
BEAT...
...ZZZ

TIRED TEACHER

So sleep is good for you. And whilst you're lying in bed you can always listen in to those chattering Neuro-phone wires as your brain tries to help you to nod off…

SLEEPY SIGNALS

Cortex to all brain areas: "I'M REALLY WIDE AWAKE. DO I HAVE TO GO TO SLEEP?"

Pineal gland to cortex: "NIGHT-NIGHT, CORTEX. SOME OF THIS NICE MELATONIN WILL CALM YOU DOWN"

SCIENTIFIC NOTE
Melatonin (mel-a tone-in) damps down the activity in the cortex. The pineal gland pumps out melatonin every night on a 24-hour cycle.

Cortex: "YAWN, I'M FEELING REALLY SLEEPY."

RAS* to cortex: "COME ON, CORTEX, TIME YOU WERE TUCKED UP. HERE'S SOME NICE SEROTONIN** TO HELP YOU SLEEP."

SCIENTIFIC NOTE
At this point your brain should lose consciousness. But you won't notice that bit. Why? Because you'll be asleep, too, stupid.

Cortex: "ZZZZ."

* That's the reticular activating system in your brain stem, remember.

** That's the "sensible" chemical that damps down your feelings. The serotonin should calm your cortex down even more.

BULGING BRAIN EXPRESSIONS

Two psychologists are chatting.

SLEEP WELL?

NO, I'M A SOMNILOQUISTIC SOMNAMBULIST

Is this dangerous?

Answer: No, but it's annoying for everyone else. Somniloquy (som-nil-o-kwee) means talking in your sleep. Somnambulism (som-nam-bew-lis-m) means walking in your sleep. So the psychologist walks and talks in his sleep. Well, could be worse: in 1993 a British businessman had to be rescued by fire-fighters after falling into a rubbish chute. He had fallen in whilst sleepwalking in the nude.

SPOT THE SLEEPWALKER

One in twenty children walk in their sleep and some adults do this when they're feeling stressed. Does your mum/dad/brother/sister/hamster sleepwalk? Here are a few signs to look out for.

A SLEEPWALKING TEACHER

EYES OPEN
BUT ASLEEP

BLANK
EXPRESSION

mumble,
mumble

ER... THE
LESS SAID
ABOUT
THIS THE
BETTER

TALKING
GIBBERISH

Mind you, some teachers act this way on a Monday morning when they are supposedly awake.

Bet you never knew!
It's quite harmless to wake a sleepwalker but it's a good idea to do it gently. After all, it's a bit confusing for someone to wake up suddenly and find themselves out of bed. On waking up, the sleepwalking person can't remember where they've been. So break the news gently, OK?

A BIT OF AN EYE-OPENER

Any sleep, even with a bit of sleepwalking thrown in, is better than no sleep at all. In the 1960s scientists kept volunteers awake to measure the effects of lack of sleep on their brains and bodies. What you are about to read is a story based on real events that happened in these tests. So try to keep awake for the next few minutes...

HORRIBLE HEALTH WARNING!

Don't try this experiment at home. You might keep parents awake and this can have a magical shrinking effect on pocket money. And, as you are about to find out, losing too much sleep is very unhealthy. For this reason scientists are no longer keen to perform this experiment.

SLEEP DEPRIVATION EXPERIMENT DIARY

by Arthur Sleep (volunteer)

Notes by Dr Irma Wake (day-shift) & Dr Hugh Kant-Dropoff (night-shift)

Monday night
I'm wide awake and feel like I could stay awake for ever! I drink coffee to keep me going. The only problem is that Dr Kant-Dropoff insists on coming to the toilet with me to check I don't doze off in there.

4a.m. Tuesday morning. Feeling a bit sleepy: I could do with some shut-eye. I fight the feeling off and play some snooker.

144

TUESDAY MORNING
Dr Kant-Dropoff writes. . .

Arthur is fine. His heartbeat and reflexes are normal. I wired him up to an EEG machine and his brainwaves are normal. I'm a bit sleepy now myself - could do with a bit of kip. Oh well, off to bed - I'm handing over to Dr Wake who will monitor Arthur during the day.

Tuesday night - I nearly dropped off tonight but Dr Kant-Dropoff rudely shook me and shouted "Wakey-wakey" in my ear. I feel really cross with him.

Dr Kant-Dropoff writes. . .

Arthur seems more tired and irritable tonight. Shouted at me at 3 a.m. after I stopped him from falling asleep.

WEDNESDAY
Dr Wake writes. . .

Arthur is slurring his words today. He keeps repeating things and he moves about slowly. He can still play chess, though, and even beat me in a game. Obviously the areas of his brain dealing with thinking are still functioning normally.

Wednesday night - I'm not talking to Dr Kant-Dropoff after last night's row. Played loud music to keep awake. I could see Dr Kant-Dropoff didn't like it - ha-ha!

145

I'm really tired all the time now. If I close my eyes I could fall asleep. Got to keep going.

Dr Kant-Dropoff writes...
Arthur has been <u>extremely</u> quiet tonight.

Thursday
I don't like the way Dr Wake shouts "rise and shine" each morning. Why does she have to be so cheerful? I mean it's not as if I've been asleep. I bet she gets a good night's sleep, though...she must have something against me. Yes, that's it: she's getting at me.

Dr Wake writes...
Arthur is clearly exhausted and his pulse rate keeps going faster and then slower.

Thursday night - My beans on
toast tasted funny tonight: I feel sure Dr Kant-Dropoff put some drug in my food. But why? WHY? Maybe he's getting back at me for playing loud music. I'll show him...

Dr Kant-Dropoff writes...
Arthur seems to be suffering from strange ideas. This is typical of people who lose too much sleep. We'll have to monitor the situation closely.

146

Friday – Refused to finish my cornflakes this morning – the milk tasted odd. Dr Wake gave them to me so she must be in on the plot with Dr Kant-Dropoff. Ha-ha! They think I don't suspect they tamper with my food.

4.15 p.m. When I stood up the floor was heaving like the sea. I must have been poisoned!

Dr Wake writes. . .

Arthur appears to be seeing things. I must contact Dr Kant-Dropoff and discuss ending the experiment.

FRIDAY NIGHT
Dr Kant-Dropoff writes. . .

Arthur has locked himself in the toilet. He keeps shouting for me to keep away and stop poisoning him. I will monitor the situation from the outside. I'm afraid he will use violence.

I'll be safe here. All quiet – I think Dr K-D's gone away. Phew, I can relax! Just close my eyes now for a minute... Zzzzzzzzzzz

---

SATURDAY MORNING
Dr Kant-Dropoff and Dr Wake. . .

We broke into the toilet and found Arthur fast asleep. He didn't stir when we moved him to a bed.

sunday evening - I've just woken up. I still feel really sleepy but all my tiredness has gone. The last few days seem like a nightmare. Did I really imagine the doctors were trying to poison me? And here they are now, all smiles with some tea and biscuits. They wouldn't harm a fly. That's the last time I miss a night's sleep.

CONCLUSION BY
Dr Wake and Dr Kant-Dropoff

Arthur seems fully recovered. His pulse, heart-rate and brainwaves are normal. The experiment proves lack of sleep can cause mistaken thoughts and cause other problems such as disorders to the pulse and heartbeat. It appears these can be put right by a longer than usual period of sleep.

Bet you never knew!
Although scientists no longer keep people awake, in one experiment volunteers were woken up as soon as they started to dream. The scientists wanted to find out how the brain would act if it couldn't dream. The poor volunteers ended up getting woken over 30 times a night as their brains tried harder to make them dream.

HOW DO YOU FEEL ABOUT NOT BEING ABLE TO DREAM?

IT'S A NIGHTMARE!

But why is dreaming so important?

Bulging brains fact file

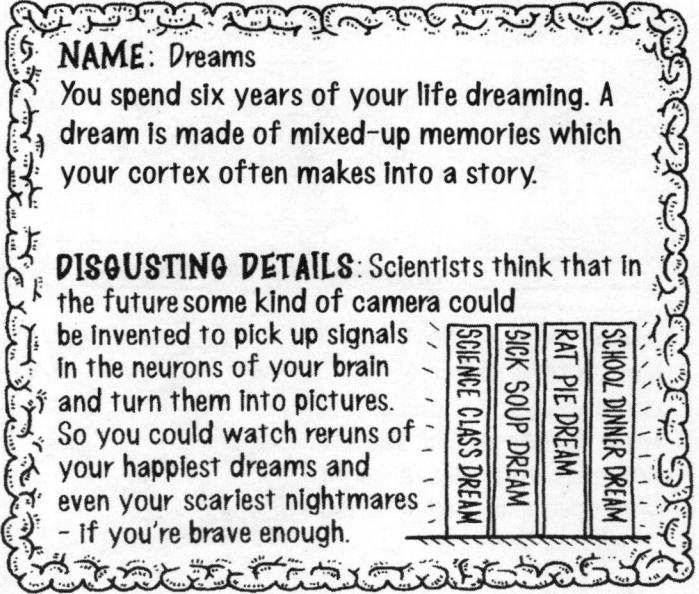

NAME: Dreams
You spend six years of your life dreaming. A dream is made of mixed-up memories which your cortex often makes into a story.

DISGUSTING DETAILS: Scientists think that in the future some kind of camera could be invented to pick up signals in the neurons of your brain and turn them into pictures. So you could watch reruns of your happiest dreams and even your scariest nightmares – if you're brave enough.

SCIENCE CLASS DREAM
SICK SOUP DREAM
RAT PIE DREAM
SCHOOL DINNER DREAM

Let's imagine it's already possible: this is how it might happen...

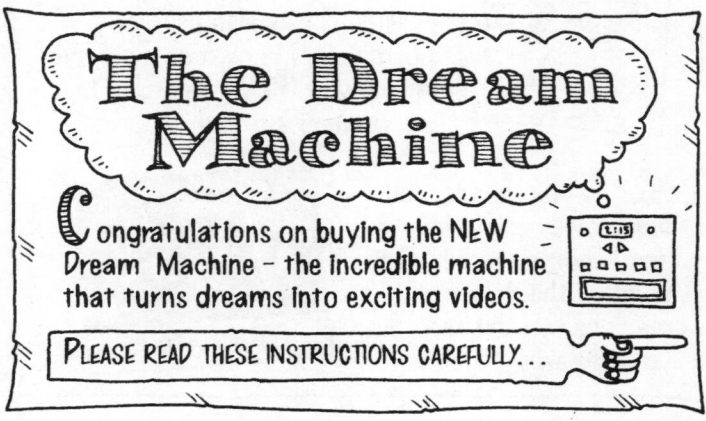

The Dream Machine

Congratulations on buying the NEW Dream Machine – the incredible machine that turns dreams into exciting videos.

PLEASE READ THESE INSTRUCTIONS CAREFULLY...

1 To set up the machine, plug it into your TV. Strap the brainwave detecting hat to your head.

DREAM MACHINE

SLEEPY PERSON

BRAINWAVE DETECTING HAT

2 Go to sleep. Nothing will happen for at least 45 minutes as your body drifts from light to deeper sleep. As you relax your mouth might drop open and start to dribble – this is entirely normal.

3 After you have been to sleep for about 45 minutes your eyes will start moving under your eyelids. This is also perfectly normal. It is known as rapid eye movement (REM) sleep and it accompanies dreaming.

4 As you dream, your brainwaves will speed up and become irregular. This triggers the dream machine to start recording your dreams.

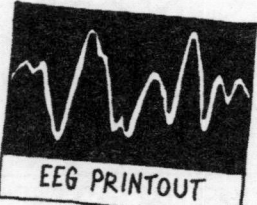

EEG PRINTOUT

5 You will not be able to move your body whilst dreaming. Your brain squirts a chemical into the brain stem that blocks nerve messages to your muscles. This is a sensible precaution to stop you sleepwalking.

SQUIRT SQUIRT SQUIRT

DON'T MOVE!

BRAIN STEM

6 Relax and enjoy your dream show. Your brain will be going into REM mode about six more times during the night. And the following morning you can replay your video and entertain the whole family with your amazing dreams!

. . . THE KILLER WOODLICE CHASED US TO THE SHORE OF THE CUSTARD SEA. WE JUMPED INTO THE PUDDING BOWLS AND MADE OUR ESCAPE USING GIANT TEASPOONS. CRUMBLE ISLAND CAME INTO SIGHT BUT WE. . .

So what do you think of this invention? It sounds really good, doesn't it? Well, here's something else that will really get your little grey cells buzzing…

BUZZ ERK!

EPILOGUE: SOMETHING TO THINK ABOUT

With its billions of neurons and synapses your bulging brain is the most complicated object in the known universe. So it's no wonder that people find it hard to get their heads round the science of the brain. Even the experts can't make up their minds.

Bishop Nemesius of Emesia (4th century AD) reckoned...

THINKING TAKES PLACE IN THE VENTRICLES

These are the fluid-filled spaces inside the brain, remember. One thousand years later Italian scientist Mondino de Luzzi (14th century) was convinced...

THE LINE OF FLESHY GORE IN THE VENTRICLES IS A WORM THAT CONTROLS THINKING

Yuck! He must have had worms on the brain.

And even modern-day scientists can have misleading ideas on the brain. For example, until the 1980s many scientists believed you could decode what the brain is thinking by looking at the pattern of neuron signals. But it's now known that this pattern varies according to your mood and your level of concentration (see page 111). This means that you can have exactly the same thought and yet each time produce a different pattern of neuron signals.

At present much of what we still don't know about the brain boils down to one awkward little word: why? Why do we have emotions? Why do we sleep?

Or, even over 200 years after Franz Gall started wondering about it...

Question, questions, questions. What do you think?

Thanks to the brilliance of the human brain, people have walked on the moon and explored the depths of the oceans. But at present we still know more about the surface of the moon or the ocean floor than the workings of our own brains. No wonder some people think we'll never find out the whole truth about our brains. They would say...

(This does make sense – just you try thinking about it!)

But, on the other hand, it's the mystery that surrounds the brain that makes brain science so exciting. And although bulging brains in tanks or dream machines are still a few years off, scientists regularly make new discoveries. They might find a new brain chemical such as serotonin that affects mood. Or perhaps a new job for an area of the brain.

For example, in 1998 scientists at the University of Iowa carried out a remarkable experiment. Healthy volunteers and people with damaged amygdalas were shown photos of faces. The volunteers thought that some faces looked untrustworthy but the brain-damaged people couldn't make these judgements. The scientists believe that in addition to shaping feelings of fear and anger the amygdala makes us distrust others. (The amygdala is part of your limbic system – see page 35 if you don't remember.) So what do you think? Would you *trust* the scientists to get it right?

Well, one thing's for sure. Scientists will never cease to search for answers to the questions posed by the brain. And it's the ability to ask questions and to seek out answers that makes us human and our brains so unique.

Now that really is something to think about!

BULGING BRAINS

QUIZ

Now find out if you're a
Bulging Brains expert!

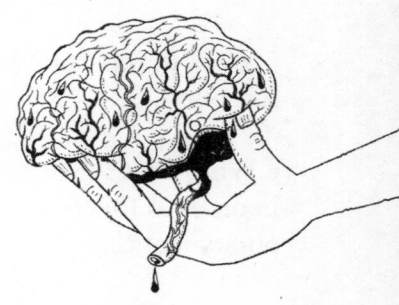

Brain strain quiz

So you've read this book and you reckon your brain in bulging with brainy know-how? Well, these no-brainer questions will show whether you really can tell your cortex from your cerebellum or whether you're a bit of a brainless blockhead…

1 What are the nerve cells in your brain called? (Clue: Not old ones, but…)

2 What is someone who studies diseases of the mind called? (Clue: Don't shrink with fear!)

3 What is somnambulism? (Clue: Take a hike sleepy head!)

4 What name is given to actions such as sneezing? (Clue: You just can't help yourself, can you?)

5 What is amnesia? (Clue: Don't tell me you've forgotten…)

6 What does the brain need one pint of every minute in order to function? (Clue: it's a treat for a guy with pointy teeth.)

7 What is the spinal cord mainly made up of? (Clue: Don't be nervous, now…)

8 What is a synapse? (Clue: It's nothing, really)

Answers:
1 Neurons
2 Psychiatrist
3 Sleepwalking
4 Reflex actions
5 Loss of memory
6 Blood
7 Nerves
8 The tiny gap between the ends of nerve fibres

Amazing memory quiz

How effective is your hippocampus (that's the part that helps process memories, remember)? Put your brain through its paces with this magnificent multiple-choice memory quiz.

1 Which baffling brain chemical helps you feel emotions?

a) Oxygen

b) Seratonin

c) Dopamine

2 How long do you retain a short-term memory for?

a) 30 seconds

b) 30 minutes

c) I'm sorry I've forgotten the question.

3 What does ambidextrous mean?

a) You can only see red and green

b) You can perform actions equally well with both hands

c) You write backwards and upside down

4 What does a CAT scan do?

a) It X-rays the brain.

b) It's a way of measuring your pet pussy's intelligence.

c) Measures nerve impulses in the brain.

5 What is the hippocampus?

a) Part of the brain that helps to form memories.

b) Part of the brain that turns light signals into pictures.

c) Part of the brain that shaped like a hippopotamus.

IT MAKES YOU THINK, DOESN'T IT?

6 In which part of your brain is your long-term memory system?
a) Brain stem
b) The bit behind your left eyeball
c) Cortex

7 Which of the following is not a reflex action?
a) Dribbling
b) Sneezing
c) Farting

SQUELCH!

8 What causes headaches?
a) Platelets in the blood stuffing up your blood vessels
b) Boring science lessons
c) Too much seratonin in the bloodstream

Answers:
1c; 2a; 3b; 4a; 5a; 6c; 7c; 8a (but b probably will too)

Brain fact and fiction

The brain can do some awesomely amazing things, but there are a lot of myths about it too (mainly because stupid scientists haven't figured out how or why the brain does certain things). Can you figure out which of these surprising statements are true and which are false?

1 Your brain is the part of your body that is most sensitive to pain.

2 Your brain is more active at night than during the day.

3 You can't tickle yourself.

4 Even a tiny amount of brain damage can never be repaired.

5 The left side of your brain controls the left-hand side of your body.

6 There is no limit to the number of thoughts that you could have.

7 You learn half of everything you know by the time you are five years old.

8 The size of your brain is related to how intelligent you are.

Answers:
1 False – there are no nerves in the brain that register pain, so doctors can perform brain surgery on a wide-awake patient – yuck!

2 True – your brain actually thinks more while you are asleep than it does even when you're in a boring science lesson.

3 True – your brain knows that you are about to tickle yourself so it basically ignores you. Talk about a party-pooper...

4 False – your brain is an amazing machine and can repair certain damage, generate new cells or compensate for injuries to some parts of it.

5 False – each side of your brain controls the opposite side of your body.

6 True – there are so many different routes for thoughts to take through your brain that you could spend your entire life having new thoughts and never run out of possible pathways.

7 True – you learn many vital things – walking, speaking, playing etc – by the time you're two!

8 False – this is complete gubbins; intelligence has nothing to do with brain size.

Beastly brain bits

Your brain is a like a mega-powerful computer and different parts do different things. Can you match the bit of your brain with its fantastic function?

1 Medulla
2 Brain stem
3 Limbic system

4 Pituitary gland
5 Cerebellum

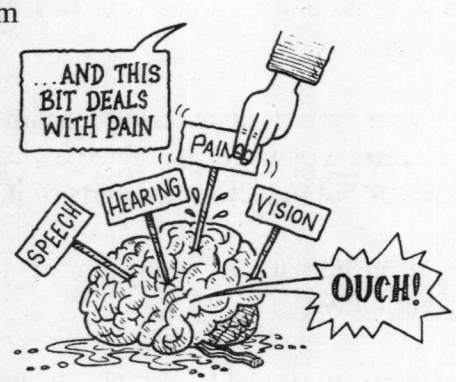

6 Hypothalamus
7 Pineal gland
8 Thalamus

a) Makes hormones
b) Controls temperature of the blood
c) Sends nerve signals to the cortex
d) Makes you vomit
e) Stops children from developing too quickly
f) Links the brain with the spinal cord
g) Controls movement
h) Controls feelings

Answers:
1d; 2f; 3h; 4a; 5g; 6b; 7e; 8c

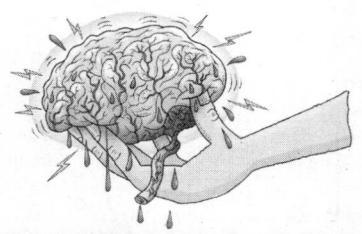

HORRIBLE INDEX

167

HORRIBLE SCIENCE

Make sure you've got the whole horrible lot!

ISBN 978 0439 94450 2

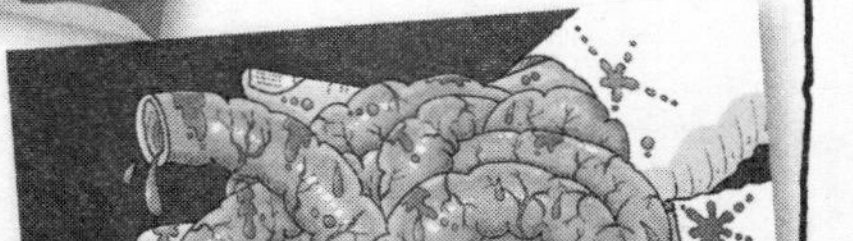

ISBN 978 0439 94445 8

ISBN 978 0439 94451 9

ISBN 978 0439 94452 6

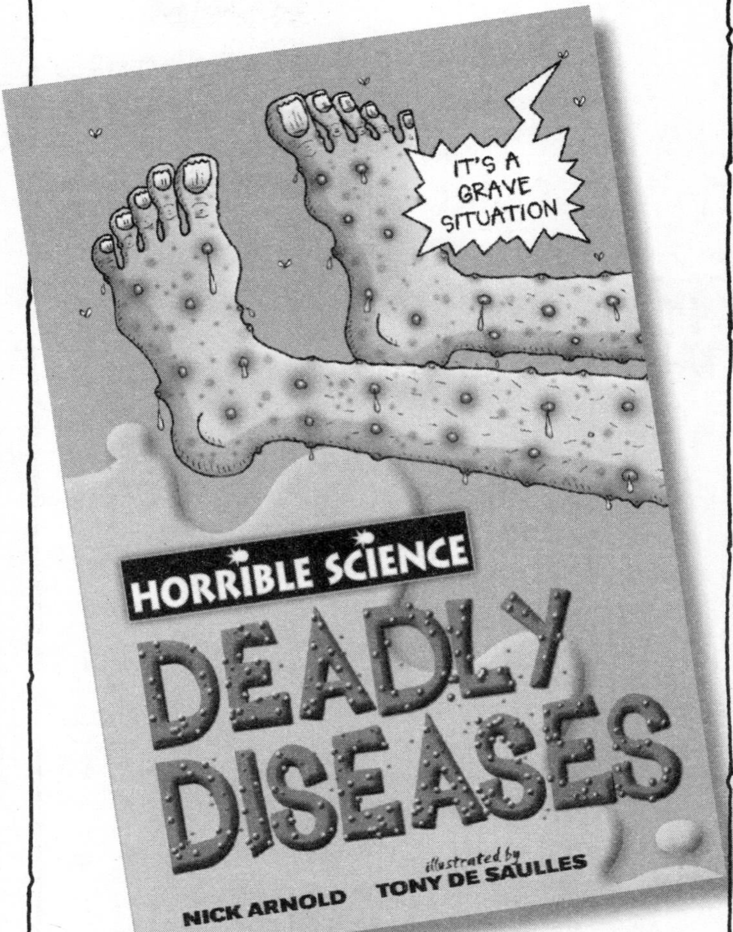

IT'S A GRAVE SITUATION

HORRIBLE SCIENCE

DEADLY
DISEASES

illustrated by
NICK ARNOLD   TONY DE SAULLES

ISBN 978 0 439944 46 5

ISBN 978 1407 10359 4

ISBN 978 0439 94408 3

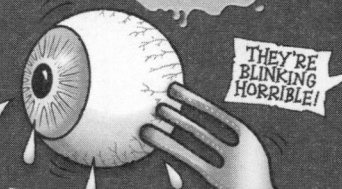

ISBN 978 0439 94407 6

HORRIBLE SCIENCE

BLOOD, BONES and BODY BITS

NICK ARNOLD

illustrated by
TONY DE SAULLES

■SCHOLASTIC

Visit Nick Arnold at
www.nickarnold-website.com

Scholastic Children's Books,
Euston House, 24 Eversholt Street,
London, NW1 1DB, UK

A division of Scholastic Ltd
London ~ New York ~ Toronto ~ Sydney ~ Auckland
Mexico City ~ New Delhi ~ Hong Kong

First published in the UK by Scholastic Ltd, 1996
This edition published 2008

ISBN 978 0439 94449 6

Printed and bound by CPI Group (UK) Ltd, Croydon, CR0 4YY

30

CONTENTS

Nick Arnold has been writing stories and books since he was a youngster, but never dreamt he'd find fame writing about body bits. His research involved inspecting sick, being sucked by thirsty leeches and encountering deadly diseases and he enjoyed  every minute of it. When he's not delving into Horrible Science, he spends his spare time eating pizza, riding his bike and thinking up corny jokes (though not all at the same time).

Tony De Saulles picked up his crayons when he was still in nappies and has been doodling ever since. He takes Horrible Science very seriously and even agreed to investigate what happens in an operating theatre. Fortunately, he's made a full recovery. When  he's not out with his sketchpad, Tony likes to write poetry and play squash, though he hasn't written any poetry about squash yet.

INTRODUCTION

Science is sickening! Extra Science homework is really rotten – but one of the most horribly sickening science subjects is the science of the body. I mean, doesn't the thought of all that blood and all those guts and bones turn your legs into jelly?

Doctors and teachers use a sickening selection of tongue-twisting names for bits you didn't even know you had. By the way – did you know that medical students have to learn 10,000 new words? And you thought English lessons were tough!

YOU'VE GOT A SEVERE CONTUSION IN THE REGION OF THE GLUTEUS MAXIMUS

IS THAT SERIOUS?

NOT REALLY – IT MEANS YOU'VE GOT A BRUISE ON YER BUM!

But science doesn't just belong to the experts – it belongs to everybody, because everybody's got a body – and you've got every right to know what's going on in yours. Why it gurgles and creaks and squelches and other tantalizing topics.

And that's what this book is about. The things YOU really want to know about YOUR body. The horrible bits. The horribly interesting bits. Here's your chance to find out what billions of germs are doing lurking in your guts. What happens when you cut a brain in half, and why doctors once covered their patients in slimy leeches. So if you find science a closed book – here's a chance to change your mind.

And once you've boned up on bones and got the inside story on your insides – who knows? You might even find the body horribly amazing. Then you could teach your doctor a thing or two. Or even blind your teachers with some really sickening scientific facts. (That doesn't mean doing nasty things to their eyeballs!) One thing is certain. Science will never be the same again!

BITS OF BODY

A DISGUSTING DISCOVERY

It was past midnight and the rain was splattering against the windowpane of the lonely attic room. By the dim light of a candle Baron Frankenstein gazed in horror at the creature that he had just put together from bits of chopped-up dead bodies. The monster was unbelievably, hideously ugly. Suddenly a shudder seemed to run through the creature's body and it stirred like a heavy sleeper about to awake...

DON'T PANIC! It's only a story. Frankenstein was written by Mary Shelley many years ago and no one has succeeded in making an entire human being out of bits of body ... yet. But just supposing you wanted to have a go, here's a bit of advice...

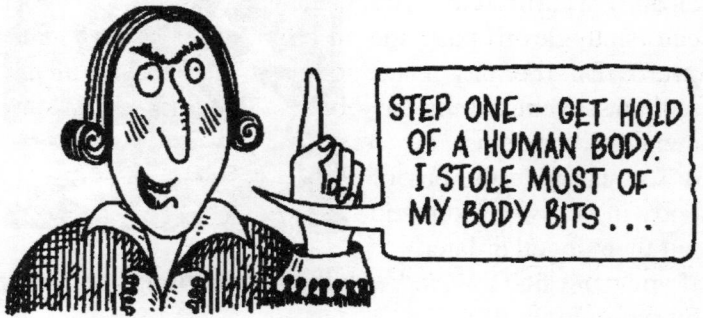

STEP ONE – GET HOLD OF A HUMAN BODY. I STOLE MOST OF MY BODY BITS ...

If this sounds too gruesome to be true, remember that in the Baron's time there was a serious shortage of bodies to cut up. In many countries this grisly practice was against the law. This was a problem because scientists could only probe the secrets of the human body by the dissection – cutting up – of dead bodies. In desperation, some scientists turned to crime.

THE BARON'S GUIDE TO BODY-SNATCHING

Body snatchers were people who went about stealing bodies. The body-snatchers knew that doctors would pay handsomely for a nice fresh corpse to cut up. Here's how to get hold of one yourself (and make some extra pocket money).

Method 1 – execute a robbery. This was the method used by Andreas Versalius, a famous sixteenth-century scientist, when he was studying medicine in the old town of Louvain in Belgium.

1 Wait until dark.

2 Go to a nearby place of execution and remove the corpses of any criminals you find.

3 Cut up the body and hide bits of it under your cloak. That way you can smuggle it past the guards on the city gates without anyone asking any awkward questions.

4 You can hide the bits of body in your bedroom and put them together later.

If you can't find any bodies lying around things get a tiny bit more difficult.

Method 2 – rob a grave. This method was used in both Britain and America in the nineteenth century.

1 Wait until dark. You will need a wooden spade for silent digging, a lantern, a canvas sheet, some ropes with hooks attached, a crowbar and a sack.

2 Go to a graveyard. Make sure you keep an eye out for angry relatives, vicars, etc, who might try to stop you digging up bodies.

3 Dig up the grave. Spread the earth on the sheet ready for you to shovel it all back again afterwards. This avoids making a mess that might give you away.

4 Lift the coffin with the hooks and lever open the coffin using the crowbar. Sssh! Keep it quiet!

5 Put the body in the sack. Fill in the hole and run for it! You should be able to do all this in an hour. Oh, and don't forget the sheet!

BODY JIGSAWS

Let's imagine that by hook or by crook you managed to get hold of some bits of body. Now you can start putting them all together to make your very own Frankenstein's monster! Unlike a normal jigsaw, you have to start with the middle bits, not the edge (the skin!). Make sure you put all the pieces in the right places and don't forget any vital parts or it won't work. If you make a mistake you will have to cut the body open and take a few bits out in order to fit the missing bit in its proper place. Here's a list of body bits to help you know what's what in your body.

Stretchy skin

A huge waterproof, germ-proof outer covering. It's better than any other kind of clothing because it actually repairs itself when it gets damaged. It also has its own heating and cooling systems. Skin wraps round the rest of your monster's body bits to keep them in position.

Fabulous fat

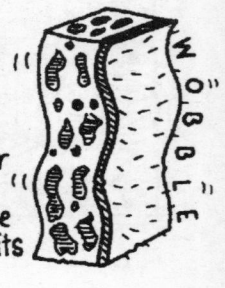

Fit a layer of fat snugly underneath the skin. Slabs of fat also slop and wobble around the tummy and hips area. Fat keeps out the cold. It acts as a convenient place for storing spare energy from all the food your monster guzzles. Your monster will use up some of the energy when it goes for its morning jog.

Eyeballs, ears and snotty nose

Very important for seeing, hearing and sniffing (in that order). In fact the really important bits of these body parts are the bits you can't see. These form the high-tech gadgetry that converts the information picked up from the senses into signals for the brain to decode. So make sure those nerves are all properly wired up.

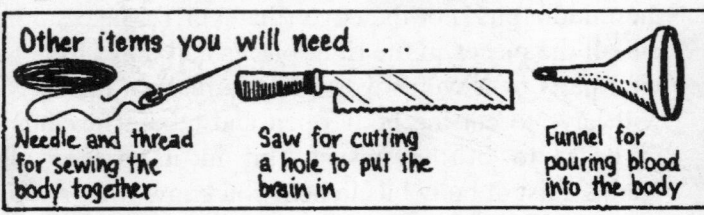

Other items you will need . . .

Needle and thread for sewing the body together

Saw for cutting a hole to put the brain in

Funnel for pouring blood into the body

10

Delicate nerves

These are the monster's signalling system. They tell the brain what's going on and transmit orders from the brain to get those lazy muscles moving. Nerves extend into every part of the body – from the top of the head to the tips of the toes. But the main nerves all join up in the spinal cord inside the backbone.

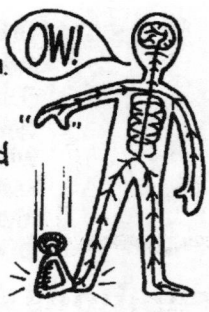

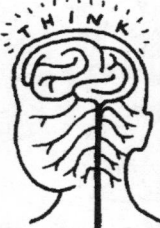

Brilliant brain

This bit acts as the boss of the monster's body. Gently plop it inside the top part of the skull, nicely protected from the outside world. It contains all your monster's memories and personality so don't bash it around too much.

Sturdy skeleton

There are 206 bones – give or take a few extra ones that some people have. Bones are very important to keep the body upright and stop it collapsing like a deflated balloon. Make sure you get the bones in the right order. This is very tricky, especially when you get to the 26 bones that make up a single foot.

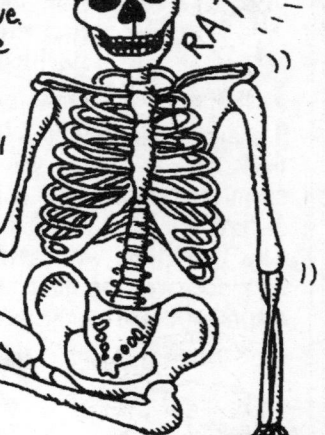

BULGE

AWFUL
UNDERPANTS

Mighty muscles

Everyone's got muscles even if they're not big bulgy ones. There are hundreds of muscles and they need to be put in their rightful places or they won't work properly. In each hand there are 20 muscles – and your monster will use 200 muscles every time it takes a step.

Tough teeth

These are the hardest parts of the body – guaranteed to tackle those rubbery school dinners. Make sure you put the teeth in their correct positions and teach your monster how to brush them regularly.

Disgusting stomach

GLUG

RUMBLE

It's a squelchy muscular bag filled with bits of half-digested food and stomach juices. Lovely! But it's vital for mashing up food so your monster will need guts to digest its dinners that means take the chemicals its body needs in its blood.

Lovely liver

It's a brownish/purplish/reddish blob about 15cm thick. Lovely. This is your monster's built-in chemical factory and it performs over 500 different jobs. It's called the liver because no one can 'liver' long without it, ha ha. Pop the liver in its place over the guts under the dome of the diaphragm (that's the breathing muscle).

WIBBLE WOBBLE

Clever kidneys

These filter the blood and take out the waste products from your monster's body. It's got two kidneys and the left one is always higher up than the right one.

Beautiful blood

It's the body's transport system, and it carries oxygen gas breathed in through the lungs and little bits of food to nourish the body. And that's just for starters. There are also white cells that fight germs and platelets that help the body heal itself. Yes - blood's got the lot. Your monster will need about 5 litres of the gloopy red stuff.

Hardworking heart

This lump of muscle is vital for pumping the blood around the body. Make sure you put the heart in its correct place - nearer the left side of the chest. Also make sure you get it the correct way round - the left-hand side of the heart pumps the blood round the body, but the right side only pumps it round the lungs.

Foamy lungs

These are like a big spongy pair of bellows in the chest that can hold up to six litres of air. Your monster needs to breathe in order to get the oxygen from the air to keep its body cells alive.

13

WEIRD BITS 'N' PIECES

Some bits of the body are well known. We've all heard about the brain and we've all heard from the stomach when it starts rumbling. But what about the not-so-well-known bits? Which of these bits are just too weird to be true? (You get double the score if you can work out where any of them fit in!)

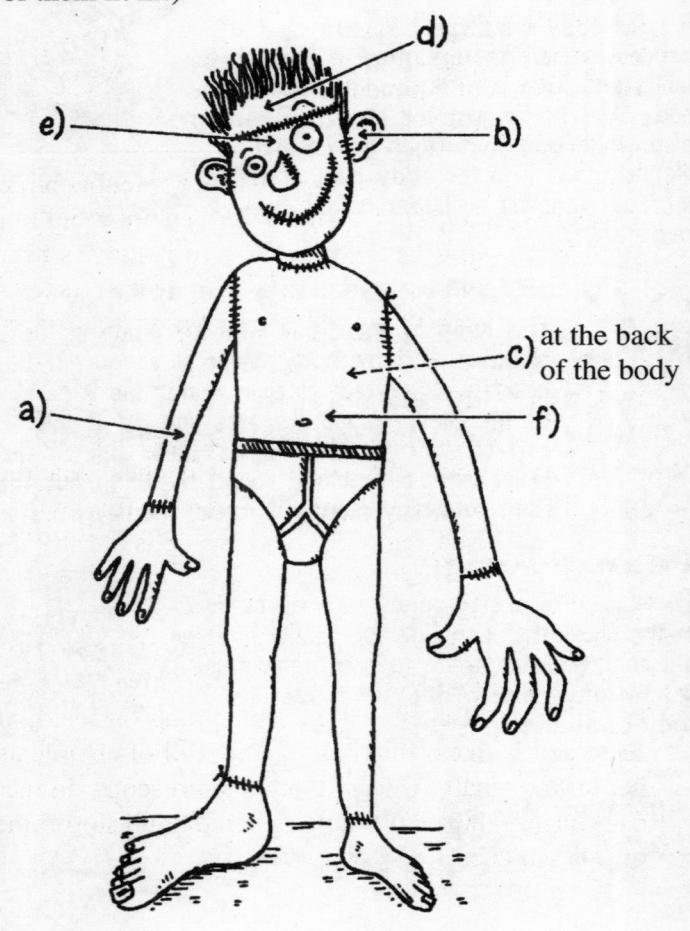

d)

e) —

b)

c) at the back of the body

a) —

f)

14

1 The oval window
2 The funny bone
3 The innomiate canal of Arnold
4 The wish bone
5 The boomerang bone
6 Fabricus's ship
7 The bicycle tendon.
8 Lane's kinks.
9 Morris's kidney box
10 The fossa of Blumenbach

IS EVERYTHING WORKING?

Whilst you are assembling your Frankenstein's monster, it's always a good idea to occasionally check that the bits of body are in good shape. You can do this by peering down a microscope to make sure the cells are still alive...

SECRET CELLS

Your monster's body is made up of about 50 million million living cells. You can tell when they are alive because there are all sorts of chemical changes going on inside them. Each cell is like a tiny ball of jelly full of chemicals and it's far too small to see without a microscope. In fact you can squeeze thousands of them into the full stop at the end of this sentence.

Inside the cell is a secret world. There are tiny objects called mitochondria (mito-con-dre-a) that produce energy, and there are pathways and little storage areas. And each cell has a nucleus that stores the information to make new cells. Sometimes the cell reproduces by pulling itself into two pieces.

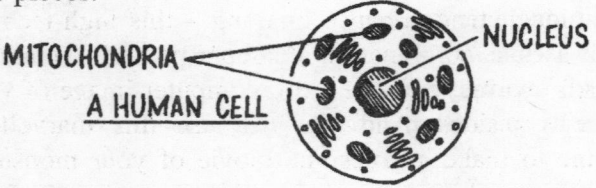

MITOCHONDRIA

NUCLEUS

A HUMAN CELL

QUALITY CONTROL

Once your Frankenstein's monster is assembled you'll need a collection of amazing but slightly gruesome tools to check whether everything is in working order inside.

You'll need *X-rays* to check whether your monster's bones are in good shape. These are high-energy rays that you can't actually see. They can pass through the body's skin, muscles and fat but not solid bone. This is why an X-ray picture can check out whether the bones are in good shape.

YOU APPEAR TO HAVE SOMEONE ELSE'S BONES, SIR!

CAT – computerized axial tomography scanner. This amazing machine scans a slice of your monster's brain using X-rays and shows the result on a computer screen. *Angiogram* (an-jee-o-gram). An X-ray picture of your monster's blood vessels after they have been injected with chemicals.

MRI – magnetic resonance imaging – this high-tech bit of kit uses a combination of super-powerful magnets and radio waves to create a 3-d computer image of your monster's insides. And you can use this marvellous machine to make a gruesome movie of your monster's heart pumping blood.

Then there's a whole collection of tubes to stick into various parts of its anatomy so you can take a look at it. These include...

Gastroscope (gas-tro-scope) A long, bendy tube with a light on the end. Ideal for poking down its throat to peer into its stomach and guts.

Opthalmoscope (op-thal-mo-scope) A bright light and viewer to see what the inside of its eyeball looks like.

Arthroscope (ar-throw-scope) A tube a bit like a telescope for peering inside your monster's joints.

Otoscope (ot-o-scope) A light a bit like a torch for shining in your monster's ear holes.

All these bits of equipment are useful because without them it's horribly hard to see what's going on inside the body. There's usually a layer of sweaty skin in the way. Let's take a longer look at it...

SWEATY SKIN

Poke around in the darker corners of your house and you may find a lovely collection of fingernails, hair and bits of skin. Bits of skin? Well – you know those pretty bits of dust that dance in the sunlight on a summer's morning? Most of them are bits of flaked-off skin – just some of the ten billion bits of skin you lose every day!

Blood, bones and body bits fact file

Name of body part: Skin

Where found: All over the outside of the body

Useful things it does: It helps to keep you at the right temperature and keep out germs.

Grisly details: It suffers from a disgusting array of skin diseases such as boils, carbuncles, etc.

Amazing features: If you removed an adult's skin it would cover about 2 square metres. A child's skin covers about 1.5 square metres. Skin is the heaviest part of your body and weighs a whopping 2.5-4.5kg, depending on your size.

DISGUSTING SKIN DISEASES

Doctors like nothing better than reading at mealtimes. And their favourite reading matter? Colourful medical magazines with pictures of skin diseases. Gulp! Here's your chance to check whether you could be a doctor. Try matching the picture to the disease.

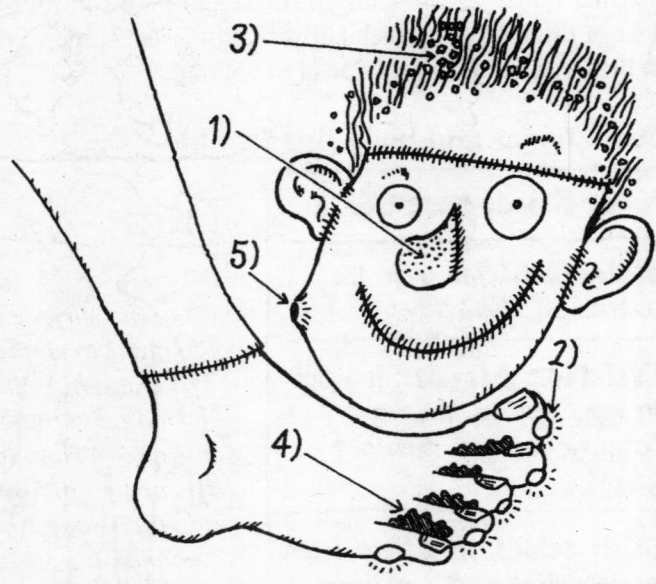

a) A fungus that grows between the toes and makes the skin peel.

b) A gland-opening that's been blocked with sweat or grease – it swells until it bursts, spraying pus everywhere.

c) Painful, itchy blotches on your toes caused by the blood supply cutting off in cold weather.

d) A build-up of dead skin cells stuck together with grease.

e) Greasy dead skin cells that turn black when they contact the air.

NASTY NOSE JOBS

If your skin disease gets really revolting you could have plastic surgery to replace some of it.

Bet you never knew!
Modern plastic surgeons make changes to the surface of the body – adding or taking away skin in order to change what someone looks like. If you've got enough money you can change almost any part of your body. But plastic surgery began in India 2,000 years ago! Criminals were punished by having their noses cut off, but one day someone found out that you could stitch some skin from the forehead or cheek over the wound so it didn't look so bad. Meanwhile in Europe ignorant surgeons were probably trying to replace a patient's missing nose with a slave's cut-off schnozzle. It wasn't until the fifteenth century that Italian surgeon Branca tried an op similar to the Indian technique. Modern plastic surgeons also use skin from the patient's own body to repair damage to the skin. These operations are called "skin grafts". They can also make changes to the surface of the body – adding or taking away skin from almost any part of the body.

But if skin can be amazingly horrible on the outside – on the inside it's also horribly AMAZING.

GETTING UNDER YOUR SKIN

Imagine walking around all day with a heavy bag of shopping from the supermarket. Well, you do – it's the weight of your skin. But your skin is well worth hanging on to – just look at what's in it! Your skin's outer layer is less than 1 mm thick, but it's packed with useful bits and pieces such as blood vessels and nerves. A area of your skin the size of a ten-pence coin has around 65 hairs, 100 oil-producing glands, 650 glands that produce sweat and 1,500 nerve sensors (see page 23). Sounds confusing? Try imagining your skin as an incredible high-tech, high-fashion space suit. Would you dare to wear it?

THE BIRTHDAY SUIT

Have YOU ever wished to slip into something more comfortable? Something that's cool in the hot weather and warm in cold weather. Try the new birthday suit. But guess what – you've got it on already! Yes, it's that suit you got for your birthday – that's the day you were born!

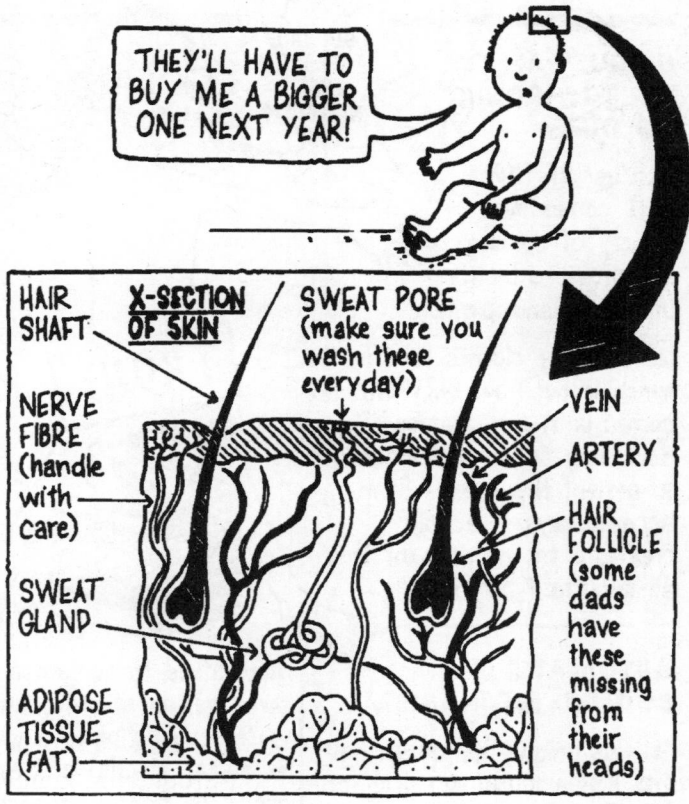

Marvel at these incredible features. Amaze your friends with THE BIRTHDAY SUIT's unique technical wizardry!

The amazing
BIRTHDAY SUIT

UNIQUE SAFETY PHOTOCHROMIC COLOURS

GET ONE FREE WITH EVERY NEWBORN BABY!

NO FADING

1. Your BIRTHDAY SUIT comes in a variety of colours all provided by its unique melanin pigments.

2. Ordinary clothes fade in the sunshine but your BIRTHDAY SUIT comes with a guaranteed darkening action under sunlight to protect the wearer from harmful rays. It actually creates extra melanin for this all-important purpose.

FRONT

CHOICE OF COLOURS

AUTOMATIC COOLING MECHANISM

3. This unique feature springs into action if the suit gets too hot. The water-cooling pipes produce sweat to cool the outside of the BIRTHDAY SUIT.

4. Every BIRTHDAY SUIT is guaranteed to contain about three million of these tiny water-cooling pipes (known as sweat glands) and each one is so tightly coiled that if you pulled it out it would be over a metre long! The total length of your pipe system is 3660km!

MANUFACTURER'S WARNING

5. The automatic cooling systems can easily lose 1.7 litres of sweat every hour in hot weather, so make sure it's well supplied with water.

6. The sweat under the arms and between the legs contains chemicals that germs like to eat. Yum! The germs make the stale sweat all yucky and smelly. (Please see Care and maintenance instruction 9 – for everybody's sake.)

7. Some people use antiperspirants to tackle the little problem above. These work by blocking the holes in the cooling systems. Fortunately they don't stop most of the sweat from escaping otherwise the BIRTHDAY SUIT would overheat.

SELF-REPAIRING MECHANISM

AUTOMATIC COOLING SYSTEM

BACK

LOW MAINTENANCE

HARMFUL RAY PROTECTION

CARE & MAINTENANCE INSTRUCTIONS

8. Your BIRTHDAY SUIT needs very little maintenance because of its unique self-repair mechanism. If it gets torn or damaged it will simply re-grow!

9. All you need to do is to gently wash the outer layer in soap and water to remove any dirt and flaky bits. Don't worry if bits drop off – the BIRTHDAY SUIT will always grow some more underneath!

25

Dare you discover … how your skin works?

For this experiment you will have to take a bath. It's OK – all the great scientists had to make sacrifices.

1 Note what happens as your skin heats up. What colour does pink skin go?
a) Red
b) Blue
c) White
2 Using a watch, time how long it takes for your skin to wrinkle up. As a result of your careful scientific observation, what do you think is causing this strange effect?
a) The heat
b) Old age
c) The water

26

HORRIBLE HAIR AND NASTY NAILS

What's the point of hair and nails? Hairs always seem to end up blocking up the bathroom plughole and nails get nasty black grime stuck underneath them. But then they're also interesting in a disgusting kind of way.

Blood, bones and body bits fact file

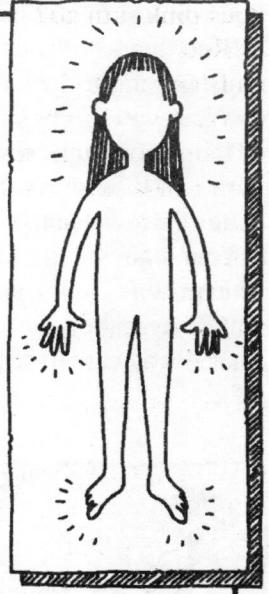

Name of body part: Hair and nails

Where found: Your body is covered by five million little hairs but your longest hairs are on your head (surprisingly!). Nails are found on your fingers and toes, but you knew that.

Useful things they do: Hair keeps you warm. Your nails stop your fingers and toes squashing up every time you touch something.

Grisly details: Hair and nails are said to continue to grow for a while on dead bodies – this isn't true!

Amazing features: Hair and nails are both made out of a hard substance called keratin. It's the same stuff that makes feathers and dinosaur claws.

HAIR-RAISING HAIR

Here's your chance to hoodwink your hairdresser with a few hair-raising facts.

1 Most people have about 100,000 hairs on their heads. Fair-haired people can have 150,000 and red-haired people have to make do with about 90,000. (I wonder who counted them all!)

2 Hair grows at about 1 cm a month or 0.33 mm a day. Hot weather makes your hair grow faster. So if you lived at the North Pole you wouldn't need your hair cut so often – and you wouldn't want it cut so often!

3 Most hairs fall out before they reach 90 cm long. It's quite normal to lose up to 60 hairs a day. Any more than that and you might start going bald!

4 Hair is horribly strong. One hair is stronger than a copper wire of the same thickness. A rope made from 1,000 hairs could lift a well-built man.

5 Your hair stands on end when you're scared because little muscles in the skin pull on the roots of the hairs. The aim is to make you look big and fearsome to an enemy. That's why cats fluff their fur when they're going to have a fight!

NAIL-BITING NOTES

Now mystify your manicurist with these nails' tails.

1 Underneath your nails is an area called the nail bed. (This is nothing to do with the bed of nails that Indian fakirs sometimes sleep on.) Your nails grow from an area called the matrix.

2 If you trap a nail in the door it will stop growing and drop off. With a bit of luck a lovely brand-new nail will grow underneath. That's OK then!

3 Sometimes toenails start burrowing into the surrounding flesh. This horribly hurtful condition is caused by not cutting the nail straight across. But cutting nails is better than biting them!

4 Nail biting doesn't exactly kill you – but it looks revolting and makes your nails sore, and it helps lots of germs leap into your mouth. It also tends to put people off their soup in posh restaurants. Especially when you chew your toenails as well!

5 If you didn't cut your nails for a year they would be 2.5 cm long.

But that's nothing compared to some people!

RECORD-BREAKERS

Longest fingernails Sridhar Chillal of Pune in India

stopped cutting his finger nails in 1952. By 1995 the nails on his left hand had reached 574 cm long.

Longest hair Mata Jagdamba of India has hair 4.23 metres long. This is amazing because, as we've already said, normally a hair will stop growing and drop out by the time it reaches 90 cm.

Longest beard Hans N Langseth of the USA grew a 533-cm-long beard. Sadly Hans is no longer with us – he died in 1927. But you'll be relieved to know that the famous beard is now a museum exhibit.

PROPERTY OF MR H.N.LANGSETH

Longest moustache Kalyan Ramji Sain of Sundargarth in India began to grow his moustache in 1976. By 1993 it was 339 cm wide.

Runner-up: A Briton, John Roy, started growing his moustache in 1939. By 1976 his moustache was 189 cm wide. But then he sat on one side of it in the bath and 42 cm of hair split off the end.

Bet you never knew!

Even with hair all over it, your skin can sense things that touch it. Oh so you DID know that! Well, bet you never knew that the human fingertips are so sensitive that they can feel an object move even if only stirs a thousandth of a millimetre. Sounds like a really touchy subject! And touch is just ONE of your five sensesational senses.

YOU'RE OUT – YOU MOVED AT LEAST ONE THOUSANDTH OF A MILLIMETRE!

COME ON DAD – IT'S ONLY MUSICAL STATUES!

SENSATIONAL SENSES

Congratulations! You're a sensitive person – how could you be anything else with your super-sensitive touch, sight, taste, smell and hearing? And whether your view of the world is happy or sad, your senses help make sense of what's going on around you. But they're also horribly incredible in their own right – in fact they're SENSE-SATIONAL.

SENSITIVE SENSES QUIZ

Which senses are too sensationally sensitive to be true?

1 Your senses are so sensitive that they only take a quarter of a second to let you know when something is happening. TRUE/FALSE

2 Your eyes can tell the difference between eight million colours. TRUE/FALSE

3 Your eyes are 1,000 times more sensitive to light than the most light-sensitive film. TRUE/FALSE

4 Some people can see ultraviolet rays produced by the Sun. TRUE/FALSE

5 Your tongue can taste a single drop of lemon juice even if it's mixed up with 129,000 drops of water. TRUE/FALSE

6 Your nose can detect a cheesy old pair of socks 200 metres away. TRUE/FALSE

7 Your ears can tell the difference between two sounds even if they are only ten-millionths of a second apart. TRUE/FALSE

8 Your ears can identify 1,500 levels of sound from high-pitched squeaks to deep booms. TRUE/FALSE

9 Some people can hear air whooshing around in the upper atmosphere. TRUE/FALSE

10 Your body can tell what time it is even if you're in a room without windows. TRUE/FALSE

Answers: 1 FALSE – your senses work much faster than that! **2 TRUE. 3 TRUE. 4 FALSE** and don't try it. **5 TRUE.** Looking at the Sun can harm your eyes! **6 FALSE** – but I suppose it depends on how strong the socks pong! **7 TRUE** – if the sounds come through separate ears. **8 TRUE. 9 Unproven and probably FALSE. 10 TRUE.**

YOUR TOUCHY SENSES

You've heard about the sensitive sensors under your skin? Well, did you know that they come in no less than FIVE sensational varieties? Each one keeps you in touch in a different way. To show you how, we need a

33

brave volunteer. Can you spot which sensor is doing the sensing in the five tests below?

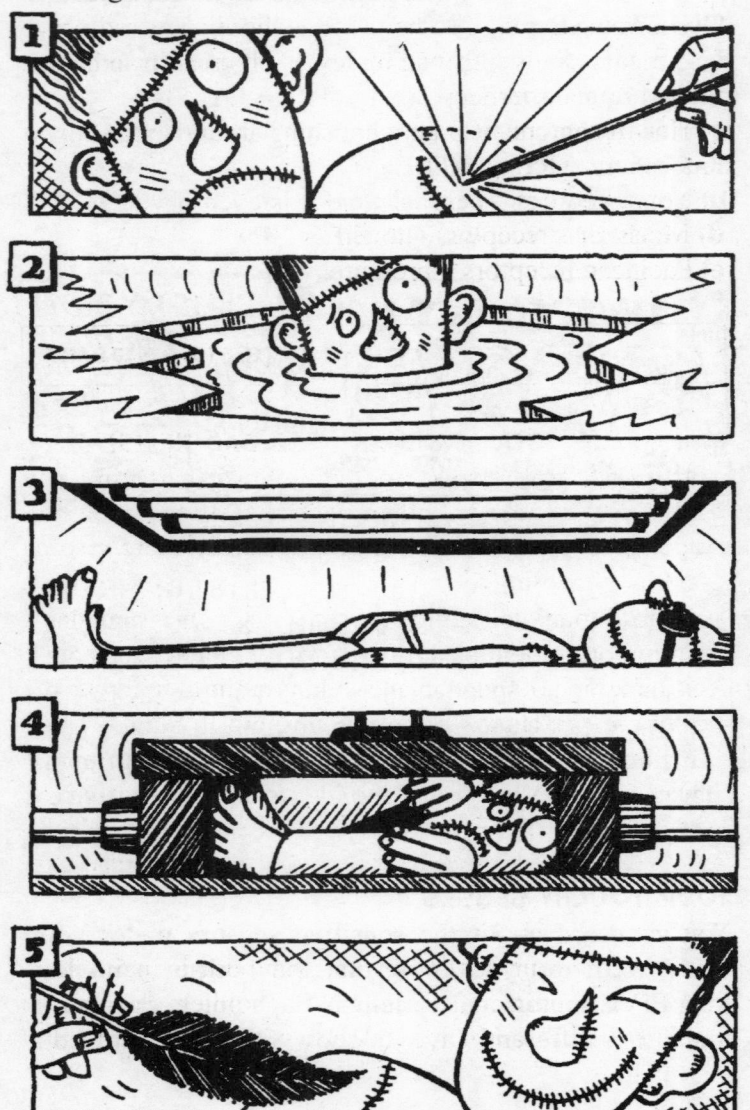

These are the sensors that you must match with the pictures. Some are named in honour of the scientists who discovered them. The person who discovered nerve endings deserves a special mention – it must have been a very painful experience.

a) Heat receptors – for heat
b) Cold receptors – cold
c) Nerve endings – pain
d) Meissner's receptors – touch
e) Pacinean receptors – pressure.

PAIN - THE GOOD NEWS AND THE BAD NEWS!

You might think that the nerve endings that bring you painful feelings are only there for the nasty things in life. And you'd generally be right. But surely there's some good in everything?

The good news – 1
You have 500,000 sensors to keep you in touch with the outside world. Hooray!

The bad news – 1
And millions of nerve endings to make you painfully aware of any horrible aches and twinges. Boo! Hiss!

The good news – 2
But luckily your brain has its own built-in painkillers called endorphins. This is why a soldier can lose a leg in battle and hop along without feeling any pain! Hooray!

The bad news – 2

Afterwards it hurts A LOT – and not only that. People who lose arms and legs often feel their missing limbs itching even when they're not there! Shame!

WHAT'S MAKING MY LEG ITCH DOC? – IT WAS CUT OFF THREE YEARS AGO!

WOODWORM!

THE PAINFUL TRUTH

Pain is there to warn us that we're getting hurt. "Stop!" say your nerve endings. "And try to be more careful next time!" It's a sensible message. So you see, a bit of pain is good for you! Sounds a bit like the sort of thing your teacher might say, doesn't it? But is that good news?

A SENSATIONAL SIGHT

Your most sensational sense is sight. After all, without it we'd all be in the dark! But did you know that your eyeballs are like tiny little video cameras full of watery jelly? Is this the sort of camera that you'd like to discover in your Christmas stocking?

THE EYEBALL CAMERA

Seeing really is believing with the incredible EYEBALL CAMERA. Now you can keep up with the speediest sporting action even at night! Just point your camera in the right direction. Wherever you go, your EYEBALL

CAMERA goes too! In fact, it's so useful it's worth using the two that you've already got – you know, those gloopy blobs that sit snugly in your eyeball sockets!

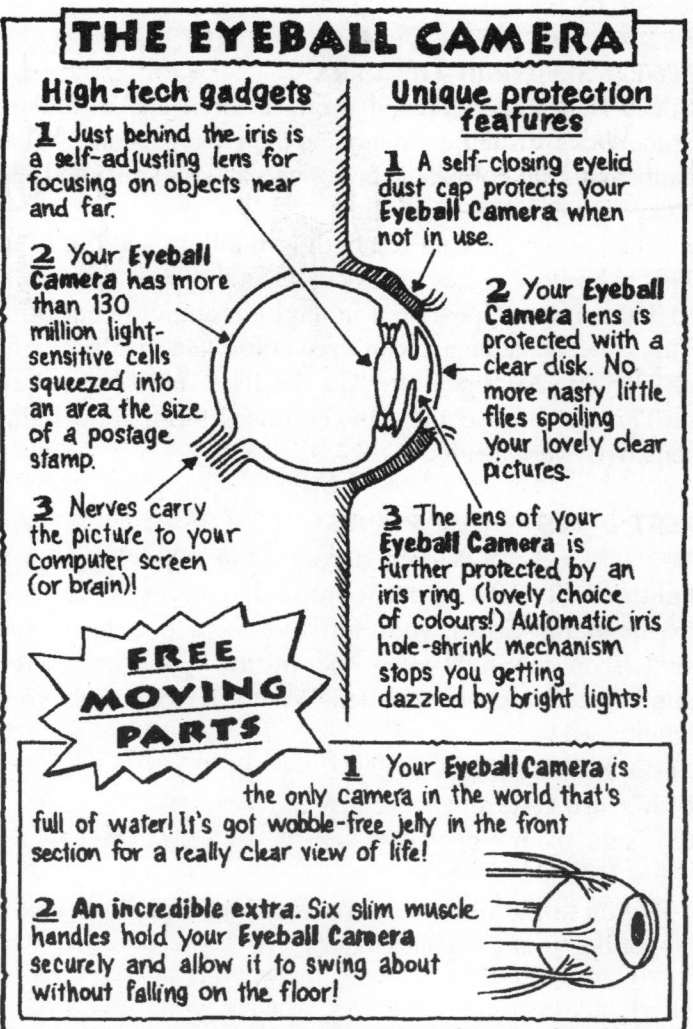

THE EYEBALL CAMERA

High-tech gadgets

1 Just behind the iris is a self-adjusting lens for focusing on objects near and far.

2 Your **Eyeball Camera** has more than 130 million light-sensitive cells squeezed into an area the size of a postage stamp.

3 Nerves carry the picture to your computer screen (or brain)!

Unique protection features

1 A self-closing eyelid dust cap protects your **Eyeball Camera** when not in use.

2 Your **Eyeball Camera** lens is protected with a clear disk. No more nasty little flies spoiling your lovely clear pictures.

3 The lens of your **Eyeball Camera** is further protected by an iris ring. (lovely choice of colours!) Automatic iris hole-shrink mechanism stops you getting dazzled by bright lights!

FREE MOVING PARTS

1 Your **Eyeball Camera** is the only camera in the world that's full of water! It's got wobble-free jelly in the front section for a really clear view of life!

2 An incredible extra. Six slim muscle handles hold your **Eyeball Camera** securely and allow it to swing about without falling on the floor!

Dare you discover ... how your eyeballs work?

Naturally you'll want to try out your sensational eyeball camera as soon as possible. So here are a few tests to try.

TEST 1 SEEING IN THE DARK

You will need a darkened room, a torch and a tomato. Shine the torch at the tomato and then away from it. What happens to the colour of the tomato as you shift the light away from it? Any idea why?

a) The tomato appears red both in the light and out of it. This is because the eye sees colour in the dark.

b) The tomato appears red in the light and grey out of it. This is because the eye can't see colours in the dark.

c) The tomato appears red in the light and blue out of it. This is because the dark confuses those little light-sensitive eyeball cells.

TEST 2 TEST YOUR PUPILS*

You will need a darkened room and a mirror with a light over it. Wait in the room until your eyes are used to the dark. Cover your left eye with one hand and switch on the light over the mirror. Your uncovered pupil suddenly goes smaller. What's happened to your other pupil?

a) It's still large.

b) It's also gone small.

c) It's got even bigger.

* Or you might like to test your teacher's pupils – you'll be getting your own back!

Hold the book close to your face and close your left eye. Focus your right eye on the left eyeball. Now slowly move the book away from your face. Why does the right eyeball vanish?

a) The eye can't focus at a certain distance.

b) There's a gap in the light-sensitive cells.

c) The light-sensitive cells get tired and stop noticing things.

Answers: 1 b) There are six million light-sensitive cone cells inside each eyeball that can see colour (either red, green or blue). But these only work in good light conditions. There are 125 million rod cells that work in dim lighting but they can only see in black and white. **2 b)** The pupils have to work together – it's a bit like being at school! **3 b)** There is a blind spot and when you look at things with it they seem to disappear. This spot is where the optic nerve connects with the inside of the eyeball.

CARING FOR YOUR EYEBALLS · EIGHT THINGS YOU SHOULD KNOW

1 You don't need to care for your eyeballs at all! Your body does it all for you.

2 Eyeballs come complete with their own windscreen-washing service – it's called "crying."

3 Fortunately you don't have to be sad to cry. You can produce tears whilst being sick, coughing, or by getting something in your eye or, preferably by laughing!

TRAGIC – SHE ONLY WON THE **SECOND** PRIZE OF £10,000!

4 Tears are also spread over your eyeball when you blink. Every blink takes 0.3–0.4 seconds – that's half an hour each day, or more than one whole year of your life. What a blinking waste of time!

5 Any tears you don't use dry up in the drainage tube that leads from the corners of your eyes to the inside of your nose. These dried-up tears form the sleepy dust you rub from your eyes every morning!

6 Each of your eyes is protected by about 200 eyelashes. Each eyelash lasts three to five months before it falls out and another grows in its place.

7 Tiny mites live in the base of your eyelashes. They have eight legs each and look like alligators! But don't worry – they won't do you any harm. In fact they are doing you quite a favour by gobbling up harmful germs!

8 If, despite all this care and attention, your eyes don't see very well – you may need glasses.

Bet you never knew!
Do you wear glasses? If you're short-sighted you may have difficulty focusing on far-away objects. Being long-sighted means, well, you can probably guess. These problems happen because your eyeballs aren't perfectly round. A pair of glasses are like extra lenses for your eyes. Well cheer up – it's easier than taking the eyeballs out and squashing them into shape!

SAVAGE SPECTACLES

One of the first people to wear "glasses" was the rotten old Roman Emperor Nero. He used a curved piece of emerald to help him enjoy the savage spectacle of lions tearing people apart at the Roman games. That sounds like really bad taste...

FAR OUT!

TERRIBLE TASTES AND SICKENING SMELLS

Here's the problem with taste and smell. They're sensational senses all right. They bring you some sensational sensations like your favourite foods and the smell of roses. But they also bring you foul bitter tastes and sickening stinks!

TERRIBLE TASTES

To find out more about taste you've got to peer into your

wet drooling mouth Better take a look now before you chicken out!

Look closely at your tongue. Say Ahhhhhh! Can you see lots of little bumps? They're crammed with 10,000 or so taste buds linked to your brain by nerves. Your brilliant buds can spot five different tastes. The sweet taste includes yummy sugary sweets, there's salt for er, salt, sour for awful acid tastes such as vinegar, umami for dribble-drooling savoury flavours such as meaty burgers or cheesy pizza. And then there's bitter for the sort of tastes that make you screw your face up.

The really tasteless question is why are you expected to taste bitter things at all? I mean – how many bitter-tasting foods do you actually like enough to eat? Well, you're not actually meant to eat most of them – spitting them out would be a lot better for you. This is because most poisons taste bitter, so the bitter-sensitive taste buds are there to warn you that you're just about to eat some vile POISON!

YOU WANT THE **BITTER** TRUTH? ...HE'S BEEN POISONED!

SICKENING STINKS

Your smelling equipment is a 2.5-cm-square patch in the top part of the area behind your nostrils. This patch has over 500 million tiny thread-like sticking-out bits called cilia (silly-ah).

Cilia have a really sickening job – they hang around in groups of eight from rod-like trunks buried in snot. (Yuck!) Smells take the form of tiny bits (called molecules) that float about in the air. When a smelly molecule lands on one of the cilia it triggers a chemical change that's passed on as a signal to the nerves.

SENSATIONALLY SENSITIVE

Your sense of smell of smell is sensationally sensitive. It's actually 10,000 times more sensitive than taste! That's OK when there's something nice to be sniffed but there are some really revolting odours around. And did you know your nose can sniff one molecule of the stinky juice squirted by a skunk even when it's mixed with 30,000,000,000 molecules of fresh air?! Yuck!

Bet you never knew!
People lump taste and smell together because...
1 They work together to help you appreciate the delicious flavour of your favourite foods.
2 In fact when you're eating your favourite fries and thinking, These are sensationally scrummy tasting chips, *you're actually smelling them!*
3 If you couldn't taste them they'd probably taste like cardboard!
4 That's what happens when you have a snorting stinker of a cold. Your nose is blocked up by snot and because you can't smell, your food is doesn't taste like it should! What a tasteless fact!

SILLY SOUND DETECTORS

Ears are eerie things. After all, just think how odd some people's ears look. And guess what? They're even odder on the inside! Just listen to this...

HOW THE EARS WORK

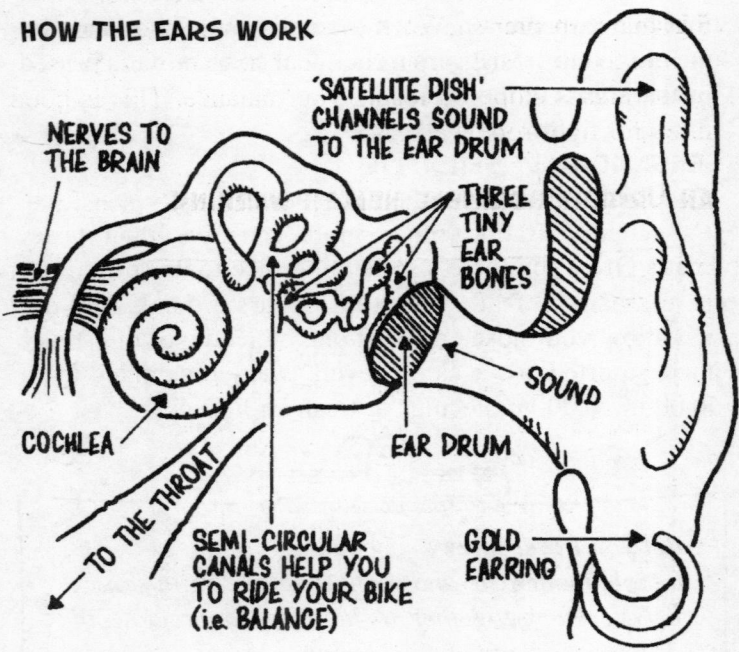

'SATELLITE DISH' CHANNELS SOUND TO THE EAR DRUM

NERVES TO THE BRAIN

THREE TINY EAR BONES

SOUND

COCHLEA

EAR DRUM

TO THE THROAT

SEMI-CIRCULAR CANALS HELP YOU TO RIDE YOUR BIKE (i.e. BALANCE)

GOLD EARRING

The ears work like a couple of satellite dishes linked up to a drum linked up to a triangle and stick linked up to a microphone with a carpenter's level attached! Simple isn't it?

1 Like satellite dishes, your ears pick up signals in the air and bounce them into the central hole. With your ears the signals in question are sounds.

2 The eardrum's a bit like a real drum. It trembles when sounds hit it.

3 The trembling eardrum makes the tiny ear bones jangle just like a triangle hit by a stick.

4 The cochlea picks up the sounds and makes them into nerve signals that go to the brain. It's a bit like a microphone picking up sounds and sending them down a wire.

5 Like a carpenter's level, the semi-circular canals are full of liquid that sloshes around as your head moves. Sensors in the canals stop you losing your balance. This is good news for tight-rope walkers!

AN URGENT HORRIBLE HEALTH WARNING

Dear Reader

Are you reading this page in a car or a ship? Well - DON'T! If you try to concentrate on something whilst moving (like now) - your semi-circular canals end up getting confused. Your brain is baffled by the confusing signals and (according to one theory) produces chemicals that make you violently travel sick!

P.S. If you already feel a bit queasy try to avoid being sick over this book. The pages might stick together.

P.P.S. Oh dear, too late.

Dare you discover ... why your ears go pop?

Try listening to yourself yawning. You may hear a few tiny tingling pops at the start of the yawn – keep trying if you don't hear them at first! So what causes them? Clue: It's something to do with your eustachian (you-station) tube – a useful little tunnel linking your mouth with the inner parts of each ear. So what's going on?

a) The tube is closing up to protect the insides of your ear from being yawned out of your head.

b) The tube contains little poppers that sound off when air goes past them.

c) The tube is opening up to allow the extra yawned-in air to reach the inside of your ear.

Answer: a) Normally the tube is closed but it opens if the air pressure increases at either end. Examples might include when you suddenly go down or up a steep hill or when you breathe in deeply.

TAKING LEAVE OF YOUR SENSES

Each one of your senses is unique and sensational in its own way. But they all have one thing in common. They all need someone or something to talk to and give them a quick answer. So they send all their information to the same place – your very baffling BRAIN.

THAT MAKES SENSE!

THE BAFFLING BRAIN

Your brain is baffling. Baffling, bemusing, bewildering, and brain-bogglingly bamboozling. For instance, how can this 1.5 kg of pinkish-grey blob be more powerful than the most powerful computer in the entire known universe? Everything it does is baffling – including its mystifying memory and strange sleeping habits.

CLICK BUZZ WHIRR

WATKINS – WHAT IS 7693271 ÷ 15134?

508·34353 SIR!

WHAT DOES THE BRAIN DO ALL DAY?

Now there's a baffling question. Unlike other parts of the body it doesn't seem to do anything exciting like squirt blood, leap about or fight germs. It just sits there wobbling nervously. It looks like a watery blancmange and it even squelches if you poke a finger in it and waggle it about.

But the brain is always busy. Even when it doesn't seem to be doing much, your brain is crackling with the electrical force of millions of nerves – just tell that to your teacher next time she accuses you of daydreaming! It fires off signals, feelings, orders, and thoughts at incredible speed. And in order to perform at such baffling speed your brain needs some strong nerves ... lots of them.

Blood, bones and body bits fact file

Name of body part: Nerves

Where found: Form a network throughout the body but mainly in the spine and connecting to the brain

Useful things they do: Take info from your senses to your brain. Bring orders from your brain to the rest of your body.

Grisly details: You can wire a battery to nerves in a chopped-off finger and make it twitch. There's one for the school science lab!

Amazing features: Nerves can carry signals at 100 metres a second – that's 10 times faster than anyone can run!

SPEEDY SIGNALS

Nerve messages are electrical signals zipping down the nerve cells and leaping from cell to cell. Phew – sounds tiring! The nerve cells don't actually touch one another. Signals are passed on by chemicals that leap the gap and spark an electrical pulse on the other side.

RECKLESS REFLEXES

Most of the signals from your nerves go to your brain
to tell it what's going on in the rest of your body.
But some messages move so fast that they make you do
things before you realize it and control it. Sounds like a
good excuse for doing something really reckless – like
breaking things!

But if reflexes are moves you make without thinking,
which of these aren't reflexes?

1 Snatching a hand away from the heat.

2 Blinking

3 Riding a bicycle

4 Sneezing

5 Getting washed in the morning.

6 Hair standing on end when scared.

7 Rolling the eyes

8 Eating breakfast

Answers: Reflexes – 1 2 4 6 7 Non-reflexes – 3 5 8

Dare you discover … how to test your reflexes?

Have you been hit below the kneecap by a doctor wielding a small rubber hammer? If so – it was probably to test the nerves that cause a reflex that works when you're walking. Here's how to do it yourself.

1 Rest one leg loosely over the other.

2 Lightly tap the upper leg just below the kneecap. What happens next?

a) The leg jerks forwards.

b) The leg jerks backwards.

c) A small purple patch appears on the lower leg.

I SAID **SMALL RUBBER** HAMMER!!

Reflexes are all right as far as they go. But to do anything interesting you need to ask your baffling brain.

Blood, bones and body bits fact file

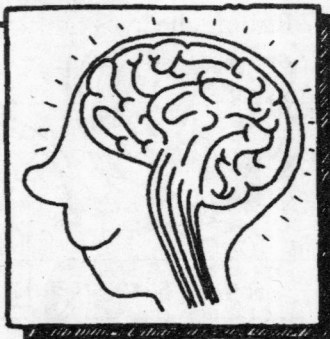

Name of body part: Brain

Where found: Inside the top part of your skull.

Useful things it does: Bosses the rest of your body about. In charge of your memories, thoughts, dreams, etc.

Grisly details: Your brain cells started dying off as soon as you were born. And they aren't getting replaced.*

Amazing features: The brain is more than 80 per cent water!

*Fortunately you've got 15,000 million cells up there ~ more than enough for a long life-time! That's:

- Three times more than a gorilla.

- Seven million times more than a stick insect.

- And about 900 million times more than a small worm that sometimes lives in the human gut.

52

TEACHER'S BRAIN TOUR

If the brain is incredibly baffling enough on the outside – the inside is even more baffling. It's like a big office building (even your teacher's is quite big) with lots of rooms filled with people doing things you don't understand. Well, here's a guided tour of your teacher's office block – I mean brain.

Note: Don't touch anything on the tour it might give your teacher a brainstorm! And don't remove any of your teacher's brain cells either – he hasn't got enough to spare!

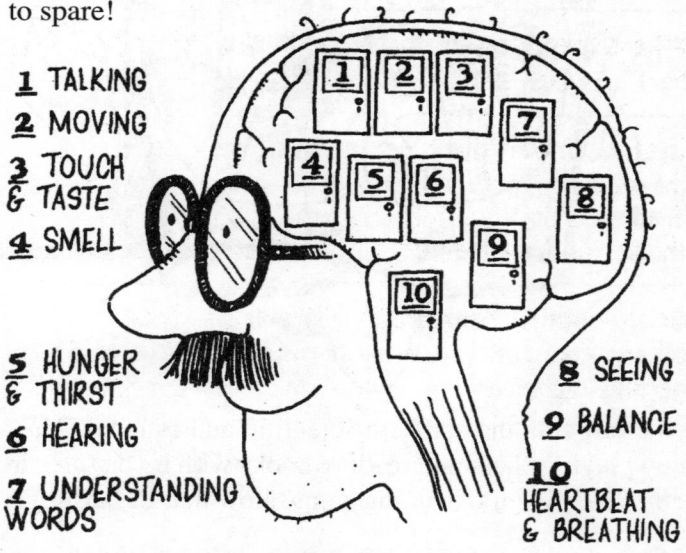

1 TALKING
2 MOVING
3 TOUCH & TASTE
4 SMELL
5 HUNGER & THIRST
6 HEARING
7 UNDERSTANDING WORDS
8 SEEING
9 BALANCE
10 HEARTBEAT & BREATHING

THE CEREBRUM (SER-RE-BRUM)

We start our tour in the big pinkish-grey wrinkly blob on top. It includes your teacher's library where his murky memories are stored. Also the boss's office where decisions are made, and offices for the speech, hearing, moving, touch, sight, understanding and feelings (probably a very small office in this case) departments.

TWO SEPARATE HALVES

Many of these offices are split into two halves linked by communication cables. In the right half the staff are artistic and emotional. They enjoy painting and arranging flowers.

In the left side the staff are scientific and rational. They enjoy playing chess and reading books with no pictures in them. (They even like doing sums. Now that IS baffling!)

THALAMUS

This is the switchboard that relays information from all your senses to the brain.

LIMBIC (LIM-BICK) SYSTEM

This is where your teacher's feelings are checked to make sure he can feel anger, fear, sadness – and even happiness.

(Yes – teachers do occasionally experience this emotion.)
The staff make sure your teacher doesn't get so happy he
walks around with a silly great grin all day.

CEREBELLUM (SERRY-BELL-UM)

Staff here control your teacher's more skilful movements.
OK – there aren't too many of these.

UNDER-BRAIN

This is another switchboard for transferring news about
reflexes happening elsewhere in your teacher's body.

HYPOTHALAMUS (HI-PO-THAL-A-MUSS)

In this broom cupboard are the controls for your teacher's
sweating, growing, sleeping and waking, thirst and hunger
control systems. There's also the control panel for the
sympathetic and parasympathetic systems. It's a big job
for a little office!

THE PINEAL (PI-KNEE-AL) BODY

This is where we end our tour...

No one is too sure what goes on in here. It stops children from developing into adults before they become teenagers and it could also be a time-control system. Perhaps it tells your teacher to wake up in the morning and stay awake though your science lesson! No – DON'T reset these controls!

BE A BRAIN SCIENTIST

Can you use your knowledge of how the brain works to predict the results of these baffling brain experiments?

Experiment 1 In the 19th century French scientist Paul Broca weighed 292 male brains and 140 female brains. He concluded that on average female brains weighed 200 g less than male brains. How would you explain this result?

a) Men are cleverer than women.
b) Boys are more big-headed than girls.
c) Men have bigger heads than women.

Experiment 2 In 1864 two French doctors were discussing what happens to the brain after the head is cut off. As luck would have it one of the doctors was due to have his head chopped off shortly. So the condemned doctor bravely agreed to try winking his right eye three times in response to a shout from his friend. But what was the result of this grisly experiment?

a) The head stuck its tongue out.

b) Nothing – because the brain was dead.
c) The head winked once.

WINK

HE DIDN'T SAY ANYTHING ABOUT OPENING HIS MOUTH!

Experiment 3 Some surgeons cut the nerves connecting the two halves of the cerebrum in order to combat brain disease. How do you think this affected the patients?
a) Each side of their body acted like a separate person.
b) They became twice as clever.
c) They died.

Answers: 1 c) Men and women and boys and girls are equally clever. Women have a similar number of brain cells squashed into a smaller head. But scientists have discovered that men and women use different parts of their brains to answer the same questions. **2 b)** Scientists believe that the brain can only live for about 11 seconds after the head is cut off. **3 a)** Amazing but true! One man tried to hit his wife with one hand whilst the other hand tried to stop him doing it!

Dare you discover … how your friend's brain works?

Reassure your friend that this experiment does not involve any pain. And they won't need to have their head cut off either. Absolutely not. But you do need to remember some rather baffling information.

• The left side of your vision is linked to the right side of the brain and vice-versa.

• The left side of the cerebrum is the half that imagines where to find something.

• The right side deals with maths questions.

1 Write down five or more baffling maths questions.

2 And write another list of five or more baffling requests to give directions from one place to another, eg from home to school

3 Don't tell your friend the aim of the experiment. Stand facing them about three paces away.

4 Ask your friend a maths question followed by a whereabouts question until you have completed both lists.

5 Watch their eye movements. What happens?

a) Their eyes roll upward before they answer the whereabouts questions and go cross-eyed with the maths questions.

b) Their eyes go right for the maths questions and left for the whereabouts questions.

c) Their eyes go left for the maths questions and right for the whereabouts questions.

HOW TO BAFFLE YOUR TEACHER

Here's how to baffle your maths teacher with your amazing brain power.

1 Ask your maths teacher the answer to the sum 4 divided by 47. Try to sound rather casual as if you've just thought up the question.

2 Make sure your teacher doesn't cheat by using a calculator.

3 After a lengthy pause for thought your teacher should be able to come up with something like 0.08 or even 0.085.

4 Smile sweetly and say:

"I don't think that's quite right. I think it's 0.0851063829 78723404255319148936170212765 9574468."

5 Pause to savour the expression of shock on your teacher's face.

6 Hopefully your teacher won't realize that this incredible feat of mental arithmetic was first performed by Professor A C Aitken of Edinburgh University.

7 Of course, if you don't happen to be a mathematical genius you'll have to learn the answer off by heart. (Tip: it's easier if you learn the numbers in groups of three or four and then string them together.)

BAFFLING LEARNING

One of the most baffling things your brain does is learning. It's incredible how they expect you to learn so much. Children at school have to learn on average TEN new words every day! But that's nothing! For example: Bhanddanta Vicittabi Vumsa of Burma learnt 16,000 pages of religious text off by heart.

Russian journalist Solomon Veniaminoff never forgot anything he learnt in his entire life!

Learning is all about remembering things. But the really baffling thing about learning is that scientists don't quite understand how memory works! Or maybe they can't remember! Long-term memory is thought to be created by making new links between brain cells but it's still very vague ... and very baffling.

THE BAFFLED BRAIN

The baffling brain is easily baffled. Just take a look at the picture below – is it a vase or are they two heads? See what I mean? Your brain just can't make up its mind.

Bet you never knew!
Brain bafflement can easily result from a bash on the head. For the brain this can be a deeply baffling experience involving loss of memory or even loss of consciousness. The damage is caused by the violent movement sloshing the poor old brain about. When one girl banged her head she started writing backwards ... and was only cured when she banged her head again cheering her favourite football team on the telly!

NO LAUGHING MATTER

Chemicals such as painkillers can also baffle the brain. Some just deaden pain without knocking you out, but the more powerful painkillers actually cause the brain to lose consciousness. So who invented these powerful drugs? Well, it's a painful story.

Once upon a time surgeons performed operations without any painkillers. They would cut off your leg or whip out vital portions of your anatomy and all you got was a gag to stop you screaming too loudly! But that was before Horace Wells got in on the act.

Connecticut, United States, 1844

Horace Wells was deeply in on the act. And he wished he wasn't. The act in question was a display of the effects of laughing-gas and Horace was in the audience. But Horace Wells wasn't really watching the show at all because he was busy being in agony. The plump, smartly dressed dentist was suffering from the most embarrassing ailment for anyone in his profession ... toothache. It was so annoying – that he, the great Horace Wells – the inventor of a wonderful new solder for fixing false teeth should have to endure this awful indignity.

He made another effort to concentrate on the entertainment. Laughing-gas, or nitrous oxide, as scientists called it, had been discovered about 70 years before. And it didn't just make you laugh. A few whiffs had even the most outwardly boring person singing, dancing, fighting, talking nonsense or even passing out. The hugely popular laughing-gas shows employed bouncers to protect the audience from the crazy antics of volunteers who breathed the gas.

Suddenly one of the volunteers went berserk. There was a struggle and the man got injured – but he didn't seem to feel any pain!

Lucky you, thought Horace Wells nursing his aching jaw. Then a little light bulb flashed inside his head and for the first time that evening he smiled. (Just a bit – you can't smile too easily with toothache.) If laughing-gas could deaden pain and knock you out ... then perhaps ... perhaps just maybe...

After the show Horace Wells approached the organizer with a somewhat baffling request.

"Could you lend me some laughing gas?"

Wells hoped to knock himself out whilst another dentist removed the aching tooth. In those days pulling out a tooth was a painful and rather bloody job involving a huge pair of tongs and a great deal of tugging. But Horace Wells breathed in the gas and didn't feel a thing!

"It's a new era for tooth-pulling!" he exclaimed in triumph as the effects of the laughing-gas wore off. Or that's what he meant to say, but since his mouth was still sore the words probably came out as:

Yes, he, Horace Wells, was about to sell the painkilling secret of laughing-gas and become rich and famous. Seriously rich.

But the painkilling project came to a rather painful conclusion. The first public use of laughing-gas by a dentist ended in disaster when the patient woke up too soon. He had received too little gas. During a later operation another patient died after receiving too much gas. A few years later Horace himself came to a painful end. He went mad as a result of breathing too much painkilling gas and in 1848 he took his own life. But he didn't die in vain. Today the idea of using a painkilling gas (not laughing-gas!) in medicine is well-established.

Fortunately you don't need to rely on gas to send you to sleep.

YOUR BRAIN'S BAFFLING BEDTIME

Every night at about the same time your brain does something remarkable – and quite baffling. It winds down its operations, pulls down the shutters and more or less switches itself off. Yes, that's right, it goes to sleep. Altogether your brain will spend at least 20 years in this odd condition. Why? Well, the really baffling bit is that no one really knows!

64

ALL YOU NEED TO KNOW ABOUT SLEEP - IN THREE EASY LESSONS

In order to make sleep less baffling – here is a course of sleep lessons. It's taught at night school, of course, and unlike ordinary school, the teachers don't mind if you nod off!

Lesson 1 – falling asleep

1 Make sure you are neither too hot nor too cold. It helps if you go to bed at the same time each night.

2 Lie very still with your eyes closed. Try counting backwards from 1,000 or imagining yourself on a lovely relaxing holiday.

3 You'll notice that you can't pin-point the moment when you fall asleep. Some people feel they are falling and twitch violently at this point so they have to start all over again!

Lesson 2 – what happens when you're asleep?

1 Here are a few things you ought to know before you fall asleep. Whilst you are sleeping...

• Your body temperature starts falling.
• Your weight drops by 28–42 g each hour.
• You can change position up to 40 times a night.
• You can wake up for less than three minutes at a time

and you probably won't remember it in the morning.

2 Don't worry about listening out for danger whilst you are asleep – your brain does this job automatically.

3 Here are some things you shouldn't do whilst asleep.

• Try not to sleep walk – about 1 in 20 children do this.

• Try not to snore too loudly. This disgusting din is made by someone sleeping on their back with their mouth open. As they breathe in, the wobbly bits at the back of their mouth start rattling noisily.

4 You can stop snorers by putting something hard and prickly (such as an old hair brush or hedgehog) into the bed. The snorer rolls onto his back and the prickles wake him up!

5 After about 90 minutes of sleep your eyeballs start twitching but the nerves to most of your muscles shut down so you can't move. You are about to enter the most baffling part of your sleep – the DREAM ZONE.

Lesson 3 – exploring the dream zone

1 Welcome to a strange world where time and space have no meaning and where nothing is impossible.

2 Dreams are caused by signals fired towards your brain by nerves underneath it. When you are awake this area screens out boring sounds – that's why you don't notice

traffic, or your teacher droning on and on and on.
Zzzzzzzzz.

3 Most dreams take 6–10 minutes but the record for the longest dream is 150 minutes! During your 20 years asleep you can look forward to watching 300,000 dreams!

4 Every night you make several trips to the dream zone.

5 Some good and bad dream news. THE GOOD NEWS: Happy dreams are three times more common than sad dreams. THE BAD NEWS: As it gets towards morning you are more likely to encounter nightmares. If you're reading this in bed you'd better save the next chapter till morning – you don't want to dream about ghastly groaning skeletons now, do you?

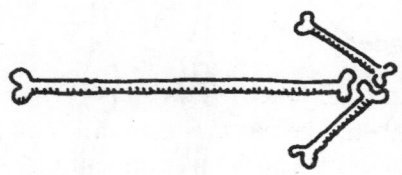

BONES AND GROANS

Spooky stories are full of groaning skeletons. But skeletons don't groan for the fun of it. No. They're groaning because that's what bones do to you. They ache and they break and if you happen to have muscles attached to your bones they ache even more! Funnily enough, bones make some scientists groan too. Well – imagine having to remember all 206 bones in the human body! Here are a few memorable groans – er, I mean bones.

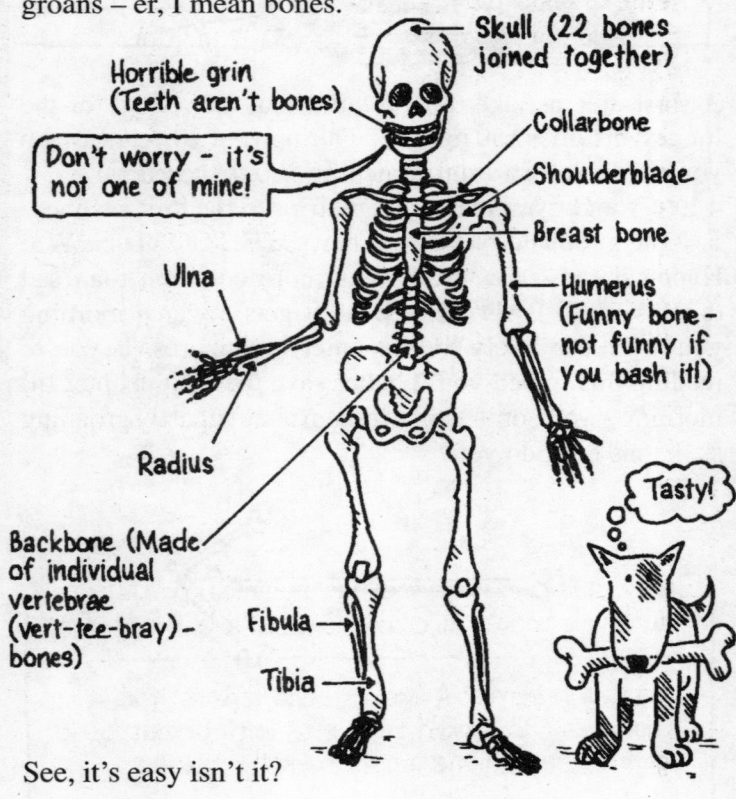

Skull (22 bones joined together)

Horrible grin (Teeth aren't bones)

Don't worry – it's not one of mine!

Collarbone

Shoulderblade

Breast bone

Ulna

Humerus (Funny bone – not funny if you bash it!)

Radius

Tasty!

Backbone (Made of individual vertebrae (vert-tee-bray) – bones)

Fibula →

Tibia →

See, it's easy isn't it?

Blood, bones and body bits fact file

Name of body part: Bones

Where found: Your bones form the skeleton that makes up about 25 per cent of your weight. Bones are made from a tough stringy substance called collagen (collar-gen), and strengthened with a mixture of hard minerals.

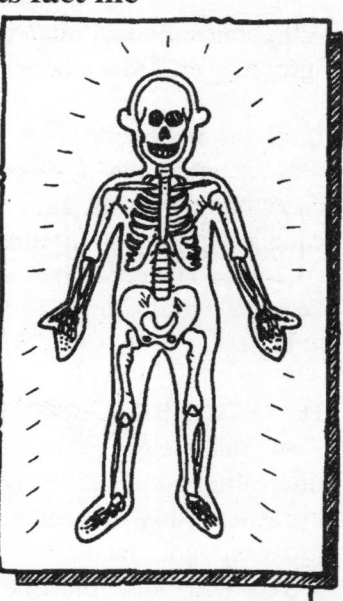

Useful things they do: They hold your body upright and give your muscles something to pull against.

Grisly details: If you took all the minerals out of your thigh bone you could tie what's left in a knot.

Amazing features: A broken bone repairs itself. As long as the broken ends are "set" or put back together – new bone grows over the break.

BONES - THE INSIDE STORY!

Some bones are solid with an area of spongy bone on the inside, others are long and hollow and their empty centres are filled with juicy jelly-like red marrow. Dogs love marrow because it's full of meaty goodness. So should you. Your marvellous marrow makes you billions of new blood cells every day.

Look at bones through a microscope and you'll see they've all got little holes in them. These tiny tunnels carry blood vessels and nerves. They're called Haversian canals (Have-er-shun) after their oddly named discoverer – Clopton Havers. It may seem odd to call these tiny tubes "canals" but it sounds better than "Clopton's bone-holes" at least.

TEACHER'S BONE-GROAN TEST

How much does your teacher really know about this interesting subject? Bone up on the answers to this ultra-fiendishly difficult test and show up your teacher's groaning ignorance!

1 You will only find one of these bones in the human skeleton. Which one?

a) The tail bone

b) The elbow bone

c) The nose bone

2 If you wanted to hold up a heavy weight what would be the strongest thing to use?

a) A stone pillar

b) A concrete pillar

c) A leg bone

3 A giraffe has seven bones in its neck. How many neck bones has a human got?

a) 3

b) 7

c) 12

4 How many bones does a baby have?

a) 206, just like a grown-up person.

b) 86

c) More than 350

5 Some Tibetan priests use the skull as a drinking cup. How much liquid do these creepy cups hold?

a) 500 ml

b) 1.5 litres

c) None – it trickles out through the eye-sockets

6 What bone forms the sticking-out bit of your ankle?

a) The bottom of the tibia

b) The ankle bone

c) The top of the heel bone

7 What is a wormian bone?

a) A wiggly little bone in the little toe.

b) An extra bone sometimes found in a baby's skull.

c) A bone infested by worms.

Answers: 1 a) Yes – that's right! We've all got tails! The coccyx (cox-sicks) is a mass of three to five joined-up bones at the end of the backbone. Fortunately it's not long enough to poke outside the body! **2 c) 3 b)** The giraffe bones are much longer! **4 c)** Lots of these extra bones join up as the baby grows up. **5 b) 6 a) 7 b)**

71

WHAT YOUR TEACHER'S SCORE MEANS:

0–3 Make no bones about it – your teacher is a bone-head!

4–5 Your teacher can teach you a few facts but only knows the bare bones of the subject.

6–7 Your teacher is probably an osteologist* (ost-tee-ol-o-gist). He or she may even have a real human skeleton at home for study purposes.

* An expert on bones.

Bet you never knew!
An osteologist studies bones looking for clues that can identify the person to whom the skeleton belonged. Do you think you could do this? Here's your chance to use your skills to solve a truly horrible true mystery.

THE WANDERING BONES

It was 7 December 1976, Long Beach, California. The TV cameraman was in for a nasty shock. He was in a haunted house sideshow filming a TV series. As he moved a gruesome dummy away from the rest of the film crew – its arm fell off! The arm was real. And there was bone underneath!

The police were called, and it soon became clear that this was no ordinary dummy – it had once been alive! The police discovered three fiendish facts. The body had been pickled in the deadly poison arsenic. It had been shot by an old-fashioned type of bullet dating from before 1914. In the body's mouth was a coin dated 1924.

The police then traced a series of former owners of the body. The former owners (who had all thought the body was a dummy) were colourful showmen who scraped a living exhibiting the gruesome specimen at funfairs. The oldest showman thought he could remember buying the body in Oklahoma. Then local history buffs dredged up a possible identity for the butchered body – Elmer McCurdy, cowboy and outlaw.

Elmer McCurdy's luck had run out at dawn on 7 October 1911. When the sheriff's men came for him he was drunk with stolen whiskey and exhausted after a night spent hiding in a hayloft. A young lad was sent up to the hiding place.

"The boys want you to surrender, Mister!" he cried.

"I'll see them in hell first!" roared the outlaw.

McCurdy died with his boots on after slugging out a desperate gun battle until his six-gun was empty. After the outlaw's death an undertaker had preserved the body and charged people to see it propped against his parlour wall!

Many people tried to buy the body but all offers were refused. Then the undertaker gave the body away to a nice man who said he was Elmer's long-lost brother.

Three months later the body appeared in a street-show in Texas.

But could the police bone experts prove that the body actually belonged to McCurdy? Here is a description of the outlaw dating from 1911. Which of the following features might you be able to check by examining the bones inside the body?

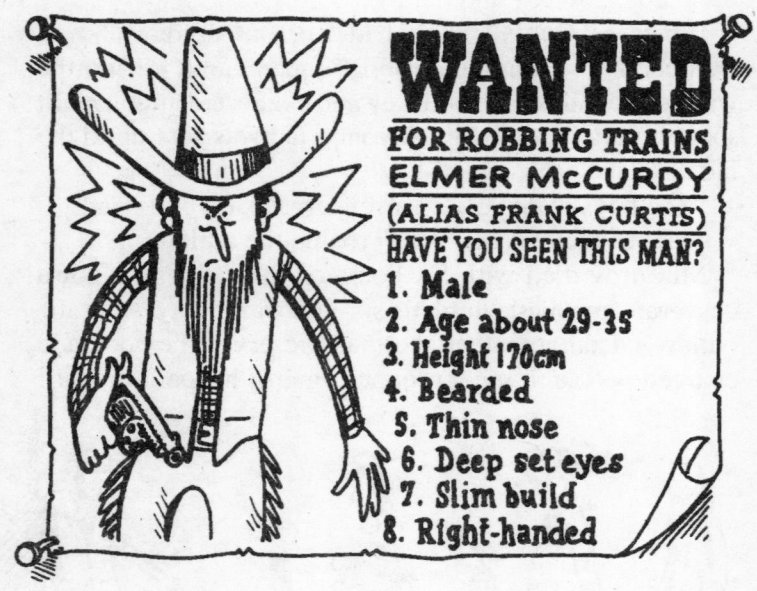

WANTED

FOR ROBBING TRAINS
ELMER McCURDY
(ALIAS FRANK CURTIS)
HAVE YOU SEEN THIS MAN?
1. Male
2. Age about 29-35
3. Height 170cm
4. Bearded
5. Thin nose
6. Deep set eyes
7. Slim build
8. Right-handed

Answers: 1 Yes, females have wider pelvic bones. **2** Yes, as he grew older some of his bones joined together. **3** Yes by the length of the thigh bones. **4 5 6** No. **7** Yes, by looking at the build of the skeleton. **8** Yes, marks on the right arm bones showed traces of more developed muscles than on the left side.

After studying the bones the scientists were certain they had the right man. The final proof came when they found that an old photo of the outlaw's head perfectly matched the shape of the skull. And so, at long last, Elmer McCurdy's body was given a decent burial – nearly 66 years after he was killed!

JOIN UP THE JOINTS

If you really want to be bone expert, you'll need to know how to fit a skeleton together. The bones in a skeleton fit together to form joints and the trick is to assemble the joints correctly. But it's not easy – there are over 200 joints to join-up!

Here are the main types of joints.

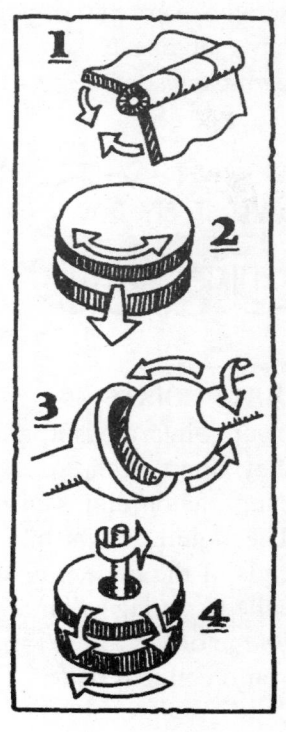

1 Hinge joints. Joints such as the knee work like door hinges, allowing the bones to move backwards and forwards. But they don't move so easily from side to side.

2 Gliding joint. The ankle bones can easily slide up and down and from side to side.

3 Ball and socket joint. As the name implies this is a ball and socket that allows arm and thigh bones to move in most directions.

4 Swivel joint. This joint allows the bone on top to move up and down and from side to side.

5 Saddle joint. The bone on top is like a jockey on a saddle. So it sways about and leans in all directions – without falling off!

LUCKY LIGAMENTS

Imagine if your arm fell off every time you threw a ball! This doesn't happen because tough cords called ligaments hold your bones together over the joint. Contortionists stretch their ligaments as they bend their bodies into horrible positions. You'd groan if you tried this! But did you know that your ligaments and joints allow you to scratch every part of your body? This is lucky if you don't have anyone to scratch your back. Try scratching your own back some time – but NOT during science class.

OVER A BIT, DOWN A BIT. OOOH YES, THAT'S GOT IT!

JUICY JOINTS

Your joints are surprisingly quiet. They don't groan – they don't even squeak. You can tiptoe softly because every major joint is cushioned in a bag of squelchy liquid. The liquid allows the joint to move smoothly and the ends of the bones are also padded with a softer material called cartilage (karta-lidge). The same stuff forms the bridge of your nose – but if you saw it in a chicken bone you'd call it "gristle".

MOANING MUSCLES

No matter how supple your joints are – you can't make a move without using your muscles. THE GOOD NEWS is that you've got over 600 of them. THE BAD NEWS is that they can make you moan in aching agony!

Blood, bones and body bits fact file

Name of body part: Muscles

Where found: Under the skin and surrounding various body bits.

Useful things they do: They're ALWAYS hard at work squeezing the food through your guts, pumping blood and so on.

Grisly details: Muscles can squeeze so strongly that they break your bones! But they have sensors to stop them squeezing that much!

Amazing features: Muscles are anchored to bones by tough tendons. A tendon won't go Twaang! unless you hang a 58-tonne weight from it!

GETTING TO GRIPS WITH MUSCLES

To get to grips with your muscles you need to take a closer look. A much closer look…

If you cut a muscle in half you can see that it's made of thick bundles of stringy fibres.

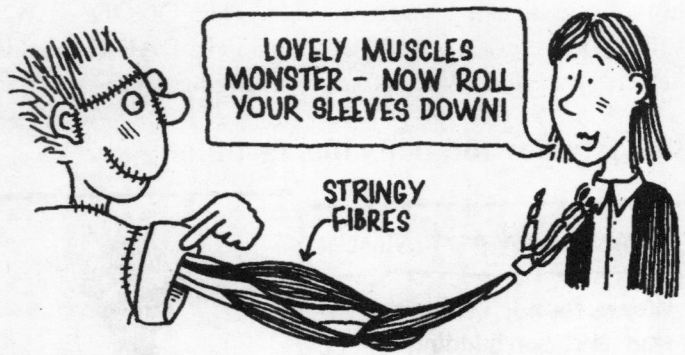

Look more closely you'll see that a fibre is made up of smaller fibres called fibrils.

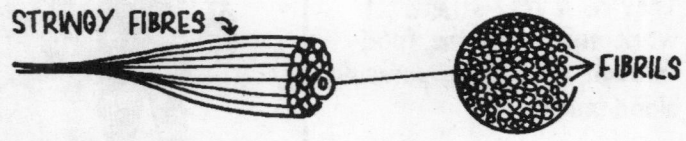

HOW TO MAKE A MOVE

1 Ask one of your nerves to send a signal to your muscles. Make sure that the tiny fibrils are shortening in response.

2 Check that your blood contains enough sugars to provide the energy to power the muscle.

3 The muscle contains chemicals that produce energy by breaking up the molecules of sugar.

But before you move a muscle there are few more things you should know...

GROANING MUSCLE FACTS

1 Muscles have complicated, instantly forgettable Latin names. See if you can remember these.

a) Gluteus maximus – bottom. Makes a nice cushion for sitting on.

GLUTEUS MAXIMUS

b) Digital flexor – wags your finger at people.

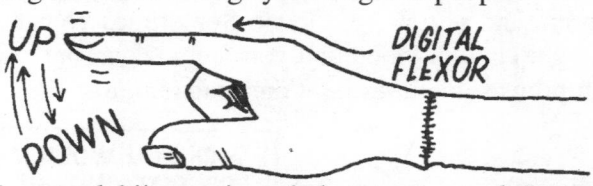

UP
DOWN
DIGITAL FLEXOR

c) Levator labii superior – helps you to snarl. Just say the word and you'll be snarling!

MUSCULUS LEVATOR LABII SUPERIORIS ALAQUE NASI

SNARL

2 Muscles can pull but they can't push. That's why muscles work in pairs. One muscle pulls one way and the other muscle pulls in the opposite direction!

3 You can watch the tendons pulling your muscles. Just spread your fingers and waggle them up and down.

4 When you stick your tongue out there's no muscle doing the pushing from behind. A muscle pulls across the tongue and this pushes the tongue forward.

5 As people get older tough stretchy fibres build up inside the muscles. That's why giants and monsters don't like eating stringy old grandparents. They prefer a succulent tender CHILD! Help!

GROANS AT THE GYM

Well, be honest, how far can you run? Or does exercise – any kind of effort – make you groan? Are you one of these people who prefer lazing around on the sofa with a big bag of popcorn? Well, if so, you'll be pleased to hear that exercise can be BAD for you! Every sport should carry a Government Health Warning.

Horrible Health Warning 1 Getting off the sofa is dangerous! Your heart suddenly has to pump blood up to your brain and not along a level. Sometimes your brain doesn't get enough blood and you feel dizzy. That's why aircraft pilots sometimes faint on a sudden turn.

I WISH YOU WOULDN'T DO THAT, CAPTAIN!

Horrible Health Warning 2 Even when you're up-and-running it's horribly hard work for your body. Your poor feet and ankles have to put up with a pressure of SIX times your body weight. The arches of your feet flop down as they hit the ground. Your fat wobbles, your brain squelches and even your eyeballs bounce slightly in their sockets!

FLOP SQUELCH WOBBLE BOUNCE

Horrible Health Warning 3 Violent exercise is especially bad for you … it can cause some especially groan-worthy pains.

a) If your heart beats more than 175 beats a minute it could get injured… Slow down gently!

I PREFERRED BEING A COUCH POTATO!

b) Stiffness. May be caused by loss of water due to sweating and build-up of a chemical called lactic acid in tired muscles . . . Slow down gently after exercise and enjoy a long drink.

c) Cramp is when your muscles squeeze painfully and you can't stop them . . . Keep the muscle warm and rest it. A nice hot-water -bottle will do!

d) Stitch. Caused by cold and running on a full stomach . . . Keep warm. Don't guzzle so much!

81

But if there's one thing worse than taking exercise it's NOT taking exercise. Look what you miss out on.

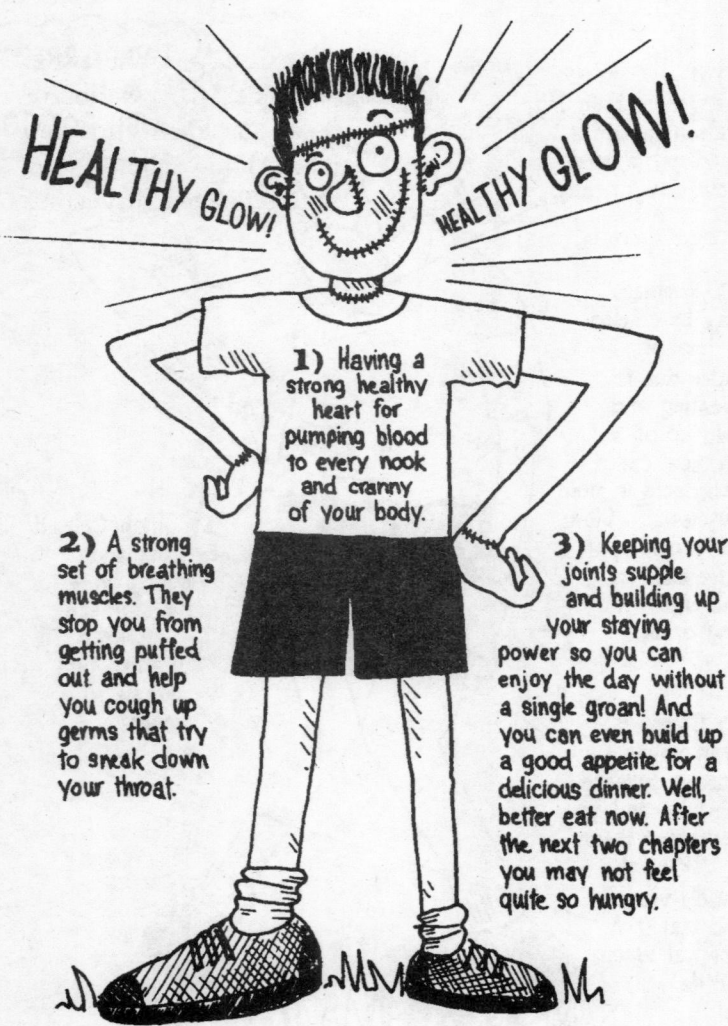

HEALTHY GLOW! HEALTHY GLOW!

1) Having a strong healthy heart for pumping blood to every nook and cranny of your body.

2) A strong set of breathing muscles. They stop you from getting puffed out and help you cough up germs that try to sneak down your throat.

3) Keeping your joints supple and building up your staying power so you can enjoy the day without a single groan! And you can even build up a good appetite for a delicious dinner. Well, better eat now. After the next two chapters you may not feel quite so hungry.

DISGUSTING DIGESTION

Could you murder a rich chocolate cake dripping with cream and icing? Does the hint of jam roly-poly and extra-thick custard make your tummy thunder? If so – you're going to find this chapter horribly tasteless. Imagine your food being chewed and squashed and squelched as it's taken into your body. It's all due to your disgusting digestive juices.

DISGUSTING DIGESTIVE GLANDS

A gland is a body bit that produces juices. At different points in your guts, glands lurk – just waiting to spray your food with digestive juices. But can you believe the horribly huge amounts of juice they produce? We're not talking little squirts here...

Gland	Daily Squirt
Saliva glands	2 litres *
Stomach	1–2 litres
Pancreas	1–1.5 litres
Liver	1 litre
Lining of guts	2.5 litres

That's over 8.5 litres every day!

* You end up gulping most of this down! Yes that's 50,000 litres of spit in a lifetime! Or enough to fill 100 baths!

Digestive juices contain chemicals called enzymes. The enzymes work horribly hard to break up the food molecules into smaller molecules that your body can absorb more easily. The hotter the body gets the faster these changes happen, until at 60°C they suddenly stop. Mind you, if you ever got that hot you'd be cooked anyway!

Dare you discover ... how enzymes work?

Rennet is a sloppy substance that contains rennin – an enzyme also found in the human stomach. Make sure it's OK for you to use these ingredients below and get someone to help you use the hob.

852 ml of fresh full-cream milk
Sugar
Rennet – available from supermarkets
Saucepan
Bowl
Tablespoon

1 Heat the milk in the saucepan and stir well until it's warm but not hot. DON'T BOIL IT!
2 Pour the milk into the bowl and stir in one tablespoon of sugar.

3 Place the bowl in a warm place.
4 Very gently stir in one tablespoon of rennet. Don't touch the bowl for ten minutes.
5 Ten minutes later ... what's happened to the milk?

HORRIBLE HINT: If your experiment has worked, the rennin will have digested the milk.

a) It's turned into a disgusting smelly yellow mixture with soggy white lumps in it.

b) It's turned into a solid wobbly mass.

c) Nothing

A HORRIBLY HEALTHY DIET

Are you a fussy eater? Your body is! To stay healthy your body has to digest a balanced diet. That means all the types of food shown below and NOT just the ones you like!

1 Fibre helps your guts grip your food and keep it moving on its long trek to the toilet.

2 Proteins help your body build and repair its cells. Ten per cent of your body is made of this stuff.

3 Carbohydrates (car-bo-hi-drates) are found in starchy foods. Once they're digested they become sugars that your cells turn into energy.

4 Sickly sweet sugars are less vital, I'm sorry to say. These sugars provide your body with easy energy. Your lazy body feeds the sugar straight to the cells.

5 Fat is a useful store of energy and it helps build body cells - often in a wobbly layer around your tummy.

A SICKENING SANDWICH

Could you combine foods that contain fibre, proteins, carbohydrates, sugars and fat in a ONE sandwich snack?

HAM AND JAM SANDWICH →

Here are some snacks to choose from…

1 A ham and jam sandwich with a fizzy drink.

2 An egg and baked beans wholemeal-bread sandwich (yuck!) and a mug of hot chocolate.

3 A chip sandwich with white bread followed by treacle pudding washed down with loads of lemonade (burp!).

4 A healthy wholemeal lettuce sandwich followed by a sugar-free nut bar and a glass of mineral water.

A HORRIBLY UNHEALTHY DIET

As if digestion isn't horrible enough just look at the horribly unhealthy things that some people eat.

1 Some people eat earth. This is horribly unhealthy because it's teeming with germs and tastes disgusting.

2 In 1927 a woman complained of stomach pains. She was rushed to hospital in Ontario, Canada. There, doctors found that she'd swallowed 2,533 metal objects including 947 bent pins.

I'VE GOT PINS AND NEEDLES IN MY STOMACH!

X-RAY VIEW

3 But the prize for the most disgusting diet must go to Michel Lotito of France. In his own country he is known as Monsieur Mangetout (Mr Eat-it-all). Starting in 1966 Mr Eat-it-all chomped his way through...

He generally ate 900 g of metal a day. All without getting indigestion. (Don't try this yourself – you might not be so lucky!)

4 The urge to eat is controlled by the hypothalamus in the brain. It tells you when you are hungry and when you are full. A scientist removed part of a rat's hypothalamus and it gorged itself until it was a horribly unhealthy fat rat.

5 At this moment millions of people are trying to lose weight by dieting. But people don't actually need to lose weight unless they are horribly unhealthy. Like William J Cobb, for example.

In 1962 William J Cobb weighed 364 kg. He was so round that he could only roll like a barrel. Not surprising – considering he was carrying 91 kg of fat! So William decided to go on a diet, and within a year or two he was down to 106 kg. He had lost the weight of three large men!

LARGE BAR OF CHOCCY

HEALTHY STICK OF CELERY

BEFORE   AFTER

6 Most people can only lose about half their normal body weight. This takes about three weeks if the person doesn't eat. Then they die – and that's a really unhealthy thing to happen!

HORRIBLY HEALTHY DIET COMPLICATIONS

To stay horribly healthy you need more than a balanced diet. You've got to eat things that you can't see or taste – like minerals for example. Luckily you don't have to go around looking for minerals to eat. Ordinary food contains minerals in tiny amounts – and that's all your body needs! For example, slurp a milkshake and you're doing your bones a favour. Milk contains the bone-building minerals calcium and phosphate. Then there are other chemicals called vitamins and they're really VITAL.

VITAL VITAMINS

Vitamins are vital because if you don't get enough of them in your diet you become horribly unhealthy. Feel more like gobbling up those greens now?

Vitamin	Found in:	Not enough causes:
A	Milk, butter, eggs, fish oil, liver.	Lots of illnesses and you can't even see in the dark.
B1 and 9 other B vits.	Yeast and wholemeal bread. Also found in milk, nuts and fresh vegetables.	Victim loses energy and can't get out of bed – sounds worse than a Monday morning.
C	Oranges and lemons. Fresh fruit and vegetables.	Loss of teeth, bleeding gums, dark spots on body. Bad breath. Yuck!
D	Oily fish, dairy products.	Bent bones and bandy legs. Bad news for footballers.
E	Vegetable oils, nuts and leafy vegetables.	Unhealthy cells – easily damaged by harmful chemicals.
K	Green veg, liver	Blood doesn't clot properly – very messy!

It took scientists a great deal of trial and error to discover the disgusting effects of lack of vitamins. But solving these medical mysteries gave them something to crow about.

The sick chickens mystery

Christiaan Eijkman was at his wit's end.

In 1884 he had gone to Indonesia to study a mystery disease. The locals called it, "I can't."

He injected animals with germs thought to cause the disease. The animals stayed healthy!

Then his pet chickens went down with the disease.

He moved them to another place and they got better!
But why?

Maybe they just needed some fresh air.

Or maybe it was due to a change in diet? In their first home the birds were eating boiled rice.

Now they were eating brown rice.

It turned out that the brown outer layer of the rice grains was rich in Vitamin B. This prevented, "I can't" or as we call it, beri-beri.

Mind you, it took Eijkman many years of experiments to prove that eating the wrong rice had made the chickens sick. As for the chickens themselves – things could have been worse. Imagine something had gone wrong with their digestive bits and pieces. They'd have been sick as parrots then! Yes, we're talking about the gruesome guts!

THE GRUESOME GUTS

Guts are gruesome. Gobsmackingly grossly stomach-churningly sickening. In fact – if you thought too much about where your food went you wouldn't feel like eating it! But if there's one thing even more gruesome than guts, it's the scientists who find guts fascinating. Oh yes, and then there's the smelly stuff that pours out the other end. Yuck!

Blood, bones and body bits fact file

Name of body part: Guts

Where found: Mostly under the chest area in the lower part of the body. (See below.)

Useful things they do: Absorb your food once it has been digested.

Grisly details: The guts form a continuous tube up to 8m long. That's longer than a huge slithery snake!

Amazing features: Your guts are held in place by the mesentery (mes-en-terry). This stops the guts slopping about and tying themselves in knots!

Dare you discover ... what's inside your mouth?

Open wide! Here's where it all begins. The gobbling, munching mouth – grinding up the goodies before they hit the guts. Imagine what it's like to be a bit of food!

TOOTH TRUTHS

The first thing you'll have to worry about are those gigantic spit-dripping jaws. They're made from enamel and they're so tough you need a diamond to drill into them. Inside each tooth there are nerves and blood vessels just like any body part. Not all teeth are the same – there are different-shaped teeth for different jobs. Here are a few that we picked up from a dentist's floor.

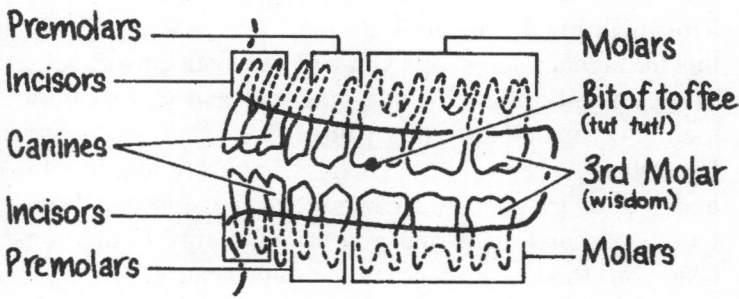

Premolars
Incisors
Canines
Incisors
Premolars

Molars
Bit of toffee (tut tut!)
3rd Molar (wisdom)
Molars

So how many teeth have you got? It depends on how old you are. You started off with 20 teeth that appeared when you were very young. As you get older these fall out and new teeth push through your gums. Here are some tooth totals – which is closest to your own number of teeth?

1 Incisors   a) 2   b) 8   c) 4
2 Canines   a) 2   b) 4   c) 8
3 Pre-molars   a) 4   b) 8   c) 12
4 Molars   a) 4   b) 8   c) 12

Can you spot any of these in your mouth?

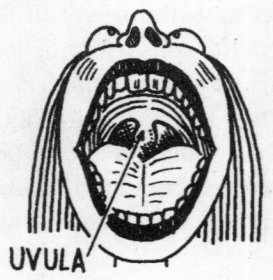

UVULA

Uvula (You-vue-la) This horrible little wobbly bit spends its time hanging around in your mouth. The name means "little grape" – can you see why? No one knows exactly why it's there but it does help you swallow.

Mouth lining If you look at this through a microscope you will see loads of soft cells. When they die they fall into your spit and you swallow them. So you end up eating yourself!

Frenulum (Fren-u-lum) This is the nasty-looking bit under your tongue. You can see the vessels that bring blood to your tongue and give it the energy to talk and taste your food (sometimes at the same time!).

Plaque A layer of germs that cluster on our teeth – they're responsible for tooth decay and bad breath! (If you find any, brush it off!)

PLAQUE

BAD BREATH

BAD BREATH

GRUESOME GOBBLING

Once you've checked your mouth – get ready to swallow. Oddly enough most of us manage to do this without thinking. This is probably because swallowing is a reflex action. But it's also a horribly complex operation – see if you can do it by following these instructions. (NOTE: try not to dribble all over your nice clean book.)

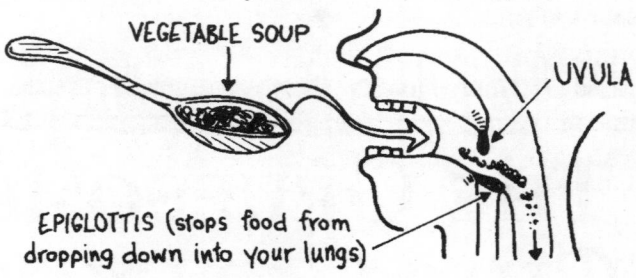

VEGETABLE SOUP

UVULA

EPIGLOTTIS (stops food from dropping down into your lungs)

1 Using your tongue, press some food you chewed earlier on to the roof of your mouth.

2 Force the food towards the back of your throat.

3 Swing up your uvula to prevent the food making a dash for freedom up your nose. On second thoughts don't worry about doing this – it happens automatically.

• NOTE 1: Try not to laugh when you eat. When you laugh your uvula swings DOWN – so you could find that the soup you've just slurped up is dribbling out of your nostrils!

• NOTE 2: Try not to breathe whilst you are swallowing. If you do your food goes down your windpipe and you have to cough it up! You've got a little lid called the epiglottis (eppy-glot-tis) that closes off the top of your windpipe to prevent this happening.

Wouldn't you like to know what really happens to your food after you swallow it? No? Go on – it's REALLY horrible!

A gruesome guts tour

Here's a gruesomely thrilling alternative to the usual boring tourist trip. Just imagine being shrunk down to the size of a pinhead and boarding a coach the size of a pea. Then imagine going on a guided tour of someone else's guts! And guess what? Your dinner's thrown in! That's if you feel like eating any . . .

The Horrible Holiday Company proudly present...

THE GRUESOME GUTS GETAWAY!

EMBARK ON THE TRIP OF A LUNCHTIME.

THE SMALL PRINT

1. If you get digested and turned into a chemical soup it's not our fault – OK?

2. There will be **no** toilet stops until the end of the tour.

1.00 pm Enter the mouth. Fasten your safety belts and close the windows securely. It's wet outside and we're about to dive down the gullet waterfall. Splosh!

GRUESOME GUTS TOURS

1.01 pm
Amazing 9 to
13-second free-fall
as we're squeezed
25cm down the
gullet!

1.02-6 pm Five-hour stopover in the
stomach. Plenty of time to admire the slimy
stomach walls with their 3.5 million digestive
juice-producing pits.

▶ Enjoy the beautiful sunset effect as a red-
hot pepper makes the stomach glow.

▶ Listen to the mighty roar of the rumbling stomach as
trapped gases squelch around amongst the food.

▶ Experience the gut-churning thrill of the stomach big
dipper as it churns and churns again every 20 seconds.
(If you feel a bit queasy, sick-bags are provided.)

6.00 pm A sudden lurch takes us from the stomach into the intestine. Then what better than a relaxing 6m cruise down the scenic small intestine? (Speed 2.5cm per minute.)

▶ Feel the lovely smooth gliding motion as we're squeezed along. The slimy gut walls help to stop the guts from digesting themselves.

▶ Marvel at the velvety insides of the intestines made up of five million tiny projections called villi.

▶ Gasp as we are covered in enzyme-rich digestive juices squirting down from the pancreas and liver.

▶ Wonder as the food chemicals are sucked into the villi.

▶ Puzzle over the mystery of the appendix. Everyone's got one of these finger-like things sticking out of their intestines. But no one knows what it's for!

10.00 pm Spend the night in the comfortable and spacious large intestines. Here the surroundings are peaceful, lie back and listen for the

relaxing gurgling of the water as it's taken out of the remains of the food and back into the body.

7.30 am (Give or take a few hours). Put on your life jacket and parachute. It's time for splash down in the toilet!

100

SOME SICKENING SCIENTISTS

Of course the first scientists who investigated the guts had to learn the hard way. That's by gruesome guesswork, sickening speculation and some awful emetic* experiments.

* WARNING TO READERS: An emetic is something that makes you throw up. Vomiting is a reflex action caused by strong squeezing of the muscles around the stomach. It could even be triggered by reading this chapter. Don't try any of these experiments at home – or at school!

EMETIC EXPERIMENTS

If you thought that science is all about spotless white coats and squeaky-clean labs…THINK AGAIN! Here are some sickening experiments you shouldn't try.

1 René Réamur (1683-1757)

Claim to fame: Famous French scientist. Expert on just about everything, including technology and industry.

Emetic experiment: Trained a kite – (that's a bird not the thing on a string) to sick up its food. Then he pored over the vile vomit to see what the half-digested food looked like.

Disgusting discovery: The meat didn't go rotten inside the bird's guts. This was because the chemicals in the bird's stomach killed the germs that made things rot.

MUST BE THAT RABBIT I CAUGHT LAST NIGHT!

2 Lazzaro Spallanzani (1729-1799)

Claim to fame: Famous Italian scientist. Expert on volcanoes, electric fish, thunderclouds and how a snail grows its head back after you cut it off.

Revolting research included:

• Forcing animals to swallow food in tubes or tied to string and then making them sick up the food so he could study how the food had changed. The animals included cats, dogs, oxen, newts, sheep, a horse and some sinister-looking snakes.

◦ Doing the same experiment on himself. Eating his own sicked-up food. He ate one bit of food three times just to see how it had changed!

◦ Making himself sick again so that he could study his own stomach juices.

Emetic experiment: Kept a container of sick in a warm place for a few hours.

Disgusting discovery: The food continued to be digested. (This was because the enzymes produced by the stomach didn't stop working.)

OH DEAR – IT MUST HAVE BEEN SOMETHING YOU ATE!

3 Claude Bernard (1813-1878)

Claim to fame: French scientist. Cut up loads of human bodies and made disgusting discoveries about blood and nerves.

Revolting research: Kidnapped dogs (or should this be "dognapped"?) for his experiments. Poked tubes into the poor pooches' stomachs to find out what was going on.

Emetic experiment: Added juice from a dog's pancreas to fatty foods.

Disgusting discovery: The fats were digested and made a greasy mess. (This was because digestive juices produced by the pancreas digest fats.)

Could you perform experiments like these? Would you want to? If your answer is "YUGGGHHH!" or "WHICH WAY TO THE BATHROOM?!" then you don't have the stomach for the job. So you wouldn't want to be at Fort Mackinac, United States in 1822...

THE STOMACH FOR THE JOB

The young man moaned in agony. A carelessly loaded shotgun had exploded – blasting a 15-cm hole in Alexis St Martin's side ... you could see all his insides. The young Canadian hunter had two broken ribs, a damaged lung and ... a hole in his stomach.

Dr William Beaumont looked at these injuries and shook his head sadly. The patient would die soon. Very soon. In those days the only treatment for this type of wound was to slap on a bandage and arrange the funeral. But against all expectations, Alexis survived the night. Weeks became months and the young man even started to get better! But he had an embarrassing problem.

The stomach hole refused to heal. So whenever he felt peckish Alexis had to bandage his tum to stop its gruesome contents from slopping out!

Oddly enough, the young man cheerfully put up with this appalling arrangement. So the devious doctor seized the opportunity to perform some gruesome gut experiments. One day he asked Alexis to swallow a bit of raw meat on a thread. Later he pulled it up again to see how it had changed. On another occasion Dr Beaumont poked a thermometer though the hole and watched it leap about as the stomach churned!

The doctor soon discovered that stomach juice is produced in large amounts when there is food in the stomach. So he drained some of Alexis's stomach juice out through a pipe and tried to identify the chemicals it contained. First of all he tasted it – YUCK! But as he wasn't sure what it was he sent it to some scientist friends.

They discovered the juice contained hydrochloric acid – a powerful dissolving chemical. This is useful for breaking down food and killing germs.

Sometimes the doctor and his patient would have a row. You've got to see it from Alexis's point of view. For two years Dr Beaumont had nursed him. But on the other hand ...well, if there's one thing worse than having a hole in your body – it's being chased around by a meddlesome medic trying to terrorize your tummy. And over the next few years Dr Beaumont took to following Alexis so he could perform even more horrible experiments!

Oddly enough these shouting matches provided Dr Beaumont with yet more sickening scientific data. He couldn't help noticing that when Alexis got cross, his stomach went all red and quivery!

At last in 1833 Dr Beaumont published his findings. It had taken 11 years of tests and tantrums. Packed full of stomach-churning pictures, the book was an overnight success. The doctor achieved fame and fortune. Yet he owed his entire achievement to one gruesome fact ... he'd had the stomach for the job!

A WEIGHTY MATTER

Three hundred years ago an Italian scientist named Santorio Santorio decided to build an incredible weighing machine. It swung from the ceiling and was big enough for his chair, desk and bed! There was even room for his prized silver chamber pot. Every day Santorio sat in the machine and recorded his weight.

For 30 years he weighed himself. He weighed himself before meals, after meals and during meals. He even weighed all his waste products.

But he still couldn't figure it out. Why did his food weigh more than the contents of his silver chamber pot?

Here's the answer. Much of the missing food turns into energy to power the body. Digested food molecules go from the guts to the blood and then off to feed billions of hungry body cells. Spare sugar and fats get carted off by a useful blood vessel to the storage place in the liver.

Blood, bones and body bits fact file

Name of body part: Liver

Where found: On top of the guts and under the diaphragm.

Useful things it does: What doesn't it do? (See below.)

Grisly details: If the liver doesn't work, waste body products build up in the skin.

Amazing features: You can lose 90 per cent of your liver and survive. That little bit of liver grows into a lovely new liver!

THE LIVELY LIVER

Yes – your liver certainly has a good time – scientists know of 500 jobs it tackles. There may be even more that haven't yet been discovered! The liver...

• Controls the amount of sugar in the blood. This is done with the aid of a substance called insulin produced by the pancreas. Too little insulin causes a disease called diabetes.

• Stores spare fat and carbohydrates.

• Makes Vitamin A

• Gets rid of old red blood cells.

• Produces digestive juices.

• Keeps you warm – all these activities produce heat!

But not all your food is used by the body. Some of it just isn't needed – so the body chucks it out!

GRUESOME GARBAGE DISPOSAL 1 - WASTE FOOD

1 Every day some of your food puts in a reappearance. It's stained brown by the liver's digestive juices – lovely.

2 This waste food is called faeces – that's Latin for "dregs" – which just about sums it up.

3 Children produce 65–171 g of the stuff every day. Some fearless scientists have discovered that faeces is 75 per cent water, and of the solid material that's left, two thirds of it is food that your body can't digest such as fibre, fruit skins and seeds. And the other third is made up of … germs!

4 Yes! Your guts swarm with billions of germs that have somehow managed to get past the acid in the stomach. Ugh! Fortunately few of them do much harm.

5 UNFORTUNATELY, they do produce gases which, added to the gases from food and drink, can reappear at either end of the body – with hilarious or embarrassing but always noisy (and sometimes smelly) results.

6 But the really bad news is that these gases include methane, a chemical that burns easily. (NOTE: please don't experiment on yourself or your teacher to prove this. One surgeon cut open a man's guts and caused a gas explosion!)

GRUESOME GARBAGE DISPOSAL 2 - WASTE WATER

Much of your food is made up of water. Cucumbers, for example, are 90 per cent water and ten per cent vegetable. Your body is over two-thirds water and water is very useful for making lots of gruesome body fluids such as tears, runny snot and digestive juices. But spare water just isn't needed so it's filtered out by your kidneys.

Blood, bones and body bits fact file

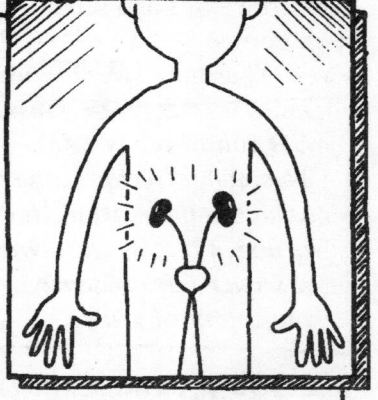

Name of body part: Kidneys

Where found: You've got two at the back of your body just below your lowest ribs.

Useful things it does: Remove spare water, unwanted salt and waste chemicals from the blood.

Grisly details: If not enough water passes through the kidneys the waste forms agonisingly painful stones.

Amazing features: Your kidneys filter up to 1,500 litres of blood every day.

HOW THE KIDNEYS WORK

The kidneys are like millions of tiny coffee filters linked up to a drainpipe.

1 Each filter takes the form of a tiny tube.

2 A little capsule at the start of each tube takes in fluid from the blood.

3 As the fluid runs down the tube, all the really useful stuff such as molecules of food escape back into the blood.

4 All the useless unwanted water plus any extra salts and poisonous wastes trickle down the drainpipe into the bladder.

5 This watery waste is urine.

Bet you never knew!
You can discover a person's state of health by studying their urine. Too much sugar in the urine is a sign of diabetes. Doctors used to taste urine to discover this! Disease may also cause a change in the colour of urine.

ARE YOU A URINE EXPERT?

Can you link the colour of these urine samples to the disease? Note: feel free to colour in the urine yourself!

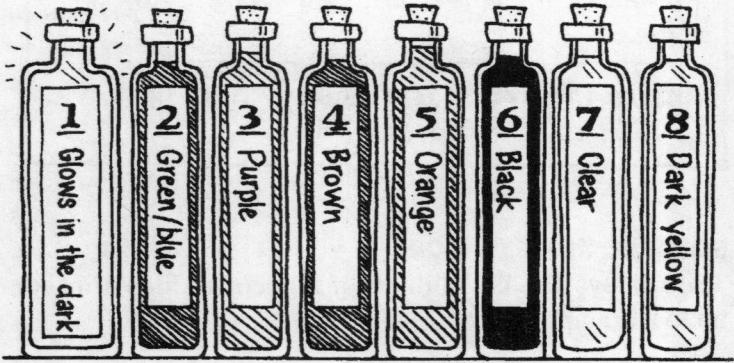

Cause of the colour...

a) The patient has been injected with blood from an animal.

b) Blackwater fever – a nasty tropical disease.

c) The patient has been eating too many food colourings.

d) The patient has been drinking a lot of liquid.

e) The patient has been eating too much beetroot or blackberries.

f) The patient is feverish and has lost a lot of water by sweating.

g) The patient has been eating too many carrots.

h) The patient is a space monster.

Answers: 1 h) **2** c) **3** e) **4** b) **5** g) **6** a) **7** d) **8** f)

Of course, your kidneys couldn't work if your blood wasn't doing its job. That's rushing round your body as fast as your heaving heart can pump it out! Warning. If the sight of buckets of blood makes you wobble at the knees it's wise to put on a blindfold before reading the next chapter.

THE BLOODY BITS

You may think that EVERYTHING to do with the body is bloodcurdling. But some bits are bloodier than others. Take, for example, blood itself and the heart that keeps it moving. But blood is also vital for life – here's why ...

Blood, bones and body bits fact file

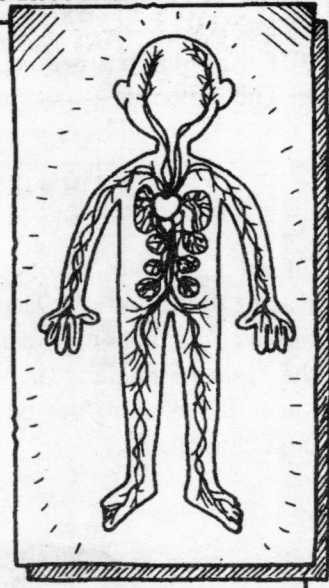

Name of body part: Blood

Where found: Throughout the body in a network of blood vessels. You've got about five litres of the red stuff.

Useful things it does: Delivers food and oxygen and other useful things your cells need to keep going.

Grisly details: You can lose one third of your blood without harm. But if you lose half – it's FATAL!

Amazing features: Blood is so full of things that it's amazing they all fit in – see below.

BLOOD - WHAT'S IN IT FOR ME?

1 Your blood is yellow! Yes it's true. If you leave a test tube full of blood for a few hours the blood cells sink to the bottom and you're left with a clear yellow fluid.

2 The yellow stuff is called plasma – it's 90 per cent water and 10 per cent chemicals such as those tasty molecules and minerals that your cells need to grow and stay healthy. Scientists have discovered how to dry plasma to a powder and turn it back into a liquid by adding water.

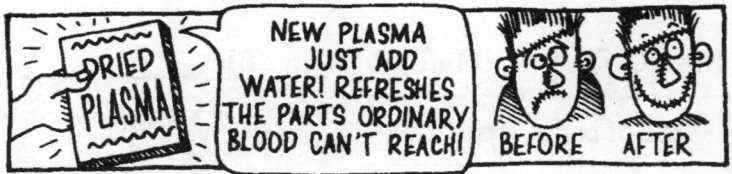

DRIED PLASMA

NEW PLASMA JUST ADD WATER! REFRESHES THE PARTS ORDINARY BLOOD CAN'T REACH!

BEFORE AFTER

3 Imagine blood as a sort of hot soup squirting through your body. It's full of sugars and other molecules from your food – which is why vampires and mosquitoes find it so tasty.

AND IT ISN'T TOMATO SOUP!

4 Blood is thicker than water. In fact it's THREE TIMES thicker. That's not surprising considering that blood is swarming with cells …here's what you get in one teeny little millimetre-sized drop!

• 7,000 white blood cells.

• 300,000 platelets – (these are little bits of bone-marrow cell that help your blood to clot).

• 5 million red blood cells.

Impressive isn't it? But that's nothing...

5 In all your body contains...

35,000,000,000 (35 million) white blood cells,

1,500,000,000,000 (1.5 trillion) platelets and

25,000,000,000,000,000 (25,000 trillion) red blood cells.

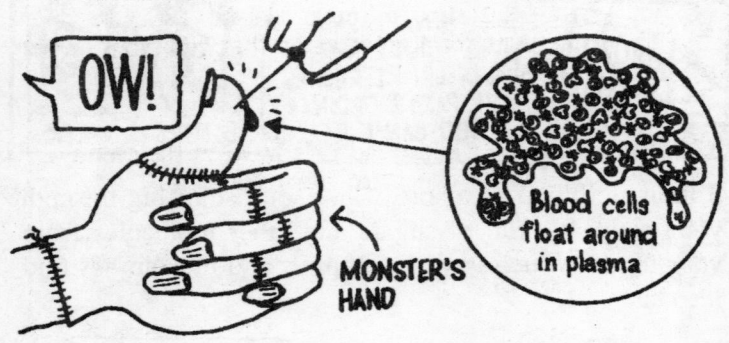

Or so the scientists say...

6 But this is only guesswork because it's impossible to count all those cells.

7 The problem isn't just the huge numbers. Every second 3 million new red blood cells are made in your bone marrow and 3 million others die. So by the time you've finally finished counting – you've got to start all over again!

8 There's plenty of room for all these blood cells. The body contains about 96,558 km of blood vessels. If you took someone's blood vessels and laid them end-to-end they'd go twice round the world. Just imagine a motorway like that!

But if you want to zoom along the blood superhighway in your very own nippy little red blood cell you'll have to learn the rules of the road.

THE BLOOD HIGHWAY CODE

 **RULE 1:** Understand the one way system. Arteries go <u>AWAY</u> from the heart and veins go <u>TOWARDS</u> the heart. <u>NOT THE OTHER WAY ROUND!</u>

 **RULE 2:** No "U" turns allowed. Valves in the veins form bottle necks that stop you reversing.

 **RULE 3:** Red blood cells travel in the centre and white cells creep along the edges.

 **RULE 4:** Make sure you can identify these other road users.

RED BLOOD CELLS   WHITE BLOOD CELLS   PLATELETS

 **RULE 5:** Make sure you don't go over the speed limits. In the big arteries over the heart it's one metre every two seconds. In the capillaries - that's the very tiny blood vessels - it's one metre every half-an-hour!

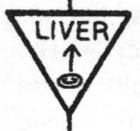 **RULE 6:** After four months all the red blood cells must report to the liver scrap yard to be broken up. All platelets to be broken up after two weeks.

 **RULE 7:** Beware of blood clots around wounds! All the platelets stick together and produce chemicals that make the plasma sticky. Other road users steer clear - unless you're a real clot!

115

If you ever get a bit short of blood you might need a blood transfusion. That's when you're given someone else's blood instead of your own. Luckily you don't have to give it back.

A BLOOD-CURDLING STORY

Three centuries ago scientists began to wonder whether it was possible to inject blood into humans. But would it work? There was only one way to find out!

One day in 1667 an audience of top British scientists gathered to watch a terrifying trial transfusion. At the centre of attention was a man who had bravely volunteered to have an extra 340 g of blood injected into his veins. The red stuff had been kindly donated by – a sheep!

1 Can you guess what happened?
a) The volunteer survived.
b) The volunteer's hair turned woolly and he died.
c) The volunteer went mad.

Answer: c) He was described as a bit "cracked in the head". But the scientists reckoned the test worth repeating and more blood transfusions were performed.

But then disaster struck. A man died after another blood transfusion in France. No one knew why! The doctor who performed the operation was accused of murder and although he was found not guilty the French government banned all transfusions.

Meanwhile the Brits carried on. In those days the technology was rather primitive. One day a doctor offered a sick old man the chance of a blood transfusion. Here's what the doctor planned to do...

• Fix a silver pipe to each end of a length of chicken gut.
• Wash the chicken gut out with warm water.
• Stick one silver pipe in the arm of a healthy volunteer.
• Stick the other pipe in the old man's veins.
• Allow the blood to flow into the old man.

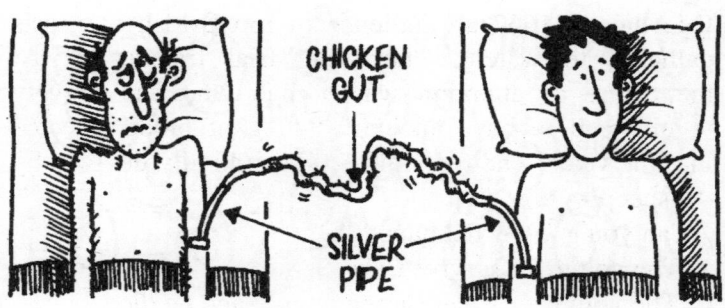

CHICKEN GUT

SILVER PIPE

2 What do you think happened next?
a) The old man said "YUCK – NOT ON YOUR LIFE!" and died soon afterwards.
b) The old man said "YES" but the transfusion bumped him off.
c) The old man said "YES" – he got better but the volunteer died!

Answer: a)

During a transfusion there was a risk of blood clots forming and blocking vital blood vessels. But what caused these killer clots? The answer emerged in 1900 when Austrian scientist Karl Landsteiner discovered that blood was divided into groups. Your blood group depends on the type of chemicals carried by your red blood cells. When red blood cells from different blood groups collide they mistake one other for germs! Germ-zapping chemicals on the outside of each cell zip into action and the cells end up glued together.

Nowadays blood can be stored in a blood bank until it's needed by someone with the same group. Blood banks don't save money but they do save lives. But sadly Karl's was not one of them. In 1943 he died of a heart attack caused by ... a blood clot.

Oddly enough while some doctors were trying to give their patients extra blood, others were trying to take it away again. These doctors thought that too much blood was bad for you.

BLOODTHIRSTY BLEEDERS

Yes – 200 years ago your local friendly doctor would do more than give you nasty cough medicine! He'd also try to open your veins to remove all that nasty bad blood!

In those days doctors had a selection of vicious looking knives especially designed for this gruesome job.

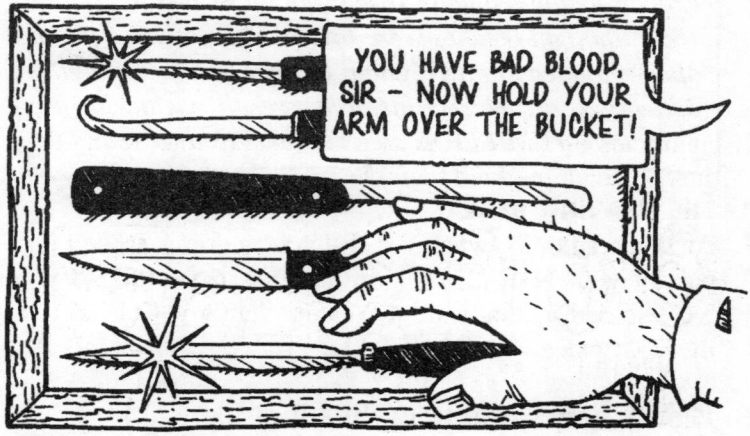

YOU HAVE BAD BLOOD, SIR – NOW HOLD YOUR ARM OVER THE BUCKET!

So you don't like the look of them? Well, don't worry – you do have another choice. Can you guess what it is?

A ROTTEN RIDDLE

What's green and yellow and dripping with slime, got 10 stomachs, has three stabbing teeth at the front end and by the time it's finished with you it's 15 cm long and GORGED WITH ALL YOUR BLOOD!?

Answer: It's a LOATHSOME leech!!!

And here's the really BAD news! Surgeons were particularly keen on using leeches to take blood from children. They reckoned it was kinder than cutting the kids with the knives!

119

THE HEAVING HEART

As you read this – whatever else you're doing, there's one part of your body that's hard at work. Especially if you were scared by that last bit. Yes, it's lucky your heart's in the right place.

Blood, bones and body bits fact file

Name of body part: Heart

Where found: The top of your heart is about 8cm to the left of your breast bone.

Useful things it does: Keeps your blood moving.

Grisly details: Your heart isn't heart-shaped – it's blob-shaped with a tangle of blood vessels on top. It's about 12cm high and weighs 250–300g.

Amazing features: It's horribly hard-working (see opposite page).

THE HORRIBLY HARD-WORKING HEART

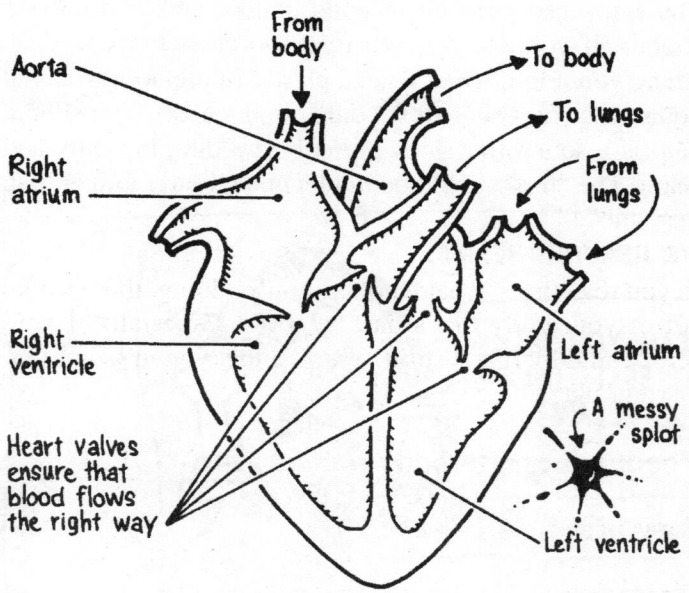

Aorta

From body

To body

To lungs

Right atrium

From lungs

Right ventricle

Left atrium

A messy splot

Heart valves ensure that blood flows the right way

Left ventricle

• Your heart is strong enough to pump blood round your body in one minute.
• Its speed is controlled by the brain and influenced by your feelings – this is why your heart beats faster before a science test. But the heart itself is powered by a built-in pacemaker that triggers the heartbeat with tiny electric shocks. So it's got to keep going!
• In just one day your heart pumps enough blood to fill a 10,000 litre tanker.
• In an average lifetime it beats 3,000,000,000 times.
• And pumps over 300 million litres of blood. That's enough to fill 5,500 large swimming pools!
• And in all that time your heart doesn't stop once, not even when you're asleep.

Dare you discover ... how your heart beats?

You will need yourself, a good pair of ears and a close friend. (If you don't want to get too close to your close friend you might want to get a plastic funnel too.) Just put your ear or funnel against your friend's heart. You should hear is a sound that goes lup-dub, lup-dub, lup-dub, and so on. The "lup" should be louder and slightly longer than the "dub".

CAN YOU MAKE IT BEAT LOUDER PLEASE?

Look at the diagram on page 121. Each of the four chambers pumps blood in the direction shown. The "lup" sound is the valves at the opening of the ventricles slamming shut. Then the ventricles squeeze the blood out and the "dub" sound you can hear is the closing of the heart valves to prevent the blood squirting backwards.

Your heart isn't the only part of your body that beats. You can feel the blood pulsing in places such as the side of your wrist just under your thumb and on the sides of your neck. What causes these pulses?

a) The arteries pumping the blood forward.

b) The arteries bulging out as a surge of blood from the heart passes by.

c) A bulge in the veins caused by the blood stopping for a moment.

You might wonder why half your heart is squirting blood to your lungs. Well, your lungs are more than a couple of wheezy wind-bags. They're needed to supply your body with oxygen, and the blood takes the oxygen round your body. And without this gas you'd be gasping!

THE GASPING LUNGS

You need your lungs like a breath of fresh air. Literally. Day after day, year after year, your lungs keep puffing away – about 600 million puffs in a lifetime. And you never need to remind them to do their job. But it's a difficult job and the facts that follow about breathing will leave you gasping.

Blood, bones and body bits fact file

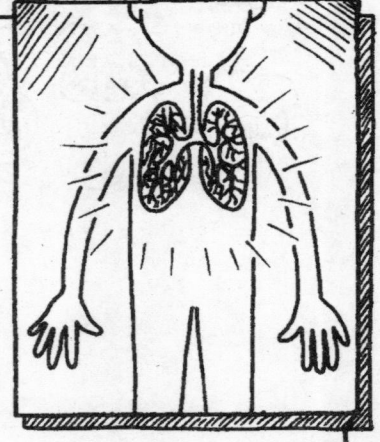

Name of body part: Lungs

Where found: In the chest on either side of the heart. The heart fits into a snug little hollow against the left lung.

Useful things they do: Breathe in air so that oxygen can get into your blood and supply your cells.

Grisly details: Once smokers get ash into their lungs they NEVER get it out again. Heavy smokers' lungs end up like tacky old tar buckets.

Amazing features: Your lungs contain 750 million little tubes and capsules. If these were laid out flat they could cover a tennis court.

BREATHING: THE INSIDE STORY

"As easy as breathing" – or so they say. But in fact there's nothing easy about breathing. Here's what happens when you try.

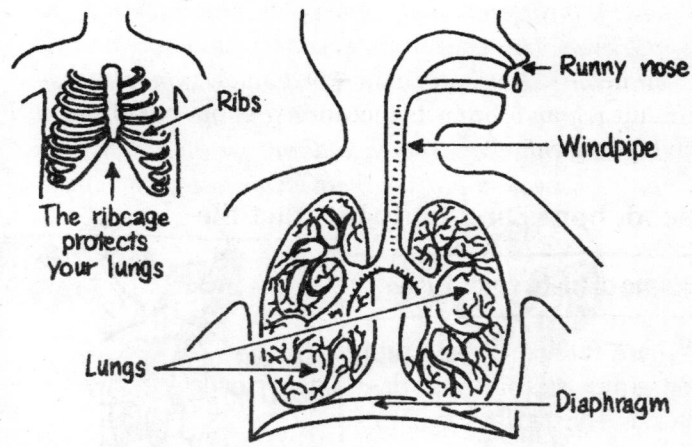

1 Diaphragm (dia-fram) pulls down.
2 Your rib cage rises up.
3 Air is breathed in through your nose and mouth.
4 The air ends up in little capsules called alveoli (al-ve-ol-i).

YOUR BREATHING SPACE

The alveoli are the places where breathing actually takes place. Oxygen gas from the air passes into the blood and hops aboard red blood cells for a free ride round the body. Meanwhile the carbon-dioxide gas (produced as a waste product by your cells and dissolved in the blood) is rushing the other way. All this takes just one third of a second. Then the breathing steps 1–4 go into reverse as the air is puffed out again. Yes, it all happens with breathless speed.

Bet you never knew!

Have you got blue blood in your veins? When red blood cells take oxygen from the lungs they're bright red. But after the cells give up their oxygen they're dark red. This is why you get dark-red blood in veins returning to the heart. If you are fair-skinned these veins appear blue! It was once said the nobility had blue blood. They stayed indoors so their skin was pale and you could see their gruesome blue veins!

WHO'S FAKING THEIR NOBILITY?

TEST YOUR TEACHER

Is your teacher full of hot air? This tricky test will leave them breathless.

Here's a clue to start them off. An adult breathes about 6 litres of air a minute.

1 A man stands in a telephone box to make a phone call. The telephone box contains about 270 litres of air, and once the door is closed no more air can get in. How long can the man speak on the phone before he faints from lack of air?

a) 45 minutes

b) 4 hours

c) 45 hours

2 A woman goes to sleep in a room 1.8 x 1.8 x 1.5 metres. The room contains about 1,300 litres of air. Would she have enough air to survive the night? (Clue: you only need about half the normal amount of air when you're asleep.)

a) Yes – and the following day too!

b) No – she'd die of suffocation.

c) Yes – just about!

3 Think about the size of the room in question 2. How much air do you need to last a lifetime?

a) Enough to fill two large airships.

b) Enough to fill a small hot-air balloon.

c) Enough to fill 339,174 hot-air balloons.

4 Why would someone die if they tried to hide in a lake and breathe through a hollow reed?

a) The lungs can't work in very cold water.

b) The water pressing against the body stops the lungs from breathing out.

c) The water gets in through the ears and drowning follows.

5 A woman has an attack of hiccupping. What part of her breathing equipment is making her hiccup?

a) Her diaphragm.

b) Her ribs.

c) Her lungs.

Answers: 1 a) This really was a problem in old-fashioned phoneboxes! **2 c) 3 a)** That's 368,000 cubic metres of air. **4 b)** You cannot do this more than 23 cm below the surface. **5 a)** It's generally caused by eating and drinking too quickly.

128

What do you think caused this dramatic cure?

a) A massive electric shock.

b) A faith healer.

c) She had an operation.

TRICKY!

Dare you discover ... how you talk?

TALKING. Some people never seem to stop. This sad affliction is particularly common amongst teachers. Naturally YOU know how to talk (and when to stop). But can you say what part your lungs play?

Halfway up your windpipe is a triangular opening. It's behind the little bump in your throat that some people call the "Adam's apple". On two sides of this opening, folds of skin stretch as you speak and wobble as air puffs past from the lungs. They're your vocal chords. The larger the chords, the deeper the sounds you can make (this is why most children have squeaky voices).

The basic sounds produced by your vibrating vocal chords are altered by the position of your tongue, lower lip and jaw. You can see how important these bits are when you try this unspeakable speech challenge.

1 Say the word "she" whilst keeping your tongue in your cheek (so you can't move it!).

2 Say the word "pie" without your lips touching one another.

3 Put your hand under your chin and try to talk without your lower jaw moving down.

DON'T WORRY IF YOU LOOK AND SOUND LIKE A JIBBERING IDIOT!

Which of the above were:
a) Possible
b) Just possible but it sounded funny.
c) Impossible
Enjoy endless fun watching your friends attempt the same challenge!

Answers: 1 b) 2 c) 3 b)

GASPING LUNGS SOUND EFFECTS
Here are a few other sounds your gasping lungs can make...

YAWNING
This may be a way of cooling your brain by suddenly taking a deep gulp of air. It can also be triggered by boring science lessons.

LAUGHING

This happens when deep breaths, caused by movements of the diaphragm, are followed by a few short puffs of air from your lungs. This can be triggered by watching your teacher fall off his bicycle.

CRYING

Your breathing is exactly the same as when you laugh. Only your feelings are different. Crying may occur as a direct result of having laughed at your teacher.

But whatever you do with your lungs there is something you ought to know first. And it's no laughing matter … here's the bad news.

BREATHING IS BAD FOR YOU

The air you breathe isn't always as pure as it could be. Especially if you live in a big city. Yes – every day you breathe in 20,000 million tiny bits of pollution, dust and dirt! THE GOOD NEWS … your body has ways of dealing with unwelcome visitors.

1 Inside your nose, windpipe and lung tubes there are tiny hairs called cilia. (silly-er). Their job is to waft all that nasty stuff back into your mouth and nostrils.

2 The snot in your nose and windpipe is a deadly dust trap. Once stuck in the snot there's no escape for the grimy gatecrashers. Have you ever noticed that when you work in a dirty place your snot turns black?!

THE BETTER NEWS

You can actually cough up dirt … this involves closing the top of your windpipe and then suddenly releasing it to allow a blast out a puff of air at 27 metres a second!

And sneeze out snot… Something tickles the inside of your nose. You suddenly relax your breathing muscles and squeeze the muscles of your lower body. The air trapped in your lungs blasts its way out through your nose and mouth. And it reaches speeds of over 160 km an hour!

THE REALLY BAD NEWS

It's not just dirt and debris that make you cough and sneeze. The air we breathe is laden with billions and billions of germs. And their whole aim in life is to invade your body and cause disgusting diseases! Atishooooooooo!

YES, THE NEXT CHAPTER IS DEAD INTERESTING . . .

DEADLY DISEASES

Remember that sneeze at the end of the previous chapter? It was more than just a puff of air. It was a million droplets of snotty spit and countless germs zooming through the air in search of a victim. And causing disgusting or even deadly diseases. So welcome to the war zone right inside your body! Amazingly, most of the time you don't even know a war's going on!

LITTLE MONSTERS

There are thousands of different types of germs but they fall into two main groups. The brutal bacteria and the vicious viruses – but they're all little monsters.

BRUTAL BACTERIA

Bacteria come in a variety of sinister shapes and sizes. Some look like octopuses, others are like sausages and others have little whip-like tails so they can swim around. Some bacteria can double their numbers every 20 minutes and increase their numbers eight times in one hour. In eight hours a single bacterium can make 16 million copies of itself!

There's something nasty in the garden shed. Something dark and invisible hiding in the corners of your school. And it's waiting to pounce. Many bacteria lurk in shadows because they're destroyed by sunlight. In gloomy weather they float on the wind as high as the clouds. And some are armed with poisonous toxins 100,000 times more powerful than the deadly poison strychnine!

ROGUES' GALLERY

The brutal bacteria include microbes that cause boils, tetanus and upset stomachs. Vicious viruses include colds, chickenpox and measles. There are hundreds of other disease-causing germs – here are a few of the more sinister specimens!

Botulinus (Bot-tu-line-us)

HABITS: Lurks in half-cooked potted meat, soil and rotting leaves.

DAMAGE REPORT: Deadly toxins. Cause double vision, sickness and death!

KNOWN CRIMES: Killed eight fishermen in Scotland in 1922. They had all eaten botulinus-infected sandwiches.

DANGER RATING: Deadly. It makes school dinners look healthy. (But don't worry, this disease is extremely rare!)

Leprosy

HABITS: You can only catch it from prolonged contact with people who already have the disease (and not everyone with leprosy has the catching sort anyway). Slow to develop. It can take years but in the worst cases it makes fingers and toes drop off.

DAMAGE REPORT: Attacks the nerves and skin.

KNOWN CRIMES: Affects several million people in hot countries.

DANGER RATING: Not so dangerous because it's difficult to catch - but very, very nasty if you've got it!

Typhus

HABITS: Lives inside lice that scratch their disgusting droppings into the human skin. Ugh!

DAMAGE REPORT: Causes a red rash, fever and death. Kills the louse too by the way - but who cares?

KNOWN CRIMES: Unlike most criminals, typhus germs actually enjoy prison. In 1750 infected lice jumped from criminals to the judges and jurors at a London trial. Three judges and eight jurymen suffered the death penalty.

DANGER RATING: Still common in many parts of the world but can be treated by drugs.

Vicious viruses

To a virus one of your body cells looks like a little planet. That's not surprising because viruses are thousands of times smaller even than bacteria. The virus touches down onto a body cell like a spacecraft landing on the moon. Then the vicious virus injects chemicals to make the cell produce hundreds more viruses. Within half-an-hour all the viruses fly off to seek more victims and the poor old cell splits like a pea pod. It's died from over-work!

Influenza

HABITS: Changes its form every year so your body's defences can't recognize it easily.

DAMAGE REPORT: Fever, aches and pains, runny nose - a few days off school.

KNOWN CRIMES: In 1918 a world-wide 'flu epidemic killed 25 million people.

DANGER RATING: No known cure. Luckily most types of influenza don't kill you - otherwise you'd need more than a few days off school.

THE BODY STRIKES BACK

Now for the good news. Your body is ready and waiting to bash germs – even if you're not! As part of its defences your body makes lots of germ-killing chemicals. How was this discovered? Well, the story's a bit of a weepie.

A tearful story

1. In 1921, scientist Alexander Fleming was breeding germs for an experiment. He had a bad cold. A drop of snot splashed the germs and they all died!

2. Fleming realized that snot must contain a germ-killing chemical. He experimented using blood plasma, spit and tears.

3. Tears were good germ killers. To get more, Fleming ambushed visitors to his lab and squirted lemon juice in their eyes! (Don't try this – it stings!)

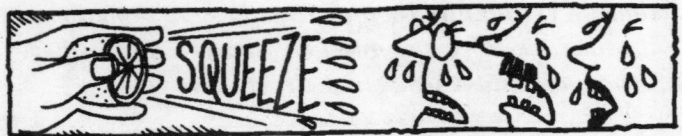

4. He even picked on small children. (He paid them afterwards.)

5. Further experiments proved that egg-white also killed germs. So Fleming started breaking eggs.

6. Then he discovered that fish eggs killed germs too. So he went fishing – oddly enough this was his hobby!

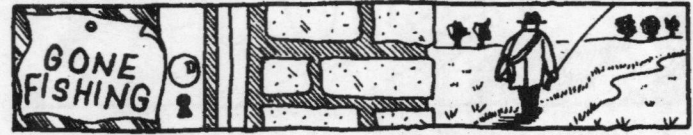

A ROTTEN RESULT

In 1965 scientists found that the germ-killing substance was an enzyme called lysozyme (lie-so-zime). It's found in all the things that Fleming tested. That's the good news. But sadly, lysozyme doesn't kill all known germs – just a few of them.

Luckily you've got a built-in army to defend you from germs. Every day they fight and die on your behalf. Recognize them? They're your wonderful white blood cells – all 35,000 million of them! Here's what they do.

Blood, bones and body bits fact file

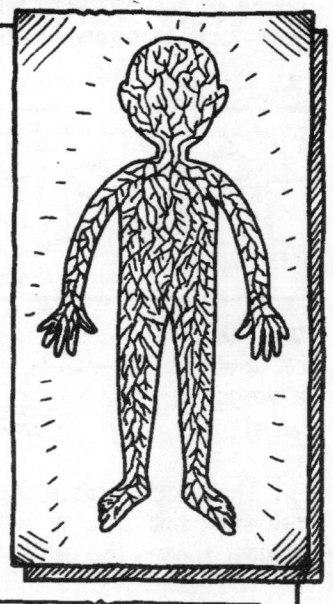

Name of body part: The immune system

Where found: A network of drainage tubes called the lymph system. Also includes your white blood cells.

Useful things they do: Fight germs and keep you healthy.

Grisly details: Pus from an infected wound consists of millions of white blood cells that have been done to death by germs.

Amazing features: White blood cells "talk" to one another using chemical substances that pass on messages such as, "Bash that virus!"

1 The tubes form a drainage system for lymph – a watery fluid that dribbles from the blood vessels.
2 Nodes: These grape-sized little lumps filter out nasty germs from the tubes. They swell up and get bigger when you're sick.

3 Spleen: Helps make white blood cells in babies.
4 Thymus makes some white blood cells.

Your battling body

Here's how your body fights back. Germs are always trying to get into your body – through your nose, in your food or through cuts and scratches.

1. But your brave white blood cells are ready . . .

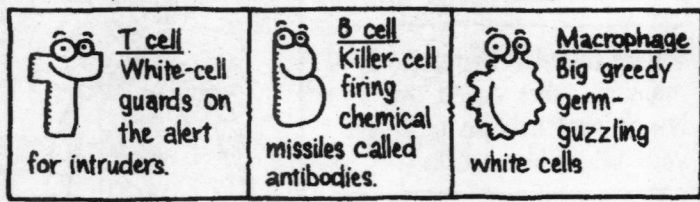

2. The T cell grabs a wriggling germ!

3. The T cell finds a B cell that makes antibodies that can stick this type of germ together. It's a desperate race against time – the germs are breeding fast!

4. The B cell fires antibodies to gum the germs together.

5. The T cell orders the B cell to make loads of copies of itself to attack any other germs loitering nearby.

140

6. The macrophage flows round the stuck-up germs. Reaches out long jelly-like arms to encircle them. Then it gobbles the germs! It can grab and guzzle 20 bacteria at a time and dissolve them whilst they're still alive! Congratulations, you win!

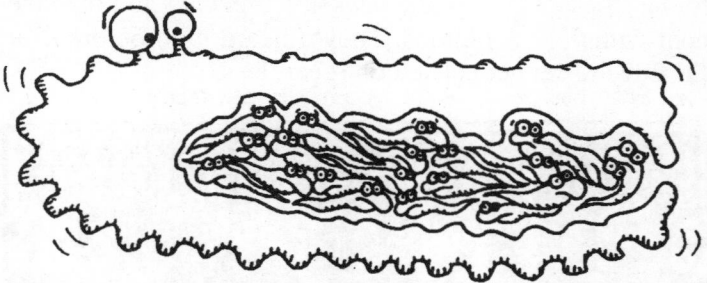

You've won if you destroy all the germs without losing too many white blood cells. It's OK to lose a few hundred thousand but lose a few billion and you're in trouble! Meanwhile bits of half-digested bacteria are left lying around on the battlefield.

HOW TO BE INCREDIBLY IMMUNE

Once you've had a certain illness, you needn't worry about getting it again – ever. Some of your white blood cells store the information about how to make the antibodies. This way, your body can store details of an incredible 18 billion types of antibody.

But sometimes your immune system needs a boost. That's why you need nasty injections. When you have a jab you are being injected with dead germs. Yuck!

These allow your body to make the antibodies needed to fight the actual full-blown disease. This painful process is called vaccination. Here's how the modern form of vaccination was developed in 1796.

JUST THE JAB

Some of the audience yawned rudely or snorted angrily. One muttered under his breath, "That Jenner's going on about cowpox again!"

These days few of the Medical Club members listened to the stocky figure in the buckskin breeches and the blue coat with yellow buttons. They'd heard it all before. But Dr Edward Jenner carried on regardless.

"Smallpox kills millions of people. It causes fever and covers the body with pus-filled spots. People lucky enough to survive are scarred for life. I believe that those who get the milder disease cowpox are protected from getting smallpox."

"Why don't you experiment?!" someone shouted.

"Yes," yelled another, "On yourself!"

"But," shouted Jenner above the uproar, "many country people also believe it to be true!"

The audience exploded with laughter – they didn't think much of country folk.

Jenner sat back down – humiliated once again. He remembered going to the doctor's as an eight-year-old boy. He was terrified of the physician and the huge needle with its thread dripping with pus from a smallpox victim. This was the traditional form of vaccination using live germs and it was very dangerous. The needle scratch was supposed to cause a mild smallpox and somehow prevent the full-blown disease. But it gave young Jenner such a terrible fever that he nearly died.

There had to be a better way. Jenner was certain that people who got cowpox from milking infected cows never got smallpox. If only he could prove it...

I MUST PROVE MY THEORY!

One day, a young milkmaid named Sara Nelmes came into the tiny garden hut that Jenner used as his surgery. The girl was in a bad way.

She'd scratched her hand and as the doctor examined her he noticed bluish raised-up spots.

"You have the cowpox, Sara?"

"Yes, sir," the milkmaid blushed. "But at least I won't get the smallpox."

Jenner smiled. "Sara, with your permission I would like to perform a small experiment."

With a needle Dr Jenner took a drop of pus from Sara's hand and then... This was the moment for which he had waited for over 20 years. He decided to inject the pus into an eight-year-old boy named James Phipps. Then Jenner saw the fear in the child's eyes and remembered his own terror of the doctor with the huge needle.

So Jenner closed his eyes and gritted his teeth as he made two scratches on the boy's arm. In the next few days James would suffer the sores and discomfort of cowpox. But would this be enough to ward off the more deadly threat of smallpox?

Six weeks later Jenner held his breath as he scratched poor James again – this time with pus from a smallpox victim. Now came the real test. There would be a two week pause and then ... what? Perhaps the boy would suffer crippling backaches, the fever and shivering and the deadly killer spots. Supposing Jenner was wrong ... the child might even die. And then the doctor would face the death penalty for murdering his young patient!

But weeks passed and James remained healthy. The child was now immune to smallpox. Some people still jeered. They sang songs about people turning into cows after a cowpox injection.

"On their foreheads, o horrible crumpled horns bud; Tom with his tail, and poor William all hairy . . ."

But Dr Jenner soon hit back with a book packed with tasteful colour pictures of pus-filled cowpox blisters. More physicians backed the doctor and soon richer people began to ask for the treatment. It proved to be "just the jab" for beating smallpox. Dr Jenner grew rich and successful but he never forgot the young boy who had made it possible. What did he give James as a thank-you present?

a) His very own thatched cottage with flowers round the door.

b) A needle made from solid gold.

c) One shilling (that's equivalent to 5p).

Answer: a)

SMALLPOX SMASHED

The virus that caused smallpox was living on borrowed time. Throughout Europe and North America governments began to organize vaccination programmes. In 1980 a determined worldwide campaign of vaccination led to a historic announcement from the World Health

Organization … smallpox had been wiped off the face of the Earth. Meanwhile, scientists had discovered vaccines for many more diseases. In 1994 all British kids were given measles jabs. Ouch!

But even if you manage to remain healthy your body never stays the same. There's always something going on even if it's a bit of a pain. Oh well – it's all part of growing up.

GROWING PAINS

You might not always like your body – but it'll grow on you. You were growing even before you were born and you spend your first 20 years getting bigger. Growing is a bit of a pain for your parents because you always need new clothes and shoes. But after you stop growing you start ageing – and that's even more of a pain!

RELATIVELY PAINFUL

Some of the biggest growing pains are caused by stupid comments from your relatives. Every Christmas they burst into your home to inspect you from head to toe and exclaim, "Haven't you grown!" At this point the best thing to do is to look rather sad and say...

HAVEN'T YOU SHRUNK?

On second thoughts – better keep quiet or you won't get any presents. Here are a few things you need to know about growing.

TALL STORIES

1 You don't grow at the same speed all the time. You grow quickly in your first two years. Then up to the age of ten your growth steadies before speeding up again in your teenage years.

2 As you grow, the proportions of your body change. For example, a baby's head takes up about 25 per cent of its length. But in an adult the head is only 12.5 per cent of its body length.

3 It's lucky these things happen otherwise you'd look pretty odd. You wouldn't want a giant-sized head – would you?

But why do people grow? If you asked a scientist this interesting question you wouldn't just get one answer – you'd get two!

1 The fairly simple answer.

2 The excruciatingly complicated but fascinating answer involving large dollops of scientific gobbledegook.

So which do you want to hear first?

THE HUMAN STRUCTURE ENLARGES WHEN TRIGGERED BY CHROMOSOMAL AND HORMONAL CHANGES, BLAH, BLAH, BLAH . . .

THE FAIRLY SIMPLE ANSWER

The speed at which you grow is affected by diet. Eat a normal balanced amount of food and you'll grow taller than if you lived off scraps that the pigs won't eat. (No, I'm not talking about school dinners!) Health is also an important factor. Some bone diseases stop people from growing properly.

THE EXCRUCIATINGLY COMPLICATED ANSWER...

The speed at which you grow is controlled by a hormone produced in your brain. So what exactly is a hormone? I'm afraid you've got to know this you before you can begin to understand the excruciatingly complicated answer...

Blood, bones and body bits fact file

Name of body part: Hormones

Where found: Made by glands in different parts of the body.

Useful things they do: Cause changes in the body. For example, some hormones give teenagers a grown-up appearance.

Grisly details: Hormones cause horrible problems (see below).

Amazing features: Cortisol (cor-tis-sol), made by the adrenal glands, is a chemical alarm clock that wakes you up!

Where to find your glands...

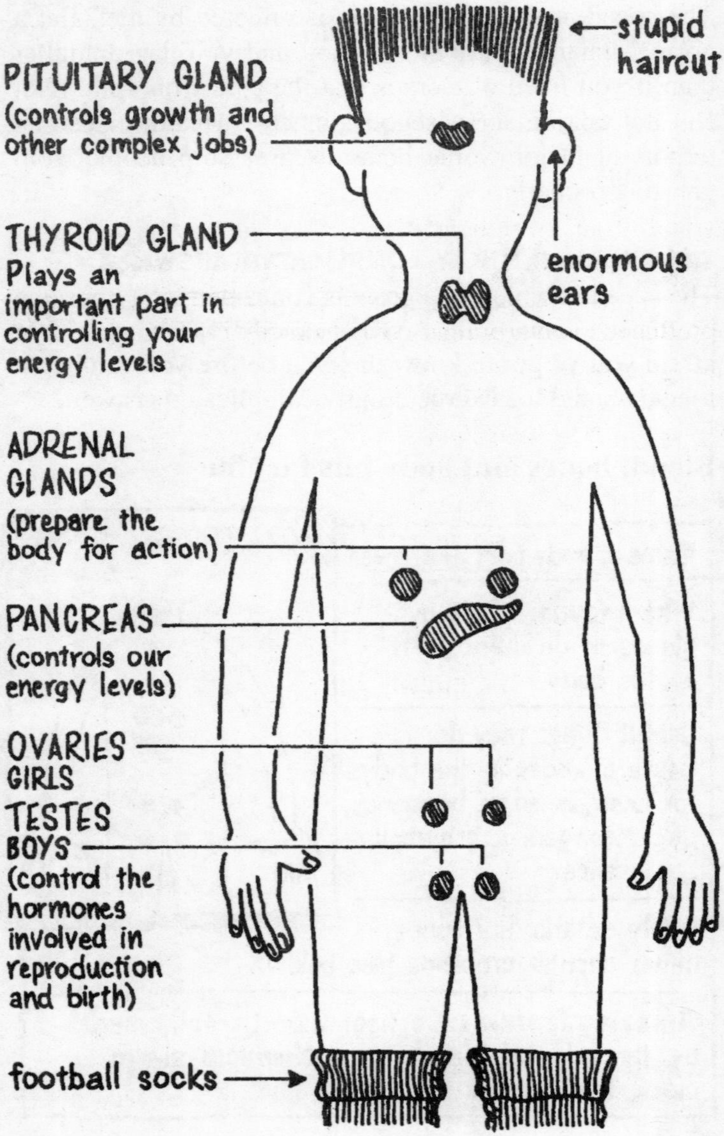

→ stupid haircut

PITUITARY GLAND
(controls growth and
other complex jobs)

THYROID GLAND
Plays an
important part in
controlling your
energy levels

enormous
ears

ADRENAL
GLANDS
(prepare the
body for action)

PANCREAS
(controls our
energy levels)

OVARIES
GIRLS

TESTES
BOYS
(control the
hormones
involved in
reproduction
and birth)

football socks →

GROWING AND GENES

Here lies the answer to the question, "Why do people grow?" The pituitary also makes the hormone that tells your body to grow! Growth hormone burrows through a cell and into the nucleus to meet – the genes. The hormone tells the genes to order the cells to grow and divide so your body can grow. So what on earth are genes? (Told you this was complicated!)

Bet you never knew!
Genes are found on 46 stringy objects called chromosomes. They contain a chemical code that tells the body what it should look like. This code stores an awesome amount of information. If you wrote out the code from just one cell in letters the size of the words in this book it would be 10,000 km long.

CHROMOSOMES

GROWING PLACES

Your relatives might think you've grown quite a bit in the last year but that's nothing to the amount of growing you did before you were born. You probably can't remember that far back – so here's what happened.

Most animals mate to make new offspring. (The only creatures that don't are tiny jelly-like things that you can only see through a microscope. They split in two – which sounds really painful.) But we humans also mate to make children. Well, just imagine your poor parents having to split in two to make your little brother!

The aim of mating is to allow the male and female parents to mix their genes up. That's why children end up looking a bit like both their parents.

The genes are carried in special cells called sperm and eggs. The male makes sperm cells in his testes and the female releases an egg cell from her ovaries. (In humans the egg cell is far smaller than a hen's egg – in fact you need a microscope to see it at all!) The male releases 250,000,000 tiny tadpole-like sperm at a time but only one of these manages to dive into the egg to make a baby.

BABY-BUILDERS

The egg now divides into two cells, and these divide to make 4, 8,16, 32, 64, 128, 256, 512, 1,024, 2,048, 4,096, 8,192, 16,384, 32,768, 65,536 cells and so on. (You continue this list if you really want!)

So from two original cells come all the cells in the body – your muscles, bones, teeth, brain, liver, eyeballs, sweat glands and everything else. This process of division and sorting goes on until the tiny ball of cells turns into a baby. A tiny, incredible, brand-new human being.

INCREDIBLE INFANCY

Now you might think that babies are pretty useless and definitely disgusting. After all, they do nothing much except sleep, dribble, throw up and other unmentionable things. But babies are incredible (just ask their mums and dads!) and babyhood is an incredible time for the body. Which of the following are too amazing to be true?

1 In the 238 days before birth a baby's weight increases 5 million times. (Lucky you don't put on weight so quickly nowadays!) TRUE/FALSE.

2 During this time a baby floats around happily in a salty pool inside its mum's womb. It turns somersaults and even scratches itself with its fingernails. TRUE/FALSE.

3 The baby is fed from the mother though a tube called the umbilical cord that passes through its belly button. TRUE/FALSE

UMBILICAL CORD

BABY AFTER 36 WEEKS

CAN'T WAIT TO STRETCH MY LEGS!

4 Babies go through a stage before they are born when they are covered in tiny hairs. TRUE/FALSE.

5 Babies have a natural sense of rhythm. They kick their little hands and feet in time to music even before they are born. TRUE/FALSE.

6 When they are born babies can't see in colour only in black and white. TRUE/FALSE.

7 Babies can taste food better than grown-ups because they have about 9,000 more taste buds. TRUE/FALSE.
8 Babies can remember faces. TRUE/FALSE.
9 A baby can tell when someone is talking in a foreign language. TRUE/FALSE.
10 Babies sleep more but dream less than adults. TRUE/FALSE.

In the first year after they are born babies can triple their weight. Within two years they can walk and talk. At five they're old enough to go to school. And after that it's downhill all the way.

MY BABY!

APPALLING OLD AGE
Age does funny things to people. The older a grown-up gets the less willing they are to admit how old they are. You might think that your teacher is about 98. But if you

dare to ask him he might well say, "I'm in the prime of life." (Teachers are ALIVE?!) Well anyway, here are a few sure signs of ageing to look out for in your teachers.

Losing hair

Lazy pupils*

Hairy ears

Deafness

Grey hair

Hairy nostrils

Dry and wrinkly skin

Jutting chin

Blotchy skin

Shuffling walk

* That's slow-moving eyes – not the pupils he teaches.

Put on weight

Trembling hands

AMAZING OLD AGE

BUT don't conclude that your poor old teacher is a clapped-out old has-been. Remember …older people (and that includes your more mature teachers) have a vast store of wisdom and learning. Many famous people have made their greatest contribution to world history in their later years.

- Genghis Khan (1162–1227) the Mongolian soldier was conquering most of the known world when he was in his sixties.
- William Gladstone (1809–1898) was Prime Minster of Britain when he was in his eighties.
- In a single year, English novelist Barbara Cartland wrote 26 books. She was 82 at the time.
- It was claimed that Shirali Mislimov of Georgia was born in 1805 and his youngest daughter was born when he was 136. And Old Shirali was still going strong at the age of 168!

THE HORRIBLE TRUTH

Nobody's perfect. And no body is perfect either. Every body ages, aches, and suffers from disgusting diseases. Sometimes its bones get broken, too. A few scientists thought they could make something better than a human body. A new improved homemade body or a machine that could replace the body.

But was it worth the effort? For all its faults, the body is the most fantastic, the most incredible machine in the entire universe. And it's all yours! Your body can do things that no machine could ever do. It can grow, and when it works harder its muscles grow too. It can walk thousands of kilometres and not wear out. The soles of its feet even renew themselves and thicken to make walking easier.

Your body can do 101 different things, and the most amazing thing of all is that you can do them ALL AT ONCE!

• You can ride a bicycle and digest your dinner.

• Kick a football and imagine you're playing in the Cup Final.

• You can listen to music and do your homework and still guzzle a packet of crisps!

The body suffers from disgusting diseases, it's true. But then it gets better. It actually heals and repairs itself. All you have to do is to give it proper food and exercise. Treat your body well and it'll last a lifetime.

Of course if you went into Baron Frankenstein's lab and saw all the body bits, the bones and bottles of blood you might say, "Yuck, how horrible!"

But you've also got to admit that the body is more than just horrible. It's horribly amazing too! And that's horrible science for you!

158

BLOOD, BONES and BODY BITS

QUIZ

Now find out if you're a
Blood, Bones and Body Bits expert!

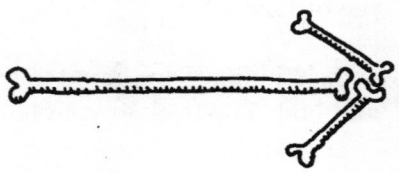

Your baffling body

Your body is the most brilliant piece of kit ever. It is so amazingly advanced that sometimes it seems too good to be true. See if you can work out which of the facts below are strange but true and which are strange but false.

1 One third of your brain cells die off every year. True or false?

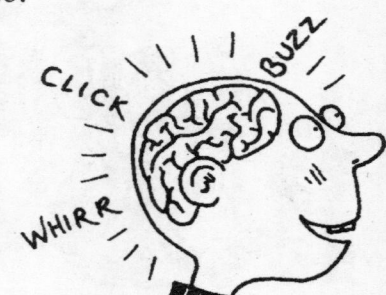

2 Your muscles can pull but they can't push. True or false?

3 Your kidneys can filter up to 200 litres of blood every minute. True or false?

4 Your brain shuts down completely while you sleep so you are unaware of any sights or sounds, or anything else that might disturb your kip. True or false?

5 You can lose half of your blood without it causing you any harm. True or false?

6 It takes less than a minute for blood to travel all the way round your body and back to your heart. True or false?

7 Everyone has exactly 206 bones in their skeleton. True or false?

8 There's a strict one-way system for blood travelling round the body. Arteries travel away from the heart and veins travel towards it. True or false?

Answers:
1 False – mind you, your brain cells start dying the moment you are born, and most of them aren't replaced!
2 True
3 True
4 False – your brain keeps listening for sounds that might suggest danger.
5 False – lose half your blood and you're as dead as a dodo's doornail.
6 True
7 False – *most* people have 206 bones, but some people have additional bones such as an extra pair of ribs.
8. True

Incredible organs

Your organs (body bits) work horribly hard throughout your life to keep you, well, alive! But do you really appreciate the hours they put in just to keep you ticking over? Take this quiz and find out just how amazing your organs are.

1 Which of your amazing organs performs more than 500 functions (and those are just the ones scientists know about)? (Clue: This could be served up in your sickening school canteen.)

2 Which of your organs is larger on the right than the left? (Clue: Take a deep breath and think carefully.)

3 What is the heaviest of all your bodily organs? (Clue: It hangs around you all the time.)

4 Which of your organs makes urine? (Clue: You have two of these wee organs.)

5 Which of your organs has to produce a new layer of mucus every two weeks to prevent it from digesting itself? (Clue: This could give you a tummy ache.)

6 In which part of the brain do you tuck away your memories? (Clue: Start at the top.)

7 Which of your bodily organs functions differently depending on your mood? (Clue: Has this one got you *beat*en?)

8 Which of your organs has no pain receptors, so surgeons can operate on it while you are awake? (Clue: This might give you a headache!)

Answers:
1 Liver
2 Lungs (the right lung is slightly larger than the left)
3 Skin (yes, the skin is an organ, and it weighs 2.5–4.5 kg depending on your size)
4 Kidneys
5 Stomach
6 Cerebrum (the top)
7 Heart (the speed at which your heart beats is affected by your feelings)
8 Brain (there are no nerves that register pain within the brain itself)

Spectacular senses

*Your senses are the
baffling body bits that
allow you to interact with
the world around you,
and provide you with a
complex cacophony of
sights sounds and smells.
But can you make sense
of the senses? Take this
quick quiz and find out.*

1 What is the chemical in your brain called that prevents
you from feeling severe pain?
a) Meissner's receptors
b) Endorphins
c) Neurofens

2 How many light-sensitive cone cells are lurking in
each of your eyeballs?
a) Six million
b) Three – one red, one blue and one green
c) 1,952

3 What function do the cilia perform in your nose?
a) They generate snot.
b) They clear mucus from the nasal passage.
c) They pass on smelly signals to the nerves.

4 Which of the following is *not* one of the five types of taste your tantalized taste buds can sense?
a) Bitter
b) Savoury
c) Umami

5 What is the medical term for being short-sighted?
a) Myopia
b) Hyperopia
c) Utopia

6 Which brilliant body part transfers information about touch to the brain?
a) Keratin in the fingernails
b) Blood vessels
c) Nerve endings

7 Which bit of your ear converts sound signals into nerve signals and sends them to the brain?
a) Earlobe
b) Eardrum
c) Cochlea

8 What two organs are linked by your eustachian tubes?
a) Eyes and nose
b) Ears and mouth
c) Mouth and eyes

Answers
1b; 2a; 3c; 4b; 5a; 6c; 7c; 8b

Fabulous body functions

Your body is made up of many amazing parts that perform all sorts of complicated tasks. Can you match the beastly body part with its fantastic function?

1 Carries information from your senses to your brain.
2 Squeezes food through your intestines.
3 Breathe in air to provide your body with oxygen.
4 Filters waste products from the blood.
5 Mashes up food so it can be digested.
6 Regulates body temperature.
7 Carries oxygen around your body.
8 Controls the amount of sugar in the blood.

a) Skin   **e)** Liver
b) Stomach   **f)** Nerves
c) Kidneys   **g)** Muscles
d) Blood   **h)** Lungs

Answers:
1f; 2g; 3h; 4c; 5b; 6a;7d; 8e

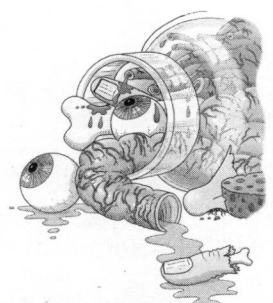

HORRIBLE INDEX

171

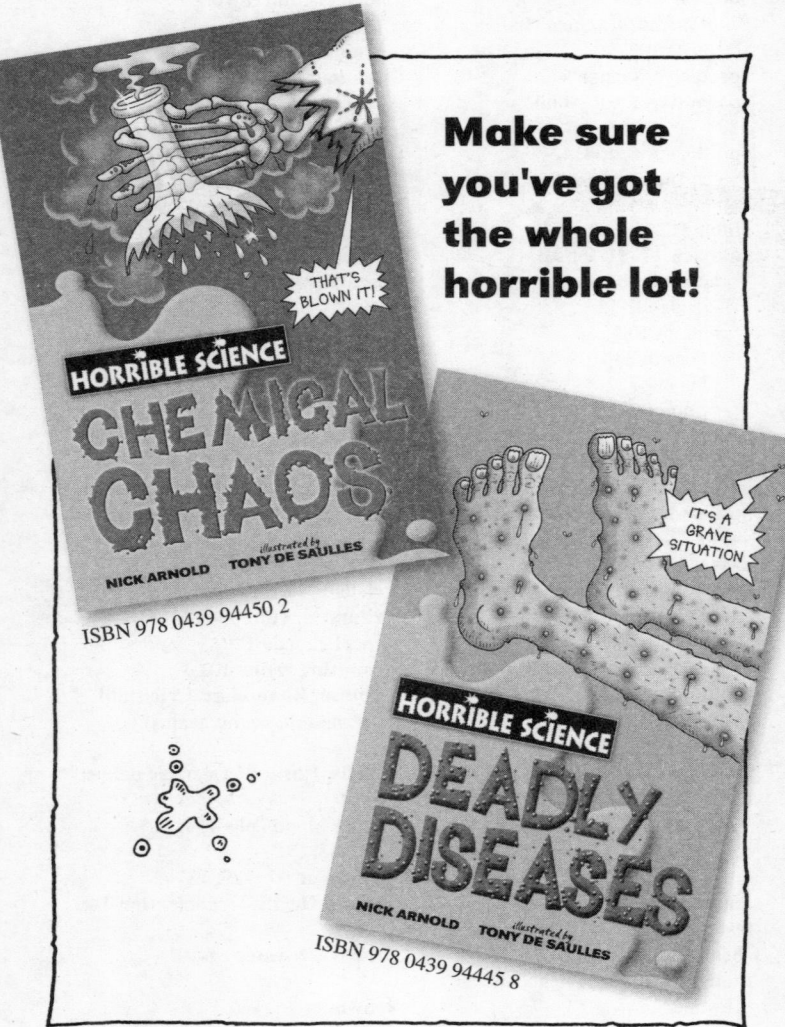

HORRIBLE SCIENCE

Make sure you've got the whole horrible lot!

ISBN 978 0439 94450 2

ISBN 978 0439 94445 8

HORRIBLE SCIENCE

I LOVE FAST FOOD!

NASTY NATURE

NICK ARNOLD   *illustrated by* TONY DE SAULLES

ISBN 978 0439 94451 9

IT TAKES GUTS!

HORRIBLE SCIENCE

DISGUSTING DIGESTION

NICK ARNOLD   *illustrated by* TONY DE SAULLES

ISBN 978 0439 94446 5

NOT A PRETTY SIGHT!

HORRIBLE SCIENCE

UGLY BUGS

NICK ARNOLD   *illustrated by* TONY DE SAULLES

ISBN 978 0439 94452 6

Science with the squishy bits left in!

Ugly Bugs • Blood, Bones and Body Bits
Nasty Nature • Chemical Chaos • Fatal Forces
Sounds Dreadful • Evolve or Die • Vicious Veg
Disgusting Digestion • Bulging Brains
Frightening Light • Shocking Electricity
Deadly Diseases • Microscopic Monsters
Killer Energy • The Body Owner's Handbook
The Terrible Truth About Time
Space, Stars and Slimy Aliens • Painful Poison
The Fearsome Fight For Flight • Angry Animals
Measly Medicine • Evil Inventions

Specials
Suffering Scientists
Explosive Experiments
The Awfully Big Quiz Book
Really Rotten Experiments

Horrible Science Handbooks
Freaky Food Experiments
Famously Foul Experiments
Beastly Body Experiments

Colour Books
The Stunning Science of Everything
Dangerous Dinosaurs Jigsaw Book

UGLY BUGS

NICK ARNOLD

illustrated by
TONY DE SAULLES

◪ SCHOLASTIC

Visit Nick Arnold at
www.nickarnold-website.com

Scholastic Children's Books,
Euston House, 24 Eversholt Street,
London, NW1 1DB, UK

A division of Scholastic Ltd
London ~ New York ~ Toronto ~ Sydney ~ Auckland
Mexico City ~ New Delhi ~ Hong Kong

First published in the UK by Scholastic Ltd, 1996
This edition published 2008

ISBN 978 0439 94452 6

Printed and bound by CPI Group (UK) Ltd, Croydon, CR0 4YY

27

CONTENTS

Nick Arnold has been writing stories and books since he was a youngster, but never dreamt he'd find fame writing about ugly bugs. His research involved being stung, crawled over and covered in slime and he enjoyed every minute of it. When he's not delving into Horrible Science, he spends

his spare time eating pizza, riding his bike and thinking up corny jokes (though not all at the same time).

Tony De Saulles picked up his crayons when he was still in nappies and has been doodling ever since. He takes Horrible Science very seriously and even agreed to investigate what happens when your body is covered in leeches. Fortunately, his injuries weren't too serious.

When he's not out with his sketchpad, Tony likes to write poetry and play squash, though he hasn't written any poetry about squash yet.

INTRODUCTION

Science can be horribly mysterious. Not just science homework – it's a mystery how they expect you to do it all. No, I mean – science itself. For example, what do scientists do all day? Ask a scientist and you'll just get a load of scientific jargon.

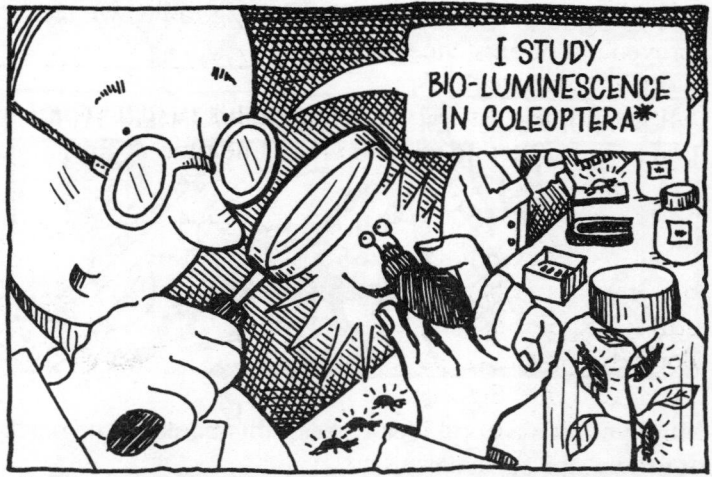

I STUDY BIO-LUMINESCENCE IN COLEOPTERA*

*ENGLISH TRANSLATION. I'M LOOKING AT BEETLES THAT GLOW IN THE DARK.

It all sounds horribly confusing. And horribly boring. But it shouldn't be. You see, science isn't about all-knowing experts in white coats and laboratories and hi-tech gadgetry. Science is about us. How we live and what happens to us every day.

And the best bits of science are also the most horrible bits. That's what this book is about. Not science, but *horrible* science. Take ugly bugs for instance. You don't need to go very far to find them. Lift up any stone and something crawls out. Look into any dark, creepy corner and there's some ugly bug lurking there. Decide on a nice early morning bath and you might discover you'll be sharing it with a huge hairy spider.

You see, ugly bugs bring science to life. Horrible life. Especially when you find out how a praying mantis catches its victims – and bites their heads off. Here's your chance to find out many more truly horrible facts about ugly bugs. And discover why for some ignorant adults an ugly bug – any ugly bug – is something to be swatted or sprayed out of existence.

Mind you, it's a good idea to keep this book out of reach of grown-ups because:
1 They might want to read it too.
2 It might give them bad dreams.
3 When you've read it you'll be far better informed than they are. You can tell them a few horrible but true scientific facts. And science will never seem the same again.

UGLY BUG FAMILIES

The worst thing about ugly bugs is that there are so many of them. There are thousands and thousands of different types. They have to be sorted out before we can even begin to get to know them. It's a horrible job – but someone has to do it. Don't worry, though, it won't be you – here's a sorting method that scientists prepared earlier.

Each type of living thing is called a species and these species are put into larger groups called genera – a bit like belonging to a club. Groups of genera make families. Confused yet? You will be.

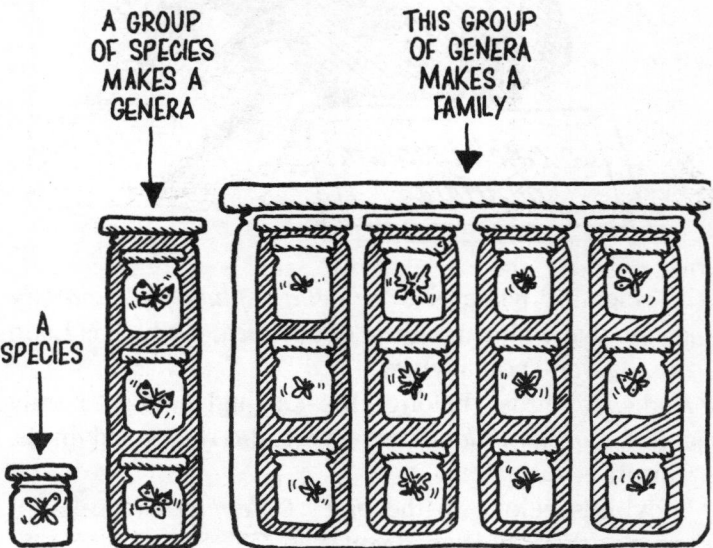

A GROUP OF SPECIES MAKES A GENERA

THIS GROUP OF GENERA MAKES A FAMILY

A SPECIES

Like any family, ugly bug family members look a bit alike. But they don't all live together in a neat little home. If they did they might start fighting over who uses the bathroom first in the morning.

Groups of related families are known as "orders". And scientists lump orders together to make huge groups called "classes". (This is nothing to do with school, even if the classes have to follow orders.)

Here's an example of what we're talking about. This little bug is a seven-spot ladybird.

MAKES ME SOUND LIKE AN ITALIAN ICE CREAM!

Coccinella septum punctata

- Its scientific name is *Coccinella septum punctata* (try saying that with a mouthful of popcorn) – which is Latin for ... seven-spot ladybird.
- And ladybirds belong to an ugly bug family called *Coccinellidae* (cock-in-ell-id-day), or ladybirds. (Surprise, surprise!)
- Ladybirds belong to the order *Coleoptera* (coe-le-op-ter-ra) – that's beetles to you.
- Beetles belong to the class *Insecta*, or insects.

Simple really! And it makes good sense for ugly bugs to be organized. There are more than 350,000 species of beetle alone. Try sorting that lot into matchboxes! So, now you know how the system works, why not flip through the ugly bug family album? First let's meet some...

IRRITATING INSECTS

Insect bodies are divided into three parts – a head, a middle bit or thorax and a bit at the back called an abdomen. An insect has two feelers (antennae) on its head and three pairs of legs attached to its thorax. Scientists have identified about a million insect species with bodies like these and there are plenty more just waiting to be discovered.

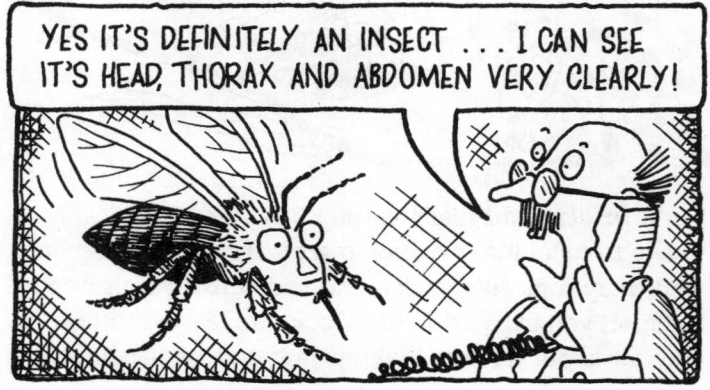

YES IT'S DEFINITELY AN INSECT . . . I CAN SEE IT'S HEAD, THORAX AND ABDOMEN VERY CLEARLY!

Earwigs At least 1,200 species. Earwigs get their name from the barmy belief that they crawl into your ears when you're asleep! They have mean-looking pincers at the back of their bodies. Males have curved pincers and females have straight ones.

Grasshoppers, crickets and locusts More than 13,000 species. They jump around and produce noises by rubbing their legs together to make themselves irresistible to the opposite sex.

Stick insects and leaf insects Over 3,000 species. Most live in tropical forests. Stick insects are so called because, well, they look like sticks, and leaf insects are so called because, you guessed it, they look like leaves. Either way they sit about all day looking like part of the furniture.

Know anyone like that? It's a clever disguise, of course, but what a life!

Beetles At least 350,000 species in this order worldwide – that's more than any other type of animal. But you'd never be able to catch them all in a jam jar. Apart from their vast numbers, many of them are known only as a single example in a museum collection.

Termites More than 2,800 species. Termites like a nice hot climate. They are small soft insects but that doesn't mean they're a soft touch. Termites build nests that look like palaces and are ruled by kings and queens. Guard-termites are so serious about their work they sometimes explode in a bid to defend the nest!

Ants, bees and wasps Well over 120,000 species in this order worldwide. All members have a narrow waist between the thorax and the abdomen. Most have wings. (Worker ants don't develop wings – they're far too busy to go anywhere.)

Mantids and cockroaches At least 6,500 species. There's a strong family resemblance in their horrible habits. Cockroaches make midnight raids on the pantry. The praying mantis sits around cunningly disguised as part of a plant, and waits to pounce on its innocent victims.

Bugs Over 100,000 species in this order worldwide. They suck vegetable juices through straw-like mouths. Nothing ugly about that, you might think, except some do like a bit of blood now and then.

Flies Far more than 120,000 species in this order. They use one pair of wings for flying (which is what they do best). They also have the remnants of a second pair of wings that look like tiny drumsticks, and are actually used for balancing. Most irritating fly habit: flying backwards, sideways and forwards round your head. OK – so you know they're incredible fliers already. Nastiest fly habit: some types of fly like nothing better than to lick the top of a big smelly cowpat. And then pay a visit to whatever you were going to have for tea.

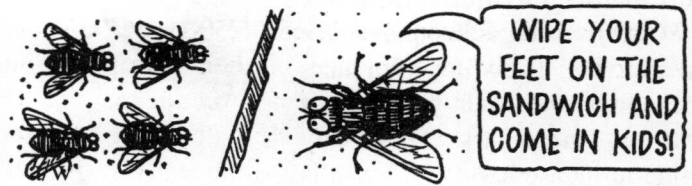

Sucking lice More than 500 species. Lice don't build their own homes. No. They live on other creatures. It's nice and warm there and you can suck a refreshing drop of blood whenever you feel like it. Lice can live on nearly every mammal – bats are one of the few exceptions. Or at least no one has ever found a louse on a bat.

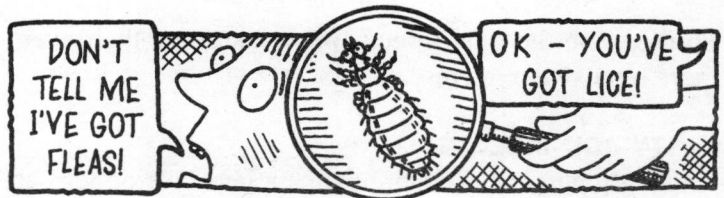

Dragonflies, caddis flies, mayflies are three different orders totalling more than 17,000 species. They start off living in water and then take to the air. Traditional names for dragonflies include "horse stingers" and "devil's darning needles". Which is odd because they don't sting horses and you can't mend your socks with them.

MAYFLY   CADDISFLY   DRAGONFLY

I DON'T LOOK LIKE A DRAGON EITHER!

Butterflies and moths Well over 180,000 species in this order worldwide. They have two pairs of wings and their young start off as caterpillars. Then they hide in a case called a chrysalis and re-arrange their body parts before emerging as butterflies or moths. It's a bit like you spending a few weeks taking your body apart in a sleeping bag. And then putting it all back together in a different order.

YOU'LL NEVER GET ME UP IN ONE OF THEM!

So these are the ugly insects, but what about their even more repulsive relatives?

NASTY NON-INSECTS

If an ugly bug has got more than six legs – or no legs at all, it isn't an insect.

Slugs and snails Over 35,000 species on land and many live in the sea. Slimy slugs and snails belong to a huge group of animals called the molluscs that even includes octopuses. But slugs and snails are the only members of the group that have tentacles on their heads.

I'D HATE TO BE A SNAIL – THEY'RE SO SLOW AND SLIMY

Centipedes and millipedes are two different classes of ugly bugs. There are about 2,800 species of centipede and more than 10,000 species of millipede. But sinister centipedes gobble up the poor little millipedes and *not* the other way round.

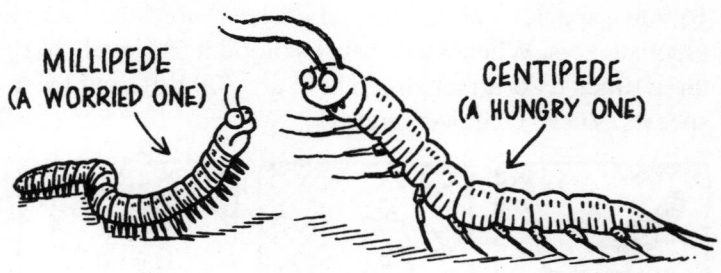

MILLIPEDE (A WORRIED ONE)

CENTIPEDE (A HUNGRY ONE)

Woodlice Over 3,500 species. They all have seven pairs of legs. Woodlice, would you believe it, belong to the same class of creature as crabs and lobsters!

I DON'T LOOK ANYTHING LIKE THAT!

WOODLOUSE

Spiders There are 37,000 species in this order but scientists think there may be up to five times that number waiting to be discovered! What a thought! Most spiders spin silken webs. They have eight legs, of course, and their bodies are divided into two parts.

MONEY
SPIDER

TARANTULA
SPIDER

Earthworms, bristleworms and leeches More than 16,000 species altogether. Leeches are the nasty bloodsuckers. When a leech sucks blood it can swell up to three times its original size. There are 300 different leech species. Yuck! One is enough!

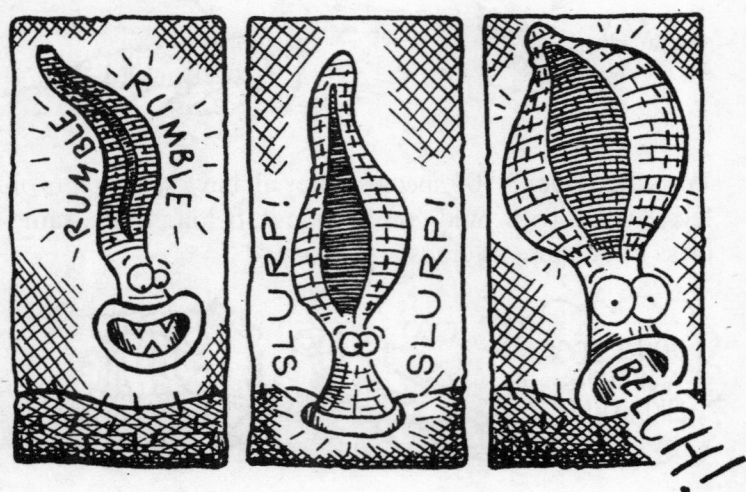

Mites There are well over 45,000 species in this order. Unlike spiders, mites have a one-piece body. Many mites are under 1 mm long but they still have some hugely horrible habits. Some eat cheese rinds and the glue in old books. Others suck blood from animals.

So there you have it. Ugly bug families *are* horribly confusing. There are so many of them and they come in a horrible array of shapes and sizes. But they've got one vital feature in common – they're HUNGRY! Take the worms, for example, they like nothing better than a breakfast of slimy rotting leaves. And some worms have even more revolting tastes.

WEIRD WORMS

You can't get away from worms. They live in soil. Bet you didn't know their slimy relatives also live in the sea? You might also find them at the bottom of ponds and even inside other creatures. There are thousands of worm species with all sorts of ugly habits. But one thing they all have in common is that they're horribly weird.

A DISGUSTING DISCOVERY

The Pacific Ocean off the Galapagos Islands, 1977

There was definitely something down there. Something strange and terrifying. Instruments trailing from the research ship far into the depths below revealed strange rises in sea temperature. Cameras lowered into the deep-sea darkness had taken pictures of strange shapes. And water samples taken from the deep stank enough to make you sick. The scientists needed to know more. Someone had to visit those remote depths where no human had ever gone before. But what would they find when they got there?

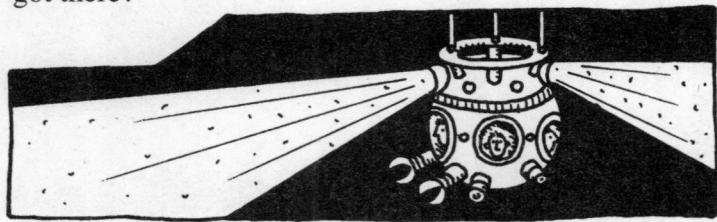

Metre by metre, the submersible slipped ever deeper into the unknown. From the observation window the scientists could make out nothing but the pitch-black freezing cold sea. The surface of the Pacific Ocean was a terrifying 2.5 km above their heads. And on every square centimetre of the submersible, a tonne of ocean pressed down. In the lights of the tiny craft the scientists could see strange volcanic rocks. But no sign of life. They shivered. Nothing could live down here in this horrible place surely? Then it happened.

The submersible's temperature gauge spun off the scale with a gigantic heat surge. The water turned from black to cloudy blue. The scientists had found a natural chimney that led deep beneath the earth's surface. Here, heated chemicals, stinking like rotten eggs, boil up from below at terrifically high temperatures.

And the hot cloudy water was alive with bacteria too small for the eye to see. The billions of bacteria billowed in vast clouds. Strange ghostly pale crabs scurried through the ooze on the sea bed in search of bits of drowned sea creatures. And there were thousands of giant clams. Then out of the darkness and confusion, the THINGS appeared.

The scientists were astounded. What were these creatures? Were they alien life forms? Why did they look so weird? The strange red tips of the creatures waved in the sea. Their bodies were hidden in long white upright tubes, each 4 metres long, and they had red blood just like humans. They were giant seaworms – the largest ever seen and of a type unknown to science. But these ugly bugs had no mouths and no stomachs. So how and what did they eat?

There was only one way to find out. The robot arm of the submersible reached out and grabbed a worm from its strange home. Back on the ship a fearless scientist sliced it open. What do you think he found inside?

a) Crabs.

b) Bits of dead animal that had floated down from the surface.

c) Beastly bacteria.

Answer: c) A slimy mass of billions of bacteria. The same disgusting chemical-guzzling bacteria that made the water cloudy. But here comes the surprise. The worms weren't actually eating the bacteria! Inside the worm's guts, the bacteria ate the smelly chemicals in the water and made new chemicals that the worms could feed off. Quite a cosy arrangement really.

WEIRD WORM VARIETIES

There are three main orders of worms. Flatworms, ribbon worms and segmented worms. So how can you tell which is which?

Weird flatworms

Surprisingly enough, flatworms get their name because they are pretty flat. Their bodies aren't divided into segments, and they're pretty slimy, too. They're probably the slimiest worm you'll come across.

For example, one type of flatworm, the parasitic tapeworm, can live inside an animal's stomach! Another, called dugesia, (dug-easi-er) picks on creatures smaller than itself and sucks them up. But if the tiddlers get a bit too big, ugly Dug wraps them up in a slimy parcel and just sucks bits off them.

PARASITIC TAPEWORM

SUCK!

Then there's the milky-white flatworm, a close relative of dugesia. It lives in water and it's almost see-through, so you can see what it ate for dinner. And when it wants to reproduce it sometimes tears itself in two!

I LOVE THIS STUFF!

SO I SEE!

Weird ribbonworms

Most ribbonworms live in the sea. Sometimes they have weird tube-like structures that shoot out from their heads to catch other unsuspecting worms and smaller creatures.

Ribbonworms can be horribly long. The bootlace worm sometimes reaches several metres. Would you like to meet a worm that's as long as your bootlace?

IMPRESSED?

Weird segmented worms

The weird worms in this gruesome group all have rounded bodies that divide into segments. Some of them are parasites, and can cause disease. Others might live in the soil, in the sea, or freshwater. They live on small plants and animals.

Bristleworms belong to this order. Maybe you've spotted them at the seaside? Some of them build tubes out of the sand and sit in them with their tentacles poking out. But uglier bristleworms crawl about looking for prey. They use their two pairs of jaws, two pairs of feelers and four tentacles to search out their food. They particularly enjoy sucking the insides out of snails. Yummy!

A sea mouse, on the other hand, has a mouse-shaped body that's all furry. Aahh, sounds quite cute, doesn't it? Except that this worm can grow up to 18 cm long and 7 cm wide. Sounds more like a sea rat!

Want to get friendly with a member of the segmented worm family? Then let's get ...

DOWN-TO-EARTHWORMS

Ugly bug fact file

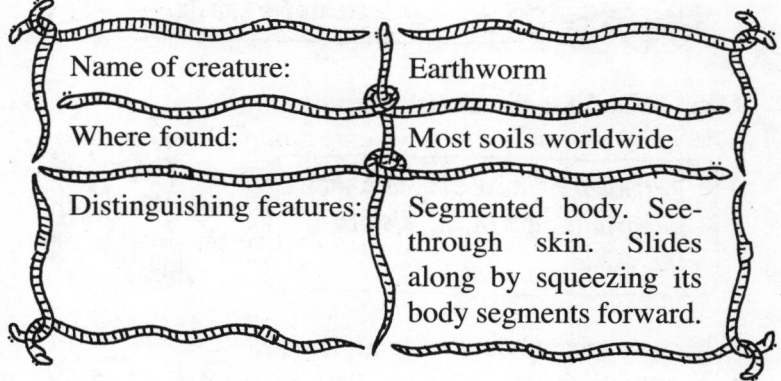

Name of creature:	Earthworm
Where found:	Most soils worldwide
Distinguishing features:	Segmented body. See-through skin. Slides along by squeezing its body segments forward.

VISUAL IDENTIFICATION

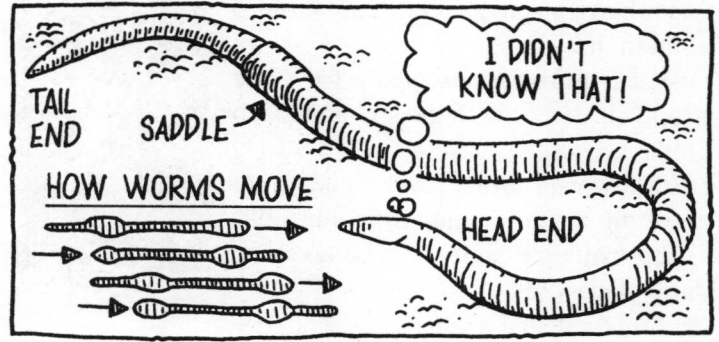

TAIL END

SADDLE

HOW WORMS MOVE

I DIDN'T KNOW THAT!

HEAD END

ARE EARTHWORMS AWFUL?

"Yes", according to people who don't like slimy wriggling creatures.

"No", according to some very famous naturalists.
In 1770 Gilbert White wrote that...

Earthworms though in appearance a small and despicable link in the Chain of Nature, yet if lost would make a lamentable chasm.

Charles Dickens liked earthworms too...

Earthworms have played a most important part in the history of the world.

What's so great about these ugly bugs?

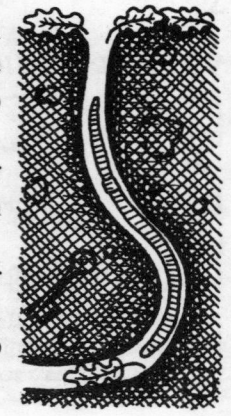

- Worm burrows mix up the soil bringing vital minerals to the surface so hungry plants can easily slurp them up.
- Worm burrows make space for water and air to mix with the soil and reach plant roots.
- Earthworms drag leaves and other rotting material into their burrows. This rotting material can be taken up by plant roots.

So you see crops grow better in soil where there are lots of earthworms. In fact in Europe and the USA there are earthworm farms that produce up to 500,000 worms a day for sale to farmers. Good old earthworms!

But earthworms are still ugly bugs, so they do have some horrible habits. After the earth has passed through their bodies it ends up in ugly earthworm-shaped piles all over your beautiful front lawn. Earthworms love to guzzle lettuce and their burrowing can damage plant seedlings. Never mind – if your earthworms turn nasty you can always use them as fishing bait.

ARE YOU AN EARTHWORM EXPERT?

You may think that earthworms are deadly dull and boring. And of course, you'd be right. But delve a little deeper into their humdrum lives and you'll discover some slimy surprises. See if you can guess these answers.

1 How many worms could you count per hectare of farmland?
a) Three
b) 65,697
c) Two million

TWO THOUSAND AND THREE . . .

2 Why on earth do earthworms have bristles? (This is true. Just try stroking one – if you dare!)
a) To help them move along.
b) To stop the early bird from yanking them out of the soil.
c) To sweep their burrows clean.

3 How on earth does a worm accidentally bury a stone?
a) The stone rolls into a hole dug by the worm to catch beetles.

b) Worms push earth up from their burrows until the stone is covered.

c) Worms tunnel under the stone. The stone falls into the tunnel.

4 How long was the longest earthworm ever found?
a) 20 cm
b) 45.5 cm
c) 6.7 metres

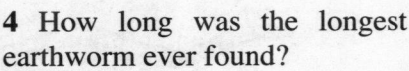

5 Worms have a part of their body called a saddle. What on earth is it used for?
a) To give rides to earwigs.
b) To carry lumps of food.
c) To make an egg cocoon.

6 What happens when you cut a short piece off the end of a worm? (No need to try this out to discover the answer.)
a) It gets upset.
b) It grows a new tail.
c) It joins back together again.

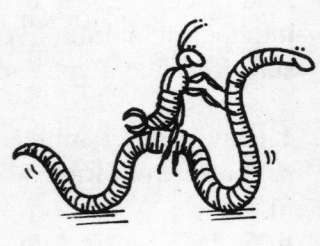
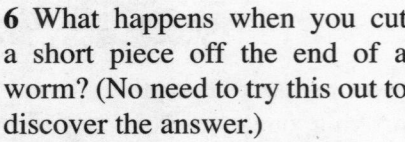

7 What on earth do moles do to worms?
a) Eat them.
b) Bite their heads off.
c) Bite their heads off *and* let them escape.

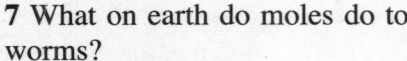

Answers: 1 c) Amazingly enough. **2 a)** *and* **b)**! **3 b)** This makes the soil level rise and things level with the soil sink down. **4 c)** It was a type of giant earthworm that lives in South Africa. This monster wriggled out of the ground in Transvaal in 1937. **5 c)** The saddle forms a slimy belt. As the worm squirms out of the belt it picks up the fertilized eggs. The belt forms a cosy cocoon for the eggs. **6 b)**. **7** Another trick question! The answer is all three! **a)** Moles love a juicy earthworm. **b)** When they're full they bite the worm's heads off and put them in their "pantry". This doesn't kill the worms, it just stops them escaping! **c)** But sometimes a worm has time to grow another head and escape!

HOW TO CHARM A WORM

You will need:

A fine day, but not too dry
A lawn or flowerbed (make sure the soil is slightly damp)
A pitchfork (optional)
A hi-fi speaker (optional)

What you do:

1 You are going to pretend to be rain.
2 You can make vibrations by jumping up and down, playing music with the speaker facing the ground,

or by sticking a pitchfork into the ground and wiggling it about a lot (this is also known as "twanging"). Alternatively, use your imagination to create your own short, sharp shower. Anyone for a spot of tap dancing? But why does this make the worms come out?

Worms like rain because they have to keep their skin moist to prevent it drying out. When they feel rain drops hitting the ground they pop their heads out to take a look.

Bet you never knew
You can "charm" an earthworm. Every summer a primary school near Nantwich, England, hosts a weird competition. It's the world worm-charming championship. Yes – it's true. What a charming traditional pastime!

SLIMY SNAILS AND UGLY SLUGS

They're covered in slime, slide along very slowly and have eyes on the end of stalks. And if that's not ugly enough, they gobble up your garden lettuce. So it's not surprising that people don't like them. But are slugs and snails really that horrible? Do they deserve their rotten reputation? Yes they do. And here's why.

Ugly bug fact file

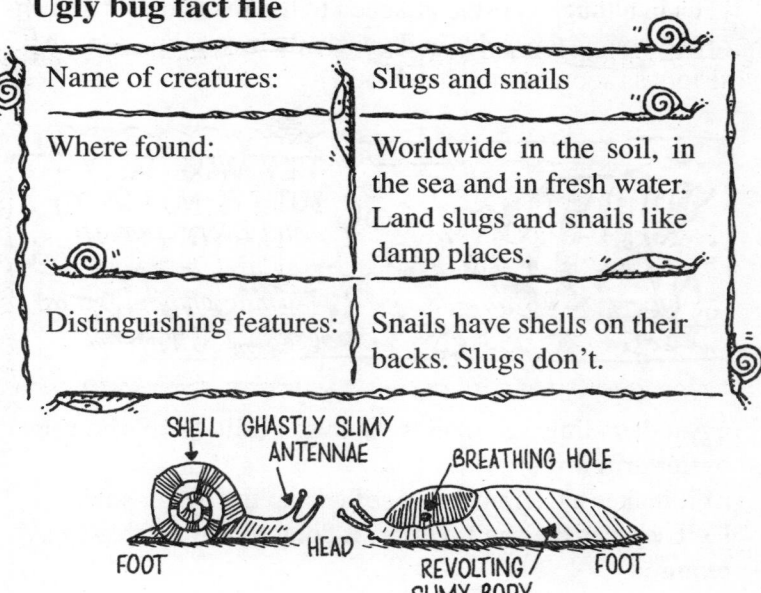

Name of creatures:	Slugs and snails
Where found:	Worldwide in the soil, in the sea and in fresh water. Land slugs and snails like damp places.
Distinguishing features:	Snails have shells on their backs. Slugs don't.

SHELL · GHASTLY SLIMY ANTENNAE · BREATHING HOLE · FOOT · HEAD · REVOLTING SLIMY BODY · FOOT

SEVEN SLIMY SNAIL FACTS YOU DIDN'T REALLY WANT TO KNOW

1 The largest snail in the world is the African Giant snail. It can be 34 cm from its shell top to its head! It eats bananas – and dead animals.

2 The garlic grass snail smells strongly of garlic. OK – it's not really horrible. But it must give snail-eating birds horribly bad breath.

3 When a snail is chomping away on your mum's prize cauliflowers, it will be using its radula – that's its tongue. The radula is so rough it actually grates its food.

4 Some sea snails on the other hand, eat meat. These snails have a few sharp teeth – well suited for catching and chomping on their prey!

5 The slimiest sea snails are dog whelks. They lay their eggs in a tough capsule attached to the sea bed. But some of the youngsters seize and guzzle their own brothers and sisters as soon as they hatch out!

THEY WERE TASTY – BUT I'VE NO ONE TO PLAY WITH NOW!

6 Another slimy sea snail is the oyster drill. Here's how an oyster drill drills:

a) It makes a chemical that softens up the oyster shell.

b) It scrapes the shell with its radula, repeating step **a)** as required.

c) It sticks its feeding tube through the hole and slurps up the juicy oyster!

7 But snails don't have it all their own way. A tiny worm lives inside the amber snail. Sometimes the worm releases chemicals that turn the snail's tentacles orange! This colourful display attracts a bird that nips off the snail's crowning glory. The worm begins a whole gruesome new life inside the bird. And the snail? It grows new tentacles. So that's all right then.

OH NO! THEY MUST HAVE TURNED ORANGE AGAIN!

UGLY SLUGS

A slug is just a slimy snail without a mobile home on its back. Come to think of it – slugs have the right idea. Have you ever seen a snail trying to get under a really low bridge? Not having a shell helps the slug to slither into nooks and crannies. But slugs have some scintillating secrets. That's if you dare discover them.

DARE YOU MAKE FRIENDS WITH ... AN UGLY SLUG?

Here's how to snuggle up to a slug. Who knows, you could be in for a horribly interesting encounter!

1 First meet your slug. You can tell where there are slugs around by the horrible silvery slime trails they leave. They like to slither about in the open on warm damp summer evenings. So just follow a tempting trail until you find your slug lurking under the leaves of a small plant.

2 Enjoy that gooey, squelchy feel between your fingers as you put your slug in a glass jar.

SQUELCH

3 Watch in amazement as your ugly slug climbs the slippery walls of the jar. It moves on a layer of slime produced by its foot. The sticky slime allows the slug to cling to the glass. Waves of movement push its foot forward. Think about it – could you climb up a glass wall on just one foot that's been dipped in something rather like raw egg?

HELP! LET ME OUT!

4 Imagine you were a bird. Would you want to eat the slug? Not likely – the slime tastes disgusting! But hedgehogs think they are horribly delicious.

5 Put your new friend back where you found him/her. That way you'll stay friends.

If you go slug hunting in your garden on a warm damp night you might meet a shield-shelled slug. (Try saying that very fast – three times!) This sinister slug gets its name from a tiny shell on the top end of its body. But can you guess what it eats? Clue: It isn't lettuce.

Answer: Earthworms, centipedes and other slugs. Delicious!

SEVEN UGLY SLUG FACTS

1 The largest British ugly slug is the great grey slug. It grows to 20 cm long!

2 But that's nothing! Some sea slugs are 40 cm long and weigh 7 kilos. They are also often brightly coloured.

3 And some of them have some horribly strange habits. Glaucus is a sea slug that floats upside down buoyed up by an air bubble inside its stomach.

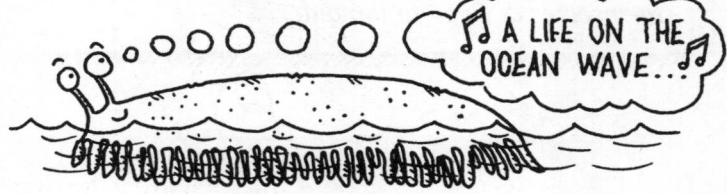

4 Meanwhile back on the farm, slugs and farmers are sworn enemies because ugly slugs eat or spoil crops. If slugs didn't eat potatoes there would be enough extra chips to feed 400,000 people for a year!

5 And land slugs have some horribly strange habits as well. Some ugly slugs can let themselves down from a height on a string of slime.

6 Like worms and snails, slugs are both male and female at the same time.

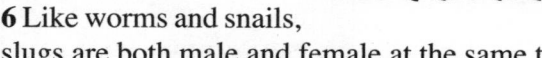

7 When slugs mate they cling together and cover themselves in slime. Then they fire little arrows called love darts at one another to get in the mood. Very romantic – if you're a slug!

Bet you never knew
An ugly slug can tell you which way the wind is blowing. It's true. A slug will always crawl away from the prevailing wind. Slugs do this to stop themselves drying out too quickly.

UNDERWATER UGLIES

Why not relax by a peaceful pond or river and forget about horrible ugly bugs? Some chance! Ugly bugs like water even more than you do. And those murky waters hide some pretty ugly undercurrents.

WINTER ~freezing.
Ugly bugs have to hide in the mud at the bottom.

SPRING ~rain.
Acid rain is very bad for ugly bugs.

SUMMER ~warm and sunny.
If the weather gets too hot the pond will dry up!

AUTUMN ~soggy.
Leaves can clog the pond. As they rot they use up all the oxygen and the ugly bugs die!

Imagine a pond as a kind of living soup. It's full of tiny plants and animals. The largest animals are always trying to eat the smaller ones, and the smaller animals are trying to eat even smaller animals, and they're all trying not to be eaten by each other. Scientists call this a food web because you get in a tangle if you try to figure out who eats who.

A pond is a perilous place to live. And its not just other animals that bugs have to watch out for. There are plenty of hazards all year round.

And at all times, horrible humans chuck in harmful rubbish and poisonous pollution. And then they drain the pond!

UGLY UNDERWATER LIFESTYLES

Every freshwater ugly bug has developed its own methods of living and eating. See if you can match each ugly bug to its loathsome lifestyle.

1 Hangs under the water surface and breathes through a tube. Grabs a passing bug in its claws and sucks out the juices.

2 Lives in an underwater diving bell made from silk and air bubbles. Eats anything that moves.

3 Hangs upside down from the surface and stores air in its shell. Eats tiny plants.

4 Walks around on the surface looking for bugs that have fallen in. Its light body and widely spaced legs ensure it doesn't break the water tension. (That's the springy top surface of the water.)

5 Lives in the water and leaps to escape. Lives off tiny plants.

6 Swims round in circles on the surface and dives to escape danger. Has four eyes – one pair of eyes above the water and one pair below. It can also fly! Eats other pond bugs.

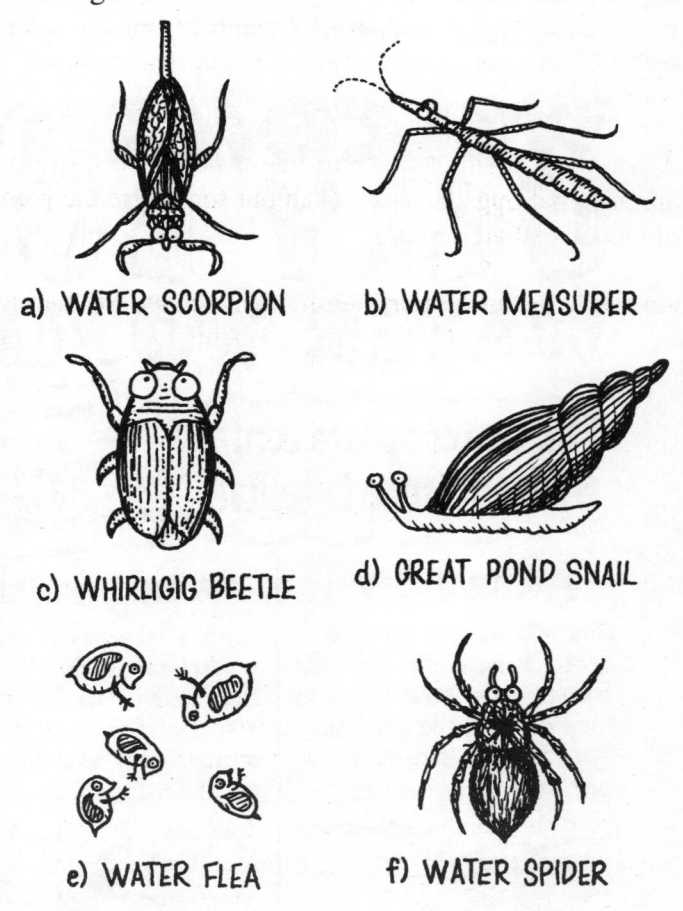

a) WATER SCORPION

b) WATER MEASURER

c) WHIRLIGIG BEETLE

d) GREAT POND SNAIL

e) WATER FLEA

f) WATER SPIDER

UGLY WATER SPORTS

As long as conditions in the pond are right and there is plenty of food, life for a pond ugly bug must seem one long holiday. Is this a holiday you could do without?

WELCOME TO UGLY BUG WATER WORLD!

The water sports centre where leisure is lethal!

The small print. We can't guarantee your safety. If you get eaten it's not our fault ~ OK?

A Great Dive!

Dive into danger with the great diving beetle. Store air bubbles under your wings to stay down for longer. Also learn to grab and guzzle any underwater edibles.

Rafting & fishing

Enjoy a lazy paddle with our resident raft spider. As you float by on your leaf raft try a spot of fishing. Just dip one of your eight legs in the water to attract little fish.

I THINK WE'LL STAY AT HOME THIS YEAR KIDS!

Power Beetle Boat racing

Race a rove beetle boat. Hang on tight as the boating beetle bombs across the water. All our beetles feature the latest jet-propelled abdomen gas engines.

Water good swim!

Learn basic backstroke with our brilliant backswimming water boatman beetle. Swimming on your front lesson taught by his assistant – the lesser water boatman.

Now you've worked up an appetite. Where better to relax than our exclusive underwater eating places?

The Caddis Fly Larva Cafe

Gravel built with silk wallpaper – it's the perfect place for a relaxing and informal meal. Book now before your caddis fly chef grows up and flies away. Vegetarian? Don't worry! The nearby Veggie Caddis Fly Cafe offers a choice of tiny slimy plants and bits of rotting leaves. <u>Warning to patrons. Beware the treacherous trout. They sometimes try to eat the cafe.</u>

Cafe

BEWARE OF THE TROUT!

HAPPY BIRTHDAY!

LOATHSOME LEECHES

Lurking at the bottom of your local pond or canal is a creature that makes the others seem quite likeable. There's no way of disguising it. These creatures are *loathsome*!

Ugly bug fact file

Name of creature:	Leech
Where found:	Worldwide in water or damp rain forests.
Horrible habits:	Sucks blood
Any helpful habits:	Used in medicine to ... suck blood (surprisingly enough)!
Distinguishing features:	Long segmented body with suckers at the back and front.

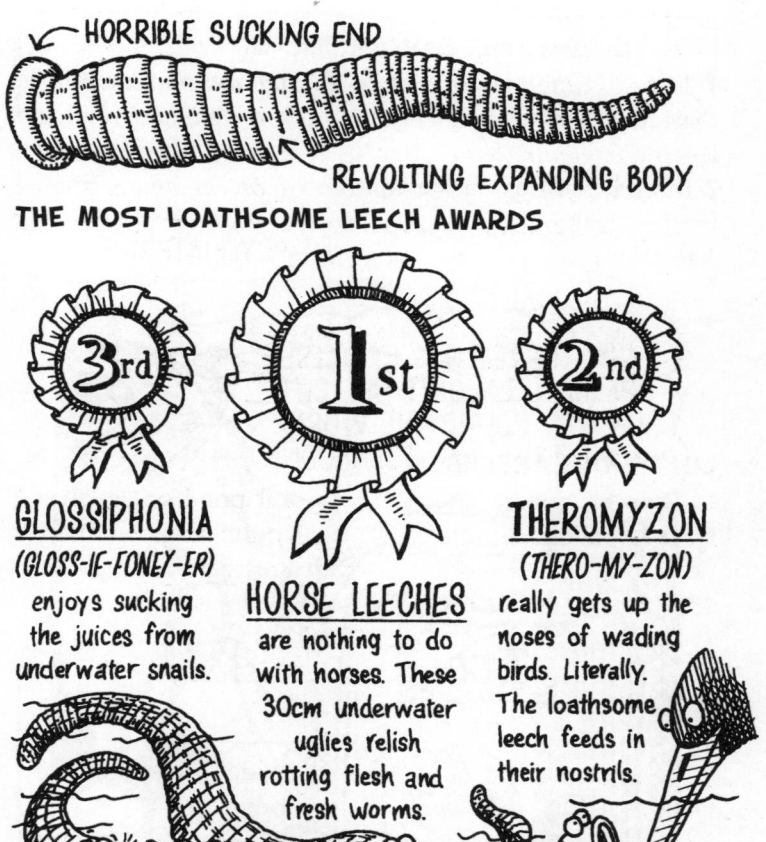

← HORRIBLE SUCKING END

REVOLTING EXPANDING BODY

THE MOST LOATHSOME LEECH AWARDS

3rd

1st

2nd

GLOSSIPHONIA
(GLOSS-IF-FONEY-ER)
enjoys sucking the juices from underwater snails.

HORSE LEECHES
are nothing to do with horses. These 30cm underwater uglies relish rotting flesh and fresh worms.

THEROMYZON
(THERO-MY-ZON)
really gets up the noses of wading birds. Literally. The loathsome leech feeds in their nostrils.

A LOATHSOME LEECH BAROMETER

But even leeches have their uses. Here is a vile Victorian invention it's best *not* to try. Simply place a leech in a jar of fresh pond water. Cover the top of the jar with a fine cloth and secure tightly. Feed your barometer on blood now and then.

HOW TO READ THE BAROMETER

1 Leech climbs to the top of the jar means that rain is expected. If the weather settles down again, so will the leech.

2 Lazy leech lies on the bottom of its jar means fine or frosty weather.

3 Restless leech shows that a storm is on its way.

CREEPY-CRAWLIES

Who hasn't looked under a stone at one time or another and seen an assortment of horrible-looking creatures? Chances are that these creepy-crawlies included centipedes, millipedes and woodlice. Now you might think that because these creatures live in the same place they'd all be mates. Well, you'd be horribly wrong. Centipedes like to eat millipedes – when they get the chance. And that's just the start of their disgusting differences!

Ugly bug fact file

Name of creatures:	Centipedes and millipedes
Where found:	Worldwide, often amongst leaf litter and rotten wood.
Distinguishing features:	Centipede: Segmented, slightly flattened body. Two jointed legs on each segment; two long feelers. Millipede: Segmented, rounded body. Four jointed legs on each segment; two short feelers.

ANTENNAE

HEAD

CENTIPEDE

MILLIPEDE

CREEPY COMPARISONS

1 Feet count Millipede means "thousand feet" – which just goes to show that some scientists can't count. Most millipedes have between 80 and 400 feet.

Centipede means "hundred feet". But once again the scientists got it horribly wrong! Some centipedes have only 30 feet.

2 Walking When a millipede walks, waves of movement pass up its body so that it glides along. When a centipede walks it raises alternate legs just as you normally do. It has extra long legs at the back so it doesn't trip up.

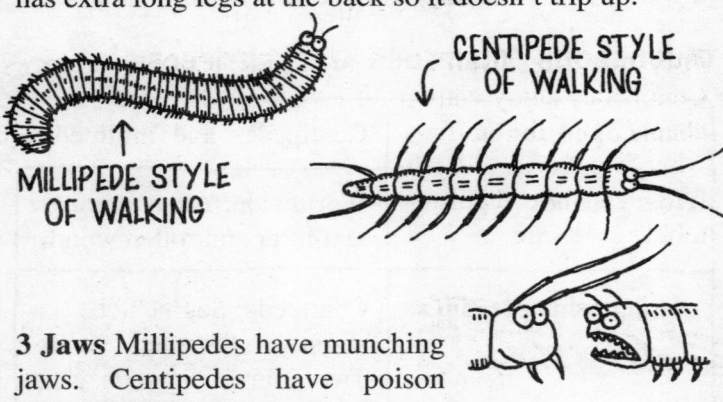

CENTIPEDE STYLE OF WALKING

MILLIPEDE STYLE OF WALKING

3 Jaws Millipedes have munching jaws. Centipedes have poison fangs. They're both pretty ugly.

4 Romantic problems Millipedes have a big problem – they can't see very well. So male millipedes have developed some strange ways of attracting a mate.

• Some bang their heads on the ground.
• Others let out a loud screech.
• Some produce special scents.
• Others rub their legs together to make sounds.

A male centipede, on the other hand, has other things on his mind. All centipedes are horribly aggressive and the female he fancies is quite capable of eating him! So first of all he walks around her, tapping her with his feelers to show he's friendly.

HE'S SO HUNKY-
I COULD EAT HIM!

MURDEROUS MILLIPEDES AND CENTIPEDES

Centipedes enjoy eating millipedes – when they get the chance. But the millipedes often put up a fight! Here's what happens... Centipede attack plan: Spear prey on fangs and inject poison. Once prey stops wriggling – nibble at leisure.

I'M A
GONNER!

Millipede defence plan: Curl up in a ball. Squirt nasty fluid from stink glands on sides of its body.

Who do you think has the best chance of winning – the menacing millipedes or the sinister centipedes?

POOH – WHAT
A PONG!

In some parts of the world, centipedes and millipedes can grow to gigantic proportions. Giant millipedes can measure up to 26 cm long.

Some of these monsters have fearsome fangs. One type of centipede in the Solomon Islands has a particularly painful bite. People have been known to plunge their hands into *boiling water* to take their minds off the pain! In Malaysia the local centipede's bite has been described by travellers as worse than a snake's. And in India there are even scarier stories of people who were *killed* by giant centipede bites.

Mind you, the millipedes aren't much better. In Haiti in the West Indies giant millipedes attack the local chickens and sometimes blind them with jets of poison! Other giant millipedes produce little puffs of poison gas. The gas kills any attacking animal.

CHICKEN TONIGHT!

But size doesn't save either the giant centipedes or the giant millipedes from a horribly gruesome death. In the African savannah giant hornbills are often seen plodding along looking at the ground. Suddenly they will nab a passing centipede in their long beak, and the centipede has no chance to bite the bird back. Scrunch, crunch, gobble and poor old deadly giant centipede has turned into another scrumptious snack for the hornbill.

Other centipedes get carried away by armies of ants. OK, the centipede can easily kill a few hundred ants but when it's 10,000 ants to one centipede, the poor old centipede doesn't stand a chance!

Giant millipedes have it tough too. Grey meerkats often feed on millipedes. Funny thing is that the meerkats always screw their faces up in disgust when they're eating. Well, who would expect a millipede to taste good?

YUCK! TASTES DISGUSTING!

TRY SOMETHING ELSE THEN!

DARE YOU MAKE FRIENDS WITH ... A MILLIPEDE?

Now for the good news. In the UK millipedes are quite harmless. Just as long as you handle them gently and as long as you don't try to make a meal of them. Here's how to make a meal for them instead, just to show what a good pal you are.

1 First catch your millipede. (And make sure it is a millipede, not a centipede!) Millipedes lurk in shady places, so try looking under leaf litter, compost or loose tree bark.

2 Pop your new friend into a small jar partly filled with earth – and a piece of a bark so it can hide.

3 Then serve up a tasty treat. A millipede's mouth would water at the thought of a ripe raspberry, a piece of potato skin, a mouldy old lettuce leaf or a little chunk of apple.

4 Place the jar in a dark secluded place.

5 Next day find out which delicious dish the millipede preferred.

6 Then it's time to say goodbye to your millipede mate. So pop your guest back where you found it. There is sure to be plenty of food and shelter there and let's hope there are no centipedes loitering nearby. Otherwise your millipede will end up on someone else's menu!

A WOODLOUSY LIFE

Along with the millipedes and centipedes, at the bottom of your garden live hundreds – no *thousands* – of woodlice. There are 50 different species of woodlice in Britain and they're all shy and nervous so make sure you read this book *quietly*. The most common species are the imaginatively named common woodlouse and the pill bug – not to be swallowed for a headache.

Ugly bug fact file

Name of creature:	Woodlouse
Where found:	Worldwide in damp, dark places where there is rotting material, e.g. slimy brown leaves.
Distinguishing features:	About 15 mm long with seven pairs of jointed legs and two feelers. Segmented armour around its body allowing it to move easily.

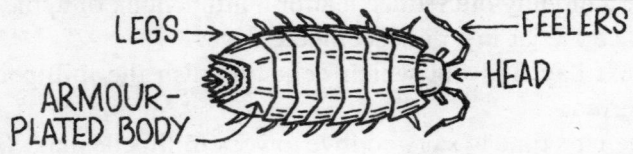

LEGS → ← FEELERS
← HEAD
ARMOUR-
PLATED BODY

48

A pill bug can roll itself into a ball (but please don't try bouncing one) – the common woodlouse can't do this. Some people think woodlice are boring. But, as always, they are wrong. Woodlice are *horribly* interesting.

TEN TERRIBLY INTERESTING FACTS ABOUT WOODLICE

1 Not a lot of people know this, but a woodlouse is not a louse! In fact, country people call woodlice some extremely un-boring names.

BIBBLEBUGS

CHOOKIES

COFFIN CUTTERS

CUD WORMS

GAMMER-SOWS

2 Woodlice have extremely interesting relatives. Crabs, shrimps, prawns, lobsters and woodlice are all part of the crustacean family. Many people are extremely interested in eating their seaside relatives. Not many people are interested in eating woodlice you might think ... but you'd be wrong.

3 This is not a horrible habit but a delicious delicacy. Salted and fried woodlice are an African speciality. They're eaten like crisps!

READY SALTED WOODLICE

4 Woodlice themselves have a horribly boring diet, though. They prefer bits of rotting plants and moulds. It's not everyone's cup of tea. But somebody's got to eat it, otherwise we'd be knee deep in the stuff. And woodlice do liven up their diet with the odd interesting dish ... like other woodlice for instance. Or their own droppings and their skin after they've shed it.

5 Woodlice start off as eggs in their mum's tummy pouch. Four weeks later they hatch as tiny woodlice. Baby woodlice live with their parents, which is an interesting way for an ugly bug to start life because most insect eggs are abandoned by their mothers. It's terrible, but true!

STAY CLOSE, MY DARLINGS!

6 And woodlice lives are full of drama and excitement. They put most TV soaps to shame. Yes. Woodlice never go to bed early with a mug of cocoa. They get to sleep all day and go out every night. And then they break into your home.

7 You're most likely to see woodlice in wet weather, because the biggest danger for a woodlouse is drying out. Interestingly, every year millions of baby woodlice come to a sad and sticky end by simply shrivelling up.

8 Some woodlice live in horribly interesting places. One variety lives inside yellow ants' nests and eats their droppings. Another type of woodlouse lives by the seaside under piles of slippery rotting seaweed.

9 Woodlice have some interesting if deadly enemies. The most dangerous of these is the dreaded woodlouse spider. Once grabbed in the spider's pincer-like grip, a woodlouse is doomed. The spider injects its poison and the woodlouse dies in ... seven seconds. Quite an interesting way to go.

10 And there are some horribly interesting woodlice pests. Such as the tiny worms that sometimes live inside them ... and kill them. Or the disgusting fly larvae that creep into a woodlouse's body and eat it from the inside out.

DARE YOU MAKE FRIENDS WITH ... A WOODLOUSE?

Woodlice may not be the masterminds of the ugly bug world, but they've learnt a trick or two about how to survive. So why not put your woodlouse to the test? Make a note of what it does, then try to work out for yourself what makes a woodlouse tick.

1 First, find your woodlouse under a stone or a log, or in a damp corner.

2 Get a piece of wood (like a ruler) and try and get your woodlouse to climb onto it at different angles. Does your woodlouse:

a) walk off in the other direction

b) easily climb onto the wood

c) struggle to get onto the wood?

3 Get a box with half the lid cut off. Find out which half the woodlouse likes best.

a) light

b) shade

4 Tip your woodlouse onto a tabletop and poke it gently with the point of a pencil. This is a pretty scary thing to do to a woodlouse (it'll be scary for you, too, if you do it on the dinner table – at dinnertime). Does your woodlouse:

a) roll up in a ball
b) run away
c) clamp down on the ground
d) pretend to be dead
e) produce a disgusting substance to put you off eating it?

5 Don't forget to pop your woodlouse back unharmed where you found it.

Did you discover ... that your woodlouse could easily climb out of danger ... it sheltered in the shade, so as not to dry out in the sun ... it had various sneaky survival tricks when it sensed it was in danger of attack?

With such a collection of tricks up its many trouser legs you'd think we'd be even more overrun by woodlice than we are. Well, we would be – if it wasn't for competition from a group of bugs so ugly that they make the woodlouse seem cuddly. Enter the Insect Invaders!

INSECT INVADERS

Seen from any point of view insects are a horribly important group of ugly bugs. Insects are the most varied, the most ruthless, the hungriest and according to some people the most disgusting life form on the planet. There may be over 30 million varieties of insect. That's TEN times more than all the other types of animal *put together.*

Not surprisingly, you can find insects virtually anywhere you look. That's if you really want to look! It's also not surprising that they have a big effect on our lives. And it's mainly as invaders – of crops, homes, schools... Nowhere is safe from the insect invaders!

WONDER WHAT WE'RE INVADING TODAY

ANIMALS OF THE WORLD

INSECTS OF THE WORLD

INSECT BITS AND PIECES

Despite their many differences, insects have the same basic features. We've caught this cute little beetle so that you can have a close look at it...

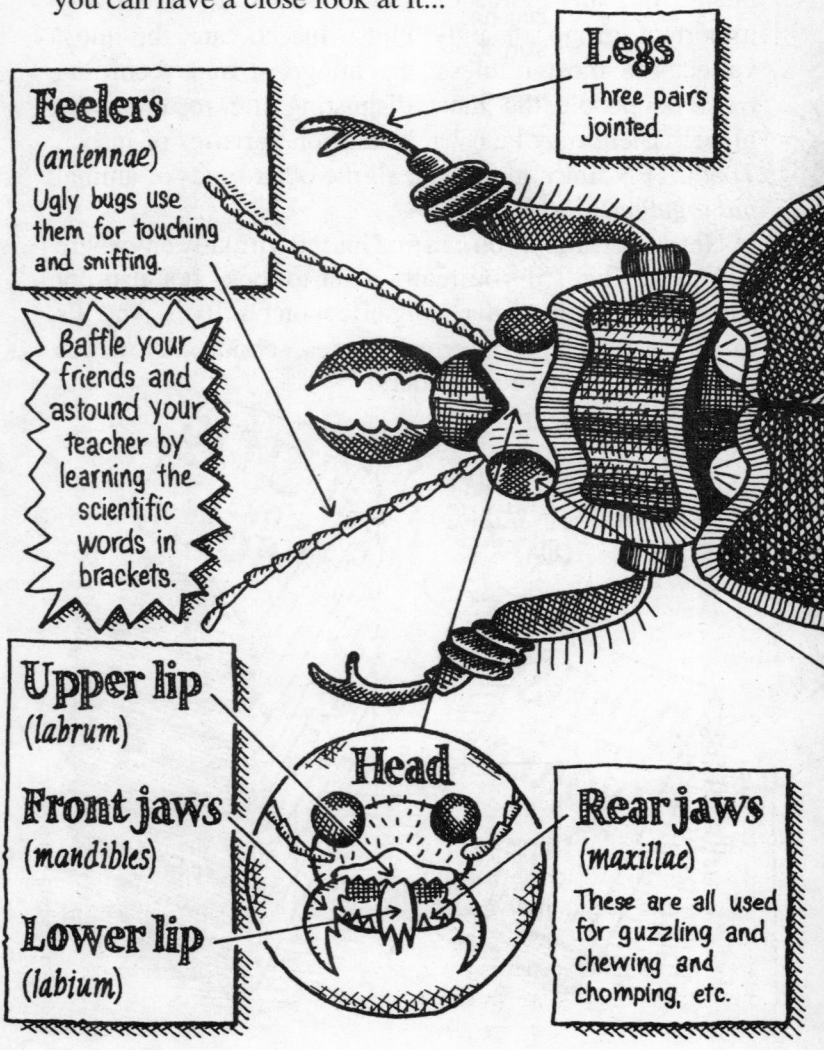

Legs
Three pairs jointed.

Feelers
(antennae)
Ugly bugs use them for touching and sniffing.

Baffle your friends and astound your teacher by learning the scientific words in brackets.

Upper lip
(labrum)

Front jaws
(mandibles)

Lower lip
(labium)

Head

Rear jaws
(maxillae)
These are all used for guzzling and chewing and chomping, etc.

Skin

Light, waterproof and tough. It doesn't stretch much and every so often the bug has to shed its skin to grow.

Breathing holes (*spiracles*)

Lead to tubes that carry air to every bit of the body.

Rear body (*abdomen*)

Contains guts and egg-laying equipment

Eyes

Insects see lots of little pictures – it's a bit like watching hundreds of TV screens except they are six sided and none gives a good picture. But they are good for spotting anything that moves and is worth eating!

Wings

Most insects have them. They go up and down and are controlled by the muscles inside the body.

REVOLTING INSECT RECORDS

1 Longest insect Giant stick insects from Borneo look like ugly old sticks. And they grow to a whopping 33 cm long.

YIKES!

2 Largest flying insect The Queen Alexandra's birdwing butterfly from New Guinea boasts a wingspan of 28 cm. But that's nothing – a mere 300 million years ago there were giant dragonflies with wingspans of 75 cm!

3 Smallest insects Cute little fairy flies are actually tiny wasps only 0.21 mm long. The good news is that they don't sting humans.

4 Heaviest insect A single Goliath beetle from central Africa can weigh up to 100 grams.

5 Lightest insect The lightest insect is a species of parasitic wasp. It would take 25 million of them to weigh as much as one Goliath beetle!

6 Fastest flying insect There's a species of Australian dragonfly that can reach 58 km (36 miles) per hour.

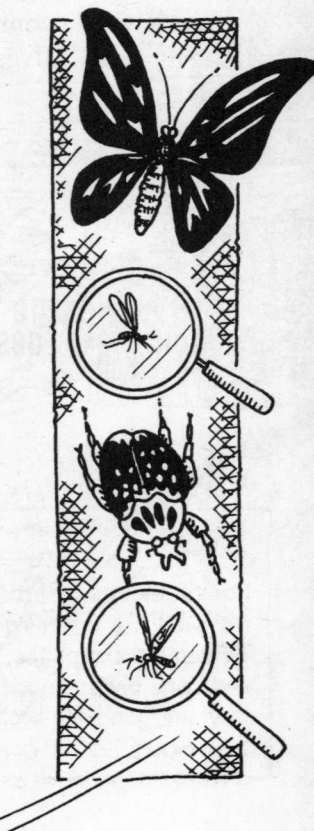

7 Fastest breeding insects Aphid females usually give birth to live young. Inside these are developing bugs. Inside the developing bugs there are more developing bugs, and so on. One female aphid can produce millions of descendants in a single summer.

I'M ALREADY A GREAT GRANDMOTHER AND I WAS ONLY BORN THREE WEEKS AGO!

LOATHSOME LIFECYCLES

Some ugly bugs only change a bit as they grow up and some change completely – so there are two types of horrible insect lives.

Lifecycle 1

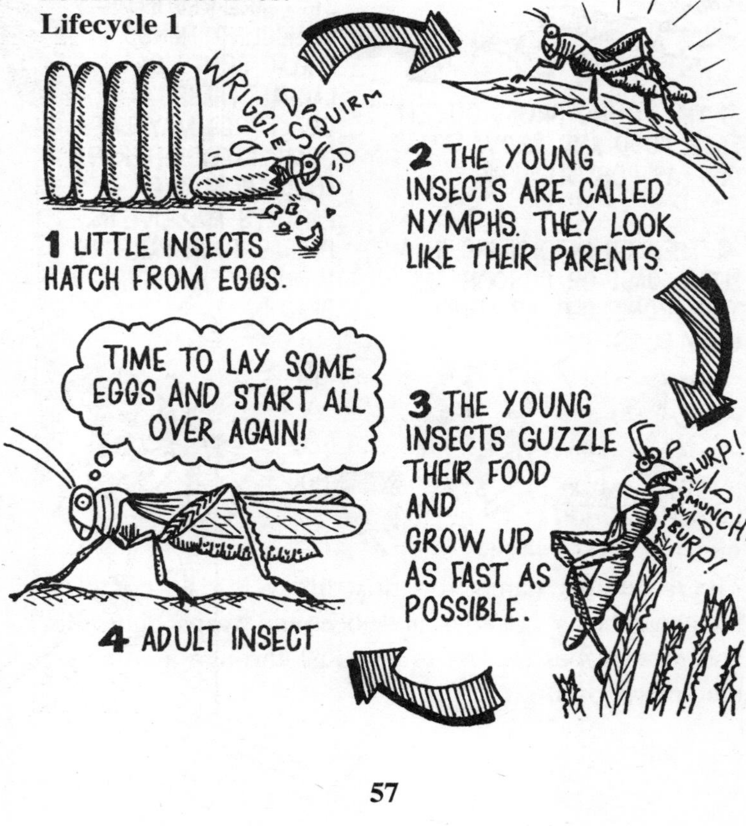

WRIGGLE SQUIRM

1 LITTLE INSECTS HATCH FROM EGGS.

2 THE YOUNG INSECTS ARE CALLED NYMPHS. THEY LOOK LIKE THEIR PARENTS.

TIME TO LAY SOME EGGS AND START ALL OVER AGAIN!

3 THE YOUNG INSECTS GUZZLE THEIR FOOD AND GROW UP AS FAST AS POSSIBLE.

SLURP! MUNCH! BURP!

4 ADULT INSECT

The scientific name for this loathsome lifecycle is "incomplete metamorphosis" (met-a-more-foe-sis). This describes a changing body. Mantids, locusts, dragonflies develop like this.

Lifecycle 2

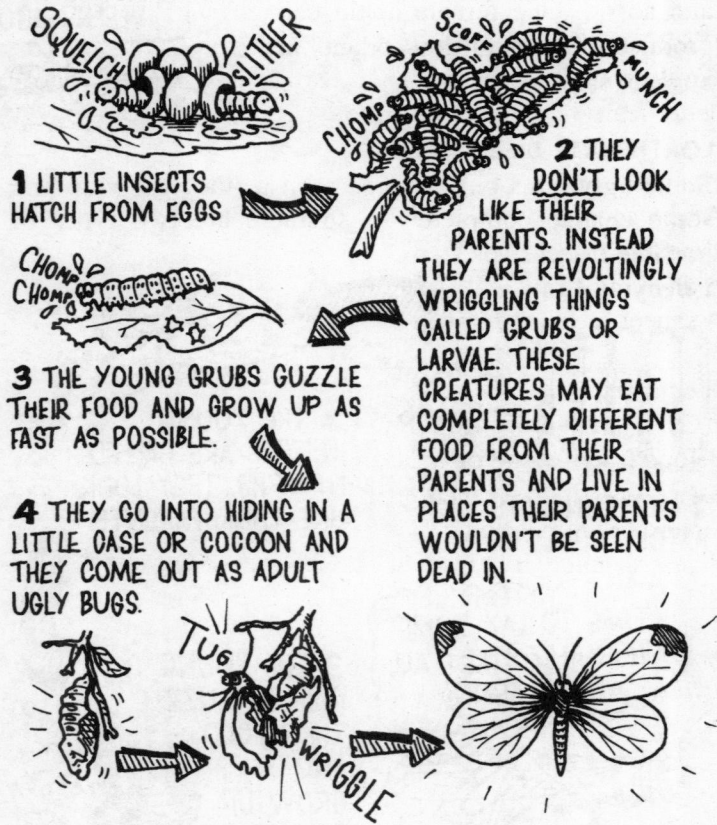

SQUELCH SLITHER

SCOFF MUNCH CHOMP

1 LITTLE INSECTS HATCH FROM EGGS

2 THEY DON'T LOOK LIKE THEIR PARENTS. INSTEAD THEY ARE REVOLTINGLY WRIGGLING THINGS CALLED GRUBS OR LARVAE. THESE CREATURES MAY EAT COMPLETELY DIFFERENT FOOD FROM THEIR PARENTS AND LIVE IN PLACES THEIR PARENTS WOULDN'T BE SEEN DEAD IN.

CHOMP CHOMP

3 THE YOUNG GRUBS GUZZLE THEIR FOOD AND GROW UP AS FAST AS POSSIBLE.

4 THEY GO INTO HIDING IN A LITTLE CASE OR COCOON AND THEY COME OUT AS ADULT UGLY BUGS.

TUG WRIGGLE

The scientific name for this lifecycle is "complete metamorphosis". Beetles, ants, bees and wasps, butterflies and moths, flies and mosquitoes go through a complete metamorphosis.

TERRIBLE TABLE MANNERS

Would you like to go to dinner with an insect? If so, you'd better learn how to eat like one.

You will need:
A new sponge
Tape
A drinking straw
A saucer of orange juice

What you do:
1 Cut a small piece from the sponge.
2 Tape it to the end of the drinking straw.
3 Try to suck up a saucer of orange juice.
Congratulations! You're eating like a fly. Flies also sick up digestive juice. It helps them to dissolve their food before they slurp it up! (Don't try this!)

TOO HORRIBLE TO WATCH

Films are full of insects – especially scary films. There are giant ants and giant flies. And it's amazing how many space monsters look like insects.

In fact, film designers often study ugly bugs to get good ideas for a really ugly monster.

But who needs made-up insect monsters when some real-life insects are far more creepy?

First prize for creepiness Diopsid flies can see round corners because their eyes are on long stalks.

Second prize for creepiness There's a type of weevil that has a neck as long as the rest of its body. And no one knows why it's so long!

HORRIBLE BEETLES

Most people think that beetles look horribly ugly. Especially big black beetles that run over your foot and seem to enjoy it. The bad news is that of all the many orders of insects, beetles are the biggest group. And it's getting bigger because scientists are always discovering new species! Amazingly enough there is only one basic design for a beetle body.

Ugly bug fact file

Name of creature:	Beetle
Where found:	Worldwide. Found just about anywhere you can imagine except in the sea, although some beetles live on beaches.
Distinguishing features:	Most beetles have short feelers. Folded forewings over the hind wings protect the beastly beetle body.

FOUL FEELERS

UGLY FACE

PROTECTIVE COVERING

CREEPY LEGS

UNBELIEVABLE BEETLES

With so many species of beetle it's inevitable that some of them are horribly amazing. And some of them have unbelievably horrible effects on human homes and food. But which of these beetles are too unbelievable to be true?

True or false?
1 The biscuit beetle eats, would you believe, biscuits. That's the bad news. The good news is that it doesn't like chocolate biscuits – only those nasty digestives you don't eat anyway. True/false

2 The cigarette beetle eats (howls of amazement) cigarettes. Its larvae especially like the tobacco and they never take any notice of the health warnings. True/false
3 The violin beetle *doesn't* eat violins – it just looks like a violin with legs. It lives amongst layers of fungus in trees in Indonesia. True/false

4 The ice-cream beetle used to live in the Arctic where it ate small flies. More recently it has become a pest of cold stores where its favourite food is tutti-frutti ice cream. True/false

5 "Tippling Tommy" is the nickname for a beetle that bores holes in wine and rum barrels. Tippling Tommy is actually a teetotaller. That's to say it never touches the alcohol inside the barrels – it prefers the wood! True/false

6 The drug store beetle is the name given to a biscuit beetle that lives in medicine cabinets. It enjoys slurping up some medicines, including many poisons! True/false

7 The giant gargling beetle is a rainforest beetle that takes a mouthful of dew and makes a loud gargling sound first thing in the morning. True/false

8 The bacon beetle beats you to breakfast every time by looting your larder in the night and munching your meats. Its favourite food is – you guessed it ... bacon! True/false

9 The museum beetle is so fond of living in the past that it lives in dusty old display cases and eats museum specimens. Its favourite food ... preserved ugly bugs. True/false

10 Deathwatch beetles live in wood. Some English churches contain families of beetles that have lived there for hundreds of years. True/false

DARE YOU MAKE FRIENDS WITH ... A LADYBIRD?

One kind of beetle that definitely does exist is the ladybird. If you've ever wanted to get to know one socially this is your opportunity.

1 First look for some tempting aphids. They can be white, brown or black "greenfly" which you'll find on your rose bushes and other plants in summer.

2 Break off a small branch or leaves swarming with aphids and place the lot in a jam jar.

3 Add a ladybird. You can find them from the late spring onwards on bushes and fences. Watch your ladybird get to work. Lovely ladybirds can gobble up 100 greenfly a day.

4 Handle your ladybird gently and let it go after lunch. Do you really want to know what happens if things go wrong and your date gets upset? Try tickling it gently with a leaf of grass. It will produce nasty tasting liquid. This will definitely put you off eating it. If you tickle it more it will roll on its back and pretend to be dead – a quick way to end your lunch date. If you upset it a lot it will bite. And beware – they *do* bite!

HOW NOT TO UPSET A LADYBIRD

During lunch you can discuss any subject with the ladybird without causing offence. This is because ladybirds don't understand English. Silly rhymes such as...

Ladybird, ladybird
Fly away home!
Your house is on fire
And your children are gone!

NOT THAT OLD CHESTNUT AGAIN!

...will not offend your ladybird in the least. This is also because:

1 Ladybirds don't have homes. A sheltered leaf is good enough for them. So it is unlikely they would be bothered if their home *was* on fire.

2 Ladybirds can fly but no ladybird would ever fly towards a fire. (Only maniac moths do that.)

3 Ladybirds don't give two hoots for their children. Once their eggs are laid, that's that!

GOT A TOUGH JOB? GET A BEETLE TO DO IT

Beetles don't only come in a horrible variety of shapes and sizes. They also have a mind-boggling array of lifestyles, and where there's a job to be done there's a beetle at the ready.

BEWARE IT'S A BOMBARDIER!

Get yourself the ultimate in personal self-defence systems! Beat off the bullies with a bombardier beetle gun. Unique self-mixing action for nasty boiling chemicals. Amazing internal heating system in abdomen heats chemicals to temperature of 100°C and fires at 500 to 1000 squirts a second!

The bombardier beetle gun is maintenance free. Just let it crunch on a few smaller insects now and then.

ELM BARK BEETLE TREE SURGEON

Unsightly elm trees getting you down? Need a bit more light? Call us now. Try our unique Dutch elm disease fungus formula - a revolting little rootless plant that terminates trees. We'll soon get in under the bark and wipe out the woody weeds!

▷ Forest felled.
▷ No job too large.
Disease established in UK - 1970s. Over 25 million elms eliminated.

BRIGHTEN UP YOUR HOME

With a firefly lantern. As used in Brazil, the West Indies and Far East. Firefly lanterns cast a soft green or yellow light from the bodies of female fireflies. Forty fireflies are as bright as one candle. They need no power or batteries - it's all done with chemicals by your friendly firefly.

THIS LOOKS LIKE A JOB FOR SUPERSEXTON!

Sexton Beetle
and Sons and Daughters

Dead? Just call in your friendly family funeral directors. No job too large. We'll bury anything even if it means ten hour shifts. Free personal limb chopping service to make burials easier. Professional after-care service. Our little grubs will look after the grave. No fee charged but they do like to come to the funeral feast. That's to feast on the dead body of course!

NEED ANY DUNG SHIFTED?

Scarab Beetle Services will get rid of the lot. Dung ball rolling and burying our speciality. What's more we'll even lay our eggs on it and get our grubs to eat it!

'Scarab beetles were round before the dung hit the ground. They had 7,000 on the job and soon got rid of it all! My savannah has never looked tidier.' A.N.Elephant, Africa.

JEWELLERY WITH A MIND OF ITS OWN

Ever wanted some jewellery that puts itself away at night? Buy some living jewel beetle jewellery as worn in many parts of the world. Choice of beautiful metallic colours including gold. Breaks the ice at parties, e.g. 'And what would your earring like to eat?' Manufacturer's warning: Don't allow your jewellery to lay eggs on your furniture. The grubs can lunch on your lounge suite for up to 47 years before turning into more jewel beetles.

BEETLE BATTLES

Beetles don't have much of a family life, but they take proper care of their property – if they don't, they'll soon find themselves in big trouble.

STAG BEETLE WRESTLING

If you were a male stag beetle, this is how you would defend your territory (your territory would be a bit of a tree branch). The aim of the game is to drop your opponent off the branch...

You will need:

A pair of giant jaws that look like deer antlers

What you do:

1 Eye up your opponent.

2 Grab him round the middle with your jagged jaws and try to flip him on to his back – that's easier said than done when he's trying to do the same to you...

3 If you lose, *you* fall off the branch and land on your back, where you risk being dissected and chewed by a waiting bunch of ... awesome ants.

AWESOME ANTS

Everyone knows about ants. They're easy enough to identify in the summer when they march into your home to inspect your kitchen. Ants can be pretty awful – they get everywhere from your plants to your pants – but they can be awesome, too, in all sorts of horrible ways.

Ugly bug fact file

Name of creature:	Ant
Where found:	Worldwide on land. They always live in nests.
Distinguishing features:	Most ants are less than 1 cm long. Narrow waist between thorax and abdomen. Angled feelers.

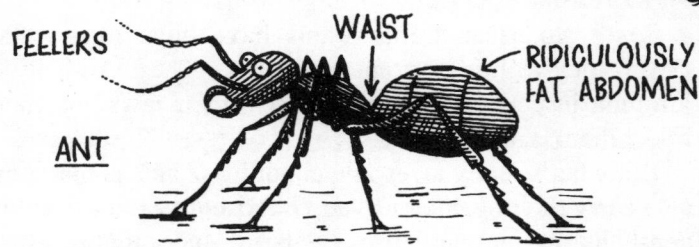

FEELERS

WAIST

RIDICULOUSLY FAT ABDOMEN

ANT

AWESOME ANT ANTICS

1 Since 1880 German law has protected red ants' nests from destruction. Why? Because the ants from each nest eat an awesome 100,000 caterpillars and other ugly pests every day.

2 Honeypot ants squeeze sticky honeydew from aphids. They're doing the aphids a favour – *they* don't need the sickly stuff. The ants keep feeding this honeydew to particular ants in their nest to make them swell up like little beads. The swollen ants then sick up the honeydew to feed the rest of the nest. Awful!

SHE'S GOING TO BE SICK ~ DINNER TIME EVERYONE!

3 Weaver ants make their own tents from leaves sewn together with silk. Their larvae produce the silk and the awesome ants use their young as living shuttles weaving them backwards and forwards! The adult ants just have to touch their larvae with their feelers whenever they need a bit more silk.

4 South American trapjaw ants have huge long jaws. (Well, they're huge by ant standards.) They catch little jumping insects called springtails in their jaws and then inject them with poison.

But what's really awesome about these ants is that they also carry their eggs, or larvae, in those gruesome jaws as gently as any mother carries her baby – isn't that nice!

5 Leaf-cutter ants grow their own crops. The ants cut up the vegetation and mix it up with their droppings to make fertilizer. Then they grow fungus on it for food. They even weed unwanted kinds of fungus from their garden and put it on their compost heap. When a leaf-cutter queen leaves to start a new nest she always takes a bit of fungus with her to start a new garden.

6 And after the hard work of farming comes the harvest. Harvester ants live in the desert where they gather seed grains and make bread by chewing it all up and removing the husks. The ants store their bread until they get hungry.

7 The Australian bulldog ant has an awfully ugly bite. Not only is the bite painful, but this appalling ant then injects poison into the wound! Thirty stings can kill a human in 15 minutes. This is probably the most dangerous ant in the world...

8 Or is it? In the jungles of Africa and South America lurks something even more awesome. It's 100 metres long and 2 metres wide. It eats anything foolish enough to get in its way. It reduces lizards, snakes and even larger animals to skeletons. And even big strong humans run for their lives rather than face it. Nothing can fight against it and live. What is this terrifying creature? Is it an ant? Well yes, actually, it's a column of 20 million army ants. The ants have no settled home. They spend their time invading places and being awesomely awful to any creature that gets in their way. If you live in South America it could get rid of cockroaches in your home, but you'd have to get yourself out of the way first.

9 Red South American Amazon ants fight fierce battles against their deadly enemies – the black ants. Red ant foot patrols are sent out to find a way into the enemy nest. They leave a trail for the main army to follow. The main army attacks and the Amazon ants use their curved jaws to slice off the heads of the opposing black ants. Some of the Amazon ants spray gases to further confuse the black ants. Then the Amazon ants retreat with their prisoners – the black ant grubs.

QUICK – EVERYONE GRAB A GRUB!

The grubs quickly pick up the smell of the Amazon ants and this fools them into thinking they're red ants too! But they aren't, and the poor befuddled black ants spend the rest of their lives as slaves to the awesome Amazon ants.

10 Marauder ants in Indonesia even build their own roads. These roads are often as long as 90 metres – and if you're ant-sized, that's *awesome*. Some of the roads even have soil roofs to protect them. And the ants have to follow a strict highway code:

A Always keep to your own part of the road. Returning ants in the middle, outwards ants at the edges.

B Move anything that gets in your way. If it's big, gnaw it. If it's small, get the younger ants to carry it off the road. If it's edible, bring it back to the nest (100 workers can shift one earthworm, 30 workers can shift one seed.)

C If you cross any other ant roads . . . kill the other ants. All ugly bugs that get in the way must be eaten alive.

Bet you never knew
There are 10,000 species af ant. But they do have some things in common.
- *An ant nest is ruled a queen who spends her life laying eggs.*
- *All the ordinary worker ants are female.*
- *Males only hatch out at mating time and they die once they have mated!*

73

AN INTELLIG-ANT MAN

Almost as awesome as the ants themselves, are some of the humans who studied them. Take Baron Lubbock, for example...

But all this was nothing compared to his life-long love affair – with insects. The barmy baron devised an awesome ant experiment...

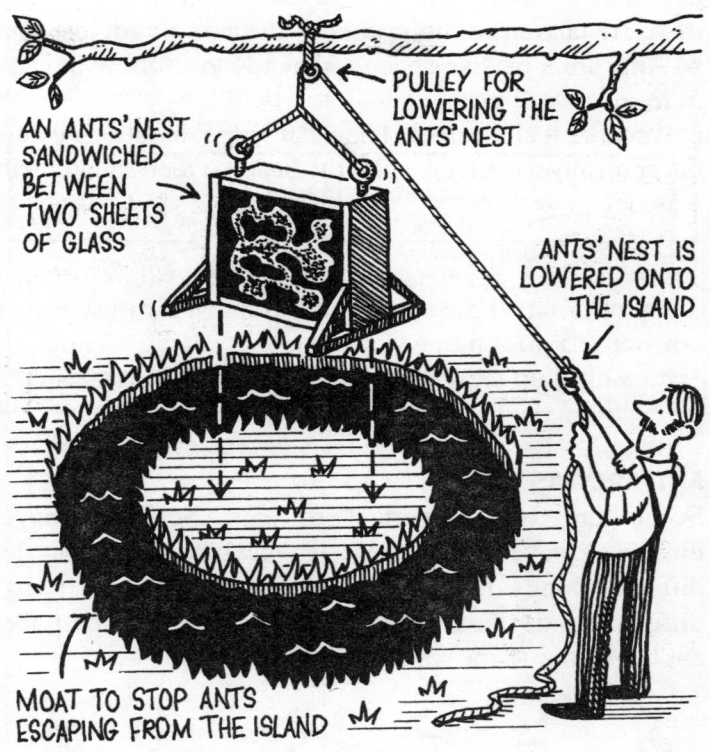

AN ANTS' NEST SANDWICHED BETWEEN TWO SHEETS OF GLASS

PULLEY FOR LOWERING THE ANTS' NEST

ANTS' NEST IS LOWERED ONTO THE ISLAND

MOAT TO STOP ANTS ESCAPING FROM THE ISLAND

and discovered...

1 Ants can be ancient. Worker ants can live for seven years, and queen ants for 14 years before they die of old age.
2 Ants respond strangely to sounds – they listen through their legs!
3 Tiny ugly bugs hide in ants' nests.

He devised another ant experiment ... with mazes, obstacle courses and a table with movable rings – all ant-sized, of course. He wanted to find out if ants had a sense of direction. What do you think he discovered?

a) We're talking ant brains here – the ants all got lost.

b) Ants are a bit like sheep – they always follow the ant in front.

c) Ants are really bright. They can judge directions using the sun's rays, even on a cloudy day – so they found their way out.

Answers: a) False. **b)** Partly true. Ants do follow one another – the leading ant makes a trail for the others to follow. **c)** Amazing but true. Ants are better at finding their way than some humans.

ANT AROMAS

Scents are very important to ants. Scientists have discovered several ant scents each of which makes ants do different things. Imagine you were a scientist observing different kinds of ant behaviour. Could you match up the ant behaviour to the smell that causes it?

1 ALARM SMELL
2 NEST SMELL
3 TRAIL SMELL
4 QUEEN BREEDING TIME SMELL
5 BIG NASTY ENEMY SMELL
6 DEAD ANT SMELL

a) THE ANTS TRY TO BURY YOU IN AN ANT CEMETERY

b) THE ANTS RUN AWAY FROM THEIR NEST

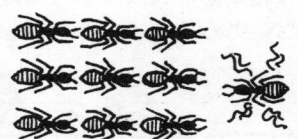

c) AN ANT ARMY IS SUMMONED

d) SOME ANTS TRY TO RUN AND OTHERS STAY TO FIGHT

e) ANTS FIGHT EACH OTHER

f) THE ANTS FIND THEIR WAY HOME

g) THE ANTS DON'T DO ANYTHING IF YOU HAVE THIS SMELL

h) MALE ANTS ARE ATTRACTED BY THIS SMELL

Answers: 1 c) 2 g) 3 f) 4 h) 5 d) 6 a)

77

SLEAZY BEES

Ants and bees belong to the same gruesome group of ugly bugs. So it's no surprise to find some bee species live in nests ruled by queens. Humans tend to say that bees are "good" because they make honey – but bees can be bad in their own horrible way. You'll get a buzz (ha ha) out of teaching your teacher their ugly secrets.

Ugly bug fact file

Name of creature:	Bees and wasps
Where found:	Worldwide. Most bees live on their own. Only a few species live in large nests.
Horrible habits:	They sting people.
Any helpful habits:	Bees make honey and pollinate flowers
Distinguishing features:	Thin waist between thorax and abdomen. Four transparent wings. Bees have long tongues and often carry yellow lumps of pollen on their hind legs.

NASTY
STINGY BIT

WAIST

BEE

TONGUE

POLLEN

INSIDE THE BEEHIVE

Bees that live together in nests are called "social bees". Well, you'd have to be social to live with *this* lot.

Quarrelling queens Usually there's just one queen in a hive. She spends her time laying eggs. But sometimes more than one queen hatches out, and things can turn rather nasty. The first queen to appear kills off any rivals.

Drowsy drones It's a lovely life for a drone. Your worker sisters keep house for you. And they even feed you. You don't have a sting because you never need to fight anyone. There's just one problem. You've got to battle with hundreds of brothers for a chance to mate. If you mate with a queen you die.

Weary workers What do the workers do? Well (funnily enough) they work. And they work. And they work. In a few short weeks the worn-out workers work themselves to death!

ME NEXT! MOVE OVER!

DON'T PUSH IN!

JOBS FOR WORKERS

clean the hive • nurse the grubs • guard the nest • fetch pollen and nectar from flowers • make honey • feed the queen • feed the grubs • feed the drones • make wax (it oozes from the worker's bodies) • build new cells using wax

HORRIBLE HONEY

So you love honey. Doesn't the thought of a lovely honey sandwich make your mouth water? And NOTHING is going to put you off it – right? RIGHT. Here's how bees make honey – complete with the horrible details.

1 Bees make honey from the sweet nectar produced by flowers. It's horribly hard work. Some bees collect from 10,000 flowers a day. They often visit up to 64 million flowers to make just 1 kg of honey.

2 That's good news for the flowers because the busy bees also pick up pollen. They even have little leg baskets to carry it. The bee takes the pollen to another flower of the same type. There, some of the precious pollen brushes on to the flower, fertilizes it and so helps it form a seed.

POLLEN BASKETS

3 Why do you think the flower goes to all the bother of making scents, bright colours and nectar. Is it all for us? No! It's to attract bees. Lots of bees means lots of flowers. See?

4 A bee uses her long tongue and a pump in her head to suck up nectar. She stores the nectar in a special stomach.

LONG
SLIMY
TONGUE

5 Nectar is mostly water. To get rid of the water, bees sick up the nectar and dry it out on their tongues – ugh.

6 Then they store the honey in honeycomb cells until they need it. That's unless humans steal it for their sandwiches!

BEEWILDER SOME BEES

It's best done on a summer's day in a garden terrace or park where there are lots of bees.

1 Put out a vase of flowers. Watch the bees find the flowers and go off to tell their friends.

2 Meanwhile you hide the flowers.

3 Back come some more bees. They are humming with happiness at the thought of all that lovely nectar and pollen.

4 But there are no flowers. Result: Bewildered bees.

BEES BEE-WARE

Bees have lots of horrible enemies. To stop them, every hive has its guards. The guards don't receive training but if they did it might look like this...

Honey-bee As long as they've got some food you let them in. If not, chase them away! Bee careful. Bees from other hives sometimes steal our honey!

Death's-head hawk moth
This nastily-named night raider flies into our hive. It licks our lovely honey with its terribly long tongue. Bee on your guard after dark!

 **African honey-badger** This hairy horror breaks open our honeycomb with its long claws. It makes shocking stinks to drive away our guards. STING ON SIGHT!

Blister-beetle grub
Bee careful when you visit flowers. This greedy grub will ambush you! It hitches a free ride to our hive. Then it hides in our cells and guzzles our grubs.

 **Mouse** Another horrible honey hunter. STING TO DEATH! Getting rid of the mouse's body is a bit of a bother. It's too big to move. Cover the body with gooey gum from trees. The gum will mummify the mouse and stop it stinking!

Humans
They only want our honey and our bees' wax for polish and candles. Sting them if they get too close. You can't pull your sting from their skin. If you try it'll drag your insides out. Never mind - you'll die a heroine!

Cuckoo bee Don't be a cuckoo and let them in. It's easy to think they're one of us. But once inside they'll lay their ugly eggs.

82

PRETTY UGLIES

What better on a summer's day than to laze about with a cool drink and watch the butterflies flutter past! And isn't it amazing that there are thousands of different kinds of butterfly throughout the world in an incredible variety of shapes and forms. Pity about their horrible habits and the even more gruesome things they got up to when they were caterpillars!

Ugly bug fact file

PROBOSCIS

BUTTERFLY

Name of creature:	Butterfly
Where found:	Worldwide. The larger butterflies live in tropical countries.
Horrible habits:	Caterpillars eat our vegetables.
Any helpful habits:	Butterflies pollinate flowers and look pretty.
Distinguishing features:	Two pairs of wings, often highly colourful. Narrow body. Long, coiled feeding tube (proboscis) attached to mouth.

THE GOOD, THE BAD AND THE UGLY

The good

1 Butterflies and many moths have amazing coloured patterns on their wings. These colours are made up of tiny overlapping scales and they help male and female butterflies to find each other before mating.

2 Butterflies and moths can detect smells using their antennae. The male Indian moon moth can scent a female over 5 km away. It follows the scent through woods – round trees and across streams – ignoring all other smells. That's like you sniffing your supper 75 km away!

3 Butterflies can smell through their feet! That way they can land on a leaf and know what type it is. Which helps female butterflies to lay their eggs on leaves their caterpillars can happily eat.

The bad

1 Newly hatched *polyphemous* (polly-fee-mouse) moth caterpillars are tiny. But they start eating straight away and within 48 hours they increase their weight 80,000 times.

That's bad news for the local greenery because the chomping caterpillars can strip all the leaves from a tree.

2 Common large white butterflies really are as common as muck. They fly across the English channel in swarms so vast that a big band of these bad butterflies once stopped a cricket match.

3 But if you're into vast swarms, the African migrant butterfly takes some beating. A scientist once tried to watch a crowd of them fly past. This was a bad idea because the procession continued for three months without stopping!

DAY 6: CAN'T GO ON MUCH LONGER...

And the ugly

1 Ugly scenes have been reported when butterflies get drunk. It's true – the juices from rotting fruit are slightly alcoholic and even one slurp is too much for a butterfly. It flops and droops around on the ground.

2 The gruesome death's-head hawk moth (last seen stealing into beehives) has a sinister skull shape on its thorax. Its equally ugly caterpillars like to nibble the poisonous deadly-nightshade plant. The noxious nightshade makes the caterpillars taste so terrible that no one in their right mind would ever want to eat them.

3 Brown-tail moth caterpillars are also pretty ugly. Their bodies are covered in sharp needle-like hairs that break off in your skin and make it itch like mad.

COULD YOU BE A LARGE BLUE BUTTERFLY?

The large blue butterfly is – amazingly enough, a large, blue butterfly. In Britain it is very rare and is currently only found in a few places in the West Country. Large blue butterflies are also found in France and Central Europe.

Like all butterflies, the large blue begins life as an egg that hatches into a caterpillar that turns into a chrysalis that turns into a butterfly. But it does horribly odd things on the way. Imagine you were a large blue butterfly. Would you survive?

1 You hatch out. How do you get rid of the remains of your egg?
a) Eat it.
b) Bury it.
c) Throw it at a passing wasp.
2 You live on a wild thyme or marjoram plant. Suddenly your plant is invaded by another large blue caterpillar that starts eating your leaves. What do you do?
a) Agree to share the plant.
b) Eat the rival caterpillar.
c) Hide until it's gone away.
3 After guzzling all the leaves you can, and shedding your skin three times, you fall off your plant. As you amble along, an ant suddenly appears. What do you do?
a) Persuade it to give you a cuddle – then give it some honey in return.
b) Grip its feelers and refuse to let go.
c) Roll over and pretend to be dead.
4 The ant takes you to its nest. It shoves you in a chamber with the ant grubs. What do you do next?

a) Make friends with them.

b) Raid the ants' food supplies and help yourself.

c) Eat the ant grubs.

5 You spend the winter sleeping in the ants' nest. Soon after you wake you hang yourself from the ceiling and turn into a chrysalis. About three weeks later you fall on the floor and crawl out of your nasty damp chrysalis. Congratulations – you're now an adult butterfly! But how do you escape from the ants' nest?

a) You have to dig an escape tunnel.

b) You crawl your way out all by yourself.

c) You pretend to be dead and an ant carries you out.

6 Free at last! What's the first thing you do?

a) Find something to eat – a dead ant will do.

b) Find a mate.

c) Dry out your brand-new wet wings.

And then you fly off to enjoy your new life! Make the best of it – you've only got 15 days to live!

MUM, WHY IS THIS ANT LICKING ME?

IT'S A LONG STORY!

Answers: 1 a) Waste not – want not. **2 b) 3 a)** It's true! The caterpillar produces its own honey-like substance. **4 c) 5 b) 6 c)**.

BARMY BELIEFS AND STRANGE SCIENTISTS

For hundreds of years no one knew exactly where caterpillars came from. And there were some pretty strange suggestions. Here's the Roman writer Pliny...

DEW FALLS FROM TREES IN SPRING AND TURNS INTO CATERPILLARS.

But no one realized that caterpillars were anything to do with butterflies. Then in the seventeenth century, the microscope was invented. All over Europe scientists started to observe insects in gruesome close-up detail.

One of these scientists was Jan Swammerdam (1637–1680) who lived in Holland. As a young man he studied medicine. But he much preferred studying insects to humans! His work was very delicate and he even used tiny scissors that had to be sharpened under a microscope. One day he cut open a cocoon and found ... mixed-up gooey bits of butterfly. Jan had proved that caterpillars turn into butterflies.

But people didn't believe him. The introduction to his insects book, written in 1669, didn't help either. Swammerdam said that the way insects changed their form was...

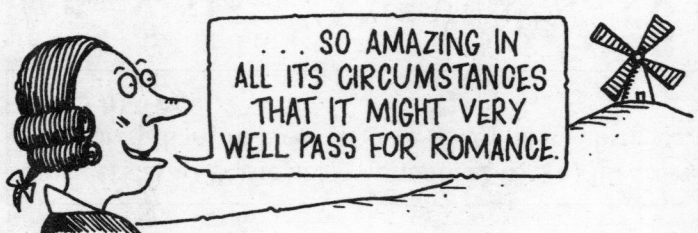

... SO AMAZING IN ALL ITS CIRCUMSTANCES THAT IT MIGHT VERY WELL PASS FOR ROMANCE.

But as more scientists studied butterflies they discovered that Jan was quite right. These scientists were the first lepidopterists – a horribly complicated name for people who study butterflies and moths.

LETHAL LEPIDOPTERISTS

Nowadays lepidopterists are mild-mannered folk who enjoy observing and photographing butterflies in what is left of their natural surroundings. It wasn't always like that.

1 In the eighteenth century, fashionable ladies wore brightly coloured butterfly and moth wings as *jewellery*.

2 Traditional butterfly hunters raced after butterflies with big nets shouting, "There she goes!" When they caught an unfortunate flutterer they plunged it into a bottle of poison and pinned it to a board – *horrible!*

3 In the nineteenth century, hunters collected hundreds of butterflies from tropical forests in New Guinea. When the butterflies soared too high they fired guns loaded with fine shot to bring them down!

4 The British collector, James Joicey, spent a fortune over 30 years paying people to collect butterflies for him. By 1927 this millionaire's son had run out of cash. But when Joicey died in 1932 his collection numbered 1,500,000 dead butterflies.

IS YOUR TEACHER A LEPIDOPTERIST?
Find out the easy way with this teacher-teasing test.

1 How can you always tell a moth from a butterfly?
a) Moths come out at night and butterflies in the day.
b) Moths rest with their wings flat. Butterflies rest with their wings upright.
c) Moths don't have knobs on their antennae.
2 How does a hairstreak butterfly avoid having its head bitten off?
a) It has a dummy head.
b) It has a head with armour on it.
c) It bites first.

3 Silk comes from the cocoons spun by the silkworm moth caterpillar. According to legend this was discovered by a Chinese Empress in 2640 BC. But how did she make her discovery?

a)

b)

c)

a) By careful scientific observation.
b) Her cat brought in a cocoon to show her.
c) A cocoon fell into her cup of tea.

4 Where does a cigar-case bearer caterpillar live?

a) In a cigar case.

b) In a little house made of bits of plants joined with silk.

c) In the fur of animals.

5 How can you tell when a butterfly is old?

a) Ragged wings

b) It goes grey.

c) Droopy feelers.

I LOOK MORE LIKE A CABBAGE GREY!

Answers: 1 c) All the others are generally true but not always. **2 a)** One head is just a decoy. A horrible hunter thinks it's bitten off the butterfly's head. Instead all it's got is a mouthful of wing. **3 c)** The hot liquid loosened the strands of silk. **4 b) 5 a)** Old butterflies have actually been around for just a few weeks. They hardly ever live much longer.

SAVAGE SPIDERS

The horrible thing about spiders is that you can't get away from them. You can see their webs on plants and washing lines and in garden sheds. And when you come home you'll probably find spiders hiding there too. Spiders aren't insects but that doesn't make them any less horrible. In fact, more people are scared of spiders than are scared of insects. Maybe it's because spiders have some seriously savage habits.

Ugly bug fact file

Name of creature:	Spider
Where found:	Worldwide. On land and in fresh water.
Horrible habits:	Paralyses prey with poison fangs and sucks out the juices.
Any helpful habits:	Keeps down the numbers of insects.
Distinguishing features:	Head and thorax joined. Separate abdomen. Four pairs of jointed legs. Eight eyes. Produces silk. Inside is a breathing organ called a book lung.

SEPARATE ABDOMEN

EYES

EIGHT HORRIBLE HAIRY LEGS

HEAD AND CHEST JOINED

Spiders can't always be savage, surely? They care for their young – sometimes. Mummy wolf-spiders often carry baby spiders on their backs. Ah, how sweet. It's a pity mum eats dad and the babies eat each other. And then there are the *really* savage bits. Read on at your own risk!

TEACHER'S TERROR TEST

Turn the tables on your teacher as you test his terror tolerance.

1 How do spiders avoid getting caught in their own webs?

a) Nifty footwork.

b) They have oily non-stick feet.

c) They slide down a line and pulley.

2 How long can a spider live?

a) Six months

b) 25 years

c) 75 years

3 When a spider sheds its skin what parts does it get rid of?

a) Its skin.

b) The front of its eyes

c) The lining of its guts and book lung (breathing organ).

4 What does a spider do with its old web?

a) Wear it.

EIGHT WALKING STICKS – HE MUST BE OLD!

b) Throw it away.

c) Eat it.

5 What does a spitting spider do?

a) It spits a poison that kills its victims as they try to escape.

b) It lassoes its victims with a 10-cm squirt of silk that ties them to the ground.

c) Nothing. It sits around looking strangely sinister.

6 How do small spiders fly through the air?

a) They use electricity in the atmosphere.

b) They inflate their bodies like tiny balloons.

c) They spin little silk parachutes.

7 What, according to legend, is the best way to cure the bite of a tarantula spider?

a) A cup of tea.

b) A lively folk dance.

c) Suck out the venom.

8 How many spiders are there in one square metre of grassland?

a) 27

b) 500

c) 1,795

9 How does a spider get into your bath?

a) It crawls up the drainpipe but can't climb out of the bath.

b) It drops down from the ceiling but can't climb out of the bath.

c) It crawls out of the taps but can't climb out of the bath.

Answers: 1 b) 2 b) Tarantulas can live this long. **3** All of these! **4 c) 5 b) 6 c)** Sometimes it's a length of silk and sometimes it's a silken loop that acts just like a parachute. **7 b)** A spider's bite is supposed to make you dance madly — that's called tarantism. The tarantella folk dance is supposed to cure the bite. **8 b)** Scientists reckon there are two billion spiders in England and Wales! **9 b)** The spider drops in for a drink of water. But the sides of the bath are too slippery for the spider to climb out again.

SAVAGE SPIDER FILE

So your teacher's terrified of spiders? Here are a few rational reasons why they're quite right to be scared.

The bird-eating spider – a terrifying tarantula

<u>Description</u>: Big. Can grow to 25cm long including legs.

<u>Lives in</u>: South America

<u>Fearsome features</u>: Scarifyingly hairy

<u>Marital status</u>: Single

<u>Horrible habits</u>: Eats birds and frogs.

<u>The bad news</u>: It has a painful bite.

<u>The very bad news</u>: Those hairs can give you a nasty rash.

<u>The absolutely appalling news</u>: People keep them as pets.

The black widow spider

Description: Body 2.5 cm long. Always in black with a sinister red mark on her underside.

Lives in: Southern USA

Fearsome features: One of the most poisonous spiders.

Marital statu : Probably a widow

Horrible habits: Eating her husband. (Streetwise males give female spiders a nice fresh crunchy bug wrapped up in silk. Just so she won't get hungry.)

Redeeming features: Rarely bites people. A shy spider who doesn't like fighting and only bites if you come across her unexpectedly.

The bad news: She hides in places where you come across her unexpectedly.

The very bad news: Such as toilet seats.

The absolutely appalling news: And her poison is absolutely deadly. It's said to be 15 times deadlier than a rattlesnake's.

The wandering spider

Description: 12cm leg-span with hairy legs.

Lives in: Brazil

Fearsome features: Said to be the most dangerous spider in the world.

Marital status: No one dare ask.

Horrible habits: Comes into houses uninvited. Wanders around biting people.

Redeeming features: Keeps your home free of bugs and burglars.

The bad news: Its bite is poisonous.

The very bad news: Nasty personality. Likes fighting and frightening. When disturbed, bites first and asks questions later.

The absolutely appalling news: Hides in clothing and shoes. Although an antidote exists, the poison can kill.

STRANGE SPIDER BELIEFS AND EVEN STRANGER SCIENTISTS

Some spider scientists had strange ideas and others were involved in strange experiments. Spider science (arachnology) started with the Greeks. But Greek writer, Philostratus, had some rather strange ideas about spiders. He reckoned that spiders spin silk to keep warm. Nice try, Phil. Mind you, the Romans weren't much better. According to Pliny, spiders appeared from seeds that grew in rotting material.

Mad Mouffet We've all heard the rhyme about little Miss Muffet who got scared away by a great big spider. But did you know that she was a real person? Her name was Patience Mouffet and she was unfortunate enough to be the daughter of strange sixteenth-century spider scientist, Dr Thomas Mouffet. Why unfortunate'? Well, her dad used to dose her with live spiders whenever she had a cold. As a special treat Patience got to eat mashed up spiders on toast.

97

Brave Baerg Dr W J Baerg of Arkansas, USA, conducted some strange experiments with the aim of discovering exactly how deadly a venomous spider bite really was. In 1922 he deliberately allowed himself to be bitten by a poisonous black widow spider! The first test was a failure – the spider wouldn't bite. So Dr B tried again and this time he was delighted to get a nasty nip. When he got out of hospital three days later the spider scientist recorded that he'd felt unbearable pain. Now, there's a surprise.

HOSPITAL TREATMENT IS REQUIRED – I THINK!

In 1958 Dr Baerg was at it again. This time he decided to test spider bites on guinea pigs and rats rather than himself. But the intrepid investigator didn't escape pain altogether. He had an unhappy accident with a Trinidadean tarantula. Baerg was lining up the hairy horror to bite an unfortunate white rat when it bit him on the finger. (That's the spider not the rat.) Luckily Dr B found that the poison didn't harm him. So he allowed himself to get bitten by a Panamanian tarantula instead and this time suffered a stiff finger. So brave Dr Baerg concluded that tarantula bites weren't so bad after all!

COULD YOU BE A SPIDER SCIENTIST?
Can you predict the result of this strange spider experiment?

In 1948 Professor Hans Peters noticed that garden spiders always spun their webs at 4 o'clock in the morning. So he fed some spiders with caffeine (that's the chemical in coffee that wakes people up) and others with sleeping pills to see what would happen. What do you think he discovered?

a) Spiders are affected just like us. The spiders stimulated with coffee woke up at 1.30 am and then worked all night. The spiders drugged with sleeping pills slept until 10.35 am.

b) Spiders are completely different from humans. The caffeine-stimulated spiders went to sleep. And the spiders drugged with sleeping pills worked harder than ever.

c) The urge to spin webs was stronger than any drug. The spiders made some odd-looking webs. But they continued to start work at 4 am.

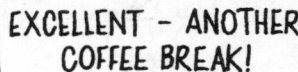

EXCELLENT – ANOTHER COFFEE BREAK!

Answer: c)

> **Bet you never knew!**
> Spiders have spun webs in space. On 28 July 1973 garden spiders Arabella and Anita boldly blasted off into space to visit the Skylab space station. Their mission – an experiment to find whether they could spin webs in zero gravity. Their first efforts were untidy. They weren't used to floating around weightless. Later efforts were more successful although poor Anita died in orbit.

WEIRD WEBS

Spiders spin silk to produce their intricate webs. The webs they make catch flies and other unlucky creatures. But the more you find out about webs the weirder they seem.

1 To make one web, spiders need to spin different types of silk.

• Dry silk a thousandth of a millimetre thick for the spokes of a web.

• Stretchy silk covered in gluey droplets for the rest. The sticky bits take in moisture and stop the web drying out.

• Other kinds of silk for wrapping up eggs and dead insects.

2 Webs come in many shapes and sizes. Have you ever seen any of these?

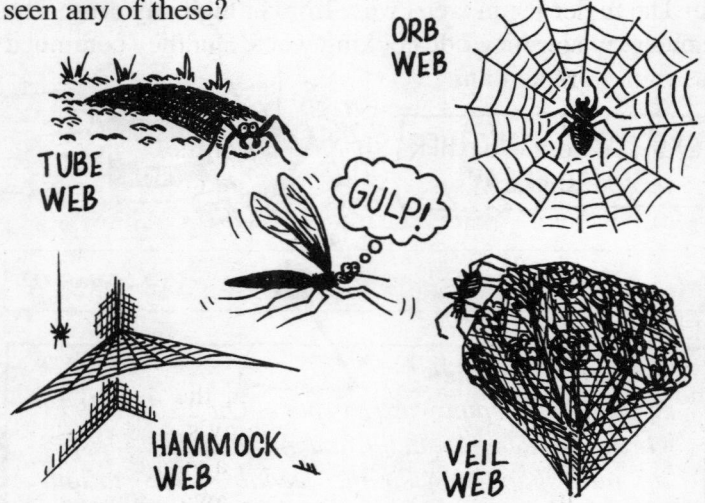

ORB WEB

TUBE WEB

GULP!

HAMMOCK WEB

VEIL WEB

3 The house spider makes a hammock-shaped web. The spider spits out bits of insect and leaves them lying around for someone else to tidy up – a horrible habit!

4 The trap-door spider digs a tunnel with a trap door at one end. The spider waits within. It grabs a passing insect and pulls it down. The door closes and the innocent victim is never seen again.

SHUT THE DOOR, LOVE – THERE'S A TERRIBLE DRAUGHT COMING DOWN THE TUNNEL!

5 The purse-web spider makes a purse-shaped web. This savage spider then stabs its victims through the web with its long poison fangs. Then before settling down to dinner it carefully repairs the tear.

6 Sinister *nephila* (Nef-illa) spiders spin giant webs up to 2 metres across to catch insects and sometimes even birds. And even fish aren't safe – in the early part of this century people in New Guinea used the silk to make fishing nets!

7 The web-throwing spider chucks its web over insects as they work under its hiding place. Then the spider drops in for tea.

8 When an insect gets caught in a spider's web, it struggles and the vibrations alert the spider. But the devious ero spider manages to sneak on to its enemy's web and bite the spider before it even realizes its got a visitor. Evil ero then sucks its victim dry and scurries away, leaving an empty spider husk sitting in its web!

9 In some places in California, spiders' webs fall like snow. The flakes are made up of mixed-up spiders' webs blown together by the wind.

Bet you never knew

It's actually possible to spin and then weave spider silk. In 1709 Xavier Saint-Hilaire Bon of Montpelier showed the French Academy several pairs of spider-silk gloves. But according to a scientist who investigated the topic it takes 27,648 female spiders to make less than half a kilogram of silk. That didn't stop more people trying to spin spider silk. In the early 1990s the US Defence Department looked into the possibility. The reason – the silk is light, strong and very springy. Ideal for making bulletproof vests!

And now you know all about these hairy horrors...

DARE YOU MAKE FRIENDS WITH ... A SPIDER?

To save spinning your own silk, try asking a spider to make some for you.

1 Cut a plastic lemonade bottle in half.

2 Add soil and twigs to the bottom half.

3 Now find your spider. Sheds and out-houses are good places to look. If you find a web the spider is normally hiding nearby. One spider is enough. Add two and one will eat the other! Be gentle, though – spiders are easily hurt!

4 Tape up the two halves of the bottle.

5 Feed your new friend with a small fly through the top of the bottle.

6 Check to see if she's spun any silk or made a web. If she has, go ahead and try knitting yourself a nice pair of spider silk gloves.

BITING BUGS

For us humans the most horrible thing about insects is the way they bite us. And suck blood and sometimes give us horrible diseases too. Maybe that's why people call a crowd of insects a "plague". Plagues are deadly diseases. In the past 10,000 years more people have died from diseases carried by insects than any other single cause. *Help!*

ROGUES' GALLERY
Here are the chief culprits.

Malarial mosquito

<u>Sex</u>: Female

<u>Habits</u>: Sucks blood before laying her eggs, while Mr Mosquito prefers plant juices.

<u>Weapons</u>: A long snout for sticking into people and a pump-action saliva gun to stop your blood setting.

<u>Last seen</u>: Sightings have been reported all over the world. Often loiters near water.

<u>Known crimes</u>: In hot countries her bite passes on germs that cause malaria. Victims suffer raging fever and feel very hot and then very cold. Responsible for one million deaths each year. Sometimes gives us yellow fever into the bargain.

<u>Danger rating</u>: Beware! Two billion people live in areas threatened by this brutal blood-sucker.

Body louse

Description: 1.5 - 3.5mm long. Has no wings.

Weapon: Blood-sucking tube

Habits: Sucks blood

Last seen: Hiding in the seams of clothes.

Known crimes: Disgusting droppings can contain germs that cause the deadly disease, typhus. Victims scratch the droppings and grisly germs into their skin.

Danger rating: Nasty. But nothing that a good bath and clean clothes can't cure.

Known associates: Head lice, or "nits", live in hair. They quite like clean hair and happily hop from head to Head. (Yes. Head teachers can get them too!)

Tsetse fly

Habits: Sucks blood. Known to drink up to three times its own weight in a single sitting. Likes a challenge - enjoys biting through rhinoceros skin.

Last seen: Many parts of Africa.

Known crimes: Its bite passes on germs that cause sleeping sickness. This deadly disease causes fever, tiredness and death.

Danger rating: In Africa 50 million people are at risk plus countless cattle, camels, mules, horses, donkeys, pigs, goats, sheep, etc. etc. etc.

Benchuca (ben-chooka) bug

<u>Last seen</u>: South America

<u>Habits</u>: Creeps up on you at night and stabs you with its pointed snout. Sucks a bit of blood and scarpers before you squash it.

<u>Known crimes</u>: Spreads Chagas' disease. Result – tired and feverish humans.

It took humans many years of painstaking research to track down the culprits of these terrible diseases and to decide what to do about them.

MALARIA MYSTERY SOLVED

In the nineteenth century Scottish born scientist Patrick Manson discovered how mosquitoes pass on malaria. Here's how he did it.

1 *1894 Manson met Ronald Ross of the Indian Medical Service.*

Hello Pat!

I think malaria is caused by tiny parasites. They live in mosquitoes.

2 *So Ross went off to India to look for them.*

3 *1897. Ross found the parasites inside a mosquito.*

Eureka!

4 *1900. Manson wanted more proof. He sent two assistants off to spend three months living in a swamp full of mosquitoes.*

Is this really such a good idea?

5 Every night the assistants went to bed in a mosquito-proof hut. They survived.

We're back!

6 Now for the ultimate test! Manson allowed his own son and another volunteer to be bitten by a mosquito that carried the parasite.

Yummy! OW!

7 They both got malaria but survived to tell the tale.

Moan!

Groan!

8 They had proof. The mosquito was guilty!

Splendid!

PLAGUE PUZZLE

Some diseases were even more puzzling than malaria. Can you piece together the gruesome clues to unravel the cause of the deadly bubonic plague?

1346 It came from the East and in the next six years 25 million people died. Peasants died in their fields, and in England three Archbishops of Canterbury died in a single year. People lived in terror of THE BLACK DEATH.

BRING OUT YOUR DEAD!

1855 The plague ravaged China. In 1894 it hit the Chinese ports and in Hong Kong the death toll soared. The harbour was crammed with steam ships. And these ships took the disease to Japan, Australia, South Africa and the Americas. The plague reached India and killed six million people in ten years.

1898 In Bombay. Dr Paul-Louis Simond of the Institut Pasteur was a worried man. The fearless French doctor had been sent to India to find the cause of the plague. Day and night he wrestled with the same fiendish puzzle. In the stricken city thousands of people were dying. All developed fist-sized bulges under their armpits followed by fever and death. But how and why?

Day after day Simond scoured the squalid streets in search of an answer. Everywhere he noticed dead rats – 75 in one house. It was extremely unusual to find so many dead rats all together in one place.

They must have died quite quickly but what had killed them? And why was it that any humans who touched the rats seemed to fall sick with the plague? These plague rats seemed to have more fleas than healthy rats. And the fleas bit people, too.

The monsoon rain buffeted the outside of the makeshift lab in a tent. Inside, Simond risked his own health as he cut up the dead rats. Then he made a dramatic discovery. In the rat's blood he found the germs known to cause the plague.

But what was the cruel connection between rats, fleas and humans? At long last the answer came. The intrepid scientist had solved the most terrifying mystery of all time. That evening he wrote in his diary in a frenzy of excitement.

But what was that crucial connection?

a) A flea bites a rat and passes on the plague. The rat bites a human and passes on the plague.

b) A flea gets plague from biting an infected rat. The flea bites a human and passes on the plague.

c) A human gets plague from an infected flea bite. The plague-crazed human bites a rat and passed on the plague.

Although Simond had the answer it took another 20 years before scientists accepted that he was right. It wasn't until 1914 that they fully understood the effects of the plague on fleas. Already vaccines were being developed against the plague and these together with insecticides and rat poisons have reduced the danger of plague epidemics in the future.

BEAT THE BUGS
Hopefully you can avoid getting a horrible disease from a biting bug. But it's hard to avoid getting bitten. Here are some danger zones.

1 Bed During the day bed bugs hide in cracks and behind wallpaper. Then at night out they pop for a midnight feast of blood.

2 Riverbanks Blackflies launch dawn and dusk raids.

3 Fields at dawn Ticks can lurk in the long grass. They prefer dogs for dinner but if one isn't handy they'll make do with you.

4 Bogs and marshes Millions of midges fly around seeking blood for breakfast. Close up they're too small to see clearly. You can't see their wings because in some varieties they beat at an awesome 62,760 strokes a minute. That's why some people call midges, "no-seeums". But you know-um when they bite you.

1 Tsetse fly trap no. 1

Remedy: Keep a pet ox.

Notes: Scientists have found that the terrible tsetse is attracted to smelly ox breath. In Zimbabwe similar smelling chemicals lured thousands of tsetses into poisoned cloth traps.

Drawbacks: Smelly ox breath. Feeding your ox. Having to take it to school with you.

2 Tsetse fly trap no. 2

Remedy: Ferment some cassava.

Notes: In Zaire people make beer from cassava roots. The messy mixture produces carbon-dioxide gas that lures the flies to their doom.

Drawbacks: People might start drinking your beer. This could cause embarrassing situations – especially at school.

3 Bed bug beaters

Remedy: Let loose an army of Pharaoh ants in your bedroom.

Notes: Pharoah ants eat bed bugs.

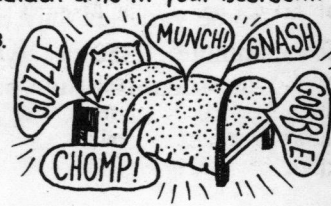

Drawbacks: How to get rid of the Pharaoh ants. Try smearing your duvet with jam. Or borrow an anteater.

PATHETIC!

4 Biting bug barbecue

Remedy: Light a really smoky bonfire.

Notes: Most biting bugs don't like smoke.

BUT IT GOT RID OF THE BUGS SIR

Drawbacks: Not a very sensible thing to do. Ever. Especially not recommended inside the home or at school.

5 Flea fighters

Remedy: Use flea mites to fight fleas.

Notes: Tiny mites infest fleas in the same way that fleas infest people. All you need to do is to capture a flea and add some mites. (You need a microscope and a steady hand to do this.)

Drawbacks: Doesn't get rid of fleas. But it does give them a taste of their own medicine.

6 Pest poisoner

Remedy: Squirt biting bugs with DDT.

Notes: In the 1940s this insecticide was used to rid the southern USA and parts of Africa and South America of malarial mosquitoes.

Drawbacks: By 1950 two types of mosquito were immune to the powerful poison. Worse still, DDT harmed bug-eating animals and the animals that ate those animals. Note- humans still spend millions of pounds each year inventing new kinds of insecticide.

A REMEDY YOU MIGHT LIKE TO TRY

Some aromatic plant oils ward off insects. You can buy these oils from herbalists or natural cosmetics shops. You could try using citronella oil on a warm summer's evening...

1 Drip a few drops of the oil on a damp piece of cotton wool.

2 Put the cotton wool in a warm place indoors.

3 When the room is full of scent open the window and dare any biting bugs to come in!

Bet you never knew!
Long before humans discovered camphor, female assassin bugs were rubbing their abdomens in camphor resin. When the females lay eggs, the eggs get coated in camphor goo. The powerful pong keeps other bugs at bay.

DEVIOUS DISGUISES

As if escaping from spiders, fish, lizards, frogs, toads, small mammals and even horrible humans wasn't enough, insects seem to spend most of their time playing hide and seek with each other. And they don't just do it for fun. Insects have to eat, after all, and they don't want to get eaten. So they use some cruel and cunning tricks to get one up on their ugly bug enemies.

Bet you never knew!
Horrible hunter, the praying mantis really does look as though it's praying. It holds its forelegs together as it waits for a tasty snack to pass by. Its forelegs have a jagged edge, just like a saw blade. The praying mantis will catch and skewer its bug lunch in just a twentieth of a second – then bite off its ugly little head!

INSECT SURVIVAL
If you were an insect, would you stay alive? Try this crash course in survival skills to help you decide.
Tactic number 1: Pretend to be something else
You've obviously got an advantage if you already look like something else – and quite a few insects do. Which of these ordinary objects might really be insects?
a) A leaf
b) A sweet wrapper
c) A twig
d) A stick

e) A thorn
f) A bird dropping

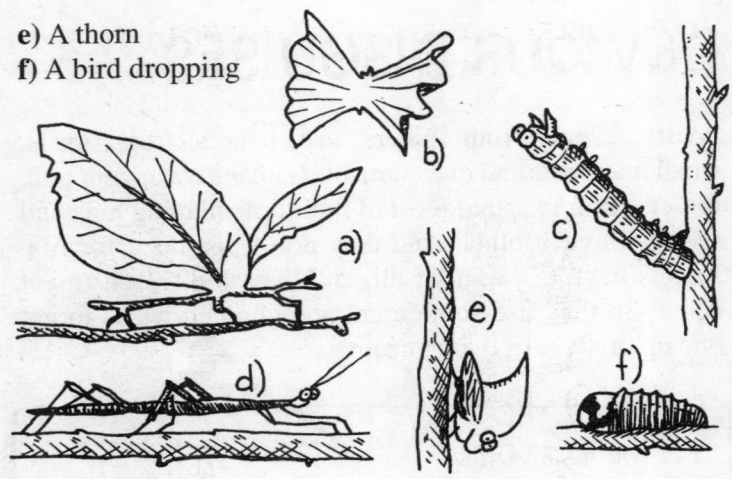

Answers: All except **b)** could be insects. See for yourself: **a)** is a Japanese leaf insect, **c)** is a European swallow-tail moth caterpillar, **d)** is of course, a stick insect, **e)** is a treehopper, **f)** is a hairstreak butterfly caterpillar.

Tactic number 2: Blend in with your surroundings
Look like your surroundings, stay still, and the hunter might just miss you. The clear-winged butterfly, for example, is invisible – it has see-through wings that make it almost impossible to spot. But you may not be such a lucky bug. You wouldn't want to be a poor old peppered moth for example...

THE PROBLEMS OF THE PEPPERED MOTH

This light speckled moth likes to hang around on light speckled trees. Perfect – not a horrible hunter in sight. Then came industry and pollution. And all the trees turned black.

BEFORE   AFTER

Suddenly the moths stood out like sore thumbs. The birds had a bonanza munching millions of moths. But some moths survived – only the ones with very dark colouring, though.

For years these dark moths had had it tough, trying not to be noticed on all those light speckled trees. Suddenly they had a bright future hiding on dark sooty ones. Or they did – until the cities started getting cleaner and the trees started getting lighter again!

Tactic number 3. Brilliant bluffs
Disguise yourself as a dangerous character and you can bluff your way out of danger.

1 Hover-flies are harmless little things. An ideal dish for an ugly bug's dinner. Or they would be if they weren't wickedly disguised as wasps! Clear-wing moths try the same trick too, but they're even better bluffers – they can make the sound effects, too!

2 Ladybirds taste terrible. On the other hand, fungus beetles taste quite nice (if you're another insect, that is). That's why fungus beetles go around pretending to be ladybirds.

3 Some butterflies even disguise themselves as other types of butterfly. In South America there are four strangely similar-looking varieties of butterfly. Only one is nasty to eat. The other three are just plain copy-cats.

4 Another great little bluffer is the hawk moth caterpillar. Its head looks fairly normal, for a caterpillar – but its rear end looks more like a snake's head!

But, beware of disguises...

REAL END   FAKE END →

5 The African dead-leaf cricket is cleverly disguised to look just like any rotten old leaf. It's got one little problem. The casque-headed frog also looks like a rotten old leaf – and this rotten old leaf likes nothing better than a cricket for its tea.

6 Best bluffer of all has to be the puss moth caterpillar. Take a look at its ugly mug! Would you want to meet that on a dark and stormy night? You'd do well to avoid this little cruel cat, as it can spit out its half-digested dinner mixed with awful acid.

Tactic number 4: Horrible hiding places
One sure way to avoid being eaten is to hide somewhere horrible. That way no one can find you and no one would want to either!

For example, the plume-moth caterpillar hides out in the sundew plant. The sundew plant eats flying insects, but the caterpillar is safe inside the plant and it gets to drink the droplets of sundew goo and munch on the sundew's insect tea.

Froghoppers hide inside a mass of foam. It looks a bit like bubble bath, but they make it themselves. The foam stops froghoppers from drying out in the sun, and it has a revolting flavour to put off horrible hunters.

DARE YOU MAKE FRIENDS WITH ... A FROGHOPPER?

1 Look for its little drops of foam on the long grass in early spring. The foam is sometimes called "cuckoo spit" – you can guess why!

JUST LEAVE ME ALONE!

2 Gently brush the foam away and you'll see a little greenish insect hiding underneath.

3 Watch carefully as it blows bubbles from the end of its body to cover itself up again. The froghopper sucks plant juices and mixes them up with its own natural bubblemaker to make the froth.

OK, so maybe the froghopper doesn't want to make friends, but you've got to admit it's got a devilish disguise.

UGLY BUGS VS HORRIBLE HUMANS

Since the day that a caveman or cavewoman first squashed a cockroach there has been a non-stop war between ugly bugs and humans. It's the biggest war the world has ever known.

You might think that humans have an advantage over insects. A human is far bigger than the biggest insect. So humans can easily squash the insect. Humans are more intelligent than insects. (Well, *most* humans are!) But if you look at what humans and insects can do for their size the picture is very different.

UGLY BUG OLYMPICS

Running *Winner:* One species of cockroach can run 50 times its body length in one second. *Loser:* The fastest human to run 50 times his own body length (about 80 metres) was about nine times slower.

The high jump *Winner:* Fleas can jump 30 cm – that's 130 times their own height. *Loser:* To match that a human would have to jump 250 metres into the air!

The long jump *Winner:* Jumping spiders can leap 40 times their body length. *Runner-up:* Grasshoppers can leap 20 times their own body length. *Loser:* To match that a human would have to leap the length of nine London buses in a single jump!

HUMAN   INSECT

Weight-lifting *Winner:* Scarab beetles can lift weights 850 times heavier than their own bodies. *Loser:* To equal that a human would have to lift eight London buses at the same time!

HUMAN   INSECT

Walking on the ceiling *Winner:* Flies. *Loser:* Humans can't do this at all.

HUMAN   INSECT

Surely though, we humans are better at some things. Like building, for example. I mean – there's the pyramids and St Paul's Cathedral and the Taj Mahal. Ugly Bugs can't match that ... can they?

> **Bet you never knew!**
> *Termites build gigantic nests. One nest contained 11,750 tonnes of sand. The termites had piled it up grain-by-grain and stuck it all together with spit! Beat that – humans!*

But who are the dirtiest, the greediest and the most destructive creatures on the planet – ugly bugs or horrible humans? You might find it difficult to choose between them.

FILTHY FLIES

They never give up. It doesn't matter how many times you let them out the window they always come back.

1 Blowflies enjoy eating rotting meat and animal droppings. They lay eggs on rotting meat and even do terrible things to your Sunday roast.

ROAST CHICKEN – ALMOST AS TASTY AS CHICKEN DROPPINGS!

2 The common housefly has common table manners. It drops in for dinner uninvited and sicks up over its food. And then it's been known to serve up a free selection of over 30 deadly diseases.

HORRIBLE HUMANS

Humans are also very persistent. Once they decide to do something they will do it even if it costs the Earth – literally.

1 Humans are the only animals that deliberately destroy their environment. Every second, humans devastate a area of forests, grasslands or swamps to build things for themselves. Each year humans burn an area of rain forest the size of Great Britain.

2 Humans also pollute the world with litter and dangerous chemicals. Every day humans dump millions of tonnes of rubbish into the sea.

3 Human beings are killers. Every hour of the day human destruction and pollution of the environment wipes out an entire species of living plant or animal.

HORRIBLE HUMANS HIT BACK

Day after day humans wage war against insects with every weapon at their disposal. But they've also discovered some surprisingly horrible uses for insects and other ugly bugs.

REVOLTING RECIPES

If you can't dispose of ugly bugs you could always eat them. That's what millions of apparently sane people do throughout the world. Would you want to try any of these dishes?

Starters
Fried and salted termites

An African treat. Tastes like fried pork rind, peanuts and potato chips all mixed up!

L'escargots

Oui, mes amis! The traditional French delicacy. (Snails to you.) Fed on lettuce. Boiled and cooked with garlic, butter, shallots, salt, pepper and lemon juice. Served with parsley. Bon appetit!

Fried witchetty grub

A native Australian delicacy – these are giant wood-moth grubs. They look a bit like fusilli pasta and swell up when fried. Delicious!

Main courses
Stir-fried silkworm pupae

This tasty traditional Chinese dish is prepared with garlic, ginger, pepper and soy sauce. Wonderful warm nutty custard flavour. You spit out the shells. Very good for high blood pressure.

Roast longhorn timber beetle

Deliciously crunchy balsawood flavour. As cooked by the native people of South America.

Fried Moroccan grasshopper

Boiled bug bodies prepared with pepper, salt and chopped parsley then fried in batter with a little vinegar. You can also eat them raw.

Blue-legged tarantula

A popular spider dish in Laos in South-east Asia. Freshly toasted and served with salt or chillies. Flavour similar to the marrow in chicken bones.

Sweets

Mexican honeypot ants
A sweet sticky treat.

Baked bee and wasp grubs
An old recipe from Somerset in England. Juicy grubs
baked in hot sticky honeycomb.

After your meal
Try one of our tarantula-fang toothpicks as used by
the Piaroa people of Venezuela.

UGLY BUGS VS HORRIBLE HUMANS: THE DEBATE

For every argument there are two points of view. And this is certainly true for ugly bugs and humans. See for yourself. Who do you sympathize with most – ugly bugs or humans?

Human point of view	Ugly bug point of view
Ugly bugs sting and bite us.	Humans trap us, poison us and experiment on us.
Ugly bugs eat our crops.	Humans destroy our food plants and plant their crops too close together so we've got nothing else to eat.
Ugly bugs creep into our homes.	Humans destroy _our_ homes.
Ugly bugs spread diseases.	Humans spread pollution and rubbish.
Ugly bugs destroy our furniture.	To us it's only wood.
Ugly bugs cost us money.	Who cares about money?
They destroy our property.	Who cares about property?

Ugly bugs just want the same things we want. Nice food and somewhere to live. The problem only comes when

125

their idea of nice food is *your* nice food, and their idea of somewhere to live is *your* bedroom.

THE UGLY TRUTH

You might think that humans are the deadliest enemies of ugly bugs. Wrong. The deadliest enemies of ugly bugs are other ugly bugs. Without ladybirds we'd be overrun by aphids. Without spiders we'd be fighting off flies.

The best way to remove an ugly bug is to get another ugly bug to do the job. When the cottony cushion scale insect invaded California it finished off entire fruit crops. Until humans brought in a type of ladybird to crush the cottony crooks.

And remember all those scary statistics about insects having millions of offspring? You'll be reassured to know that the weight of insects eaten by spiders in a year is greater than the combined weight of all the people on earth. And if ugly bugs really *were* our enemies do you think we'd stand a chance? Nope. Quite apart from the fact that there's a million of them to every one of us they can do horribly ugly things that we wouldn't even want to dream about.

But there's another side to ugly bugs. All ugly bugs are horribly incredible. Horribly interesting. And amazingly enough some ugly bugs are even horribly useful to humans.

We rely on ugly bugs to make plants fruit and to eat up rotten plant rubbish. Without insects we'd have no honey and no firefly lanterns. No silk, no jewel beetles and no beautiful butterflies. Admittedly we wouldn't have plagues and half-nibbled vegetables either. Ugly bugs make the world a worse place. But they make the world a better place too. And that's the ugly truth!

UGLY BUGS

QUIZ

Now find out if you're an
Ugly Bugs expert!

Insect identification

So – you think you know your moths from your millipedes and your crickets from your cockroaches? Take this quick quiz and see if you could be an incredible entomologist or a baffled butterfly-brain.

1 How can you tell a male earwig from a female earwig?
a) Males have curved pincers and females have straight ones.
b) Males have four pairs of legs and females have three.
c) Females have longer eyelashes.

2 Which of these insufferable insects follows insect trails?
a) Fly
b) Grasshopper
c) Ant

3 What kind of creature is a dog whelk?
a) A dog
b) A spider
c) A snail

4 How can you tell a centipede from a millipede?
a) A centipede has 100 legs and a millipede has 1,000.
b) A centipede has two legs on each segment, a millipede has four.
c) A centipede is 1 centimetre long and a millipede is 1 millimetre long.

5 Which one of the following is part of the same family as a slug?
a) Octopus
b) Spider
c) Caterpillar

6 Which two types of insect are ruled by queens?
a) Ant and bee
b) Ant and beetle
c) Ant and flea

7 What is a fly's second pair of wings for?
a) Flying (of course!)
b) Balancing
c) Keeping away predators

8 What insect will emerge from a chrysalis?
a) Caterpillar
b) Butterfly
c) Bee

Answers:
1a; 2c; 3c; 4b; 5a; 6a; 7b; 8b

Mysterious mating rituals

Attracting a mate can be a right song and dance for ugly bugs. There are many horrible habits for finding the right partner in the insect world, but which of the following are true and which are false?

HE'S SO HUNKY—
I COULD EAT HIM!

1 Male millipedes bang their heads on the ground to attract a mate.

2 Stick insects can lay eggs without mating.

3 Male ants mate four times a year.

4 Grasshoppers attract a mate by rubbing their antennae together.

5 Dragonflies mate while flying.

6 Praying mantises eat their own mates.

7 The male Indian moon moth can scent a female more than 5 km away.

8 The male bee that mates with the queen becomes the king of the hive.

Answers:
1 True
2 False – but it's tough for the boy stick insect to find a mate because their eyesight and sense of smell are poor and the girls are disguised as, well, sticks.
3 False – male ants only hatch in mating season, it's all girls together for the rest of the time.
4 False – they rub their back legs together to make that noise you always hear at night in warm countries.
5 True.
6 True – but their name comes from the fact that they look like they're *praying*, not because they *prey* on their mates.
7 True.
8 False – male bees die after mating with the queen.

Fiendish food facts

Bugs might be slippery, slimy, stinging, scratching species, but their eating habits are even more devilishly disgusting. See if you can match the creepy creatures below with their favourite foul foods.

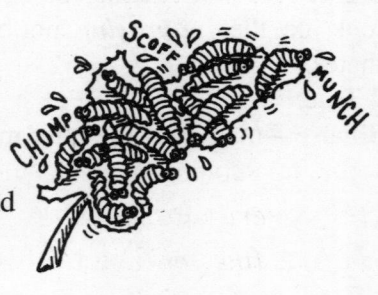

1 Leech
2 Centipede
3 Woodlouse
4 Sexton beetle
5 Black widow spider
6 Death's head hawk moth
7 Harvester ant
8 Cockroach

a) Mould
b) Bread
c) Blood
d) Its mate
e) Millipede
f) Honey
g) They'll eat anything but they don't like the kind of soap that makes your eyes sting.
h) Dead bodies

Answers:
1c; 2e; 3a; 4h; 5d; 6f; 7b; 8g

Nutty naturalists

Naturalists have travelled the world finding out about curious creatures of all shapes and sizes. Here's a letter one daring bug hunter might have written, but it got a bit soggy with seawater. Can you figure out the missing words to reveal his dramatic discoveries?

Darling Mummy,

I have to say I'm awfully homesick (not to mention seasick) on this long voyage, but I have seen some awesome animals and incredible insects! The first thing I saw when we landed were some curious cone-shaped structures that turned out to be (1)_____ nests. I studied these creatures carefully. Their bodies had three sections with (2)_____ pairs of legs attached to the middle section, called the (3)_____, and they were most fascinating, guarding their palace like soldiers and stinging me when I got too close – ouch.

I then wandered into some nearby woods and it seemed like everywhere I turned there were weird and wonderful creatures. I saw a shimmering (4)_____ and odd bugs covered in what looked like armour. I shall call these (5)_____ because I found them underneath logs. There were beetles rolling balls of (6)_____ like their lives depended on it. And the spiders! Great big fat ones, their (7)_____ legs all covered in hair! I even saw a (8)_____ emerge from a chrysalis. Stupendous!

I must end here. I went for a swim in a pond to cool off and now I'm covered in blob-like bugs that seem to be sucking my blood...

Your son, Charles

a) Three
b) Dragonfly
c) Dung
d) Butterfly
e) Woodlice
f) Ant
g) Eight
h) Thorax

Answers:
1f; 2a; 3h; 4d; 5e; 6c; 7g; 8d

HORRIBLE INDEX

137

140

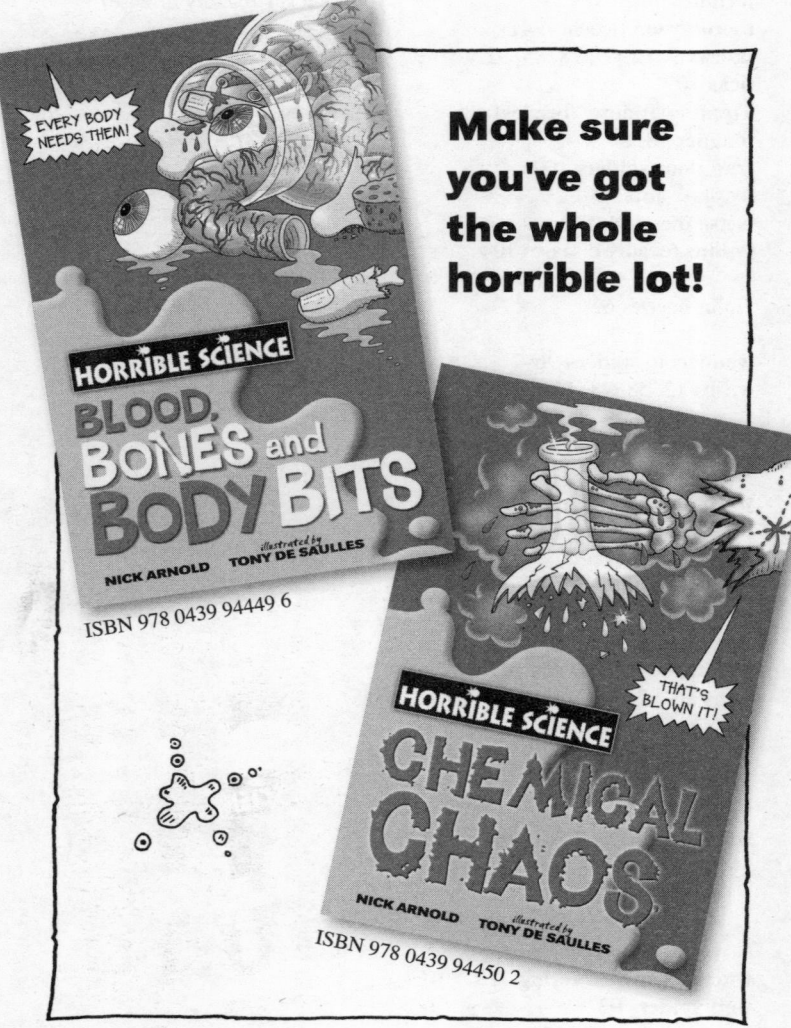

HORRIBLE SCIENCE

THE TERRIBLE TRUTH ABOUT TIME

NICK ARNOLD   illustrated by **TONY DE SAULLES**

SCHOLASTIC

www.horrible-science.co.uk

www.nickarnold-website.com
www.tonydesaulles.co.uk

Scholastic Children's Books,
Euston House, 24 Eversholt Street,
London NW1 1DB, UK

A division of Scholastic Ltd
London ~ New York ~ Toronto ~ Sydney ~ Auckland
Mexico City ~ New Delhi ~ Hong Kong

First published in the UK by Scholastic Ltd, 2002
This edition published 2009

Text copyright © Nick Arnold, 2002
Illustrations copyright © Tony De Saulles, 2002

ISBN 978 1407 10958 9

Page layout services provided by Quadrum Solutions, Ltd, Mumbai, India
Printed and bound by CPI Group (UK) Ltd, Croydon, CR0 4YY

17

The right of Nick Arnold and Tony De Saulles to be identified as the author and
illustrator of this work respectively has been asserted by them in accordance
with the Copyright, Designs and Patents Act, 1988.

CONTENTS

THANKS!

WELL, THERE'S
NO PRESENT
LIKE THE TIME!

Nick Arnold has been writing stories and books since he was a youngster, but never dreamt he'd find fame writing about time. His research involved timing snails and being kidnapped by aliens and he enjoyed every minute of it.

When he's not delving into Horrible Science, he spends his spare time eating pizza, riding his bike and thinking up corny jokes (though not all at the same time).

Tony De Saulles picked up his crayons when he was still in nappies and has been doodling ever since. He takes Horrible Science very seriously and even agreed to test a time machine. Fortunately, he has made a full recovery.

When he's not out with his sketchpad, Tony likes to write poetry and play squash, though he hasn't written any poetry about squash yet.

Introduction

Everyone knows about time. We have spare time, we gain time, we lose time. We mark time, keep time, play for time, but in the end time waits for no one. You can tell the time from a clock, but few people can handle the really tricky time questions.

See what I mean…?!

So, where do you look for the truth about time? Well, you could ask an expert. But you might need a brain as big as an elephant to understand their answers...

But there is another way you could read this book! It tells the greatest mystery story ever: the story of how some people tried to find the truth about time by measuring it and experimenting with it, and others have even dreamt of travelling through it...

Any good book will carry you away to other times and distant places. But this book takes you far, far further on a trek through time and space to seek out some of the strangest science ever. You'll also meet some seriously suffering scientists. But hold on – I mustn't tell you everything now! You'd best read on and find out the Terrible Truth for yourself...

IT'S ABOUT TIME

Here's a terribly tricky thought:

TIME IS LIKE AN ONION...

No, I don't mean that the topic of time has a bitter taste and gives you bad breath and makes you cry! I mean, like an onion, time has layers; layers of knowledge and mystery. And you'll be pleased to know that we'll be exploring all these layers and uncovering some fascinating facts like...
- How it's possible to be late for everything and get away with it.
- What happens if you fall into a black hole.
- And the TERRIBLE TRUTH mentioned in the title.

But let's start outside our onion (it's better than starting in the middle!). You probably learnt about time when you were little, and no wonder! Time affects us all – we measure our lives by time, we plan our days by time, and we're always running out of time. Especially on a Sunday evening when the weekend's almost over and the dog needs to go walkies.

But now for a question that makes scientists froth at the mouth. You see, the answer's terribly complicated...

OK, OK – I'll try to answer it myself…

Terrible time fact file

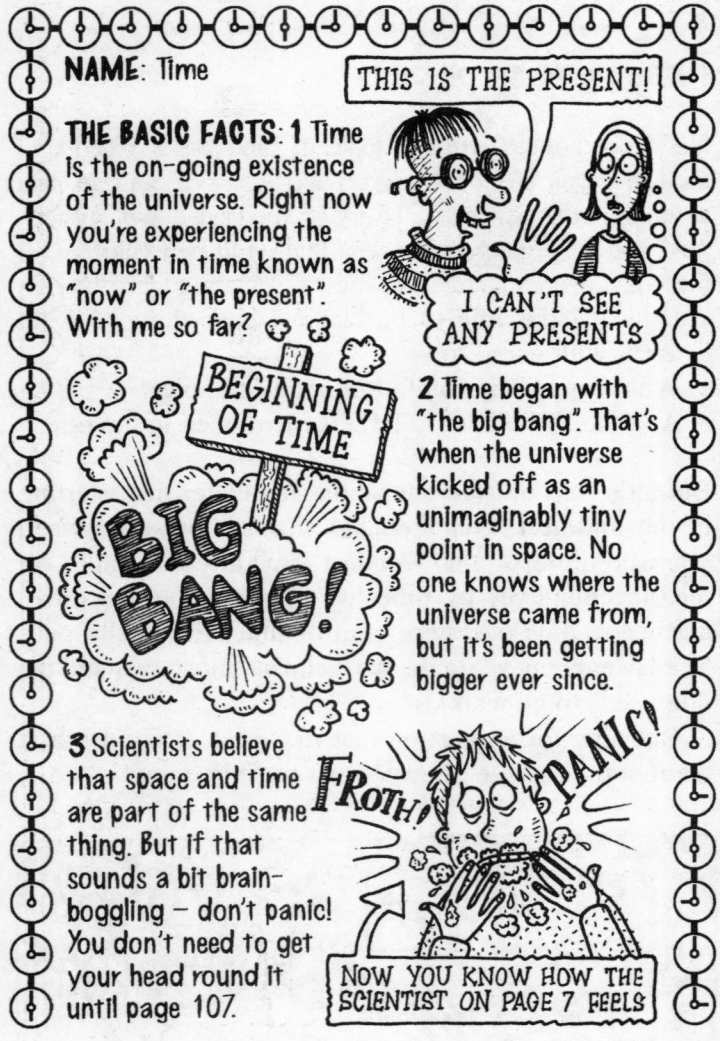

NAME: Time

THE BASIC FACTS: 1 Time is the on-going existence of the universe. Right now you're experiencing the moment in time known as "now" or "the present". With me so far?

THIS IS THE PRESENT!

I CAN'T SEE ANY PRESENTS

BEGINNING OF TIME

BIG BANG!

2 Time began with "the big bang". That's when the universe kicked off as an unimaginably tiny point in space. No one knows where the universe came from, but it's been getting bigger ever since.

3 Scientists believe that space and time are part of the same thing. But if that sounds a bit brain-boggling – don't panic! You don't need to get your head round it until page 107.

FROTH! PANIC!

NOW YOU KNOW HOW THE SCIENTIST ON PAGE 7 FEELS

TERRIBLE DETAILS: Many of life's misfortunes can be put down to being in the wrong place at the wrong time. Ever missed a train, a plane, a bus or a boat? Ever turned up for a fancy dress party on the wrong day? You'll know *exactly* what I mean!

IT'S TOMORROW BUT YOU CAN WAIT IN THE LIVING ROOM.

Bet you never knew!

1 The smallest amount of time that can possibly be measured is 0.00000000000000000000000000000 00000000000001 of a second – that's six hundred million billion billion billion billionths of a minute. This teeny-weeny fragment of time is called "Planck time". It's not to be confused with…

a) A plank of wood.

b) Walking the plank – that's how pirates were said to get rid of their victims.

c) Being as thick as a plank.

9

It's actually named after German scientist Max Planck (1858–1947) who made the calculation. Mind you, although Planck time is less than the blink of a gnat's eyelid, it's probably twice as long as it takes most children to open their Christmas presents.

2 The largest amount of time is the existence of the universe – roughly 13.7 billion years. That is a very long time – I mean, in that time 195 million people might have lived one after the other. That's if people had been around at the start of the universe!

So people have had stacks of time to wonder what time is and how it all began. Unfortunately, without this book to help them, they had to come up with their own ideas.

There are stories about time from all over the world – here's one from ancient Greece…

A TERRIBLY SICKLE STORY

The god of time was called Kronos*. He was the son of the god of the sky and the goddess of the Earth.

*Kronos means "time" in Ancient Greek.

One day Kronos had a big row with his dad. He took a sickle, that's a tool with a curved blade, and chopped his dad into bits.

I'VE TAUGHT HIM A SHARP LESSON.

And then he locked Kronos in an unimaginably terrible fiery pit in the underworld for ever.

THIS PLACE IS THE PITS!

I RECKON THEY ALL NEEDED FAMILY COUNSELLING.

Isn't that a pleasant little bedtime tale? To this day the old year is often pictured as an old man (known as Father Time) with a sickle, and the new year as a baby – and these characters were once Kronos and Zeus. Careful with that sickle now!

Today we know that these stories were as sensible as trying to teach opera to a tom cat – but they do show how people tried to make sense of time. Scientists, of course, have taken a more scientific approach – and we will too, in the next chapter. But you'd better hurry – the next chapter is starting now!

WAIT FOR ME!

TERRIBLY MESSED-UP TIME

The really odd thing is that you can't see time passing – but you can see things happening as time passes. Every day the sun appears to move across the sky at night as the Earth spins in space, and the moon moves across the sky at night for the same reason. The seasons change more slowly. And even more gradually, people grow older.

NOW   20 YEARS' TIME   200 YEARS' TIME

We're used to all this – aren't we? I mean, you'd be utterly stunned if things happened the opposite way round and people magically grew younger. Mind you, I bet anyone over 40 reading this would be thrilled if their wrinkles disappeared and their grey hairs faded without the aid of special shampoo!

Dare you discover ... how to see things happening backwards?

You will need:
This book
Yourself

13

What you do:

1 Photocopy this tasteful picture and cut out the man's head and body. (That's cut out the photocopy, not your nice new book.)

2 Place the cut out head and body on one piece of paper about 4 cm apart.

3 Roll the second piece of paper widthways to make a tube. Put the tube to your left eye and point it at the head whilst looking at the man's neck with your right eye.

You should find:

The man's head and body seem to join together. What's happening is your brilliant brain is uniting the different images seen by each eye – but it does seem as if time is running backwards.

So could you imagine time running backwards? It would be like watching a movie backwards. People would leap to their feet after an explosion and the car chases would be in reverse gear. Well that brings us to part 1 of our terrible time story...

Private eye, MI Gutzache will do anything as long as it's for money, and he's about to test a time machine for odd-ball inventor, Professor N Large. But the test goes wrong ... can you spot the problem?

M.I. GUTZACHE IS LOST IN TIME

Gutzache's report

So what's a New York private eye like me doing helping out in some kind of half-ass experiment? I wish I knew. The reasons go back in time and I haven't the time to go into them. I'd done some jobs for the Prof in the past and wished I hadn't. But the pay was good and the dollars did the talking.

So there I was in the Prof's sinister science lab. I was strapped into his lousy invention like salami in a sandwich. He said it was a time machine – I guess that made me the time-machine guinea pig.

The Prof threw a switch and next thing I knew I was tucked up in bed in the Prof's spare room. I had a hunch something was wrong – but I just didn't know how wrong. I couldn't put my finger on it – but I found out soon enough.

I backed out of bed. A few jigsaw pieces fell into place – I'd lost control of my body! It had a mind of its own and that mind wasn't mine. My body wanted to move backwards – so I humoured it. At least it knew where it was going – and that was more than I did...

The next bit is kind of personal and dirty, but the Prof said "spill the beans" and I do as I'm paid. I backwards shuffled into the bathroom. I grabbed my toothbrush and turned the taps but the water flowed up from the drain. Big globs of frothy spit-like slime flew into my mouth with wet splutt sounds.

I was kind of shocked. I tried to brush my teeth – but my mouth felt foul.

"Hey, Gutzache," I thought shakily. "Get a grip buddy!"

Feeling kind of confused, I wiped my face and hands on the towel and tried to wash. The towel made me wet and more scummy water rose from the drain and leapt into the taps. I figured the Prof could use a good plumber!

I tugged the toilet chain and then opened the lid. The pan had been used and I didn't like what I saw – but I dropped my pants and sat down. Then the contents of the bowl rose up and got sucked into my body! It was the worst moment of my life, but worse was to come...

The paper was dry as I pushed it on to the roll. I stood up. The water looked clean – but I felt dirty. The case had gotten to my nerves.

"Hey, Gutzache," I thought, "you're a detective, you've gotta figure it out!"

To cut a long story slightly less long, I changed into my clothes and somehow got downstairs – all backwards, of course. I was scared I'd fall but my body knew the steps. I could hear the Prof's voice. He wasn't talking no English I'd ever heard.

THGIN-DOOG!

I figured it was Ancient Icelandic.

The Professor insisted on talking in this language all the time and the real weird thing was, I was talking back to him in the same tongue. I hadn't a clue what we were saying, but whatever it was it sure made sense to the Prof.

Then I found myself seated at the table for some kind of meal. And it was soon after this that I cracked the case. It was the cat that blew the cover on the entire operation.

The Prof had been bumbling around picking bits of china out of the trash and arranging them on the floor. He was muttering some clap-trap – something like: "YRROS OS M'I RAED HO!"

For some dumb reason the Professor picked up the cat and put her on the table. Then a real weird thing happened. The bits of china flew together on the floor and rose in the air like a freaky flying saucer landing right in front of me. It hit the cat's foot. And the cat took off backwards like some kind of kitty helicopter and touched down on the floor!

I've seen a few wacko things but I ain't seen nothing like that. And then I figured that I had. Last night the kitty jumped on the table and knocked my mug on the floor. Then I knew the worst. I was re-living yesterday! Time was going backwards!

I felt kind of bloated. I could feel half-chewed food rising up in my gullet and into my mouth and my spoon scooping it out of my mouth and OH HELL – it had to be the snails I ate last night! They looked just as bad second time around. In fact they looked almost as bad as I felt. I was giving up food  from my stomach and putting it back on my plate!

I was eating … backwards!

And so the day went backwards. I made a backwards flight in a backwards-flying plane. I recalled the moment when the greasy airline dinner and air turbulence made me barf.

 I was praying it wouldn't happen and it did – backwards!

It was as bad as last time and worse. I grabbed the sick bag and the puke kinda leapt out at me. I got to catch it in my mouth and gulp it down my throat. I ended up at home in bed. It was morning. I was sleepy. It had been the worst day of my life – the wrong way round! And that's when I woke up back in the time machine…

The Professor writes…

I fixed the fault and I apologized to Mr Gutzache on behalf of myself and my cat, Tiddles. It seems Mr Gutzache experienced time running backwards although his brain was working normally. Mr Gutzache didn't feel much like his supper that evening – and, oh dear, I thought he liked snails!

Oh no, looks like the story has upset our scientific adviser for this book, self-taught time expert, Norbert Nerdworthy. I should explain that Norbert spends most of his time in his bedroom researching time science – and he's most particular about details…

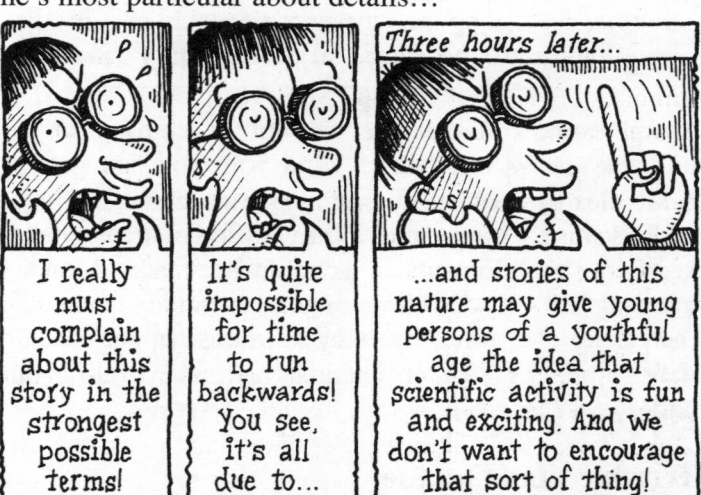

I really must complain about this story in the strongest possible terms!

It's quite impossible for time to run backwards! You see, it's all due to…

Three hours later…

…and stories of this nature may give young persons of a youthful age the idea that scientific activity is fun and exciting. And we don't want to encourage that sort of thing!

Hmm – Norbert's got a point! Many scientists believe that time can't go backwards because of a very important scientific rule. This rule only works in one direction – forwards into the future. It's to do with the increase of muddle…

TERRIBLE EXPRESSIONS

A scientist says: Do you say…?

MY EXPERIMENT HAS GAINED ENTROPY (EN-TRO-PEE)

GAINED A TROPHY? WELL DONE!

Answer: Only if you're proud of your ignorance. Entropy is science-speak for "muddle" – a hugger-mugger; higgledy-piggledy, confused, chaotic, messy, muddled, disgustingly disorderly dog's dinner. Scientists use the word to refer to the amount of muddled-up matter in a place – it could be muddle in an experiment, or the universe.

Scientists reckon that the amount of entropy in the universe grows over time. Mind you, you can get the basic idea by looking in your very own home! Do your socks vanish without trace? Do you find someone else's knickers or underpants in your drawers on a Monday morning? If so, you'll know what I mean about muddle increasing over time! But why does this happen? Could it be a plot by sinister scientists to make us lose our underwear? Er, no.

Terrible time fact file

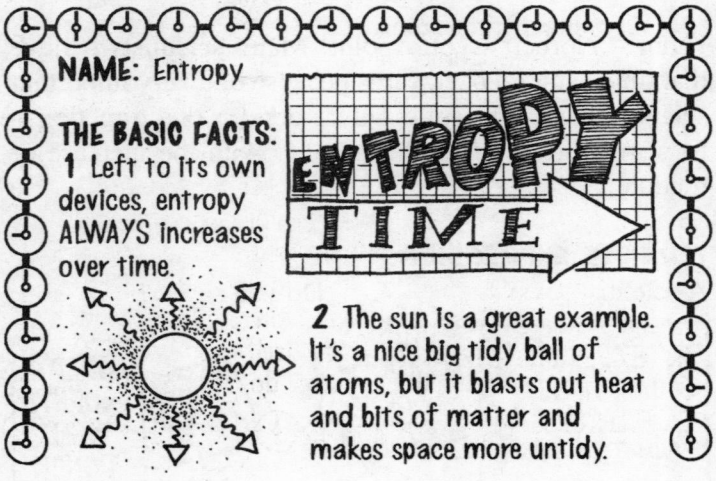

NAME: Entropy

THE BASIC FACTS:
1 Left to its own devices, entropy ALWAYS increases over time.

2 The sun is a great example. It's a nice big tidy ball of atoms, but it blasts out heat and bits of matter and makes space more untidy.

3 Entropy also increases over time in this lovely mug of hot chocolate topped with ice cream...

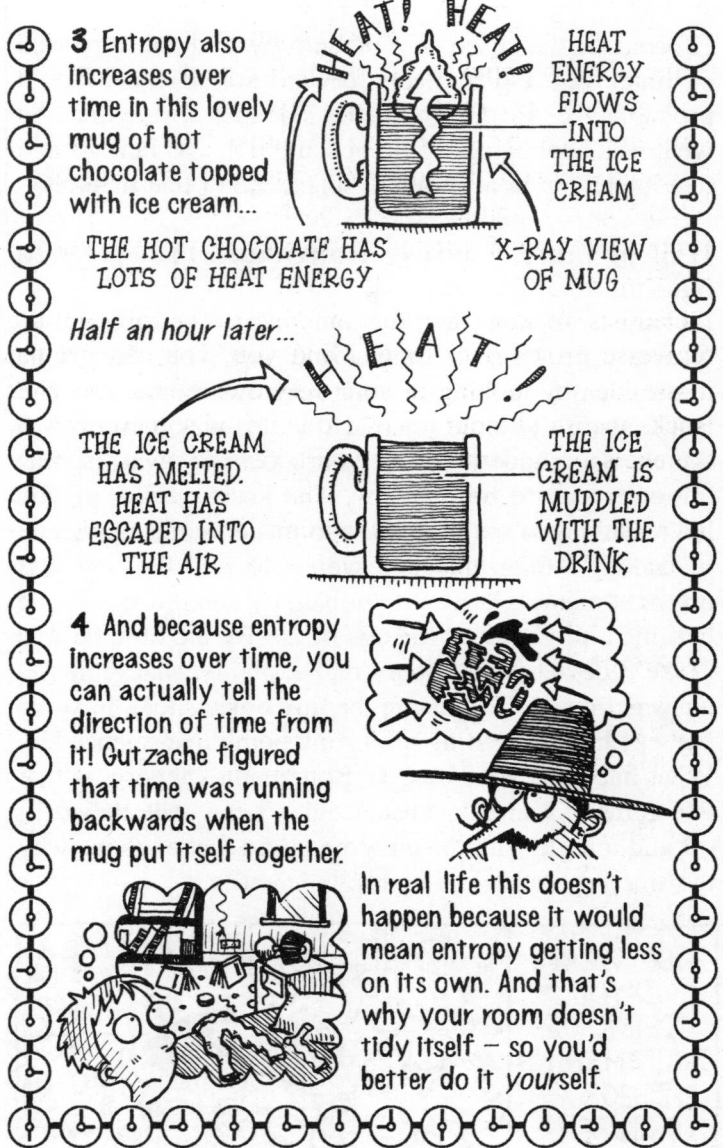

HEAT! HEAT!

HEAT ENERGY FLOWS INTO THE ICE CREAM

THE HOT CHOCOLATE HAS LOTS OF HEAT ENERGY

X-RAY VIEW OF MUG

Half an hour later...

HEAT!

THE ICE CREAM HAS MELTED. HEAT HAS ESCAPED INTO THE AIR

THE ICE CREAM IS MUDDLED WITH THE DRINK

4 And because entropy increases over time, you can actually tell the direction of time from it! Gutzache figured that time was running backwards when the mug put itself together.

In real life this doesn't happen because it would mean entropy getting less on its own. And that's why your room doesn't tidy itself – so you'd better do it *yourself*.

Of course, the discovery of entropy and the direction of time was a giant leap forward for science. You'd probably like to think that the scientist who explained what was happening would become rich and famous and live happily ever after. Well, science ain't that nice...

Hall of fame: Ludwig Boltzmann (1844–1906)
Nationality: German

Ludwig Boltzmann was big and bearded and miserable. Naturally he wasn't born that way any more than some teachers are born strict or some scientists are born boring. But Ludwig did once say that since he was born on Ash Wednesday and missed the Mardi Gras festival, he was always going to be unhappy. And so it proved. If you have hankies to spare, prepare to make them soggy...

Ludwig's mum and dad were rich and the boy was bright at maths. He went to university and did so well he became a professor at the age of 25. By the time he was 28 he'd developed a theory that explains what atoms in a gas get up to. (Atoms are the tiny objects that make up matter.) Imagine letting off a stink bomb in a science lab. What happens, according to Boltzmann's theory, is that the atoms of a smelly substance don't stay still, they drift off and mingle with the air atoms. And that explains why the smell spreads. And entropy increases.

1 Boltzmann's theory suggests that it's possible for an ice cream left in a warm room to actually stop melting and start to freeze again … but it's not very likely. Mind you, if someone sits on your ice cream it's even less likely to re-freeze.

2 Boltzmann wasn't too interested in the wider meanings of his big breakthrough. He didn't have too much time for philosophers and he thought that one famous thinker, Immanuel Kant (1724–1804), was actually playing a joke on his readers.

By 1877 Ludwig had figured out the maths behind entropy. Atoms get muddled because there's more chance of muddle developing than order. There's more chance of the ice cream on a mug of hot chocolate melting than staying cold. There's more chance of the stink bomb stink filling the room than staying in one corner. Now was he right, was he right or was he right?

Many scientists thought that he was wrong. Ludwig's ideas depended on atoms, but at that time no one had proved that atoms existed and many scientists didn't believe in them. For these scientists, Ludwig's ideas were as welcome as a clothes moth at a fashion show. And it didn't help that Ludwig didn't make friends easily. He looked odd and had a strange, squeaky voice. He was bad tempered and argued a lot, too. Soon, a gang of heartless scientists were queuing up to bully Boltzmann.

Sometimes science can be worse than horrible – it can be cruel, too. For 30 years, Ludwig put up with the scorn and sneers of other scientists and became more and more miserable. And soon after Ludwig developed his great theory, his life began to fall apart. His young son died and he was turned down for a top job. One student remembered that Ludwig was so sad you could hear his heart-rending groans out in the street.

Then, in 1900, an obscure clerk in a Swiss office told his girlfriend that he was sure that Ludwig Boltzmann was right about atoms. In 1905 he explained why. The young clerk's name was Albert Einstein (1879–1955) and he used maths to prove beyond doubt that atoms did exist.

But Ludwig never read the article. By then he was nearly blind and suffering from splitting headaches. For a while he'd been thought mad and was locked up in a mental hospital. His wife, Henriette, wrote to their daughter, Ida:

Father gets worse every day. I have almost lost any confidence in the future.

Ludwig and his wife went on holiday. Henriette went for a swim and stopped on the way back to collect her husband's suit from the dry cleaners. When she returned to the house, she found that Ludwig had taken his own life. He was 62 years old.

Ludwig Boltzmann once wrote:

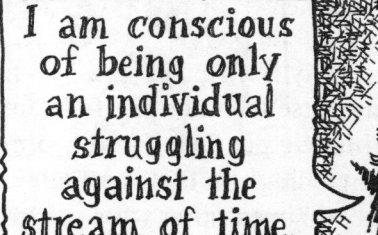

I am conscious of being only an individual struggling against the stream of time.

It was a chillingly accurate prediction.

Time had not been on Ludwig's side. If he'd made time to read Einstein's article he might have cheered up a bit. If his wife had got back to the house in time he might not have died. And if Ludwig had lived just a year longer there is no doubt that he would have won the Nobel Prize and been recognized for the genius that he truly was.

OK, you can blow your noses now but don't get too down, readers. The next chapter is all about how we make sense of time and you're sure to have … the Time of Your Life! (Unlike poor Ludwig!)

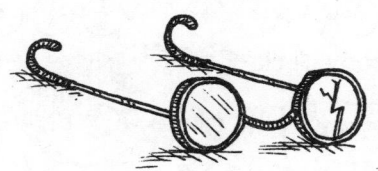

THE TIME OF YOUR LIFE

Ever noticed how time seems to speed up when you're enjoying yourself? Isn't it incredible that when you're playing your favourite computer game, or surfing the Net with your mates, time simply zips by?! And when you're waiting your turn at the dentist's, listening to that whining drill

going neeeeeeeeeeeeee! – time drags on FOR EVER!

The thing is, when you're wrapped up in what you're doing you stop noticing time, and when you're not doing anything you enjoy, you do notice it. And that's what this chapter is all about – how we humans and assorted furry friends and plants sense time.

It's a skill, you know. Imagine you're standing on a pavement. There's a giant lorry crashing down the road but it's some way off. You reckon there's enough time to cross. Phew – you make it! Ever wondered why you don't get squished? It's all thanks to your ability to judge time using your brain's built-in timers. But don't take my word for it – just clock these facts!

Terrible time fact file

NAME: The body clock

DON'T BE ALARMED!

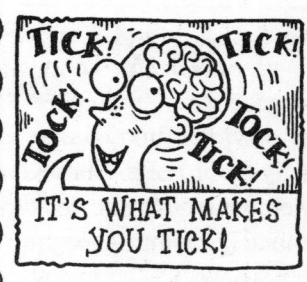

IT'S WHAT MAKES YOU TICK!

THE BASIC FACTS:

1 Your brain marks time in an area called the hypothalamus (hy-po-thal-a-mus). Here, a blob of cells no larger than a grain of sand fires regular signals like a clock.

2 Thanks to its brilliant built-in timer your brain can perform vital tasks such as controlling your body temperature, feeling hungry and sleeping on a roughly 24-hour cycle.

PUT A WARM JUMPER ON!

EAT SOMETHING!

GO TO BED!

3 As a result your body is at its best in the late afternoon and early evening when your temperature rises and your muscles are at their strongest.

TERRIBLE DETAILS:

In the early hours of the morning the body is at its weakest. Heart attacks and death are more likely at this time.

FRET!

WORRY!

Fancy being shut away in a gloomy cave without daylight or even a clock? That's the fate of volunteers in experiments to find out how the body copes without time clues. In 1989, Stefania Follini moved into "Lost Cave" in New Mexico, USA. She lived there for 18 weeks and, without knowing it, began following a 28-hour day. After six weeks she lost all sense of time and began to stay awake for 30 hours at a stretch. The long days didn't seem to do her any harm but she reported feeling sad and tried to cheer herself up by chatting to mice and frogs.

OK, SO THAT'S ENOUGH ABOUT ME. WHAT D'YOU GUYS LIKE TO GET UP TO?

I guess the experiment shows that the body needs light and dark to re-set its clock and, as you can find out below, the brain has ways of sensing light.

TERRIBLE EXPRESSIONS

A scientist says: Do you say…?

WOW! GIVE ME FIVE! I'M INTO RHYTHM AND THE CIRCADIANS ARE A COOL GROUP!

I'M INTO CIRCADIAN RHYTHMS…

Answer: Only if you want the scientist to "beat" you up! The circadian (sir-kay-dee-an) rhythm is the approximate 24-hour rhythm followed by the body (and other animals and plants).

Well, I hope your circadian rhythms are reaching their peak right now ... because it's quiz time!

BODY-TIME QUIZ TIME

1 Your brain senses light because it's linked to your eyes by nerves. But during the long dark Arctic winters your body's timer goes wonky and people can't sleep. What's this condition called?

a) Bug eye.   **b)** Big eye.   **c)** Big head.

2 Nerves relay light info to a brain area that makes a sleepy substance. This sends you to sleep at night. What's it called?

b) The pineal gland.

a) The pineapple gland.

c) The peanut gland.

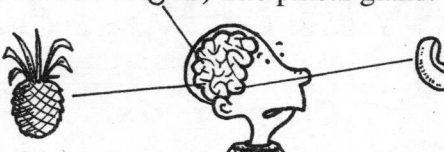

3 Besides the circadian rhythm, the body runs on other cycles that scientists don't fully understand. How often do we reach our peak of germ-fighting powers?

a) Once a week.   **b)** Every ten years.   **c)** Once a month.

4 What's it called when the body's circadian rhythm gets out of sync with daylight after a long flight?

a) Gut lag.

b) Old lag.

c) Jet lag.

And while we're talking about jet lag, if you suffer from the condition you might be interested in a treatment that really seems to work. The travel book below is based on one man's real-life experience.

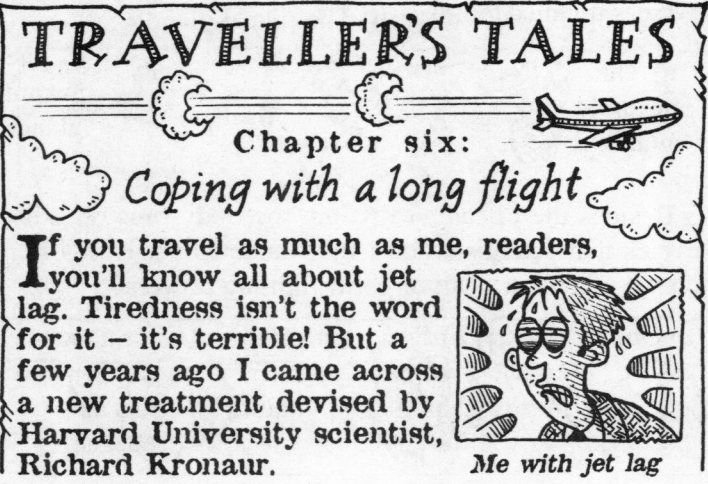

TRAVELLER'S TALES

Chapter six:
Coping with a long flight

If you travel as much as me, readers, you'll know all about jet lag. Tiredness isn't the word for it – it's terrible! But a few years ago I came across a new treatment devised by Harvard University scientist, Richard Kronaur.

Me with jet lag

Richard used pulses of bright light to re-set my body clock. Sounds weird – but it works!
And all I had to do was avoid morning sun on my flight from the USA to England.
That's when I hit upon the idea of wearing welder's goggles. When I arrived at Heathrow Airport, I was very flattered by the attention I was getting. Maybe folks thought I was a movie star! I was smiling and waving until I got arrested by the security guards for looking like a shady character.

STAGGER A SCIENTIST

Next time you see a scientist, tip-toe up to him or her and tap them on the shoulder…

IS IT TRUE THAT TIME SEEMS TO SPEED UP THE OLDER YOU ARE?

ER....

Answer: Yes, or as a scientist might say "probably". Older people grumble that the years roll by faster and faster. Perhaps as a person gets older their brain slows and everything that happens seems faster in comparison, so they think that time is passing more quickly.

In one test people listened to two sets of beats and had to decide which one was faster. Children did better at judging the difference between faster beats and older people did better with the slower beats. Perhaps children have faster brains and feel time is passing more slowly than older people. Of course, this explains why children claim science lessons last for ever whilst their elderly teachers think the lessons are too short...

Bet you never knew!
Speedy creatures like flies may see time passing even more slowly than children. Some scientists think that when a fly watches TV, its brain works so fast to put together an image of what's going on that it can actually make out the dark bits in between the TV pictures. A TV can show 60 frames a second and our dull plodding brains put them together to see a moving picture and miss the boring dark bits – but flies may not.

Mind you, many animals and plants – even vegged-out potatoes – are better at telling the time than some people. In fact, you can even use them as clocks! We'll be back after the commercial break...

THE HORRIBLE SCIENCE

Old Curiosity Clock Shop

(PET DEPARTMENT)

BORED OF YOUR TIRED-OUT TICK-TOCK?
WHY NOT INVEST IN A *LIVING* TIME-TELLING PET?!

THE OYSTER CLOCK

Guaranteed to open its shell for up to four minutes every hour as long as the tide is high! Mind-boggling moon sensors pick up the pull of the moon's gravity that causes tides and tells your oyster clock when the tide is high. Yes, with this *pearl* of a clock – the world is your oyster!

THE SMALL PRINT: If you get bored of your clock you can always slurp up its insides with a nice garlic sauce!

THE FRUIT-FLY ALARM CLOCK

Finding it hard to get up in the mornings? Why not try the fruit-fly alarm clock? These little bugs manage to emerge for their first flight at dawn – even if they're kept in the dark and their parents and parents' parents, and so on (15 sets of parents here) never saw daylight either!

THE SMALL PRINT: You'll enjoy being woken by the fruit flies crawling up your nostrils, dying in your tea and practising aqua-aerobics in your cornflakes but don't ask us to catch them — we're outta here!

INTO BUGS? YOU'LL GET A BUZZ FROM THE HONEY-BEE CLOCK!

Leave out marmalade at a certain time each morning and the bees will come round to inspect it at the same time each day, regular as clockwork.

THE SMALL PRINT: And best of all they're at a price that won't sting your pocket — even if they will sting the rest of your body.

INTO GARDENING?

Let our multi-plant clock tell you what time it is...

❀ Spotted cat's ear opens at 6 am.

❀ Passion flowers open at noon.

❀ Evening primroses open at 6 pm.

They smell nice and come at a price you won't sneeze at!

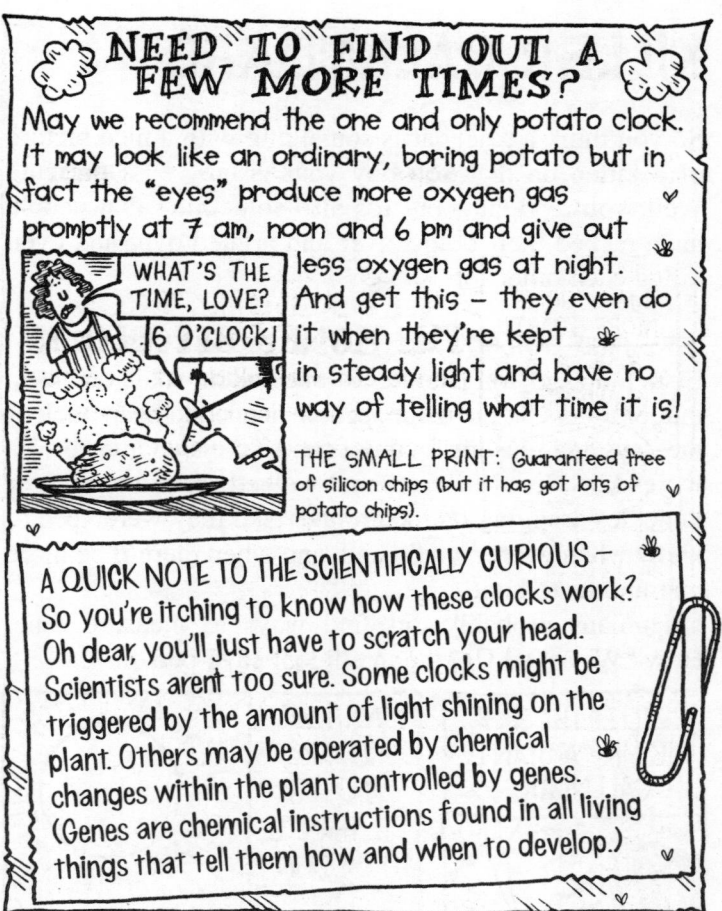

NEED TO FIND OUT A FEW MORE TIMES?

May we recommend the one and only potato clock. It may look like an ordinary, boring potato but in fact the "eyes" produce more oxygen gas promptly at 7 am, noon and 6 pm and give out less oxygen gas at night. And get this – they even do it when they're kept in steady light and have no way of telling what time it is!

WHAT'S THE TIME, LOVE?

6 O'CLOCK!

THE SMALL PRINT: Guaranteed free of silicon chips (but it has got lots of potato chips).

A QUICK NOTE TO THE SCIENTIFICALLY CURIOUS – So you're itching to know how these clocks work? Oh dear, you'll just have to scratch your head. Scientists aren't too sure. Some clocks might be triggered by the amount of light shining on the plant. Others may be operated by chemical changes within the plant controlled by genes. (Genes are chemical instructions found in all living things that tell them how and when to develop.)

Well, as you've just found out, we humans are quite good at keeping track of time but to do it well we really need a clock. And it's much the same thing with longer lengths of time, like weeks and months and years. With them it helps if you have a diary or calendar handy. So why not make space in your diary to read the next chapter?

KILLER CALENDARS

So you think a calendar is something with a nice picture of a kitten on that you buy your granny as a present? Well, you're right – but it's also something that people have racked their brains over and argued over and even killed each other for!

LET'S FIND OUT HOW ALL THIS CALENDAR FUSS BEGAN

Even long ago, long before anyone had invented bicycles, indoor toilets or television, people needed to keep track of the days and seasons. In those far-off days your ancestors wore skins, lived in caves and walked around with their knuckles dragging on the ground. And they were keen to know when winter would end, and when there'd be more mammoths to hunt.

Humans probably did find ways to measure time. How? We asked Ug, the intelligent cave-person:

- In summer the sun rises towards the north-east and sets towards the north-west. The days are long and the sun feels hot.

- In spring and autumn the sun rises in the east and sinks to the west. The midday sun is lower than in the summer.

- In winter the sun rises in the south-east and sets in the south-west. The days are short and cold. And I bet cave-people had to wear their sensible thermal underwear. That's right, itchy-scratchy fashion-disaster mammoth-fur underpants!

There are four special days to mark the passing year...
- The summer solstice is the longest day (usually 21 June)*. On that day the noon sun reaches its highest point in the year.
- The winter solstice is the shortest day (usually 21 December)*. The noon sun is now at its lowest point in the year.
- The equinoxes in the spring and autumn (21 March and 21 September) are when day and night are equal in length.

* If you happen to be reading this in the southern half of the Earth these two dates are the other way round.

Now you might be wondering why the sun bothered to make the days different lengths. I mean, was it some kind gesture to help those thicko cave-people sort out the correct time of year?

In fact, it's all down to the fact that the Earth is spinning at an embarrassingly wonky angle...

The Earth whizzes round the sun, taking one year to make the trip.

This means that the northern and southern halves of the Earth take it in turns to lean towards the sun. And that's why when it's winter in Lapland it's summer in Australia...

And people soon figured out that we've had a full year when the sun is at exactly the same point in the sky at noon as it was the previous year...

But we humans want to measure shorter lengths of time than years. I mean, just imagine the terrible results of just having years! Buses and trains would only run once a year, you'd only get one holiday a year and certain members of your family really would spend a year in the bathroom.

Fortunately, nature provides a way of cutting the year into smaller bits. Know what it is? I'll give you a clue: you don't have to ask for the moon ... but it helps!

Yes, the moon circles the Earth ROUGHLY once a month – you can watch the moon's progress as it seems to change shape from a crescent to a circle and then back again. Clever old moon!

Dare you discover … how the moon changes shape?

You will need:
The crescent moon (it's up there somewhere!)
A calendar or diary
A compass

What you do:
1 Note down which direction the horns of the crescent are pointing…
2 Look at the crescent moon in about two weeks' time.

What do you notice?
a) The horns are pointing in the opposite direction!
b) The horns are pointing in the same direction.
c) The horns are pointing upwards like a giant smiley face.

Answer: a) The moon shines because it reflects the sun's light. The moon appears to change shape as it travels round the Earth and gets the sunlight from different directions. When the moon is waxing (growing towards a full moon) the horns point west. And when it's waning (getting thinner) the horns point east. With me so far? (The horns can point up but they still appear to be tilted east or west.)

Special extra bonus point for clued-up calendar counters. There are a couple of days when the moon can't be seen, followed by what people call the "new moon". So what the heck's going on?

a) The moon moves too far from the Earth for us see it properly.

b) The position of the moon means that it gets no sunlight – so we can't see it.

c) The moon is only out during the day – and it's hard to see.

> **Answer: c)** Daylight is normally too bright for the moon to show up.

OK, so the moon zooms around the Earth and you can be sure what it's up to and when the new moon will appear. So it sounds a real cool idea to use the appearance of the new moon to start a month. Well, early people probably thought so...

Possibly the world's earliest calendar proved horribly fatal for a French eagle 13,000 years ago. Scientists have found an eagle bone with strange markings that could be a record of the changing moon.

Of course, other scientists disagree, violently claiming that it's just a load of grotty old scratches...

But now for a deeply shocking announcement ... ahem!

For thousands of years people used the moon to measure months. The moon told them when to plant and harvest crops and when to pay taxes. But all these millions of people were doing things on the wrong days: the moon had fooled them, cheated them, hoodwinked them, deceived them and made them look as daft as trying to fight a tiger armed only with a pair of false teeth. And here's why...

HA HA HA! MOON MONTHS DON'T FIT INTO THE SUN YEAR!

In the year 2000, the Earth took 365 days, five hours, 48 minutes and 45 seconds to go round the sun, and the moon took 29 days, 12 hours, 44 minutes and 2.9 seconds to go round the Earth. And that means – as they found in ancient China and Greece and Arizona and lots of other places – that if you try to fit 12 moon months into a sun year you're left with a few days over. So your calendar is going to be out by that number of days each year.

Well, you've got to do something with the spare days. And so it was that people like the Babylonians (who lived in the land now known as Iraq), the Greeks and the Romans all ended up slotting the extra days into extra months every few years. Sounds complicated? You bet!

I could tell you all about the many different types of calendar that developed in different parts of the world over thousands of years. But I'm not going to because...

a) You might not be interested.
b) This book would be 1,596 pages long and only read by geeky calendar nerds like Norbert.

So instead I'm going to tell you about the amusingly odd bits…

AMUSINGLY ODD CALENDAR FACTS

1 Religious calendars for Christians, Jews, Muslims and Hindus are still based on the moon. This is why Easter Sunday is officially the first Sunday after the first full moon after the spring equinox.

2 There is probably no scientific reason why a week should last seven days. It seems that in ancient Babylon people quite fancied the number seven and so it's remained.

3 One of the earliest references to the calendar was in a poem by Greek poet Hesiod in 800 BC. The poet lists all the work he had to do during the year in order to tell off his lazy brother for not doing any. Yep, lazy brothers are not a modern invention.

4 In the ancient Aztec calendar there's a cycle of 52 years, at the end of which time was believed to die. In order to stop the world ending, Aztec priests would rip out the beating heart of a victim and burn it in a fire.

ROTTEN ROMAN TIME RECKONING

The ancient Roman calendar belonged to priests. No one else was allowed to see the calendar until 304 BC. Then the rule was relaxed after a brave Roman rebel stole a copy of the calendar and showed it to the people.

> ### *Bet you never knew!*
> The Romans invented our month names. Until 713 BC the year had ten months and then they added January and February. The names September, October and November meant "seventh month", "eighth month", "ninth month" and so on – very imaginative – I DON'T think! "But hold on, isn't September the ninth month?" I hear you exclaim. Well, not for the Romans – their year started in March. But we're still using the old names even though they're now wrong.

But the Romans had a worse calendar problem. Right from the start the priests could add extra months to the year whenever it suited them. If this custom existed today there would be terrible results at work … and school.

JULES ROOLS OK

Thanks to the priests adding extra months to some years, by 46 BC the calendar was out of step with the seasons. People weren't sure when to bring in the harvest or pay taxes.

But when the going gets tough, the tough get going. And no one was a tougher go-getter than superstar General, and all round big-head, Julius Caesar (100–44 BC).

HAIL, CAESAR!

But it's not even raining!

Friends, Romans, Countrymen, lend me your ears!

But they're stuck to our heads.

I'm going to reform the calendar!

I've been talking to some Egyptian scientists — thanks, guys!

We're going to make the year 365.25 days instead of 354.

HUH?

The 0.25 of a day will result in an extra "leap" day every four years. These years will be known as "leap years".

The new calendar seemed to tick along just fine. But there was a problem – the year turned out to be 11 minutes longer than the time the Earth took to go round the sun. Now that doesn't sound too bad. I mean, what's 11 minutes between friends – huh? Trouble is the next year the calendar was out by another 11 minutes and so on. And if you don't have a calculator handy I'd better say 11 minutes a year equals ONE WHOLE DAY every 134 years – or 11 days in 1,500 years. So it wasn't long before Christmas and Easter and everyone's birthday ended up on the wrong days!

Over the next 1,300 years quite a few scientists sussed that the days were wrong. And the experts passed on the bad news to the Pope. (As boss of the Church, the Pope was the only man with the power to put things right.) For some reason some of these experts had silly names ... for example, there were Notker the Stammerer, Notker the Peppercorn and Notker the thick-lipped (all no relations).

But the most famous expert of the lot was a monk named Roger Bacon (1214–1292) – or Friar Bacon to use his official job title. Now I could tell you a lot about Roger but I'm not going to because I've just discovered a long-lost book about him by his best friend! Oh hold on, it might be a forgery...

Roger Bacon –
the monk behind the myth
by Friar Egg

"Friar Bacon" – just saying that name makes me think of breakfast – why didn't he have a sensible name like me? But then people say I'm not the brightest monk in the bunch. The other monks call me "Half-cracked Egg" – I can't think why!

ME

Anyway, that's enough of me – I want to tell you about my monkish mate Roger!

Our boss, the Prior, didn't like Rog. And Rog didn't like him – always arguing they were. I mean, Rog reckoned he knew how to teach the young monks better than anyone and the boss didn't like that. So Roger was picked on and given all the rotten jobs no one else wanted to do. Naturally I gave Rog moral support by not getting in his way when he was scrubbing out the toilets.

THE PRIOR

PONG!

47

Then one day – oh, it must have been in 1266, Rog got a letter that put a grin on his face. He heard that an old mate of his named Guy had just been elected Pope. And guess what – this Guy wanted Rog to tell him all his ideas about everything!

Dear Rog
Please tell me everything!
Guy

But then Rog realized he hadn't written anything down – he'd been too busy cleaning out the pigpen and cutting the other monks' toenails.

Well, Rog got to work and this time the boss didn't dare stop him – not when the Pope commands and all that. And after two years of working night and day Rog finished it – it was a weighty work! I know, I dropped it on my toe – ouch!

ARGH!

"What shall I call it, idiot-features?" asked Rog.

He always used this friendly tone of address with me – me being his mate and all that.

"Well, it's a major work," I said, ruefully rubbing my pet corn.

THUMP!

"Love the title!" shouted Rog, giving me a friendly punch and sending me sprawling.

And that's what he called it – "Major Work".

Now, I can't say exactly what was in it 'cos it's got lots of pages and no pictures and I haven't started it yet. But I know that Rog was a bit rude about the Church for letting the calendar go all out of sync. Rog said that the calendar's 11 minutes out a year – and that means that Easter is always on the wrong day.

Anyway, Rog gave a copy of the book to his servant, John, and sent him to Rome to give it to the Pope. Well, when John got back he said it was a tough journey and he nearly got robbed a few times. But he made it to Rome in the end. Trouble was the Pope had died and no one else wanted to read Roger's book.

HE'S DEAD!

Now, my mate Rog, he never gave up without a fight. He wrote to all the top people in the Church to tell them where they were going wrong about the calendar and everything else. And boy did they take notice of him! They took SIZZLE! so much notice of him that they locked him up in prison for 15 years.

By the time they let him out he was a frazzled friar, or you might say a bit of a burnt-out Bacon. Sadly he died soon after and everyone's forgotten him except me – his true monk-mate – Friar Egg.

Of course, Bacon was right and even the Church wasn't powerful enough to change the way the Earth moved. By 1582 the calendar was almost two weeks wrong and things were getting serious – or should I say too darn silly for words...

HAPPY EASTER, YOUR HOLINESS!

BUT IT'S CHRISTMAS, YOUR MAJESTY!

Bet you never knew!
1 The year had been accurately measured by several scientists outside Europe. Arab scientist Abu Allah Mohammed Ibn Jabir al-Battani (850–929) used astronomical observations to get it right to within 28 seconds.
2 In central Asia, Ullagh Beg (1394–1449) was a prince with an interest in astronomy and an odd ambition to become a science teacher (how weird can you get!). He set up his own university so he could teach science, and spent a fortune building his own observatory so he could study the stars. In fact, Ullagh proved to be a star star-gazer who measured the year to within 25 seconds of its true length. Sadly, his son was less of a star. He plotted against his scientist dad and sliced open his head with a sword. That wasn't a "slice" thing to do – was it?

Anyway, back in Europe one of the world's greatest unsung heroes was about to make his appearance. This person should be more famous than Mickey Mouse but sadly no one can even decide what his name was...

Hall of fame: Luigi Lilio otherwise known as Aloysius Lilius (that's his name in Latin) (1510–1576) Nationality: Italian

If you just said "Luigi who?" I don't blame you. In fact, I bet that 99.99999% of the readers of this book have never heard of him! Some people are incredibly famous for doing nothing important – kicking a football, singing a few songs, acting in movies – but so what? Luigi Lilio is unbelievably un-famous for doing something STUPENDOUS. Something so incredibly important that it affects every day of our lives.

He invented our modern calendar.

And here's how he did it...

Luigi was a retired doctor and university teacher living quietly in southern Italy when one day in the early 1570s he had an incredible idea:

IT'S TIME TO GET THE CALENDAR RIGHT!

In a rush of excitement the old doctor sat down and wrote down his brilliant brainwave in a book. Then he packed up his belongings and travelled to Rome to tell the Pope. Soon afterwards he died.

And that, you might well think, should have been that. After all, if they didn't listen to brainy Bacon why should anyone listen to laid-out Luigi especially seeing as he was dead. But Luigi had a secret weapon: his brother, Antonio. And Antonio battled to get the Pope and other important people to take his brother's plan seriously. At last, in 1578, he succeeded.

As popes go, Gregory XIII (1502–1585) wasn't exactly pope-ular. He taxed the people heavily and spent the money on big celebrations and grand buildings whilst poor folk went hungry. But he did sort out the calendar mess. Or more accurately he set up a group led by German astronomer Christopher Clavius (1537–1612) to do the job for him. And they backed Luigi Lilio's plan.

You see, Lilio's plan had one big advantage: it was simple and it was common sense. Er – hold on that's actually two. We'd best let Luigi speak for himself…

WE TAKE TEN DAYS FROM THE CALENDAR — THAT'S ALL WE NEED TO DO TO HOLD EASTER AT THE TRADITIONAL TIME OF YEAR. WE STOP THINGS GOING WRONG AGAIN BY CANCELLING THE LEAP YEAR THREE TIMES IN EVERY 400 YEARS.

Er – can you explain this, Norbert?

This meant that any year that ended "00" was not a leap year unless you could divide it by 400. And that's why 2000 was a leap year but 1900 wasn't. Riveting stuff, don't you think, readers?!

Luigi's plan worked! Well, not quite, as it was still one day out every 3,300 years, but hey – who cares! Well, obviously some people do...

TUT, TUT –
ONE WHOLE
DAY!

Gradually the new calendar spread throughout Europe and America. In parts of what is now Belgium and the Netherlands the authorities decided to miss the extra ten days over Christmas. So Christmas was cancelled! No doubt children cried and mean-minded parents secretly rejoiced. By 1949, when China adopted the calendar it had swept the entire world and you can be sure that it was named after the one person who made it all possible. That's right ... good ol' Pope Gregory

It's called the "Gregorian Calendar" and not the "Lilian Calendar" because Luigi was dead and buried. In fact the Pope's office even lost their original copy of Luigi's book. So remember folks – if you want to be dead famous, it's a bad idea to be too dead before your wonderful ideas are taken up by important people who become famous instead of you.

HEE, HEE!

DATING DISASTERS
Of course, the calendar can tell us what day of the year it is – but it doesn't keep track of the years. The idea of numbering the years was invented by an obscure

priest named Dionysius Exguus (500–560). But everyone called him "Little Dennis" either because he was a bit lacking in the height department or he didn't have much to say for himself.

Anyway, Dennis invented the term "AD" (now often called CE or Common Era). AD stands for anno Domini, "the year of our Lord". It was meant to number the years since Jesus was born, but it didn't. And why not?

1 Today's historians think that Jesus was born in 4 BC. Oh, what's wrong now, Norbert?

BC MEANING "BEFORE CHRIST" (NOW OFTEN CALLED BCE = BEFORE COMMON ERA) WASN'T ACTUALLY IN USE UNTIL AFTER 1615.

YAWN!

YAWN!

2 Dennis started off with year one and not year zero – he can't be blamed for this since the idea of a number zero didn't reach Europe (from India via Arabia) for another 200 years.

THEY'RE GONNA LOVE THIS!

ZERO

EUROPE

INDIA

YEAH, WE'VE GOT ZERO TO GIVE THEM!

A TERRIBLY SHOCKING THOUGHT

Er – hold on! I've just thought of something! That means history teachers and history books have been wrong about dates for over 2,000 years! Even the dates in this book are wrong! It means that the real Millennium celebrations should have been in 1996 and the WHOLE WORLD missed the big day! OOPS!

Bet you never knew!
You may have heard of the Chinese practice of naming years after animals – the year of the rat, the year of the tiger and so on. But did you know that the year you were born in is supposed to give you certain qualities? Good teachers are born in the year of the monkey – but younger readers are advised not to share this fact with their educators...

YOU'RE A BORN MONKEY, SIR!

But anyway, the calendar was sorted. Mind you, some people went on inventing their own calendars with terrible results. I mean, look what happened in France in 1792! After the French Revolution in 1789 the new leaders wanted to change the calendar to something they thought was more logical. No doubt the papers were full of it – especially when things went terribly wrong...

The Daily Revolution

5 April 1794

CROOKED CALENDAR-CHANGER GETS CHOP!

All Paris turned out today to see Philippe Fabre D'Eglantine lose his head. The potty ex-poet hit the big time two years ago when he backed a scatter-brained scheme to change the calendar.

YESTERDAY

The new calendar was introduced by law and made the year ten months and the day ten hours. But a bid to make the week ten days long flopped after people complained about getting one day off in ten. Fabre's enemies said he stole money and took bribes. His career came a cropper and he faced the chopper!

At the execution the time-tinkering traitor was calm and kept his head right until the end. As time ran out he handed poems to the crowd. Typical author — anything for a bit of free publicity!

TODAY

The new calendar was scrapped in 1805 but by then most people had been ignoring it for years. The idea of changing the clock time was even less successful: it had as much chance of catching on as a wig in a hurricane. And now we're on the subject of clocks it's time to discover some crazy old timers...

No, I meant the time-keeping machines in the next chapter!

CRAZY CLOCKS

Where would we be without clocks? You wind up your clock – (well, the old-fashioned type) and then it winds you up by waking you up in the morning and reminding you how late you are. But clocks are crucial and this chapter explains why...

STOP THE CLOCK!

Our whole lives are bound up with measuring time in halting hours, meandering minutes and swiftly speeding seconds. I mean – can you name one sport that doesn't depend on clocks to time speeds or the length of a game? Yep – you even need a clock for snail racing...

...AND AFTER A SLUGGISH START, MR MOLLUSC WINS BY A FRACTION OF ... AN HOUR. ER ... 35 MINUTES, ACTUALLY.

You may like to know that the hour, the second and the minute were invented in Babylon over 4,000 years ago. Mind you, without a clock, hours, seconds and minutes are as useful as a diving suit in the desert – but around this time (1500 BC) the world's first time-measuring device came out of the shadows. Some people still have one in their gardens. Don't go away – we'll be back after this commercial break...

For an extra £999,999.99 we'll put ancient Egyptian picture writing on your obelisk just like the original. Then everyone can read about your heroic deeds and the battles you've won!

THE SMALL PRINT – Since the Earth's orbit round the sun is an ellipse (like a squashed circle) and not a circle, the sun takes longer to cross the sky on some days than others. And this means your clock won't always be accurate.

TERRIBLE EXPRESSIONS

A time expert announces:

I HAVE A HUGE GNOMON IN MY GARDEN...

Do you say...?

OH YEAH – MY AUNTIE BERYL'S GOT MILLIONS OF GNOMES IN HER GARDEN!

Answer: Only if you want to upset our expert and that might be bad for your 'elf – I mean health. For your information, a gnomon (no-mon) is an upright object that casts a shadow to tell the time – like our obelisk.

MESSAGE TO YOUNGER READERS

What's that? Your penny-pinching parents won't buy you an obelisk? Oh shame! Oh well, why not make your own sundial? OK, it's not as grand as the one in the advert but it's cheap and cheerful and you don't need any slaves to build it! And when you've made the sundial there's another clock to make too...

Dare you discover ... how to make your own clock?

1 The sundial

You will need:
A piece of card
A torch
Some scissors
A ruler

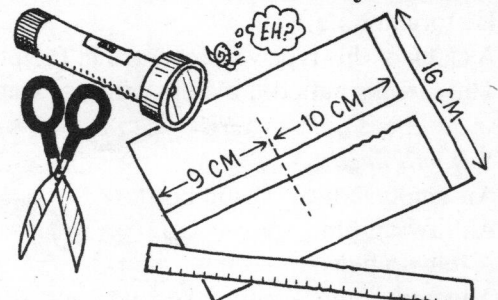

What you do:
1 Cut out the "T" shape and fold it as shown.

2 Place the ruler over the flat part of the shape.
3 Darken the room and switch on the torch. Move the torch in an arc like the sun rising and moving across the sky.

You should find:
The lower the sun (WHOOPS, I mean torch), the longer the shadow. In most parts of the Earth the midday sun appears lower in the sky in the winter and higher in the summer – so a sundial can also tell you what time of year it is.

61

2 The water clock
Historical note
A clock of this type was invented in Egypt around 1350 BC. The Greeks called it a clepsydra or "water thief".

You will need:
An empty 2-litre plastic bottle
A drawing pin
A felt-tip pen
A watch or clock with a second hand

What you do:
1 Using the drawing pin, make a hole about 2.5 cm (1 inch) above the base of the bottle. Place the bottle by the sink to avoid unwanted floods and friction with your family.
2 Fill the bottle to the top with water and mark the water level. Time a minute. Mark the new water level as the bottle empties through the hole into the sink. Time another minute and carry on until you get bored.
3 Read the rest of this book in between marking minutes.

You should find:
The minute marks get closer together as the water gets lower and empties more slowly from the bottle. Of course, a cold night might freeze the clock and dirt could block the hole.

Wherever clocks were installed they began to take over peoples' lives. Ancient Greek thinker Aristotle (384–322 BC) complained that when people went to the theatre they didn't follow the play because they were watching the public water clock. In Athens, people used a huge water clock to find out when boring politicians ran over the time allowed for their speeches.

In 100 BC an ancient Greek wrote…

When I was young there was no other clock for me but my belly. For me it was the best and most accurate clock, at its call we ate, unless there was nothing to eat…

He added that since those funny newfangled sundial thingies had become popular people ate their lunch when the sundial told them it was lunchtime, and that meant they got really hungry whilst they were waiting. Do you know the feeling?

Bet you never knew!
The first clocks appeared in the 1280s. No one knows who invented them but they were so inaccurate they only had one hand – to count the hours. The key to building a clock that could tell the right time turned out to be a neat little gizmo…

THUD!

CLUNK! CLANK!

RATTLE!

TERRIBLE EXPRESSIONS

A clock expert says:

I NEED AN ESCAPEMENT

Do you say…?

WHY, WHO'S AFTER YOU?

Bet you never knew!

From the 1650s the time-keeping part of the clock was a swinging weight (or "pendulum") or a wheel that rocked to and fro under the control of a small spring. Both moved at a regular rate. Of course these old timers are valuable antiques now and not to be confused with old-time humans who are still into rock and swing.

CLOCK THIS!

1 Before the first pendulum clock, astronomers timed stars moving across the sky by forcing children to swing pendulums and count the exact number of swings. In those days "having a go on the swings" was far less popular.

2 The power for a pendulum clock comes from weights that slowly descend in stages controlled by the swinging pendulum. This means that the traditional grandfather clock doesn't work in space, as there's no gravity to pull the weights down.

3 And the sea is just as bad. The inventor of both the pendulum and the spring clocks, Dutch super-scientist Christiaan Huygens (1629–1695), tried for 20 years to build a clock that would keep good time at sea. But to keep time a pendulum needs to swing at a fixed rate and that's hard when the ship is being tossed around like a rubber duck in a paddling pool. And springs and other metal parts were affected by heat and cold.

Well, that's tough, because seafarers didn't just need accurate clocks to find out what time it was, they needed them to find out where they were at sea. And bad time-keeping could prove dangerously deadly, as we'll see in the next chapter… Don't be late!

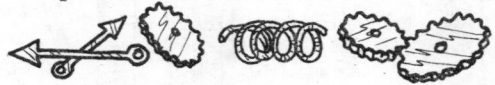

THE WRONG TIME AND PLACE

Finding out where you are at sea is a PROBLEM. Once you're out of sight of land there's not much to put on your map except a pretty blue colour and the word "SEA", so you need a device to tell you where you are.

That device proved to be the clock and Norbert is about to explain how to use it. I ought to say that when he isn't at home glued to his computer screen, our geeky pal enjoys a bit of messing about in his dinghy…

HOW TO FIND OUT HOW FAR EAST OR WEST YOU ARE AT SEA IN THREE EVER-SO-EASY STAGES WITH NORBERT

You set an accurate clock to the correct time.

THAT'S 08.01 AND 35 SECONDS TO BE PRECISE.

I'M SAILING WEST

– BUT HOW FAR HAVE I GOT?

The clock tells Norbert the time at the port.

IT'S 12.01 BACK THERE

And the overhead sun means it's 1200 hours on board Norbert's dinghy.

The difference between the two is one minute. The sun seems to move from east to west at 20.1 km per minute.*

SO I'VE SAILED 20.1 KM! RIGHT – TIME FOR MY SANDWICHES ...

* This figure is roughly correct for much of North America, Europe, Asia and Japan.

... FISHPASTE AND CABBAGE ARGH!!!

Sounds simple. But as I said, back in the olden days, clocks didn't keep good time at sea. So inventors looked at other ideas even if they were a bit daft...

LOOPY LONGITUDE METHODS

We've invited the inventors to show off their plans. And Norbert is going to explain their drawbacks ... ready, guys?

1 The Telescope Helmet

INVENTOR: Italian mega-genius Galileo Galilei
DATE: around 1611

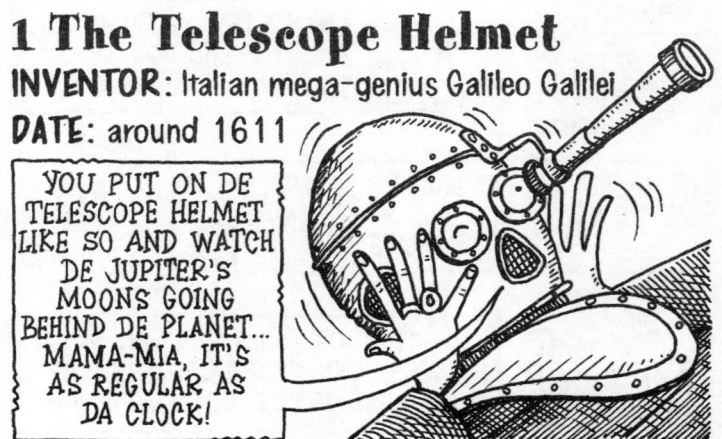

YOU PUT ON DE TELESCOPE HELMET LIKE SO AND WATCH DE JUPITER'S MOONS GOING BEHIND DE PLANET... MAMA-MIA, IT'S AS REGULAR AS DA CLOCK!

What do you reckon, Norbert?

Well, I suppose it's a good idea but I'm not really sure if it will work. You see, it's hard to spot a planet when the ship is tossing about in the ocean. I tried it once and jammed the telescope in my earhole! And if it's cloudy then it's impossible! Also the time taken for light to reach us from Jupiter varies with the planet's position so you can't set your clock by it. Fascinating stuff, though!

2 The Powder of Sympathy

INVENTOR: Sir Kenelm Digby

DATE: 1687

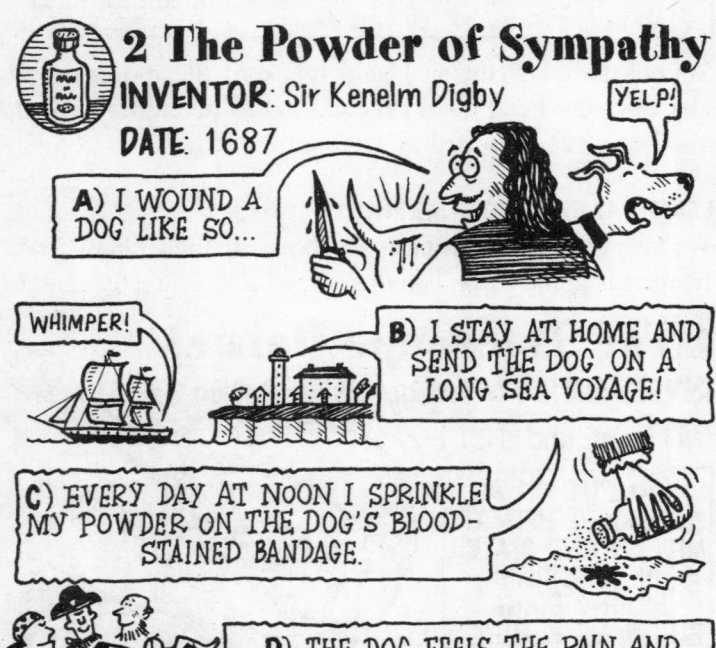

YELP!

A) I WOUND A DOG LIKE SO...

WHIMPER!

B) I STAY AT HOME AND SEND THE DOG ON A LONG SEA VOYAGE!

C) EVERY DAY AT NOON I SPRINKLE MY POWDER ON THE DOG'S BLOOD-STAINED BANDAGE.

HOWL!

D) THE DOG FEELS THE PAIN AND HOWLS — AND THIS TELLS THE SHIP'S CREW WHEN IT'S NOON AT HOME!

I've spent the last eight hours looking through all my time books and the Internet for this powder and I am forced to conclude that it does not exist! I think this idea must be a hoax!

An urgent warning from the author
Don't try this at home, readers. It's cruelty to animals and may result in a long prison sentence and a badly bitten backside!

3 The signal-ships plan

INVENTORS: William Whiston and Humphrey Ditton
DATE: 1713

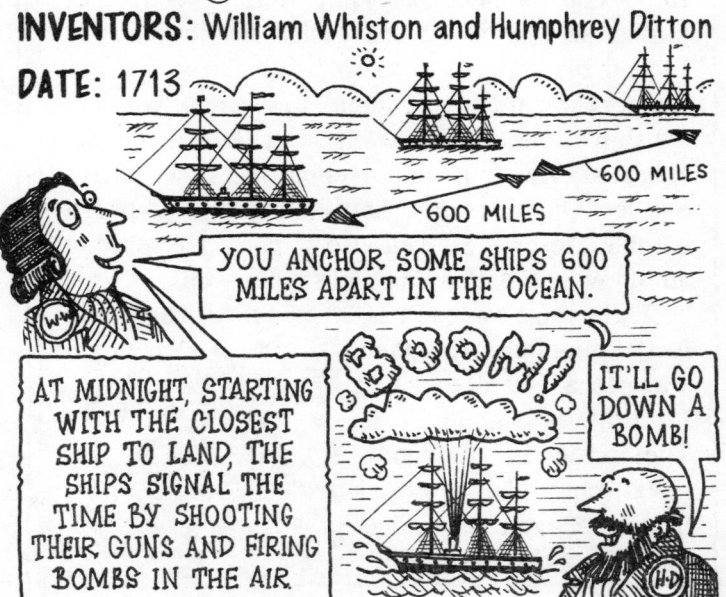

600 MILES

600 MILES

YOU ANCHOR SOME SHIPS 600 MILES APART IN THE OCEAN.

AT MIDNIGHT, STARTING WITH THE CLOSEST SHIP TO LAND, THE SHIPS SIGNAL THE TIME BY SHOOTING THEIR GUNS AND FIRING BOMBS IN THE AIR.

BOOM!

IT'LL GO DOWN A BOMB!

Oh dear, oh dear, oh dear! I've never heard of such twaddle! I've done a lot of digging out facts and found out that oceans are too deep to anchor in. In bad weather guns and bombs wouldn't be heard or seen. And it would prove difficult to keep the ships supplied with food. I'm afraid this idea is a bit of a "bomber", ha ha!

Bet you never knew!

In 1707 a fleet of English ships was sailing home after a battle. Admiral Sir Clowdisley Shovell was looking forward to a hero's welcome when a sailor warned him that the fleet was further west than the ship's captain believed. They were in danger of hitting the rocks of the Scilly Isles! But the Admiral backed his captains who said that the sailor was wrong. Crew members weren't allowed to work out the ship's course and Shovell ordered the man to be executed. The following evening the ships hit the Scillies. One man from Shovell's ship lived to tell the tale. Admiral Shovell also staggered ashore but an old woman killed him and stole his ring.

Three ships sank and 2,000 men died. They were lost at sea after losing their way at sea. But all they had needed was a good clock. The pride of England's navy went to the bottom of the sea because its leaders didn't know the right time.

ERK!

EEK!

ARGH!

Stunned by the disaster, in 1714 the British Parliament offered a reward of £20,000 for anyone who could invent a way to solve the problem of measuring longitude to an accuracy of 48.27 km (30 miles).

IMPORTANT NOTE

**In those days, £20,000 was worth a fortune.
In today's money it's more than
TEN MILLION POUNDS. It was the greatest
prize in the history of science.**

Bet you never knew!
Lines of longitude are imaginary north-south lines that mark off how far east or west you are on a map.

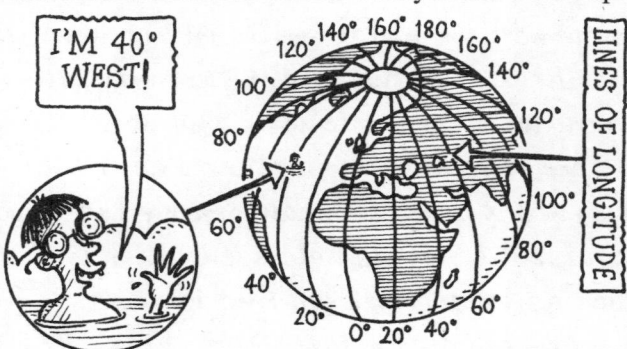

The prize looked hard to win. As Norbert explained, the ideas put around at the time had less chance of making it than a balloon in a pin factory. But there was still the hope of building a clock that kept time at sea. And one man was determined to do it and win the prize.

Hall of fame: John Harrison (1693–1776)
Nationality: British

When John was a young lad he fell ill and his parents placed a watch on his pillow so he could listen to the ticking. In those days watches were rare and expensive and the boy was enthralled by this strange machine. He was fascinated by science too and even copied out an entire book of science notes. Would you be that dedicated?

John's dad was a carpenter and the boy learnt the trade. When he was just 19, John built a wooden clock that was so finely made that everyone who saw it had to agree that the young man had a special talent for making things. Here's what John's notebook might have looked like…

1726 ~ Pesky things - pendulum clocks! The pendulum metal swells in hot weather and shrinks in the cold. Either way, the pendulum changes length and won't swing to time. Anyway, my brother and I have designed a pendulum containing two metals. The metals hold each other in place as they swell up. And it works! The new pendulum loses just one second a month! I reckon we're onto something here!

It was an incredible achievement! With no training and little money two young men had built the most accurate clock ever known! John decided that he could win the Longitude Prize. But would his skill be enough?

It took John four years to draw up his clock plans and then he went to London to see the Board of Longitude – this was the committee Parliament had set up to award the prize. In London John met Edmond Halley (1656–1742), a leading member of the Board. Halley sent John to see George Graham – the finest watchmaker in London. But what would the expert make of John's plans?

The expert was impressed. John and George Graham talked for ten hours – non-stop! And the watchmaker loaned the young man cash to build his clock. But it took John five more years of work before the clock was ready. No doubt his notebook was full of it...

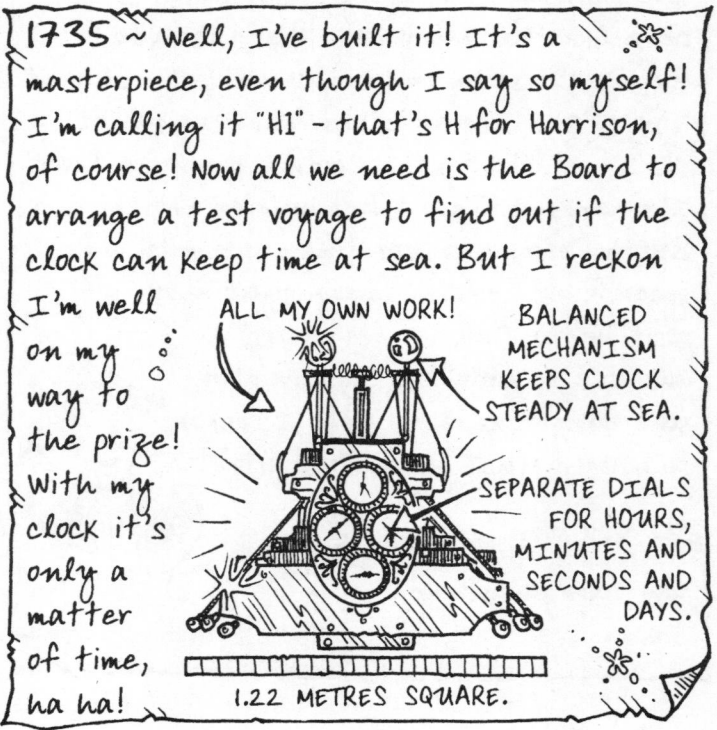

1735 ~ Well, I've built it! It's a masterpiece, even though I say so myself! I'm calling it "H1" – that's H for Harrison, of course! Now all we need is the Board to arrange a test voyage to find out if the clock can keep time at sea. But I reckon I'm well on my way to the prize! With my clock it's only a matter of time, ha ha!

ALL MY OWN WORK!

BALANCED MECHANISM KEEPS CLOCK STEADY AT SEA.

SEPARATE DIALS FOR HOURS, MINUTES AND SECONDS AND DAYS.

1.22 METRES SQUARE.

After months of delay the Board agreed to test the clock by sending it and John on a sea voyage to Lisbon, Portugal. Here's a letter John might have written to his wife, Elizabeth.

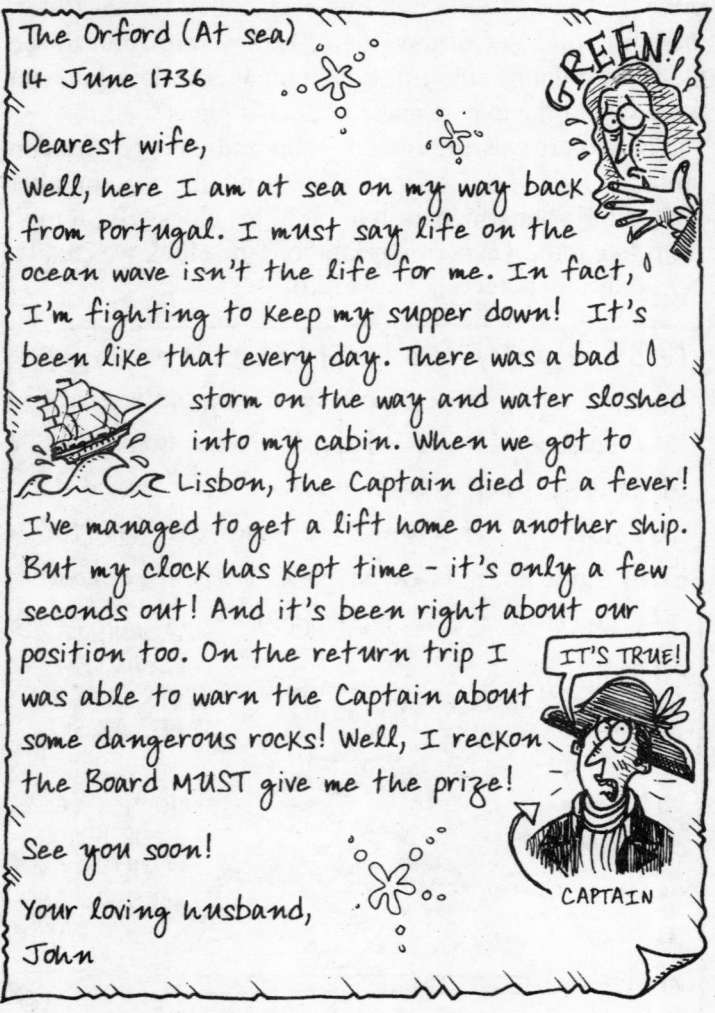

The Orford (At sea)
14 June 1736

GREEN!

Dearest wife,
Well, here I am at sea on my way back from Portugal. I must say life on the ocean wave isn't the life for me. In fact, I'm fighting to keep my supper down! It's been like that every day. There was a bad storm on the way and water sloshed into my cabin. When we got to Lisbon, the Captain died of a fever! I've managed to get a lift home on another ship. But my clock has kept time - it's only a few seconds out! And it's been right about our position too. On the return trip I was able to warn the Captain about some dangerous rocks! Well, I reckon the Board MUST give me the prize!

IT'S TRUE!

See you soon!

Your loving husband,
John

CAPTAIN

But the Board said the test didn't count. John should have gone to the West Indies – so why did they send him to Lisbon? In any case, you might think John was too honest for his own good. He said the clock needed improving – and he began to build a new one. At least this time the Board gave him some cash up front.

Let's take another peek in that notebook…

1741
Well, that was a mistake and a half! It's taken me four years to build H2 and it's even heavier than H1!
It's more accurate and can withstand high and low temperatures.

H2

And yes, the scientists at the Royal Society have tested it by shaking to prove that it can stand up to a voyage. But that's not good enough for me!
I KNOW I CAN DO BETTER!

Once more John began making a new clock. This time the work took even longer. Another 18 years in fact!

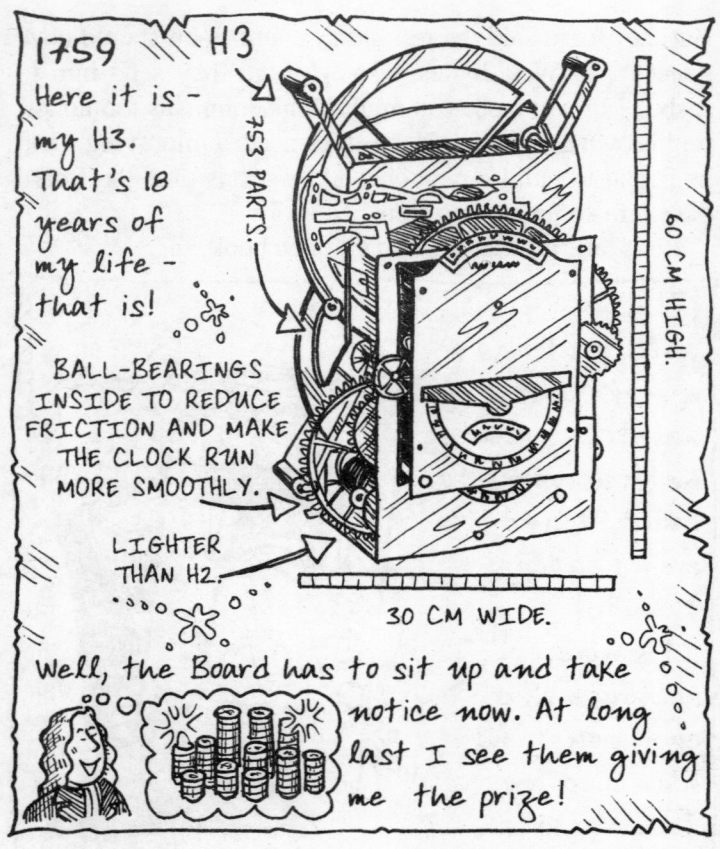

Meanwhile, the Board had been looking at plans by astronomers to use the moon to find longitude. The idea was to predict when the moon appeared to pass certain stars on certain days as seen from London. Mariners could clock the time when this happened (using a clock they re-set at noon) and compare this to the London time. And they could use the time difference to work out the distance east or west of London.

You might think this is terribly complicated – and you'd be right – but the scientists on the Board liked the idea. They thought it was more scientific than using a humble clock. But John was busy working on yet another clock...

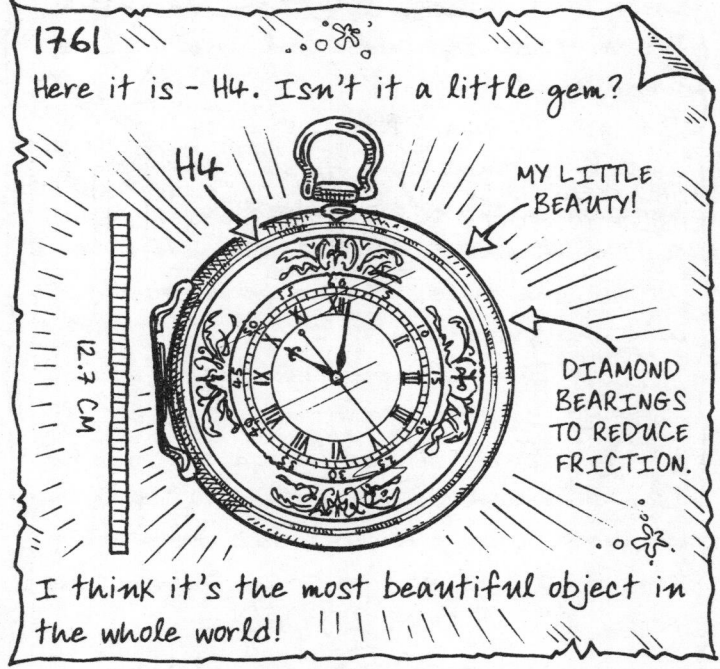

1761

Here it is – H4. Isn't it a little gem?

H4

12.7 CM

MY LITTLE BEAUTY!

DIAMOND BEARINGS TO REDUCE FRICTION.

I think it's the most beautiful object in the whole world!

The new clock – the "watch" as John called it – was a miracle. Nothing like it had ever been seen before, and it seemed impossible that such a small thing could measure time with the accuracy the Board demanded. The Board wasn't impressed, but in the end agreed to test the clock on a voyage to the West Indies. By now John was too old to travel and so he waved goodbye to the two most precious things in his life – his watch and his son, William. Here's a letter that William might have sent his father...

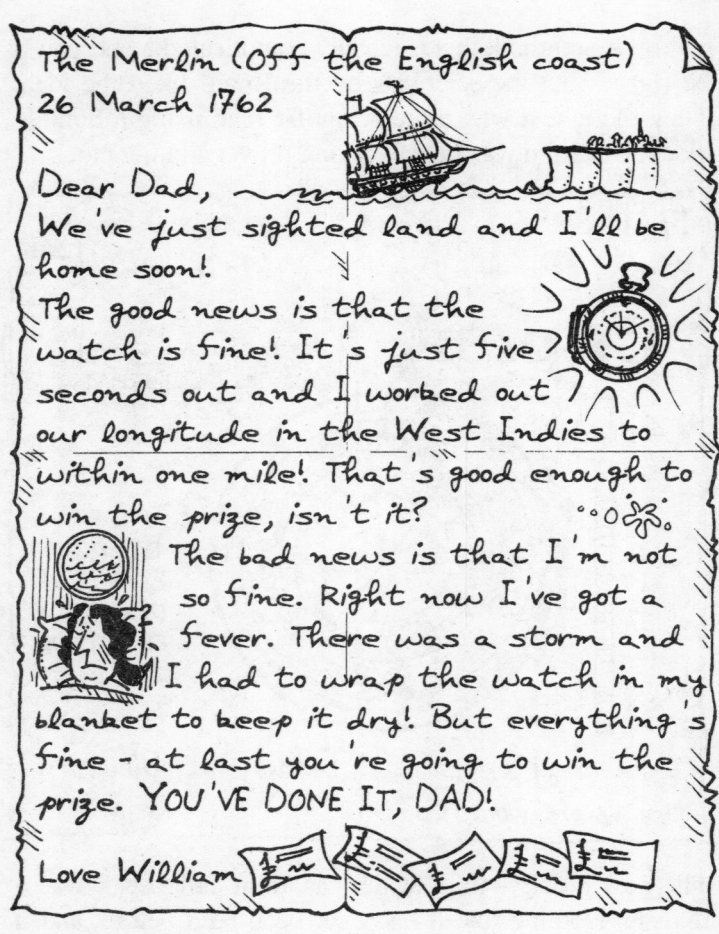

The Merlin (Off the English coast)
26 March 1762

Dear Dad,
We've just sighted land and I'll be home soon!
The good news is that the watch is fine! It's just five seconds out and I worked out our longitude in the West Indies to within one mile! That's good enough to win the prize, isn't it?

The bad news is that I'm not so fine. Right now I've got a fever. There was a storm and I had to wrap the watch in my blanket to keep it dry! But everything's fine – at last you're going to win the prize. YOU'VE DONE IT, DAD!

Love William

Some chance! The Board came up with a new excuse and said that William hadn't tested the watch properly. So he had to take the watch back to the West Indies and do it all over again! And this time Nevil Maskelyne would be there too. Maskelyne was an astronomer and a supporter of the rival moon method. Here's how the papers might have reported the new test…

THE CLOCKMAKER'S TIMES

July 1764

CRUCIAL CRUNCH CLOCK CRUISE

W. HARRISON

John Harrison is scenting success in his long longitude prize quest. The veteran clockmaker proudly told how his son, William, sailed for a second time to the West Indies, where his "watch" kept near-perfect time.

Rival timer, Nevil Maskelyne botched his observations of the moon after a row with William. "He wasn't exactly over the moon," reported William.

N. MASKELYNE

John Harrison had done everything to win the prize – but still the Board dragged its feet. It must have been incredibly, unbelievably frustrating. And then disaster struck. Still smarting from the row with William, Nevil Maskelyne became Astronomer Royal, that's the top British astronomer, and joined the Board. Would he take his revenge on John? Here's John's notebook again…

1766

I've spent 40 years trying to win this prize. I even spent six days showing experts how my watch works – before they took it away and ordered me to build a new one ... from memory! And now this...

This morning, Maskelyne turned up with a gang of men to take away my other clocks. He says the Board wants him to test them. When the workmen laid rough hands on the beautiful wooden cases I was shaking with fear and fury. Then a clumsy oaf drops my H1 in the gutter with a horrible jangling crash. I shuddered to see the work of 40 years jolting and bumping away on the back of a dirty old cart. I'VE HAD IT UP TO HERE! Sorry about the tear stains ... I don't think I'll ever get over this...

By now John was an old man. He couldn't walk or see too well. The only thing that kept him going was the hope that somehow one day he would get justice and win the prize. But Maskelyne claimed that the clocks didn't keep good time. Odd that – they did well enough in all those tests at sea. Meanwhile the astronomer boasted that his charts of the moon's position had solved the longitude problem for good.

Was this the end of John Harrison's dream?

A TIMELY QUESTION

John was running out of time – he was 74 years old and not expected to last much longer.

So how do you think his story ends?

Well, let's find out, shall we?

William went to see King George at his castle and told His Majesty about his father's long battle to claim his reward. Surprisingly the King was interested in science and clocks and already knew some of the facts. But he couldn't believe how badly John had been treated.

When William finished his story, His Majesty was visibly moved and turned away muttering, "These people have been cruelly treated."

The King promised to put things right and ordered a new set of tests. The watch kept near-perfect time. In June 1773, Parliament passed a law to award John a generous cash reward.

John was 80 years old and near the end of his life. He never lived to see clocks based on his designs taken in ships all over the world and never knew how many thousands of lives they saved.

Today, millions of visitors come to marvel at John's clocks at the National Maritime Museum, Greenwich. And John Harrison is honoured as the greatest clockmaker of all time.

Of course time's moved on since those days and we must too. So let's get really up to date and check out how time is measured in modern times...

Get ready to say "COR!" rather a lot.

MAKING GOOD TIME

Building a clock that could help you find your location proved to be just the start. Today time is organized and mapped across the whole world and measured with super-accuracy to billionths of a second. And there have been bucket-loads of shiny-new time inventions – like the 24-hour clock.

THE TERRIBLY CONFUSING 24-HOUR CLOCK

Can you make sense of the 24-hour clock? That's the one where 5 pm is known as 1,700 hours and so on? If you can't, you may like to know who's to blame for it...

Well, here he is now: Sandford Fleming, the great time expert. He's about to make a discovery on a station platform at Bandoran, Ireland in 1876. He's so keen to catch a vital train that he's turned up three hours early. But we'll leave him to discover the terrible truth in his own good time...

That'll be the 5.35 AM, sor! Ye'll be having another 12 HOURS to wait.

Harumph! I'll miss my ferry to England!

The trouble about being in a hurry, sor, is that you never have time for anything important...

SHUT UP!

Sandford spent the next 12 hours trying to think up a way to prevent this kind of maddening misunderstanding. And his simple solution was the 24-hour clock – a clock that made it clear whether the time was morning or afternoon (that's if you can understand it!).

If Sandford had done nothing more in his life than invent the 24-hour clock, he'd have merely changed the lives of millions of people all over the world for ever. But he did MORE, much, much more and that's why he deserves a place in our Horrible Science...

Hall of fame: Sandford Fleming (1827–1915)
Nationality: Scottish-born Canadian
As the ship rolled and tossed and pitched in the mountainous seas, the frightened passengers hugged and prayed. Meanwhile, on the heaving deck, as the freezing spray stung his face and fierce wind tugged his clothes, a youthful scientist calmly measured the wind speed and direction.

It looked like young Sandford Fleming's dream of leaving his native Scotland for Canada had ended before it had begun. He sealed the letter in a bottle and tossed it overboard hoping that someone somewhere would find it and send it to his family. And in fact they did. A few months later the Fleming family learnt of the death of their son in a storm.

Except that he was still alive...

At the last moment the wind had dropped and the ship had made it to Canada. Young Sandford could begin his climb to fame and fortune as a top railway planner. And the secret of his success? Well, you might say it was talent... Sandford was good at his job as a surveyor (someone who maps the route of railways) and he was a talented artist who designed Canada's first postage stamp.

Or you might say that Sandford had energy. I mean this guy never stopped! He belonged to 70 scientific societies, and when he was on a ship he would walk 4.8 km round the ship every day to keep fit. And he later got involved in a project to lay a telegraph cable across the Pacific Ocean – I expect that was light relief.

But I think that Sandford's secret was to do with time. He knew how to make the most of it. He had this idea that he should never waste a second. Even when he wasn't working he was practising his drawing or designing a new kind of roller skate or writing articles about the science of rocks. And when he wasn't striding round a ship he was writing a newspaper for the other passengers.

So time was very important to our pal Sandford, and that's why he was so annoyed about being stuck in a station for 12 hours, and that's why he used the time to think up some seriously scintillating ideas.

THE TIMELY TIME-ZONES IDEA

Sandford began to think that the whole world should be divided into time zones based on the spinning of the Earth. It took him two years to work out the details. The idea was that there would be 24 time zones. Each zone would cover 15° of the 360° of longitude or one hour of the sun's passage across the sky. And the time would be the same everywhere in a zone.

Time zones were a great idea and the reason was big and dirty and made an odd puffing sound. No, I'm not talking about your grandpa – it was the steam train! Before time zones, travelling by train was as tricky as cutting a gnat's toenails. Just imagine what TV travel shows would have made of it – that's if they'd had TV in those days!

Here at Buffalo, New York, there are three different railway company times and a separate local time. Which means that...

WE'VE JUST MISSED OUR TRAIN!

Time zones would make it simpler for railway companies to keep their trains running on time. What's more, people could do business abroad by telegraph (and later by phone) more easily because they could work out the time in other countries. So, at last, in 1884, after arguments about where to have the 0° line and where to start the day, Sandford's idea was taken up by the leading nations of the world.

Here's a map showing the time zones. Which one do you live in?

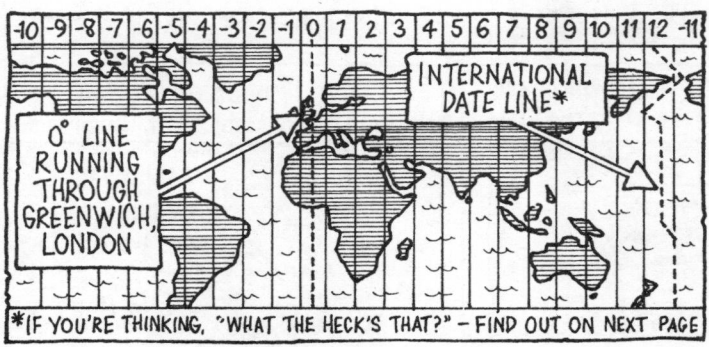

-10 -9 -8 -7 -6 -5 -4 -3 -2 -1 0 1 2 3 4 5 6 7 8 9 10 11 12 -11

INTERNATIONAL DATE LINE*

0° LINE RUNNING THROUGH GREENWICH, LONDON

*IF YOU'RE THINKING, "WHAT THE HECK'S THAT?" – FIND OUT ON NEXT PAGE

And here's how they work: the 0° line runs through Greenwich, London. East of Greenwich, each time zone is one hour ahead of Greenwich time. As you travel west each time zone is one hour behind Greenwich time.

The really mind-wobbling bit is when you get to the International Date Line. This line is 180° west of Greenwich in the middle of the Pacific Ocean. It's 12 hours ahead of Greenwich going east but 12 hours behind Greenwich going west. And that raises the interesting question of what day is it on the Date Line? Can it be two days at once? We've sent Norbert and his dinghy (at great expense) off to investigate.

So that's your answer, folks! On the Date Line, you get two days side-by-side, 24 hours apart. And that's why they call it the "Date Line"!

> ### *Bet you never knew!*
> In the USA, a teacher named Charles Dowd was thinking along similar lines to Sandford. Dowd suggested solving the train timetable problem by splitting the USA into time zones. But everyone ignored his ideas. However, in 1883 leading US rail companies hit on the same solution. Sadly, in 1904, the teacher who dedicated years of his life to getting trains to run on time was run over ... by a train. And if Dowd was unlucky in life he was unlucky in death too. His memorial was a bronze plaque in a church. In 1976 the church burnt down and the plaque melted.

TERRIBLY WEIRD FACTS ABOUT TIME ZONES

1 The International Date Line zigzags to avoid land. One zigzag was drawn on the map to avoid the Morrell and Byers islands near Hawaii – until someone discovered that the islands didn't exist. They were a map-maker's mistake!

2 In the USA, some towns refused to join a time zone. Detroit was close to a line and kept changing its mind about which zone to be in. This meant that the time kept changing too.

3 In 1852, Britain moved from local time to time based on the time at the Royal Observatory in Greenwich. Lots of people were upset at losing their local time and there were big arguments. In Birmingham, scientist Abraham Osler (1808–1903) cunningly re-set a public clock to London time when no one was looking. In Bristol, an old councillor didn't accept the new time. He spent years being 14 minutes late for everything.

THE ULTIMATE EXCUSE FOR BEING LATE ALL YOUR LIFE

Have you ever wanted to be late and get away with it? Yes, just imagine – you could laze about and roll up for things whenever you felt like it! And you could go to bed late and get up late whenever it suited you! Interested? Read on! All you do is smile sweetly and explain:

IMPORTANT AND TERRIBLY URGENT SCIENTIFIC NOTE

Saying this may result in further questioning/torture sessions, so you will need to know what your local time is. This is the time in terms of the sun's position in the sky as opposed to the time zone time that everyone else is trying to follow.

Dare you discover ... what your local time is?

You will need:
A map that shows time zones
A ruler
A pocket calculator

What you do:
1 Find out where the eastern border of your time zone is.
2 Find out where you are on the map.
3 Using the ruler, measure how far west you are from this border. Then use the calculator and the scale of the map to work out how many kilometres (or miles) this is.

You should find:
As you know (it's on page 67), the sun seems to move across the sky at a regular speed. So all you do is divide the distance in kilometres by 20.1 and you have the number of minutes your local time is behind the official clock time. These are the number of minutes you're allowed to be late. Worth a try – isn't it?

Er – hold on, looks like Norbert's back – what's up?

The sun moves at 335.28 metres (1,100 ft) per second if you want to be astoundingly accurate!

I'm at the west end of this soccer pitch. My local time is now 0.22 seconds behind the east end! Hmm — fascinating!

SIT DOWN! YOU'RE SPOILING THE GAME!

An important announcement for teachers from the publishers

We apologize for the disruption caused by younger readers of this book who are turning up late for classes and claiming that the class clock is wrong. The author responsible is now in hiding.

An important announcement for anyone who thinks that it's possible to get away with being late for things

We have just heard that teachers have worked out that if the local time is later than the clock time then that means that classes can go on later than the clock says...

STOP PRESS ~ We have just heard that children are now claiming that clock time is perfectly OK when it comes to going home from school...

Well, I think it's safe for me to creep out of hiding. I just wanted to say that nowadays we can measure time (time zones and local time) pretty accurately. And we've got some really whizzy watches to help us. I mean, even that oh-so-ordinary-looking watch on your wrist is a little marvel.

WATCH THIS!

A quartz watch works by running electricity from a battery through a tiny piece of manufactured quartz. (Quartz is a substance found in rock.)

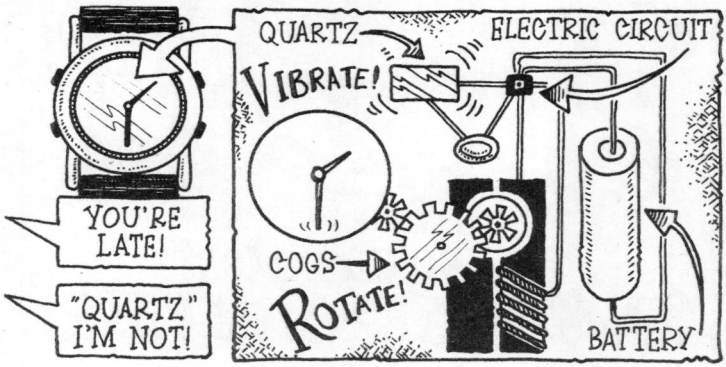

The quartz wobbles (vibrates) exactly 32,768 times a second. In this way it keeps time and produces pulses of electricity to control the motor that turns the watch hands.

Bet you never knew!
The quartz inside your watch makes a high-pitched whine as it vibrates. This would drive you crazy if your ears were sensitive enough to hear it.

We'll be taking a short break now but don't stop reading – we'll be back in a tick-tock!

Never mind, you can put it on your Christmas list…

At this moment I can guess what you're thinking: you're thinking that time is sorted. Time is tamed and measured and made sense of. After all, we've got watches and time zones and everyone's sure what time it is!

Er, no...

NO?

Yes, you know that bit about a day lasting 24 hours? Well – it's not quite true...

Bet you never knew!

The Earth's spin is slowing because of the dragging effect of the sea's tides! This makes each day 0.00000002 seconds LONGER than the day before! Does this explain why Friday afternoons drag on for so long? Anyway, it means even if the world had managed to celebrate the Millennium in the right year we'd have still fired those fireworks and popped those party poppers at the wrong time!

TUT, TUT! YOU'VE MISCALCULATED THE CORRECT DAY FOR YOUR CELEBRATION, YOUNG MAN — GO HOME!

Fortunately, the world now has a marvellous bit of science kit to help us keep track of those awkward little milliseconds and keep time so exactly that there are absolutely NO arguments. In fact it's only one second wrong in THOUSANDS of years!

It's called an atomic clock.

AWESOME ATOMIC CLOCKS

Here's how an atomic clock works…

GRANDFATHER CLOCKS MEASURE TIME WITH THE SWING OF A PENDULUM, ATOMIC CLOCKS USE THE VIBRATION OF THE CAESIUM ATOM.

TICK! TOCK! TICK! TOCK! TICK! TICK!

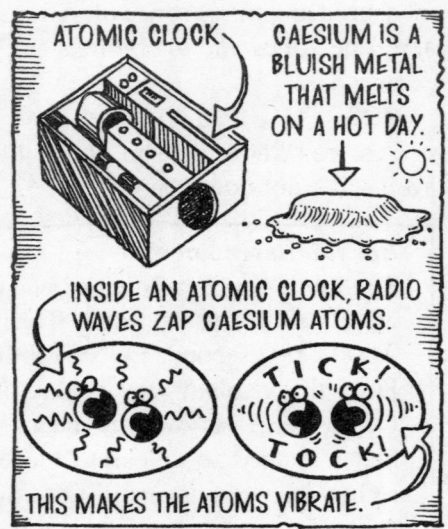

ATOMIC CLOCK

CAESIUM IS A BLUISH METAL THAT MELTS ON A HOT DAY.

INSIDE AN ATOMIC CLOCK, RADIO WAVES ZAP CAESIUM ATOMS.

TICK! TOCK!

THIS MAKES THE ATOMS VIBRATE.

The atomic clock was invented by US scientists in 1948, and clocks were built in the USA and Britain. They were a great success and in 1967 the nations of the world agreed to base time on the wobbling caesium atom.

Today, one second is officially reckoned to be 9,192,631,770 vibrations of caesium and one hour is now 33,093,474,372,000 (around 33 TRILLION) caesium wobbles. (It might seem longer if you happen to be waiting for a train in the rain.) Time is now clocked by a worldwide system of 50 atomic clocks coordinated by an International Bureau in Paris. And it's as accurate as measuring the distance to the moon to the width of a human hair. Impressive – huh?

This is far more accurate than the Earth's wobbly, ever-changing movements in space. So to keep the official time in line with the Earth, an extra or "leap" second can be added. Yes, Norbert?

So nowadays we're not really measuring time in terms of the Earth spinning in space. It's more to do with a fidgety atom that can't keep still. But you might be wondering why anyone, apart from Norbert, wants to measure time to the nearest billionth of a second. Well, scientists do. Science is about accuracy of measurement and that includes time. And as you'll find out on page 105, time experiments need to be clocked really, really accurately.

Navigation systems on planes also need accurate time-keeping. Being one billionth of a second out may mean that you're 30 cm off course. And then you might land in a swamp full of hungry alligators instead of on the runway.

So the next time you fly you'd better hope that the caesium atoms are wobbling to time.

> **Bet you never knew!**
> In 2001, US scientists created a clock that uses light waves to keep time. And it's only one second out every 15 BILLION YEARS. That ought to keep the alligators hungry!

So that's it...

Thanks to those tireless ticking atoms we can measure time exactly. And like a stream, time always flows past at the same speed and we can all set our watches without worrying that time will ever run slower. No way! Or as Norbert might say...

You see, the dramatic discoveries of a certain scientific superstar, whom we've already met, have chucked everything back into the melting pot. In fact, time really CAN slow down. It all depends on how fast you're moving...

And if that sounds maddeningly mind-mashing you'd best switch your grey cells to overdrive for the next chapter...

Yippee, it's fasten your seat belt time!

TERRIBLY SPEEDY TIME

As I was just saying, the rate at which time passes depends on your speed. And the inventor of this incredible idea? Albert Einstein, of course!

To understand what Einstein was on about we'll need to get to grips with his Special Theory of Relativity. And if you thought I just said "the special theory of relatives and tea" you really do need to read on. Albert dreamt up the theory in 1905, the same year in which he proved the existence of atoms.

But wait! I've just heard that our pal MI Gutzache is experiencing the effects of Einstein's Theory! We'll find out what's happening to him in a second, but first there's a word I've just got to explain…

TERRIBLE EXPRESSIONS

A scientist says:

I'M GOING TO MEASURE THIS MASS…

Do you say…?

ISN'T THAT A KIND OF DONKEY?

STAGGER!

WOBBLE!

Answer: NO! That's an ass – you ass! Mass means the amount of material that makes something up. Just remember that something that has a lot of mass tends to be pretty MASS-ive in size…

As you're about to find out, mass is a vital idea when it comes to understanding time and space...

M.I. GUTZACHE IS LOST IN TIME (and space)

The story so far...

Fearless private eye MI Gutzache is recovering from a time-travel experiment that went wrong. That night he woke up suddenly...

I knew the Prof had company – and the company wasn't invited. The Prof was snoring but I figured I could handle the situation. I crept into the lab. The Prof's dumb cat followed. But we weren't alone. A little green guy with tentacles was snooping around the machine! Then he blasted the machine with his ray gun.

I knew he wasn't your average two-bit hoodlum, but I decided to play it cool. "Hey, lil' fella," I hissed, "ain't you on the wrong planet?"

Well, I figured ET didn't like my tone. Before I could do nothing he knocked me out with a blast from his ray gun. And next thing I knew I was aboard his flying saucer. Well, I guess that was bad – but the little schmuck kidnapped the cat, too!

When I came to we were in space. The sky was big and black and the stars were kinda shiny. I'd never seen so many stars and the Earth looked mighty small.

Meantime that low-life cat was licking her butt and scratching her fleas. The little green guy said he was Oddblob from the planet Blurb and his orders were to trash the time machine because we humans are too dumb to use the technology wisely.

Well, I kinda took exception…

"Now listen up, wise guy!" I snapped. "This dumb animal here is what you might call stupid. But I'm as smart as the next alien!"

Well, that kinda got Oddblob thinking and he said that in that case I might figure out some simple rules of time and space discovered by a guy named Einstein…

"How fast is the light from our laser headlight?" asked the little fella.

I reasoned for a while and figured I'd cracked the case. It turned out I knew nothing.

"Ha ha – trick question!" I replied. "It's the speed of light plus our speed."

The alien gave me a dirty look. "Foolish humanoid!" he sneered. "It's still only the speed of light! Light shines at the same speed no matter how fast you're moving. Albert Einstein should have told you that!"

SCIENCE NOTE
The speed of light is about 300,000 km per second. That means that in one second a ray of light could zoom around the Earth more than SEVEN times!

Then I got kinda mad and started hollering.

"Hey, back off, pal! I never knew this Einstein fella!"

Well, Oddblob wasn't having any of it and what happened next made my stomach heave.

"Einstein predicted the results of travelling at 75% of the speed of light," he said nastily and powered up his engine.

The news was bad. For one thing, I have a motion-sickness problem. But there was no way out and I was the fall guy. The flying saucer shot forward – the stars seemed to leap towards us. I knew we were going fast. My stomach knew it too. Why hell, even the cat looked unwell.

"Our craft appears shorter in the direction of travel," announced Oddblob, showing me a picture on his display screen.

"Our mass increases," he added.

All this science sounded kind of heavy.

SCIENCE NOTE – Gutzache's got it right for once! In Earth's gravity we can measure mass in terms of weight.

The alien hadn't finished. He was showing me some kind of alien movie of the Prof's clock on Earth. His green face wore a smug look – but my face was green for another reason.

"And our ultra-accurate Blurb time-measurer slows down compared to your primitive Earth clocks."

The alien sure knew his stuff! The hands on the Prof's clock were in speeded-up motion. But I had motion problems of my own…

"Do you have a travel-sickness bag?" I gasped, but the alien was still talking science.

"We do not notice because everything is slower. My two brains and your single primitive brain work slower. If you could be heard on Earth your voice would sound s-l-o-w-e-r a-n-d d-e-e-p-e-r."

I put my hand over my mouth and sweated, slowly.

"I can't hold it much longer!" I warned.

Oh no! It looks like Norbert isn't too happy about the story…

There is no proof that aliens exist at all — and as for aliens visiting Earth, this is an unlikely suggestion that rightly belongs in a work of science-fiction!

OK, Norbert, scientists don't believe aliens have visited Earth but most reckon that our galaxy has so many stars that there must be life somewhere. And I should add that the way that time slows down when you travel fast – that is TRUE and scientists have proved it happens … honest!

COULD YOU BE AN EINSTEIN? – PART 1*

* (Part 2 of this quiz is on page 118)

Can you predict the result of the following experiments…?

1 Muons are tiny bits of matter that exist for two millionths of a second. What do you think happened when scientists made them in the lab?

a) The faster they moved the less time they lasted.

b) The faster they moved the longer they lasted.

c) The slower they moved the longer they lasted.

2 In 1971, two US scientists took atomic clocks on round-the-world trips on planes. What did they find?

a) They landed half an hour before they set off.

b) Time actually slowed down a bit whilst they were in the air.

c) Time speeded up whilst they were flying.

"BIG DEAL!" I hear you exclaim and I'm not too surprised. It's not very much is it? A plane can only fly at one-millionth the speed of light – so if you spent your whole life whizzing about in planes you'd only live one millisecond longer than if you'd stayed on the ground.

THIS IS YOUR CAPTAIN SPEAKING. I HOPE YOU'VE ENJOYED TRAVELLING AT THE SPEED OF LIGHT THE BAD NEWS IS THAT WE'VE TRAVELLED TWO WEEKS INTO THE FUTURE AND YOUR HOLIDAYS ARE ALREADY OVER!

DISGRACEFUL!

IT ALWAYS GETS THEM GOING!

BUT WE'VE ONLY JUST SET OFF!

HUH?

HA HA!

But cheer up, you can time travel into the future without leaving the ground … in fact you're forced to!

HOW YOU AND ME AND YOUR PET CAT ARE ALREADY TIME TRAVELLERS

Thanks to the time dilation effect, you and me, your cat and your pet goldfish, and everyone on planet Earth is a time traveller! It's true – at this exact second the Earth is whizzing through space as it loops around the sun, while the sun and the Earth are zooming round the galaxy and the galaxy is sailing around in our local friendly group of galaxies. Feeling dizzy yet?

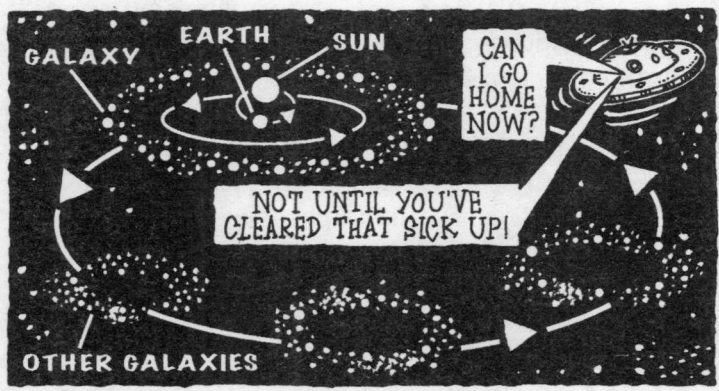

In all we're moving at 350 km per second. That's also a tiny fraction of the speed of light – but it's enough to make each second on Earth last one-millionth longer than it should. And that means if you came from a very sluggishly slow boring planet and spent your life on Earth, when you went home you'd travel 40 minutes into the future!

Time for a quick re-cap. We've looked at how going fast can make time slow down. But Einstein's Special Theory of Relativity went on to change the whole way in which scientists look at time. And we'll be changing our view too, in the next chapter.

SPACED-OUT SPACE-TIME

Do you remember how I said that time is a bit like an onion and this book would peel away the layers and explain what time is really about?

Well, we've just about reached the centre of the vegetable (but don't fry it yet). And this book is about to turn mind-squelchingly head-explodingly brain-boggling ... (YOU HAVE BEEN WARNED!)

BRAIN-BOGGLING SPACE-TIME

You've heard of space? You've heard of time? Well, in this chapter we're not going to be talking about space and time because in fact time and space go together like toes and ankles. Yep, folks, they're part of the same thing! Scientists call it "space-time" and if your head just turned full circle on your neck, you'd do well to spend some time in the space of the next few pages...

HOW TO GET YOUR HEAD ROUND SPACE-TIME IN THREE (FAIRLY) EASY LESSONS

1 You may know that our world has three directions (or dimensions). There's up-and-down, side-to-side, and front-to-back...

Over the page our ever-helpful artist has drawn a three-dimensional dog to explain what I mean... Thanks, Tony!

2 In space-time you have to imagine time as the fourth dimension (or direction) in space. Scientists draw a special diagram to show you where you are in space-time:

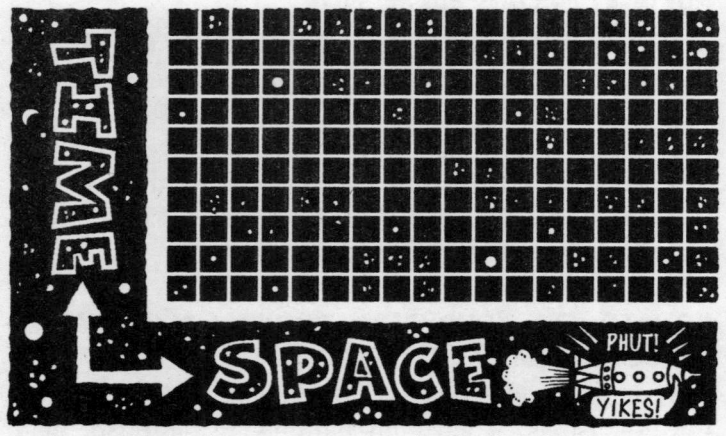

3 Now, the whole point of space-time is that if you're planning a trip in space you really need to know your position in space and the time. And here to show you how space-time works are the adventures of Captain Smirk on the star-ship Terrible.

CAPTAIN'S LOG

STAR DATE: 2090 — 201 days

We're still working on the engine.

A QUICK NOTE FROM THE AUTHOR
Notice anything, readers? The spacecraft has moved on in time by one day but it hasn't moved in space because it's still broken down!

You might be wondering where I got this idea of space-time. Did I discover it myself? Oh yeah – I wish. In fact, the idea of space-time came from Albert Einstein's old maths teacher! And he's on the TV show where the guests are late, long-gone and even a bit gone off…

Dead brainy: Hermann Minkowski (1864–1909)

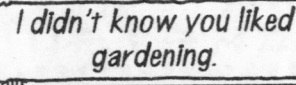

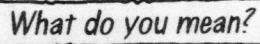

IMPORTANT AND URGENT NOTE TO YOUNGER READERS

Don't get any ideas. Missing your maths class and copying your friend's work doesn't make you a genius!

So how did you discover space-time?

AFTER READING EINSTEIN'S SPECIAL THEORY OF RELATIVITY, I REALIZED THAT THE BEST WAY TO EXPLAIN HOW TIME SLOWED DOWN WHEN YOU WENT FAST WAS THAT TIME AND SPACE ARE PART OF THE SAME THING.

And do you remember what you said in 1908?

I SAID, "HENCEFORTH SPACE BY ITSELF AND TIME BY ITSELF, ARE DOOMED TO FADE AWAY INTO MERE SHADOWS, AND ONLY A KIND OF UNION OF THE TWO WILL PRESERVE AN INDEPENDENT REALITY."

WOW! And have you got a message for your most famous pupil?

WHERE'S YOUR MATHS HOMEWORK, YOU LAZY DOG?!

It took time for word about Einstein's Special Theory of Relativity to filter through and meanwhile the man himself was still a clerk. In 1907 he was turned down for a teaching job that wasn't even paid! The following year he got a job teaching science but just three students turned up to his classes! By now, though, he was working on some terribly tricky maths of his own…

The Special Theory of Relativity was all about what happens if you go fast, but it didn't say anything about gravity. So now Albert was looking for a theory that combined the idea of space-time with gravity. It was even harder than it sounds…

For one thing, the maths proved tougher than Albert had bargained for … sounds familiar? Maybe he should have showed up for those maths classes after all! After a few years of struggling with the fiendish figures he admitted:

In desperation, he wrote to his friend, Marcel Grossmann, for help – yes, that's the same friend who had let Albert copy his maths notes:

With the help of Marcel's maths, Albert came to realize that gravity happens because space-time is actually being pulled towards an object. Eureka! Albert had hit on his greatest scientific discovery – the Theory of Relativity…

EINSTEIN'S TERRIBLE JOKE

Unlike some scientists, Albert had a sense of humour. In 1949 he said: "When you sit on a red-hot cinder a second seems an hour. That's relativity."

Readers keen on time travel are advised not to try this experiment – it has nothing to do with relativity. Unlike the facts you're about to read…

Terrible time fact file

NAME: Einstein's Theory of Relativity

THE BASIC FACTS: 1 By 1915, Einstein had proved that any object with mass pulls space-time towards it in the same way that a cat sleeping on your bed makes a dip in the covers.

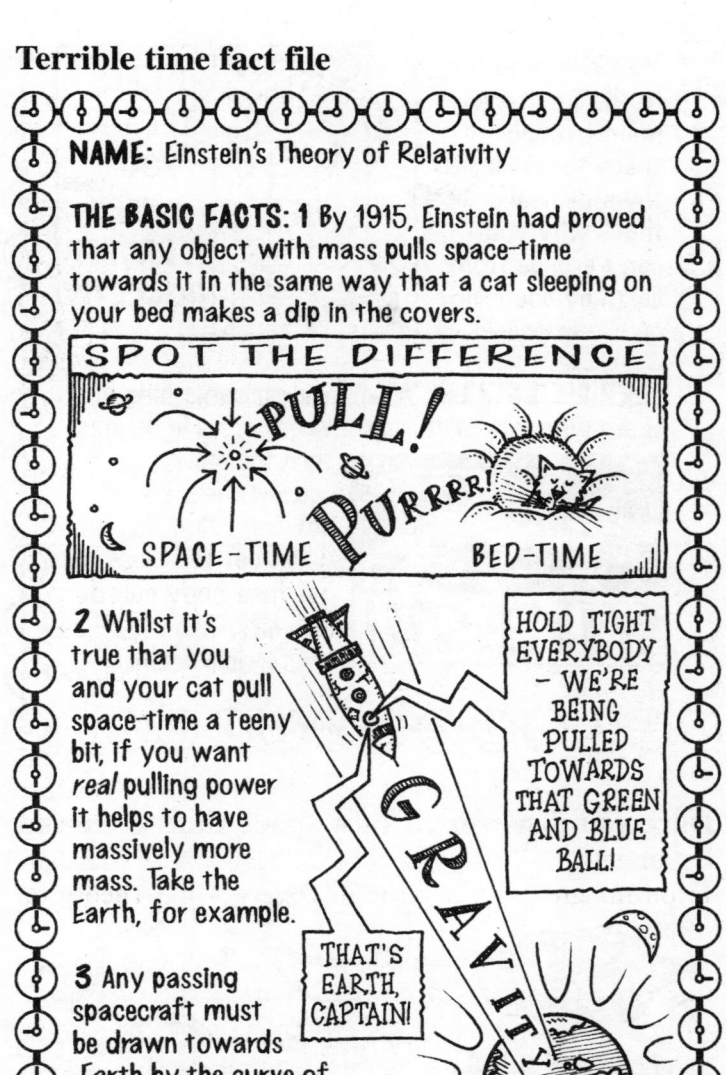

SPOT THE DIFFERENCE

PULL!

& PURRRR!

SPACE-TIME   BED-TIME

2 Whilst it's true that you and your cat pull space-time a teeny bit, if you want *real* pulling power it helps to have massively more mass. Take the Earth, for example.

HOLD TIGHT EVERYBODY – WE'RE BEING PULLED TOWARDS THAT GREEN AND BLUE BALL!

GRAVITY

THAT'S EARTH, CAPTAIN!

3 Any passing spacecraft must be drawn towards Earth by the curve of space-time. This is the effect we call "gravity".

115

The closer you get to the Earth the more strongly space-time is pulled towards it and that's why you can't escape from Earth by bouncing on a trampoline!

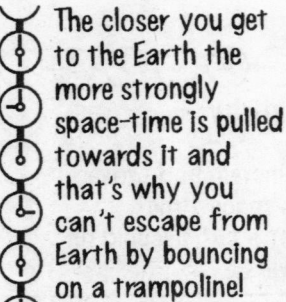

I KEEP TELLING YOU... I NEED A PROPER ROCKET!!!

TERRIBLE DETAILS: When you get something in space with lots of mass squished into a little area

YIKES!!!

then the pull on space-time is so powerful that anyone who goes too close will get their body pulled into bits. (Page 130 has the terrible details.)

Dare you discover ... how space-time is curved by mass?

You will need:

A PLASTIC NET BAG FOR VEGETABLES OR THE NET COVERING A SMALL BOX OF FRUIT

A BOWL WITH A RIM THAT CAN BE COVERED BY THE NET

SCISSORS

A LARGE ELASTIC BAND

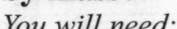 A TABLE-TENNIS BALL

A RUBBER BALL

116

What you do:

1 Cut the net open (younger readers may need help here).

2 Place the net over the top of the bowl (this is going to be space-time).

3 Secure it with the elastic band.

4 Place the rubber ball on the net. Remove it and place the table-tennis ball on the net.

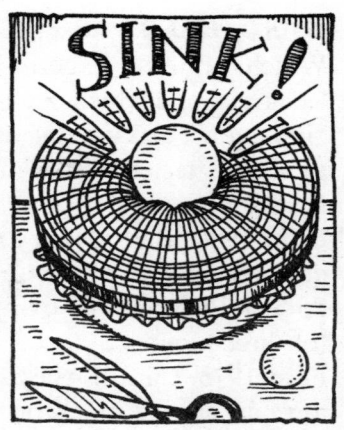

You should find:

The rubber ball has more mass and makes a steeper dip in your space-time. The table-tennis ball forms a larger, more gentle dip. Put both balls on the net and you can imagine they're two planets and create some terrible inter-planetary disasters as they're pulled together! It's all in the cause of science, naturally...

GO-SLOW GRAVITY

One result of this effect is that an object with lots of mass, like the Earth, actually makes time slow down the closer you get to it. That may sound odd but once again scientists have devised experiments that prove Einstein was right...

Which of these experiments actually proves General Relativity and which one is made up and so proves zilch, zippo, nowt and nothing at all?

a) Clocks tested on the moon run faster than clocks on Earth.

b) In 1999, Barry Antley of the University of Duodong delayed the start of the new year on his atomic clock by three milliseconds by living in a hut on top of a mountain for three months.

c) In 1975, Carroll Alley of the University of Maryland took an atomic clock on an exciting all-expenses-paid flight 9 km in the air. He found that at this height time runs a few billionths of an hour faster.

Answers: a) and **c)** prove the theory because they show that when gravity is weaker time passes more quickly. **b)** is made up. Gravity is slightly weaker on a mountain top so time actually goes a little faster. This means if you lived your life in the mountains your life would be a fraction of a second shorter than if you lived by the sea.

And here's why gravity makes time slow down. The pull of gravity actually robs light of some of its energy. You can test this idea by running up six flights of stairs. As you battle against gravity you might find yourself losing energy too! Now imagine you're looking down on a massive planet. As light struggles up from the surface, anything taking place down there would seem to be happening more slowly.

The more mass the object has, the slower time goes. In fact if you survived on the sun for a week you'd be a second younger than if you'd stayed at home. Mind you, your survival chances would be less than a choccy bar in a microwave oven.

But there are some things in the universe that have such powerful gravity that they actually STOP time in its tracks! I'm talking about black holes in space. Their pulverizing power was predicted by a sick scientist with a disgusting disease...

Hall of fame: Karl Schwarzchild (1873–1916)
Nationality: German

Karl was the eldest of five sons. He was a happy lad (oddly enough considering he had four horrible little brothers). His mum was cheerful and his dad was hard working and the whole family rubbed along just fine.

Unlike the rest of the family, who were keen on art and music, Karl became interested in science and saved up his pocket money to buy a telescope. His best friend was the son of one of his dad's pals, who happened to be an astronomer. Soon Karl became madly keen on astronomy and maths and by the age of 16, he was writing scientific articles.

After studying at the Universities of Strasbourg and Munich, Karl became a Professor and worked on measuring the brightness of stars from photographs. His hobbies were all fairly dangerous – he liked nothing better than ballooning, mountaineering and skiing, but he survived all that. He was one of Germany's top astronomers and everything would have been hunky-dory if it hadn't been for the war.

In 1914, Germany went to war with Russia, France and Britain and the ultra-patriotic Karl joined the army. The fact that he was too old to be a soldier didn't bother him. The army used his talents to work out how best to aim long-distance shells in order to kill the most people, but things really went wrong when Karl was moved to Russia. There, he picked up a sickening skin disease that caused huge blisters and made his skin rot.

To take his mind off his pustules Karl read about Einstein's Theory of Relativity and began to have ideas.

Here's a letter that he might have written to Einstein…

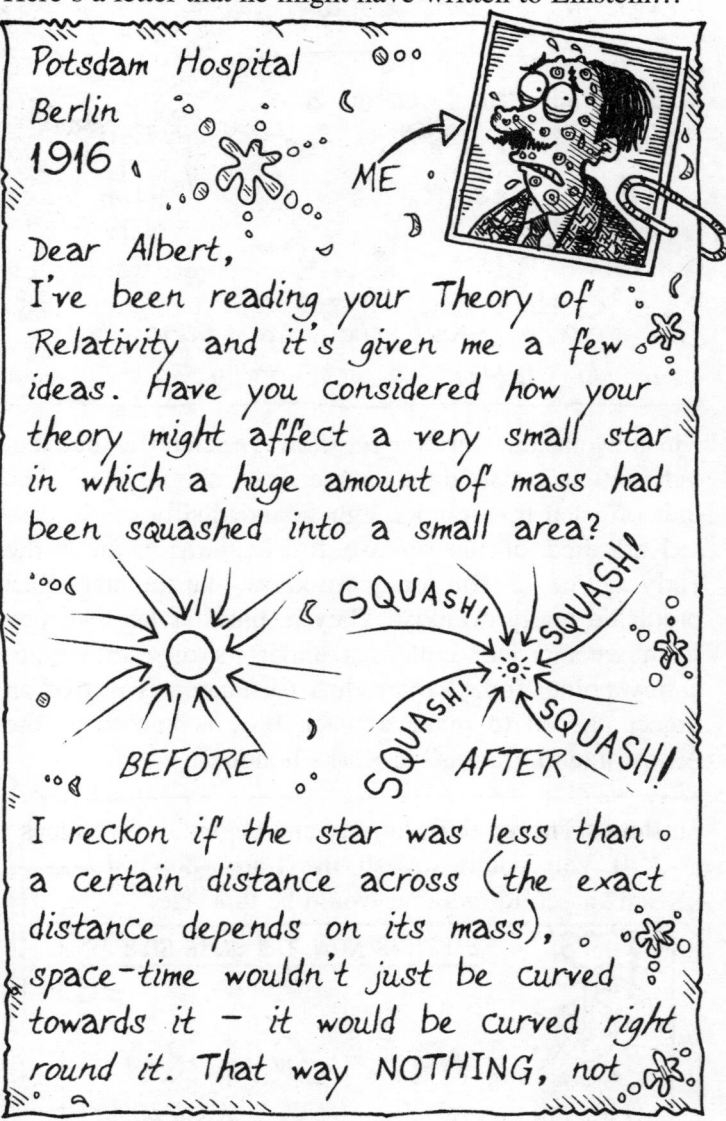

Potsdam Hospital
Berlin
1916

ME

Dear Albert,
I've been reading your Theory of
Relativity and it's given me a few
ideas. Have you considered how your
theory might affect a very small star
in which a huge amount of mass had
been squashed into a small area?

SQUASH!

SQUASH!

SQUASH!

SQUASH!

BEFORE

AFTER

I reckon if the star was less than
a certain distance across (the exact
distance depends on its mass),
space-time wouldn't just be curved
towards it — it would be curved right
round it. That way NOTHING, not

even light could escape from it!

Sorry I can't come and see you — I'm not too well at present.

Karl

PS Sorry about the scabs and pus on this letter...

Einstein read out Karl's suggestion to a scientific meeting, but most scientists didn't agree. Why should they? The idea of a star that trapped light sounded silly.

Karl died of his disease four months later at the early age of 42. But today we know that the stars Karl predicted really do exist. They're black holes and they form when a star collapses under its own gravity to a tiny point. Today, the radius (distance across) of an object needed to make a black hole is known as the "Schwarzchild radius" in Karl's honour.

Bet you never knew!
1 If you could squash the Earth down to its Schwarzchild radius it would be this size...

HELP!

EARTH IS NOW THE SAME SIZE AS

0.88 cm   A FLY   A NUT   A BIG BOGEY

At this point the Earth would turn into a black hole! The sun would become a black hole if you squished it into a space 2.9 km across. And if you fancy a jumbo-sized black-hole all you have to do is squeeze 500 sun-sized stars into our solar system.

2 Prepare yourself for a shock and try not to let this spoil your day. Scientists reckon there's a HUGE BLACK HOLE in the centre of our galaxy! The black hole is 11.25 billion km across! But before you look for a fast rocket out of here I'd better add that it's a big fat well-behaved black hole that's eaten every star near it and is now dozing peacefully like a big contented cat snoozing after supper. Anyway, we won't be going anywhere near it for billions of years.

But here's the interesting thing. If we could go near the black hole we could find the secret of travelling into the future. And with that scary suggestion it's time to tread carefully into the next chapter. By the way, it's all about time travel and I've got a terrible feeling that MI Gutzache and Tiddles might be heading for a black hole! Are they on a one-way trip?

TIME TRAVEL FOR BEGINNERS

Time travel is not a new idea…

London, 1895
My dear friends,
Everything I told you is true! I am
a time traveller and I really did visit
the far future. And that story I told
you about how we humans end up as
two races - a tribe of beautiful but
weak beings and a mob
of hairy flesh-eating
monsters - is true!
PLEASE BELIEVE ME -
I AM NOT MAD! Those monsters
wanted to EAT ME!
So you wanted to know how I
escaped? Well, I shut myself in the
monsters' temple and started up my
machine. But I panicked, didn't I? In
the dark, I set the wrong date on
my machine and went far into the
future to the time when the
sun has died and all life
on our planet has ended.
Once again I escaped with
my life - but only just!
And you, my dear friends, told me to
rest and recover but I wanted to

124

visit the past. So now I'm sitting in my little brass machine and setting the dials to whiz backwards in time. I know it's dangerous but I've just got to do it! And, my friends, if you read this letter it must mean that I never came back. Let this be my goodbye... So long!

The Time Traveller

And the time traveller was never seen again and perhaps he ended up as a dinosaur's dinner. But don't worry – it's only a story! Mind you, ever since writer HG Wells penned the tale in 1895, people have dreamt of travelling through time. In a moment, we'll find out if time machines really are possible but first you may be shocked to find out that there is a way to see the past happening in front of your eyes! And there's no risk of being a tyrannosaur's tea-time treat either. It's easy when you know how!

All you do is wrap up warm and go outside somewhere dark on a starry night (younger readers should take an adult with them and make sure the adult doesn't get lost or scared). And just gaze at the stars. Aren't they lovely? Who needs boring street lights when we have the stars for free?

Because the universe is so big, the light from many stars has taken hundreds or thousands of years to reach us. Even our next-door-neighbour star, Proxima Centauri, is about 40,000 billion km away. And that's so far that its light takes 4 years and 73 days to reach us. So when you look at the stars, you don't see them as they are now – you see them as they were in the past when the light left the star. Get the idea?

THE STARS ARE SO WONDERFUL!

AND OUT OF DATE

And yes, that means if you had a really big telescope (bigger than anything that's ever been invented) you might spot weird-looking aliens, wearing embarrassing alien fashions, sporting dreadful alien haircuts, dancing to awful alien disco music 30 years ago. And aliens with their really big telescopes might gaze in horror at your dad's disco dancing 30 years ago!

Yep, you've got it – you and the aliens would both be looking backwards in time!

WHAT ON EARTH DO THEY LOOK LIKE?

WHAT ON ZIGVORX DO THEY LOOK LIKE?

Since nothing can move faster than light we'll never get more up-to-date info about the stars, and any aliens living around them can't get up-to-date info on us. This means that any aliens who tune into our TV signals (they spread out into space at the speed of light) have to make do with boring old black-and-white films and early episodes of Star Trek. And if we ever picked up alien TV (assuming that aliens have TV) we'd be watching their awful old programmes.

But of course, looking at an out-of-date view of the stars (and the out-of-date stars on alien TV) isn't half as much fun as real "I was there" time travel. And didn't I mention that a black hole might come in handy here? And didn't I warn you that MI Gutzache and Tiddles would get uncomfortably close to one??

M.I. GUTZACHE IS LOST IN TIME

The story so far…

MI Gutzache and Tiddles have been abducted by an arrogant alien with two ultra-brainy tentacle brains. Gutzache has been taken unwell…

I felt better after I'd chucked my guts – but the little green guy didn't take it too well.

I had to clean out the craft with some kind of super-sucker alien sponge and just when I'd finished, that dumb useless feline started barfing too. Out of sympathy, I figured.

Well, I guess that made the alien kinda mean 'cos shortly after he tried to rub us out.

He was peering at his control panel and his tentacles started to twitch. I knew he was up to no good. He pulled his ray gun and stuck it under my nose.

"Our sensors show a black hole ahead," he said. "No humanoid has ever entered a black hole. YOU and your fellow earth creature will be the first to try this experiment. Get into the escape craft…"

Then the alien displayed some kind of simulation to show us what to expect. I watched it all and wished I hadn't…

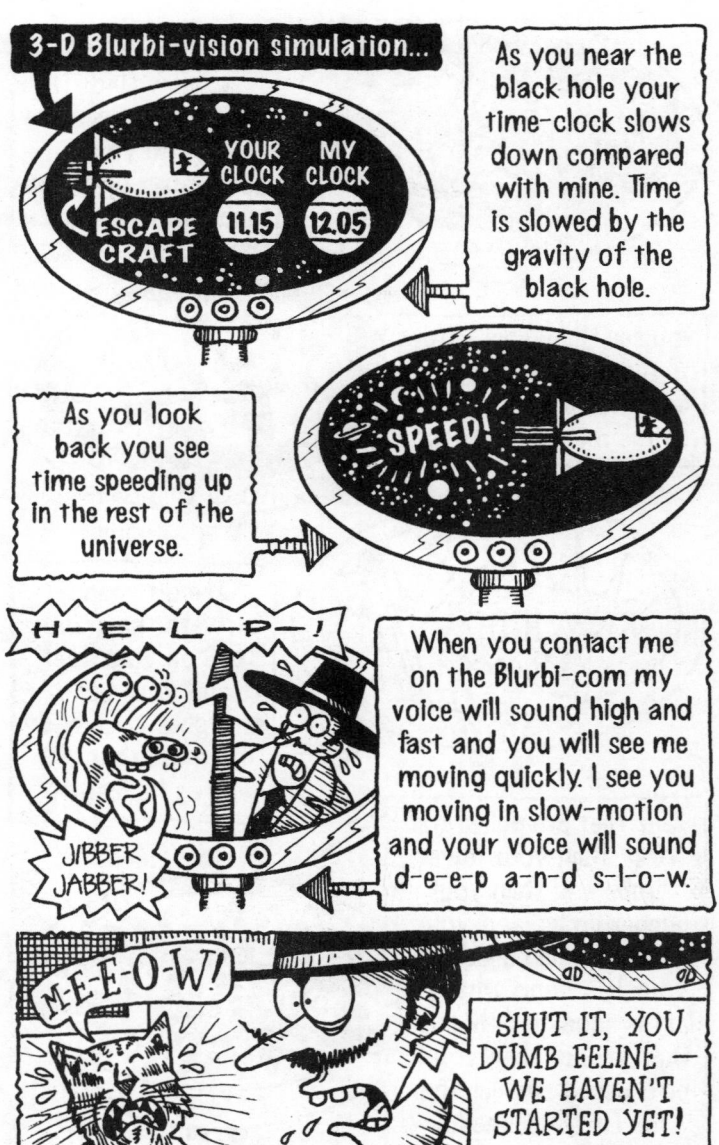

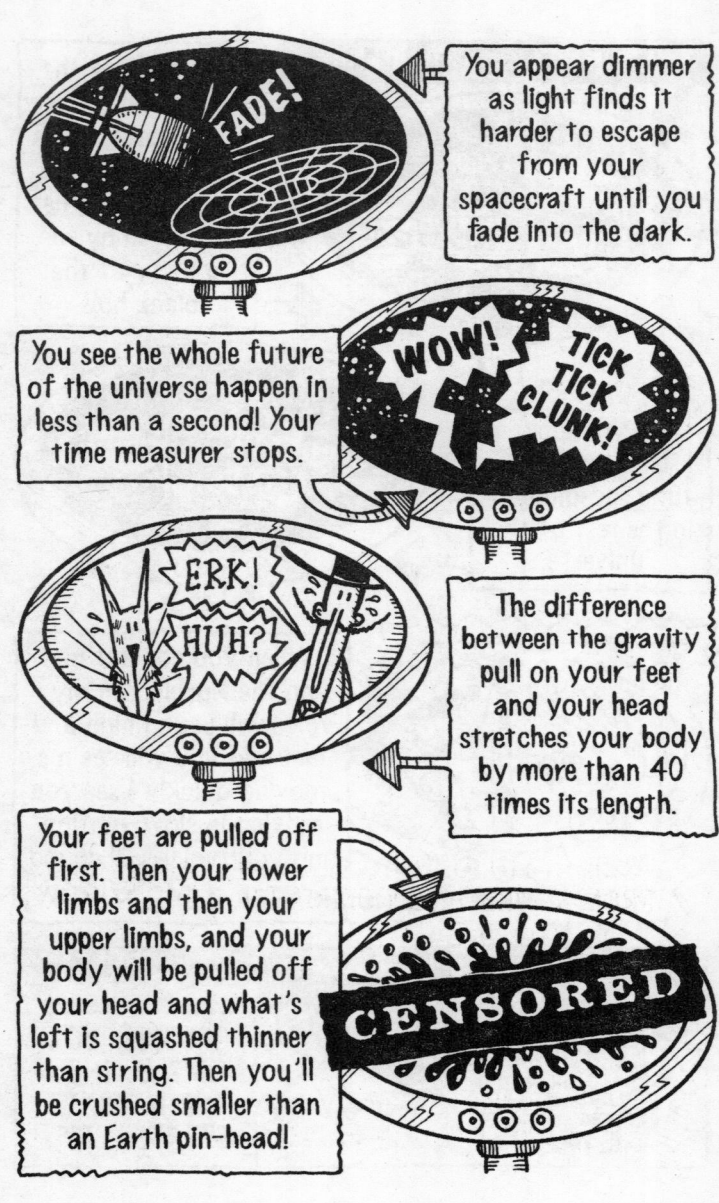

The alien sure wasn't kidding. I figured we were spaghetti – and pasta wasn't my thing. The black hole was no holiday trip. There was no way me or that mangy low-life feline were gonna try it. We both wanted out and that meant staying put.

I was just cooking up a sob story about my aged mom in New York when Dame Fortune dealt a helping hand.

The timing was good. Oddblob didn't like it – but these were orders and the heat was off.

"You'd better take us home, pal!" I told him.

The alien looked glum.

"Our fast space-flight slowed time. Earth is now ten Earth-days in front of us!" he said.

I was just trying to get my head round this when the little green guy brightened up. "I have decided to travel back in time by travelling faster than light," he announced.

Then he bustled about the controls making happy sounds. I guess he liked speeding. Well, we just had time to fasten our safety belts when my stomach shot forward and the stars and space blended into a whirl like froth on a coffee. I grabbed the cat and the cat grabbed me and Jeez her claws were sharper than mine!

I gritted my teeth in pain and looked for the traffic cops. I felt sick but I'd already shot my supper.

"Have you a licence for this thing?" I asked the little guy, but I guess he missed my drift.

And then I figured that if we were going back in time we could hit any year I fancied. Time to cut a deal.

"Hey, buddy!" I said. "Take me back a few years, I could solve the Mississippi mud-pie murder mystery! I could win the lottery!"

But the alien wasn't playing ball...

"FORGET IT, EARTHLING!" he replied.

Just then a comet crashed into a mighty big space rock – except we saw it backwards! The comet kinda leapt from the rock.

It put itself together and flew off as good as new! Even that dumb-schmuck cat looked surprised.

In less time than it takes to tell, Oddblob guided the flying saucer back to Earth, arriving at the Professor's house on the night we left. The Prof didn't spot the alien but he sure was mad at the busted time machine. I knew I was in the frame and I sure took the rap...

Uh-ho – Norbert's not too happy about the story and he's wagging his finger.

Oh dear, naughty, naughty! I must point out in the strongest possible terms that NOTHING can go faster than light and no one can go backwards in time!

WAG!

Oh, er, sorry, Norbert! He's got a point, readers. Remember when Oddblob's spacecraft went fast the first time (it's on page 102)? The craft's mass increased. Einstein's calculations for the Special Theory of Relativity show that mass and energy change into each other at high energies. As the huge energy of going fast turns into mass it becomes harder to go faster. If you really could go as fast as light you'd have more mass than the entire universe!

This would mean two things…

1 You have a serious weight problem and would need to go on a cosmic crash diet.
2 You actually need endless energy to go this fast and there isn't that much energy in the whole universe.

So, many scientists think you can't travel faster than light.

I hope you've been making notes on all this…

But – and OK I'll come clean, it's a BIG "but" – some scientists reckon that there may be ways of sneaking around the cosmic light-speed limit. And just imagine if you could! As you know, the faster you go, the slower time passes compared to Earth. So if you could go faster than light, it's possible that your clock would actually run backwards compared to Earth time! And that actually means you'd be returning in the past – just like in the story!

This idea is explained in a traditional limerick recited by frisky freaky physicists at scientific parties:

There was a young lady named Bright
Whose speed was far faster than light
She set out one day in a relative way
And returned the previous night!

BUT IS IT REALLY, HONESTLY POSSIBLE TO TRAVEL THROUGH TIME?

Well, it's best to take the question in two parts. If you're talking about travelling forward in time, as you've found out, the answer is "yes". We're moving forward into the future anyway and to do some serious forward time travel all we need to do is to solve the problem of going really fast through space. And we can always slow time by going near (but not too near!) our local friendly snoozing black hole.

As for travelling backwards in time, scientists are divided (most would say "NO"). The scientists who would say "YES" or "MAYBE" have their own rather complicated favourite ideas. We'll be back after the commercial break…

FANCY A NICE COOL STROLL?

IT'S COOL, MAN!

VISIT OUR FREEZING LIGHT VORTEX! Light slows down as it spirals around inside a giant cylinder at a temperature just above ABSOLUTE ZERO (that's as cold as anything ever gets). Time turns into space and space turns into time and you can walk back through time!

BUT WE DID THIS YESTERDAY, MUM...

TODAY **IS** YESTERDAY, SON, AND TOMORROW CAN BE TODAY... IF WE COME BACK AGAIN IN 24 HOURS!!!

WARNING! It's cold in this time machine so don't forget your thermal undies and a hot water bottle!

THE SMALL PRINT: 1 Neither of our time machines will take you back to before the time machines were made – so dinosaur safaris are out! **2** The machines are based on genuine time-travel ideas but even if the machines were ever built, they might not work (money not refundable). **3** If they do work they might be dangerous but, hey – it's an adventure!

What's that? You didn't understand some of the words in these adverts? Well, you'd best read this…

TERRIBLE EXPRESSIONS

A scientist says:

I'VE FOUND A WORMHOLE.

Do you say…?

SO WHAT, MY GARDEN'S FULL OF THEM!

Answer: Only if you want to dig it! A wormhole is a kind of short-cut in time and space where a spinning black hole forms a kind of tunnel. And no, it's not the home of a giant flesh-eating space worm – it's FAR MORE DANGEROUS! Like a black hole, it could pull you to bits and gobble up the odd planet, so you've got to treat it with a bit of respect.

HOW TO BUILD YOUR OWN TIME MACHINE

1 First, make a wormhole by creating a black hole and whizzing it around.

2 Take one end of the wormhole for a fast space-flight. You can pull it along by tempting it with a nice juicy planet – Jupiter will do.

3 Thanks to time dilation, when you return to Earth 50 years will have passed, but you can get back to the year when you set off by jumping into the wormhole and leaping out the other end!

It may sound loopy but you've made a loop in time. Don't be scared – it's safe! If you don't touch the sides of the tunnel you won't suffer the black-hole effect!

HI, MUM... GUESS WHAT? I'M GOING TO HAVE FOUR CHILDREN ... THREE GIRLS AND A BOY!

THE BAD NEWS

It's NOT that easy, as Norbert is desperate to point out. OK, Norbert you can put your hand down now.

Tut, tut — this is nonsense! You see, there's not enough energy on Earth to make a wormhole! Anyway how would you stop one closing up? Oh dear, I'm getting quite hot under the collar about this!

Scientists are discussing these problems at this very minute and a few horribly complicated ideas for holding open the wormhole have been suggested. Trouble is, they use types of energy that may not even exist – so don't pack for that last-minute bargain time-travel holiday just yet!

Mind you, one day it might be as easy to time travel as hopping on a bus. In fact, it might be easier because there may not be any buses by then! But would we want to travel backwards in time? If you did manage to go back to before you were born, things do get rather impossible…

IMPOSSIBLE THINGS THAT COULD HAPPEN TO TIME TRAVELLERS

1 A half-crazed time traveller might kill their granny…

PROBLEM: But if she killed her granny, then the time traveller couldn't have been born! By the way, why is it that time science books always feature the granny-killing case? Have some scientists got something against grannies?

2 The time traveller might meet her younger self…

PROBLEM: So who is the real person?

3 And she might tell herself how to make the time machine.

PROBLEM: So where did the idea come from?

Some scientists think there might be ways round these problems. Others think there aren't – but then scientists don't always agree on things. So, what do you think? And if you're not sure, why not have a think about it?

Finished thinking? OK, let's move swiftly on and imagine you could travel forwards in time – that's FORWARDS not backwards. How far could you go? Does time go on for ever? Or will time screech to a grinding halt at some future date? Try not to let it keep you awake at night...

As I said on page 8, scientists reckon that time began with the start of the universe – before then there was no space-time and so no time. So that means we're actually looking at how the universe might end.

So what do you think? Will the universe go on growing for ever or will it suddenly reach a maximum point and start shrinking and coming together in a massively messy squished-up crunch?ws: it's exciting! Bad news: but very messy!

By the end of the 1990's scientists had figured out the shocking secret. The light from very ancient and distant star blasts proved to be dimmer than they expected and that could only mean that not onlyl was the universe getting bigger (but of course) – it was growing faster than ever!

Scientists reckon that mysterious dark energy produced by empty space is super-sizing the cosmos – but whatever the cause, the universe is going to get even bigger and even emptier.

The universe won't stop growing not even when all the stars have burnt out and the black holes have leaked into nothingness. And time will go on and on – even though eternity does look rather boring. But maybe that's a good thing – scientists will need plenty of time to argue about time...

I think we'd better leave them to it.

EPILOGUE: THE END OF TIME

Everyone who has ever lived or will ever live is affected by time. And some people find the whole idea of time so amazing that they spend years trying to understand or measure it, or just get their heads round it. Think of John Harrison, or Sandford Fleming, or Luigi Lilio…

This book is called Terrible Time and right at the start I promised to tell you the ultimate terrible truth about time. Have you been wondering?

Well, here it is: As soon as we wake up we look at the clock and because time is part of every day life we think we know what it is. We track time with clocks and measure it with incredibly accurate atomic clocks... We come up with theories about time and even dream of travelling through time. But ultimately we don't understand time at all! We're not sure where it came from or where it's going. We can't say how it operates or why it only goes in one direction.

THE TERRIBLE TRUTH IS THAT TIME IS STILL A MYSTERY!

For anyone trying to make sense of time, that really is terrible! And that's why for scientists time remains the ultimate challenge. When Albert Einstein was a very old man he wrote:

We are in the position of a little child entering a huge library whose walls are covered to the ceiling with books in many tongues... The child does not understand the languages... He notes a definite plan in the arrangement of the books, a mysterious order which he... only dimly suspects.

Some people get this feeling every time they open a science book (but hopefully not this one!). In case you're wondering, Albert was talking about the ultimate mysteries of the universe. Including, of course, time.

But one thing's for sure. Slowly, scientists are unravelling time's riddle. And the answer is out there. Somewhere in the universe, somewhere in the cold and dark amongst the glittering stars is the key to the mystery. And one day we'll find it … OH YES, IT'S ONLY A MATTER OF TIME!

ONLY A MATTER OF TIME? WELL, YES, THAT'S ONE THEORY. BUT I SUGGEST THAT ESSENTIALLY THE PRIMARY EXPLANATION IS PROVIDED BY THE INFINITE MASS OF...

SHUT UP!

THE TERRIBLE TRUTH ABOUT TIME

QUIZ

Now find out if you're a
**The Terrible Truth
About Time** expert!

Now you've been on trip through time, how much have you taken in? Could you be an intrepid time traveller, or are you as baffled as a walrus without a wristwatch? Take these quick quizzes and find out the terrible truth...

The truth about time

Time can be tricky, and crazy scientists have come up with some incredible ideas about it throughout history. Take a tick and try to tell whether the following statements are the terrible truth or just a load of science fiction.

1 The concept of hours, minutes and seconds were invented around 4,000 years ago.
2 In the Southern Hemisphere, the summer solstice occurs in December.
3 It takes the Earth 365 days to move round the Sun.
4 The rate at which time passes depends on how fast you're moving.
5 Everything in the awesome universe is three-dimensional – made up of two dimensions of space and one of time.
6 The space-time continuum is a concept invented by sci-fi freaks in the late twentieth century.

7 It might be possible to travel in time using strange strings that stretch across the universe.

8 There's a place on Earth where you can jump back and forth between days in a matter of seconds.

Answers:

1 TRUE. The Babylonians invented these brilliant breakdowns of time, but as clocks weren't invented until much later, there was no way of keeping track of them, so they were a pretty useless concept.

2 TRUE. Summer and winter are reversed in the Southern Hemisphere, so while you're wrapped in your winter woollies, people who live in the southern half of the Earth are sunning themselves on the beach in December.

3 FALSE. It actually takes 365.25 days – that's why there was such a muddle by the Middle Ages, and people were celebrating Easter on the wrong day.

4 TRUE. But you won't notice it at the piddling speeds you travel on Earth – even in a plane, only if you had a rocket ship that could travel close to the scary speed of light.

5 FALSE. Freaky physicists reckon there are FOUR dimensions – three of space and one of time.

6 FALSE. The space-time continuum might sound like the stuff of sci-fi movies, but it is a real thing. Scientists use it to refer to the way space and time are connected.

7 TRUE. Well, it's an idea, anyway. Some scientists think there are things called cosmic strings in space. Objects attached to them could travel at incredible speeds and allow them to pop into a different time.

8 TRUE. You could hop from Sunday to Monday and back again if you were hanging around the International Date Line. Actually, you'd have to swim because it's in the middle of the ocean.

Useful units of time

Over the centuries (each one a horrible 100 years), people have found all sorts of different ways of dividing time into blocks – probably to make sure they didn't spend any longer than they had to in their Horrible Science lessons. Can you match the mysterious measurements below with the lengths of terrible time they refer to?

1 Minute
2 Attosecond
3 Halek
4 Millennium
5 Centisecond
6 Fortnight
7 Jiffy
8 Friedman

a) 1,000 years
b) Six months in the future
c) 60 seconds
d) 14 days
e) 1/250th of a second
f) The time it takes for light to travel the length of three hydrogen atoms

g) 1/18th of a minute
h) 1/100th of a second

Answers:
1c; 2f; 3g; 4a; 5h; 6d; 7e; 8b

Scary space-time

For many years, people have looked to the sky for the answers about time, and asked impossible questions such as how old is the universe? How long does it take for light from the stars to reach Earth? Do aliens spend as much time in the bathroom as your older sister? So, stare into space and see if you can answer the questions below.

1 What do strange scientists call the weird places in space where time has stopped? (CLUE: The deepest, darkest places in the universe)
2 What bizarre bodies in space let us take a sneak peak into the past? (CLUE: Brilliantly bright balls)
3 Through what strange space in space might you be able to slip into the past? (CLUE: Made by giant invertebrates?)
4 What theory thought up by Albert Einstein explains how space-time works? (CLUE: It's nothing to do with your auntie and uncle)

5 What do freaky physicists call the beginning of time? (CLUE: It's an explosive theory)

6 What is the one thing in the universe that nothing could overtake in a race? (CLUE: Come on, you're a bright spark...)

7 Which cosmic object do we use to measure months on Earth? (CLUE: A question to howl at?)

8 If a crazy scientist started wittering on about 'acceleration caused by the curvature in the space-time continuum', what would he be referring to? (CLUE: An attractive force)

Answers:
1 Black holes
2 The stars
3 A wormhole
4 Relativity
5 The Big Bang
6 Light
7 The moon
8 Gravity

Curious clocks and calendars

Since humans first stepped out of their caves, they've been trying to figure out ways of measuring time – it's been a confusing old business and no mistake. Have you managed to keep track of time? Take this quick quiz and find out...

HAPPY EASTER, YOUR HOLINESS!

BUT IT'S CHRISTMAS, YOUR MAJESTY!

1 What do we earthlings call the shortest day of the year?
a) The winter solstice
b) The winter equinox
c) The winter wibble

2 Where will you find the International Date Line?
a) In Greenwich, London
b) In the Lonely Hearts section of your local newspaper
c) In the Pacific Ocean

3 What do we call every fourth year, in which February has 29 days – a trick introduced by genius Julius Caesar?
a) Leap Year
b) Long Year
c) Lucky Year

4 Which part of your brain controls your amazing body clock?

a) The hippocampus
b) The hippoptamus
c) The hypothalamus

5 Which clever clocks are the most awesomely accurate on Earth?
a) Quartz clocks
b) Atomic clocks
c) Sundials

6 What are the strange sections of the Earth called in which the time is the same no matter where in the section you are?
a) Time sectors
b) Time zones
c) Timepieces

7 Which ingenious invention in the seventeenth century allowed clocks to keep time much more accurately than ever before?
a) The escapement
b) The second hand
c) The caesium atom

8 Which cool calendar, introduced in the sixteenth century, is still widely accepted today?
a) The Greenwich Calendar
b) The Perpetual Calendar
c) The Gregorian Calendar

Answers:
1a; 2c; 3a; 4c; 5b; 6b; 7a; 8c

Meet the time travellers

Well, not time travellers, exactly, but all the strange scientists below took terrible trouble to investigate time. Can you match each one with their disturbing discoveries and awesome inventions?

DON'T I KNOW YOU FROM SOMEWHERE?

1 This German genius did some monumental maths and figured out what the teeniest, tiniest measure of time could be.

2 This crazy clockmaker spent his whole life trying to solve the problem of telling the time at sea.

3 Missing a train made this man mad enough to invent the 24-hour clock.

4 This confused character came up with the idea that things get more muddled as time passes.

5 This awesome astronomer predicted the existence of big bad black holes in the universe.

6 A forlorn and forgotten figure, this Italian astronomer actually invented the modern calendar.

7 This terribly time-obsessed physicist proved that time and space and gravity were all connected through his really radical relativity theories.

8 This peculiar priest coined the expression anno Domini (AD) to number the years since Jesus was born.

a) Sandford Fleming
b) Karl Schwarzschild
c) Dionysius Exguus
d) Max Planck
e) Albert Einstein
f) Ludwig Boltzmann
g) John Harrison
h) Luigi Lilio

Answers:
1d; 2g; 3a; 4f; 5b; 6h; 7e; 8c

HORRIBLE INDEX

157

SPACE, STARS AND SLIMY ALIENS

NICK ARNOLD

illustrated by
TONY DE SAULLES

■SCHOLASTIC

www.horrible-science.co.uk

www.nickarnold-website.com
www.tonydesaulles.co.uk

Scholastic Children's Books,
Euston House, 24 Eversholt Street,
London, NW1 1DB, UK

A division of Scholastic Ltd
London ~ New York ~ Toronto ~ Sydney ~ Auckland
Mexico City ~ New Delhi ~ Hong Kong

First published in the UK by Scholastic Ltd, 2003
This edition published 2008

Text copyright © Nick Arnold, 2003
Illustrations © Tony De Saulles, 2003, 2008

ISBN 978 1407 10614 4

Printed and bound by CPI Group (UK) Ltd, Croydon, CR0 4YY

26

The right of Nick Arnold and Tony De Saulles to be identified as the author and
illustrator of this work respectively has been asserted by them in accordance with
the Copyright, Designs and Patents Act, 1988.

CONTENTS

WHO'S LEFT THIS REVOLTING, SMELLY SLIME TRAIL? READ ON TO FIND OUT...

Nick Arnold has been writing stories and books since he was a youngster, but never dreamt he'd find fame writing about outer space. His research involved staring at stars, being turned down for astronaut training and trying to burp in space – and he enjoyed every minute of it.

When he's not delving into Horrible Science, he spends his spare time eating pizza, riding his bike and thinking up corny jokes (though not all at the same time).

Tony De Saulles picked up his crayons when he was still in nappies and has been doodling ever since. He takes Horrible Science very seriously and even agreed to jump into a black hole. Fortunately, he has made a full recovery.

When he's not out with his sketchpad, Tony likes to write poetry and play squash, though he hasn't written any poetry about squash yet.

INTRODUCTION

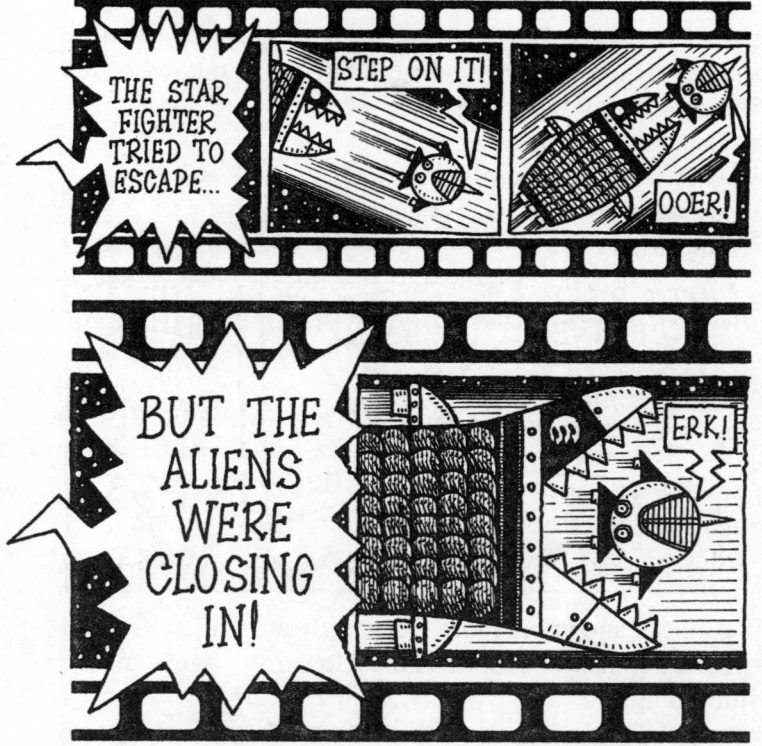

Space movies are great, aren't they? Don't you just love the speeding spacecraft, perishing planets and slimy slobbering aliens. And isn't it a pity when some tedious teacher says, "Oh, but it's all made-up"? But what they don't tell you is that real-life outer space is even more scary than the scariest space movie!

In a moment, we'll blast into space to boldly go where no science book has gone before. Our mission is to find out why space is so scary. And why just going for a walk in space without your spacesuit can make your guts explode and your eyeballs plop out of your head.

Then, if we survive outer space, we'll be peering at putrid planets and sizzling stars and mad moons. Horrible places, the lot of them. And we'll be finding out fearsome, foul and funny facts such as…

• How the Sun *sings*.
• Why you can't burp in space.
• Which stars turn you into slime.
• And why your body bits are made of blown-up stars.

Yes, these and many more facts really are true … er, hold on … our space expert, Luke Upwards, wants to say something…

Oh all right! Scientists aren't sure if aliens exist. And if you must know, I made up the alien story in this book.

Mind you – we will be looking at our chances of meeting real-life aliens.

But the rest is really real – even if it sounds like it's off on another planet. And hopefully you'll feel that space is an out-of-this-world subject and you'll be encouraged to find out more. And who knows? Maybe one day you'll become an astronaut and live your own true-life space adventures.

So who needs movies? Just grab your popcorn and settle down in your seat. The show is about to begin!

SPLATTERING SPACE

Earth is a small blue ball floating in a big black sea. And the big black sea is as dark and dangerous as a bad-tempered black bear in a coal cellar! Later on we'll find out how deadly dangerous space really is – but first it's time to check out the basic background bits.

So what's floating about up there?

Space, stars and slimy aliens fact file

NAME: Stuff in space

THE BASIC FACTS: Here are the main things that you might see in space...

COOL!

Stars – balls of super-hot gas like the Sun that blast heat and light (see page 21 for the sizzling details). Nearly all stars are hugely bigger than planets but in 2005 scientists found a pathetically weedy star not much bigger than Jupiter. Galaxies – swirling whirls of billions of stars.

ASTRONOMICAL!

WHAT ON EARTH IS THAT?

Planets and dwarf planets – big spinning balls of rock and gas that orbit (whizz round a star). One orbit is a year and one spin is a day. Dwarf planets such as Ceres, Pluto and Eris are smaller than planets.

Solar System —
the Sun and planets,
etc, that orbit it.

Moons — rocky
objects that orbit
planets and
dwarf planets.

BY JUPITER!

Asteroids — large space rocks that orbit the Sun.
Most of them hang out in an area called the
Asteroid Belt. (The details are on page 91.)

ROCK ON!

COMET

Comets — balls of ice and rock that orbit the Sun
on the edge of the Solar System. Some comets fly
close to the Sun. (For more details, why not steer
your spacecraft to page 128.)

SLIMY SECRETS: Some stars aren't lucky stars if
you go too near them. These twinkling terrors
could cook you to a puddle of slime. (If you're
interested and feeling really brave you can turn to
pages 26–29 for the dangerous details.)

THIS "STAR
TREATMENT" ISN'T
ALL IT'S CRACKED
UP TO BE...

But there's more to space than planets and galaxies – a whole universe in fact. Fortunately there's a way to squeeze the whole universe into three minutes…

WELCOME TO THE THREE-MINUTE UNIVERSE TOUR…

Get ready to switch on your imagination because you're going to do more imagining than you've ever imagined before. We're going on a three-minute tour of time and space. Don't forget to put on your spacesuit and set your watch to Planet Splott time…

ERK!

WARNING! YOU'D BEST PUT ON A CRASH HELMET BEFORE READING THIS NEXT BIT!

FIRST STOP: THE BIG BANG

It's 13.7 billion years ago and the universe has popped out of nothing. It started as a tiny point of heat and energy but in less than one second it's bigger than a galaxy. In the first 20 minutes many of the atoms that make up you formed in the brain-boggling heat. Maybe it's a bit too hot – let's get out of here!

SECOND STOP: QUAKING QUASARS

It's ten billion years ago and the universe is much bigger – it never stopped growing. The first galaxies have formed and early stars are more violent than a bear in a honey shop. Black holes have formed in the centre of the new galaxies and they rip matter apart as it whirls towards destruction. Some horribly hungry holes can gobble 1,000 stars in a year and blast energy two trillion times brighter than the Sun. Astronomers call these blasts quasars. Hmm – maybe this isn't a good spot for a picnic.

THIRD STOP: THE MILKY WAY

We're floating in space billions of kilometres from our own galaxy – the Milky Way. Isn't it lovely? Aha – that's Earth down there.

If you're on Earth and a long way from streetlights, the Milky Way looks like milky drool dribbled across the night sky by a giant baby… Except it's not milk. It's stars. About 200,000 billion stars, in fact. And they're bunched together because you're seeing them from the side (look at a dish and you'll get the idea).

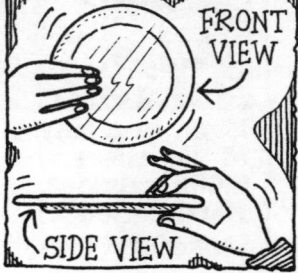

11

The Milky Way is just one of over 40 galaxies called "the local group". And the local group is one of 400 galaxy groups known as the Local Supercluster (but that's not as local as your local supermarket). You might like to know that we're in an interesting-sounding gas cloud called the "local fluff" which is part of an area known as the "local bubble".

FOURTH STOP: EARTH

In 1990 scientists launched the Hubble telescope to see the stars from space and they tried peering at a speck of sky the size of a stick-insect's eyeball on the end of your out-stretched fingertip... You might think they found one measly star. But they found more ... much, much more.

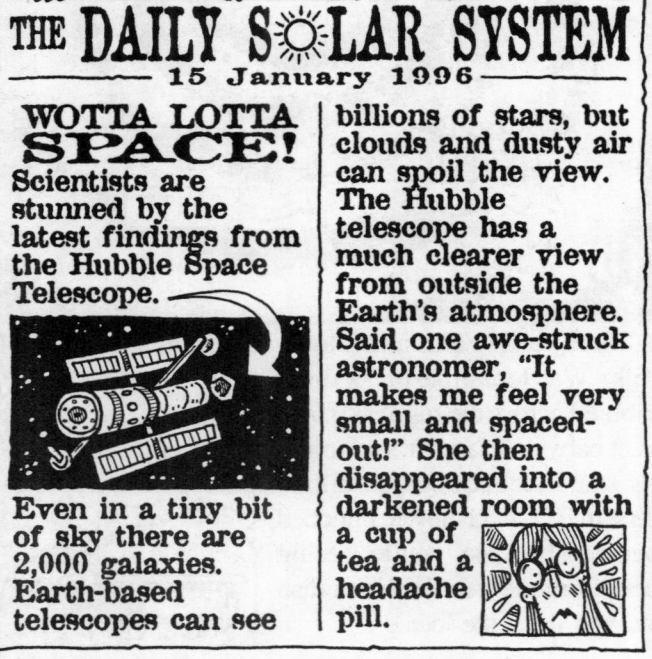

THE **DAILY S☼LAR SYSTEM**
— 15 January 1996 —

WOTTA LOTTA SPACE!

Scientists are stunned by the latest findings from the Hubble Space Telescope.

Even in a tiny bit of sky there are 2,000 galaxies. Earth-based telescopes can see billions of stars, but clouds and dusty air can spoil the view. The Hubble telescope has a much clearer view from outside the Earth's atmosphere. Said one awe-struck astronomer, "It makes me feel very small and spaced-out!" She then disappeared into a darkened room with a cup of tea and a headache pill.

Two thousand galaxies could mean 200,000 BILLION stars and those were just the galaxies Hubble could make out... But the amazing truth is that scientists reckon that space is nearly all empty, er, space. If the universe was 30 km wide and 30 km high, all the stars and galaxies and planets and slime ice-cream from Planet Splott would scrunch into an itsy-bitsy grain of sand.

FIFTH STOP: THE UNIVERSE IN ONE MILLION BILLION YEARS TIME

It's dark. It's cold even by space standards because most of the stars have spluttered out. Even the longest-lived stars eventually burn out or get sucked into black holes. There is scarcely any energy around for living things to consume. The trouble is that energy is always being lost as heat and now the universe is too big and matter is too scattered for gravity to pull together new stars. Eventually even the black holes will disappear. It's all very sad and dreary – scientists have even got a nice cheerful name for how the universe will end – heat death. Maybe it's time to go home for a nice hot drink.

THE MIND-BLOWING MYSTERIOUS UNIVERSE

Having toured the universe in three minutes you might think that astronomers know it all – but they don't. Here are some maddening mysteries to mull over...

Where has 96 per cent of the universe got to?

According to scientists the stars and planets, etc. we can see should only amount to 4 per cent of the universe. The other 96 per cent seems to be hiding. The experts that 22 per cent of the universe could be objects such as black holes that we can't see or detect but where's the rest got to? Some boffins reckon there could be undiscovered particles out there – all very mysterious.

Why is the universe growing so fast?
In the 1990s scientists were shocked to find that the universe wasn't behaving itself. It was growing too fast to fit their theories. According to the experts this is due to a mysterious power called dark energy that pushes things apart. It would be handy if they were right since dark energy could be the missing 74 per cent matter of the universe … and yes, you did read that right because you can actually make matter from energy.

Why aren't we over-run with aliens?
There could be one billion planets in the Milky Way like Earth. So why aren't slimy aliens crawling out of our plugholes? Well, they might be too distant to contact us. I mean, the universe is many trillions of kilometres across and we can't send them our address and expect a postcard…

Earth
The Solar System
Orion arm
(that's one of the swirling sticking out bits)
The Milky Way
The Local Group
The Local Supercluster
The Universe
OOPS Sorry I've forgotten the postcode.

Dear Earthlings
Found you at last! Must pop round for tea sometime!
Love the Aliens XXX

A radio or light signal would be quicker. They whizz along at 300,000 km per second or 9.46 million million km per year – I guess they're so fast because they're travelling light. Scientists call this distance a "light year". But the Milky Way is 100,000 light years across and a chat with aliens could take 10,000 years. And I bet your phone bills would be ASTRONOMICAL.

Mind you, that hasn't put off some scientists. A series of SETI projects (SETI = Search for Extra-Terrestrial Intelligence) searched for alien radio signals but so far without result. Maybe aliens aren't smart enough to build radios? Or maybe they don't want to know us?

What's that? You want to go looking for aliens … and dark matter and dark energy and you can't wait to leap into your spacesuit and go and see space?

Not so fast! You don't think you'd be allowed to whizz off in a multi-billion dollar spacecraft just like that, do you? You need *years* of training before you're allowed near one of those things. But while you're waiting for your training to start, you can always read our super sci-fi space story. And guess what? The first

episode shows what space is *really* like…

Oddblob's Alien Adventure

GREETINGS. MY NAME'S ODDBLOB FROM THE PLANET BLURB... I USED TO BE A SPACE EXPLORER, BUT NOW I'M IN THE INTERGALACTIC ADVENTURE HOLIDAY BUSINESS. HERE'S MY BROCHURE...

> Get away from it all with

ODDBLOB'S ADVENTURE TOURS

Relax in our luxury chauffeur-driven spacecraft on a guided tour of the SOLAR SYSTEM!

🌀 Brilliant brainy guide (with two brains) – that's me – Oddblob.

🌀 Action, adventure and fun for all the family!

🌀 All types of alien welcome, just so long as you pay and don't eat each other!

🌀 NINE planets, one Sun and lots of moons to explore!

🌀 Stunning, super space walks (spacesuits provided).

"These tours are the best holidays in the galaxy!" Oddblob the Blurb (no relation)

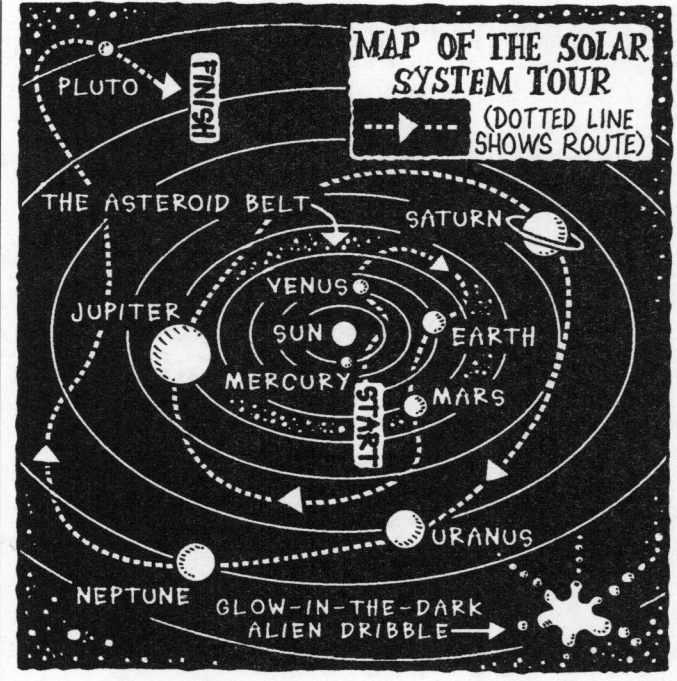

The small print

1 Oddblob will warn you about the dangers of each planet you visit. So you mustn't blame him if you get killed.

2 If you leave the spacecraft, you must remember to put on a spacesuit. If you forget you'll spend your final seconds wishing you had a better memory.

IMPORTANT SCIENCE NOTE

Hmm – sounds like Oddblob's spacecraft is faster than anything known on Earth. Our human spacecraft would take years to travel between the planets. For example, the unmanned Voyager 2 craft was launched in 1977 and didn't get to Neptune until 1989 – that's 12 years later!

My story begins when I took a booking from a family of aliens. They wanted to tour the Solar System, but they were a bit messy... They even left alien dribble on my brochure.

Here's the alien family. Slobslime is a Snotty from the Planet Splott. And she's not the smartest alien in the universe.

And here's her baby, Sloppy. She lives in an egg-pod, but in 100 years time she'll hatch into an adult Snotty like Slobslime.

On the first day of the aliens' holiday I tried to get them used to living in space.

Things went wrong from the start. Our first outing was a walk in space, but Slobslime had forgotten some vital equipment...

Seconds later, Slobslime suffered the effects of being in space without a spacesuit.

Space can be colder than −100°C. That's cold enough to freeze skin solid. Sunlight can be hotter than 120°C, hot enough to burn the skin to a crisp. Slobslime was frozen like a slime-lolly on one side and roasted to a slime-crisp on the other.

With no air to press on Slobslime's body from the outside, the air in her body pushed outwards. Soon her guts, lungs and eyeballs were about to go pop. Without air pressure all her blood and body juices began to boil like slimy green soup.

Deadly rays, known as radiation (ray-de-ay-shun), from the Sun blasted Slobslime. Soon she'd be cooked from the inside like a blurbi-turkey in a microwave With seconds to spare I pulled Slobslime to safety and, after a few hours of body repairs in my spacecraft's sick bay, she was back to her old slimy self.

ANOTHER IMPORTANT SCIENCE NOTE

It looks like Snotties have incredible powers of healing and recovery. Any human who did this would certainly be killed!

So you see, there are a loads of dangers in space – but at least the stars look great. As the Hubble Space Telescope showed, you get a lovely clear view. But you don't have to go into space to see stars… Instead, you could bang your head (though that's not a good idea!).

Or you could point your telescope at the next chapter.

STAGGERING STARS

It's easy to stare at the stars but it's not so easy to explain them. You might even come up with some curious questions…

HOW ARE STARS MADE?

HOW DO STARS WORK?

ARE THEY ALL THE SAME?

OK, OK – here are some answers. Let's start at the beginning (it's better than starting at the end). How are stars made? To find out, I've arranged an exclusive interview with our local friendly star – the Sun…

21

THE SUN'S SECRET STORY

by our reporter Randall Scandal

He's definitely the biggest star in our Solar System – a legend in his own lifetime. When I met the Sun, he was in a sunny mood in his exclusive home in the centre of the Solar System. For a big 4.6-billion-year-old ball of hydrogen gas, he didn't look at all bad.

Randall: How did you become such a big star?

Sun: I remember it like it was yesterday. Though it wasn't yesterday – it was 4.6 billion years ago.

Randall: So how did it all begin?

Sun: At the time I was nothing. Just a big cloud of dust and gas floating around in space. I was a bit of a drifter.

Randall: But you pulled yourself together?

Sun: You bet I did? I'm not too sure what happened since I wasn't feeling too bright at the time but I figure some superstar blew up and gave me a nudge. Anyhow I started pulling gas and dust into a ball. I was having a ball when I got my act together and landed my STARRING role!

22

Randall: So what happened?

Sun: As I got bigger, I got hotter – that's when I really shone!

Randall: So what was the secret of your success as a star? What really makes you tick?

Sun: Well, I guess if you're a star, you must have what it takes…

Randall: What's that?

Sun: Enough gravity to crush your hydrogen gas into a substance called helium. Star quality – that's what I call it!

Randall: And that gives you energy?

Sun: Some of the hydrogen gets turned into heat and light energy. It certainly keeps me going!

Randall: But in the early days, success didn't come easy – it took a few million years before you became a star.

Sun: Yeah, it was hard work!

Randall: And meanwhile your planets were forming…

Sun: Yeah – that was the outer part of my cloud. They're part of my dazzling success.

Randall: I know, I've got sunburn.

Well, the Sun's got a good memory! The Earth and the other planets really did start off as bits of dust and gas. The bits pulled together to form small rocks. And the small rocks clumped into bigger rocks and then mini-planets. The mini-planets smashed together and the bits joined up to form the planets as they are today.

Now for the question that I bet you're asking at this very second. What was doing all this pulling and smashing of dust and gas and rocks to make stars and solar systems? Without it, we wouldn't be here, so I guess it's a matter of some gravity. Hey, that's the answer – it's a force called gravity!

GREEDY, GRASPING GRAVITY

Gravity is vital for getting a handle on space and everything in it and you've got to know about it to make sense of the rest of this book. But it's a bit *scientific*.

ARGH! NOT AGAIN!

WARNING –
SCIENCE FACTS
COMING UP!

Space, stars and slimy aliens fact file

NAME: Gravity

1 Gravity is a force made by everything in the universe.

2 The force pulls on everything else as it reaches across space.

GRAVITY!

3 The Earth's gravity pulls you towards it and your gravity pulls the Earth towards YOU!

4 The further you go from Earth the weaker its pull becomes. But gravity still works billions of kilometres away. That's why the Sun's gravity stops the planets zooming off into space.

SLIMY SECRETS: The bigger and heavier you are, the stronger your gravity is. That's why the Earth (being bigger than you) pulls you down towards it when you jump. Possibly with painful results...

IT'S CRUNCH TIME!

OK, so that's the nitty-gritty of gravity. In a moment, you'll get the chance to see stars with your very own eyes. But first I've got some nasty news about big stars, roughly about ten times the size of the Sun. These heavyweights have horrible habits...

25

SINISTER SUPER-STARS' SECRETS

Big stars are bad news. Would you believe it – before they're even *born* these murderous mega-stars in the making are already causing chaos in the cosmos! Stars of all sizes form in huge clouds of dust and gas (as in the Sun's story on page 22). But as a big star takes shape, it zaps smaller wannabe stars with gas and blasts them to bits.

Big stars are greedy gas guzzlers too. They make more heat and crush hydrogen into helium faster than smaller stars like the Sun. And, after 11 million years, the star crashes inwards – pulled by the force of its own gravity!

The centre bounces out again ... only to hit the outer part of the star which is still falling in!

The BIG BASH bursts the star to bits in a blast brighter than ONE HUNDRED BILLION stars! It's called a supernova and it's a real super-star show-stopper. And that, you might think, is that... After all, the sinister super-star is blown to itsy-witsy bits. Or is it?

You know those horror films where the monster is supposed to be dead but suddenly comes back to life? Well, it happens in real life with big stars...

After the blast, the centre of a star carries on shrinking. But it doesn't die – it turns into a scary mini-monster. It's known as a neutron star.

It's just 20 km across. And you might think that's too small to be dangerous. But here's what happens if you get too close to it...

The neutron star is incredibly heavy. This gives it GIGANTIC gravity. If you landed on a neutron star, the gravity would make your body so heavy that a tiny flake of dried snot would weigh ONE MILLION TONNES. This could make a very large hole in your hankie.

Would you fancy a neutron-star holiday?

Horrible Holidays present...

The Neutron Star Hotel

Check into our out-of-this-world ONE-STAR hotel...

WELCOME!

GASP!

Unique atmosphere! It's so heavy that it's only 2.5 cm high. At least you can enjoy an all-day lie-in as you struggle to breathe!

Work-out in our exclusive gym. Just lifting your head uses more energy than climbing Mount Everest.

URRRRRGH!

You'll want to come back as soon as possible. And even if you don't – the gravity will pull you back!

Some neutron stars are known as pulsars. They spin so fast that the whole star can turn 360° in less than a second. And they blast out beams of radio waves like whirling flashing space sirens.

But there is one type of neutron star that makes that seem rather relaxing. I'm talking about the mean, murderous magnetar.

The magnetar is like a giant magnet – but you wouldn't want one on your fridge. If a magnetar was where the moon is, its force would rip away every bit of magnetic metal on Earth and wipe clean your dad's classic music cassette collection. And that's the nice bit…

The fearsome force would turn all the humans on Earth into slime soup by re-arranging every bit of matter in their bodies. And that really is no laughing matter!

But, for really big stars – those weighing more than 20 Suns – an even more frightening future is in store. Something that makes the magnetar look warm and fluffy. With these really big stars, the bit left after the supernova blast shrinks into … A HORRIBLE BLACK HOLE! Visiting a black hole could spoil your "hole" day – but if you wanna try it…

Horrible Holidays present…

The Black Hole Hotel

Why not "drop-in" for a "hole" lot of fun?! It's more than just a hole, it's a hole in the universe. And you'll find its pull hard to resist! Once inside, you'll enjoy a quick break! Well, several breaks, as your body is pulled into long stringy bits and squished smaller than a pinhead and never seen again… You'll be thrilled to bits…

YES, VERY LITTLE BITS!

Oh, so you don't fancy spending your holidays in a hole? And you'd rather clean a toilet with your toothbrush... Oh well, cheer up!

THERE'S A STAR IN EVERY BODY!

You see, those exploding giant stars aren't all bad news. Bet you never knew that much of your body is made of bits of blown-up stars! Here's your very own incredible insides story...

Like every other star, giant stars spend time happily crunching hydrogen into helium. But not always. When the giant star is overheating and about to go pop, it crushes more and more bits of matter together and starts churning out other substances. The oxygen in your lungs, the iron in your blood and the carbon in your body were all made by an exploding star billions of years before you were born.

And now, at long last, it's your chance to have stars in your eyes. Yes, folks – it's star-staring time!

THE HORRIBLE SCIENCE STAGGERING STARGAZERS' CLUB

Every night sees the most eye-popping show in the universe. It's called the stars and here's your chance to join a brainy band of star spotters who are setting out to explore the universe using their eyeballs. Welcome to the Staggering Stargazers' Club!

Stuff needed for stargazing

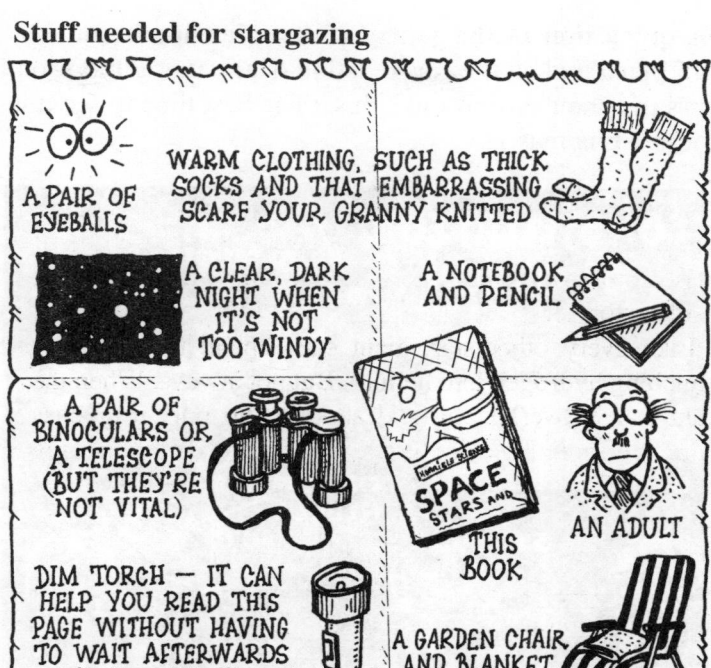

A PAIR OF EYEBALLS

WARM CLOTHING, SUCH AS THICK SOCKS AND THAT EMBARRASSING SCARF YOUR GRANNY KNITTED

A CLEAR, DARK NIGHT WHEN IT'S NOT TOO WINDY

A NOTEBOOK AND PENCIL

A PAIR OF BINOCULARS OR A TELESCOPE (BUT THEY'RE NOT VITAL)

SPACE STARS AND — THIS BOOK

AN ADULT

DIM TORCH — IT CAN HELP YOU READ THIS PAGE WITHOUT HAVING TO WAIT AFTERWARDS FOR YOUR EYES TO GET USED TO THE DARK

A GARDEN CHAIR AND BLANKET (NOT VITAL)

IMPORTANT NOTE

Don't leave home without your adult. Also, do remember that adults get scared easily so don't wander off and leave them!

Here's what to do...

1 Take your equipment (including your adult) to a dark place away from street lights.

2 Look up at the sky. If you sit in the garden chair you can pretend to sunbathe – or should I say "star-bathe"? If you feel cold, you can snuggle under the blanket.

Got all that? Great!

Here's our first space spectacle coming right up!

A quick tour of the galaxy without leaving home

1 Take a look at the constellation (star pattern) of Orion. It's the one that looks like this. (The best time to see it is after Christmas.)

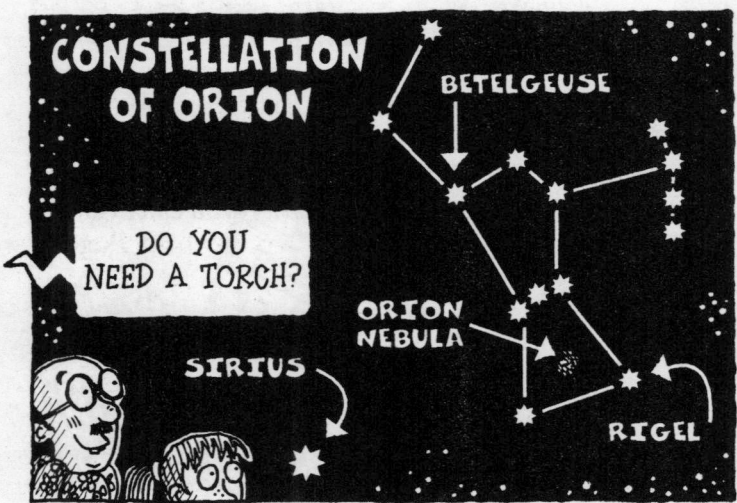

2 Can you see Sirius – the brightest star in the sky? It's about 8.6 light years away from us and 23 times brighter than the Sun. The only reason why you're not screaming, "AARGGGGH ME EYEBALLS!" is that Sirius is so far away, not much of its light is reaching us.

3 Now back to Orion... Stars can be different colours. Cooler stars can be red and hotter stars are bluish-white. Most star colours are too faint to see clearly, but you can see some in Orion if you look carefully:

- Rigel is a giant, hot, blue-white star up to 900 light years away and 40,000 times brighter than the Sun.
- Betelgeuse is at least 600 times bigger than the Sun and thousands of times brighter. Luckily for us it's

over 420 light years away. It's a "red supergiant" star – you might be able to make out its tasteful orangey-colour. It's a kind of gruesome glimpse into the future of our Sun at the end of its life when it'll swell up and fry the Earth to a frazzle. (See page 137 for the red-hot details.)

- The Orion Nebula looks like a little twinkling cloud – you'll only see it if the sky's really dark. It's over 1,300 light years away and is part of a bigger, darker cloud that's 100 light years across. It's a sort of nursery where cute little baby stars are born – you can even see the baby stars twinkling. Who's a pretty baby then?

Note to readers in the southern half of the Earth

Orion can be seen from all over Earth except for the South Pole. But in countries south of the Equator, it'll appear upside-down compared to how it's shown here. So you could put the map upside-down. Or if you want to do things the hard way you could stand on your head to stare at the stars!

And instead of looking for Sirius, you might like to check out Canopus. It's here:

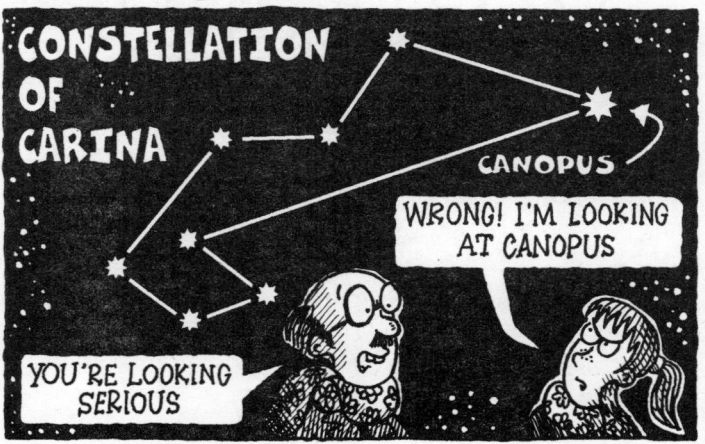

This giant star is 12,000 times brighter than the Sun and so far away its light takes 300 years to reach us. And that's a long way to come for a flying visit. So long! Have FUN!

> **Bet you never knew!**
> In 2001, astronomers found a huge boozy-woozy cloud of alcohol drops floating near the centre of our galaxy. Certain sozzled scientists are now trying to book spaceflights to get there.

But we're not. You see we're heading for the most important star of all. It's the star at the centre of our Solar System and the star we all depend on for light and heat. And if you "tan" the page, you'll find that the next chapter is a red-hot read!

THE STUNNING SUN

The Sun is an ordinary, yellow star like millions more in the Milky Way. But it's still powerful and stunning. And the stunning Sun's sunshine is incredibly important for all of us on Earth...

Six stunning Sun statistics

1 The Sun is so hot that a pinhead heated in its centre would give off enough heat to kill a person 160 km away.

2 Imagine an iceberg 2.5 cm thick. The Sun's hot enough to melt the ice in 2 hours and 12 minutes, even though the iceberg is 150 million km from the Sun.

But just think... The Sun blasts heat in all directions all the time.

So imagine that you built a wall of ice 2.5 cm thick around the Sun at a distance of 150 million km.

Even though your wall would be 949 MILLION km long – the Sun could melt it *all* whilst you're enjoying a nice film. SCORCHING!

3 Every second, the sizzling Sun guzzles 564 million tonnes of its hydrogen fuel. I bet its gas bills are gigantic! Every minute, 235 million tonnes of hydrogen turn into energy. That's equal to ONE MILLION elephants blowing up every second! SENSATIONAL!

4 The Sun (and the Solar System, including us) are spinning around the centre of the Milky Way at something like 230 km a second. Reckon that sounds fast? It is. But it still takes 225 million years to do one lap – called a cosmic year. So far, the Sun's managed 20 laps – so it's 20 cosmic years old. STAGGERING!

I'M 20 COSMIC YEARS OLD.

AND I'M ABOUT 7 COSMIC SECONDS OLD.

MR GRIMES (AN ANCIENT SCIENCE TEACHER)

5 The Sun "sings". Yes – *really*! The Sun's surface wobbles in and out. Waves of wobbling pass over the Sun's surface like the waves of air called sound waves. Sadly we can't hear the Sun's song. There's no air to carry the sound and, anyway, it's too deep for our Earthling ears to hear. But scientists have used a computer to make a similar sound and then made the sound higher-pitched so we can hear it. It's a deep rumbling noise – like a hungry hippo with a grumbling tum. SURPRISING!

6 The Sun gives off radio waves. These are just another form of energy, like light or radiation. Maybe the singing Sun could cut a single and play it on its own radio station? SHATTERING!

But the most stunning Sun fact of all is that without the Sun's heat and light, it would be night all over Earth for ever. It would soon start to get very cold and all the plants would die. And then all the animals that live off plants would die too and we humans would have nothing to eat. It doesn't bear thinking about – as any bear will tell you...

But despite the fact that the Sun is so obvious and important, we can't look at it...

Hmm – the Sun sounds a bit dangerous. And now for the next episode of our sci-fi space story. Will the aliens get sizzled by the stunning Sun?

Oddblob's Alien Adventure

We set off for the boring, yellow star known as the Sun. I told the Snotties that we wouldn't get too close to the star. If we did, our flying saucer would turn into a frying saucer, *snirk snirk**. Instead, my plan was to keep a safe distance and switch on our light filters so that we wouldn't get blinded.

On the way to the Sun, Sloppy became bored…

I had to explain that the Sun is easy to see because it's large and bright (unlike Sloppy who is neither large nor bright). But as any super-intelligent Blurb knows, it's a long way away. Afterwards, Sloppy played a game of snotball with my pet robot blurbi-dog, Roverbot.

* Ha ha! in Oddblob's language.

BLURBI—DATA

BY COSMO THE COMPUTER

☀ NAME: The Sun

☀ SIZE: 1,392,000 km across

☀ SIZE COMPARED TO EARTH: One million times larger

☀ GRAVITY COMPARED TO EARTH: 28 times stronger

☀ LENGTH OF DAY: Like a planet, the Sun spins in space but takes 28 Earth days to turn round once

☀ ATMOSPHERE: Super-heated gas called the corona. Steer clear of it - it's 2 million$^{\circ}$C

☀ WEATHER FORECAST: It's going to be UNBEARABLY HOT. The Sun's surface is about 6,000°C and its centre is 15 million$^{\circ}$C! It's also going to be windy - but the wind isn't made of air. It's bits of atoms blasted from the Sun. There's also lots of deadly radiation.

☀ TRAVEL TIPS: Keep your distance. But if you must go close, wear super-thick blurbi-shades and sunscreen and make sure your spacecraft has a really thick heat shield.

As we hovered at a safe distance, I pointed out the most interesting sights.

•Bumpy bits – The surface of the Sun looks like a sweet Earth fruit called an orange. The bumps are the tips of rising currents of hot gas.

• Sunspots – Those simple-minded Snotties reckoned the Sun had snotty-pox spots! I told them they were sunspots – holes in the surface made by magnetic forces. They were 1,500°C cooler than the Sun's surface but still blistering hot!

• Solar flares – These are a bit like a Snotty's slimy sneeze only the snot is bits of hydrogen. They can reach Earth and knock out primitive Earthling electrical equipment. That's the flares, not the Snotties' sneezes, snirk, snirk.

WARNING BY COSMO!

Solar flares are hot enough to bake a Blurb. If my sensors spot one, I'll warn you. But beware - the flares zoom at 400 km a second. So you'd better move fast, Oddblob!

From 20 million km away, Cosmo's super-sensitive sensors scanned the Sun's insides...

BLURBI X-RAY OF THE SUN

CORE

CHROMOSPHERE

PHOTOSPHERE

CONVECTIVE ZONE

RADIATIVE ZONE

SWEAT!

CHROMOSPHERE - This is the inner atmosphere. It's 10,000 km deep.

PHOTOSPHERE - This is the surface of the Sun. It's 300 km deep.

CONVECTIVE ZONE - This is the area where hot gases rise up from the core. It's 200,000 km deep.

RADIATIVE ZONE - 380,000 km thick.

CORE - 380,000 km across. Heat energy is made here.

It was too hot to go any closer to the Sun, but we did enjoy a blurbi-barbecue.

Now for a fascinating fact… The Sun makes up 99.86 per cent of all the matter in our Solar System. It doesn't sound much, but the teeny leftover 0.14 per cent includes the most incredibly interesting bits of the Solar System … the planets!

And right now we're off on a tour of the planets – from melting Mercury to perishing Pluto and all the weird worlds in between. So turn the page and climb aboard…

HOT AND HORRIBLE PLANETS

Anyone stupid enough to mess about on Mercury or visit Venus has less chance of escaping than a balloon in a pin factory. These planets are so hot and horrible that they would turn a person into goo in a fiery flash. You wouldn't send your worst enemy there … would you?

HERE WE GOO…

A suffering scientist has been sent to Mercury by her worst enemy. She soon discovers that the planet moves in a weird way with an eerie effect on the days…

MY TRIP TO MERCURY by Ivana Coldrink (sorry about the scorch marks)
I arrived on Mercury this morning just in time to watch the Sun rise. It climbed in the sky and as it climbed it seemed to get bigger.
Around noon, I was about to eat my sandwiches when I noticed that the Sun had started to move backwards. I was so surprised that I forgot to eat, and my sandwiches turned into burned toast.
A little later, the Sun changed its mind and went forwards again. At the end of a very long day, it set in the evening but now it's reappeared! Suffering space rocks! What's going on?

Oh well, Ivana – you've got to suffer for science and this science sounds seriously scintillating. Here's what's happening…

SO WHAT'S UP WITH THE SUN?

As Mercury orbits the Sun, it travels in a shape called an ellipse. It looks like this...

When Mercury is closer to the Sun – the Sun looks bigger. When the planet moves away from the Sun – the Sun looks smaller. And because a day on Mercury lasts 59 Earth days – and that's most of a Mercury orbit (88 Earth days) – the Sun can change size during one day. With me so far? Great! Now for the backwards bit...

On Earth, the Sun appears to cross the sky every day as the planet spins in space. But just imagine if our planet were spinning a lot slower. Well, then the Sun would seem to move slower. And if our orbit were faster than the speed the Sun seemed to move, the Sun would appear to go backwards. That's what happens with the slowly spinning Mercury! See what I mean?

Hmm – Mercury sounds mad. Oh well, let's catch up with our space story and see if Oddblob can make sense of mixed-up Mercury...

Oddblob's Alien Adventure

We set off for Mercury. It's the closest planet to the Sun – a quick hop of about 58 million km.

BLURBI—DATA

- NAME: Mercury
- SIZE: 4,900 km across
- SIZE COMPARED TO EARTH: Three times smaller across
- GRAVITY COMPARED TO EARTH: A little over one-third. That means you would be one-third your Earth weight, Oddblob.
- MOONS: None
- LENGTH OF DAY: 58 Earth days and 12 hours
- LENGTH OF YEAR: 88 Earth days
- ATMOSPHERE: Hardly any
- WEATHER FORECAST: Too hot AND too cold. During the day it's 427^{0}C - that's hot enough to melt a tin of blurbi-baked beans.And there's no escape from the Sun's radiation. At night, it's -183^{0}C.
- TRAVEL TIPS: It's not a sensible place to go - but if you really must visit Mercury, you'll need your spacesuit, your blurbishades and extra-thick thermal socks for those long cold nights.

As we swooped over Mercury, I pointed out the main tourist attractions. This didn't take very long as there weren't many.

- Cliffs – 3 km high.
- The Caloris Basin – a crater 1,300 km across.
- The deep craters have ice in them.

The Snotties pestered me to let them go skating in the craters. But I decided to move on 50 million km to Venus. I hoped it would be more interesting. And it was, but not in a nice way...

BLURBI–DATA

◑ NAME: Venus

◑ SIZE: 12,100 km across

◑ SIZE COMPARED TO EARTH: A bit smaller

◑ GRAVITY COMPARED TO EARTH: A little weaker

◑ MOONS: None

◑ LENGTH OF DAY: 243 Earth days

◑ LENGTH OF YEAR : 225 Earth days. No, Oddblob I am not blowing my blurbi-chips! The planet spins so slowly that one Venus day lasts longer than one Venus year! And just to confuse you a bit more Venus spins backwards compared to all the other planets...

◑ ATMOSPHERE: Choking clouds of carbon-dioxide gas. The atmosphere is heavy enough to crush you flat and the clouds are full of acid that could dissolve what's left of you.

Then there are the volcanoes ... they're not erupting at present - but they might start at any moment.

◑ WEATHER FORECAST: Today's going to be hot, 500°C to be exact, just the same as every day. It's the hottest place in the Solar System (not counting the Sun).

◑ TRAVEL TIPS: I'd rather crash my computer chips than go to Venus!

Despite Cosmo's advice, I decided to land, even if we stayed in the spacecraft. But the Snotties wanted to go outside…

At this point Roverbot decided to go walkies…

This gave me the chance to point out the dangers of…

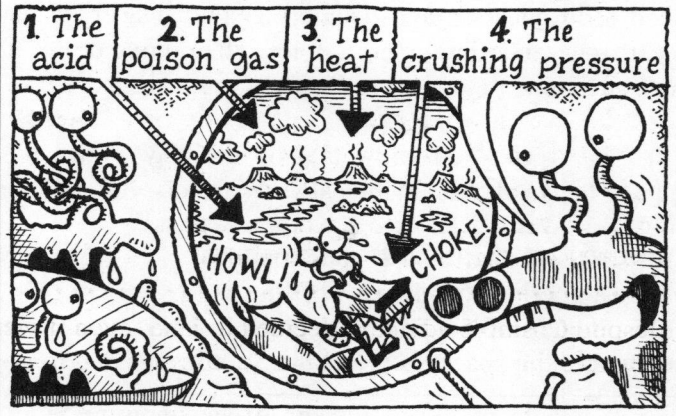

1. The acid	**2.** The poison gas	**3.** The heat	**4.** The crushing pressure

HOWL!

CHOKE!

After I'd rescued Roverbot with the spacecraft's robot arm, he seemed rather upset and took it out on me…

YOUCH! YOU UNGRATEFUL DOGGY!

CHOMP!

But if Venus the planet is vicious and violent, Venus the god was vile! The Mayan people of Central America thought the planet was a god (not a goddess as the ancient Greeks believed). And Mayan priests spent lots of time looking at the planet to see what their god was up to. Was he moving? What time of day did he appear?

COULD YOU BE A MAYAN ASTRONOMER?

This quiz is based on real events. It's the year 562. You're the priest astronomer to King Sky-witness of Calakmul. But are you an awesome astronomer or a feeble fortune-teller?

Here are the rules:

Read each question and decide on your answer. If you get it right, award yourself a point. Then move on to the next question.

1 It's 29 April. You know that on this day Venus will appear to stand still in the sky. What do you tell the king?

a) It's a good day to bash your enemies.

b) It's a good day to do a bit of shopping.

c) It's a bad day – you'd best go to bed and hide under the duvet.

> **Answer:**
> **a)** The god Venus is in charge of war and disaster. If he's hanging about in the sky (as seen from Earth) it's a good time to ask for his aid.

2 The king's army captures the rival city of Tikal with its king, Double Bird. What do you do with him?

a) Lock him in a small room and make him do hard sums.

b) Agree with him that life is very unfair and let him go.

c) Crush him under a wheel-shaped rock and cut his heart out.

> **Answer:**
> **c)** He was a sacrifice – a little thank-you prezzie for Venus.

3 Also captured was a royal prince named Animal Skull. He's only a boy. What do you do with him?
a) Drown him in a pot of custard. Then eat the custard.
b) Make him king and excuse him from going to school.
c) Tikal, I mean *tickle* him to death with a feather duster.

Answer:
b) But the boy has to do what you tell him to.

4 What do you do with King Double Bird's army?
a) Treat them to a slap-up supper.
b) Pull out their fingernails and cut out their hearts.
c) Send them to work in the royal chocolate factory.

Answer:
b) Venus likes sacrifices – he's a real "hearty" character.

What your score means...
0–1 You're far too nice to be a Mayan astronomer.
2–3 You might act a bit strangely if you had a stone heart-cutting knife in your hands. You're not a science teacher by any chance?
4 You're a menace to society and you'd make a great Mayan astronomer.

If you really want to be a Mayan astronomer, here's your chance to view Venus with your own eyeballs. (Just leave the stone knives at home!)

Don't forget the things you need from page 31!

Viewing Venus

Here's what to do…

1 Look out for Venus in the west, two hours after sunset. (You should be able to see the planet for about half the year – so if it's not there it'll turn up in a few months.)

2 Venus looks like a brilliant bright star. It's so bright because the Sun's light reflects off the planet's deadly choking clouds. Isn't that pretty?

Did you find Venus easily? Hopefully you did. But, in the past, viewing Venus has presented plenty of puzzling problems. It even wrecked some astronomers' lives.

This is the story of poor Guillaume Le Gentil. In 1761, this French scientist was keen to see a transit of Venus. That's when the planet moves across the face of the Sun as seen from Earth. With me so far?

For astronomers, a transit is something special. It's the chance of a lifetime to measure how big and far away Venus is compared to the Sun. A transit was due in 1761 and the best place to see it was India – so Guillaume sailed off to India. But his plans flopped faster than a bungee-jumping hippopotamus. If Guillaume had sent his scientific buddies letters they might have sounded like this (complete with a dodgy French accent)…

1761 (In India)

To ze French Academy of Sciences
Bonjour, guys!

I hev some good news and some bad news. Ze good news is that I hev seen ze transit and ze weather was sunny so I saw everything. Zoot allors! Eet was gobsmacking! Ze bad news is that owing to ze war with Britain I couldn't

DARN!
DARN!
DARN!
DRAT!

land – so I 'ad to watch ze transit from my ship and I couldn't set up my scientific equipment.

Ze weather is terrible. It eez pouring with rain but I hev decided to stay in India to wait for ze next transit. It's not due for another eight years but at least I'll be in ze right place zees time!

Au revoir!
Guillaume

PS Zere is green mould growing on my wig.

After seven years of waiting, Le Gentil did some calculations. To his dismay, he found that he'd get a better view from Marianas Island in the Pacific Ocean. So he set off for the island as soon as he could. But, once again, his luck was out…

1769

Bonjour, guys! ....○ ✺
Darn! Darn! Darn! I em in
manila in ze Philippine Islands
and I hev just found out zat I
hev meesed ze only ship zat
goes to marianas Island. I asked
when ze next one goes and it won't be for
another THREE years!

Oh well, mustn't grumble, as ze British say.
I reckon I weel still get a good view of ze
transit from 'ere.

Au revoir!
Guillaume

I em'ere

PS Ze bugs hev eaten a
huge hole in ze backside
of my trousers.

But the Academy had other ideas. They decided that Le
Gentil would get a better view back in India. So he was
sent back the way he had come – with fateful results…

1769

Bonjour, guys!
Darn! Drat! Curses and FRILLY KNICKERS! I
sailed to ze India like you told me to. I got
zere in time. I set up my telescope. I was so
excited I couldn't sleep. I'd been waiting
EIGHT long years for zees! Ze next
day ze Sun was shining. I was all
ready for ze transit and then… ze sky
clouded over and I did nat see a thing!
And now I hev just 'eard zat in manila where

I wanted to stay zere was a blue sky and everyone saw the transit. And the next transit isn't due for another 100 years! ARRGGGH! I em jumping up and down on my mouldy wig!

Yours crossly
Le Gentil

1770

Bonjour, guys!

You do remember me – don't you? Eez me – Guillaume and I'm home! I hed a terrible voyage back from India. Well, it was three voyages actually – I kept getting shipwrecked. My trousers are all cut to pieces and my wig is washed overboard.

Well, when I got 'ome, everyone thought I was dead and my 'orrible family were just dividing up all my belongings.

Au revoir

Guillaume

PS My family says I should thank my lucky stars I em still alive. Grr – don't mention ze stars or planets or I will scream – ARGH!

Oh dear... Well, you'll have no trouble seeing this next planet. You probably see it every day and you might well be an expert on it! Yes, it's time to get down to Earth!

DOWN TO EARTH!

If I were an alien looking for somewhere to live, I'd
certainly choose Earth. After all, it's the only planet with
running water, air and the chance of finding a decent
pizza. But enough of me – it's time for another episode
of our slimy space story. Let's find out what the aliens
think of Earth…

Oddblob's Alien Adventure

Earth would be a perfect planet to live on if it weren't
overrun by those annoying half-witted humans. Mind
you, when we landed on Earth, the Snotties acted
almost as half-wittedly as the humans…

BLURBI-DATA

- 🌍 NAME: Earth
- 🌍 SIZE: 12,700 km across
- 🌍 MOONS: One   the Moon
- 🌍 LENGTH OF DAY: 24 Earth hours
- 🌍 LENGTH OF YEAR: 365.25 Earth days
- 🌍 ATMOSPHERE: 78% nitrogen, 21% oxygen. The
rest is other gases including 0.038% carbon
dioxide (increasing with human pollution).
- 🌍 WEATHER FORECAST: It's going to be hot
around the Earth's middle and well below
freezing at the poles (each end). A large
amount of water will fall from the sky in
the form of small drops. Earthlings call
this rain.

🌍 TRAVEL TIPS: Human scientists have invented a portable roof. This item of equipment is carried in the hand and protects the head from rain. It's called an Um-brell-a. It's worth taking one of these with you if you go out. Some life forms on Earth are extremely unfriendly and fierce and might try to eat you.

BEWARE OF THESE!!!

SHARK

TIGER

CROCODILE

As we approached Earth, I pointed out a couple of interesting features...

• Earth is mostly blue because of its water – 71 per cent of the planet is covered in masses of water known as seas. Even the clouds are made of tiny drops of water floating in the air. As usual, the half-witted humanoids have got it wrong – they should be calling their planet Water rather than Earth or maybe Planet Damp and Drippy, snirk, snirk.

• Earth teems with life. You can see it from space – for example, huge areas of land are covered in giant green life forms known as trees. Despite their size, trees do not appear to be dangerous and have never been known to chase anyone.

WE COME IN PEACE!

Slobslime and Sloppy had never seen Earth's life forms and they hadn't been listening to my talk on trees...

Then Slobslime met her first human.

The human had a dangerously fierce Earth creature with her…

On Earth, there are billions of tiny life forms called microbes – these can cause disease. Slobslime seemed to have fallen ill.

Well, I think Earth's lovely. OK, so I'm biased, but everyone who sees Earth from space is amazed at how pretty the planet looks with its shiny blue seas and its fluffy white clouds. Earth reflects so much sunlight it seems to glow in the dark...

Here's what astronaut Jim Lovell said back in 1968:

The vast loneliness up here is awe-inspiring, and it makes you realize just what you have back on Earth. The Earth from here is a grand oasis in the big vastness of space.

EARTH'S ULTIMATE SECRET

Apart from its beauty, you might not think that Earth's that special. Of all the planets in our Solar System, it's the third hottest planet with the fifth-fastest spin. It's the fifth heaviest planet and it has the fourth-strongest gravity. So what makes the Earth so special?

Notice anything?

Earth's in the middle of every list! Being the Solar System's Mr Average is what makes Earth special! It means that Earth isn't too hot or too cold for life. And it means that Earth's gravity is just right for all the life forms that live on it.

Including you and me.

But it doesn't stop there. Earth has other fantastic features that make it safe for life. My shady pal, Honest Bob, has moved into the second-hand planet business and he's keen to sell you the Earth. Can you spot what's wrong with his advert?

We'll be back after this commercial break...

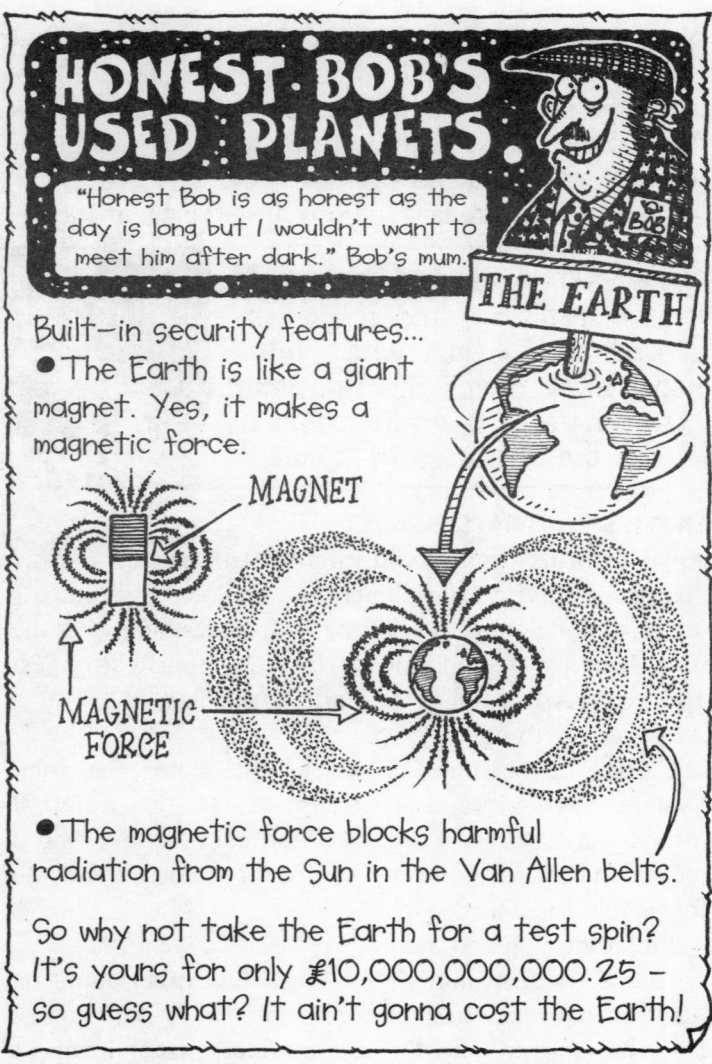

HONEST·BOB'S USED PLANETS

"Honest Bob is as honest as the day is long but I wouldn't want to meet him after dark." Bob's mum.

THE EARTH

Built-in security features...
• The Earth is like a giant magnet. Yes, it makes a magnetic force.

MAGNET

MAGNETIC FORCE

• The magnetic force blocks harmful radiation from the Sun in the Van Allen belts.

So why not take the Earth for a test spin? It's yours for only £10,000,000,000.25 – so guess what? It ain't gonna cost the Earth!

So would you buy the Earth off Honest Bob? Hope not! As far as I know, the Earth isn't actually for sale! Let's ask Luke Upwards about the rest of Honest Bob's claims...

HONEST BOB IS BEING SURPRISINGLY... HONEST. ALL THE DETAILS HE GIVES ARE CORRECT!

Honest Bob was right about the Earth's defences against the Sun. But what's this? It looks like Izzie Starrs who works with Luke has a joke she wants to share with us...

WHERE DO YOU FIND THE VAN ALLEN BELTS?

IN SPACE?

ROUND VAN ALLEN'S TROUSERS!

PATHETIC!

Bet you never knew!
The Van Allen belts, named after US scientist James Van Allen who found them in 1958, are between 1,000 and 25,000 km from Earth. The Sun's radiation gets trapped by the Earth's magnetic field in the belts. But if a spacecraft broke down there, the astronauts would be revoltingly roasted by the radiation.

Now let's take Honest Bob up on his offer to take the Earth for a spin. We can because...

Shock horror news! Earth is moving!

Right now, you're whizzing through space at about 30 km a second (that's about 108,000 km an hour) as Earth whizzes around the Sun. In fact you've actually whizzed 300 km since the start of this sentence. And what's more, you, me, the cat and the goldfish and the entire Earth are *spinning* too!

HOW TO ENJOY A FREE ROUND-THE-WORLD TRIP WITHOUT GETTING OUT OF BED

All you have to do is stay in bed all day at a point on the equator (the imaginary line around the Earth's middle). As the Earth spins in space you'll move with it. In one day, you'll travel a distance equal to going around the world. That's right – you enjoy a free 40,000 km space ride at 1,670 km an hour, *without getting out of bed!*

Now let's imagine you pushed your bed to the North Pole (or the South Pole if you prefer sleeping upside down. Just make sure that duvet's really thick!) While you stay in bed all day, your bed will go around in a little circle like an ice skater in a tight spin. Confused? Hopefully this will help:

If you're at the North Pole, you can look up and see the Pole Star directly above your head. All the other stars seem to go around it in a circle as the Earth spins in space. Of course – you don't have to go to the North Pole to see the Pole Star. Anywhere in the northern half of the Earth will do...

THE HORRIBLE SCIENCE STAGGERING STARGAZERS' CLUB
First collect the things you need from page 31!
Peer at the Pole Star
Here's what you have to do...
1 Head for a dark place away from street lights.
2 Look up at the sky. Find the constellation called the Big Dipper or the Plough. The lovely romantic star names in the Plough are Arabian.

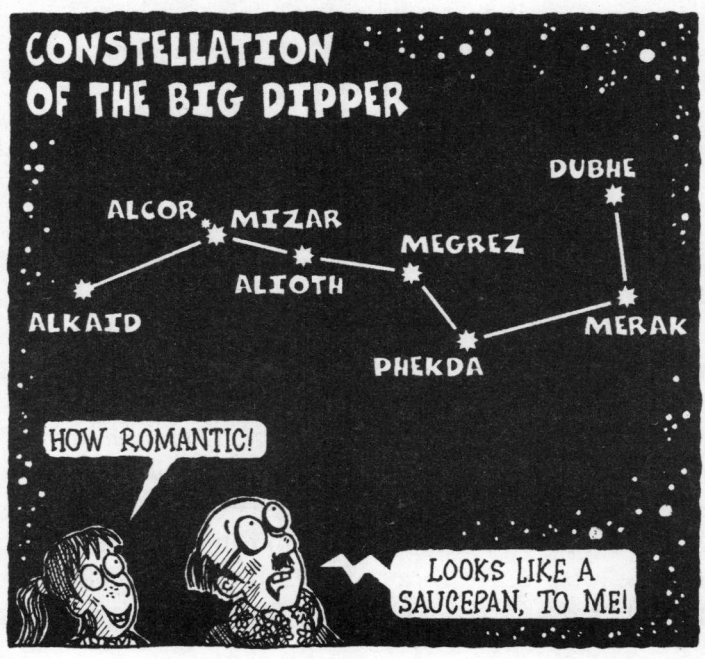

CONSTELLATION OF THE BIG DIPPER

DUBHE
ALCOR · MIZAR
MEGREZ
ALIOTH
ALKAID
MERAK
PHEKDA

HOW ROMANTIC!

LOOKS LIKE A SAUCEPAN, TO ME!

Follow the line from Merak to Dubhe upwards and you're peering at the Pole Star.

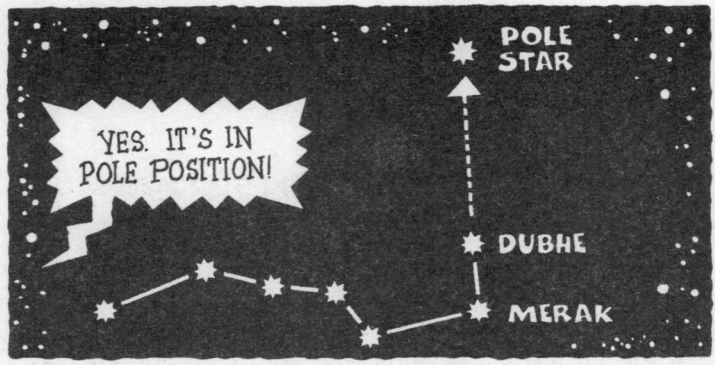

POLE STAR

YES. IT'S IN POLE POSITION!

DUBHE

MERAK

3 Can you see Alcor? It helps if it's a dark night! A thousand years ago the Arabs reckoned that you had good eyesight if you could spot Alcor.

4 The Pole Star is a giant star 2,000 times brighter than the Sun but, as luck would have it, it's a nice safe 480 light years away.

5 Since the star always appears directly over the North Pole – you can always tell which direction is north, even at night!

> ***Bet you never knew!***
> *Earth's spin has an embarrassing wobble. And that means by the year AD 14,000 the North Pole will be pointing to a different star. DRAT – this book will be out of date! But after another 12,000 years, we'll be pointing at the Pole Star again and you can blow the dust off this book and read it again!*

Hold on – if you live in the southern half of the Earth you may be a bit miffed because you can't see the Pole Star. Don't be cross – you can stare at the Southern Cross instead!

Check out the Southern Cross

1 Here's where to look for it…

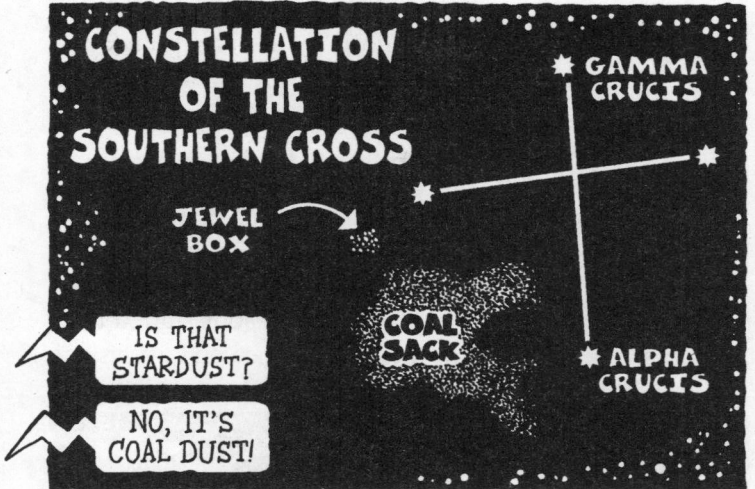

2 If the long arm of the cross were five times longer, it would end up above the South Pole.

3 Now here's a shock (I don't think). The Coal Sack is nothing to do with dirty lumps of coal and you won't find jewels in the Jewel Box. The Coal Sack is a big, dark cloud of gas and the Jewel Box is a group of distant stars.

Mind you, it doesn't matter where you live in the world – there's one thing in space everyone can see. Yes – you'd better turn that page fast or we'll miss our flight to the Moon!

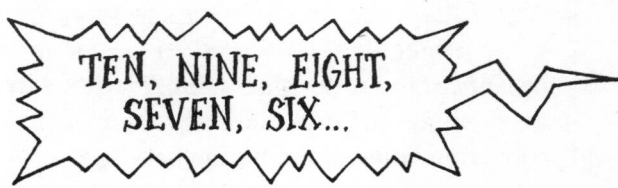

THE MADDENING MOON

The Moon's story started four billion years ago when the Earth got hammered on the head by a small planet and the weather changed. And here's the whole head-banging history...

The big bash

When Earth was whacked by a Mars-sized planet, the big bash blasted red-hot rocks into space. Gravity grabbed the rocks and rolled them into a ball and – BINGO! – the Moon was made. And that's how the seasons started too.

You see, Earth was knocked off balance and ever since it's been leaning over at an interesting angle of 23.44°.

So when the Earth goes round the Sun, the northern and southern halves of the planet take it in turns to lean towards the Sun and have summer. And now we've got the seasons sorted, it's time for another instalment of our slimy sci-fi story...

Oddblob's Alien Adventure

As we neared the Moon, I asked Cosmo the computer for some info on the place. But first I had to clean the green slime off his computer chips. Grrr – those slobbering slime-slopping Snotties!

BLURBI—DATA

NAME: The Moon

SIZE: 3,476 km across

SIZE COMPARED TO EARTH: A quarter its width

GRAVITY COMPARED TO EARTH: One sixth

LENGTH OF DAY: Nearly 28 Earth days

LENGTH OF YEAR: 365 Earth days and 6 Earth hours

ATMOSPHERE: Nothing much...

WEATHER FORECAST: The weather's going to be either too hot or too cold. During the day it's 110°C and blasted by radiation from the Sun. At night, it's 170°C. But at least there'll be no rain because there's no water, and no wind because there's no air.

TRAVEL TIPS: Wear spacesuits and leave the umbrella in the spacecraft.

From space we had a great view of the Moon and I showed the Snotties the most interesting sights.

• Craters – The Moon's craters were made by crashing exploding space rocks. There are about 300,000 craters and those slug-brained Snotties tried to count them all. Some craters are thousands of metres deep and their bottoms never see the Sun. They could contain ice.

...EIGHT, NINE, TEN, ELEVEN, TWELVE, THIRTEEN, FOURTEEN...

DON'T BOTHER!

• The Earth – When you're on the Moon, the Earth looks much bigger and brighter than the Moon does when seen from Earth. This is because the Earth is bigger than the Moon.

• The "seas" – Sadly, these are silly Earthling names for masses of dark rock that melted when giant space rocks hit the Moon 3.8 billion Earth years ago. No chance of space surfing, I'm afraid!

Baby Sloppy heard me say "seas" and thought we were going to the seaside…

Because the Moon is smaller than the Earth, the gravity is weaker. This means that everything weighs one-sixth of its Earth weight. This came as a surprise to the Snotties…

Hmm – the Moon sounds cool! Sadly, NASA has just told me that I'm too unfit to be an astronaut, so I guess I'm stuck looking at the Moon. Never mind – staring at the Moon can be loads of fun! Especially if you're a member of…

Make eyes at the Moon

Things to look for…

1 What shape is it?

Possible shapes

CRESCENT   FULL   GIBBOUS

IMPORTANT SCIENCE NOTE

The shapes depend on the angle the Sun is shining on the Moon as it orbits the Earth. The new Moon appears as a skinny sliver so close to the Sun that it's hard to make out. And it grows into a big round Moon before shrinking back into a crescent.

2 What time is it?

The new Moon rises at sunrise and sets at sunset. When the Moon is waning (getting thinner) it rises at midnight and sets at midday.

The full Moon rises about sunset and sets about sunrise. So the higher the full Moon is in the sky the later it is.

3 Can you see any details?

Here are three things you can spot without a telescope…

COPERNICUS — A 93-KM-WIDE CRATER

IT'S VERY PEACEFUL HERE!

SEA OF TRANQUILLITY WHERE THE FIRST HUMANS LANDED IN 1969

TYCHO — A ONE BILLION-YEAR-OLD CRATER

Note to readers in South America, Australia, New Zealand and southern Africa

You'll see the Moon like this:

No matter where you are on Earth, you'll only ever see one side of the Moon. And no, it's not because the Moon doesn't want us to see the other side… It's because the Moon only turns once as it circles the Earth. To show how this works, Luke Upwards is sitting in my swivel chair as Izzie Starrs walks around him. Luke's pretending to be the Earth and Izzie's the Moon. Hey – you might like to try this at home too!

Like the Moon, Izzie makes one turn each time she goes around Luke. Hmm – in that time Luke ought to make 28 of the turns we call "days". I'll just whizz him round. OH YUCK! Luke's been space-sick!

Well, by now you may be feeling you've mastered some of the Moon's maddening mysteries. But does that make you an awesome astronomer? Or are you simply spaced-out? Find out with these cosmic quizzes...

COSMIC QUIZ 1

Mad Moon scientists have come up with some incredibly idiotic ideas about the Moon. Which idea did I make up?

1 William Pickering (1858–1938) and George Darwin (1845–1912): The Moon was thrown off the Earth as it spun in space billions of years ago. The hole left by the Moon is the Pacific Ocean.

PEAR-SHAPED? HE MUST HAVE BEEN BANANAS!

2 Frédéric Petit (1810–1865): There are TWO moons, the second one is very small.

3 Peter Hansen (1795–1874): The Moon is pear-shaped.

4 Hans Hörbiger (1860–1931): The mountains on the Moon are made of ice. There have been lots of moons, but they crashed to Earth and wiped out the giants who lived there.

Answers:
1 TRUE And they weren't too wrong – as you'll remember from page 64.
2 TRUE In the 1850s a lot of annoyed astronomers got eye-strain searching for the second moon. No one's found it yet.
3 FALSE Wrong! Ha ha! As if the Moon was pear-shaped! NO – Peter Hansen said the Moon was

egg-shaped and the end that we can't see is covered in jungle. So there!

4 TRUE He must have been as barking mad as a dog up a tree! Maybe that's why nasty Nazi leader Adolf Hitler hailed half-crazed Hans as the world's greatest scientist.

You might think that these theories were as daft as the man who ate the skin and threw away the banana. And, of course, you'd be right – but could *you* do any better?

COSMIC QUIZ 2

Which two items have been found on the Moon?

a) Germs that normally live up your nose.
b) Dust that smells of garlic.
c) Multicoloured bits of glass.
d) Slimy green lettuce.

WHAT'S IN A NAME?

The first scientist to peer at the Moon through a telescope, Italian super-scientist Galileo Galilei (1564–1642), thought the Moon had "seas". And he even gave these places names…

Seas that you might like to visit on the Moon…
• The Bay of Rainbows
• The Lake of Dreams

Seas that you might want to avoid…
• The Ocean of Storms
• The Marsh of Decay
• The Lake of Death

THE PUZZLING PLACE-NAMES TORTURE TEST…

Certain places on the Moon and the planets are named after places and people from Earth. This is handy for staggering a scientist.

Questions to ask…

1 ARE THE ALPS IN EUROPE?

"Yes," they say – quite rightly, since the Alps *are* in Europe.

You say, "No, they're on the Moon!" This is also true, since the Alps *are* mountains on the Moon.

If they say, "It's in the Middle East", you can say, "No, it's a desert on Mars." This is just as true. And now the quiz gets crueller…

You can say, "Not the famous composer – I mean the 644-km-wide crater." Mercury's craters are named after famous arty people and that's why Mark Twain and Leonardo da Vinci *are* on Mercury. Just to confuse your victim, you could add that Beethoven is also an asteroid.

Mind you, even the chilly dark side of the Moon is cosy and cheerful compared to our next stop. Living on this planet must be as jolly as a blocked drain. And is it really the home of monsters – or is that just an ugly rumour?

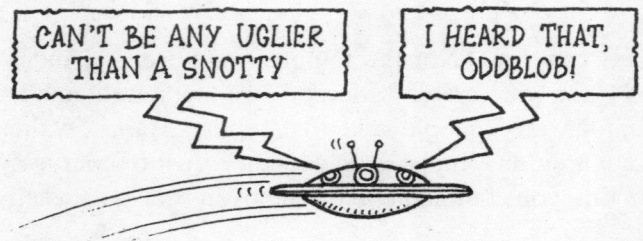

CAN'T BE ANY UGLIER THAN A SNOTTY

I HEARD THAT, ODDBLOB!

MONSTERS ON MARS?

Mars is the must-see planet for monster hunters. In this chapter, you'll stumble across monster scenery, monster stories and who knows what else? You might even find a few microscopic Mars monsters squirming and slithering over the next few pages...

Yes, there's something about Mars that really wakes folk up – it's even been known to work on people who haven't woken up for years. In 1997, people all over Earth watched a live TV broadcast from Mars on the Internet. No, they weren't glued to an alien TV station – a camera on the Sojourner space probe sent pictures that were transmitted on the Internet.

Actually the live show was more of a dead show. Nothing appeared to happen on Mars and there was nothing to see except hundreds of rocks and a pretty pink sky. There would have been more life in a graveyard at midnight, but even so, one billion people gazed at the scene in awestruck amazement.

The really exciting part of the mission was when a man named Brian Cooper used virtual-reality software to drive a radio-controlled robot car named Rocky about on MARS! Would you like a Rocky for Christmas?

See you after the commercial break.

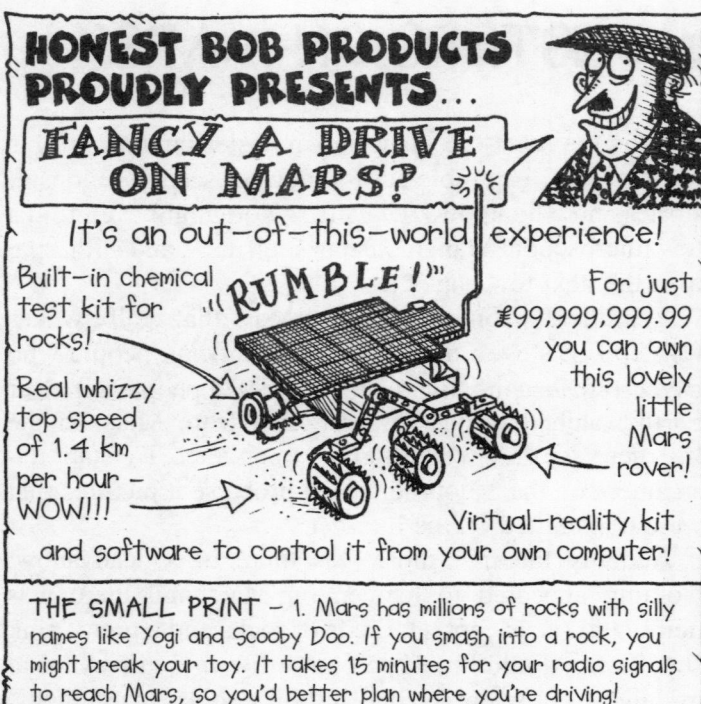

Oh well, it was fun while it lasted. Sadly, I've just heard that spoil-sport NASA scientists won't let me drive a robot car on Mars. But if that's got you interested in visiting the planet, I guess you've got a choice…

a) You could hang about waiting for a manned flight – there'll be one in a few years and, who knows, they might let you come along for the ride.

OR

b) You could try this experiment now and get an idea of what to expect on Mars…

Dare you discover ... how to cause a Martian dust storm?

You will need:

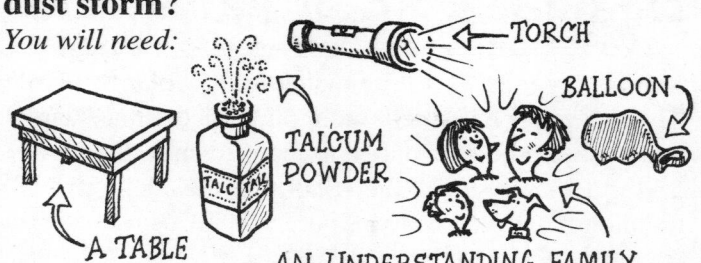

TORCH
TALCUM POWDER
BALLOON
A TABLE
AN UNDERSTANDING FAMILY

What you do:

1 Darken the room or wait until dark. Switch on the torch and place it so that it shines on the table from the side.
2 Sprinkle the table with talcum powder.
3 Blow up the balloon and let out the air a few times.
4 Now blow up the balloon and place the mouth of the balloon so that the escaping air blows over the top of the table.

You should notice:

The dust swirls out in a big cloud, billows into the air and floats about like a 100 per cent genuine Martian dust storm. Great, isn't it? In fact, just like on Mars, the dust storm starts when the wind blows bits of dust against each other that knock into more dust, etc.

> **WARNING TO YOUNGER READERS**
> *Ask permission before blanketing your home in a talcum powder dust storm. If you don't, you might be sent to Mars or possibly to your bedroom, until the dust settles!*

And now it's time for another slimy slice of sci-fi story action. This time the aliens explore Mars...

Oddblob's Alien Adventure

Mars is my most favourite planet in the Solar System! The scenery is massively more magnificent than Earth and there are no half-witted humans to spoil the view! I decided to show the Snotties the delights of mountaineering on Mars. And I asked Cosmo for the background basics...

BLURBI-DATA

🌑 NAME: Mars

🌑 SIZE: 6,800 km across

🌑 SIZE COMPARED TO EARTH: Half Earth's diameter

🌑 GRAVITY COMPARED TO EARTH: Not much more than one third as much

🌑 MOONS: Deimos and Phobos - they're only a few km across

🌑 LENGTH OF DAY: 24 Earth hours and 37 Earth minutes

🌑 LENGTH OF YEAR: 687 Earth days

🌑 ATMOSPHERE: Just a few wisps of carbon dioxide

🌑 WEATHER FORECAST: It's going to be very cold (about 30⁰C) but at least it won't rain. After all, it hasn't rained for four billion years. There's a chance of a dust storm that could last days. Don't worry, Oddblob the winds are weak because there's so little air. It won't be windy enough to blow you away.

🌑 TRAVEL TIPS: Soil chemicals can dissolve your space boots and some of your 24 toes.

As we came in to land on Mars, I showed the Snotties the superb scenery…

GET A LOAD OF THIS LOT...

• The Mariner Valley is the vastest valley in the Solar System. It's 6.4 km deep and 241 km wide – four times deeper and six times wider than that crack in Earth known as the "Grand Canyon". It's long enough to stretch across the puny Earthling country known as the United States of America.

• There are river valleys and lakes where water flowed on Mars billions of years ago. Some rivers were more than 24 km wide and 100 metres deep.

• Deimos and Phobos were probably asteroids that were pulled in by the gravity of Mars. Phobos, the slightly larger moon, rises in the west and sets in the east and goes across the sky in 4.5 Earth hours. Deimos is so titchy it looks like a bright star.

• Mons Olympus is the Solar System's highest mountain. It's a volcano 483 km wide and 25 km high – twice as wide as Earth's widest volcano and three times as high as Earth's most massive mole-hill, I mean mountain.

THAT'S WHERE WE'RE GOING TO CLIMB!

GULP!

We decided to climb Olympus Mons starting at the top! Well, *really*! (Talk about tourists taking life easy – anyone would think they're on holiday!) To get enough energy, the Snotties snacked up on slime ice cream first.

Just then Sloppy decided she wanted to visit Deimos. Deimos is so small its gravity is very weak. We were almost weightless there!

Suddenly, Slobslime suffered a gut gas problem! In the weak gravity this was enough to blast her into space.

But Roverbot rushed to her rescue…

Five facts not many people know about Mars moons

1 The gravity in Deimos is so weak you can take off into space just by riding a bike. And Slobslime's super-strong bottom burp is sure to result in a blown-off blast-off.

2 If you want to see what Deimos looks like from Mars, try this exciting experiment. Ask a friend to hold a potato at one end of a football pitch. Seen from the other end of the football pitch, the potato looks the same size as Deimos as seen from Mars. Not very big, in other words. (If you're feeling cruel, you can wander off and leave your friend holding a potato for hours.)

3 Actually, Deimos even *looks* like a potato, although it won't make tasty French fries.

SPOT THE DIFFERENCE
POTATO
DEIMOS

4 Each time Phobos orbits Mars, it spirals lower – dropping 18 cm every 100 Earth years. In 40 million years, the moon is due to hit Mars with messy results for any humans or aliens living there at the time.

5 In the 1950s, Ukrainian scientist Iosif Shmuelovich Shklovskii said that the moons of Mars were made by super-smart Martians. But in 1971, US space-probe photos proved that Phobos was just a large rock and the red-faced scientist said that he'd been joking.

BLUSH!

ALIEN INVADERS

So what about those alien invaders and Mars monsters? Well, at present, we aren't sure that there are aliens in the Solar System at all. But some past astronomers have been mad-keen on the idea of Mars aliens. And some of them thought there may be life on Venus too. But, as I'm sure you've guessed, these claims were a bit too barmy to be believable…

CHEEKY CLAIMS
by Barmy Boffins

TEDIOUS TRUTH
by Luke Upwards

1 Swedish scientist Svante Arrhenius (1859–1927)  said Venus was covered in swamps. Some scientists reckoned dinosaurs could live there.

1 There's no water on Venus and it's hot enough to turn dinosaurs into instant tasty dino-dinners.

2 In the 1830s, German astronomer, Franz von Paula Gruithuisen said Venus appears brighter every 47 years because the aliens light lamps in honour of their new emperor

2 You'll know why Venus shines from page 50. Scientists aren't too sure why the brightness changes (if it does). But it's nothing to do with alien emperors.

But those spaced-out scientific suggestions sound normal compared with the most crazy, cheesy alien claim ever!

THE NEW YORK SUN
27 August 1835

GIANT BEAVER BOUNDS ABOUT ON MOON!
Sir J.H.

OUR ARTIST'S IMPRESSION OF THE BEAVER

Top astronomer Sir John Herschel has spotted a giant beaver on the Moon! "It walked on two feet and it didn't have a tail," gasped the awe-struck astronomer. Sir John said that the Moon is covered in trees and he's seen herds of hairy bison that waggle their ears, and ape-like humans with wings. "There's something unearthly about the whole scene – oh yes, silly me, that's because it's not Earth!" added Sir John.

A MESSAGE FROM THE EDITOR

Gee-whizz, we'd sure like to thank all you folks who've been buying our paper. We were on the edge of going bust, but since we started reporting these Moon discoveries, we've become the biggest-selling paper on the planet – yee ha!

And the truth? The staggering stories had been cooked up by reporter Richard Adams Locke (1800–1871). The real Sir John Herschel was in South Africa. When he got to hear of the *Sun*'s tall tales, he was confused, but then he started to laugh very loudly.

BUT WHAT ABOUT THE MARS MONSTERS?

Oh yes, thanks for reminding me! The most famous astronomer to believe in aliens on Mars was Percival Lowell (1855–1916). Now, as you can see from these dates, Percy's been pushing up the pansies for quite a few years. But I'm pleased to say that he's agreed to appear on the only TV show where the broadcast is live even if the guests are dead...

That planet you said existed beyond Neptune...

YES! I SPENT YEARS LOOKING FOR IT, BUT I COULDN'T FIND IT!

THERE'S ONLY DWARF PLANETS SUCH AS PLUTO. And you know those canals you saw on Mars?

YES, THEY WERE DUG BY BRAINY ALIENS TO BRING WATER TO THE DESERTS ON MARS.

You know you built a special telescope to see them and spent years mapping them...?

Y-E-S?

You were seeing things! Spacecraft have landed on Mars and proved they don't exist!

THIS IS SO EMBARRASSING – I WISH I WAS DEAD!

You are dead!

The rotten reality is that when the two US Viking spacecraft landed on Mars in 1975 and 1976, they found that Mars is missing the basics for life. The sort of things you'd like to find in your home – warmth, water and air – don't exist on Mars. Trust Honest Bob to tell you the bad news – and sell you the planet into the bargain...

HONEST BOB'S USED PLANETS

"Honest Bob was a lovely kid – as long as he was asleep he did nothing wrong" – Bob's mum.

MARS

REALLY COOL!

IDEAL SIZE!

NO DAMP!

LOVELY COLOUR!

- OK, so it's got 4.6 billion years on the clock. But that's what you might call a genuine antique – and it's real old too!
- It's not too big! I mean, it's cosy – some folk don't like a big planet.
- Real smart red colour to it. I deny that it's rust. OK – so the rocks are a bit rusty – but hey, that's all part of its character.
- It's a bit cold, but as my mum always says, a bit of cold won't kill you. Well, it will, but it's kinda healthy too!
- OK, so the planet's kinda dry at present, but at least you won't get rising-damp problems.

Why not take a trip to Mars and look at it for yourself? You'll love it!

LOW COST!

At only **£700,000,000.12** – I'm robbing myself (instead of robbing you – OOPS pretend I didn't say that!).

THE TRUTH ABOUT HONEST BOB'S CLAIMS...

Don't be fooled by all that claptrap about "cosy" Mars. The terrible truth is that Mars is too small for its own good. Billions of years ago, Mars had lots of air and water. The cosy air blanket kept Mars warm enough for running water. But because Mars is smaller than Earth, the planet's gravity wasn't strong enough to hang on to the air. Ultraviolet rays from the Sun split the water into gases that wafted off into space. And that's why a visit to Mars is presently as pleasant as a pyjama party in a deep freeze.

What's that, Luke?

Luke Upwards writes...

> But give Bob his due — he's right about the rust. Iron in the rocks has rusted and that's why people call Mars "the red planet". If you get to see Mars from Earth, you'll find it even looks red from here!

SO MARS ISN'T TOO NICE RIGHT NOW - BUT IS THERE ANY CHANCE OF LIFE?

Surprisingly the answer isn't "NO", it's "hmm..." Well, that's what I think. But maybe you should judge for yourself? Yes, all you need to do is put on a judge's robe (a dressing gown will do fine). Take a chair in your very own courtroom  (or even your bedroom) and listen to the arguments from our two top scientist-lawyers...

Putting the case for **LIFE ON MARS** is Izzie Starrs.

And putting the case against LIFE ON MARS is Luke Upwards.

Over to you, Luke!

Luke: Life on Mars? No way! I mean, there's no water and it's too cold. When the Viking spacecraft did robot tests on the soil, they couldn't prove that there was life.

Izzie: Objection, your honour! The tests showed chemical changes that might have been caused by microbes.

Luke: It was just a chemical reaction!

Time out to think it over: WHAT DO YOU THINK?

OK – now it's time for the case for life on Mars…

Izzie: So Mars is pretty dry now – but it once had lakes and rivers and where there's water, there's life. Maybe there's ice or even water deep underground. And maybe there are microbes hiding there. Microbes on Earth aren't too fussy – they're at home in ice and deep underground.

MICROBES

Luke: Objection, your honour – she keeps saying "maybe"!
Time out: WHAT DO YOU THINK?

Izzie: In 1996, some scientists found fossil microbes in a rock from Mars. Here's exhibit A.
Luke: Objection! That's just a grotty old lump of rock. These so-called fossil microbes are too small to have been real microbes.

Izzie: But they could be hairs that the microbes used to swim about. Chemical changes in the rock could have been caused by microbes!
Time out: WHAT DO YOU THINK?

Luke: OK – you asked for this! In 1932 a scientist said he'd found microbes in a rock from Mars. They were found to be microbes from human snot. Here's Exhibit B.

Izzie: That's gross!
TIME FOR OUR LAWYERS TO SUM UP...
Luke: There's no way that there's life on Mars. Even if there were once life (and there's no proof), it doesn't mean there's life now!

Izzie: It's possible that rocks with microbes in them could have been blasted from Mars and landed on Earth and brought life to Earth. We might have started off as aliens from Mars!

Luke: Are you calling me an alien from Mars?

Izzie: Well, you're slimy enough!

Hey, break it up, guys! It's only science and there's nothing at stake except our whole understanding of life and the way we see our place in the universe. Er – OK, that sounds rather a lot. OOOH DEAR! I bet that hurt, Luke!

Bet you never knew!
In 1995, scientists Michel Mayor and Didier Queloz at Geneva University spotted a tiny wobble in the star called 51-Pegasi. They found out that this was caused by the gravity of a huge planet that was orbiting the star. Since then, scientists have found scores of planets. And many stars have planets like our own Solar System. (In 2003, they even found a planet that was about to be swallowed up and blasted by a giant star.) So all in all, there's a great chance of alien life lurking somewhere out there…

BUT THERE'S STILL NO PROOF!

TIME TO ROCK ON

These arguments look set to run – so let's make a run ourselves ... to the asteroid belt. Asteroids are rubbly leftovers from when the solar system formed...

HUH?

WELCOME TO THE ASTEROID BELT PLEASE DRIVE CAREFULLY

But not that close together! There are over one million asteroids but they're separated by millions of kilometres of space. And here's a few more facts to get you rocking...

Space, stars and slimy aliens fact file

NAME: Asteroids

ANOTHER POTATO AHEAD, CAPTAIN!

THE BASIC FACTS: 1 Most asteroids are shaped like, er, rocks.

2 The asteroid belt contains the dwarf planet Ceres. Found by Italian Guiseppe Piazzi in 1801, Ceres is 950 km across. There's hardly any atmosphere but there are rocks, ice and maybe an ocean under the ice. Some scientists think it might be home to alien life.

3 There are enough asteroids out there to make a planet the size of the Moon, or even bigger.

IT'S TRUE, WE'VE JUST GLUED THEM ALL TOGETHER!

(GLUE)

THE MOON

4 Unfortunately, Jupiter's gravity knocked the asteroids together and smashed them to bits so they didn't get the chance to make a planet. Poor little darlings!

5 In 2000, scientists found an asteroid shaped like a dog's bone.

6 Some asteroids are in two lumps loosely stuck together by gravity. Others even have their own mini moons the size of footballs.

SLIMY SECRET: Do YOU wanna be rich? Many asteroids contain valuable minerals such as iron and platinum. They're worth billions. Send a spacecraft to fetch one and you'll be the richest person in the Solar System. (Honest Bob's working on it right now!)

THE NAME GAME QUIZ

With so many asteroids zooming around up there, is it any wonder that astronomers are running out of names for them! Which two items from this list *haven't* had asteroids named after them?

1 Mr Spock, the character from the 1960s TV series – *Star Trek*.

2 A type of pudding.

3 A shipping company.

4 A pop group.

5 A well-known brand of washing powder.

ASTEROID AND CUSTARD

YUMMY!

HUH?

MADE UP

1 There IS an asteroid called Mr Spock but it was named after an astronomer's ginger cat! The cat was named after the TV character – so you can have half a point if you said TRUE.

5 I guess this idea didn't wash with astronomers.

TRUE

2 Halawe is a sweet eaten in the Lebanon. It's a tasty blend of sugar, ground sesame seeds and lemon juice. But if you sink your teeth into Halawe the asteroid by mistake, your teeth will fall out!

3 Hapag was a German shipping company.

4 Yes, it's the only place in the universe that you can still see the famous 1960s pop group The Beatles together. So let's have a big cheer for asteroids Lennon, McCartney, Harrison and Starr. Shame they can't sing.

Phew – at last we're safely through the asteroid belt. Now for the big one. It's time to hit Jupiter! Well, let's hope we don't actually *hit* the planet. That might be a teeny-weeny bit fatal...

JUPITER

LET'S GO!

GIANT JUPITER AND SHOW-OFF SATURN

If Jupiter were human, he'd be a big bullying crook and the moons would be his gang. So, let's meet the roughest, toughest gangster gang in the Solar System.

THE JUPITER GANG

BIG J → EUROPA

IO →

CALLISTO GANYMEDE

Yes, Big J's a planet-sized bully. He's so awful, the cosmic cops are after him…

THE MEMOIRS OF DETECTIVE PLANET OF THE SSPD

Yeah, I remember Big J. He was a nasty big-time crime boss over on the wrong side of the Solar System. You couldn't miss him - he had this big red spot on his face and I figure he'd been eating too many asteroids because his waist sure was bulging.

Now, Big J was a big, mean fella - I mean he had real gravity. He had a gang of four big moons. There are also loads of smaller moons, but they were small

94

fry – little more than
hangers-on. Anyhow, we got
complaints that Big J was
turning the heat on one
of his own gang members,
a moon called Io. Poor Io
was melting inside thanks
to Big J's gravity, helped out by the
rest of the gang. What a crowd of sickos!
Then the finger was pointed at Big J for
picking up asteroids by gravity and
firing them in the general direction of
Earth. Yessir – Jupiter was the meanest
critter I ever met in my years of cosmic
crime-fighting. He was always armed and
dangerous. He had a radiation gun. Hey –
don't ask me how it works, I'm just a
cop. Big J picked up radiation from the
Sun using some kind of magnetic force.
And this low-life scumbag planet blasted
all the moons around him! He even blasted
his next-door neighbour, Mr Saturn! The
best thing to do with Big J was to lock
him away and throw away the key!

GET THE MESSAGE?

Jupiter is more antisocial than a slug in a salad bar.

And now it's time for another incredible instalment of
our sci-fi space story. In their tour of the Solar System,
the aliens have reached Jupiter...

Oddblob's Alien Adventure

Jupiter is dangerous. The very idea of going there gave
both my brainy brains a hammering headache. But, for

some stupid reason, those half-witted Snotty space tourists wanted to take a closer look. Too close for safety!

BLURBI—DATA

- NAME: Jupiter
- SIZE: 140,000 km across
- SIZE COMPARED TO EARTH: 1,321 times bigger
- GRAVITY COMPARED TO EARTH: About 2.5 times stronger
- MOONS: Four big ones and loads of little ones   probably asteroids trapped by Jupiter's gravity
- LENGTH OF DAY: Nine Earth hours and 51 Earth minutes
- LENGTH OF YEAR: 11.8 Earth years
- ATMOSPHERE: Mainly hydrogen with a bit of helium. My sensors detect hydrogen crushed by the pressure of gravity into a liquid. And there's nowhere to land.
- WEATHER FORECAST: Hold on tight, Oddblob

it's going to be stormy. One storm, the Great Red Spot, has been blowing for 300 years and I forecast it'll be blowing today. Don't think that you'll be safe away from the planet. The radiation around Jupiter is strong enough to blast a Blurb.

◉TRAVEL TIPS: Avoid this planet!

THAT'S WHY WE CAN'T GO THERE

And with that I pointed out the things we could see from a safe distance.

ARE YOU **SURE** THIS IS A SAFE DISTANCE, ODDBLOB?

• Bulging middle – Jupiter spins so fast that it bulges a bit in the middle.

• Dark bands of clouds caused by areas of cooler gas that sink towards the planet.

SINK! SPIN! WHIRL! BULGE!

• Great Red Spot – The winds in this stormy area are strong enough to flatten a skyscraper. Sometimes the spot turns grey – maybe Jupiter uses anti-spot cream, snirk, snirk.

Hmm – bulging middle, big red spot. Jupiter reminded me of Slobslime, except she had a big green spot. By now, the Snotties had lost interest in Jupiter and were eyeing up Europa with all three of their eyes.

We decided to land on Europa for a spot of space skating. Snotties are fond of this sport because they can glide along without much effort…

At this very moment, an asteroid crashed into Europa and made a hole in the ice. And, of course, Slobslime fell in!

The ice is many kilometres thick, but beneath it there is an ocean up to 100 km deep. After Slobslime fell in, the ice quickly froze above her in the cold of space. There was only one thing we could do … and that was nothing!

In the end I had to rescue Slobslime to shut Sloppy up. So I fired the spacecraft's engine to melt the ice and grabbed Slobslime from the water.

The icy cold instantly froze Slobslime into a block of ice. And while she was melting I decided we'd all had enough of Europa.

IMPORTANT SCIENTIFIC NOTE

Like the ocean on Ceres, Europa's ocean might be home to life. There could be alien microbes or giant worms (similar to creatures that lurk in Earth's deep oceans). But Oddblob didn't even look for them... What a shame!

AMAZING MOONS

Even without the worms, Jupiter's moons are awfully odd. So here's a really odd thought to amuse you. What would Jupiter moons *taste* like? Welcome to the Solar System's first cosmic cook book!

The Cosmic Cook Book

Hi to all you intergalactic gourmets! If you're feeling hungry, why not treat yourself to these tasty recipes … they're cooked just the way old Jupiter likes 'em!

Io pizza

Ingredients:
Several million tonnes of rock
Sulphur (according to taste)
Hydrogen

1 Mix the ingredients and place close to (about 421,600 km away from) a pre-heated Jupiter with its gravity and radiation going full blast.
2 Leave for 4.6 billion years, while Jupiter cooks the mixture until the rocks melt.

WARNING ~ The mixture will get very hot (up to 500°C in places) and its insides will bubble up to the surface. They'll stink of rotting eggs but it's all part of the flavour!

Europa slushy-melt

Ingredients:
Several million tonnes of rock
Enough water to fill all of Earth's oceans
Alien microbe slime and giant worms
(if you like that sort of thing)

1 Form the rock into a ball and pour on the water.
2 Freeze until the outside is frozen solid but the inside is still runny.

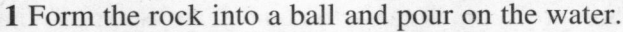

For a more crunchy mixture, try the Callisto method. You freeze the ice a little more and crack it a bit. Or you can simply mix the rock and ice into a ball (the Ganymede method).
It really is that simple. Enjoy your moons and *bon appetit*!

BURP!

Oh, so you didn't fancy munching one of Jupiter's moons? I guess it's time to make our escape from Jupiter and shoot off to Saturn. And by some curious coincidence, the next episode of our space story is set there...

Oddblob's Alien Adventure

Slobslime thawed out of her ice block in time to see Saturn. Of course, the brainless alien was confused by the rings.

WOW — THAT'S AN EARTHLING IN A HAT!

With a big sigh, I asked Cosmo for the low-down on Saturn. With an equally big sigh, Cosmo replied...

BLURBI-DATA

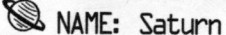

🪐 NAME: Saturn

🪐 SIZE: 120,500 km across

🪐 SIZE COMPARED TO EARTH: 764 times bigger

🪐GRAVITY COMPARED TO EARTH: Only 1.16 times as much. That's because Saturn is mostly made up of light gas with weak gravity. The whole planet is light enough to float on water!

🪐MOONS: I had a dreadful job trying to count them. There are about 22 above 20 km in size, but there could be more that my sensors missed. The big one (5,150 km across) is called Titan

🪐LENGTH OF DAY: 10 Earth hours and 38 Earth minutes

🪐LENGTH OF YEAR: 29.5 Earth years

🪐ATMOSPHERE: Hydrogen and helium, like Jupiter

🪐WEATHER FORECAST: EXTREME WEATHER WARNING! The winds reach 1,800 km an hour. There's no solid surface to land on and there's a danger of being seasick or airsick or both. Probably at the same time.

🪐TRAVEL TIPS: Take a giant windbreak and a large supply of sick bags.

We got a great view of Saturn's rings and I told the Snotties about how there were thousands of rings and how each one is made of shiny bits of ice and rock. They may have come from a crashed comet. Moons move between the rings and their gravity holds the rings together...

BITS OF ROCK AND ICE VARY IN SIZE!

Then I realized that the Snotties weren't listening.

I decided to wake up those snoring Snotties…

We Blurbs love blurbi-kite-flying. Unfortunately, the winds of Saturn proved just a bit too strong…

Lucky old Oddblob! Don't you wish you could see Saturn's rings close up? Of course, you can see the real thing if you happen to be looking through a really good telescope. But if you don't have a really good telescope, here's the next best thing:

Dare you discover ... Saturn's rings?

You will need:

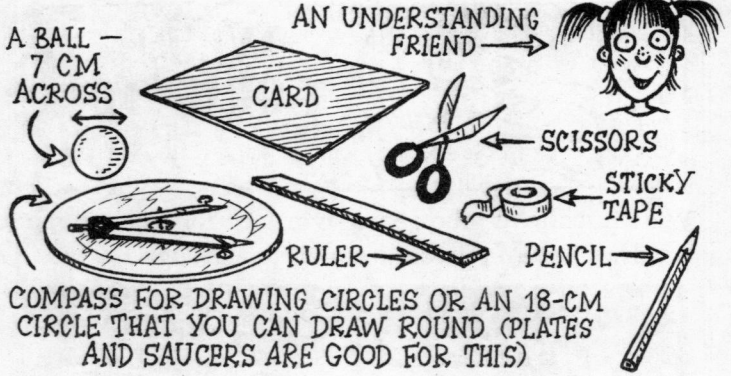

A BALL — 7 CM ACROSS

CARD

AN UNDERSTANDING FRIEND →

← SCISSORS

STICKY TAPE

RULER →

PENCIL →

COMPASS FOR DRAWING CIRCLES OR AN 18-CM CIRCLE THAT YOU CAN DRAW ROUND (PLATES AND SAUCERS ARE GOOD FOR THIS)

What you do:

1 Using the compass, or an object to draw round, draw a circle on the card 18 cm across. The circle should be 11 cm wider than the ball. Cut the circle out.

2 Cut out the inside of the card circle to make a card ring.

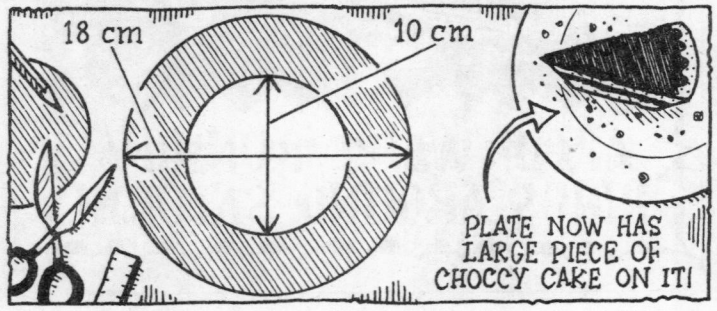

18 cm   10 cm

PLATE NOW HAS LARGE PIECE OF CHOCCY CAKE ON IT!

3 Stick your card ring to the ball with sticky tape.

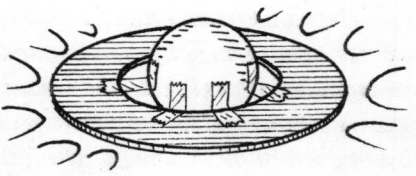

4 Well done, you've just made Saturn! Ask your friend to hold it in their hand and stand 15 metres away from you. They should start by holding the planet level and then at an angle.

You should notice:

When the rings are held level you can't see them. They're too thin and far away. The real Saturn's the same. Saturn spins at an angle, and every 15 years the rings cannot be seen from Earth. In fact, we're looking at Saturn sideways on.

But they appear when seen from any other angle...

THAT MOON'S THE LIMIT

But let's drag our eyeballs away from the rings. I've got some BIG news! Honest Bob's just sold me a ticket to the biggest night out in the Solar System. It's the Saturn's Odd Moons Awards. They're like the Hollywood Oscars in space!

All the stars are out in force for this glittering galactic event! And the awards for the oddest moon prizes for Saturn are as follows...

THE CRAZIEST MOON couple award goes to ... **Janus** and **Epimetheus**. Hey, what's up with these guys? Every four years they swap orbits. Are they getting bored or something?

THE UGLIEST MOON award goes to ... **Tethys**. This moon has a crack running halfway around it. Anyone know a planet plastic surgeon?

THE MOST TASTY-LOOKING MOON award goes to ... **Hyperion**. It's shaped like a giant hamburger. Fast food anyone?

THE BEST-DRESSED MOON award goes to ... **Iapetus**. This moon is wearing a lovely stripy black and white zebra-style outfit. Very trendy – give us a twirl!

And now for the one we've all been waiting for! The award for THE MADDEST MOON ON SATURN...

And the winner is ... TITAN with its hazy orange nitrogen atmosphere, ice mountains, methane seas and volcanoes blasting water and ammonia (a substance found in rotten wee). It even rains methane. No other moon has anything like this. You can find methane in cow farts but Titan must be the ultimate loony moo-moon!

> I'D LIKE TO THANK EVERYONE WHO'S HELPED ME IN THE LAST FOUR BILLION YEARS, ESPECIALLY SATURN. JUST BECAUSE I'M -180°C SOME PEOPLE THINK I'M A BIT COLD. BUT I'M REAL FRIENDLY AND OFFER A WARM WELCOME, JUST SO LONG AS YOU DON'T MIND FREEZING TO DEATH.

And I do hope you don't mind a bit of freezing. You see, the remaining planets on our tour of the Solar System are chilly and cold with a c-c-capital C! D-dare you take a look?

YOU CAN BORROW ONE OF MY BLURBI BOBBLE-HATS!

ODDBALL OUTER PLANETS

The wonderful thing about the Solar System is that you can be really weird and wacky and way out and no one seems to mind. And they don't come weirder, wackier or further-out that those kooky, chilly planets – Uranus, Neptune and the puny dwarf planets beyond…

Take Uranus, for example. This planet is seriously way out. It's way out from the Sun by about 2,871 million km. And it's so weird and way out that instead of spinning, it tumbles head over heels through space like an out-of-control acrobat. I bet even Honest Bob would find Uranus a hard planet to sell…

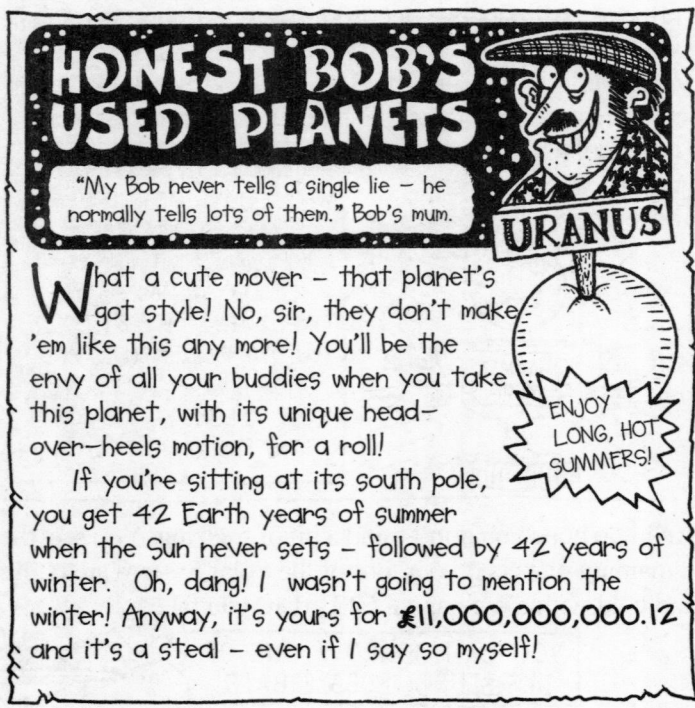

HONEST BOB'S USED PLANETS

"My Bob never tells a single lie – he normally tells lots of them." Bob's mum.

URANUS

What a cute mover – that planet's got style! No, sir, they don't make 'em like this any more! You'll be the envy of all your buddies when you take this planet, with its unique head-over-heels motion, for a roll!

ENJOY LONG, HOT SUMMERS!

If you're sitting at its south pole, you get 42 Earth years of summer when the Sun never sets – followed by 42 years of winter. Oh, dang! I wasn't going to mention the winter! Anyway, it's yours for £11,000,000,000.12 and it's a steal – even if I say so myself!

Hmm, Uranus sounds kinda fun! Let's get back to our sci-fi space story as the aliens whizz towards the planet… What will Oddblob make of oddball Uranus?

Oddblob's Alien Adventure

We were nearing the end of our tour of the Solar System and I wasn't going to be sad to see the Snotties go. I wondered how I'd ever clean that sticky green slime out of my spacecraft!

The next planet we were going to visit was Uranus, but it was just going to be a fly-by. Cosmo had the details – and landing was a bad idea…

BLURBI-DATA

⊜ NAME: Uranus

⊜ SIZE: 52,000 km across

⊜ SIZE COMPARED TO EARTH: 6.3 times larger

⊜ GRAVITY COMPARED TO EARTH: A bit less

⊜ MOONS: Five main moons and at least 1.5 smaller ones

⊜ LENGTH OF DAY: 1.7 Earth hours and 1.2 Earth minutes

⊜ LENGTH OF YEAR: 84 Earth years

⊜ ATMOSPHERE: Hydrogen and a bit of helium. Methane in the upper clouds gives the planet a greenish look.

⊜ WEATHER FORECAST: It's going to be a bit blowy. But the winds are only 300 km per hour. It's a gentle breeze compared to Saturn.

⊜ TRAVEL TIPS: There's nowhere solid to land. So let's not try.

To be honest, I didn't like Uranus. Its colour reminded me of a spacesick Snotty. The moons looked as boring as an unwanted Blurbi-mas present. I showed the Snotties the best bits – and it didn't take long…

• Uranus has rings like Saturn. But they're only 1.6 km thick and made of black rocks, so they're hard to spot.

• One of the moons – Miranda – has grooves that look like racetracks. That's groovy – snirk, snirk. One of these is called the chevron! Miranda was probably smashed apart by an asteroid and pulled itself back together by gravity.

HOW TO FIND A PLANET IN ABOUT 23 EASY STAGES

Now, here's a quick question to bamboozle your brain. How many astronomers does it take to discover a planet?

Well, in the case of Neptune, the answer is "quite a few"… But that's not too surprising because, from Earth, Neptune looks like just another star. It's as hard to spot as a needle in a … pin factory.

After a long search, Neptune was eventually tracked down by young scientists, John Couch Adams (1819–1892) and Urbain Le Verrier (1811–1877). We've put them in two rooms, so they can tell their stories separately. These stories begin in 1841, when no one knew that Neptune existed…

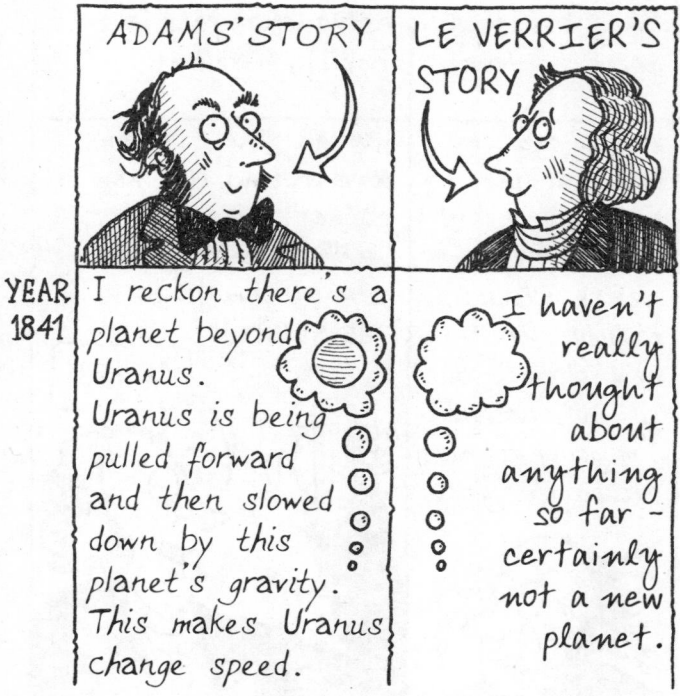

ADAMS' STORY

LE VERRIER'S STORY

YEAR 1841

I reckon there's a planet beyond Uranus. Uranus is being pulled forward and then slowed down by this planet's gravity. This makes Uranus change speed.

I haven't really thought about anything so far – certainly not a new planet.

	ADAMS' STORY	LE VERRIER'S STORY
1845	I've worked out where the new planet is! I'll ask astronomer, George Airy, to find it for me.	I reckon there's a planet beyond Uranus and I know where it is. I've written about it in a scientific journal. I'll ask top astronomers in Paris to find it for me.
1846	Grr — he's not looking! I've called round to see Airy three times but he's never at home.	Grrr — they're not looking for the planet either so I'm sending my ideas to some astronomer pals in Berlin, Germany.
LATER IN 1846	Airy's read my ideas at last and he's asked ace astronomer James Challis to look for the new planet. But so far, nothing. I'm going to miss out on the glory! 	Hurrah! The Germans have found the new planet. It's just where I said it was. I'M GOING TO GET THE GLORY!!!  CHEERS!

So who actually discovered Neptune? Was it…?

a) Adams. He was the first person to suggest where the planet was.

b) Le Verrier. He made sure the planet was spotted. And in science the credit for a discovery goes to the first person to write about it in a scientific journal – which was Le Verrier.

or **c)** German astronomers Johann Galle and Heinrich d'Arrest. They were the first to find Neptune.

Well, Luke?

Most astronomers would say Adams *and* Le Verrier. But some people would say the answer's **d)** Galileo! The incredible Italian spotted Neptune through his telescope long before anyone else, but he thought it was a star rather than a planet.

Anyway, you'll be pleased to know that when Adams and Le Verrier actually met they became friends, despite not speaking each other's language. (Hmm – Le Verrier was said to have been the rudest man in France, so it may have helped that Adams didn't know what he was saying…)

*WE'VE TRANSLATED HIS FRENCH INTO ENGLISH

113

Now, you might think that discovering Neptune sounded a tricky business. But the details of the discovery were even more mixed-up than I've made out so far. It's almost as if Neptune *didn't want to be found*!

YEAH — LEAVE ME ALONE!

Before Adams, lots of people thought there was a planet beyond Uranus, but none of them found time to look for it.

COULDN'T BE BOTHERED, MORE LIKE!

James Challis did see Neptune but he thought it was a star. On the evening that he would have got his best view of the planet, he was drinking tea with a friend.

HA, HA! YOU MISSED YOUR CHANCE, MATE!

The boss of the Berlin Observatory, Johann Encke (1791–1865), also missed out on seeing the planet because he was at a party.

"SPACED OUT" ON CHAMPAGNE, I EXPECT!

And now back to our space story. Will the aliens have trouble finding Neptune?

Oddblob's Alien Adventure

With the aid of Cosmo's hyper-speed multi-dimensional navigation systems, I had no difficulties in finding Neptune. The planet looked like Uranus. In fact, it looked enough like Uranus to fool the Snotties…

I pointed out that Neptune's methane clouds are easier to see. Pah! – any alien can spot the difference! I asked Cosmo for the facts. And I made sure the Snotties paid attention.

BLURBI-DATA

- NAME: Neptune
- SIZE: 48,000 km across
- SIZE COMPARED TO EARTH: 58 times larger
- GRAVITY COMPARED TO EARTH: A bit stronger than Earth - and Uranus
- MOONS: Eight, but at 2,705 km across, Triton is the only large one

🌑 LENGTH OF DAY: 16 Earth hours and 6 Earth minutes

🌑 LENGTH OF YEAR: 165 Earth years

🌑 ATMOSPHERE: Mostly hydrogen, some helium and a smidgen of methane

🌑 WEATHER FORECAST: EXTRA EXTREME WEATHER WARNING! It's going to be more stormy than Saturn! Expect winds of 2,000 km an hour - so put that kite away, Oddblob! There'll be methane-snow high in the atmosphere, but it'll melt before it lands.

🌑 TRAVEL TIPS: If you dare go near Neptune, Oddblob, I'll erase all your computer games!

Once more we hovered at a safe distance while I pointed out the tourist attractions...

• Neptune has four rings (they're dark and hard to see).

• There's a storm the size of Earth called the Great Dark Spot that travels round the planet backwards.

• There's a cloud called the Scooter that blows around the planet faster than the Spot.

CRASH! BOOM! SCREAM!

...TODAY'S WEATHER FORECAST — CLOUDY, STORMY WEATHER WILL BRING SCATTERED SHOWERS FOLLOWED BY ... CERTAIN DEATH!

• Triton is the only moon in the Solar System that orbits in the opposite direction to its planet's spin. The pink south pole is made of frozen nitrogen and the rest of the moon is covered in ice.

When the Snotties heard about Triton's ice, they wanted to go there. They enjoyed skating on Europa so much that they wanted to skate on Triton. But Cosmo warned us that Triton is –235°C. It's the coldest place in the Solar System and it could be too cold to visit safely. But did the Snotties listen?

As it happened, the Snotties had great fun skating on the frozen moon. And, for once, there were no problems… Until it was time to leave…

A few hours later…

But just then…

As luck would have it, the spacecraft was parked on a nitrogen geyser. This is a hole where liquid nitrogen blasts from the ground. It's like a hot-water geyser on Earth. The blasting nitrogen turned to gas – it was enough to throw us into space and get our engines going.

And so we set off to the dwarf planet Pluto…

The first thing to say about Pluto is that it's *really* far away – on average, 5,193 MILLION km. No wonder the US astronomer who found it, Clyde Tombaugh (1906–1997), had to check 45 million stars over 13 years to see which one moved like a planet. I bet he got a stiff neck.

SPOT THE DISCOVERER OF PLUTO

AN INTERESTING IDEA FOR YOUNGER READERS

Mind you, there's one thing harder than finding a new dwarf planet – and that's thinking up a name for it! Imagine you had to think up names for places near you. Perhaps you'd name them after your friends...

You could name a putrid-smelling pond after your brother or sister. And you could name a dismal dump after your teacher (or is that a rubbish idea?).

But someone's sure to challenge your choice of names...

Things were much the same with the dwarf planet Clyde Tombaugh found...

At that time everyone thought it was a full-sized planet and everyone had an idea what to call it. Remember Percival Lowell from page 84? Well, his wife wanted the new discovery to be named Lowell after him (it's better than Planet Percy). Then she decided it ought be called Constance after herself.

Astronomers hated Constance's idea. The other planets had been named after ancient Roman gods like Mars and Jupiter.

LIKE THE NEW PLANET, I'M BEAUTIFUL AND MYSTERIOUS...

IT'S A PITY SHE'S NOT 5,900 MILLION KM AWAY!

← ANGRY ASTRONOMERS

Things were just turning nasty when someone in England came up with a better name. Incredibly that someone was just 11 years old. She was a girl named Venetia Burney.

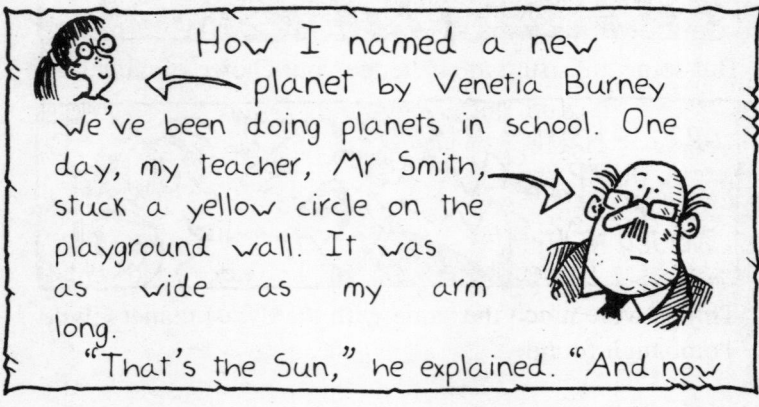

How I named a new planet by Venetia Burney

We've been doing planets in school. One day, my teacher, Mr Smith, stuck a yellow circle on the playground wall. It was as wide as my arm long.

"That's the Sun," he explained. "And now

we're going for a walk to find out how far away the planets are."

Mr Smith led us across the playground. He was counting out the paces. He walked so fast, his shoes started squeaking. When he reached 30, he bent down and laid a teeny little seed on the ground.

"That's Mercury," he announced, puffing a bit. "Cor - isn't it little?" we said, squinting at the tiny seed.

And that's how I learned that the planets are really small compared to the Sun. And they're a long way apart. The Earth turned out to be a squishy pea on the pavement outside the school. We looked back at the Sun and it looked quite small now. Then my friend Amy trod on the pea by mistake.

"You've just squashed the world!" I said. "Aarggh - a giant foot's just landed on top of us and splatted us flat!"

We headed all the way down the street and across the park until we reached Saturn. There seemed no end to the Solar System. Mr Smith was puffing like a train and his shoes sounded like a couple of noisy mice having a fight. His face was the colour of a sweaty tomato and he was mopping his forehead with a spotted handkerchief.

"1,019 paces!" gasped Mr Smith. "And this golf ball's Saturn."

We couldn't even see our Sun circle but Mr Smith said that, from the real Saturn, the Sun would just look like a bright star.

"I bet it's cold on Saturn," said Amy with a shiver.

Our teacher was examining his watch. "We'll have to leave it there - Uranus is twice as far from the Sun as Saturn. And Neptune is three times further."

I was glad Mr Smith didn't make walk to Neptune.

PHEW!

In the afternoon, Mr Smith taught us about the ancient Roman gods. And that's how I knew that the planets were named after gods, but I noticed that some gods didn't have their own planets.

where's my planet?

JUPITER   VENUS   MERCURY   PLUTO

I first heard about the new planet a few weeks later. Mum, Dad, Grandpa and me were having breakfast. As usual, Grandpa was reading the newspaper aloud and, as usual, the news was boring. I was munching my toast loudly so that I wouldn't have to listen. Dad gave me an annoyed look.

"Don't eat so loudly, Venetia," he said.

But just then, Grandpa read something about a new planet and my ears pricked up.

"It's a wonderful discovery," Grandpa was saying. "But astronomers don't know what to call it. The new planet is a very long way from the Sun..."

And that's when I had my great idea.

"I think Pluto would be a good name for it!" I said.

"Don't speak with your mouth full!" said Mum sharply.

I knew Pluto was the Roman god of the underworld and I thought the underworld must be cold and dark like the planet.

But Grandpa was looking at me with interest.

"Well, bless me!" he exclaimed, laying his newspaper on the table. "What a good name for the planet! I must make a note of it. I'll call on my old friend

Mr Turner at the University Observatory and see what he thinks of it."

Mr Turner liked the name so much he sent a special telegram to Mr Tombaugh, the astronomer who found the planet. And all Mr Tombaugh's astronomer friends liked the name so much they decided to use it.

Thinking up planet names is easy! I can't wait for the next planet to be discovered. But there's NO WAY I want to walk there!

Mr Tombaugh

Bet you never knew!
If Venetia's teacher had made the children walk to Pluto, they'd have found a pinhead over 3.7 km from the school. No wonder the real Pluto was so hard to track down! But it was harder because Pluto's orbit is so awesomely odd. It's a stretched-out ellipse that takes Pluto up to 7,390 million km from the Sun.

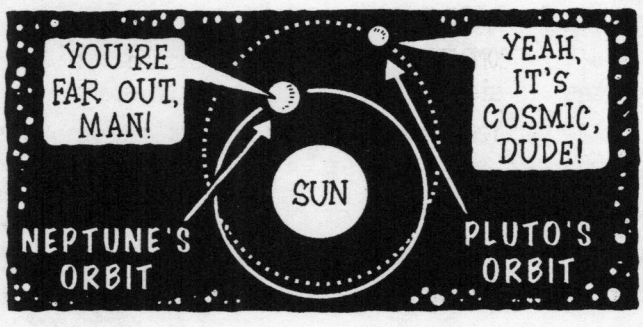

YOU'RE FAR OUT, MAN!

YEAH, IT'S COSMIC, DUDE!

SUN

NEPTUNE'S ORBIT

PLUTO'S ORBIT

Meanwhile, out in space, the huge distances are really getting to the Snotties...

Oddblob's Alien Adventure

We spent half the day travelling to Pluto. And, after five minutes, the Snotties were showing signs of boredom.

IT'S BOR-WING!

When, at last, Pluto came in sight, the Snotties weren't impressed.

IS DAT IT?

YOU'VE BROUGHT US SIX THOUSAND MILLION KM TO SEE THAT?

I asked Cosmo for details. The Snotties were right ... Pluto was pathetic!

BLURBI-DATA

- ○ NAME: Pluto
- ○ SIZE: 2,300 km across
- ○ SIZE COMPARED TO EARTH: You could fit 160 Plutos inside the Earth with room to spare
- ○ GRAVITY COMPARED TO EARTH: Next to nothing
- ○ MOONS: Three. The largest, Charon, takes one Pluto day to go around the planet. If you're on Pluto, the moon is always in the same place in the sky.

- ☉ LENGTH OF DAY: Six Earth days and ten Earth hours
- ☉ LENGTH OF YEAR: 248 Earth years
- ☉ ATMOSPHERE: A bit of methane and nitrogen
- ☉ WEATHER FORECAST: It's going to be VERY COLD for ever! In fact, when the planet is furthest from the Sun, the whole atmosphere freezes and falls to the ground. It's worse than a cold shower on Triton!
- ☉ TRAVEL TIPS: Take a spacesuit and plenty of hot drinks.

Pluto had peace and quiet and no danger of sunburn. It was my kind of place. But as we whizzed over the reddish frozen surface I could see that snot-brained snottie's eight hearts weren't set on landing...

Well, if you don't fancy skating on Pluto here's a dance that scientists perform to explain why Pluto and Charon always face each other...

Dare you discover ... the Pluto spin?

What you need:

Two people, ideally an adult parent or teacher, and you! (The adult is going to be Pluto and you are going to be Charon.)

Some groovy music

What you do:

1 Pluto should put both their hands round Charon's hands and hold tight.

2 Put the music on...

3 Start swinging round and round...

Hold your partner by the hands
And start swinging round and round!
ROUND AND ROUND AND ROUND YOU GO
'Cos you're spinning like old Pluto!

You should notice:

Wheee! This is FUN! Charon's swinging around in a bigger circle than Pluto. Pluto's gravity is strong enough to swing Charon in a bigger circle and hold it in position.

The snotties have had enough but there's plenty more to see. In fact Pluto is just one of thousands of frozen-rocky thingies in the Kuiper-Edgeworth belt including the dwarf planet Eris. And here's what they missed. Eris is 2,500 km across, has one moon and takes 557 years to orbit the Sun – so baby Sloppy would have to wait forever for her birthday slimy-cake.

Other similar-sized mini-planets beyond Neptune include Orcus, Sedna and Quaoar (Kwah-o-ar) – all found in the early 2000s. Quaoar was a god of the Tongva tribe who used to live in the Los Angeles area of the USA. That's funny – I thought it was the sound you make when a dentist tells you to "open wide".

Well, that's all for now, folks! As far as the Solar System is concerned, you've had your lot. It was great while it lasted but there's not a lot more to see unless you count the Oort Cloud. Scientists think this is an area of giant balls of ice and rocks that could stretch two light years from the Sun. Once again they're massively more spaced-out than the crazy cartoon shows!

CRUEL COMETS

The Oort cloud sounds fantastically faraway but those snowballs can come a bit closer to home. When this happens we call them "comets". Here's what happens...

1 A distant star gives a comet a nudge with its gravity.

2 The nudge sends the comet whizzing in the direction of the Sun.

3 As the comet nears the Sun, it starts to melt and the solar wind blows a tail millions of kilometres long behind it. As the comet flies away from the Sun, the tail streams in front of it.

Every year Earth whizzes through clouds of melted comet dust and rock. Then, we see free light shows called meteor showers as the dust and rock burns up in our atmosphere. The meteors make tiny whizzy flashes of light high in the night sky. And it's really exciting counting them and trying to guess where the next one will appear. Here are the best times to see them…

You can see the meteors anywhere in the sky and especially in the eastern half.

Of course, these bits of comet are too small to harm Earth. For that we'd need to be smashed by something really big. Something like an asteroid ... but there's not much danger of that! Er – hold on – let's check the sci-fi story. What's happening on Oddblob's spacecraft...?

Oddblob's Alien Adventure

BLURBI-MESSAGE

A HUGE ASTEROID IS HEADING FOR EARTH. THIS COULD BE THE END OF LIFE AS WE KNOW IT!

OH THAT SOUNDS INTERESTING...

OOPS – I spoke too soon! You'd better turn the page now ... otherwise you'll miss the end of the world!

CAN WE GO AND WATCH, MUM?

THE END-OF-THE-WORLD MOVIE SHOW

There's nothing movie makers like more than a nice Earth-shattering disaster. Something with a budget of billions and big bangs and stunning special effects. But what's the true picture? Are we really going to be destroyed from space? And, oh yes, what's going to happen in our sci-fi space story?

Well, you'll be delighted to know that the answers to all these questions are in this chapter ... so read on!

The first thing to say is that most movies about the Earth being wiped out from space are rubbish. The science is WRONG with a capital W – they just couldn't happen in real life.

SPOT THE SILLY SCIENCE SCREEN QUIZ

Here's a selection of movies from Honest Bob's Used DVD store.

1 Which five really could happen and which three sound like silly science and couldn't ever happen in a Pluto year of Sundays?
2 Which of these five movies could come true some time in the next hundred years?

a) THE PLANETS OF DOOM

Heave in HORROR as the planets line up and their gravity causes earthquakes and storms on Earth! The end of the world is due at 8.08 pm on 5 May 2000 – so you'd better hide under your bed!

b) INVASION OF THE SLIMY ALIENS

THEY CAME FROM ANOTHER WORLD TO STEAL OUR PIZZAS AND TURN US INTO JELLY BABIES!

c) THE GOBBLING GALAXY

ARGH!

HELP!

YIKES!

EEK!

Gasp in horror as a giant galaxy gobbles our Milky Way and Earth is hurled into a black hole! It's a hole lot of horror!

THE SPLATTERING STAR d)

WE'RE GONNA DIE LAUGHING!!!

IT'S A QUIET DAY ON EARTH... Suddenly a star blows up and blasts Earth with radiation that turns our atmosphere into laughing gas!

e) THE SIZZLING SUN

Experience the ultimate suntan as you see the Sun turn into a red fireball and melt Mercury and vaporize Venus and eat up the Earth. This movie's really red-hot!

f) "THE" "SMASHING" "METEOR" "SHOWER"

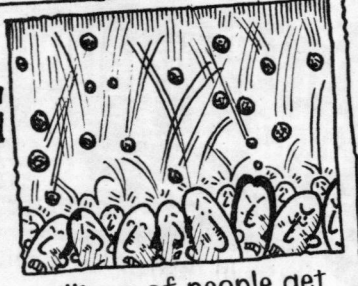

Tremble in terror as millions of people get hit on the head by stunning space rocks!

g) THE CRUSHING COMET CRASH

Shudder and shriek as a huge comet crashes into Earth and blasts billions of people to bits.

h) ASTEROID ATTACK

Shout with shock as the Earth is smashed by a giant space rock and all life is wiped out!

OOER!

Answers:

1 Scientifically possible movies – c), d), e), g) and h).

Impossible movies – a), b), f).

2 The movie that might happen in real life in the next hundred years is h).

Now, I bet you want to know why some of the movies are possible and why some of them are as likely as a vegetarian vampire bat... Well, with Luke's help, I've got the answers. Let's start with the movies that just couldn't happen.

THREE WAYS THE EARTH WON'T GET WIPED OUT...
1 The planets lining up
In 2000, the planets appeared close together as seen from Earth. Some people were afraid their gravity would pull on the Earth and cause disaster. So, what happened? Not a lot. The effect on us was weaker than the gravity of the Sun and the Moon.

2 Alien invasion
As Luke was quick to remind me, there's no proof that aliens exist. But if they do, how would they get to travel hundreds of light years through space? And if they could, why would they bother to invade us? If they're that smart, they could make everything they want for themselves using chemicals in space.

AND REMEMBER...
IF ALIENS DO
EXIST, THEY'D
SEE YOU AS AN
ALIEN, TOO!

ERK! A
HIDEOUS
ALIEN!

3 Meteor showers

You may be stunned to read that 20,000 tonnes of space rocks fall on Earth every year – they're mostly lumps of smashed-up asteroids. As they whizz though the air, they're called meteors and if they land they're called meteorites. But don't worry – nearly all meteors burn up before they hit the ground. The only creature ever killed by one was a dog in Egypt in 1911.

FOUR WAYS THE EARTH COULD BE WIPED OUT (BUT NOT FOR MILLIONS OF YEARS)

1 Eaten up by a black hole

In this movie, the Milky Way gets eaten by another galaxy, something that really is possible! Galaxies called (and I love this name!) cannibal galaxies actually pull other galaxies in using gravity and swallow them up. In fact, our Milky Way is a cannibal galaxy because it's currently gobbling up a little galaxy called the Sagittarius Dwarf!

As for our chances of being gobbled, there's a big galaxy called the Andromeda galaxy heading our way at 643,600 km per hour. We'll probably join it to make a bigger galaxy. Many galaxies (including the Milky Way) have black holes in their centres and when the big scrunch happens, some stars could be knocked into the black hole of either galaxy. Panicking yet? Well, DON'T... Andromeda's not due to arrive for THREE BILLION years. So there's plenty of time to finish this book and find somewhere to hide!

2 Splattered by a giant star

If a giant star blew up close to us it would be curtains. Radiation from the blast really could turn our air to nitrous oxide or laughing gas. Sounds fun, doesn't it? Trouble is, the radiation would cook us alive and boil the oceans. But don't go racing off in any rockets just yet. There are no stars near to us that are set to blow – so we're safe for hundreds of millions of years.

3 Sizzled by the Sun

The Sun's too small to blow like a giant star, but it's going to get bigger until it cooks Earth. Here's the sizzling story...

As the Sun uses up all its hydrogen gas fuel, the Sun's centre (or core) shrinks.

What's left of the Sun's core squashes together and heats up.

This makes the outer parts of the Sun swell like a balloon.

As the Sun grows, it cools from white-hot to red-hot. But it's still hot enough to bake us like a burned burger. The outer part of the Sun is lost into space and the core shrinks to a small glowing burned-out star called a white dwarf. Panicking yet? Don't – the big blow-out isn't due for another five billion years.

4 Crushed by a comet

Comets are stony snowballs – so living on Earth is a bit like dodging a gang of snowball-chucking bullies. Except that some of the snowballs are more than 5 km across… But most comets miss us by millions of kilometres and we only get hit by a comet every half a billion years or so.

That still leaves one movie that might just possibly come true…

ASTEROID ATTACK!

Earth gets whacked by an asteroid big enough to wipe out humans every hundred million years – so that's not too often. But scientists reckon Earth's been bashed by three million asteroids of all sizes in its life. There are hits big enough to crush cities every hundred years or so. Luckily, they've missed our cities…

Luke Upwards is so impressed with the science in the *Asteroid Attack!* movie that's he's bought it from Honest Bob.

Oh well, Luke, at least you can read our space story. Just to remind you, the asteroid is heading for Earth. It's moving at twice the speed of a bullet. And it means business...

Oddblob's Alien Adventure

We tuned into an Earthling TV station to find out what the humans were doing...

AN ASTEROID IS HEADING FOR EARTH!

AT 10 KM WIDE, IT'S BIG ENOUGH TO END LIFE ON EARTH AS WE KNOW IT!

10 KM

IT LOOKS LIKE THE ASTEROID WILL HIT US WITH THE FORCE OF ALL THE WORLD'S BOMBS. DON'T PANIC! IT'S NOT THE END OF THE WORLD. WELL, YES IT IS...

IT'LL LOOK LIKE THIS

AND NOW FOR THE WEATHER FORECAST...

HOT

FOR 1,000 KM ROUND THE BLAST ZONE IT'LL BE VERY HOT. IN FACT IT'LL BE SO HOT THAT HAIR WILL CATCH FIRE AND EYEBALLS WILL MELT... YIKES — I'M OUTTA HERE!

I figured it would be fun to watch the blast from a distance. But the Snotties didn't like my idea.

For some reason, they thought we had to stop the asteroid. I was just about to blast it with my blurbi-laser when Cosmo stopped me...

BLURBI-DATA

ODDBLOB, LEAVE THAT BUTTON ALONE! You'll blow the asteroid to bits but the flying bits of rock will hit Earth and do even more damage. Here are some Earthling scientists' ideas we could try...

1 Set off a bomb NEAR the asteroid to knock it off course.

2 Put a rocket on the asteroid and knock it to one side.

3 Whack it with a giant air-filled pillow (this idea was suggested by a scientist in 2002).

We didn't have bombs or rockets or giant pillows. So I thought we could sit back and enjoy the show. But Slobslime had other ideas...

For the first time in 1,000 Earth years, Slobslime had had an idea. And what's more – it actually worked!

HURRAH – THE ALIENS HAVE SAVED EARTH!
They really are space stars! I wonder what will happen when they get home?

Oddblob's Alien Adventure

I returned to a hero's welcome on Planet Blurb. Unfortunately, the Snotties seemed to be bigger heroes than me.

We were invited to a grand party ... but at least I didn't make a fool of myself!

THE END

EPILOGUE: THE SKY'S THE LIMIT

And so we return to our own blue shiny Earth. OK, so I know it's a bit wet – but as far as the Solar System goes, there really is no place like home. After all, it's the only planet we humans can live on... And now you've seen what the others have to offer, maybe it's the only planet you'd *want* to live on!

Younger readers may think that space reminds them of their worst teacher. It's big and dangerous and it goes on and on for ever. But space is also beautiful and brain boggling. And, best of all, there's much, much more to find out. This book started with a movie and it ended with a story. But the *real-life* adventure of space is just beginning. In the future, there are sure to be millions of...

- New planets to explore.
- New stars to study.
- And perhaps even new friends to meet...?

SPACE, STARS
AND SLIMY ALIENS
QUIZ

Now find out if you're a
Space, Stars and Slimy Aliens expert!

WOW – THAT'S STAGGERING!

So, you've glided through galaxies and bumped into black holes, but how much have you learned about the magnificent mysteries of the universe? Take these tests and find out if you're a galactic genius or a simple snottie-brain.

Understanding the universe

You've taken a whistle-stop tour of the universe – studied the stars, peeked at the planets, avoided asteroids and come into contact with comets – so now let's see how much you remember.

1 In which galaxy will you find the Sun?
a) The Milky Way
b) Andromeda
c) Splott

2 Why are black holes called black holes?
a) They were named after the person who discovered them – Billy-Bob Black.
b) They are dark holes in space.
c) No light can escape them, so they always look black.

3 What is a red dwarf?
a) A small, cool, middle-aged star.
b) A small person who's been in the Sun too long.
c) A small planet on the edge of the Solar System.

4 What form do galaxies take?
a) Triangle
b) Spiral
c) Circle

5 What unit of measurement do astronomers use for distances in space?
a) Earth diameters
b) Light years
c) Mercury miles

6 What is the name of the group of galaxies to which we belong?
a) The Milky Way Group
b) The Terrestrial Group
c) The Local Group

7 What is the name given to the moment the universe was formed?
a) The Big Bang
b) The Catastrophic Crunch
c) The Enormous Explosion

8 What is the Oort Cloud?
a) A region of space inhabited by aliens.
b) A region of space completely made up of black holes.
c) A region of space filled with large lumps of rock and ice.

Answers:
1a; 2c; 3a; 4b; 5b; 6c; 7a; 8c

Strange space words

From black holes to binary stars and comets to chromospheres, scientists have a medley of mysterious words to describe all the things in the universe. See if you can match the definitions to the correct space name.

1 Brown dwarf
2 Corona
3 Magnetar
4 Nebula
5 Supernova
6 Quasar
7 Pulsar
8 Constellation

a) The awesome atmosphere of the Sun.

b) A spectacular star explosion.

c) A cool collection of shapely stars.

d) A neutron star that sends out regular radio waves.

e) A stunted star – too small to work properly.

f) A curious cloud of dust and gas from which stars are formed.

g) The mysterious middle of a distant galaxy.

h) A magnificent magnetic neutron star.

Answers:
1e; 2a; 3h; 4f; 5b; 6g; 7d; 8c

Postcard from Planet Earth

During her pitstop on Planet Earth, Slobslime decided to send a postcard to her friends back on Splott (Earth is the only planet with post boxes). Unfortunately, Slobslime is seriously stupid and forgot some of the words. Fill in the blanks to make sense of her nonsense note.

Dear Slurpy and Snodhood,

We've just stopped off at yet another weird world and I can tell you for sure - there is life on other planets! There are strange beings called 1)_____ inhabiting the 2)_____ galaxy. They look pretty primitive actually (they only have two arms and two eyes). Seventy-one per cent of the planet's surface is covered in 3)_____, so I'm surprised they're not all fish. They breathe in a gas called 4)_____ that floats all around them in the 5)_____, and they stick to the surface of the planet by a freaky force that they call 6)_____. It's a dangerous world here and no mistake. Everywhere you go there are billions of tiny 7)_____ that can kill you dead, though they're too small to see (even with my three eyes). This poxy planet only has one measly 8)_____ - and no one even lives there! Sounds dull, but that's where we're off to next.

See you in a few light years.
Lots of love
Slobslime

a) Gravity
b) Oxygen
c) Moon
d) Humans
e) Milky Way
f) Seas
g) Atmosphere
h) Microbes

Answers:
1d; 2e; 3f; 4b; 5g; 6a; 7h; 8c

The Sun and other stunning stars

*Our Sun seems like a pretty ordinary star at first
glance: average size, average colour, average
age. But in fact our Sun and all the other stars in
the universe are amazingly interesting. Have a
look at these freakish facts and figure out which
are true and which are false.*

1 There are more stars in the universe than there are
grains of sand in the whole of the Britain.
2 Green stars are the largest and hottest.
3 A comet's tail always points away from the Sun.
4 It takes eight minutes for light from the Sun to reach
Earth.
5 The brightest star in the sky is the bizarrely named
Betelgeuse.

6 The places where baby stars are born are called stellar nurseries.

7 The Sun is one thousand times larger than Earth.

8 The Sun makes up nearly all the mass of our Solar System.

CAN WE GO AND WATCH, MUM?

Answers:

1 FALSE. There are more stars out there than there are grains of sand ON EARTH.

2 FALSE. Stars might vary in colour from white to red, but there are no green ones! Blue-white stars are the hottest.

3 TRUE. The gas and dust melted off the comet, which form the tail, are pushed away from the Sun by the solar wind.

4 TRUE. Which means that if you see the Sun go out, it actually happened eight minutes ago!

5 FALSE. The brightest star is Sirius. Its name means "scorching" and it's twice as bright as any other star in the night sky.

6 TRUE. Stellar nurseries are the parts of nebulae where stars burst into life.

7 FALSE. The Sun is ONE MILLION times larger than Earth.

8 TRUE. The mass of the Sun makes up 99.8 per cent of the Solar System's mass.

Planetary puzzles

Our Solar System is a strange family, and each weird world is different from the next. Can you identify these peculiar planets by their crazy characteristics?

1 The temperatures on this backwards-spinning planet – nicknamed the morning or evening star – are so high they could melt lead!

2 The moons Deimos and Phobos orbit this rusty rock – home to the highest mountain and the longest valley in the Solar System.

3 This gassy, ringed planet might be 764 times bigger than Earth but if you put it in a bath of water, it would float!

4 This small planet snuggles closer to the Sun than any other. It also has the most terrible temperature extremes. The nights are a bone-chilling -183°C.

5 Tumbling through space rather than spinning neatly like the others, this queasy-looking planet has no solid surface, but at least 20 moons.

6 This massive planet has an unfortunate facial feature called the Great Red Spot – a storm that has been raging for more than 300 years.

7 The third planet from the Sun, this water-covered rock has a single moon and an atmosphere made up mostly of nitrogen.

8 The moon Triton orbits this far-out planet in an opposite orbit. It also has a cloud called Scooter that swirls swiftly around the surface.

Answers:
1 Venus
2 Mars
3 Saturn
4 Mercury
5 Uranus
6 Jupiter
7 Earth
8 Neptune

HORRIBLE INDEX

158

HORRIBLE SCIENCE

ANGRY ANIMALS

NICK ARNOLD

illustrated by
TONY DE SAULLES

■SCHOLASTIC

www.horrible-science.co.uk

www.nickarnold-website.com
www.tonydesaulles.co.uk

Scholastic Children's Books,
Euston House, 24 Eversholt Street,
London NW1 1DB, UK

A division of Scholastic Ltd
London ~ New York ~ Toronto ~ Sydney ~ Auckland
Mexico City ~ New Delhi ~ Hong Kong

First published in the UK by Scholastic Ltd, 2005
This edition published 2009

Text copyright © Nick Arnold, 2005
Illustrations copyright © Tony De Saulles, 2005

ISBN 978 1407 11026 4

Page layout services provided by Quadrum Solutions Ltd, Mumbai, India
Printed and bound by CPI Group (UK) Ltd, Croydon, CR0 4YY

21

The rights of Nick Arnold and Tony De Saulles to be identified as the author and
illustrator of this work respectively have been asserted by them in accordance
with the Copyright, Designs and Patents Act, 1988.

CONTENTS

Nick Arnold has been writing stories and books since he was a youngster, but never dreamt he'd find fame writing about angry animals. His research involved howling with wolves and dining with komodo dragons and he enjoyed every minute of it.

When he's not delving into Horrible Science, he spends his spare time eating pizza, riding his bike and thinking up corny jokes (though not all at the same time).

Tony De Saulles picked up his crayons when he was still in nappies and has been doodling ever since. He takes Horrible Science very seriously and even agreed to make a sketch *inside* a crocodile. Fortunately, he has made a full recovery.

When he's not out with his sketchpad, Tony likes to write poetry and play squash, though he hasn't written any poetry about squash yet.

INTRODUCTION

Most people like animals but some animals don't like us. Of course I'm not talking about the kind of playful pets you might like to find tickling your toes. I mean the sort of angry animals that would happily bite off your arm and scoff it for supper. Beastly beasts like these...

Nasty-looking crowd, aren't they? In this wild book I'll be telling you what makes animals attack us and how not to get killed if they do. You can expect more hairy moments than a mammoth's hairdressing salon. In fact this book is *so* dangerous I had to invent an expert to help us – someone stupid enough to tackle a touchy tiger with the tummy rumbles. So let's hear it for top TV naturalist Will D Beest and his clever pet monkey, Mickey...

Will is going to help us find the world's cruellest creature and present it with this lovely trophy…

So enjoy the rest of this book! You're sure to shudder at the bloody bits but you'll also get a shocking new view of nature and maybe a new view of people too! So are you brave enough to read on? OH DON'T BE A CHICKEN! GO ON – I DARE YOU!

THE BEASTLY BASICS

Now I bet you'd love to rush to the nearest jungle and track down the world's cruellest creature. Well, you can't – you see, there's a problem. There are up to 50 MILLION types of animal on Earth (scientists call them 'species') – so how on Earth do we find the beast we're looking for?

Well, here's a few simple questions to help us arrange the animals and plan where to look...

1 What major group of animals does the species belong to?
2 What does it eat?
3 Where does it live?

And here are one or two useful science words...
vertebrate = ver-tee-brate = animal with a backbone
Invertebrate = in-ver-tee-brate = animal without a backbone. They're a bit spineless - ha ha.

THE HORRIBLE SCIENCE ANIMAL GROUP GUIDE
Presented by Mickey the Monkey and various animals...

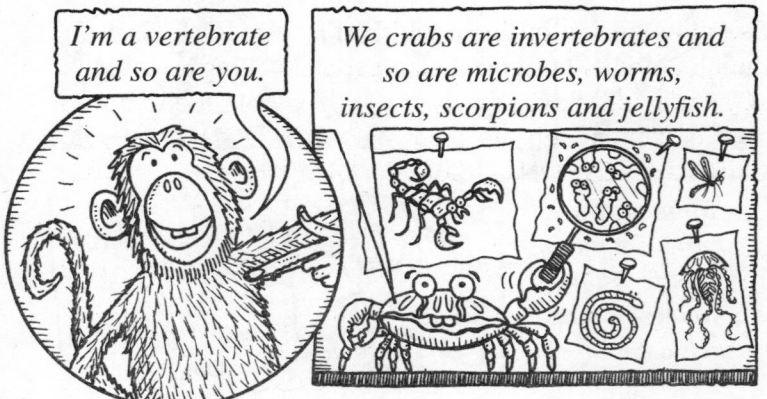

I'm a vertebrate and so are you.

We crabs are invertebrates and so are microbes, worms, insects, scorpions and jellyfish.

The main groups of vertebrates are fish, amphibians, reptiles, birds and mammals.

We fish swim in water and breathe through gills.

We frogs are amphibians. We live on land but grow up and breed in water.

I breathe through lungs so I'm not a fish.

Oh yikes – they eat monkeys!

Reptiles include crocodiles like me and snakes. We all have scaly skin and lay eggs with leathery shells.

If it's got feathers, wings, no teeth and less than five toes, it's a bird.

If it's got feathers, five toes and no teeth, it's probably Will's granny with a feather duster!

Mammals are hairy creatures that feed their young on milk, such as monkeys.

And let's not forget elephants, bears, tigers, lions, wolves and - ahem - humans!

8

Well, that monkey's certainly got brains! Now I hope you haven't got a sicky stomach because the next bit's about how to sort out animals according to what they eat. And it's going to be terribly tasteless even if the facts are easy to digest…

DISGUSTING DINNER-TIME DETAILS

Like you, every species of animal has a favourite food…

• Meat-eaters eat meat (hey who said science was hard!). The posh name for them is *carnivores* and the animals they eat are called their *prey*. Your pet cat and dog are carnivores and so are tigers. (Mind you, a tiger would happily chomp on your cat and dine on your dog so you'd best keep them apart.)

• Meat-eaters that eat dead animals are called *scavengers*. They like food with a bit of body. Many carnivores eat any dead animals they find – even if they're manky and maggoty. Full-time scavengers include vultures.

• Plant-eaters eat plants. (I bet you bought this book to find that out!) Brainy biology boffins call them *herbivores* and examples include elephants, hippos and your pet guinea pig.

9

• Animals that eat plants and animals are called *omnivores*. (By the way, I expect you're an omnivore – otherwise known as a steak and salad scoffer.)

• Creatures that eat insects are *insectivores*. I bet they love their grub(s). Examples include aardvarks (they're a species of African mammal, just in case you're wondering).

FOUL FEEDING-TIME QUIZ

OH NO! Will's attempt to feed the animals at the Anytown Zoo has turned into a disaster! All the animals have been given the wrong food! Can you match the food to the animal that eats it?

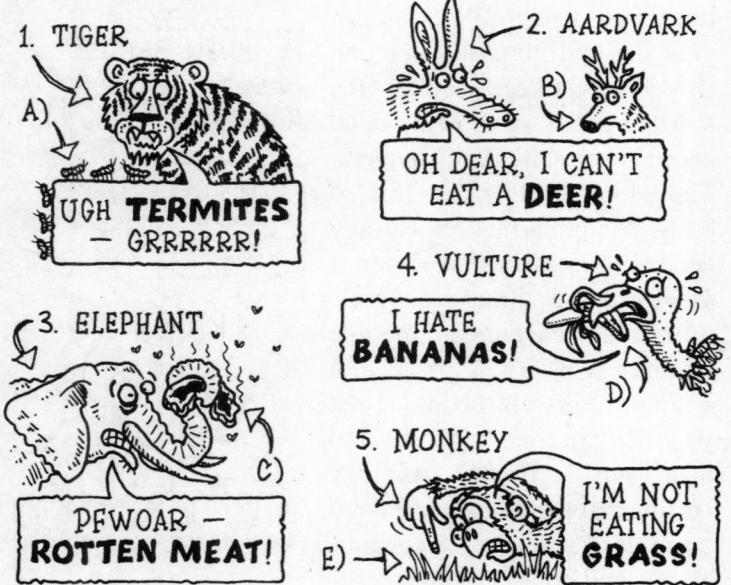

Meat-eaters scoff plant-eaters, plant-eaters scoff plants and so on. Scientists show these feeding choices in special diagrams called food chains or food webs (this is nothing to do with spiders' webs or webbed feet). Confused? Here's some fantastic food facts to feed your brain...

Angry animals fact file

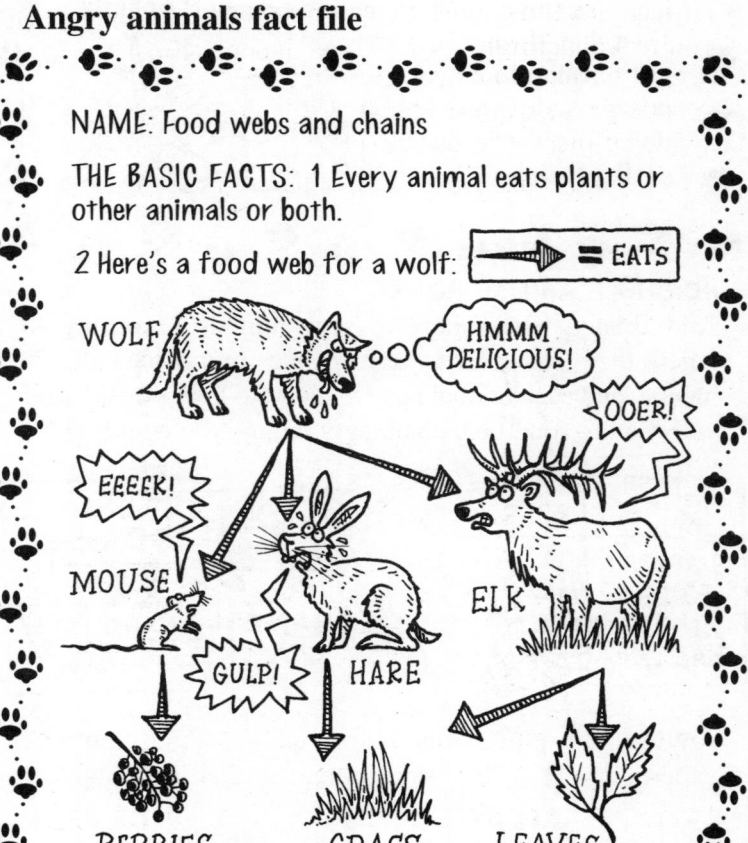

NAME: Food webs and chains

THE BASIC FACTS: 1 Every animal eats plants or other animals or both.

2 Here's a food web for a wolf: ➤ = EATS

WOLF — HMMM DELICIOUS!

OOER!

EEEEK!

MOUSE

ELK

GULP! — HARE

BERRIES   GRASS   LEAVES

3 A single set of links in a food web is called a food chain, but it's nothing to do with bicycle chains or the things that ghosts rattle.

THE ANGRY DETAILS: Food chains mean animals depend on one another...
• If the plant-eaters die, the meat-eaters die too because they've got nothing to eat.
• If the meat-eaters die, the plant-eaters increase their numbers and guzzle all the plants. Then they die because they've got nothing to eat. So I guess meat-eaters are doing them a favour by eating them!

YEAH, THANKS A LOT!

HORRIBLE ANIMAL HOMES

And finally, here's how to sort animals according to where they live… Every animal lives in a place called a habitat, and each animal is well-suited to living there. So if you want to sound breathtakingly brainy, you could say…

EVERY SPECIES IS ADAPTED TO LIFE IN ITS HABITAT.

SIMPKINS — I'M SPEECHLESS!

MR BOTTOMLY THE BIOLOGY TEACHER

Anyway, to prove this point, we've set up an evil experiment. Here are three animals in their habitats.

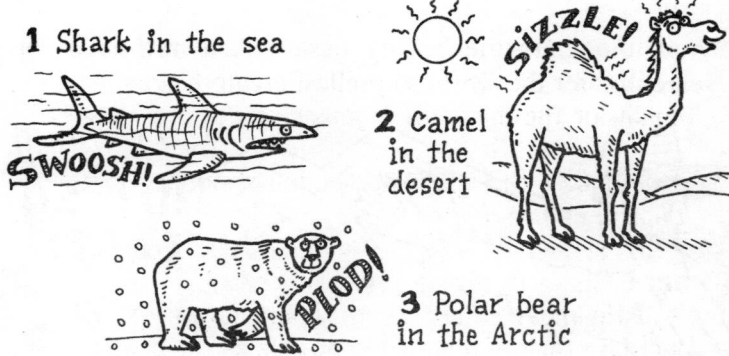

1 Shark in the sea

SWOOSH!

2 Camel in the desert

SIZZLE!

3 Polar bear in the Arctic

PLOD!

But what if we moved them around? The shark's in the Arctic, the polar bear's in the desert, and we've chucked the camel in the sea…

1 The shark's gills are adapted to breathing oxygen dissolved in the water. In the air it's gasping and now it's frozen solid. Anyone fancy shark fishfingers?
2 The polar bear's thick fur is adapted for life in the cold. It's over-heating right now.
3 The camel is adapted for life without too much water but it's sunk in the sea. Hmm – maybe we should have given it a snorkel and flippers…

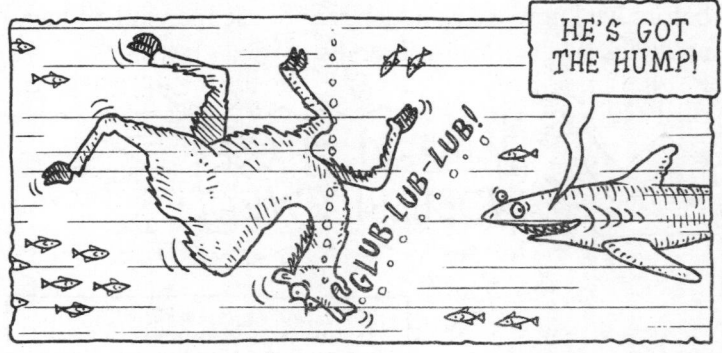

HE'S GOT THE HUMP!

GLUB-LUB-LUB!

Well, those are the beastly basics. And now let's get searching for the world's cruellest creature...

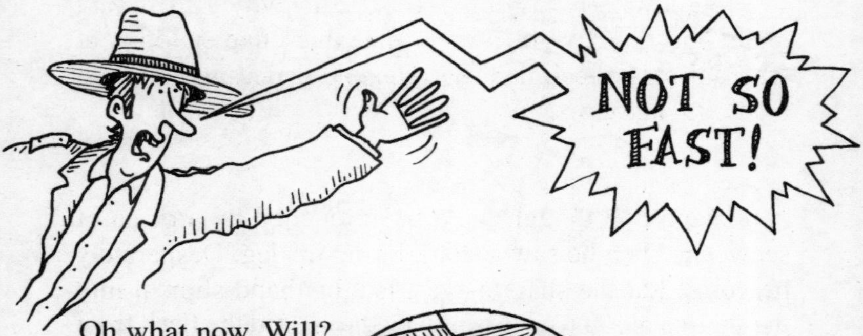

NOT SO FAST!

Oh what now, Will?

YOU HAVEN'T EXPLAINED WHY ANIMALS ATTACK US.

IT'S PROBABLY BECAUSE HUMANS ANNOY US...

OOPS – silly me! We can't go looking for animals until we know *why* they attack us. I mean, they might attack us before we know we're in danger. 'Scuse me whilst I have an attack of the n-n-n-n-n-erves...

GIBBER! SHAKE! WOBBLE! SWEAT!

DON'T WORRY, READERS, NICK WILL BE FINE IN A MINUTE AND WE CAN GET ON WITH THE NEXT CHAPTER...

ANGRY ANIMAL ATTACKS

I'm ok now, I really am. The reason why I'm hiding under the duvet right now is that this chapter looks at why animals attack us. These people ended up getting a bit scrunched-up...

South Africa, 1960
A teenage boy thought he'd been touched by a piece of seaweed. Then he saw a shark biting his leg. Desperately he gouged at the shark's eyes. But his hand slipped into the shark's mouth and its sharp teeth stripped the flesh from his fingers. Moments later the shark let him  go but as the boy tried to escape, the killer fish bit his side. The terrified boy swam for his life through a cloud of his own blood...

Northern Australia, 1981
Blood spurted from the man's body as the huge crocodile tried to pull him into the deep water. Bravely, the 12-year-old girl leapt into the river and grabbed the man's arm. She gritted her teeth – she wouldn't let go even as the man screamed in pain when the croc's jaws bit deeper into his flesh...

Kenya, Africa, 1900s
The little girl sang as she ran barefoot over the dusty earth. She never saw the lion stalking her through the long grass and making ready to spring.  The next thing she felt was the blow that threw her to the ground, the sharp teeth biting her leg and the ROAR that seemed to fill the whole world...

You'll be pleased to know that the boy swam to the shore, and the 12-year-old girl pulled the man from the water and drove him to safety, and the little girl was rescued from the lion. But other victims weren't so lucky. So why do people get attacked? Are we really that tasty? We asked Will D Beest…

In fact Will's given us *loads* of answers…

1 Meat-eaters (carnivores) usually kill to eat. Some meat-eaters set out to hunt humans but others only attack if they mistake us for their usual prey. Well, that's their excuse. Meanwhile, some brave scientists have studied why tigers and lions eat us, and you can snap up their findings on page 103.

2 Herbivores aren't best pleased about being eaten, so they try to fight back. And herbivores sometimes attack us if they think we're trying to attack them.

3 Many animals attack us if they think we're trying to invade their territory (that's the area where they live and feed).

4 Animals are more likely to attack us if they're angry.

• Injured animals are sure to be more bad-tempered. This is why teachers with toothache are especially dangerous.

• Caged animals are often stressed and likely to attack anyone who ventures into their cage. That's why I wouldn't get too close to Mr Bottomly right now…

5 Male animals are extra-grumpy in the breeding season because they often have to fight with other males to win a mate. And they might take their bad temper out on us.

6 Female animals often try to protect their young if you go too close to them.

7 Male animals may try to protect their families.

8 Larger animals are always bad-tempered when they're hungry. Plant-eaters often get hungry if humans take all the best grazing land for their sheep and cattle.

To make matters worse, loads of different animals seem willing to have a go at us. In the next quiz there are five creatures that have attacked humans and two that are as harmless as a toy puppy. So which is which?

THE HAIR-RAISING HARMLESS AND HARMFUL QUIZ

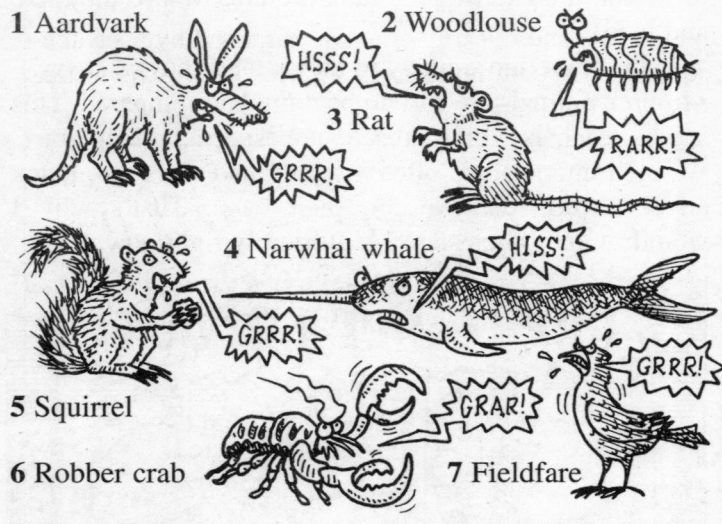

1 Aardvark

2 Woodlouse

HSSS!

RARR!

3 Rat

GRRR!

4 Narwhal whale

HISS!

GRRR!

5 Squirrel

6 Robber crab

GRAR!

GRRR!

7 Fieldfare

Answers:

1 HARMFUL In 2001 a Scottish tourist in Africa was tossed in the air by an angry aardvark. The tourist broke four ribs. It must have been real 'aard luck.

2 HARMLESS Woodlice eat rotting wood so they're only a menace to your teacher's wooden leg.

3 HARMFUL Rats attack sleeping people (this makes the humans ratty too). But according to scientists it's nothing personal. Rats eat other dead rats and they think a sleeping person is a bit on the dead side too. Mind you, that's no excuse for putting your pet rat in your sister's bed…

4 HARMLESS (as long as you don't upset it) Despite its spiky horn, the narwhal has never spiked a human. The word "narwhal" means "corpse whale" and comes from its habit of swimming belly-up.

5 HARMFUL When wacky inventor Mike Madden tested his bird-feeding hat – complete with built-in bird house and nut tray – he was attacked by a savage squirrel. Mike suffered neck injuries (this is honestly true so stop shaking your head).

6 HARMFUL Talking about nuts, it's said that in 1957, 26 sleeping people were killed on a Red Sea island by robber crabs who mistook their heads for coconuts. Now that's what I call shell-shock!

7 HARMFUL (sort of) So you think a cute little bird like a fieldfare wouldn't harm you? You're right! But when people get too close to fieldfare nests, the beastly birds bombard them with poo. Anyone fancy fighting off 50 filthy flapping fouling fieldfares?

A VERY IMPORTANT ANNOUNCEMENT...

I've just received a very important email from the Cruellest Creature Competition judges.

> *The Cruellest Creature Competition Judges' Ruling*
> We've received hundreds of entries for the Cruellest Creature Competition, but to save time we're only considering...
> • Animals with backbones.
> • Animals that kill lots of people.
> Hope your readers aren't too disappointed!

Well, it looks like bees, wasps, jellyfish, spiders and scorpions are out of the running because they don't have backbones. And it's goodbye to birds and loads of small creatures because they hardly ever kill people. Oh dear – these animals are angry at being left out!

Time to make our escape. Tell you what, let's dive into the next chapter!

Er, maybe not...

SAVAGE SHARKS

First up in our crazy quest for the World's Cruellest Creature is the great white shark. Now I bet you can't wait to get your teeth into some savagely shocking slaughter-in-the-water shark stories … but because this is a respectable educational book we're going to have a few facts instead.

Oh, all right – I'll tell you the bloody bits on page 24!

Angry animals fact file

NAME OF CREATURE: Great white shark

TYPE OF ANIMAL: Fish

DIET: Carnivore — eats fish and mammals such as cute seals and dolphins and the odd not-so-cute human.

NUMBER OF PEOPLE KILLED*: Great white sharks kill fewer than two people per year. (On average, all types of shark only kill about 12 people a year.)

WHERE THEY LIVE: Cool oceans all around the world. For some strange reason they like to hang around islands where seals live. Any guesses why?

* All figures in this book are estimates and may vary from year to year.

SIZE: Females are larger than males and they can be up to 4.5 metres long. Some great whites grow to over 6 metres and can weigh 3 tonnes.

FEARSOME FEATURES:

Lateral line (see page 30).

Rough skin made from the same material as teeth.

Gills.

OOER!

Tail beats from side to side.

Skeleton made of cartilage (it's the same stuff that makes up your nose and ears).

Bet you never knew!
In 2003 scientists in Canada found that fish send messages by farting bubbles. Herring keep in touch at night using high-pitched bottom burps. No one knows if sharks have musical bottoms but you're welcome to find out ... if you dare!

OOPS – PARDON!

22

Anyway here are some shark facts that we do know – well, some people know them…

FOUR FACTS THAT NOT A LOT OF PEOPLE KNOW ABOUT GREAT WHITE SHARKS

1 Great white sharks hatch from eggs whilst still inside their mums. They keep alive by eating unhatched eggs. That's right – they gobble up their unborn brothers and sisters.

2 A great white shark has a "belly button" … on its throat! It's the mark where the yolk of the egg is connected to its body.

3 Once it's born, a baby great white shark has to hide from adult sharks who might try to eat it. Even the baby's mum might try to munch it. And you thought you had it tough…

4 As a great white shark grows older it gets greyer on top and bigger round the middle – just like some humans! Of course, the sharks are fairly grey on top already – the colour helps them to blend in with the dark sea when seen from above.

RUTHLESS RELATIVES

So you thought your relatives were bad? Wait 'til you meet some of the other human-killers in the shark family! They're not into happy families, but they might want to play "SNAP" with you…

Name: Bull shark
Size: 2.1 to 3.5 metres long.
Lives: Warm seas close to coasts; sometimes swims up rivers.
Dreadful danger: The brutal bull shark chomps any humans it finds in the river. This antisocial habit makes it a bigger killer than the great white.

Name: Tiger shark
Size: 3 to 6 metres long.
Lives: Warm oceans just like the ones people like to swim in.
Dreadful danger: The terrible tiger shark isn't too fussy about food and will happily eat a human. This gives a totally new meaning to the phrase "feeding the fish".

Now, I suppose you're wondering what it's like to be attacked by one of these savage sharks.

Well, it's no fun at all… In 1994 South African surfing champion Andrew Carter was grabbed by a shark. He said: "I remember its power. I felt like my bones were being crushed."

Andrew screamed as the water turned red around him, but oddly enough like many shark-bite victims, he didn't feel much pain. As the shark opened its jaws to take a bigger bite, Andrew shoved his surfboard into the shark's giant gob. A lucky wave carried Andrew to shore.

He was indeed lucky. The shark attacked Andrew's friend Bruce and bit off his leg. Bruce died of his injuries.

Now for another savage shark story – this is how the paper might have reported it. In bite-sized chunks, naturally…

The **Matawan News**

12 July 1916

CRACKPOT CAPTAIN'S SHARK SCARE STORY!

Captain Thomas Cottrell says he's spotted a shark in the creek just 100 metres from our town. "I saw its dark grey shape in the water!" puffed the potty pensioner as he hurried into town to alert locals. But everyone laughed at the oddball old-timer.

Capt. Cottrell

The News says...

WHAT A FISHY TALE! So old Captain Cottrell's seen a shark? Like heck he has! Matawan folk won't be panicked by this far-fetched fishy tale. Our town is 16 km from the sea and the creek is too shallow for sharks. So grab your towels and enjoy a dip! Yes — let's ignore that strange old sea dog!

The **Matawan News**

14 July 1916

STOP THESE SHOCK SHARK SLAYINGS!

Matawan is reeling after the savage shark attacks that killed two local lads and injured another. First the fearsome fish seized young Lester Stilwell when he was swimming with friends.

At first no one knew it was a shark, and when have-a-go hero Stanley Fisher tried to rescue Lester's body the fearsome fish bit Fisher's leg off. He died later in hospital.

As terror gripped the town, men piled into boats and dropped dynamite into the creek to blast the shark to bits.

But the shark bit back. As Joseph Dunn and his friends tried to flee the water — the savage shark chomped the young lad's leg.

The News Says...

SORRY READERS!

We would like to apologize for the misprint in the News of two days ago. When we said "enjoy a dip" we actually meant to say "that shark's gonna let rip!"

The facts of this story are true, but modern experts aren't too sure what species of shark carried out the attack. Some sharks were caught near the scene but no one knew which one was the killer. Most people blamed a great white, which had bones in its stomach, but a bull shark may have been the guilty fish.

And while we're talking about being eaten by a shark you might be feeling a trifle peckish. If so, here's a revolting recipe to relish...

THE HORRIBLE SCIENCE COOK BOOK
Shark Stomach Soup

This soup is based on items that were really found in sharks' stomachs…

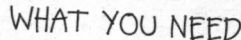

INGREDIENTS
A horse's head
Bits of bicycle
A human arm
One dog's backbone
One whole goat (make sure it's 100 per cent dead!)
Shark's stomach juices
Salt and pepper

WHAT YOU NEED
A big pot
A clothes peg for your nose – your soup is going to pong!

A supply of sick bags

WHAT YOU DO

1. Stir the ingredients in the big pot. Or you could pour them into a shark's stomach.
2. Heat gently until the sickening stink is so bad you can't bear it any more.
3. Serve your soup before the neighbours complain and enjoy the sight of all your friends throwing up.
4. Pour the rest of the soup down the toilet.
5. Go into hiding.

Bet you never knew!
The human arm belonged to an Australian gangster named James Smith. It turned up inside a tiger shark in 1935. One of Smith's crooked mates confessed to killing the criminal and dumping his body in a metal box. He cut off Smith's arm because it stuck out of the box…

SHOCK HORROR – HERE'S SOME GOOD NEWS ON SHARK ATTACKS!

The GOOD news – your chances of being hurt by a shark are about 20 times more teeny than a termite's toenail. The number of people bitten by sharks in the USA every year is about one quarter of the number who have to go to hospital in New York after vicious hamster attacks. You've actually got ten times more chance of being killed by a falling coconut than being killed by a shark.

The BETTER news – great white sharks often attack because they mistake us for seals. They usually only bite us to find out a bit more about us (or do I mean a "bite" more about us?). Some scientists think that sharks aren't keen on our taste and that's why they often take just one bite and then swim off.

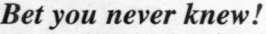

Bet you never knew!
US shark scientist David Baldridge tested how fussy sharks can be. He lowered a rat into a pool of sharks but the sharks refused the rat.

HORRIBLE HEALTH WARNING!
Lowering your pet hamster into a pool of sharks is strictly against the law!!!

So are sharks dangerous? You bet! Sharks bite first and ask questions afterwards (well, come to think of it, they don't ask questions at all). What's more, even a friendly nibble from a great white can bite you in half like a jelly baby. Anyway, despite the danger, Will D Beest wants to show us how a great white shark attacks its prey. Now is that stupid – or what?

*Yes, it really is called chum. This is the usual method of attracting sharks.

DRAT! The attack was too fast to tell you what was happening. Fortunately we have the technology to show you an action replay…

1 The shark sniffs blood in the water 0.5 km away.

2 The lateral line on its side feels movement in the water 100 metres away.

3 The shark scents the dead fish.

4 When it's 25 cm away the shark senses electrical currents in the water. The shark shoots its jaws forward to grab a bigger bite and then it…

5 Bites! Each triangular tooth is rammed into the victim.

6 The shark often draws back after the first bite to allow its victim to bleed to death. Fortunately in this case, the "victim" was a rather silly rubber ring.

THE SAVAGE SHARK SURVIVAL QUIZ

Naturally you're far too sensible to be caught by a great white shark, aren't you? And that's why you've just been signed up for this cruel quiz…

> ## WARNING!
> IF YOU LOSE THE QUIZ YOU GET EATEN BY A SHARK!!!

You're having the holiday to end all holidays – but will it prove to be the end of YOU?

SHARK ISLAND
POPULATION ~~136~~ ~~135~~ 134

GRORK!

1 Where's the safest place to swim?
a) Next to the Shark Island Fishing Competition – I can watch it underwater.
b) Next to the seals. I'll love playing with them.
c) Close to the lifeguard's hut.
2 What's the safest thing to wear?
a) My bright yellow stripy swimming cozzie (it'll scare the sharks away) plus my lucky charm for extra good fortune.
b) A suit of armour.
c) An ordinary swimming costume.
3 What's the best anti-shark protection?
a) A bottle of shampoo.
b) My shark-blaster bomb-stick.
c) My pet dolphin.

ANTI SHARK

4 Anything else you've forgotten?
a) My surfboard – I could surf
a wave and escape the shark.
b) A dead sheep to feed the
shark with – that way it won't
be hungry for me.
c) Nothing.

5 The shark attacks you – what's the best thing to do?
a) Reason with it in a calm
but firm tone of voice.
b) Stick my finger in its
eye or punch its nose.
c) Scream very loudly and
wave my arms in the air.

Answers:
1 c) The lifeguard could help you. Anywhere with
juicy dead fish or seals is going to be a magnet for
great whites.
2 c) Experts call yellow "yum-yum yellow" because
the colour seems to attract sharks. They could mistake
the stripes for a stripy fish. The armour is a bad choice
because it causes electrical currents that sharks sense.
Oh yes – and you could sink to the bottom of the sea
and drown. Mind you, shark scientists do wear a kind
of armour called chain-mail to protect themselves
against smaller sharks.
3 a) Shampoo contains sodium lauryl sulphate – a
chemical that puts sharks off when you squirt it into
their mouths. I expect they "hair off" in the opposite
direction. The bomb could injure a shark and make it
more dangerous. In the 1950s US scientists tried to
train Simo the dolphin to fight sharks, but scared Simo

scarpered from larger sharks. Sounds like a sensible Simo to me.

4 c) The surfboard is seal-shaped when seen from underneath so it might draw sharks. Experiments by US scientist A. Peter Klimley show that sharks hate sheep so they won't eat it. It was a woolly-minded idea anyway...

5 b) If a shark grabs you, fighting back is your only chance.

WHAT YOUR SCORE MEANS

5 Shark survivor! You're clued up and know exactly what to do. There's NO WAY you'll end up as a shark snack!

3–4 Careful now! You made a few silly mistakes and you could be chancing your arm ... or possibly your leg!

1–2 Accident waiting to happen. You've got it coming!

0 YOU'RE A DEAD LOSS! Well, dead actually.

Bet you never knew!

1 In 1957, after a series of savage shark attacks, the South African government ordered a warship to drop underwater bombs on the sharks. They probably wanted to give the animals a short shark shock – but it didn't work. The attacks continued.

2 Talking about fighting sharks ... in ancient Hawaii prisoners were forced to fight hungry sharks armed only with a shark's tooth. I expect the fights took place at tooth-hurty in the afternoon (or is this just tooth horrible tooth think about?).

OOH – I'M TERRIFIED!

Well, no matter if you're a secret shark scientist or a fully fledged selachophobic (that means someone who's scared of sharks), you've got to agree that sharks must be strong contenders for the Cruellest Creature Competition – but wait, here's a late entry…

WANTED FOR CRUEL CRIMES

The Red-bellied Piranha Fish

Last seen: Lurking in South American rivers.

Crimes include stripping animals to their bones in a few murderous minutes, turning especially nasty if they get trapped in a drying-out lake.

Known associates: Some species of piranha fish are vegetarian. I bet they could terrify a healthy fruit salad.

BEWARE! The piranha is a fearsomely fierce fish so don't dip your toe in the river to find out what will happen. And DEFINITELY DON'T bring one home to make friends with your pet goldfish...

BUBBLES BEFORE   BUBBLES AFTER

Hmm – so you think your school's bad? I bet you'd want to be expelled from a school of piranhas even faster! But what's this? The judges don't seem to agree…

> *The Cruellest Creature Competition*
> *Judges' Ruling*
> Actually, piranha fish aren't so cruel after all – in fact they're big softies...
> *1* They're scared of shadows.
> *2* They might munch a toe or two – but there's no proof that piranhas have ever killed a human.
> The piranha fish have been DISQUALIFIED from this competition.
> The Judges

But just when you thought it was safe to go back into the river, something else raises its ugly head...

You can turn the page now, but be careful where you put your fingers!

CRAFTY CROCODILES

The creature in this chapter could put you off messing about on the river for life – well, your life won't last five minutes if you get too close. It's true! Just look at these crucial crocodile facts…

Angry animals fact file

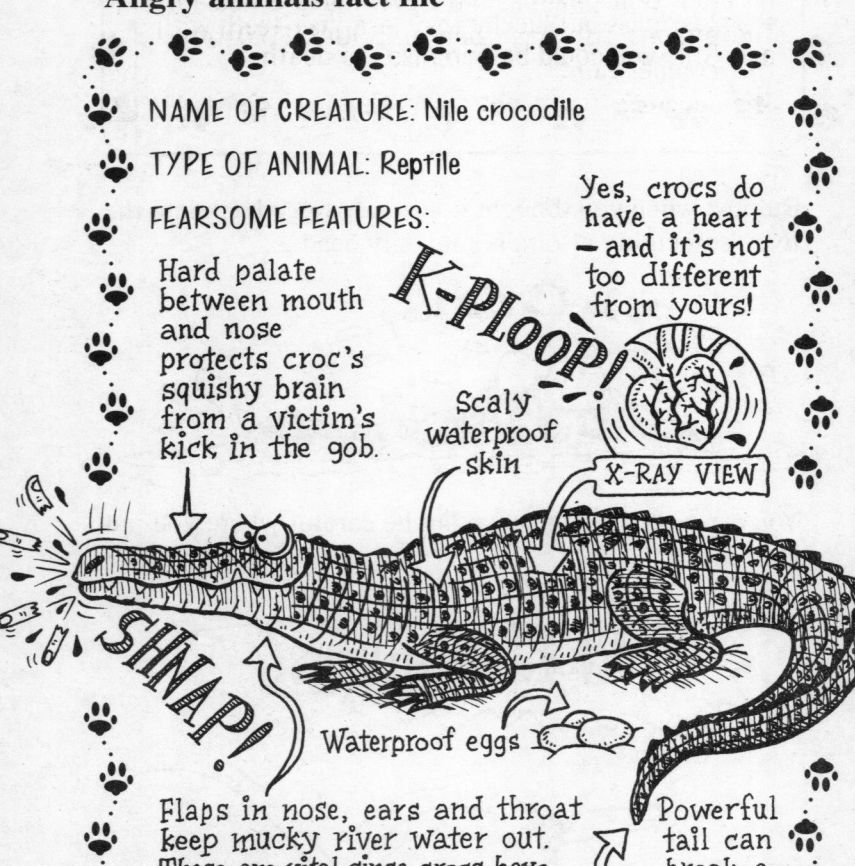

NAME OF CREATURE: Nile crocodile

TYPE OF ANIMAL: Reptile

FEARSOME FEATURES:

Hard palate between mouth and nose protects croc's squishy brain from a victim's kick in the gob.

K-PLOOP!

Yes, crocs do have a heart – and it's not too different from yours!

Scaly waterproof skin

X-RAY VIEW

SHNAP!

Waterproof eggs

Flaps in nose, ears and throat keep mucky river water out. These are vital since crocs have no lips to seal their mouths.

Powerful tail can break a deer's legs.

DIET: Carnivore – eats fish, mammals, birds and anything it can scrunch. Crocs only need to feed once a week – but they can still kill a human.

NUMBER OF PEOPLE KILLED: Several hundred per year.

WHERE THEY LIVE: Rivers and lakes in Africa and Madagascar.

SIZE: Up to 4.88 metres long. The bigger crocs are the older ones but luckily they lose their teeth with age. Still, you could be "gummed" to death.

Bet you never knew!
Most reptiles don't have voices, but crocs do. Their roars sound like distant thunder – I'd hate to hear them singing in the bath first thing in morning!

RUTHLESS RELATIVES

You'll be delighted to read that most other species of crocodiles and alligators never attack humans. But you'll be less delighted to learn that some of these cruel creatures happily harm humans…

Name: Alligator
Size: Males are up to 3.66 metres long.
Lives: South and Central America, southern USA, China.
Dreadful danger: American alligators are relaxed reptiles when it comes to humans. In the USA they only kill about one person a year. Mind you, that doesn't make them safe. If you bathed in their rivers they'd probably turn your bath-time into barf-time.

Name: Saltwater crocodile (known to its friends as "saltie").
Size: Up to 6 metres long.
Lives: Rivers and coasts in southern Asia and the Pacific including Australia. They've been spotted up to 970 km from land.

Dreadful danger: These angry animals reckon their stretch of the river belongs to them and trespassers will be eaten. We're talking about two people per year in Australia and many more in the rest of the world.

SPOT THE DIFFERENCE COMPETITION
Can you spot THREE differences between these pictures?

CROC ALLIGATOR

Answers:
1 The crocodile has a more pointed snout.
2 You can see a lower tooth on each side of the croc's jaw.
3 The croc buries her eggs in a nest of sand. The alligator makes her nest from rotting plants.

CRUEL CROCODILE CHILDHOOD

And now for a tale of woe that will have you shedding tears by the bucketful (crocodile tears, naturally).

A few years ago crocodile scientists discovered that mother crocodiles have a caring sharing side. Yes, they're really kind-hearted crocs.

Having laid and buried about 60 eggs, Ma Croc patiently hangs about for three months waiting for the babies to hatch. This is vital since many creatures, including lizards, birds and monkeys, like nothing better than a crocodile-egg omelette. But Mother's there to protect her nest...

When they're ready to hatch, the cute little baby crocs call to their mum and gently, oh so gently, she digs them from the sand. With tender care she carries them to the river in her giant jaws. Ahhh isn't that sweet... I just hate to tell you that most of the those ever-so-cute baby crocs get guzzled by lizards and fish and snakes and yes, other crocs. In fact 99 per cent of them don't get to grow up. Oh dear.

TASTY!

Bet you never knew!
1 Alligator mums care for their young in a similar way, but they take the babies to a special pool known as a 'gator hole. And I bet the hole's a hole lot safer.
2 Alligator nests get re-used over the years, slowly growing into swampy islands. Trees grow on the islands and birds called egrets nest in the trees. Ma Alligator keeps other creatures away from the nest, so it's only fair that when a baby bird falls from the nest the reptile gets a little reward ... oh well, it's a cheep-cheep snack.

Crocs and alligators sound completely cruel and I certainly wouldn't want to be a croc dentist. But there was a zany zoologist (a scientist who studies animals) who would have loved the job. Unlike other naturalists of his time, Charles Waterton (1782–1864) didn't want to hear about animals from travellers – he wanted to study them in their natural habitats. Wacky Waterton enjoyed wrestling with a cayman (that's a relative of the crocodile). But was he quite as strange as everyone said?

GOODBYE MAGAZINE

1851

MY CHAT WITH CRANKY CREATURE-CRAZY CHAS

By roving reporter Randall Scandal

I'd heard a lot about nutty naturalist Charles Waterton – much of it deeply worrying. "Beware!" warned one of his friends. "He may pretend to be a dog!"

They weren't joking – unlike Charles who started joking as soon as I entered his house...

Randall: Nice to meet you Mr W-AAAAAGGH!... OUCH my ankles!

Waterton: GRRRRRR – bow-wow – ruff, slobber!

I kicked Mr Waterton, who began to whimper. When he had recovered, he invited me to lunch. This proved to be bread and watercress (all he ever eats). But I wasn't too hungry because there was a dead gorilla on the dining table.

RS: What's that dead gorilla doing on the dining table?

CW: I'm cutting it up – would you like to look at the liver?

RS (turning green): I'm not too fond of liver.

After lunch Mr Waterton took me on a tour of his house to scare me with his collection of home-made monsters, created from bits of animal bodies. This was followed by a hop along a high wall. The interview continued up a high tree.

RS: What are we doing up a tree?

CW: I come here to watch birds and wildlife on the ground. I like to talk to the birds.

After the fire brigade rescued me from the tree, the interview continued on the ground.

RS: You're famous for your travels in South America where you studied the local animals. Is it true that you tried to make a vampire bat to drink your blood?

CW: Yes, but the bats weren't biting. I had more luck with the flesh-eating bugs. I made notes on how I felt as they bored into me.

RS: You mean the bugs were boring?

CW: No – they were quite interesting, actually.

RS: So how did you catch a cayman in South America?

CW: I wanted to study a cayman close up. So in 1819 I paid some natives to catch one using a rat as bait. But the cayman was rather upset at being caught and no one dared to go near it.

RS: Except you...?

CW: Catching the beast was easy – if I can just demonstrate...

At this point Mr W asked me to crouch like a crocodile. A moment later he jumped on my back and forced my arms backwards.

RS: OUCH – get off me!

CW: So you see it was quite easy... Excuse me I have an itch.

Suddenly Mr W leapt off me and began to scratch the back of his head with his big toe. After this disgraceful display, Mr W offered to show me how he caught a giant snake using the braces that held up his trousers. A few hours later, he untied me and I made my escape...

I would like to finish my report by saying that everything they say is true, and Mr W is as utterly nutty as a squirrel's pantry! I need a holiday!

OK, so I made up Randall, but all these freaky facts about Charles Waterton are truthfully true.

Bet you never knew!

1 Charles Waterton was one of the first people ever to turn his garden into a nature reserve. In Waterton's garden, no one was allowed to harm any animal except rats.

THAT'S UNFAIR!

YES – I SMELL A RAT!

2 The animals seemed to love creature-crazy Chas as much as he loved them. It's said that a flock of birds followed his body to its grave. And don't be unkind – they didn't want to EAT it!

HE PUT BREAD OUT IN THE WINTER, BLUB!

R.I.P. C. WATERTON

SOB! AND HALF A COCONUT ON A BIT OF STRING!

Speaking personally, I don't think it's terribly sensible to wrestle with caymans or crocodiles. And if you tried to wrestle with these celebrity crocs you might end up missing some vital body bits…

TOP OF THE CROCS

WHAH!

At number 5…

Sweetheart (Yes, that's an odd name for a huge flesh-eating reptile but read on and all will be revealed.)
   Home: Sweet's Look-out Billabong, Australia. (Told you!)
      Hobbies: Crunching outboard motors.
Fate: Apart from biting boats, Sweetheart never did anyone any harm but sadly the saltie (that means saltwater croc, remember?) died when scientists tried to knock him out to move him away from people.

Solomon

Home: A wildlife park in Australia.

Hobbies: Eating and basking in the sun.

Fate: One day in 1997, wildlife-park worker Karla Bradl was showing Solomon the saltie to some tourists when the cunning croc chomped her leg. Karla's dad (the park boss) jabbed the croc's eyes until it let go and luckily Solomon was old and partly toothless. In fact, Karla had just said: "If I ever get grabbed, I'd rather it be this one!"

I expect Solomon felt a bit down in the mouth. But you'll be pleased to hear that Karla's dad refused to let Solomon be killed saying "...he wouldn't bite anything with bones in it." Except his daughter of course!

Kwena

Home: Okovango Swamp, Botswana, Africa.

Hobbies: Gobbling goats (and people).

Fate: When Kwena was killed in 1968, the 5.8 metre killer croc had two goats, half a donkey and half a woman in its stomach.

We've nearly reached Number One – but first…

Bujang Senang

Home: Lupar River, Sarawak, Borneo.

Hobbies: Football and eating people. (To be honest, I'm not too sure if the croc even liked football, but the local team named itself after the revolting reptile.)

Fate: In the 1980s and 1990s this crafty croc crunched dozens of people but always managed to hide from hunters. And a witch doctor's bid to catch the croc by magic spells spelled failure.

AND NOW FOR THE BIG NUMBER 1 – AND IT REALLY IS BIG...

Gustave

Home: Burundi, Africa.

Hobbies: Scaring hippos and eating people.

Fate: Terrified locals claimed the gigantic 1 tonne croc had eaten over 300 people. In March 2003 an international team of scientists tried to trap the croc in a giant cage or using spring traps. But the crafty croc dodged the traps ... until one day he disappeared, never to be seen again. Maybe he'd gone to a croc-and-roll concert...

I hope you're hungry for crafty croc and artful alligator attack facts because here's a cruel quiz to chew over. My mate Honest Bob has five facts – but beware! Bob's as dodgy as a second-hand dodgem car. The facts get more and more freaky. Can you spot where the facts stop being true and start being false? Over to you, Bob!

HONEST BOB'S "CAN YOU BELIEVE IT?" QUIZ

TRUE/FALSE

1. In 2001 a Florida alligator tried to eat ... a live horse!
2. In 2001 a camper in Australia woke to find himself in bed with ... a crocodile!
3. In 2002 an African crocodile was bitten by ... a man!
4. In 2004 a group of children took an alligator ... to school by bus!
5. In 2005 a teacher was attacked on the toilet by ... an alligator that lived in the sewer!
6. In 2005 scientists found a fossil crocodile ... with wings!

Answers:

1 TRUE You'll be pleased to hear that the horse survived its injury and is now in a stable condition – geddit?

2 TRUE The crafty croc had crawled into the man's sleeping bag but another camper frightened it away.

3 TRUE Mac Bosco Chawinga was grabbed by the croc but escaped after biting its snout – and that's snout too funny if you're a croc.

4 TRUE The children tied the alligator up with clothes but I bet their teachers were terrified.

5 FALSE Alligators don't live in sewers although they can be swept into them by heavy rains. If the teacher had been bitten he'd have nipped in the toilet, been nipped on the toilet and nipped out even faster!

6 FALSE No croc ever had wings. Oh don't tell me you fell for *that!!!*

All this talk of ruthless reptiles raises quite a queasy question. How exactly do crocs and alligators attack humans? Oh dear, I'm sure you don't want to know – it's really *very* gruesome…

BUT WE DO!

Well, I've got a uneasy feeling that Will D Beest is about to find out.

WILL D BEEST IN … CROC CRACK!

This man has a death-wish…

Nonsense! It's quite safe for an expert like me.

Crocodiles only attack if they're hungry... or think we're attacking their young. Or protecting their territory.

An attacking croc floats slowly closer...

OOER — SPOT THE CROC!

The croc dives and grabs its victim...

Time to go!

SPLOSH!

AGGGGGGH!

The croc rolls its body to tear off flesh — it's called a death roll.

HE'S IN A ROLL LOT OF TROUBLE!

Ouch, I bet that hurt, Will! When Australian wildlife ranger Charlie Finn was attacked by a saltie, the cruel croc grabbed his arm. Charlie said later: "I heard the sounds of bones crunching. It was pretty horrible." The croc went into a death roll, but luckily it let go of Charlie's chewed arm.

Still, this is all scientifically fascinating, and whilst Will's recovering in hospital, we've asked the croc that did the damage to tell us about his eating habits...

CRUNCH-TIME FOR CROCS

We crocodiles drown our prey – including humans. That way they don't fight back and we can guzzle them at leisure.
Like sharks, we can't chew. We rip off bits of body and gulp them down.
Sometimes we leave the body to rot until it's soft and squishy enough to bite off bits more easily.
The acid in our stomach is strong enough to dissolve bones.

Hey – why's that crocodile getting all the attention?

Cos he's more interesting than you!

And now for the disgusting details that you'll probably wish you hadn't read before supper. At least one chewed-up croc victim was still alive when he was left to rot and he managed to get away. But most victims are dead and end up being dissolved by the croc's super-strong stomach juices. When crocs have been cut open, all that remains of some victims are their finger and toenails. Well, it's good to know crocs don't chew their nails...

Bet you never knew!
Some people in history quite liked crocs. They must have been total croc-pots, er, crackpots.
1 In the 1860s King Litunga Sipopa of Barotseland in Africa enjoyed feeding crocs with executed criminals. You could say "Cruel king's cross crocs crunched crooks' corpses" – but I bet you can't say that with a mouthful of people, er, I mean popcorn.

2 The ancient Egyptians worshipped crocs, and a crocodile-headed monster named Ammut gobbled up the hearts of bad people in the land of the dead. Of course the real crocs gobbled up good people in the land of the living too.

WELCOME TO THE LAND OF THE DEAD... HOW DID YOU DIE?

I WAS EATEN BY A CROC!

Mind you, most people aren't too fond of crocs. And many human-killing crocs are hunted, killed and even eaten. Can you believe that crocodile tastes like a cross between fish and beef? I bet you could even make one into a fishcake-flavoured beefburger!

Bet you never knew!
In 1995 a pair of crocs were blamed for eating children in Cameroon, Africa. The wretched reptiles were dressed up as humans – complete with silly wigs – and burnt alive.

More often crocs and alligators are hunted for their skins and have ended up as posh shoes and handbags. By the 1960s nearly all the alligators in the USA had been wiped out by hunters. So does that mean that crocs are out of the running for the Cruellest Creature Competition? Are we more of a danger to them than they are to us?

We've just had another late entry to the competition...

Angry animals fact file

NAME OF CREATURE: Komodo dragon

TYPE OF ANIMAL: Reptile (to be more exact, it's a giant monitor lizard)

DIET: Carnivore. Eats anything it can sink its jaws into. It's especially keen on wild boar and deer but it'll happily munch on us.

NUMBER OF PEOPLE KILLED: They eat a tourist every few years.

WHERE THEY LIVE: A few islands in Indonesia including Komodo.

SIZE: About 2.6 metres long.

FEARSOME FEATURES:

Disgusting bad breath (makes your dog look like a toothpaste advert)

Teeth for tearing flesh

Sharp claws

So, could killer komodo dragons be crueller than crafty crocodiles? Whilst we're waiting for the judges to decide, here's a problem page for komodo dragons... Wow – take a look at this. These dragons are really *beastly* to each other!

THE DAILY DRAGON
problem page...

Hi!

Are you a dragon in difficulties? Why not drop a line to your favourite animal agony aunt, Daphne Dragon?

Dear Daphne
I'm a baby komodo dragon with a terrible problem. My parents have bad breath and they want to kill me. What should I do?

Little Nipper

Dad

Mum

Dear Little Nipper
Your problem is perfectly normal. All komodo dragons want to eat their babies once they leave their nest. As for the bad breath – it's healthy for us dragons to have loads of germs in our mouths. They get into any creature

we bite and kill them. And we sniff out their rotting bodies (that's why no dragon should ever use mouthwash).

PS If you really don't want to be eaten try hiding in a tree or rolling in poo. The disgusting stink will put your parents off eating you. It worked for me!

Dear Daphne

I've never eaten with other dragons before and I've heard we can eat each other. Are there any table manners I should remember?

Hungry Snapper

Dear Hungry Snapper

Table manners?! You must be choking, er joking! Simply start with the guts, eat fast and don't be fussy. I'm especially fond of an over-ripe deer with a side order of maggots. If you don't like the maggots you can lick them off the meat and if they crawl up your nose you can sneeze them out! Bon appetit!

COME TO THE DEAD BUFFALO DINER!!!
All our meat is guaranteed rotten!

Everything you can eat in ten minutes is FREE!
Live maggots extra!——>

THE SMALL PRINT After ten minutes another dragon might turn up and eat you...

Well, those dragons sound completely cruel to me … but it looks like the judges disagree!

> ### The Cruellest Creature Competition Judges' Ruling
> Although komodo dragons do kill humans, they don't kill enough people to take part in the competition. The dragons are DISQUALIFIED!
> The Judges

So it's disappointment for the dragons and cheers for the crocs. But are the crocs cruel enough to win the coveted cruel creatures cup? Well, the competition's getting tough. I mean look at the creatures in the next chapter – you can't trust these slippery characters. They're real snakes in the grass. I'm not joking – they really *are* snakes in the grass!

SINISTER SNAKES

Pssst! Listen carefully. Whilst you read this chapter it's best to remain completely still. This chapter is all about the most deadly snakes on the planet, and if you move too fast they might get upset and you'll be hissss-tory. So no fidgeting, OK?

Now it so happens that Honest Bob is writing a best-selling children's book on snakes (well, it's a best-seller according to Bob). But Bob's book isn't exactly truthful – can you spot at least FIVE fibs in it?

THE KIDDIES BOOK OF
SNAKES
by Honest Bob

PRAISE FOR THIS BOOK
"This book is a work of ultimate genius if I say so myself!" Honest Bob (no relation).

Chapter 1 **Types of Snakes**
Snakes – Ugh! Poisonous snakes love to bite and eat humans. This book tells you how horrible snakes are and it's all TRUE (probably). There are thousands of species of deadly snake and here are the most deadly!

1. THE ELEPHANT–BITING SNAKE
It hides in rivers and grabs an elephant by the trunk when it comes to drink. The snake kills the elephant with a deadly bite and sucks its blood, but sometimes the elephant falls dead on the snake and squashes it flat. Serves it right!

SPLOOSH!

2. THE HOOP SNAKE

This American snake grips its tail in its mouth and rolls along like a hoop. There's no hoop of escaping it! As my old mum says, "what goes around comes around!"

3. THE COACHWHIP SNAKE

If the hoop snake doesn't get you, the coachwhip will. This American snake gallops faster than a horse. And when it catches you, it wraps its body around you and whips you to death with its tail.

Take it from me, kids, the best thing to do with snakes is to kill them stone dead before they kill you even more stony dead. But BEWARE – their mate will try to kill you in revenge!

OH NO! I've haven't read so much rubbish since *Teachers Are Nice to Their Pupils* by Biggy Lyer. So how many fibs, porkies and whoppers did you spot? Why not re-read Bob's book and double-check before reading on?

Answers:

FIB 1: "... love to ... eat humans" Poisonous snakes can't eat humans – their jaws are too small to swallow us whole and their teeth can't bite off bits of body. They mostly eat small animals such as rats and birds.

FIB 2: "There are thousands of species of deadly snake" Like heck there are! Out of more than 2,500 species of snake only about 50 are deadly to humans.

FIB 3: "The elephant-biting snake" The Roman writer Pliny (AD 23–79) wrote about this snake – but it doesn't exist. And by the way, no snake sucks blood.

FIB 4: "The hoop snake" is a Victorian myth. No snake moves like this.

FIB 5: "The coachwhip snake" *is* a real snake, but it attacks with a good old-fashioned bite. No snake whips its victims and no snake moves faster than a horse. In fact, the real coachwhip snake can't even out-run a child! ADVANCED LEVEL BONUS POINTS You can win an extra point for spotting each of these especially-hard-to-spot fibs...

• "Poisonous snakes love to bite ... humans." No they don't. Mostly they try to escape and only bite if they feel trapped or try to defend their eggs.

• "Their mate will try to kill you in revenge!" Snakes don't seek revenge. How are they supposed to find out who killed their mate anyway?

We wanted to ask Bob about the fibs in his book but he's gone for a long holiday in Peru. Oh well, at least Bob's book shows us some of the barmy beliefs that people have about snakes. In a moment we'll be finding out real-life poisonous snake secrets, but first let's meet a ruthless reptile that likes to get wrapped up in its work...

SICKENING SQUEEZERS

Some snakes, such as boa constrictors and pythons, wrap themselves around their victims. Will is showing Mickey how an African rock python attacks its prey. Take care, Will!

WILL D BEEST IN ... PYTHON PRESSURE

It's all in a day's work for a top TV star!

Pythons mostly eat small animals such as bats...

...and monkeys.

Pythons sink their jaws into their prey and squeeze it so it can't breathe.

The python has picked up Mickey's scent on my clothes...

SQUEEZE!

OWWW – I'b dot a bunkey!

AGGGGH – HELP!

Will's in a tight spot...

I think we'd better move on swiftly to somewhere a bit safer… Oh dear, this page isn't safer at all!

Angry animals fact file

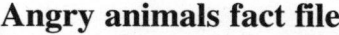

NAME OF CREATURE: King cobra

TYPE OF ANIMAL: Reptile

DIET: Carnivore. Eats other snakes and lizards.

FEARSOME FEATURES:

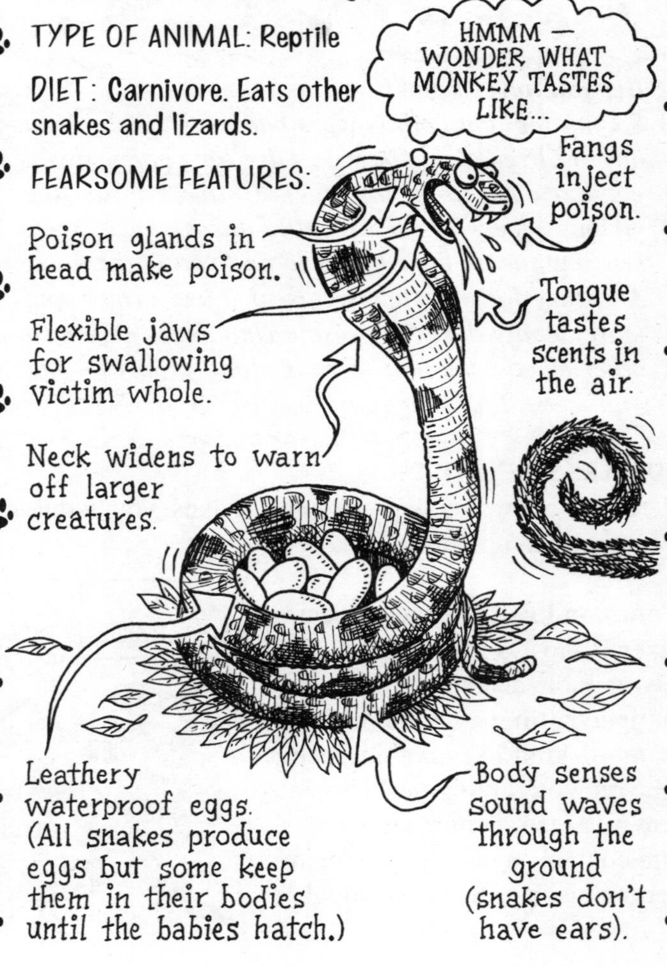

Poison glands in head make poison.

Flexible jaws for swallowing victim whole.

Neck widens to warn off larger creatures.

HMMM — WONDER WHAT MONKEY TASTES LIKE...

Fangs inject poison.

Tongue tastes scents in the air.

Leathery waterproof eggs. (All snakes produce eggs but some keep them in their bodies until the babies hatch.)

Body senses sound waves through the ground (snakes don't have ears).

59

NUMBER OF PEOPLE KILLED: The total number of people killed by all types of snakes could be as high as 60,000 per year. Many of them are killed by cobras! Oh yikes!

WHERE THEY LIVE: India and south-east Asia.

SIZE: Up to 5.6 metres long.

Bet you never knew!
So you thought cobras were bad news? Pah – you haven't lived! And you won't live long either if you get too close to a pit viper. Unlike cobras, the vicious vipers (such as rattlesnakes) have heat-sensing pits on their heads to find you in the dark. And they have hollow fangs to inject larger and more deadly doses of poison. (In cobras and most other snakes the poison runs along grooves – but that doesn't mean a cobra bite is "groovy".)

RUTHLESS RELATIVES

Here are a few more poisonous snakes you wouldn't want to wake up with…

Common krait (12 other species)
Size: Up to 1.8 metres long.
Lives: India and southern Asia.
Danger-rating: The Indian common krait likes nothing better than crawling into your bed whilst you're asleep. Unfortunately its bite contains a deadly nightmare nerve poison… Sweet dreams!

A CRATE OF KRAITS

Rattlesnake

Size: Up to 2.4 metres (eastern diamondback).

Lives: North America.

Danger-rating: There are 29 species and they're all poisonous. They kill fewer than 15 people in the USA every year, though.

Sea snake

Size: Up to 90 cm long.

Lives: Indian and Pacific Oceans.

Danger-rating: Rarely bites humans although it does enjoy chasing divers. Its bite is the most poisonous of any snake. Fancy a dip?

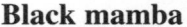

Black mamba

Size: Up to 4.3 metres long.

Lives: Africa south of the Sahara Desert.

Danger-rating: Its poison can kill in 20 minutes. In the 1970s South African snake expert Jack Seale spent weeks sharing a small room with a black mamba. He said the secret of survival was not to move quickly... Lucky he didn't need the toilet in a hurry then.

The spitting cobra

Size: Up to 2.5 metres long.

Lives: Africa – south of the Sahara desert.

Danger-rating: Low. OK, so if you dried the poison and injected

it into 165 humans they'd all die. But this snake *spits* its poison (how come you knew that already?) and it can't hurt if it lands on your skin. The bad news: if the poison hits your eyes it can dissolve your eyeballs. The very bad news: the snake aims for the eyes. The yikes-I-need-a-clean-pair-of-pants bad news: it's a very good shot.

Dare you discover ... if you're as accurate as the spitting cobra?

You will need:

A water pistol (Make sure you fill it with water and not snake poison!)

An eyeball. (If you don't have a spare eyeball here's one we've borrowed. You can trace it and draw it on a piece of card.)

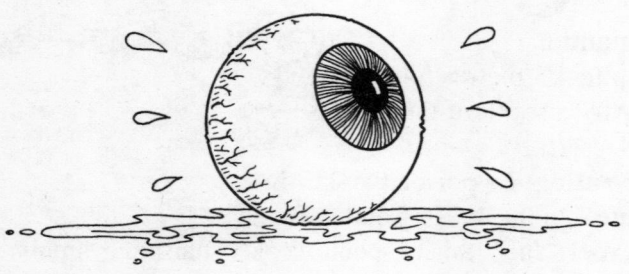

A measuring tape
Blu Tack

HURRY UP – I
NEED IT BACK!

What you do:

1 Stick the eyeball to the wall 1.5 metres up with the Blu Tack (this is best done outside).

2 Measure 2.5 metres from the wall.

3 Crouch down and try to hit the eyeball with a jet of water.

You should find:
This is tricky for you but easy for a sinister spitting cobra.

HORRIBLE HEALTH WARNING!
You should only use water pistols for this experiment and that means NO SPITTING. And no spitting at your pet snake/teacher either!

Is your teacher a herpetologist (that's the posh name for a snake scientist)? If so, they may have a cobra named Colin which they feed small furry animals (so that's what happened to Hamish the school hamster!). Anyway here are some strange snake secrets that they probably don't know…

SEVEN STRANGE SNAKE SECRETS

1 Even your most scary school teacher can't out-stare a snake. Snakes can't blink because they don't have eyelids. See-through scales protect their eyes.

2 Ever wondered how sea snakes eat really spiny fish without them getting stuck in their throats? Me neither – but apparently they gulp the fish and then force the spines out through their own bodies. I guess they must be prickly characters!

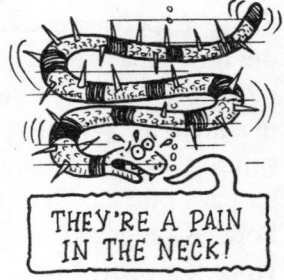

THEY'RE A PAIN IN THE NECK!

3 It's possible to eat snake eggs. The trick is to choose the smooth ones. The crumpled ones contain baby snakes and their bite can be poisonous. So if you eat the wrong egg you'd best scramble.

4 Although snakes taste smells using their tongues, some species have nostrils too.

5 Snakes take baths. Before they shed their skin they take a dip to make their skin moist. Then they unroll their skin along the length of their body. It's a bit like Will D Beest taking off a sock – but without the cheesy whiff.

PHWOAR!

6 A snake can decide how much poison to give you. The crosser the snake the more you get!

7 And talking about poison, US scientists have found that cottonmouth snake poison is ideal for shifting stubborn stains. Of course it shifts stubborn humans too. Anyone want to test the vile venomous cleaner? If the test goes wrong at least you'd suffer a clean death.

STRANGE SNAKE SCIENTISTS

Snake experts are trying strange snake experiments all the time…

• Kenyan-based fang fancier Constantine Ionides invented a pair of goggles to protect his eyes from spitting cobra poison, kept a pet puff adder named Popkiss and ate a gaboon viper for Christmas dinner. He even raced a black mamba to find out how fast it was – luckily it proved slower than the barmy boffin.

THEY NEED WINDSCREEN **VIPERS**, MR IONIDES!

• Our old pal Charles Waterton (last seen riding on a crocodile) once let a rattlesnake loose at a scientific meeting. I bet the scared scientists were even more rattled than the rattlesnake.

So it's not too surprising that lots of snake experts have been bitten by the snakes they tried to study. Take John Toomey, for example...

NAME: John Toomey **DATE:** 1916

JOB: Zookeeper at Bronx Zoo, New York

INJURY: Bitten by a rattlesnake

CONDITION: Desperate. Another zookeeper tried to suck out the poison but the swelling has spread all over Toomey's body. He's in extreme pain and throwing up all the time.

MEDICAL FORECAST: He's a goner without a doubt...

NOTES: Toomey's life was saved by Brazilian snake expert Dr Vital Brazil. By an amazing chance, Dr Brazil just happened to be in New York and just happened to have some of his newly invented snakebite remedy with him. Toomey was the first person saved by the cure.

Bet you never knew!
Scientist Karl Schmidt wasn't so lucky. In 1957 he was studying a snake called a boomslang. The bad-tempered boomslang bit careless Karl with just one fang. But the bite was deadly and the suffering scientist died the next day.

A SNAKEBITE SURVIVOR'S STORY

So, how does it feel to be bitten by a poisonous snake – is it really as bad as it sounds? Well, no. Actually, it's a whole lot WORSE!

In 1987 British snake expert Jack Corney (1924–2003) was collecting poison from a rattlesnake for scientists to study. Jack knew what he was doing but as he held the snake by the back of its neck the killer creature bit his thumb.

"Don't panic," Jack said to himself grimly. "Freeze your mind." He knew that if he let himself feel scared, his heart would beat faster and pump the poison more quickly around his body.

Carefully he replaced the snake in its box and wrapped a bandage tightly around his bitten arm. But he was too late. As the poison took hold Jack began to gasp for air. His injured arm swelled to three times its size. The pain was an unspeakable agony. Jack gritted his teeth and rang for help.

In hospital Jack's heart stopped, but he still could hear and feel as the doctors fought for his life. One doctor held Jack's wrist and tried to find a pulse as another stuck a needle in his arm.

"We're losing him," said one doctor.

"He's gone."

Jack felt as if he was drifting out of his body. Then everything went black.

Suddenly Jack's eyes opened. He was looking at a clock. Where was he? What had happened? Slowly and painfully he realized that he was still in hospital and three hours had passed. He later found out that his heart had stopped for three minutes and it had only started to beat again at the last moment before death. For five days he was more dead than alive, and even when he began to get better his arm was useless for weeks. Then Jack went back to work studying snakes.

He was bitten several times after that. Ten years later Jack remarked...

"Some people think I'm mad doing this job..."

Now I wonder why they thought that?

Obviously you don't want to mess about with poisonous snakes – so here are a few snake experts' safety tips, just in case you find yourself in snake country...

Expert snake safety tips - don't leave home without them!

1. Always wear long trousers and boots. They protect you against bites from small snakes.

2. Always step on top of logs rather than over them. There may be a snake hiding on the other side.

3. If you see a snake always keep a safe distance - the snake can't strike more than half its length.

4. Make sure the snake has a way to escape.

5. Stay calm - I said DON'T PAAAAAAANIC!

Hmm, poisonous snakes certainly sound like the odds-on favourites for the Cruellest Creature Competition. They kill more humans than sharks and one snake even shot a man... Well, I don't care if you don't believe me – IT'S TRUE!

Bet you never knew!
In June 1996 a Chinese hunter named Li from Shanxi Province was feeling bored. He came across a snake and thought it might be fun to prod it with his gun. The surprised snake coiled around the gun, pulled the trigger and blasted Li in the bum. He died soon afterwards ... shot by a snake!

Mind you, the Cruellest Creature Competition is still wide open and our next cruel chapter features a creature that's horribly big, scoffs buns and lets out loud trumpets. And NO – I'm not talking about your teacher!

BIG BAD BEASTS

I'm delighted to tell you that Will D Beest has almost recovered from his unfortunate encounter with the python. And here he is to introduce this chapter…

Thank you, Will. The first animal we'll be looking at is a creature that kills hundreds of people every year. It's a jumbo-sized menace…

Angry animals fact file

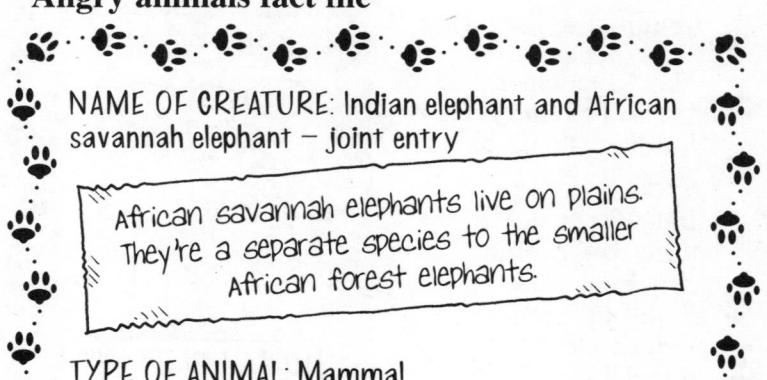

TYPE OF ANIMAL: Mammal

DIET: Herbivore. Elephants eat just about any plant food...

- They pull up grass with their trunks and uproot trees, eating everything including the bark and roots.
- Elephants can guzzle more than 200 kg of greenery a day, so imagine what a herd of elephants would do to your school cabbage patch.

NUMBER OF PEOPLE KILLED: Evil elephants kill about 200 people in India alone. But savannah elephants are worse-tempered.

OOER!

FEARSOME FEATURES:

Trunk = the elephant's nose and upper lip, used for drinking, sniffing and picking things up.

SAVANNAH ELEPHANT

Tough, leathery skin.

"Lip" on upper end of trunk is handy for holding small objects.

Tusks = extra-long front teeth used for digging for food and fighting. (Female Indian elephants don't have tusks.)

Smaller ears than African elephants.

INDIAN ELEPHANT

WHERE THEY LIVE: The Indian elephant lives in India (oddly enough) and South-east Asia. And I bet you'll be trumpeting with amazement to read that both types of African elephant live in Africa, south of the Sahara Desert.

SIZE: Indian elephant: up to 3 metres high at the shoulder.
Savannah elephant: up to 3.2 metres high at the shoulder.

EXTREME ELEPHANT ATTACKS

In 1952 a hunter named JC Hunter (no, I'm not making this up as I go along) said: "I have often been chased by elephants. It is like running from a nightmare ... not a second goes by but you expect to feel that snaking trunk round your neck."

And when the elephant catches you, things get far, far worse – but I'm sure you won't want to read these upsetting details...

OH YES WE DO!

Well don't say I didn't warn you! The elephant picks up the human with its trunk and throws them to the ground or bashes their brains out against a tree. And then the enraged elephant splats them flat with its big heavy feet. I think you'll agree that's a nasty way to *goo*.

WHAT'S THAT SMELL?

SNIFF!

I TROD ON SOMEONE NASTY.

People who train elephants have to be extra careful, because the big brutal beasts get angry without warning. In the 1900s an elephant named Mandarin performed in a US circus. One day a new trainer started work. Mandarin had been taught to place his foot on the previous trainer's head. But guess what happened when the new trainer tried that trick?

HURRY UP — STEP ON IT!

Bet you never knew!

A US circus elephant that killed a cruel trainer in 1916 was hanged by the neck until she was dead. It's said that the elephant's owners tried to electrocute her but the jumbo-sized shock just left her a bit dazed.

So are you a cool clued-up elephant expert who'd know what to do if an elephant decided to pay your school an unfriendly visit? Or would you be cowering in a cupboard along with your terrified teacher? Try our teasing quiz and find out!

COULD YOU BE AN ELEPHANT EXPERT?

Which of the two possible answers is correct? You've got a one in two chance of being right so it's OK to guess!

1 How can you tell when an elephant is growing up?
a) Its voice breaks.
b) It gets spotty and wants to stay out late.

2 Older elephants suffer from worn teeth. Because they can't eat too easily they get hungry and grumpy and violent. What did Thai scientist Dr Somsak Jitniyom give Morokot the toothless elephant in 2004?
a) False teeth.
b) Milkshakes.

3 How do farmers in Zimbabwe stop elephants from eating their crops?
a) They pay boys to throw stones at them.
b) They burn a mixture of chilli and elephant poo.

4 Why did elephants flatten an Indian army base in 1996?
a) They jumped up and down on an ants' nest and the ground shook so much the buildings fell down.
b) They got drunk.

Answers:

1 a) Austrian scientists found this out in 2003.

2 a) Yes – it's a CHEW story!

3 b) Elephants sniff out crops 10 km away. The terrible tuskers march in and munch the lot, and the poor farmers starve. But the spicy stink of chilli and poo puts them off. Believe it or not, elephants hate chilli and that's why you'll never find an elephant in a Mexican restaurant. By the way, throwing stones at an elephant is even less sensible than using a python as a skipping rope.

4 b) They were drunk on rotting fruit that contained alcohol. When the boozy beasts raided the camp's drink store a brave soldier tried to stop them, but they flattened his hut. The answer isn't **a)** because elephants can't jump.

I SAID, **HALT!**

WHAT YOUR SCORE MEANS...

4 CONGRATULATIONS – you're an excellent elephant expert and I bet you've got a jumbo-sized brain!

2–3 You might get into a flap if an elephant flapped its ears at you.

0–1 Oh dear – you'd best keep away from elephants. Help, where's your teacher's cupboard?!

Mind you, if elephants can be evil you might think these horrible herbivores are worse. Read on now and decide which is cruellest – the terrible tuskers, battering buffalo or horrible hippos...

BATTERING BUFFALO

Cowboys call them "buffalo", but actually they're North American bison. Whatever they are, they're awesomely powerful beasts. A male bison can be 2 metres high from the top of its hump and twice as long, and its skull is even thicker than a school bully's. The skull's said to be bullet-proof (and it's certainly bully-proof)...

Although buffalo rarely kill humans, they will fight back if they think they're being attacked. In 1799 US farmer Samuel McClellan shot at a herd of buffalo that had invaded his farm. The buffalo were starving because humans had taken their grazing land. When Sam stupidly stabbed the leading male buffalo the others overran his house and flattened his family. There's a famous old song that goes...

Oh give me a home where the buffalo roam!

But I don't think that's what it meant. And I don't suppose the buffaloes wiped their feet either...

Bet you never knew!
US General George A Custer (1839–1876) is famous for being killed by Native Americans at the Battle of Little Big Horn. But a few years earlier Custer was nearly killed by the big horn of a buffalo instead. He was out hunting when a brave bison attacked him. The gun-toting general panicked and shot his own horse. Hmm – he sounds like a cowardly Custer to me.

75

HAIR-RAISING HIPPOS (OR HIPPOPOTAMI IF YOU WANT TO WAKE EVERYONE UP IN SCIENCE CLASS)

We're going to find out what makes these angry animals awesomely awful by letting loose a herd of them in a school swimming pool...

You can see what makes a hippo such a menace if you peer into its giant gob.

WOW! It's the biggest yawn of any animal — even bigger than when I nod off in Mr Bottomly's biology class!

50 cm long teeth

Baby hippos are born underwater

SNORE~GLUG GLUG!

Hippos snooze underwater and come up for air in their sleep.

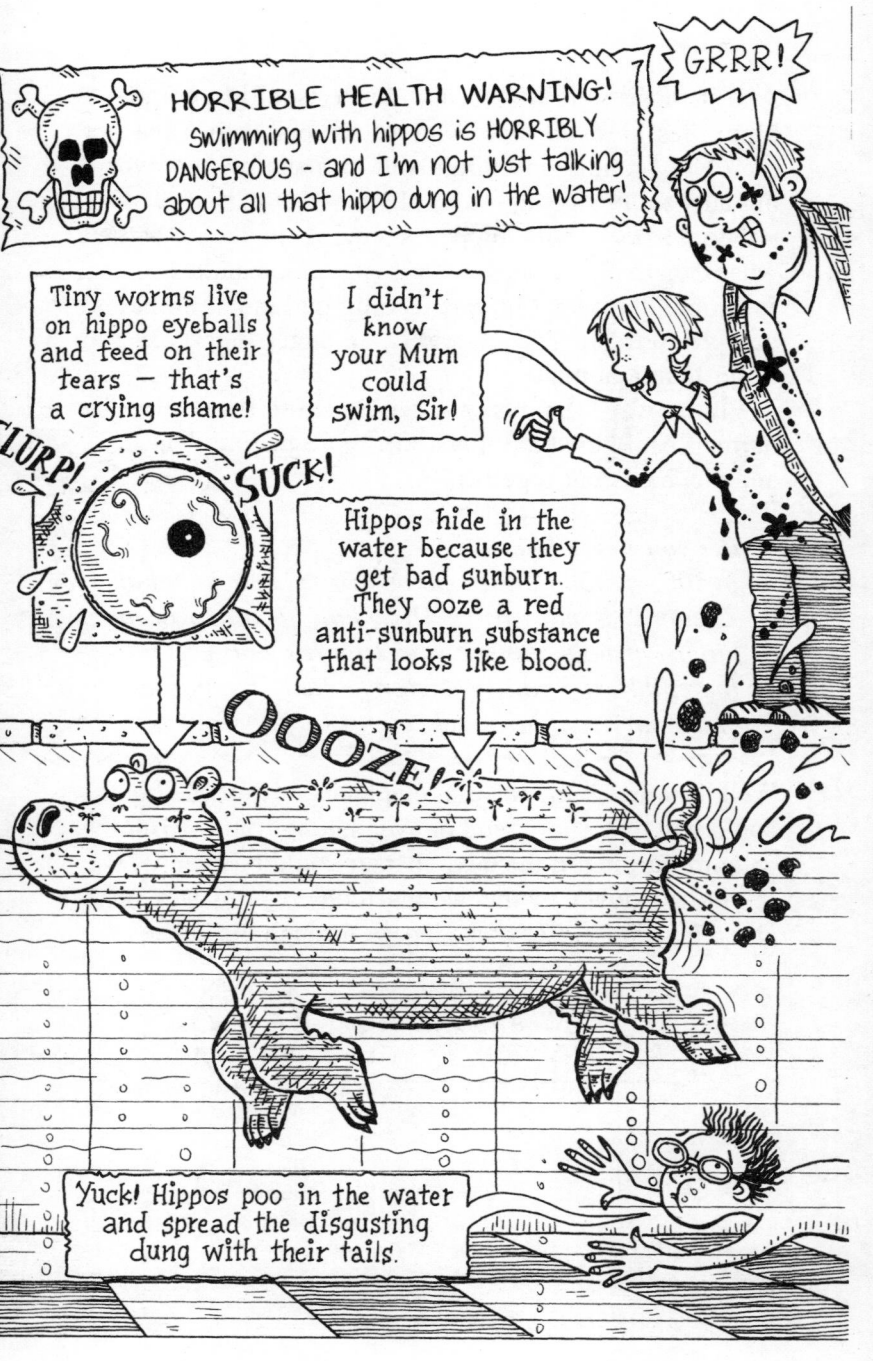

And if those teeth look scary, worse is still to come – a hippo has an even more vicious temper than a teacher on a wet Monday morning. And to make matters worse humans are *always* upsetting them.

• People don't spot hippos snoozing in the river and whack them on the nose with their canoe paddles.

• People don't spot hippos feeding on land at night and bump into them. The trouble is, an angry hippo can run faster than a human!

Either way, the result is a dreadful death for the human. And horrible hippos kill more people than lions and elephants put together.

Bet you never knew!

In 2002 a hippo-attack victim arrived in hospital in Zululand, South Africa. His whole face had been bitten off and all that was left was one eyeball. Incredibly, the patient doctors called "the miracle man" survived the attack.

Well, if you ask me the evil elephants or horrible hippos could win by a short head or even a long trunk... But the creature lurking in the next chapter could be even worse. If you go down to the woods today you're sure of a *horrible* surprise. Let's take a peek through the keyhole...

ER – HAS ANYONE GOT ANY HONEY?

BEWARE OF THE BEARS

Mr Bottomly has a deeply embarrassing secret…

Mr Bottomly by day

The bear is a crepuscular omnivore, blah, blah…

bear

Mr Bottomly by night

Night, night, Mr Wuffles

Oh dear, this is shocking – but a lot of people honestly think bears are cute cuddly teddies. Huh! If you tried to cuddle a real bear you'd suffer a grisly grizzly fate…

Angry animals fact file

NAME OF CREATURE: Brown bear (known in North America as the grizzly)

TYPE OF ANIMAL: Mammal

DIET: Bears are omnivores and insectivores. They eat everything – and I mean EVERYTHING! If you don't believe me, just wait 'til you get to page 87!

NUMBER OF PEOPLE KILLED: Less than five a year in the USA.

WHERE THEY LIVE: Wild areas of North America, Russia and Eastern Europe.

SIZE: About 1.3 metres to their big hairy shoulders.

FEARSOME FEATURES: Sense of smell is 100 times more sensitive than a human's.

Coat can be brown... or black or even blond. (Best not ask this grizzly if she's a "natural blonde".)

Grumpy bad temper.

"Hump" on back called a roach.

GRRR!

14 cm claws.

Different types of teeth for biting and slicing meat and chewing plant food.

Grizzlies can have two or three cubs every three years.

Powerful legs can run at 50 km per hour.

RUTHLESS RELATIVES

Black bear
Size: Up to 1.7 metres long (they're smaller than brown bears).
Lives: North American forests.
Danger-rating: They kill a human every five years or so. Because they often live closer to humans they attack us more often than brown bears.

...AND WE'RE "TREE-MENDOUS" CLIMBERS!

Polar bear

Size: Up to 3 metres tall on their hind legs. Polar bears are the biggest meat-eaters on land. (If you meet one in the dark it won't be all white on the night.)

Lives: On and around the Arctic Ocean.

OF COURSE WE'RE THE BIGGEST MEAT-EATERS... THERE AREN'T ANY PLANTS!

Danger-rating: On average, polar bears kill a person every three years or so in North America. They kill even more rarely in Russia.

We fitted Will D Beest and Mickey with centrally-heated thermal pants and sent them off to check out the dangers...

WILL D BEEST IN ... POLAR PERIL

I'm starring in this Arctic adventure!

IT'S PANTS!

Polar bears ambush seals when they come up to breathe...

B-b-b-b

SEAL BREATHING HOLE

Oh dear! Looks like Will's in a hole lot of bother. He'll bear-ly escape with his life, but he's bear-ing up well, and bear-ing in mind... (Aggggh! I can't bear these bear jokes – The Editor.) Anyway, Will was so busy being mugged by the bear that he forgot to tell us that bears prefer scoffing seals to people. You see, seals have more juicy, energy-rich fat – or blubber – than us...

So I guess we humans aren't filling enough for them...

Polar bears prowl the streets of Churchill in Canada. Believe it or not, a polar bear once even walked into a local club. The manager told the blundering bear it wasn't a member, so it walked out again. At Halloween local children aren't allowed to dress as ghosts because they might be mistaken for polar bears and shot with a knock-out dart.

OF COURSE I'M NOT WEARING A GHOST COSTUME!

Talking about polar bears, did you know that they're all left-handed? Or did I make that up? Your teacher might know – so here's your chance to torture your teacher with a queasy quiz featuring all kinds of bears (it's purely in the interests of entertainment – I mean education!).

TEACHER'S TERROR TORTURE TEST

Test rules

1 The answers to this quiz are either TRUE or FALSE.

2 They're designed to be incredibly hard.

3 If you're soppily soft-hearted you can let your teacher ask the class before he decides...

4 For every wrong answer your teacher loses a point.

5 Whenever his score totals ZERO or less he has to sit on a giant whoopee farting cushion.

TRUE OR FALSE?

1 Polar bears are left-handed.

THAT'S WHY WE HAVE POOR HAND-WRITING!

2 In 2003 a polar bear in a zoo in Argentina was dyed pink.

IT MADE ME SEE RED!

3 Bear brains have a built-in cooling system.

IT'S IMPORTANT TO KEEP A COOL HEAD!

4 Bears don't go to the toilet all winter.

ROLL ON THE SPRING!

5 Some bears pee whilst doing handstands.

OK SO I HAVEN'T GOT THE HANG OF IT YET!

6 Brown bears stink of rotten fish.

YOU DON'T SMELL TOO GOOD YOURSELF!

7 The best thing to do if you're attacked by a brown bear is climb a tree.

ANYONE GOT A LADDER?

Answers:

1 TRUE – polar bears probably shake hands with their left paws, but other bears can be left- or right-handed.

2 FALSE – pink polar bears, ha ha – as if! No, the polar bear was dyed *purple* by an antiseptic spray. Now isn't that a colour to "dye" for?

3 TRUE – the blood vessel that goes to the brain is designed to lose heat to cooler veins heading in the opposite direction. Hot-headed bears also lose heat through their noses.

4 TRUE – bears don't poo or pee for six months when they're hibernating (sleeping through the winter). So how long can your teacher last? Hmm – on second thoughts, don't ask!

5 TRUE – pandas pee on trees to mark their territory. Standing on its front paws helps the panda pee higher and so fool other pandas that it's bigger. Don't try handstands in the toilet – they can result in unfortunate accidents!

6 FALSE – they have a kind of soggy doggy smell.

7 TRUE – but only if it's an adult bear. Their claws are the wrong shape for climbing.

So how did your teacher get on? If he lost he'll be in a beastly bad-temper as he bounces on the farting cushion like a kangaroo fed on beans. But if he won he could be a secret bear boffin and he won't be too miffed when you take your pet bear to school. "Pet *bear*?" I hear you gasp. Why yes – here's how to look after one...

THE HORRIBLE SCIENCE
Bear Care Guide

It's great being a baby-bear owner. Just follow our advice for hours of bear fun and games!

Lesson 1 Bear bed-time

It helps to stay awake at the same time as your bear. Your bear is crepuscular (that's a posh word meaning active at dawn and dusk) and you'll have to be too. So you'll have an early start - yawn! But if you get tired you can always take an afternoon nap in your science lesson!

SORRY, MISS, BUT I'M CREPUSCULAR!

Lesson 2 Making your bear feel at home

Don't expect your bear to help with the housework. If it's as badly behaved as the naughty black bears that break into homes in the wilds of North America,

IT WASN'T ME, MUM!

it'll smash all the china, leave muddy paw-prints everywhere and poo in your brother's bed. Your family might be a bit put out and your bear might be put out too. That's put outside to sleep, and you'll be sent to join it. Oh well, wild bears sleep on a bed of leaves and moss and they're comfy enough!

Lesson 3 Feeding your bear

Like all mammals, baby bears drink their mum's gloopy milk. But when it's four months old, your bear cub will want to sample adult bear foods such as...

Bear de-luxe menu

Meat (cat food).

Small furry animals (the cat).

Berries (bears get berry hungry!).

Juicy leaves (Dad's prize-winning lettuce).

Honey (especially honeycomb with wriggling grubs).

Fish (Bubbles the goldfish).

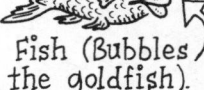

Ants (wood ants taste like gooseberries — just take my word for it!).

During the building of the Trans-Canada highway, bears raided the builders' stores. The greedy grizzlies actually ate dynamite, but DON'T try feeding your bear on explosives!

Lesson 4 School-time is play-time!

Your bear is sure to rule the school. All your friends will want to pet your pet and give it their unwanted school dinners (yes, bears really do eat anything). And it's bound to be very educational when your bear trashes the classroom. I'm sure your teacher will want to join in the fun by being chased round the football pitch and having his bottom whacked by the bear's paw ... followed by a spot of bear wrestling!

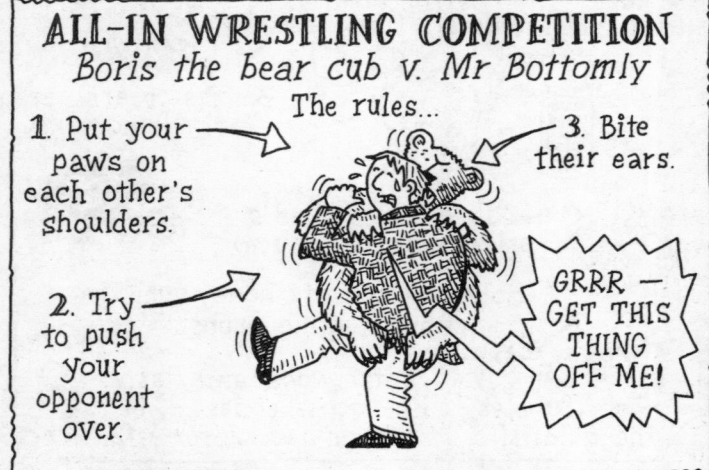

ALL-IN WRESTLING COMPETITION
Boris the bear cub v. Mr Bottomly

The rules...

1. Put your paws on each other's shoulders.

2. Try to push your opponent over.

3. Bite their ears.

GRRR — GET THIS THING OFF ME!

Of course this is all harmless fun. But you'd better stop your bear behaving as badly as black bears in US National Parks...

• Jumping on car roofs to break open the door and steal food.

• Chasing people with food until they panic and drop it - and then scoffing it!

— BLACK BEAR

NO YOU CAN'T HAVE MY STICKY BUN!

After a day of bear fun your teacher's sure to be in a good mood. In fact he'll probably reward you and your pet with a long holiday! This is also known as "being expelled".

Lesson 5 A nice long rest

Your bear will get sleepy in the autumn and want to hibernate all winter. Simply help your bear dig a huge sleeping den in the garden. I'm sure your dad will be delighted if you dig up his boring old prize-winning vegetables ... and if you're still banned from the house you could always move in with your bear! There's only one problem - bears snore! Oh well, you'll just have to grin and BEAR it!

SNORRRE!

A RATHER-TOO-LATE WARNING FROM THE AUTHOR

Baby bears are dangerous. They're strong enough to hurt people and trash your home, and you shouldn't have one as a pet. It's lucky you didn't take our Bear Care Guide too seriously!

Oh you did? And you're sending me the bill? Gulp – I'm off to join Honest Bob in Peru!

Bet you never knew!
In the 1990s a Hungarian couple bought a cute white puppy. They became a bit worried when their pet grew very big and smashed up their home. And they were even more alarmed to discover their puppy was really a polar bear!

GRRR!

ER... WALKIES?

But if baby bears can do dreadful things to your furniture, just think what an adult bear could do to YOU! I mean, look at what happened to poor old Hugh Glass. In 1823 Hugh was part of an expedition exploring the wilds of North America...

My Diary by Hugh Glass
August 1823

I'm in a mess. I'm covered in scratches and my leg is broken. I guess it was my fault. I should never have gone into the forest by myself. I never meant to go disturb that mother bear, but she thought I was hunting her cub and attacked me. I had to kill her – but she darn near killed me first...

One week later
All the others have gone but John Fitzgerald and
Jim Bridger were left behind to
look after me ... until I die. I
heard them last night. John was
whispering that I was a goner and all they had to
do was sneak off and say I was already dead.

One day later...
When I woke up this morning, John and Jim were
gone. They've taken all my belongings.
   "Grr — I ain't finished yet!" I told myself angrily.
   So I put a splint on my broken leg and wrapped
myself in the bear's skin. My wounds were
so rotten I had to roll in maggots. The
hungry little varmints ate the bad bits off
me. Then I began to crawl. I'm heading for Fort
Kiowa — but it's 320 kilometres. Will I make it?

GASP!

Eight weeks later...
I'm STARVING. I've been living off rotten dead
buffalo and berries and snakes, but I won't give
up. Some days the pain drives me crazy. If I ever
find that John and Jim I'LL KILL THE PAIR OF
THEM! That's if I live that long! I've just reached
the Cheyenne River and I've just about reached the
end of my tether... What now???

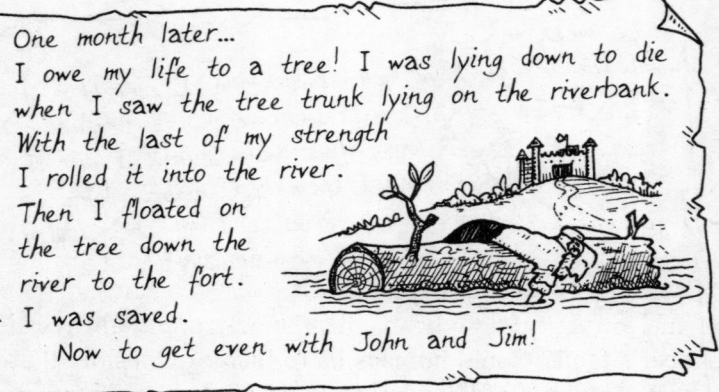

One month later...
I owe my life to a tree! I was lying down to die when I saw the tree trunk lying on the riverbank. With the last of my strength I rolled it into the river.
Then I floated on the tree down the river to the fort.
I was saved.
Now to get even with John and Jim!

You'll be pleased to hear that when Hugh Glass caught up with John and Jim he forgave them. In fact Hugh was lucky. Lucky to find his way to safety and even more lucky to survive the bear's attack. A bear can kill a human with a blow of its paw – and it all takes less than 30 seconds.

COULD YOU BE A SCIENTIST?

In 1984 US scientist Doug Dunbar sprayed a new anti-bear pepper spray in a bear's face. What happened?

a) The angry animal chewed up the scientist.

b) Nothing. The bear simply walked away.

c) The angry animal sneezed gloopy bear-snot all over the scientists.

ACHOO!

UGH! IT'S YOGI, I MEAN, **BOGEY** BEAR!

Answer:
a) Mind you, it took a few tries before the scientist made a bear angry enough to attack and test the spray. Before then the bears wandered off, so there's half a point for **b)**.

So, bears are quite hard to annoy, it seems. That's interesting. Could it be that bear attacks aren't always the bear's fault? Could humans be to blame? Consider these facts: rangers in Yellowstone Park, USA, once stopped a woman dabbing honey on her child's face so a bear could lick it off. Another man put a bear in his car to take a photo of it sitting next to his wife. So who was more brainless – the humans or the bears? We've asked a brainy bear to explain the bear's point of view to a rather brainless human…

 **Bear's** point of view

 **Human's** point of view

You disturb us when we're resting and frighten our cubs.

You act like bears with sore heads!

You humans take our territories to graze your animals.

You bears eat our animals.

Then you shoot us!

Hey, lighten up, buddy! It's only sport! You bears steal our food.

93

Well we're starving because you've taken our territories. Got any chocolate?

NO!

OK, I'll eat you...

KEEP AWAY FROM ME YOU BEASTLY ANIMAL!

So maybe bears aren't so cruel?

Maybe they're not even front-runners for the Cruellest Creature Competition?

What do *you* think?

Tell you what – you can always make up your mind after the next chapter. Now – who's brave enough to feed our next group of angry animals? Oh thanks, Will!

HERE KITTY, KITTY!

HE'LL DO ANYTHING FOR PUBLICITY!

CRUEL BIG CATS

Please answer the following questions…

1 Do you live with a cat?

2 Does your cat enjoy playing with half-dead mice, staring hungrily at the budgie and sinking her claws into the postman?

If you answered "yes" to both of the above questions it's quite likely that you own a cruel cat. But even the cruellest cat is a cutesy-pie kitten compared to this lot…

No wonder they didn't want the cat food. Er, has anyone seen Will?

Angry animals fact file

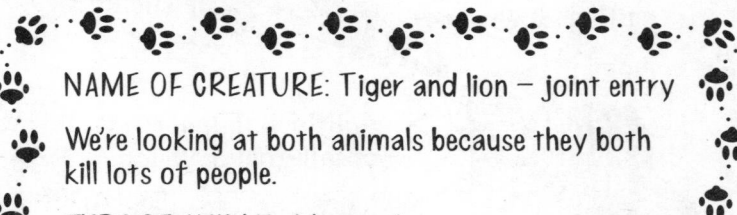

NAME OF CREATURE: Tiger and lion — joint entry

We're looking at both animals because they both kill lots of people.

TYPE OF ANIMAL: Mammal

DIET: Meat, meat and more meat — ideally large four-footed creatures. Lions like wildebeest and zebra. Tigers eat several species of Indian deer. Oh yes, and neither species minds munching a human…

NUMBER OF PEOPLE KILLED: Each year lions kill hundreds of people in Africa and tigers kill over 100 people in India.

WHERE THEY LIVE: Lions live on open plains in Africa (with a few in India). Tigers live in forests, mainly in India and Nepal with a few in South-east Asia, China and Russia.

SIZE: Lions and tigers grow up to 2.7 metres long including their tails.

FEARSOME FEATURES:

Paws the size of a man's head.

LION

Greasy waterproof coat.

Canine teeth for biting prey.

Claws as thick as a man's thumb for pulling down prey.

GRRR!

Flesh-slicing back teeth.

TIGER

Slightly bulging eyes for all-round vision.

Stripy coat to blend in with long grass and forest.

Soft paws for silent creeping.

RUTHLESS RELATIVES

Although lions and tigers look different, they're part of the same group of animals – scientists call them the *Panthera,* or roaring cats. (Your cat isn't a roaring cat – she's a mewing cat. Especially when she wants more supper and she's trying to make you feel sorry for her.) But here's some roaring panthera you really wouldn't want to meet on a dark night…

Jaguar
Size: Up to 1.9 metres long.
Lives: Forests in South America.
Danger-rating: Rarely attacks humans but does enjoy sinking its fangs into a victim's brain. Maybe it's hungry for knowledge…

Puma
(alias the cougar or mountain lion and I bet if one attacked you, you might like to call it other names).
Size: Up to 2.4 metres long.
Lives: Wild parts of North and South America.
Danger-rating: Can attack people but deaths are very rare.

Leopard

Size: Up to 2.5 metres long (including tail).

Lives: Plains in Africa and forests in India.

Danger-rating: They normally hunt monkeys and antelopes but they have a horribly antisocial habit of breaking into huts and grabbing people in their sleep. And a leopard can knock the spots off a human in a fight.

GRRR – WHERE'S THE MONKEY FROM PAGE 94?

Bet you never knew!
In 1998 a puma calmly strolled into the office of a plastics company in the USA. It scared the secretaries and terrified the typists until a brave employee locked it in an empty office. Well, I hope the office was empty…

GOOD DAY AT THE OFFICE, DEAR?

As you've just found out lions and tigers live in different places, but let's imagine a lion cub and tiger cub met for a chat. OK, I realize this is going to take a bit of imagining…

Tiger cub HELLO!   Lion cub HI!

TC: Mum feeds me.

LC: Mum and Gran and Mum's sisters feed me. We're called a pride – well, Mum's proud of us!

TC: We only feed every few days.

LC: So do we – blimey I'm starving!

TC: Mum lets me eat first.

LC: Huh – you're lucky! I have to eat last.

TC: I never see my dad.

LC: My dad rules the pride.

TC: My mum made a chemical message in her wee to attract my dad.

LC: So did my mum. Grown-ups are s-o-o disgusting!

TC: My dad makes a Aoooom! sound to warn off other tigers.

LC: My dad roars.

TC: If a new male tiger takes over my dad's territory he could kill me.

LC: If a new male takes over the pride he could kill me.

WE HAVE IT TOUGH!

TC: Fancy a game of chase?

LC: OK – you're IT!

Actually, lion and tiger cubs don't play for fun. Well, that's according to boring old scientists who haven't had fun for 50 years. Instead, the scientists say the cubs are practising adult skills such as hunting and fighting. Sadly, human cubs aren't allowed to practise vital fighting skills with their brothers and sisters.

But talking about hunting, there was an awful lot of that going on in Tsavo, Africa, in 1898. In that year a pair of man-eating lions ate more than 130 African and Indian workers who were building a railway. Here's how one of the workers might have described the danger. Read on if you think you're up to scratch…

30 November 1898

My dear sister

Here I am in Tsavo, helping to build a railway - but there's a terrible problem. Many of my friends have been eaten by a pair of lions. All we hear is a scream in the night followed by the sound of crunching bones, and in the morning all that's left is a head … or a hand and puddles of blood.

Our boss Colonel Patterson built thorn hedges around the camp and posted guards. But the lions are as fearless as demons. My friends whisper that the lions can't be killed - they call them The Ghost and The Darkness. We were so scared that we took to sleeping in a tree. But we were too heavy and now the tree's fallen down! I'm really scared I'll be the next victim…

Pray for me!

Your brother, Govinder

30 December 1898

My dear sister

Much has happened since my last letter. Colonel Patterson built a giant wooden trap and caught one lion.

But some policemen who were helping him tried to shoot the animal. They shot off the lock by mistake and the lion got away!

Then Colonel Patterson's boss came to see what was happening and the lion attacked him and tore up his best suit. This big boss was not happy, especially when the lions ate his pet goats (all except one which the Colonel shot by mistake).

GRRR!

Next the Colonel built a wobbly platform from sticks. He told us he would wait on top of it every night until he could shoot the lions. A few nights later a lion showed up but just then an owl landed on the Colonel's head. The Colonel still managed to fire his gun and hit the lion.

He was most pleased. Yesterday the Colonel was even more pleased after he tracked down and shot the second lion.

We workers are happy too because we no longer have to fall asleep wondering whether we will wake up in the lion's jaws. Hooray for Colonel Patterson! I think we all deserve a holiday!

Your brother,
Govinder

I PROPPED THE DEAD LION UP WITH STICKS!

Of course there are still man-eating big cats in Africa,
and Will D Beest was air-brained enough to want to take
a closer look. Here's Mickey to take up the story...

WILL D BEEST IN ... BIG CAT, BIGGER TROUBLE

This opens up a big ugly can of worms... Why do lions, tigers and leopards attack us? Is it because they don't like us? The answer is NO – or as a scientist would put it...

The main reason why big cats eat us is because they're hungry and we're easy to catch. They could be hungry because...

• They're too old and toothless to catch their usual prey.
• They have been injured in fights with other animals or humans.
• Humans have driven away their usual prey in order to graze their farm animals.

In other words it could be our fault if a big cat turns to eating people. But just to complicate the picture…
• Not all big cats eat people – even if they're hungry.
• Some big cats eat people when they're not obviously starving.
• Some female man-eating big cats train their cubs to eat people too.

And now for a few purr-fectly horrible big cat stories…

FIVE BEASTLY BIG CAT BITES

1 When a tiger grabbed elephant driver Subedar Ali, the young man prayed to all the gods he could think of. The tiger ripped flesh from the top of Ali's head and nearly bit his fingers off. But Ali's elephant picked him up in its trunk and pulled him to safety. Officials at the Corbett National Park, India, wanted to shoot the tiger but Ali begged for the animal to be saved. His wish was granted. The tiger was sent to a zoo and Subedar Ali visited it to say "hello".

2 In 1870 James Robinson's Circus visited Middletown, Missouri, in the USA. A ten-piece band played a cheery tune on top of the lions' cage. But the roof was weak. With a bang and a crash the band fell into the lions' cage and seven of them were eaten. So I guess the lions got a taste for music…

DROP IN ANYTIME!

3 In 1937 an English vicar called Harold Davidson was sitting in a cage with a lion named Freddie. (The vicar was trying to make some money after losing his job.) But when the clumsy cleric trod on his tail, Freddie began to feast on the priest with fatal results.

4 Despite the danger, thousands of people keep big cats as pets. In Brazil they're kept as guard dogs – er, cats – and burglars have been eaten. (I wonder if they were beefy burglars, cheesy burglars or even veggie burglars.)

5 In 2003 a man in New York kept a tiger, an alligator and a kitten as pets. But the tiger decided to eat the kitten. The oddball owner tried to save the kitten and got bitten. The big animals ended up in zoos, the man ended up in hospital, and the kitten ended up in shock.

EATEN B-B-B-Y MY OWN R-R-RELATIVE... F-F-F-F-FREAKY!

Well, it does look as if we humans have made the problem of man-eating worse – so does that mean man-eating big cats aren't cruel creatures? And if they are, could they be more savage than sharks and more sinister than snakes? Or more wicked than the creatures in our next blood-curdling chapter?

Read on for the howl truth…

HOWWWWWL!

IS THAT YOU, WILL?

WICKED WOLVES

Fairy stories are full of wolves dressing up as grannies or scaring little pigs, but real wolves are much more dangerous and far more fearsome. In fact, if you ask me, we've found our Cruellest Creature Competition winner! To prove it, I'm going to turn out the lights and tell you a terrible tale about a werewolf – a human who turned into a wolf. WARNING – this could be a bit scary!

The Horrible Science Book of
SCARY TALES
FOR NASTY BOYS AND GIRLS

THE EVIL WOLF-MAN

Are you sitting uncomfortably? Then I'll begin. A long time ago in the cold, bleak Auvergne Mountains of France there lived a nasty nobleman by the name of Count Vargo. This cruel count enjoyed attacking people for fun and he was so evil that even his own mother didn't have a good word to say about him. One day Count Vargo attacked a young girl. Hearing the girl's screams, her two brothers rushed to her rescue. The lads bravely fought the Count off and as the villain ran away into the forest, one of them cursed him.

"The whole of nature will be against you, Count Vargo!"

The cruel Count merely laughed – but within minutes his laughter turned to a scream of terror. Without warning a huge wolf leapt from the bushes. The fearsome beast seized Count Vargo in its sharp slobbery jaws.

"Help me – save me!" shrieked the Count.

An old man heard the Count's cries and set his dog on the wolf. But the wolf tore the dog's throat out. Then, with an evil howl that sent shivers down the old man's spine, the wolf loped off into the forest.

The Count lay in a puddle of dark red blood. He was still alive but the old man was afraid that the wolf would return. He dared not take the Count to safety until dawn.

Count Vargo recovered from his wounds, but he was a changed man. He began to chew on raw flesh and one night he disappeared. And that's when the howling began. The howls rang through Mercoire Forest and terrified the peasants. Some of them reported seeing a giant wolf. The frightened peasants whispered that the creature was none other than Count Vargo who had become a werewolf – a human that becomes a wolf.

Then the killings began... Men and women were found torn apart. This was no ordinary wolf. Time after time, hunters fired at the beast. And time after time the bullets seemed to strike the wolf only for the beast to escape – unharmed! Perhaps the curse had come true and the Count was the enemy of all other creatures!

Soldiers and hunters searched for the wolf. No one could find it. Even the bravest bloodhounds yelped and cringed in terror when they picked up the beast's scent. All that winter and the following spring, the killings continued, until no one dared to leave their homes. At last, the king sent his huntsman, Antoine de Beauterne, to kill the wolf. Patiently, the huntsman mapped the area, searching for the beast's lair. Then, he led a band of men and dogs to the dark ravine where he thought the wolf lived.

There was a horrible silence. No bird dared to sing. But something was watching from the bushes. Something big and cruel and angry. Then, all at once, the wolf charged. Antoine fired his gun. All the men fired. Their bullets struck the beast again and again, but it didn't fall until its evil heart had bled dry.

At last the wolf was dead, and as for Count Vargo … he was never seen again. But you can be sure he died unhappily ever after!

SO WHAT'S THE BORING OLD TRUTH?

In 1765 a huge wolf killed more than 100 victims, and it was said to be Count Vargo. A second beast was shot in 1767. But scientists don't believe in werewolves and many experts think the creatures were wolf-dog cross-breeds. Hmm – maybe it's time we focused on the facts scientists agree with…

Angry animals fact file

NAME OF CREATURE: Wolf

TYPE OF ANIMAL: Mammal

DIET: Carnivore. Wolves hunt small mammals on their own and band together to kill big animals such as elk.

NUMBER OF PEOPLE KILLED: Wolves sometimes kill people (mostly in India).

WHERE THEY LIVE: North America (mainly in Canada and Alaska), Russia, Eastern Europe and parts of Asia and India.

SIZE: Male wolves grow to 2 metres long and 85 cm high.

FEARSOME FEATURES:

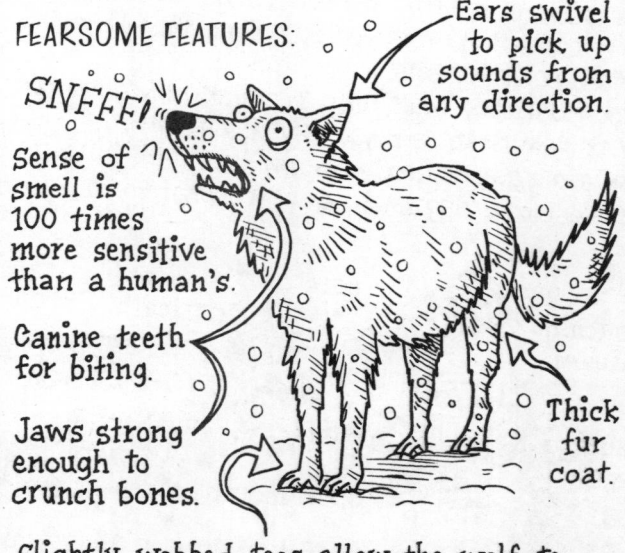

Ears swivel to pick up sounds from any direction.

SNFFF!

Sense of smell is 100 times more sensitive than a human's.

Canine teeth for biting.

Jaws strong enough to crunch bones.

Thick fur coat.

Slightly webbed toes allow the wolf to run on snow without sinking too much.

RUTHLESS RELATIVES

Wolves belong to a group of animals called canids, which includes red wolves, coyotes, foxes and dogs. From this group, only wolves and dogs kill humans (see page 115 for the deadly doggie details). But in the USA coyotes are said to give cats nervous breakdowns by staring at them through windows and breathing on the glass (no, honestly, I didn't make that up!).

Canids often live in family groups, and a wolf family is called a pack. So how would you get on in a wolf pack? And could it be any worse than life in your own pack, er, family?

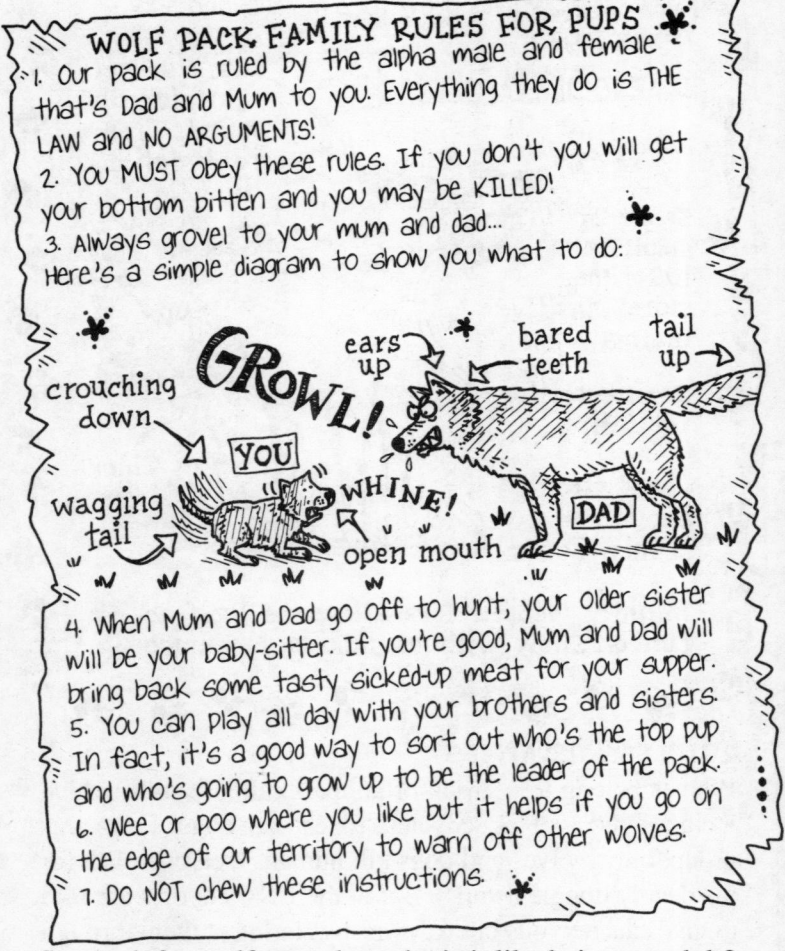

WOLF PACK FAMILY RULES FOR PUPS

1. Our pack is ruled by the alpha male and female that's Dad and Mum to you. Everything they do is THE LAW and NO ARGUMENTS!
2. You MUST obey these rules. If you don't you will get your bottom bitten and you may be KILLED!
3. Always grovel to your mum and dad... Here's a simple diagram to show you what to do:

crouching down
GROWL!
ears up
bared teeth
tail up
YOU
WHINE!
wagging tail
open mouth
DAD

4. When Mum and Dad go off to hunt, your older sister will be your baby-sitter. If you're good, Mum and Dad will bring back some tasty sicked-up meat for your supper.
5. You can play all day with your brothers and sisters. In fact, it's a good way to sort out who's the top pup and who's going to grow up to be the leader of the pack.
6. Wee or poo where you like but it helps if you go on the edge of our territory to warn off other wolves.
7. DO NOT chew these instructions.

So much for wolf pups, but what's it like being an adult? Let's take a look at this wolf newspaper...

The Daily Wolf

IN TODAY'S NEWS:
▶ Win a wolf whistle
▶ Wolf spotted in sheep's clothing
▶ Little Red Riding Hood had it coming — a wolf speaks out

WOLF & WOLF

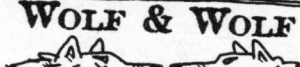

ESTATE AGENTS

We'll keep the wolf from your door!
Looking for a territory to hunt in?

LOVELY BIG TERRITORY IN CANADA

500 square km — and lots of elk to munch! Just the right size for your growing pack!
Also included — deluxe wolf meeting place
• Lots of half-chewed animal bones for pups to play with
• Den for the pups to be born in (OK, it's a hole in the ground but it's a palace for us wolves!)

Just published...
THE WOLF HAPPY HUNTING GUIDE

Find out how to choose the weakest elk in the herd, pull it down and rip it to pieces — it's all down to team-work!

YOU ARE THE WEAKEST ELK... GOODBYE!

"This book really gave me something to get my teeth into. And there weren't too many howling mistakes."
AN Other-Wolf

Just released... **THE WOLF PACK'S GREATEST HITS**
Listen to one of the greatest packs of our time howling out their most famous songs ... including their chart-topping classic the haunting and heart-warming
"HOWWWWWWWWL — GET OUT OF OUR TERRITORY YOU OTHER WOLVES OR WE'LL RIP YOU TO BITS!"
"Strangely moving — in fact I'm moving to safety right now!" A wolf music critic

If you ask me, wolves sound rather dangerous – and anyone who wants to howl at wolves has the brains of a jellyfish...

WILL D BEEST IN ... WOLF WARNING

Will and Mickey are in Canada finding out about the world of wolves...

As a top TV naturalist I'm used to danger...

Will he ever learn?

If I howl at wolves, they'll howl back.

Here comes trouble...

HOWOOL!

HOWL!

Trouble is, the wolves think I'm another wolf — they may attack.

Now he tells me...

A wolf can scent me 2.5 km away so I'm masking my scent by rolling in rotten fish. Wolves do this to confuse elk.

This plan stinks!

GRRR!

YIKES — I forgot about the grizzlies!

I must say, wolves sound cruel to everyone including other wolves. And if they're as cruel as they're cracked up to be they're a DEAD cert for the Cruellest Creature award. But are they? Well, one thing's certain – humans have killed millions of wolves. Hundreds of years ago, wolves were found all over North America, Europe and most of Asia. But humans have wiped them out in many countries.

- The last wolf in Britain was shot in 1743.
- Nearly every wolf in the USA was killed by the 1920s.
- Wolves were wiped out in France by 1927.

And yet in all that time humans were welcoming millions of wolves into their homes! No, seriously, readers – it's true!

Bet you never knew!
Many scientists believe that dogs are descended from wolves that people once kept to help with hunting. And wolves and dogs still have a lot in common. Both animals show their feelings by making the same sounds and adopting the same positions.
• They bark to sound a warning, wag their tails when friendly and growl when they're cross.

• Does your dog whine and try to lick you when it wants feeding? Wolf pups do this to get their parents to feed them. If you sicked-up some meat your dog might even want to lick it up.

113

- *If your dog whines and grovels when you're cross with it, it probably thinks you're its pack leader.*
- *Does your dog insist on sniffing and peeing on lampposts and leaving you-know-whats in certain places? Well, he's acting like a wolf marking his territory (your dog probably thinks you own your home town).*

For 10,000 years humans have bred dogs to look different from wolves. And we've developed a very close friendship with dogs … *most* of the time.

BARKING MAD QUIZ

Which of these three so-called dog facts are true and which one is a shaggy dog story?

1 In 2003 a Japanese company invented a machine that translates dog sounds into human speech.

2 A Brazilian doctor trained his pet dog to help with surgical operations.

3 A dog was once a king in Norway.

Answer:
1 TRUE – Japanese toy maker Takara has created a device called Bowlingual that picks up the sounds made by dogs, works out the sound patterns and turns them into a message. They've made a similar device for cats.

2 FALSE – Would you want a doggie doctor or a Fido physician? I hope not – dogs can be DANGEROUS!!!

3 TRUE – According to legend, King Eystein conquered his enemies and made them choose his dog as their ruler. I bet the dog made everyone else bow-wow to him.

FIDO THE FEARSOME

Most dogs have been bred and trained *not* to attack humans, but some of them can be a menace…

1 Parts of the USA and Europe have been terrorized by wild dogs (mostly unwanted pets). These prowling packs include all types of dogs but they're usually led by big dogs such as Alsatians.

WANTED FOR MURDER

THE DOG GANG

ARTIST'S IMPRESSION OF THE RING-LEADER

In 2001 these horrible hounds raided Staten Island Zoo, New York, and killed two wallabies, four deer and a pair of peacocks.

Reward $50 AND ALL THE DOGGIE BISCUITS YOU CAN EAT.

2 In the USA, every year about 18 people are killed by dogs and about 300,000 need hospital treatment. In fact, deadly dogs kill and injure more people than sharks, snakes, bears and mountain lions put together!

3 In 2001, wild dogs known as dingos killed a boy on Fraser Island, Australia.

4 Some breeds, such as pit-bull terriers, have been bred to fight other dogs. In most countries dog fights are against the law but in 2002 thieves in California tried to steal a litter of pit-bull puppies to train them to fight. Unfortunately they stole chihuahua puppies by mistake…

I guess those thieves were dogged by misfortune and now they're in the doghouse.

So where does all this leave our Cruellest Creature Competition? Is the treasured trophy going to the dogs – or are we barking up the wrong tree? Well, don't go away – I'VE JUST HEARD WE'VE GOT A RESULT!

AT LAST – THE NEWS YOU'VE ALL BEEN WAITING FOR…

Welcome to the Anytown Zoo! We're here to announce the winner of the Horrible Science Cruellest Creature Competition. All the animals in this book are here except for the great white shark (no one's been brave enough to invite him).

And here to make the announcement is Will D Beest...

And the winner is...

Well, why not turn the page and find out who's won?

Surely not?

You're kidding!

I don't BELIEVE it!

Gasp!

THE WORLD'S CRUELLEST CREATURE?

And here to receive the award is Honest Bob.

Oh dear, there are scenes of uproar in the hall. Will's looking upset, the animals are angry and Bob's run off with the trophy. We asked Will why he's so unhappy at the result...

I think Will's got a point. So I asked the judges to explain their decision...

Is that really true? Let's see if the judges are right. Do humans really kill more dangerous animals than they kill us? Well, the figures are a bit sketchy – but here's a fascinating figure about sharks...

DEATHS PER YEAR SCOREBOARD
Humans v Sharks (all species)
Humans = 12
Sharks = 100 MILLION

And look at all the crocodiles and buffaloes and bears and tigers and lions and wolves that humans have killed over the years. OK, we'd better agree with the judges on numbers. But what about us being able to wipe out other animals. Surely that's a bit over the top?

Er, no it's not...

Remember all that stuff about food webs and habitats? (Take a look back to page 11 if you don't.) Food webs mean that animals depend on each other for food. But when humans take over a habitat the food

119

web unravels faster than your granny's knitted jumper. And since the big carnivores at the top of the food chains need lots of herbivores to hunt, they're in great danger of going hungry. Let's visit Wolf Forest in North America...

OK, so I made up Wolf Forest – but many of the animals in this book are going hungry as humans take over their habitats. We've seen it with elephants and bears and lions and tigers. And when the wild animals eat the humans' livestock or crops the humans turn nasty and the animals are in danger…

Bet you never knew!
In 2008, 16,928 species were in danger of dying out – including one-eighth of all birds, more than a fifth of all mammals, and one in three amphibians. More than 100 species are dying out every week, and that's just in the world's rainforests.

Let's see what this means for some of the animals in this book. I've invented a machine called an Extinct-o-meter. All you do is press the button for each animal and find out how many are left. If the animal's in danger of becoming extinct (dying out) a siren sounds…

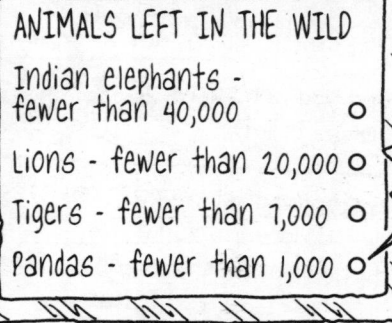

ANIMALS LEFT IN THE WILD

Indian elephants – fewer than 40,000 ○

Lions – fewer than 20,000 ○

Tigers – fewer than 1,000 ○

Pandas – fewer than 1,000 ○

Neeeeeeeeeeegh!

Is this really necessary?

Hmm – it really does look as if humans could wipe out some species of animals in this book. It's a good thing no one's shooting animals for money and selling off their body bits… Oh dear, look what I've just found!

Honest Bob's Animal Body Bits shop

All our products are guaranteed illegal, so if you see any cops you don't know me – right?*

Brighten up your home and scare the cat with a traditional **tiger-skin rug**. Warning – keep clear of the sharp teeth!

ORIENTAL MEDICINES

Bear bile slurp – lovely **bear's gall bladder** (that's the bit that stores digestive juices from the liver). It's good for your guts and your heart.

Delicious **tiger-bone tonic wine**. It's good for your joints and it boosts your brainpower!

Tiger skull. Sleep on it and you won't have nightmares (traditional Chinese belief).

Lovely **leopard-skin coat**. You'll feel a million dollars in this luxury coat – so that's what I'll charge you!

Genuine wild **crocodile-skin shoes** and matching handbags. Ideal for the snappy dresser!

*DON'T worry, readers, Bob's a con-artist – so he's not selling real animal body bits!

Do you like elephants? You'll love this tasty **elephant meat**. Yes, you can tuck into jumbo–sized steaks.

Trendy ivory jewellery. Made from real **elephant tusks**.

NASTY NOTES

1 In 2005 experts claimed that poachers in India were killing one tiger every day.

2 Tiger bones do have some painkilling powers – but then so do other animal bones. Bear gall bladders also have medical uses, but man-made substances work just as well.

3 Some people like to eat wild animal meat including the flesh of monkeys and chimps. Can't understand it myself – I mean who'd want to munch a monkey?

HMMMM! MONKEY AND CHIMPS – I MEAN, CHIPS!

DON'T EVEN JOKE ABOUT IT!

Time to sum up. It looks like the judges are right. Some humans are a menace to the animals in this book – but does that make us cruel creatures? Surely we humans have a kinder, gentler side?

I've got a feeling we might find out in the next chapter. Let's hope so – it's the last one!

EPILOGUE: CARING FOR CREATURES

The first Cruellest Creature Competition was held over 500 years ago. In 1459 Count Cosimo de Medici of Florence wanted to find out which animal was fiercest.

But things didn't turn out that way...

The animals were well-fed and, like any well-fed animals, they weren't too keen to fight and risk injury. In fact the cruellest creatures proved to be the humans who set up the terrible test.

Our Horrible Science Cruellest Creature Competition was won by humans, but that doesn't mean we're all cruel. After all, some people really care about animals...

Remember Charles Waterton? Or Subedar Ali trying to save the tiger that attacked him? And *you're* not cruel to animals, are you? Right now many people are trying to save wild animals. Here's an inspiring story that sums up the best and worst about people...

NOW YOU'RE TALKING!

THE BUMPED-OFF BISON

Two hundred years ago the North American plains were thick with bison. You could travel for days and see them all around you. Scientists think they were the biggest herds of wild animals ever. Within 100 years nearly all the bison were dead. Many had been shot by hunters ... for FUN!

WHERE ARE YOU, MUM?

BEFORE

MUM?

AFTER

In Europe all the bison had been slaughtered long ago … except for one herd in the forest of Bialowieza in Poland. In 1914 a battle was fought in the forest and nearly all the bison were killed.

But that's not the end of the story…

In the USA and Europe some bison survived in zoos. Slowly they bred and today bison have returned to the North American plains and the forest of Bialowieza.

This last bit is terribly important. All over the world scientists are studying wild animals in their habitats and trying to find ways to protect them…

• Most countries have already banned the hunting of the animals in this book.

• An international agreement called CITES (Convention on International Trade in Endangered Species) attempts to stamp out the trade in rare animal body bits.

• Zoos are trying to breed rare wild animals in safety. Even if they die out in the wild, some will survive in captivity.

• Some experts think that hunting is a good way to protect habitats – just so long as it's strictly controlled. Many experts are against all hunting.

• More and more tourists visit wild places and some experts hope that the money tourists spend can be used to protect habitats and save their wild animals.

So humans aren't all bad. Some of us might be cruel creatures, but many more of us are caring creatures. And let's hope we're clever enough to choose the best way forward. Happy Horrible Science everyone!

Clever creatures? You're joking!

ANGRY ANIMALS

QUIZ

Now find out if you're an
Angry Animals expert!

So, you've dodged deadly darts from spitting cobras, battled with bears and wrestled with the gruesome tale of Count Vargo. But are you fully up to speed with the world's cruellest critters? Take the quizzes below and find out!

Beastly basics facts

From vertebrates to invertebrates, there are an eye-watering 50 million species on Earth. Don't worry – we're not going to ask you to name them! What you need to do is cast your eye over these frighteningly fiendish questions about our beastly buddies (complete with curiously kind clues)...

1 What's the proper name for meat-scoffing animals? (CLUE: They'd love chilli con *carne*)

2 How does the cute little fieldfare bird protect its nest? (CLUE: You'd need a good wash afterwards!)

3 What do scary scavengers such as vultures like to chow down on? (CLUE: They're not worried about 'best before' dates!)

4 Which fearsome reptile has a nerve-shredding roar like 'distant thunder'? (CLUE: They only need to feed once a week)

5 Why do snakes pick up sound waves from the ground? (CLUE: They can't wear glasses)

6 Why do hippos ooze a red, oily substance from their skin? (CLUE: Look up for an answer!)

7 What kind of bear eats more meat than any other wild animal? (CLUE: They might keep it in the freezer)

8 What would happen to plant-eating animals if all the world's meat-eating creatures died? (CLUE: It's dead simple)

Answers:
1 Carnivores
2 The winged warrior defends its habitat by pooing on trespassers!
3 Dead animals
4 Crocodiles
5 They have no ears
6 The poor mites suffer from sunburn
7 Polar bears
8 The plant eaters would increase their numbers and guzzle all the plants until they ran out of food. They too would then die.

Savage sharks

How would you fare if you were to dip your toe into shark-infested waters? Would you lose a limb in a blood-drenched attack, or would your fishy knowledge save you from a toothy encounter? It's time to find out.

1 Great white sharks kill fewer than two people per year. What's their favourite feast?

a) Seals

b) Sea horses

c) Shire horses

2 Great whites hatch from eggs while still inside their mums – so what do they munch on while waiting to be born?

a) The gruesome remains of unfortunate sailors.

b) Their un-hatched brothers and sisters.

c) Chips.

3 An American scientist once proved that sharks were fussy eaters by using a furry critter as bait. What was the creature that the cunning killing machines turned their noses up at?

a) A meerkat

b) A tabby cat

c) A rat

4 What's the name for the mix of fish blood and guts used to attract sharks in the wild?

a) Chum

b) Blood broth

c) Cuppa Sick

5 Sharks can sniff blood in the water from far away. But *how* far, exactly?

a) 100 miles

b) 0.5 miles

c) 100 cm

6 How did South Africans try and drive away sharks from their shores in 1957?
a) They dropped bombs into the water.
b) They dropped eggy stink-bombs into the depths.
c) The dropped cows into the water.

7 What is a selachophobic?
a) Someone who's scared of sharks.
b) Someone who loves sharks.
c) Someone who clears up shark poo in aquariums.

8 Where would you find cartilage – the stuff that makes up a shark's skeleton – in your own body?
a) In your ears and nose.
b) In your toenails.
c) Slopping around in your stomach.

Answers:
1a; 2b; 3c; 4a; 5b; 6a; 7a; 8a

Sinister snakes

Serpents are a slippery bunch – just as you're getting to grips with one, another, even more deadly, species slinks along and ruins your whole day. Some of the world's worst snakes have slithered along to introduce themselves. Can you work out who's who?

1 Like many of my serpentine siblings, I can inject poison through my fangs, but I'm ssssupremely sssspecial because of my neck – it widens to warn off larger creatures.

2 I live in India and southern Asia and can grow up to an impressive 1.8 metres long. My favourite trick is to crawl into the beds of unsuspecting human victims and deliver a deadly nightmare nerve poison.

3 Me and all of my 28 American relatives are poisonous – but that's not what makes us exceptional. Our most fearsome feature is a shaft of dry skin that makes a distinctive noise when shaken…

4 I may be slim and short (just 90 cm), but I pack the deadliest bite of any serpent. Luckily for humans, I rarely target the divers who disturb my sub-aquatic slumber.

5 Kick up the sand in Africa and you'll probably find all four-and-a-half metres of my thick, black length curled up in the scorching sun. Don't take me on, though – my poison can kill within 20 minutes!

6 I live in Africa, south of the Sahara Desert, and while I might not have the deadliest venom in the world, my method of delivery is truly terrifying. If you get in my bad books, I'll sling a gob of poison your way that will dissolve your eyeballs.

7 I mostly eat small animals such as birds and bats, but if I come across anything bigger, I have a particularly neat way of putting them into a tight spot. I'll sink my jaws into them, coil myself around them and … sque-e-e-eze.

8 Don't think for one minute that you're safe from snakes in Britain. Mess with me when I'm enjoying a snooze in the sun and I'll give you a bite that'll make you feel rotten for hours.

a) Sea snake
b) King cobra
c) Spitting cobra
d) Common krait
e) Rattle snake
f) Adder
g) Python
h) Black mamba

Answers:
1b; 2d; 3e; 4a; 5h; 6c; 7g; 8f

Big bad beasts

Below are some notes from the eighteenth-century explorer, Sir Percival Bottomly-Higginbottom. Infuriatingly, some of the words are missing! Fill in the gaps to make sense of the old boy's animal ramblings.

Dear Diary,

Today I witnessed my first Savannah Elephant. It stood well over 1)_____ metres high and was pulling up grass and roots with its enormous trunk – the locals tell me it can consume a massive 2)_____ of greenery every day.

It reminded me of the North American bison I saw last year. That was an impressive beast, and no mistake. The one I saw was built like a steam locomotive and had a 3)_____ that was thick enough to withstand a bullet.

Perhaps the most imposing creature I've encountered thus far is a hippopotamus. A fearsome blighter with teeth 4)_____ long, it has tiny worms living in its 5)_____. Ghastly!

Next month I hope to catch up with the brown bears of North America. Now, they are a sight to behold. They have claws 6)_____ long, can run at speeds of up to 7)_____ and kill 8)_____ poor souls every year.

Toodle-pip!

a) 50 cm
b) Three
c) 50 km/h
d) 14 cm
e) Eyes
f) Five
g) Skull
h) 200 kg

Answers:
1b; 2h; 3g; 4a; 5e; 6d; 7c; 8f

Wicked wolves fact or fiction

It's now been proved beyond all doubt that, despite what happened in Little Red Riding Hood, wolves cannot dress themselves in clothes and pass themselves off as humans. Even the really clever ones. But which of the following facts are true of our canine cousins, and which are nothing more than fairytale fodder?

1 Wolves possess webbed toes.

2 Their sense of smell is 100 times more sensitive than a human's.

3 Their eyes can pop out of their heads to enable them to look around trees.

4 Domestic cats in the USA have been given 'nervous breakdowns' by wolves staring at them through windows and breathing on the glass.

5 Male wolves can grow up to two metres high.

6 Some wolves employ crude tools such as sharpened stones to help them kill their prey.

7 There are wild wolves living in remote parts of Great Britain.

8 Wolves can smell prey some 2.5 km away.

Answers:

1 TRUE. Their feet are slightly webbed – it enables them to run on snow.

2 TRUE. Imagine being able to smell your pongy little brother from the other side of the school!

3 FALSE. Although their eyes can't pop out of their head, their ears do swivel to pick up sounds from any direction.

4 FALSE. Coyotes, not wolves, are responsible for cat-bothering in the USA.

5 FALSE. Not two metres – that'd be truly MASSIVE. They can grow up to 85 cm (which is terrifyingly huge, nonetheless!)

6 FALSE. They don't need tools when they've got fearsome canine teeth!

7 FALSE. Sorry! The last wild wolf was shot in Britain in 1743.

8 TRUE. Petrifying, isn't it?!

HORRIBLE INDEX

141

HORRIBLE SCIENCE

DEADLY DISEASES

NICK ARNOLD

illustrated by
TONY DE SAULLES

■ SCHOLASTIC

Visit Nick Arnold at
www.nickarnold-website.com

Scholastic Children's Books,
Euston House, 24 Eversholt Street,
London, NW1 1DB, UK

A division of Scholastic Ltd
London ~ New York ~ Toronto ~ Sydney ~ Auckland
Mexico City ~ New Delhi ~ Hong Kong

First published in the UK by Scholastic Ltd, 2000
This edition published 2008

ISBN 978 0439 94446 5

Printed and bound by CPI Group (UK) Ltd, Croydon, CR0 4YY

30

CONTENTS

Nick Arnold has been writing stories and books since he was a youngster, but never dreamt he'd find fame writing about deadly diseases. His research involved catching colds, grappling with germs and trying out plague cures and he enjoyed every minute of it.

When he's not delving into Horrible Science, he spends his spare time eating pizza, riding his bike and thinking up corny jokes (though not all at the same time).

Tony De Saulles picked up his crayons when he was still in nappies and has been doodling ever since. He takes Horrible Science very seriously and even agreed to draw malaria-carrying mosquitoes. Fortunately, he has made a full recovery.

When he's not out with his sketchpad, Tony likes to write poetry and play squash, though he hasn't written any poetry about squash yet.

INTRODUCTION

Are you well?

If so, GREAT. If not, maybe you need the *Horrible Science* treatment! Take one copy of this book and read it in large doses – after food. (Reading it before meals can ruin your appetite.) You're bound to feel better because laughter is a great healer!

(AND THAT'S JUST THE CONTENTS PAGE)

And if you're not ill you ought to read this book anyway to maintain a healthy sense of humour.

This book is especially effective against SLUMP disease (that's Science Lessons Upset Mystified Pupils). Sufferers of this common condition often slump over desks and feel a strong urge to sleep. And sadly, SLUMP disease can prove deadly ... deadly boring, that is.

INFECTIOUS PATHOGENS, BLAH BLAH, MUMBLE, DRONE.

I'M BORED

I'M DEAD BORED

I'M DEAD

Well, if you're a SLUMP sufferer, cheer up! This book contains medically proven ingredients such as sick jokes and sickening stories and seriously sick facts to fight SLUMP disease by boosting your brain power. This treatment is so successful that afterwards you can test your teacher and dumbfound your doctor with your deadly disease discoveries! Read about fiendishly foul phenomena like the nurse who drank diarrhoea...

...and the scientist who died of the disease he was studying...

...and the doctors who *killed* one another because they argued over a disease.

Feeling better yet? You will soon. Just keep on reading!
But be warned…

WARNING!

SIDE EFFECTS OF THIS BOOK CAN
INCLUDE SNORTS OF LAUGHTER AT
EMBARRASSING MOMENTS, AND
FEELING AN URGE TO TRY
REVOLTING EXPERIMENTS.

Well, what are you waiting for…?

THE SICKENING FACTS

DISEASES COULD WIPE OUT THE HUMAN RACE!

It sounds sickening – but is it a fact? Well, you can check on your survival chances later on, but now it's time for a story to get your brain juices going…

THE INVASION

The aliens landed on a Saturday at about 7.30 pm.

Alex and his parents were having tea when they arrived. Huge dark green shapes loomed at the windows, lumbering like bears. There was a crash as an alien vaporized the door with its heat gun. It had two staring eyes like a giant squid and tentacles around its mouth.

"ARGGGH!" screamed Alex.

"Blimey!" said his dad.

"Hello, vicar," said his mum, searching for her glasses.

"Ulla ulla ulla!" said the alien, opening its razor-sharp fangs.

All three humans turned to run. There was a whooshing sound followed by a nasty burning smell as one of the aliens microwaved the cat.

Within hours the army had sealed off the area. The roads were clogged with people trying to flee. Everyone was unsure where to go, everyone was scared. It was worse than the first day at a new school.

"Don't panic!" shouted the general through a battered army megaphone. "We'll stop them!"

Just then a red haze appeared glowing against the sky. It was a cloud of gas billowing and tumbling like thick smoke. Ahead of the gas, soldiers from an advance patrol came running and stumbling and choking and falling.

"Gas masks!" ordered the general.

"Er … sorry, sir, we left them at the base!" stammered his sergeant.

"Then we'll have to make a rapid strategic withdrawal!" barked the general.

"Come again, sir?" asked the sergeant.

The general swung round bellowing "THAT MEANS RUN, YOU BLITHERING IDIOT!"

Soon the whole country was in uproar. All the roads were jammed with cars trying to escape the gas that hung in little wisps and unexpectedly seeped under doors. There was no TV because the aliens had knocked out the electricity system, but at least the schools were closed. Alex and his parents found themselves hiding in a sewer.

"I need some fresh air!" gasped Alex as he clambered towards the entrance.

"This living room needs a good clean," said his mum (who still hadn't found her glasses).

"You'll need more than fresh air if the gas gets you!" warned his dad, but the boy wasn't listening.

Alex sniffed the air. It seemed fresh enough. Well, it would after the sewer. So he decided it was safe to look for food and crept cautiously down the road. Suddenly he froze – an alien patrol had appeared round the corner! There was nowhere to hide. Alex closed his eyes and waited to be microwaved.

But the aliens ignored him.

They stumbled and shuffled past saying something like...

"Ulla, urgle, gurgle!"

Thick orange dribble slobbered from their mouths and their tentacles were droopy.

Taking courage, Alex followed the aliens into a field where he saw an awesome sight. Several spacecraft were leaning at drunken angles. All around lay aliens, many dead but a few twitching. There was a vile smell like rotting school-dinner cabbage.

The boy couldn't believe his eyes.

The aliens were sick, they were being destroyed.

But how and why?

Just then an alien sneezed a big glob of purple snot. Alex realized that the aliens had the most appalling, stinking colds. The invaders hadn't been defeated by the army or by anything that humans could do. No, they were beaten by humble common-or-garden germs.

Cool story?! It was inspired by a novel, *War of the Worlds* by H G Wells (1866–1946), in which diseases halt an alien invasion. Bet you never knew that hovering over every 6.4 square cm of ground there are 4,000 microbes looking for somewhere to land, someone to attack. And if you live in a big city there'll be about 400,000 germs hovering over your head! It's enough to make your hair curl.

No wonder the aliens never stood a chance!

So what about us? Are we going to be wiped out like the aliens? Well, germs certainly give us a tough time – you can be *dead* sure of that. But before we delve into their murky world – here's a chance to check your existing knowledge.

ODD DISEASES QUIZ

1 Which of these animals does NOT get colds?
a) Teachers.
b) Ferrets.
c) Fish.

2 Which of the following animals does NOT get flu?
a) Pigs.
b) Ducks.
c) Woodlice.

3 Which of the following treatments is USELESS against germs?
a) Feeding a maggot on diseased flesh.
b) Smearing a wound with honey.
c) Plonking a dollop of bat's poo on a wound.

4 Where will you NEVER find germs?
a) The moon.
b) Mars (that's the planet not the choccie bar).
c) A school dinner.

5 Which substance is USELESS for killing germs?
a) Moon dust.
b) Custard.
c) Toilet cleaner.

Answers: 1 c) If fish got colds their paper hankies would go soggy.

You may be interested to know that in the 1930s a scientist discovered that ferrets get colds after a ferret sneezed on him and he developed the illness.

2 c) Ever seen a woodlouse sipping lemsip?

In fact, you can catch flu from pigs and even ducks (that's when you need a quack doctor!). You can breathe these germs in or, even worse, the germs pass out of the animals' faeces (poo) into water. If humans drink the water we fall ill too. Sickening, eh?

3 c) The poo is crawling with germs. Doctors in Washington DC, in the USA, covered an injured girl's germ-infected leg with 1,500 maggots. The maggots ate the germs and diseased flesh but left the healthy bits. Honey is great for killing germs – the sugary stuff dries them out. That's why honey keeps for months in a cupboard after you've opened it. Mind you, if you want to keep your family sweet don't go smearing their honey on your scabby wounds and then putting the knife back in the pot.

4 b) Scientists tested Martian soil for germs in 1977 and found none. School dinners are full of germs and scientists have even found germs on the moon! In the 1970s astronauts brought back a piece of an old lunar-landing vehicle left on the moon in 1967. Inside the protective casing of the vehicle's camera, the scientists found germs from snot that had got into material when it was made. *The germs were still alive!*

5 b) Germs happily scoff custard. Toilet cleaner contains bleach, a highly effective germ-killer. And scientists in Houston, USA, have found that moon dust actually contains chemicals that kill germs – trouble is your local chemist probably doesn't sell moon dust and if they did it would cost £5 million a gram!

A NOTE TO THE READER

This is a little book about a big subject. There are thousands of different diseases. There are nasty diseases, smelly diseases and diseases you can't even tell your mum about. Some are caused by poisonous chemicals and others by worms in the guts. To fit them all in a book you'd need a book the size of a bookcase. So to save space, this book deals only with the deadly diseases caused by tiny living things – microbes.

DON'T WORRY, IT'S NOT CAUSED BY MICROBES...

...JUST WORMS IN YOUR GUTS

So how are you feeling now? Maybe a bit shivery, or perhaps a bit sick? Perhaps these germs might be doing something nasty to *you*? Could it be that you've already got one of the deadly diseases we'll be looking at in this book?!

SHIVER!

SHAKE!

SWEAT!

TREMBLE!

We've hired Dr Grimgrave – the most miserable doctor in the world (he really ought to read a *Horrible Science* book to cheer himself up!) – to tell you the worst...

DR GRIMGRAVE'S GUIDE TO SYMPTOMS

So how are we today? Deadly disease, eh? Well, I'll need to examine you ... do you have any of these symptoms? If you aren't sure, I can arrange a consultation but not for idiots and time-wasters. Being a doctor could be enjoyable if it wasn't for all those whinging, sick people one has to see.

VIOLENT COUGH

Coughing is normal. I encourage my patients to cough into a handkerchief because it's the body's way of removing mucus

OFTEN A LOVELY GREEN COLOUR

(snot) caused by an infection. A violent cough, fever and huge lumps under the armpits and black spots on the skin may be a sign of one form of plague. Rapid burial in earth may be the most effective treatment here.

Dear reader
We apologise for the poor quality jokes. Dr Grimgrave is not known for his sense of humour.

DEADLY DIARRHOEA

Severe diarrhoea turns from brown to green and becomes paler when it contains the gut lining. This could be a sign of cholera. If untreated, there is continuous diarrhoea until the victim's body dries out. My old colleague, Dr Twinge caught cholera and he nearly dried of it.

ESSENTIAL EQUIPMENT

SOMETIMES LOOKS LIKE **BIGPOX**, HA HA!

PUS-FILLED PUSTULES

Spots are caused by minor infections resulting in a build-up of pus. Violent fever, muscle pains and spots filled with pus covering most of the upper body were a symptom of smallpox. In severe cases large chunks of flesh die and fall off the victim's body – most unhygienic.

DANGEROUS DRIBBLING

IT'S A MOUTH-WATERING EXPERIENCE!

Uncontrollable salivation can be a symptom of rabies. Other signs include fear of water, and an inability to swallow. By the time the disease reaches this stage there is no cure. Honestly, what do these patients expect me to do ... heal them?

17

BRIGHT YELLOW SKIN

The liver fails and chemicals escape and build up under the skin — jaundice, we doctors call it.

(I always think that if the liver is bad you should try onions — they improve the taste no end. Ha ha.) Jaundice and black vomit are signs of yellow fever. I have a sample of this remarkable regurgitation in my private medical collection. ➤

FEEL LIKE DEATH AND *LOOK* LIKE A BANANA!

BLACK SICK

PLEASE NOTE: you're unlikely to have these deadly diseases. Most mild diseases can be treated by taking a painkiller and going to bed and allowing the body to heal itself. That way you don't bother me, your doctor. Now, if you'll excuse me, I've got work to do...

We'll be getting to grips with the gore and pus later on, but first a question: what actually *causes* all these deadly diseases? Yep, I'm sorry, but it's time to look at some deadly disease germs, and you can catch them in the next chapter...

GRUESOME GERMS

Take a peek down this microscope and you'll see them…

Not much to look at, maybe, but they're the nastiest and deadliest killers the human race has ever known. Just take a look at their files…

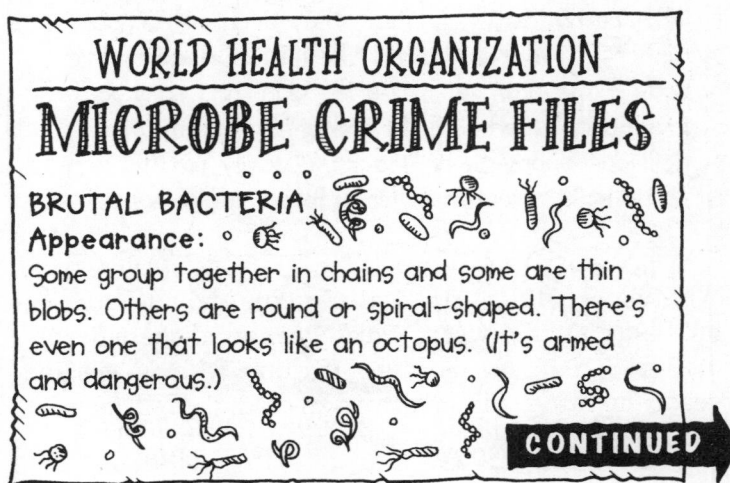

CONTINUED ➜

Size:
Most bacteria are 0.5 – 1.5 micrometres in size. (Up to 10,000 bacteria can stretch across your thumbnail – you'd better wash your hands afterwards!)

Horrible places they live:
Everywhere! Bacteria particularly like dirty places, like sewers or mounds of poo. Millions live in your guts (where they do no harm except make chemicals that make farts smelly).

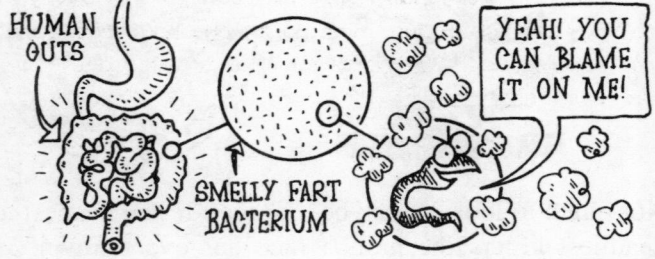

HUMAN GUTS

SMELLY FART BACTERIUM

YEAH! YOU CAN BLAME IT ON ME!

Favourite food:
They're not fussy. In fact, they even eat school dinners! They particularly like bits of dead or live body if they can get inside the skin. And many bacteria love human blood with its comforting warmth and delicious gloopy sugar snacks. (Luckily for the germs, there isn't *too* much sugar in blood, unlike honey!)

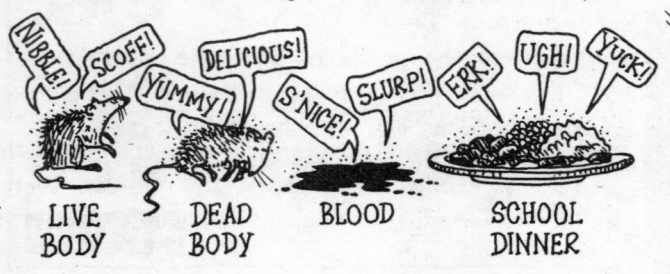

NIBBLE! SCOFF! YUMMY! DELICIOUS! S'NICE! SLURP! ERK! UGH! YUCK!

LIVE BODY   DEAD BODY   BLOOD   SCHOOL DINNER

Nasty habits:

Make deadly chemicals called toxins (tock—sins) that can stop human nerves working so the person can't move. The toxins kill by stopping the victim's breathing or disrupting their heartbeat. These bacteria are heart—less!

Brutal behaviour:

If they're warm and well—fed, bacteria happily increase in numbers by splitting in half. (Yeah — they're split personalities.) They can do this every 20 minutes, so in just nine hours one bacterium (one of these things is a bacterium, two or more are *bacteria*) can produce 100 million copies.

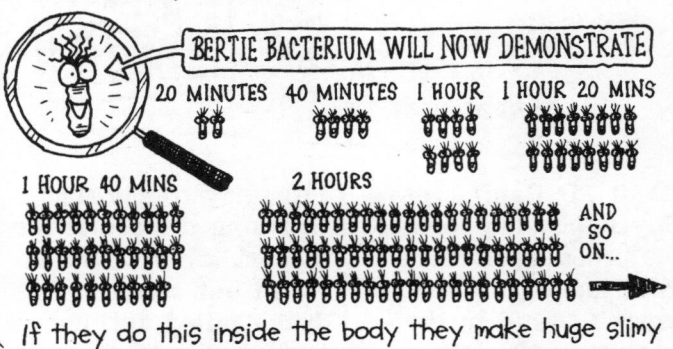

BERTIE BACTERIUM WILL NOW DEMONSTRATE

20 MINUTES   40 MINUTES   1 HOUR   1 HOUR 20 MINS

1 HOUR 40 MINS   2 HOURS   AND SO ON...

If they do this inside the body they make huge slimy lumps that break up the body's vital organs and cause death. Yikes!

TERRIBLE TB

By now you might be wondering what bacterial diseases are lurking in wait for you. The answer is *plenty*. For example, besides the plague and cholera, there's tuberculosis (ter-burk-u-lo-sis) or TB. Trust Dr Grimgrave to break the news gently...

HEALTH NEWS

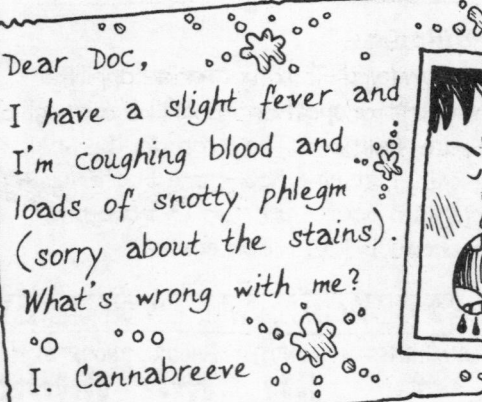

Dear Doc,

I have a slight fever and I'm coughing blood and loads of snotty phlegm (sorry about the stains). What's wrong with me?

I. Cannabreeve

Dear Mr Cannabreeve,
My hobby happens to be breeding bacteria and judging by the ones I found in the stains on the letter — you have TB.

I'm sorry to say that this lung disease is the biggest killer in the world but a course of drugs called antibiotics should save you.*
PS Don't call me Doc.

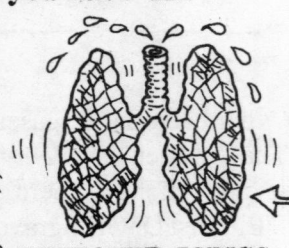

Your body is trying to clear your lungs of the Tuberculosis bacteria.

INFECTED LUNGS

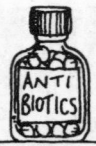

* For more information on antibiotics see page 68.

Mind you, if you think that sounds bad – just wait until you see the next section of the MICROBE CRIME FILES.

MICROBE CRIME FILES - PART 2

VICIOUS VIRUSES

Appearance: Weird-looking – some are like lunar landing craft and others look like anti-ship mines covered in spikes.

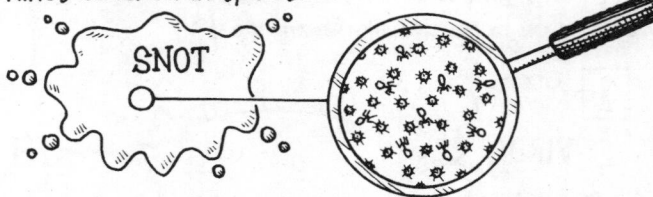

SNOT

Size: 17 to 300 nanometres. You could fit a chain of ten *million* viruses across your thumbnail (though you'll need a steady hand and a lot of patience).

ANTI-SHIP MINE | DEADLY | DEADLIER

VIRUS

Horrible places they live: Viruses have no proper bodies to protect them from heat or cold and that's why they live inside cells. (No, not *police* cells, silly, I mean the tiny living blobs of jelly that make up our bodies.)

Favourite food: Viruses don't eat or breathe. In fact, some scientists reckon they're not even alive! Think of viruses as vampires – creatures neither dead nor alive that prey on unsuspecting humans. No wonder they're a pain in the neck!

Nasty habits: The virus sticks to a cell and hijacks the control system of the cell and forces it to make copies of the virus. When the cell is worn out it dies and the viruses go in search of another victim. (For more details see page 111.)

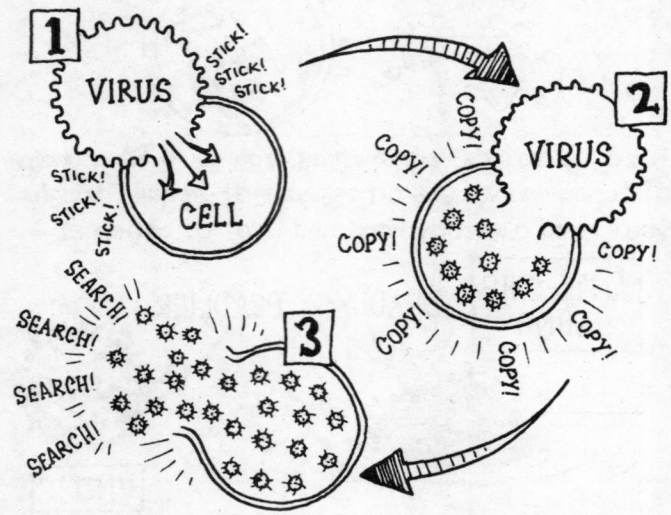

Vicious behaviour: Viruses often spread in tiny drops of spit that spray out of the mouth when we cough or sneeze. This danger is not to be sniffed at. Here are some interesting notes that I wrote on my hankie...

SNOTTY SNEEZY FACTS

1 One sneeze can contain *six million* viruses! Next time a cold makes you sneeze try counting them!

2 Millions of microscopic snot lumps shoot out of your nose and mouth at over 100 km per hour. If your sneeze was a gust of wind it would be strong enough to snap twigs off trees!

3 Within seconds the water in the snot dries out encasing the germs in hard dry snot-like tiny bullets (but too light for anyone to feel). If someone's in the way some snot might go down their throat or up their nose and some might go on their hands and they might then put their fingers in their mouth. And that's how your germs get into someone else.

WOULD YOU LIKE TO BORROW MY HANKIE?

NO THANKS!

MICROBE CRIME FILES – PART 3

REVOLTING IN-BETWEENIES

No, that isn't their scientific name. These are actually living things that are smaller than bacteria and bigger than viruses – the best known are rickettsia (rick-ket-see-a).

CONTINUED ➤

Appearance: Tiny blobs of colourless jelly.

Size: 0.5 micrometres across. You could fit 20,000 in a line across your thumbnail. (Now where did you put those viruses?)

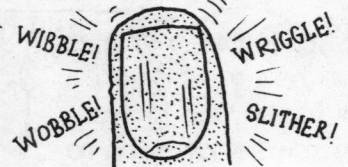

NOW YOU KNOW WHY MUM SAYS, "DON'T PICK YOUR NOSE!"

Horrible places they live: Rickettsia live inside insects like ticks and lice. Typhus rickettsia live inside blood-sucking lice that lurk on unwashed bodies. Maybe that's why they spread lousy diseases? The germs emerge in lice poo or eggs which enter the human body through the skin when it is scratched.

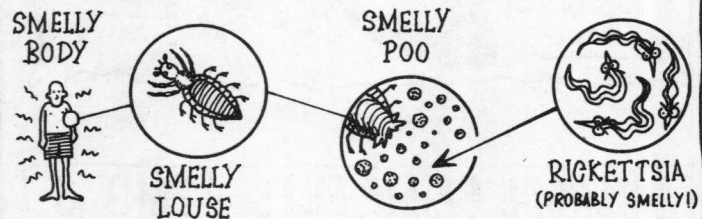

SMELLY BODY

SMELLY LOUSE

SMELLY POO

RICKETTSIA (PROBABLY SMELLY!)

Because the rickettsia are so small they can hide inside body cells and this makes them hard to find.

Nasty habits: Typhus rickettsia cause the disease typhus fever.

Bet you never knew!

The posh scientific name for typhus rickettsia is Rickettsia prowazeckii *(rick-ket-see-a prow-a-zecky). If this germ had friends they could always call it Ricky. It's named after American scientist Howard T Ricketts (1877–1910) who found the germ in 1909 and Stanilaus von Prowazeck (1875–1915) who studied it in 1915. And guess what? Both men caught typhus and died horribly. Well, looks like the germ discovered them too.*

I FOUND IT AND STAN STUDIED IT...

R.I.P. H.T. RICKETTS 1877-1910

R.I.P. S.V. PROWAZECK 1875-1915

...AND WE'RE BOTH SICK TO DEATH OF IT!

SO WHAT IS TYPHUS FEVER?

Dr Grimgrave knows the dreadful details...

HEALTH NEWS

SICK? NEED ADVICE?

Write to Dr Grimgrave and if he's not too busy he might bother to reply to your questions...

Dear Dr Grimgrave,
The day before yesterday I had backache. Now I've got a splitting headache, fever and I think I'm starting with a rash. I can't sleep. Am I going to die?
  Yours,
          Vera Sicke

Dear Ms Sicke,

Yes, probably. You have typhus and you may die of heart failure caused by germ toxins. But the rash might turn to sores which might rot and if your fingers and toes are infected they might drop off. If so, could you spare them for my private medical collection?

IF YOU COULD SPARE FIVE FINGERS, THAT WOULD *REALLY* BE GIVING ME A HAND

If you want to get better, I'd recommend antibiotics, which should stop the disease developing.

Now if you'll excuse me, my patients are getting impatient.

IF YOU CAN'T SLEEP TRY LYING ON THE EDGE OF THE BED ~ YOU'LL SOON DROP OFF

Now back to those files...

MICROBE CRIME FILES ~ PART 4

PUTRID PROTOZOA

Appearance: Blobs of colourless jelly. Protozoa look a bit like human cells and that makes them rather hard to spot inside the body. Imagine trying to find a toffee in a chocolate factory.

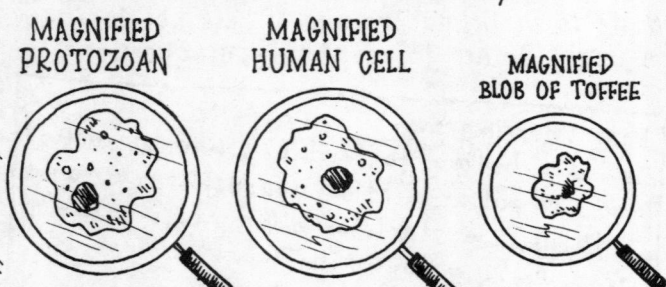

MAGNIFIED PROTOZOAN

MAGNIFIED HUMAN CELL

MAGNIFIED BLOB OF TOFFEE

Size: Most are less than 0.5 millimetres across. (So you'd need at least 20 big-uns to stretch across that grubby thumbnail.)

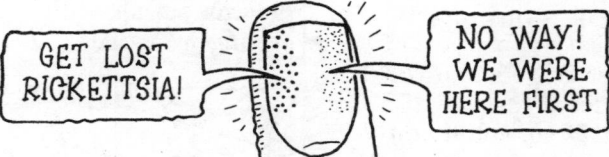

Horrible places they live: Often make themselves at home inside other creatures – in places such as guts or blood where they cause disease by making toxins.

Nasty habits: It depends on the disease. Take malaria for example – this disease is caused by protozoa with as much conscience as a gang of piranhas in a goldfish bowl.

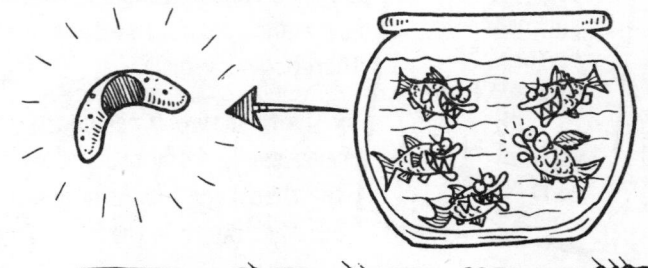

Deadly disease fact file

NAME: Malaria

THE BASIC FACTS:

1 The protozoa are spread by Anopheles (a-noff-fa-lees) mosquitoes.

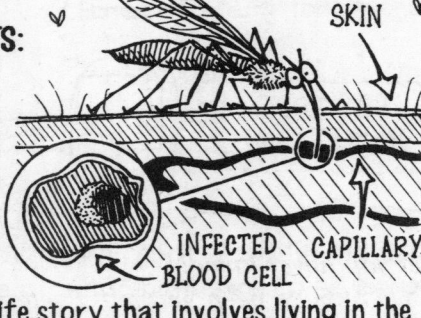

HUMAN SKIN

INFECTED BLOOD CELL

CAPILLARY

2 The protozoa have a complex life story that involves living in the mosquito's stomach and spit-making glands and moving into the blood when the mosquito bites a human.

3 There, the protozoa make toxins and guzzle red blood cells (the vital carriers of oxygen to the rest of your body) and this is what causes the malaria.

DEADLY DETAILS: **1** You've got a choice of four varieties of malaria, each caused by a different protozoan.

MALARIA MENU

TYPES 1-3: muscle pain, headache, fever, sweats.

TYPE 4: As above but with a side-order of blocked blood vessels and muscle spasm.

2 With all four you get muscle pains, terrible headaches, violent fever and ice-cold sweats. And then it gets worse.

3 The first two types cause fever every 48 hours and with the third type it's 72 hours. But the fourth is the...

4 REALLY nasty version. Around half the victims die as dead blood cells block blood vessels in the brain. Muscle spasms follow, so bad that the victims sometimes bite their tongues in half!

FINK I'FE GOK THE FORF HYPE!

Bet you never knew!
1 There have been germs – bacteria, viruses and protozoa – for millions of years. They're some of nature's great survivors – which is more than you can say for their victims. Scientists have found fossilized dinosaur bones that had been attacked by bacteria. I expect the dinosaur was an Ouchmybonesaresaur.
2 Every day you shed ten billion flakes of dead skin – they just drop off your body as fresh skin forms underneath. You can see a few of these bits if you turn a dirty pair of black trousers inside-out. At least two-thirds of these foul flakes carry bacteria and viruses.

3 So when you clean your room you stir up these bits and breathe in your own skin and germs!

COULD YOU BE A DOCTOR?

A patient has a boil on his nose. The boil is caused by bacteria and the red swelling is full of lovely golden pus.

Oh well, it could be worse – it could be a boil on the foot. Then you'd have pus in boots! Anyway, what forms this substance?

a) It's gas given out by the bacteria.
b) It's blood sucked in by the bacteria.
c) It's a mixture of dead blood cells and dead bacteria.

HORRIBLE HEALTH WARNING!

DON'T squeeze the boil. This allows more germs into the body and you may squirt pus in your eyeball. Yuck!

Answer: c) The blood cells died heroically fighting the bacteria.

Want the full story? It's in a top-secret deadly-disease-fighting document. And it just so happens we've got a copy and it's in the next chapter...

YOUR BATTLING BODY

Fancy a fight? Well, your body does. Every day it's spoiling for a fight – with germs! And here, as promised, is a unique glimpse of those top-secret military battle plans...

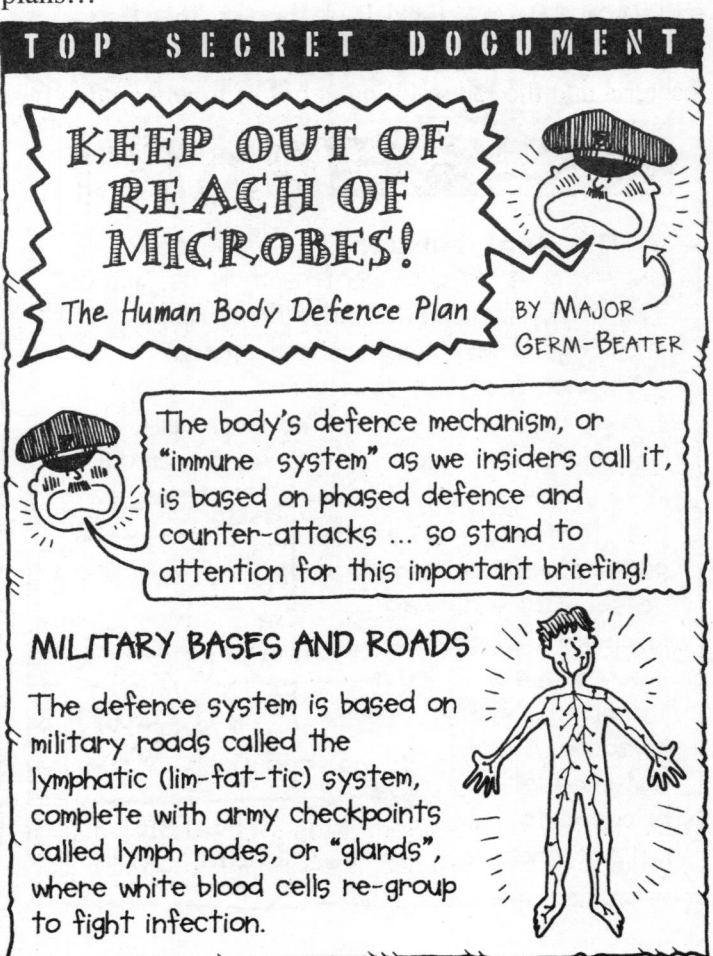

TOP SECRET DOCUMENT

KEEP OUT OF REACH OF MICROBES!

The Human Body Defence Plan

BY MAJOR GERM-BEATER

The body's defence mechanism, or "immune system" as we insiders call it, is based on phased defence and counter-attacks ... so stand to attention for this important briefing!

MILITARY BASES AND ROADS

The defence system is based on military roads called the lymphatic (lim-fat-tic) system, complete with army checkpoints called lymph nodes, or "glands", where white blood cells re-group to fight infection.

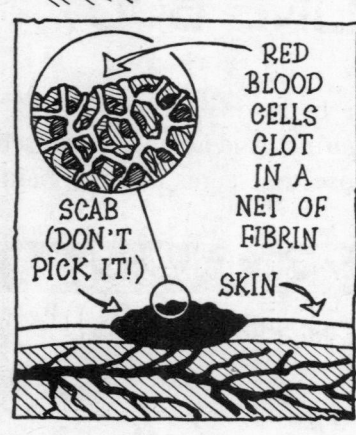

RED BLOOD CELLS CLOT IN A NET OF FIBRIN

SCAB (DON'T PICK IT!)

SKIN

LINES OF DEFENCE

1 Skin barrier

I'd like to see the germ who can burrow through this thick leathery wall! Trouble is, humans do insist on scraping or cutting their skin and allowing germs in.

2 The snot barrier

Known to us defence professionals as "mucus". The sticky snot of the nose or windpipe or guts bogs down attackers and contains a substance that kills some germs. Our front-line troops deployed here are the mast cells. They're under orders to release a chemical they store called histamine (his-ta-meen). This widens gaps between cells in blood vessel walls – allowing killer white blood cells (see opposite) to leave the blood and fight the invaders. Meanwhile, watery snot is released to flush out the enemy!

ARGH!

FLUSH THEM OUT!

ALL NOSE-PICKERS SHOULD BE COURT-MARTIALLED!

Some humans pick snot from their noses and eat it. This disgraceful habit allows germs caught in the mucus to enter into the guts where they can cause diarrhoea if not dissolved by acid in the stomach.

3 Bloody warfare

a) As a result of the gaps forming between cells, the blood vessels naturally get larger and more blood rushes to the area making it feel hot. That's why body parts, where there are germs, appear red and swollen.

b) Germs can die if they get too hot – so we aim to make 'em sweat by heating up the blood! White blood cells send chemical signals to the brain, which responds with chemicals that cause

HEAT!

the body's cells to make energy faster. This gives off extra heat. The skin turns pale as blood is retained deep within the body so it doesn't lose heat to the air. Humans call this "fever" – I call it a jolly good tactic!

All army units must counter-attack with every weapon at our disposal!

WHITE BLOOD CELL ARMY UNITS...

The T-cell army
T = top secret code for thymus (thi-mus) area where the army is recruited and trained.

This army is made up of three operational units...

THYMUS

1 The killer cells are combat personnel with orders to search out and destroy all germs. All body cells believed to be hiding germs are to be eliminated without mercy!

2 T-helper cells are highly trained intelligence and communications specialists. They identify germs and produce a chemical signal alerting the B-cell army (see opposite), and order the killer cells to move in.

3 T-suppressor officer corps'. Their job is to stop the others getting carried away and attacking in too great numbers. This could result in damage to the body as, inevitably, civilian body cells will get killed in the fighting. Yes, it's tough – but this is WAR!

THE B-CELL ARMY
B = top secret military code for bone marrow training centre where the army is recruited and trained.

BONE MARROW

1 Each B-cell is trained to identify enemy antigens. That's military jargon for any invader of the body. ("Antigen" – just saying that word makes me feel dirty!) Each B-cell is covered with chemicals like tiny keys that lock into chemicals on the outside of a particular antigen. And since we have millions of different B-cells there's every chance that for any antigen we'll have a B-cell to fit it. You can rely on the B-cell army to get to grips with the enemy.

2 Specialized B-cells are based in the lymph node bases ready to make antibodies. If an

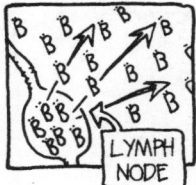

LYMPH NODE

antigen is detected, the bone marrow training centre will send millions of B-cell reinforcements with the right key to search out antigens wherever they're hiding.

THE ANTIBODY WEAPON SYSTEM
These are guided missiles used by our troops to lock on to antigens and destroy them. Each antibody is designed to cover an antigen and gum it up so it can be engulfed by the tank corps (see next page).

WHITE BLOOD CELL TANK CORPS

Our tanks – we call them macrophages (mac-ro-fay-ges) – capture the gummed-up enemy bacteria by grabbing them in their mechanical arms and pulling them inside. All prisoners are to be dissolved alive! Remember – WAR IS NOT A TEA PARTY!

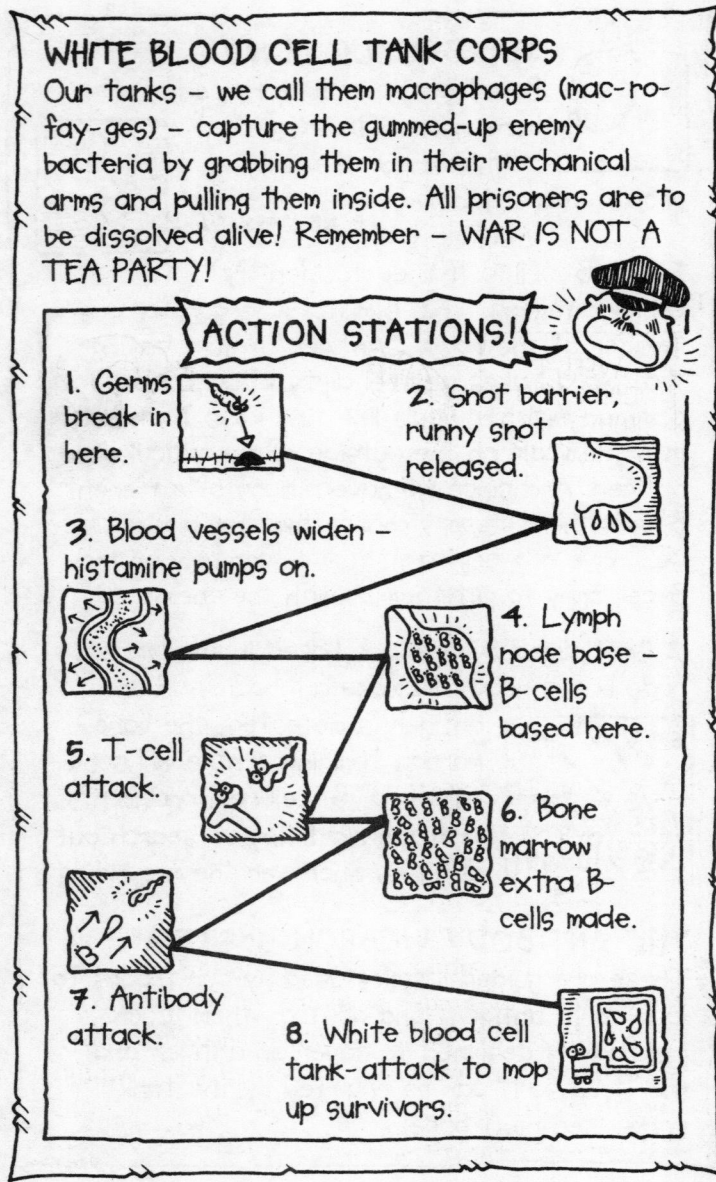

ACTION STATIONS!

1. Germs break in here.

2. Snot barrier, runny snot released.

3. Blood vessels widen – histamine pumps on.

4. Lymph node base – B-cells based here.

5. T-cell attack.

6. Bone marrow extra B-cells made.

7. Antibody attack.

8. White blood cell tank-attack to mop up survivors.

DEADLY EXPRESSIONS

A scientist says...

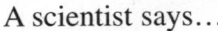

I'M INTO INTERFERON

Do you say...?

WELL, I THINK YOU SHOULD MIND YOUR OWN BUSINESS, BEAKY-NOSE.

Answer: He said ''interferon'', not *interfering*. All cells make interferon (in-ter-fear-ron) if attacked by viruses. It doesn't save them but in ways we don't understand this chemical stops the virus from multiplying.

Bet you never knew!
Your defences against disease can make you ill!
Asthma sufferers are unusually sensitive to little bits
of chemical like pollen from flowers or pollution
from cars. When they're breathed in, the mast cells
in the lungs that make histamine go into overdrive.
And although this substance widens the blood vessels
it actually narrows *airways and causes breathing*
problems. It's enough to make you gasp!

You're probably an expert in what viruses can do to the human body. Yes, you are! If you've ever had a cold you'll know *exactly* how it feels. The bad news is that after hundreds of years of medical research even the cleverest doctors still can't cure a cold. The good news is that the body cures itself anyway. Here's how it's done...

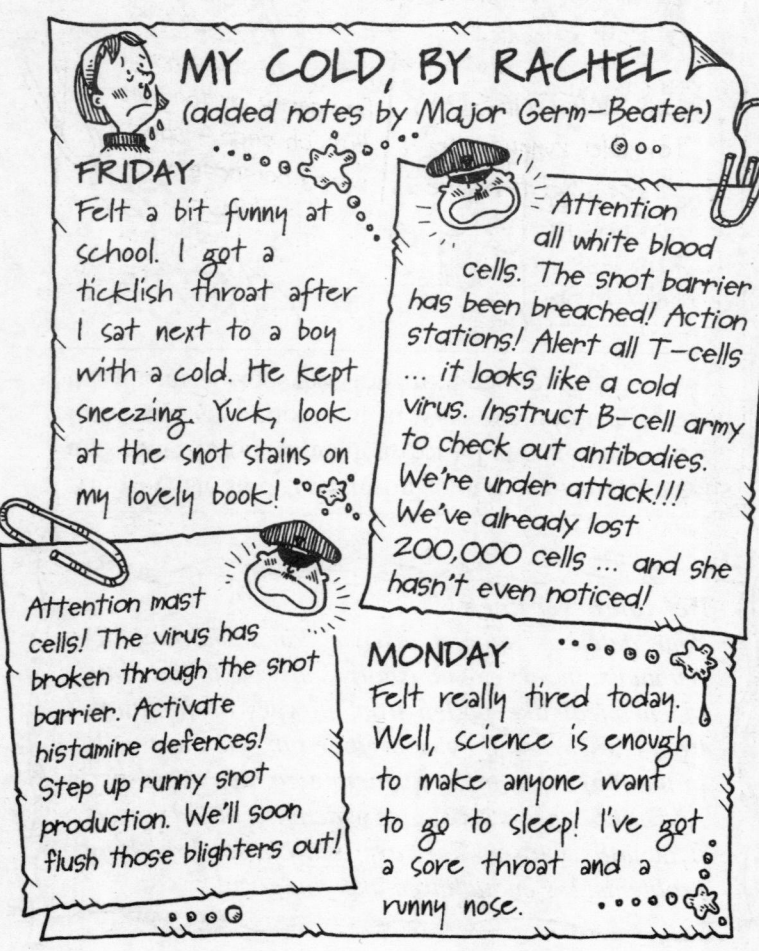

MY COLD, BY RACHEL
(added notes by Major Germ-Beater)

FRIDAY

Felt a bit funny at school. I got a ticklish throat after I sat next to a boy with a cold. He kept sneezing. Yuck, look at the snot stains on my lovely book!

Attention all white blood cells. The snot barrier has been breached! Action stations! Alert all T-cells ... it looks like a cold virus. Instruct B-cell army to check out antibodies. We're under attack!!! We've already lost 200,000 cells ... and she hasn't even noticed!

Attention mast cells! The virus has broken through the snot barrier. Activate histamine defences! Step up runny snot production. We'll soon flush those blighters out!

MONDAY

Felt really tired today. Well, science is enough to make anyone want to go to sleep! I've got a sore throat and a runny nose.

TUESDAY

I woke up today with a sore nose. It felt all bunged up. Had to go to school — worst luck. Felt chronic!

Histamine defences working well. White blood cells to the affected nose region.

WEDNESDAY

Terrible runny nose, I feel light-headed. Mum says I've got a fever. No school today.

Runny nasal discharge has germs on the run! But, oh dear – she's wiping her nose with used hankies and stuffing viruses back up her nostrils! Fever defence working well.

THURSDAY

I just feel like going to sleep. I'm so tired.

"Sleep" she says! Pah! We in the immune system NEVER sleep. We've been fighting non-stop for days. Phew!

FRIDAY

I'm tired and washed out.

Not half as much as us! We've lost millions of dead white blood cells ... but, we've won – well done chaps!!

SATURDAY

I'm feeling better! Just in time for the weekend!

All thanks to us!

41

Once you've had a disease caused by a virus or bacterium the general rule is that you shouldn't get it again. A scientist would say you're immune to that illness. (Yes, I know you get colds all the time but that's because each cold is caused by a slightly different virus.)

Deadly disease fact file

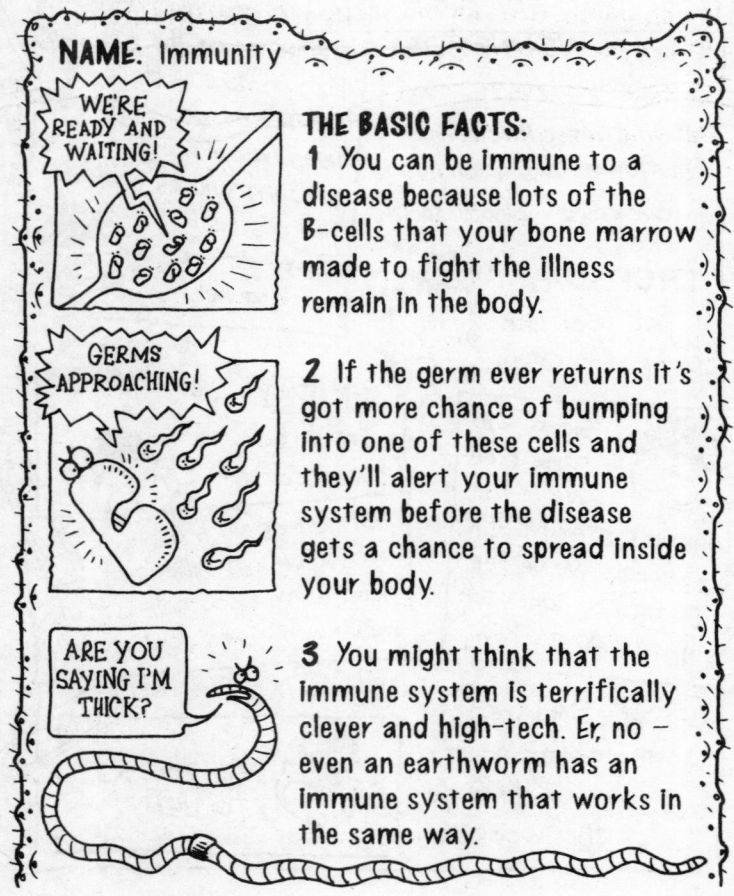

NAME: Immunity

WE'RE READY AND WAITING!

GERMS APPROACHING!

ARE YOU SAYING I'M THICK?

THE BASIC FACTS:

1 You can be immune to a disease because lots of the B-cells that your bone marrow made to fight the illness remain in the body.

2 If the germ ever returns it's got more chance of bumping into one of these cells and they'll alert your immune system before the disease gets a chance to spread inside your body.

3 You might think that the immune system is terrifically clever and high-tech. Er, no – even an earthworm has an immune system that works in the same way.

DEADLY DETAILS: If lots of people in an area are immune to a disease it can't spread widely, but if most people aren't immune then it will become a huge tidal wave of illness – an epidemic.

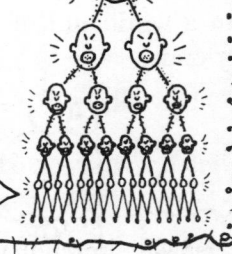

COUGH!

| INFECTED PEOPLE MULTIPLY IN THE SAME WAY AS BACTERIA | → |

Bet you never knew!
When an epidemic struck the cities of ancient Turkey an ugly person was chosen to be sacrificed to the gods. They ate a barley loaf, dried figs and cheese, and they were beaten with fig branches. Afterwards, the chosen person was burnt alive and their ashes scattered in the sea. Oddly enough, this practice didn't stop the epidemic and no, your teacher wouldn't have been the victim so stop daydreaming and read on...

So why aren't there epidemics everywhere? Come to think of it why aren't we all *dead*? Well, a few hundred years ago, as you'll discover later, there *were* massive outbreaks of disease but today many diseases are under control – thanks to the work of the people in the next chapter. Who are these wonderful people? Well, some people call them "miracle workers". Let's go meet them.

ANXIOUS ANTIGEN

GULP!

MEDICAL MIRACLES

In a world full of deadly diseases you can rely on two friends.

1 YOUR IMMUNE SYSTEM   **2** YOUR DOCTOR

Though if your doctor's Dr Grimgrave you'll have to make do with your immune system. Anyway, talking about medics, it's time to meet the people who dedicate their lives to fighting deadly diseases…

SPOT THE SCIENTIST

Let's imagine your school has been hit by a mystery ailment – the dreaded "Green Teacher Disease". Teachers and (I'm afraid) pupils, are turning green and developing smelly purple boils.

SCHOOL CLOSED DUE TO OUTBREAK OF GREEN TEACHER DISEASE!

A team of scientists is desperately trying to find a cure. Here they are…

① IMMUNOLOGIST
(im-mu-nol-lo-gist)
Studies how the immune
system fights the disease.
The immunologist is looking
at blood samples from the
sufferers to discover if
they're making antibodies
to fight the disease
antigens. An immunologist
knows the difference
between an antibody and an
antigen (check back to
page 37 if you're not
sure).

ABSENT-MINDED
LOOK.

TEST-TUBE
CONTAINING AN
INTERESTING
BLOOD SAMPLE.

② BACTERIOLOGIST/VIROLOGIST
Bacteriologists (back-teer-re-ol-lo-gists)
study bacteria and virologists (vi-rol-lo-
gists) study (that's right!) viruses – and
between them they are trying to find the

REMEMBER THESE?
FROM PAGES 19-24

VIRUS

BACTERIA

germs that cause Green
Teacher Disease. (They could
be bacteria or viruses – we
don't know yet.) Both
scientists want to search
for the germs in samples of
blood and skin and snot and diseased matter
from the purple boils. The bacteriologist
will try to spot the germs through a
microscope but since viruses are far
smaller than bacteria, the virologist will
use the more powerful electron microscope
for her work.

CONTINUED

45

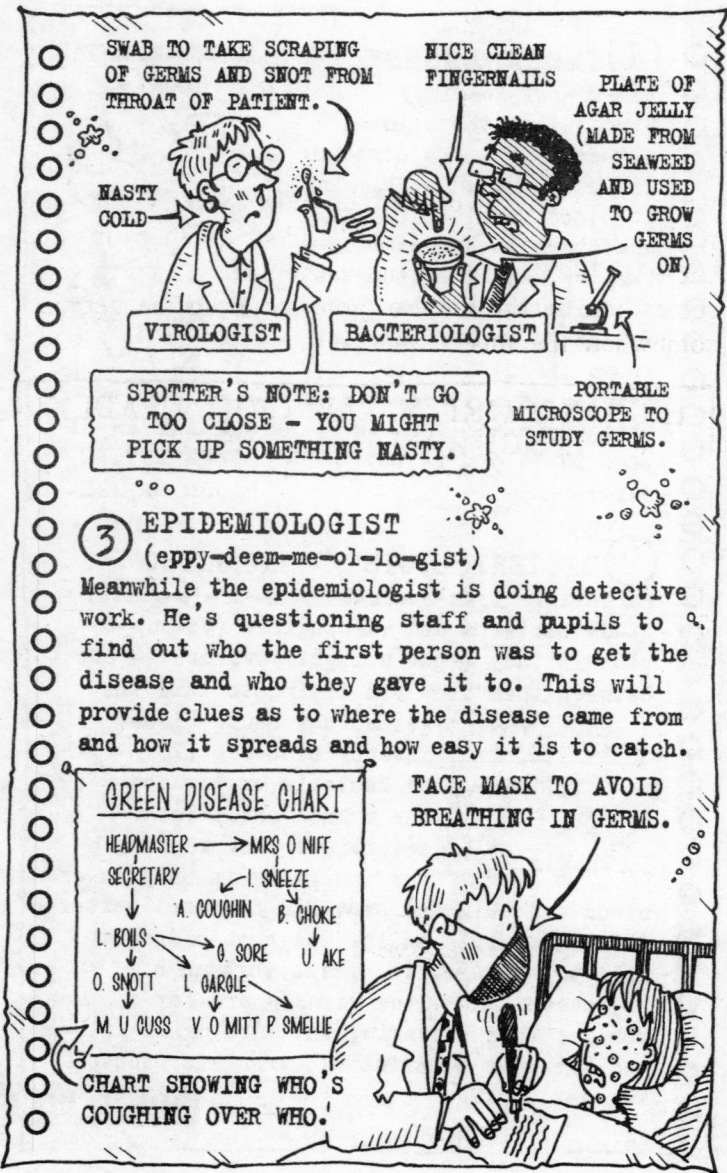

SWAB TO TAKE SCRAPING OF GERMS AND SNOT FROM THROAT OF PATIENT.

NICE CLEAN FINGERNAILS

PLATE OF AGAR JELLY (MADE FROM SEAWEED AND USED TO GROW GERMS ON)

NASTY COLD

VIROLOGIST

BACTERIOLOGIST

SPOTTER'S NOTE: DON'T GO TOO CLOSE — YOU MIGHT PICK UP SOMETHING NASTY.

PORTABLE MICROSCOPE TO STUDY GERMS.

③ EPIDEMIOLOGIST
(eppy-deem-me-ol-lo-gist)

Meanwhile the epidemiologist is doing detective work. He's questioning staff and pupils to find out who the first person was to get the disease and who they gave it to. This will provide clues as to where the disease came from and how it spreads and how easy it is to catch.

GREEN DISEASE CHART

HEADMASTER ⟶ MRS O NIFF
SECRETARY ⟶ I. SNEEZE
A. COUGHIN   B. CHOKE
L. BOILS ⟶ G. SORE   U. AKE
O. SNOTT   L. GARGLE
M. U CUSS   V. O MITT   P. SMELLIE

FACE MASK TO AVOID BREATHING IN GERMS.

CHART SHOWING WHO'S COUGHING OVER WHO.

WHERE THEY WORK

All these scientists work in university laboratories and in specialist research institutes such as the Pasteur Institute in Paris or the Center for Disease Control in Atlanta, USA. Immunologists also work in hospital laboratories where they advise doctors on how well patients are resisting diseases. Scientists who work with germs that cause deadly diseases are in danger. They need to work somewhere where they're protected from the germs – somewhere like this...

HIGH-SECURITY LAB (FOR DEADLY INCURABLE DISEASES)

SCIENTISTS WEAR SPACESUITS TO PROTECT THEIR SKIN FROM ANY GERMS IN THE AIR

ATCHOO!

AIR SUCKED INTO THE LAB IS PREVENTED FROM LEAVING. THIS STOPS GERMS FROM FLOATING OUT OF THE LAB.

SCIENTISTS BREATHE THROUGH AIR HOSES ATTACHED TO THE CEILING.

THICK CONCRETE WALLS DESIGNED TO WITHSTAND EARTHQUAKE OR BOMB DAMAGE WITHOUT ALLOWING GERMS TO ESCAPE.

X-RAY VIEW OF LAB

COULD YOU BE A SCIENTIST?

So how would you get on as a germ scientist?

1 Have you got the right gut instinct? In 1982 Australian scientist Barry Marshall became convinced that the painful ulcers some people get in their stomachs were caused by bacteria. It was a gut instinct all right – but certain germs always seemed to be in the victims' stomachs. Barry decided on an experiment…

What did he do?

a) He cut open a healthy patient's stomach and added the bacteria to see what would happen.

b) He tried growing the germs in a bowl of school dinner custard. The slimy custard was the closest he could get to the slimy insides of the stomach.

c) He drank the disgusting bacteria and stuck a viewing tube called an endoscope into his own stomach to check what they were up to.

2 In 1948 scientists were searching for a person who was spreading the germs that caused the deadly disease typhoid in their poo. How did they find the person?

a) They placed an advert in the paper.

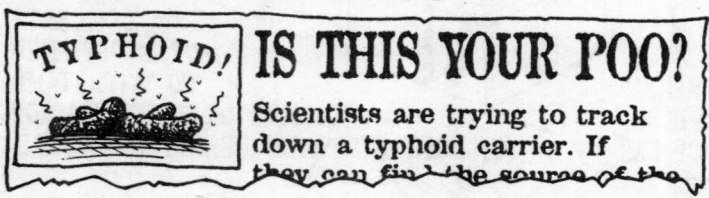

b) They tested everyone in town for the disease.

c) They ran tests on the sewage and found the germ and then tested all the sewage pipes, crawling through the sewers until they found the toilet that the person was using.

HOW DID SCIENTISTS DISCOVER THAT GERMS CAUSE DISEASE?

It's a good question because germs can be quite hard to investigate. They come in a confusing number of varieties and none of them carry signs saying:

EARLY IDEAS

Some ancient doctors suspected that unseen creatures caused disease. Roman medic Marcus Terentius Varro

(116-27 BC) reckoned that disease was caused by tiny living things that were too small to see. He was right, of course, but he couldn't prove it.

But despite Varro's ideas most ancient doctors thought the gods caused disease. We've brought together two of them to argue their cases...

Four hundred years ago doctors thought that diseases were caused by revolting smells. Luckily this isn't true, otherwise your brother or sister's trainers could spark a major health alert.

Even after the microscope was invented in 1609, scientists refused to believe that tiny germs could kill a person – it was like saying ants could slay elephants.

The first clue that germs were less innocent than they seemed came in the 1860s when French scientist Louis Pasteur (1822–1895) investigated a disease that attacked silkworms (the caterpillars that spin silk). Pasteur found the disease was caused by protozoa and that a nasty bacterium caused silkworm diarrhoea. But you couldn't just collar a particular germ and say "Oi, you're nicked for causing this 'ere illness." For one thing, there are loads of germs which made pinning the blame on one of them a bit hit or miss.

A pushy doctor was to change all that…

Hall of fame: Robert Koch (1843–1910)
Nationality: German

Young Robert Koch had 13 brothers and sisters. Can you
imagine how he suffered? Thirteen brothers and sisters
all trying to boss you around.

Well, anyway, Robert was a clever lad and his
science-minded granddad and uncle encouraged him to
build up a collection of dead insects and other grisly
specimens. Later, at the University of Gottingen, one of
his teachers persuaded young Robert to take up medicine
and he became a doctor, first in the Army and later on in
Wollstein, Germany.

But he became more and more interested in germs. He
turned his consulting room into a lab and in 1871, his
wife gave him a microscope for his birthday.

Can you guess what he wanted it for? No, not for
searching the cat's fur for fleas. He used it to take an even
closer look at germs.

And so Koch came to study an especially disgusting disease called anthrax. This causes revolting sores on the lungs and can kill humans and animals.

Koch used dyes to stain some bacteria so he could see them clearly under the microscope. He next proved that it really was these bacteria that caused the diseases by injecting them into some cute little mice and making them ill. (I suppose they could have been saved by mouse to mouse resuscitation.)

SUDDENLY I DON'T FEEL HUNGRY

CHEESED-OFF MOUSE

COULD YOU BE A SCIENTIST?
What did Koch feed his anthrax bacteria on?

a) Chocolate

b) Wood shavings

c) The watery jelly-like stuff from the inside of an eyeball mixed up with blood.

CLUE: Think of where anthrax bacteria might like to eat.

Answer: c) At this point agar jelly hadn't been invented. The anthrax germs happily multiplied on the tasty gloop. (Of course, anthrax is a disease of animals so the germs fed on bits of animal.) By the way, Koch invented agar jelly a few years later.

Koch had proved for the first time ever that germs cause disease in humans. And he used his work to develop four postulates.

MY POSTULATES ARE FAMOUS...

Do you say...?

ARE THEY PAINFUL?

Answer: A "postulate" has nothing to do with pustules. It's a posh word for a suggestion. Now my postulate is that you read on and stop asking silly questions!

Koch's suggestions were important because they outlined a new approach to studying disease. Here's Robert Koch back from the dead to explain them.

R.I.P. R. KOCH 1843-1910

COME ON, IT'LL ONLY TAKE FIVE MINUTES

Oh – a quick warning. As a result of his discoveries he did become rather big-headed...

DEAD BRAINY: THE GREAT ROBERT KOCH

I, the great Robert Koch, will explain my four postulates that have changed the history of the world. I will use as my example the severe sore throat that I have developed since I've been dead. I've been dying for a cough in my coffin.

In order to prove that a germ causes disease…

Postulate 1. You must find the germ living in the body in the same place as the disease. I took a swab of my throat and discovered this bacterium.

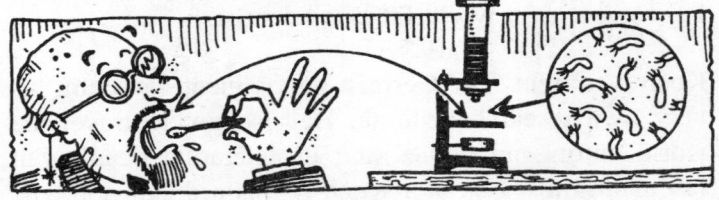

Postulate 2. You must be able to grow the germ so that it divides several times. I have succeeded in growing the germ in a plate of beef soup that has been cooked into a jelly.

Postulate 3. By giving the germs to a healthy animal you make the animal sick. I have succeeded in doing this to a rabbit.

Postulate 4. You must next find the germs living inside the animal. I have taken a sample from the rabbit and found the germs have multiplied in its throat.

THIS EXPERIMENT IS A PAIN IN THE NECK - I MEAN THROAT!

This proves that although I have been dead for some time I am still a great world-famous scientist.

Koch was right. The German government gave him his very own research institute. He also got to travel the world cutting up bodies and investigating deadly but fascinating diseases. For Koch it was a dream job. His two greatest discoveries, in 1882 and 1884, were the germs that cause the deadly diseases TB and cholera. (You can find out more on pages 21 and 96.) In 1905 Koch was awarded the Nobel Prize for his work.

POSTULATE 5 - I THOROUGHLY DESERVE IT!

BOAST!

Between them, Koch and his rival, Frenchman Louis Pasteur, encouraged a whole new group of scientists to plunge into the world of deadly diseases and go searching for the germs that caused them. And the scientists had a powerful new weapon to fight infection: vaccines. Here's all the vital facts you need to know about those necessary jabs...

PASS YOUR SCIENCE TEST WITH HORRIBLE SCIENCE

1 What is a vaccine?

It's a sample of weakened germs. The germs can be weakened by keeping them low on food or heating them to a temperature that they find uncomfortable. Either way, the germs should find it hard to multiply – yes, a bit like some kids in a maths test, ha ha.

2 How does a vaccine work?

By injecting the germs into a person you can get their immune system (B-cells and T-cells) to recognize the germ and get ready for a bit of fisticuffs. Of course the weakened germs aren't a threat, but if the same germs get into the body the white blood cells will be ready and waiting.

ARGH! THEY'RE WAITING FOR US!

3 How were vaccines discovered?

In 1796 Edward Jenner (1749–1823) discovered how to use pus from the sores made by the milder disease, cowpox, to prevent smallpox. Although Jenner didn't understand about immunity, the virus that causes cowpox is similar to smallpox so the body can use immunity against one to fight the other. Jenner was on the right lines even if his scratch wasn't a true vaccine because he didn't use actual smallpox germs. Then, in 1879 Louis Pasteur investigated chicken cholera. (Any guesses what animal this disease infects?)

Pasteur went on holiday leaving a sample of the germs in a nice tasty broth – lucky no one ate it whilst he was away. On his return, Pasteur was amazed to find that when he injected the disease into, yes, you got it, chickens – the birds *didn't* fall ill. As Pasteur found out, the weakened germs made the chickens immune to the disease. Bet that gave him something to crow about!

NEW DRUG FACTS

The doctors soon had another weapon. Scientists were rapidly discovering that certain substances killed bacteria but not the living cells of the body that they lived amongst…

1 The first germ-killing substance was salvarsan, found by German scientist Paul Ehrlich (1854–1915) in 1909. Ehrlich had been searching for new germ-killing substances and salvarsan was effort number 606. And I thought third time was supposed be lucky, not 606th!

2 Many early germ-killing drugs were actually dyes. German scientists noticed that the dyes stained and killed bacteria and left human cells untouched. One famous example was prontosil found by Gerhard Domagk in 1932 (1895–1964). Unfortunately the red dye turned the patient bright red!

3 Within four years French scientists had found that the germ-killing part of the drug was actually a substance called sulphonamide (sul-fon-a-myde) that had already been discovered in 1908. So poor Domagk was left red in the face.

4 Scientists began to develop new drugs based on the sulphonamide chemicals and by 1947 they had made over 5,000 varieties!

Oddly enough though, some of the most powerful germ-killing substances are made not in test tubes but in living cells. Wonderful chemicals that rescue people from the jaws of death. Why not inject a bit of life into your day and read the next chapter?

It could prove a lifesaver...

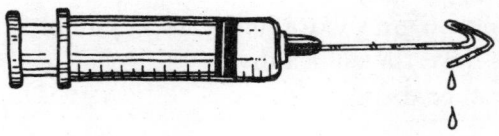

LUCKY LIFESAVERS

Doctors have two more weapons in the battle against deadly disease: antitoxins and antibiotics. And if you thought I said "ant-tick-tock" (an insect alarm clock?) you'd better read this next bit...

AMAZING ANTITOXINS

Antitoxins are antibodies from a person or animal that has had a disease. They can be injected into another person to help them fight the disease, a process also known as "serum therapy". This breakthrough was made by two scientists working for Robert Koch, German Emil von Behring (1854–1917) and Japanese Shibasaburo Kitasato (1852–1931).

SERUM THERAPY? I DON'T GET THE POINT

YOU WILL!

COULD YOU BE A SCIENTIST?

The scientists injected toxins from a deadly kind of bacteria called tetanus into a rabbit. The rabbit hadn't received enough toxin to kill it and it made antibodies to the toxins. The scientists then injected these into mice. They then gave the toxins to the mice.

What happened?

a) The mice grew extra long ears and nibbled lettuce.

b) The mice stayed healthy.

c) The mice died.

Answer: b) The rabbit antitoxins protected the mice. In 1894 Von Behring used this technique to get a horse to make antitoxins that could be given to children to fight the deadly disease diphtheria.

A NOTE TO THE READER...

Homework can be a problem – especially when you haven't done it. Nowadays, teachers are quite sophisticated and no longer believe perfectly reasonable excuses like:

What you need is a new set of excuses – like you're suffering from a deadly disease. If you're lucky you might even get the next six weeks off school! Anyway, free with this book you get a set of sick notes. Simply copy them out and fill in your name in the spaces and post them to your teacher!

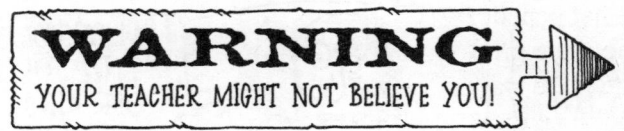

SICKENING SICK NOTE 1: DIPHTHERIA

Dear teacher,
I'm really scared about poor little me
.... I've s/he's got
disgusting, oozing throat sores and now
they've formed a horrible thick slimy
layer. It's TERRIBLE! Poor ....
can't drink soup without it dribbling
out of her/his nostrils! Her/his
condition is dreadfully desperate - s/he
can hardly breathe! The doctor says
it's diphtheria - so I hope you'll
understand that .... hasn't done
any ~~of my~~ homework.
Signed,

A concerned parent

Sickening sick note notes

1 With diphtheria, the bacteria make toxins that poison the nerves and stop them from working. This can lead to heart failure and death.

2 And if that doesn't happen the victim is slowly suffocated by the slimy germs. No wonder the Spanish call the disease "garrotillo" from "garrotte" – a form of strangulation.

CHOKE A LOT?

I'M SUFFOCATING AND YOU'RE OFFERING ME SWEETS?

3 But on the plus side you do get a few days off school … and maybe more!

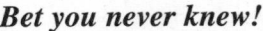

Bet you never knew!
The diphtheria antitoxin saved thousands of lives, but it was hard to make and wasn't available in every hospital. And sometimes the disease would strike in remote places where there was no antitoxin. This is what happened in Nome, Alaska, in 1925 when an outbreak of diphtheria led to a terrifying race against time…

THE MIRACLE DOGS
Nome, Alaska, January 1925
Anna was dying. The nine-year-old girl had little time left but mercifully she didn't know it. Her breathing was uneasy as the diphtheria took a grip. Outside, the wind howled and snow banked up above the windows. It seemed as if the little hospital was lost in a world of ice under the dark skies of winter.

Dr Curtis Welch paced up and down the ward. The worry lines pinched his forehead and his eyes hurt because they hadn't closed for two nights. Five times the town's radio telegraph operator had called for help for the sick children in his care. All had diphtheria and they needed antitoxin desperately.

But when would help come?

Already four children were dead, slowly smothered by the germs that bred in their throats. Twenty children were sick, of whom Anna was the worst. And Dr Welch knew that without antitoxin the disease would kill them all, one by one.

He glared angrily at the swirling snow. If only the weather would ease, a supply might get through! But it kept on snowing – for hour after hour. The snow looked set to fall for ever.

Next morning, Americans read in their newspapers of the plight of the children. In churches all over the nation people offered prayers. A supply of antitoxin was sent to the railhead town of Nenana – but this was 674 miles from Nome.

Meanwhile in Nome the Board of Health committee was arguing about how to get hold of the lifesaving medicine. Planes were the answer, declared the Mayor. Some people nodded their heads but mining boss Mark Summers, disagreed.

"The planes are grounded for the winter. But my sledge dog drivers are the best. Hell – if anyone can get through they can!" he exclaimed.

"So when can we expect the antioxin?" asked Dr Welch eagerly.

"I guess nine days, but maybe more."

"Nine days – for pity's sake – those kids don't have nine days!"

Mark Summers shook his head.

"These guys do the impossible but they ain't miracle workers."

Dr Welch felt like swearing. The exhausted doctor dared not tell his nurses about the delay. One of them was Anna's mother. She could see that her daughter was burning up with fever and every so often she would creep into the kitchen and sob quietly. Yes, Anna was fighting every step. But now her body was tired, desperately weak, and the germs choked her throat until she couldn't swallow. Dr Welch knew that time was running out fast.

And outside it was still snowing...

Within days the Alaska state authorites organized a relay of dog drivers. Despite the terrible weather twenty men offered to help – passing on the medicine at agreed handover points. The best of these was Mark Summers' top driver Leonhard Seppala and it was he who travelled the furthest.

On the night of 1 February it was the turn of Gunnar Kaasen to race through the blizzard. All the tough driver could hear was the panting of his dogs and the creaking of their harness and the hiss of the sledge runners and the endless howl of the ice-laden storm.

With grim pride Gunnar noted that his 13 dogs were pulling well, especially the lead dog, Balto. Gunnar had his doubts about the strong black and white huskie – was he really lead dog material? But Balto never hestitated – he seemed to know the way even as the blizzard worsened and Gunnar could scarcely see the handlebar of his sledge.

Suddenly a blast of wind caught the sledge. It lifted and rolled sideways. The dogs yelped as they tumbled in a jumble of paws and fur and twisted harness. The precious container of antitoxin fell from the sledge into deep snow. Frantically Gunnar picked himself up and untangled the dogs. Where was the antitoxin? He dug desperately in the snow with his numb, clumsy frozen hands. Surely the medicine phials were broken? Then all this would be for nothing...

At the hospital at Nome, Anna's mother watched her daughter's face by the light of an oil lamp. The child's face was so deathly pale that she looked like a waxwork – except for a thin film of sweat. Every few seconds Anna would draw a painful breath. And once her eyes opened. She gazed at her mother and said:

"I feel terrible. I'm not dying, am I?"

And Anna's mother had kissed and hugged her daughter, saying, "Hush darling, don't talk. I'm here."

66

After what seemed an age, Gunnar found the precious container still in its fur wrapping. But his thoughts were wandering as if they had a life of their own. He thought of the other drivers. Some dogs had dropped dead with cold and some of the drivers had arrived at their relay stations with their faces blackened by frostbite. Gunnar felt the stinging cold chewing at his cheeks as the sledge raced onwards. His mind slid in and out of consciousness. He knew he could die out here.

Suddenly as if by some strange miracle the snow stopped falling. With cold-stiffened hands, Gunnar removed his goggles. A little distance away he could make out buildings half-buried by snow.

Where was he? Nome? No, impossible. Yes – yes, YES! They had reached Nome! The streets were deep in snowdrifts but a few early risers stood and watched in amazment. Suddenly they began to clap and cheer with delight. Slowly Gunnar made his way towards the people. But as he reached Balto he stumbled and fell, exhausted in the snow.

Soon a small crowd had gathered. They were hugging Gunnar and petting the dogs, especially Balto, who stood silent with exhaustion, too weary to wag his tail.

All the nurses were there except one who stood by Anna's bedside with tears streaming down her face.

"You're safe now," she whispered to the unconscious girl. "You're going to live."

Bet you never knew!

The newspapers hailed a miracle. In just five incredible days the drivers and their dogs had beaten the weather to deliver the precious medicine. Not a single dose of antitoxin had been lost. Today children in Central Park, New York play around a statue of Balto but the glory belongs to all the drivers, most of them native Athabaskan and Inuit, who risked their lives to save the children of Nome.

AMAZING ANTIBIOTICS

Three years later a scientist discovered an amazing substance called an antibiotic that killed bacteria (but not viruses). The substance was made into a new drug called penicillin that could literally snatch people from the jaws of death, and its discoverer won the Nobel Prize and became an international superstar. His name was Alexander Fleming (1881–1955) and he's so famous your teacher will know all about him – won't she/he?

Well, *won't* she/he? Let's find out...

OF COURSE I KNOW ALL ABOUT ALEXANDER FLIM, ER, FLOM, ER, FLAM, ER...

FLEMING!

TEST YOUR TEACHER

1 How did Fleming get his first medical job?
a) His natural genius impressed other scientists.
b) He was a crack rifle shot.
c) The other scientists needed someone to make tea.

2 During the First World War Fleming treated wounded soldiers in France. What experiment did he perform to help them?
a) He used slug juice to heal wounds.
b) He made a model wound and filled it with germs to test whether germ-killing chemicals worked properly.
c) He tried to use cold tea to kill germs.

3 What was Fleming's favourite hobby?
a) Gardening.
b) Painting pictures using germs.
c) Collecting used tea bags.

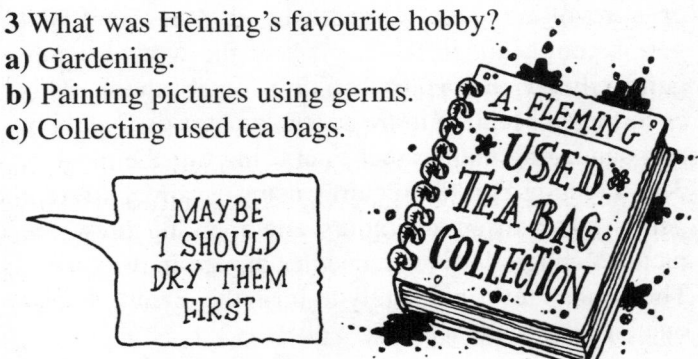

MAYBE I SHOULD DRY THEM FIRST

A. FLEMING USED TEA BAG COLLECTION

4 In 1921 Fleming discovered the germ-killing chemical in mucus. How did he make this breakthrough?
a) A dollop of snot fell from his nose on to a sample of germs.
b) He made the substance by mixing chemicals in a test tube.
c) He found that tea leaves didn't rot when they were wrapped in a snotty handkerchief.

69

Answers: 1 b) No, Fleming DIDN'T shoot his boss at the job interview! The hospital where Fleming was a student had a prize-winning rifle team. Fleming was a member of the team and his bosses were keen for him to stay.

2 b) Fleming melted some glass into the shape of a revolting deep jagged wound. He found germs could lurk in the corners of the wound where germ-killing chemicals couldn't reach them. This encouraged Fleming to treat wounds by washing them and bandaging them rather than using the chemicals.

3 b) Fleming painted pictures using germs. Different germs have different colours and Fleming drew the pictures in agar jelly with needles dipped in the germs. The germs grew on the jelly to form the picture. Fancy one on your wall?

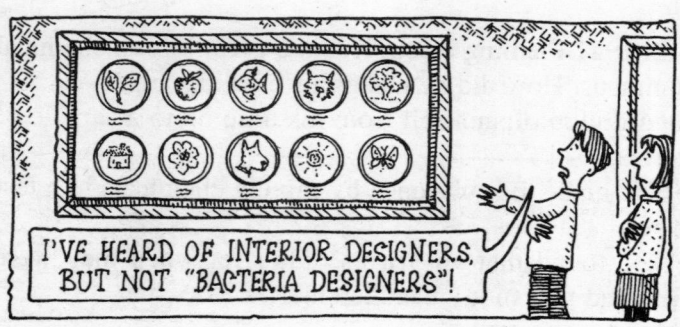

4 a) One day Fleming had a cold and snot from his runny nose fell on some germs and killed them.

(Unfortunately the germ-killing chemical, lysozyme, wasn't powerful enough to make into a drug but Fleming became interested in natural germ-killers.)

What your teacher's score means

0–1 Lucky the school inspectors didn't hear about this.

2–3 Fair, but remind your teacher that a higher score will be required the next time you test them.

4 Too good to be true.

Note all the **c)** answers seem to be about tea and if your teacher kept saying "**c)**" it's probably because she's longing for a tea-break. This attitude is not acceptable in one who is supposed to be educating the young.

A MOULDY OLD STORY

It's a fact that raw penicillin is made by a rare type of mould that Fleming found growing on one of his agar plates. The story has often been told but here's a *Horrible Science* exclusive – the mould gets to tell its *own* story!

MY STORY

BY PENNY CILLIUM

Surprised you want to talk to *me*. Me being an 'umble mould and all that. In all these years no one's ever asked for *my* side of the story, even though it was me and me mouldy friends what made this stuff millions of years before humans got their hands on it. Well, anyway 'ere's what *really* happened.

I first saw the light of day in St Mary's hospital, back in 1928. A scientist was researching moulds and I started my life as a little spore what blew upstairs and landed on a plate of jelly in Fleming's lab. *Strawberry or lime?* I asked meself. Sorry, just a mouldy joke. The jelly was boiled seaweed. But I'm not fussy – if it's food, it's food.

Fleming was growing bacteria from an infected boil on the plate – but I soon put a stop to that. Well, I mean, I know I'm only 'umble but would *you* want someone oozing boils over your dinner? So I squirted some germ-killing stuff we moulds make and that kept the germs away. Success on a plate, I thought.

So where was Fleming whilst I was hard at

GRRR!

72

work? Well, I'm only an 'umble mould and no one tells me nothing but I found out later he was on holiday. Scotland to be exact – very nice! And get this ...

me
when he comes back he only dumps me in a bucket of disinfectant! Lucky, I was on top of the pile of other plates otherwise no one would have heard of penicillin!

Wasn't till a pal of his dropped by and spotted me that Fleming got interested. That's when the trouble started – he started doing tests and one of his mates nibbled me to see if I was poisonous! Wish I had been!!! In the end Fleming used me juice to kill unwanted germs on his precious germ dishes. And that was me life for years – cleaning up for a lazy scientist! I'm only 'umble, but well, would you want to spend yer life washing dishes?

Years later humans learnt how to make my juice stronger using chemicals and people started saying what a hero lazy old Fleming was for finding me! Fleming and his mates got a Nobel Prize and a slap-up dinner – but did I get invited? I'm only 'umble – I'd have been happy to eat the mouldy old food scraps no one wanted! After all, that's a feast for me! But I was left stuck on that jelly dish and then can yer believe it? – I got shoved in a *museum*. Well honestly – there's gratitude for yer!

SO WHAT HAPPENED NEXT?

After Fleming spotted the mould and realized it could kill germs he got excited. The problem, as we've seen, was that Fleming's mould juice wasn't strong enough to kill germs in the body. Fleming tried investigating bits of mouldy old cheese and old books and creaky old boots and household dirt, looking for more moulds with germ-killing powers. But he never found any.

WANTED! ANYTHING MOULDY. THE MOULDIER THE BETTER!

PASS ME THAT CHEESY OLD SOCK, PLEASE.

Penicillin only saw the light of day because German-born scientist Ernst Chain (1906–1979) was looking for a germ-killing substance and read an article Fleming had written about his discovery. Chain found a way to concentrate the mould juice and make it more powerful by treating it with chemicals. Now the mould juice could really prove its worth. A little girl at St. Mary's Hospital was dying from a diseased bone marrow but huge doses of penicillin cured her in just one amazing night. By morning she was sitting up in bed feeling much better!

YESTERDAY I WAS DYING AND TODAY I'M DYING... TO GO HOME!

Chain and his Australian boss Howard Florey (1898–1968) took their idea to America, looking for help to produce penicillin on a massive scale. They found backers in a government lab in Peoria, Illinois, where scientists grew the mould on waste from corn-processing. Then local fungi expert "Mouldy" Mary Hunt found another mould growing on a melon in a local market.

It turned out that this mould, a relative of the one that Fleming had found, was even better at making germ-killing juice! And for ten years, until scientists learnt how to make the drug in a test tube, this mould supplied the world with penicillin.

AMAZING MOULD FACTS

1 Yep – there's no doubt about it, moulds are good for you. Well, some are. In the Ukraine and parts of England mouldy slices of bread were used as traditional bandages. And yes, the mould stopped germs from infecting the wounds.

2 You might never have been treated with penicillin but if you've ever eaten Stilton cheese you've *eaten* it. That's because a mould related to the one that makes the drug gives stilton its delicious pongy flavour.

THE SMELL WILL MAKE YOU SICK, BUT THE MOULD WILL MAKE YOU BETTER

REVOLTING STINK!

3 Scientists have since found more mouldy antibiotics. One type are the cephalosporins (cef-fal-lo-spoor-rins) made by a kind of fungus. They were found by scientist Giuseppe Brotzu (1895–1976) by a seaside sewage pipe. The fungi were greedily scoffing the rotting poo. But NO, paddling in sewage doesn't always guarantee a great scientific discovery so don't try it.

4 Another antibiotic was discovered by a team of boffins led by American scientist Selman Waksman (1888–1973). Glory-hunting Selman was so keen he tested over 10,000 (yes, you did read that right, TEN THOUSAND) suitable microbes. But it was actually his student Albert Schatz who found the promising bacteria … in the throat of a chicken.

WHOOPEE!

GROAN!

So would you volunteer to poke around in a chicken's gullet? Or would you turn chicken? In the end Waksman was the winner. He was awarded the Nobel Prize in 1952 – which was a bit odd because he hadn't been around when Schatz made his dramatic diccovery. It sounds a bit like fowl play to me!

DEADLY EXPRESSIONS
A scientist says…

IT'S STREPTOMYCES
(STREP-TOE-MY-SEES)

Do you say…?

IT'S
STEPPED
IN YOUR
WHAT?

Answer: No. It's the name of the microbe Waksman found.

Streptomyces proved good for bumping off the bacteria that cause TB and other deadly diseases such as plague. These horrific germs make the other microbes you've seen so far seem warm and caring!

Wanna know more? I hope so cos THEY'RE LURKING IN THE NEXT CHAPTER

RAGING PLAGUE

This is a story about a human, a rat, a flea and a bacterium. It tells how the bacterium made everyone's lives (and deaths) a complete misery and how between them they killed hundreds of millions of people and caused hundreds of years of misery. Would you fancy a dose of plague? Why not read on – it's the most painless way to find out!

SICKENING SICK NOTES 2: THE PLAGUE (AKA THE BLACK DEATH)

Dear teacher,
TERRIBLE NEWS! My poor little
.... had the Black Death last
night so s/he didn't do ~~my~~ any
homework. It all began with an
agonizing headache and fever and then
~~my~~ her/his lymph nodes filled with
germs and pus and swelled to the size
of apples! S/he was in AGONY!
Horrible lumps of bacteria formed under
her/his skin causing black blotches – I
don't know what to do! He/she might
die and then ~~I~~ he/she might not go to
school for ages!
Signed,
~~Me~~ A con very concerned parent.

Sickening sick note notes

(Don't forget to read this bit!)

1 Plague is caused by a bacterium called *Yersina pestis*. But this tiny pest is far from tiny in its effects. If the disease isn't treated with antibiotics at least one third of its victims *die* in five days.

2 Sometimes plague attacks the brain and blood and sometimes it dissolves the lungs. The victims cough germs everywhere and spread the disease.

3 Whatever happens, death is usually caused by the toxins that the germs make and huge lumps of germs breaking up vital bits of the body.

Sounds like fun, I DON'T think. But how does this horrible disease spread? Well, let's imagine a rat, a flea, a human and the bacterium all kept diaries… (OK – this *is* going to take quite a leap of imagination, or in the flea's case quite a hop.)

DEADLY DIARIES

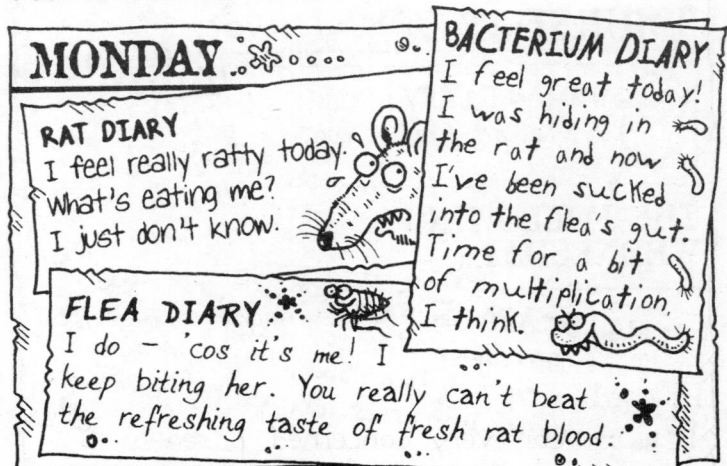

MONDAY

RAT DIARY
I feel really ratty today. What's eating me? I just don't know.

FLEA DIARY
I do – 'cos it's me! I keep biting her. You really can't beat the refreshing taste of fresh rat blood.

BACTERIUM DIARY
I feel great today! I was hiding in the rat and now I've been sucked into the flea's gut. Time for a bit of multiplication, I think.

FLEA DIARY
I feel sick – I can't keep nothing down. Every time I suck blood I end up sicking it up! Silly me – must have drunk some dodgy blood – I'm hopping mad with myself!

WEDNESDAY

BACTERIUM DIARY
Too right, pal, and now there's thousands of us blocking your gut so you can't eat properly. Well, all I can say is ... that flea's got guts!

FLEA DIARY
Still feeling peckish though. So I'm biting everything in sight trying to find some blood I can keep down.

BACTERIUM DIARY
Ha ha, every time he does that we get into another body.

THURSDAY

HUMAN DIARY · Ouch, wretched fleas! Hop it!

BACTERIUM DIARY
OK gang let's move into our human victim.

THE FOLLOWING WEDNESDAY...

HUMAN DIARY
I feel terrible. I've got fever, I'm throwing up all the time, I've got huge lumps under my arms. Er, gotta dash!

BACTERIUM DIARY
So you should - you've got thousands of us in every drop of your blood. Hey gang - let's go and check out the old lungs.

FRIDAY

HUMAN DIARY I've got stinking breath and I'm coughing up blood.

BACTERIUM DIARY
Hmm, don't reckon this one will last much longer. It's about time we found another victim ... anyone fancy a nice juicy rat?

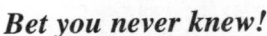

Bet you never knew!
1 Rats actually find the plague more deadly than humans but who cares about them? Actually, I've heard some teachers have pet rats and cuddle these vicious rodents and call them soppy names like Tufty – but it's hard to imagine.
2 Although the main way the flea passes on the bacteria to humans is through bites, other methods include...
a) Rubbing flea poo into the open wound made by the bite. (Flea poo always contains bacteria.)
b) Crunching a flea in your mouth. The flea blood is full of bacteria and if it gets on your tonsils the bacteria can sometimes ooze into your blood. Lovely!

So that's how the bacteria can get into your body. But where did the plague come from? Who got it first – the rats, the fleas or the humans? Well, the loathsome life story of the plague is about to be revealed…

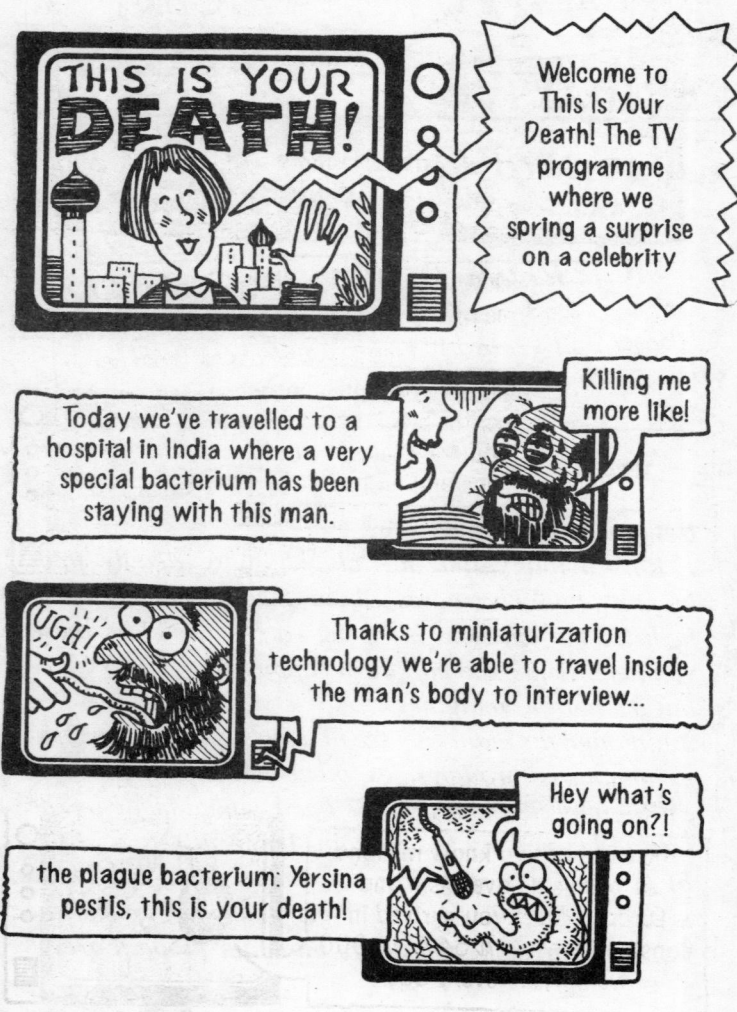

Your early life was rather obscure wasn't it? It's thought that you lived in Central Asia.

Well, yes it was over 100,000 years ago but my memory's a bit hazy now. I do remember being happy living amongst the wild marmots in their warm burrows.

They never got a nasty disease?

No, I got on well with them. Well, all right, their immune systems stopped me multiplying but they couldn't wipe me out.

Then you teamed up with your long-suffering partners the black rat and its fleas. Together you travelled the world living in ships and houses.

Er yes, but we've never got on very well.

And here they are...

Grrr — you make us sick — we're going to get you!

Er hi guys!

Yeah — it was a busy time.

You soon got to know millions of people all over Asia and Europe. When you arrived in Constantinople in AD 542, 10,000 were dying every day.

You made many return trips to Europe and Asia, in 1348 for instance, when over 50 million people died.

Oh yes – happy days!

The death toll was so terrible that the war then raging between England and France had to be put on hold.

Just doing my bit for world peace.

And of course you kept coming back every few years.

Well, yes, my public needed me!

But they hated you, they feared you – YOU KILLED THEM!

Yeah, OK – so I did. Now clear off BEFORE I KILL YOU!

THE PUTRID PLAGUE

Every few years the plague struck cities all over Europe killing old and young, rich and poor. And wherever the plague went it spread sorrow, misery and death. Often people fled their homes to get away from the disease and families split up.

IT'S THE PLAGUE. FLEE!

DO THEY MEAN ME?

Of course the authorities did all they could do to fight the menace (which wasn't a lot). Which of these anti-plague rules are genuine?

PLAGUE RULES OK?
Answer TRUE or FALSE.

To fight ye plague…

1 All ye cats and dogs must be killed (and that goes for ye – Tiddles).

2 Everyone coming from plague-stricken areas must spend up to 40 days in isolation from the rest of ye town.

3 Everyone who hath the plague is to be made to take a nice hot bath twice a day on pain of ye death.

4 Paint a red cross on ye door and order ye entire family to stay at home. Leave food and medicine on ye doorstep and send ye old women to check if they be dead yet.

5 If anyone sneaks out they will be executed in front of their own house.

6 Anyone with ye plague is to be given £100 on condition that they leave town at once.

7 If ye fall sick of ye plague ye house will be burnt down and all ye belongings burnt.

Answers: 1 True. In London in 1665 plague killed 75,000 people and all the cats and dogs were killed to stop the plague spreading. In fact, cats and dogs do actually suffer from the disease but killing them did little good because, of course, the fleas carried on biting humans and spreading the disease.

2 True. This precaution was developed in Ragusa (now in Croatia) in 1377. It became known as quarantine and when it was properly enforced it stopped the plague from spreading.

3 False. In 1348 doctors at the University of Paris warned that bathing opened up pores in the skin and would let diseases into the body. This was "pore" advice. But nowadays children are still forced to take a bath on pain of death.

4 True. This is what happened in London in 1665. Unfortunately when we say "old women" we're not talking sweet white-haired old dears – we're talking killer grannies. The old women often robbed the dead and strangled those who weren't quite dead enough. In 1348 gravediggers committed this grisly crime in Florence, Italy.

5 True. This was a rule from Scotland. In 1530 a tailor was hanged in front of his house for going to church when his wife was ill. Luckily the rope broke so the man was kicked out of town instead.

6 False.

7 True. Queen Elizabeth of England (1533–1603) ordered the belongings of sick people to be burned – this was sensible because the fire killed the fleas. The same is true for burning houses, a measure used in Hawaii in 1899. Unfortunately the fire lit in one house got out of control and destroyed 5,000 more. I expect the person responsible got a warm reception.

Bet you never knew!
In the English village of Eyam in 1665 a bundle of cloth sent from the plague-stricken city of London brought fleas and the plague. Within four days the man who had received the cloth was dead. Bravely, the villagers decided to quarantine their village, letting no one in or out so that the plague wouldn't spread. Then one by one, they died. By the following spring, of the 350 villagers, just 84 were left alive. But thanks to their bravery the plague spread no further.

Of course, the true causes of plague hadn't been discovered yet. But doctors tried every cure you can think of and a few that you'd never think of in a thousand years. Needless to say they were as useless as an odour-free stink bomb.

☠ HORRIBLE HEALTH WARNING!

Did you hear me? I said they were U–S–E–L–E–S–S. So don't even *think* of trying any of these cures on yourself or your little brother/sister/pet plague rat. Some of these "cures" were DANGEROUS!

87

Ye Olde Plague Cure Book

Chapter One

WEAR YE RIGHT GEAR
(1348 version)

Doctors all over Europe are wearing ye latest anti-plague gear. Ye high-tech clobber will keep ye plague away!

Beak full of nice smelling herbs

Mask

Wand for checking a victim's pulse

Long leather gloves

Leather gown

SCIENTIFIC NOTE
This gear didn't stop the fleas biting the doctor and causing plague.

88

Chapter Two
A BREATH OF FRESH AIR

As everyone knows, ye plague be caused by some kind of nasty smell in ye air. So it helps if you...

Light ye bonfires or set off ye cannon. Smoke gets rid of ye smell. Smoking tobacco is _good_ for ye because it gets rid of smells. Everyone should smoke including ye children.

HISTORICAL NOTE: Cannons and tobacco were seventeenth century, the others were 1348. Children were beaten by their teacher at Eton College, England, for _not_ smoking.

WHACK!

BUT SMOKING IS **BAD** FOR YOU!

DING! DONG!

To get ye air moving in a healthy way try letting birds fly round ye room or ringing a few bells. If ye don't have ye gunpowder or ye birds or ye bells ye needs to fart into ye bottle and uncork it to let out ye odour. Ye whiff will chase out ye foul air that causeth plague (and ye friends too). If ye have not ye bottle why not simply stick ye head down ye blocked toilet?

YE FARTY PONG!

89

Chapter Three

BATHING IS GOOD FOR YE

No, we do not mean baths in <u>water</u> -
everyone knoweth that they be <u>terribly</u>
bad for ye. No, ye modern 1348 way
to ward off ye plague is to bath in...

a) Vinegar

b) Your own pee
(if any be left
over ye can drink
it twice a day)

c) Goat's pee

Chapter Four

GOOD HEALTHY SKIN: REMEDIES FROM YE SEVENTEENTH CENTURY.

If ye hath the plague ye must take
care of ye skin, so...

1 Take one toad and crush it and smear
ye slimy juices all over ye plague sores.

2 Rub the rump of a dead
chicken on ye plague sores.

3 Apply the guts of a
puppy to ye forehead.

Chapter Five

MARVELLOUS MEDICINES

Now it be time for ye medicine. That'll cure ye plague in the twinkling of an eyeball! Well, maybe.

1 Eat some crunchy dry scabs from ye plague victim's sores. They be delicious washed down with a bowl of fresh pus. (Fourteenth century)

Scabs

pus

2 Fancy something with a bit more bite? Here be a traditional seventeenth-century recipe...

a) Take the brains of a young man that hath died violently.

b) Mash well and add some wine.

c) Add a generous dollop of ye horse dung and leave to rot for a year.

NOT TO BE TAKEN BEFORE 1666

That'll doeth ye trick!

SCIENCE CLOSES IN ON THE PLAGUE GERMS

In 1855 plague was on the move again. It hit the Chinese province of Yunnan and over the next 40 years killed 100,000 people. When at last it reached the coast of China it attacked ports such as Hong Kong, and ships took the rats, the fleas, the bacteria and the plague all over the world.

Between 1896 and 1917, in India alone, over *ten million* people died. Something had to be done!

By now scientists understood that germs cause disease and thanks to Koch they knew how to perform tests to discover which germ caused a particular disease. Or so they reckoned...

In 1894 a team of scientists from Robert Koch's Institute went to Hong Kong to find the plague germ. They were led by renowned scientist Shibasaburo Kitasato (remember him from page 60). But there was another scientist in the field, Swiss-born Alexandre Yersin (1863–1943) who had worked for Louis Pasteur and had since been travelling and making maps in Vietnam. But who would make the key breakthrough?

Here's how Yersin might have recorded the next few days...

YERSIN'S DIARY 1894

SATURDAY ~ Got to Hong Kong today. Phew, it's hot - had to carry all my own bags to the humble boarding house where I'm staying. Kitasato and his 30 assistants have taken over a posh hotel in the centre of town. Well, he's welcome to it. Huh, who needs a posh place ... haven't got any nice clothes to wear anyway.

MONDAY ~ Went to the local hospital today looking for a plague victim to study and got kicked out! Seems everyone reckons that Kitasato is going to find the germ. Then the man himself turns up in his smart white suit and looks at me as if I'm something the cat brought in. OK, my armpits were a bit sweaty and I guess I could have done with a shave this morning. "You're too late, Yersin!" he sneers with a smug smile. "I've already found the germ. It was simple, I grew it from the finger of a dead plague victim!"

WEDNESDAY ~ Everyone thinks Kitasato has found the germ - but I'm not so sure. I mean, whoever heard of anyone getting plague in their finger? Lungs maybe, or lymph nodes but a finger? Anyway there's a gang of English sailors burying the dead bodies and I'm bribing them to let me cut out the rotting swollen lymph nodes from the bodies. It's smelly work, but hey ... I'm a scientist, I'm used to it. S'cuse me while I throw up!

FRIDAY ~ I've found it!!! The lymph nodes are full of fat little germs! Now all I have to do is grow them. But am I on the right track or am I wasting my time? Maybe Kitasato was right after all!

SATURDAY ~ Today I injected my germs into a healthy rat. Lucky my landlord, Yu Pai-now, doesn't know there's a rat in my room. Now all I can do is wait. Will the rat get the plague?

WEDNESDAY ~ The rat's still healthy ... oh rats! Not even a sniffle!

THURSDAY ~ No, wait, the rat's got swollen glands. He's acting as if he's drunk – he's got the plague! He's very ill. Oh yes, yes, YES – I'm so very happy!

Yersin had found the germ that causes plague and that's how it came to be named *Yersina pestis*, in his honour. Back in France he was able to make an antitoxin to the germ's toxins and two years later he was back in Hong Kong to try it out. For the first time in history people were actually cured of the plague! Today, although the plague is still around – wild animals in Asia and parts of the United States carry the disease – it can be beaten by drugs and antibiotics. The plague is still feared but it's no longer a mass killer.

Mind you, if the plague seems a pain in the guts wait till you read the next chapter...

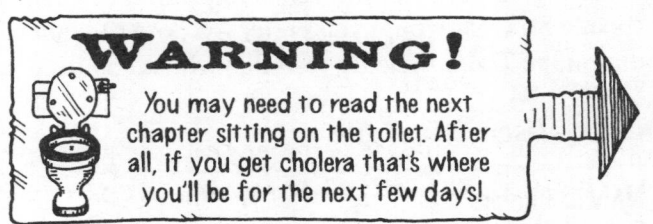

WARNING!
You may need to read the next chapter sitting on the toilet. After all, if you get cholera that's where you'll be for the next few days!

CRUEL CHOLERA

Fancy a bite to eat? Well, you'd better enjoy it now because as you read this chapter you may find your appetite disappearing. And it'll be all down to the vicious little bug that causes cholera.

WHAT'S IN A NAME?

Here's a Greek word that your teacher doesn't know: "kholera" means diarrhoea in Greek. So next time you have a bad case of the trots tell your teacher you've got a dose of cholera and you might get six months off school! But calling cholera "diarrhoea" is like calling the *Titanic* a "boat". So what would you prefer – a dose of cholera or a trip on the *Titanic*? Better read this whilst you decide...

Deadly disease fact file

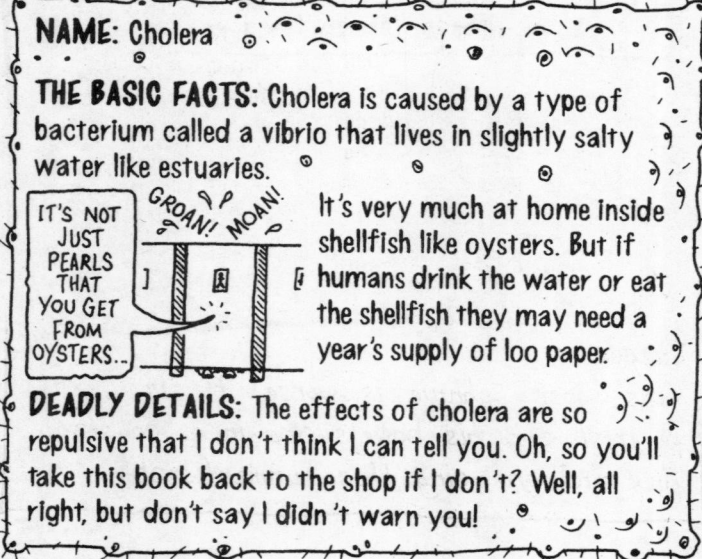

NAME: Cholera

THE BASIC FACTS: Cholera is caused by a type of bacterium called a vibrio that lives in slightly salty water like estuaries.

IT'S NOT JUST PEARLS THAT YOU GET FROM OYSTERS..

GROAN! MOAN!

It's very much at home inside shellfish like oysters. But if humans drink the water or eat the shellfish they may need a year's supply of loo paper.

DEADLY DETAILS: The effects of cholera are so repulsive that I don't think I can tell you. Oh, so you'll take this book back to the shop if I don't? Well, all right, but don't say I didn't warn you!

A DISGUSTING DIARY

Here's the journal of a Victorian lady recording the illness of her husband. Our old chum Dr Grimgrave has added his up-to-date medical comments...

Monday

1832

Oh alas! My poor Johnnie is sick. He has vomited many times and has (dare I mention this unseemly word even in the privacy of my own diary?) diarrhoea. Yet he has eaten nothing today, and prior to falling ill he had drunk but a little water. Oh woe is me! Oh woe is Johnnie!

Dr Grimgrave writes...

The stupid woman should stop blubbering and summon a doctor.

The water was crawling with cholera germs. Their toxins stop the patients bowels from doing their job of soaking up digestive juices. All these juices, containing water and minerals vital to health, are flowing out of him as diarrhoea. Without prompt treatment the patient will end up a "stiff" as we say in the medical profession.

Tuesday

Alas, poor Johnnie is worse! He is feverish and his bowels are in a constant flux and producing those unmentionable fluids. He is thirsty but sicks up anything he drinks and — horrors! — his skin has turned BLUE! And he is in agony from cramps. I called the doctor and he said he had to take blood from my beloved because he has too much! But alas — my Johnnie's blood has turned into black syrup!

Wednesday

Alas, my Johnnie is up with the angels. His skin had turned purple, then dark blue and black. And his poor dead face resembles a skull. But wait — even as I write he moves... ARGGGH! His dead body is jerking and twitching!

Dr Grimgrave writes...
That doctor should be struck off! The patient is drying out — he needs *more* liquid — not *less* blood! The drying out causes the cramps and black blood — which in turn explains the blue skin. The diarrhoea contains tiny bits of guts — hmm — I think this calls for closer examination.

Dr Grimgrave writes...
Well, the patient died as I predicted.
The lack of vital body salts is
resulting in signals from the dead
nerves which in turn keep the dead
muscles moving for a few hours.
Hmm – it's a dead fascinating
post-mortem phenomenon.

Sounds horrible? Sounds so horrible that you'd run a mile to get away from this disease? Well, if you don't feel like running a mile you could always take a nice relaxing holiday in some of the cholera hot-spots.

HORRIBLE SCIENCE HOLIDAYS present
A HOLIDAY WITH A DIFFERENCE
THE CHOLERA EXPERIENCE

Visit some of the most spectacular and beautiful
parts of the world and spend hours and hours on the
toilet (don't forget to pack the loo paper!). You'll be
dying to get away!

Paris 1832
Enjoy the colour of the Paris
carnival. Marvel at the revellers
with their delightful painted
faces and bright costumes.

CONTINUED →

SMALL PRINT

1. The revellers with blue faces are actually suffering from cholera but everyone thought it was just make-up until they started dying in the streets.

2. If you're not French it might be a good idea to make yourself scarce. The crowd blamed foreigners for poisoning the victims and started killing them!

3. For the REAL cholera experience why not try one of the cures suggested by Dr Francois Megendie. You lie down and he slaps 50 slimy blood-sucking leeches on your body. Note – it doesn't work, but hey, it's an experience!

FANCY A BIT OF ADVENTURE?

Try a trip to Russia in the 1890s. Experience the thrill of being a suspected cholera sufferer.

The law says that if you have cholera all your belongings are taken away and you're imprisoned in a military barracks to stop the disease spreading.

1. Life in the barracks is very harsh and you don't get much food. But at least it's cheap and cheerful.

2. If you try to escape you'll be whipped.

THINK I'LL COME BACK NEXT YEAR

YOU'LL STILL BE HERE NEXT YEAR

No wonder a traditional Russian curse said "May you get cholera." You can try this one out on the school bully … if you dare.

COULD YOU BE A DOCTOR?

YOU are famous Victorian physician John Snow (1813–1858). You're well known for pioneering the use of the painkiller chloroform in operations and now you're interested in cholera.

In 1854 cholera breaks out in London. Thousands die, including 700 in one small corner of Soho. The people here live in slums and 54 people share an outside toilet. (How do they all fit in?)

The toilet is oozing its disgusting contents into the drinking water of the nearby pump. All the cholera victims have drunk the water. You believe that the germs that caused cholera got into the water from the toilet.

1 What do you do?

a) Take away the toilet for testing.

b) Take some water from the pump for testing.

c) Take away the pump for testing.

2 Your tests show that there are germs in the water. What do you do next?

a) Drink the water to see if you get cholera.

b) Give the water to an enemy to see if they get cholera.

c) Take the handle off the pump so no one can use it.

Answers: 1 b) When people with cholera used the toilet the germs made their way into the drinking water. The disease was slow to develop because some sufferers used potties and emptied them out of the window. It was messy if diarrhoea landed on your head but at least it kept the germs out of the water supply.

AND THAT'S SUPPOSED TO MAKE ME FEEL BETTER?

2 c) The epidemic stopped. (It was ending anyway but the important thing was that it didn't flare up again.) Snow had proved the link between cholera and dirty water.

Of course, the world sat up and took notice and Snow became a national hero! *Didn't he?* Come off it: *Horrible Science* ain't no fairy tale! No one took any notice and when John Snow died aged 44, his discovery was forgotten. Forgotten, that is, until super-doc Robert Koch took an interest in cholera.

KOCH-YA!

In 1883 cholera struck the Egyptian city of Alexandria but by the time Koch reached Egypt the cholera had all but disappeared. I bet he was gutted! Never one to miss out on research, he tried giving germs to crocodiles to see if they got cholera. If they had, they'd have shed crocodile tears!

Meanwhile Louis Pasteur had sent two assistants, Emile Roux and Louis Thuillier, to Alexandria to find the cholera germ. Unfortunately, they tried to grow germs in a broth rather than on a plate of jelly and this made it hard to sort out the many different types of germs in the broth. The two scientists became confused but Thellier still managed to catch cholera and die. Science can be tough sometimes.

Koch went to East Africa and then to Calcutta, India, in search of cholera. In Calcutta he found thousands of people suffering from the disease. Naturally, he was delighted.

He cut open ten dead bodies and tested their festering diarrhoea and vomit and local water. He found vibrio germs in all of them, proving beyond doubt that the bacteria caused cholera.

Scientific note:
Actually, Italian scientist Fillipo Pacini described finding the cholera germ in the guts of victims as early as 1854 – but no one realized that the germ actually caused the disease and Pacini's discovery was forgotten.

WARNING! REALLY REVOLTING FACTS AHEAD.

TWO REALLY REVOLTING CHOLERA STORIES
1 Even after Koch's discovery there were some who refused to believe that the disease was caused by a germ. German scientist Max von Pettenkofer (1818–1901) thought that the disease was caused by chemicals. To prove his theory he actually *drank* a revolting mixture of germs taken from the diarrhoea of a cholera victim. Von Pettenkofer got mild diarrhoea which he claimed was nothing to do with the cholera. Yeah, right.

NOT BAD, PERHAPS A LITTLE MORE PEPPER

2 Actually this experience was not unique. A nurse told John Snow how one night she was tired after a long day nursing cholera patients and she felt like a drink. She was exhausted and dazed and picked up a large cup of tea and gulped it down. Only then did she realize that it wasn't a cup of tea she was drinking … it was a potty full of diarrhoea! Amazingly, the nurse survived.

But hold on – why didn't Max and the nurse get cholera? Well, they were being protected by their stomachs. Yes, the human stomach makes a strong acid that dissolves most of the cholera germs. Wanna know more?

Dare you discover 1 … how stomach acid protects guts?

You will need:

Three glasses or jars
Yeast (the dried variety is fine)
Vinegar
Baking powder
Sugar
Three teaspoons

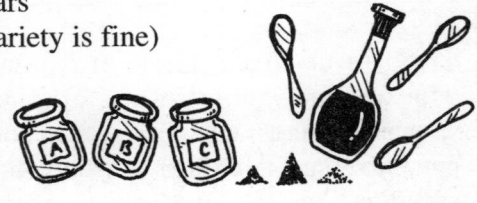

What you do:

1 Label the three glasses A, B and C.
2 Fill each with warm water and add three tablespoonfuls

of vinegar to B and C. Then add a heaped teaspoonful of baking powder to C and stir well until most of the froth has gone.

3 Add a teaspoonful of yeast and a heaped teaspoonful of sugar to each jar. Stir well.

4 Place the glasses in a warm place for an hour.

What do you notice?

a) Each glass contains milky beige-coloured liquid, and if I put my ear to the glasses I can hear a fizzing noise.

b) A and C are like this but not B.

c) Only B is like this, A and C are a disgusting shade of green.

> **Answer: b)** In A and C the yeast is multiplying like cholera germs and the fizzing is carbon-dioxide gas that is given off as the yeasts feed. The acid vinegar in B has killed most of the yeast and the sample is now a vile green colour. The acid in C was weakened by the baking powder. When your stomach acid is weak, perhaps because you've drunk lots of water, cholera germs survive to wreak havoc in the guts. Sickening – eh?

Dare you discover 2 ... how to make cholera cures?

If you get cholera you're going be very interested in finding a cure. Here are two possibilities...

Cure A

You will need:
A tea bag
Some mustard
A mug
A teaspoon

What you do:
1 Fill the mug with boiling water. (Grab an adult and ask them to help.)
2 Dunk the tea bag quickly in the water.
3 Add a level teaspoon of mustard and stir well.
4 Allow five minutes to cool and try a sip. (OK, you can sniff it instead!)
Note: if you don't like it you could always add milk and give it to the adult saying:

Cure B
What you need:
A mug
Some sugar
Some salt

What you do:

1 Fill the mug with boiling water. (Apologize to adult for the horrible trick you played and ask for help.)

2 Add a heaped teaspoonful of sugar and a quarter of a level teaspoon of salt and stir well.

3 Allow five minutes to cool, and then taste.

Which cure do you think works best?

a) A

b) B

c) They're equally useful but work in different ways.

Answer: b) Cure **A** is a traditional Spanish remedy and, like many old remedies, it's useless. Cure **B** is based on a mixture invented in Dacca, Bangladesh and Calcutta in the 1960s. It's designed to replace lost sugars and salts in the body and the boiling kills cholera germs in the water. This treatment has saved thousands of lives – it reverses the drying out so that the patient's white blood cells can kill off the cholera germs.

Today, cholera is still going strong in many parts of the world. Every so often the disease goes on a world tour, spread by ships that take polluted water into their ballast tanks (tanks of water that are used to stop the ship rolling in the sea) and released elsewhere. So although the disease can be cured, it's still a force to be reckoned with.

Mind you, if you think this sounds bad, in the next chapter you'll meet a whole new gang of disease-causers. They're a gang that cause really deadly diseases so you're sure to find them sickening.

Better put on that spacesuit...

VICIOUS VIRUSES

Your granny is wrong – small parcels don't always mean nice things. This chapter is about viruses – tiny things, far smaller even than bacteria. These tiny objects can ruin your life *for ever*. Fancy a closer look? Well, you'll *need* to look closer – a lot, lot closer.

Here they are…

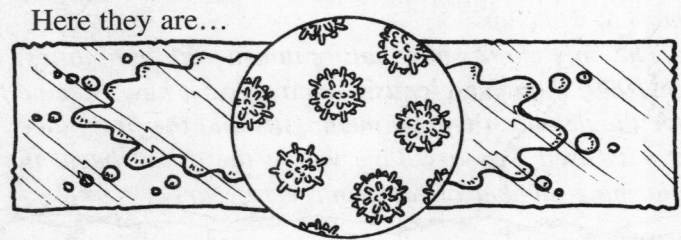

A virus is basically a chemical called DNA (or, if you want to be teacher's pet, deoxyribose nucleic acid) surrounded by another chemical called a protein. DNA, as its long name suggests, is an incredibly complicated substance.

COULD I HAVE MORE INFORMATION ON THE STRUCTURE OF DEOXYRIBOSE NUCLEIC ACID, SIR?

TEACHER'S PET

It's found in all living cells and contains millions of chemical codes that control the cell's chemistry and affect how it grows and develops. Remember that viruses hijack the cells in your body and use them to make more viruses (see pages 23–5, if you've forgotten). Well, now for the deadly details…

Deadly disease fact file

NAME: Viruses

THE BASIC FACTS ABOUT WHAT THEY DO:

1 They sneak into the body through a cut or get in through the mouth or nose.

SNEAK!

2 They land on a cell and lock on to it using their protein outer coats.

VIRUS *LAND!* *CELL*

SQUEEZE!

3 They squeeze their DNA through the cell wall or creep in with other chemicals that are being taken into the cell.

COPY! COPY! COPY! COPY!

4 They make for the nucleus where the cell's DNA is stored and activate the DNA chemically to program the cell to make lots more viruses. (This takes about half an hour.)

DEADLY DETAILS:

SEEK! SEEK!

1 When the cell runs out of juice it dies and the viruses seek another victim!

2 There are five million red blood cells in one drop of blood and each can hold 1,000 viruses – so there's plenty of room!

VICIOUS VIRUS FACTS

1 One of the body's few defences is to kill the cells that viruses infect. Unfortunately this can sometimes make things worse. The Hepatitis B virus hides inside liver cells. The immune system kills the liver cells but you need your liver to live and sometimes the body ends up killing itself! That's dead unlucky.

2 There are actually viruses called bacteriophages (back-teer-rio-fay-ges) that attack bacteria. Doesn't your heart just bleed for the little darlings?

3 When viruses copy their DNA inside a human cell they often make mistakes – known as mutations (mu-tay-shuns). Whilst some of these mistakes can harm a virus others can make it better at infecting you. For example, they make chemical changes in the outer coat that disguise the virus so that the body's defences don't spot it. Sneaky, eh? As a result, it's hard for scientists to devise vaccines for diseases caused by these viruses … diseases like flu.

FOUL FLU

Have you had flu? Sorry, silly question…

Flu is short for "influenza", which actually comes from the word "influence" and reflects an old belief that flu was caused by the influence of the stars. Well, you can thank your lucky stars if you don't get it…

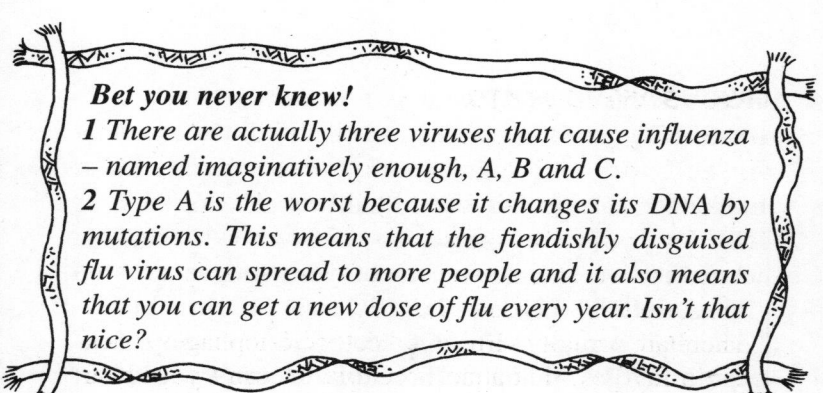
Like a cold, flu is spread by coughing or sneezing
droplets of spit – oh, so you knew all about that? Well,
did you know that you can even spread colds and flu by
talking?

Dare you discover ... how speaking spreads flu?

You will need:
Yourself
A good supply of spit (drink a glass of water first)
A mirror

What you do:
1 Press your nose against the mirror.
2 Say the word "SPIT" loudly.
3 Say "DRY" loudly.

Which letters leave the most spit on the mirror?
a) "SPIT"
b) "DRY"
c) Neither, I never spit when I talk!

> **Answer: a)** The movement of your tongue as you speak letters such as the "P" and "T" in "SPIT" actually sprays spit. Of course, the drops of spit could be hiding millions of flu viruses. Maybe you could share this interesting information with a teacher who sprays spit as they talk. Or maybe not...

TEACHER'S TEA-BREAK TEASER

Feeling cruel? Oh good. Well, wait until your teacher gets the flu and when she drags herself into school (most teachers seem to think it's a shame if you get sent home because there's no one to teach you) hammer on the staffroom door. Smile sweetly at your suffering school teacher and ask...

THE DAILY GLOBE

31 December 1918

FATAL FLU FEAR!

This year everyone has been talking about the worldwide flu epidemic. In the USA it's said that 500,000 have died, in the UK 200,000 and in India perhaps 20 million. It's even worse than the Black Death!

Dead bodies

THE FLU CAN KILL IN 48 HOURS! In India trains have been reported full of dead passengers and in some cities the streets are full of dead bodies. Here in America many cities have banned meetings in a bid to stop the disease spreading. Cinemas have shut down and churches are closed (except for funerals).

Bodies are buried standing up to save space.

PUBLIC HEALTH ADVERT

- **❀** Have you got the flu?
- **❀** Do YOU have a fever, headache, cough, has your skin turned blue or purple, are you coughing up blood? Looks like you've got the flu. Well, that's tough.
- **❀** *Don't* go out ... please!
- **❀** And *definitely* don't go near us!
- **❀** *Do* phone a funeral director – they're getting rather booked up just now.

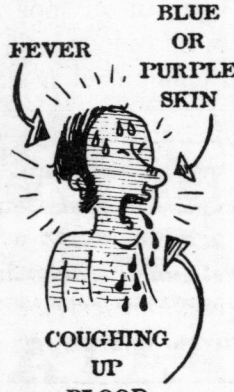

FEVER

BLUE OR PURPLE SKIN

COUGHING UP BLOOD

Doctors' advice
We asked 20 different doctors for advice and received 21 different suggestions including ... drink coffee, take painkillers, drink alcohol, drink small doses of poison such as arsenic, eat potatoes, breathe wood-smoke, and pull your teeth and tonsils out (that'll help clear your throat).

☠ HORRIBLE HEALTH WARNING!

All these remedies were tried and they were all USELESS, so next time your little brother/sister gets flu, DON'T pull their teeth out or anything. Otherwise you'll end up in an unhealthy situation.

Bet you never knew!

1 The flu has been so deadly because it weakens the victims so much that bacteria can attack their lungs and cause the disease known as pneumonia. This results in fever, and difficulty breathing as the lungs fill with pus. Pneumonia can kill but nowadays it can be cured with antibiotics.

2 In the 1950s, American scientist Johan Hultin decided to find some of the 1918 virus. He went to a town in Alaska where the bodies of flu victims had been buried deep in the frozen ground. He dug up several preserved bodies and removed their lungs and tried to infect a ferret with the virus.

GLAD WE WEREN'T AROUND IN 1918 WITH THAT NASTY VIRUS

Unfortunately, it turned out to be dead. (That's the virus not the ferret – the ferret was no doubt relieved.)

3 After his retirement, Hultin returned to the village and dug up some more bodies. This time a team of US scientists led by Jeffrey Taubenberger studied the DNA of the virus and concluded that it came from pigs and then spread to people. It sounds a really horrible way to make a pig of yourself.

TEACHER'S TEA-BREAK TEASER

Still feeling cruel? Yippee, cos today, having shaken off her flu, your teacher's gone down with a cold! That's tragic! Once again she's dragged herself off her sick bed to come and teach you lot. Hammer boldly on the staffroom door. Your teacher will appear, clutching a dripping hankie. Smile sweetly and ask:

Answer: Originally, perhaps – and that's neigh kidding! Scientists have discovered that one type of cold virus is similar to a virus that affects horses. They believe that humans caught the disease thousands of years ago from their trusty steeds. Perhaps that's why your teacher's a little hoarse?

A VERY SMALL DISCOVERY

You might be wondering how scientists managed to discover viruses when they're so tiny. Well, the answer is that scientists didn't see viruses until 1930 when the electron microscope was invented. This brilliant bit of kit uses a beam of tiny blips of energy called electrons to show up tiny objects such as viruses. Sometimes it pays to think small! Before then scientists like Louis Pasteur realized that there was something causing viral diseases and they knew that it was very small because it went through the finest filters.

There was one particular virus called rabies that Pasteur struggled to make a vaccine for. It was a battle that was to have a dramatic and shocking conclusion…

Deadly disease fact file

NAME: Rabies

THE BASIC FACTS: Rabies is a virus that attacks animals such as dogs, foxes, bats, squirrels ... and humans. The disease drives the animals crazy – the dogs become mad, the bats go batty and the squirrels turn a bit nutty.

WOOF GRRR! FLAP GRRR! SQUEAK GRRR!

DEADLY DETAILS:

1 The virus heads for the brain where it blocks the nerve signals that cause swallowing. Swallowing becomes incredibly painful. Spit full of viruses dribbles out of the mouth.

2 Other symptoms are a terror of water (because the victim fears drinking because of the pain of swallowing) and violent fever.

3 Luckily, the virus is slow-moving and there's time to inject a vaccine and antibodies to defeat the virus before it reaches the brain.

A MATTER OF LIFE OR DEATH

Paris, 1937

It was late afternoon when the young American woman arrived at the gates of the Pasteur Institute. There was no one about except an old man sweeping the yard.

"Good afternoon, Mademoiselle," he said politely. "Can I help you?"

"Oh no," she said. "I merely came to see…"

"Oui," said the old man proudly. "We get many visitors like yourself, but there is no one around now." He was a thin old man with a flat cap and grey stubble on his chin.

Just then there was a rumble of thunder and it began to rain heavily.

"Oh no!" exclaimed the young woman looking crossly at the sky.

The old man shrugged. "It is impossible! I cannot work with this rain. Mademoiselle, may I offer you a cup of coffee?"

"Why yes, thank you," she smiled.

The old man led the way to a cramped room, part caretaker's shed and part storeroom of dusty laboratory supplies.

"You are interested in the great Louis Pasteur perhaps?"

"Well, I'm training to be a teacher and next semester we're doing a project on him."

The old man beamed, his eyes were misty with pleasure.

"Ah, but that is wonderful. I remember Monsieur Pasteur well."

"No kidding – you knew *the* Louis Pasteur!" said the woman in amazement.

"Oui. Perhaps you would like to hear a story about Monsieur Pasteur?"

And as he busied himself with making the coffee, the old man launched into his tale.

"It was in 1885 that Pasteur was studying the disease rabies. You are familiar with this disease?"

The young woman shuddered and nodded.

"Well, Pasteur was experimenting with a vaccine made from rabbits. Rabbits that died of rabies. Pasteur dried their backbones that were, of course, full of the virus.

He did this to weaken the virus and then he could inject it into dogs and, voilá, the dogs were protected from the rabies."

"One day a young woman knocked at his laboratory door. She had her son with her – boy named Joseph Meister who two days before had been savaged by a rabid dog."

"A *rabid dog*! Hey – that's terrible. Was the kid in a bad way?"

The old man took his time answering, carefully pouring the coffee into two chipped mugs.

"The boy had been bitten on his hands, on his legs – everywhere! He was not expected to live. Pasteur knew that he had to try the vaccine on the boy or he would die.

"I remember the scene like it was yesterday. It was evening, the blinds were drawn in the laboratory, and there was a smell of chemicals. Pasteur was there in his velvet cap, offering advice as a doctor injected the boy with vaccine. Injected! Pah – it was more like being stabbed in the belly! Of course the boy was scared, very, very scared. But he was brave and did not cry out."

The old man stirred his coffee.

"And after the injection all anyone could do was wait. Wait and wait to see whether the injection would work. Wait to see if the boy would live ... or die."

There was a long silence broken only by a rumble of thunder.

"And did the boy die?" asked the woman anxiously.

"No – he did not. In fact, he is alive and well! Mademoiselle, I shall pretend no longer – the boy in the story was me. My name is Joseph Meister!" The old man's voice shook. "Louis Pasteur saved my life. That night I promised myself that I would serve Pasteur in any way I could. And I have worked here all my life – so you see, I kept my word."

His voice was stronger now and full of pride. And the face of the old man who was Joseph Meister wrinkled into a smile as he slowly sipped his coffee.

MORE VICIOUS VIRUSES

Viruses come in all shapes and sizes (though they are all fairly tiny). Here are two that you might have come across, and as usual Dr Grimgrave has all the bad news...

HEALTH NEWS

Dear Doc,
You've got to help me. My face has swollen up - it's really painful and I feel sick. Will I die?
Fay C. Ake

Dear Ms Ake,
You're suffering from the viral disease – mumps. It's caused by a virus that infects the spit-making glands on the sides of your face. It gets better on its own so go to bed and take painkillers or keep the area warm. Until then you've just got to face it.
Dr Grimgrave

SWOLLEN GLANDS

Dear Doc,
Thanks for your advice. I rested for two weeks and I feel a lot better – my appetite is back and I'm eating like a horse!
Fay C. Ake

Dear Ms Ake,
Eating like a horse are you? Well, you'll only get indigestion if you don't sit down and use a knife and fork like everybody else.
Dr Grimgrave

Dear Doc,
I'm feeling sick and achy and feverish and my back and chest and forehead are covered in itching pus-filled spots.
I. B. Spottie
PS Sorry about the stains on this letter.

> **Dear Mr Spottie,**
> You have chicken pox. It's a common virus and easy for an experienced doctor like me to spot. The best thing to do is rest and wait for the spots to become scabs and dry out. Don't bring them to me – I already have some in my collection. And don't pick them or they'll scar. At least you won't get chicken pox again, because your body will be immune to the virus.
> Goodbye!

Don't pick them!

Mind you, in the next chapter there's a virus so vicious and so nasty it'll make you *long* for chicken pox. Are you brave enough to read on ... or are you about to turn chicken?

CLUCK! CLUCK!

YELLOW DEATH

There are over 150 names for yellow fever and some of them aren't very nice. For instance, you could call it "yellow breeze" or "yellow jack" or (just so long as it isn't a mealtime) "black vomit".

Bet you never knew!
In Jamaica in 1740 Dr John Williams announced yellow fever was different to blackwater fever. This is a fever (surprise, surprise) in which your pee turns brown or red (but not usually black). Local doctor Parker Bennett disagreed and challenged Williams to a duel. In the fight both doctors were killed.

SCIENTIFIC NOTE

Williams was dead, but he was dead right. Blackwater fever is actually caused by another disease, malaria, attacking the kidneys (see page 152). The pee gets its colour from blood. Mind you, yellow fever is even worse! Would you care for a dose? Could it be worth it to get off school? ...

SICKENING SICK NOTE 3: YELLOW FEVER

Dear teacher,

I'm so worried about ~~me~~ ....
~~I'm~~ s/he's bright yellow! First s/he
had a flushed face, fever and aching.
And now the poor dear is in terrible
pain and bringing up black vomit and
bleeding from the ears and nose. The
doctor says it's yellow fever and I'm
at the end of my tether - I'm so
scared! So please excuse ~~me~~ her/him
for not doing any homework.

Signed,

blood →

sick

An extremely concerned parent

Sickening sick note notes

1 The black colour is congealed blood.
2 The disease is spread by the aedes (a-ee-dez) mosquito.
We trapped one of the little villains and extracted a
confession...

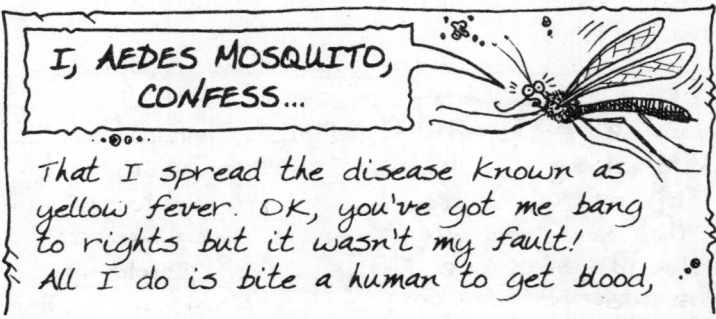

I, AEDES MOSQUITO,
CONFESS...

That I spread the disease known as
yellow fever. OK, you've got me bang
to rights but it wasn't my fault!
All I do is bite a human to get blood,

I mean, I'm a mosquito right - that's me job. I only take a drop and don't mean no harm. I'm usually around at dusk if anyone wants to donate blood. It's not my fault if the blood sometimes has the virus that causes yellow fever. I mean, how am I supposed to know? It's not as if the victim is bright yellow! Well, OK they are - but I'm hungry. So I bite another victim and they get sick. Well, that's sad. You're not going to squash me, are you? Are you?

If the yellow fever virus could be caught and put on trial for crimes against humanity here is what the charge sheet might have said.

CHARGES AGAINST THE YELLOW FEVER VIRUS

1 That on or about the seventeenth century you crossed the Atlantic from Africa inside mosquitoes in ships bound for America. That you infected the sailors so that sometimes most of them were dead by the time the ship reached land.

2 That once in South America you killed off millions of innocent monkeys that had no immunity to you.

3 That you caused deadly epidemics in the Americas, Caribbean and even parts of Europe. For example, in 1802 you killed 23,000 French troops in Haiti and in 1821 you killed one in six people in Barcelona, Spain.

4 You caused such terror that in the 1840s the people of Memphis, USA considered abandoning their fever-ridden city and burning it to the ground.

DAFT DOCTORS

1 As usual, the doctors were confused about yellow fever. To begin with they thought it was caused by – surprise, surprise – bad smells.

In the 1790s in Philadelphia, a city ravaged every year by the disease, Dr Benjamin Rush blamed rotting coffee beans in the docks. But this theory wasn't worth a bean.

2 A certain Dr Firth was so sure that the disease couldn't be caught like flu he actually *drank* the disgusting black vomit made by a sufferer and *injected* himself with the victim's blood. Although by rights he should have got the disease, it didn't actually develop – perhaps because the virus was weak. Still, don't try this at home.

But scientists were closing in on the yellow fever and in 1900 George M Sternberg (of the US army) sent an elite team of scientists to Cuba to investigate the disease. Would they succeed when so many had failed? They were led by army doctor, Walter Reed. Here's what his reports to Sternberg might have looked like…

FOUR AGAINST THE YELLOW DEATH

Havana ~ June 1900

Dear George

I've just met the others for a chat.

A.A. There's Aristides Agramonte - he's from round here and an expert on yellow fever - in fact he's been studying it for two years!

J.C. James Carroll was born in England but as you know he's been in the US army for years. He's quiet and hard-working.

J.L. Then there's Jesse Lazear, a pal of Agramonte. He's a bit posh but deep down he's a friendly guy.

Oh and me, Walter Reed, the leader. We're getting on fine. W.R.

Well, let's hope we can find the cause of yellow fever. At present we HAVANA clue - geddit? First thing we're going to do is check out this guy Carlos Finlay. He's a local doctor who reckons the disease is spread by infected mosquitoes, but he can't prove it.

Kind regards, Walter C.F.

July 1900

Dear George,

Strange things are happening at the army base. A soldier died of yellow fever whilst locked in the guard house. But the other prisoners didn't get the disease. Some soldiers have slept in the beds of yellow fever victims, complete with dried sick and poo on the sheets (soldiers ain't too fussy). But they didn't get the disease either! Blistering bedpans! Know what I'm thinking? I figure you can't get yellow fever by person-to-person - or even person-to-body-waste contact like an ordinary disease.

So maybe Finlay's right and it's something to do with them pesky mosquitoes? Jesse Lazear's been catching mosquitoes and letting them bite volunteers but so far no one has gone down with yellow fever - BLAST!

I'll keep you posted, Walter

September 1900

Dear George,

As you know I'm back in the States but I've kept in touch with the others and can report a success - sort of.

Carroll and Lazear were in the lab and Jesse was showing off how to get a mosquito to bite a person.

"Don't think this one's hungry," said Lazear.

131

"Maybe it'll take a bite of me?" said Carroll, and sure enough it did. Well, shiver my stethoscope! Blow me if Carroll's not got yellow fever!

Mind you, I shouldn't joke - he could die.

Well, we've got to try this experiment again. We've still got the mosquito and its little tummy is rumbling. Luckily, there's a very stupid soldier at the base called William Dean and he's volunteered to be bitten!

CHOMP!

Derrr

Five days later...
I've just heard Dean's got yellow fever! He says it must have been something he ate! That proves the mosquito spreads yellow fever. Success at last!

Walter

DEADLY DISCOVERIES

1 The scientists had proved the mosquito spread yellow fever but fate was to play a cruel trick. A few days later Lazear was also bitten (quite by accident) and although Carroll and Dean survived the disease, Lazear did not. Sadly, he was not the only scientist to be killed by this deadly disease.

2 Japanese scientist Hideyo Noguchi (1876–1928) was already a famous and successful germ hunter when he decided that yellow fever was caused by bacteria. Sadly he was wrong – the disease is caused by a virus. In 1928 Hideyo was studying yellow fever in Africa when he died ... of yellow fever. His last words were "I don't understand." Too true – he didn't.

3 In 1927 Irish doctor Adrian Stokes (1887–1927) was in Africa trying to prove a link between yellow fever and monkeys when he caught the virus. He continued to experiment on monkeys using himself as a guinea pig, and proved that mosquitoes can pass the disease between monkeys and humans. Then he died.

4 Scientists didn't develop a vaccine to yellow fever until 1936. In that year a virus taken from a young African called Asibi was shown to be weakened so much that it no longer caused disease, but it made the body develop immunity. Since then the vaccine made from Asibi's virus has saved millions of lives.

GALLOPING GORGAS
Armed with the vital information that the aedes mosquito spreads yellow fever, scientists set about attacking the new enemy. None was more determined than US Major Walter Gorgas. With him it was all kind of *personal*.

When Gorgas had been a young officer his Colonel's daughter fell ill with yellow fever and the Colonel ordered Gorgas to speak at the girl's funeral. In fact, she recovered but Gorgas got the disease and the girl nursed him. They fell in love and got married.

In the 1880s a French attempt to build a canal across the Isthmus of Panama (the narrow bit between North and South America) failed when 52,816 labourers got yellow fever. In 1904 the Americans decided to have a go...

In 1904 Gorgas, by then a top army doctor, was ordered to Panama by the President to beat yellow fever. Gorgas sent thousands of men into the battle. He wanted oil poured on all open water so the mosquito couldn't lay eggs and bushes burnt so that the mosquito couldn't hide.

Gorgas had to face opposition from his bosses in the US Army.

Colonel Goethals complained:

EVERY MOSQUITO KILLED COSTS THE US GOVERNMENT TEN DOLLARS!

ONE OF THOSE TEN DOLLAR MOSQUITOES MAY BITE YOU!

By 1906 Panama was free of yellow fever and the canal was completed in 1913. For the first time ever, humans had taken on a deadly disease on its own ground … and won!

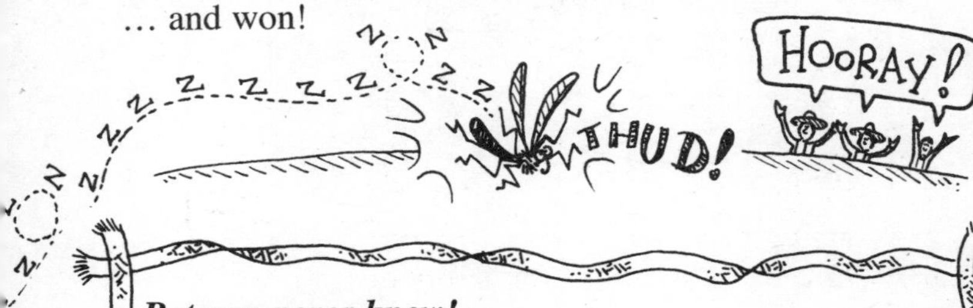

HOORAY!

Bet you never knew!
Today, yellow fever is still lurking in the tropics (the warm regions of the world) but it's no longer a massive killer. That's the good news – but one of its revolting relatives, dengue fever, is spreading. This disease is also spread by aedes mosquitoes and it's known as "breakbone fever" because it feels like all your bones and joints are breaking apart. Fancy a break off school, then?

SOME GOOD NEWS AT LAST...

It's typical. Just when we think we're beating a disease another one pops up. It's a bit worrying, isn't it? Well, here's a bit of good news. There's one deadly disease that we've beaten fair and square – for *ever*!

You'll find the next chapter a real shot in the arm...

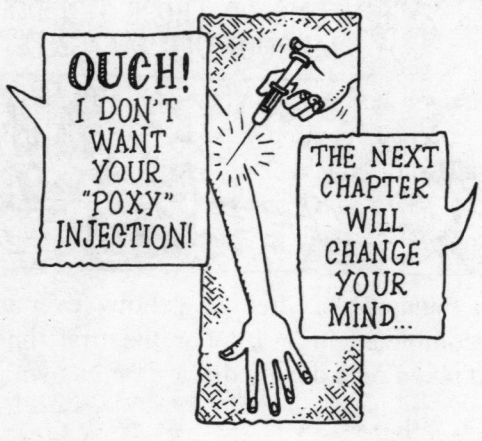

SMALLPOX SMASHED

For thousands of years a war has been raging between microbes and humans. It's a war without mercy on either side, and millions of humans and trillions of germs have died. But at last, after thousands of years of sickness and suffering, humans won a great victory – over smallpox. So what was this deadly disease like?

If you've ever had measles then you'll know what *that's* like. Can you imagine measles ONE HUNDRED times as bad? If not, you'd better read this…

SICKENING SICK NOTES 4: SMALLPOX

Dear teacher,

I don't know what to do! The doctor says my poor .... has smallpox! It began with a violent raging fever and throwing up and agonizing muscle pains from head to toe and later a horrible rash. Now the fever is worse and the rash is a mass of huge pus-filled spots! Germs have attacked the spots and ~~my~~ his/her skin is rotting and falling off! I can't stand it and nor can poor .... Please excuse ~~me~~ him/her from all science lessons - *for ever!*

Signed,

Very worried parent

Sickening sick note notes

1 Like measles, smallpox is caused by a virus. The brick-shaped smallpox virus is called variola.

2 The virus can be spread by touching the scabs and by infected breath. If there was an outbreak of smallpox at your school they'd have to close down the whole school for months.

3 Unfortunately, I mean luckily, no one gets smallpox any more (for reasons you're about to discover) so your teacher might not believe your sick note and then she might realize that all the others were made up too.

THIS IS YOUR DEATH!

In its time smallpox killed millions of people. I wonder what the *This Is Your Death* people would make of it?

WELCOME TO THE TV PROGRAMME THAT PUTS THE LIFE BACK INTO DEATH.

Today we're at a high security laboratory to meet a celebrity who has touched the hearts of people around the world — and other parts of their bodies too. We've shrunk down to interview the smallpox virus — Variola major, this is your death!

THIS IS YOUR DEATH!

Wow! I don't get too many visitors here!

No one knows where you came from. But in your time you've been very close to royalty. Indeed, it's said you made a killing from your connections with them. Here are your royal chums... Come in Your Majesties!

I sure did.

GRRR!

Ramases V of Egypt (died 1157 BC), Mary II of England (died 1694), Peter II of Russia (died 1730) and Louis XV of France (died 1774).

Luis I of Spain (died 1742), two Emperors of Japan (both died 548) and the Inca Emperor Huayna-Capac (died 1526).

Er – nice to see you again guys.

Numerous people were left scarred by your scabs, including George Washington.

Yes, I've left my mark on history.

Your impact was worldwide. In Ethiopia in 1886 people who got smallpox were left to be eaten by hyenas.

GRRR!

I've always had a soft spot for animals!

SINISTER SMALLPOX STORIES

One of the first to study smallpox was Arab doctor, Abu Bakr Mohammed ibn Zakaria (860–932), known as al-Rhazes, who described the differences between smallpox and measles on the basis of observing the sufferers. Just in case you're wondering…

1 Measles makes you sneeze in the early stages and this gives you a red nose.

2 Measles spots are smaller than smallpox spots and don't form scabs.

3 With measles you also get white spots in the mouth.

Rhazes wrote 200 books, mostly about philosophy and religion – but his religious views fell foul of a powerful mullah (Islamic priest). The mullah ordered Rhazes to be beaten with his own book until either the book broke or his head broke.

Unfortunately, Rhazes' head wasn't as thick as his book and he got brain damage and went blind.

SMALLPOX GOES WEST

When smallpox arrived in America in 1521 it triggered the greatest disaster in human history, something that made the Black Death look like the Teddy Bear's Picnic. The disease was brought over by Europeans. Many Europeans had had the disease and their bodies were immune to it but the native Americans had never encountered smallpox (or other European diseases such as measles and flu) and so they had no protection.

And they had no more idea of how to cure the disease than the Europeans. The native treatment, sweating the disease out and then jumping into icy water, only hastened death. (Mind you, some schools still practise this technique – it's known as the "swimming lesson".)

For over 200 years smallpox happily rampaged through the Americas like a caterpillar in a cabbage patch. In all, one hundred *million* people may have died.

The defeat of smallpox began with a custom that developed separately in China and Turkey. It was called inoculation and it involved giving a person a mild dose of the disease to boost their immunity. It's a bit like vaccination, but this time the virus is alive. A remarkable woman worked to spread the custom around the world...

Hall of fame: Mary Wortley Montague (1689–1762) Nationality: British

Mary had every reason to hate smallpox. She was a beautiful and talented young woman of 26 when the disease struck. And it left horrific scars on her face. Before then her dad had tried to marry her off to an incredibly boring man named Clotworthy. (I didn't make that bit up, honest!) When Mary refused, her dad locked her in the house and got her sister to spy on her. (Little sisters can be vicious…)

Anyway, Mary escaped with her rich pompous boyfriend, Edward Montague, who became ambassador to Turkey.

And it was there that Mary came across inoculation. Here's what she might have written to her friend, Sarah Chiswell, in England…

Adrianople, 1717
Dear Sarah,
I've come across this wonderful method for preventing smallpox! Every year an old woman comes round asking if anyone would like the smallpox cure.

If anyone's interested the old woman puts some smallpox pus in a nutshell and puts this on the end of a pin. Then she scratches their skin and dabs a bit of pus into the wound. In a few days each person falls ill with a mild fever and spots and then they get better and never get smallpox. Wow! Of course, there's a down side. You've got a one in four chance of getting full-blown smallpox, and if you get it you'll probably die. But hey – it's only a one in four chance and I can't wait to try it out on my son and daughter.
Love,
    Mary

Mary's children survived. Back in England in 1718, Lady Mary suggested the treatment for the daughters of her friend the Princess of Wales. The Princess wasn't so sure so Mary suggested a horrifying experiment. Six criminals awaiting execution were given a deadly choice...

Would YOU be dying to take part? Anyway, the criminals survived (actually one had had smallpox and was immune anyway but he didn't let on) and the royal children were safely inoculated too. Mary became famous although not everyone liked her bossy manner. The poet Alexander Pope wrote some rude verses about her so she bought his book and used it to line her potty. And then she boasted that she plopped her poop on Pope.

TEACHER'S TEA-BREAK TEASER

Important note: if you try this teaser and you get expelled you're on your own, OK.

Rap smartly on the staffroom door. When it squeaks open give your teacher a sunny smile and enquire:

SMALLPOX GOES WEST (AND THIS TIME FOR GOOD)

In 1796, Jenner developed cowpox vaccinations to fight smallpox (remember that bit from page 57). So it was now possible to stop people getting smallpox. And unlike plague the disease didn't hide in wild animals and unlike yellow fever it wasn't spread by insects. The virus only lived in people and if everyone was vaccinated then the virus would die out. In 1966, following a suggestion by Russian scientists, the World Health Organization set out to do just that.

Led by US doctor Donald Henderson, 650 WHO health-workers scoured the world for smallpox. In Brazil a doctor was kidnapped but before he was released he insisted on vaccinating his captors against the disease.

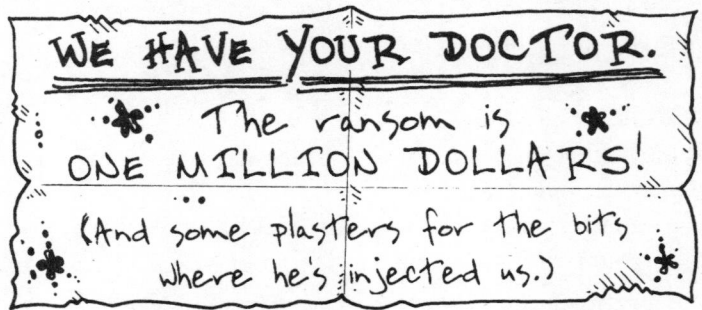

WE HAVE YOUR DOCTOR.

The ransom is ONE MILLION DOLLARS!

(And some plasters for the bits where he's injected us.)

Another doctor was killed by a native American arrow. Eventually the disease was found only in Somalia and Bangladesh and then in 1980 there came the long-awaited announcement. Smallpox had been wiped off the face of the Earth (though a few samples were kept for research). For the first time in millions of years humans had destroyed a deadly disease!

Well, that was the good news. But meanwhile new deadly diseases were appearing – but where were they coming from? And why did they have to be so *nasty*? Are they really out to get us? Read on and find out…

NASTY NEWCOMERS

I'm afraid the facts about some of these new diseases make rather miserable reading. Dr Grimgrave is happily putting together a dossier on some of the worst offenders…

HORRIBLE HEALTH WARNING!

READERS MAY LIKE TO PUT A HANKIE OVER THEIR NOSE AND MOUTH AT THIS POINT. YOU DON'T WANT TO RISK CATCHING ANYTHING NASTY, DO YOU?

ROGUE'S GALLERY

WANTED FOR MURDER

BACTERIAL DISEASES

LEGIONNAIRE'S DISEASE

 <u>First known appearance:</u> Philadelphia, USA, 1976.

<u>Known crimes:</u> Killed former members of the American Legion staying at a hotel. Since then has appeared all over the world. I would

A NOTE FROM DR GRIMGRAVE
I object to the light-hearted presentation of serious factual information. Anyone would think that this book is a publication of a humorous nature.

like to study it further but
unfortunately none of my patients
has caught it.

Method of operation: Attacks the
lungs and causes fever.

Known associates: Lives
inside a protozoan that
lives in shower heads and
air-conditioning systems.

Danger rating: Still rare
and can be treated with
antibiotics.

LYME DISEASE

First known appearance:
Studied by scientists at
Old Lyme, Connecticut,
USA 1975.

Known crimes: Attacked a group of
children in the town, they all
recovered. Since then has appeared
all over the USA and parts of
Europe, China, Japan and South Africa.

Method of operation: My colleague Dr
Gripe got this illness and it caused
him a few gripes I can tell you. He
suffered fever, rash, stiff neck,
aching joints and years of pain. But
luckily he was a patient patient.

Known associates: Lives
inside tiny biting bugs
such as deer ticks. The tick
collects the virus by biting
mice and can pass it on to
humans by biting them.

TICK

Danger rating: Not fatal – can be treated with antibiotics.

VIRUSES

EBOLA

First known appearance: Sudan and Congo Republic, Africa, 1976.

Known crimes: Kills between 50 and 80 per cent of victims.

Method of operation: Spread by contact with body fluids such as blood and vomit. Symptoms include violent headaches, bleeding from the ears, eyeballs and bottom. Hair and fingernails drop off. Certainly a fascinating disease, I watched a programme about the symptoms whilst eating supper last night.

Known associates: None.

Danger rating: Very rare even in Africa. All outbreaks have been contained.

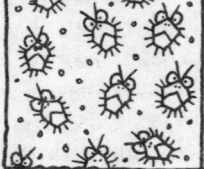

AIDS

First known appearance:
Africa, probably in the
1950s. There are actually
several varieties of the
HIV virus (Human Immuno-
deficiency Virus) that cause the
disease known as AIDS (Acquired
Immune Deficiency Syndrome).

Known crimes: If left untreated, kills
99.9 per cent of all its victims.

Method of operation:
1 Hides inside the DNA
of the T-cells where
it's impossible for
the immune system to
find it.

> Horribly complicated
> – to get your head
> round it you might
> like to check back to
> page 111.

2 After several months or
even years, for unknown reasons, the
virus starts to attack more T-cells.

Basically what happens is that the
virus kills more and more T-cells
until the immune system can't fight
off germs such as TB bacteria.

Known associates: It's these other
deadly diseases that actually kill
the patient.

Danger rating: Deadly, but because
the virus is spread by contact with
body fluids such as blood, it's
quite hard to get. You can't get it
from someone coughing over you or
even from sharing a toothbrush or a
toilet with a sufferer, like some
idiots claim.

SO WHY ARE WE GETTING ALL THESE NEW DISEASES?

Ask two scientists and you'll be given three different answers (at least).

THE CLIMATE IS GETTING WARMER AND THIS MAKES IT EASIER FOR INSECTS THAT SPREAD DISEASE TO BREED.

AND AS PEOPLE TRAVEL MORE THEY TAKE GERMS WITH THEM. THIS MEANS THAT DISEASE CAN SPREAD FASTER.

AND DON'T FORGET MANY PEOPLE NOW LIVE CLOSE TOGETHER IN BIG CITIES WHERE DISEASES CAN SPREAD EASILY.

As usual with science there's no simple answer. But there's one explanation that many scientists support. Many of the new diseases are spread by animals. AIDS and ebola have been found in monkeys, Lyme disease is spread by ticks and so on. What seems to be happening is that as humans settle in wild areas of the world and cut down forests we pick up diseases that have existed there for thousands of years. That's probably how we first got the plague from the cute furry animals that normally carry it.

So it's all our fault? Charming!

Depressing reading, eh?

Well, cheer up – it gets worse. You know all those lovely diseases that we've been talking about and which you might have thought were beaten by modern medicine? Well, some old favourites have been crawling out of the dustbin of history. Take the lung disease TB…

TB: THE BAD NEWS…

To cure TB you take antibiotics for up to a year. But most people feel better after a few months and the drugs are expensive so it's easy to give up the treatment. This is a massive mistake because it means that the remaining TB germs are the strongest and the most able to survive the drugs, and they can stage a comeback. In many parts of the world TB is now resistant to antibiotics. So today millions of children need to be tested for TB. (If you're a budding actor you could say "TB or not TB, that is the question.")

MALARIA: MORE BAD NEWS

In Africa, 3,000 people die of malaria every day and it's getting worse. It's reckoned that a person gets bitten by an infected mosquito every *30 seconds*. (That person must be getting sick of it by now! Sorry, sick joke.)

In many parts of the world the mosquitoes that carry the disease can't be killed by sprays. The reason is the same as for the TB germs: the mosquitoes' bodies have learnt to deal with the poisons. And the protozoa that cause the disease are increasingly able to survive anti-malaria drugs.

Here's something to take your mind off it…

COULD YOU BE A DOCTOR?

You're in Dr Grimgrave's waiting room. You've got a splinter in your little finger. (Let's hope he's in a good mood and doesn't cut it off!) The other patients aren't in the pink of health. Can you work out what's wrong with them…?

CLUE: Try looking back at the diseases mentioned in this book.

1 SKIN IS PURPLE-BLUE. JUST ABOUT TO DASH TO THE TOILET.

2 LICE. SPLITTING HEADACHE AND FEVER. RASH.

3 BRIGHT YELLOW SKIN. VIOLENT FEVER. BOWL OF BLACK SICK.

4 SWOLLEN FACE. FEELING SICK.

NEXT!

SOME GOOD NEWS AT LONG LAST!

Science *is* fighting back... Here's an exclusive peek at some of the latest high-tech drugs that are heading our way. Yes, here in one of Dr Grimgrave's medical magazines!

MEDICAL NEWS

NEW DRUG BREAKTHROUGHS!

RESISTANT BACTERIA

ANTIBIOTIC PROBLEMS

Scientists are always working to develop new drugs. This week we report on the latest developments...

Amazing antibiotics

When bacteria have become resistant to an antibiotic scientists want to know why. It's usually because the bacteria make a chemical that sticks to the antibiotic and stops it working. As one drug company representative said: "It's a real sticky problem." One response is to add a chemical to the antibiotic that sticks to the bacteria chemical and stops *it* working.

Designer DNA

Scientists are trying to attack the DNA in a virus.

That's the chemical that controls how the virus develops (some viruses use a simpler chemical called RNA but the effect is the same).

The idea is to make a protein chemical that can stick to the DNA and stop it working. This stops the virus from multiplying.

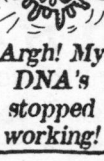

Argh! My DNA's stopped working!

WANTED FOR MEDICAL COLLECTION

Dead body parts showing signs of unusual disease. Rare pustules, blisters and sores particularly welcome.
Contact:
Dr Grimgrave,
The Surgery,
Much Moaning.

BRAND-NEW BREAKTHROUGHS!
Thanks to genetic engineering we can make bacteria produce large amounts of vital chemicals such as antitoxins or interferon. (As all readers know, interferon is the vital substance that stops viruses multiplying.)
Another area of research is artificial antibodies called monoclonal antibodies. Grown in

cells kept in laboratories, these chemicals can be used like antibodies to block toxins.

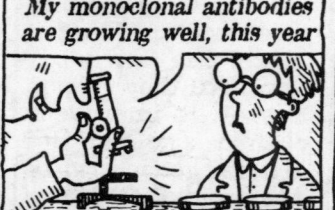

My monoclonal antibodies are growing well, this year

Next week

▶ Would we doctors be happier without patients?

▶ Fascinating gory operations in full colour.

▶ Our "long-running" series on body fluids features an in-depth report on diarrhoea and vomit.

WARNING!

The next bit won't just scare the socks off you – it might scare your toe nails off too!

Bet you never knew!
Have you ever had a really bad nightmare? Well, if you're a virologist chances are your worst nightmare would be about H5N1. It's a kind of flu that bumps off birds in huge numbers. But the scary thing is that it could change its DNA and do the same thing to us. It would be like 1918 all over again only even more nasty. Whenever the virus appears scientists try to kill all the birdlife to stop it spreading. In 1997 they killed all the chickens in Hong Kong. So far the virus hasn't spread widely amongst people. We've been lucky ... so far.

But will the next time be the *last time*? Perhaps, lurking somewhere out there is a germ so nasty, so vicious that it could wipe out life on this planet! Better read on and find out!

EPILOGUE:
A SICKENING FUTURE?

So will a new disease appear and wipe us out?

The answer's no so please DON'T PANIC!

Even if there were such a disease (and some diseases are pretty anti-social as you've just found out), it's *not* going to destroy us and here's why. Doctors now have the knowledge and the technology to keep people healthier than they've ever been before.

YOU'RE LATE FOR YOUR CHECKUP, MRS WHEELER!

SORRY DOC, MY MOUNTAIN BIKE GOT A PUNCTURE COMING DOWN CRAGGY FELL

You can shiver at deadly diseases but you don't have to be scared of them. Most can be cured if treated quickly.

So even if a new deadly disease appears we know enough about diseases to ensure that it won't keep spreading. We know about techniques such as vaccination and antibiotics that can fight it. The truth is that although the battle against deadly diseases hasn't been won altogether – we're still gaining ground.

And there's more. For a disease to wipe us out it would have to kill us before scientists could devise any kind of treatment. Of course a few diseases *do* kill quickly – think of the 1918 influenza. But most diseases aren't that rapid – for a horribly good reason. If people died in five minutes then the germs would be buried with their first victim and never spread. And being buried alive is a nasty fate – even for a germ.

But if the disease spreads over a period of months and years then there would be time for some people to come into contact with just a few germs and get a mild dose of the disease. These people would fall ill and recover and so develop immunity.

And there's an even better reason why we should be OK. *Human nature*.

This has been a book about death and suffering and pain. But in the worst times you can sometimes glimpse the best in people. People like the scientists who risk their lives and sometimes die to conquer a particular deadly disease. Or the volunteers who agree to take part in experiments that might leave them sick or dying.

Or the doctors who work round the clock to keep their patients alive, or Gunnar Kaasen and the other sledge drivers who raced to save children from diphtheria.

Ultimately, people try to help one another. It's the best way for us all to survive, and it's the reason why, whatever happens, humans will continue to fight and win the battle against deadly diseases. And that's the not-so-horrible truth!

DEADLY DISEASES

QUIZ

Now find out if you're a
Deadly Diseases expert!

GULP!

Ghastly germs and vampire viruses

You carry germs around with you every day, but how much do you really know about them? Try these true or false questions to see if you're a germ genius or a disease dunce.

1 Germs are carried on bad smells. True or false?

2 A fever is the body's way of heating up germs so much that they die. True or false?

3 Interferon is a chemical that stops viruses from multiplying. True or false?

4 Once you've had a disease caused by a bacteria or a virus you won't get it again. True or false?

5 Picking your nose and eating the snot helps build up antibodies that can prevent colds. True or false?

6 Viruses can be spread by simply shaking hands with an infected person. True or false?

7 Your nose runs when you have a cold because your body is trying to get rid of the cold germs. True or false?

8 A vaccine is actually a dose of a disease. True or false?

Answers:

1 False – germs are everywhere. It's more likely that they're the cause of bad smells than the result of them!

2 True – the fever heats the germs until they die.

3 True – the body produces interferon naturally, but stupid scientists don't know how!

4 True – the antigens stay in your body and will attack the disease if it comes back.

5 False – not only is picking your nose disgusting, it's also bad for you. The germs in the snot can get into your guts and give you a runny tummy.

6 False – viruses are spread through scratches in the skin or on tiny drops of spit like those that fly out of your granny's mouth when she's speaking.

7 True – your snot contains all the nasty stuff that your body is trying to get rid of.

8 True – but it's a very mild dose, just enough to get your body working to create the antigens to protect it from the disease in the future.

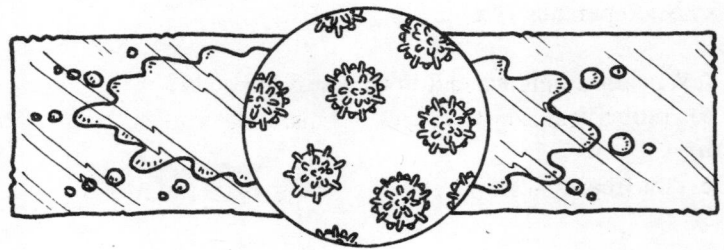

Battling body quiz

So, you think you've figured out the way your battling body works? Try these quick questions to see if you're fit to lead the charge against enemy invaders...

1 Where in the body are blood cells made?
a) Bone marrow
b) Snot
c) Intestines

2 What is a macrophage?
a) A type of computer program
b) A type of protein
c) A type of white blood cell

3 What is pus made of?
a) Dead bacteria and cells
b) Slugs and snails
c) Snot and mucus

4 What do scientists call invaders of the body?
a) Antibodies
b) Antigens
c) Antifreeze

5 Where won't you find germs?
a) In your baby brother's nappy
b) In your lunchbox
c) On the planet Mars

6 How often do bacteria split in half?
a) Every 20 minutes
b) Every three days
c) Every third Tuesday of the month

7 What type of enemy invaders can antibiotics cure?
a) Maggots
b) Viruses
c) Bacteria

8 What are rickettsia?
a) Germs that give you bendy bones and bandy legs.
b) Deadly disease bacteria that live inside cells.
c) Viruses shaped like TV aerials.

Answers:
1a; 2c; 3a; 4b; 5c; 6a; 7c; 8b

Shocking symptoms

Have you learned enough to be able to work out what icky illness someone has just by their symptoms? Look at the list below and match the symptoms to the deadly disease.

1 Violent coughing, boils on the skin
2 Fear of water, mad dribbling
3 Coughing blood, snotty phlegm
4 Sneezing, runny nose, sore throat
5 Oozing sore throat, sense of suffocating
6 Muscle pains, pus-filled spots on the skin
7 Fever, headache, vomiting, rash on the skin
8 Fever with cold sweats, muscle spasms

a) Tuberculosis
b) Diphtheria
c) Malaria
d) Plague
e) Smallpox
f) Rabies
g) Common cold
h) Meningitis

Answers:
1d; 2f; 3a; 4g; 5b; 6e; 7h; 8c

Crazy cures

It's not enough just to identify the disease, though – you have to cure them too. Look at the list of diseases below. Can you figure out what cures dastardly doctors came up with in the past?

1 Cholera
2 Diphtheria
3 Typhoid fever
4 Plague
5 Smallpox
6 Rabies
7 Common cold
8 Flu

a) Rub toad's blood all over your body
b) Burn the wound with a red-hot iron
c) Eat chicken soup
d) Sweat the disease out then jump into iced water
e) Cover the body with blood-sucking leeches
f) Drink poison
g) Drink brandy every hour
h) Shave your head

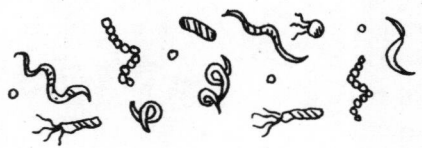

Answers:
1e; 2g; 3h; 4a; 5d; 6b; 7c; 8f

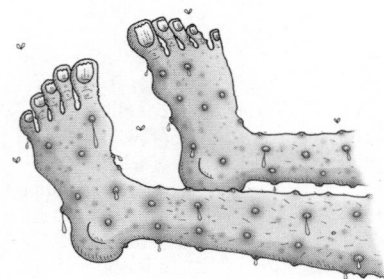

HORRIBLE INDEX

169

170

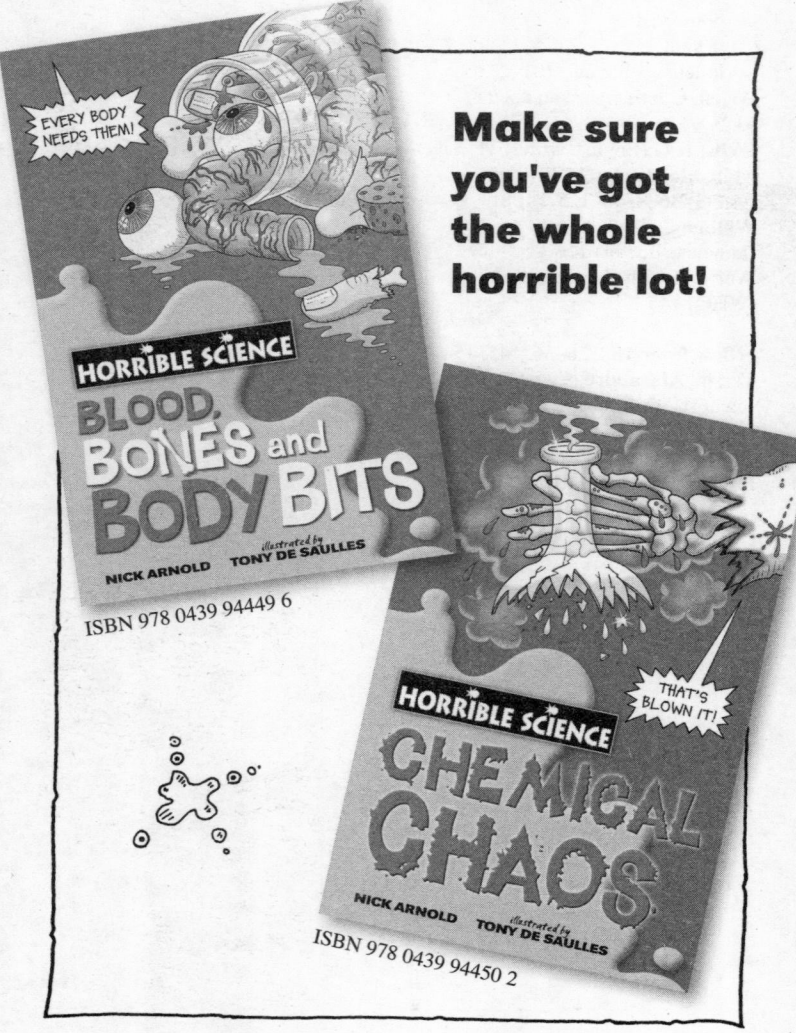

ISBN 978 0439 94451 9

ISBN 978 0439 94445 8

ISBN 978 0439 94452 6

Horrible
Handbooks
to collect!

ISBN 978 1407 10359 4

ISBN 978 0439 94407 6

ISBN 978 0439 94408 3

HORRIBLE SCIENCE

CHEMICAL CHAOS

NICK ARNOLD

illustrated by
TONY DE SAULLES

■SCHOLASTIC

Visit Nick Arnold at
www.nickarnold-website.com

Scholastic Children's Books,
Euston House, 24 Eversholt Street,
London, NW1 1DB, UK

A division of Scholastic Ltd
London ~ New York ~ Toronto ~ Sydney ~ Auckland
Mexico City ~ New Delhi ~ Hong Kong

First published in the UK by Scholastic Ltd, 1997
This edition published 2008

Text copyright © Nick Arnold, 1997
Illustrations © Tony De Saulles, 1997

All rights reserved

ISBN 978 0439 94450 2

Printed and bound by CPI Group (UK) Ltd, Croydon, CR0 4YY

28

The right of Nick Arnold and Tony De Saulles to be identified as the author and
illustrator of this work respectively has been asserted by them in accordance with
the Copyright, Designs and Patents Act, 1988.

CONTENTS

WHOOPS - FORGOT
MY GLOVES!

ACID

Nick Arnold has been writing stories and books since he was a youngster, but never dreamt he'd find fame writing about Chemical Chaos. His research involved being blown up, sucking helium out of balloons and cooking up revolting substances and he enjoyed every minute of it.

When he's not delving into Horrible Science, he spends his spare time teaching adults in a college. His hobbies include eating pizza, riding his bike and thinking up corny jokes (though not all at the same time).

Tony De Saulles picked up his crayons when he was still in nappies and has been doodling ever since. He takes Horrible Science very seriously and even agreed to test out some of our explosive experiments before drawing them. Fortunately, his injuries weren't too serious.

When he's not out with his sketchpad, Tony likes to write poetry and play squash, though he hasn't written any poetry about squash yet.

INTRODUCTION

Chemistry can be summed up in a single word – "UGH!".
It's that part of science to do with chemicals and test tubes.
"Ugh!" is the best word for it! It's the most *horrible* part
of Horrible Science.

And why is it so horrible? Well – if you find science
confusing you'll find chemistry as clear as mud. It can
cause chaos in your brain.

For starters, there are those chaotic-sounding chemical
names. Like poly methyl metha crylate* (say polly me-
thile-me-tha-cry-late). *That's the acrylic in your jumper,
if you didn't already know.

THAT'S AN ATTRACTIVE
POLYACRYLONITRITE
GARMENT YOU'RE WEARING!*

*TRANSLATION – I LIKE YOUR ACRYLIC JUMPER

These long words are mainly Latin or Greek. Fine for
ancient Romans – but horribly confusing for the rest of
us. Sometimes chemistry turns totally chaotic. That's
when chemists talk their own chaotic code language.

THIS H_2O HASN'T YET
REACHED 100°

I REQUIRE SOME
$C_{12}H_{22}O_{11}$

THIS LACTIC ACID
SMELLS UNPLEASANT

5

TRANSLATION:
1 The water hasn't boiled.
2 Pass the sugar.
3 Lactic acid = sour milk: the milk's gorn orf!

Even a chemist's brain seems pretty chaotic. How else would they come to investigate soggy cornflakes? (Chemists have reported that a cornflake with more than 18 per cent milk content is just too soggy to study.)

But funnily enough that's what this book is about. Not the bits you learn in school – but the funny bits and the fascinating bits, the bits you really want to find out about … nasty bubbling green mixtures, vile and sometimes poisonous potions, test tubes, horrible smells, bangs, blasts and dodgy discoveries.

And who knows, *Chemical Chaos* might just help you see through the confusion that is chemistry. Then you might just end up causing chaos in your chemistry teacher's day, by getting your own experiments to work...

CHAOTIC CHEMISTS

Chemists are curiously chaotic. Their knowledge of chemicals used to be chaotically confused and their messed-up experiments caused chaos too. The first chemists were called alchemists and they were pretty chaotic. And strange.

Imagine it's a particularly boring chemistry lesson, and you are feeling ver-r-ry sleepy. The next thing you know you are in a mysterious room... You see an old man reading a book. He is surrounded by oddly-shaped flasks, the stumps of candles and dirty beakers. On a nearby table there are bottles of ink, tatty goose feather pens, oily rags and old musty books – full of ancient dust and secrets. In the chaotic shadows stand row upon row of bottles filled with weird potions. On the floor lie the rat-nibbled remains of several meals. The old man laughs to himself. Then in a thin crackly voice he reads a magical spell...

EYE OF NEWT,
WING OF BAT,
FOOTBALL BOOT,
TAIL OF CAT!

Confused? Don't worry this is NOT your chemistry teacher! You've just slipped back 500 years to meet your local chemist. Except 500 years ago chemists weren't called chemists – they were called alchemists.

A note to the reader

Dear reader, as far as this book is concerned a chemist is NOT a shop where you buy pills. A chemist is someone who studies chemicals. O.K.?

APPALLING ALCHEMISTS

As far as we know, alchemy started in Ancient Greece and China. It's a mixture of chemical knowledge, magic and philosophy about how materials are formed. On a more practical level, alchemists tried to turn cheap metals into gold. Here's one of their more unusual recipes.

YE OLD ALCHEMIST'S RECIPE FOR MAKING GOLD.

1. Take some alum (that's a compound of aluminium, sulphur, potassium and oxygen).

2. Add some coal dust, pyrites (iron ore) and a few drops of mercury (the runny metal found in thermometers).

3. Mix well.

4. Stir in an ounce of cinnamon (spicy-tasting tree-bark) and half a dozen egg yolks. Keep stirring until the mixture is gooey.

5. Then add a generous dollop of fresh horse dung. Keep stirring.

6. Finally, add some sal ammoniac. (This is a poisonous mixture of ammonia and chlorine found in volcanoes.)

7. Bake well in a hot oven for six hours. The result should be pure gold. If you're lucky.

A note to the reader:

Although some people poked fun at its more curious notions – alchemy was fashionable. Even kings wanted to try it. It has been suggested that the British King Charles II was poisoned by the mercury he used for alchemy experiments. His scientist pal Sir Isaac Newton used this substance for experiments and it's said he went mad for two years.

Bet you never knew!
One famous alchemist was the Arab writer Geber (or Jeber). Now old Geb had lots of ideas but he was a lousy writer. In fact, his boring books of experiments gave rise to the word "gibberish". Sadly, Geber wasn't the last scientist to come out with a load of old gibberish.

Here's another alchemist's trick you shouldn't try.

TO WARM A LIQUID

Surround a jar of the liquid with horse manure. Germs in the dung cause chemical reactions which produce heat. This really works – but if you do want to keep your tea warm try a thermos flask – it's less smelly!

GET-RICH RUTHERFORD?

Despite many failures the alchemists kept going. They believed a substance called the "philosopher's stone" would turn cheap metals into gold. No one knew what the philosopher's stone was exactly or where to find it. But alchemists were convinced that the person who found the stone would live for ever. Of course, no one ever discovered the real answer. Until quite recently...

In 1911 New Zealander Ernest Rutherford (1871–1937) found out how to change metals into gold. This involved the metals' atoms, which are the minuscule objects that make up all substances. To make the gold, you zap bits off the atoms with a high-energy ray. By changing the atoms you can change the metal they form.

But Rutherford had bad news for alchemists:

1 Atoms are so tiny they're easy to miss with your zapping ray.

2 The easiest metal to turn into gold is platinum. But that's even more expensive than gold!

I WONDER IF YOU CAN TURN GOLD BACK INTO PLATINUM?

3 So if you want gold it really is cheaper to buy some from your local jeweller!

CHAOTIC CHEMISTS OF THE PAST

By 1700 scientists were becoming curious about chemicals for reasons other than alchemy. They dropped the "al" bit as well, and called themselves "chemists" instead. "Al" only means "the" in Arabic anyway. But many people thought chemistry was a strange idea. One scientist, Justus von Liebig (1803–1873) was told off at school for not doing homework. His teacher asked him what job he wanted to do and Justus said he wanted to be a chemist whereupon…

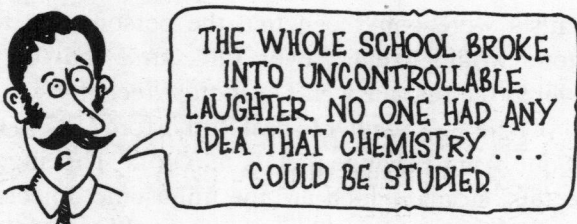

THE WHOLE SCHOOL BROKE INTO UNCONTROLLABLE LAUGHTER. NO ONE HAD ANY IDEA THAT CHEMISTRY… COULD BE STUDIED.

One man played a vital role in begining to change their minds. His name was Antoine Lavoisier (1743–1794). Some people even called him the "Father of Modern Chemistry". But in 1789 revolution swept France and Lavoisier found himself in a seriously chaotic situation.

AN ENEMY OF THE PEOPLE?

It was a time of terror but no one dared use the word. No one was safe from arrest. In the Square of the Revolution there were daily executions for the old women to watch as they sat knitting in the spring sunshine.

MERCY!

WHY DO THEY ALWAYS SAY "THANKYOU"?

"Pass me ze papers," said the Public Prosecutor to his newly-appointed clerk. "Yes, the ones about Citizen Lavoisier."

The young man hurriedly searched his desk. It was unwise to waste the Prosecutor's time. The Prosecutor, Antoine Fouquier-Tinville, was always in a hurry.

"*Merci* – thank you," said the Prosecutor, and he hastily examined the paper. "Aha, Antoine Lavoisier – the collector of taxes..."

"He's a great scientist too..." ventured the clerk.

"WHO dares say so!" screamed the Prosecutor.

The clerk dropped his quill pen and papers in a shower of ink. "I mean, I didn't mean that!" he stammered. "I meant Lavoisier is a great traitor! Oh, silly me!"

"Well," said the Prosecutor, "let's see what the file says." He began reading the document in the harsh voice he used to terrify prisoners in court:

"Antoine Lavoisier. Born 1743 and brought up by his aunt, father and grandmother... Hmm – he was a swot at school. Spent one year in which his only lessons were science and maths. Pah! Two more years learning nothing but philosophy. Pah! Pah! Wrote his first scientific paper at the age of ten – what a little creep! Later found gypsum has water in it and mineral water has tiny bits of salt. Very useful ... I *don't* think. Ha, ha!"

"I ... I know," said the clerk from the floor in a small

13

voice, "that Lavoisier is a traitor … but … he did find that water contains hydrogen and oxygen chemicals. Then he discovered gases in the air. Then he found you can't destroy chemicals – only change them around and then…"

"Stop, you fool!" spat the Prosecutor. "Do you think I need ze chemistry lesson?! Ah – here's the juicy bit. In 1768 Citizen Lavoisier became a tax collector. One of his friends said, 'The dinners he will give us will be so much the better!' All the *tax* collectors are the enemies of the people. Thanks to the revolution they're in prison now!"

The Prosecutor smiled unpleasantly. "Let's see if they enjoy their fine dinners without their heads on!" He drew his finger across his throat and made a choking sound.

"Excuse me – I've got some papers to file!" said the clerk as he fled the room in panic. He just missed a thin man in a green coat. The visitor was plainly dressed apart from his white powdered hair. He certainly didn't look like the most powerful man in France. But that's who he was.

"Citizen Robespierre," said the Public Prosecutor with a false smile. "This is indeed a pleasure and an honour. The papers await your signature."

"More enemies of the people?" enquired Robespierre. He seated himself without being asked and read the document. "Lavoisier. Yes, I remember him. He supported the revolution at first. Helped with the new metric weights too. He did good work for France running gunpowder factories before the revolution. He would be a great loss."

The Prosecutor frowned. He was unsure if Robespierre was testing his loyalty and replied nervously, "Our revolutionary hero, Citizen Marat, called Lavoisier a traitor in his newspaper articles."

"Yes, I know," said Robespierre. "But Marat was a failed scientist and Lavoisier was rude enough to say so. That's why Marat hated him so much."

"So. You mean us to spare Citizen Lavoisier?"

Robespierre merely smiled coldly and gazed out of the window. The pen was poised like a dagger in his hand.

Antoine Lavoisier's trial began on 8 May, 1794. The scientist looked pale and tired after six months in prison. He pleaded for more time to finish a vital chemistry experiment. Would Robespierre take pity on him? What do *you* think the verdict was?

a) GUILTY. The Judge said, "The Republic has no need for scientists." and Lavoisier was beheaded that afternoon.
b) NOT GUILTY. The Judge said, "The Republic should spare the life of such a great scientist."
c) GUILTY. The Judge said, "But we'll give you a month to finish off your experiment."

Answer: a) One of Lavoisier's friends said, "It took them only an instant to cut off that head, and another hundred years may not produce another like it." Two months later Robespierre lost power and was put to death. Fouquier-Tinville was executed the following year. And Lavoisier's work lives on…

CHAOTIC CONTEMPORARY CHEMISTS

Nowadays, there are thousands of chemists. In the USA alone there are over 140,000 chemists trying to discover new chemicals! Some are looking for ultra-light metals or new kinds of plastics. Others are looking for new food ingredients or medical drugs. Here's where they work.

A CHEMISTRY LAB

At first sight all these bits and pieces look a bit funny. But they all have their uses.

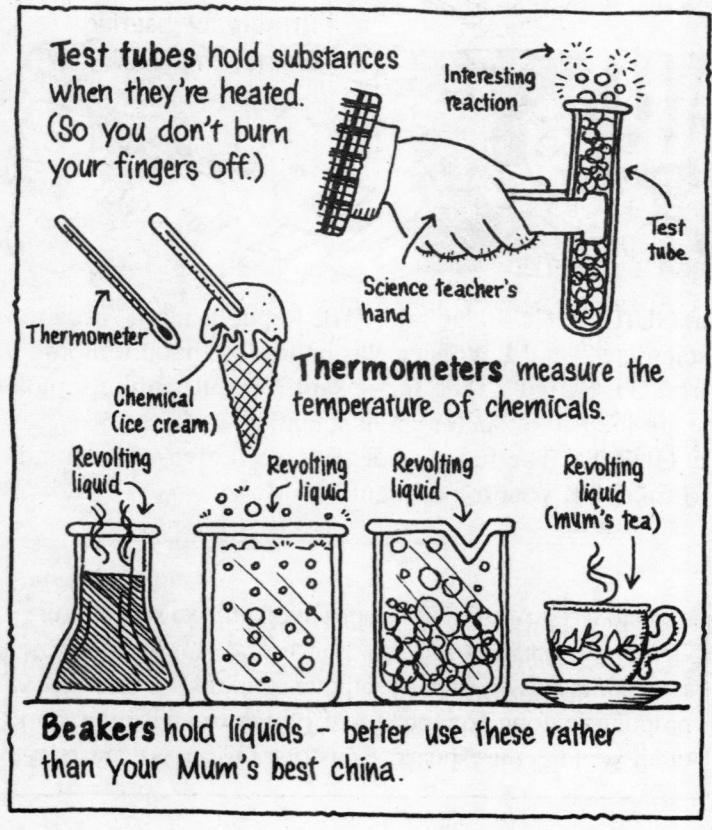

Test tubes hold substances when they're heated. (So you don't burn your fingers off.)

Interesting reaction

Science teacher's hand

Test tube

Thermometer

Chemical (ice cream)

Thermometers measure the temperature of chemicals.

Revolting liquid

Revolting liquid

Revolting liquid

Revolting liquid (mum's tea)

Beakers hold liquids – better use these rather than your Mum's best china.

Flasks are for mixing chemicals in. They're usually conical in shape - that means they're shaped like a cone - and have flat bottoms.

A mess

Flask

Funnels for pouring mixtures into flasks without slopping them all over the floor (see above).

Funnel

No mess

Filter paper

Fold here

Fits in funnel

Filter paper - a paper sieve for separating solid chemicals from a liquid. The runny bit passes through paper and solid lumps get caught. It's a bit like making filter coffee really.

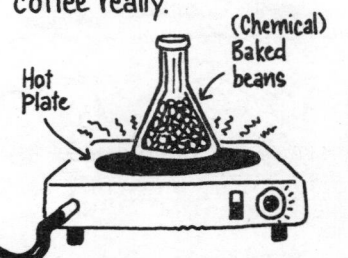

(Chemical) Baked beans

Hot Plate

Hot plates - a bit like cooker tops. Ideal for heating and cooking dinner too.

Droppers for measuring little drips of chemicals.

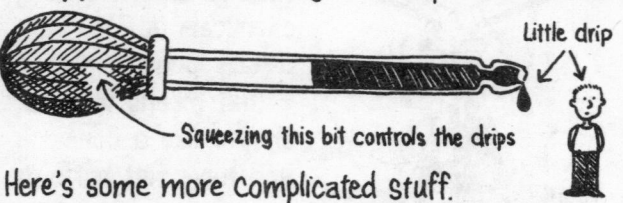

Little drip

Squeezing this bit controls the drips

Here's some more complicated stuff.

A gas chromatograph
Inside this mysterious machine are chemicals that absorb and so separate out the chemicals in your favourite stinky gas. That way you'll know what goes to make up that lovely pong.

A spectroscope allows you to spot a chemical from a pattern of lights and colours given off when it is heated up. It's a bit like watching your very own colour TV.

Bet you never knew!
These days robots do many of the boring jobs in a lab such as testing samples. Pity they can't get robots to do science homework, too!

Dare you discover … your own secret substance?
If being a chemist sounds like fun here's your chance to make a laughably easy discovery.

You will need:
2 teaspoonfuls of cream of tartar (available from supermarkets)
1 cup of salt
2 cups of plain flour
2 cups of water
2 tablespoonfuls of cooking oil

What you do:
1 Mix the flour and salt in a large saucepan.
2 Add the water and mix well.
3 Add the cream of tartar and the cooking oil and mix well.
4 Ask an adult to help you heat the saucepan on a low heat and stir it until the mixture thickens. Leave to cool.
Like any other inventor you'll need to find a use for your new discovery. That's up to you – here's a few daft ideas.

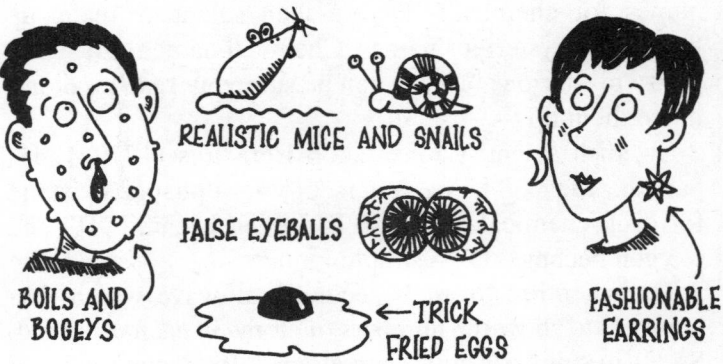

REALISTIC MICE AND SNAILS

FALSE EYEBALLS

BOILS AND BOGEYS

←TRICK FRIED EGGS

FASHIONABLE EARRINGS

Finally, you'll need to dream up a name for your new substance … any suggestions?

CHAOTIC CHEMICAL EXPRESSIONS

Were chemists just having a laugh when they thought up names like polyvinylidenechloride? What do you think they were talking about?

ER!

YOU HAVEN'T WRAPPED THEM IN POLYVINYLIDENECHLORIDE, DAD

WHAT'S IN A NAME?

So, how do scientists decide on a name for all these new substances? And do they have to be so long and complicated?

1 In 1787 Lavoisier suggested that scientists should agree names for chemicals. Before then scientists made up their own mysterious names. Chemical names still sound pretty mysterious but you can be sure your teacher didn't make them up.

2 Swedish scientist Jöns Jakob Berzelius (1779–1848) had the idea of using letters of the alphabet to stand for each chemical atom. So hydrogen became "H" and oxygen became "O" – simple innit?

3 The scientific Swede's second brainwave was to use numbers to show the numbers of atoms in each chemical. So H_2 means "two hydrogen atoms". Brilliant – eh?

4 When you get two or more atoms joined together it's called a molecule. $2H_2$ means two lots of two hydrogen atoms and H_2O is a molecule of the two hydrogen atoms and an oxygen atom joined together.

5 In fact H_2O is just the chemists' code for plain boring old water.

But anyone can be a chemist. In fact, you may be one without even realizing it. And if that sounds incredible – consider this: you use chemistry every time you cook or wash up. Shocking, isn't it?

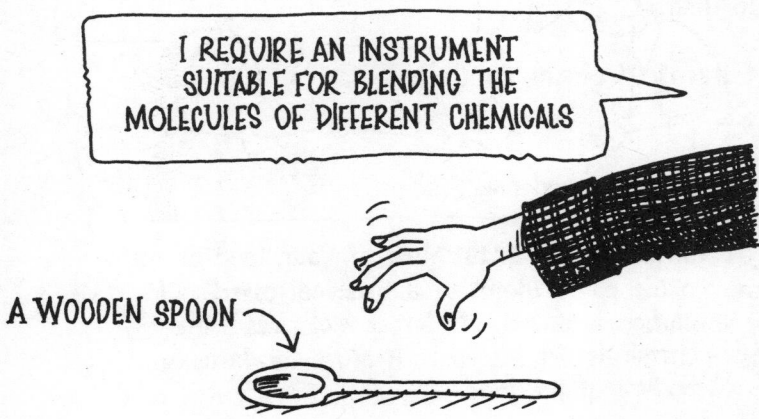

I REQUIRE AN INSTRUMENT SUITABLE FOR BLENDING THE MOLECULES OF DIFFERENT CHEMICALS

A WOODEN SPOON

CHAOTIC KITCHEN CHEMISTRY

How can cookery possibly be chemical? Actually, it would be impossible to cook without chemistry. It's what cooking's all about – from the suspect substances that call themselves school dinners, to the revolting reaction that makes your dad's homemade rice pudding stick to its dish.

Chemical chaos fact file

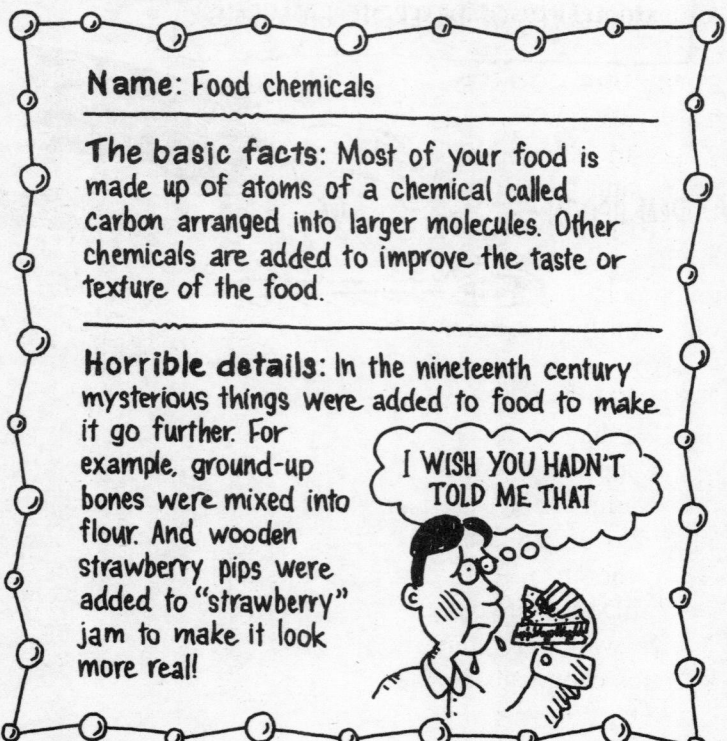

Name: Food chemicals

The basic facts: Most of your food is made up of atoms of a chemical called carbon arranged into larger molecules. Other chemicals are added to improve the taste or texture of the food.

Horrible details: In the nineteenth century mysterious things were added to food to make it go further. For example, ground-up bones were mixed into flour. And wooden strawberry pips were added to "strawberry" jam to make it look more real!

I WISH YOU HADN'T TOLD ME THAT

KITCHEN CHEMISTRY LAB

It's a strange thought, but your kitchen is a bit like a chemistry lab.

THE SOUP HASN'T REACHED THE OPTIMUM TEMPERATURE YET

CONCAVE COMBINATION UTENSIL (BOWL)

HEAT ENERGY CONDUCTOR (COOKER)

METALLIC CHEMICAL COMPOUNDER (SPOON) →

SPOUTED RECEPTACLE (JUG)

METALLIC SMALL SOLIDS MANIPULATOR (TONGS)

Some machines in your kitchen are mysteriously similar to instruments used by scientists.

PRESSURE COOKER

This works by allowing water to boil at a higher temperature than usual, so it cooks things faster. But it's similar to a machine called an autoclave that kills germs on scientific instruments.

THERMOS FLASK

This is handy for keeping your soup hot or a drink cold on a summer's day. But the flask was originally invented by a chemist. In 1892 Sir James Dewar invented the double-walled container to keep his chemicals cold.

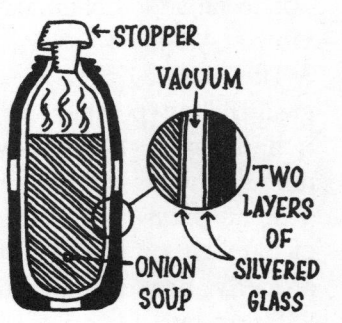

← STOPPER

VACUUM

TWO LAYERS OF SILVERED GLASS

ONION SOUP

COOKER

This is simply a machine for heating food chemicals to produce the chemical reactions that we call cooking.

Here are some fascinating food facts to impress your friends during school lunchbreak. (You'll impress them even more if you can work out what you're eating.)

SIX MIXED-UP FOOD FACTS

1 The burning sensation you get if you eat chilli peppers is due to a chemical called capsaicin (cap-say-kin). According to experts the best remedy for a fiery mouth is a generous helping of ice cream! That's tragic!

2 The smell of raspberries found in most yoghurts is due to an added chemical called ionone. It's made from violets. Aah!

3 The bubbles in a cooked cake mixture are made by gas! Baking powder contains an acid and a chemical rich in carbon. When they're heated, a chemical reaction produces a gas called carbon dioxide.

4 Salad dressing is an emulsion. No, that's not a type of paint. It's a mixture of two chemicals that don't mix properly. Leave a salad dressing for a few hours and it will turn into a layer of oil above a layer of vinegar.

5 Vinegar is made from wine that has gone disgustingly sour. This chemical reaction is caused by the waste products produced by germs. Yuck!

6 Toast is bread in which the carbon has been partly burnt. The smoke that sometimes pours from the toaster is made from tiny bits of carbon.

Teacher's tea-break teaser

If you are very brave (or foolhardy) knock on the door of the staffroom and try this question on your teacher.

Answer: It does make a difference. Milk contains a chemical called casein (case-in). When tea mixes with milk, chemicals called tannins in the tea can break down the casein into smaller molecules. If you add the milk to the tea it means that more casein gets broken down. This makes the tea taste of boiled milk. That's why chemists in the know add tea to milk and not the other way around!

AMAZING CHANGES

Like tea-making, cooking is about heating chemicals until they change in some way. For example, chips cook at 190°C (374°F) and meringues need several hours at 70°C (158°F). But what causes these dramatic changes?

Try these terrible trick questions on your unsuspecting cookery teacher!

1 When you are trying to boil milk why does it suddenly go "whoosh" and try to leap out of the pan?

2 The boiling point of cooking oil is hotter than the temperature needed to melt a frying pan. So how can you fry food?

Answers: 1 The milk contains fat globules that form a layer on the top of the liquid as it heats. At about 100°C the milk under the fat layer is a frenzy of boiling bubbles. Suddenly the fat layer splits allowing the milk to whoosh! **2** The food contains water that boils at its usual temperature. This boiling water cooks the food and the oil doesn't boil at all.

FOUL FERTILIZERS

Even your vegetables are not free from the mysterious activities of the chemical industry. There's a whole array of herbicides, insecticides, fungicides and pesticides sprayed on the growing plants to deter ugly bugs and weeds. Then there are *fertilizers* to make crops grow.

HOW DARE YOU! I WOULDN'T TOUCH THE STUFF!

Phosphorous may be poisonous for humans but it's good for making fertilizer chemicals called phosphates. One traditional type of naturally phosphate-rich fertilizer is guano. It's found several metres deep on islands off the coast of Peru. And the origin of this special substance … do you really want to know? Old seabird droppings full of digested fish bones. Oh yes – bones are rich in phosphates and ground-up bones are ideal for growing plants.

HERE HE COMES – GET READY WITH THE BUCKETS

Nowadays fertilizers are made by mixing sulphuric acid with phosphates found in rocks. But the chemists have not just stuck to fertilizers. Some *foods* were practically invented in a test tube.

A SLIPPERY STORY · MARGARINE

French Emperor Napoleon III organized a competition to invent a cheap butter-substitute for poor people.

Scientist Hippolyte Mége-Mouriez reckoned that anything a cow could do HE could do better.

Can you make a spread that's better than butter? If so, let me know.
Emperor Napoleon
(Emperor Napoleon III)
P.S. BIG PRIZES

In 1869 he came up with his magic marg ingredients:

UGH!

INGREDIENTS
beef fat
skimmed milk
ice
pigs' stomach
juices

METHOD

1 Simply heat the beef fat to the body temperature of a cow.
2 Gradually pour in pigs' stomach juices.
3 Stir in the water and milk.
4 Now churn the ingredients together in a handy barrel.
5 Add ice to cool the mixture.
6 Squelch it all together.

Mouriez hoped to get rich and he opened a factory to make margarine. Unfortunately, war broke out between France and Prussia and his factory had to close down.

GONE TO WAR, BACK IN TWO YEARS.

BLUB

Two years later the idea was bought by a couple of Dutch merchants. Soon they were churning out margarine and profits.

In 1910 a shortage of animal fat led to the use of vegetable oils or smelly fish oil.

LOOKING AT THE INGREDIENTS

Most foods you can buy in a supermarket have the ingredients on the side. Some sound a bit weird. Margarine, for example usually contains...

- hydrogenated oils
- emulsifier
- antioxidants
- vitamins
- water

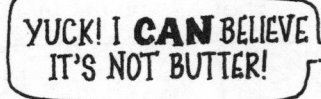

Emulsifiers are chemicals with two ends. One likes oils and one likes water. So this marvellous molecule cleverly joins the water and the oil molecules together.

Antioxidants stop the margarine going off, or rancid. Sage and rosemary plants include natural antioxidants often used by food manufacturers.

Hydrogenation means adding hydrogen molecules to the margarine. This makes the marg harder and more like butter.

Vitamins are a group of different chemicals you can get from different foods. Vitamins keep your body healthy. Margarine doesn't contain some vitamins so they are added to make it healthier to eat.

CHAOTIC CHEMICAL COOKERY

Besides margarine, lots of chemists have made food from chemicals you definitely wouldn't want to eat.

1 Alexander Butlerov (1828–1886) found that formaldehyde (for-mal-de-hide) can be treated to make a type of sugar called glucose. Formaldehyde is a horrible smelly chemical used to preserve bits of dead body.

2 During the Second World War German chemists discovered how to make fat from oil – not cooking oils but the sort of oil you put in a car! Mmm, tasty!

ONE CAN DOES 2 CARS OR 950 FRIED EGGS

AUTO ÖL

Dare you discover ... some chemical cookery?

Try creating a little bit of chemical chaos in your kitchen with these experimental recipes.

1 *Yucky yeast* Yeast is no mere chemical. It's ALIVE! Yes – yeast is a tiny fungus like the mould that grows on stale bread. Ugh! Yeast is harmless but its horrible relatives can cause skin infections and some diseases of the lungs and guts.

You will need:
Some dried yeast (you can get packets from supermarkets)
Teaspoon and tablespoon for mixing
A small bowl and glass
Sugar
Warm water

What you do:
1 Mix a sachet (that's 7 grams) of yeast with a small glassful of warm water.
2 Stir in a teaspoonful of sugar until it dissolves.
3 Leave the bowl in a warm place for an hour and check what's happened.

a) The mixture has turned bright red.
b) The liquid froths up and has a funny smell.
c) Small crystals have formed in the mixture and it stinks.

Answer: b) The yeast eats up the sugar and produces alcohol and carbon dioxide – that's the froth. This is also what happens when people make wine from grape juice.

2 *Terrific toffee* Sugar is a complicated compound (mixture) of chemicals including carbon, hydrogen and oxygen atoms. Many sweets are simply sugar that's been heated to a particular temperature. For example, fudge is made at 116°C (241°F), caramel at 120°C (248°F) and the hottest of all … toffee. Here's how to make it.

You will need:
An adult to help you
25 g butter
100 g castor sugar
7.5 ml water
A sugar thermometer
A tablespoon and saucepan
A bowl of ice-cold water
Some chopped apple with skin attached
Enough cocktail sticks for every bit of apple

What you do:
1 Stick a cocktail stick in each of the chopped apple pieces.
2 Mix the sugar, water and butter in the saucepan.
3 Heat the mixture to 160°C (320°F). Stir it gently. Notice how the sugar turns into a brown, melted, gungey mass on the way.
4 Dip some apple in the mixture. Be careful – it's very hot! Then dip the apple into the cold water for about 20 seconds to cool it down.
5 Eat it!

And after that there's nothing else for it – you've got to wash up. It's a mystery where half the washing-up comes from. Never mind, even the really great scientists had to do this. And luckily, there's lots of chemical cleaners to help you!

SQUEAKY CLEANERS

There's bound to be a few squeaks of protest when it comes to washing greasy dishes or getting soggy in a boring old bath. But it's got to be done, so where would we be without cleaning chemicals? Somewhere disgustingly dirty – that's where!

Chemical chaos fact file

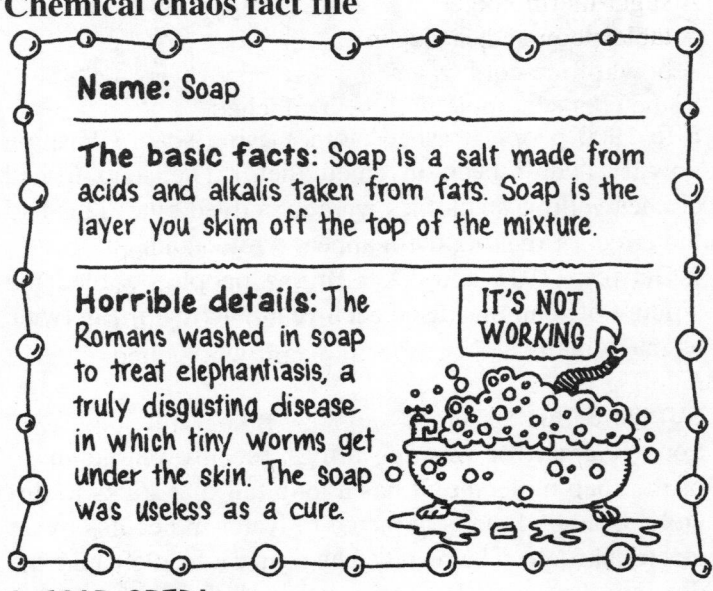

Name: Soap

The basic facts: Soap is a salt made from acids and alkalis taken from fats. Soap is the layer you skim off the top of the mixture.

Horrible details: The Romans washed in soap to treat elephantiasis, a truly disgusting disease in which tiny worms get under the skin. The soap was useless as a cure.

IT'S NOT WORKING

A SOAP OPERA

1 The first soap was mixed-up fat and wood ash. It was probably invented when someone's cookery went chaotically wrong.

2 Soap was used in France about 2,000 years ago by an ancient people called the Gauls. They claimed that soap made from goat fat kept their hair nice and shiny.

3 Eighteenth-century soap was made by mixing boiling fat and soda. The soda rips the fat molecules apart and soap results. Mind you, too much soda dissolves your skin! Nasty.

4 Luckily, before 1853 soap was so heavily taxed that many people couldn't afford to use it.

5 In 1900 people washed clothes using soap. (Washing powder hadn't been invented then.) The soap turned clothes yellow, so clothes were then dyed blue. This had the effect of making them appear white again.

6 Between 1911 and 1980 British people doubled the amount of soap they used each year. Did that mean twice as many baths?

SUPER SOAP

Soap is great for washing things because of the shape of the soap molecule. It has a long tail that sticks to dirt and a head end that's attracted to water molecules by an electrical force. The result? The soap molecule yanks the dirt into the water. Then you can wash the dirt away.

Dare you discover … a slippery soap experiment?

You will need:
Two mirrors
A bathroom
Soap

What you do:
1 Rub one mirror with a thin layer of soap.
2 Run the hot tap. Only one of the mirrors steams up.
Which one is it … and why?

a) The soapy mirror steams up because soap attracts the water in the steam.

b) The soapy mirror doesn't steam up or get wet because the soap stops the water getting to the glass.

c) The soapy mirror gets wet but doesn't steam up. The soap stops the water in the steam forming droplets on the glass.

Answer: c)

DETERGENT - WHAT'S IN IT FOR YOU?

The first detergents were developed by the Germans during the First World War. They were made from soap powders and salt. During that war the Germans had a smelly problem owing to a shortage of soap, so they used

35

detergents instead. But these were useless – you had to rub really hard before you got any froth. But as luck would have it – the new detergent worked wonders on their woollies!

DETERGENT
USELESS ON SKIN BUT GREAT ON JUMPERS!

EATING UP THE DIRT

It's amazing what they fit in a box of washing powder. For example, "biological" washing powders include enzymes. These are chemicals often found in living creatures that speed up reactions between other chemicals. Washing powder enzymes help to gobble up nasty stains such as blood and egg and disgusting little bits of food. The enzyme molecules stay the same.

WASHING POWDER ENZYME

BLOOD AND EGG – SCRUMMY!

ACTION-PACKED POWDERS

Here are some other things you'll find in a packet of washing powder.

Builders – these are nothing to do with construction workers! These are chemicals that remove dirt and stop it sticking to anything else in the wash.

Anti-rusting chemicals stop rust from eating away your washing machine's vital innards.

Conditioners stop the grains of powder sticking together and help them to dissolve in the washing water.

Optical brighteners are chemicals that soak up ordinary light and reflect back bluish light. This makes your undies appear whiter than white. Just a clever chemical trick, really.

Dirt-bouncers are other chemicals that give dirt a tiny electrical force, making it bounce off your washing.

HORRIBLE SCIENCE HEALTH WARNING

...AND DON'T MISTAKE IT FOR SHAMPOO LIKE I DID

Some cleaning materials such as caustic soda and oven cleaner contain horribly unpleasant chemicals. They dissolve germs – but make sure you stay clear of them. They're very good at dissolving fingers too!

CHEMICAL CHAOS IN THE BATHROOM

Your bathroom is brimming with amazing chemicals.

1 The water in your taps contains salts. It also contains calcium and magnesium salts dissolved from rocks in the ground.

2 If there is a lot of calcium and magnesium in the water it is called "hard water" and forms a revolting scum when you try to lather soap.

3 Boiling hard water changes the dissolved chemicals into chemicals that won't dissolve. That's how you get a disgusting deposit of limescale. Limescale is actually calcium carbonate – the same chemical found in chalk. You may find it lurking inside electric kettles too.

4 The first toilet cleaners were made from explosives! They were invented in 1919 when heating engineer

Harry Pickup was removing explosive waste from an ammunition factory. He dropped some in a toilet and found that the substance – nitrecake – is brilliant at cleaning. Flushed with his success, Harry opened a factory and soon became rich.

5 Talcum powder comes from volcanoes. Yes – it's true. Talc is a chemical called magnesium silicate. It's found in rocks that have been chemically changed by underground heat.

6 Toothpastes sometimes contain pumice which is another rock produced by volcanoes. (You may find pumice lurking in your bathroom anyway. It's used for scrubbing away at hard skin.)

7 Toothpaste is designed to brush away germs and stray bits of food. The first toothpastes were made from gritty substances such as chalk and jeweller's polish. They certainly wore away those nasty little stains – but they wore away people's teeth too!

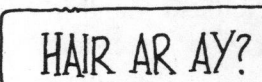

Dare you discover ... how to make your own toothpaste?

You will need:
Salt
Sugar
A bowl and spoon

What you do:
1 Mix the salt and sugar with a little water to make a paste.
2 Try it on your teeth.

Note: These ingredients really were used in the nineteenth century to make toothpaste. But don't you try them more than once. The sugar's not good for your teeth. In fact, you'd better use some proper toothpaste to remove your home-made version! Some experiments should never be repeated.

Toothpaste is just one of a huge array of strange but useful substances dreamt up by chemists. Funnily enough, chemical chaos often led to some amazing accidental discoveries.

DODGY DISCOVERIES

A chaotic combination of muddles, mishaps and mix-ups – that's how many a vital substance has been discovered. Scientists have to keep their minds open to anything that might happen during an experiment, but sometimes they might set out to answer one question, and end up solving another.

CHAOTIC CHEMISTS' COMMENTS...

Here's how some chaotic chemists describe their discoveries. Test them out on your science teacher.

"No great discovery is ever made without a bold guess."

Sir Isaac Newton (1642-1727) discoverer of gravity and big fan of alchemy.

"Failure is the mother of success."

Hideki Yukawa (1907-1981) who discovered what some of the tiny bits of atoms are made of.

"The most important of my discoveries have been suggested by my failures."

Sir Humphry Davy (1778-1829) discoverer of many new chemicals.

Many surprising substances all owe their discovery to happy accidents.

EIGHT DODGY DISCOVERIES

1 Teflon, the stuff used to coat non-stick pans was only used for this purpose after 1955 because the inventor's wife was a bad cook. She kept getting her food stuck to the bottom of the saucepan.

2 *Tracing paper* was invented by mistake in the 1930s because a worker at a paper factory put too much starch in a vat of wood pulp. The result was strong but see-though paper.

3 *Paper tissues* were designed as a new kind of make-up remover. In 1924, they were sold as disposable handkerchiefs after people wrote in saying the pads were ideal for blowing their noses.

4 *Vulcanized rubber* Early rubber boots melted in hot weather. But in 1839 Charles Goodyear spilt some boiling rubber and sulphur. He found that the resulting sticky mess didn't melt so easily.

5 *Silly Putty* the bouncy modelling clay, was discovered in 1943 when scientists attempted to make artificial rubber from silicon. The substance was no good for tyres but the chemists had a lot of fun playing with it. A sharp-eyed salesman spotted the opportunity to develop a new toy and sold 250,000 Silly Putty balls in three days.

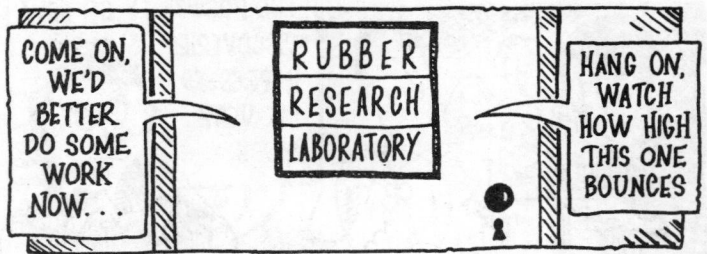

6 *Lubricating oil* was first sold in 1690 as a cure for the painful joint disease rheumatism. The chaotic idea was that if it makes hinges move easily then it could do the same for the joints!

7 Leo Baekeland (1863–1944) discovered a new plastic through a chaotic accident. He made some fascinating chemical blobs by mixing phenol and formaldehyde. The blobs were a new kind of plastic – Bakelite. Mind you, legend has it he made the same discovery by spilling formaldehyde on his cheese sandwich!

8 *Dyes* made from chemicals in coal were discovered accidentally in 1856 by a young whiz-kid – William Perkin (1837–1907).

A colourful character

1. When Perkin was twelve a friend showed him some chemistry experiments.

THE POSSIBILITY OF NEW DISCOVERIES IMPRESSED ME VERY MUCH.

2. Young William decided to try a few chemistry experiments and a few years later enrolled in the Royal College of Science.

ROYA OF SC

REVOLTING BLACK SLUDGE

3. One Easter holiday he was doing chemistry homework in his dad's garden shed. He was trying to make the medical drug, quinine, using a coal tar chemical as raw material. The result was a revolting black sludge.

4. Many scientists would have given up at this point but Perkin was intrigued. So he added alcohol, and some lovely purple crystals appeared.

5. This type of purple was a brand new colour. Nothing like it had ever been seen before. So Perkin tried making the crystals into a dye. They turned out to be ideal for dying silk.

WHAT AN INTERESTING ELECTROMAGNETIC REFLECTION

6. Perkin sent a sample of dyed silk to a Scottish firm and received a letter in return.

Dear William

If your discovery does not make the goods too expensive, it is decidedly one of the most valuable that has come out for a long time.

Yours faithfully,
Pillars of Perth

CRIKEY!

What could be more encouraging?
7. Young William talked his dad into putting up the money for a factory to make the purple dye he called "mauvine".

8. Mauve turned out to be popular and fashionable. Soon everyone wanted to wear it. It was even used for stamps.

9. William became so rich that he was able to retire at the ripe old age of 35. He built a new house complete with private lab.

10. In 1869 he invented a red dye but a German scientist had beaten him to this discovery by one day!

11. In 1906 a celebration was held to commemorate the discovery of mauve. It was attended by the world's most distinguished scientists and business tycoons. And the guest of honour was 68-year-old William Perkin.

12. Sadly Perkin died soon afterwards. The excitement had been too much for him!

Meanwhile scientists were experimenting with plastics to find more man-made substances. And making more discoveries . . . by accident.

Chemical chaos fact file

Name: Plastic

The basic facts: Plastics are long chains of molecules based on carbon atoms. They're often made from chemicals found in petrol, but some come from coal, natural gas, cotton or even wood. Plastics are strong but bendy because the molecules are tangled up.

Horrible details: Nowadays some plastics are designed to rot in soil. They are made from carbon-dioxide and water inside microscopic germs. The plastic is removed and the germs are boiled away!

> PETE'S PLASTIC COFFINS "THEY'RE ONLY £2, AND THEY ROT UNDERGROUND!"

FANTASTIC PLASTICS QUIZ

It's amazing the sheer variety of things that can be made from plastics. Which of these items do you think are made from plastics, and which sound too comical to be true?

1. DRUMHEADS

2. BOOK COVERS

3. DRINK CARTONS

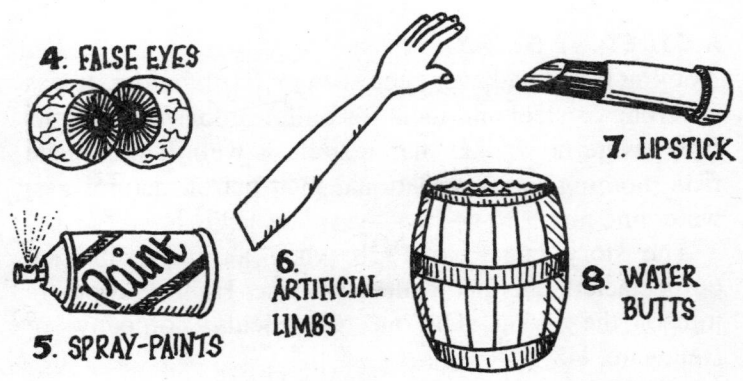

4. FALSE EYES

7. LIPSTICK

6. ARTIFICIAL LIMBS

5. SPRAY-PAINTS

8. WATER BUTTS

Answers: 1 TRUE – polyester. **2** FALSE – a resin based lacquer stops the cover getting soggy if you spill a drink over it. Don't try this! Not on your Horrible Science book anyway. **3** TRUE **4** TRUE – they contain acrylic so they don't break if they fall out of the eye socket! **5** TRUE – they contain acrylics. **6** TRUE **7** FALSE **8** TRUE

CHAOTIC CHEMICAL EXPRESSIONS

A chemist tells his best friend: My underwear is made from polyhexamethylene adipamide (polly-hexa-meeth-ile-ne-adi-pam-ide).

Is this dangerous?

Answer: No – he's got nylon underpants.

Bet you never knew!
You're probably wearing plastic clothes! Many materials used in clothes such as polyester, acrylic, viscose and nylon are made from plastics. But nylon was discovered by accident, too. Here's what happened.

A STRETCHY STORY

Nothing like it had ever been seen on Earth before. It was as strong as steel and ideal for bullet-proof vests. Yet its fibres were no thicker than a spider's web. It was made from nothing more sensational than petrol, natural gas, water and air.

The story began in 1928 when a mild-mannered, bespectacled chemist called Wallace Hume Carothers joined the giant DuPont Chemicals company at Delaware, USA.

"Young man," said Company Vice-President Charles Stine. "I've got a special job for you. We're looking at ways to make silk from minerals."

Most of us would say, "Yikes, that's a tall order!" But Corothers looked thoughtful. "I'll need to look at polymers. I mean those stringy molecules that make silk so strong and flexible. I wonder if it's possible?"

"I guess the best way," said Carothers, "is to invent some new molecules."

"Well – that's your job, son. Just give it whatever it takes."

Carothers' lab was a chaotic maze of oddly-shaped flasks. There were tripods, jars filled with strange fluids and glass bottles with unreadable labels. But this is where he felt at home and where he made his great discovery.

After five years of research Carothers came up with his own substance – nylon. It was useless! Nylon was a clear plastic blob at the bottom of a test-tube. But it wouldn't melt unless you heated to a high temperature. So how could it be made into fibres suitable for a fabric?

Carothers turned his attention to polyesters. One day Julian Hill, one of Carothers' assistants, was mucking about with some polyester in a test-tube. He was amazed to find that he could pull strands of it out on a rod – like gungey mozzarella cheese on a cooked pizza.

'Let's wait till the boss goes out,' he told the others. 'I wanna try a little test.'

They pulled the stringy polyester as far they could. It must have been a strange sight as they managed to stretch it several metres down a corridor.

But this process locked the polyester molecules into place to form strong fibres. Maybe they could do the same for nylon? Yes, they certainly could.

This dramatic breakthrough made it possible to create amazing new fabrics. Carothers' reaction when he got back wasn't recorded but he might well have said, "It's good to see you're working at full stretch. Ha ha!"

Nylon stockings were launched at the World Trade Fair in 1938. A female audience heard Charles Stine declare, "It's the first man-made organic textile fibre … yet it's more elastic than any common natural fibres."

And the best news of all: nylon was going to be a lot cheaper than silk so more people could afford it. The audience were delighted and erupted into wild applause. They shouted and cheered until the ceiling shook. But Carothers wasn't there to see it…

A FATAL FINALE

In 1936 he had fallen into despair following the death of his sister. The following year he took his own life with a dose of the deadly poison cyanide. He was only 41 years old.

MORE MAN-MADE MARVELS

Within a few years the world would be at war and nylon was to prove itself a vital war-winning material. It was used to make countless parachutes and the used parachutes were then recycled to make stockings.

Nowadays, nylon is used to make not only stockings but everything from ropes and carpets to toothbrush bristles. Yet nylon is just one of hundreds of man-made substances. From A-Z they range from acrylic paints and zinc oxide (particularly useful for treating nappy rash).

Funnily enough – all these chemicals have something in common. They're made from atoms – those pesky little things that make chemists curious. Yup – it's time to get down to basics.

YOU'RE ALL JUST
A LOAD OF
OLD ATOMS!

AWESOME ATOMS

Atoms are awesome. Awesomely small that is. And awesomely important. After all, everything in the universe is made of them ... including you.

THE INCREDIBLE SHRINKING TEACHER

The machine stands ready. It's an awesome jumble of tubes and lasers all polished and ready for use. All that's required is a brave and perhaps foolhardy volunteer to venture into the unknown. This person will experience the awesome power of the incredible shrinking ray – and hopefully live to tell the tale.

The volunteer is ready. A person with nerves of steel. In the cause of Horrible Science she is about to embark on what might prove to be a one way trip. This heroic volunteer is none other than ... your science teacher.

She stands under the ray and seems to be disappearing. Soon she is no larger than a doll and she's still shrinking. In the blink of an eye she's become FIFTY times smaller. Now she's small enough to fit in your pocket! Then ... is it an ant or a gnat? No, it's your teacher – and she's smaller than ever. Now she's FIVE HUNDRED times smaller. Hey – where's she gone now?

The smallest object you can see is about one tenth of a millimetre long. Your teacher is now tinier than this. If you had a microscope you might still see your teacher if she was 400 times smaller. But already she's too small for this. Now she's smaller even than the tiniest droplet sprayed from an aerosol can – 1/50,000th of a mm! And that's pretty small!

Your incredible shrinking teacher is falling, plunging headlong towards a mass of balls churning like a stormy sea. Every ball looks like a tiny planet surrounded by clouds of chaos. She's arrived in the weird world of atoms.

IT'S A SMALL WORLD
- You can stretch one million atoms in a line and they'd just about cover the full stop at the end of this sentence.
- If you squeezed them a bit you'd fit one billion billion – that's 1,000,000,000,000,000,000 atoms – onto a pin-head.
- You can fit 600,000,000,000,000,000,000,000 (that's six hundred billion trillion) atoms into a thimble.

But if atoms are so small, how do we know they exist?

Hall of fame: Democritus (c. 460–370 BC) Nationality: Greek

This ancient Greek was known as "the laughing philosopher" – no one knows why. He was certainly laughed at by some people for suggesting the existence of atoms. Here's his idea…

CUT A PIECE OF CHEESE IN HALF . . . CUT THE CHEESE IN HALF AGAIN AND AGAIN. EVENTUALLY YOU'LL GET A PIECE TOO SMALL TO CUT IN HALF. THAT'S AN ATOM!

In those days, few people imagined that atoms really existed so people poked fun at Democritus. But hundreds of years later he was proved right – so maybe he got the last laugh.

Bet you never knew!
Nowadays scientists can see atoms and even photograph them using a scanning tunnelling microscope. This brilliant bit of gizmo measures the electrical force between atoms at a single point. It produces amazing images that look strangely like table tennis balls!

INSIDE AN AWESOME ATOM

Here's an interesting thought: imagine your incredible shrinking teacher ventures inside an atom. Here's what she sees.

1 An atom is a blob of matter called a nucleus surrounded by electrons. The electrons are tiny bits of electrical energy.

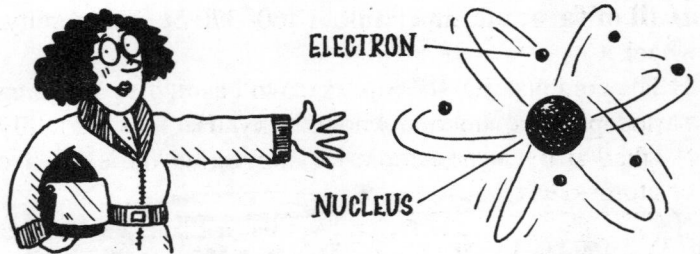

ELECTRON

NUCLEUS

2 Electrons zoom chaotically so that by the time you've spotted where they are they've moved somewhere else.

OOER!

3 Mind you, the electrons can't go just anywhere. They're found in layers known as atomic orbitals.

Dare you discover ... how to watch atoms in action?

You will need:
Some water cooled in the fridge for two hours
Food colouring
A large glass

What you do:
1 Fill the glass half full with hot water.
2 Add a few drops of food colour and mix it up.

3 Fill the rest of the glass with the cold water. What happens?

a) Nothing at all. The bottom half of the water stays where it is.

b) The cold water at the top seems to be slipping down to mingle with the warm water in the bottom half.

c) The warm water seems to be moving upwards.

HMMM VERY INTERESTING

Answer: c) The warm water molecules are moving faster than the colder molecules. As they move apart they rise upwards. So you're seeing billions of atoms on the move.

The first problem for a chemist studying atoms is to work out how the atoms in a substance fit together. Now, the usual answer to this is to do lots of careful scientific experiments and then repeat them just to make sure they got it right. But one man had a different approach...

Hall of fame: Friedrich August Kekulé (1829–1896)
Nationality: German

At school Kekulé was good at drawing and he studied to be an architect. one day he went to a chemistry lecture by Justus von Liebig and got really excited about the subject although they never got on very well. So there you have it – you can still make a great discovery even if your teacher isn't your favourite person. According to the story Kekulé told many years later it all began when he was working as a research assistant in London.

A Dream Discovery

1. 1854. Kekulé was dozing on a double-decker bus.

2. All of a sudden he saw atoms dancing about.

3. Then he woke up.

4. But the dream had given him a nifty idea.

5. He decided to make model atoms using little balls joined by sticks.

THIS IS FUN!

That's how he figured out that carbon atoms can join together in straight chains to make new substances. It opened up a whole new field of chemistry. And all because of a dream!

6. 1863 Ghent, Belgium. Kekulé had another dream. He'd been writing a book whilst suffering a nasty dose of flu.

7. But he was also worrying about a tricky chemistry problem.

Benzene = a chemical in coal = 12 atoms. How are they arranged?

8. He dozed off and dreamt about snakes. Well, why not?

9. One of the snakes bit its own tail.

OUCH!

10. Kekulé awoke with a bright idea.

BENZENE IS RING-SHAPED

11. But many people thought this was a daft idea . . .

DREAM ON, KEKULÉ!

Today some experts think that Kekulé fibbed about his dreams to grab the glory for the benzene discovery from scientists who made the breakthrough before him. But it's definitely true that Kekulé spent years proving that benzene was indeed a ring of atoms. This dream discovery made it possible to develop new chemical dyes and thousands of other useful substances. Could you complete your chaotic chemistry homework in your sleep?

A DREAM COME TRUE!

ELEMENTARY CHAOS

Atoms come in over one hundred varieties. These different varieties are known as elements. For years chemical knowledge was in chaos as confused chemists tried to classify these chemicals. The idea of elements was invented by a boring British scientist – John Dalton.

Hall of fame: John Dalton (1766–1844) Nationality: British

John Dalton wasn't exactly a laugh-a-minute kind of bloke. He would drone on non-stop for hours about science, science and more science. And if that reminds you of a science teacher you know, you won't be too amazed to learn that John was a science teacher, too. They really did start young in those days. John was only 12 when he started teaching.

BORING INDEED! YOU CAN STAY BEHIND AND SHARPEN THE QUILLS

Like most other scientists, John knew that water could be broken down into hydrogen and oxygen. But those chemicals couldn't be broken down further. So he called them "elements" and said that each was a type of atom. People poked fun at John. But they were soon laughing on the other side of the faces. Scientists found that their experiments proved John right. He became famous and now there's even a statue of him.

ALWAYS KNEW I WAS RIGHT!

CHAOTIC CHEMICAL ELEMENTS

You can find 92 elements on Earth. More elements are made in nuclear reactors or created by scientists out of tiny bits of matter. But the heavier man-made elements have the rather irritating habit of falling apart after a second. Here's your very own chaotic guide to elements that don't do this.

CHAOTIC ELEMENTS SPOTTER'S GUIDE

Name of element:
ALUMINIUM

Where found: in soil and rocks

Crucial characteristics: a light and useful metal. It's used to make tank armour, saucepans, kitchen foil and folding chairs. You can even make clothes out of it!

HATS TOO

Name of element:
CARBON

Where found: in diamonds, benzene, coal and the "lead" in your pencil.

Crucial characteristics: the most common atom in the human body, which is a bit weird, because people don't look anything like lumps of coal.

I DO

Name of element:
LEAD

Where found: This isn't the lead in your pencil. Real lead is a grey metal often found on old church roofs.

Crucial characteristics: it's quite a nasty poison if you happened to eat it by mistake. It's also very heavy so don't go dropping it on your teacher's toe.

Name of element:
CALCIUM

Where found: milk, chalk and marble and also in bones and the plaster used to set broken bones.

Crucial characteristics: if you burn calcium it gives off a lovely red flame. But that's no excuse for setting fire to your teacher's plastered toe!

OOH LOVELY!

Name of element:
CHLORINE

Where found: in salt, sea water and rock salt.

Crucial characteristics: it's very good for killing germs, but not very nice if it gets up your nose.

Name of element:
COPPER

Where found: in rocks under the ground.

Crucial characteristics: lots of uses including electrical wires and the rivets that hold your jeans together. Air pollution caused by cars and industry causes a chemical reaction that turns copper green That's why the copper plated Statue of Liberty in New York looks a bit sea-sick.

GET ME A BUCKET

Name of element:
GOLD

Where found: in rocks under the ground.

Crucial characteristics: gold is good to make into jewellery – that's why people drape it round their necks. It's also worth lots of dosh.

Name of element:
HELIUM

Where found: in the air

Crucial characteristics: used to fill balloons. It's lighter than air so the balloons float skywards. Breathing helium makes your voice sound like Mickey Mouse. This happens because your voice passes faster through helium than ordinary air. So it sounds higher and squeakier!

Name of element:
HYDROGEN

Where found: it's the most common element. Stars such as the sun are made of hydrogen. So is 97 per cent of the known universe.

Crucial characteristics: hydrogen is also the lightest element so it floats upwards. This was why hydrogen gas was once used in balloons. It's also burnt as a rocket fuel. Hydrogen sulphide is a gas that stinks of rotten eggs. But don't confuse it with a stink bomb – it's poisonous.

Name of element:
IRON

Where found: much of the earth is made of iron. You find it in rocks and the soil.

Crucial characteristics: you can use iron to make railings. It's also found in the chemical that gives blood its tasteful red colour.

Name of element:
OXYGEN

Where found: it's the most common element on Planet Earth.

Crucial characteristics: it's really lucky that over one fifth of the atoms in the air are oxygen. Without them we'd be more than a little bit dead. Some people think that if they breathe pure oxygen they'll live longer. They must be confused because scientists believe that breathing too much oxygen is bad for you. They say it damages the body, especially the nerves and lungs.

Name of element:
PLUTONIUM

Where found: it's found in nuclear reactors but nowhere else in nature.

Crucial characteristics: Plutonium is incredibly poisonous. It looks like metal but it turns green in the air. And damp air makes it catch fire! The man who discovered plutonium in 1940 kept a lump of it in a matchbox. Weird.

Name of element:
SILVER

Where found: in underground rocks.

Crucial characteristics: a really useful shiny metal much prized for dangling around the neck, making the shiny backs of mirrors and really posh cutlery. In the last 50 years people have lost 100,000 tonnes of silver coins. Where have they all got to? That's what I'd like to know.

I'VE NO IDEA – HONEST!

Name of element:
SULPHUR

Where found: sulphur is a smelly yellow chemical spat out of volcanoes in choking clouds.

Crucial characteristics: at one time it was known as brimstone and mixed with treacle. It was used as a medicine for children. The medicine tasted disgusting so it was probably spat out by the choking children too.

ODD ELEMENTS QUIZ

Some of the more obscure elements are ever so odd. Which of these are too strange to be true?

True or false

1 The element phosphorous was discovered by an alchemist whilst he was examining the contents of his own urine.

2 The elements yttrium, erbium, terbium and ytterbium are all named after a quarry in Sweden.

3 The element dysprosium was discovered in 1886. The Greek name means "really smelly".

4 The element selenium was discovered by the Swedish scientist Berzelius. Sadly, he didn't realize it was poisonous until it poisoned him!

5 The element cadmium was discovered when it accidentally got into a bottle of medicine.

6 The element krypton was named after the planet that Superman comes from.

7 The scientist who discovered beryllium named it after his wife – Beryl.

8 The element Astatine is so rare that if you searched the entire world you'd only find 0.16 grams of it.

9 Technetium was first found in caterpillar droppings.

10 Lutetium is named after the ancient Roman name for Paris.

Hall of fame: Dmitri Mendeleyev (1834–1907)
Nationality: Russian

Other scientists had difficulties. But Mendeleyev lived a real-life soap opera. His father was a teacher who went blind. His mother ran the family glass factory and brought up 14 children. But when Dmitri was 14 the factory burnt down.

Dmitri went to St Petersburg to study chemistry. He discovered the Periodic Table by writing the elements on cards and arranging them as in his favourite card game – Patience. In 1955 element 101 was named mendelevium in his honour. So Dmitri ended up in his own Table!

IT LOOKS VERY COMPLICATED

YES, IT DID REQUIRE SOME PATIENCE

THE COMPLICATED BIT

So that's it. All you need to know is the Periodic Table and which elements join together. Simple, really? Er – no. Just to add a little chaos – chemicals are always changing and getting mixed up. Confused? You soon will be. See you in the next chapter!

CAN I HAVE SOME WATER, MUM?

WOULD YOU LIKE IT AS ICE, LIQUID, OR GAS, DEAR?

CHAOTIC CHEMICAL CHANGES

Everything changes – this fact is so well known it's a cliché. But WHY exactly do things change? Well, with chemicals it's mainly due to the effects of heat or cold. This can result in a few chaotic chemical mix-ups.

Bet you never knew!
You might think that water is runny, iron is solid, and oxygen is a gas. Wrong, wrong and WRONG again! In fact ANY chemical can be a solid, a liquid or a gas. It just depends on how hot the chemical is at the time. Below 0°C (32°F) water is the solid object we call ice. Above that temperature water turns into ... well ... water and above 100°C (212°F) water boils and turns into a mixture of gas and tiny droplets – you'd probably call it steam.

SOLID SECRETS

Have you ever wondered why some solid objects are bendy and others are very tough? Well, have you ever pondered why your auntie's best china is always breaking and why her rock cakes are ... just like rocks? Here's the answer.

- In every solid object the atoms are bonded together. But what's important is the way the atoms are arranged.
- If they're in stretchy strings the object will be stretchy like an elastic band. You can squash them together quite easily.

- In very hard materials such as diamonds the atoms are arranged in a very tight and very strong framework.

- In softer materials such as graphite – pencil lead – the atoms are arranged in loose layers that rub off easily when you write.

- In china the atoms are closely packed and joined tightly together. But if just one atomic join breaks the china will crack!

- In a metal the atoms are surrounded by a crowd of jostling electrons. (They're a bit like teachers in a playground at break-time.) The electrical force of the electrons keeps the atoms in place. But each atom can move a bit and that's why you can bend metal – if you're very strong!

GO ON, IT'S EASY!

MELTING MOMENTS

Here are some impressive facts about melting and freezing water.

1 In Northern Canada some lakes freeze solid. The freezing starts with a single ice-crystal that grows and grows. So each frozen lake becomes a giant ice-crystal.

2 As water freezes it expands and crushes anything it traps with a force of 140 kg per square cm. That's enough to sink a ship or crush a man to death!

3 You get snow and hail when water molecules join and freeze in the sky. Hailstones occur when lumps of ice swirl around in a cold cloud getting larger and larger. In June 2003 a hailstone as large as a soccer ball fell on Nebraska, USA.

OW!

4 You can make snowballs because snow is partly melted ice and slushy so you can squash the snow together. If it's really cold, as in the Antarctic, the snow is hard and powdery.

So you can't have a snowball fight at the South Pole.

5 Here's what happens when you melt ice… When they are stuck together as ice the water molecules are fairly still although they do wobble a bit.

6 It's only when a chemical is really cold that the molecules stop moving completely. This temperature is -273.15°C (-459.67°F), absolute zero.

7 As ice melts the molecules take in heat energy and wobble about more and more. Then they wobble free and start floating around.

WOBBLING MOLECULE

MELTING ICE CUBE

YIPPEE!

FREE AT LAST!

8 As they heat up even more, they move faster and faster until they take a flying leap into the air and become a gas.

Bet you never knew!
1 Different chemicals melt and turn into gases at different temperatures. It's all to do with the bonds between atoms in the chemical. If these bonds are strong you need loads of heat energy to break them apart. So their melting point is higher.
2 All gases need to be very cold before they become liquids. To make liquid oxygen you need to cool it to -188.191°C (-306.74°F). And to make solid oxygen it needs to be a very chilly -218.792°C (-361.83°F)! Luckily, our weather isn't that cold or we'd have nothing to breathe. And that would cause chaos!

TEST YOUR TEACHER

Of course, anything can be a liquid – if it's the right temperature. Terrorize your teacher with this terribly tricky test.

1 Over hundreds of years glass sinks slowly to the bottom of a window frame. Does that make glass a liquid or solid?

2 The black displays that you get in some calculators are made out of crystals – are they a liquid or solid?

3 Is school custard a liquid or a solid?

NOT SURE – I'LL CHEW IT OVER

4 If you cool helium gas to -271°C (-455°F) it can be poured and it even climbs up the sides of a beaker. Is it liquid or solid?

Answers: 1 It's a liquid! **2** Trick question. They're special molecules that exist somewhere in-between. **3** It's a liquid called a colloid – that's a liquid with lots of little oily drops in. Yuck! You can squash custard powder mixed with water into a solid – if you're brave enough, that is! **4** Another trick question. It's a supercool liquid which explains why it acts rather oddly.

MIXED-UP MIXTURES

Much of our planet is made up of mixed-up chemicals. Take a breath of air. In one gulp you'll get a chaotic combination of oxygen, nitrogen and hydrogen and a few other gases thrown in for good measure. All these atoms are completely mixed up, but guess what? The funny thing is that nothing happens, there's no reaction between them, so you don't notice them all.

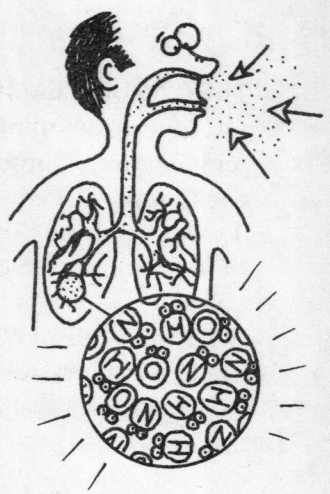

When you mix two gases or two liquids, the atoms of each chemical often spread out until they are thoroughly mixed. But some mixtures don't mix properly.

If a liquid is heavier than water it may sink to the bottom of a glass of water and not mix with it at all. Try out this chaotic chemical cocktail...

You will need:
A tall glass
Water (adding a few drops of food colouring might make it more interesting)
Oil
Syrup (in roughly equal amounts)
Umbrella (optional)
Straw (optional)

What you do:
1 Pour a similar amount of each of the three liquids into the glass.
2 Sit around and wait for something to happen.
3 Check your answer against these three possibles...

a) The liquids all mix together.

b) The water stays at the top, the oil sinks to the middle and the syrup to the bottom.

c) The oil rises to the top, the water stays in the middle and the syrup sinks to the bottom.

Answer: c) Unless you've gone chaotically wrong somewhere.

Bet you never knew!

If you mix up a solid substance with lots of water, the solid sometimes dissolves. But why does this happen? A water molecule is two hydrogen atoms joined to an oxygen atom. Funnily enough, the electrons of the hydrogen atoms have been stolen by the oxygen atom. This gives the hydrogen atoms a positive electrical force and the oxygen atom a negative force. Molecules innocently floating about in the water are caught between the forces and RIPPED APART! Sounds painful.

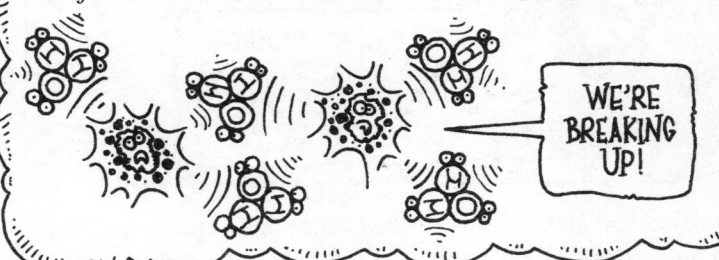

WE'RE BREAKING UP!

UN-MIXING MIXTURES

Not only can you mix up chemicals, much of the time you can un-mix them too. For example, if a substance is mixed with water you can boil off the water and you're left with the original chemical. Talking about un-mixing things from water – one scientist had a very funny idea about this. He was Germany's Fritz Haber and here's his story…

Hall of fame: Fritz Haber (1868–1934) Nationality: German

Fritz Haber was a short and sharp-looking man, and in old photographs he is always immaculately dressed. Born a merchant's son he dedicated his life to chemistry and the service of his country. Yes – Fritz was Germany's secret weapon.

Before the First World War (1914–1918) Fritz invented a new way to make a chemical called ammonia. This had good and bad results.

• The good news: the ammonia was used to make cheap fertilizers. Very handy for helping plants to grow.

• The bad news: it was used to make explosives. Very handy for blowing people up in the First World War.

Eventually the Germans lost the war. The country was in a mess and nearly penniless. And that's when Fritz had his funny idea.

FRITZ GOES GOLD HUNTING

If you really want to raise a few billion dollars don't wash your dad's car on a Sunday afternoon. Go prospecting for gold instead! There's gold in that there sea – millions of tons of clinky-clanky yellow stuff! Think about it … 71 per cent of the Earth is covered by oceans with 97 per cent of all the world's water. Imagine millions of streams scouring gold from rocks and crevices and rivers washing it down to the sea!

But there's one teeny little problem. The gold is in tiny little atoms and grains. They're mixed up with trillions of tonnes of water, salts and all the 70 or so other chemicals you get dissolved in the sea.

In the previous 50 years no fewer than 50 scientists had come up with inventions for removing the gold. And they ALL failed!

But Fritz and his fellow scientists were all keen to have a go. So they chartered a luxury ocean liner called the *Hansa* and set sail in search of gold-rich seawater. The plan was to boil off the water and use other chemicals to separate the gold from the solid dregs.

But after three voyages and eight years they gave up. Here's the cause of their chaos. If you searched a billion buckets of seawater you'd find traces of gold in only 40 – if you were LUCKY! There's loads of gold in the sea but there's even more seawater. And getting the gold ain't worth the effort.

But that's not the last we'll hear of Fritz. He pops up rather nastily in the next chapter.

IT'S A GAS!

Without gases there'd be chaos. We'd have nothing to breathe and balloons would fall out of the sky. Gases can be chaotic – especially when they poison people or explode! But they're interesting, too. Sometimes they're even funny – take nitrous oxide, for example, better known to you as laughing gas.

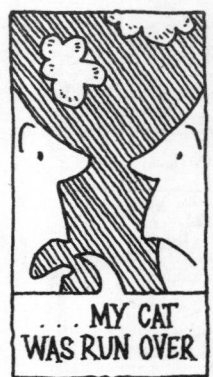
...MY CAT WAS RUN OVER

...THE CAR WAS STOLEN

...AND OUR HOUSE BURNT DOWN!

Chemical chaos fact file

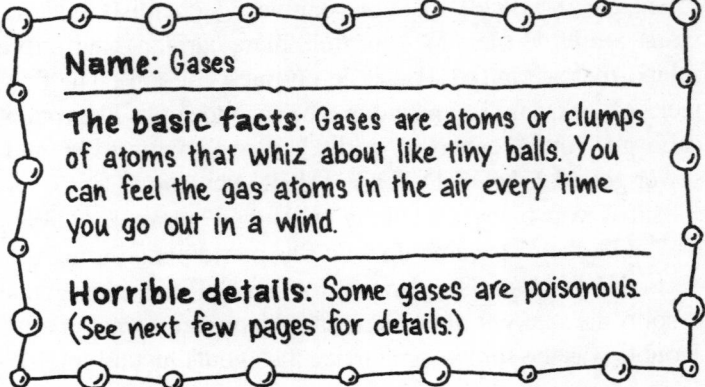

Name: Gases

The basic facts: Gases are atoms or clumps of atoms that whiz about like tiny balls. You can feel the gas atoms in the air every time you go out in a wind.

Horrible details: Some gases are poisonous. (See next few pages for details.)

STINK BOMBS

Some chemists don't smell too good. This must be true otherwise they wouldn't produce such stinky substances. Any smell is caused by gas molecules which we sniff in the air. Now *you* can kick up a bit of a stink using...

There are thousands of stinks known to chemists but the worst are ethyl-mercaptan (e-thile-mare-cap-tan) and butyl seleno-mercaptan (bu-tile see-le-no-mare-cap-tan). The first reeks of leeks and is poisonous. The second stinks like rotten cabbage, rotten cabbage, garlic, onions, burnt toast and sewer gas ALL MIXED TOGETHER! Phwoar!

But if you fancy something even more nasty, try "Who me?" US chemists came up with this putrid pong during the Second World War. The plan was for French Resistance agents to spray the stinky stuff on German solders to embarrass them! Trouble was the stinky spray made the agents just as smelly.

Dare you discover … gas experiments?

1 Want to grab a bit of gas?

You will need:
A balloon

What you do:

1 Blow up the balloon and pinch the end with your fingers.

2 Squeeze the balloon.

What happens?

a) As you squash more the balloon gets harder to squeeze.

b) As you squash more the balloon gets softer.

c) The balloon stays the same.

2 Make your own gas

You will need:
A narrow-necked bottle half-filled with water
A balloon (use the same one!)
2 alka-seltzer tablets crushed into powder
Funnel

What you do:

1 Blow the balloon up and release the air a few times to make it softer.

2 Use the funnel to pour the powdered tablets into the bottle.

3 Quickly stretch the balloon over the neck of the bottle.

4 Very gently swirl the water around in the bottle.

What happens?
a) The balloon is sucked into the bottle.
b) There is a small explosion.
c) The balloon inflates slightly.

3 Bubble trouble
You will need:
A bottle of fizzy mineral water, lemonade or cola.

What you do:
Give the bottle a really good shake for two minutes. *Slowly* open the top and notice what happens.
a) Nothing
b) Loads of bubbles form and gas escapes.
c) Bubbles appear then sink to the bottom.

Answers: 1 a) Billions of gas atoms are squashed together. The harder you squeeze, the harder those atoms push back! **2 c)** The tablets react with water to make carbon-dioxide gas. The molecules of this gas are made from one carbon and two oxygen atoms joined together. **3 b)** The fizz comes from carbon-dioxide bubbles. The gas is dissolved in water under pressure. Removing the top reduces pressure and allows bubbles to form.

Bet you never knew!
Just as in experiment 3 gas bubbles form in the blood of deep sea divers as they surface. The "bends" as they are called can have fatal results! To prevent this, divers spend time in a pressurized chamber so their bodies get used to the change in pressure.

WHAT A GAS!

The air is mainly made of nitrogen. Some plants use this to help them grow though it doesn't do much for us. But the oxygen and carbon dioxide in the air are worth gassing about.

Hall of fame: Joseph Priestley (1733–1804)
Nationality: British

Priestley's friend Sir Humphry Davy said:

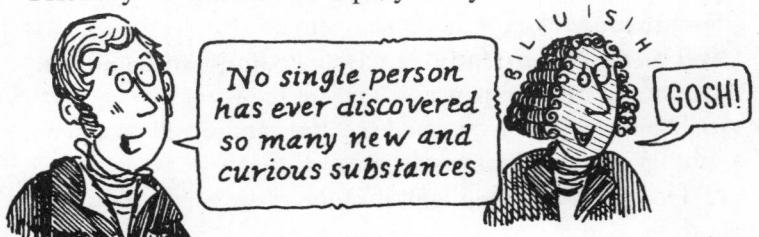

No single person has ever discovered so many new and curious substances

BILIUISH GOSH!

(Not since the first scientific analysis of school dinners anyway.) Joe could speak nine languages but he was useless at maths. In the 1790s Priestley disagreed with the Government and his political enemies sent a mob to smash up his lab. The shaken scientist did a runner to the USA. Could you think like Priestley? Try explaining the results of one of his famous experiments.

A LOAD OF HOT AIR
1 In 1674 scientist John Mayow put a mouse in a jar with a candle.

2 The mouse fainted as the candle burnt out.

3 In 1771 Priestley burnt a candle in a jar until the flame went out. Then he added a sprig of mint to the jar.

4 The plant stayed healthy.

5 A few months later Priestley added a mouse. This time the mouse stayed awake.

6 Finally the scientist added a candle in the jar again. The candle burnt normally, the plant stayed healthy and the mouse stayed awake.

So how do you explain these results?

a) The mouse produced a gas that the plant used. The candle also used this gas.

b) The plant used a gas made by the candle and produced another gas that the mouse used.

c) The candle made a gas that the mouse and the plant both used.

Answer: b) Yes – the plant used the carbon dioxide to make food and produced oxygen so that the mouse could breathe.

In 1774 Priestley heated mercuric oxide to make a colourless non-smelly gas. He put this gas in a jar and added a mouse. The mouse seemed happy and relaxed. So Priestley sniffed the gas.

AHA! THE RODENT SEEMETH CONTENTED

Which gas was it?

a) The gas produced by the plant.

b) The gas produced by the candle.

c) The gas produced by the mouse.

Answer: a) In 1783 Priestley's friend Lavoisier (later to lose his head) found that the gas from the candle was the same gas breathed out by the mouse. Its name is carbon dioxide. Lavoisier called Priestley's other gas – the one made from mercuric oxide – "oxygen".

Bet you never knew!
Joseph Priestley invented fizzy drinks. He put together a home-made machine from a washing tub and a few wine glasses and bubbled carbon dioxide through water. The water tasted fizzy and you could flavour it with fruit juices. But Priestley stored the gas in a pig's bladder and funnily enough some people complained that the drink had a "piggy" flavour.

TRICK QUESTION FOR YOUR TEACHER.
Who discovered oxygen – Priestley or Lavoisier?

Answer: Neither. Oxygen had been discovered some years before by Swedish scientist Karl Scheele.

Hall of fame: Karl Scheele (1746–1786) Nationality: Swedish
Karl Scheele discovered new chemicals such as oxygen, chlorine and nitrogen. But life wasn't much of a gas for

this sad scientist. Owing to a publishing mix-up the book describing his discoveries wasn't printed for 28 years! Meanwhile, other chemists had discovered the same chemicals. And to make matters even worse, Scheele died after being poisoned by a chemical he discovered but never got the credit for!

A MAD MACHINE

Meanwhile scientists investigated hydrogen gas. The lighter-than-air hydrogen was ideal for filling balloons but early flying machines were fearsomely fatal. In 1785 French balloon pioneer Pilâtre de Rozier was killed trying to fly this chaotic contraption. A faulty valve probably caused the crash.

In 1819 balloonist Sophie Blanchard was killed when her hydrogen balloon caught fire. Some of the watching crowd cheered. They thought the blaze was part of the act.

THE LAST LAUGH

Sir Humphry Davy (1778–1829) was 19 when he discovered laughing gas, or nitrous oxide as the chemists call it. He thought there was something funny about the gas when he sniffed it. And he felt so good that he burst into gales of laughter.

Laughing gas shows became a popular form of entertainment. You could see people sniffing the gas and making fools of themselves. In 1839 a chemist described how people breathed the gas out of pigs' bladders:

Some jumped over tables and chairs, some were bent on making speeches, some were very much inclined to fight . . . As to the laughing, I think it was chiefly confined to the lookers-on.

And the funny thing was that people under the influence of the gas didn't seem to feel any pain.

THE DABBLING DENTIST

Ambitious American dentist Horace Wells (1815–1848) experimented unsuccessfully with laughing gas as a way of knocking people out for operations. Later he went mad and killed himself. Meanwhile his former partner William T Morton the proud owner of a false teeth factory, was experimenting with another chemical – ether.

Following the advice of a professor called Charles Jackson, Morton tested the gas on his pet dog and then on himself. Mind you, I don't suppose he noticed that he'd knocked himself out. Next he tried it on a patient. Success! Sadly, this story has a painful ending. Ether is quite cheap and easy to make. So to make money Morton said he'd invented a brand new substance.

He coloured the ether pink and added perfumes to it so no one would recognize it. Then he sold the bottles to doctors at ludicrous prices. He thought he'd be laughing all the way to the bank. But when the doctors found out they'd been cheated, they lost all confidence in Morton.

Morton exchanged a lot of hot air in his arguments with Charles Jackson over who had discovered ether. One day the inventor read a magazine article crediting Jackson with the discovery. He was so cross he had a fit and died. Meanwhile, Jackson had been acting rather oddly. After a visit to Morton's grave he went mad and had to be locked up.

In the last fifty years laughing gas has come back into fashion. It has been widely used as a painkiller in hospitals.

So I suppose Horace Wells got the last laugh.

And if you think this story sounds chaotic, wait till you get wind of these nasty niffs...

THE MOST HORRIBLE GAS COMPETITION

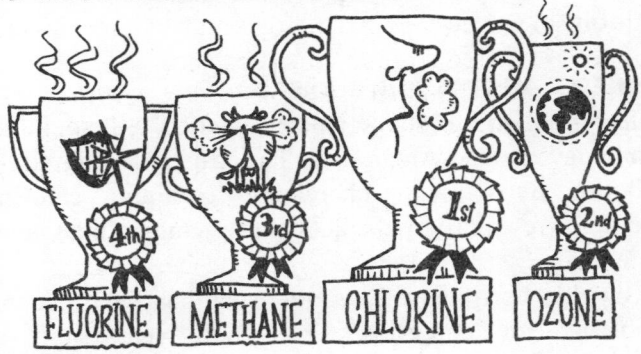

FOURTH PRIZE

Fluorine Five scientists tried to make this gas – all were poisoned. Eventually French scientist Henri Moissan (1852–1907) succeeded using platinum equipment. Platinum is one of the few materials fluorine doesn't dissolve.

Nowadays, tiny safe amounts of fluorine atoms are found in the chemicals called fluorides in toothpaste that help protect teeth from decay. That's OK, but too much fluoride actually discolours teeth.

THIRD PRIZE

Methane gas bubbling from marshes catches fire to make the ghostly lights called will-o'-the-wisps or jack-o'-lanterns. You'll also find methane in cows' farts (and humans') – *and* the gas that people use for cooking. It's true!

SECOND PRIZE - RUNNER UP

Ozone gas molecules are formed by three oxygen atoms joined together. They smell of new-mown hay and were discovered when a scientist noticed a funny pong in his lab.

Ozone kills germs. It also kills people if they breathe too much of it. Luckily most ozone is 25 km up in the air where it forms a useful barrier against the sun's harmful rays.

WINNER (JUST NOSING AHEAD)

Chlorine In the 1980s scientists spotted a hole in the ozone layer over Antarctica. The gap was caused by pollution by CFCs – chemicals containing chlorine. The hole grew until by the 2000s it was bigger than North America.

But this horrible yellow-green gas has been causing problems for centuries. Over 600 years ago an alchemist bubbled chlorine though water and said it was good for salad dressings. WRONG. Chlorine is horribly poisonous.

WOW! IT'S TURNED BLUE – I WONDER WHAT IT TASTES LIKE

In the First World War German scientist Fritz Haber developed chlorine gas as a horrible weapon of war...

A BREATH OF AIR

"Tell me about it," Billy pleaded.

Arthur McAllsop hunched his shoulders against the cold drizzle and shook his head. "I've told you son – it's not a nice story."

"You said you'd look after me."

"Yeah, I did. Listen son, just keep your head down and you'll be alright."

"Well, I need to know about it. Can't have been too bad – you're still here aren't you?"

A flare cut through the night. Billy blinked in the sudden blaze of light. He looked so young – just 16 and his first time away from home. Must have lied about his age.

Arthur sighed. There was nothing for it. The boy would find out soon enough.

"We were near Ypres, I expect you've heard of the fights there in 1915. Well, it was a quiet sort of day – warm for April. Nothing much to bother us all day. We were having a nice cup of tea when it happened."

"What happened?" asked Billy.

"Gas," said Arthur. "The gas attack. It was like a yellow fog rolling down. Well, luckily the wind blew the worst of it away. We didn't have gas masks then."

"Did you get gassed?"

"Only a bit. It was like a horrible sore throat and I couldn't stop coughing. But I was lucky – I was still alive."

"That night it poured with rain. The shelling didn't let up. Not for one moment. Chaos. You couldn't hear yourself talk. We had nothing to eat, no sleep. After we came out of the line everything was a mess. The gas had turned all the grass yellow. And there were no birds in the trees."

There was a long silence. It was a quiet night and if you listened hard you could hear voices from the enemy trenches. Orders in a foreign language. Then came a crack of rifle fire and the whine of a stray bullet.

"Arthur, you don't think they'd use gas on us?"

Both men sniffed the air. The trench smelled of mouldy earth. Muddy water squelched on the duckboards beneath their army boots.

"No Billy – we'll be all right. They put the gas in shells now. They don't blow up but they do go plop! So if one plops you'd better put your gas mask on double-quick!"

It was getting lighter and a chill dawn breeze set the barbed wire twanging. Soon it would be time to stand to – then they could eat breakfast.

The soldiers heard the approaching shell. It whistled through the air like a train getting louder and louder. They both crouched, instinctively ducking their heads.

Waiting for the bang that never came. Instead the shell fell in the mud of No Man's Land with a gentle plop.

Billy turned white.

"Gas," he cried in a choking voice. "GAS!"

In seconds the word was passed down the line. Half-awakened soldiers groaned and cursed – fumbling with the clumsy gas masks they wore around their necks.

Only one man did nothing. A man who had already seen the worst of gas warfare and knew what to expect.

"Don't be silly, Billy!" cried Arthur McAllsop. "It's a dud shell. Gas shells don't whistle like that!"

Bet you never knew!
1 By the end of the First World War more then 125,000 tonnes of gas had been released by both the British and the Germans.
2 The first gas masks were rifle cleaning cloths soaked in urine (the water in the urine was supposed to absorb the gas). Yuck!
3 Eventually the soldiers were given gas masks that absorbed the gas in layers of charcoal.
4 In 1975 Dr Buddy Lapidus used this idea to invent odour-eating insoles. The charcoal eats up nasty smelly foot odour like a little gas mask!

But gases aren't the only deadly chemicals. Metals make murderous weapons, too.

MARVELLOUS MURDEROUS METALS

What's hard, shiny and doesn't bounce when it hits the floor? No, it's not your teacher's bald head, although it could be – it's a metal! Where would we be without metals? Think of the chaos it would cause. We'd have no coins, cars or computers for a start. But then we'd also have less in the way of murderous weapons. Let's face the facts…

Chemical chaos fact file

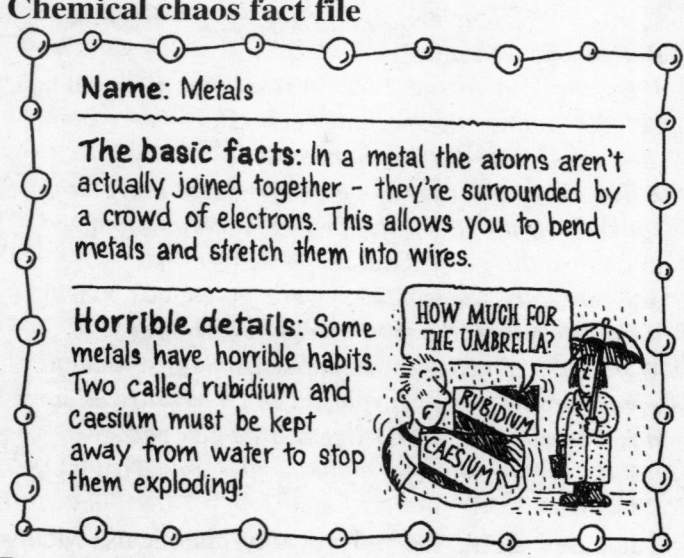

Name: Metals

The basic facts: In a metal the atoms aren't actually joined together – they're surrounded by a crowd of electrons. This allows you to bend metals and stretch them into wires.

Horrible details: Some metals have horrible habits. Two called rubidium and caesium must be kept away from water to stop them exploding!

HOW MUCH FOR THE UMBRELLA?

RUBIDIUM

CAESIUM

But metals have many amazing secrets too!

MARVELLOUS METAL FACTS

1 Some metals can float on water – for example, sodium does until it reacts with the water to make hydrogen gas.

2 Mercury is a metal that is actually a liquid at room temperature. You can see it in your thermometer. As the mercury heats up, it expands up the scale. Mind you – one Russian winter the thermometers all froze at -38°C. If your school ever gets that cold it's time to go home!

3 Gallium melts so easily that if you put some in your hand it collapses into a greasy puddle!

HONEST MISS –
IT JUST COLLAPSED
IN MY HAND

4 Tantalum is a rare grey metal used to make plates that cover holes in the skull.

5 Nowadays, platinum is more valuable than gold. But the funny thing is that in the sixteenth century the Spanish government thought the metal could be made into fake coins. So they dumped their entire stock of platinum in the sea!

6 In 1800 William H Wollaston (1766–1828) invented a way to re-shape platinum into long threads so it could be made into new shapes. The cunning chemist was raking in cash like crazy from his invention and made sure no one else found out. The secret was revealed after he died. Well – he didn't need the money any more!

7 Titanium is a metal that doesn't melt easily. This is good for making fast aircraft because their wings get very hot due to air molecules rubbing over them at high speed.

8 Scientists have suggested making artificial legs out of titanium. At least they won't buckle under in the heat of the sun!

SENSATIONAL SILVER

Silver is so widely used it's difficult to believe that anything could be so useful. Which of these silver adverts are too stupid to be true?

a) **PROBLEMS WITH PAINFUL JOINTS?** Take these real silver pills. Genuine cure promised.

b) **Are your knuckle joints wearing out?** Replace them today with this lovely silver set. Invest for the future!

c) Jet engine for sale – genuine solid silver bits in it.

d) **Problems with germs?** A silver water tank kills germs and keeps your water fresher for longer.

e) **LOVELY SILVER SOLAR PANELS.** Now you can live on the sunny side of the street.

f) **BURNS ARE A PAIN!** Take this soothing silver lotion. Guaranteed healing!

Answers: All are TRUE except b)!

AMAZING ALUMINIUM

Apart from silver, aluminium is one of the most useful metals known to man. But aluminium was once amazingly difficult and expensive to make. The French Emperor Napoleon III had his cutlery and baby's rattle made out of aluminium just to show how wealthy he was!

Hall of fame: Charles M Hall (1863–1914) Nationality: American
Paul L T Héroult (1863–1914) Nationality: French
One day Charlie heard his teacher say,

So the go-getting young American decided to have a go. Soon he was hard at work on his main piece of equipment . . . a grotty old gas stove in a woodshed.

Against all the odds – Charlie succeeded! The trick is to dissolve aluminium-rich bauxite in a chemical called cryolite. Amazingly this discovery was made at the same time by Frenchman Paul Héroult. Both inventors were exactly the same age and both worked in similarly chaotic chemistry labs! And here's the really bizarre bit. They were born and died in the same year too! Aluminium may be amazing, but it's not...

AS GOOD AS GOLD

Yes – GOLD. It's the stuff that dreams are made of. Royal crowns, pirate treasure, ancient coins. For thousands of years men have fought, struggled and died to get their mits on this magical metal. And sometimes they've made complete fools of themselves...

FOOL'S GOLD

Sir Martin Frobisher (1537?–1596)
was nobody's fool. The tough-talking
Yorkshireman was everyone's idea
of an explorer – brave, weather-
beaten and determined.

In 1576 Frobisher sailed off in search of a sea route to
Asia across the north of Canada. Sir Martin didn't find
the fabled route but he did visit the icy wilderness of
Baffin Island. And there he made a stunning discovery.

It was a lump of rock that glittered in the chilly
northern sun! Back in England two experts confirmed it,
"Yup – it's gold." Chaos soon ensued because everyone
wanted to grab a share.

The next year, Frobisher returned to the island with a larger
expedition. It was no picnic – they braved icebergs and gales
that could tear a ship to pieces. On land there were polar
bears strong enough to kill a man with a single blow. But it
was worth the danger. Working with picks in the freezing
cold, they hacked away 197 tonnes of the golden rock.

The following year Frobisher headed an armada full
of excited adventurers. This time the ships returned laden
with an incredible 1,180 tonnes of the glittering prize. It
was worth a fortune – enough to make them rich beyond
their wildest dreams. Or so they reckoned…

Then the bubble burst. There was no gold on Baffin Island. It was just iron pyrite – a common-as-muck mixture of iron ore and sulphur that you can find anywhere. Some unkind people called it "fool's gold". Sir Martin and his crew became a laughing stock.

Would you have been fooled by iron pyrite? Here are a few tips to make sure you get the right stuff.

BECOME A GOLD PROSPECTOR

1 Panning for gold

Swirl a load of sand and water in a pan. Carefully swill the water and floating sand from the pan. Any gold will settle to the bottom of the pan as golden grains or nuggets.

2 Testing for gold

Scrape your golden nugget on a dark rock called a touchstone. If it leaves a streak of gold it's genuine.

3 Dig a gold mine

It takes time to dig your own mine. Some mines are thousands of metres deep so don't dig into your garden unless you're sure there's real gold lurking in the rocks beneath. You have got real gold in the rocks beneath your garden? OK, then, here's how to get at it.

Getting the gold . . .

1 You'll need to spend a lot of money on machines, etc. One million pounds should cover it.

2 Smash thousands of tonnes of rock with heavy machines. Check every bit of rock to make sure you don't chuck away the golden nuggets by mistake. (You wouldn't see the funny side of this.)

3 Then smash them up in a giant cylinder filled with ball-bearings. (It's much quicker than using a potato masher.)

4 Mix the rock powder with the deadly poison cyanide plus water to make a slimy mess. (Don't try this in the living room.)

5 Leave the slime to settle in a tank. Then remove any bits of rock. Check for gold.

6 Add zinc dust to the slime. This separates out the cyanide from any gold there.

7 Melt the gold with a chemical called borax. The borax sticks to any unwanted chemicals and floats to the top of the mixture. Carefully skim this off.

8 A bit of further processing and you end up with a bar of 99.6% gold. It's as simple as that! (NOT)

Now you've gone to all this trouble to get gold, what do you do with it? Oddly enough, you might put it back underground – in a bank vault. That's where half the world's gold ends up!

Bet you never knew!
In the 1920s gold was used in medicines to kill off the lung disease tuberculosis, but it poisoned the patients too. Yes, there's a mean side to metals. In fact, you could call them murderous.

MURDEROUS METAL POISONS

Lead is dangerous. Sixteenth-century ladies used white lead face powder to improve their complexions. After a few years the poison ruined their skin – it absorbed the lead and gave them blood poisoning. But the ladies didn't know why their skin was ruined so they used extra lead to cover up the damage!

YEAR 1   YEAR 2   YEAR 3   YEAR 4

But the most poisonous metal in the world is arsenic. Many years ago this substance was used to make fly papers. Flies stuck to the paper and came to a sticky end once the arsenic got to work. Unfortunately a few humans went the same way too.

Mind you, poison isn't the only way that metals can murder people. Metals make lethal weapons too.

Murderous metal weapons

1. The first iron weapons were made from meteorites that fell from outer space.

2. Ancient people worked out how to heat iron-ore to make metal, but it wasn't very strong.

3. Iron needed to be mixed with another metal before it was really strong. In 1400BC people first added carbon to iron to make it stronger.

ONE PORTION OF CARBON

4. Meanwhile soldiers fought with bronze swords. But they often bent in battle!

HA HA HA

5. Iron swords were much harder, sharper ... and more deadly.

SWOOSH

And that wasn't all. There followed iron guns and iron cannon firing iron cannon balls. This led to more chaos on the battlefield and buckets of blood being spilt. And oddly enough, there's iron in blood too.

> **Bet you never knew!**
> There's metal in your blood! Italian scientist Vincenzo Menghini (1704–1759) discovered this vital fact. He added iron filings to the food he fed dogs. The aim was to find where the iron would go. It turned up in the dog's blood. Iron in the red blood cells attracts oxygen atoms allowing blood to carry oxygen round the body. Some spiders have copper instead of iron in their blood. As a result they have blue blood.

CHAOTIC CHEMICAL EXPRESSIONS

ARGHH!
HYDRATED IRON-OXIDES.
IT'S $Fe_2O_3H_2O$ AGAIN!

IS THIS THE END OF THE WORLD?

Answer: No. Her car's got a spot of rust.

A ROTTEN REACTION

One big problem with iron is that it joins up with oxygen atoms to make rust. That's right – rust is a compound of iron and oxygen atoms. And rusting is speeded up by water and salt. This is why rusty old ships sail the salty seas.

And rusting is just one of many rotten reactions.

RUST IS A MIXTURE OF IRON AND OXYGEN ATOMS – WATER AND SALT ACCELERATE THE PROCESS, BLAH BLAH...

SHUT UP AND KEEP BAILING MAN!

ROTTEN REACTIONS

What have rusting and rotting got in common with photography? Give up? They're all based on chemical reactions. But what exactly is a chemical reaction?

Chemical chaos fact file

Name: Chemical Reactions

The basic facts: A chemical reaction is when atoms join together – or joined-up atoms split apart so new chemicals appear.

Horrible details: Rusting isn't the only rotten reaction caused by oxygen. Oxygen mixed with butter or margarine over time makes them revoltingly rancid! It's enough to wipe the smile off anyone's face.

GAG SPLUTTER

QUICK REACTIONS

Normally, when atoms bump into one another they bounce apart again. But if they're moving fast they can stick together before they have a chance to rebound. The outer groups of electrons decide what happens next... Sometimes atom kindly gives the other its electrons.

When this happens an electrical force sticks the atoms together like metal to a magnet. This is an ionic bond and it's more common in salts and other minerals.

Sometimes, the atoms share electrons. The electrons whiz round both atoms. When atoms join together like this it's called a covalent bond.

These bonds tend to form between non-metals – often gases or liquids. With both types of bond a new chemical is created.

PREDICTABLE REACTIONS

So atoms bump together and decide to join up. It sounds hit or miss doesn't it? But it isn't. Do you remember Mendeleyev playing Patience in the chapter, "Elementary chaos"? Thanks to Mendeleyev's Periodic Table, scientists can predict what happens. It's so simple. It just depends on the number of electrons an atom has in its outer atomic orbital – that's the outer layer that electrons can move in. If you have an adverse reaction to this, you shouldn't try this puzzle.

ROTTEN REACTION PUZZLE

Here are the atoms you'll be using to work out the puzzles.

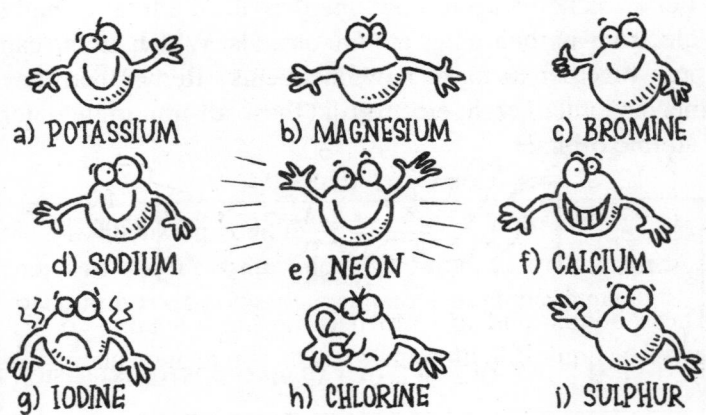

a) POTASSIUM   b) MAGNESIUM   c) BROMINE
d) SODIUM   e) NEON   f) CALCIUM
g) IODINE   h) CHLORINE   i) SULPHUR

First puzzle

How many outer electrons does each atom have? Read the clues below then work it out for all the atoms above.

Clues:

1 Sulphur has six electrons – that's three times more electrons than calcium. But between them they've enough to make a new chemical.

2 Neon has the same number of electrons as sulphur and calcium combined.

3 Magnesium has twice as many electrons as sodium and potassium.

4 Sodium and chlorine have enough electrons to make a chemical called sodium chloride. That's salt to you.

5 But sodium has only half as many electrons as calcium.

6 All the other atoms have one less electron than neon.

STOP MOANING. I'VE ONLY GOT HALF AS MANY AS YOU

YES, BUT HE'S GOT TWICE AS MANY AS BOTH OF US

Second puzzle

For two chemicals to combine they need a total of eight electrons in their outer atomic orbitals. Which atoms can join together to make new chemicals? Remember, they need a total of eight electrons in those all-important outer atomic orbitals.

Answers: First puzzle a) 1 **b)** 2 **c)** 7 **d)** 1 **e)** 8 **f)** 2 **g)** 7 **h)** 7 **i)** 6

Second puzzle Potassium/sodium + bromine/iodine/ chlorine • Magnesium/calcium + sulphur • Neon can't join with any other atom.

110

MY $Cu + Ag\ NO_3$ HASN'T BECOME $Cu(NO_3)\ 2Ag$ BOO HOO!

IS THIS FATAL?

Answer: No. His photos haven't come out.

GET THE PICTURE!

You might think these chemical reactions are a bit remote from everyday life. Surely you'd never normally have a hand in a reaction? But if you took a photo with a traditional light-based camera – you would need a chemical reaction to get the picture!

1 The first photographers used light-sensitive silver chloride paper. Energy from light causes a reaction that turns the silver chloride black.

2 Light showed up as dark on the photograph. Dark patches showed up as white.

3 To be in a photo you had to sit still and wait for the chemical action to work. This could take hours and meanwhile you had to keep a totally straight face!

GOSH IS THAT THE TIME? NOW JUST STAY STILL FOR AN HOUR WHILE I HAVE MY LUNCH

4 Unfortunately the chemicals continued to react to light so you had to look at your photographs in the dark!

111

5 This problem was overcome when inventors discovered a chemical that removes silver chloride from the photograph.
6 Twentieth-century black-and-white film had quick light-reacting silver bromide salts. This meant you could take action-photos.

7 Some of these salts were so sensitive to light you could take a photo from Earth of a candle flame on the Moon!

ELECTRIFYING REACTIONS

One incredibly useful type of reaction is electrolysis. It was developed by scientific superstar Michael Faraday.

Hall of fame: **Michael Faraday** (1791–1867)
Nationality: British
Michael had a tough childhood. His family were so poor that one day he was given a loaf of bread…

He couldn't afford books but he got interested in science after reading books that he was supposed to be binding for a bookseller. He asked Sir Humphry Davy to take him on as an assistant. As luck would have it, Davy was temporarily blinded during a particularly chaotic chemical experiment. So Faraday got the job.

Faraday investigated the process of electrolysis using different chemicals. Basically, you mix compounds with ionic bonds with water and run electricity through the solution. The atoms are pulled towards one or other of the two electrical terminals. The chemical gets torn apart!

Bet you never knew!
One use for electrolysis is in electroplating. You electrolyse a compound containing metal and a thin layer of the metal forms over an object. It's used to make silver-plated jewellery, for example. In 1891 sinister French surgeon, Dr Varlot, used the technique to cover a dead body in metal. The result of this revolting process was to wrap the body in a 1-mm layer of copper. He then put the gruesome object on display. I bet he got a few shocked reactions.

QUICKER AND SLOWER REACTIONS
Some reactions take a second – but others take millions of years. Luckily for chemists, many reactions are speeded up by heat. This makes atoms move a lot faster so they bump together more often. But you can slow down reactions by cooling. That's why food (and dead bodies) can be kept cold to prevent the reactions that make things go rotten.

Dare you discover ... how to stop a reaction using another reaction?

You will need:
An apple cut in half (ask an adult to do this bit)
Some lemon juice.

What you do:

1 Place the two halves cut side up. Sprinkle lemon juice over one of them.

2 After a few minutes the half without the juice is brown. It's a reaction between chemicals in the apple and oxygen in the air. An enzyme in the apple speeds it up.

3 What happens to the half with the lemon juice on it?

DON'T TOUCH MY EXPERIMENT, MUM!

YUCK!

FESTERING APPLE

a) The apple goes black.
b) The apple stays the same.
c) The apple dissolves.

Answer: b) The acid in the lemon juice stops the enzyme working and slows the reaction.

But acids have their gruesome side too. See the next chapter for the grisly details.

ACID DROP?

APPALLING ACIDS

They lurk in lemons and vinegar and tea leaves and even car batteries. Some of them have killer molecules that rip apart other nicer chemicals. It's appalling what they can get up to. Can you face the facts. . .?

Chemical chaos fact file

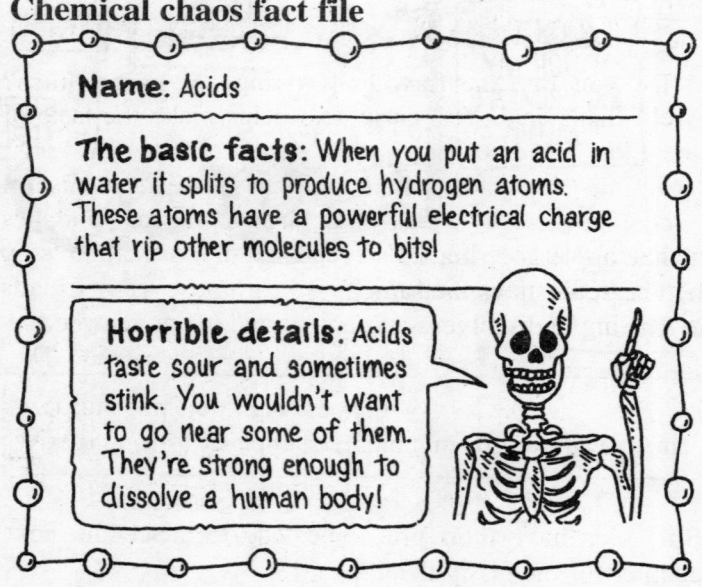

Name: Acids

The basic facts: When you put an acid in water it splits to produce hydrogen atoms. These atoms have a powerful electrical charge that rip other molecules to bits!

Horrible details: Acids taste sour and sometimes stink. You wouldn't want to go near some of them. They're strong enough to dissolve a human body!

But not every acid is quite so appalling. Sometimes they can even be useful...

USEFUL ACID FACTS

1 Amino acids are molecules that join to make proteins. Most of your body is made of proteins.
2 Ascorbic acid is another name for Vitamin C. This useful chemical is found in fresh fruit and prevents the

deadly disease, scurvy. The vital vitamin was discovered by two different chemists and they spent the rest of their lives arguing over who was first!

3 Do you like the flavour of orange or lemon juice? Well, that's acid. Yes, citric acid helps make the taste of the juice.

4 Alginic (al-jin-ick) acid is found in seaweed. It's useful for keeping cakes moist and when added to bandages helps to stop bleeding! It's even used in ice cream to stop the ingredients separating. You can amuse your friends by telling them their ice cream started off as seaweed!

5 Salicylic (sallis-sill-ick) acid is used to make aspirin. Yes – the miracle pain-killer is an acid. It was first found in willow bark. People once chewed the wood to reduce fevers. Don't try this – it tastes disgusting.

6 Horribly useful acids were once used to produce leather. These tannic acids from acorns or poisonous hemlock bark killed the germs that made leather rot. The acids are also found in many other substances including tree bark or even a cup of tea, and luckily they don't harm people. But other acids are completely useless.

APPALLING ACID RAIN

What do these places have in common – the Acropolis, Athens, St Paul's Cathedral, London and the Lincoln Memorial, Washington? Give up? They're all being dissolved ... by RAIN! Industry and traffic produce sulphur-dioxide gas. This makes rain more acid. In 1974 rain fell on Scotland that was as acid as lemon juice. That must have left people feeling rather sour.

Volcanoes make the problem worse. In 1982, the volcano El Chichin in Mexico belched out thousands of tonnes of acid gas!

Acid rain eats away at buildings old and new. Even your school is in danger! Oh well, every cloud has a silver lining.

It kills trees by the million.

It does terrible things to fish. They don't grow and the acid dissolves their bones!

Acid rain doesn't dissolve people. But funnily enough, it can turn your hair green. It reacts with copper in water pipes to form copper sulphate, which causes the interesting colour change.

CHAOTIC CHEMICAL EXPRESSIONS

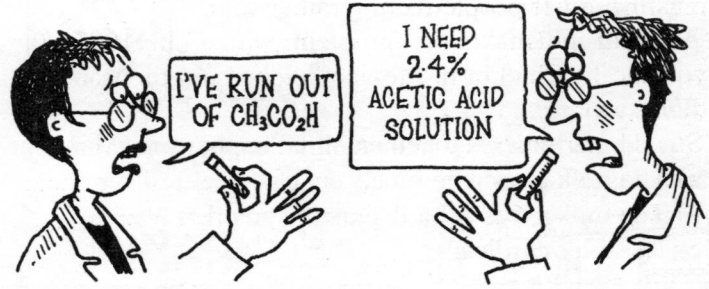

What's their problem?

Answer: No vinegar for their chips.

Dare you discover ... some simple solutions?
Dissolving a bone
You will need:
A stiff bone with no cracks in it. No need to go to too much trouble – a chicken bone will do.
Vinegar

What you do:
Cover the bone in vinegar and leave it for 12 hours.
What do you notice about the bone?

a) It's gone green.
b) It bends easily.
c) It's only half its original size.

Answer: b) The calcium in the bone has been dissolved by the acid.

SOUR SECRETS

You will need:
15 drops of lemon juice
A cup of milk

What you do:
Stir the ingredients together. What happens next?
a) The milk goes pale blue.
b) The milk gives off a disgusting smell.
c) The milk curdles.

Answer: c) The milk curdles because its protein molecules are clumped together by the acid in the lemon juice.

BOTTLED EGG

You will need:
A fresh egg
Some vinegar
A glass
A bottle with a wide neck

HOW DO THEY DO THAT?

What you do:
1 Soak the egg in the vinegar for two days. The egg will look the same but the shell will be thinner and softer.

2 You can carefully squeeze the egg into a bottle. Ask your friends to guess how you did it.

Bet you never knew!
You've got acid in your stomach. This fact was discovered by William Prout (1785–1850) in 1823. The hydrochloric acid kills germs and dissolves your food. So why doesn't it dissolve people too? Well the funny thing is – sometimes it does – that's when people get ulcers. The slimy stomach wall usually stops this happening but too much acid can cause indigestion.

SINISTER SULPHURIC ACID

It's oily, colourless and turns things to sludge, but it's got nothing to do with school dinners. It's sulphuric acid – a chemical so powerful that it has to be watered down before it can be used safely.

So why bother making sulphuric acid? Well, it does have its uses. For example, you can use it to make fertilizers for plants. If you add acid to paper it becomes see-through. It's often added to toilet paper. Fortunately the acid is washed off later otherwise it could be appallingly uncomfortable. But that's not the only thing sulphuric acid can do...

THE ACID TEST

An acid test is when you use a specially-treated paper called litmus to detect acid. The paper goes red if there's acid around. But in 1949 the acid test was one of lies versus truth and the issue was murder!

In 1949 businessman John Haigh was charged with murder. He had disposed of his victim's body in an appallingly horrible way by dumping it in sulphuric acid. Haigh had boasted to police that there would be nothing left. As he said at the time:

HOW CAN YOU PROVE MURDER IF THERE'S NO BODY?

But Haigh was wrong. The acid had not destroyed the evidence. There were a few grisly tell-tale bits remaining – and a complete set of plastic false teeth. These were promptly identified by the dentist of the murdered woman.

I'D RECOGNIZE THAT GRIN ANYWHERE

Haigh then admitted getting rid of five more bodies using the same method. He went on trial at Lewes Assizes. The jury took 18 minutes to reach their verdict and John Haigh was executed.

APPALLING ACID POISONS

1 Rhubarb leaves contain poisonous oxylic (ox-al-ic) acid. It's there to poison any hungry caterpillar that fancies nibbling it. Luckily, there's less poison in the stalk and it's destroyed when it's stewed..

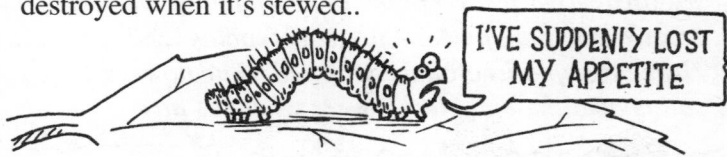

I'VE SUDDENLY LOST MY APPETITE

2 Bee stings contain acid and that's why they hurt. You can neutralize a bee sting with bicarbonate of soda because this is alkaline.

3 But if you put bicarbonate of soda on a wasp sting it'll hurt more than ever. Wasp-sting poison is a base not an acid! And if you want to know more about bases you'll need some basic base facts.

Chemical chaos fact file

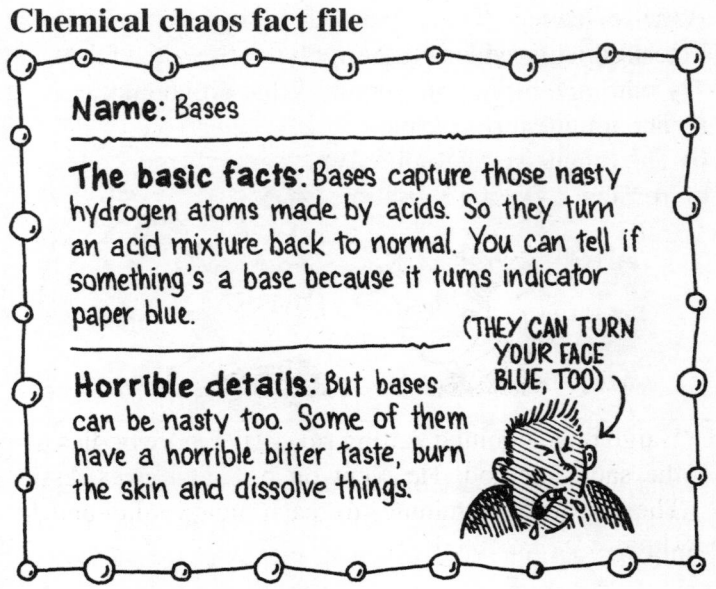

Name: Bases

The basic facts: Bases capture those nasty hydrogen atoms made by acids. So they turn an acid mixture back to normal. You can tell if something's a base because it turns indicator paper blue.

Horrible details: But bases can be nasty too. Some of them have a horrible bitter taste, burn the skin and dissolve things.

(THEY CAN TURN YOUR FACE BLUE, TOO)

Dare you discover … the secret of sherbet?

You will need:

50 g citric acid crystals (You can buy them from a chemist's shop.)

25 g bicarbonate of soda

175 g icing sugar

What you do:

Mix all the ingredients thoroughly.

Try putting a bit in your mouth. What do you notice?

a) The tongue turns purple.

b) The tongue starts to dissolve.

c) You feel a fizzing sensation.

Answer: c) The acid lemon juice and the alkaline bicarbonate of soda react together to produce carbon-dioxide gas. If you add sherbet to a drink you can make it taste fizzy.

124

SALTY SECRETS

When you mix an acid and a base they react to make
... a salt. A salt isn't simply the stuff you put on your
french fries. If you look closely at a salt you'll see
an arrangement of tiny shapes. It's a collection of
crucial crystals.

CRUCIAL CRYSTALS

Here's a question to mystify your teacher: What have metals, gems, bones and computer chips got in common?

A SMASHING DISCOVERY

In 1781 René-Just Haüy was having a rather chaotic time. He dropped a calcite stone on the floor. It shattered into identically shaped pieces. Intrigued, he smashed the broken bits even more with a hammer. This produced smaller fragments that were still of the same intricate shape. He was looking at crystals!

Chemical chaos fact file

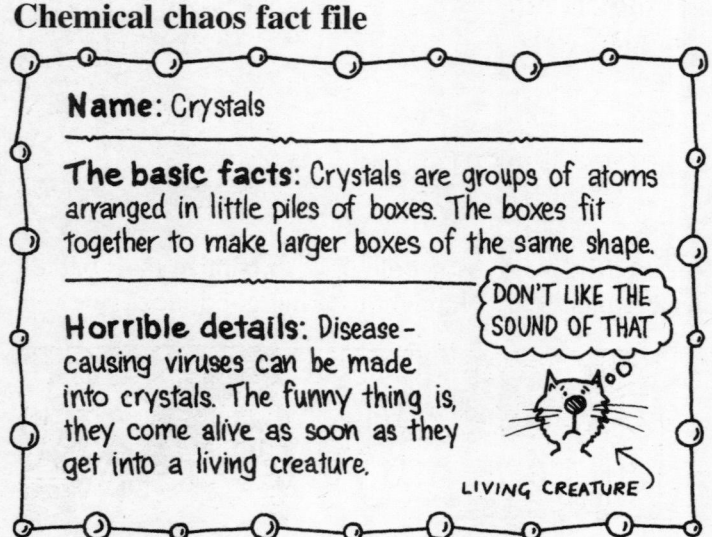

Name: Crystals

The basic facts: Crystals are groups of atoms arranged in little piles of boxes. The boxes fit together to make larger boxes of the same shape.

Horrible details: Disease-causing viruses can be made into crystals. The funny thing is, they come alive as soon as they get into a living creature.

DON'T LIKE THE SOUND OF THAT

LIVING CREATURE

A SICK DISCOVERY

This discovery was made by Wendell M Stanley (1904–1971). He infected some leaves with the tobacco mosaic virus. He mashed up the dried leaves and found that the virus had turned into nasty needle-like crystals.

Bet you never knew!
Salt is made up of crystals. If you look at salt through a microscope you'll see them as a pile of little boxes.

SALTY SECRETS

1 Salt contains the elements sodium and chlorine. Both chemicals are poisonous but strangely a little salt is vital for your health!

2 In the Middle Ages people used to baptize their babies in salt water. It was thought to bring good luck.

3 In France an unpopular tax on salt helped to trigger the French Revolution and the execution of thousands of people.

4 Salt is a major problem in parts of Asia. As swampy land dries out salt is left in the soil and kills the plants.
5 But that's nothing to the Dead Sea. This inland lake is the saltiest place in the world. It's so salty no fish can live there!

CRUCIAL CRYSTALS QUIZ

Crystals can be used for loads of crucial jobs but some of their uses you wouldn't believe. Which of these is too incredible to be true?

1 Diamonds were used to make spacecraft windows for a trip to Venus.

2 Diamonds are used to make lenses for protective goggles.

3 Rubies have been used to make lasers.

4 Crystals are used in some hospitals to kill germs.

5 Scientists are investigating using energy locked up in the atoms of crystals to power space craft.

6 Crystals were used in early radio sets.

Answers: 1 TRUE. The diamonds didn't heat up in the planet's fiery atmosphere. **2 FALSE 3 TRUE.** The atoms in the crystals take in energy and let it out in one intense beam of light. **4 and 5 FALSE 6 TRUE.** The crystals were used to control electrical currents inside the radio.

Bet you never knew!
The colours in gems are due to tiny amounts of other chemicals. For example, a bit of chromium turns a crystal pink. A bit more chromium makes a ruby red. Most diamonds don't contain other chemicals and that's why they're clear.

CRUCIAL DIAMOND FACTS

1 Diamonds are made from carbon atoms. Intense heat and pressure 250 km below ground force the atoms into a cage-like shape.

2 Diamonds are so hard the only thing that cuts them is …

another diamond. Their strength makes diamonds ideal for cutting all kinds of metals. You'll also find diamonds on the end of dentists' drills (that's if you dare look)!

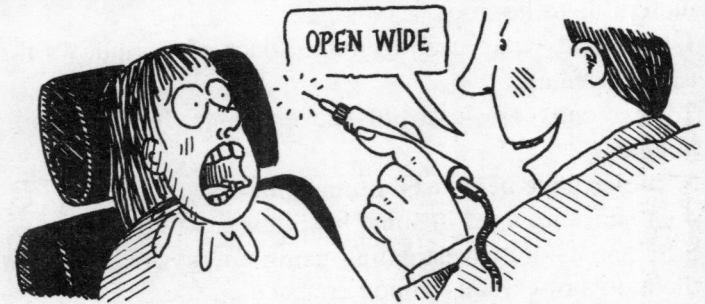

3 The gems are sometimes spat out by volcanoes. This is why diamond mines are dug into volcanic rock.

4 It was Lavoisier who discovered that diamonds are made of carbon. He used a giant magnifying glass that focused the rays of a hot sun onto a diamond. Suddenly it disappeared in a puff of carbon-dioxide gas. The carbon in the gas came from the diamond.

5 Some scientists think that diamonds form inside certain types of stars. If you could find a way to get your hands on them you could become the richest person in the Solar System.

6 Diamonds are so mysterious that it's not surprising that there are many diamond myths. But BEWARE – some diamonds are cursed with deadly misfortune. Here's the sinister story of just one famous gem.

A DEADLY DIAMOND

It was a large blue diamond – unmatched in its beauty and rarity.

No one knew its origin. Some whispered that it was the eye of an Indian goddess – stolen from a temple. And perhaps it was cursed too.

It was sold to the French King and was worn by Queen Marie Antoinette. In 1793 she was executed and her priceless stone was stolen!

In 1830 the gem was sold in a London auction. It was bought by a banker – Henry Hope. But Hope died penniless with his business empire in ruins.

A young Prince bought the diamond for his girlfriend. He later shot her.

A Turkish Sultan bought the stone. A few weeks afterwards he was forced to give up his throne.

A wealthy Greek bought the diamond but he was killed when he drove his car off a cliff.

The next owner was an American millionairess who wore the diamond in a necklace. Her husband went mad and two of her children died in tragic accidents.

The next owner of the necklace wisely gave it to a museum. And that's when the story should have ended.

But in 1962 a museum curator took the diamond to Paris for an exhibition … in his pocket! His plane landed four hours late and the man's car was involved in an accident. The curator wasn't hurt but he never took the stone anywhere again.

Mind you, diamonds can threaten disaster for other reasons too.

A CUT ABOVE THE REST

Premier Diamond Mine, South Africa, 26 January 1905
Frederick Wells couldn't believe his eyes. Embedded in the wall of the freshly dug pit was a prize worth dying for. A huge diamond weighing perhaps

500 grams – that's as big as a man's fist. In a few moments the dazed mine boss was frantically digging out the diamond with his penknife.

It was the largest diamond ever found and it was fit for a king. So the government bought it for $750,000 to give to King Edward VII of Britain as a birthday present.

HAPPY BIRTHDAY DEAR YOUR MAJESTY, ♪ ♪ HAPPY BIRTHDAY TO YOU ♪ ♪

Now came the tricky bit. The diamond was a rough stone. For its true beauty to shine, the stone had to be split in pieces and each piece carefully cut and polished.

So it was sent to Mr J Asscher – the most famous diamond cutter in Amsterdam. For months Asscher studied the gem trying to guess how it would split. If he was right, the diamonds would be objects of priceless value. But if he was wrong the gem would shatter into fragments. The King would lose everything – but then so would Asscher. His business would be ruined because no one would ever trust him with their diamonds again. He would be a laughing stock and a famous failure.

With shaking hands Asscher set the gem against a wedge. He made a tiny notch in what he hoped was the right spot. He took a chisel and slowly and painstakingly placed it at the precise angle in the notch. His mouth was dry and there were tiny beads of sweat running down his forehead. His hand trembled violently as he picked up a mallet. This was the moment of truth…

Would the diamond shatter? Would it split to perfection? Asscher would never forget the next few moments…

He hit the chisel with all his strength.

The steel chisel shattered.

The diamond was too hard.

Asscher was led away to hospital. He was laughing like a madman and his nerves were shattered – even if the diamond wasn't.

HA,HA… I'M SHATTERED… HA,HA…
WHAT A GEM… CHISEL SHATTERED
WHAT'S FOR TEA?.. ICED GEMS?
…MOTHER… MY BEST CHISEL…

Meanwhile, just thinking about the priceless gem made his skin crawl. But he was determined to try again.

After weeks of treatment Asscher felt well enough to return to work. At last the dreaded day dawned. This time a doctor was on hand to provide first aid.

Asscher closed his eyes and clenched his teeth. He gripped the chisel in one sweaty hand.

Then he struck…

The diamond split cleanly in just the right place. But Asscher was lying on the floor. He had fainted!

The Cullinan diamond was cut into 105 beautifully polished diamonds – each one worth millions of pounds. Two of these are in the English crown jewels. The finest and largest diamond is the Star of Africa which holds pride of place in the royal sceptre.

DIY DIAMONDS

Not surprisingly, many chemists have tried to make their own diamonds. But chaos often ensued. For example, Scotsman J B Hannay blew up his laboratory in 1880 after heating carbon in an iron tube.

Henri Moissan, the discoverer of fluoride, knew that diamonds are sometimes found in meteorites. So he decided to make his own shooting star. He melted a lump of iron with carbon in the middle. But he didn't find any diamonds.

Eventually, scientists learnt how to make diamonds. You've got to heat graphite to 1,500°C (2,732°F) under massive pressure. Thousands of tiny crystals appear. But it takes a week of this treatment to make even a small diamond.

Dare you discover ... how to make your own crystals?

You will need:
A beaker
Salt and warm water
Food colour

What you do:
1 Mix the salt and water in the beaker so that the salt dissolves.
2 Add the food colour.
3 Leave the mixture in a warm, sunny place for about two days. Sit back and wait for a reaction.
So what happens?
a) You return to find priceless gems have formed in your beaker.

THE ANSWER'S CRYSTAL CLEAR TO ME NOW

b) The mixture evaporates down and coloured crystals appear.
c) You can fish some shiny lumps out of the beaker with a spoon.

Bet you never knew!

Buckminsterfullerene is the name given to a form of carbon discovered in 1985. It forms hollow crystals in the shape of footballs. They're named after Richard Buckminster Fuller (1895–1983) an American architect who designed domes of this shape for factories and exhibition buildings. Buckminsterfullerene is a bit of a mouthful, so scientists call the shapes "bucky balls" for short. They sound very rare and exotic – but they're not. You'll find them in boring old soot.

Mind you – there's a lot of soot wafting about in the next chapter. It's made by combustion (that's the posh word for burning) and fiery explosions!

I KNOW

BANGS AND BURNING

Burning and explosions are nothing out of the ordinary. They're just chemical reactions that get … a bit out of hand. For centuries people have found bangs and burning useful. Read on for an explosive story.

A BURNING ISSUE

Thousands of years ago one of your ancestors made the greatest discovery of all. Fire. Without it school dinners would be even worse – just raw veg and very tough meat. There'd be no heat and no electricity because this form of power depends on burning coal or oil. There'd be no metals because there would be no metal smelting (apart from gold, that is!). And your school would be built of mud because without fire you can't make bricks and glass.

Chemical chaos fact file

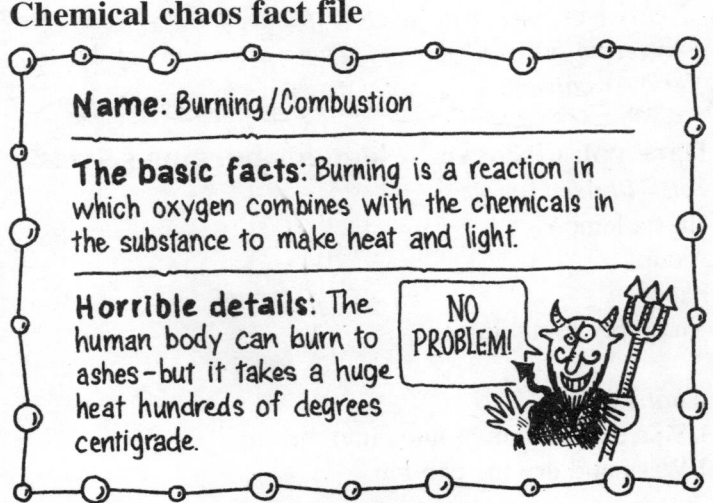

Name: Burning/Combustion

The basic facts: Burning is a reaction in which oxygen combines with the chemicals in the substance to make heat and light.

Horrible details: The human body can burn to ashes – but it takes a huge heat hundreds of degrees centigrade.

NO PROBLEM!

CHAOTIC CHEMICAL EXPRESSIONS

YOUR FACIAL HAIR IS UNDERGOING A LUMINOUS EXOTHERMIC GASEOUS REACTION

WHAT'S UP?

Answer: His beard's on fire.

Bet you never knew!
1 Fire sucks in air to make light and heat.
2 A flame gives off heat and light energy. The yellow bit of a candle flame consists of unburned carbon from the candle.
3 Gas can burn with a clear flame if there's enough oxygen to burn all the gas. There are no messy bits of leftover carbon.

Dare you discover ... lemon's burning secret?

You will need:
Half a lemon
A cup
Paper
An empty fountain pen

What you do:
1 Squeeze the lemon juice into the cup.
2 Wash and dry the pen nib.

3 Dip the pen in the lemon juice and write a few words on the paper.

4 Hold the paper in front of a warm radiator. The writing appears on the page. Why?

a) The heat makes the paper whiter so you can see the writing.

b) The heat makes the paper darker so that the writing shows up.

c) The heat makes the lemon juice darker so you can see it.

Answer: c) Lemon juice burns at a lower temperature than paper. This fact is very useful for sending your own secret messages.

FEARSOME PHOSPHOROUS

One chemical that burns easily is phosphorous. For centuries doctors prescribed this poisonous chemical as a medicine. The doctors thought that it must be good for you because it glows in the dark! Then an inventor discovered phosphorous matches.

HORRIBLE SCIENCE HEALTH WARNING

Matches are useful for starting fires. Luckily, none of the experiments in this book involves burning down your school. So to avoid scenes of chaos and other dire consequences leave the matches safely in their box.

STRIKE A LIGHT

In 1826 John Walker, a chemist from Stockton-on-Tees, England was stirring potassium carbonate and antimony with a stick. When he scraped the stick on a stone floor to get rid of the chemical blob on its end, the stick caught fire. John Walker had met his match.

John decided to sell his new inventions and strike it rich. At that time people carried tinder boxes containing flint and steel to make sparks and a bit of dried fungus to burn. Now everyone had money to burn on the new matches!

But the new matches were deadly. If the air got warm and moist, the matches burst into flames. They sometimes set fire to people's pockets and made poisonous fumes. A few customers got more than their fingers burnt.

And there was an even more terrible price to pay. Phosphorous slowly poisoned the girls who made matches. Entering the body through rotten teeth it caused a ghastly bone disease nicknamed "phossy jaw".

When these facts came to light social reformers campaigned to ban the matches. In 1888 the workers went on strike (that means not working, not striking matches, silly). But people didn't stop using the matches until they were banned in 1912.

Nowadays we use "safety matches". They were developed as early as the 1840s. Basically you've got two reactive chemicals – potassium chlorate on the match head and red phosphorous on the striking surface. Since the chemicals don't mix until the match is struck they should be safe enough. But early matches had a mix of potassium chlorate and another dangerous chemical, and they had an embarrassing habit of exploding all by themselves.

PERHAPS I'D BETTER TAKE ANOTHER LOOK AT THE MIXTURE

Nowadays in Britain alone people use one hundred billion matches every year! That's enough wood for 70,000 trees.

MAD MACHINES - THE SELF-IGNITING MATCH

Here's a marvellous match-saving (and tree-saving) invention. A nineteenth-century French scientist made this bell-shaped box.

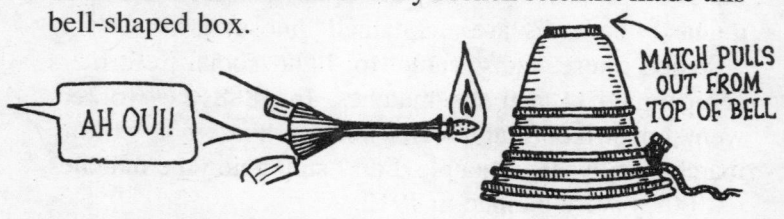

MATCH PULLS OUT FROM TOP OF BELL

AH OUI!

As you pull out the match, a spark sets fire to the chemical inside the box. Return the match to its hole and the flame goes out. Brilliant!
JUST WATCH WHERE YOU USE IT!

Chemical chaos fact file

Name: Explosions

The basic facts: Explosions are just a type of burning.
1. "Low" explosives produce rapid burning and lots of gas. The gas blasts outwards causing the explosion.
2. "High" explosives use chemical reactions to do this faster.

Horrible details:
Explosives blow people up.
Oddly enough though,
most explosion injuries are
caused by flying objects
rather than the blast itself!

KABOOM

Hall of fame: Sir Humphry Davy (1778–1829)
Nationality: British

Sir Humphry on schooling…

I'm glad I wasn't worked too hard. It gave me more time to think for myself.

Now let that be a lesson to teachers everywhere. In fact, Davy taught himself science and he must have done a good job. Within five years of reading his first chemistry book he was a Professor of Chemistry at the Royal Institution!

In 1815 he went to Newcastle to investigate the problem of explosions in coal mines. After studying samples of the gas, he found that the explosions were caused by the intense heat of the flame. So he designed a lamp:

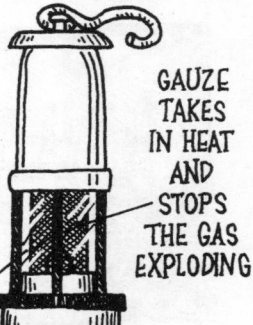

GAUZE TAKES IN HEAT AND STOPS THE GAS EXPLODING

STRONG GLASS PROTECTS FLAME FROM GAS

But as mines were getting safer, a soldier's life was getting more dangerous.

A POTTED HISTORY OF GUNPOWDER

1 A seventh-century Chinese alchemist described how to make gunpowder from sulphur, saltpetre and charcoal.

2 Saltpetre is found in rotting pig manure. Early gunpowder makers boiled the disgusting mess and then cooled it to make saltpetre crystals.

3 Licking the mixture checked the crystals for unwanted salt. Eurk!

4 For six centuries the Chinese guarded their secret. Then Europeans somehow managed to steal the recipe and invented cannon.

And muskets that could fire through armour…

And bombs to put under city walls…

5 Wars would never be the same again. The problem with gunpowder was that it filled battlefields with thick smoke. So you couldn't see anything…

6 Nowadays gunpowder is found in fireworks and a similar chemical is used to preserve tinned meat.

IT'S LOVELY GEORGE, WHAT IS IT?

BLEE

A FIREWORK OF COURSE

Bet you never knew!
One type of explosive was invented after another bit of chemical chaos. Christian Schönbein (1799–1868) was experimenting in his kitchen when he spilt a mixture of nitric and sulphuric acid. So he snatched his wife's apron to mop it up. Keen to avoid an explosive situation with his wife the chaotic chemist left the apron to dry. It dried ... and exploded! Schönbein had discovered nitro-cellulose – the world's first exploding fabric.

BANGS AND BLASTS!

1 The bang in your Christmas cracker is caused by mercuric fulminate. In 1800, its discoverer was injured during a lecture as he tried to show it off. Luckily, you only get a tiny bit in a cracker or your party would go with a very loud bang!

2 Another explosive is TNT – otherwise known as trinitrotolulene (try-nite-tro-toll-you-lene). One TNT molecule will produce a blast one thousand times its size. It just takes a little shock to set it off. Mind you – a blast like that will give you more than a little shock.

3 Amazingly, one kilogram of butter stores as much energy in the bonds between its atoms as the same quantity of TNT! But butter tastes nicer on toast and it doesn't blow up either.

THE MAN WHO MADE A BOMB

Dynamite was discovered by Swedish inventor Alfred Nobel. The blasting power comes from nitroglycerine which is an oily mix of glycerine and acids used by Schönbein. Although he became one of the world's richest men, Alfred Nobel wasn't a bundle of laughs. He was tormented by a guilty conscience. Here's what his diary might have looked like.

✑ *1865* ✑

Dear Diary

It's _all_ got out of hand. Explosives are fantastic and fascinating and fun, and I've never been afraid of them . . . but today I've discovered just how dangerous, dreadful . . . and deadly they can be. There was this explosion in the factory.

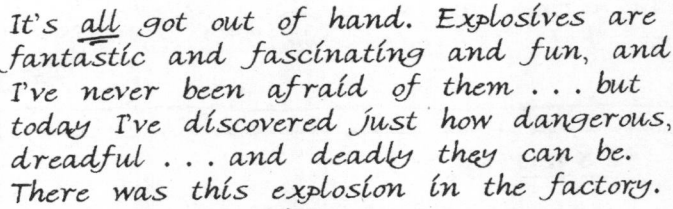

All my work's destroyed. And, most terrible of all, my brother is dead. That's what explosives really do. They kill people. It's horrible. And now I'll never see my brother or speak to him again.

I'll never touch explosives again, either! If only Dad hadn't got me started, what with his underwater mines, I'd never have thought about playing around with that nasty nitroglycerine stuff.

No, that's it, finished. No more loud bangs for me, not even so much as a pop. I'm going to forget all about the amazing effects of playing with chemicals, loud bangs, fireworks, sparks flying . . . It's just too dangerous. But it's so fascinating, too, maybe I could just play around a little, from time to time. I could try and do something good with explosives. Maybe I could invent one that didn't do anyone any harm. I could invent a safe explosive. Yes, that's it, that's what I'll do!

✑1866✑

I'm brilliant! I've cracked it. I've invented a safe explosive that will definitely make the world a better place. They'll use it in mines and, well, anywhere, really. And the brilliant thing about it is that it won't blow up if you accidentally drop it. It's so simple to make. I just mixed that nasty nitroglycerine with kieselguhr (made from the ground-up skeletons of tiny sea creatures). That was all! The kieselguhr absorbs the chemicals in the nitroglycerine. Then you fire an explosive cap to set it all off. I'm going to call my new invention - "dynamite".

<u>Disaster</u>! My wonderful life-saving invention has gone horribly wrong. It's out of control. It's made me rich beyond my wildest dreams, but what good is the money when they use my invention for weapons of war? I wish I'd never discovered it. I want to be remembered for good deeds, not bad.

But if I can't get it right, maybe someone else can. I'm going to use my fortune to fund a really special prize. It will be presented every year, and given to people whose inventions do truly great things for science, the arts . . . and peace. That should make the world a better place . . . shouldn't it?

But can chemicals really make the world a better place?

CHEMICAL CHAOS?

Chemicals cause chaos – if we don't look after them properly, if they explode at the wrong moment, or if we let them loose without knowing what they'll do to the environment. So are we cooking up a chaotic chemical catastrophe? Or is it just the chaos of invention?

As ever, it's always the bad news that hits the headlines first. (You don't hear so much about the exciting new discoveries that happen all the time.)

A DEADLY DISASTER!

11 December 1979
Just before midnight, 106 train wagons of dangerous chemicals jumped the rails in Mississauga, Ontario, Canada.

One wagon contained 90 tonnes of chlorine, 11 others were full of easy- to-burn propane gas. Witnesses report scenes of chaos with massive fires raging out of control. One carriage exploded at once and another was blasted 750 metres away.

A quarter of a million people were forced to flee their homes as the chlorine wagon began leaking deadly fumes. Firefighters on the scene are working round the clock in a desperate bid to plug the leak. Their first attempts have failed to make the area safe. Meanwhile the evacuees wait anxiously for news of when they can return to their homes . . .

Luckily, the first explosion had thrown the chlorine high into the air and away from nearby cities. The locals were not in any danger, but it was days before the experts could confirm the air was safe. Others haven't been so lucky. Although the chemical industry has strict safety standards, horrible accidents can happen. In Bhopal, India, in 1984 2,000 people were killed by a poison gas cloud following an explosion at a chemical factory. And there's more bad news...

A STICKY SITUATION

Imagine crude oil – it began as the rotten bodies of plants and animals squashed under the ground millions of years ago. It's thick, black, sticky and very messy and people risk their lives to get at it. They drill holes in the beds of stormy oceans and venture into barren deserts.

And why? Because oil is horribly useful. You can make it into substances such as petrol to power cars, bitumen to surface roads and the raw ingredients of plastics.

Trouble is – like many chemicals, oil causes chaos when it gets out of human control. Oil spills wipe out wildlife and turn golden sandy beaches into black, slimy wastelands. And car exhausts cause problems too.

HOW'S THIS FOR PROGRESS...?
The 1900s...
Smog made from coal smoke and fog caused pollution in cities. In Britain smoky coal fires were banned in the 1950s.

The 2000s...
Smog made from car exhaust fumes caused pollution in cities. What do you think should be done about it?

THE GOOD NEWS

Although chemistry seems horribly chaotic at times, chemistry is also incredibly creative. The creative ideas of chemists can make most people's wildest dreams look rather tame. Just imagine a spacecraft made from a material that resists temperatures of 10,000°C (18,032°F) without melting.

If your reaction is to say, "What will those science fiction writers think of next?" you'll be amazed to know that this substance already exists. It was invented in 1993. And here are a few more substances that seem too good to be true.

FANTASTIC FACTS

Chemists have invented...

1 A superacid called fluoro-antimonic (flewer-ro-anti-mon-ic) acid, which according to some experts could have ONE HUNDRED TRILLION TIMES the dissolving power of concentrated sulphuric acid. Keep your fingers clear of that!

2 In the 1970s chemists developed a cornstarch-based substance known as Super Slurper. It was so good at mopping up spills that it could soak up hundreds of times its own weight in water.

I'M IMPRESSED

3 A new sweetener that's up to 3,000 times sweeter than sugar. It's called talin and it's made from the fruit of the West African Katemfe plant.

TOO MUCH SUGAR, DEAR?

4 Crystals called zeolites in the shape of tiny sieves that separate individual atoms in a chemical. They're a compound of aluminium, silicon, water and metals.

And there's more good news...

Chemists can actually use their chemical knowledge to tackle the chaos of chemical pollution.

1 Many of the world's cars contain catalytic (cat-a-lit-ic) converters. The metal honeycomb shape is coated with platinum. This traps the nasty chemicals produced by the car's engine and breaks them down into harmless chemicals such as water.

2 Ordinary petrol contains lead – added to stop the car engine making knocking sounds. Unfortunately lead in car exhaust fumes is enough to take your breath away. Don't forget lead is poisonous! So chemists have developed lead-free petrol and you can use it in your catalytic converter.

3 Every year people chuck thousands of tonnes of plastics in deep holes in the ground. What a waste. But in 1993 a factory opened in Britain that turns plastic back into the oils that they were made of originally. So now you can make old plastic into new plastic.

4 You remember that hole in the ozone layer caused by chlorine-based gases? They were used to put the squirting power into aerosol cans. But they've been banned and chemists have developed safer gases to use instead. So now you can spray on deodorant without causing a stink for the environment.

THANK GOODNESS FOR THAT!

THE CHAOTIC TRUTH

It's not chemicals that cause chaos – it's *humans*. We make chemicals. We store them, we use them – ultimately we are responsible for what they do.

We can use them for good or allow them to cause chaos and destruction. The decision is ours. Here's what one chemist had to say on the subject. Pierre Curie (1859–1906) and his wife Marie (1867–1934) discovered the element radium. Pierre said:

We might still consider that in criminal hands radium might become very dangerous . . . (but) I am among those who believe that humanity will derive more good than evil from new discoveries.

We hardly know what lies in the future. Except that out of the chaos of chemistry will emerge even more amazing and incredible inventions. And the future will be more fantastic and hopefully brighter than ever before. And that's the chaotic truth!

CHEMICAL CHAOS

QUIZ

Now find out if you're a
Chemical Chaos expert!

Chaotic chemical quiz

If you've been paying attention while reading this book, you'll be as clever as those cunning chemists you've met along the way. Take this quick quiz to see just how much you've learnt.

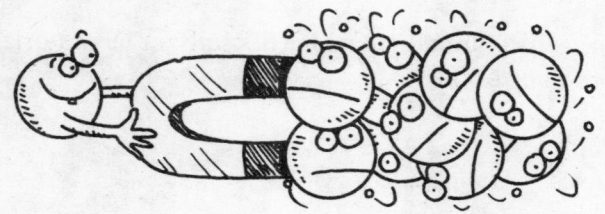

1 What three forms can chemicals come in?
a) Crystal, plasma and steam.
b) Solid, liquid and gas.
c) Fire, air and water.

2 Why is it possible to bend metals?
a) The atoms aren't actually joined together.
b) The atoms are joined together loosely.
c) Most metals have some rubber in them.

3 What is an ionic bond?
a) A bond made of iron.
b) A type of superglue.
c) A bond where electrical force binds atoms together.

4 What is vinegar made from?
a) Wine that has gone sour.
b) Apple juice mixed with yeast.
c) Grape juice and carbon dioxide.

5 Which precious gems are used in lasers?
a) Rubies
b) Pearls
c) Golden nuggets

6 How many chemical elements occur naturally
on Earth?
a) None – they are all created artificially in laboratories.
b) More than 1,000
c) 92

7 What is an emulsion?
a) An acid found in seaweed.
b) An alkali found in soap.
c) A combination of chemicals that don't mix properly.

8 What do atoms share in a covalent bond?
a) Protons
b) Electrons
c) Crystals

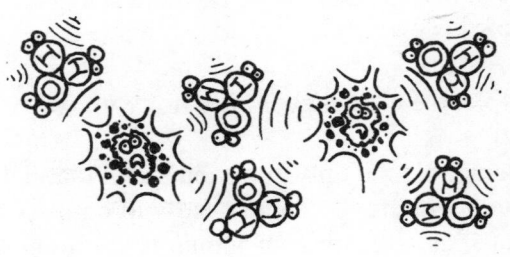

Answers:
1b; 2a; 3c; 4a; 5a; 6c; 7c; 8b

Amazing elements

Super scientists can tell which element is which by their potty properties, but could you do the same? See if you can identify these crazy chemical elements by their characteristics.

1 This pongy element is vomited by volcanoes when they erupt.

2 This is the most common element in the universe. It can be found everywhere, from enormous oceans to the scalding sun.

3 This element hates air pollution. In fact it goes green at the thought of it...

4 Without this element you wouldn't be able to breathe (but at least there'd be no more horrible science lessons).

5 This explosive element can mix fire with water.

6 This element is the only common metal that is liquid at room temperature. It can be deadly to humans but you might stick some in your mouth if you're not feeling well...

7 This element flows through your veins and is what makes you see red when you cut yourself.

8 This light gaseous element can't be seen or smelt but if you breathe it in you'll have some squeaky symptoms!
9 This ghastly green gas has been used to kill germs – and people.

10 This light but strong element is very useful. You can do everything with it, from assembling aircraft to wrapping up your sarnies!

Answers:
1 Sulphur
2 Hydrogen
3 Copper
4 Oxygen
5 Plutonium (it catches fire when wet)
6 Mercury (it's used in thermometers!)
7 Iron
8 Helium
9 Chlorine
10 Aluminium

Intriguing ingredients

Chemistry isn't just something that occurs in your school laboratory. It's part of your daily life. Can you match the everyday items below to their ingredients?

1 Washing powder
2 Your baby brother
3 Talcum powder
4 Tap water
5 Ice cream
6 Aspirin
7 Salt
8 Orange

a) Magnesium silicate
b) Salicylic acid
c) Sodium and chlorine
d) Enzymes
e) Carbon
f) Ascorbic acid
g) Calcium and magnesium
h) Alginic acid

Answers:
1d; 2e; 3a; 4g; 5h; 6b; 7c; 8f

Luckless Lavoisier and his daring discoveries

Crazy chemist Antoine Lavoisier may have been chopped down in his prime in the fearful French Revolution, but before he lost his head, he did many incredible experiments. Here is a letter he might have written to his wife – can you match the missing words to make sense of his discoveries?

Darling Marie-Anne,

It's official! Your little Tony is truly one of ze most splendid scientists in the world. I have been locked in my lab doing all sorts of amazing experiments and I've made discoveries that will put all those other cocky chemists to shame. Hah! My burning experiments have revealed that (1)_____ contains two gases – (2)_____ and (3)_____. The first of these combines with the substance being burnt! Next I turned my attention to water. And what should I find? The same chemical can be found in it! Only this time it's mixed with (4)_____. Well, my curiosity revealed other fascinating facts. Did you know that ze (5)_____ in ze ring Grandma left you is actually a (6)_____ form of (7)_____? Oui – that rock is just a plain old lump of (8)_____. Am I ze greatest scientist ever, or what?

Got to stop now, ma cherie – some rascally revolutionaries are at the door...

Antoine

165

a) Diamond
b) Air
c) Crystal
d) Coal
e) Hydrogen
f) Oxygen
g) Carbon
h) Nitrogen

Answers:
1b; 2f; 3h; 4e; 5a; 6c; 7g; 8d

HORRIBLE INDEX

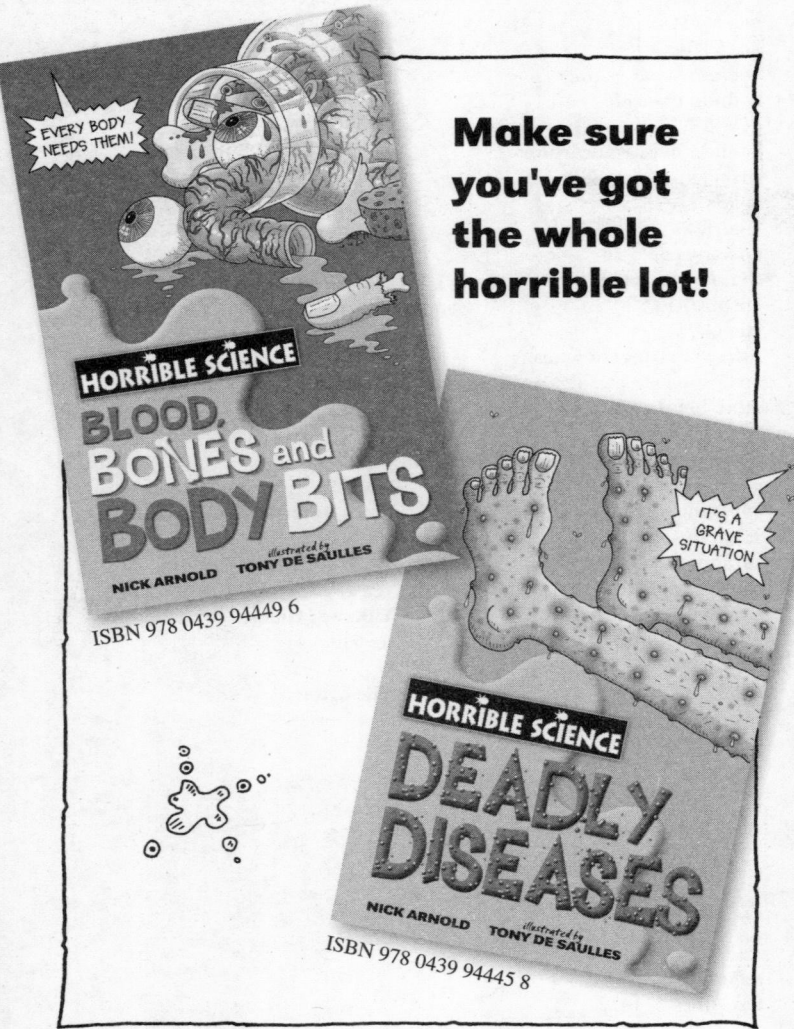

HORRIBLE SCIENCE
NASTY NATURE

I LOVE FAST FOOD!

NICK ARNOLD   illustrated by TONY DE SAULLES

ISBN 978 0439 94451 9

HORRIBLE SCIENCE
DISGUSTING DIGESTION

IT TAKES GUTS!

NICK ARNOLD   illustrated by TONY DE SAULLES

ISBN 978 0439 94445 8

HORRIBLE SCIENCE
UGLY BUGS

NOT A PRETTY SIGHT!

NICK ARNOLD   illustrated by TONY DE SAULLES

ISBN 978 0439 94452 6

Horrible Handbooks to collect!

ISBN 978 1407 10359 4

ISBN 978 0439 94407 6

ISBN 978 0439 94408 3

HORRIBLE SCIENCE

Science with the squishy bits left in!

Ugly Bugs • Blood, Bones and Body Bits
Nasty Nature • Chemical Chaos • Fatal Forces
Sounds Dreadful • Evolve or Die • Vicious Veg
Disgusting Digestion • Bulging Brains
Frightening Light • Shocking Electricity
Deadly Diseases • Microscopic Monsters
Killer Energy • The Body Owner's Handbook
The Terrible Truth About Time
Space, Stars and Slimy Aliens • Painful Poison
The Fearsome Fight For Flight • Angry Animals
Measly Medicine • Evil Inventions

Specials
Suffering Scientists
Explosive Experiments
The Awfully Big Quiz Book
Really Rotten Experiments

Horrible Science Handbooks
Freaky Food Experiments
Famously Foul Experiments
Beastly Body Experiments

Colour Books
The Stunning Science of Everything
Dangerous Dinosaurs Jigsaw Book

HORRIBLE SCIENCE

SHOCKING ELECTRICITY

NICK ARNOLD

illustrated by
TONY DE SAULLES

■ SCHOLASTIC

Visit Nick Arnold at
www.nickarnold-website.com

And visit Tony De Saulles at
www.tonydesaulles.co.uk

Scholastic Children's Books,
Euston House, 24 Eversholt Street,
London, NW1 1DB, UK

A division of Scholastic Ltd
London ~ New York ~ Toronto ~ Sydney ~ Auckland
Mexico City ~ New Delhi ~ Hong Kong

First published in the UK by Scholastic Ltd, 2000
This edition published 2008

ISBN 978 1407 10536 9

Printed and bound by CPI Group (UK) Ltd, Croydon, CR0 4YY

21

CONTENTS

A BATTERY HEN

SHOCKING JOKE

Nick Arnold has been writing stories and books since he was a youngster, but never dreamt he'd find fame writing about shocking electricity. His research involved swimming with an electric eel and collecting static electricity in his hair and he enjoyed every minute of it.

When he's not delving into Horrible Science, he spends his spare time eating pizza, riding his bike and thinking up corny jokes (though not all at the same time).

Tony De Saulles picked up his crayons when he was still in nappies and has been doodling ever since. He takes Horrible Science very seriously and even agreed to test how electricity runs through lightning. Fortunately, he has made a full recovery.

When he's not out with his sketchpad, Tony likes to write poetry and play squash, though he hasn't written any poetry about squash yet.

INTRODUCTION

Phew! It's the end of another day...

Mind you, science is boring – especially the science of electricity. That's SHOCKINGLY boring. So the alien monster probably got bored out of its two tentacle brains.

R E P O R T   B Y

Oddbl⊗b the Blurb

►**STAR-DATE**: Present

MISSION: Observation of humanoid activity on planet known as "Earth".

GALAXY CO-ORDINATES:
0001.1100.0011100.0

BACKGROUND: Juvenile humanoids or "children" are subjected to factual information by adult humanoids at a gathering known as a "science lesson". Tests reveal that 99 per cent of data is forgotten by the children. This can result in a primitive display of aggression by the adult humanoid.

J.H.

A.H.

PRESENT ACTIVITY: Monitoring of "science lesson" in a primitive shelter known as a "school".

BRAINSCAN VIDEO

TODAY'S TOPIC IS ELECTRICITY

DRIBBLE! DOZE! YAWN!

NOTES: Juvenile humanoids enter an altered state of awareness known as "snoozing".

6

Are your science lessons this bad? Does learning about electricity leave you in shock? Well, if science makes you suffer then reading this book could change your life. These pages are buzzing with shocking facts about electricity and humming with shocking stories including: the scientist who got struck by lightning, the surgeon who gave an electric shock to a gory human heart and the scientist who had a man *killed* to win an argument. After all, who needs *boring* science when you can have HORRIBLE Science?!

So what are you waiting for? Why not plug in and switch over to the next page!

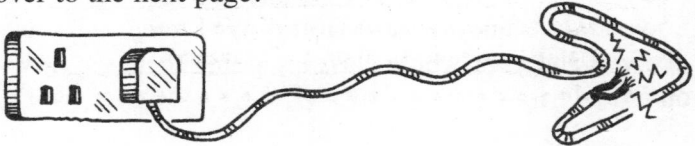

SHOCKING ELECTRICAL POWER

This book is guaranteed free from electrical failure. Er – well, that's probably because it doesn't run on electricity unlike lots of other things – like toasters and televisions and fans and fridges. Where would we be without electricity? Well, you could be on a HORRIBLE SCIENCE HOLIDAY – just take a look at this:

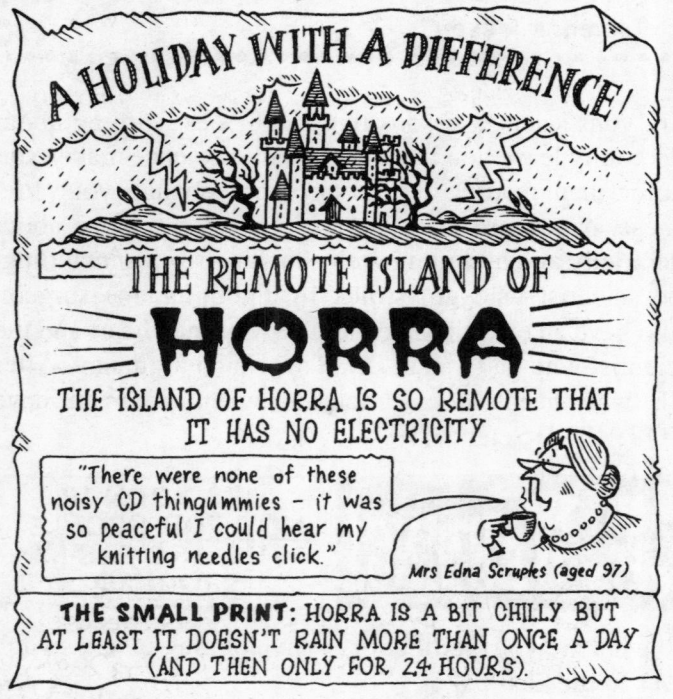

A HOLIDAY WITH A DIFFERENCE!

THE REMOTE ISLAND OF

HORRA

THE ISLAND OF HORRA IS SO REMOTE THAT IT HAS NO ELECTRICITY

"There were none of these noisy CD thingummies - it was so peaceful I could hear my knitting needles click."

Mrs Edna Scruples (aged 97)

THE SMALL PRINT: HORRA IS A BIT CHILLY BUT AT LEAST IT DOESN'T RAIN MORE THAN ONCE A DAY (AND THEN ONLY FOR 24 HOURS).

So you don't fancy a bit of Horra? Well *tough* – it looks like you and your whole class are going there anyway – on a field trip.

Horra Towers
Horra

Dear Coastal Rescue
Please rescue us from Horrible Horra!
This island has <u>NO ELECTRICITY</u> and no
electric heaters. It's <u>FREEZING</u> cold and we're
taking turns to warm ourselves
on the island's cat. All we've
got to eat is cat food because
our food supplies have been lost. And it's not
even hot cat food because there aren't any
electric cookers.

Our only light is a smelly candle — 'cos
light bulbs need electricity. And it's <u>MEGA-
BORING</u> here 'cos there's no TV, no videos,
no computer games, and no CD player 'cos,
yeah, you guessed it — they all need <u>ELECTRICITY</u>.
And our teacher, Mr Sparks, is making us do
extra homework. He says as a reward we can
listen to him playing his squeaky old mouth organ.
Laugh, we nearly cried.
You've got to come before
we all die!!!! Pleeeeeeease!
Lots of love,
Class 5e

PS The cat would like some fresh fish for supper.

9

Yep, life without electricity sounds as much fun as cleaning a toilet with a toothbrush. But what do you actually know about this vital form of power? Heard any of these facts before?

FOUR SHOCKING FACTS ABOUT ELECTRICITY

1 You can make electricity from farts. It's true – by burning methane gas (found in some farts) you make heat which can be used to power generators and make electricity. Methane is also found in rotting rubbish, and in the United States there are 100 power stations based at rubbish tips that burn the gas.

2 Lightning is a giant electrical spark (look out for the striking facts on page 58). One place that's safe from a lightning strike is inside a metal object like a car. The lightning runs through the metal but not through the air inside – so if you avoid touching the metal yourself you're safe. Much safer than sheltering in an outdoor toilet, for example.

SO YOU CAN MAKE ELECTRICITY FROM FARTS, EH?

PHWP!

...HMM

3 Sometimes electrical power can surge when the power station pumps out too much electricity. (Imagine a huge wave of power surging into your sockets.) In 1990 people in the English village of Piddlehinton (yes, that's the name) were shocked when a power surge blew up their cookers and TVs.

4 The biggest power cut in history hit the north-east United States and Ontario, Canada in 1965. Thirty million people were plunged into darkness, but luckily only two were killed in the confusion.

Now you can test your knowledge further in this quickie quiz. It's bound to spark your interest.

SHOCKING QUIZ
1 Which of these machines *doesn't* need electricity to work?
a) The toilet
b) The telephone
c) The radio
2 Why is it that the victim of a huge electric shock gets thrown through the air? (No need to test this on family pets or frail elderly teachers.)
a) The force of the electricity lifts them off the ground.
b) The electric current runs through the nerves and

makes the muscles jerk violently so the victim leaps backwards.

c) Electricity reverses the force of gravity and makes the body weightless for a second.

3 Your teacher gets struck by lightning in the playground during a storm. Why is it dangerous to be in the playground at the same time?

a) You might have to give your teacher the kiss of life.

b) The playground will be wet from rain. The electric current from the lightning can spread through the wet surface and give you a nasty shock.

c) The hot lightning turns playground puddles into dangerous super-heated steam.

Answers:

1 a) Even if the radio doesn't work off mains electricity it will be powered by electricity from a battery. When you're chatting on the phone to a friend the receiver turns your voice into electric signals that travel down the wire to your friend's phone where they're changed into sounds again. Got all that? Toilets aren't powered by electricity but you may be interested to know that in 1966 inventor Thomas J Bayard devised an electrically powered wobbling toilet seat. The idea was that pummelling the bum prevents constipation. Sadly, people poo-poohed the idea and the seat went off the market.

2 b) This is handy because the person is usually thrown a safe distance from the object that's giving them the shock. Another effect of a violent shock to the muscles and nerves is to make you poo and pee ... resulting in shockingly smelly underwear.

3 b) Electricity can pass through water – which is why it is extremely silly to put any electrical machine (not designed for it) near water or to touch power sockets or switches with wet fingers.

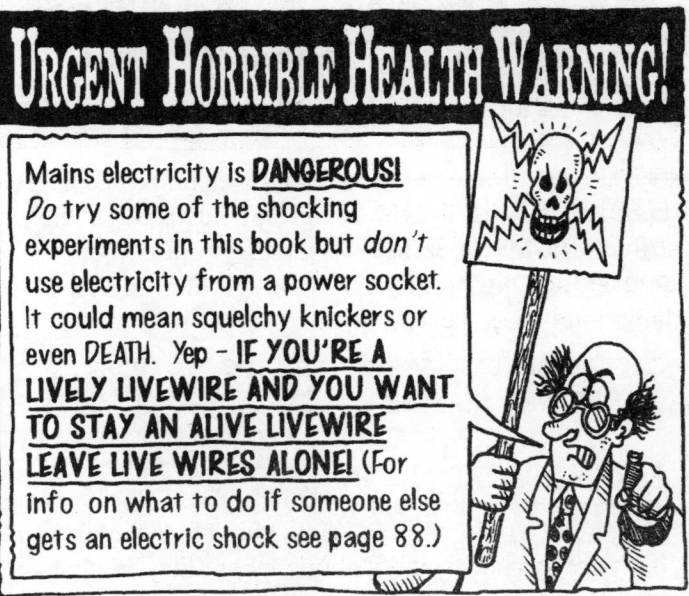

URGENT HORRIBLE HEALTH WARNING!

Mains electricity is **DANGEROUS!** *Do* try some of the shocking experiments in this book but *don't* use electricity from a power socket. It could mean squelchy knickers or even DEATH. Yep – IF YOU'RE A LIVELY LIVEWIRE AND YOU WANT TO STAY AN ALIVE LIVEWIRE LEAVE LIVE WIRES ALONE! (For info on what to do if someone else gets an electric shock see page 88.)

But before you get stuck into those experiments here's an important and interesting question: What on Earth is electricity actually *made of*? If you don't know read on – the answer's in the next shocking chapter!

13

SHOCKING ELECTRICAL SECRETS

OK, so what *is* electricity made of? Hands up who knows…

ART TEACHER — UM?

ENGLISH TEACHER — ERR?

HISTORY TEACHER — HUH?

SCIENCE TEACHER — ME, ME, ME!

Oh dear, it looks like Mr Sparks, the science teacher, knows the answer:

ELECTRICITY IS A RANGE OF PHENOMENA DERIVED FROM A FORM OF ENERGY ASSOCIATED WITH STATIC OR DYNAMIC CHARGES. CHARGES MAY BE CHARACTERIZED AS POSITIVE OR NEGATIVE IN RELATION TO THE NUMBER OF ELECTRONS IN A CHARGED SUBSTANCE.

BOAST! BRAG! SHOW OFF!

Well, thank you, Mr Sparks. Anyone understand that?

No? OK, let's try again. Everything in the universe is made of titchy bits called atoms and most atoms are surrounded by a cloud of even smaller blips of energy called electrons.

AN ATOM
MAGNIFIED
MILLIONS
OF TIMES →

ELECTRON

MR SPARK'S
DRIBBLE
(LIFE SIZE)

The electricity in your power sockets is actually *made of* moving electrons and the *power* of electricity comes from the force the electrons give out.

Let's imagine an atom as a family...

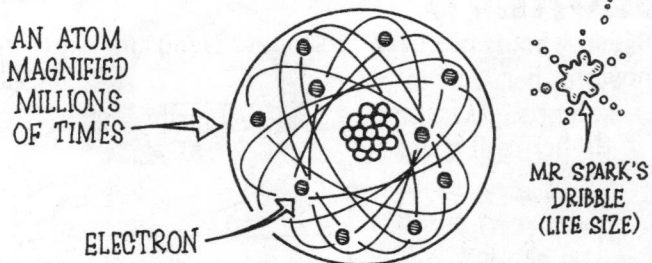

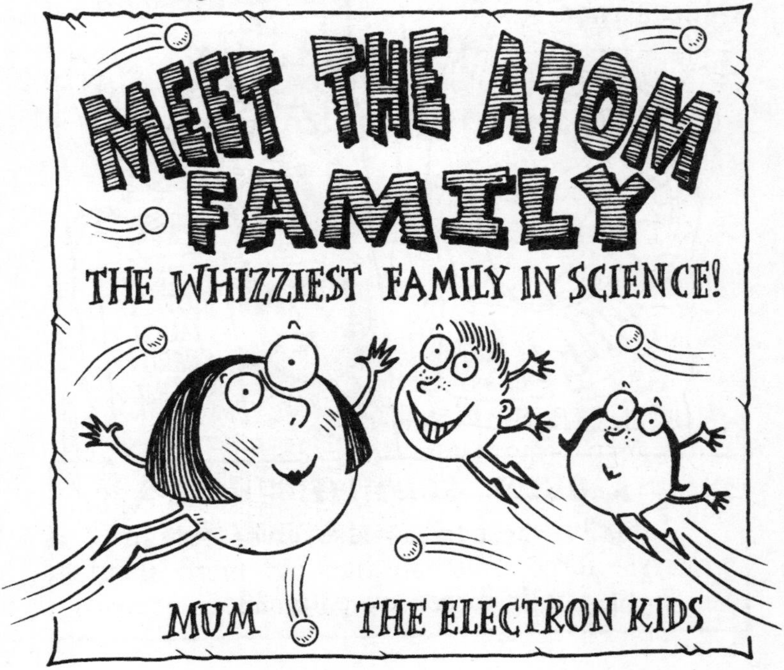

MEET THE ATOM FAMILY
THE WHIZZIEST FAMILY IN SCIENCE!

MUM   THE ELECTRON KIDS

Mum is the centre of the Atom family ~ everything revolves round her. Actually scientists would call her *a nucleus*.

DON'T YOU CALL **ME** NAMES!

The electron kids whiz around Mum.

WHEE!

WHEEE!

Each electron constantly gives out its energy as an electric force.

THEY'VE GOT SO MUCH ENERGY AT THEIR AGE!

A QUICK SCIENTIFIC NOTE

Actually, the nucleus also gives out an electric force. You can find out more about both forces on page 26.

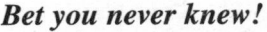

Bet you never knew!
Electrons really are tiny. An electron is ten thousand times smaller than the nucleus. If you had a very steady hand you could put 1,000,000,000,000 (one thousand billion) electrons in a line and even then you wouldn't have quite enough to stretch across a pinhead!

IT'S A WOBBLY LINE, SMITH. START AGAIN

IT'S A NUMBERS GAME

- Got a torch? All right then, switch it on and start counting – 1, 2, 3...
- That dim feeble light in your torch bulb uses 6,280,000,000,000,000,000 – (6.28 billion billion) electrons *every second*. Just to give you some idea of how massive this number is...
- A school day has about 23,400 seconds – if you don't believe me try counting them! So if you wanted to get to a million you'd have to count non-stop for another ten days.

...EIGHT HUNDRED AND SEVENTY TWO THOUSAND, THREE HUNDRED AND NINETY ONE...

- If you kept counting for another 32 years and 354 days (and that means counting whilst eating and sleeping and going to the toilet) you'd eventually reach one billion (if you hadn't died of boredom).

- Not gobsmacked yet? Well, get this... In order to count those electrons used by your dim and feeble little torch *in just one second* you should have started counting well before the Earth was formed 4,600 million years ago!

A NOTE TO THE READER...

What we call an "electric current" is actually a stream of electrons flowing through a wire – this is measured in amps. Can you imagine what it would be like to *swim* in this stream? Here's a story about a person who did just that. He's an odd-job worker called Andy Mann – good name, eh? It all began when Andy got a shrinking feeling and was made to feel very very small...

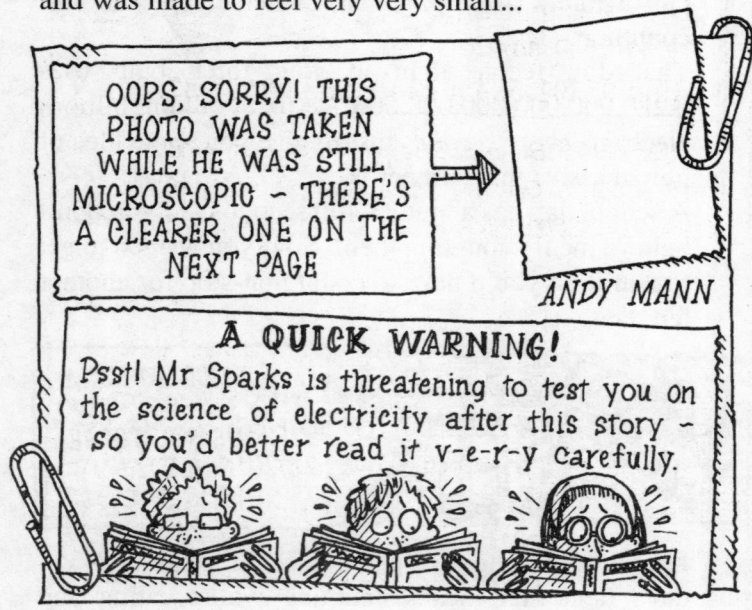

IT'S A SMALL, SMALL, SMALL, SMALL WORLD

Here's me story and I want cash up front, OK? Me name is Andy Mann - Andy by name, handy by nature, geddit?

ANDY MANN
General Repairs,
Plumbing, Electrics,
Brickwork

*Need a handy man? -
Andy's your man!*
No job too small!

(Ring 01201 5843673 mobile 09123 87690)

You can call me anytime but not when there's darts on the telly. Yeah, I was telling you what happened - it all started when I went round to Professor Buzzoff's house to do a job. Just a bit of sanitary engineering as we say in the trade - well, she had a blocked toilet pipe.

Anyway, imagine me surprise when she said I had to wear this protective suit.

"All right," I said - thinking the toilet might be a "stinker", as we say in the trade.

19

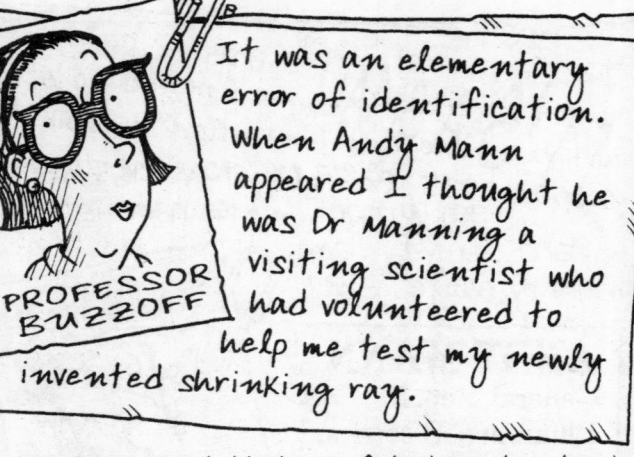

It was an elementary error of identification. When Andy Mann appeared I thought he was Dr Manning a visiting scientist who had volunteered to help me test my newly invented shrinking ray.

PROFESSOR BUZZOFF

Dr Manning - huh! The Prof told me to stand under this machine. It didn't look much like a toilet and I was about to say that the wiring looked a bit dodgy and did she want it seeing to when she flicked a lever. Then she started getting bigger and the room started getting bigger. But hold on ... *it was me getting smaller!*

ER!

EH?

OOER!

YIKES!

ERK!

Well I know me card says no job's too small, but this job was looking, well ... a bit too small. So I went on shrinking until I got sucked into an electrical wire. "Wire am I here?" I asked meself.

There was a malfunction in the diminisher unit. By the time I managed to de-activate the ray Andy had shrunk to 0.000000025 mm, almost as small as an atom. And to make matters worse he had vanished inside the machine. Obviously this was a situation of some danger.

Yeah well, it was dangerous all right. The first thing I saw was these weird balls and I thought blimey they're atoms. And there was these tiny blips buzzing round the atoms. They were so fast they looked like a blurry mist. Well, the Prof later said they were electrons. The wire looked like this huge tunnel with atoms round the sides and there was electrons flowing through it like a river. Then I got swept away by them electrons. They was like rubbery peas and I had to swim for my life. Was I scared? Yeah, I was wetting meself. How d'you get out of this electric current Andy?

Well, me being a skilled electrician (all jobs considered by the way), I knew that an electric current is made by electrons all flowing one way. And those electrons was fast. Luckily they missed me or I would have been KILLED until I was DEAD!

Fascinating! The electrons were zapping at 1 million metres per second, and electrical signals can zip along at nearly the speed of light! Meanwhile I frantically tried to reset the shrinking ray to make Andy bigger. I switched on the light to help me see.

CLICK!

Yeah well, guess what happened? The wire got narrower. All the electrons squashed

SWEAT

together and they slowed down and started rubbing against the atoms around the sides - yeah, and me. Phew - it was hot! Well, it's friction innit? Rubbing makes heat like when you rub your hands together.

ATOMS

ELECTRONS

Blobs of light started flying around - and then it hit me. *I WAS INSIDE THE LIGHT BULB.* Yeah - the one she'd just switched on. Mind you, I wasn't feeling too bright.

Of course, I didn't know that Andy was in the bulb. We scientists call the friction Andy describes "resistance" and the blobs of light Andy saw are called "photons" (fo-tonns).

PHOTON
MAGNIFIED
MILLIONS
OF TIMES

They're given off by the electrons as they try to cool down. It must have been a scientifically fascinating experience.

Yeah fascinating, Prof - shame I was about to DIE! Me protective suit was melting and I reckoned I'd be melting soon! I was boiling hot and sweating buckets. "This is it, Andy," I said to meself, "I'll never get to see the darts final!"

Just then me mobile rang. I didn't feel too chatty ... but I answered it anyway ... might as well say goodbye to someone.

RING!

I observed Andy's business card and remembered he had a mobile phone. So I called his number. I was shocked to discover that he was inside the light bulb and switched it off immediately. The switch stopped the flow of electrons and the light went out.

Just in time! The wire started to cool down - but I wasn't out of the woods yet - I mean out of the wire. I mean how was the Prof s'posed to get me out? Maybe I was going to stay tiny all me life. How was I s'posed to live? I couldn't even go outside cos an ant might tread on me and squash me flat! ARGH!

It took me three hours to enlarge the bulb wire in small steps and each time I cut out the portion of wire that contained Andy until eventually he was free. Then I was able to enlarge him back to his correct size. Of course, he was rather annoyed...

I'M IN THIS BIT!

Annoyed? I was fuming! First she sticks me in a light bulb and nearly cooks me - then she brings me back to me old size - exactly. Not six foot two - I mean I always wanted to be six foot two, didn't I?

HERE WE GO...

...AND BIGGER

...BIGGER

GRRR. IS THAT IT?

And guess what? She only goes on about that bunged up toilet and then I really blew a fuse! Just wait till she sees me bill - that won't be tiny!

I BET *SHE'LL* WANT TO SHRINK AWAY THEN!

A quick note

Good news! We've managed to lock Mr Sparks in the stationery cupboard so there won't be a science test – Phew!

BANG! BANG!

LET ME OUT!

But just in case he manages to escape here's a quick crib sheet with all the science test answers on.

Electricity Test
Answers

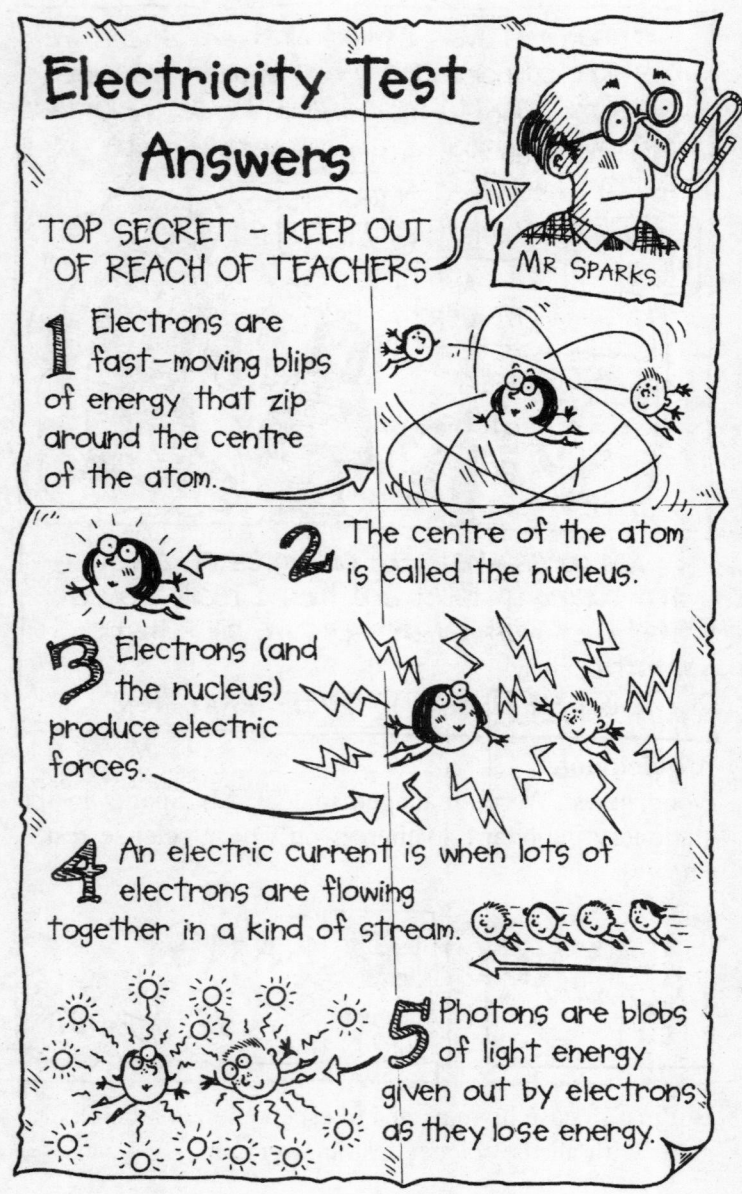

MR SPARKS

1 Electrons are fast-moving blips of energy that zip around the centre of the atom.

2 The centre of the atom is called the nucleus.

3 Electrons (and the nucleus) produce electric forces.

4 An electric current is when lots of electrons are flowing together in a kind of stream.

5 Photons are blobs of light energy given out by electrons as they lose energy.

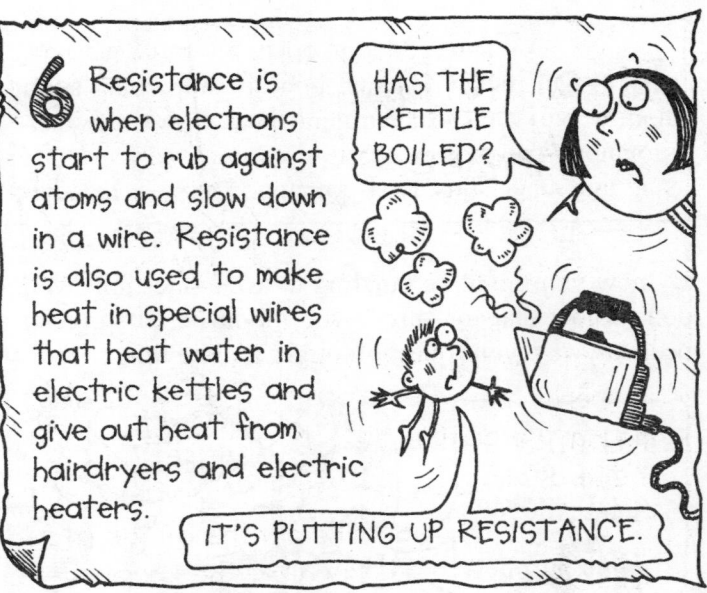

6 Resistance is when electrons start to rub against atoms and slow down in a wire. Resistance is also used to make heat in special wires that heat water in electric kettles and give out heat from hairdryers and electric heaters.

HAS THE KETTLE BOILED?

IT'S PUTTING UP RESISTANCE.

SHOCKING EXPRESSIONS

DO YOU KNOW ANY GOOD CONDUCTORS?

Do you say...?

WELL THERE'S MY MUSIC TEACHER. BUT SHE'S A TERRIBLE CONDUCTOR – THAT'S WHY THE SCHOOL ORCHESTRA IS SO BAD.

By now you might be bursting to ask a question. Well, I don't know that for sure – you might be bursting for a pee. Anyway, your question might go like this...

Well, why not discover the next electrifying chapter and find out...?

SHOCKING DISCOVERIES

One of the most amazing things about science is the way scientists calmly tell us that tiny things exist even though no one has ever seen them.

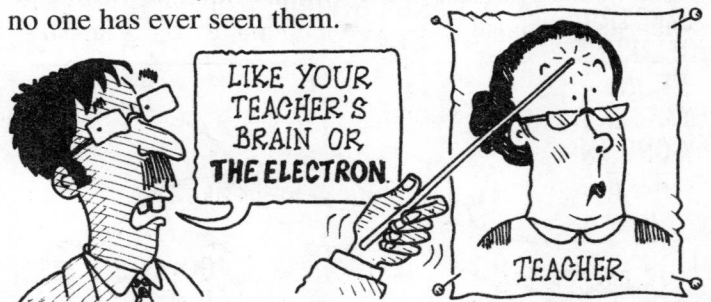

Well, lets face it they're both far too tiny to see even with the most powerful microscopes. But here's the amazing story of how it was discovered (that's the electron not your teacher's brain)...

TWO REALLY BIG BREAKTHROUGHS

By 1880 scientists knew how to make it and they knew how to store it (see page 55) but they didn't know what electricity was actually made of. In that year scientist William Crookes built a new machine to help him find the answer...

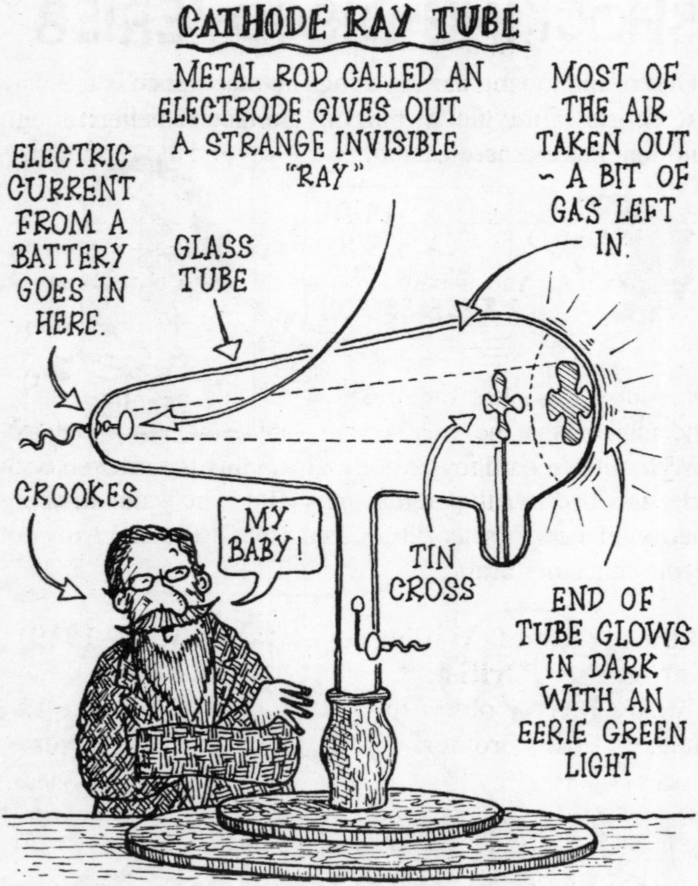

CATHODE RAY TUBE

METAL ROD CALLED AN ELECTRODE GIVES OUT A STRANGE INVISIBLE "RAY"

MOST OF THE AIR TAKEN OUT ~ A BIT OF GAS LEFT IN.

ELECTRIC CURRENT FROM A BATTERY GOES IN HERE.

GLASS TUBE

CROOKES

MY BABY!

TIN CROSS

END OF TUBE GLOWS IN DARK WITH AN EERIE GREEN LIGHT

QUICK SCIENTIFIC NOTE...

By taking the air out of the container Crookes was getting rid of atoms in the air that might get in the way of the invisible ray. We now know that the "ray" was in fact a stream of electrons shooting out from the battery.

COULD YOU BE A SCIENTIST?

So what do you think made the green glow?

a) The gas glowing as it's hit by the electrons.

b) The glass tube glowing where the electrons hit it.

c) A chemical reaction between the gas and the chemicals in the glass.

> **Answer: b)** The electrons hit the atoms of the glass and heated them up until they gave out energy in the form of light photons.

Of course, Crookes didn't know all this and he didn't understand what he was seeing. And as you're about to discover it was hard for Crookes to explain his work to other scientists because they didn't trust him. The problem was that, unlike most scientists, Crookes believed in *ghosts*. Here's his story...

Hall of fame: William Crookes (1832–1919) Nationality: British

Crookes was the oldest of 16 kids. (Would you like 15 cheeky little brothers and sisters breaking your things?)

WHERE'S MUM?

HAVING ANOTHER BABY, I EXPECT.

Obviously this could drive a person to desperate measures and maybe that's why Crookes became a chemistry teacher. But eventually he inherited a fortune. (So at least he could afford Christmas presents for everyone.)

He retired from teaching and set up his own private chemistry lab for exciting experiments.

But some of his investigations shocked other scientists. In those days many people believed that the spirits of the dead came back as ghosts and could be summoned by people with special abilities called mediums. Crookes decided to find the truth by careful scientific observation…

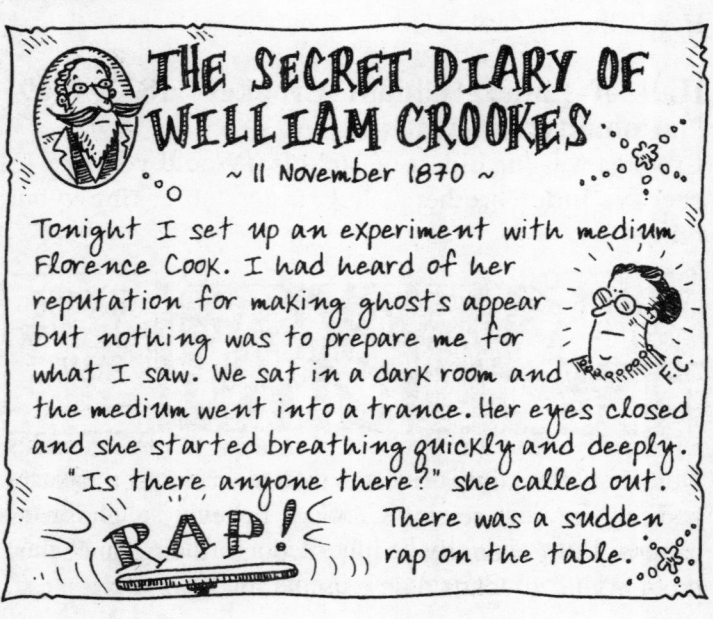

THE SECRET DIARY OF WILLIAM CROOKES

~ 11 November 1870 ~

Tonight I set up an experiment with medium Florence Cook. I had heard of her reputation for making ghosts appear but nothing was to prepare me for what I saw. We sat in a dark room and the medium went into a trance. Her eyes closed and she started breathing quickly and deeply. "Is there anyone there?" she called out. RAP! There was a sudden rap on the table.

"Rap once for yes," demanded the medium.
Bang!
"Are you a spirit?"
Another rap.
"Can you make yourself visible?"
I asked, sounding rather scared.
A cold wind blew through the room. The curtain fluttered and I saw a vague white shape. I blinked in horror - it was a woman with a ghostly pale face. She drifted round the room and I almost managed to touch her unearthly form.
"Who ... what are you?" I gasped. The ghost moved her pale lips. In a faint voice she replied: "My name is Katie, I have a message for you..."
The medium gave a sudden cry. She was pale and sweaty now, and when I looked again the ghost had vanished. So what was the message? I can't wait for the next session!

But had he seen a real ghost? Crookes' fellow scientists were less than impressed with his work as a spectre inspector. Most scientists don't believe in ghosts (I suppose they can see right through them) and they thought that Crookes didn't stand a ghost of a chance of proving anything. Instead the investigation ruined Crookes' image as a sensible scientist.

One scientist who didn't give up on Crookes was John Joseph Thomson (1856–1940), a professor at Cambridge University. JJ, as his friends called him, was useless at experiments and usually broke his equipment (but blowing up the school lab is not always a sign of genius as I'm sure your teacher will point out). Luckily for JJ, when he became a professor he had people to do the hands-on work for him.

JJ thought the "ray" Crookes had reported might be made of tiny blips of energy and to find out more he repeated one of Crookes' tests of using a magnet to bend the ray. He worked out how strong the magnetic force had to be to bend the ray and using complicated maths he calculated the weight of the blips that he thought made up the ray from the angle it was bent. Try doing that for your maths homework!

It turned out the ray really *was* made of tiny blips and they were far lighter than the lightest atoms. Thomson calculated how much energy each blip carried and realized that it matched the lightest atoms. Thomson reckoned rightly that each atom carried at least one and usually far more of the blips. The tiny blips, of course, were electrons.

Bet you never knew!

Electrons make things feel solid. You see, the electrical force made by an electron pushes other electrons away. Solid objects are made of atoms and electrons tightly packed together and so when you squash them they push apart slightly and this makes the object feel solid. Just think – if it wasn't for electrons, sitting on a chair would be like sitting on a slimy school dinner blancmange. You'd sink through it and end up sprawled on your bum.

ELECTRONS – WHO NEEDS 'EM?

SPLOSH!

Electric forces can do lots of other interesting things. They can even make your hair stand on end! And you can find out how in the next chapter – it's bound to set a few sparks flying.

I'D BETTER READ ON...

SHOCKING STATIC ELECTRICITY

Have you ever got an electric shock when stroking the cat or trying on a woolly jumper? Yes? CONGRATULATIONS – you've encountered static electricity. But "static" is definitely the wrong word. After all "static" means staying still...

So you'd think that in static electricity the electrons must be lazing around reading comics. WRONG! Actually, although the electrons aren't all flowing together in an electric current, they're still whizzing around as usual. And in static electricity the electrons also get to fly through the air and make sparks and give scientists nasty shocks and many other exciting things.

Wanna know more?

Before you can understand the secret of static you need to get your brain-box round the electrical forces made by an electron and the atom nucleus. This quickie experiment should help...

Dare you discover ... how electric forces work?

You will need:
Two magnets

What you do:
Put them close together.

What happens...?

a) The magnets spring apart or pull together depending on which way round they are.

b) The magnets are *always* drawn together.

c) The magnets can be placed together but you don't feel any force between them.

Answer: a) When the magnets spring apart you can imagine that they are two electrons. As you may recall from page 35 the electrons are pushed apart by their own forces.

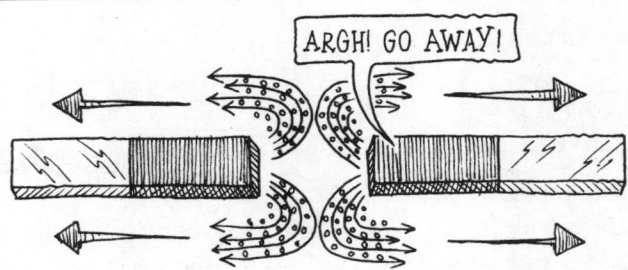

When the magnets pull together you can imagine they're like an electron and a nucleus. This time their forces actually pull them together! (It's all to do with complex interactions between the two forces and no, I don't understand this either.)

LET'S PULL TOGETHER!

SCIENTIFIC NOTEs

1. The force between the nucleus and the electrons actually helps to hold the atom together. To be accurate the force made in the nucleus is made by tiny bits in the nucleus called protons.

2. Actually, the force we call magnetism really is made by electrons! Turn to page 111 if you don't believe me.

SHOCKING EXPRESSIONS

Two scientists are talking...

I GOT A NEGATIVE CHARGE

I GOT A POSITIVE CHARGE

Are they comparing hotel bills?

Answer: No, they're talking about their experiments. To avoid confusion, scientists call the electrical energy carried by the electron a NEGATIVE charge and the electrical energy carried by the nucleus a POSITIVE charge. And you'll be positively thrilled to know these terms will be coming up a lot in the next few pages.

Now here's another glimpse of our pals the Atom family as they show you how they make static electricity...

THE ATOM FAMILY IN... STATIC SUSPENSE

The adventure begins with a scientist who is about to make static electricity.

WE'LL NEED A BALLOON AND A CAT.

1 We rub the balloon on the cat's fur ten times or more.

THAT'S QUITE NICE, ACTUALLY.

2 The Atom family are living on the cat's fluff.

The atoms of the balloon are rubbing electrons free from the atoms of the cat fluff. Here's a close-up view of what happens to them...

3 The electrons are now stranded on the balloon's surface. Of course this means there's a lot of electron energy (negative charge, remember?) on the balloon.

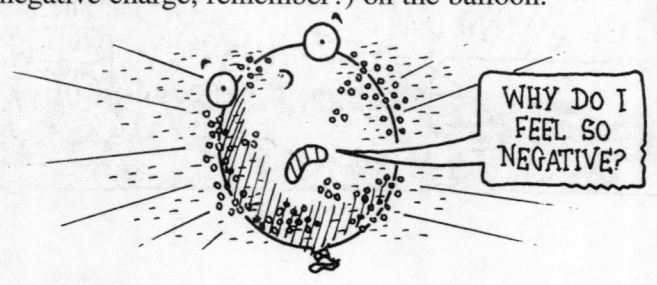

4 The powerful negative charge made by the electrons results in a negative force that tries to pull on the atoms of the cat's fluff.

5 Meanwhile on the cat's fluff, the atoms that are missing their electrons are positively charged. And together their positive electrical forces try to pull the electrons back.

6 These forces make the cat's fur stand up on end as they try to pull the balloon and cat together.

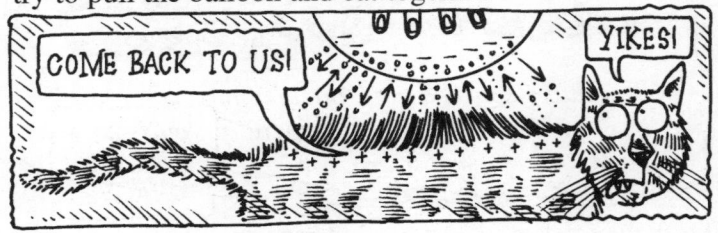

7 When the balloon is brought nearer to the cat's fur the missing electrons are yanked back to their atoms. You can even hear this happen as a quiet crackle.

Bet you never knew!
Ancient Greek boffin Thales of Miletus (624–545 BC) made static electricity by rubbing amber (a kind of fossil tree gum) with an old bit of fur (I hate to think what happened to his pet cat). The amber could then pick up feathers.

HE USED TO PURR WHEN I DID THIS

BIT OF OLD FUR

STROKE!

AMBER

Well, if that's sparked your interest maybe you'd like to try that experiment too (hopefully your cat will manage to keep her fur on).

Or maybe you'd like to try this experiment...

Dare you discover ... how to make clingfilm move?

You will need:

Two pieces of new clingfilm 10 cm x 2 cm

A clean dry comb

Blutak

Some clean hair – you might possibly find some on your head. (If not maybe you could ask the cat nicely.)

What you do:

1 Hold a piece of clingfilm in each hand. Try to bring the two pieces of clingfilm together. Notice what happens.

2 Stick a piece of clingfilm to the end of a table so the clingfilm hangs downwards. Now comb your hair quickly and strongly four times. Quickly point the teeth of the comb towards the strip of clingfilm and hold it close but not touching. Notice what happens.

Well, what does happen?

a) The two pieces of clingfilm are drawn together. But the clingfilm doesn't want to touch the comb.

b) The pieces of clingfilm don't want to touch but the clingfilm does want to touch the comb.

c) A spark flies between the clingfilm and comb but nothing happens between the two bits of clingfilm.

Answer: b) The atoms of the clingfilm are short of electrons. This means they are positively charged and give out positive forces. Remember how two negative forces push each other away? Well, two positive forces also push against each other and that's why the pieces of clingfilm move apart. The comb rips electrons off your hairs and the force from these electrons (negative charge) pulls in the positively charged atoms in the clingfilm.

SUPER STATIC

Static electricity is shockingly useful. For example, did you know that photocopiers use static electricity to copy documents?

Here's what happens...

1 A bright light shines on the picture to be copied and its image reflects on to a mirror and through a lens on to a metal drum. Got all that?

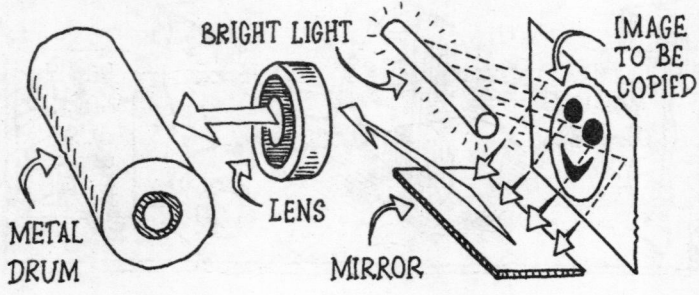

BRIGHT LIGHT

IMAGE TO BE COPIED

METAL DRUM

LENS

MIRROR

2 The drum is coated with a substance called selenium (see-leen-nee-um) that gives off electrons when light shines on it.

3 This means the areas of the drum that get most light (in other words the brighter parts of the original) lose negatively charged electrons and become positively charged. Yep – it pays to think positive!

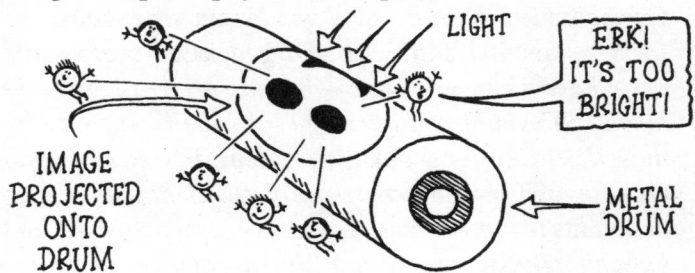

4 Positively charged toner powder gets sprinkled on the drum and sticks to the dark areas which are still negatively charged. (Hope you're taking notes on all this.)

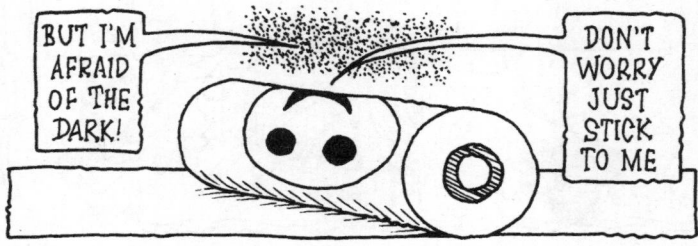

5 Paper now goes over the drum and the toner sticks to the paper to make a copy of the original picture.

I NEED ANOTHER 300 COPIES

PHOTOCOPIED IMAGE

ERK! ARE YOU **POSITIVE?**

PAPER

6 A heater softens the toner and squashes it on to the paper.
7 *Finito* – one perfect photocopy!

Bet you never knew!
The photocopier was invented by US inventor Chester Carlson (1906–1968) who made his first copy in 1938 using tiny statically charged moss seeds. He must have been ex-static – ha ha. After all, it had taken four years of tinkering with smelly chemicals that filled Chester's flat with rotten farty egg whiffs. On the way his marriage broke up, his research assistant resigned, and countless firms refused to back him. But after more than 20 years of improvements photocopiers became popular and Chester became a multi-millionaire.

HE STARTED WITH JUST ONE DOLLAR BILL

THEN HE PHOTOCOPIED IT 3 MILLION TIMES!

But Chester's discovery wouldn't have been possible without the work of earlier scientists who investigated static electricity. Did you know some of the most shocking static electricity experiments were performed by a scientist called Stephen Gray (1666–1736)? And can you believe he conducted these experiments on ... helpless children. Now read on for the whole shocking story...

A SHOCKING STORY

London 1730

"You new here?" asked Joe.

The thin little girl with the dirty face nodded dumbly.

"And that's why you were following me about just now?"

The girl nodded again.

Joe chewed his lip as he pondered what to do. He didn't want some little kid following him around all day but he could see the new girl was scared of being in the children's home.

They sat down cross-legged on the bare dusty floor and he asked her name.

"Hannah." the girl whispered as if scared to raise her voice.

"Well Hannah, it's not so bad in here. Look, I tell you what, here's a story to take your mind off it."

The girl leaned forward expectantly.

"Is it a true story?"

"It's true all right," said Joe. "I was working for this scientist and guess what – he did experiments on me!"

"You mean it – actual science experiments?" asked the girl.

"Stop asking questions and I'll tell you. It happened one day when this old scientist geezer came to the children's home and asked for a kid to help him with his work. He was fat and rich and his name was Mr Gray, Mr Stephen Gray.

"Well, the supervisor collared me and took me to Mr Gray's place. Real posh it was with heavy curtains and a smell of polish and silver on the table. And guess what? Mr Gray gave me a slap-up meal! Said I looked as if I could do with feeding! I had beef and onions and dumplings and potatoes and gravy and three helpings of pudding. Heaven it was."

Joe glanced at Hannah and sure enough she was drooling. "I want to work for Mr Gray too!" she said hungrily.

"Mr Gray's servant came in. She was this really old grim-looking woman named Mrs Salter, and she said 'If the boy eats any more he will break his cords.' *Cords*? I thought. Well, that made me a bit scared. Maybe this Gray bloke was going to tie me up and then he was going to *kill* me. *Maybe he was going to chop my body up and eat me!*

"Mr Gray must have seen my expression because he patted me on the head and said 'Don't worry Joseph, it won't hurt much.'"

"Did it hurt?" asked Hannah fearfully.

"Well," said Joe bravely, "I'm still alive, ain't I? Anyway, Mr Gray took me into this room and I was gobsmacked. It was stacked with all these scientific gadgets, like glass rods, a set of metal balls – I didn't know what they was for – and flasks and telescopes.

"Mr Gray picked up a telescope. 'I used to be an astronomer till I did my back in bending over that telescope. Well, now I'm into electricity.'

"'What's electricity?' I asked, and Mr Gray told me all about this weird force. Well, don't ask me to explain it. I couldn't get me head round it.

"'Is that anything to do with them metal balls?'
I mumbled stupidly.

"'Ah yes – interesting they are,' said Mr Gray. 'I
proved that it doesn't matter if a ball is hollow or solid
– it can still store the same amount of static electricity. I
think the force must be stored on the outside of the ball.
And I learnt how to electrify objects and that brings us to
our experiment.'

"He nodded to Mrs Salter and quick as a flash she
looped silk cords round my shoulders and legs and waist.
I was too surprised to say anything. But I yelled loud
enough when they hoisted me into the air. I thought me
dinner was going to come up all over the floor.

"Mr Gray put his finger on his lips. 'Don't shout,
Joseph. We're only going to electrify you.'

"'But I don't want to be electrified!' I yelled.

"Mr Gray looked troubled. 'But it's for science, Joseph
and anyway, I'll pay you sixpence.'

"Well, that settled it. I'd have done it for a penny.

"I felt really weird like I was swimming – or maybe
flying in the air with my arms outstretched on either side.
Mrs Salter rubbed my clothes real hard with a glass rod

– blimey was she strong! Meanwhile Mr Gray put some tiny bits of paper on three metal plates on the ground under me.

"'Now, Joseph,' said Mr Gray, 'reach out your hands and pick up those bits of paper.'

"'I can't do that!' I cried. My arms were too short to reach the paper and just to show him I tried. And something magic happened. The bits of paper flew towards my fingers – they looked just like confetti at a wedding.

"'Bravo!' shouted Mr Gray clapping his big fat hands and I was so chuffed I gave him a mid-air bow.

"'Can I come down now?' I asked. Mr Gray nodded and his servant reached out to untie me. There was a sudden crack and I felt a sharp pain. It was agony!

"'Oh dear,' said Mr Gray, 'you seem to have received an electric shock. Never mind here's your sixpence.'"

"You really got a whole sixpence?" asked Hannah, her eyes widening.

"Yes," said Joseph proudly.

"That's a lot of money. I've never seen one. Can I see it? Can I touch it?"

Joe held the shining silver coin and the girl touched his hand.

"Ow!" she yelled. "You stung me!"

"Don't worry," said the boy with a careless wave of his hand. "It's just an electric shock."

Dare you discover ... how Joe picked up the paper?

You will need:

A piece of polystyrene (to represent Joe)
A woollen jumper or pair of nylon tights
A few tiny bits of paper (the circles of paper from a hole punch are ideal)

What you do:

1 Rub the polystyrene on the fabric a few times.
2 Hold the polystyrene near the bits of paper.

What happens?

a) The bits of paper jump on to the polystyrene.
b) You get an electric shock.
c) The polystyrene is pulled gently towards the paper.

Answer: a) When Joe was rubbed with the rod, the glass removed electrons from his clothes and skin. This gave the atoms that made them up a positive charge. The electrons in the paper were pulled towards him and this pulled the paper too. When Mrs Salter touched Joe electrons from her skin also rushed on to Joe and gave him a shock.

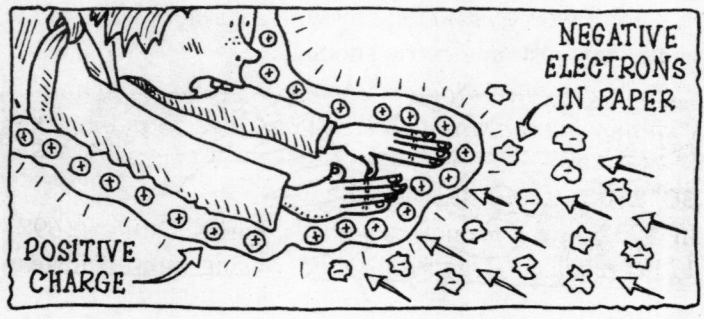

Oh, by the way, Hannah didn't get a shock because Joe was still electrified – it's just that skin sometimes collects an electric charge (for example when you walk over a carpet). That's why you can get a shock by touching people.

IT'S SUCH A SHOCK TO MEET YOU!

Bet you never knew!
Besides electrifying a boy, Gray found he could electrify hair and feathers. It's even said that he sent electricity along gold-painted cow guts. (Don't ask me what he was doing painting cow guts gold!)

SIXPENCE? I'LL WANT A LOT MORE THAN THAT, PAL!

He investigated different conductors (and if you don't know what they are check back to page 28 at once!).

SO WHAT HAPPENED NEXT?

In 1732 brave French scientist Charles Dufay (1698–1739) repeated Gray's experiment using himself instead of a boy. According to one story, when Dufay's assistant tried to touch him, the scientist got a shock that burnt through his waistcoat.

The scientist found the experience thrilling – or should I say electrifying (ha ha) – and insisted on repeating it in the dark so that he could see the spark made by the static electricity.

Dufay's experiments proved that anything could be electrically charged by rubbing except for liquids, metals and a grisly lump of meat. Dufay didn't realize this, but since these substances are good conductors of electricity, electrons tend to run through them rather than sticking around to build up a powerful negative electric charge.

Within a few years scientists developed brilliant machines that could make and store static electricity if it was needed for experiments. (In those days mains electricity hadn't been invented.) Would you fancy owning one of these machines? Of course you wouldn't use it to give nasty shocks to your teacher/brother/sister would you? WOULD YOU?

A SHOCKING CATALOGUE

Amaze your friends and shock your enemies with this incredible range of static electricity generators from SPARKY-JOLT LTD.

You'll love a Leyden Jar!

Developed by Dutch scientist Pieter van Musschenbroek (1692–1761) this stylish jar stores static electricity.

METAL BALL

METAL CHAIN

WATER IN GLASS JAR

STATIC ELECTRICITY PASSES DOWN METAL CHAIN INTO JAR AND CAN'T ESCAPE.

SHOCKING SAFETY WARNING!

Touch the metal ball at the top and you'll get a painful electric shock. This shocking discovery was made accidentally by Musschenbroek's assistant. Ouch!

D'YOU MEAN THIS BIT?... ARGH!

X-RAY VIEW OF GLASS JAR WITH METAL LINING BOTH INSIDE AND OUT

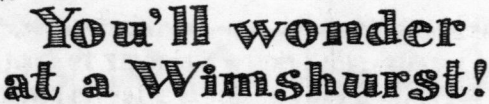

You'll wonder at a Wimshurst!

Named after its inventor James Wimshurst (1832-1903), this wonderful piece of electric wizardry makes static electricity when the glass and metal discs rub together.

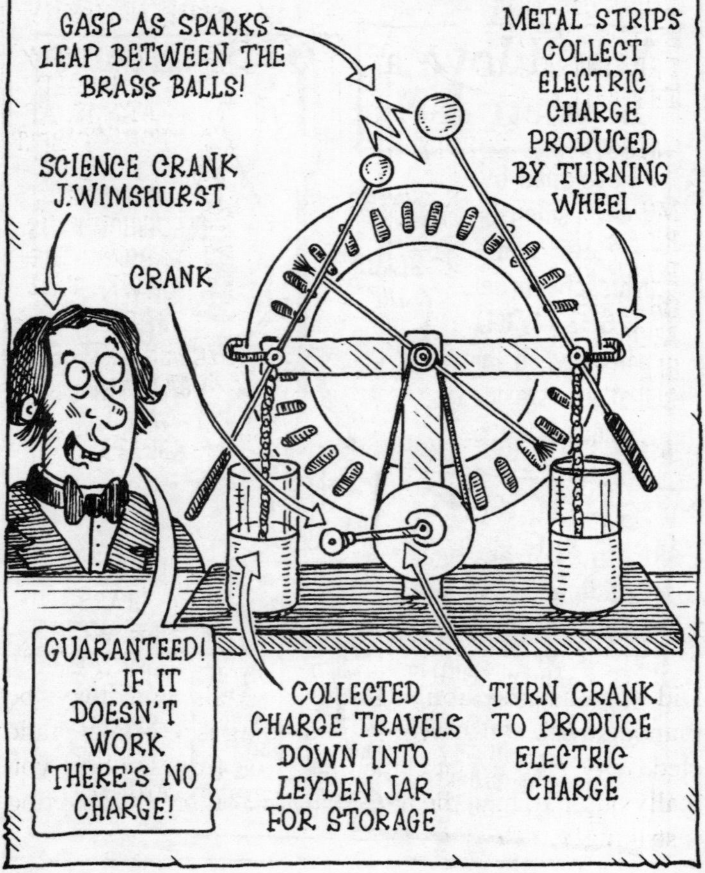

GASP AS SPARKS LEAP BETWEEN THE BRASS BALLS!

METAL STRIPS COLLECT ELECTRIC CHARGE PRODUCED BY TURNING WHEEL

SCIENCE CRANK J.WIMSHURST

CRANK

GUARANTEED!
...IF IT DOESN'T WORK THERE'S NO CHARGE!

COLLECTED CHARGE TRAVELS DOWN INTO LEYDEN JAR FOR STORAGE

TURN CRANK TO PRODUCE ELECTRIC CHARGE

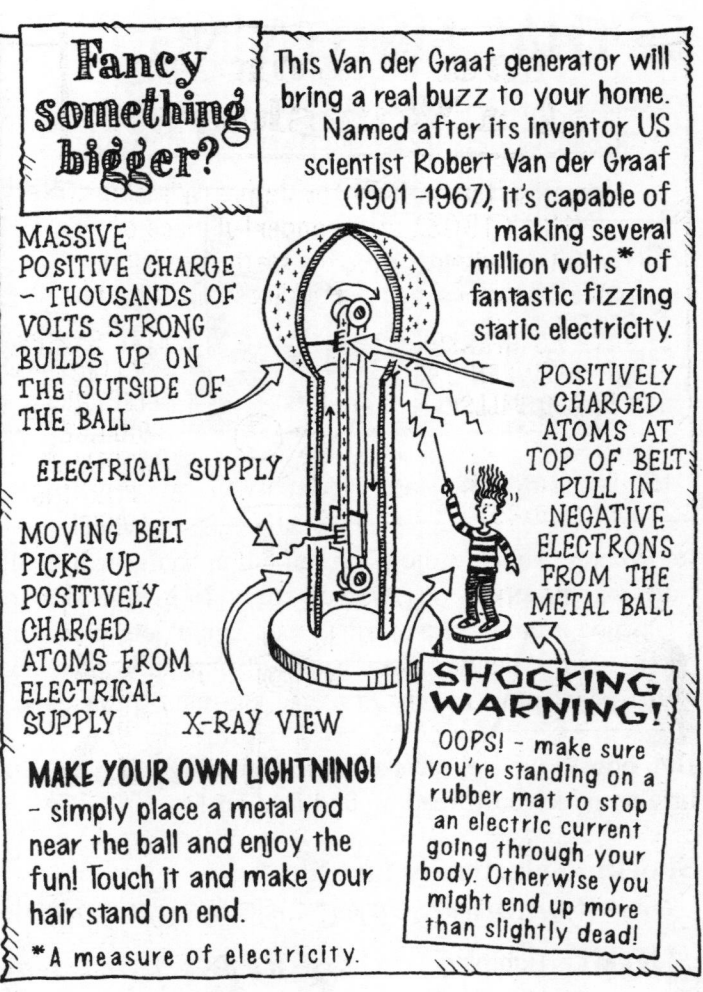

Fancy something bigger?

This Van der Graaf generator will bring a real buzz to your home. Named after its inventor US scientist Robert Van der Graaf (1901-1967), it's capable of making several million volts* of fantastic fizzing static electricity.

MASSIVE POSITIVE CHARGE - THOUSANDS OF VOLTS STRONG BUILDS UP ON THE OUTSIDE OF THE BALL

ELECTRICAL SUPPLY

MOVING BELT PICKS UP POSITIVELY CHARGED ATOMS FROM ELECTRICAL SUPPLY

X-RAY VIEW

POSITIVELY CHARGED ATOMS AT TOP OF BELT PULL IN NEGATIVE ELECTRONS FROM THE METAL BALL

SHOCKING WARNING!

OOPS! - make sure you're standing on a rubber mat to stop an electric current going through your body. Otherwise you might end up more than slightly dead!

MAKE YOUR OWN LIGHTNING! - simply place a metal rod near the ball and enjoy the fun! Touch it and make your hair stand on end.

*A measure of electricity.

Did anyone mention lightning? Well, you may be thunderstruck to discover that lightning is a form of static electricity. And if that came like a bolt from the blue you really ought to read the next chapter. You're bound to find it striking!

LETHAL LIGHTNING

TEACHER'S TEA-BREAK TEASER

Try this shockingly tricky question on your teacher...

Clue: it's to do with static electricity.

Answer: Sometimes when oil tanker holds are being cleaned with high pressure hoses, atoms in the water rub together really fast. This makes static electricity that results in lightning sparks. The sparks can set fire to petrol fumes in the hold and blow up the tanker!

But how do water drops make lightning? If you're a bright spark you'll read on and find out!

Shocking electricity fact file

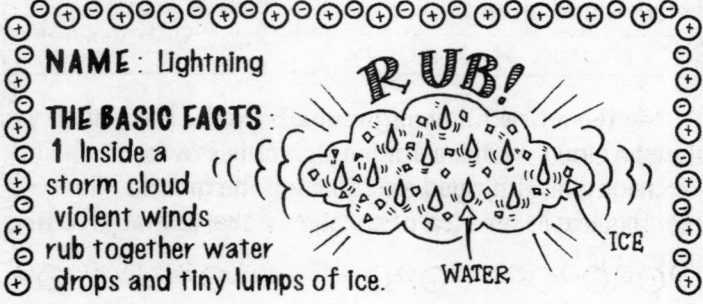

NAME: Lightning

THE BASIC FACTS:
1 Inside a storm cloud violent winds rub together water drops and tiny lumps of ice.

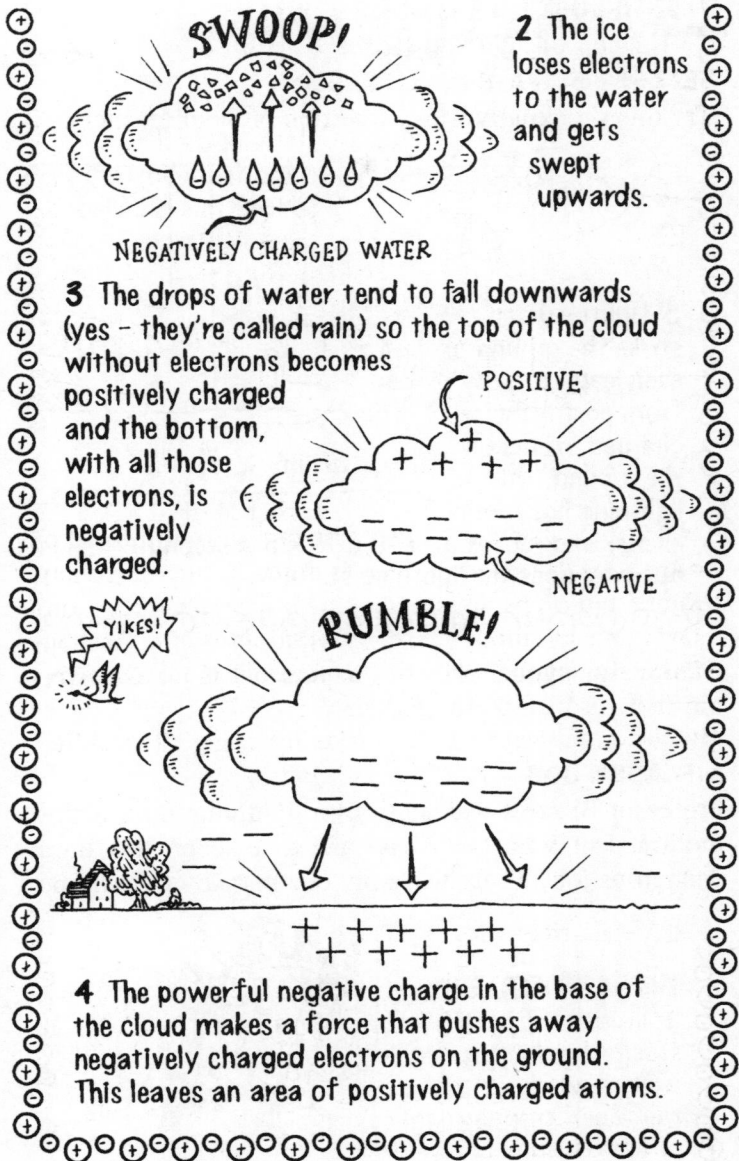

SWOOP!

NEGATIVELY CHARGED WATER

2 The ice loses electrons to the water and gets swept upwards.

3 The drops of water tend to fall downwards (yes – they're called rain) so the top of the cloud without electrons becomes positively charged and the bottom, with all those electrons, is negatively charged.

POSITIVE

+ + + + +

– – – – –

NEGATIVE

YIKES!

RUMBLE!

+ + + + + + + + +

4 The powerful negative charge in the base of the cloud makes a force that pushes away negatively charged electrons on the ground. This leaves an area of positively charged atoms.

THE SHOCKING DETAILS:

1 A bolt of lightning strikes at 1,600 km a second.

BOOM!

2 Lightning can flash inside the cloud from bottom to top. This is called sheet lightning.

CRACK!

3 Lightning can strike the ground or even leap upwards from positively charged atoms on the ground. This lightning has more energy and moves at 140,000 km a second! But why does the lightning strike?

+ + + + +

Obviously anyone who tries to find out is taking a very big risk – a VERY BIG RISK.

A FLASHY JOB

Professor Buzzoff wanted to film lightning in ultra-slow motion. But who could she ask to take on this ultra-dangerous job? There was only one person in the frame.

LEAVE IT OUT, PROF – I'M NOT DOING NO MORE SHRINKING!

I assured Andy that no shrinking was required and that I would join him on the shoot. After a brief discussion about money he agreed to take the job.

I took the job cos I'm a dab hand with camcorders. I do weddings, funerals, whatever (all offers considered). So filming lightning seemed a cinch - I mean, it's all over in a flash, innit? So there I was filming the clouds and waiting for a flash of lightning and I cricked me neck looking up and got a right soaking. "Water rotten job!" I said to meself...

Andy didn't have too long to wait. When the negative charge at the bottom of the cloud reaches a certain power, the lightning appears as a bright blob under the cloud. This is actually a ball of negatively charged electrons.

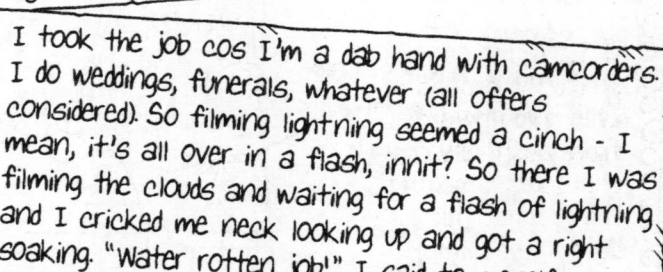

A stream of electrons flashes downwards, drawn by the pulling force of the positively charged atoms on the ground. What we call the streak of lightning marks the path taken by the electrons through the atoms of the air. On the way, the lightning hits atoms in the air making them give off heat and light. The lightning appears much brighter.

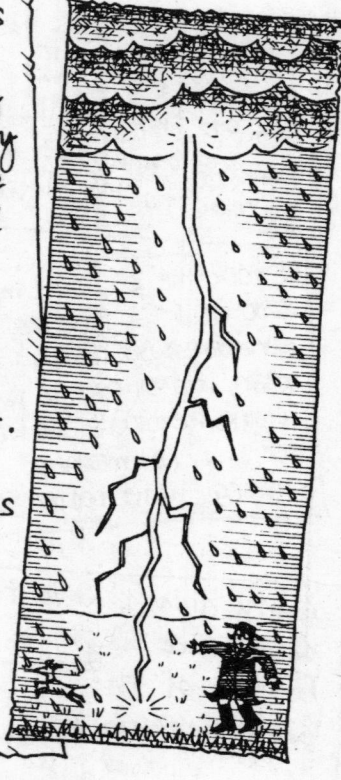

The lightning hits the ground. The bolt of lightning is up to 1 cm wide.

The lightning heats up the air around it very quickly, then it cools again very quickly. This creates shock waves in the air that our ears hear as thunder. As Andy was taking this picture I became aware that another bolt of lightning was forming in the cloud under which he was standing. . .

Did someone say "All over in a flash"? Didn't realize it would be over for _me_ in a flash. I was too busy filming the Prof (who was jumping up and down pointing to something high above me) to see the next streak coming. Fast as lightning it was. . . . Argh!

THIS IS A NEWS FLASH. ANDY MANN HAS BEEN STRUCK BY LIGHTNING! WE'LL BE HEADING OVER TO THE HOSPITAL IN A FEW MINUTES TO CHECK ON HIS CONDITION.

So YOU'RE not scared of lightning? And you fancy making some lightning in the comfort of your own home? OK – here's how; but try not to fire your lightning at little brothers or sisters or the cat – Tiddles has suffered enough!

Dare you discover ... how to make lightning?

You will need:

A radio with the aerial extended

A balloon

A thick jumper (no not a stupid kangaroo – I mean a *woollen* jumper). A woollen rug or scarf will also do.

What you do:

1 Wait until it gets dark or sit in the coal cellar with the lights out. This experiment works best in complete darkness.

2 Rub the balloon on the wool about ten times. Put it near or touching the aerial.

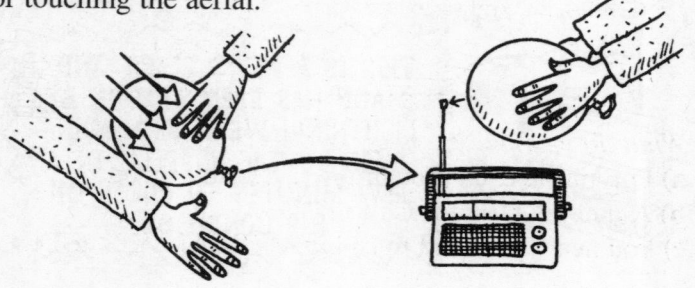

What do you see?
a) The radio comes on without you touching it – it's spooky.

...AS I WAS SAYING ON PAGE 63, ANDY MANN IS IN A STATE OF SHOCK!

b) An eerie glowing ball of light appears and floats round the room – scaring the life out of your pet budgie.
c) Tiny sparks.

Dare you discover ... how to hear lightning?
You will need:
The same equipment from the first experiment

What you do:
1 Switch the radio to AM and make sure it's not tuned to any station.
2 Turn the volume down very low.
3 Repeat the first experiment and listen.

HMMM!

What do you hear?
a) Pop music even though the radio isn't tuned.
b) A quiet pop (but it isn't music).
c) You hear the sound in **b)** but it's REALLY LOUD.

Hall of fame: Benjamin Franklin (1706–1790)
Nationality: American

Benjamin Franklin packed so much into his life it's a wonder that he had time to eat or sleep. He was a...

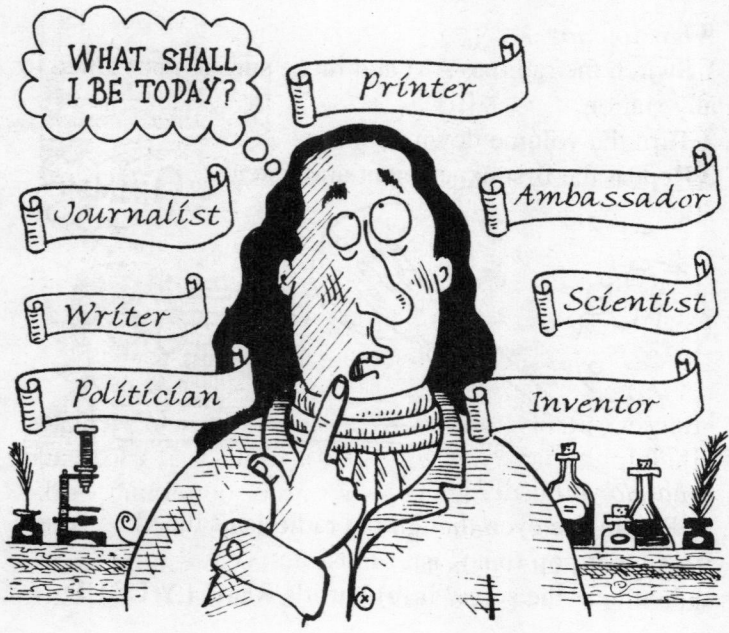

Young Ben was the youngest of 17 children – can you imagine how terrible that must have been? Sixteen older brothers and sisters bossing you around and getting their baths first so you have to make do with their filthy scummy bath water? Ben had just three years of schooling but that must have seemed too long because he hated maths and failed all his tests. But worse was to follow – he had to spend the next seven years working 12 hours a day for no pay for one of his older brothers. Would you swap school for this?

Ben learnt the art of printing in his brother's shop. Then suddenly at the ripe old age of 15, he found himself a *newspaper editor.*

Ben's brother had been locked up for saying rude things about important people in the newspaper he printed. So Ben took charge of the newspaper and that must have been really cool. He could have printed wicked articles about computer games and rollerblading. If they'd been invented then, that is.

Ben eventually fell out with his brother and went to Philadelphia, arriving with just a small loaf of bread to eat and no money at all. Luckily, he soon found work as a printer and became pals with the British Governor who ruled the city in those days. But the Governor played a shocking trick on young Ben. He sent him to London to learn more about printing but after Ben set sail he realized that the Governor hadn't given him the money he'd promised.

Ben's big break came in 1732. He was back in Pennsylvania after a spell as a printer in London and he published an almanac – a sort of calendar with wise sayings. It was an instant smash-hit! The sayings are so well-known and wise you might have heard your granny use them...

Actually, Ben Franklin *didn't* take his own advice. When he lived in Paris in the 1770s he enjoyed lots of late-night parties, but he still remained healthy and rich, and as you're about to find out he was wise too. Mention this to your granny ... *if you dare*!

Ben made so much money he retired from printing and got interested in science and inventing things. Amongst other things he invented a new kind of wood-burning stove, extendable grippers for taking things off high shelves (and raiding the biscuit jar) and a musical instrument made of a glass bowl with a wet rim. The glass bowl turned round and if you touched the rim with your fingertips it made a sound.

Bet you never knew!
Benjamin Franklin was interested in everything – including farting. He set up a competition to discover a drug that could be mixed with food to make pleasant perfumed farts. Although such a discovery is not to be sniffed at, sadly there were no winners.

But Ben's greatest discoveries were to do with electricity. In 1746 he went to a science talk on electricity and he was so thrilled by it that he bought up all the lecturer's equipment and started doing his own experiments.

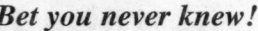

Bet you never knew!
Franklin was a great scientist and he wasn't afraid to suggest new ideas. He was the first to suggest that static electricity might be based on positive and negative charges. (He didn't have too much proof of that but he was right of course.) Unfortunately Ben reckoned that electricity flowed from positive areas to negative areas. He was wrong – negatively charged electrons flow towards the positively charged atoms.

Like other experimenters, Franklin made sparks from electrically charged Leyden jars and the sight of the spark and the tiny crack it made reminded him of lightning. Could lightning be a giant electrical spark? Ben wondered. And if so, how could he prove it?

His first plan was to put a metal rod on top of a church steeple and draw off some of the electric charge from a thunder cloud. But the church steeple he had in mind hadn't been built and within a few months a French scientist followed Ben's plan and performed the test. It proved that lightning was indeed made of electricity – but it was really dangerous. If lightning hit the metal pole anyone close by would meet a shocking end. As Russian scientists Georg Richmann found out to his cost...

The St. Petersburg Times

RUSSIAN RICHMANN ROASTED!

by ace reporter Hall D. Frontpage

Top scientist Georg Richmann has been struck dead by lightning. The Russian boffin was seen rushing home to perform a dangerous experiment. Richmann, 42, wanted to measure the strength of the electric charge of a bolt of lightning. Today the Times talks to his long-time friend Mikhail Lomonosov.

"I tried to warn him. I said 'Georg, Franklin says electricity can jump from the lightning rod.' But did he listen? Silly idiot only put a metal ruler up close to the rod. He had a thread on the ruler and he wanted to measure how far the charge would lift the thread up.

"Yeah - it was a shocking error!

A giant spark shot out of the rod. It bounced off the ruler and struck Georg dead. I was thunderstruck! So was Georg and well, when I saw what the bolt had done to Georg, I bolted too. A pretty sight it was not."

Scorched shape in carpet shocks servants

By that time, Benjamin Franklin had conducted his own experiment on lightning. Of course, it was extremely dangerous, as you've just discovered. So did Ben share Richmann's fate and end up a fried Franklin-furter?

71

BENJAMIN FRANKLIN'S NOTEBOOK

1 October 1752

Dark overcast day, really thundery, looks like rain. Great! It's ideal weather for my kite flying test. I've made a special kite from an old silk handkerchief.

HANDKERCHIEF (BIT OF DRIED SNOT)

STRING WITH KEY ON THE END

METAL SPIKE TIED TO KITE

SILK THREAD (SILK CAN'T CARRY AN ELECTRICAL CHARGE)

My plan is to fly the kite in a thunderstorm and pick up some electricity from the clouds, which will run down the string and charge up the key. But will it work? It's not the danger of getting killed that bothers me — it's getting killed in public. I think I'd die of embarrassment. So it's just me and my son and we're going to a nice quiet field where no one can see us.

Three hours later. . .

This is really frustrating. There's no decent thunderclouds blowing our way — my lad's really bored. Oh well, better give up. No — hold on, here comes one.

72

Now to get this kite in the air! Wow! The threads on the string are standing on end — I figure they're electrified. I'm electrified too — with excitement. Let's put my hand near that key — better not touch it — OUCH!!! I got a painful electric shock. I'm so happy YES! YES! YES! Let's put a Leyden jar up to the key. There's a spark jumping into the jar — it's the static electricity I've been studying. Well that proves it. I've managed to draw electricity from the clouds and I'm still alive!

HORRIBLE HEALTH WARNING!

Franklin and his son were dead lucky — but they could have been unlucky and dead. If the kite had been struck by lightning then Ben would have been a has-Ben sorry, a has-been. Don't ever, EVER fly a kite in a thunderstorm or near high-voltage power lines.

Following this success Ben was soon hard at work designing an invention that would prevent lightning from striking your house and giving the cat a nervous breakdown.

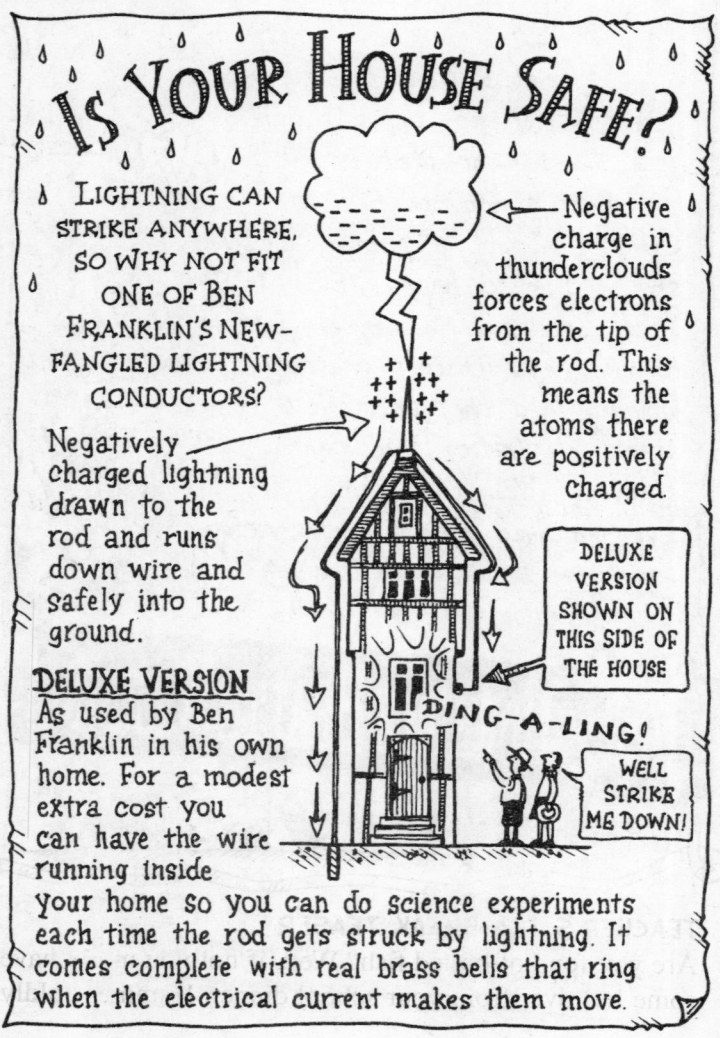

Ben's discoveries made him famous. In those days North America was ruled by Britain but in 1776 Ben helped write the American Declaration of Independence. (It's said his co-authors had to keep an eye on Ben to stop him putting in silly jokes.) Ben became America's ambassador in France and won French support for the new nation.

Now back to lightning...

Bet you never knew!

In Victorian times some people carried lightning conductors on the end of their umbrellas. The device consisted of a metal rod on the spike of the umbrella, with a metal wire attached down which the lightning would run (and hopefully away from the petrified person holding the brolly). It worked in the same way as a full-sized conductor and was designed to keep its owner safe in a storm. But was this a smart idea? I mean, these umbrellas attracted lightning – would you put up with one?

WARNING!
PURCHASERS WERE ADVISED NOT TO USE THE METAL WIRE TO WALK THE DOG

TEACHER'S TEA-BREAK TEASER
Are you fond of boiled fish? Well, if not you might have some left over from your school dinner. Hammer boldly

on the staffroom door. When it squeaks open, smile sweetly, and shove the revolting fish dish under your teacher's nose saying...

I WAS JUST WONDERING IF THIS IS WHAT HAPPENS TO A FISH IF THE SEA IS STRUCK BY LIGHTNING?

FISHY PONG

Answer: It depends on how close the fish was. As you know, electricity can travel though water. Any fish close to the strike would get a massive electric shock and the heat from the strike would probably boil it too. The heat turns the water to steam and makes an explosion that can be heard underwater for many kilometres. Any divers close by would probably be deafened.

BOOM!

COD HELP US!

LIGHTNING ADDITION QUIZ

This quiz is really easy. In fact, you can probably go through it like greased lightning, ha ha. All you have to do is to add up the numbers.

1) How many times does lightning strike somewhere in the world in a second? The answer = 14 + 86

2) What is the record number of times a person has been struck by lightning? The answer = answer **1)** – 93

3) Lightning is hotter than the surface of the sun. By how many times? The answer = answer **2)** – 1.5

4) In 1995 lightning struck a football match. How many were blasted by a single bolt? The answer = answer **3)** + 11.5

Answers:

1) 100. Luckily it isn't the same spot – after all, lightning never strikes twice in the same place, so they say. Mind you, some people do seem to get more than their fair share of lightning strikes…

2) 7. US park ranger Roy Sullivan was struck *seven* times. That's at seven *different* times – not all on the same day. That really would have put him off his tea. In 1942 he lost his toenail (he must have been cut to the quick); in 1969 his eyebrows were burnt off; the following year his shoulder was burnt; in 1972 and 1973 his hair caught fire – "hair we go again", as he might have said; in 1976 his ankle was injured; and in 1977 his chest was burnt ... but I expect he was getting used to it by then.

3) 5.5. Lightning can be 30,000°C (54,000° F) and the surface of the sun is a rather tepid 5,530° C (9,980° F). No wonder a lightning strike can melt solid rock – and that's not your auntie's rock cakes we're talking about here. (They'd probably survive intact.)

4) 17. The victims were all parents and children from Kent, England. They all survived, but some of them suffered nasty burns.

Now, how about poor old Andy Mann – is he badly burned too? Is he *still alive*? Let's grab a bunch of grapes and rush over to the hospital.

A CHECK ON ANDY MANN

The good news is that Andy is sitting up in his hospital bed and watching the darts final on TV. The bad news is that he's suffered a few injuries.

PATIENT RECORD

NAME: Andy Mann   **Age:** 35

GENERAL NOTE: This patient has a severe attitude problem. He has been complaining loudly about a Professor Buzzoff.

SYMPTOMS: The patient shows signs of having been struck by lightning.

1 There are burn holes in his clothes and his sideburns are frazzled.

2 A leaf-like pattern of dead flesh on his skin shows where the lightning has burnt through it.

3 Since it's easier for the lightning to run over his body than to push through his skin and enter his body, this is what happened. Bleeding between his toes shows where the electricity left his skin and entered the ground.

Although the lightning was hot enough to kill him, as is common in a lightning strike, it didn't stay long enough to do fatal damage.

4 The patient was knocked out for about a minute. This was caused by the force of air pushed ahead of the lightning bolt. He was lucky not to suffer broken bones.

<u>PROGNOSIS:</u> If the lightning had actually gone through the patient's body the shock of being struck by lightning might have made his heart stop and resulted in death. As it is – he's lucky to be alive but should make a full recovery.

HUH ~ ME LUCKY? ME BOILERSUIT'S RUINED, ME EARRING'S MELTED, AND THERE'S AN OLE IN ME 'AT. AND I BET ME SIDEBURNS WON'T GROW BACK NEITHER. TELL THE PROF I WANT DAMAGES AND DANGER MONEY!

So you've been warned. Electricity can do shocking things to the human body. Oh, so you want to know more? Well, if you want to check out the gruesome details you can – just carry on reading...

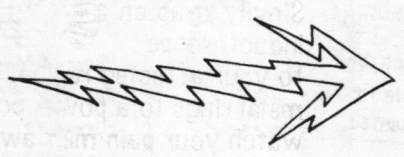

SHOCK TREATMENT

Getting a massive surge of electricity running through your body is no picnic, as we've seen, but that didn't stop certain doctors using electricity to help people get better. Are you shocked? You will be. We'll be back after the commercial break...

ELECTRIC ADVERTS

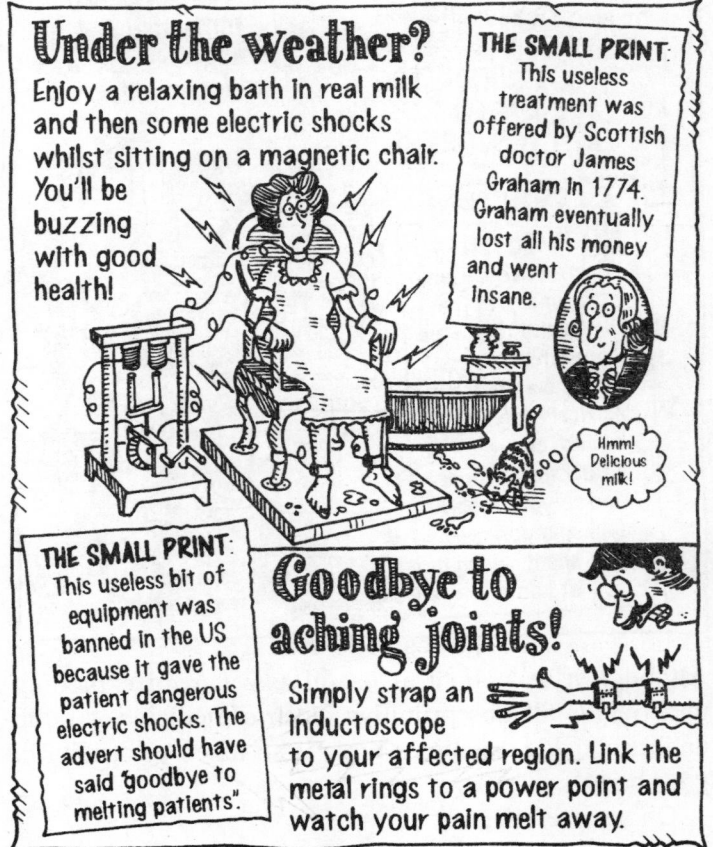

Under the weather?

Enjoy a relaxing bath in real milk and then some electric shocks whilst sitting on a magnetic chair. You'll be buzzing with good health!

THE SMALL PRINT: This useless treatment was offered by Scottish doctor James Graham in 1774. Graham eventually lost all his money and went insane.

Hmm! Delicious milk!

THE SMALL PRINT: This useless bit of equipment was banned in the US because it gave the patient dangerous electric shocks. The advert should have said "goodbye to melting patients".

Goodbye to aching joints!

Simply strap an inductoscope to your affected region. Link the metal rings to a power point and watch your pain melt away.

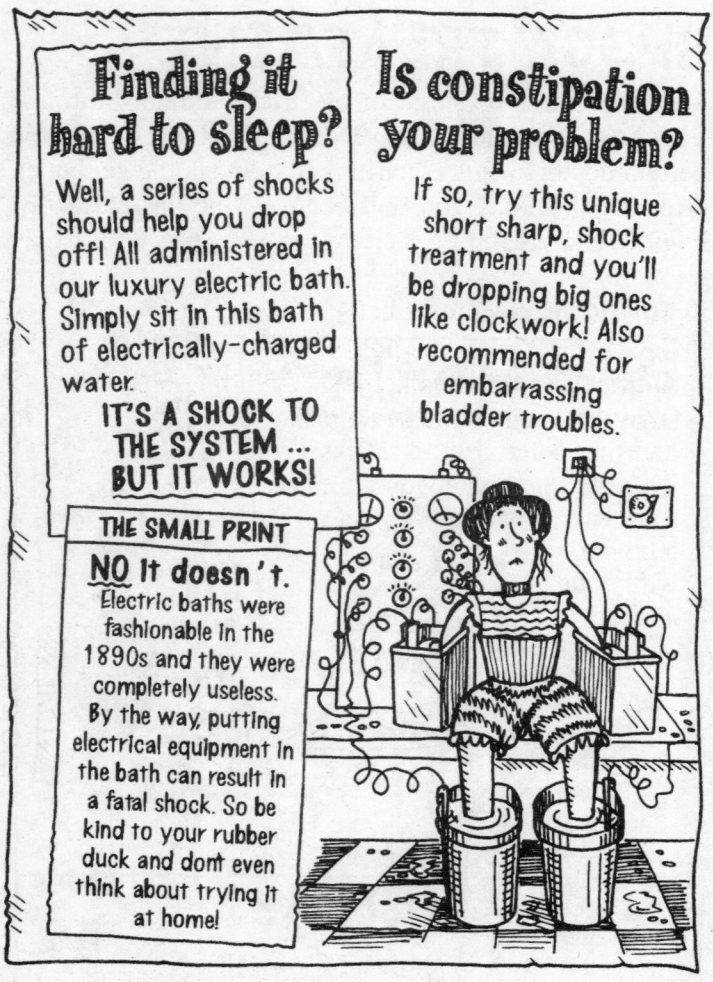

Finding it hard to sleep?

Well, a series of shocks should help you drop off! All administered in our luxury electric bath. Simply sit in this bath of electrically-charged water.

IT'S A SHOCK TO THE SYSTEM ... BUT IT WORKS!

THE SMALL PRINT

NO It doesn't. Electric baths were fashionable in the 1890s and they were completely useless. By the way, putting electrical equipment in the bath can result in a fatal shock. So be kind to your rubber duck and dont even think about trying it at home!

Is constipation your problem?

If so, try this unique short sharp, shock treatment and you'll be dropping big ones like clockwork! Also recommended for embarrassing bladder troubles.

Although it was about as useful as a pair of exploding underpants, all this primitive electric medicine is quite understandable, seeing as there is so much electricity in your body.

Oh yes there is...

Shocking electricity fact file

NAME: Electricity in the body

THE BASIC FACTS: **1** Your body contains enough electricity to light the fairy lights on a Christmas tree. No, DON'T wire your little brother/sister to the lights and check this detail. The electricity is found mainly in the nerves.

2 A nerve signal is made by positively charged atoms that flood into the nerve.

NERVOUS SYSTEM

NERVE SIGNAL

THE SHOCKING DETAILS:
Some animals sense electric forces. And some people and animals have much more than their fair share of electricity.

HEY! YOU'VE GOT MORE THAN YOUR FAIR SHARE!

BATTERY

THIS IS NOTHING! READ ON AND YOU'LL BE REALLY SHOCKED...

THE HORRIBLE SCIENCE LIVING ELECTRICITY COMPETITION

Class one - Nasty Nature

Yep, it's true that some animals can sense electrical forces - and the bad news is that this can make them vicious. Here are the most horrible examples...

3rd Prize:
HAMMERHEAD SHARK

3rd

Lives: Warm oceans

Sharks like the hammerhead can sense the electrical pulses in the nerves of their victims. To do this the hammerhead uses senses in its oddly-shaped bonce. But the shark is too good at its work because it also senses the electrical waves given off by submarine microphone cables (used to listen out for other subs) and attacks them! With shocking results ... for the shark that is.

ERK!

Joint 2nd prize
HONEY BEE

Lives: Every continent except Antarctica

Bees actually build up a negative electrical charge on their hairy little bodies. It comes from friction with the air atoms as the bees buzz busily around.

This charge vacuums up positively charged pollen grains from flowers that the bee has been feeding from. But the charge is disrupted by the forces made by an electric lawnmower or strimmer. So the brassed-off bees "charge" off to sting the gardener.

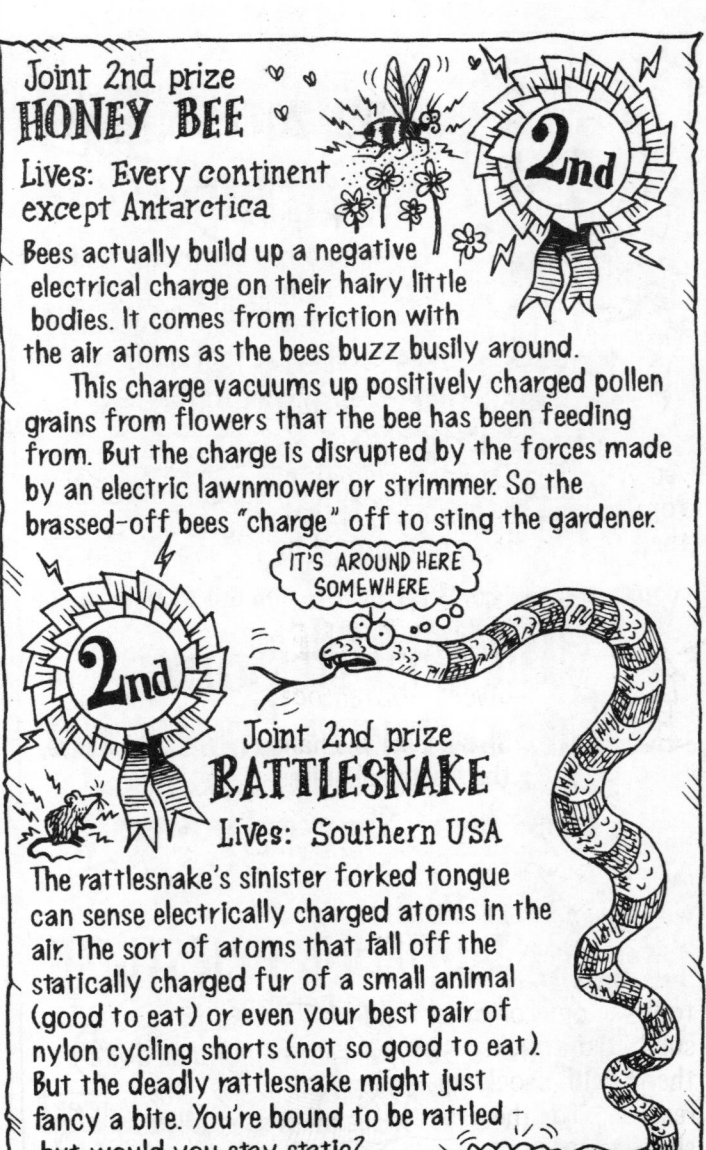

IT'S AROUND HERE SOMEWHERE

Joint 2nd prize
RATTLESNAKE

Lives: Southern USA

The rattlesnake's sinister forked tongue can sense electrically charged atoms in the air. The sort of atoms that fall off the statically charged fur of a small animal (good to eat) or even your best pair of nylon cycling shorts (not so good to eat). But the deadly rattlesnake might just fancy a bite. You're bound to be rattled – but would you stay static?

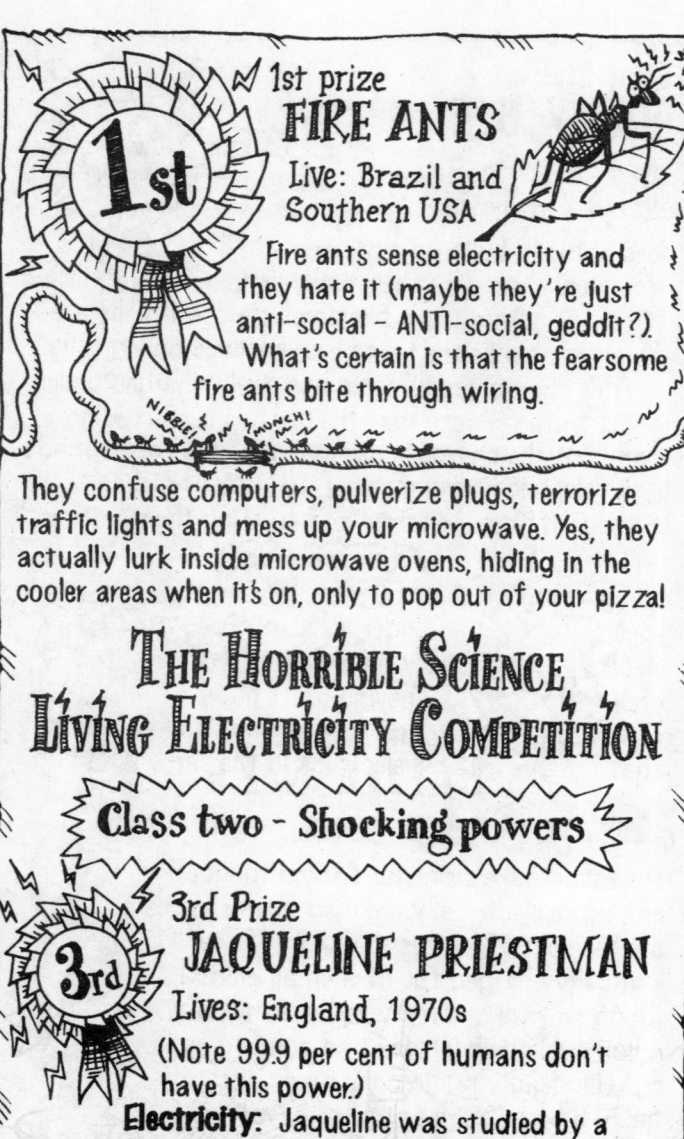

1st prize
FIRE ANTS

Live: Brazil and
Southern USA

Fire ants sense electricity and
they hate it (maybe they're just
anti-social – ANTI-social, geddit?).
What's certain is that the fearsome
fire ants bite through wiring.

NIBBLE! MUNCH!

They confuse computers, pulverize plugs, terrorize
traffic lights and mess up your microwave. Yes, they
actually lurk inside microwave ovens, hiding in the
cooler areas when it's on, only to pop out of your pizza!

THE HORRIBLE SCIENCE LIVING ELECTRICITY COMPETITION

Class two – Shocking powers

3rd Prize
JAQUELINE PRIESTMAN

Lives: England, 1970s

(Note 99.9 per cent of humans don't
have this power.)

Electricity: Jaqueline was studied by a
scientist from Oxford University and found to have

ten times more electricity in her body than normal.

Shock value: Could make TVs change channels without touching them and power sockets explode. For some unknown reason she stopped being electric when she ate green vegetables. So greens really are good for you!

2nd Prize
ELECTRIC CATFISH

Lives: African rivers

Electricity: Makes 350 volts in a special muscle just under its skin. The electricity is made by moving positively charged atoms to one end of its body. This causes an electrical current in the same way that a movement of electrons in the same direction makes an electrical current (see page 141).

Shock value: Enough power to kill a fish but that didn't stop the ancient Egyptians eating it. Would you risk an electric shock from your supper?

THE TASTE IS SHOCKING!

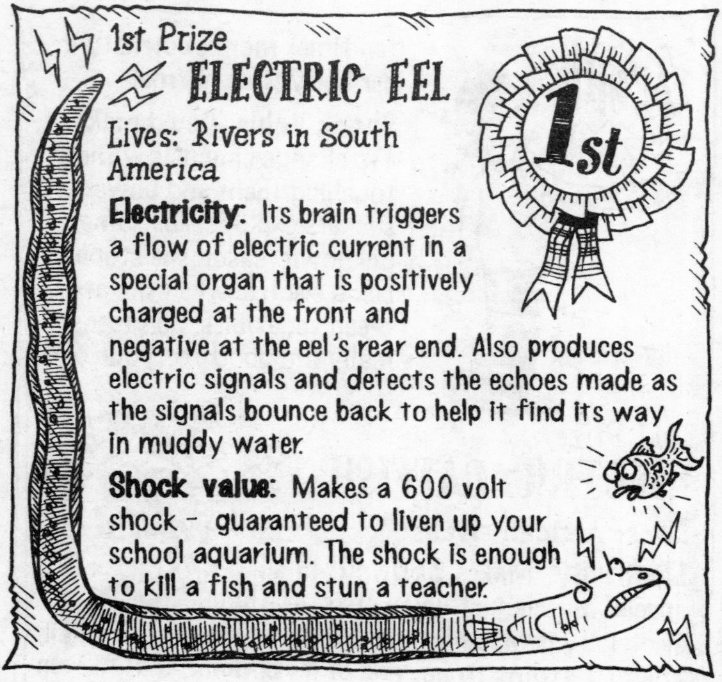

1st Prize
⚡ ELECTRIC EEL

Lives: Rivers in South America

Electricity: Its brain triggers a flow of electric current in a special organ that is positively charged at the front and negative at the eel's rear end. Also produces electric signals and detects the echoes made as the signals bounce back to help it find its way in muddy water.

Shock value: Makes a 600 volt shock – guaranteed to liven up your school aquarium. The shock is enough to kill a fish and stun a teacher.

SOME SHOCKING FIRST AID

Imagine your teacher actually did suffer an electric shock. Would you know what to do? Well, you're about to find out...

THE HORRIBLE SCIENCE GUIDE TO FIRST AID

Mr Sparks the science teacher is performing a dangerous electrical experiment. YIKES HE'S RECEIVING A VIOLENT ELECTRIC SHOCK!!!

Nasty! So what are you going to do to help? YES ... you've got to do *something*.

 GULP!

CLICK! ON OFF

1 Switch off the power. If you touch Mr Sparks before you do this you might get an electric shock too.

2 Even now don't touch Mr Sparks – you might still get a shock. Use a rubber or wooden object such as a ruler to knock away the electric wire.

HURRY!

3 Send someone to ring for an ambulance. Mr Sparks will need complete rest and a check-up. Oh well, looks like you can go home early from school. And having saved his life, chances are he'll be so grateful he'll let you off homework for the rest of term. Yeah right, dream on...

Bet you never knew!
If the victim is holding the electrified object the muscles of their hand will squeeze so they can't let it go. According to one story a pop star was holding his microphone when it gave him a severe shock. He couldn't let it go and ended up on the floor yelling loudly. Everyone thought it was part of the act!

HAVE A HEART

The most important electrical charge in your body is the signal (similar to a nerve signal) that controls your heart beat. It's made by an area of muscle in the upper part of the heart. The signal makes the heart muscle squeeze in a regular rhythm.

The heart can be monitored using a brilliant gizmo called the electrocardiogram (e-leck-tro-car-de-a-gram) developed by Dutch scientist Willem Einthoven (1860–1927) in 1903. Metal electrodes on the chest pick up electrical pulses from the nerve signals that control the heart. The pulses pass along a wire stretched between the poles of a magnet, making the wire bend very slightly. The machine displays this bending as a pattern on a screen.

But if this rhythm ever breaks down it's SERIOUSLY BAD NEWS. The condition is called ventricular fibrillation (ven-tric-ular fib-brill-la-tion). The heart flutters helplessly like an injured bird and stops pumping blood. The blood brings life-giving oxygen (a gas taken from the air by the lungs) to the body and without it the body will die in minutes. *And the shocking truth is that this terrifying condition can be triggered by an electric shock.*

Bet you never knew!
But the heart can be re-started. Incredibly, the best way is to give it an electric shock. Yes, you did read that right – another electric shock!

For reasons that scientists don't quite understand, the shock stops the fluttering of the heart so it can re-start itself. This fact was discovered in an especially tragic fashion. Read on for the heart-rending details...

STRAIGHT FROM THE HEART
Arizona, USA, 1947
"Here we have an interesting case. A 14-year-old male with a chest that hasn't grown properly for several years – making him unable to breathe normally. Am I going too fast?"

Top surgeon Claude Beck glanced at the medical students who were taking notes and, as usual, following his morning ward round like a flock of white-coated gulls after a fishing boat.

Beck had short greying hair, a square face, a square jaw and looked you squarely in the eye even when he had bad news to announce. And right now he was gazing straight into the eyes of his young patient.

"I wish I could tell you the op will be a cinch son, but it's an involved procedure. We've got to separate your ribs from your breastbone so you can breathe normally. Still I reckon we'll pull it off." Mickey's eyes were huge and dark and the rest of him looked thin and pale under his crew cut.

"And then?" he whispered anxiously.

"You'll be right as rain."

Mickey struggled to ask another question but he was short of breath and the surgeon and his students had already moved on. So later he asked a nurse about Dr Beck.

"Oh yes, Mickey," she smiled. "He's a real expert. Why, he's so clever he's even gone and developed a machine to re-start hearts using electric shocks. It's called a defibrillator. He's been testing it out on dogs. So don't you worry – you're in good hands."

Beck did indeed pull it off. The operation went just fine and after two hours the ribs were separated. The tricky part was over and the surgeon sighed with relief as he carefully sewed up the wound. Then, without warning Mickey's heart stopped beating. The unconscious boy gave a gentle sigh as his life ebbed away.

There was no time to think – and only seconds to act.

"Cardiac arrest!" yelled Beck, grabbing a scalpel and slicing through the stitches holding the side of the wound. There was just one thing he could do, one terrible option. He pulled aside the bone and muscle and grabbed the boy's heart. It was quivering like a hot bloody jelly.

"Ventricular fibrillation!" he snapped. Already he was gently squeezing the heart in his hands – willing it to start pumping blood on its own. Willing the boy to come back to life. For 35 minutes the surgeon frantically massaged the heart between shots of drugs designed to stimulate the muscle – but he knew that he was only buying time. There was just one hope.

"Fetch my defibrillator!" he ordered. "I'm going to try to shock the heart."

He glanced at the white, strained face of the anaesthetist. She was shaking her head.

"But," she protested. "It's never been tested on humans – only dogs."

"We've got to try it," said Beck desperately. "If not..."

The porter quickly wheeled Beck's machine, a mass of wires and dials, into the operating theatre and plugged it into the mains.

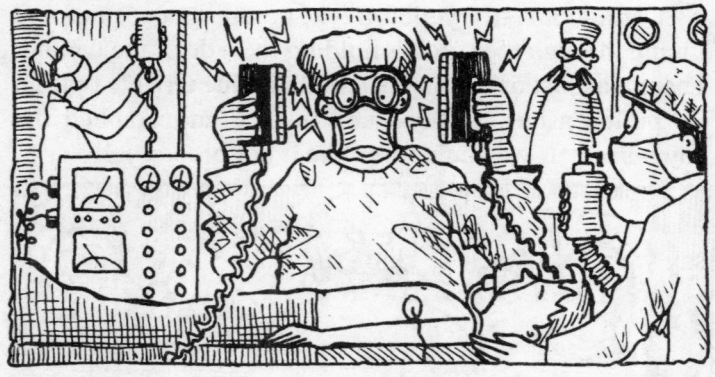

Beck placed the silver electric paddles to the boy's heart and fired 1,000 volts of electricity. The paddles jumped under Beck's hands but the heart was still, lifeless.

"We're losing him!" shouted the nurse.

Sweat ran down Beck's forehead and into his surgical mask. Once more he was frantically squeezing the slippery heart in his hands. Twenty-five agonising minutes passed, Beck's arms were aching but he dared not stop. More drugs were injected but still the heart would not beat. Perhaps it would be easier to let the boy die, Beck reasoned, knowing he could easily stop. But something drove him on.

"I'll try again," said the surgeon grimly, applying the paddles to the heart with shaking hands. Another jolt of electricity, longer this time, and 1,500 volts made the paddles jump.

There was a long tense silence.

"It's working!" said Beck, his voice hoarse with relief. The heart was pulsing and beating blood strongly and normally as if nothing had happened. And the nurses, the anaesthetist, the whole theatre staff broke into wild cheering.

Later that day Mickey was sitting up in bed.

"I'm starving," he complained. "The food here is shocking."

The nurse smiled, her eyes glistening with happiness and relief. "Well, Mickey," she said, "I think I can safely say we've all had a shocking time."

SHOCKING MEDICINE

1 Beck's defibrillator became a standard item of equipment in hospitals where it has saved tens of thousands of lives. Then, in 1960 US doctors developed a battery-powered version that could be used in ambulances. And today there are even small defibrillators that can be implanted inside the body. These fire tiny jolts of electricity into the heart if its rhythm breaks down.

2 The pacemaker is a similar device. Like an implanted defibrillator it runs off a battery outside the body but

unlike a defibrillator it produces regular shocks to keep the heart beating normally. In 1999 surgeons implanted a tiny pacemaker – the size of a 50 pence coin – to boost the heart of a three-week-old baby.

HIS NAPPY NEEDS CHANGING EVERY DAY BUT NOT HIS BATTERIES

PACEMAKER

3 In 1995 surgeons equipped a British woman with a battery-operated machine that helped her stand up. The woman's nerves had been damaged in a car accident and the machine fired electrical signals to her undamaged nerves to make her muscles move.

Have you spotted what these inventions have in common? No? Well, here's a clue – it's metal, it's full of chemicals and produces energy. No – it's not a can of fizzy drink! It's a battery, and without it most machines would be so much scrap metal. Well, by some shocking coincidence the next chapter's all about batteries – so why not read on? You can stretch yourself on the sofa and relax as you read. It's sure to re-charge your batteries – ha ha.

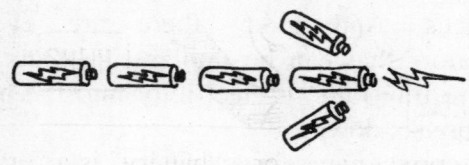

BULGING BATTERIES

Remember those kids on the Island of Horra? Bet they wished they'd brought a few batteries with them! Batteries are a great way of storing electricity so you take it with you and use it to power torches and radios and toy cars and walking, talking, crying, peeing dolls ... whatever you want. But how do they work?

TEACHER'S TEA-BREAK TEASER

All you need is a battery and a big grin. Knock on the staffroom door and when it creaks open hold up the battery.

Your teacher will probably say "It's a battery you little idiot!" Then you can shake your head sadly.

Yes, the correct name for a "battery" is a "dry cell". It's called that because the chemicals inside are in a paste and not in a liquid as they were in the first batteries, or cells. The word "battery" actually means a number of cells put together to make power, as in a torch. Anyway, we'll go on using "battery" in its everyday sense.

Shocking electricity fact file

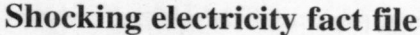

NAME: Battery (dry cell)

THE BASIC FACTS: A battery is a way of storing electricity in the form of two chemicals. The chemicals mix and a chemical reaction makes an electric current (for more details see page 107).

PERSONAL STEREO

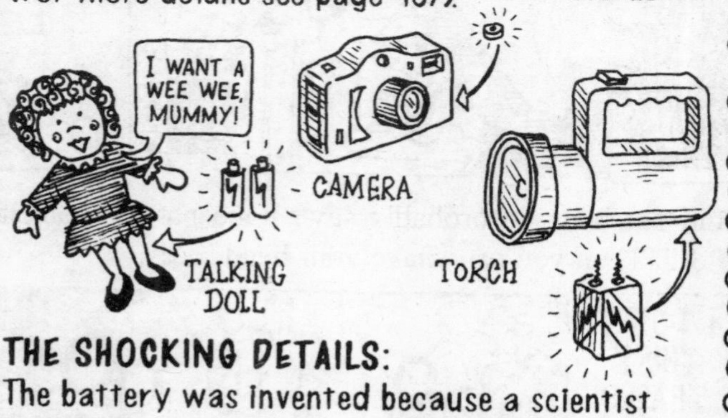

I WANT A WEE WEE, MUMMY!

CAMERA

TALKING DOLL

TORCH

THE SHOCKING DETAILS:
The battery was invented because a scientist noticed a dead frog's leg come to life and another scientist did horrible things to his own eyeballs. Oh yes, it's shocking ... but it's true.

SEE PAGES 101-107 FOR THE WHOLE GRISLY STORY

Hall of Fame: Luigi Galvani (1737–1798) and Alessandro Volta (1745–1827) Nationality: Italian

This is the story of two Italian scientists who started off as friends and ended up deadly enemies, and on the way both made major contributions to the science of electricity.

ALESSANDRO'S STORY...

The clever boy was educated by priests. His teachers were so impressed by him they tried to bribe him to train as a priest by giving him sweets.

But Alessandro's family didn't want their son to be a priest and took him away from school. (If only all families were so understanding!) Young Alessandro became interested in science and became a science teacher at Como and later a professor at Pavia University.

Alessandro got interested in electricity when he invented a pistol fired by an electric spark produced by static electricity. This set fire to methane gas contained in the pistol. Remember methane – it's the gas found in farts and rotting rubbish. And no, before you ask, you can't use exploding farts to shoot people.

Luigi's story

Young Galvani trained to be a doctor and later lectured in medicine at the University of Bologna whilst working as a doctor. He made a study of bones and later kidneys without making any startling discoveries.

But in the 1780s he became interested in nerves and made an electrifying breakthrough. Anyway, here are the letters that Luigi and his buddy Alessandro wrote to one another (beware, they could well be forgeries).

Bologna University 1780

Dear Aless,

You'll never guess what's happened! I was cutting up a frog's leg - as you know I'm researching nerves - and something shocking happened. There was a spark and the frog's leg twitched!

MY METAL SCALPEL

FROG'S LEG

METAL SHEET UNDERNEATH

Well, I checked and the frog was definitely dead. Oddly enough, the leg only seems to twitch if you touch it with metals. Bone or glass, for example, don't work. So I tried an experiment - I fixed some frog legs with brass hooks to the iron bars outside my lab windows and get this! The legs were all twitching merrily like a line of high-kicking dancers. The neighbour's cat got a real shock!

I think the frog's muscle contains electricity which forms a current through the metal. I think this electricity is the spark of life itself -

already some of my fellow scientists are trying to bring dead bodies back to life by giving them electric shocks – no success there I'm afraid! But I'm still really excited – in fact I'm galvanized. Nice word that!*

Your mate, Luigi

* A NOTE TO THE READER

Yes, the word "galvanized", meaning to get a sudden surge of energy, was inspired by Galvani's experiment. Well, as you can imagine, Volta was galvanized into making his own experiments...

Dear Luigi

That's a really interesting discovery but I'm sorry to say I don't think you're right about electricity in the body. First of all I gave an electric shock to a live frog. The frog trembled but it didn't jump. "Why not?" I asked myself. I decided to investigate whether electricity makes our senses work. So I gave my tongue and eyeballs and ears electric shocks to see if I started tasting, seeing and hearing things that weren't there. I didn't – and yeouch, it hurt!

Then suddenly I realized the shocking truth. I reckon it's the metals you used that made the electric current and it simply ran through the frog's leg and made it twitch. Since then I've actually managed to make electricity flow between two metals like this...

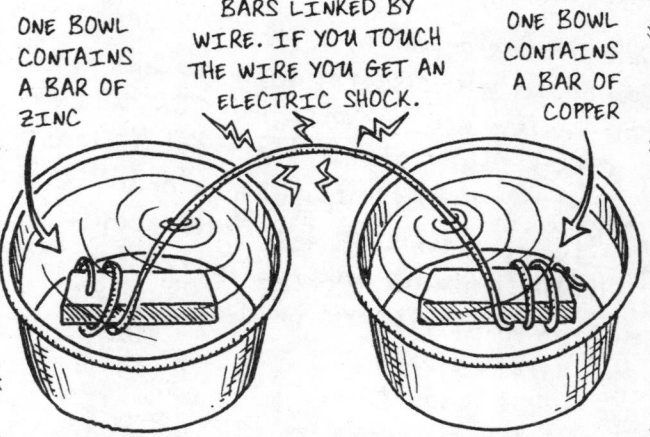

ONE BOWL CONTAINS A BAR OF ZINC

BARS LINKED BY WIRE. IF YOU TOUCH THE WIRE YOU GET AN ELECTRIC SHOCK.

ONE BOWL CONTAINS A BAR OF COPPER

TWO BOWLS OF SALTY WATER (I HAVE FOUND BY EXPERIMENT THAT THE ELECTRIC CURRENT TRAVELS MORE EASILY THROUGH SALTY WATER.)

So there you have it...
Your pal,
Alessandro

SCIENTIFIC NOTE

1 Volta was right. Like any animal or human body the frog's leg was mostly salty water and electricity can travel through this mixture. But Galvani wasn't totally wrong – after all, the nerves do send a kind of electrical signal (check back to page 83 if you're not sure what I'm talking about).

2 Volta was right about his experiment too. Electrons flow from the zinc to the copper and this forms an electric current. But Galvani wasn't impressed.

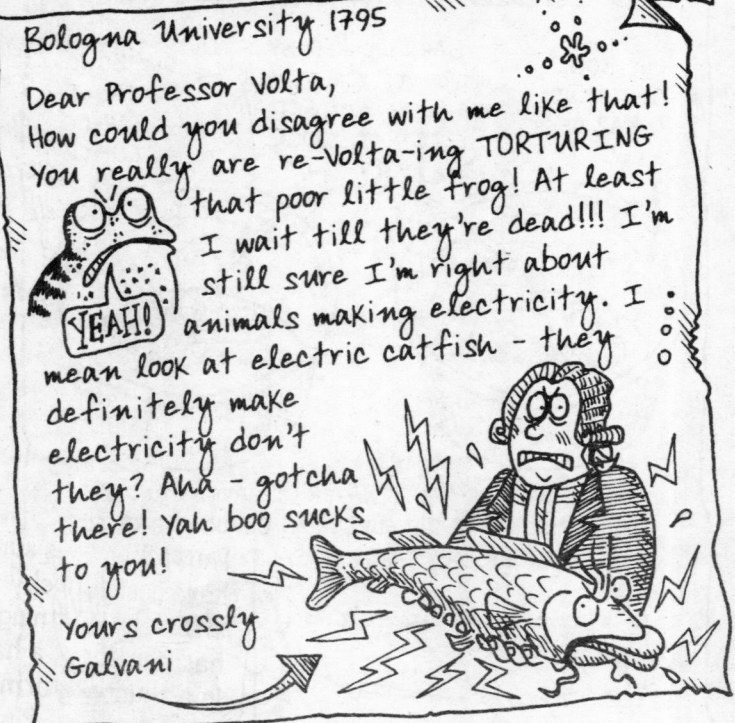

Bologna University 1795

Dear Professor Volta,
How could you disagree with me like that! You really are re-Volta-ing TORTURING that poor little frog! At least I wait till they're dead!!! I'm still sure I'm right about animals making electricity. I mean look at electric catfish - they definitely make electricity don't they? Aha - gotcha there! Yah boo sucks to you!

Yours crossly
Galvani

YEAH!

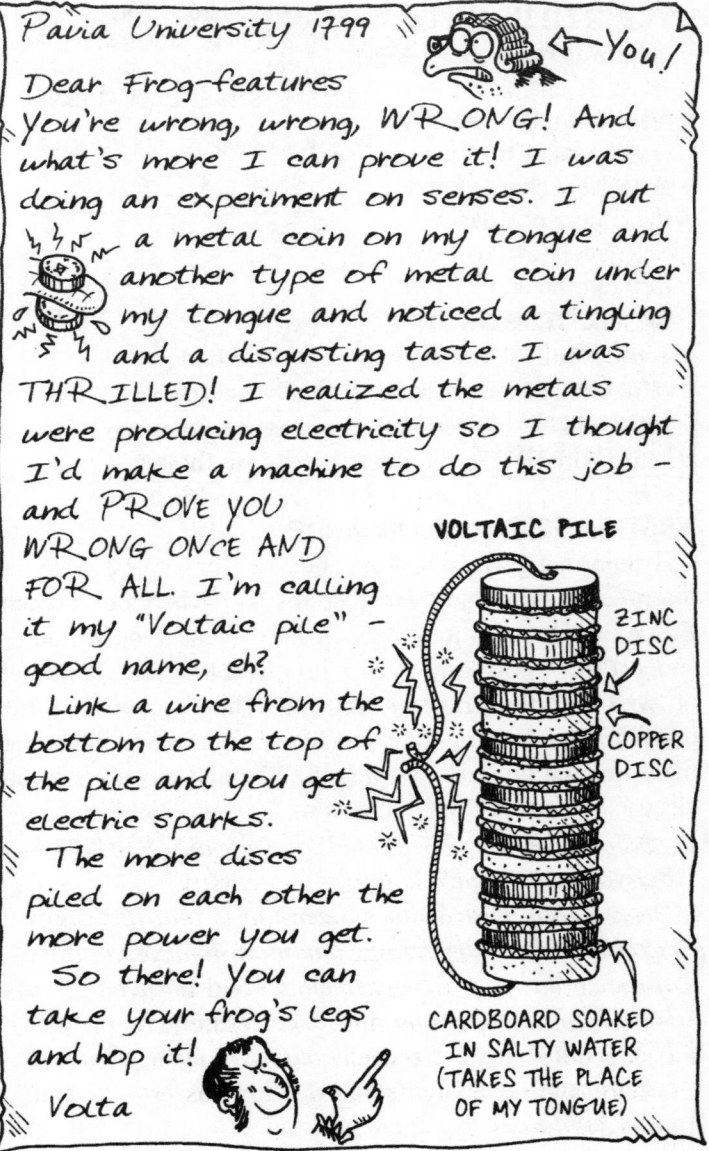

Pavia University 1799

← You!

Dear Frog-features

You're wrong, wrong, WRONG! And what's more I can prove it! I was doing an experiment on senses. I put a metal coin on my tongue and another type of metal coin under my tongue and noticed a tingling and a disgusting taste. I was THRILLED! I realized the metals were producing electricity so I thought I'd make a machine to do this job - and PROVE YOU WRONG ONCE AND FOR ALL. I'm calling it my "Voltaic pile" - good name, eh?

Link a wire from the bottom to the top of the pile and you get electric sparks.

The more discs piled on each other the more power you get.

So there! You can take your frog's legs and hop it!

Volta

VOLTAIC PILE

ZINC DISC

COPPER DISC

CARDBOARD SOAKED IN SALTY WATER (TAKES THE PLACE OF MY TONGUE)

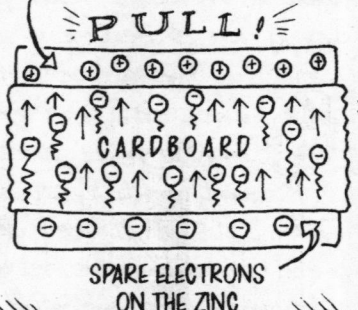

THE FORCE FROM THE POSITIVELY CHARGED COPPER ATOMS PULLS THE ELECTRONS TOWARDS THE COPPER. THIS MAKES AN ELECTRIC CURRENT.

POSITIVELY CHARGED COPPER ATOMS

PULL!

CARDBOARD

SPARE ELECTRONS ON THE ZINC

WHAT HAPPENED IN THE END?

Galvani never gave up his idea and he never forgave Volta for disagreeing with him. He lost his job when the French Emperor Napoleon took over in Italy because he wouldn't support the French, and died a disappointed man. Volta got on well with the Emperor who made him a count and his invention made him famous. Today the volt, a unit that measures the amount of "pressure" behind electrons in an electric current, is named after him.

Bet you never knew!
The problem with Volta's invention is that the soggy cardboard kept drying up. The more familiar battery of today (the dry cell – remember?) was invented in 1866 by French inventor Georges Leclanché (1839–1882). It uses a mixture of chemicals to make chemical reactions that result in electrons flowing from the zinc inner container to the carbon rod.

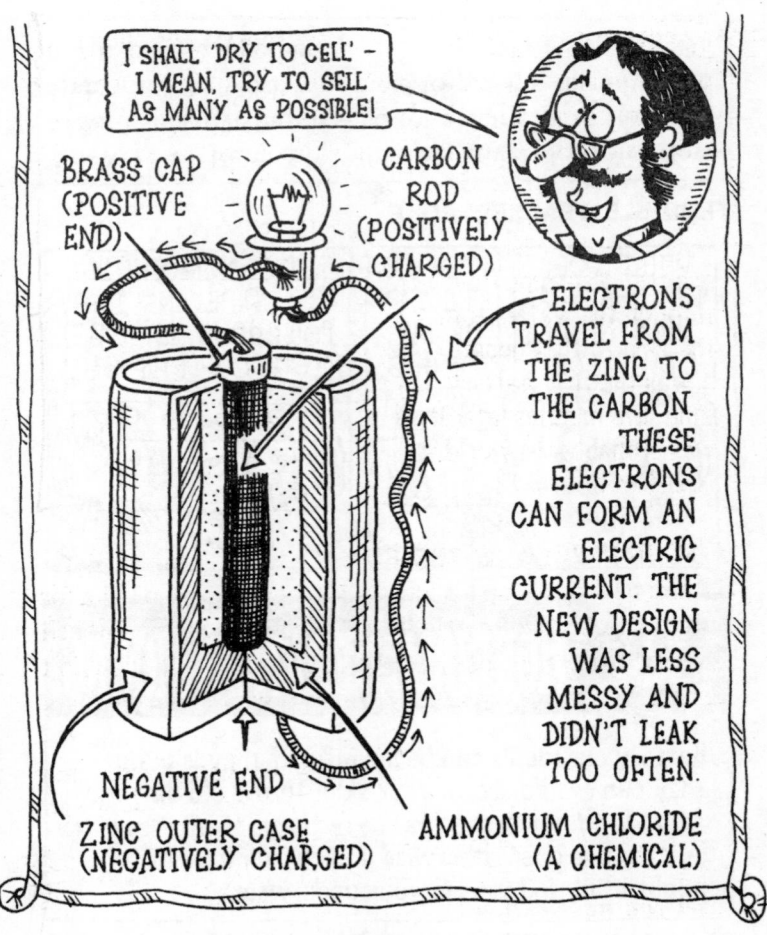

COULD YOU BE A SCIENTIST?

Which way round do the batteries go in a torch? Yeah, OK you can try it out – or you could think about which way the electrons move. Is it...

a) Positively charged end to positively charged end?

b) Negatively charged end to negatively charged end?

c) Negatively charged end to positively charged end?

Answer: c) Remember that negative electrons flow towards positive atoms — so for electricity to flow and your torch to work you have to put the negative and positive ends together.

TERRIBLE TEACHER JOKE

WHAT DOES THE CHEMICAL SIGN NH₄CL STAND FOR?

IT'S ON THE TIP OF MY TONGUE.

IT'S AMMONIUM CHLORIDE AND IT'S POISONOUS SO YOU'D BETTER SPIT IT OUT!

☠ HORRIBLE HEALTH WARNING!

Battery chemicals can be harmful. If they leak out they can even dissolve your skin! Throw old batteries away (and not in the fire) or recharge them. Never try cutting one open otherwise your burning curiosity might result in burns in your underwear.

BRILLIANT BATTERIES

The brilliant thing about batteries is that you can use them anywhere. On the beach and in the car and in the toilet. And there's plenty of choice of batteries each using different chemicals to produce electrons and make an electric current.

HOW DO YOU SWITCH IT OFF?

RiNG RiNG

I DON'T KNOW – THE INVENTOR DIED IN 1892

One of the most interesting battery-powered machines is the battery-powered car – no not a toy one, a real one. By the 2000s scientists were developing cool cars that could drive hundreds of km without a recharge. Japanese students even built one car that could zoom at 122 km (76 miles) per hour even though it was powered by ordinary AA batteries. Mind you, back in 1985 things were very different. A battery car was launched with massive hype. But was it more hype than horsepower?

SATISFY YOUR DRIVING AMBITION!

YOU DON'T NEED A DRIVING LICENCE TO OWN A SINCLAIR C5! INVENTED BY INVENTOR SIR CLIVE SINCLAIR, THIS BATTERY POWERED TRICYCLE CAN GO 32 KM WITHOUT BEING RECHARGED!

READ ON FOR MORE INFORMATION

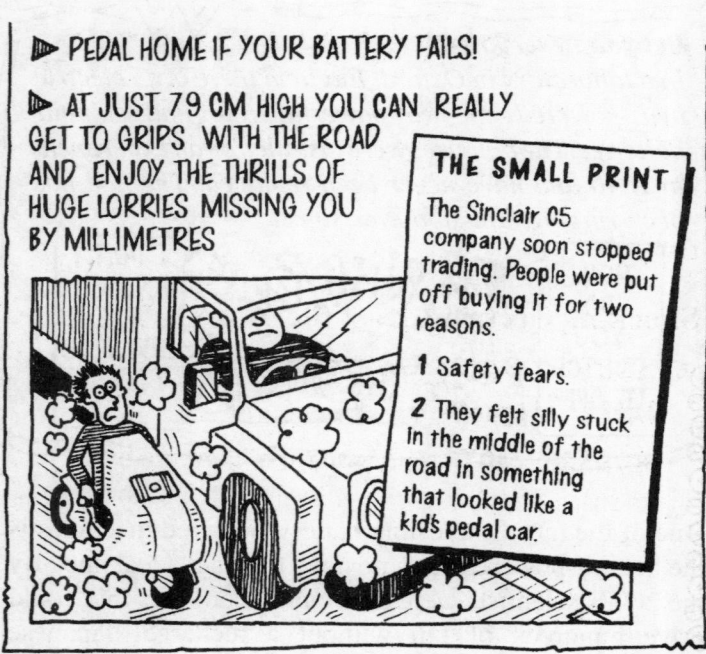

▷ PEDAL HOME IF YOUR BATTERY FAILS!

▷ AT JUST 79 CM HIGH YOU CAN REALLY GET TO GRIPS WITH THE ROAD AND ENJOY THE THRILLS OF HUGE LORRIES MISSING YOU BY MILLIMETRES

THE SMALL PRINT

The Sinclair C5 company soon stopped trading. People were put off buying it for two reasons.

1 Safety fears.

2 They felt silly stuck in the middle of the road in something that looked like a kid's pedal car.

So there you have it, batteries are a great way to produce the electrical force to get things on the move. Even a Sinclair C5. But there's another kind of force too that's found in the C5's electric motors and indeed in any other electric motor.

And it's made by our old friends the electrons...

Wanna know more?

Well, read on, you're bound to feel drawn to the next chapter. It's mysteriously attractive ... just like a magnet!

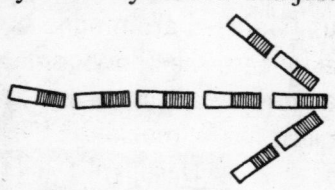

MYSTERIOUS MAGNETISM

Are you finding this book hard to put down? I expect it's the magnetic force coming from these pages. If you can *force* yourself to read the next few pages you'll find out what magnetism is and how it's made. Let's face a few facts...

Shocking electricity fact file

NAME: Magnetism

THE BASIC FACTS: **1** Magnetism is made by magnets. (Well, knock me over with a feather duster!)

2 *What we call magnetism is actually the same force as the electric force made by electrons – that's why the posh scientific name for the force is electromagnetism (e-leck-tro-magnetism).*

MAGNET

FORCE MADE BY ELECTRONS

REMEMBER THIS ON PAGE 41?

3 What this means is that every atom which has electrons is very slightly magnetic.

THE SHOCKING DETAILS:

QUESTION: But if atoms are magnetic and atoms are everywhere then how come everything isn't magnetic? How come you're not stuck to your bed in the morning? (No you're not, it just *feels* like you are.)

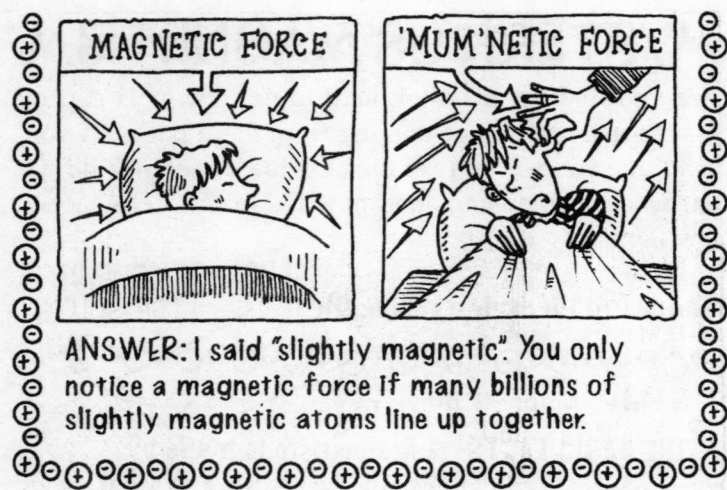

ANSWER: I said "slightly magnetic". You only notice a magnetic force if many billions of slightly magnetic atoms line up together.

MAGNETISM: THE INSIDE STORY

So how do you line up all those atoms? I mean, you'd need a tiny pair of tweezers and loads of patience and it would still take for ever.

THERE'S GOT TO BE AN EASIER WAY...

Well, you'll be pleased to know that inside a magnet this lining up is done quite naturally by those nice helpful atoms.

1 Inside a magnet the atoms line up to form little boxes (about 0.1mm across) called domains (doe-mains). Inside these boxes the electrons can combine their forces to make what we call a magnetic force.

2 A magnet has two ends called north and south poles.

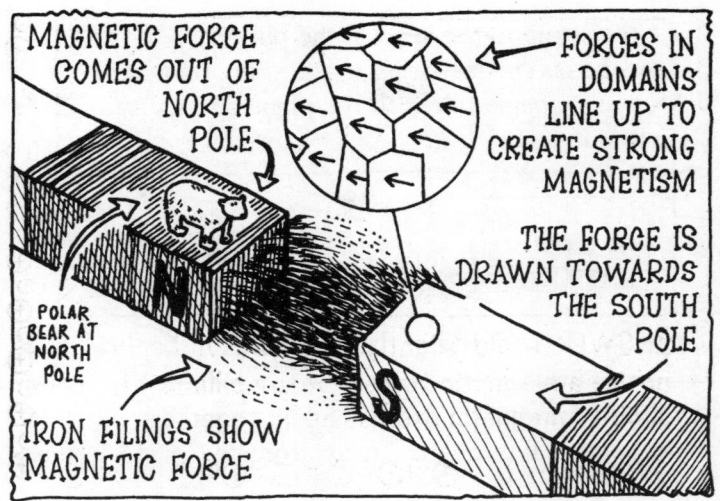

MAGNETIC FORCE COMES OUT OF NORTH POLE

FORCES IN DOMAINS LINE UP TO CREATE STRONG MAGNETISM

THE FORCE IS DRAWN TOWARDS THE SOUTH POLE

POLAR BEAR AT NORTH POLE

IRON FILINGS SHOW MAGNETIC FORCE

Dare you discover ... how to make a magnetic plane?

You will need:
A piece of tissue paper 2 cm x 1 cm
Sticky tape and scissors
A metal pin
A magnet (This should be as strong as possible – you could use several magnets in a line.)
A piece of thread 30 cm long.

What you do:
1 Thread the pin through the paper so it looks like a little plane (the paper being the wing).

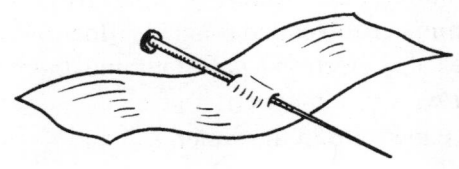

113

2 Tie the string to the head of the pin.

3 Tape the end of the string to the side of a table.

4 Move the magnet near to the plane and try to make it fly without touching it.

What do you notice?

a) If I move the magnet away from the plane it stays flying.

b) The closer the magnet is to the plane the better it flies.

c) The magnet will only work if it's a certain way round.

Answer: b) The closer you are to the magnet the stronger its force. The area around a magnet that is affected by its force is called a "magnetic field". (Mind you, don't tread in any magnetic cow pats!)

Dare you discover ... if magnetism works underwater?

(No, you don't need a diving suit for this experiment.)

You will need:

A glass of water

A magnet

A paper clip

What you do:

1 Plop the paper clip in the water.

2 Place the magnet up against the *outside* of the glass.
3 Now try to use the magnet to bring the paper clip to the top of the glass without touching the paper clip and without getting the magnet wet.

What do you notice?
a) It's easy.
b) I can't move the paper clip at all.
c) The paper clip only moves when I hold the magnet *over* the water. This proves that magnetism works through water but not through glass.

Answer: a) This proves that magnetism works through glass and water.

Dare you discover ... how magnetic tape works?
Did you know that tape recorders work using magnetism? Yes, it's true. To find out more try this fascinating experiment.

You will need:
A cassette tape
A cassette recorder and microphone
A magnet

What you do:

1 Talk into the microphone. No, it doesn't really matter what you say – why not try a few farmyard impressions?

2 OK, that's enough farmyard impressions – I said THAT'S ENOUGH FARMYARD IMPRESSIONS!

Now rewind and play the tape. Rewind the tape and stop in the middle of your recording.

3 Now sweep the magnet across the tape four times.

4 Rewind and play the tape.

What do you notice?

a) My voice blanks out in the middle. My lovely recording is ruined!

b) The tape is LOUDER than ever and all the neighbours are complaining.

c) My voice sounds like an alien's.

Answer: a) The microphone turns your voice into electronic pulses and these are turned by a magnet into magnetic signals that rearrange the tiny bits of metal chemical on the tape to make a recording. Easy-peasey! Your magnet muddled up these chemicals so that the tape recording was lost.

Don't you DARE even *think* of using your mum and dad's classic tape collection for this experiment! Oh I see, it's too late. Well beware – your parents might use a magnet to grab your pocket money.

MAGNETIC QUIZ

1 Some Canadian coins are magnetic. TRUE/FALSE

2 Magnetism can be used to suck out diseased parts of bone marrow (the juicy pink bit that dogs love). TRUE/FALSE

3 An ultra-powerful magnet can pull the eyeballs out of your head. TRUE/FALSE

4 Magnetism stores information in computers. TRUE/FALSE

5 In Siberia people fish by chucking iron filings into lakes. When the fish have eaten the filings they are caught using magnets. TRUE/FALSE

6 There's a magnet inside your school bell and/or your school fire bell. TRUE/FALSE

7 Magnetism can power a full-sized train. TRUE/FALSE

Answers:

1 True. Canadian dimes are made of nickel – a metal that can be naturally magnetic.

2 True. In the mid-1980s British scientists discovered how to treat lumps of diseased bone marrow inside bones with chemicals coated in magnetic material. The chemicals stuck to the affected areas inside the bone. It was then possible to draw the diseased lumps out in tiny bits using powerful magnets. Hungry yet, Fido?

3 False. Human eyeballs aren't magnetic but magnets *are* used to remove tiny bits of metal from eyeballs after accidents.

4 True. For example, a floppy disk stores computer code like a tape recording as magnetic chemicals on its surface. The "read" head of the computer turns magnetic pulses from the disk into electric signals inside the computer. The hard disk is a series of magnetic disks that store information.

5 False.

6 True. The ringing that wakes you up at the end of a science lesson is made by a hammer hitting a bell. The hammer is yanked by a powerful magnet in the bell that responds to an electric current set up when someone presses the button.

7 True. In the 1990s Maglev trains were built in Japan and Germany. The train is lifted off the rail using powerful magnets. As the train glides forward, powerful magnets on board make electrons move in the reaction rail underneath the train. This creates an electric current which gives off a magnetic force that pulls the train forward. Fancy one for Christmas?

A FORCEFUL TALE

Magnets have a long history. About 2500 BC, according to legend, a Chinese Emperor guided his army through fog using a rock containing magnetite (also called lodestone). Well, stone me. He probably used a sliver of the rock hung from a thread.

Magnetite is naturally magnetic so a sliver of it points towards the north and can be used to make a compass, a device described by Chinese scientist and astronomer Shen Kuo (1030–1093) in 1088.

Chinese sailors used the compass to steer a course at sea, a technique that spread to Europe and the Middle East within 100 years. But although sailors happily used compasses, no one bothered to do experiments with magnets until a doctor called William Gilbert (1540–1603) came on the scene.

WONDERING WILLIAM

Little is known about William's early life. But he studied medicine and eventually became Royal Doctor to Queen Elizabeth of England.

HOW IS YOUR ROYAL ILLNESS – I MEAN HIGHNESS?

But just two years later the Queen died, so William's medicines must have been a dead loss. Anyway, he was the first person to investigate magnets in a scientific way. For example, people thought that if you rubbed a magnet with garlic the pong would drive the magnetism away. (Sounds reasonable – after all it can have this effect on your friends.) But Gilbert found the treatment didn't work.

THIS EXPERIMENT STINKS!

MY RESULTS ARE NOT TO BE SNIFFED AT

Gilbert was fascinated by the way that a magnetic compass pointed north and wanted to know why. At last he realized that the whole Earth is a magnet! He found this out by putting a magnetic compass needle on a small rod. The needle pointed north of course but it also dipped slightly downwards. This suggested that magnetism must come out of the Earth at some point far to the north and Gilbert reckoned (rightly) that the Earth itself is a GIANT magnet. I guess that's one magnet that would be too big for your fridge.

FIVE MAGNETIC EARTH FACTS

1 A sea of melted metal surrounds the Earth's core. If you fancied a dip you'd be crushed and burnt – but fortunately no human has ventured this deep.

2 Currents swirl around in the metal and the huge masses of electrons set up powerful electric and magnetic forces.

3 The magnetic forces come out of the ground at the South Magnetic pole, sweep round the Earth and enter the ground at the North Magnetic Pole.

4 Yes, you did read that right – it's the *opposite* of an ordinary magnet! In line with other magnets we really ought to say that the North Magnetic Pole is near the South Pole and the South Magnetic Pole is near the North Pole – that would bamboozle your Geography teacher! The reason for the confusion is that the north pole of a compass magnet happened to get its name because it points towards the North Magnetic Pole, which is towards the geographic south. Lost yet? You will be.

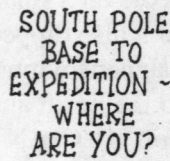

5 The direction of the magnetic force has flipped round about 300 times in the last 4,600 million years. (Don't ask me why or when it will happen next – no one knows!) This would make a compass needle point south instead of north and if it happened on a school trip you're bound to get lost. And then your teacher would really flip!

Talking about expeditions – d'you fancy a holiday?

Sun is like a big explosion firing out bits of atoms.

WOW! COR! FAB! COOL!

These bits are sucked into the Van Allen belts by the earth's magnetic force.

OUR SPACECRAFT

They hit atoms in the upper atmosphere which give out blips of light (photons) to make lovely displays of coloured lights. These are called the Northern and Southern lights because you can only see them near the north and south poles.

THE SMALL PRINT

SOMETIMES THE SUN FIRES VAST AMOUNTS OF EXTRA ELECTRONS. THEY SET OFF HUGE MAGNETIC WAVES IN THE VAN ALLEN BELTS THAT BOOST THE EARTH'S MAGNETIC FORCE. IF OUR METAL SPACECRAFT GETS CAUGHT IN ONE OF THESE SURGES YOU MIGHT FEEL SPACE SICK OR EVEN A BIT SPACED-OUT.

THE "SOUTH MAGNETIC POLE" TOUR

No, this isn't the actual South Pole (the base of the Earth) this is the place where magnetic forces actually come out of the ground. (Australian explorer Sir Douglas Mawson [1882-1958] was the first to get there in 1909.) You too will gasp in amazement as your compass needle wildly swings round.

Sir D.M.

TURN OVER FOR DETAILS

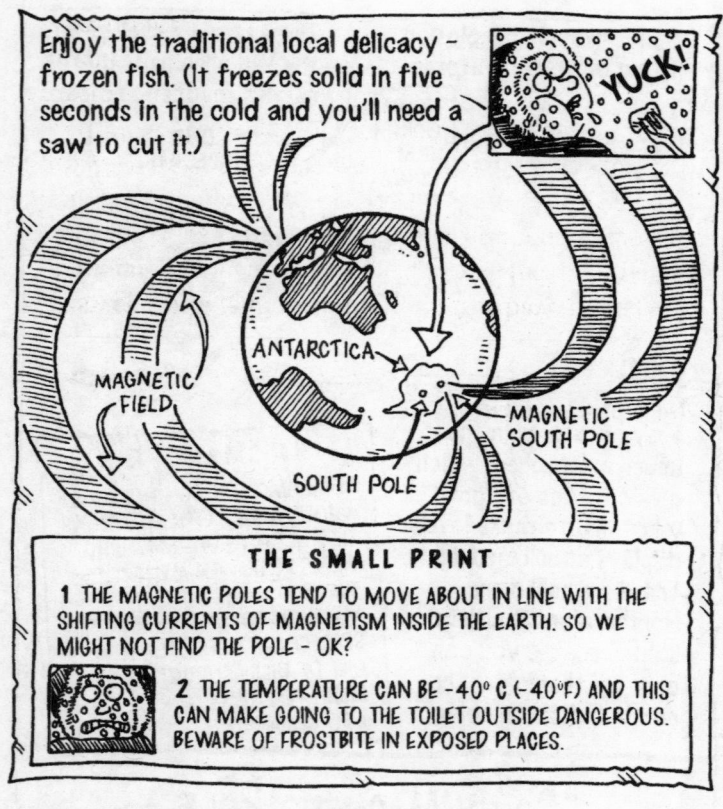

Enjoy the traditional local delicacy – frozen fish. (It freezes solid in five seconds in the cold and you'll need a saw to cut it.)

YUCK!

MAGNETIC FIELD

ANTARCTICA

MAGNETIC SOUTH POLE

SOUTH POLE

THE SMALL PRINT

1 THE MAGNETIC POLES TEND TO MOVE ABOUT IN LINE WITH THE SHIFTING CURRENTS OF MAGNETISM INSIDE THE EARTH. SO WE MIGHT NOT FIND THE POLE – OK?

2 THE TEMPERATURE CAN BE -40° C (-40°F) AND THIS CAN MAKE GOING TO THE TOILET OUTSIDE DANGEROUS. BEWARE OF FROSTBITE IN EXPOSED PLACES.

COULD YOU BE A SCIENTIST?

In 1995 American scientist Robert Beason stuck magnets to the heads of bobolinks (small American birds that normally fly south-east in the autumn). Beason then opened the birds' cages. What did the birds do?

a) Nothing. Their poor little magnetic heads were stuck to the metal floor of their cages.

b) They flew in roughly the right direction but they were slightly off course.

c) They flew in completely the wrong direction.

Bet you never knew!
You can destroy the power of a magnet by "killing" it – that's the actual word scientists use. It sounds rather sinister, like some dreadful murder. Well, if it was a crime would you know how to solve it?

THE CASE OF THE MURDERED MAGNET...

THE CASE FILES OF OFFICER LODESTONE, NYPD.

Following a tip-off from some kids, we busted the flat of a science teacher. Judging by the still-warm cup of coffee he had only been gone a few minutes. The flat was a mess and I felt dirty just being there.

The magnet was lying face down on the table.

THE VICTIM

THE SUSPECT

CONTINUED...

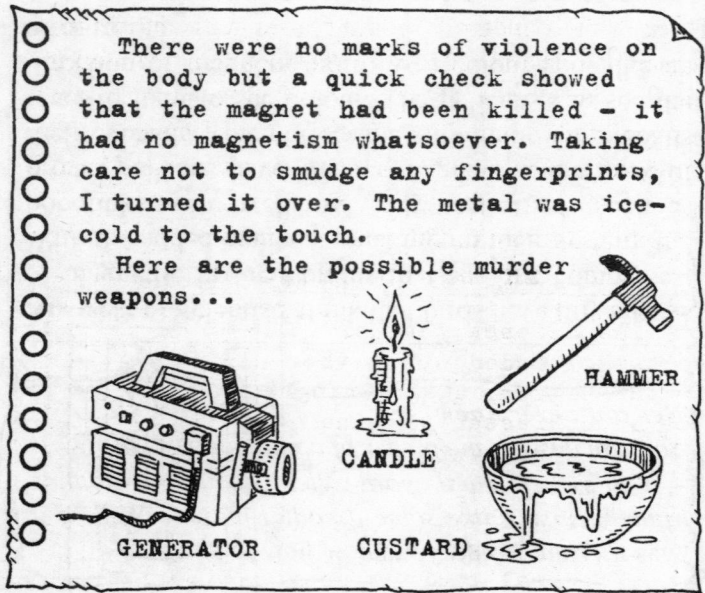

There were no marks of violence on the body but a quick check showed that the magnet had been killed — it had no magnetism whatsoever. Taking care not to smudge any fingerprints, I turned it over. The metal was ice-cold to the touch.

Here are the possible murder weapons...

CANDLE

HAMMER

GENERATOR

CUSTARD

Your mission ... is to find out how the magnet was killed. *Was it by...*

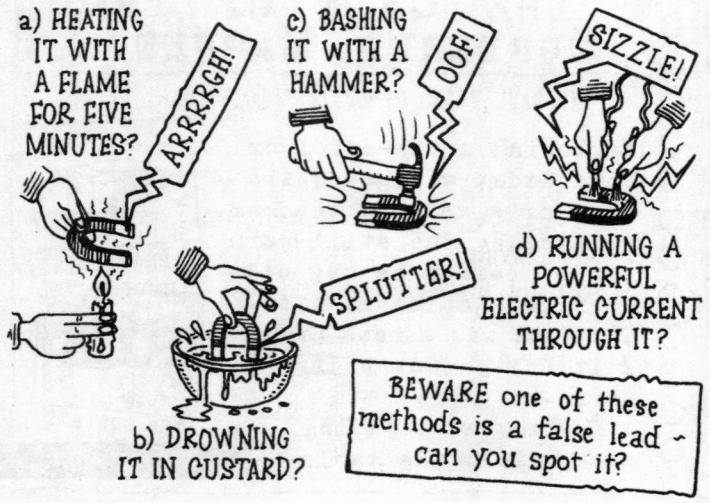

a) HEATING IT WITH A FLAME FOR FIVE MINUTES?

ARRRRGH!

c) BASHING IT WITH A HAMMER?

OOF!

SIZZLE!

d) RUNNING A POWERFUL ELECTRIC CURRENT THROUGH IT?

SPLUTTER!

b) DROWNING IT IN CUSTARD?

BEWARE one of these methods is a false lead - can you spot it?

Three of these methods would rearrange the atoms in the domains so the magnetic forces no longer pointed in a single direction. This would mean that the magnet lost its power. Read the case notes again ... you may find some more clues. OK – ready for this? The answer is **d)** and **b)** is useless!

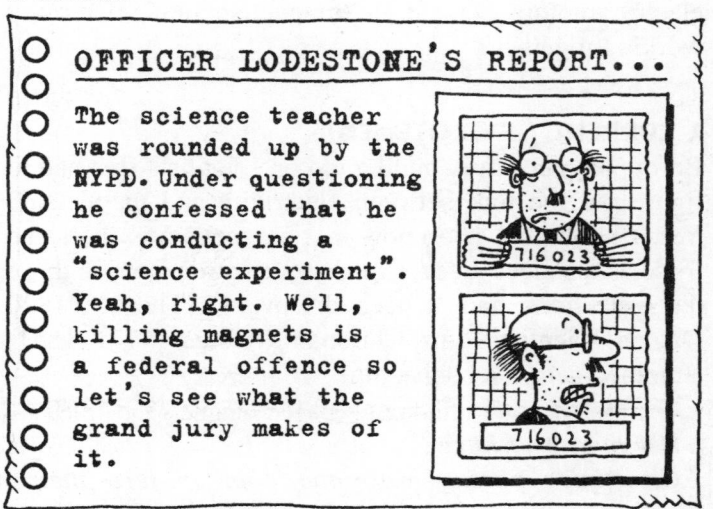

OFFICER LODESTONE'S REPORT...

The science teacher was rounded up by the NYPD. Under questioning he confessed that he was conducting a "science experiment". Yeah, right. Well, killing magnets is a federal offence so let's see what the grand jury makes of it.

716 023

716 023

What's that? Did you say "It doesn't sound too serious to me"? WELL, IT IS!!! You can't just go around killing magnets because magnets are vital and important. Vital to make THE MOST IMPORTANT MACHINE ON THE PLANET. A machine that literally powers the modern world. Wanna know more?

Well, why not "motor" on to the next chapter?

MIGHTY MAGNETIC MOTORS

Clean, silent, powerful. Electric motors power all sorts of things from washing machines to milk floats and the only time anyone notices them is when one doesn't work or gives their owners a nasty shock. But did you know that electric motors depend on magnetism and electricity working together?

A CURRENT OF EXCITEMENT

Before anyone could build a motor, scientists first had to figure out the link between electricity and magnetism. Yes, I know that you know that magnetism is the same force as the electric force made by electrons, but in those days electrons hadn't been discovered. Then in 1820 Danish scientist Hans Christian Oersted (1771–1851) stumbled across a connection.

Bet you never knew!
Christian's parents were too poor to feed their children so they gave Christian and his brother away to the neighbours. (No, your parents are unlikely to give your brother/sister to the folk next door so stop daydreaming and get on with this book.) But the boys managed to educate themselves from books. They did so well they were allowed into Copenhagen University, where Hans became a Professor.

Anyway, Hans wondered if an electric current had any effect on a compass needle. One day during a lecture he placed a compass needle near a fixed electric wire. The needle mysteriously swung away from the wire as if pushed by an invisible finger.

Oersted wasn't quite sure why this was happening but realized he'd stumbled across something really IMPORTANT.

COULD YOU BE A SCIENTIST?

You've been reading this book (unlike poor Oersted) so you can work out what was going on. What was it?

a) The electric force given out by the wire was pulling the magnetic compass needle towards it.

b) The force given out by the electrons in the wire was pushing the magnetic compass needle away.

c) The compass needle was moving as a result of static electricity.

> **Answer: b)** The electric force is also a magnetic force – that's why it's called electromagnetism (remember that word from page 111?). And the forces made by electrons push against each other – remember that too? Well, the two forces pushed against each other as usual. This had the effect of pushing the compass needle away. (The wire would have moved too if it wasn't fixed.)

So the force from an electric current can make a magnet move and, as you're about to find out, this is exactly the principle behind an electric motor. Wanna know more?

Shocking electricity fact file

NAME : Electric motor

THE BASIC FACTS : **1** Every type of electric motor uses the electromagnetic force to make a wire loop move. Here's how…

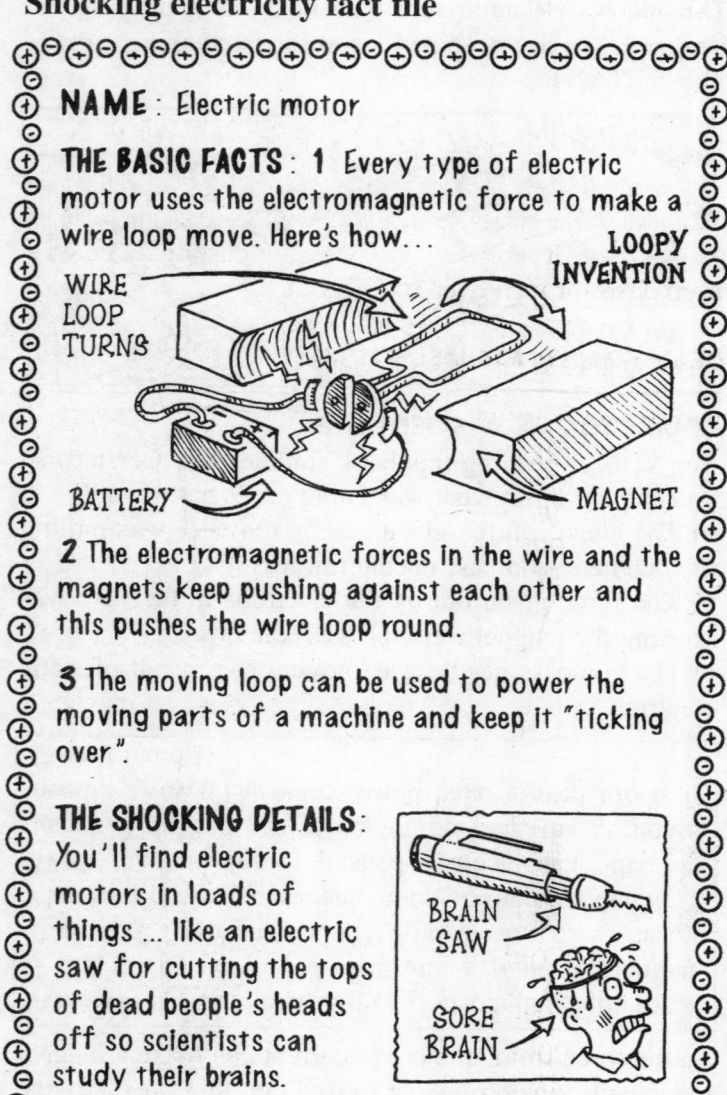

LOOPY INVENTION

WIRE LOOP TURNS

BATTERY

MAGNET

2 The electromagnetic forces in the wire and the magnets keep pushing against each other and this pushes the wire loop round.

3 The moving loop can be used to power the moving parts of a machine and keep it "ticking over".

THE SHOCKING DETAILS: You'll find electric motors in loads of things … like an electric saw for cutting the tops of dead people's heads off so scientists can study their brains.

BRAIN SAW

SORE BRAIN

THE MOTOR RACE

The race was on to combine electricity and magnetism to make a working electric motor. But the basic idea was thought up in 1821 by scientist Michael Faraday (1791–1867). Faraday actually built a machine to show this and it was the first ever electric motor. In a first for *Horrible Science* we've actually persuaded the great scientist to explain how it works. (This is quite amazing since he's been dead for well over 100 years.)

DEAD BRAINY: MICHAEL FARADAY

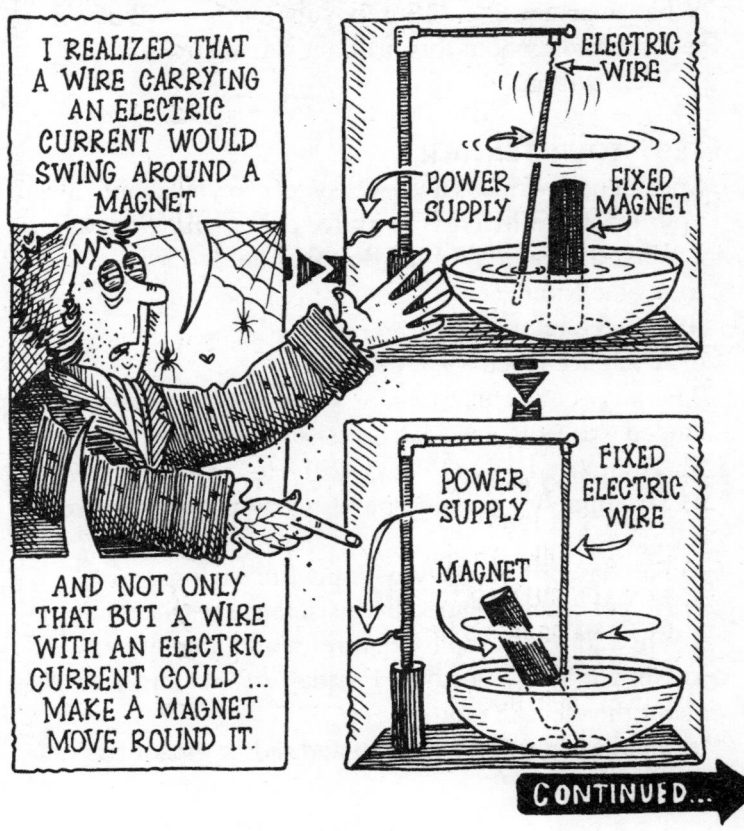

I REALIZED THAT A WIRE CARRYING AN ELECTRIC CURRENT WOULD SWING AROUND A MAGNET.

ELECTRIC WIRE

POWER SUPPLY

FIXED MAGNET

AND NOT ONLY THAT BUT A WIRE WITH AN ELECTRIC CURRENT COULD ... MAKE A MAGNET MOVE ROUND IT.

POWER SUPPLY

FIXED ELECTRIC WIRE

MAGNET

CONTINUED...

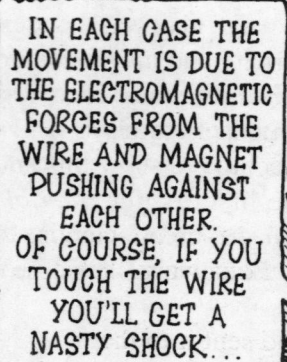

IN EACH CASE THE MOVEMENT IS DUE TO THE ELECTROMAGNETIC FORCES FROM THE WIRE AND MAGNET PUSHING AGAINST EACH OTHER. OF COURSE, IF YOU TOUCH THE WIRE YOU'LL GET A NASTY SHOCK...

ARGH! I NEARLY KILLED MYSELF!

M.F. HAS FORGOTTEN THAT HE'S BEEN DEAD FOR OVER 100 YEARS

What an achievement! Surely your teacher will be able to tell you more about this brilliant scientist.

Well *surely*?

TEST YOUR TEACHER

Special note – this is a very easy test so you should award your teacher a MINUS mark for every *wrong* answer.

1 What did Faraday's dad do? Was he...

a) A blacksmith?

b) An ice-cream seller?

c) A science teacher?

2 Faraday began his career as a bookbinder's assistant but landed a job as lab assistant to top scientist Sir Humphry Davy (1778–1829). How did he do it?

a) Sir Humphry sacked one of his assistants and created a vacancy.

b) Faraday bribed Davy with his life savings.

c) He got recommended by his science teacher.

3 Why did Sir Humphry quarrel with Faraday?

a) Sir Humphry accused Faraday of stealing his ideas about the electric motor.

b) Faraday borrowed his pen and didn't give it back.

c) Sir Humphry was jealous because Faraday was a better teacher than he was.

4 What was Faraday's favourite hobby?

a) Work – especially setting up science experiments.

b) Going to parties.

c) Teaching children about science.

5 Other scientists made machines based on Faraday's work but found it hard to make them work. What did Faraday do?

a) Made copies of the machine and sent it to them.

b) Wrote them rude letters with the word IDIOT scrawled in big letters.

c) Organized a special training day for them.

6 As an old man what problem did Faraday suffer from?

a) A weak memory.

b) Embarrassing hairy ears.

c) He lost his voice so he had to give up teaching.

7 When the Chancellor of the Exchequer came to Faraday's lab and asked what use electricity was how did Faraday reply?

133

Answers: All the answers are **a)** so it should be easy enough to add up your teacher's score.

1 Faraday's dad was always ill and the family was very poor.

2 Faraday had already got a job as a secretary after giving Davy a beautiful handmade book of notes on Davy's lectures. Yes, producing marvellous homework does pay off sometimes.

3 Like many scientists Davy was very sensitive about who gets the glory for discoveries. Davy and his scientist pal William Hyde Wollaston (1766–1828) had worked on a motor that didn't work. Faraday had benefited from their ideas but hadn't mentioned them when he wrote about his discovery.

4 Faraday had few friends and no social life. But he wasn't sad – he was a genius. Obviously, your teacher has no such excuse. You can award half a mark for **c)** because Faraday enjoyed teaching at the Royal Institution where he worked and even set up Christmas lectures for children.

5 That's the kind of man he was.

6 This came after an illness in 1839 that Faraday said affected his head. It might have been poisoning by the chemicals he used for experiments.

7 And sure enough in 1994 the British government plonked Value Added Tax on electricity.

What your teacher's score means

-7–0 Your teacher's ignorance is SHOCKING. Order them to take the rest of the term off in study leave. Oh well, you'll just have to amuse yourself in science lessons.

1–3 Passable. Could do better.

4–7 Check your teacher's drawer for a copy of this book. If you find one disqualify your teacher AT ONCE! By the way, if your teacher keeps saying **c)** she is totally absorbed in her job and needs a nice long holiday. Of course, you'll have to take one too.

Bet you never knew!
All Faraday's motor did was run around in circles and not do any work. Do you know anyone like that? The first working electric motor was made by Joseph Henry (1797–1878) in 1831. Henry was another remarkable scientist. He started his career as a watchmaker and then wrote plays before getting interested in science. He was not a greedy man and when he got a science job working for the Smithsonian Institute he refused a pay rise for 32 years.

IF YOU DON'T STOP TRYING TO GIVE ME A PAY RISE...I'LL GO ON STRIKE!

Dare you discover ... how to make your own electric motor?

You will need:

A compass OR a needle
A magnet
A 25-cm length of thread
Some blu tak
Sticky tape
A 1.5-volt battery (HP11)
A piece of kitchen foil 28 cm x 6 cm
A grown-up to help. (Yes, they have their uses.)

What you do:

1 If you don't have a compass, stroke the needle with the magnet 30 times. This turns the needle into a magnet too.
2 Secure the needle to the end of the thread with a small blob of blutak in the middle so it hangs sideways in the air.

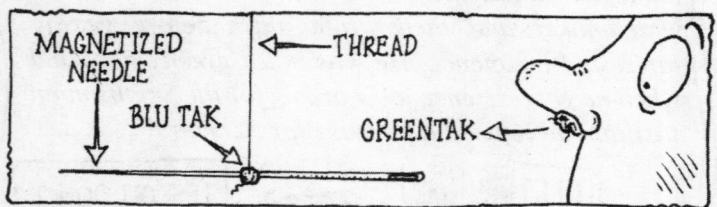

MAGNETIZED NEEDLE
BLU TAK
THREAD
GREENTAK

3 Stick the other end of the thread to a table top with more blu tak.

ANOTHER NUTTY EXPERIMENT!
BLUTAK
TABLE TOP

4 Fold the foil in half lengthways and then fold it again lengthways. Make sure you don't tear the foil.

5 Use sticky tape to stick one end of the foil to the positive end of the battery and the other end to the negative end. This makes a circuit for an electric current to run through.

6 Now, EITHER ... hold the battery horizontal and pass the foil loop from side to side over the face of the compass.

OR put the foil loop round the needle and move the foil up and down without touching it.

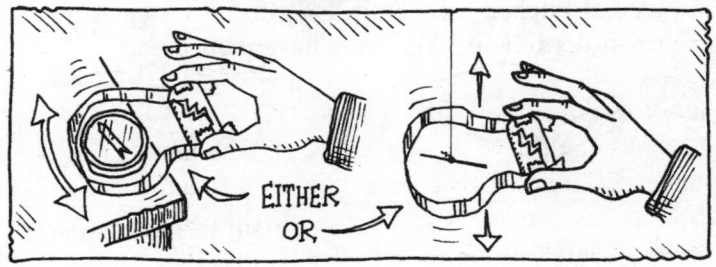

What do you notice?

a) The needle starts to glow with a strange blue light.

b) The needle twists round.

c) The needle jumps up and down.

Answer: b) The compass needle turns round and round and the needle twists around. Either way the magnetic field produced by the wire moves with the wire. This keeps pushing away and then attracting the magnetic needle – just like a real electric motor!

SPOT THE ELECTRIC MOTOR QUIZ

Which of the household objects on the next page contains an electric motor? (No, you're NOT allowed to take them apart to find out.) Here's a clue instead – if it's got moving parts it's got an electric motor.

HUM!

TURN!

SPIN!

WIND!

BLOW!

Answer: All of them!

Just take a look at this...

1 Ever wondered why fridges hum sometimes? (NO, it's not 'cos they're happy.) Specially cooled chemicals are pumped around pipes at the back that pass into the fridge and freezer areas.

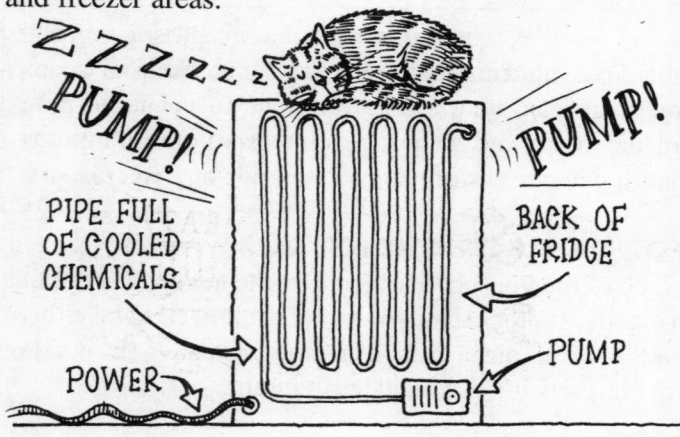

Z Z Z z z z

PUMP!

PUMP!

PIPE FULL OF COOLED CHEMICALS

BACK OF FRIDGE

POWER

PUMP

2 In a microwave oven the food goes round on a turntable driven by an electric motor.

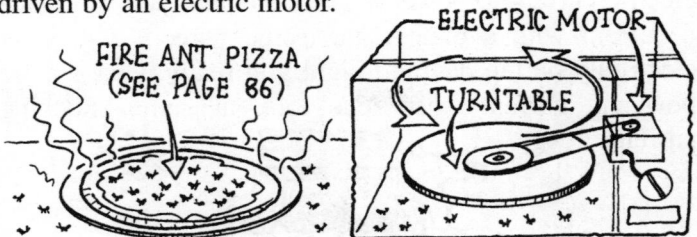

FIRE ANT PIZZA
(SEE PAGE 86)

ELECTRIC MOTOR
TURNTABLE

The motor also drives the fan that is used to reflect microwaves on to the food.

3 The CD player uses a laser beam to scan tiny pits on the underside of the CD. The laser beam jumps lightly as it scans the pits producing a reflected flickering pattern that the CD player turns into electric pulses that an amplifier can turn into sounds. Got all that? Well, the laser couldn't scan anything if the CD wasn't spinning and this is powered by an electric motor.

4 The DVD player is a bit like a CD player – only for sound AND images such as your favourite movies. Once again you need a electric motor to spin the disc so that it can be scanned by a laser beam.

5 A hairdryer is simply a coil of wire that heats up by friction as electrons crush through it (just like a light bulb – see page 21).

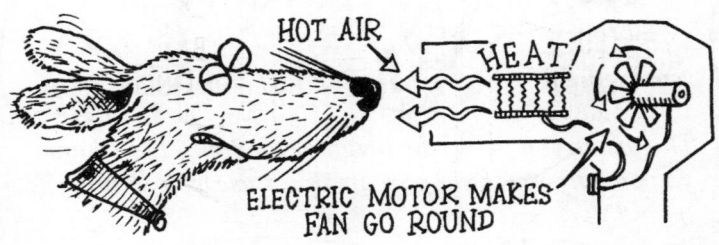

HOT AIR
HEAT!
ELECTRIC MOTOR MAKES FAN GO ROUND

Mind you, an electric motor is pretty useless without an electric current to power it. And although you can make a current with a battery and some wire, if you want electricity on tap day and night you really need a more powerful current – so let's look at some shocking currents.

No, I mean *electric* currents... Amazingly enough, people have argued and died over the best way to make an electric current.

Bet you never knew!
Chances are you've actually generated your own electricity – if you own a bike dynamo, that is. The movement of your wheels makes a magnet go round. The magnet gives out a moving electromagnetic force that pushes electrons through the dynamo wire to light up your lamp.

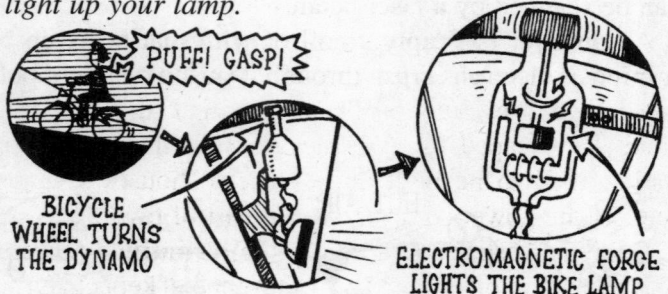

BICYCLE WHEEL TURNS THE DYNAMO

PUFF! GASP!

ELECTROMAGNETIC FORCE LIGHTS THE BIKE LAMP

The faster you pedal the brighter the light. Let's hope your penny-pinching parents don't use you to power their TV!

HIGH POWER - HIGH STAKES

Soon power generation became big business. And when electric power was launched in America in the 1880s the stakes were very high indeed. Leading the way were two power-hungry tycoons, Thomas Edison (1847–1931) and George Westinghouse (1846–1914).

Edison was a wealthy inventor with a multi-million-dollar power business complete with 121 power stations. He championed **direct current**, which means the electric current simply flows along a wire from the power station to your house. The problem was that the electrons gradually escaped through the wires so that the power stations had to be built quite close to houses and you needed one power station for each part of town.

George Westinghouse backed **alternating current**. The power station pumped out a current that kept changing direction. This made shock waves rush through the electrons in the wire at 300,000 kilometres (186,000 miles) a second. The advantage of this type of current was that it could be boosted using a device called a transformer and pumped into the wires at a massive 500,000 volts. And although electrons still leaked out of the wires there were more than enough to be carried long distances. At the other end of the wires a second transformer simply reduced the power to a safer level.

Westinghouse planned to take over Edison's business empire. But Edison insisted that alternating current was dangerous. Things were about to turn nasty ... shockingly nasty...

CRUEL CURRENTS

New York News
August 1888

BAN THESE SHOCKING TESTS!

Professor HP Brown, a consultant hired by Edison, has been organizing *HP Brown* shocking tests on cute fluffy animals to show the dangers of alternating current. The tests involve shocking dogs and cats. When asked where he got the animals Brown turned red and said, "They just volunteered." He refused to say whether he's paid anyone for the animals.

NEW YORK NEWS

December 1888

A SHOCKING WAY TO GO!

New York State is to execute murderers. This follows embarrassing incidents when hangings have gone wrong and people have had their heads pulled off by the rope. The first victim to be

electrocuted is to be William Kemplar a fruitseller convicted of killing his girlfriend. Thomas Edison says the execution will prove the danger of alternating current.

W. Kemplar (before the murder)

STOP PRESS!

Westinghouse is shocked that his alternating current is going to be used to kill someone. Kemplar says he's shocked too and he's appealing, claiming the execution is too cruel. We expect him to be even more shocked if the execution goes ahead.

W. Kemplar (Yesterday)

NEW YORK NEWS

A DEAD LOSS

Kemplar is dead. His appeal was rejected after Thomas Edison claimed that electrocution wasn't such a bad way to go, because it kills nice and quickly. But the execution in the newly-designed electric chair went horribly wrong. Kemplar survived the first shock and took another jolt of over a minute resulting in smoke and sparks coming out of his body. The execution was a shocking sight

and a doctor present said: "I've heard smoking is bad for you but this is ridiculous!" before disappearing into the toilet.

WHAT HAPPENED NEXT?

Well, Westinghouse won. High voltage alternating current was the only way to move electricity any distance and in 1893 Westinghouse unveiled a powerful motor. It used alternating current and magnets that acted on first one side and then the other side of a metal loop. The motor was designed by a brilliant Croatian-born inventor named Nikola Tesla (1856–1943).

Some people thought Tesla was mad because he became a lonely old man who talked to the pigeons that lived in his New York apartment. Well, just imagine if one of the pigeon's had written Tesla's story. OK, I realize that's pretty unusual ... books by pigeons tend to be about flying.

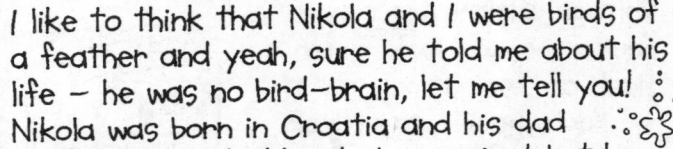

TESLA AS I KNEW HIM...
By Percy Pigeon.

I like to think that Nikola and I were birds of a feather and yeah, sure he told me about his life — he was no bird-brain, let me tell you! Nikola was born in Croatia and his dad wanted him to be a priest but he wanted to be a scientist. So he talked his dad into letting him go to college. Mind you, he ruffled his teacher's feathers in a lesson on electric motors. Announced he could build a better electric motor — but no one believed him.

N. TESLA

Anyway, Nikola was in a park when he got the idea for this motor. He was reading poetry (why wasn't he feeding the pigeons?) and he drew the design on the ground with a stick. He built the machine the next year and soon after he went to America to work for this Edison guy. Nikola went there with four cents in his pocket, some plans for a flying machine he never got round to building, and his electric motor.

ELECTRIC MOTOR

But things didn't work out. Edison didn't like alternating current (whatever that is) which is how Nikola's machine worked, and he didn't like Nikola either. So, Nikola got himself hired by Edison's rival Westinghouse. He dreamt up a new transformer for making high voltages (whatever that is) and

TRANSFORMER

Westinghouse marketed the machine. Old Nikola was an amazing guy. His lab was full of giant lightning flashes given out by his high-voltage alternating currents. I reckon he was looking for a flash of inspiration.

Yeah, people say Nikola got weird. But all he said was he was in touch with aliens and that he'd invented a death-ray to shoot down planes. Sounds sensible to me! I mean planes are a menace to high flying pigeons. Anyway Nikola was my idea of a nice guy — generous with the breadcrumbs and he didn't even blow a fuse when I got my aim wrong and pooed on his head.

Time was when the electric motor was the height of high technology. But those were the days when even your most ancient teachers were still running around with squeaky little voices and teddy bears. Today we have electric machines that, although still powered by electric motors, can do a lot more than simply go round and round. Machines that calculate sums and help you play really cool high-tech computer games. Machines stuffed full of wonderful, interesting electronics. Devices that control the flow of electricity and make it do useful work.

So if you want to do some useful work take a look at the next chapter … it's AWESOME.

AWESOME ELECTRONICS

Electronics is really about one thing. Getting electrons in an electronic current to perform fancy tricks inside machines by the use of clever gadgets and circuits.

CLEVER CIRCUITS

What is a circuit? Well, for an electrical current to flow it's got to have somewhere to flow to. A circuit is simply a wire arranged in a circle for the current to flow along and on the way there might be switches and bulbs and various electrical gadgets. Here's your chance to test your teacher's knowledge of circuits.

TEACHER'S TEA-BREAK TEASER

You will need a bird. No, not a real pigeon like Percy – a toy bird will do. All you do is tap gently on the staffroom door. When it opens, smile innocently and ask:

HOW COME BIRDS CAN PERCH ON A HIGH-VOLTAGE WIRE AND NOT GET ELECTROCUTED?

Answer: If the bird's going to get a nasty shock the electricity must flow through its body. But electricity must have somewhere else to go before it can flow – as in a circuit. So if Percy isn't touching the ground or a pylon at the same time as touching the wire he's safe.

CRUCIAL CIRCUIT TRAINING

To discover more about circuits, let's imagine a unique fitness centre, and remember those sparky electron kids from the Atom Family? Well, now they're being put through their paces by fearsome fitness fanatic, A Tomm.

THE ELECTRON FIZZICAL TRAINING CAMP

Crazy circuits

In our first event, the electrons race round a series of race tracks and light up bulbs and sound buzzers.

The first race is the series circuit – it's a nice, gentle warm up. The electrons must run from their battery hut round the wire, through the bulbs, and back to their battery. But so many electrons are crawling through the bulb wire that the rest get held up so they don't go too fast. A. Tomm isn't impressed.

SERIES CIRCUIT

The second race is the parallel circuit. This is tougher and faster. A. Tomm has rearranged the wires so that there are two separate wires for each bulb. This means half the electrons can go one way and half can go the other so there's less of a bottleneck and the race is faster.

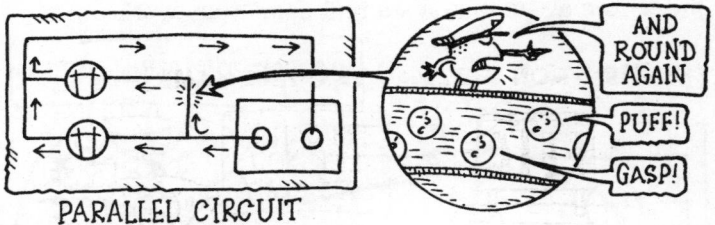

PARALLEL CIRCUIT

Super switches

Are you ready to make the switch? The electrons sure better be! In this exercise they'll have to get past the dreaded electrical switch. The switch is a springy piece of metal. When the switch is on the springy piece of metal is held down so the electrons crawling through the wire can crawl through it too. But they better be quick because when the switch is off the metal springs up and breaks the circuit. Leaving the electrons stranded!

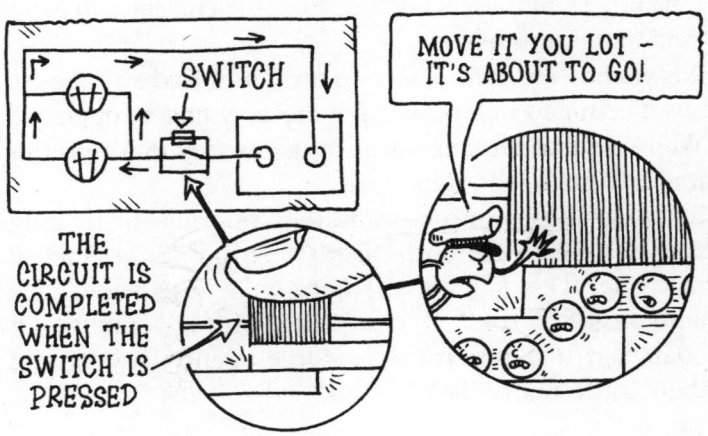

Fizzing fuses

Or should we call it frazzled fuses? In this heat (and boy, is it hot!) the electrons have to crawl though a narrow piece of wire. The resistance they get as they crawl through makes a lot of heat. If too many crawl in together the wire may melt so it's a real dangerous work-out.

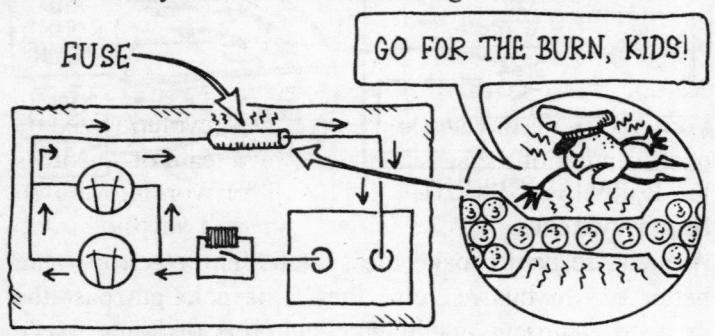

FUSE

GO FOR THE BURN, KIDS!

AND HERE ARE THE FULL FIZZICAL FACTS...

1 You get circuits everywhere electricity flows – so in your house a circuit runs round your light switches in each floor with separate circuits serving your power plugs. (Just imagine all those wires inside the walls!) As long as any of these switches is on, the current will flow. And that brings us to...

2 Switches. Besides power points you'll find switches in any electrical machine whether mains or battery operated. Well, how on Earth else are you going to turn it on – ask it nicely?

3 You get fuses in plugs and they're great for making sure too much current doesn't rush into an electrical machine. The number of amps in a fuse shows the amount of current it can take before it melts. Of course, if it did melt the machine wouldn't work and then you'd really blow a fuse!

That's why it really is a bad idea to use a single power socket to run your radio, TV, video and CD player on. The machines would use so much power that they'd melt the fuse!

SUPER SEMI-CONDUCTORS

From the 1950s onwards electronics was revolutionized by the invention of the semiconductor by a team of scientists led by William Shockley (1910–1989) working at Bell Laboratories, USA. A semiconductor isn't anything to do with a semi-detached house, a semicolon or a semicircle. It's actually two slices of an element (type of atom) called silicon – you can imagine it as a slice of holey Swiss cheese on a slice of bread.

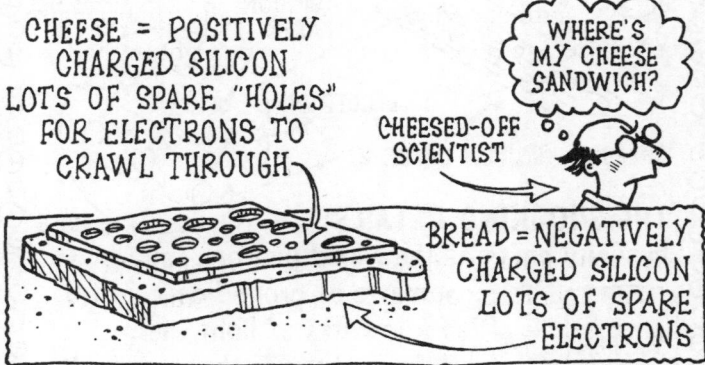

CHEESE = POSITIVELY CHARGED SILICON LOTS OF SPARE "HOLES" FOR ELECTRONS TO CRAWL THROUGH

WHERE'S MY CHEESE SANDWICH?

CHEESED-OFF SCIENTIST

BREAD = NEGATIVELY CHARGED SILICON LOTS OF SPARE ELECTRONS

The electrons are quite happy crawling from the bread to the cheese but they can't return from the cheese to the bread. This means you can use a semi-conductor to control the direction that electrons flow. And then they can even be used to make power from the sun!

Shocking electricity fact file

NAME : Solar power

THE BASIC FACTS : A solar cell is simply that tasty cheese on bread semiconductor. Sunlight is made up of those tiny blips of light called photons.

1 Photons knock electrons in the bread free of their atoms.

2 Free electrons go off to explore the cheese.

3 More electrons move from the bread to take their place. This makes an electric current.

SUN

BREAD/TOAST-
(SILICON
LAYER 1)

ELECTRIC
CURRENT

ELECTRON

CHEESE ~ (SILICON LAYER 2)

HOLE

THE SHOCKING DETAILS:

In sunny parts of the world just one square metre of ground gets 2,000 kilowatts of light energy from the sun. That's enough to boil a kettle for six weeks. Mind you, if you did try that you'd boil the kettle dry before you got a cup of tea!

I'D RATHER HAVE A GLASS OF COLD WATER

SUPER SOLAR POWER

Amongst the uses found for solar power are a way to make power for spacecraft, experimental cars that can travel at 112 km per hour (70 miles per hour), and a solar-powered hat invented in 1967 by US inventor W Dahly. It used solar power to drive an electric fan hidden inside the hat to keep the wearer's head cool.

ARGH! MY HAIR'S CAUGHT IN THE FAN!

Sadly the invention proved a flop. I guess it didn't have too many fans.

Now back to semiconductors – did you know that without them a computer wouldn't work?

SUPER SILICON CHIPS

No, this is nothing to do with French fries. The chip is a semiconductor found in computers and many other gadgets. On its surface are hundreds and thousands of tiny switches called transistors. Each transistor is like a set of traffic lights at a road junction.

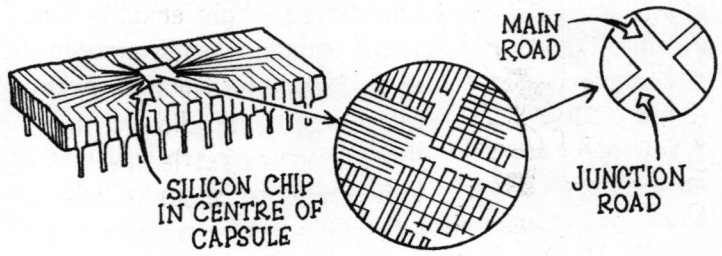

SILICON CHIP IN CENTRE OF CAPSULE

MAIN ROAD

JUNCTION ROAD

Electrons can only go along the "main road" if the current is also flowing for the "junction" road. By switching this "junction" current on and off very fast the transistor makes a current of one-off electrical pulses on the "main road" that make up basic computer code.

SILICON SECRETS

1 A silicon chip is made of silicon. (So how come you knew that already?) Anyway you can find silicon in sand. Yes, it's true, the insides of your computer probably started off loafing about on a beach somewhere.

2 Chips are shrinking. At the end of the 1960s the smallest silicon chip was 200,000 atoms across. By the end of the 1970s the smallest chip was 10,000 atoms across and by the end of the 1980s they were ten times smaller. And yet the finished chip is as complicated in its plan as a large city.

...3 BILLION DOLLARS TO DEVELOP THIS TINY CHIP, CARTER...AND YOU JUST DROPPED IT!!!!

Incredibly, it's now possible to make a chip a few dozen atoms across ... and in the future? Well, actually that's about as far as you can go. If you made a chip smaller its circuits would have corners too tight for electrons to flow round.

3 You might be wondering how you can get all that detail on a chip too tiny to hold. Actually, the boring fiddly work of adding the different types of silicon and aluminium to carry the current is done by robots. The only thing we humans need to worry about is getting dust or dandruff or dried snot in the chips and ruining them. (Of course robots don't have this problem.)

4 Nowadays silicon chips are found in loads of machines and not just computers. You can find silicon chips controlling DVD players and Play Stations, and Andy Mann's mobile phone and even walking, talking, peeing dolls. Yes – it really is chips with everything!

MIND YOU, IT STOPPED WORKING WHEN I DROPPED SALT AND VINEGAR ON IT!

There's a gap of 2,600 years between old Thales rubbing a lump of amber with a bit of fur to the latest up-to-the -minute silicon chips. Although it's a long time the vast leaps forward in technology are even more astonishing. But where's the tide of technology taking us? Are we heading for an electronic wonderland or could we slip back to the dark ages? What kind of shocks await us?

Better read on and find out...

THE FUTURE

EPILOGUE: A SHOCKING FUTURE?

In the olden days before electricity life was hard and cold and comfortless and slow. But that was then and today the world of electricity and electronics is buzzing with new ideas.

Some ideas are exciting, some are important and some are rather silly. Which ones do you think will take root, and which will quietly disappear like the solar-powered hat and the wobbling toilet seat? And what will they think of next? Let's switch on the TV.

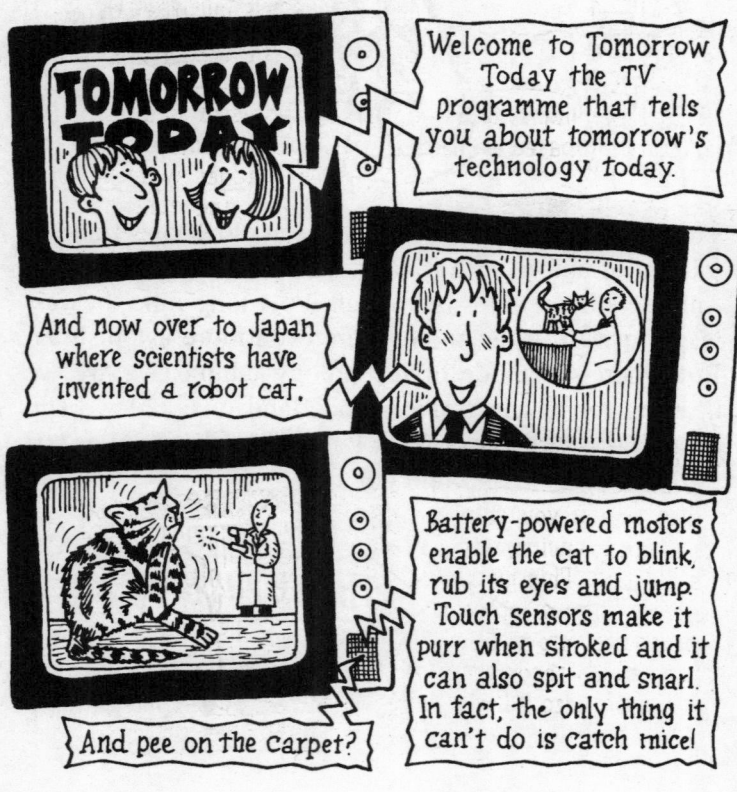

Researchers from IBM have created a computer screen that gives you a picture as good as the very best TV. It works like the display of a calculator which uses liquid crystal blocks that give out light when an electric current runs across them.

The screen has no fewer than 5.5 million pixels (dots of light) powered by 15.7 transistors and 4.21 km of wiring.

Gosh!

That's nothing. A British university Professor has had a silicon chip-based control device implanted into his arm. The gadget switches on lights and computers without the professor having to touch them!

Any volunteers for this op?

And finally you can relax and unwind with a TV box. This nifty device turns a laptop computer into a TV and video recorder with full video editing facilities.

Besides new gadgets, scientists are working on longer-term research which might in time lead to new technology and more new gadgets. So what does the future hold? We've asked Tiddles the robot cat (alias Mystic Mog) to gaze into her mysteriously cloudy bowl of milk. Here's what she saw...

1 It's life ... but not as we know it

In 1952 Stanley Miller at the University of Chicago fired an electric spark through a mixture of gases. He was trying to copy the effect of lightning on gases in the air thousands of millions of years ago. His experiment had a remarkable result: amino acids – complex chemicals found in living things – formed from the gases. Scientists are still looking at ways in which electricity in the form of lightning may have given rise to life on Earth.

Prediction 1

Scientists find out how to make a new kind of life-form in a test tube using electricity and chemicals.

2 Powering ahead

Scientists in different parts of the world are developing plans to use the power of tides to make electricity. Although their plans vary they all depend on using the water rushing through narrow channels to drive turbines. In the 2000s other scientists were looking at building a huge chimney in the South African desert. Warmed by the hot sun, air will rise up the chimney and power generators to make electricity.

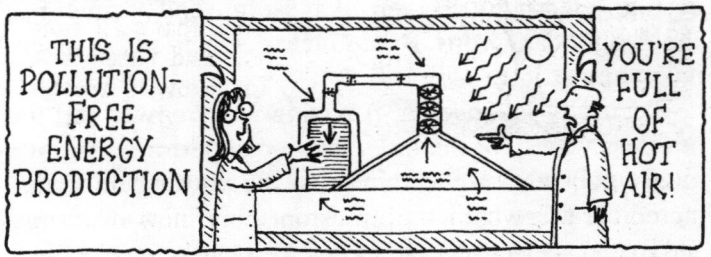

Prediction 2

One of these plans will come off and create a new technology which can make electricity for nothing *for ever.*

3 Real cool power

As long ago as 1911 Dutch scientist Heike Kamerliingh-Onnes (1853–1926) found that at very low temperatures, say just above -273° C (-459° F) metals like the mercury in a thermometer become superconductors. This means they lose their resistance to electricity – isn't that super! In 1957 a team led by US scientist John Bardeen (1908–1991) calculated that superconductor atoms wobble less when they are very cold allowing electrons to swim between the atoms without being knocked off course.

Prediction 3

Scientists invent a substance that allows electricity to run through it easily at room temperature. This opens the door to a new generation of electric machines that need scarcely any power to run.

Despite the promise of future progress most people still find electricity mysterious, but hopefully having read this book you won't be one of them. All most people know is that electricity is terribly useful and sometimes shockingly dangerous. But of course, electricity is much, much more.

Electricity is amazing. Amazing in its power and the limitless variety of the tasks that it can perform. And it's totally gobsmacking to think that the power behind this incredible force comes from astonishing blips of energy and matter – electrons and atoms. Yep, the same electrons and atoms that help a pelican find its way home and make your heart beat and give shape and substance to everything in the universe. Including you.

And that's the SHOCKING TRUTH!

SEE YA!

SHOCKING
ELECTRICITY

QUIZ

**Now find out if you're a
Shocking Electricity expert!**

Electrical impulses are everywhere. In the Earth, in the clouds – even in your horrible science teacher. Without electricity there'd be no light bulbs, no television, nothing fun at all. Take these quick quizzes to see how much you really know about this fatal force...

ASTONISHING ELECTRONS

If your brain is fully switched on by this book, you'll know by now that electricity is made of electrons – tiny blips that spend their lives whizzing around the nucleus of atoms. But what do you really know about these powerful particles and their amazing effects?

1 What charge does an electron have?
a) Positive
b) Negative
c) Dangerous

WHY DO I FEEL SO NEGATIVE?

2 What is the name of the particle given out by electrons as they lose energy and slow down?
a) Pooton
b) Proton
c) Photon

3 What is static electricity?
a) A form of electricity in which the electrons stop moving completely.
b) A form of electricity in which electrons are transferred from one thing to another. changing the electrical charge of each.

c) A form of electricity that looks all fuzzy through a microscope.

4 How can you rearrange the atoms in a magnet so that it doesn't work any more?
a) By frying it over a strong heat.
b) By drowning it in salty water.
c) By slicing it in half with a chainsaw.

5 How do batteries make an electric current?
a) By removing all the positive charges from the metal casing.
b) By mixing two chemicals together.
c) By squashing together lots of tiny magnets.

6 What happens when you hold an electrified object?
a) Your muscles squeeze together so you can't let go and you'll probably die a horrible death.
b) It interrupts the electrical impulses in the heart and you'll probably die a horrible death.
c) The electricity fries your brain and you'll definitely die a horrible death.

7 Where is the safest place to shelter during an electric storm?
a) In a car.
b) Under a tree.
c) Under an umbrella.

8 How fast can electrons move?
a) About the speed of sound.
b) About the speed of a horse.
c) About the speed of light.

HORRIBLE ELECTRICITY FACTS

Electricity flows all around us (as well as inside us), but it took scientists a long time to get to grips with it, and along the way they made some messy mistakes. Below are some silly statements about electricity – can you figure out if these fascinating force facts are true or false?

1 Electricity flows from positively charged areas to negatively charged areas.
2 You can make electricity from farts.
3 Animals like sharks and bees can detect electrical pulses in humans.
4 Electricity always finds the quickest route to the ground.
5 Electricity can travel through metal wires.
6 Electric shocks aren't always bad – they can be used to re-start the heart if it stops beating.
7 The Earth is just one great big magnet.
8 The human body contains enough electricity to light the fairy lights on a Christmas tree.

Answers:

1 False. It's the other way around (although brilliant Ben Franklin got this wrong too...).

2 True. Farts contain the gas methane, which can power generators.

3 True. And it can make them pretty angry!

4 True. Which is why it's not a good idea to stand under an umbrella in a lightning storm – the metal in the umbrella will attract the electricity and channel is straight to the ground – through you!

5 False. Ha ha. Trick question – in fact, electricity travels through a field around the wire.

6 True. Doctors use a shockingly clever machine called a defibrillator that passes an electric current into the heart to restart it.

7 True. The Earth's core is surrounded by a massive sea of melted metal that sends out electric and magnetic forces.

8 True. But don't worry – if you weren't a bundle of electric pulses you'd be, well, dead.

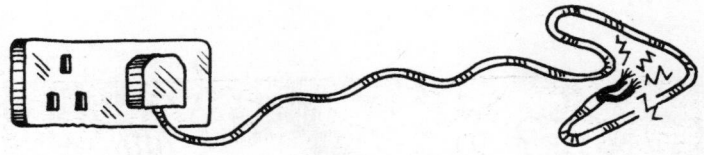

STRANGE SCIENTISTS

They say it takes all sorts, but the silly scientists who helped us understand electricity were some of the strangest ever. Experiments with electricity can be horribly dangerous, and some of these fantastic physicists diced with death. Just take this quiz and find out for yourself...

1 What natural force did barmy Benjamin Franklin investigate in his most famous experiment? (Clue: It was certainly enlightening.)

2 What did John Joseph Thomson use to bend the ray of electrons in his cathode ray tube experiment? (Clue: It was an attractive experiment.)

3 What kind of electricity did ancient Greek Thales of Miletus experiment with? (Clue: It was certainly hair-raising.)

4 What amazing invention did Robert Van de Graf come up with? (Clue: It generated some interest at the time.)

I'D BETTER READ ON...

5 What happened when Luigi Galvani attached his dead pet frog to the iron bars on his windows? (Clue: It made the silly scientist jump!)

6 What substance did Alessandro Volta find to be the best conductor for passing an electric current between two pieces of metal? (Clue: Water surprise!)

7 What magnetic mystery did William Gilbert solve while playing around with his compass? (Clue: He remained well-grounded despite his discovery.)

8 What magnificent machine did mad Michael Faraday build? (Clue: He was driven to it.)

Answers:
1 Lightning.
2 A magnet.
3 Static electricity.
4 An electrical generator.
5 The frog's legs jumped around as if it was still alive.
6 Salt water.
7 That the Earth is magnetic.
8 The electric motor.

MYSTERIOUS MEASUREMENTS

There are all sorts of ways of measuring electricity and most of the units of measurement are named after the strange scientists who discovered them. You've met some of them in this book, so now see if you can match the mad measurement with its meaning.

1 Amp
2 Volt
3 Watt
4 Ohm
5 Farad
6 Watthour
7 Coulomb
8 Henry

a) A measure of electrical resistance.
b) A measure of electrical storage capacity.
c) A measure of electric current.
d) A measure of electrical energy.
e) A measure of reaction to changes in the magnetic field.
f) A measure of electrical pressure.
g) A measure of electrical charge.
h) A measure of electrical power.

Answers:
1c; 2f; 3h; 4a; 5b; 6d; 7g; 8e

HORRIBLE INDEX

170

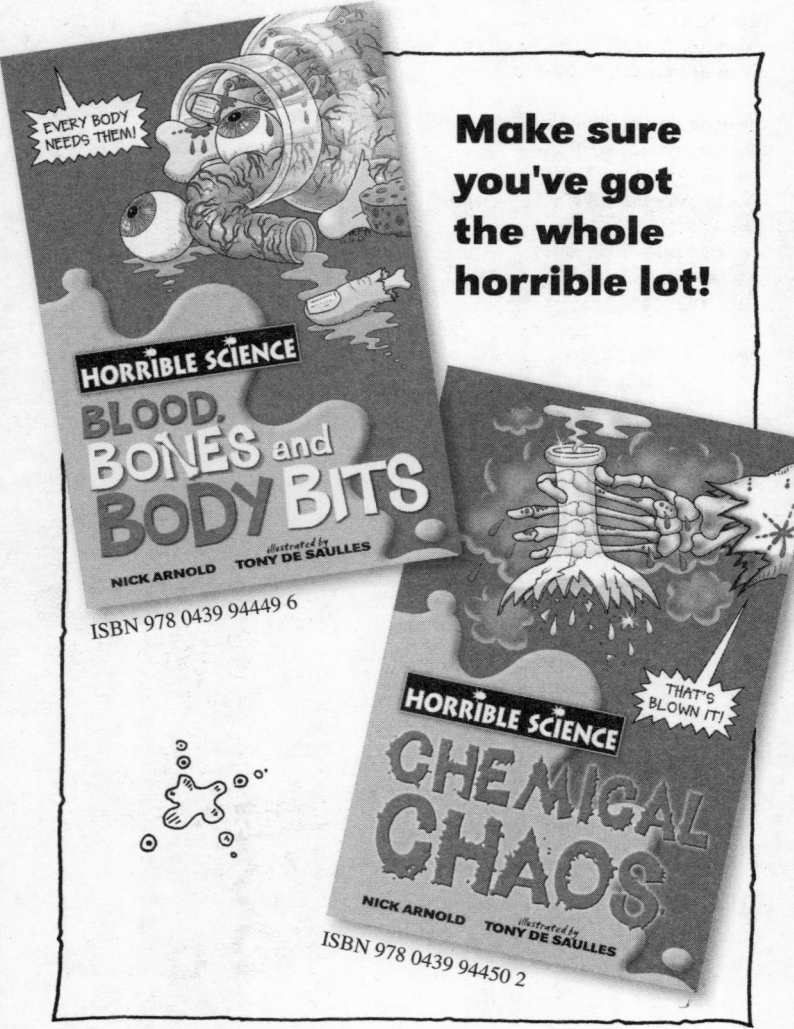

HORRIBLE SCIENCE
NASTY NATURE

I LOVE FAST FOOD!

NICK ARNOLD   *illustrated by* TONY DE SAULLES

ISBN 978 0439 94451 9

HORRIBLE SCIENCE
DISGUSTING DIGESTION

IT TAKES GUTS!

NICK ARNOLD   *illustrated by* TONY DE SAULLES

ISBN 978 0439 94445 8

HORRIBLE SCIENCE
UGLY BUGS

NOT A PRETTY SIGHT!

NICK ARNOLD   *illustrated by* TONY DE SAULLES

ISBN 978 0439 94452 6

HORRIBLE SCIENCE

KILLER ENERGY

NICK ARNOLD

illustrated by
TONY DE SAULLES

■SCHOLASTIC

www.horrible-science.co.uk

www.nickarnold-website.com
www.tonydesaulles.co.uk

Scholastic Children's Books,
Euston House, 24 Eversholt Street,
London NW1 1DB, UK

A division of Scholastic Ltd
London ~ New York ~ Toronto ~ Sydney ~ Auckland
Mexico City ~ New Delhi ~ Hong Kong

First published in the UK by Scholastic Ltd, 2001
This edition published 2009

Text copyright © Nick Arnold, 2001
Illustrations copyright © Tony De Saulles, 2001

ISBN 978 1407 10960 2

Page layout services by Quadrum Solutions Ltd, Mumbai, India
Printed and bound by CPI Group (UK) Ltd, Croydon, CR0 4YY

18

The right of Nick Arnold and Tony De Saulles to be identified as the author and
illustrator of this work respectively has been asserted by them in accordance
with the Copyright, Designs and Patents Act, 1988.

CONTENTS

Nick Arnold has been writing stories and books since he was a youngster, but never dreamt he'd find fame writing about killer energy. His research involved building his own steam engine and entering an Iron Man Competition and he enjoyed every minute of it.

When he's not delving into Horrible Science, he spends his spare time eating pizza, riding his bike and thinking up corny jokes (though not all at the same time).

Tony De Saulles picked up his crayons when he was still in nappies and has been doodling ever since. He takes Horrible Science very seriously and even agreed to sketch radioactive atoms. Fortunately, he has made a full recovery.

When he's not out with

his sketchpad, Tony likes to write poetry and play squash, though he hasn't written any poetry about squash yet.

INTRODUCTION

I hope you're not easily scared, because ... you're about to meet a huge, horribly powerful MONSTER!

It's a very, very old monster (yes, it's even older than your science teacher). In fact, it's so incredibly ancient that it's as old as time itself. And the amazing thing about this monster is that it's always around but no one has ever seen it – *well not until now that is*!

The monster's name is ENERGY...

The Energy Monster gets everywhere. It makes stars shine and bonfires burn, and it moves everything from the slowest slug to the speediest spacecraft. But don't go thinking that the Energy Monster is a helpful gentle giant. No way! Take a deep breath and read on ... if you dare!

Sometimes the Energy Monster is a cruel, crazed, KILLER that destroys humans in hundreds of horrible ways. Of course, ordinary science books don't dwell on these disgusting details but this is a *Horrible Science* book – and that means you can read the killer energy info you *really* want to know, such as…

• Why this lucky man is bursting into flames because of a fart…

• Why this man is eating greasy fat for breakfast…

• And why this scientist is getting rats drunk…

• Plus, the ULTIMATE FATE OF THE UNIVERSE (and whether it'll spoil your holiday this year).

HORRIBLE HEALTH WARNING!

This book contains foul facts, rude words and blood-thirsty cartoons. This material may shock teachers and other sensitive persons.

SHOCK! HORROR!

Hopefully, though, you're made of sterner stuff. Now, have you got enough energy to turn the page?

ER...WELL, OK THEN

THE ULTIMATE POWER

Is your brain powered up? Well, this killer question will get it going so fast that steam could blast out of your ears. Ready? OK, here it is...

What do the following have in common?

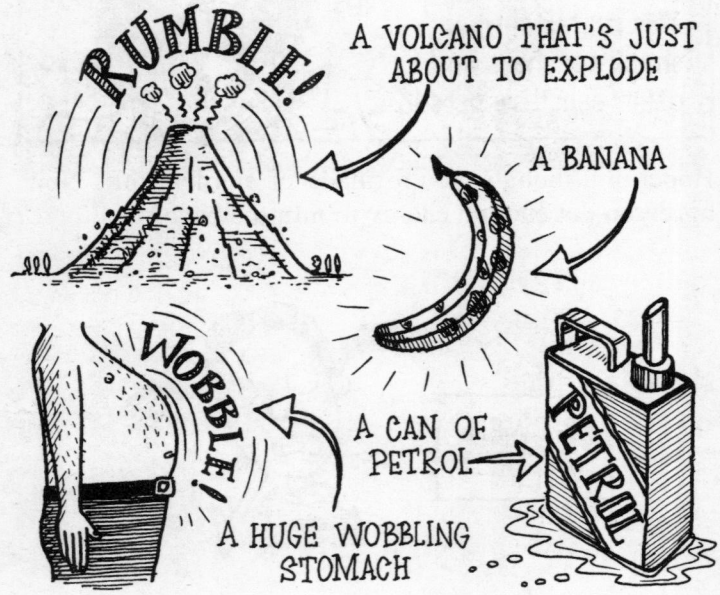

RUMBLE!

A VOLCANO THAT'S JUST ABOUT TO EXPLODE

A BANANA

WOBBLE!

A CAN OF PETROL →

PETROL

A HUGE WOBBLING STOMACH

Give up?

Well, they all store *energy*...

The volcano stores movement energy. And when the volcano explodes you'll need lots of movement energy to run away. Bananas are great energy stores which is why some tennis players eat at least six every match. Petrol is a fuel so it's "fuel" of energy, and the bulging belly contains fat which is yet another food energy store...

Now at this point we were going to ask a teacher to tell us what energy is. But we couldn't find one who knew … see what I mean?

Honestly … do I have to explain *everything* round here?

Killer energy fact file

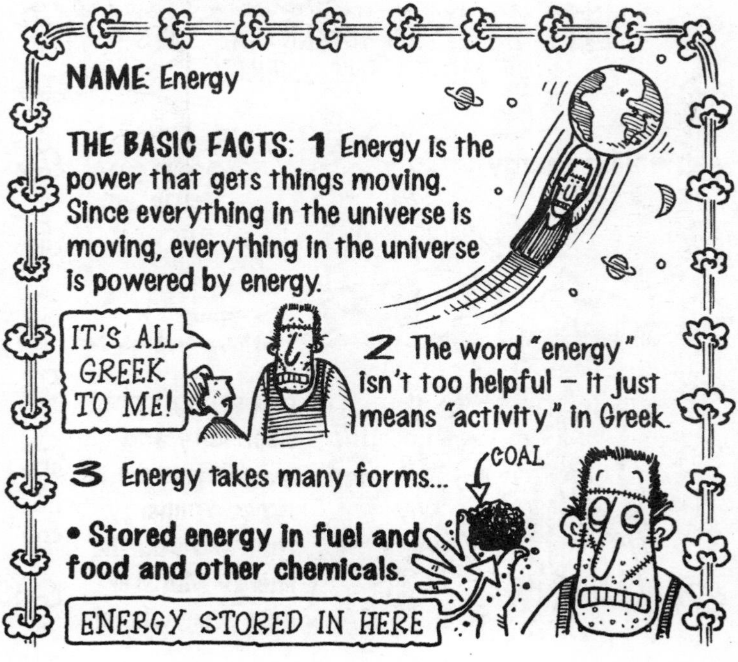

NAME: Energy

THE BASIC FACTS: 1 Energy is the power that gets things moving. Since everything in the universe is moving, everything in the universe is powered by energy.

IT'S ALL GREEK TO ME!

2 The word "energy" isn't too helpful – it just means "activity" in Greek.

3 Energy takes many forms…

COAL

• Stored energy in fuel and food and other chemicals.

ENERGY STORED IN HERE

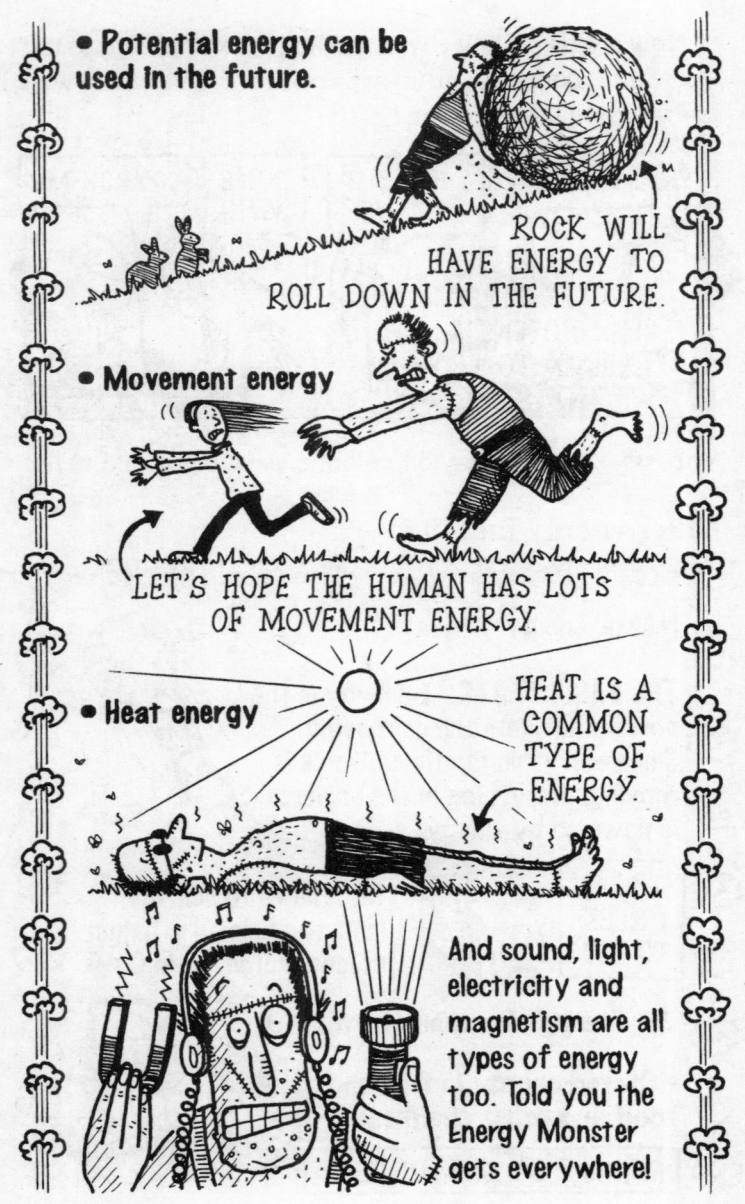

• Potential energy can be used in the future.

ROCK WILL HAVE ENERGY TO ROLL DOWN IN THE FUTURE.

• Movement energy

LET'S HOPE THE HUMAN HAS LOTS OF MOVEMENT ENERGY.

• Heat energy

HEAT IS A COMMON TYPE OF ENERGY.

And sound, light, electricity and magnetism are all types of energy too. Told you the Energy Monster gets everywhere!

KILLER DETAILS: Every execution method uses energy in one form or another. As you can see...

KILLER BLADE HAS POTENTIAL ENERGY TO FALL AT ANY SECOND

With me so far?

So energy gets things moving and takes different forms. But someone had to figure this out. As you can imagine, scientists in the past had some really wrong ideas about energy. Here are four scientists to argue their points of view…

THE GREAT ENERGY DEBATE

Famous Greek philosopher, **Aristotle** (384–322 BC)

Not-so-famous Greek philosopher, **Anaxagoras** (500–428 BC)

German scientist, philosopher, mathematician, historian and all-round know-all, **Gottfried Leibniz** (1646–1716)

German scientist, **Georg Ernst Stahl** (1660–1734)

11

Things have the energy to move because they are guided by a great unseen mind called the nous.

That's rubbish — an invisible substance called pneuma makes things move.

Well, I can't see it!

That's 'cos it's invisible — dim-wit!

GRRRRR!

You're both wrong — living things move because they have the spirit of life inside them.

These ideas were as sensible as attacking a lion's mane with a razor, running five miles to escape, and then shouting: "HOW'S THAT FOR A CLOSE SHAVE!"

It took scientists until the 1850s for a number of them (working separately) to begin to make scientific sense of energy. And then they came up with the Laws of Thermodynamics (that's ther-mo-dy-nam-ics). And if you thought I said "thermal underwear" you really need to read the next chapter to find out what the heck I'm going on about...

LAYING DOWN THE LAWS

In this chapter you'll find out about the Laws of Thermodynamics. They sound dead posh and impressive but actually they're horribly easy to understand. (Don't tell anyone how easy, and with luck your friends will think you are a scientific genius!)

Killer energy fact file

NAME: The Laws of Thermodynamics

THE BASIC FACTS: 1 "Thermodynamics" means "moving heat". The laws tell you what heat energy does and how it links up with other forms of energy.

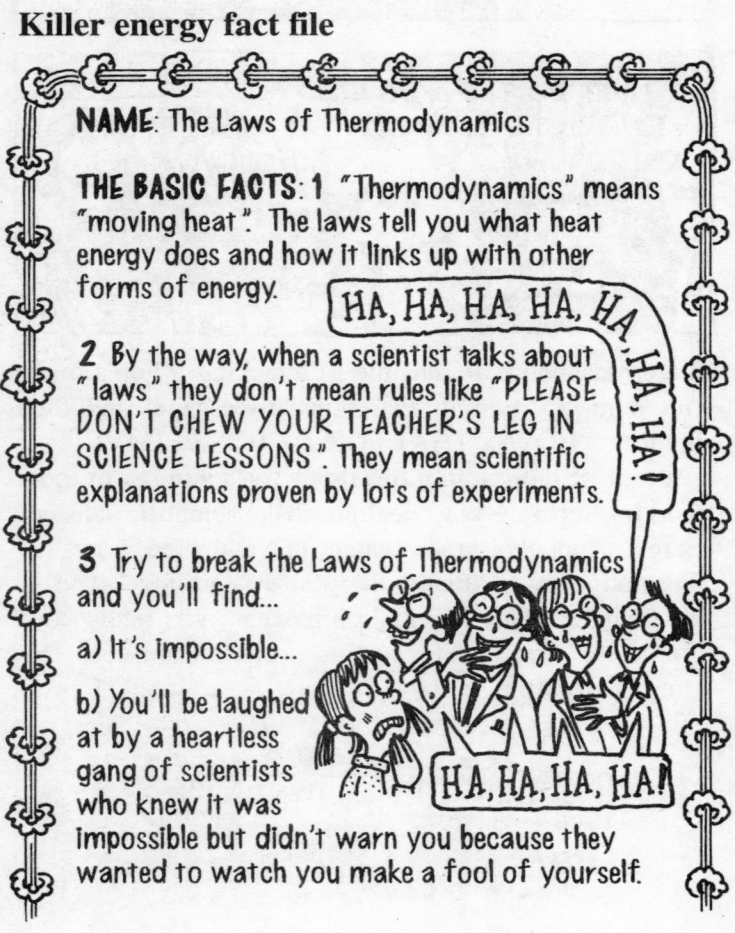

HA, HA, HA, HA, HA, HA, HA!

2 By the way, when a scientist talks about "laws" they don't mean rules like "PLEASE DON'T CHEW YOUR TEACHER'S LEG IN SCIENCE LESSONS". They mean scientific explanations proven by lots of experiments.

3 Try to break the Laws of Thermodynamics and you'll find...

a) It's impossible...

b) You'll be laughed at by a heartless gang of scientists who knew it was impossible but didn't warn you because they wanted to watch you make a fool of yourself.

HA, HA, HA, HA!

KILLER DETAILS: The search for these laws drove one scientist into madness. Let's hope you're more fortunate...

THERMO DIE MANIC! DON'T PANIC! RAVE! JIBBER!

SO, WHAT DO THE LAWS SAY?

Meet Harvey Tucker, the BIGGEST journalist in Australia – well, he's certainly the largest (and the laziest).

G'DAY SPORTS!

Later on he'll be investigating energy (that's if he can be bothered). But for now, we've managed to persuade Harvey to report on how the Laws work...

THE LAWS OF THERMODYNAMICS

Well, I wasn't too hot on thermo ... heat energy, but no worries – I surfed stacks of info from the Internet.

Phew — it's hard yakka! Anyway, here's the low-down...

LAW ONE
Energy can't be made or destroyed. But heat energy can be used to power movement energy and movement energy can turn into heat energy. Streuth! That's fair dinkums. If I did some work I'd have more movement energy and this would make me feel more heat energy. So I'd best sit here with my lager and save my energy — BURP!

HEAT ENERGY —— POWERS —→ MOVEMENT ENERGY

←— CAN TURN INTO ——

LAW TWO
Heat energy always moves from hot things to cold things. So heat from the sun is warming up my cold lager. Well, talk about stating the blithering obvious! If heat went from cold places to hot places my lager would *cool* down in the sun — well, that *would* be the day! I'm fair cooked already!

HOT SUN

HEAT ALWAYS MOVES IN THIS DIRECTION

COLD BEER

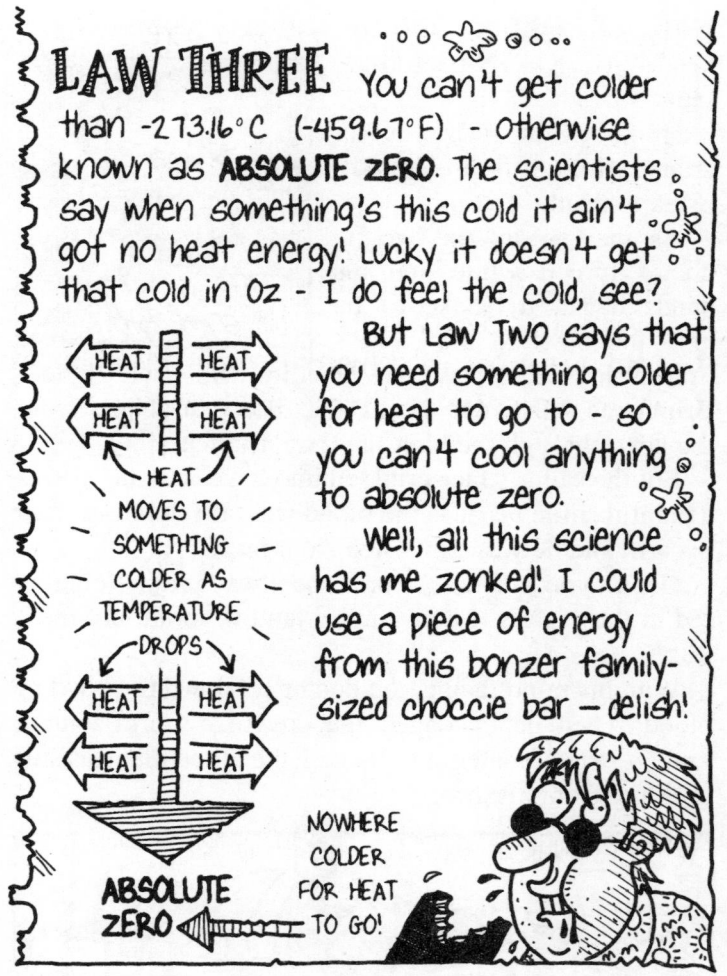

LAW THREE You can't get colder than -273.16°C (-459.67°F) - otherwise known as **ABSOLUTE ZERO**. The scientists say when something's this cold it ain't got no heat energy! Lucky it doesn't get that cold in Oz - I do feel the cold, see?

But Law Two says that you need something colder for heat to go to - so you can't cool anything to absolute zero.

Well, all this science has me zonked! I could use a piece of energy from this bonzer family-sized choccie bar — delish!

HEAT | HEAT
HEAT | HEAT

HEAT MOVES TO SOMETHING COLDER AS TEMPERATURE DROPS

HEAT | HEAT
HEAT | HEAT

ABSOLUTE ZERO NOWHERE COLDER FOR HEAT TO GO!

We'll be taking a look at Laws Two and Three in the next two chapters, but for now we'll stick to Law One. Did you know that a scientist who worked on the first law got his ideas from *blood*? Yes, it's true!

Read on for the bloodthirsty details...

Hall of Fame: Julius Robert von Mayer
(1814–1878) Nationality: German

"Ach mein Gott – I hev cut an artery! Hold still or you vill bleed to death!"

As he spoke the young doctor turned white and his hands began to shake as he held the bowl to the sailor's brawny arm. The bowl was steadily filling with blood. Bright red, glistening blood, the kind that squirts from the heart through the high-pressure arteries.

But the sailor's face crinkled into a weak smile. It was a painful smile because the blood was still draining from his arm and he was exhausted from fever.

"Don't you fret, doc – our blood always comes out this red in these parts. I don't understand it, mind, but there it is."

With his mind racing, the doctor set down the bowl of blood. Then he bandaged the crewman's arm with a grubby strip of material to staunch the blood that was still trickling from his arm.

In 1840 doctors like Mayer believed the best way to treat disease was to drain blood from their patients' veins. But when Julius tried to do this in Java he found the blood was bright red, even in veins where it's usually dark red. Julius Mayer was about to make a great discovery.

It nearly destroyed him.

Julius was not a lucky person. He didn't do well at school and he was expelled from university for joining a secret club that was frowned on by his teachers. (Today's teachers are a bit more understanding, so you may escape being expelled for joining the Horrible Club.)

Mayer was allowed back into university the following year. He studied medicine and became a ship's doctor – and that's how he came to be in Java in 1840. Seeing the red blood got him thinking. Here's how Mayer might have made sense of the puzzle in letters to his best friend – his brother…

Jakarta, Java 1841
Dear Fritz,
Remember the red blood I mentioned in my last letter? I do, I can't stop thinking about it, and now I've got an idea!
1. Bright red blood contains oxygen. The body needs oxygen in order to live – that's why we breathe!
2. The blood in the sailor's veins was bright red with oxygen. Since veins carry blood back from the body this means the sailor's body is using less oxygen than usual.

OXYGEN

3. I think the body uses oxygen to keep warm. But when it's hot (like here — sorry about the sweat stains!) the body needs less heat so it uses less oxygen.
Yes, I think I've cracked it!
What do you think?
Your bruv,
Jools

MORE OXYGEN

LESS OXYGEN

Jakarta, Java 1841
Hi Fritz,
It's me again....
Don't know what's got into me — but I've suddenly had loads of WONDERFUL NEW IDEAS!
1. I think the body needs food as well as oxygen to make heat. It's a bit like a fire that needs fuel and oxygen to burn properly.

FOOD + OXYGEN

2. This means energy must switch from one form to another. Yes, I reckon energy must be stored in food and turn into heat and movement energy inside the body.

Am I hot on the trail – or is my brain over-heating? I can't wait to get home and tell everyone!
Your very excited bruv,
Jools

Mayer was right not once but TWICE!! He'd made not one but TWO brilliant breakthroughs! He'd figured how the body uses energy *and* he'd got the idea for the First Law of Thermodynamics. (Remember, it showed the link between heat and movement energy.) Of course, all the other scientists were thrilled and Jools became famous and lived happily ever after ... didn't he?

Excuse me – this is *Horrible Science* not some sloppy-soppy little fairy tale! Mayer wrote an article and sent it to a science magazine but they didn't reply. No one believed him because he hadn't done any experiments to prove his ideas. So Mayer studied science for months and months until he knew enough to re-write the article in more scientific language. But by the time the article was published other scientists had put forward the same idea.

21

There were heated rows over who'd thought of the First Law first...

Bet you never knew!
1 One of the rival scientists was a Briton, James Joule (1818–1889). James's family was so rich he never had to go to school (he even had a top scientist, John Dalton (1766–1844), as his very own personal teacher).

AND I'D LIKE THE NEXT THREE WEEKS OFF, DALTON!

YES, CERTAINLY MASTER JAMES

(You could ask your parents to let you off school and pay for your own teacher, and if you happen to be dreaming they might even say "YES!")
2 James had a private lab for energy experiments. In 1843 he found out, by measuring the temperature of water turned by a paddle, that movement energy can be turned into heat energy.
3 Today, scientists measure energy in joules. One joule gives you enough energy to lift an apple one metre – can you do this?

GO ON!

UUUUGH!

YOU CAN DO IT!

Now back to miserable Mayer...

Julius Mayer's luck hadn't turned. He fell in love and got married but five of his seven children died of disease. Revolution broke out in Germany, and Fritz supported the revolution, but Julius was arrested for opposing it. He was soon released but fell out with his brother. Julius grew increasingly miserable about his lack of scientific success. One unhappy day, he decided to take his own life. He failed but his family thought he was mad and he spent ten years locked in mental hospitals.

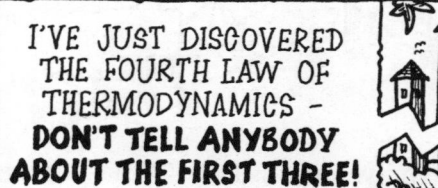

I'VE JUST DISCOVERED THE FOURTH LAW OF THERMODYNAMICS — **DON'T TELL ANYBODY ABOUT THE FIRST THREE!**

It was only years later that scientists came to realize that the First Law of Thermodynamics was correct. At last, when Mayer was a broken old man, the Royal Society, Britain's top science club, gave him a gold medal. But talking about the First Law – here's an experiment that shows it in action. Go on, give it a go – it's easy!

Dare you discover ... the First Law of Thermodynamics?

You will need:

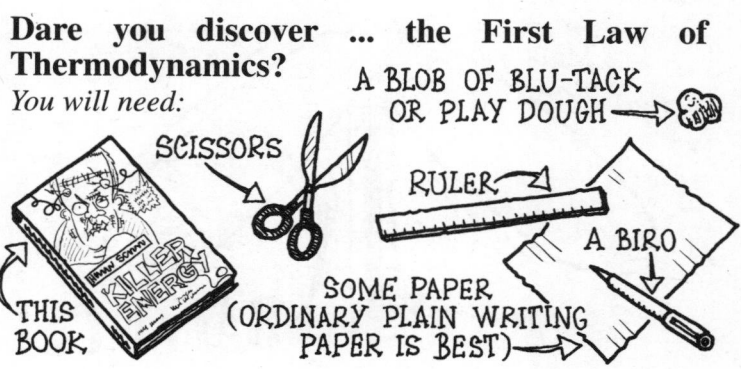

A BLOB OF BLU-TACK OR PLAY DOUGH

SCISSORS

RULER

A BIRO

THIS BOOK

SOME PAPER (ORDINARY PLAIN WRITING PAPER IS BEST)

What you do:

1 Place the paper over this shape and trace round it. Draw in the fold line using the ruler.

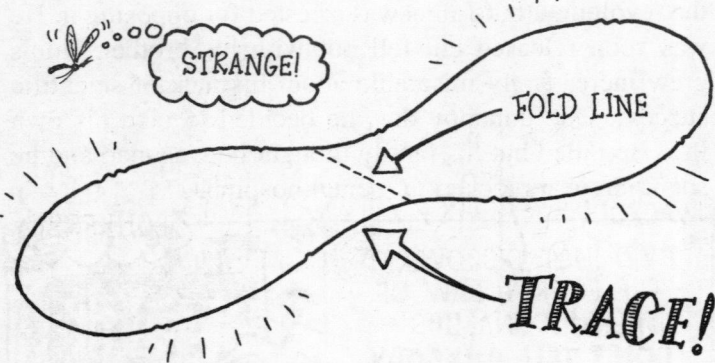

2 Cut out the shape you've drawn. DON'T cut out the shape from your *Horrible Science* book, *especially* if it comes from the library! Fold one side of the shape along the line. Unfold the shape.

3 Stick the blu-tack on a table and stick the pen in it, so it's standing on end. Make sure the pen is upright (use the ruler to check).

4 Turn the shape upside down and balance it on the point of the biro so that the sides point downwards at about 45° – carefully does it!

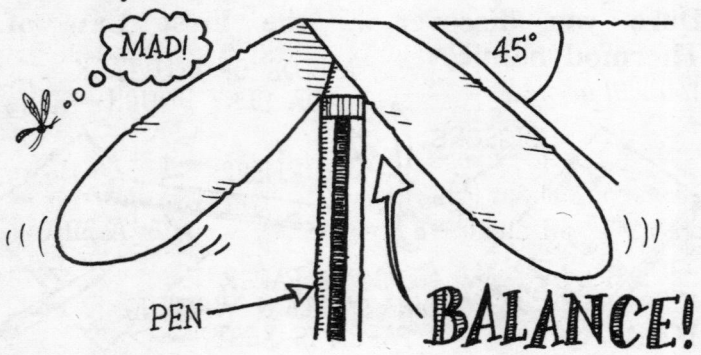

5 Watch what happens to the shape for a minute or two. Then place your hands on their sides on the table to make a circle round the biro. (If your hands are cold you need to rub them until they're warm.)

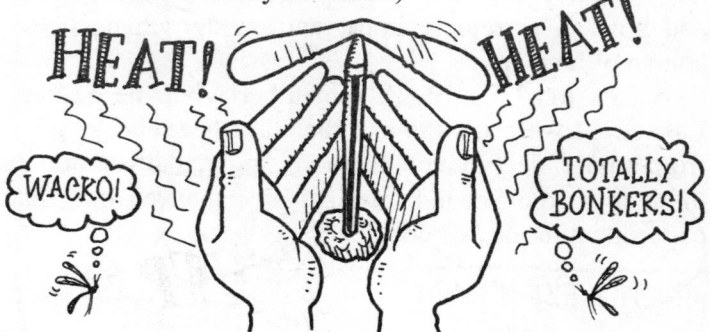

What do you notice?

a) The shape rocks backwards and forwards.

b) The shape whizzes into the air.

c) The shape moves around and then stops. When I put my hands near it the shape moves round faster than before.

Answer:
c) The shape is powered by heat energy! It might move at first because of draughts in the room or wobble as it balances on top of the pen. But it really gets going when the hot air rises off your hands. This proves the First Law is right when it says that heat energy can make things move.

But talking about heat – it just so happens that the next chapter is all about this cosy topic ... will you warm to it?

HORRIBLE HEAT

This chapter lets you into some sizzling heat secrets, including how the Second Law affects the entire universe and how an extremely important sausage changed the course of history...

What's that? You don't remember what the Second Law says? Well, it's the one that says heat energy goes from a hot object to a cooler area. And actually, come to think of it, the Second Law actually sneaked into that experiment in the last chapter.

IN THE EXPERIMENT HEAT ENERGY PASSED FROM A HOT AREA — YOUR HOT, STICKY HANDS — TO A COOLER AREA — THE AIR.

YIKES!

And as I said, the Second Law has a HUGE effect on the whole universe. Take this nice hot cup of tea...

IS MY TEA READY YET?

The Second Law says all the time the cup of tea is losing heat energy. In other words, it's cooling down. If you blow on the tea, it will cool even faster.

Your breath blows away the air warmed by the hot tea and the heat energy flows more quickly into the cooler air.

BLOW!

In half an hour the tea is disgustingly lukewarm.

LUKEWARM!

OI, WHERE'S MY BLOOMIN' TEA?

In an hour, it's stone cold.

STONE COLD!

OH YUCK!

The only way to make the tea hot is to heat it up again – in other words to add more heat energy!

And what's true for the tea is also true for everything in the *entire universe*. Yes, the Second Law says that *everything*, from galaxies to gravy, from hippos to hotwater bottles, is forever cooling down. Your body is losing heat and so is an alien starship on the other side of the cosmos.

*WE'RE LOSING HEAT, CAPTAIN!

*IT'S THAT BLASTED 2ND LAW, AGAIN!

And the only way to keep anything hot is to chuck in more heat energy. And that means you'd better eat your dad's revolting rice pudding and digest it and turn it into heat to replace the heat energy you lost today.

And that rotten old Second Law has some even worse news for you on page 141. But first it's time to find out a bit more about a real hot topic...

Killer energy fact file

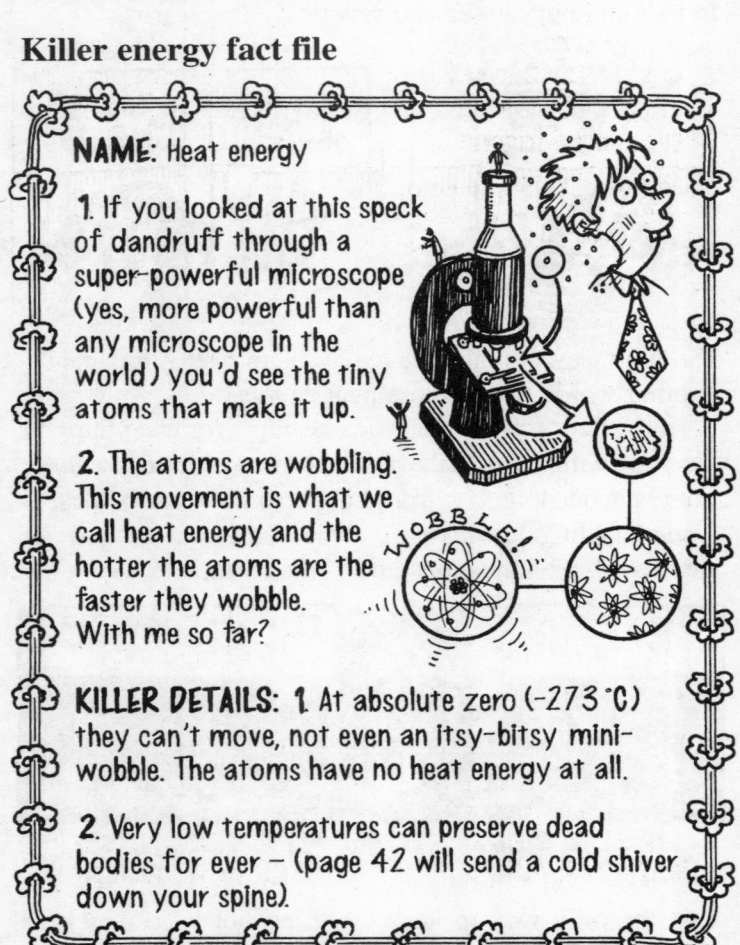

NAME: Heat energy

1. If you looked at this speck of dandruff through a super-powerful microscope (yes, more powerful than any microscope in the world) you'd see the tiny atoms that make it up.

2. The atoms are wobbling. This movement is what we call heat energy and the hotter the atoms are the faster they wobble. With me so far?

WOBBLE!

KILLER DETAILS: 1. At absolute zero (-273°C) they can't move, not even an itsy-bitsy mini-wobble. The atoms have no heat energy at all.

2. Very low temperatures can preserve dead bodies for ever – (page 42 will send a cold shiver down your spine).

NOT SO HOT THEORIES...

You can't expect scientists to grasp all this straight away and early ideas about heat were definitely on the tepid side. Here's Swiss scientist Pierre Prévost (1751–1839).

Of course this "caloric" was a load of hot air, but Prévost wasn't proved wrong until American scientist Benjamin Thompson, Count Rumford (1753–814), took on a boring job. He worked as Minister for War in Bavaria, Germany, and he was watching a cannon being bored by a drill. The cannon got very hot and, if you believed in caloric, you might think that the cannon would run out of the hot stuff after a while. But it didn't!

So Rumford realized that heat can't be a substance – it must be a form of energy that was picked up from the rubbing of the drill in the same way that rubbing your hands makes them feel warmer. In 1798 Rumford proudly announced his discovery at a meeting of the Royal Society and ... no one took any notice.

They must have been bored...

TERRIBLY TACKY THERMOMETERS

The measurement of heat energy is called temperature (I hope you're suitably impressed by this fact). But early scientists had a problem measuring heat as no one had got around to inventing the thermometer. After combing dozens of scientific junk shops we've uncovered a selection of ancient thermometers…

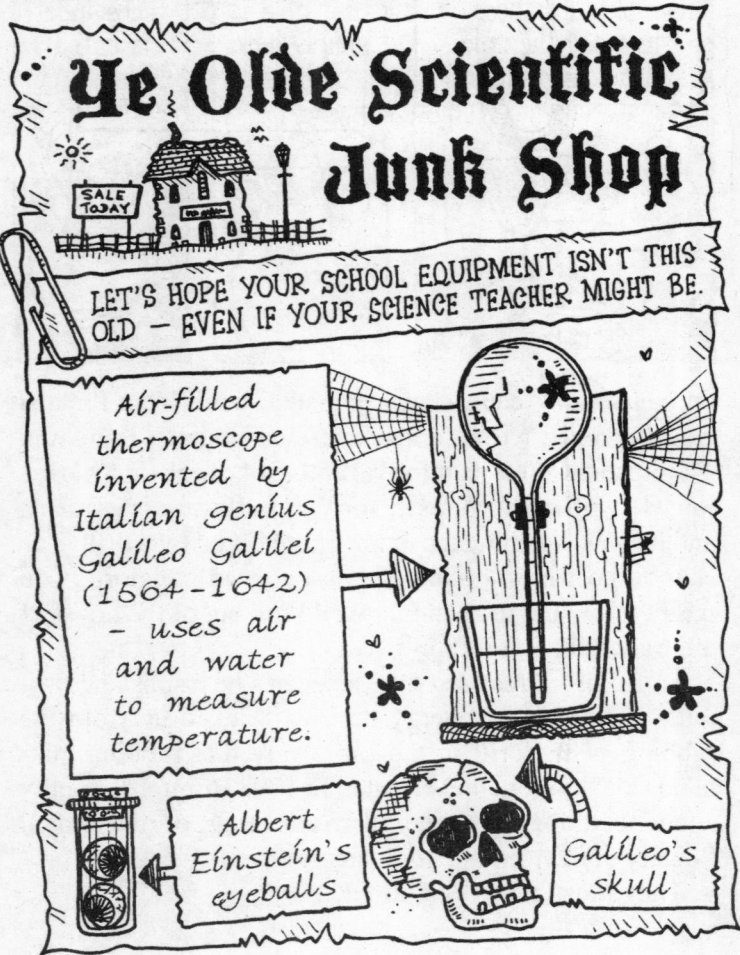

Ye Olde Scientific Junk Shop

SALE TODAY

LET'S HOPE YOUR SCHOOL EQUIPMENT ISN'T THIS OLD — EVEN IF YOUR SCIENCE TEACHER MIGHT BE.

Air-filled thermoscope invented by Italian genius Galileo Galilei (1564-1642) - uses air and water to measure temperature.

Albert Einstein's eyeballs

Galileo's skull

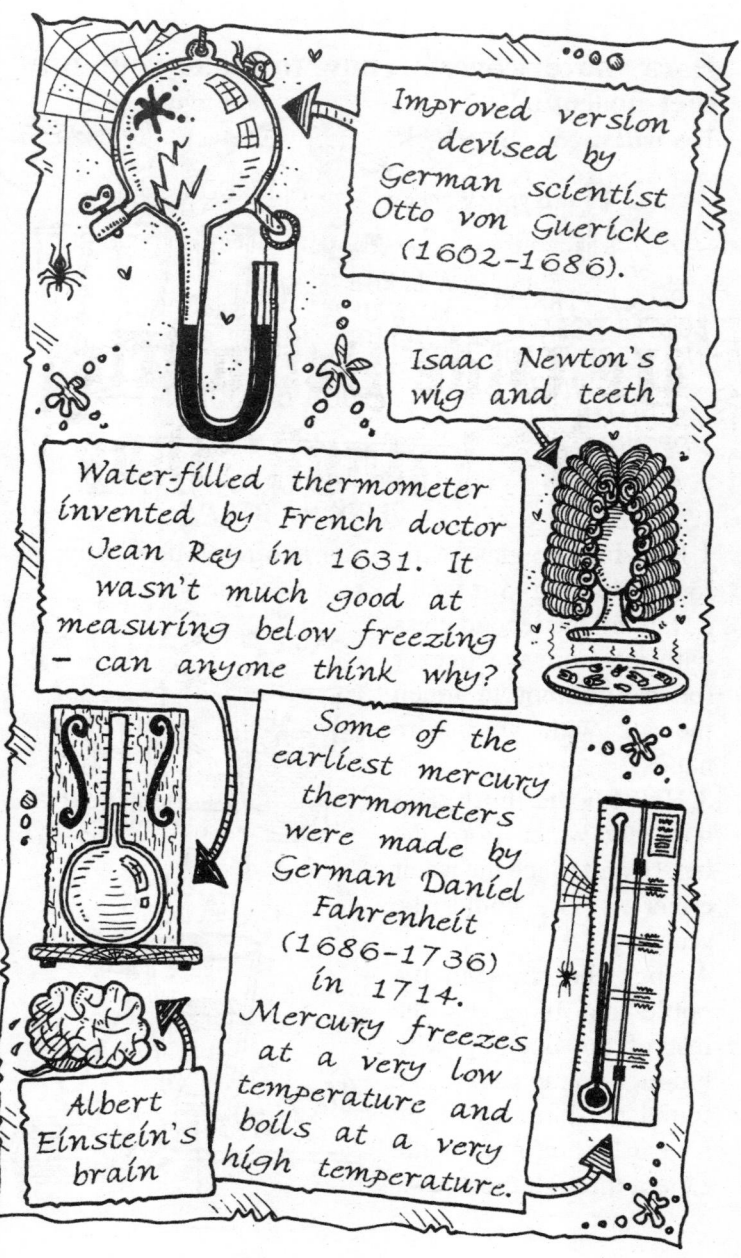

Improved version devised by German scientist Otto von Guericke (1602-1686).

Isaac Newton's wig and teeth

Water-filled thermometer invented by French doctor Jean Rey in 1631. It wasn't much good at measuring below freezing — can anyone think why?

Some of the earliest mercury thermometers were made by German Daniel Fahrenheit (1686-1736) in 1714. Mercury freezes at a very low temperature and boils at a very high temperature.

Albert Einstein's brain

Dare you discover . . . how to make your own thermoscope?

You will need:

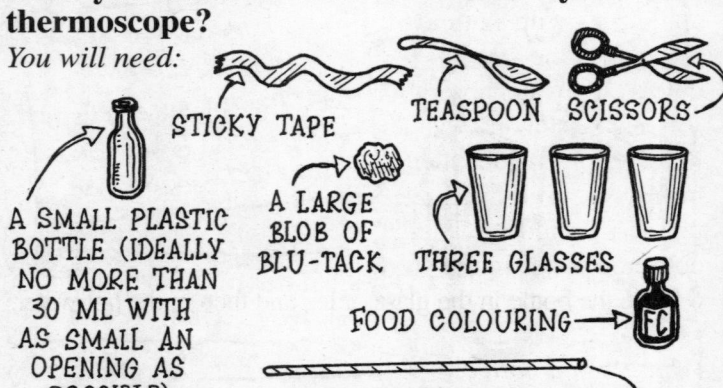

STICKY TAPE   TEASPOON   SCISSORS

A SMALL PLASTIC BOTTLE (IDEALLY NO MORE THAN 30 ML WITH AS SMALL AN OPENING AS POSSIBLE)

A LARGE BLOB OF BLU-TACK

THREE GLASSES

FOOD COLOURING → FC

A LIGHT-COLOURED PLASTIC DRINKING STRAW

What you do:

1 Half-fill one glass with water and add a few drops of food colouring. Stir well.

2 Half-fill the second glass with ice from the freezer (be careful not to touch the ice with your bare hands).

3 Half-fill the third glass with hot water from the tap. (Don't touch the water either – it could be scalding!)

4 Stick the straw in the bottle and block up the rest of the opening with blu-tack. Wrap sticky tape round the blu-tack so no air can get into the bottle except through the straw.

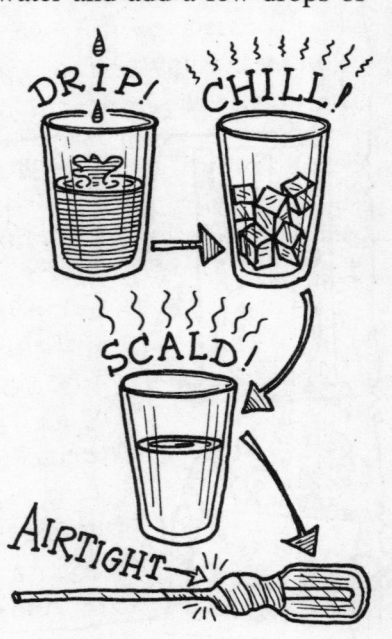

DRIP!   CHILL!

SCALD!

AIRTIGHT →

5 Gently squeeze the bottle and turn it upside-down so the end of the straw is in the coloured water. Coloured water will flow up the straw. Now stop squeezing the bottle and put it the right way up. You should see a band of coloured water in the straw.

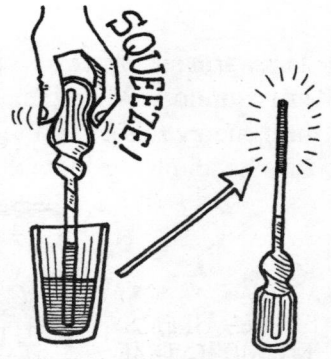

6 Place the bottle in the glass of ice and then in the hot water.

What do you notice?
a) The water in the straw goes up in the ice and down in the hot water.
b) The water in the straw goes up in the hot water and down in the ice.
c) The water in the straw becomes lighter in the ice and darker in the hot water.

Answer:
b) Remember those wobbling atoms on page 28? When you heat up the air in the bottle, the atoms have energy and try to move off in all directions – think of a class of energetic kids running outside at break-time.

The warm air atoms push up the straw and they push the water up too. When the air is cold the atoms have less heat energy so they don't want to go anywhere – think of kids huddling together for warmth on a cold day.

The pressure of the air pushing down on the straw from above pushes the water level down.

TRICKY TEMPERATURE FACTS

1 Scientists still had a problem. They had thermometers but they couldn't agree on a scale to measure temperature. Scientists made up their own measurements – and this no doubt led to heated arguments.

2 The first widely used measure of temperature was invented by our pal Daniel Fahrenheit – can you guess what it was called?

3 Fahrenheit decided that the coldest temperature he could make by mixing chemicals in his lab was 0°. This meant that water froze at 32° and the temperature of the human body was 96° (that's three times 32°). But Fahrenheit hadn't got it right – the body is around 98.6° so his carefully planned scale was wrong.

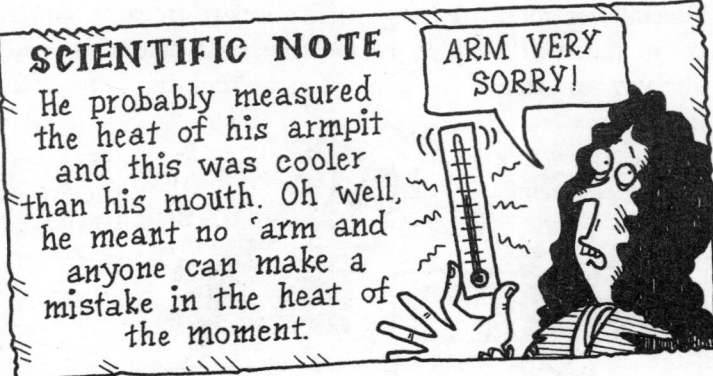

4 Fahrenheit's scale is now used in the USA but the rest of the world uses a measurement invented by a Swedish scientist named Anders Celsius (1701–1744). It's sometimes called centigrade but the official name is the Celsius scale after its inventor.

Anders was the son of a Professor of Astronomy and he grew up interested in maths and science. He loved exploring and went on two trips to the north of Finland. There he studied the northern lights and made observations that proved the Earth was slightly flattened at the North Pole.

5 Anders suggested a scale of 100° with water boiling at 0° and ice melting at 100°. Yes, you did read that right – Anders Celsius put his scale the wrong way round but another scientist reversed it after his death. Oh well, I guess they had a "measured" approach to science.

But talking about freezing, there's lots of freezing going on in the next chapter. In fact the next chapter's cold enough to freeze a cup of tea rock-hard *in one millisecond*!

Are you wrapped up *really* warm?

THE DEAD FREEZING CHAPTER

If science leaves you cold you might be gob-smacked to hear that science really can be cool – in fact *supercool*! Yes, this chapter and the next one are about losing heat energy and the science of low temperatures.

THE BIG FREEZE-UP

Remember the Third Law of Thermodynamics – the one that says that you can't get colder than absolute zero? (See page 17 if you don't.) Bet you never knew that one scientist who worked on this law went to university when he was just *ten years old*. He's been dead for ages but we've zapped him with energy for one last interview…

Dead Brainy: William Thomson, Lord Kelvin (1824–1907)

Welcome back to the land of the living, your lordship.

IT'S GOOD TO BE BACK!

So what's it like to be dead?

I'M BURIED IN LONDON IN WESTMINSTER ABBEY NEXT TO ISAAC NEWTON. I'M HAPPY TO BE SEEN DEAD WITH HIM…

You began your career by going to university at the age of ten.

WELL, I'M NOT ONE TO BOAST BUT SCHOOL SCIENCE WAS JUST TOO EASY FOR ONE OF MY GIANT INTELLECT.

Your first maths discovery was read to a science meeting by someone else — why didn't you read it yourself?

I WAS ONLY TEN AT THE TIME — IT MUST HAVE BEEN PAST MY BED-TIME.

You eventually became a Professor at Glasgow University...

me talking to a student

YES, I WAS GETTING ON A BIT BY THEN — I WAS ALL OF 22

And how long did you stick the job?

1842 1899

FIFTY-THREE YEARS — UNTIL I RAN OUT OF ENERGY

You studied electricity and heat and worked on the Second and Third Laws of Thermodynamics...

YES, THEY WERE BEING HOTLY DEBATED AT THE TIME.

Using maths you calculated that you couldn't cool anything below absolute zero.

0° KELVIN

YES, IT'S KNOWN AS 0° KELVIN — GOOD NAME, EH?

You advised on the laying of the first telegraph cable across the Atlantic Ocean and made a fortune.

YES, I WAS "CABLE" TO ANSWER EVERY QUESTION.

Of course, you made some mistakes in your scientific work...

EH?

You claimed that the sun's heat comes from burning coal.

I WONDER IF IT'S RUN OUT YET?

Bet you never knew!

1 A degree on the Kelvin scale is the same as a degree Celsius but unlike Celsius, the Kelvin scale starts at absolute zero. The scale is used for scientific measurements of the heat energy of atoms and it's named after the great man because he suggested it.

2 Thomson was made Lord Kelvin for his services to science. He took his title from a small river in Glasgow (I expect the locals call it "a wee burn"). So today scientists use the name of a wee burn in Scotland every time they measure temperature.

SPOT THE DIFFERENCES...

THE KELVIN – A WEE BURN

A HOT PLATE WITH A LOT OF KELVIN

LORD KELVIN WITH A WEE BURN

WELCOME TO THE CHILL-OUT ZONE

So would you like to experience absolute zero (almost)? Well, what you need is a holiday in space...

Bet you never knew!
Away from the sun's heat, space is only a degree or two above absolute zero. It's so cold that pee ejected from a space loo freezes instantly into a pretty stream of golden crystals. When asked what was the most beautiful sight he had seen, one returning astronaut replied:

THE URINE DUMP AT SUNSET

For some chilled-out scientists this sort of thing is brrrrrilliant. They cool atoms for super-cool experiments by trapping them with magnetic forces. Did you know that electricity runs through the chilled-out atoms with scarcely any friction? Well that's just the start of the weird stuff...

THE **ICE IS NICE** COMPANY

P R E S E N T S...

Fancy a cool thrill?

Buy this super-cooled helium (it's the same gas they put in high-flying balloons) but it's cooled to −272.2° C (−485° F).

Amaze your friends and terrify the cat as it turns into a liquid and starts climbing the sides of the jar.

THE SMALL PRINT
Don't drop your cat in the helium or you might end up with a frozen pet!

Fancy an ice-cream?
Can't wait hours for it to freeze? Try using this super-cold liquid nitrogen at −196° C (−393° F)! In 1997 a British scientist used this substance to make ice-cream in ten seconds! Children who sampled the ice-cream said it was "very nice" and a chef said:

IT'S NOT VERY RICH OR CREAMY, BUT IT DEFINITELY TASTES LIKE AN ICE-CREAM.

THE SMALL PRINT
The nitrogen won't spoil the taste. When it meets air it turns into nitrogen gas and floats away – and that's fine, because air is mostly nitrogen gas.

By the way, if you're thinking of making the ice-cream you should know that if you stick your finger in liquid nitrogen it'll freeze solid and break off. I guess that's what they call "a cold snap" – or do I mean ice-scream?

But talking about dipping bodies in liquid nitrogen, did you know that some people are planning to preserve their dead bodies in just this fashion?

Fearless reporter Harvey Tucker is just about to find out more. . .

HARVEY TUCKER'S BIG ADVENTURE

Fearless - me? Aw come off it! Okay - I'll come clean...

I've been writing for *Living on the Edge Magazine* for yonks. I've described how I bungee jumped from helicopters, dived with great white sharks and jogged across deserts. Lies, darn lies! The closest I've come to a shark is watching the Discovery channel on TV.

Well, they're dangerous aren't they?

But when the magazine's editor found out about this she wasn't too sympathetic. She gave a nasty little smile and sent me off to write an in-depth undercover feature on cryogenics - that's when bodies get deep frozen.

ANGRY EDITOR

Frankly I wasn't too tickled - I do feel the cold. But we Tuckers always bounce back and I soon hit on a real beaut plan! I decided to disguise myself as a dead body! My mate Sally Smart offered to pose as the bereaved rellie and do the natter — she's a real sport! All I had to do was lie back and listen. So I snacked up on five jumbo packets of crisps and vegemite sandwiches so I wouldn't feel too peckish in my coffin.

SALLY

So there I was at the body store of the Frozen Funerals company concentrating on being dead.

"What we do," said the doc, "is drain the body of blood and fill it up with antifreeze and other chemicals..."

I felt a mite uncomfortable. For one thing, I didn't like what I was hearing – for another being dead made me feel mighty hungry.

Meanwhile the doctor continued:

"Then we preserve the bodies in liquid nitrogen. By removing the heat energy we kill germs before they can rot the bodies. And then, when science has found a cure to whatever carried off dear departed Harvey – he can be thawed out and brought back to life..."

Dear departed Harvey – hey, I wasn't going to be anyone's "dear departed"!

Sally sounded as doubtful as I felt.

"But don't the chemicals damage the bodies and don't ice-crystals form inside them and wreck them beyond repair?"

I had forgotten that Sally was the magazine's science expert. The medic sounded a bit miffed...

"Er, yes, that's a general problem, but we're sure science will come up with a cure for this damage in the future ... er ... hopefully."

43

Whilst they were yacking, I risked opening an eye and taking a butchers at the body store. I could see bodies in flasks – a chill ran through my veins.

I felt as cold as the bods.

"How much does it cost?" Sally was asking.

"That depends," replied the doc. "It's $100,000 for the full body but only $50,000 for the head – it's a cut-price offer."

Cut off – what?! Well, I freaked didn't I?

"Forget it, mate!" I yelled sitting up in my coffin.

The doctor screamed and ran off and Sally gave me a frosty look. She's been really cold to me ever since.

ARGH!

Cryogenics is popular in the USA and many bodies and heads have already been frozen. Some people have had their pet dogs preserved – I guess they're frozen Fidos. But some companies operating the service have gone bust and had their assets frozen (maybe it's the chilly economic climate) and the bodies thawed out with smelly results. I'm sure it's a thaw point all round.

Of course, you don't need to find a vat of liquid nitrogen to find a frozen body – there are plenty of well-preserved bodies in the polar regions at the ends of the Earth. Why not turn to the next ice-cool chapter and find out how they got there and what happens to the body when it gets low on vital heat energy. Yes, read on, you're about to make a chilling discovery…

KILLER COLD

This chapter is warmer than the last one, but it's still freezing cold. Later chapters will be hot enough to fry your fingertips but for now you're more likely to freeze them off! This chapter is full of cool killer facts about how lack of heat energy freezes water ... and people.

COULD YOU BE A SURGEON?

You're a surgeon. Your patient has a swelling blood vessel in his brain. Soon the blood vessel will burst and cause a killer build up of blood pressure. Your patient could die – *what can you do*? Better hurry up and decide...

a) Cut open the patient's skull and squirt the brain with liquid nitrogen to freeze it up and stop the blood moving.

b) Cut open the skull and pack ice cubes around the brain to reduce the swelling.

c) Pack the patient's body with ice until their body temperature is low, remove half their blood and then operate on the brain.

Answer:
c) Cooling the body slows it down so it needs less oxygen from the blood. (In fact, cooling can be used to treat severely injured people by giving their bodies a chance to heal naturally.) By draining the blood you reduce swelling and gain time to operate on the blood vessel. In the 1960s a Japanese brain surgeon chilled the brains of patients to 6° C (43° F), drained their blood and operated before warming the brains up with nice hot blood. I expect he needed a cool head.

45

Fancy going there for a holiday? Well, if so you'll enjoy chilling out in a hotel built out of solid ice! There really is such a place … here's how they might advertise it.

HAVE AN 'ICE DAY! AT THE **ICE HOTEL** ▽▽ NORTHERN SWEDEN ▽▽

❄ A real cool place to stay!

❄ You're sure of a frosty reception! → HI!!

SORRY, WE DON'T DO HOT COCOA!

❄ Break the ice at the ice bar (yes the bar's made from ice too!) and the drinks are always on ice (they're served in containers made of ice).

❄ Relax in your luxury bedroom!

✴✴✴✴ THE SMALL PRINT ✴✴✴✴

1. Your bedroom and your bed are solid ice! Central heating might melt the hotel so your bedroom has to be freezing. You do get a comfy mattress and sleeping bag and we promise not to laugh if you wear a bobble hat in bed!

SHIVER! SHAKE!

ICE HOTEL

2. Don't bother coming back - by the spring the hotel will have melted but we'll build a new one next winter we promise!

46

So what's this got to do with energy?

Killer energy fact file

NAME: Ice

HEAT!

THE BASIC FACTS:

1. As water cools it loses heat energy to the air.

LOCK!

2. At 0°C (32°F) the groups of atoms (molecules as scientists call them) that make up water lock together.

"WOBBLE!"

3. Ice still has heat energy and the frozen water molecules are still gently wobbling.

KILLER DETAILS: 1. If you added up all the heat energy in an ice cube there'd be enough to produce a flame hotter than a burning match.

2. When you make a snowball you crush the ice-crystals together and this movement energy turns to heat energy that melts some of the ice. The squishy water makes the ball easy to mould.

GRRR!

BEWARE – if the snowball hits your teacher he might go in for the kill!

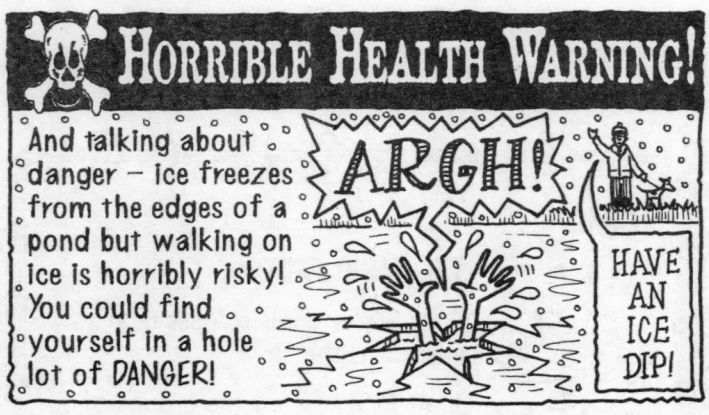

HORRIBLE HEALTH WARNING!

And talking about danger – ice freezes from the edges of a pond but walking on ice is horribly risky! You could find yourself in a hole lot of DANGER!

ARGH!

HAVE AN ICE DIP!

TEACHER'S TEA-BREAK TEASER

It's break-time. With luck your teacher will just be getting some milk from the fridge to put in her tea when you knock on the staffroom door…

IF THE SECOND LAW OF THERMODYNAMICS SAYS HEAT ALWAYS GOES FROM A WARM PLACE TO A COLD PLACE, HOW IS IT POSSIBLE FOR FRIDGES TO MOVE HEAT OUT FROM THE COLD FRIDGE TO THE WARM ROOM?

WHAT?

Answer:
Even if your teacher understands what you're talking about, explaining the answer will take her all break by which time the Second Law will have made sure that her tea is colder than a shivering Siberian snowman. But you could be in hot water!

48

HOW A FRIDGE WORKS

Fridge tubes contain a chemical that turns into a gas in the part of the tube that's inside the fridge. For this to happen the chemical needs heat energy so it sucks heat from the inside of the fridge.

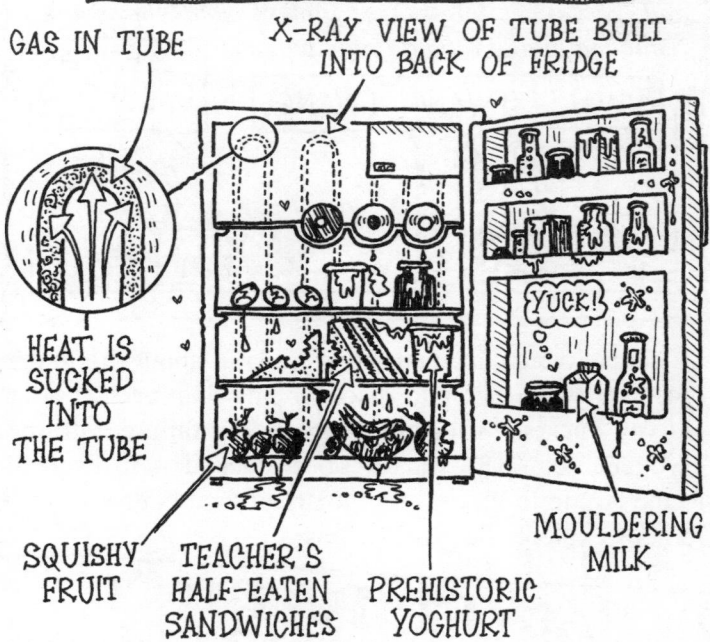

~THE STAFFROOM FRIDGE~

GAS IN TUBE

X-RAY VIEW OF TUBE BUILT INTO BACK OF FRIDGE

HEAT IS SUCKED INTO THE TUBE

YUCK!

SQUISHY FRUIT

TEACHER'S HALF-EATEN SANDWICHES

PREHISTORIC YOGHURT

MOULDERING MILK

In fact, fridges actually heat things up more than they cool things down! The gas is squashed into the tubes at the back of the fridge by a pump and this makes it form a liquid and release the heat energy it took from inside the fridge. And if you count the heat given out by the pump motor, fridges actually produce MORE heat than they ever suck out of your ice-cream.

Ice is noisy – and I don't mean when you crunch it in your mouth. Water movements under ice in the Arctic and Antarctic Oceans can put the ice under strain. This results in loss of energy in the form of sound (and a tiny amount of heat). Explorers report hearing noises like grunts, squeaks, groans, the sound of birds singing and kettles boiling. One witness said the sounds reminded him of a banjo playing…

Of course there's loads more to find out about life in the cold, and who better to discover this than ace reporter Harvey Tucker? After his embarrassing failure with the cryogenics company Harvey's been packed off in disgrace to the Arctic to report on a polar survival course run by famous explorer Fergus Fearless…

HARVEY TUCKER'S BIG ADVENTURE

I told her I can't stand the cold! Adventure - my bum! I was stranded hundreds of miles from a decent bar. I was cold, I was hungry…

SHIVER!

yes, definitely cold and hungry and I couldn't think of anything else. I must have been a grape short of a bunch! Even my snot was freezing! Two long icicles stuck out of my nostrils!

I decided to open a tin of toffees — you need a spot of tucker for heat energy. But they were so cold and hard they nearly cracked my teeth! I tried to clean the frozen toffee off my teeth but my toothpaste had frozen solid! This place was the pits!

Well, I decided to skip the survival course — you won't catch me snacking off frozen fish and building igloos. So I read my book. It's by some glum old pommie medic, and I thought there's sure to be some nifty natter about cold that I could use in the article.

DISEASES I HAVE KNOWN
by Dr H. Grimgrave

Chapter 14
EFFECTS OF THE COLD

Only idiot patients think you can catch colds by getting too cold. In fact, cold kills the germs that cause colds. But every year I'm snowed under by tiresome

CONTINUED

timewasters who claim they caught colds by being snowed under. I'm only a doctor but they still expect me to cure them!

Frostbite is a more likely outcome for people who get lost in snow. Blood vessels in the skin close to keep heat energy in the body. The nerve endings that feel things stop working, which is why extreme cold causes numbness: it's known as frostnip. Oxygen doesn't reach these areas and, of course, they begin to die. In severe cases this can cause blisters and blackening.

AFTER A WHILE THE AFFECTED AREA STARTS TO ROT AND SMELL.

Recently, my colleague Dr Sneak went on a skiing holiday. The silly idiot forgot his thermal socks — and developed frostbite in his big toe. It was just "toe" bad, ha ha.

I advised him on the telephone to avoid rubbing the toe — this may damage it.

DR SNEAK

"The thing to do," I said, "is to bathe the toe in warm water and see a doctor."

"But I am a doctor!" he protested.

So I told him to see a *proper* doctor.

In severe frostbite the affected bits actually drop off (these patients need to pull themselves together, ha, ha). Or the frost-bitten bit may be amputated (or "chopped off" as vulgar persons say). Any readers who have lost fingers and toes would be welcome to donate them to my private medical collection. I might pay a small  fee just so long as it doesn't cost an arm and a leg.

More lethal than frostbite is cooling of the body (hypothermia [hi-po-ther-me-a] as we doctors term it). Of course, every winter I get an avalanche of malingerers who think feeling a bit chilly is going to kill them — no such luck I'm afraid! I'm always cool to them. Drink hot drinks and wrap up warm — that's my advice. Physical exercise helps — I always order a five mile run for children who complain of the cold. They generally stop snivelling after the first four miles!

Real hypothermia is likely to affect idiots who go out in the cold without warm clothing and they deserve everything they get. As their bodies cool they shiver violently. They think they're hot and feel like removing clothing.

TYPICAL IDIOT

As the brain cools it sees things. One idiot even rang me and said he thought he was a pack of cards! I told him I'd deal with him later. People suffering from hypothermia need to be warmed up slowly to avoid further damage to the body. But of course what they really deserve is a good roasting!

Well, cop that! Reading about hypo-what's-it gave me the shivers – AH NO! shivering's a sign of hypo-thingie! I snuggled in my sleeping bag and felt hot – isn't that hypo too? I decided to build my strength by eating a mega-de-luxe family-sized pizza but it had frozen rock-solid! The cold crept up on me until it seemed to chill the marrow of my bones. I wrote my farewell letters – goodbye cruel world! But then...

"Hold on!" I thought, "Fergus Fearless might have a web-site to tell me how to stay alive – it's worth a bo-peep."

FERGUS FEARLESS TELLS YOU
HOW TO SURVIVE IN
THE ARCTIC

BEWARE FROSTBITE If you can't touch your thumb with your index finger you're in trouble – that's why this gesture traditionally means "I'm OK". Try putting your hands in your armpits to warm them up. Stamp your feet and put your feet on the tummy or in the armpits of an understanding friend.

THE TOILET Unless there's a blizzard it's safe to go outside because the vital bits are well supplied with heat energy in the form of warm blood, so they don't get frostbite as quickly as fingers and toes. *WARNING:* hungry husky dogs and polar bears sometimes attack explorers when they're on the toilet.

WEE!

54

H-E-L-P! As soon as I read these words I needed the dunny! But, oh no, it was too dangerous! This place had got on my quince! So I got on my radio blower for help. And whilst I was waiting to be rescued, I crunched my way through the rest of the frozen toffees. It seemed a shame to waste 'em!

Bet you never knew!

1 Frostbite was a killer condition for early explorers who were trying to reach the North and South Poles. One day American Robert Peary (1856–1920) took off his boots and eight of his toes fell off. He later remarked:

A FEW TOES WERE NOT MUCH TO GIVE TO ACHIEVE THE POLE

Do you agree?

2 In 2000 a museum received an unusual donation. Major Michael Lane sent them five of his own fingers and eight of his toes. They had been lost to frostbite when he was climbing Mount Everest in 1976. "I don't think it was quite what they were expecting," remarked the gallant mountaineer.

3 In 1991 frostbite claimed both the hands of heroic Korean climber Kim Hong Bin on Mount McKinley, USA – but he made it to the top using his legs and teeth.

So you've read this chapter and you're an expert in dealing with deadly lack of heat energy (or "cold" as non-scientists say)? But before you move on to the next chapter, why not try your hand at this killer quiz? Could you survive the ultimate challenge and reach the North or South Pole?

COULD YOU BE A POLAR EXPLORER?

1 It's so cold that your breath has frozen and covered the inside of your hut with ice. What do you do?

a) Put up with it.

b) Melt the ice with a blow-torch.

c) Open a window.

2 Which food would give you the most energy?

a) Chocolate.

b) Spinach.

c) Greasy lumps of fat from a dead animal mixed with toffee and banana breakfast cereal.

3 You're starving hungry but you have no food left. You need food to keep warm – what do you eat first?

a) Your traditional Eskimo-style socks.

b) Your dogs.

c) Your little brother/sister.

4 When travelling to the South Pole what's the best place to store fuel for heat and cooking?

a) In blocks of ice.

b) In jars sealed with corks.

c) In jars with leather seals.

Answers:

1 a) It's all you can do. **b)** would use up vital fuel and may set fire to your hut and **c)** would make it colder.

2 c) When explorers Dave Mitchell and Stephen Martin walked to the North Pole in 1994 they actually ate this. The fat, or suet as it's called, gives you more energy for its weight than most other foods. Fancy a munch?

3 b) Choose a dog that seems weaker than the others. When you've eaten all your dogs you could eat **a)** because they're made of animal hair. WARNING: eating your brothers and sisters is cruel and may result in a long prison sentence.

4 b) Using ice to store fuel is really fuel-ish … er … foolish because you'll need fuel to make a fire to melt the ice to get at the fuel. In 1911 a British expedition led by Robert Falcon Scott (1868–1912) used **c)**, and a rival team led by Norwegian Roald Amundsen (1872–1928) used **b)**. Amundsen got to the South Pole first. Scott's leather seals froze and dropped off and the Brits ran out of fuel and died of cold. Their frozen bodies still lie in Antarctica where they perished.

The unlucky explorers were killed by the killer science of fuel and lack of heat energy. As any scientist will tell you, fuel is a form of stored energy and, by some power-fuel coincidence, the next chapter will have you firing on all cylinders… It really is a gas!

HORRIBLY POWERFUL FUEL

Without fuel – or the energy stored in fuel – the world would grind to a chilly halt. Fuels like gas, oil, coal and petrol store the vital energy that keeps you warm and cooks your supper…

GOOD OLD FUEL!

…and fuel may well get you to school on time…

HORRIBLE FUEL!

TROUBLE IN STORE

But fuels are just one way in which energy can be stored. Here are some other ways to store energy which are just about to cause disaster for the world's most accident-prone teacher.

HI!

THE ADVENTURES OF PUT-UPON PHIL

And the dynamite stores chemical energy... of course it's quite safe...

BOOM!

THAT'S IT – I QUIT!

THE FUEL FACTS

For thousands of years the only fuel for most people was wood to burn in fires. Open fires provided light and heat to roast a juicy hunk of dead mammoth. But around 3000 BC an Egyptian invented the candle. No one knows this person's name but it was a *flaming* good idea – here's how it worked.

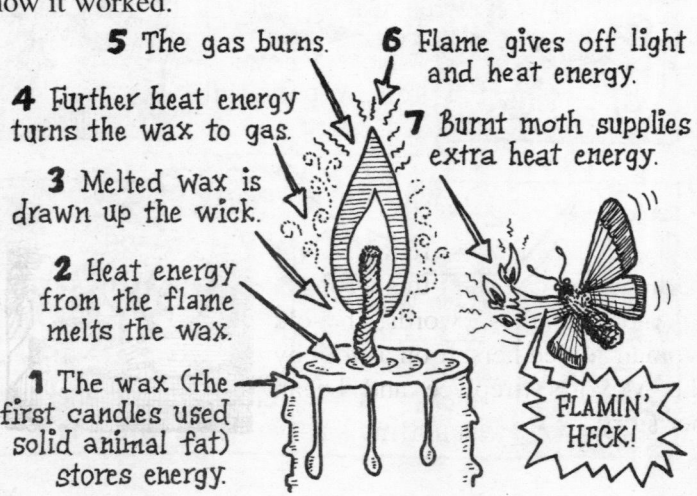

5 The gas burns.

6 Flame gives off light and heat energy.

4 Further heat energy turns the wax to gas.

7 Burnt moth supplies extra heat energy.

3 Melted wax is drawn up the wick.

2 Heat energy from the flame melts the wax.

1 The wax (the first candles used solid animal fat) stores energy.

FLAMIN' HECK!

Now the great thing about candles is that you can move them around, so they were really useful to take with you to bed if you were scared of the dark in the days before electricity. But you still need to make a flame to light the candle. Traditionally, people struck pieces of metal and flint to make sparks, but what was needed was a striking new idea...

In the 1850s Swedish inventor John Lundstrom invented the matches still used today. The energy is stored in the side of the box in the form of phosphorus (fos-for-rus). This substance burns when heated by the energy of the match striking the side. (If the match doesn't light it's probably on strike, ha ha.)

Anyway, phosphorus was discovered in 1669 in a revolting fashion. This story may shed some light on the subject.

A GLOW IN THE DARK

Hamburg, Germany 1677
"Yes, Herr Obermeyer, I'll tell you everything. Since you're the Mayor perhaps you can right this wrong."

And with these words, the old woman settled herself on a stool by the Mayor's fireplace and began her story.

61

"Sir, I'll be honest. My master, Hening Brandt, is not a good man. He is rude to us servants and grovels to people richer than himself. He married his first wife for her money, and by the time she'd died he'd spent it on science experiments. Aye, I'm not one to gossip but it's said he married the present Frau Brandt for her money too. He's always trying to make gold from cheap metals. What's that? He's an alchemist? Why yes, that's what he calls himself...

"One dark evening I was passing my master's laboratory. I was taking a clean suit to his room – oh dear, what a mess my master makes of his clothes with all those chemicals! And the smells from that room are better left imagined! He had buckets of – how can I put it politely? It was wee – rotting in some experiment."

The old woman screwed up her face in disgust.

"Of course we servants weren't allowed to clean in there, but the stink was horrible enough!

Then I heard his voice. Thinking he was calling me, I crept to the door. But my master was talking to himself...

"'It glows!' I heard him say 'It's the secret of how to make gold and I've found it in wee!'

"I peered into the room. It was dark but I could see his fat excited face in a strange light that came from a glowing flask. Then he saw me and in a second he had me by the throat. He slapped my face once, twice – for all his fat he's a big strong man. He told me that he'd do terrible things if I dared to tell anyone what I'd seen. I promised I wouldn't – I had to didn't I?

"And true to my word I've kept his secret for six years. I always think that a good servant sees everything and says nothing. And all that time my master tried to make gold from the substance. He tried and failed and tried and failed until he had spent all his wife's money.

"We began to be pestered by alchemists who wanted the secret of the glowing substance. How they heard of it I can't say – but my master had taken to boasting of his discovery in taverns. And to think – he had sworn *me* to silence!"

There was a crack, and shower of sparks leapt up the chimney from a log on the fire. The woman gave a little gasp and looked up in alarm as if expecting to see her master's angry face. Then she continued her story.

"One night my master was visited by a Herr Krafft. He offered to give my master money in return for the secret. But my master was sly as well as greedy. He wouldn't tell Herr Krafft how he made the glowing material but he promised to sell what he had. He added with a low laugh that he could make plenty more.

"I wanted to tell Herr Krafft that the substance was made of wee but I was afraid of my master's temper. So I sat quietly with my sewing. Suddenly there was a pounding on the door.

"It was Herr Kunckel, he was an alchemist who had called to see the strange substance a few days before. Herr Kunckel also wanted to buy some of the chemical but my master told him rudely that he'd failed to make any more. I heard my master whisper, 'yes, it's made of wee, now go away!'

"Then, looking flustered, he came back and closed his deal with Herr Krafft.

"After Herr Krafft left, my master began to dance. Soon he was slapping his legs and laughing fit to burst.

"His friend the innkeeper came round and my master ordered me to fetch wine. After a bottle or two my master was drunk. His fat face shone red and shiny in the firelight and his voice was loud and slurred as he boasted of how he had tricked Herr Krafft and Herr Kunckel.

"The innkeeper leaned forward and prodded my master's belly.

"'So what's this substance made of – you old crook?'

"My master exploded with laughter until his chins wobbled.

"'Wee' he snorted, 'left to rot and heated until it's just a white powder at the bottom of a flask – then heated again! Two hundred thalers – just think of it – two hundred silver thalers for a pot of wee!'

"My master laughed until he rocked backwards and forwards. Then he wiped his wet lips and clumsily tapped his nose.

"'Remember, old friend, not a word of this.' he hissed.

"Well Sir, I am sure you've heard what happened next – it was the talk of Hamburg. Herr Kunckel made his own glowing substance. And they do say that Herr Krafft made a fortune showing it to kings and queens all over Europe. And now Kunckel and Krafft are telling everyone that *they* discovered the chemical! My master was in a foul mood for days – he's been unbearable! And that's why I am here to testify that my master, Hening Brandt, made the discovery first.

"A good servant never offers an opinion but I must add a word of my own. Sir, I wish this substance had never been found! It's like an evil genie making men cruel and selfish and greedy so that they trick one another and tell lies. What's that? How can I prove what I say is true?"

The woman looked troubled.

"I'm only a poor serving woman – I have only my word – and this…"

She opened her bag and slowly drew out small flask. The flask contained a powder that shone with the ghostly glow of green fire.

Bet you never knew!

1 When phosphorous atoms combine with oxygen in the air, the atoms give out their stored energy in the form of light. Although phosphorus is poisonous it was made into pills to cure stomach and lung diseases. The pills were useless and the people who ate them felt sick and began to glow in the dark.

HOW ARE YOU FEELING AFTER TAKING THE PHOSPHORUS PILLS?

A LITTLE LIGHT-HEADED!

2 In 1890 a girl was smeared with phosphorus so that she could pretend to be a ghost during a seance (a gathering where ghosts are supposed to appear). The poison killed the girl, so perhaps she became a genuine ghost.

Today few Europeans and Americans use candles and open fires. (Mind you, it's rumoured that in power cuts mean-spirited teachers wrap themselves in woolly scarves and teach by the light of candles. Anything to avoid sending their pupils home.)

But mostly we rely on gas or electricity produced from coal, gas or oil. Now I expect you're keen to find out about these vital forms of energy, so we've invited an expert to answer your questions...

HORRIBLE SCIENCE QUESTION TIME
With Bernard Boyle of the Energy Department

Was it made out of dinosaur bones?

PLANTS

COAL

No, but a fossil fuel is made of ancient living things. Coal's made from giant plants that slowly rotted in swamps 275 million years ago. I've brought some to show you...

THAT'S COOL!

Why is it black?

Yes, I know it's coal.

Over time most of the plants rotted and what's left is mainly black carbon.

OOPS!

Oil and gas are fossil fuels too. They're made from the rotting remains of tiny sea creatures that sank to the sea bed hundreds of millions of years ago. Germs turned some of the remains into gas and some into oil.

So my dad's got sea creatures in his car?

Sounds fishy to me!

Does your cookery teacher cook on gas?

I dunno we've never tried to cook her...

All fossil fuels burn well. In power stations they're burnt to release heat energy to heat water and make steam...

Does it boil?

It's *Professor Boyle* to you! Oh you mean the water — yes!

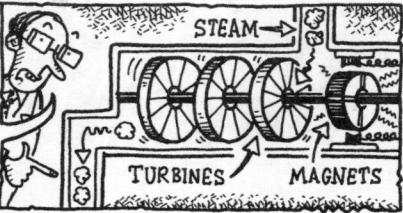

The steam turns the blades of a turbine round. The turbine turns a powerful magnet and makes an electric current.

STEAM →

TURBINES   MAGNETS

The problem is that the fossil fuels and especially oil will be running out by the 2060's.

Did you say oil be running out?

No, I'll be here for another two hours!

GROAN!

Bet you never knew!
When it's pumped out of the ground by an oil rig, oil is a disgusting thick green-black slime called crude oil. Crude oil's full of chemicals such as paraffin and petrol and butane (used to fuel camping stoves). In the 1860s rock oil (a mixture including petrol) was sold as a medicine for toothache and corns. Yes, tank goodness you don't have to drink that!

Do you say...

Answer:
DON'T YOU DARE!!! The killer scientists might attack you! A rhino-analyst studies smells in cooking gas. The actual gas doesn't smell, so smelly sulphur chemicals are added to the gas to make it pong so that people notice if they leave their gas taps on – this is called "stenching".

Although gas is often removed from rocks where there's oil, a cooking and lighting gas can also be made from coal. And I bet you never knew that this fact was discovered by a ingenious inventor with a terrible taste in hats...

Hall of Fame: William Murdock (1754–1839)
Nationality: Scottish

Mrs Murdock was furious...

"Ye greet daftie – luik wat ye've done to ma best china tea pot! It's ruined – ye greet muckle lump! It's nay guid noo! Ye've nay sense – tho ye be ma ane laddie!

(Mrs Murdock probably used other words that were too rude to repeat in a respectable book like this.)

Young William bowed his head and was just mumbling something about science experiments when the tea pot whizzed past his ear and smashed to pieces on the black iron stove behind him.

But he had actually made a vital discovery. By heating coal (yes, in his mum's tea pot) he had found out that you can make a gas that burns to produce heat and light energy. But then William always was a practical lad. Already he had built his own tricycle out of wood to get to school on time. This was surprising because:

1 He was keen to get to school.

2 The bicycle hadn't been invented yet!

When William was 23, he heard about a factory in England where they made the most powerful steam engines in the whole world. He was so excited that he *walked* hundreds of kilometres to the Soho Works in Birmingham to ask for a job. The boss, Matthew Boulton, was about to show William the door when the young man's hat fell off. It hit the floor with a solid clunk, as well it might since it was made of wood. Yes, the hat was one of William's inventions and it proved the lad was no wooden head.

For the rest of his life William worked for Matthew Boulton and his partner, Scottish steam engine inventor James Watt (1736–1819). He repaired steam engines all over the country but still found time to invent a steam-powered carriage and a method of using fish skin to remove cloudiness from beer (if your dad's into home brew this could spell doom for your pet goldfish).

William developed his coal gas idea. He began by heating coal in a tank and pumping it round pipes where the gas could be lit from special gas taps. First William lit the cottage in Cornwall where he was working and then the Soho works. Boulton was delighted by the discovery but he stopped William patenting his idea. Eventually other people copied him and he made no money from it.

THE FUEL CRISIS STARTS TO BITE

Remember what Bernard Boyle was saying about fossil fuels running out? You may have heard people talking about it. There's enough coal underground to keep us warm and cosy until about 2160 but by the 2000's oil and gas were running out in a hurry and the world was guzzling them like they were going out of fashion. For some scientists the answer was to think small – I mean very, very small...

Killer energy fact file

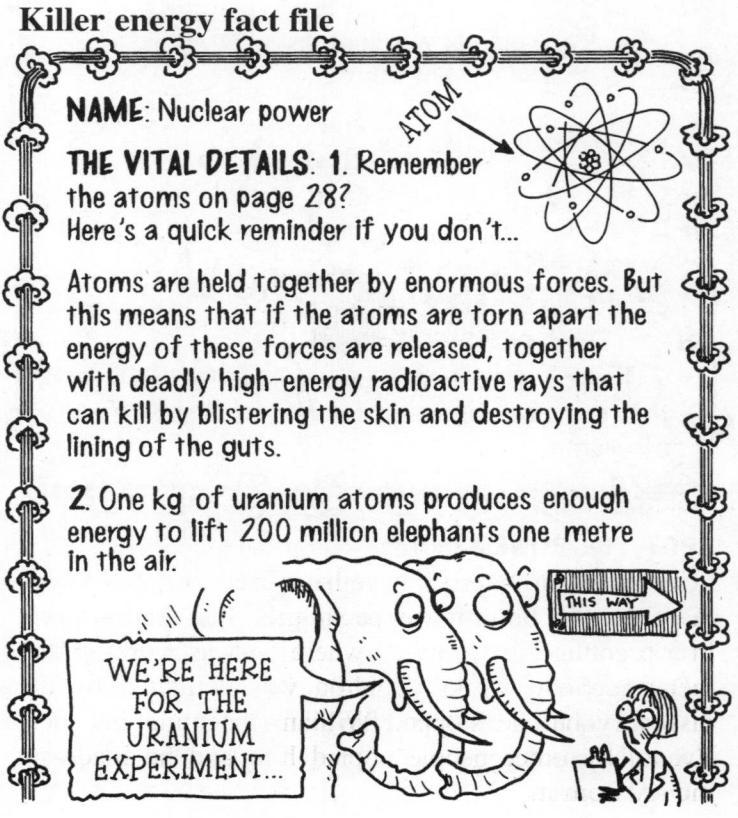

NAME: Nuclear power

THE VITAL DETAILS: **1.** Remember the atoms on page 28?
Here's a quick reminder if you don't...

ATOM

Atoms are held together by enormous forces. But this means that if the atoms are torn apart the energy of these forces are released, together with deadly high-energy radioactive rays that can kill by blistering the skin and destroying the lining of the guts.

2. One kg of uranium atoms produces enough energy to lift 200 million elephants one metre in the air.

WE'RE HERE FOR THE URANIUM EXPERIMENT...

THIS WAY

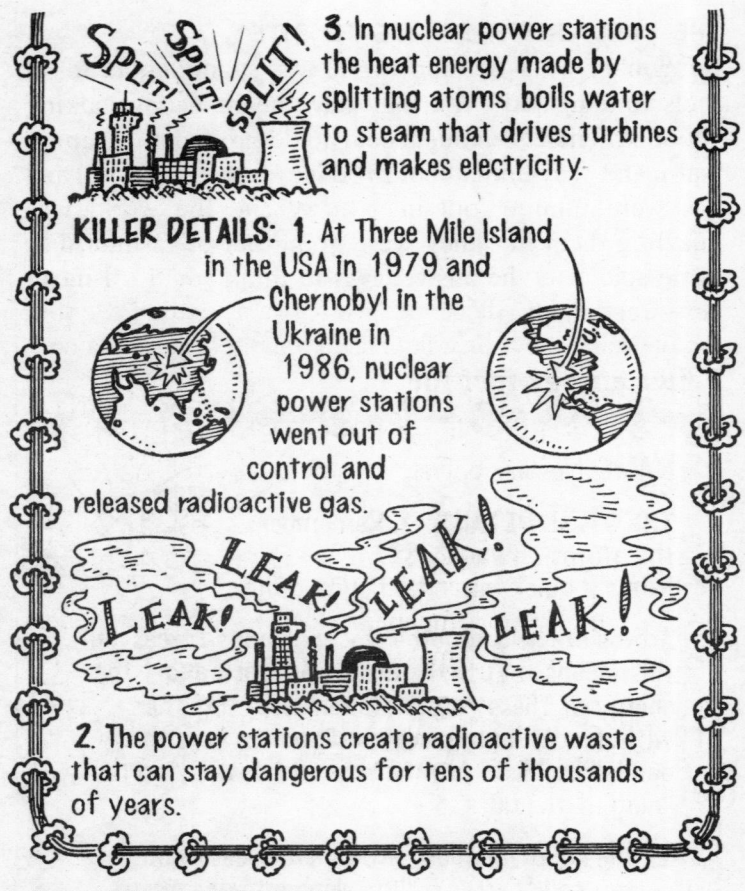

3. In nuclear power stations the heat energy made by splitting atoms boils water to steam that drives turbines and makes electricity.

KILLER DETAILS: 1. At Three Mile Island in the USA in 1979 and Chernobyl in the Ukraine in 1986, nuclear power stations went out of control and released radioactive gas.

LEAK! LEAK! LEAK! LEAK!

2. The power stations create radioactive waste that can stay dangerous for tens of thousands of years.

SPOT THE POWER QUIZ

Some unusual materials have been used to make power. Have you the brain-power to spot the fuel that no one's ever tried?

1 Dead cows
2 Waste cooking oil from chip shops
3 Smelly rotten eggs
4 Used nappies

Answer:

3 But who "nose" what might happen in the future? As for the others, in 2000…

1 Some English power stations were making electricity from burning the remains of diseased cows. I suppose that's what they call moo-clear energy.

2 A man in Manchester, England ran his car on oil from his local chip shop that had been changed chemically into diesel oil. I suppose he could have run it on oranges but then he'd have run out of juice, ha ha.

4 French cement companies were burning the nappies to fire their cement-making kilns.

You can also make power from wind, waves, tides and solar power (that's the heat and light of the sun). These natural types of energy are called "renewable" because there's always more of them being made. And deep within the Earth there's another type of renewable energy: here's how YOU can tap into it…

HOW TO BUILD YOUR OWN
GEOTHERMAL POWER STATION

INTRODUCTION

Geothermal power uses the mass of molten rock thousands of metres under your feet to make heat energy. This power actually makes it possible to grow bananas in Iceland (in heated greenhouses)

MOLTEN ROCK

HEAT!

PLANET EARTH

so why not have a bash at building your own geothermal power station!

- No more nasty energy bills!
- Piping hot water for ever!
- No cost except for the few 100 million that you spent building your power station.

Some of these instructions may not be totally sensible. You're advised to read them carefully first!

WHAT YOU WILL NEED...

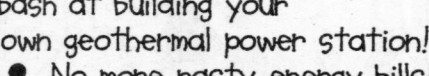

TWO DRILL RIGS

HEAVY LIFTING GEAR, BULLDOZERS, BUILDING MATERIALS, ETC.

SEVERAL KILOMETRES OF PIPES

VERY RICH, UNDERSTANDING PARENTS

AN OLYMPIC SIZED SWIMMING POOL OR PRIVATE LAKE.

HOT ROCKS

HOUSE
PIPES

POOL

BOILING WATER

INSTRUCTIONS

1. Set up your drill rigs and drill 7 km down until you reach some rocks that are hot enough to boil water.

2. Don't forget to push down the pipes into the holes after your drills.

3. Remember to link up the pipes from your second bore hole with the hot water system of your house. I expect your friend's parents will be delighted to have their homes plumbed in too!

4. Now for the FUN bit! Link up the pipes to your first rig to the swimming pool and turn on the taps so the water rushes down into the first bore hole.

5. Superheated hot water will rush up the second bore hole and into your hot water system! Warning: you might need to adjust the pressure or your radiators may explode!

WHOOPS!

THE SMALL PRINT
If molten rock oozes from your bore holes you've created a volcano that could bury your neighbourhood and school under thousands of tonnes of red hot lava. This may be a good moment to leave the country.

If your geothermal power station doesn't work there's a simple way to tackle the energy shortage: use less energy. Simply switch off those electrical gadgets left on stand-by – that'll save lots of power and I am sure that your dad won't mind losing the chance to video Trainspotter's Weekly. *Then you could turn down the heating and put on a warm jumper instead.*

And if you're cold you can rub your hands together. Remember how the drilled cannon made heat on page 29? Yes, that's right – in the same way, your hands rub together and the rubbing force (known as friction) turns movement energy into heat energy – easy-peasy!

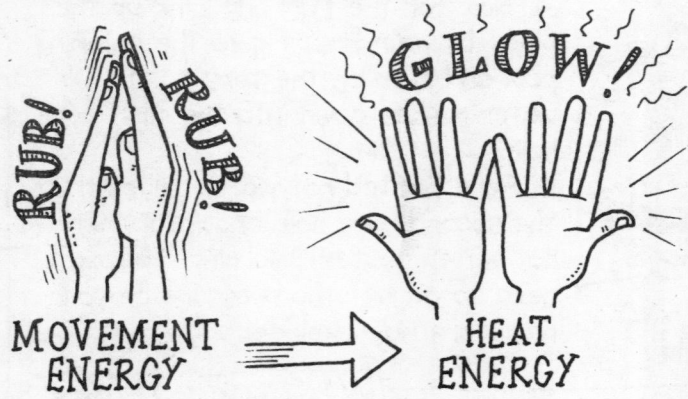

Mind you, you'll find plenty of movement energy in the next chapter. In fact, it's just about to move off *now*!

THE POWER TO MOVE YOU

Look out the window and you're sure to see something moving. You might see a cat chasing a mouse, or a dog chasing the cat, or children chasing the dog ... or the neighbours chasing the children or maybe everyone being chased by a killer Tyrannosaurus.

Well, they've all got something in common and it's called...

KILLER EXPRESSIONS

I STUDY KINETIC ENERGY

Do you say...

MY CAT'S GOT LOADS OF KITTY ENERGY!

Answer:
Don't show off the paw state of your knowledge. Kinetic (ki-net-tic) energy is the scientific name for movement energy. That's right – every move you make is powered by kinetic energy.

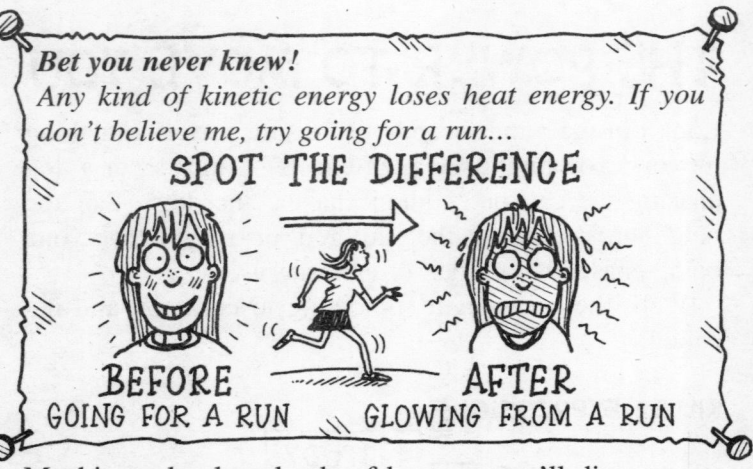

SPOT THE DIFFERENCE

BEFORE
GOING FOR A RUN

AFTER
GLOWING FROM A RUN

Machines also lose loads of heat, as you'll discover on page 90.

Kinetic energy moves caterpillars and cars and comets and ... well, everything, really. It even powers monster waves known as mega-tsunami (meg-a-tu-nar-me). Vast landslides into the sea provide kinetic energy for killer waves. They sweep across the ocean and arrive at the opposite shore half a kilometre high! But DON'T PANIC! Waves this big happen once in tens of thousands of years. Anyway, here's how to make your own model mega-tsunami ... without wrecking your house too badly.

Dare you discover ... how movement energy works?

You will need:

ARGH!

A TORCH

HELP!

A WASHING UP BOWL OF WATER
(IDEALLY THIS SHOULD BE PLACED IN THE KITCHEN SINK AND NOT OVER YOUR BROTHER/SISTER'S HEAD.)

What you do:

1 Wait until it's dark. Switch on the torch and hold it about 60 cm above the bowl.

2 Set the mixer tap so that a drop of water falls into the basin. (Or you could pick up a drop on your finger and let it fall from about 30 cm into the bowl.)

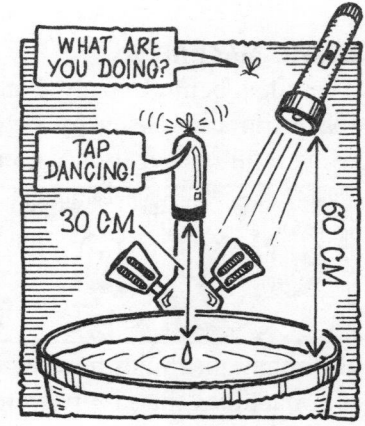

What do you notice?

a) Ripples spread out from the middle and then disappear.

b) Ripples move inwards from the side.

c) The ripples spread out to the sides and then move back.

Answer:

c) Did you spot the faint returning ripples? The kinetic energy of the falling drop makes ripples of movement energy through the water. The ripple loses energy to the sides and this makes it appear fainter as it returns to the centre.

Bet you never knew!
Sound energy is waves (like water waves) of movement energy in the air caused by noise – like your favourite music.

SHUT THAT KINETIC ENERGY!

MAGIC MACHINES

The idea behind many hand-operated machines is to make life a bit easier by saving us energy. For example, using a tin-opener uses less energy than the alternative…

But many machines need even less human energy. These are machines that are powered by fuel energy, and right now it's time to meet the grand-daddy of all these types of machine…

HI-TECH MAGAZINE AD 100

HAVE A BALL!

Enjoy a spin with this exciting steam powered toy designed by Hero of Alexandria.

Movement energy of escaping steam makes the ball spin round.

Steam forced into pipes from boiler

Water heated up in boiler

Fire makes heat energy

This idea might have set Roman technology steaming ahead. Just think – the Romans might have built steam trains and steam ships … but they didn't. As the magazine said, no one knew what to do with steam engines and the Romans weren't that bothered about saving muscle energy. Not whilst they had lots of slaves to do all the hard work.

It took another 1,600 years for an inventor named Thomas Savery (1650–1715) to reinvent the idea. One evening he drank a bottle of wine. He was too drunk to throw the bottle away – so he chucked it on the fire. Steam puffed from the bottle and Savery was just sober enough to see that the remaining wine was turning to steam. So the boozy boffin pulled the bottle from the fire and stuck it in water to cool it down and then, to his amazement, the water was sucked into the bottle!

But what was going on?

COULD YOU BE A SCIENTIST?

So what do *you* think was causing this effect?

a) As the bottle cooled it grew slightly larger and this made room for the water.

b) As the air cooled it took up less space so the water flooded in.

c) The hot wine was pulling in the water by a mysterious force.

> **Answer:**
> **b)** When air has heat energy it pushes outwards, remember? As the air cools it takes up less space.

Savery worked this out and designed engines for pumping water from mines. Over the next 80 years inventors like Thomas Newcomen (1663–1729) and James Watt improved the steam engine until it could power any kind of machinery, and transport like trains and ships. The world was transformed, and all because a tipsy scientist had a lot of bottle.

Here's one of Watt's inventions – Watt an invention, eh? It's a wonderful way to turn heat energy into movement energy (that's the First Law of Thermodynamics from page 16).

☕WATT STEAM ENGINE☕

③Piston passes movement energy to wheel

④Drive belt transfers movement energy to machinery.

WHAT'S THIS MACHINE, WATT?

THIS IS WHAT I CALL MY WATT STEAM ENGINE

WHAT D'YOU MEAN WATT, WATT?

WHAT? WHAT WATT?

SPIN!

②Heat energy boils water to steam. Steam has movement energy.

①Energy stored in the form of coal. Coal burned to make heat energy.

A FEW FACTS TO GET STEAMED UP ABOUT...

1 Inventors were fascinated by steam engines. In the 1730s an 11-year-old boy named John Smeaton (1724–1794) was taken to see one of Newcomen's machines. He was so excited he built a model steam engine and used it to pump out his dad's goldfish pond. Don't try this at home!

You'll be pleased to know that John survived the punishment he got from his dad and grew up to be a famous engineer who built canals and lighthouses.

2 Inventors like William Murdock built steam carriages that ran on the road like cars today. In 1801 Murdock's pal, inventor Richard Trevithick (1771–1833), built his own steam carriage and took it for a spin. It broke down, but the inventor managed to fix it and went to the pub to celebrate. Unfortunately he left the fire on – the boiler boiled dry and the engine exploded. That must have been a BLASTED nuisance!

3 In 1894 inventor Hiram Maxim (1840–1916) built a giant plane with wings 38 metres across powered by steam engines. The engines weren't powerful enough to get the heavy plane flying. The plane managed to get a few centimetres into the air before crashing into a crumpled wreck. I expect Maxim got a bit steamed up about the accident.

But the most successful use for steam power turned out to be the steam turbine. As you discovered on page 69 – turbines are used to make electricity in power stations. But that proved to be the least of their uses – as you're about to find out:

Hall of Fame: Charles Parsons
(1854–1931) Nationality: Irish

Young Charles was born with a silver spoon in his mouth. NO, he didn't get a valuable bit of cutlery stuck in his gob! He was born filthy rich. His dad was a science-mad astronomer who happened to be the Earl of Rosse and owned his own castle. In 1845 the Earl built the world's largest telescope – at an astronomical cost. But the 15 metre monster proved a real big mistake since you could only use it when the sky was clear and in that part of Ireland it was usually raining.

Young Charles was too rich to go to school – so like James Joule he had his own personal teacher. Charles became interested in science and began to invent machines. He built a steam-powered carriage and gave his brothers rides. One day he took his aunt for a ride but she fell off the machine and died.

Charles joined a company that built steam engines. He enjoyed his work so much that when he got married his idea of a romantic honeymoon was dragging his bride off to watch the testing of his newly invented turbines on a miserably cold lake. Charles came away with a lot of scientific data and his wife came away with a nasty dose of fever.

In the 1880s Charles developed his idea for the turbine. The idea was very simple: hot steam energy powered small turning blades. In fact, the blades turned very fast and Charles realized that they could be used to turn a propeller and power a ship. Here's what happened next…

The secret diary of Rear-Admiral Lord Blewitt

1894 ~ I've just had a visit from that inventor chappie Parsons. Perfect crack-pot, just like his father! I've never heard such piffle and humbug! He says he can build a ship that sails at 34 knots - that's faster than any ship afloat! Parsons says he's got a working model but I told him in no uncertain terms that nothing is faster than an ordinary steam engine. Personally, though, I can't see what's wrong with wind-power - it was good enough when I was a boy!

1895 ~ Yet another letter from that blasted nuisance Parsons. He's been pestering my fellow admirals with his half-cracked ideas. Can't he take NO for an answer? That fellow should be keel-hauled and flogged with the cat! His letter is full of scientific balderdash. He says he's built an actual boat now and he wants to show it off to us.

That's out of the question!!! We admirals have more important things to do - like going for cruises!

1896 - Please excuse the shaky writing - I am in a state of shock. Today was Fleet Review Day. Every year we admirals watch proudly as our great fleet steams past and raise a glass of port to Her Majesty's good health! But not today. Oh no...

Blow me if the whole proceedings weren't completely ruined by a little boat dashing past at 34 knots! I was so taken aback I began to splutter and my false teeth fell out! Poor old Admiral Snuff was so upset he spent the whole day peering through the wrong end of his telescope!

I took a look through my own glass and saw that confounded blighter Parsons on the fast boat. He was actually grinning and waving! If I'd had my way our warships would have blown him out of the water! But, er ... no one could catch him, actually! I'm afraid he left even our fastest ships astern.

My fellow admirals are talking about ordering these new-fangled turbines. It seems that our entire navy has just become out of date! I have a real sinking feeling about all this...

You'll be pleased to know that Parsons became rich and famous although he later wasted most of his money trying to make diamonds out of graphite – that's the substance used to make pencil lead. Oh well, no doubt he thought he was on the write lines.

THE ULTIMATE FREEBIE

Mind you, for hundreds of years scientists having been trying to build an even more powerful machine. A machine that *never* needs any new energy! A machine that once it starts will never, ever stop! I suppose that's what our hungry reporter pal Harvey Tucker would call "the ultimate free lunch". Scientists call it "perpetual motion".

BUT HOLD ON, DIDN'T YOU SAY ON PAGE 16 THAT THE SECOND LAW SAYS THAT EVERYTHING LOSES ENERGY IN THE FORM OF HEAT AND THAT MEANS YOU HAVE TO KEEP PUTTING MORE ENERGY INTO IT?

A VERY ALERT READER

Hey, that's right! And what's more, as I said earlier, movement energy leads to a loss of heat energy and this means that sooner or later any machine will always run out of energy. In 1824 French scientist Nicolas Carnot (1796–1832) worked out that steam engines will never work perfectly for this reason. But I didn't say that perpetual motion worked, did I? Mind you, it took a while for scientists to figure this out...

THE SCIENTIST'S FRIEND

Problem Page with Professor Frank Helper

Are you a scientist with an embarrassing problem? Do you feel it would help to talk to someone who cares? If so write to me and no one need know your secret except, of course, our 567,000 readers! This week — perpetual motion...

Dear Frank,
I've built this perpetual motion machine but it doesn't work. It's a bit worrying, me being a famous architect and all that. Am I a bit of a plonker?

Villard de Honnecourt
(14th century)

Dear Villard,
You certainly are! Your wheel will always stop owing to friction between the wheel and axle which turns the movement energy of the wheel into heat energy. Perhaps you ought to throw your energy into architecture?

Dear Frank,
I'm a science-mad nobleman. I'm also a big supporter of King Charles in his battles with Parliament and I've been arrested and imprisoned a few times — but that's enough about me. Anyway, I've built this perpetual motion wheel operated by falling balls — see my drawing. It spins for ages but

CONTINUED ➔

then it stops. Why? Why? My
head is spinning
faster than
my wheel —
help me!
Yours nobly,
Edward Somerset
The 2nd Marquis
of Worcester (1601–1667)

Dear Marquis
The falling balls
have no effect
on your
lordship's wheel.
The wheel — er,
I mean real —
reason it stops
is friction. See
my answer to
Villard.

Dear Frank,
I've gotta this
bellissima perpetual
motion machine!
It's powered by
de wind power and
it's perfectissimo
except for one tiny
detail — it wonna
work! I'd be humbly
grateful for
ever for
your most kind advice.

Marco Zimara (Italy 1500s)

TURNING SAIL SQUEEZES
DE BELLOWS TO MAKE
MORE OF DE WIND.

WIND BLOWS THE
SAILS ROUND

Dear Marco,
My most kind advice is, forget it! Your
machine is a load of hot air! The sails lose
energy from friction and don't have enough
energy to squeeze the bellows. So I'm afraid
you're out of puff, pal.

Yes, perpetual motion is about as likely as a puppy dog that doesn't pee in your slippers. Italian mega-genius Leonardo da Vinci (1452–1519) put it a bit more elegantly:

Oh you students of eternal motion! How many futile things have you created while searching for it.

And old Leo ought to know – he built his own machine which (please don't faint with surprise) didn't work.

Italian scientist Gerolamo Cardano (1501–1576) used maths to figure out that perpetual motion was impossible. Gerolamo led an exciting life. He was brought up by his strict grandmother who was cruel to him when he was naughty. (I hope your granny is a bit less vicious!) Gerolamo became a doctor and a scientist who claimed (rightly) that fire isn't a substance as people thought at the time, but then he found himself facing a fearsome fiery fate...

In 1570 he was arrested by the Church for using his interest in astrology (star signs) to speculate about religion. He was threatened with torture and burning to death unless he confessed he was wrong. Should he confess? It was a burning question. Clever Cardano did the sensible thing and he was released.

But later on his son murdered someone and had his head chopped off. Gerolamo fell out with his second son and asked the government to banish him to another city as "a youth of evil habits". Hopefully your dad is a bit less strict with you!

So there you are – perpetual motion is impossible. The laws of energy just won't allow it.

But what's this?

PERPETUAL MOTION AT LAST!!!

COME AND SEE THE PERPETUAL MOTION MACHINE INVENTED BY ME, JOHANN BESSLER OTHERWISE KNOWN AS "OFFREYEUS" USING THE LATEST 1680s TECHNOLOGY.

Yes, Offreyeus the great healer, doctor, fortune teller, gun-maker, painter, watchmaker and all-round genius has done it!

ALL MY OWN WORK!

ADMISSION ONE MARK.

WOW!

The machine has been examined twice by Germany's greatest scientists and pronounced genuine!

You've seen the machine now buy the book, it's 600 pages all about me and how clever I am!

OFFREYEUS'S TRIUMPHAL PERPETUAL MOTION MACHINE

"What a load of ... book!"
Saxony Times

"This is the most ... book I have ever read!" Kassel News

A NOTE TO THE READER
Don't worry - the Laws of Thermodynamics haven't been broken. Just read on and you'll see why...

CONFESSION

I, Gretel Braun, the servant girl of Johann Bessler, confess that my master is a crook and his machine was built to trick foolish people out of their money. He spent his wife's savings building this machine but he wouldn't let anyone look at its insides — not even the scientists who said it was genuine. And why? Because there's a handle next door that turns the wheel! I should know — I had to crank that flipping handle every time people came to see the machine.

Ouch my poor back!

PS Please don't execute me — I was only doing my job!

Yes, Johann's machine relied on good old-fashioned muscle power. And that brings us to the next chapter. Actually I'm not going to tell you what's in it because I don't want to spoil the surprise.

But here's a hint… It's hot, it's sweaty and it's all yours…

HOT, SWEATY BODY BITS

This chapter is about how your body uses energy. Yes, this is the chapter in which the going gets tough. And you know what that means? The tough get going – and Harvey Tucker slobs out with a bucket of popcorn in front of the telly...

Killer energy fact file

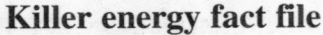

NAME: Your body and energy

THE BASIC FACTS: 1. The body is a living machine for turning the stored energy in your food into movement energy to move your muscles.

2. Actually only one-quarter of the energy that your muscles use is used for movement – the rest becomes heat energy and escapes from the body.

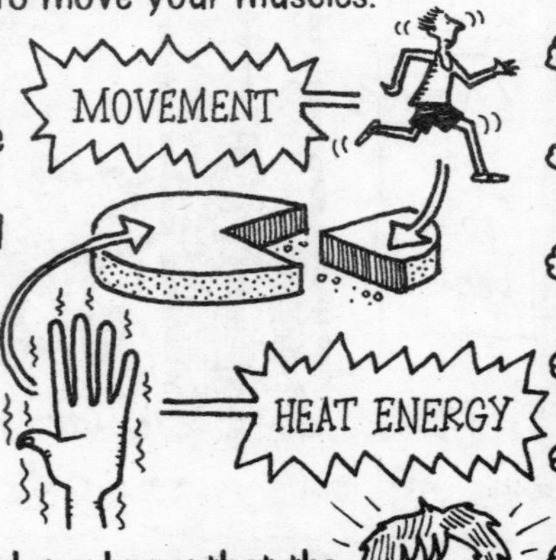

MOVEMENT

HEAT ENERGY

KILLER DETAILS: Did you know that the energy in your body is made by tiny creatures that were once killer germs? It's true!
Read on for more dreadful details...

GULP!

WORKING UP A SWEAT

Tough exercise is all in a day's work for athletes. In 2000, marathon runner Tegla Laroupe from Kenya said she took up running because she had to walk 10 km to school and was punished if she was late. Soon she was running 192 km a week. That's like running to school and all the way home again and all the way to school a second time. And doing it all again in the afternoon. And doing this every school day.

Wanna try it?

And speaking of exercise, here's a few killer holidays Harvey Tucker wouldn't be seen dead on (well, if he tried them he might be dead on them)...

DYING FOR A DANCE?

YOU COULD BE DYING FOR EVER AT OUR OLD-TIME 1930S AMERICAN DANCE MARATHON.

Yes, you have to dance until you drop – the winner is the person who stays on their feet for longest.

RULES ~ 1. No sleeping. 2. You *must* keep moving. Anyone not dancing fast enough gets wet towels flicked at their legs! 3. You have 15 minutes rest in each hour – so make sure you go to the toilet and receive life-saving medical treatment in this time.

4. If you die during the dance marathon you get disqualified.

IMPORTANT ANNOUNCEMENT
We've just found out that dance marathons have been BANNED in the USA since 1937 after several people went mad with tiredness. This holiday has been cancelled! Anyone who has booked will get a full refund ... that's if they can find where we've hidden the money.

Mind you, in the 1940s, dance marathons continued to be held in secret…

SICKENING SHIP SHINDIG SUNK!

NEW YORK NEWS

Cops raided an illegal dance marathon. The dancers might have been prancing to prison but the organisers herded them still dancing onto vans. After a can-can in the van it was a quick hop to the docks and a shuffle to a ship to take them outside US territory. But once at sea it was take your partners for the fling (your lunch) as seasickness had the dancers fox-trotting for the sides. Said one dancer, "It's heaving out there, 'scuse me gotta dash!"

HORRIBLE SCIENCE

FITNESS HOLIDAYS

DANCE MARATHONS TOO *SOFT* FOR YOU?
WHY NOT TRY THE

WESTERN STATES ENDURANCE RUN?!

YOU'VE GOT TO RUN 161 KM (100 MILES) IN
LESS THAN 30 HOURS. YOU HAVE TO RUN UP
MOUNTAINS AND AVOID RATTLESNAKES.

WARNING!
YOUR BODY WILL DRY OUT
IN THE HEAT AND YOU MAY
LOSE 7% OF YOUR WEIGHT.

← START
FINISH

AND WHILE YOU'RE AT IT, WHY NOT TRY THE

HAWAII IRONMAN COMPETITION?

SPLASH!

PEDAL!

STRIDE!

1 Swim	2 Cycle	3 Run a marathon
3.86 km	180 km	42.2 km
(2.4 miles)	(112 miles)	(26.2 miles)

WARNING!
WE'VE ALLOWED A DAY FOR THE *WHOLE COMPETITION* SO
YOU'D BEST HURRY OR YOU'LL MISS YOUR FLIGHT AND
HAVE TO SWIM HOME ACROSS THE **P**ACIFIC **O**CEAN.

But all this energy raises a sensational scientific suggestion – how exactly do our bodies turn stored food energy into action-packed movement energy? How can a stodgy old school dinner help you turn in a world athletic running record? (And we're not talking about getting the squirts and having to dash for the loo.)

FIRST THE THEORIES...

1 Three hundred years ago scientists believed the muscles contained gunpowder that exploded to make them move. This idea wasn't as silly as it sounds because gunpowder is a form of stored energy and the muscles do use stored food energy (see below if you don't believe me). Of course, the idea was soon exploded.

2 French chemist Antoine Lavoisier (1743–1794) was interested in burning and breathing and pointed out that you breathe more when you work hard. Well, blow me if he wasn't right! Lavoisier reckoned that some kind of burning was going on in the lungs to change food into energy.

3 Then another scientist, Joseph Lagrange (1736–1813) said that if the lungs burnt food they'd catch fire. Hopefully your lungs won't do this – not even when you've eaten a really hot chilli.

4 German scientist Justus von Liebig (1803–1873) reckoned that the body's vital force moved the muscles.

But none of these clever and very thoughtful scientists grasped the truth. The answer to how the body uses energy is a small detail – how small? Oh, about 0.02 mm across. It's called a cell, and to find out more why not read this rare copy of HOW YOUR BODY WORKS by the famous Dr Jekyll and Mr Hyde. Apparently Dr Jekyll's quite nice but when he drinks a potion he turns into a blood-crazed killer monster...

HOW YOUR BODY WORKS

by Dr Jekyll and Mr Hyde

INTRODUCTION

Dr Jekyll writes... Dear Reader Welcome to our little book about how the body works. We're sure you'll enjoy reading its fascinating facts and looking at its ever so interesting diagrams...

Dr J

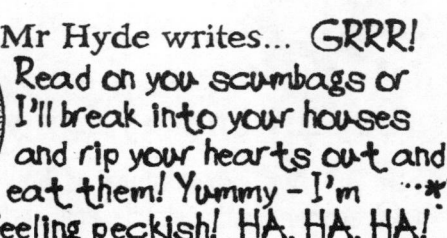

Mr H

Mr Hyde writes... GRRR! Read on you scumbags or I'll break into your houses and rip your hearts out and eat them! Yummy – I'm feeling peckish! HA, HA, HA!

Chapter 1: Feeding your cells

Dr Jekyll writes...

Your body is made up of trillions of human body cells that need energy to put together proteins. These are chemicals that build into all the useful bits that make up the body. Every cell is a teeny-weenie living machine that makes power in hundreds of tiny units called **mitochondria** **(mi-toe-con-dree-a).** Mitochondria make energy using glucose — it's a very tasty type of sugar found in foods such as flour, bread,

INSIDE VIEW OF CELL

cereal and sweet things like dainty little pastries...

AGGGGH! I'll stuff Dr J's pastries up his NOSTRILS!!!! Your cells grab glucose from your blood — so if you want extra glucose why not DRINK SOMEONE'S BLOOD WHEN IT'S HOT AND STEAMING! HA, HA!!!

Chapter 2:
Useful energy for your body

There are two explanations of how the mitochondria make energy — the simple one and the one with scientific details. Of course being a scientist I prefer...

Well I HATE details 'cos they're BORING. Anyone who wants details is gonna get MINCED UP FOR CAT FOOD! Anyway, your mito-thingies do it automatically so who's bothered — EH, EH? ...

I've drawn a nice clear diagram to make the process easy to understand.

HOW CELLS MAKE ENERGY

GLUCOSE (made by mitochondria) + OXYGEN (from breathing) → WATER | CARBON DIOXIDE | HEAT | ATP

CELL   MITOCHONDRIA   GLUCOSE! GLUCOSE! GLUCOSE!

ATP, or Adenosine Triphosphate (A-deen-o-sin Try-fos-fate) as we scientists call it, is a lovely little chemical energy store that goes wherever it's needed in the cell to make energy to power your muscles or make new bits of the cell...

And the old bod can make energy without oxygen, like when someone tries to run away from me. But they can't get enough oxygen to their cells and they're gasping. HA HA HA! Their stupid cells try to make energy without oxygen but can't make as much ATP and SO I GRAB THEM AND PLAY MARBLES WITH THEIR EYEBALLS! HA! HA HA!

MIGHTY MYSTERIOUS MITOCHONDRIA

1 Inside you right now are about 10,000,000,000,000,000
(ten million billion) mitochondria busily churning out
energy to keep your body going. But they're so small that
you can fit one billion of them inside a grain of sand.

2 Mitochondria look like very tiny brown-red worms and
when they make more of themselves they spilt in half.
Scientists think that mitochondria were once germs that
moved into cells a billion years ago. At first they were a
pest but somehow the cells and mitochondria worked out
how to live together...

OKAY, SO I PROVIDE FOOD AND SHELTER...

YEAH, AND I MAKE YOU ENERGY.

IT'S A DEAL!

And now every time you eat and every time you breathe you are doing it to feed alien life-forms hiding in your body!

3 You get your mitochondria from your mum. That's because the mitochondria in your cells are descended from a tiny egg made by your mum. Actually your energy level depends on lots of things like health and diet, but basically you get your energy from your mum!

MASSIVE MUSCLES

The part of your body that *really* needs energy is your muscles. It doesn't matter whether your muscles are bulging and beefy or you look like a stick insect on a diet. Your muscles are where your body turns stored chemical energy from ATP into movement energy.

And now for some facts you can muscle into...

Killer energy fact file

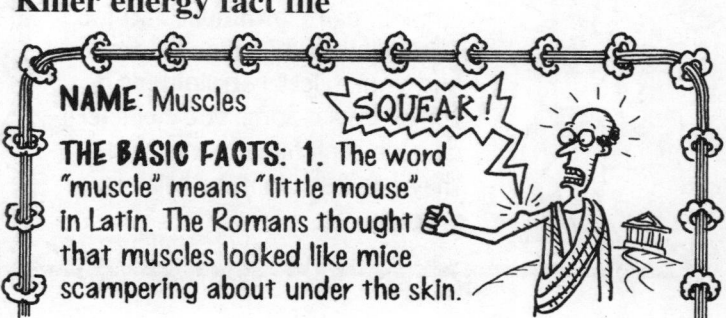

NAME: Muscles

SQUEAK!

THE BASIC FACTS: 1. The word "muscle" means "little mouse" in Latin. The Romans thought that muscles looked like mice scampering about under the skin.

2. All muscles are made of fibres that shorten in response to nerve signals from the brain. When the fibres relax so does the muscle.

3. Here are the main types of muscle.

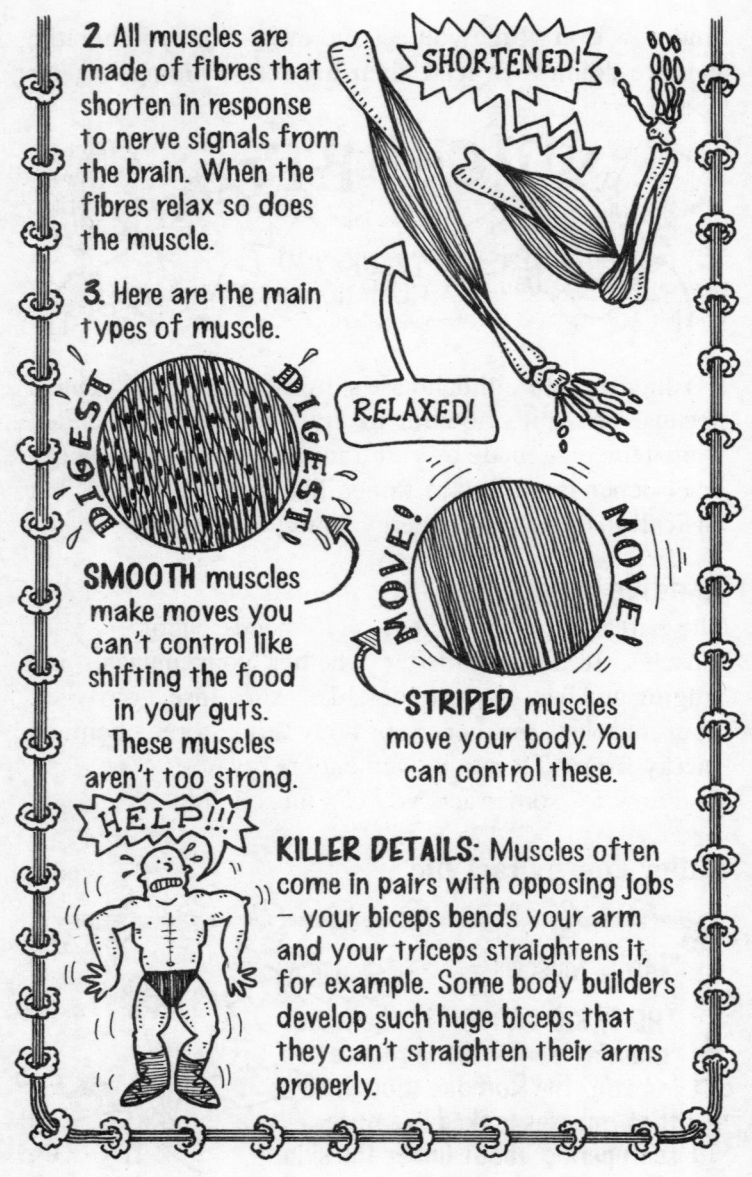

SHORTENED!

RELAXED!

DIGEST! DIGEST!

MOVE! MOVE!

SMOOTH muscles make moves you can't control like shifting the food in your guts. These muscles aren't too strong.

STRIPED muscles move your body. You can control these.

HELP!!!

KILLER DETAILS: Muscles often come in pairs with opposing jobs — your biceps bends your arm and your triceps straightens it, for example. Some body builders develop such huge biceps that they can't straighten their arms properly.

So you've got your head around how your body makes energy from mitochondria to muscles? Well, that's fab! Hopefully you've still got enough energy to try this rather exhausting quiz...

SEVEN SUPER-ENERGY QUIZ QUESTIONS

You should be able to race through this quiz because each question has just TWO possible answers. I just hope you're not in two minds about it!

1 Babies are more likely to have this than adults – what is it?

a) Built-in central heating.

b) Cold blood.

2 How much heat energy does your body give off when you're watching telly for an hour?

a) As much as an electric heater.

b) As much as a light bulb.

3 Which of these statements is correct?

a) Lazy people live longer than hard-working people because they use up less energy.

b) Hard work never killed anyone (as Dr Grimgrave likes to remind us).

4 Why do children seem to have more energy than adults?

a) Children make energy faster than adults.

b) People of all ages produce the same amount of energy but adults prefer slobbing about.

5 Why do some people get overweight?

a) They eat more than they should.

b) Their bodies burn up food more slowly and spare food is stored as fat.

6 When does your brain use most energy?

a) In a science test.

b) When it's dreaming.

7 Why do people feel tired in the morning?

a) Their bodies are weak because they haven't eaten all night.

b) Their brains need glucose.

Answers:

1 a) Yes, babies really have central heating! They have a type of fat called brown fat (which adults have far less of). Mitochondria in the fat process fuel in a way that makes extra heat and this helps to keep the baby warm.

2 b) If you go for a run your body gives off the heat of ten light bulbs. In seven minutes of playing squash you can make enough heat to boil one litre of water.

3 b) Sorry, Harvey Tucker! Answer **a)** was suggested by US scientist Raymond Pearl (1879–1940) who wrote an article in 1927 entitled "Why lazy people live longest". But Pearl didn't take his own advice – he penned 700 articles and 17 books and he still lived to be 61.

4 a) Children's mitochondria are going at full blast making energy for an active lifestyle and a growing body. As a person gets older they slow down. And by the time they're as ancient as your more mature teachers, all their get up and go has got up and gone.

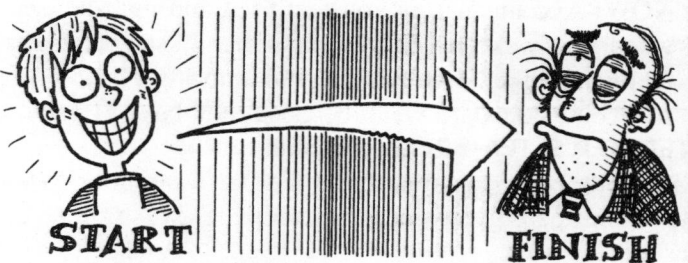

START   FINISH

5 a) Overweight people often make *more* energy than thinner people (it takes a lot of energy to shift a big body). The idea that overweight people don't eat too much comes from surveys where overweight people have fibbed about their eating habits. Now you might think that fat people eat more because they're greedy, but scientists have found that overweight people seem to take longer to feel full than thinner people.

6 b) If you fall asleep in your science test and start dreaming, your brain actually uses *more* energy than when you're awake! You may like to share this information with your teacher if she catches you sleeping during the test…

ZZZZ, HUH? OH ER, I'VE JUST BEEN POWERING UP MY BRAIN, MISS!

7 b) The brain needs glucose to make energy. Your blood contains just one hour's supply of glucose but your liver stores glucose in the form of a chemical called glycogen (gly-co-gen) to keep you going. But by morning your brain is hungry and it wants its glucose NOW! And that's why you feel tired and light-headed when you wake up. If you miss breakfast you might feel like a bike – two tyred to stand up – ha, ha.

TEACHER'S TEA-BREAK TEASER

At about 3 p.m. tap smartly on the staffroom door. When the door opens give your teacher a wide-awake smile and ask…

IS IT TRUE YOUR ENERGY LEVEL DROPS AT THIS TIME OF DAY?

MUMBLE, GROAN…

Answer:
Yes it does. Scientist Robert Thayer of the University of California interviewed lots of people.
Here's your teacher's day based on his findings…

7 am: Wake up feeling groggy…

SCIENCE, BLAH, BLAH, HOMEWORK, WITTER…

11 am: Energy levels have increased…

3 pm:
Energy
levels low...

7 pm:
Energy levels
pick up.

11 pm: Energy
levels dipping
to bed-time

Tired people tend to be more bad-tempered and the best treatment is exercise. In fact, I should have warned you earlier…

☠ HORRIBLE HEALTH WARNING!

Beware of KILLER TEACHERS! Yes, a tired teacher can be more dangerous than a tiger with toothache!

KILLER TEACHER GETTING MUCH NEEDED EXERCISE BY CHASING PUPIL.

Of course your teacher may try to revive themselves with a nice hot mug of tea. But inside that mug of tea something interesting is going on. The heat is spreading – it's heating up the cup, it's warming your teacher … and eventually it'll warm up the rest of the universe.

What on Earth's going on…?

It's time to turn up the *heat*.

KILLER HEAT

Earlier we talked about cold (lack of heat energy) but now it's time for heat. Time for this book to warm up to its boiling, burning climax. Yes, it's time to get as hot as the hottest place in the universe!

But first a question to fire your imagination…

> ## HOW CAN HEAT SPREAD ACROSS THE COSMOS?

Whoops – that's a tricky one! We've asked Bernard Boyle back to answer your questions – let's hope he can keep his cool…

HORRIBLE SCIENCE QUESTION TIME

Today I'm going to tell you how heat energy spreads…

Is that "spreads" like margarine?

I expect that's 'eat energy.

Since heat is really just wobbling atoms it can spread from atom to atom as they knock into one another and start wobbling faster and faster. We scientists call this conduction (con-duck-shon).

A substance that allows heat to pass through it easily is called a good conductor — examples include metals.

My grandpa was a good conductor...

For heat?

No, the number 92 bus.

An insulator is a bad conductor. Examples include air, plastic and this rather trendy but sensible woolly jumper I'm wearing.

Heat can also spread through convection (con-veck-shon). That's the word for when hot air or water atoms' molecules move apart because they've got heat energy.

Why do they do that?

This makes the air or water lighter than the same amount of cold air or water. And so the hotter substance rises.

Shouldn't our teacher rise? He's full of hot air!

Finally, heat can spread through radiation.

RADIATION

Is that when people get zapped with high energy rays?

113

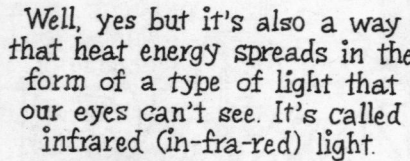

Well, yes but it's also a way that heat energy spreads in the form of a type of light that our eyes can't see. It's called infrared (in-fra-red) light.

INVISIBLE RAYS

It's what you're feeling when you feel hot in the sun. Now if you'll just turn to page 99 of my book...

That's right, INFRARED.

Did you say we're in for a read?

CONDUCTION IN ACTION

Conduction and insulation are so common I bet you come across them all the time. Yes, common as muck they are ... *and I can prove it!*

Bet you never knew!
Manure heaps steam in cold weather. The heat energy is actually made by billions of microbes cheerfully scoffing the delicious dung. But manure itself contains lots of air, water and bits of half-digested plants – all good insulators so that quite high temperatures can build up inside the heap until it's hot enough to steam. Fancy a steam in one?

In the Second World War the Germans invaded Russia and in November 1941 they were poised to capture the Russian capital, Moscow. One night the temperature crashed. Thousands of soldiers were frost-bitten and their rotten feet had to be chopped off. The Germans wore boots shod with iron nails that conducted heat away from their feet. The Russians wore felt boots. Felt is a type of pressed wool. It's a good insulator and keeps the heat in. The Russians won and the Germans were left feeling sore about de-feet.

And talking about insulation...

Dare you discover ... what a sock does to ice?

You will need:

A sunny windowsill or bright lamp

Sock (it doesn't have to be clean but you may feel cheesed off if it smells)

Two ice cubes

Two saucers

Gloves to protect fingers from ice

What you do:

1 Put on gloves. Place one ice cube on one saucer.

2 Put the other ice cube in the sock and wrap the sock around it tightly. Place the sock on the second saucer.

☠ HORRIBLE HEALTH WARNING!

If you borrowed your dad's sock, beware – he might find it and put it on whilst the experiment is in progress. Any plans to increase your pocket money might be put on ice!

3 Place the ice cube and the sock 15 cm from the light bulb.

YOU MAY NEED BOOKS TO RAISE THE ICE TO THE RIGHT HEIGHT.

HMMM! I SMELL CHEESE!

4 Leave the experiment for 45 minutes.

What do you notice?
a) Both ice cubes have melted.
b) The ice cube in the saucer has melted but the ice cube in the sock hasn't.
c) The ice cube in the sock has melted but not the ice cube in the saucer.

Result
b) The ice cube in the sock should be only half-melted. Like any material, the sock is a good insulator – but if an object is already cold the insulator can keep it cold too! Here's what happened:

HEAT ENERGY

LAMP

MOST HEAT ENERGY SOAKED UP BY SOCK, ICE STAYS COOL →

INSULATED SNOW PERSON KEEPS COLD LONGER.

ANYONE SEEN MY JUMPER?

COULD YOU BE A SCIENTIST?

In 1960 the US Air Force carried out tests on volunteers to find out the greatest heat a human can survive. It turned out to be 260° C (500° F) – hotter than boiling water, hotter than a cooking steak. (I expect the volunteers were real hot-heads.) What were they wearing?

a) They were in the buff, raw, nip, nuddy or any other word that means that they wore no clothes.

b) A full set of clothing.

c) Flame proof underpants.

Answer:

b) A person can stand 60° C (140° F) *more* heat when wearing clothes because the clothing insulates the skin from the heat.

Bet you never knew!
At the World Sauna Championships in Finland people sit in a hot sauna room at temperatures up to 43° C (110° F) – this is as hot as some deserts! The aim is to sweat dirt from the skin but everyone wears swimming costumes because the organizers say it would be rude if they didn't.

Mind you, a heatwave can be as hot as a sauna. Killer heatwaves often strike the southern USA – in 1980, for example, thousands of people died as temperatures soared above 37.7° C (100° F). In Dallas, Texas the official in charge of stopping cruelty to children said:

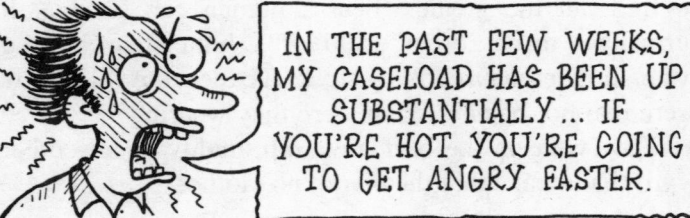

IN THE PAST FEW WEEKS, MY CASELOAD HAS BEEN UP SUBSTANTIALLY ... IF YOU'RE HOT YOU'RE GOING TO GET ANGRY FASTER.

Yes, I'm sorry to say that hot-tempered parents were taking it out on their children. So, BE WARNED. It's not a smart idea to ask for extra pocket money when your dad's sweltering.

I'LL TAKE THAT AS A "NO", THEN

But, talking about heatwaves, there's one place where the weather is *always* boiling. It's one of the hottest places on Earth – it's so hot that the heat kills people *all the time*. One early visitor called it:

THE NEAREST TO A LITTLE HELL ON EARTH THAT THE WHOLE WICKED WORLD CAN PRODUCE.

It's California's Death Valley and *Living on the Edge Magazine* was after a fearless, super-fit, ultra-brave reporter to write a feature on the region. They couldn't find one, and so…

HARVEY TUCKER'S BIG ADVENTURE

I was summoned to the editor's office but I had my excuses ready.

"I can't go!" I moaned. "Please don't send me back to the Arctic I'll get hypo-what's it and lose all my toes!"

The editor folded her arms and shook her head.

"Cut the cackle, greedy-guts. You're not going to the Arctic and you won't get hypothermia. Sunstroke, sunburn, fever maybe, but no hypothermia!"

And she gave me my next assignment - a feature on the effects of heat in Death Valley. "Death Valley" — it's the kind of name that gives me a cold shiver — or should I say a hot shudder?

But as my old dad used to say, we Tuckers are like a bad pork pie - you can't keep us down! So I thought, "No sweat — I'll just go and check out the scenery," and I threw myself into planning. (Well, for five minutes — then I watched the game on TV.) Then I packed my sunnies, 26 tubes of sunblock, 15 jars of suncream, my laptop, a crate of cold drinks and six family-sized boxes of ice-cream. That should keep me going! Then I dressed up in my home-made heat protection suit...

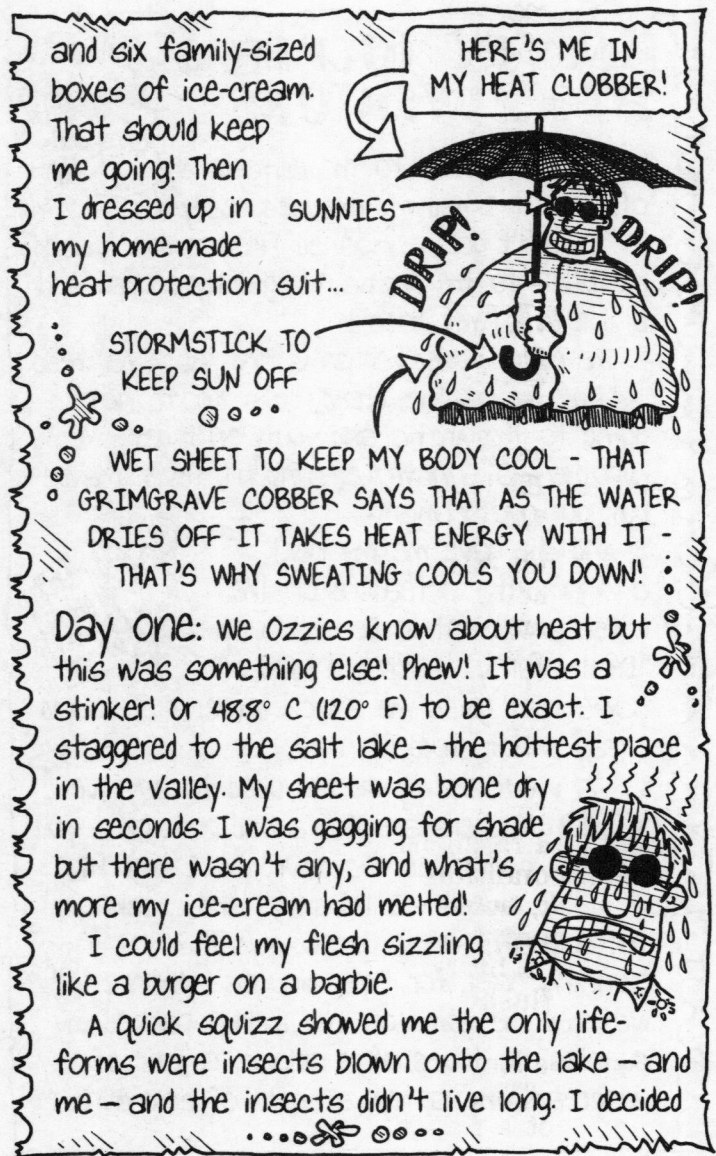

HERE'S ME IN MY HEAT CLOBBER!

SUNNIES

DRIP! DRIP!

STORMSTICK TO KEEP SUN OFF

WET SHEET TO KEEP MY BODY COOL - THAT GRIMGRAVE COBBER SAYS THAT AS THE WATER DRIES OFF IT TAKES HEAT ENERGY WITH IT - THAT'S WHY SWEATING COOLS YOU DOWN!

Day one: We Ozzies know about heat but this was something else! Phew! It was a stinker! Or 48.8° C (120° F) to be exact. I staggered to the salt lake – the hottest place in the valley. My sheet was bone dry in seconds. I was gagging for shade but there wasn't any, and what's more my ice-cream had melted!

I could feel my flesh sizzling like a burger on a barbie.

A quick squizz showed me the only life-forms were insects blown onto the lake – and me – and the insects didn't live long. I decided this place was real sticky — and so was I. So I huddled under my stormstick and had a go at some research. I downloaded some info from the Internet — but my laptop melted! So I took a gander at my book — maybe old Dr G has something more to say about heat...

DISEASES I HAVE KNOWN
by Dr H. Grimgrave

Chapter 21
THE EFFECTS OF HEAT ON THE BODY

Too much heat is as bad for you as too much cold. The body sweats until it dries out and heats up. The chemicals that make it up begin to break down. This process is known as heatstroke.

In the village of Much Moaning, where I practice, we don't get too many cases of heatstroke. This is unfortunate as heatstroke is a fascinating medical condition. Last week, however, an idiot complained of feeling a bit hot.

"Am I flushed?" he asked.

"Don't be stupid man!" I told him. "You're a person, not a toilet."

SWEAT!

IDIOT FEELING
A BIT HOT

The effects of heatstroke are easily summed up: fever, vomiting, headache, thirst, confusion, dry skin...

FEVER

HEADACHE

CONFUSION

THIRST

DRY SKIN

VOMITING

IDIOT WITH HEATSTROKE

... loss of consciousness and death.

So let that be a warming ... er ... *warning* to you. Sometimes the victim faints after feeling giddy.

In my days as an army doctor the soldiers would walk into lampposts during long, hot, marches. Their heart beat slowed and they couldn't pass water, or "urinate" as we doctors say.

The treatment is to rest in a cool place (I shut the soldiers in a cool food store) and drink lots of liquid. Water is the cheapest option, I find. Most doctors will tell you that victims of heatstroke should avoid hard work. Personally I take the view that hard work never killed anyone so I made them peel potatoes to make chips for my supper. It's a fried and tested remedy, ha ha.

"That's it" I thought "I'm crook, I've got heatstroke!" Just then I saw a sticky-beak scientist go swanning past — they study heat out here. She ordered me to drink 45 litres of water a day or my body would dry out! Too right — I was dripping with sweat. So I drank all my drinks — they were fizzy so I spent the next six hours burping.

At last I found a motel with air-conditioning. Heaven!

I jumped into my cozzie and dived into the pool and stayed there until sunset with just my nose sticking out of the water.

Days 2-10

Still recovering so I spent the next few days bludging by the pool — the motel had a nice line in ice-cold lager, cold slushy milkshakes and 64 flavours of ice-cream — ace tucker! (I felt I ought to sample them all to decide which I liked best.) I was sure the magazine wouldn't go to the knuckle about the bill!

SOME HOT NEWS JUST IN...

The Earth is heating up and causing killer climate chaos. There have been deadly droughts and fatal floods and the woeful warmth is melting ice from the land and raising sea levels and causing more floods. And here's why...

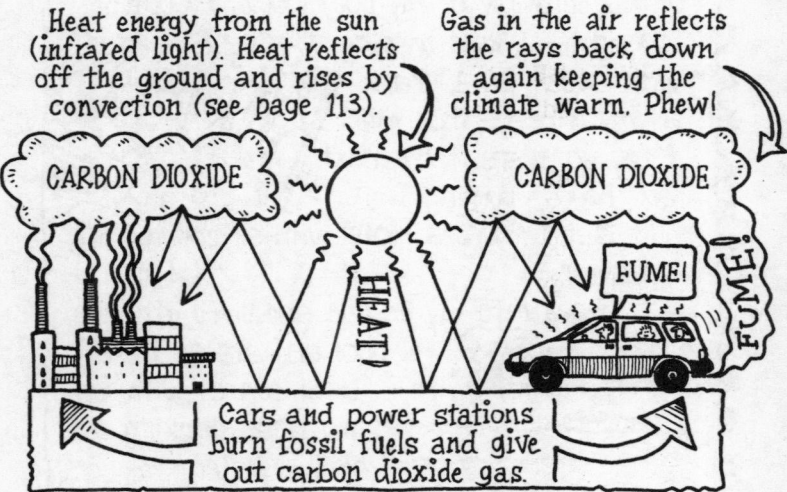

Heat energy from the sun (infrared light). Heat reflects off the ground and rises by convection (see page 113).

Gas in the air reflects the rays back down again keeping the climate warm. Phew!

CARBON DIOXIDE

CARBON DIOXIDE

HEAT!

FUME!

FUME!

Cars and power stations burn fossil fuels and give out carbon dioxide gas.

This is sometimes known as the "greenhouse effect" because the gas traps heat like the glass of a greenhouse. Okay – so any old science book will tell you this. But did you know that another gas causing global warming is methane? And a major cause of methane is farts – especially cows' farts (they blow-off more than humans) and also the farts of wood-eating insects called termites.

PARDON! FART! PARDON! PARDON!
PARDON! FART! FART! FART!

The greenhouse effect was discovered before it even became a problem. The possibility was pointed out by Irish scientist John Tyndall (1820–1895). Tyndall was a fantastic science teacher (yes, they do exist!). In one lecture at the Royal Institution in London he used the science of energy to play a cello … without touching it!

COULD YOU BE A SCIENTIST?

OK, so how did he manage *that*?

Was it…

a) Energy from laser beams.

b) The movement energy of air blasting from an elephant's trunk.

c) Sound energy travelling along a pole from someone playing a piano in the basement.

TOO HARD, JUMBO!

Answer:
c) Sound energy passed along the pole and moved the cello's strings.

Sadly, Tyndall was poisoned accidentally by his wife when she gave him too much of the medicine he was taking.

Mind you, in the next chapter you'll find killer temperatures that make global warming seem a bit chilly. Can't you just hear the crackling and roaring from the next few fiery pages…

It's gonna be HOT.

Is the fire brigade ready?

FEARSOME FIERY FURNACES

Put heat energy into something and three things can happen.

1 If it's solid it might melt into a liquid like Harvey's ice cream and his laptop a few pages ago.

2 If it's already a liquid it might turn into a gas – like water when it boils.

3 Or it might burst into flames **BURN!**

Scientists call the first two effects a "change in state". Basically what's going on is that heat energy is making the atoms wobble so fast they break free of neighbouring atoms. If they stick close to their neighbours the substance is a liquid – but if they go off in search of adventure they're a gas.

Fire is different ... actually the posh scientific word is combustion (com-bust-tee-on).

Killer energy fact file

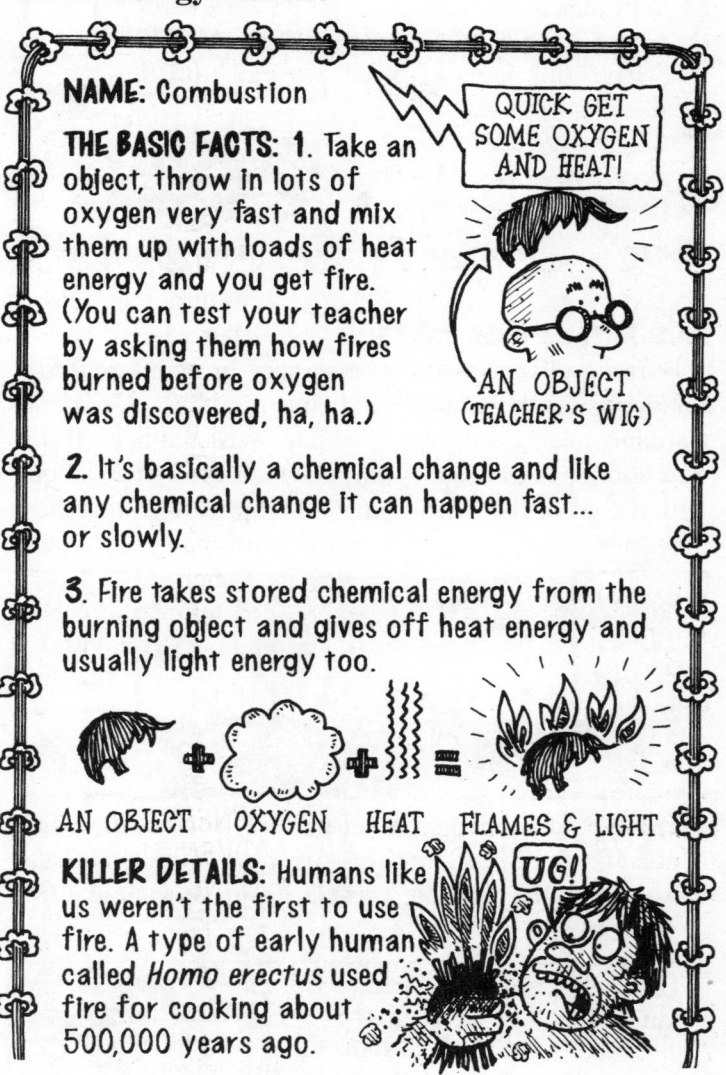

NAME: Combustion

THE BASIC FACTS: 1. Take an object, throw in lots of oxygen very fast and mix them up with loads of heat energy and you get fire. (You can test your teacher by asking them how fires burned before oxygen was discovered, ha, ha.)

QUICK GET SOME OXYGEN AND HEAT!

AN OBJECT (TEACHER'S WIG)

2. It's basically a chemical change and like any chemical change it can happen fast... or slowly.

3. Fire takes stored chemical energy from the burning object and gives off heat energy and usually light energy too.

AN OBJECT   OXYGEN   HEAT   FLAMES & LIGHT

KILLER DETAILS: Humans like us weren't the first to use fire. A type of early human called *Homo erectus* used fire for cooking about 500,000 years ago.

UG!

Scientists have found traces of their fires near Beijing, China — so was this the first-ever Chinese takeaway? And ever since we've been finding horrible uses for fire...

SWEET AND SOUR MAMMOTH – FASCINATING!

FIVE FATAL FIERY FACTS...

1 Burning alive was the punishment in many countries for opposing the Church or being a witch – Gerolamo Cardano nearly suffered this fate – remember? If the executioner felt kind they might smear the victim's body with a kind of fast-burning tar called pitch to finish them off faster.

FANCY SOME PITCH?

TAR VERY MUCH!

2 In England women were burnt alive if they killed their husbands or clipped bits of silver off coins. The last woman to suffer this fate was Christian Murphy in 1789. A witness said

She behaved with great decency, but was most shocked at the dreadful punishment she was about to undergo.

No wonder she was shocked – if she'd been a man she'd have got off with a nice quick hanging.

3 Burning wasn't the only method in which fire helped to get rid of people. In ancient China criminals were fried in oil. The English King Henry VIII (1490–1547) ordered that people found guilty of poisoning should be boiled alive.

4 Archaeologists have studied skeletons from Herculaneum, a Roman town destroyed by a volcano in AD 79. The people had been killed by superheated gases and the archaeologists found that their brains had boiled whilst they were *still alive*.

5 People who think that humans can burst into flames for unknown reasons (this is called spontaneous human combustion) have blamed the mystery fires on fart gases such as methane that burn easily. Scientists explain this burning question in terms of sparks from static electricity but either way it must be a nasty way to glow, er, go.

And now for more burning questions…

COULD YOU BE A SCIENTIST?

The human body burns at around 600–950° C (1112–1710° F) but some victims of spontaneous human combustion have been found burnt to ashes leaving their surroundings untouched.

How is this possible?

a) The fire was hot and quick-burning and burnt itself out.

b) The fire made the bodies explode from inside.

c) The fire burned like a candle, consuming the body's fat at high temperatures, but it didn't spread.

Answer:
c) Non-fatty bits like the legs are often left amongst the ashes. In 1986 a scientist from Leeds University, England, set fire to a dead pig to produce similar results. Crispy bacon, anyone?

Bet you never knew!
It was once thought the victims were drunken people and the fires were made hot by alcohol burning inside them. So scientist Justus von Liebig (remember him from page 100?) tried soaking bits of dead body in alcohol and setting them on fire. They didn't burn. He then got rats drunk and set them on fire but they didn't burn either.

☠ HORRIBLE HEALTH WARNING!

Getting your pet hamster drunk and setting it on fire is extremely cruel and dangerous. Anyone who tries this experiment may find themselves locked away until they are no longer a menace to hamsters. *Hic!*

COULD YOU BE A SCIENTIST?

In the Pacific Islands, India, Japan, Greece and many other parts of the world people do fire walking. They walk across glowing embers at 649° C (1200° F) in their *bare feet* without scorching their clothes or burning their feet.

How is this possible?

a) It's all to do with the conduction of heat.
b) They have flame-proof skin on their feet.
c) They're protected by magical charms.

Answer:

a) The embers are carbon or stones which are poor conductors of heat. This slows the speed at which the heat gets to a walker's feet. The feet themselves are wet or sweaty and this also slows the heat. And the walkers usually move too quickly for their feet to burn. Mind you, it's still a brave feet ... er ... *feat*.

☠ HORRIBLE HEALTH WARNING!

Don't try anything like this – you might not be so lucky.

But talking about burning bodies – having recovered from his ordeal in Death Valley, Harvey Tucker is now facing his sternest challenge yet ... can he stand the *heat*?

HARVEY TUCKER'S BIG ADVENTURE

"I'm giving you one last chance, you wussy," snapped the editor. I guess she was feeling very hot under the collar about the huge bill that I had run up at the Cool 'n' Comfy Motel.

"You're going to report on the Fire Brigade training course or I'll clobber your lights! And this time there's going to be no telly, no Internet, no motels. Just you..."

"Just me?" I gulped.

"Yes – and I want your article about it on my desk next Tuesday or you won't be worth a burnt crumpet!"

"Where do I get a sick note?" I wondered.

Day one:

No sweat! All we did in the morning was sit on comfy chairs and listen to fire officers telling us about what to do in a fire. Nifty stuff like if your chip pan catches fire put a damp cloth over it and turn the power off. I could murder a plate of chips!

Lunch:

All this listening was hard work! I went to the canteen and ate six helpings of beans, sausages, eggs and, yes, chips. Fire-fighters are big eaters and even I was chockers!

Afternoon: Things got queasy in the arvo. The Fire Officer started blathering about burns and scalds. You've got to rinse them under cold running water and get medical advice if they're bad. Then he showed gross piccies of burn injuries. They're worse if the burn goes though the skin so there's no skin left. Also the heart and kidneys can shut down as blood moves towards the wound.

Then we looked at piccies of burned dead bods. Well, everyone else did — I covered my eyes. If you carry a burnt bod the guts can fall out and the arms and legs drop off.

I needed some air.

I took a dekko at the canteen to check out the tucker — sausages again. I left in a hurry clutching my mouth — I felt fit to chunder!

"Well, Harvey mate," I thought, "this is as bad as it gets."

I was wrong...

The Fire Officer announced that tomorrow we'd be tested on how to survive in a real burning building!!! What a choice — if I stuck the course I might catch fire — if I didn't I'd be fired anyway!

Day 2

The day started bad and that was the best bit...

"The main danger," said the Fire Officer, "is flashover or backdraft. Imagine an explosion of heat at 1000° C (1832° F). It's hot enough to burn the clothes off your back and split your bones

open. It's so hot that
even a jet of water from
a hose turns to steam."

I imagined it – and closed my eyes
and tried to think of food. This
usually calms me down but for
some reason I started thinking
about flaming Xmas puds!

After a real 'mis' hour of waiting and ten visits
to the dunny it was my turn. At the training
school they have a real-sized building
that they stage training fires in.
I found myself in the bedroom...
"Close the door!" yelled the Fire
Officer through his megaphone.

I did as I was told but smoke
began to ooze under the door.
"Block the gap with a wet
towel!" he instructed.
I found a towel – it

HELP!

was dry so I called for help.
"There's a tap in the basin!"
"I can't see it – there's too much smoke!" I yelled.
It's true I couldn't even see my fingers. But
then I found the tap – I wet the towel and
stuffed it under the door. Then I wet myself –
with water from the tap, you'll understand. I
thought it might stop me bursting
into flames.
SPLASH! "Get out of the building, Tucker!"
barked the Fire Officer.

I crawled to the window and looked down. The ground seemed a long way off.

"Now what?" I called anxiously.

"Throw some bedding out the window and jump!"

I did as I was told – well, all except the last bit.

"What are you waiting for, you lily-livered drongo?!" yelled the Fire Officer, coming close in order to see through the smoke that was (despite my efforts) gushing out the window.

I couldn't answer because I was spluttering.

So I jumped. It was easy and it helped that the Fire Officer was there to catch me. Well, I'm not sure he meant to catch me but he should be out of hospital in the next few weeks...

ARGH!

GETTING HOTTER...

If there's one thing worse than a flashover, it's a firestorm. A huge killer fire that sucks air from its surroundings in hurricane force gusts and sucks in humans too. Temperatures can reach 800° C (1472° F) – hot enough to melt glass and lead. And the heat is enough to spread the fire as houses nearby get so hot they burst into flames. And the fire consumes all the air in the area and kills anyone who isn't burnt to death.

But the firestorm is not the hottest temperature you can get by any stretch. It's *nothing* compared to the heat belted out every day by our friendly neighbourhood star...

Killer energy fact file

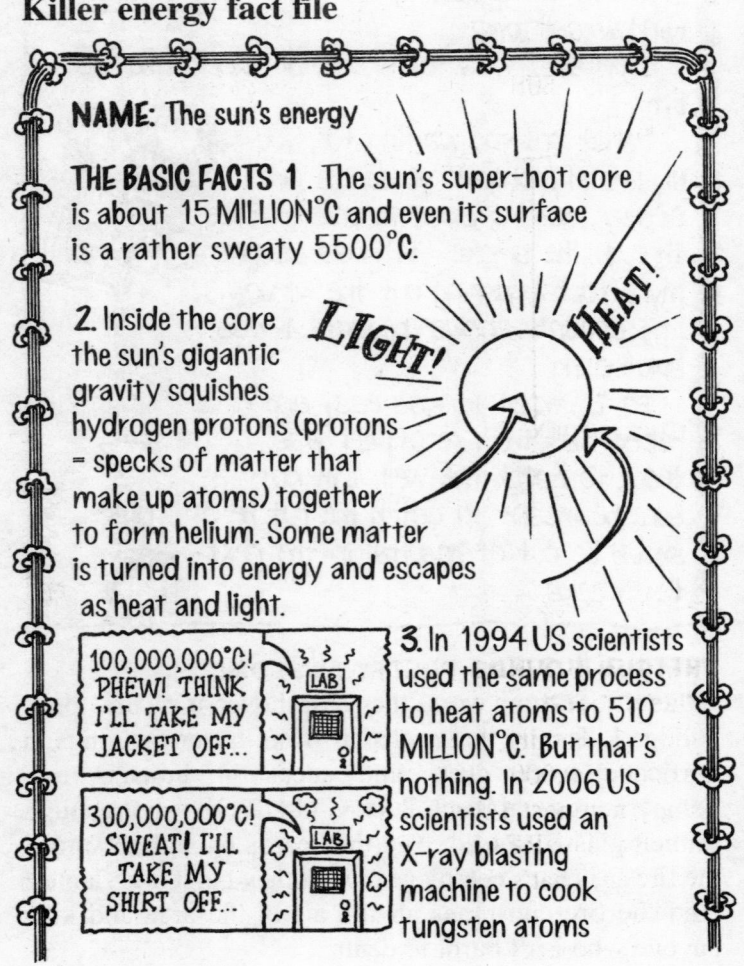

NAME: The sun's energy

THE BASIC FACTS 1. The sun's super-hot core is about 15 MILLION°C and even its surface is a rather sweaty 5500°C.

2. Inside the core the sun's gigantic gravity squishes hydrogen protons (protons = specks of matter that make up atoms) together to form helium. Some matter is turned into energy and escapes as heat and light.

LIGHT!

HEAT!

100,000,000°C! PHEW! THINK I'LL TAKE MY JACKET OFF...

LAB

300,000,000°C! SWEAT! I'LL TAKE MY SHIRT OFF...

LAB

3. In 1994 US scientists used the same process to heat atoms to 510 MILLION°C. But that's nothing. In 2006 US scientists used an X-ray blasting machine to cook tungsten atoms

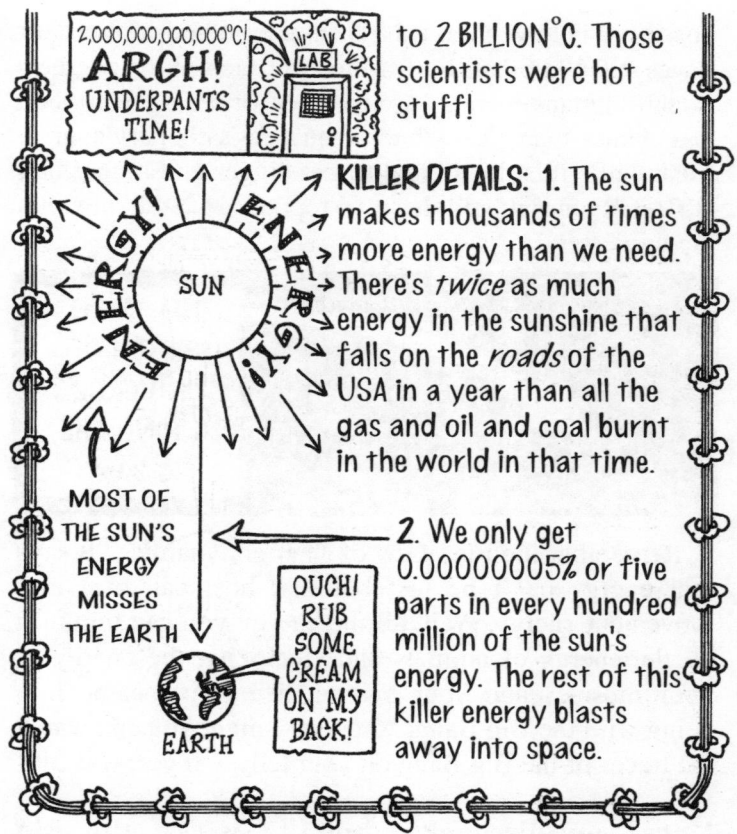

2,000,000,000,000°C!

ARGH!
UNDERPANTS
TIME!

LAB

to 2 BILLION°C. Those scientists were hot stuff!

KILLER DETAILS: 1. The sun makes thousands of times more energy than we need. There's *twice* as much energy in the sunshine that falls on the *roads* of the USA in a year than all the gas and oil and coal burnt in the world in that time.

ENERGY!

SUN

MOST OF THE SUN'S ENERGY MISSES THE EARTH

2. We only get 0.00000005% or five parts in every hundred million of the sun's energy. The rest of this killer energy blasts away into space.

OUCH! RUB SOME CREAM ON MY BACK!

EARTH

THE SUN SOUNDS PRETTY AWESOME – DOESN'T IT?

Well, it's nothing special. Just an average star amongst 100,000,000,000 (100 billion) others in an average galaxy amongst 100 billion other galaxies in the known universe. For REAL energy you need to go back to the Big Bang. That's the start of the universe about 15 billion years ago.

All the energy in the universe was stuffed into a tiny dot smaller than an atom. And it was so hot no one can possibly say how hot it was. Even after it had cooled a bit it was still 10,000 million million million million degrees. Lucky humans weren't around then or we'd have stood less chance than a baby budgie on a cat's cookery course. Meanwhile this dot started to get bigger and bigger and BIGGER and it still hasn't stopped ... and now it's the universe!

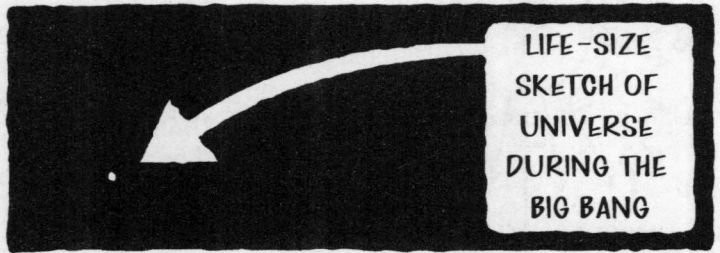

LIFE-SIZE SKETCH OF UNIVERSE DURING THE BIG BANG

Remember the First Law of Thermodynamics? It says that energy can't be lost but that heat can turn into movement energy. Well, all the energy you can think of, all the energy of animals and electricity, the energy in your muscles and your beating heart, first came into being with the Big Bang. And every night you can watch the traces of the Big Bang on your telly. Oh yes, you can!

Dare you discover ... how to watch the Big Bang on TV?

You will need:
A TV
What you do:
1 Switch on the TV.
2 Switch it to a channel that hasn't been tuned in to any station.

What do you notice?

a) The screen shows strange alien forms.

b) There are hundreds of little dots of light dancing around.

c) There are strange patterns that look like explosions.

> **Answer:**
> **b)** The dots are made by microwaves – yes, the same type of energy that would zap the milky bar in a microwave oven – but these microwaves have been around since the Big Bang.
> The microwaves are the last lingering echoes of that gigantic energy drifting for ever through the cold empty darkness of space. And they're far more interesting than some TV programmes I could mention.
> And so we end this chapter with…

Didn't you say on page 6 that you were going to tell us the fate of the universe?

THAT VERY ALERT READER FROM PAGE 90

Oh, I'm sorry it must have slipped my mind! Well, it's just a small detail but the ultimate fate of the universe is…

OOPS – sorry readers we seem to have run out of space for this chapter – you'll have to read on to find out…

A POWER FOR GOOD?

Energy is everywhere – in the singing of the birds and the swaying of the grass. It makes us warm and comfortable and it's the killer monster in a raging fire. It's in turning the pages of this book and every wisp of steam from a kettle. Energy is the pulse of the universe and without it the universe would die.

The Big Bang and the Laws of Thermodynamics supply clues about the future. In particular there's a miserable message in the Second Law – yes, the one about heat energy always being lost. Here's how Scottish scientist James Clerk Maxwell (1831–1879) summed it up:

If you throw a tumblerful of water into the sea you cannot get the same tumbler of water back again.

Sounds reasonable – and if you don't believe me you can always try it next time you're at the seaside…

WHERE'S MY DRINK?

What Maxwell was saying was that the amount of confusion and muddle in the universe is always growing.

It's like drops of water mixing in the sea and it'll *never* sort itself out on its own. It makes sense. Think of your bedroom – I bet you it *never* tidies itself on its own!

Now look at energy. The universe started off as a tidy little dot of energy all squashed neatly in one place. But now it's an untidy hotch-potch of hot stars and cold space and it's getting worse. The Second Law says that energy is always getting lost in the form of heat energy. So where does all this heat energy go? Well, the Second Law has the answer: heat always heads for the coldest place it can find – and that, ultimately, is outer space.

And once heat energy drifts off into space no one can ever get it back – never, ever, ever. And that means one day all the energy in the universe will have turned to heat and floated off into space. The stars will sputter out like candle flames and the planets will die of cold. Eventually even the dusty remains of the stars and planets will turn to heat energy and drift away.

The universe will be a thin cold soup of tiny bits of atoms floating about in the dark emptiness. Time will go on but nothing will ever change, and nothing will ever happen again. It'll be worse than a wet winter weekend when the telly's broken down.

SPOT THE DIFFERENCE COMPETITION

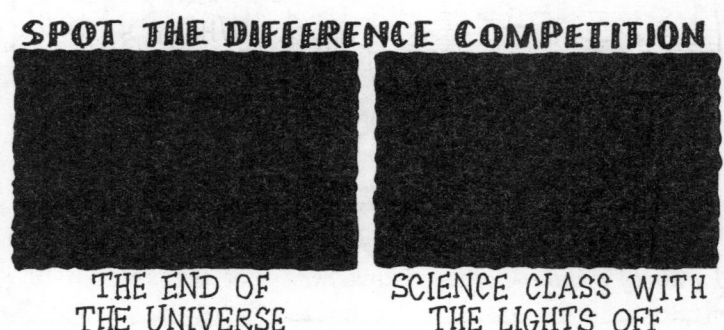

THE END OF
THE UNIVERSE

SCIENCE CLASS WITH
THE LIGHTS OFF

And in the end the loss of its energy will kill the universe – if it doesn't die of boredom first!

But let's look on the bright side. For one thing, it's not going to happen before the weekend. Scientists think it will take about 1,000,000,000,000,000,000,000,000,000,000 (one thousand billion billion billion) years. And they've got plenty of time to find a way to get the heat energy back or perhaps find a nice new universe for us to live in.

Or we might discover a new kind of power. People who believe that UFOs are alien spacecraft claim that they might work through some kind of anti-gravity force. This would have to get its energy from somewhere, and perhaps one day we'll find out…

Bet you never knew!
In 1878 inventor Thomas Edison (1847–1931) wanted to invent anti-gravity underwear that floated around in mid-air! A drawing of the time shows a dad towing his floating children.

But wait, would YOU fancy turning up at school in a pair of ground-defying knickers?

More urgently (and seriously) we're still running out of oil and gas energy and cooking our planet with the greenhouse effect. As usual, scientists are thinking up lots of answers, but whatever is done it's bound to involve developing renewable forms of energy like the sun's power and geothermal, wind and wave energy. These aren't going to run out like fossil fuels and don't give off gases that cause global warming.

But as the world fills up with people and more people travel in space we're going to need lots more energy. So here are some possibilities for the future...

SUPER-SUN SATELLITE SOARS!

Scientists are thrilled at the success of a giant satellite going round the sun. The satellite picks up power and beams it to Earth in the form of microwave rays. Said one beaming boffin, "We've taken a real shine to this project!"

POO POWERS PLANET PROBE!

It was revealed today that the interplanetary spacecraft is powered by fuel cells fuelled by germs eating rotting astronauts' poo.

Scientists in Michigan State University, USA began working on this project in 2000. A scientist said, "We thought the idea stinks – but it's proved to be out of this world."

FART!

SUPER-CELL SPARS SPEED-SPURT!

Super-cell spars speed-spurt! Car makers hailed the ten millionth car driven by a tiny fuel cell invented back in 2000 at University of Pennsylvania, USA. The cell can make electricity and power cars from a wide range of fuels. Our motoring reporter says that it can go for thousands of kilometres and not go past its cell by date.

10 MILLIONTH CAR TO BE CELLED — I MEAN, SOLD!

TINY FUEL CELL

One thing's for sure: science has come a long way in understanding energy. And perhaps one day human cleverness will find a way of turning killer energy into a power for good.

I'LL DRINK TO THAT!

KILLER ENERGY

QUIZ

Now find out if you're a **Killer Energy** expert!

Are you feeling energized? Plug in the power, crank up the grey matter, and have a go at these awesome energy quizzes to find out.

Energy in everything

Energy is everywhere, changing from one form to another, but have you got to grips with all the different types? Match the freakish forms of energy below with their strange sources.

1 Potential energy
2 Heat energy
3 Electrical energy
4 Chemical energy
5 Kinetic energy
6 Gravitational energy
7 Nuclear energy
8 Sound energy

a) The energy you generate when you're snoring in your Horrible Science lesson
b) The energy that causes lightning during a storm

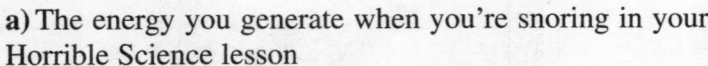

c) The energy in use when you're riding your bike

d) The energy at work when you fall off your bike…

e) The energy packed into your banana and peanut butter sandwich

f) The energy in the stretched elastic band just before you flick it at your teacher

g) The energy created when atoms bash into each other at supersonic speeds

h) The energy you lose in sweat when you run for the bus

Answers:
1f; 2h; 3b; 4e; 5c; 6d; 7g; 8a

Fantastic fuel

Without fuel life would be very different. You wouldn't be able to watch boring TV documentaries with your mum and dad. The dentist's drill wouldn't work. You wouldn't be able to get to your Horrible Science lessons on time by driving to school. But if you think life would be more fun without fuel, take this quick quiz and think again…

1 We rely on fossil fuels for millions of everyday things, but which of the following is a fossil fuel?

a) The sun

b) Natural gas

c) Cow poo

2 ATP is the type of chemical fuel your body stores in case you want to move from the sofa to the kitchen to raid the biscuit tin. But what does ATP stand for?

a) Adenoidal Tuppawareplate

b) Adenosine Triphosphate

c) Add The Power

3 How many elephants could be lifted 1 metre in the air by the power of 1 kg of awesome uranium atoms?

a) 200 million

b) 200

c) 2 (and baby ones at that)

4 A French cement company found a way of using radical recycling in their processes. What is the fantastic new fuel they're using to fire their kilns?

a) Used nappies

b) Used toilet paper

c) Snotty tissues

5 Which curious chemical fuel is stored on the side of matchboxes and combines with the air to burn brightly but briefly when struck?

a) Oxygen
b) Gold
c) Phosphorus

6 Which type of radical renewable fuel is pumped from the ground and uses the heat from masses of molten rocks below the Earth's surface?
a) Hydroelectric
b) Geothermal
c) Methane

7 What sweet ingredient can be used to make the biofuel ethanol?
a) Sugar cane
b) Candy floss
c) Honey

8 Which fossil fuel is used to make the petrol we put in our cars?
a) Cow farts
b) Coal
c) Oil

Answers:
1b; 2b; 3a; 4a; 5c; 6b; 7a; 8c

Horrible heat and killer cold

Strange scientists spent years figuring out how heat and cold affect things. They came up with some crazy ideas along the way – and some unbelievable discoveries. Can you figure out if these fascinating facts are the chilling truth or just a lot of hot air?

1 Your horrible human body gives off enough heat in half an hour to boil a saucepan of water.
2 Everything in the awesome universe is getting hotter and hotter.
3 It's so cold in space that when astronaut pee is ejected from a rocket toilet it freezes immediately.
4 Your muscles turn 90 per cent of your food fuel into kinetic (movement) energy – the rest turns into heat energy, which turns you red in the face.
5 Icebergs can sing.
6 Your slimy saliva boils at three times the temperature of ordinary water.
7 You'll almost certainly catch a cold if you spend too long in the snow.
8 Goose bumps are your body's way of warming up.

Answers:
1 TRUE. Who needs electricity to make a cuppa when you can just cuddle the kettle?
2 FALSE. Everything is constantly losing heat. To keep things toasty you have to add heat energy.

3 TRUE. That's a *wee* bit of space trivia for you…

4 FALSE. Only a quarter is used to make you motor, all the rest is sticky sweat.

5 TRUE. They probably wouldn't win too many talent shows, but the noise they make when they grind together is a bit like a cool chorus.

6 TRUE. Don't try sticking your tongue in a saucepan though.

7 FALSE. Extreme cold *kills* germs, so you won't suffer from sniffles at the South Pole.

8 TRUE. Goose bumps make your hairs stand on end, which helps trap your body heat.

Meet the scientists

Over the centuries scientists have carried out many amazing energy experiments and have blown hot and cold over the laws of thermodynamics. Sometimes they got it right – and sometimes they got it really wrong. From the clues below, can you match the brilliant brainbox with his discovery?

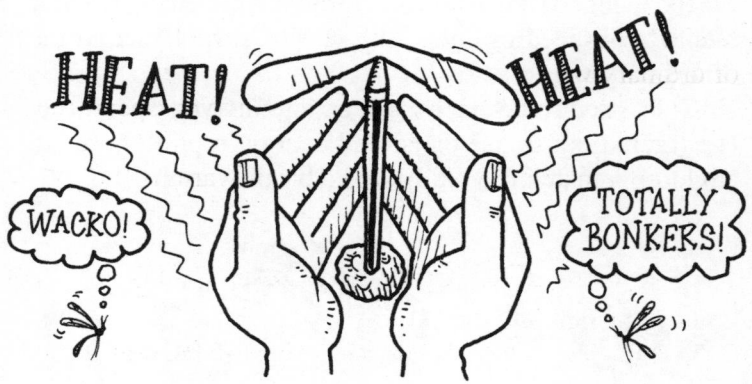

1 Noticing a cannon heating up while being bored by a drill, this stunning scientist realized that heat wasn't a substance – it was energy caused by the rubbing of the drill (sadly, everyone thought his discovery was boring!)

2 A lot of hot air drove this impatient inventor to figure out how to use steam to pump water from mines (he was *steaming* drunk when he made the discovery).

3 An amusing accident with a teapot resulted in this strange Scottish scientist discovering that burning coal released a gas that could be used to produce heat and light energy (it certainly *fuelled* his imagination as an inventor).

4 This German genius of a doctor made the stupendous discovery that stuffing your face with food gave you enough energy to move (it was *bleeding* obvious, really).

5 We remember this fancy physicist by the temperature scale that bears his name. He discovered how cold it had to be to freeze water, and how hot the human body was (although he got that last bit wrong).

6 This amazing mathematician calculated that nothing can be chillier than absolute zero. For being so brilliantly bright, he was allowed to put his name to another scientific scale. (Pretty cool, huh?)

7 By using steam to turn a turbine, this Irish inventor sent ships speeding round the seas (it *revolutionized* the energy industry).

8 This Swedish inventor made an illuminating discovery – he figured out to use the stored energy in phosphorus to light up a match (he really was a bright *spark*).

a) William Thomson, Lord Kelvin
b) Charles Parsons
c) Benjamin Thompson, Count Rumford
d) Daniel Fahrenheit
e) John Lundstrom
f) William Murdock
g) Julius Robert von Mayer
h) Thomas Savery

Answers:
1c; 2h; 3f; 4g; 5d; 6a; 7b; 8e

Confusing renewable energy

From deep underground and high in the sky, nature has provided the means to generate amazing energy in ways that might save our precarious planet. Untangle these energy anagrams to identify the fantastic renewable phrases.

1 PEARL SALON (2 words)

CLUE: Put one of these on the roof of your house to harness the heat of the super sun.

2 GAMER HOTEL (1 word)

CLUE: This type of energy bubbles and burps its way up from deep within the Earth.

3 UNBID WINTER (2 words)

CLUE: The air causes this incredible invention to twist and turn and generate electricity.

4 CLEAR INFUSIONS (2 words)

CLUE: This powerful process uses energy from atoms in a chain reaction.

5 CORRECTLY HID YETI (1 word)

CLUE: The power of running water makes this type of amazing energy.

6 WEAVE PROW (2 words)

CLUE: You'll see that the sea plays a big part in creating this energy.

7 LEADING TYRE (2 words)

CLUE: The effects of the moon help with this watery renewable power source.

8 BOIL FUSE (1 word)

CLUE: Stuffing the tank of your car with sugar, perhaps?

Answers:
1 Solar panel
2 Geothermal
3 Wind turbine
4 Nuclear fission
5 Hydroelectricity
6 Wave power
7 Tidal energy
8 Biofuels

HORRIBLE INDEX

HORRIBLE SCIENCE

VICIOUS VEG

NICK ARNOLD

illustrated by
TONY DE SAULLES

SCHOLASTIC

www.horrible-science.co.uk

www.nickarnold-website.com
www.tonydesaulles.co.uk

Scholastic Children's Books,
Euston House, 24 Eversholt Street,
London, NW1 1DB, UK

A division of Scholastic Ltd
London ~ New York ~ Toronto ~ Sydney ~ Auckland
Mexico City ~ New Delhi ~ Hong Kong

First published in the UK by Scholastic Ltd, 1998
This edition published 2008

Text copyright © Nick Arnold, 1998
Illustrations © Tony De Saulles, 1998

All rights reserved

ISBN 978 1407 10615 1

Printed and bound by CPI Group (UK) Ltd, Croydon, CR0 4YY

21

The right of Nick Arnold and Tony De Saulles to be identified as the author and
illustrator of this work respectively has been asserted by them in accordance with
the Copyright, Designs and Patents Act, 1988.

CONTENTS

...AND HOW LONG HAS THIS APPLE PIP BEEN STUCK BETWEEN YOUR TEETH, MR SMITH?

Nick Arnold has been writing stories and books since he was a youngster, but never dreamt he'd find fame writing about Vicious Veg. His research involved swinging from vines, grappling with strangling plants and dancing in fairy rings and he enjoyed every minute of it.

When he's not delving into Horrible Science, he spends his spare time riding his bike, eating pizza and thinking up corny jokes (though not all at the same time).

Tony De Saulles picked up his crayons when he was still in nappies and has been doodling ever since. He takes Horrible Science very seriously and even agreed to sketch foul-smelling plants that ponged of rotting flesh. Fortunately, he has made a full recovery.

When he's not out with his sketchpad, Tony likes to write poetry and play squash, though he hasn't written any poetry about squash yet.

INTRODUCTION

Some science books tell you about plants. You can learn nice little facts about leaves, seeds, fruits and pretty little flowers. But this book is different. It's about plants all right, but it's also about Horrible Science!

So if your science lessons are like this…

*AN-GEE-O-SPERMS = PLANTS WITH FLOWERS

And the only excitement is when someone actually drops off to sleep and your teacher turns vicious…

Maybe you need a helping of Horrible Science. Then you can ask your teacher a few vicious questions…

WHAT ABOUT BUG-EATING PLANTS?

DO THEY REALLY TURN THEIR VICTIMS INTO SLIME?

WHICH PLANTS MAKE POISONOUS GAS?

DO PLANTS REALLY STRANGLE ONE ANOTHER? AND THEN SUCK OUT THEIR JUICES?

ERR?

Now, doesn't that sound a bit more interesting? *Horribly* interesting? And guess what? It's all TRUE. With facts like these at your fingertips you'll be able to show your friends you're a budding scientist, and turn your teacher green with envy.

...THEN THE TRAPPED BUGS ARE DIGESTED ALIVE INSIDE THE PLANT!

COR! WOW! GREAT! BRILL!

FUME! SEETHE!

So there you are. There really is a lot more to plants than silly seeds, fancy flowers and limp leaves. Plants have loads more vicious secrets and many VILE, VILLAINOUS, VIOLENT and VICIOUS tricks. And by some spooky coincidence that's what this book is about – VICIOUS VEG (that's vegetables to you – it's another word for plants). So what are you waiting for? Why not "leaf" through a few pages? You might even find that plant science starts to grow on you...

THE VICIOUS VEGETABLE WORLD

Welcome to another world. This is a green and terrifying world where horrible things happen every day. A world where death is an ugly tendril slowly reaching out to strangle its victim. A world where the only rule is kill or be killed and the only aim is to stay alive. Welcome to the vicious world of veg.

Unlike animals, plants can't run away, and they can't hide from danger. And danger is everywhere. Take a look at this peaceful country scene. Looks quiet, doesn't it? Maybe a little boring?

Well, you couldn't be more wrong. Just imagine that you're a plant. Bigger plants are stealing your light. Without light you may die.

Trees are grabbing light from all the plants.

Your roots are fighting the other plants for moisture.

Millions of munching bugs want to guzzle you alive.

Imagine seeing a whole day in a speeded-up film. You'd see your leaves twisting and turning as they follow the sun as it moves across the sky. You'd see the plants

9

around you slowly strangling one another and trying to poison visiting bugs. Like I said, plants are vicious, and we know all about this vicious world thanks to plant scientists. Here's the first of them – a curious Greek named Theophrastus.

Hall of fame: Theophrastus (371–287 BC)

Nationality: Greek

Theo is famous because he was the first botanist – that's a person who studies plants. Other people either ate them or grew them, but Theo preferred to study plants very closely and he went on to describe them in a very organized way.

Nothing is known of Theo's early days but he seems to have spent his life working as a teacher in Athens. He was a pal of brainy philosophers such as Plato and Aristotle and he wrote more than 200 books in his own write, I mean right. Including a book on plants. In it Theo described over 500 plants such as bananas and flowers from as far afield as India.

10

He really did a good job of describing them but he also believed a few tall tales. For example, it's said that old Theo reckoned that a scorpion could be killed by being stroked with a wolfsbane plant and then brought back to life with a touch of the white hellebore plant.

And talking about far-fetched fantasies – it's said Theo lived far longer than the dates given here. It's said he finally threw in his gardening gloves at the ripe old age of 107. Who says greens aren't good for you?

COULD YOU BE A BOTANIST?

So you want to be a botanist? Well, beware. Being a botanist isn't about tiptoeing through the tulips and talking to the trees. Botany is a tough outdoor science. It's more likely to involve exploring horrible places such as stinking swamps in search of rare and vicious plants. And sinking up to your neck in mud that reeks of rotten eggs, and being eaten alive by blood-sucking bugs.

But that's only the start of the horrible things that can happen to botanists. In the nineteenth century botanists travelled all over the world collecting plants and seeds for scientific study, and they faced all kinds of terrible dangers...

THE ORINOCO NEWS

The voice of South America   1801

MYSTERY BUG ATE OUR COLLECTION

News just in from botanists Alexandra von Humboldt and Aimé Bonpland somewhere on the Orinoco river. These two brave botanists claim that vicious bugs unknown to science have scoffed most of

their plant collection. Said Humboldt, "We found thousands of brand new plants. Unfortunately, the bugs discovered the plants too." In a bid to make the bugs back off the botanists smeared themselves in alligator fat. Sounds a fat lot of good for our battling botanists.

THE HAWAII HERALD

1834

DARING DOUGLAS DEAD!

Plant hunter David Douglas is dead. Reports say he fell into a pit trap containing a wild bull while he was looking for rare plant specimens. A police spokesperson said, "The bull was pretty wild at being in the trap."

Douglas, 36, shot to fame when he found thousands of previously unknown plants in North America. These included the Douglas fir - now named after him. Daring Douglas had travelled thousands of miles and had an earlier brush with death when his canoe capsized and he nearly drowned. Here was one botanist who wasn't scared to walk on the wild side.

CROOKED CACTUS COWBOYS CAUGHT

The sheriff's office today reports that three cactus rustlers have been rounded up following a tip-off from a botanist. The rustlers, who were armed and dangerous, were taking cacti from the desert without a permit. Stolen cacti fetch huge prices from collectors in Europe and Japan but the ruthless rustlers are wiping these prickly plants out. They take huge numbers and cacti are getting scarce. And because these giant greens are so slow growing it will take ages before new cacti can grow and take their place. A botanist in the State Conservation Department said, "Cacti rustling sure is a prickly problem."

VICIOUS PLANT TYPES

So you know the dangers and you're still keen to be a botanist? Well, you're going to need a bit of vital info to get you started. We'll start off with the basics. So you reckon you'd know a plant if you bumped into one? Well, now you can cultivate your knowledge a bit more...

Vicious veg fact file

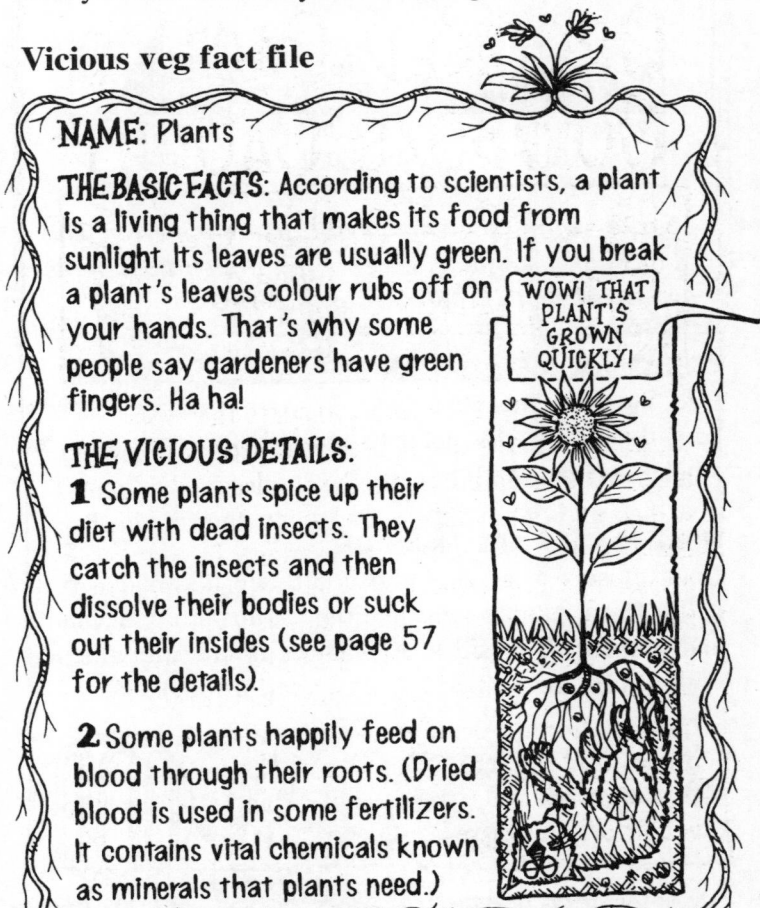

NAME: Plants

THE BASIC FACTS: According to scientists, a plant is a living thing that makes its food from sunlight. Its leaves are usually green. If you break a plant's leaves colour rubs off on your hands. That's why some people say gardeners have green fingers. Ha ha!

WOW! THAT PLANT'S GROWN QUICKLY!

THE VICIOUS DETAILS:

1 Some plants spice up their diet with dead insects. They catch the insects and then dissolve their bodies or suck out their insides (see page 57 for the details).

2 Some plants happily feed on blood through their roots. (Dried blood is used in some fertilizers. It contains vital chemicals known as minerals that plants need.)

15

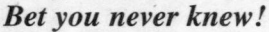

Bet you never knew!

Blood is only one ingredient of some traditional fertilizers. Here's a genuine revolting recipe...

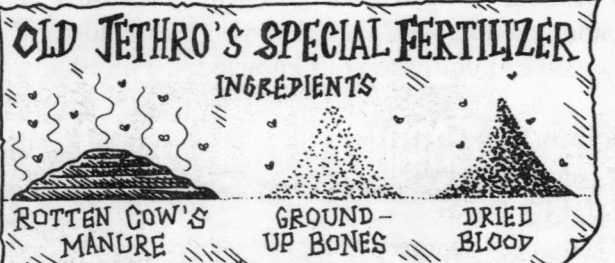

OLD JETHRO'S SPECIAL FERTILIZER

INGREDIENTS

ROTTEN COW'S MANURE · GROUND-UP BONES · DRIED BLOOD

These revolting ingredients are rich in minerals. The plants can take the chemicals in through their roots and use them to grow and stay healthy.

COULD YOU BE A BOTANIST?

OK, now for the next stage in your training. There's something else you need to know before you can get stuck into that swamp.

WHAT PLANTS ARE MADE OF

Look closely at a plant and you'll see it's made up of cells. These minute jelly-like objects make up all plants and animals. The sides of plant cells are strengthened with a substance called cellulose (cell-u-loze).

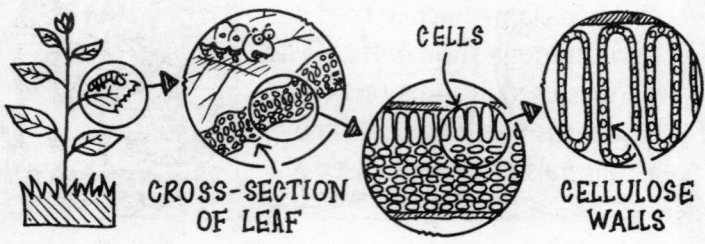

CROSS-SECTION OF LEAF · CELLS · CELLULOSE WALLS

Cellulose is the stuff that makes greens stringy. It makes up the roughage in your diet which helps your body move your half-digested food through your guts. Most cellulose ends up in your poo. (Just in case you were wondering.)

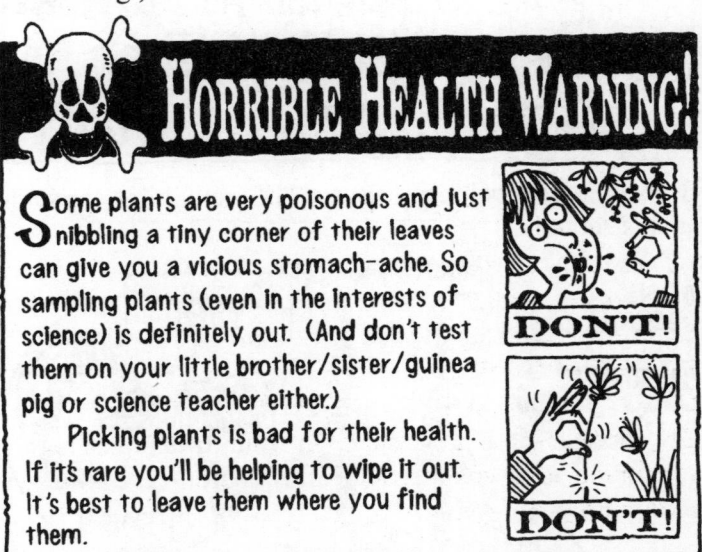

HORRIBLE HEALTH WARNING!

Some plants are very poisonous and just nibbling a tiny corner of their leaves can give you a vicious stomach-ache. So sampling plants (even in the interests of science) is definitely out. (And don't test them on your little brother/sister/guinea pig or science teacher either.)

DON'T!

Picking plants is bad for their health. If it's rare you'll be helping to wipe it out. It's best to leave them where you find them.

DON'T!

HAVE YOU GOT THE VITAL EQUIPMENT?
Magnifying glass for looking at really small plants such as this duckweed.

WOW! THAT'S SMALL!

↑ 0·3 mm ↓

DUCKWEED

DUCK WEE

Microscope for looking really closely at plants and for checking out even tinier plants such as algae.

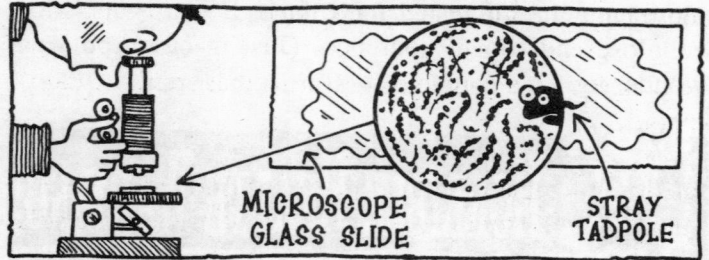

MICROSCOPE GLASS SLIDE

STRAY TADPOLE

Binoculars for looking at the tops of really big trees such as this sequoia.

GIANT SEQUOIA TREES IN CALIFORNIA*

MIAOW!

DON'T JUMP, PUSS!

*These beautiful trees are the largest on Earth. One heartless person reckoned that if just one giant sequoia was cut down it could make five billion matchsticks.

NOTEBOOK, PEN AND CAMERA TO RECORD PLANTS WITHOUT PICKING THEM

VEGETATION OBSERVED ON EXPEDITION

VEGETATION EATEN ON EXPEDITION

Have you got all that? And you can't wait to start your career as a brainy botanist? Great – here's a handy identification guide to get you started.

We'll start with a couple of lifeforms that aren't actually plants...

Baffling bacteria (Number of species [individual types] is unknown. It's thought that 90 per cent of them are still unknown to science.)
Chances are you've got a few million of these crawling on you. Don't panic! We all have – 'cos bacteria are everywhere. You'll find them lurking about in the depths of the ocean as well as in the depths of your toilet. Bacteria are tiny blobs of matter so small that millions can fit on the point of a drawing pin (just don't go sitting on the drawing pin). That's because some vicious bacteria cause disease although many others are quite harmless. Some even live in your guts and make vitamins K and B to keep you healthy.

Foul fungi (70,000 species)
Fungi don't have chlorophyll – that's the green stuff that plants use to make food from sunshine – and they guzzle animals and plants, either dead or alive. When they feed, they turn their victim into a nourishing soup and slurp up the juices. Tastee! Foul fungi include the mildew in your bathroom, the mushrooms swimming in your soup and the mould on your school dinner. (See page 94 for more details.)

Here are the main groups of plants...

Awesome algae (more than 30,000 species)

You'll find algae everywhere – from Antarctica to your local pond where they give the water that lovely muddy green colour. The sea in particular is alive with algae. Some are revolting tiny slimy squirming things that are smaller than a pinhead and others are enormous, like the giant seaweeds 60 metres long found off the coast of California, Japan and New Zealand. Yes, that's right, seaweeds are algae too.

Bet you never knew!

Algae can poison the sea. Algae guzzle the chemicals found in the sewage that humans dump in the sea. Well, there's no accounting for taste, is there? Sometimes algae multiply uncontrollably and form huge blooms of vicious algae that use up the oxygen from the water and suffocate fish. (Oxygen, by the way, is the gas that humans and animals need to breathe to stay alive.) Some algae make chemicals that can poison humans swimming in the water, or dogs drinking it. The only things that aren't killed are certain kinds of bacteria. But they make horrible rotten egg smells. Fancy a dip?

Loathsome lichens (more than 25,000 species)

A lichen isn't a single plant at all. It's a sort of double act with algae and fungi living together so closely that they seem to be the same plant. The fungi are good at sucking up water, dissolving rock and getting at minerals. The algae can make sunlight into food. It all sounds very cosy. So why are lichens loathsome? Well, it's just an opinion really. Swedish scientist Carl Linnaeus (1707–1778) made up the system of Latin names for plants that is still used. But Carl didn't like lichens for some reason. He called them: "... the poorest vegetable rubbish."

Drippy liverworts and mosses (more than 23,000 species)
These are actually different types of plants but they enjoy (if enjoy is the right word) a similar lifestyle. Basically this involves sitting around in a damp shady spot and staying as wet as possible. Sounds like fun – I don't think. But they have a rather unusual life story...

● The adult plant makes lots of tiny spores (they're like scaled-down seeds without food stores).
● These DON'T develop into adult plants. Instead they form small leaf-like objects.
● These tiny plants make special male and female cells that join together.
● They grow into a new adult plant.

Sounds a load of bother. Botanists call this "alternation of generations" – which means big plants making little plants making big plants and so on. If this happened to humans your parents would be 1 cm long and you'd be normal size. But at least there wouldn't be any arguments over pocket money!

COMMON TYPE OF LIVERWORT

COMMON TYPE OF MOSS

...AND I'LL HAVE NEXT WEEK'S IN ADVANCE

WHATEVER YOU SAY, SON!

Gigantic gymnosperms (around 750 species)
Gymnosperm (Jim-no-spurm) means "naked seed" in Greek. This simply means that seeds on these plants are open to the air rather than wrapped up in a flower.

Well-known gymnosperms include all pine trees, yew trees and a rather ancient species of plants called a cycad that was once munched by dinosaurs. Those cycads must be the oldest salads in the world – yes, even older than that limp lettuce you get with your school dinner.

TREES

Trees aren't a proper group of plants. A tree is just a giant plant with a woody stem to hold it up. (We can't have trees flopping over, can we?) The woody stuff is a substance called lignin that's dumped in the centre of the tree.

This means at school you probably sit on a lump of lignin. And in days gone by your vicious teacher might have whacked you with a length of lignin. The living part of the tree is the bit under the bark – which is why trees can be hollow and yet still be alive. Trees are big because they continue to grow all their lives. Imagine if you kept on growing. You could end up 300 years old and 100 metres tall. (You'd need a *giant* zimmer frame to help you to walk!)

Amazing angiosperms (up to 400,000 species)
These are flowering plants, remember? They are a huge plant group that includes just about everything that people might grow in their gardens. And just about everything that would ever turn up in a school dinner salad (excluding the odd caterpillar).

Flowering plants produce flowers (howls of amazement) as a way of spreading their pollen to other flowers of the same species. After they've received the pollen, some parts of the flowers turn into fruits and seeds (see page 107 for the amazing details). Then we humans or just about any other hungry creature get to munch them. Mind you, the plant gets the last laugh. More often than not the seeds pass through the animal's guts and reappear later with a nice dollop of dung to help them grow.

So as you can see, plants come in all shapes and sizes. Some look fairly ordinary but they're all really gobsmacking. I mean just read on and you'll see why...

GOBSMACKING GREENERY

Some people think plants are boring. But they couldn't be more wrong. And here's the most amazing fact of all. Plants are the *main* form of life on Earth. In fact, the Earth ought to be renamed Planet Plant. (Planet Vegetable or Planet Turnip would sound a bit too ridiculous!)

PLANETARY PLANT FACTS

Imagine you're an alien looking at Earth from your spacecraft. At first, you might think that plants actually ruled the Earth. I mean, take a good look. Spot any humans? Nope – they're too small. But you can see plants, can't you? Loads of them.

See that huge smudge of green on the northern part of the world? That's millions and millions of trees that make up the vast pine forests that stretch across Asia from Norway to Canada. And those greeny blobs in South America, Africa and South-east Asia? They're rainforests. OK, there are fewer forests since humans started cutting them down for roads and farms. But you get the idea.

So the Earth is absolutely teeming with plants. If you weighed every living object on Earth you'd find that 99.9 per cent of this massive weight is plants. And only 0.1 per cent is made up of animals (and that includes big heavy animals like overweight elephants).

OK, so if plants are so amazingly widespread that means teachers must know loads of gobsmacking plant facts. Right? Here's your chance to find out. Does your teacher have green fingers? Or is their knowledge rather weedy?

TEST YOUR TEACHER

Even a chimp can get one third of these questions right because there are only three possible answers. So how will your teacher get on?

1 How much ground can one grass plant cover?
a) One square metre.
b) As much as a small garden.
c) As much as a large field.

2 How long can a seed survive before it dies?
a) Ten months
b) Ten years
c) Ten thousand years

3 Some types of plants puff out gas from their leaves. This is taken in through the leaves of another plant of the same species (type of plant). The gas carries a message but what is it?
a) I lurve your flowers.
b) Make more fruit.
c) BEWARE – hungry giraffes on the rampage.

4 Where might you find a plant growing?
a) Between your toes.
b) Inside a solid rock.
c) Underneath the snow in the Antarctic.

5 What do some plants do if you breathe on them?
a) Turn your breath to a poisonous gas and puff it back at you.
b) Wilt
c) Turn your breath into sugar and eat it.

6 What substance is NEVER made by trees?
a) A red fluid that looks suspiciously like blood.
b) Dew
c) The stuff they use to make chocolate.

7 How do some plants keep warm?
a) Central heating
b) Hairy leaves
c) By shivering

8 What do some plants do when they're thirsty?
a) Grow special windows in their leaves that let the sun in without letting water out.
b) Cut bits off their own bodies.
c) Cover themselves in a sort of cling-film.

9 Which of these objects might just be a plant in disguise?
a) A bird's dropping
b) A weird mushroom-shaped object
c) A pebble

Answers:

1 c) A single plant can really grow this big. Scientists have found that a field of fescue (that's a type of grass) is often a single plant. This can be hundreds of years old and still growing strong.

2 c) Amazing but true. In 1982 Japanese scientists found a 10,000-year-old magnolia seed in an old storage pit. They planted it and the incredible seed sprouted into a healthy plant.

3 c) Yes – acacia trees say it with flowers. Or more accurately with their leaves. When an African acacia is attacked by a hungry giraffe its leaves make a foul-tasting poison to put the giraffe off. They also puff out ethylene (eth-ey-lene) gas. Nearby acacia trees take in the gas through tiny holes in their leaves called stomata (sto-mart-a) and start making the poison as well.

4 Trick question – it's **b)** AND **c)** but *not* **a)**. Mind you, if your feet are *really* dirty you might find anything growing between your toes. Some people suffer from athlete's foot fungi (check out the vicious details on page 97) but these aren't plants.

As for **b)** some algae in Antarctica live inside sandstone rock. The algae get in through cracks in the rock. They're kept alive by sunlight that filters through see-through grains in the rock. And you might find a plant in **c)** because other Antarctic algae live in snow. They swim around in the snow using special swimming hairs and make a kind of antifreeze to stop their bodies from freezing up. They'd be quite at home in your favourite ice cream.

5 c) Your breath contains carbon-dioxide gas. A plant takes this in through their stomata and turns the carbon into sugar. The plant uses the sugar as energy to grow. It might send some to its flowers to make nectar. If a bee makes the nectar into honey you might end up eating the carbon from your own breath. Hmm.

6 b) Although you might find drops of dew on trees the dew is actually tiny drops of water that form in the air. So dew is not made by plants.

a) The red stuff is a kind of gum that oozes from the Australian bloodwood tree if you cut its bark. The gum protects the cut as it heals, and you can guess how it got its name. Yep, it's ideal for vegetarian vampires. Aborigines use the juice to heal wounds and as a gargle for sore throats.

c) Chocolate is made from the crushed seeds of the cacao tree.

7 b) Edelweiss plants have hairy leaves to keep them warm in the cold air of the Alps where they grow. Lobelia flowers on Mount Kenya in East Africa grow on a hairy stem. The hair protects the flowers from freezing just like a little fur coat.

COPY CAT!

8 Ha ha – this is another teacher-torturing trick question. Plants do *all* these things. Give your teacher ONE mark for saying "all of them". But a miserable half a mark for suggesting either **a)**, **b)** or **c)**.

a) Window plants in the Namib desert in south-west Africa make special see-through crystals to protect their leaves from the hot sun. It's a bit like wearing sun cream.

b) Plants lose water through their stomata. The Namibian quiver tree grows a wall inside its trunk to cut off a branch. The branch has to fall off. That means there are fewer leaves to lose water.

c) Many plants protect themselves from drying out by pumping out a waxy layer from their stomata. This covers the leaves and stops them from losing water.

9 It's another viciously vile question. The answer is **a)** AND **c)** but *not* **b)**. The weird object in **b)** is a stromatolite made of mud and a type of bacteria that contains chlorophyll. But these bacteria aren't counted as plants. Stromatolites are found on some beaches in Australia and sculpted by the sea into a mushroom shape. **a)** is an anacampseros (anna-camp-ser-ros) plant that lives in dry areas. And animals don't scoff it because it looks like a bird dropping. Fancy finding one in your salad? **c)** is a pebble plant from the deserts of Africa. It disguises itself to look like a pebble to stop animals eating it. Well, stone me.

What your teacher's score means:
9 Impossible. NO teacher in history has ever scored this high ... unless they've been secretly peeking at this book. If so, confiscate the book *at once*. You can't have your teacher knowing more than you, can you?
7–8 BEWARE. Your teacher is a secret botanist. Signs to look for are green fingers, dirt under the fingernails, half-crazed expression, always talking about plants, knowing all the Latin names of plants, etc.
4–6 Average – could try harder. Just a common or garden teacher, really.
0–3 This is sad. Your teacher obviously needs to turn over a new leaf and do some extra botany homework.

One of the most gobsmacking things about plants is the way they eat. And do plants like to eat! They feed themselves all day long ... just like some humans, really. But their eating habits can be very different. Read on for the vicious details.

GREEDY GREENERY

Imagine you had ultra-powerful hearing. If you went outside you'd be able to hear a quiet slurping noise that would be the sound of thousands of plants busily guzzling their food.

But plants don't eat stuff like cream cakes. Oh no – a plant can make a meal of just three simple ingredients. Water, air and sunshine.

OK, so you don't believe me? Well, read on and find out for yourself…

VICIOUS VEG EXPRESSIONS

Doesn't she need a camera?

Can you imagine what it would be like if all you had to
do when you wanted to eat was to lie about in the sun.
Life would be brilliant, wouldn't it? You could laze about
and scoff a scrumptious snack whenever you felt like it.
This incredible process was discovered by a desperately
shy scientist who managed to needle just about
everyone.

Hall of fame: Jan Ingen-Housz (1730–1799)
Nationality: Dutch

You could tell young Jan was going to do something
brainy when he grew up, he was that kind of kid. Clever.
But no one guessed he was going to be a scientist. Young
Jan himself wanted to be a doctor. He studied at universities
in Belgium and Holland and sure enough he went on to
be a successful doctor.

He went to England in 1764 and heard about the new-
fangled science called inoculation. This was a way of

stopping people from getting the killer disease smallpox. Doctors pricked them with a needle and thread that were coated with smallpox germs taken from the gory pus of a sick person. The idea was that by giving a few germs to a healthy body the body would learn how to protect itself from the killer disease. But the operation was risky – it sometimes went horribly wrong. The needle might carry too many germs and cause the patient to develop full-blown smallpox and die.

Well, Jan got busy with his needle and in a few months he had inoculated over 700 people. The British king, George III (1738–1820) was so impressed he sent Jan to Austria with instructions to inoculate the Austrian royal family. It was a horribly dangerous job for Jan. If he got it wrong he might kill the Empress of Austria with his needle!

SORRY, I'M HAVING T-T-TROUBLE THREADING THE N-N-N-NEEDLE

But the operation was a success. The Empress stayed healthy and she never caught smallpox. As a result Jan was given loads of expensive presents.

In the 1770s, during a stay in England, Jan became interested in the gases plants made. This had nothing to do with inoculation and it all came about because Jan read about the work of scientist Joseph Priestly (1733–1804), who found out that plants seemed to make and soak up mysterious gases. So Jan decided to do some experiments of his own.

He eventually proved that plants take in the gas we now call carbon dioxide and spray out oxygen. He then went on to prove that this only happened in green parts of the plant that were exposed to light. BINGO! Jan had discovered photosynthesis. He later proved that plant cells also take in oxygen and give out carbon dioxide. So plants also "breathe" just like us.

Jan was interested in lots of other areas of science and he went on to design a machine (which he never got round to building) to help patients with breathing problems by giving them pure oxygen.

PRECIOUS PLANTS
Now here's the really BIG news. Without photosynthesis we'd all be as dead as an oven-ready dodo.
1 Plants make oxygen by photosynthesis and we breathe it in. And 70 per cent of the Earth's oxygen comes from

the sea. This vital gas is made by trillions of algae that float around in the waves. So it's basically plants that keep us humans alive.

2 No animal can do without oxygen for more than a few minutes. And if you added up all the oxygen used by all the animals on Earth in just one second it would come to 10,160 tonnes. That's an awful lot of puffing and panting.

3 Scientists reckon there's enough oxygen around to last us about 3,000 years. After that, without plants to make more oxygen we'll all be gasping. Now 3,000 years might sound like a really long time. But it's nothing compared to the three billion years that plants have been around on Earth.

And plants are vital for other reasons too.

4 Just imagine getting up in the morning. Horrible thought, isn't it? But it would be far tougher if you didn't have any energy at all. The energy that gets you up came from the food energy in that lovely burger and fries that you had for supper.

5 And all of that came from plants. Plants? Well, yes…

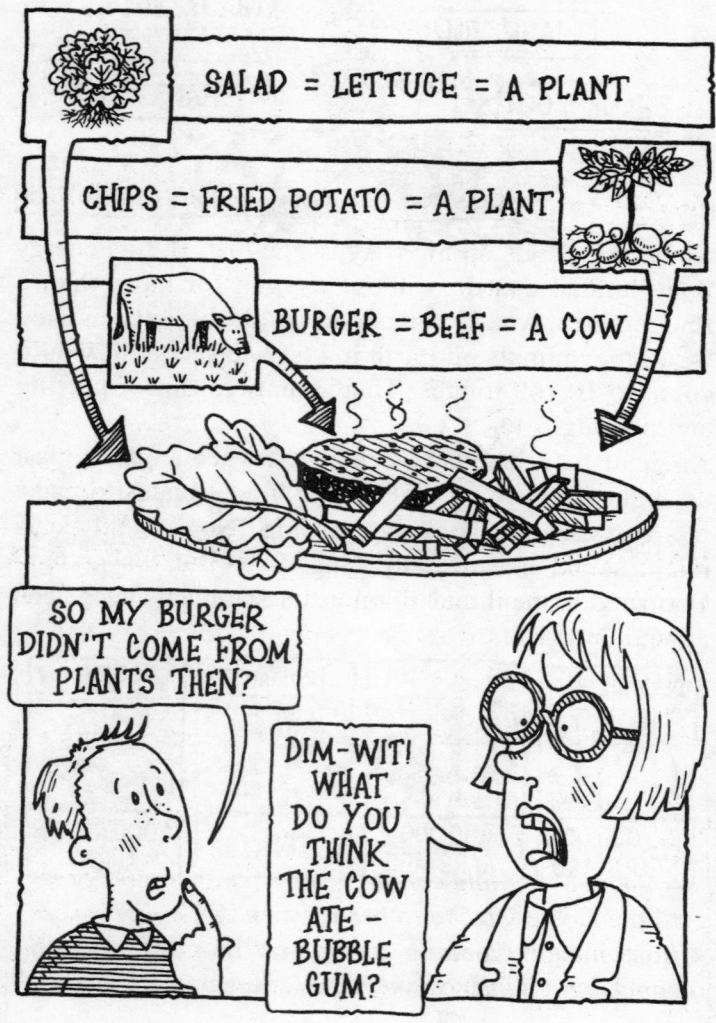

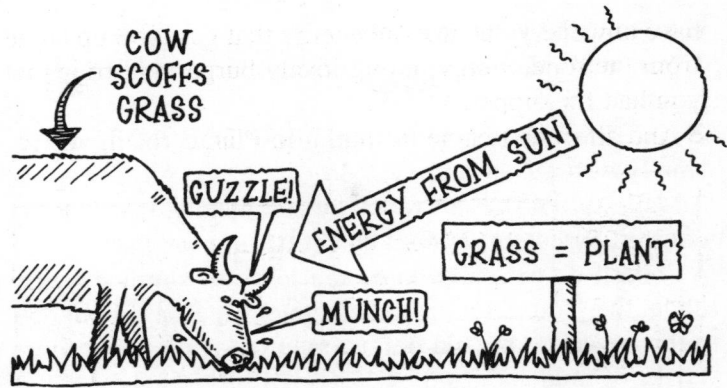

Some grass ends up in a smelly cow pat. But its energy doesn't go to waste.

Poo rots into soil and is eaten up by greedy fungi and grass. And so all the food in plants (and the cow and the fungi) was originally built up using photosynthesis.

Bet you never knew!
The power to cook your supper in a microwave or electric cooker comes from electricity. This may have come from burning coal at a power station. And guess what? Coal also comes from plants. Yes, coal is made from ancient plants (a few species of which are still knocking around) called clubmosses and horsetails.

How to make your own coal...

1 You will need one giant horsetail – say 40 metres in height.

2 Cut down the horsetail and allow it to rot in warm, smelly water. A swamp will do.

3 Make sure it doesn't rot away completely. It should be covered by layers of more half-rotted horsetails.

4 Squash down really hard, and leave to simmer gently under the ground for a good length of time, say about 350 million years. Oh, and don't forget to keep adding more layers of mud and sand.

5 Remove from the ground and burn.

You should find that with all this squashing your horsetail has turned into hard, black coal. But coal is simply carbon from the carbon dioxide taken in by the horsetail by photosynthesis all those years ago. Worth the wait wasn't it?

POWERFUL PLANT PLANS

Let's take a closer look at a typical plant:

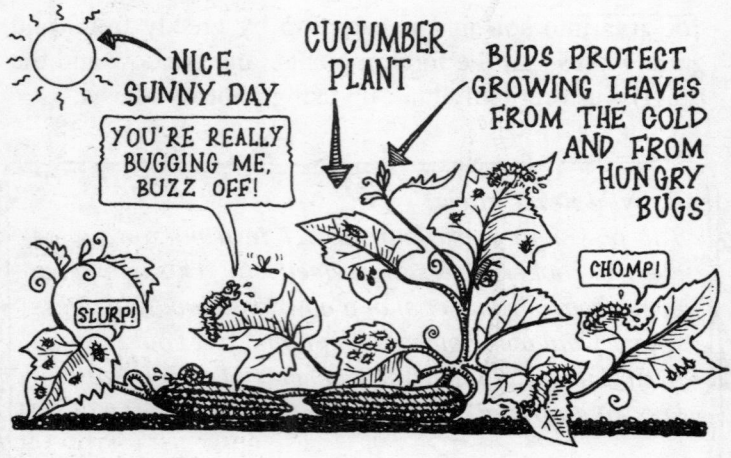

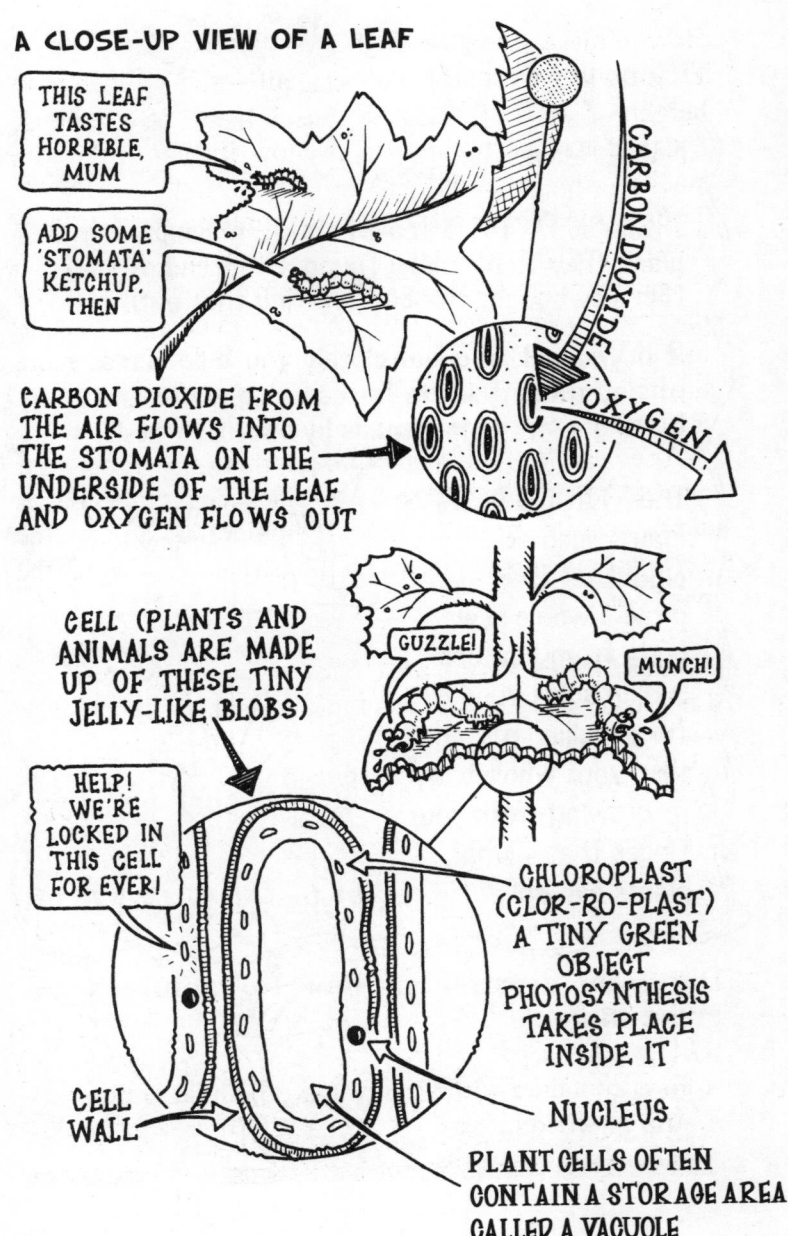

A CLOSE-UP VIEW OF A LEAF

THIS LEAF TASTES HORRIBLE, MUM

ADD SOME 'STOMATA' KETCHUP, THEN

CARBON DIOXIDE

OXYGEN

CARBON DIOXIDE FROM THE AIR FLOWS INTO THE STOMATA ON THE UNDERSIDE OF THE LEAF AND OXYGEN FLOWS OUT

GUZZLE!

MUNCH!

CELL (PLANTS AND ANIMALS ARE MADE UP OF THESE TINY JELLY-LIKE BLOBS)

HELP! WE'RE LOCKED IN THIS CELL FOR EVER!

CHLOROPLAST (CLOR-RO-PLAST) A TINY GREEN OBJECT PHOTOSYNTHESIS TAKES PLACE INSIDE IT

NUCLEUS

CELL WALL

PLANT CELLS OFTEN CONTAIN A STORAGE AREA CALLED A VACUOLE

41

Vicious veg fact file

NAME: Leaves

THE BASIC FACTS: 1 Leaves are the green part on a plant. They're normally found at the end of stalks. (Bet you bought this book to find that out!)

2 If you look at a leaf closely you'll see a maze of tiny tubes. They're for carrying water and carting away sugars made by photosynthesis.

THE VICIOUS DETAILS: Plants such as the piggyback plant can grow a whole new body from just one leaf. Imagine your finger falling off. And then your whole body re-growing from your finger. That's what plants can do!

WHERE DID IT FALL OFF?

DOWN THERE!

Dare you discover ... how to capture some green slime?

What you need:

A glass container with a screw top (a jam jar is fine)

A strip of wood or bark

A plant spray

42

What you do:

1 Spray the wood with water.

2 Find some of that powdery green algae that lives on tree trunks. Scrape some on to your damp strip of wood.

3 Place the wood in the jar and seal the lid.

4 Leave in a light place for a few days.

What happens next?

a) The green stuff turns yellow.

b) The green stuff starts to spread.

c) The green stuff glows in the dark.

Answer:
b) The algae are using carbon dioxide from the air, sunshine and the water you gave them to make sugars. This gives them the energy to grow. If a), it needs a bit more light and possibly water. If c), you have found an alien life form. Beware, because it might start squishing out of the jar and frightening the cat.

AMAZING LEAF FACTS

There's nothing thrilling about this leaf? Well, get your teeth into these fantastic facts…

1 The leaves of the sensitive plant are surprisingly… sensitive. If you touch them the stem bows down to the ground and the plant folds into a spike. This puts off most hungry animals – well, it would, wouldn't it? Have you ever had a salad that tried to escape?

2 What happens is that the touch triggers an electrical current inside the leaf. This empties all the liquid out of cells in the base of the leaves and makes them collapse. So remember this plant is sensitive and don't go upsetting it by saying cruel things like "vinaigrette dressing".

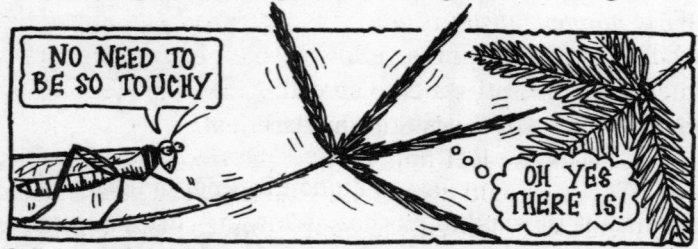

3 Some of the biggest leaves belong to a species of arum plant. Its huge leaves are 3 metres wide. Some travellers use them as tents but you can also eat them. (Note: It's a bad idea to nibble holes in your tent.)

4 Talking about huge leaves – Amazon water lily leaves are 2 metres across. They're so strong that the first gardener to grow them, Joseph Paxton (1801–1865), dressed his daughter as a fairy and photographed her sitting on a leaf. Bet she felt a right idiot. (This won't work with normal-sized water lilies.)

CHILD SITTING ON GIANT
AMAZON WATER LILY

CHILD SITTING ON
NORMAL WATER LILY

5 Ever wondered why leaves turn pretty colours and fall in autumn? Well, amazingly, the leaves are pushed out by the tree! In cold countries it's tough for trees in the winter. They find it hard to suck up water from the cold soil. It's a bit like you trying to suck ice cream through a straw. So the trees shut up shop. There's no use keeping those useless water-losing leaves.

6 Those pretty colours come from leftover and unwanted chemicals in the leaves. The valuable green colour from the chloroplasts gets sucked back into the tree whilst more waste chemicals pour into the leaf.

7 And when the leaf falls it's like the tree is going to the toilet – or should that be lav-a-tree? The tree makes chemicals that loosen the stalk from the branch. So it flutters gently down to earth. And by some revolting coincidence that's exactly where we're heading.

REVOLTING ROOTS

To understand plants you need to go back to your roots. That's to say, take a look below the surface of plants and see what's going on in the cold dark soil, and probe its revolting secrets. Hope you've got a really strong stomach.

REVOLTING DOWN-TO-EARTH DETAILS

Try to imagine soil as an entire world – a secret underground city full of tiny rooms. That's what you see through a microscope. Each tiny grain of soil is surrounded by stuff called humus, rather like a chocolate-coated nut (no, don't try to eat soil – it tastes disgusting – read on to find out why).

Humus is made up of tiny rotting lumps of plants and animals and poo all mixed together. Oh, and not forgetting bacteria – billions and trillions of bacteria. A large pinch of soil – just four cubic centimetres – holds five billion bacteria. That's almost as many bacteria as there are humans on Earth.

DOWN-TO-EARTH BACTERIA

REALLY DOWN-TO-EARTH SCIENTIST

If these bacteria were the size of a person, that pinch of soil would be the height of a skyscraper 10,000 floors high. If you spread all the muck you'll find in just 28 grams of fine soil it would make a thin layer covering four hectares – that's the size of a small city. And all this slime binds the tiny grains of soil together and stops them from blowing away.

It sounds gross but this secret unseen world is a happy hunting ground for millions of tiny bugs called mites. And there are also larger bugs and squirming worms as well as fungi all happily hunting and scrunching one another. Then there are plant roots blindly searching for minerals and water in the soil. (Minerals are chemicals that plants need to grow and stay strong and healthy, remember? They include potassium, phosphorus and nitrates.)

Bet you never knew!
Stinging nettles grow well in soils rich in phosphorus. This chemical is also found in bones. So a thick clump of nettles may mean that a dead body lies buried underneath.

POOR JIM, HE HATED NETTLES

And there are an awful lot of roots underground. One little winter rye plant less than one metre tall has nearly 623 km of roots in just 0.06 cubic metres of soil. In fact, if you stretched out all the plant roots in just one average-sized garden they'd stretch all the way round the moon *and* back again.

THE ROOT OF THE PROBLEM
If it wasn't for their roots plants would really be falling down on the job. Let's take a slightly different look at that cucumber plant…

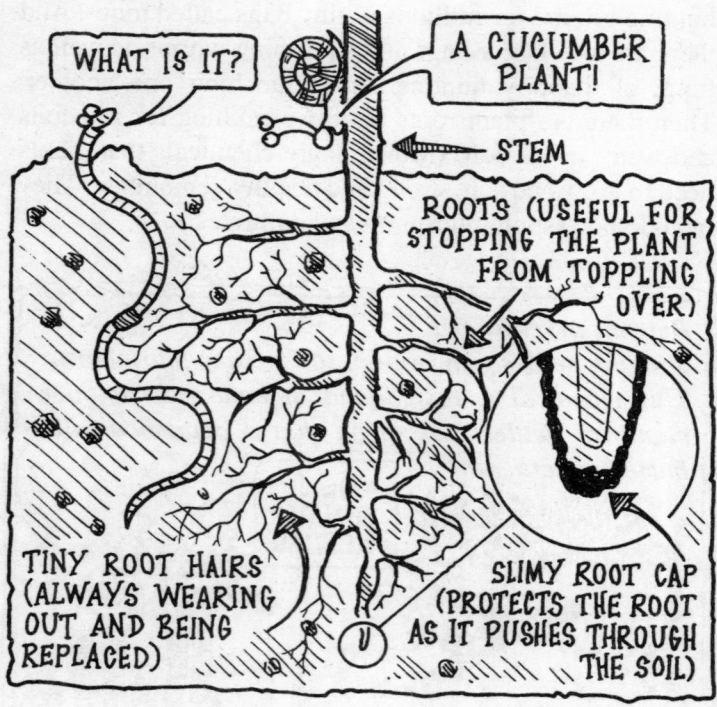

WHAT IS IT?

A CUCUMBER PLANT!

STEM

ROOTS (USEFUL FOR STOPPING THE PLANT FROM TOPPLING OVER)

TINY ROOT HAIRS (ALWAYS WEARING OUT AND BEING REPLACED)

SLIMY ROOT CAP (PROTECTS THE ROOT AS IT PUSHES THROUGH THE SOIL)

The root hairs suck up water and minerals. These are sucked up to the leaves though tubes called xylem (zy-lem). Sugar made by photosynthesis moves around in other tubes called phloem (flow-em).

And here's an X-ray view of the cucumber plant's stem.

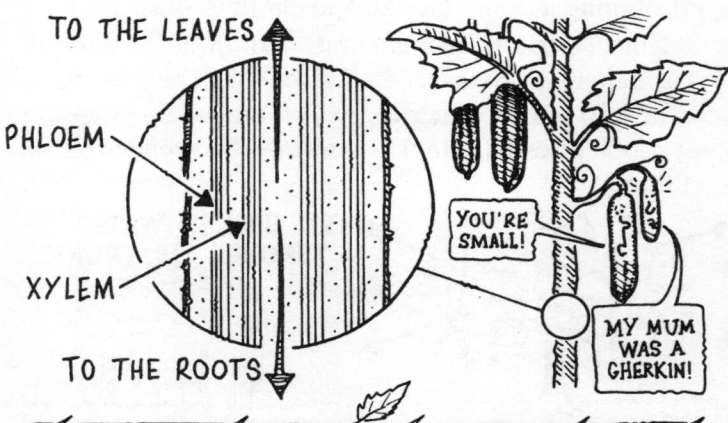

TO THE LEAVES

PHLOEM

XYLEM

TO THE ROOTS

YOU'RE SMALL!

MY MUM WAS A GHERKIN!

> **Bet you never knew!**
> Some plant roots actually improve the soil. Roots of plants called legumes (related to peas), contain bacteria that turn nitrogen gas from the air in the soil into nitrate chemicals that other plants use once the legume has died.

VICIOUS VEG EXPRESSIONS

IT'S TRANSPIRATION!

Shouldn't that be perspiration?

No, she's talking about her plant. Transpiration is when plants soak up water through their roots and lose it through the stomata in their leaves. This ensures a stream of water to their leaves for photosynthesis. It's a bit like you slurping a drink through a really long straw.

Plants lose huge amounts of water through transpiration. An average-sized lawn – 15.2 x 6 metres – can lose 50 tons of water every year and a large tree can lose 1,000 litres in a single sunny day. No wonder plants get thirsty.

TREE SUCKING WATER UP THROUGH ITS TRUNK

(ELEPHANT DOING THE SAME THING)

Dare you discover ... transpiration?

What you need:
A plant
A polythene bag
An elastic band

What you do is:
1 Cover a branch and a few leaves with the polythene bag.
2 Secure the edges of the bag with the elastic band so that air can't get into the bag.
3 Leave it in a sunny place for four hours.

What do you notice?
a) The bag has been sucked in.
b) The bag has been blown outwards.
c) The inside of the bag is covered with tiny water droplets.

COULD YOU BE A BOTANIST?

1 You're looking for plants near the Arctic Circle and you find some pretty flowers growing in the decaying skeleton of an animal. Why are they there?

SPOOKY!

a) The flowers were there first and the animal died on top of them.

b) The flowers were poisonous. The animal ate the flowers and died.

c) The animal died first. The flowers sprouted later and fed on the nourishing rotting bones.

2 You find these roots growing on a seashore. Why are they sticking upwards? (Roots normally grow sideways or downwards.)

SPIKY!

a) To breathe air.

b) To stab passing animals and suck their blood.

51

c) To stop mud being washed away by the sea and so build up some nice solid soil for the plant to grow on.

Answers:

1 c) The soil is very poor but the rain has washed nourishing minerals from the dead body into the soil. So the flowers flourish. The skeleton also protects the plants from the biting wind.

2 a) They're a type of mangrove root. They stick out of the water to take in air. When the tide comes in they stop taking in air and the plant has to hold its breath until the tide goes out.

Mind you, the next chapter might leave you bit breathless. The plants you're about to meet are extra *vicious*. They are quite capable of using fiendish traps and tricks to capture bugs and small animals and then ... dinner time!

DON'T LET THEM GET US!

VICIOUS BUG-EATING VEG

Plants sit around doing nothing. Animals eat the plants. It's the law of nature. Well, not necessarily. Some plants bite back … and they eat animals. Welcome to the nightmare world of bug-eating vegetables…

Vicious veg fact file

NAME: Bug-eating plants

THE BASIC FACTS: In some swampy areas there aren't enough minerals to feed plants. The soil is especially low in the nitrates that plants need to grow. Plants help themselves to extra nitrates by scoffing insects.

THE VICIOUS DETAILS: Some bug-eating plants look pretty. The Australian pink petticoat plant looks like a tiny pink petticoat. (How sweet!) But an unwary bug that crawls inside finds itself in a trap and is digested … alive.

> HAVE YOU GOT ANTS IN YOUR PANTS?

> NO. I'VE GOT BUGS IN MY PETTICOATS!

THE LOST LUNCH-BREAK

Imagine a vast table-shaped mountain 2,700 metres high. It's so high and so steep that waterfalls cascade down its sides and turn to steam before they hit the ground. The summit of this mountain is lost in dense, gloomy clouds. This is the sinister and mysterious realm of Roraima in South America. What horrible secrets does it hide?

One British botanist was determined to find out. He was brave, or perhaps a bit foolish. His name was Everard Im Thurn (1852–1932). When Everard wasn't busy with his botany, he had a full-time job with the regional government. This is what his diary *might* have looked like (OK – it probably didn't)…

Everard's diary
1884

Day 1

A piece of luck! I've found a way up the cliffs of Roraima on a sloping ledge. OOPS - it's a bit slippery up here. Mustn't look down -it's 2,744 metres. Was this such a good idea? I hate heights!

Day 2

Terrible weather - pouring with rain. But at least I made it. YES! Here I am at the top - wonder what I'll find? Bound to be thrilling, maybe there are dinosaurs roaming around! Let's go for a walk. WHOA! That was close.

All the rocks up here are covered in slippery, slimy black algae. And there are massive cracks in the rock 30 metres deep. I nearly fell into one. The rocks are awesome. Some look like mushrooms and some like ruined temples. I've even found one that looks like my old science teacher! That was scary, I can tell you! It's still raining.

Day 3 - Morning
Still raining. Found a little pool a few centimetres across. Just large enough to wash in . . . realized too late it was a bromeliad. That's a plant that makes a little pool by catching water in its leaves. (There's plenty of that - it's STILL raining.) Anyway this was a plant with a difference. The pool was full of digestive juice and dead insects. So it looks like the plant is eating insects that drown in the pool. WOW! - wait till I tell the lads back home about this.

Afternoon - still raining!
Looked more closely at the bromeliad
and found tiny plants and creatures
actually living in the pool. Somehow
they aren't getting digested. The tiny
plants are bladderworts and they're
eating the animals by sucking them
into little pockets in their leaves and
digesting them! A bug-eating plant
inside a bug-eating plant. This place
is seriously weird. IT'S GREAT!
Pity I'm soaked through.

Day 4
Still raining - sigh!
Looks like I've accidentally discovered
a new kind of pitcher plant. It works
a bit like the bromeliad I found, by
trapping insects in a pool of
water and leaving them to
rot. Of course the pitcher
plant is a different shape...

  I guess the pitcher plant feeds on
the rotting bodies. Fascinating.

Later. . .
I'm not feeling too good. Don't think
it's the pitcher plant, though. Think
it's all this rain. I'm sure I'm
getting a cold. ATISHOOO!
I feel awful. Time to go home. . .

Bug-eating plants seem horribly mysterious, don't they? I mean – how exactly do they catch their victims? And what do the vicious vegetables do next? Are you brave enough to read all the revolting details? Go on, you know you want to…

MYSTERIES OF BUG-EATING PLANTS
THE SUNDEW PLANT

Found all over the world from Australia to the USA. A sundew plant works like this…

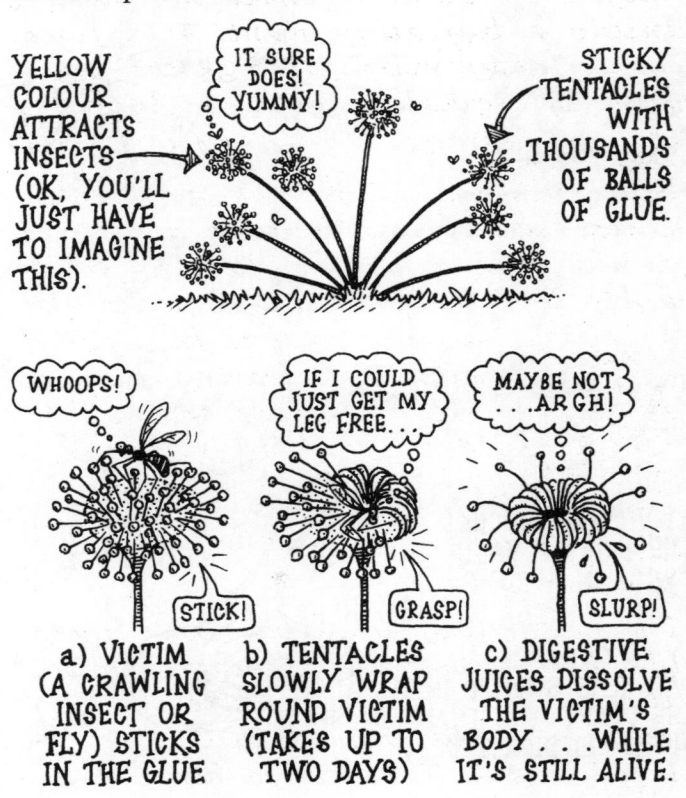

YELLOW COLOUR ATTRACTS INSECTS (OK, YOU'LL JUST HAVE TO IMAGINE THIS).

IT SURE DOES! YUMMY!

STICKY TENTACLES WITH THOUSANDS OF BALLS OF GLUE.

WHOOPS!

IF I COULD JUST GET MY LEG FREE...

MAYBE NOT ...ARGH!

STICK!

GRASP!

SLURP!

a) VICTIM (A CRAWLING INSECT OR FLY) STICKS IN THE GLUE

b) TENTACLES SLOWLY WRAP ROUND VICTIM (TAKES UP TO TWO DAYS)

c) DIGESTIVE JUICES DISSOLVE THE VICTIM'S BODY...WHILE IT'S STILL ALIVE.

THE WATERWHEEL PLANT

Found in Europe, Australia and Africa.
The waterwheel plant lives in ponds and eats tiny pond creatures.

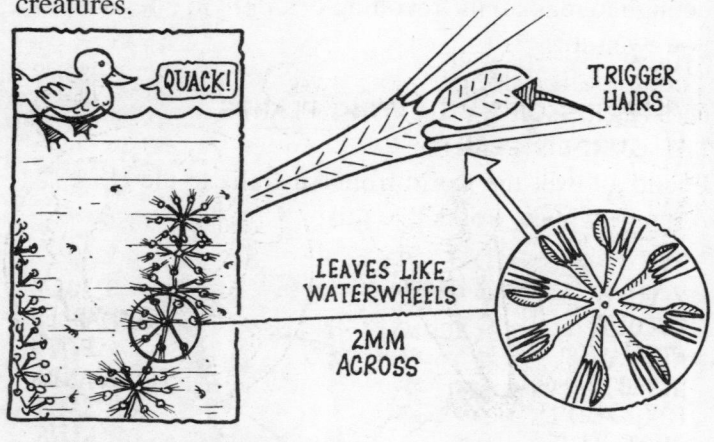

QUACK!

TRIGGER HAIRS

LEAVES LIKE WATERWHEELS

2MM ACROSS

And here's what happens...

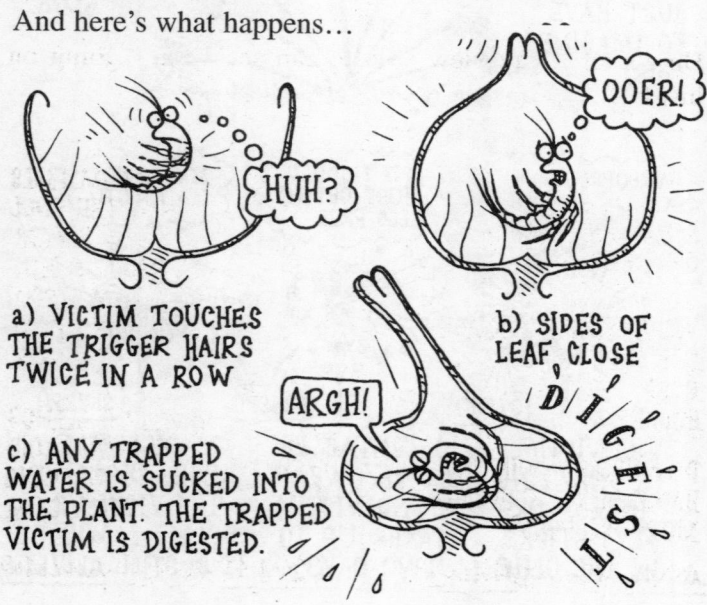

HUH?

OOER!

a) VICTIM TOUCHES THE TRIGGER HAIRS TWICE IN A ROW

b) SIDES OF LEAF CLOSE

DIGEST!

ARGH!

c) ANY TRAPPED WATER IS SUCKED INTO THE PLANT. THE TRAPPED VICTIM IS DIGESTED.

THE PITCHER PLANT
Found in the USA, South America and Australia.

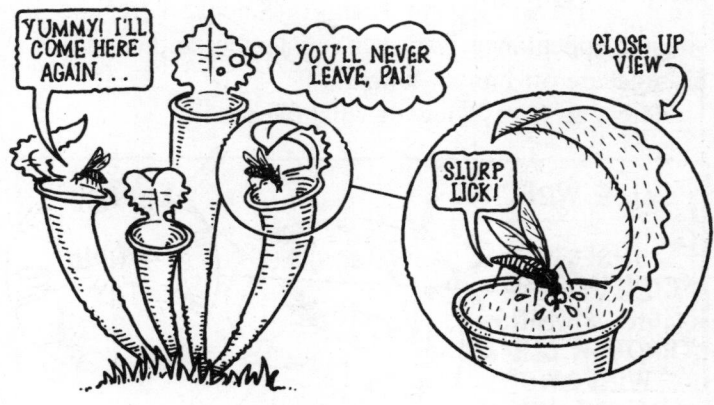

Here's an X-ray view so you can see what's going on inside…

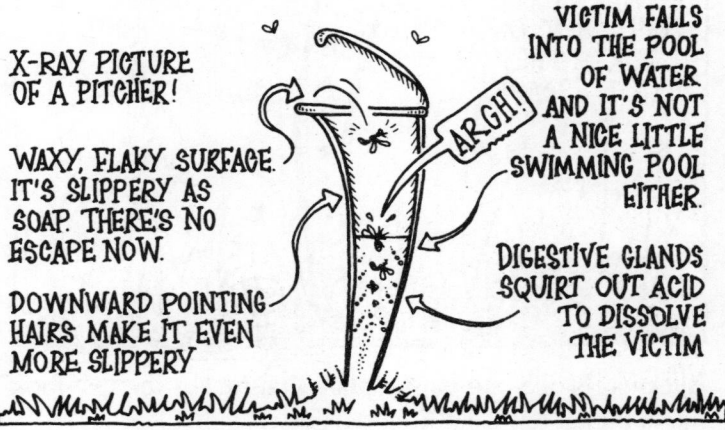

THE COBRA LILY

Found in the USA.

Looks like a deadly cobra snake rearing up and about to strike. Stupid little insects crawl into the "mouth" of the "snake". Have they no brains? (Scientists reckon its sinister appearance is just a sinister coincidence, not a bid to scare off hungry animals.)

Here's an X-ray view of what happens…

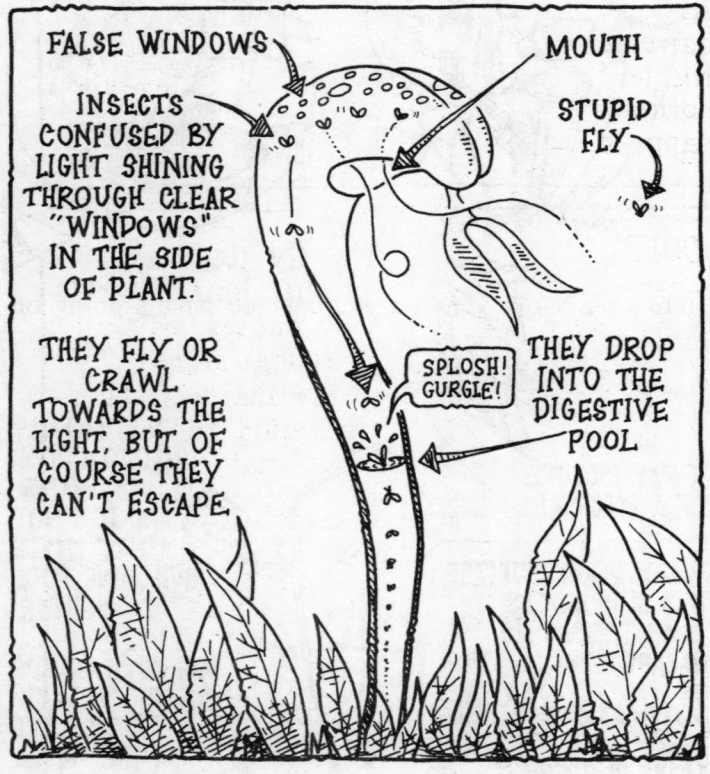

FALSE WINDOWS

MOUTH

INSECTS CONFUSED BY LIGHT SHINING THROUGH CLEAR "WINDOWS" IN THE SIDE OF PLANT.

STUPID FLY

THEY FLY OR CRAWL TOWARDS THE LIGHT, BUT OF COURSE THEY CAN'T ESCAPE.

SPLOSH! GURGLE!

THEY DROP INTO THE DIGESTIVE POOL

But there's one bug-eating plant that makes the rest look like a bunch of sweet little daisies…

THE VENUS FLY-TRAP

Don't panic! You won't find one of these lurking at the bottom of your garden. They only grow in the swamps of North and South Carolina, USA. Here's how they catch their prey...

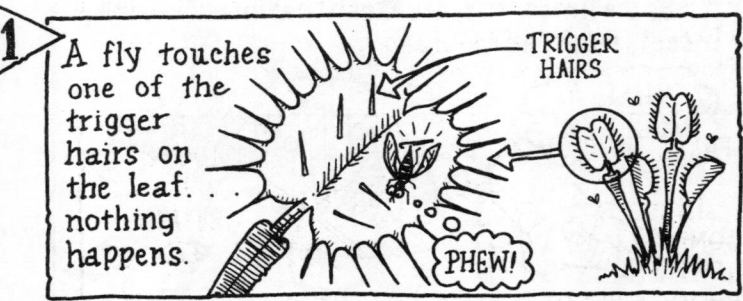

1 A fly touches one of the trigger hairs on the leaf... nothing happens.

TRIGGER HAIRS

PHEW!

2 OOER!

The fly touches another hair. Yikes! This causes an electrical signal inside the leaf. All the liquid rushes out of special cells and the leaf folds.

3 Half a second later ... the spikes on the leaf edge trap the insect. Yes, it's a plant with what looks like a pair of jaws. The fly is trapped!

I WANT MY MUM!

MUNCH!

Within half an hour the fly is squeezed tight by the leaves. Then it's digested while it's still alive! The vicious vegetable takes two weeks to complete its murderous meal.

Sometimes the fly-trap catches a big insect such as a wasp.

WHAT A WHOPPER!

BUZZ BUZZ

But the insect is too big to digest. The fly-trap runs out of digestive juice. Bacteria eat the insect's dead body and they kill the leaf as well. But the fly-trap lives to bite another day.

ERK!

VICIOUS USES FOR A BUG-EATING PLANT QUIZ

All around the world people have found that bug-eating plants can be useful. Which of these uses are true and which are as impossible as a botanist who doesn't like salads?

1 Portuguese sundew plants were traditionally used in Portugal and Spain to control flies. The nice sweet smell attracts buzzing beasties in the home. The insects crawl over the sticky leaves and get covered in gluey slime. Soon their breathing holes block up and they die a horrible lingering death. TRUE/FALSE

2 Butterwort (a sticky-leafed plant that catches insects in a similar way to a sundew) was used in many parts of Europe for catching lice that had infested people's beds. TRUE/FALSE

I SLEPT BETTER WHEN THE BED WAS INFESTED WITH LICE

3 You can also use butterwort to curdle milk. The plant's juices make the milk clump into stringy lumps called curds that you can eat. (Careful now, don't eat the leaf by mistake!) TRUE/FALSE

4 The trumpet pitcher got its name because it can be played just like a trumpet. In the seventeenth century musicians would play dried trumpet pitchers as a form of street entertainment. TRUE/FALSE

5 Sundew juice squeezed from the leaves was a traditional remedy for warts and corns. You simply squeezed the juice over the warts and corns and they would dissolve like magic. TRUE/FALSE

OH WELL, THE WARTS AND CORNS HAVE GONE!

Answers:

1 TRUE. One sundew plant can catch three flies per tentacle. After that the tentacles die.

2 TRUE. People put butterwort leaves between the sheets. But they could cause nightmares ... would you fancy being tucked up with a bug-eating plant?

3 TRUE. Simply dip the leaves in milk to make the delicious stringy curds. As eaten by the Lapp people of Scandinavia.

4 FALSE.

5 TRUE. But boring scientists reckon that the remedy doesn't work. It's just a corny old wives' tale.

Now here's a use for a bug-eating plant which is all too true ... and horrible. Can you believe that some botanists have actually *drunk* the disgusting goo from a pitcher plant? If you fancy a quick swig – here's how to...

MAKE YOUR OWN PITCHER PLANT COCKTAIL

1 Take one pitcher plant (huge choice of sizes available)

2 Add:

- Some digestive juices strong enough to dissolve eggs and meat.
- 20–30 half-digested bits of dead insect
- Several hundred thousand tiny swimming algae
- A few worms
- Tadpoles
- A family of red spiders

(The last four manage to live in the fluid without getting digested.)

3 Mix well. Leave for a few days. Serve warm.

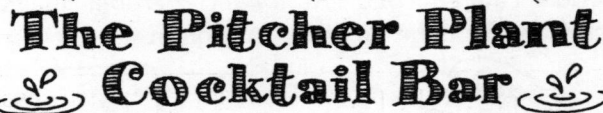

The Pitcher Plant Cocktail Bar

Slake your thirst with a Pitcher Plant Cocktail – our staff are dying to serve you!

Delicious range of pitcher plant cocktails. Speedy service. Our secret acid recipe delivers a fully digested midge cocktail in just a few hours (flies take a few days).

🐛 Cocktails served warm and fresh with just that extra tingle of acid.

🌿 Huge choice of pitcher shapes – over 60 species to choose from – claret decanters, champagne glasses, etc.

🌿 Standard size holds 2 litres

🌿 Rajah pitcher – share one with your friends (up to 3.5 litres). Choice of regular flavour and mousy flavour (if you're lucky you'll find a tasty half-digested mouse at the bottom).

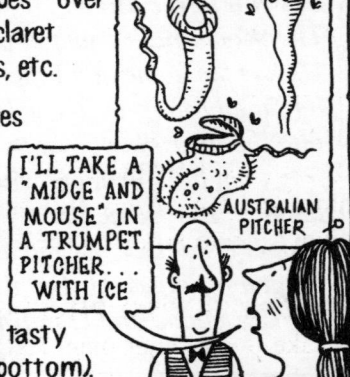

HANGING PITCHER   TRUMPET PITCHER

AUSTRALIAN PITCHER

I'LL TAKE A "MIDGE AND MOUSE" IN A TRUMPET PITCHER... WITH ICE

Here's what the scientists had to say…

British naturalist Alfred Wallace (1823–1913) said:

We found it very palatable, though rather warm, and we all quenched our thirst from these natural jugs.

American Paul Zahl of the *National Geographic* magazine drank from the plant on an expedition in the 1960s:

It tasted good though warm.

But he added that he didn't like the gluey bit at the bottom. Fancy a slurp?

Bet you never knew!
The 90-cm-high trumpet pitcher plant from southern USA is the home of a little green frog. The frog spends its time lurking in ambush. It waits for insects to fall into the horrible goo at the bottom of the pitcher. The frog then licks them up with its disgusting long, sticky tongue. But sometimes the frog loses its grip on slippery sides of the pitcher, falls in itself, and ends up getting digested. For the pitcher this must be like ten Christmas dinners all rolled into one.

TERRIBLE TABLE MANNERS

Fancy sharing your home with a bug-eating plant? Not any more, you don't.

HORRIBLE HEALTH WARNING!

Reading this section aloud at mealtimes can seriously damage your chances of getting birthday or Christmas presents for about 100 years.

1 Some insect grubs can survive living in the pitcher plant's deadly ooze. They feed off the bits of insect body in the pitcher and seem quite happy with their horrible home. In some plants these grubs are in turn eaten by larger grubs.

2 The pitcher doesn't mind these lodgers – in fact their disgusting droppings are rich in nitrates and they all go to feed the plant. And the grubs that eat bits of insect help to keep the pitcher clean and tidy.

3 The twin-spurred pitcher plant goes one better by providing a cosy little room for a gang of ants. The ants guzzle some of the pitcher's victims but some insect bits plop back into the pool. And when they're cut up they're easier to digest.

4 Some vicious seeds also eat bugs. Sounds bizarre, doesn't it? Well, get this. Shepherd's purse seeds swell up with water until their outer covering bursts open. Underneath there's a slimy layer. From now on any bug that bumps into the seed gets stuck in the slime and slowly digested. The seedling grows and grows – nourished by its tasty new food supply.

5 The most surprising thing about bug-eating plants is that they don't really need to eat bugs at all! Deprived of their insect food they don't die they just stop growing.

But plants aren't just vicious to bugs. They're vicious to one another too. Warning! Readers looking at the next chapter might find themselves turning a sickly green colour. (If you are affected place a wastepaper basket over your head and no one will notice.)

Read on ... at your peril!

I FIND THE CLASSROOM LIGHTS TOO BRIGHT, SIR

...AND MY HEAD FEELS COLD, SIR

VICIOUS BATTLING VEG

You might think it's easy being a plant – but it's not. Life is tough and it *can* be murder. At best, it's a jungle out there and life is one long vicious battle for survival. The signs are everywhere. Look closely at this leaf and you'll see the horrible ravages of hordes of peckish bugs and foul fungi.

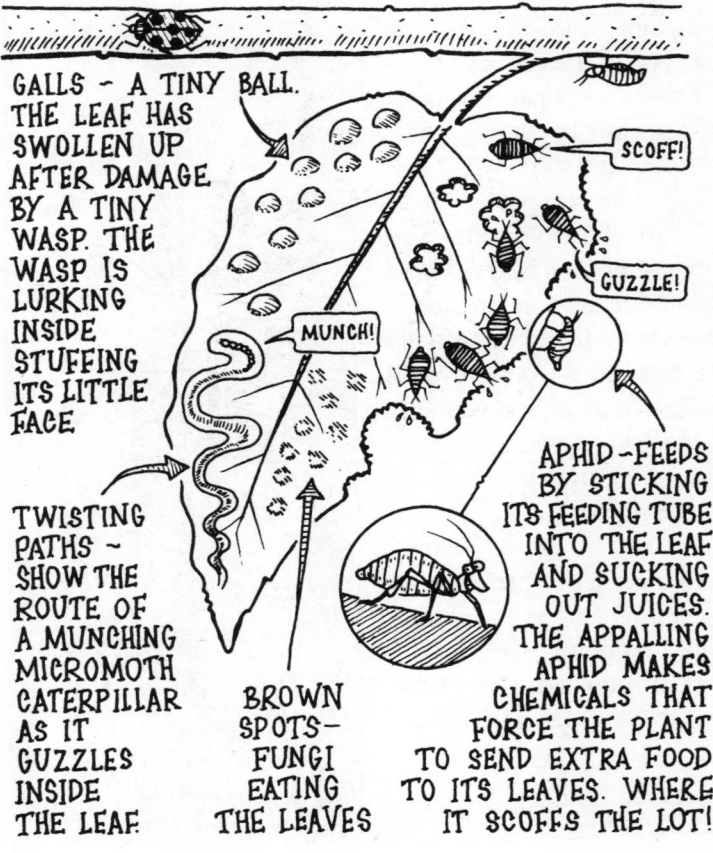

GALLS – A TINY BALL. THE LEAF HAS SWOLLEN UP AFTER DAMAGE BY A TINY WASP. THE WASP IS LURKING INSIDE STUFFING ITS LITTLE FACE

SCOFF!

GUZZLE!

MUNCH!

TWISTING PATHS – SHOW THE ROUTE OF A MUNCHING MICROMOTH CATERPILLAR AS IT GUZZLES INSIDE THE LEAF

BROWN SPOTS – FUNGI EATING THE LEAVES

APHID – FEEDS BY STICKING ITS FEEDING TUBE INTO THE LEAF AND SUCKING OUT JUICES. THE APPALLING APHID MAKES CHEMICALS THAT FORCE THE PLANT TO SEND EXTRA FOOD TO ITS LEAVES. WHERE IT SCOFFS THE LOT!

THE JUNGLE OF DEATH QUIZ

So life can be perilous for plants. It's no good sitting in the soil and waiting for the sun to shine and the rain to rain and hoping that everything will come up smelling of roses. If you're a plant you'll only survive if you're meaner and more murderous than any other lifeform. In other words you've got to be VICIOUS or you're compost.

So how would you measure up to the meanest and greenest in the plant world? In this cruelly challenging quiz you'll have to fight for your life against savage snails, invading insects and crafty caterpillars.

Are you ready? Remember, there's no peeping at the answers and no going back!

Will you survive THE JUNGLE OF DEATH?

HOPE THERE'S SOME LEFT WHEN WE GET THERE!

1 Watch out! There's a huge savage slimy snail rasping its jaws on the underside of your leaves. What do you do?

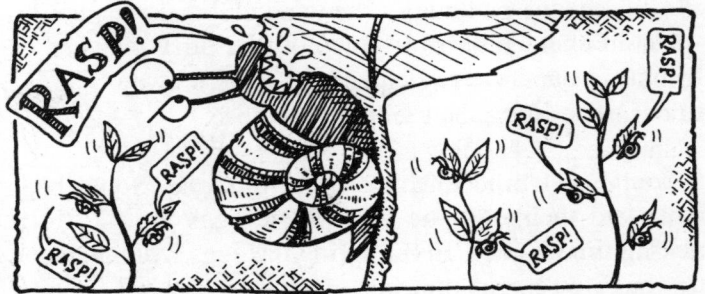

a) Make slippery slime under the leaves. The snails would slide off your leaves.

b) Grow spikes on the undersides of your leaves to neatly kebab the snail.

c) Allow the snails to feed. Don't panic! The snails will never eat all your leaves and what's left will grow again.

2 Cut-throat caterpillars are crunching your leaves. If you don't stop them they'll eat you alive. What's your plan?

a) Drop off the affected leaves – that'll take the caterpillars with them. And good riddance!

b) Grow extra-thick leaves. The leaves would be too thick and chewy for the caterpillars to bite through.

c) Make a gas. It's an SOS signal to passing wasps.

3 You're surrounded! On every side there are insects that want to eat your leaves. You've got to raise your own army to fight them off. Which are the best creatures to use? Better decide right now!

a) Ants – good for attack.

b) Woodlice – good for defence.

c) Rats – bigger than insects.

4 Action stations – DANGER! A vicious half-starved rabbit is attacking your leaves! How can you fight it off?
a) Quickly grow a tendril. The wind will make the tendril wave around. This will frighten off the furry monster.
b) Open your flowers suddenly to scare it away.
c) Hit back. Sting the rabbit on the nose.

5 You've got time to think about this one. Some bugs have laid their eggs on you. These eggs are like little ticking time bombs. In the spring the eggs will hatch and the bugs will start stuffing themselves on your tender spring leaves. What's your plan?
a) Don't produce any new leaves in the spring.
b) Produce new leaves unexpectedly early or unexpectedly late so the bugs don't know when to hatch.
c) Make poisons in the new leaves.

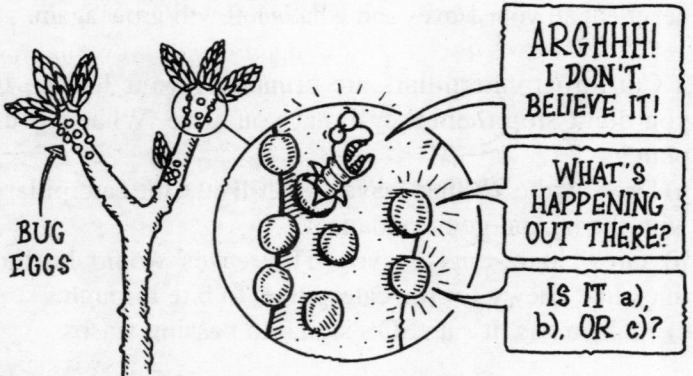

BUG EGGS

ARGHHH! I DON'T BELIEVE IT!

WHAT'S HAPPENING OUT THERE?

IS IT a), b), OR c)?

6 Danger from the air! They're landing. An army of aphids. They've come to suck juices from your leaves. You've only got minutes to fight back. Quick, what will you do?
a) Send extra juices to your outer leaves so the aphids go and feed there. Then set up an ambush.

b) Send extra juices to the leaves where the aphids are feeding. The aphids will drink until they swell up and go pop. It's messy but deadly.

c) Pump the juices out of your leaves. The aphids will go away because they will have nothing to feed on. That's right, starve them into surrender.

7 More insect invaders are marching up your stem. This time they're beetles and they mean business. They're biting your leaves to pieces. You've got to act now . . . or DIE!

a) Try to fold up your leaves so the beetles get trapped inside.

b) Pump water out of the tiny holes in your leaves and try to wash the beetles away.

c) Make a gas that smells like a female beetle. If they're males they'll try and find the female and leave you in peace.

73

Answers:

1 b) If you were an Amazon water lily you'd do this to water snails. Spikes are a good way to beat off hungry animals. Tropical screw pines have sword-shaped leaves. The barbs on the leaves mean that any creature that gets too close gets skewered. Even ordinary grass has tiny blades made from a chemical called silica. That's why careless humans sometimes cut themselves on grass.

IT'S **YOU** WHO WAS SUPPOSED TO BE CUTTING THE **GRASS**

2 c) Rose bushes defend themselves in this way. The wasps scoop up the caterpillars and take them back to their nest. There the caterpillars are torn apart and fed to the wasp grubs as a tasty tea-time treat. That'll teach them.

3 a) Ants are ideal. The South American ant plant actually provides a cosy little chamber inside its stem for the ants to live. The plant eats the ants' droppings and the ants kill any insect that comes near. So everyone's happy – except the insects that get killed.

4 c) Stinging nettles do this. Their leaves are covered in tiny hairs. If the hairs are touched poison pours out. A rabbit's nose is very sensitive and rather than risk a sting the cowardly bunnies avoid the nettle. In fact, dead nettles (which don't have a sting) keep the bunnies at bay and avoid getting eaten because they look like stinging nettles. It's a vicious disguise.

5 b) You have to be a viciously cunning oak tree to make this work. The bugs never know when there'll be leaves to eat. If the bugs hatch out too soon they'll starve and if they arrive too late the oak leaves will have had time to make poisons to defend themselves. (So there's half a point for **c**).)

6 a) It's a vicious trick. High flying ladybirds can spot the aphids on the outer leaves and chew them up for supper. And serves 'em right!

7 c) This is a typically vicious trick by the cucumber plant. The cunning cucumber keeps its cool and the bothered beetles beat it.

Now add up your score…
Give yourself *one* point for each correct answer.

Score 5–7. YOU HAVE CONQUERED THE JUNGLE OF DEATH. Congratulations! You'd make a blooming brilliant plant. Nothing can touch you – the insect invaders don't stand a chance.

Score 3–4. Although you have a budding talent you're still a bit green. With a bit of luck you'll live to grow another day.

Score 1–2. Drooping daisy. You won't last long in the jungle of death. You're not vicious enough – better stick to being a human.

TEACHER'S TEA-BREAK TEASER

Hammer boldly on the staffroom door. When your teacher comes to the door smile sweetly and enquire:

YOU KNOW THAT YOUR TEA CONTAINS TANNIN – WHAT DOES YOUR TANNIN DO TO AN INSECT'S MOUTH PARTS?

ERK!

Answer:
Tannins are bitter chemicals made by many types of plant including roses, oak trees and tea plants. They protect the plant from aphids. The tannins gum up an aphid's mouth parts so it starves to death. Although tannins also give tea its slightly bitter taste, they don't gum up human mouth parts – worse luck. If they did your teacher would be speechless after every tea-break.

Bet you never knew!
On top of all their other problems plants can also be attacked by viruses. These tiny objects are far smaller even than bacteria. They're the same things that give you colds and flu. Plants get them from the bites of hungry bugs like aphids. But they don't get blocked or runny noses or sneezing – oh no. It's far worse. If a virus such as mosaic leaf attacks our cucumber plant (see page 40) its leaves would become discoloured and it would die. There's no cure!

And if that isn't bad enough some vicious vegetables are keen to make a meal of any plant that gets in their way. These plants are REALLY VILLAINOUS!

VEGETABLE VILLAINS I HAVE KNOWN

THE CASE NOTES OF CHIEF INSPECTOR GARDEN

Whenever I look at these notes I am shocked by the sheer inventiveness and viciousness of these vegetable villains. Clearly society should not tolerate these vegetable riff-raff.

NAME: the Strangler Fig

LAST SEEN: South America

KNOWN CRIMES: strangling trees One day I came across the dead body of a mature tree. I deduced immediately that foul play was involved and I was soon proved right. On closer examination I realized that the cause of death was due to strangulation and thirst and the blocking of light. It seems that the victim was powerless to run away or hide.

METHODS USED: The villainous vegetable had climbed up the tree and wrapped its branches around the victim's trunk tighter and tighter.

ROOT
TREE
STRANGLER FIG
I CAN'T BREATH!

Five years later it had sunk its roots into the ground and stolen the victim's water supply. It must have been a terrible way to grow — er, go.

ARGHH!

UNFORTUNATE VICTIM

NAME: Dodder

LAST SEEN: sightings reported worldwide

KNOWN CRIMES: murdering countless plants

DODDER

METHODS USED: the dodder usually loiters in the undergrowth. Waiting for a victim, I shouldn't wonder. Then quite without warning the victim is grabbed by the dodder's tendrils. The victim is usually then stabbed in several places by the tendrils which suck out its insides. A most vicious criminal.

NAME: The Corpse Flower
(alias the Indian pipe)

LAST SEEN: lurking in the forests of
north-west America

DESCRIPTION: ghostly pale and
corpse-like, 25 cm high

KNOWN CRIMES: its roots make
unprovoked attacks on harmless
underground fungi
and suck out
their juices.

METHODS USED: my
enquiries have
established that
the crime occurs
because water in
the fungi juices
is quite
naturally
drawn towards
the thicker
liquid in the
corpse flower's
roots by a
natural
process,
called osmosis
(os-mo-sis).
Be that as it
may - this
villain is
deadly.

I HAD TO GET
TO THE ROOT OF
THE PROBLEM...

SLURP!

SUCK!

NAME: Christmas tree

(Note: The name is due to the fact that the tree flowers around Christmas. But the public should be warned this is no ordinary Christmas tree. Members of the public are requested not to place presents under it. The villain will probably try to eat them.)

LAST SEEN: Western Australia

DESCRIPTION: a tree with pretty orange or gold flowers. Many people have been fooled by this pretty, innocent exterior.

KNOWN CRIMES: roots seek out roots of other plants.

METHODS USED: Woody fangs sink into other plant roots followed by the tubes that divert the other plant's water into the Christmas tree.

Beware: this character is dangerous — approach with extreme caution. Has even been known to attack underground phone cables.

THE SECRET DIARY OF A KILLER CUCUMBER

Now you might think that faced with a vicious killer plant the other plants might curl up and die. Well, surely they're defenceless, aren't they? Not necessarily. Some plants fight back. Take the cucumber plant we were looking at earlier, for example. It looks harmless enough, but appearances can be deceptive. Just imagine if it could keep a diary of its life. OK, so you're *really* going to have to stretch your imagination for this.

Here's what it might say...

Spring – April

ARGH!

This is disgraceful. The gardener's gone and planted me outside. Next to all these bullying geranium plants. I want to go back to that nice warm greenhouse.

Blast him!

Two days later...

The geraniums are trying to get me. Their roots are pumping out poison gas. Lucky all this gas doesn't harm me. It's all to do with the incredible mix of chemicals in my roots that can soak up poisons and re-use them.

But I'm still not putting up with it!
I'm going to swallow up
the gas in my roots.
That'll sort 'em!

TEE HEE

me

A few hours later...

Now I'll get my revenge. I'll make the
geraniums' gas into
a more deadly mixture
of my own. And send it
right back to them.

ARGH!

Two weeks later...

I don't like the way those tomatoes
are looking at me. Their roots are
taking too much water from
the soil. It's got to stop.

The enemy

Three hours later...

This will teach them. The soil is full of
tiny nematode worms. Ugly little brutes.
The soil is too dry for them to be
active so they're asleep at the
moment. This gas will wake them
up. The worms don't like the gas
so they slither towards the
tomatoes. Yeah, go get 'em, you worms.

Three weeks later...
The tomatoes are weak and wilting and so are the geraniums. Hooray, I win! Now for a bit of serious growing.

DROOP!

Another three weeks later...
Hmm, I'm getting a bit tall. I need something to climb on to stop me falling over. Those tomato plants will do. I'll just stick out a tendril.

GOTCHA!

GROAN

Three days later...
Now I'm going to climb and climb.

Dare you discover ... how to make a plant attack you?

You will need:
A lot of bravery
A pea plant, our pet cucumber plant,
a passion flower or any plant with tendrils
A pencil

What you do:
Gently stroke the tip of the tendril with the pencil.

What does the tendril do?

a) It grabs the pencil and snaps it in half.

b) The tendril draws back suddenly.

c) It slowly bends.

HORRIBLE HEALTH WARNING!

Don't be too slow. If you hang around for more than a few days the plant will twine its tendrils around your neck. That's what happens to a nearby plant as the tendril plant grabs it. Better run away before it's too late.

Bet you never knew!

One good way for a plant to defend itself against insects or animals is to make itself poisonous so it can't be eaten. Do you like the lovely, cool, refreshing taste of mint? Its flavour is actually due to a poison in the leaf that affects your nerves. Of course, it's not strong enough to harm you. It just switches on the nerves that sense cool things on your tongue. So that everything tastes cool and refreshing. But for insects the chemicals are just too poisonous and they die.

A FEW THINGS YOU SHOULD KNOW ABOUT VICIOUS PLANT POISONS. HERE IS THE NEWS.

THE BAD NEWS

SOME PLANT POISONS ARE DEADLY POISONOUS TO HUMANS AND THEY HAVE HORRIBLE EFFECTS ON THE BODY

THE GOOD NEWS

MOST PLANT POISONS ARE DESIGNED TO BUMP OFF INSECTS. THEY'RE NOT SO HARMFUL TO US. IN FACT, A TINY DOSE OF SOME POISONS CAN BE GOOD FOR YOU. THEY CAN BE MADE INTO USEFUL MEDICINES.

The calabar bean was once used in trials. The accused person had to eat the poisonous bean. If they died they were considered guilty, if they lived they were innocent. Of course, the bean had no idea whether or not you deserved to die. The trick was to gulp it down and then sick it up again before the poison had a chance to work.

P-PLEASE, DON'T MAKE ME...

EAT IT! OR YOU WON'T GET ANY PUDDING

The mandrake root is poisonous. There were once a lot of strange superstitions about it because it looked a bit like a man. One idea was that the mandrake screams when it's dug up. In Roman times dogs were used to dig up the roots because the Romans thought anyone who heard the mandrake's scream would die.

Deadly nightshade is also known as "belladonna" which means "beautiful lady". This is because women used to put the poison in their eyes to make their pupils (the black bits in the centre of the eye) bigger and more beautiful. *Don't* try this at home. Oddly enough, a tiny drop is used today to make a drug that widens the pupils during eye surgery.

BEAUTIFUL DEAD BEAUTIFUL DEAD

The poison curare comes from the bark and roots of the strychnos (strick-nos) tree. It's used by native Americans to tip their deadly arrows and it works in seconds. Oddly enough a little curare is used to relax a patient's muscles during operations on the guts.

And talking about poisonous plant drugs...

Hall of fame: William Withering (1741–1799)
Nationality: British

William was rich, bad-tempered and boring. Although he worked as a doctor his favourite hobby was botany. In 1776 he wrote a massive, boring book that described hundreds of species of British plants. (William's other hobbies were dog breeding and playing the flute – but they aren't relevant to our story.)

Naturally, William had lots of scientist pals. They all used to meet together on nights of the full moon and called themselves the Lunar Society. It was a sensible arrangement because they could all see their way home by the light of the moon but local people called them "lunar-tics" because of their odd ideas.

YOU'VE HEARD OF SUNDIALS – WELL, I'VE INVENTED A MOONDIAL

HE CALLS IT A 'LUNAR-TIC-TOC'

William had a few of these himself. He was convinced that the poison from foxgloves could cure the deadly disease dropsy. Foxglove is a pretty pink flower about 1.5 metres high. It was also known as "bloody man's fingers" and "dead man's bells". Why? Because foxglove is deadly poisonous. So how could a poison be a medicine? Here's the story of William's great discovery.

One day he visited an old woman who was sick with dropsy. "I'll be better soon," she cackled, "thanks to my secret herb tea."

William was too polite to say, "What a load of old rubbish – you're a gonner I fear, my dear."

But that's what he probably thought. After all, dropsy

was a very painful disease that made the lower body swell up to horrible proportions. There was no known cure.

But the next week the old woman was skipping about the house and getting on with a bit of spring cleaning. William was gobsmacked and insisted on buying some of the amazing tea for further study.

He found out that the active ingredient was foxglove leaves. Only a small bit, not enough to kill the person who drank it. So he tested foxglove tea on some of his patients. He noted one particular case of a retired builder with dropsy…

There were only two little difficulties...

1 People who took the treatment found their heartbeat very fast and they wanted to pee all the time.

2 If you took too much foxglove you died. One famous victim was the former prime minister Charles James Fox (1749–1806), who died after a cure went wrong. So you could say, "foiled physicians failed to fix Fox with foxgloves".

In 1785, William Withering wrote a book about the foxglove and doctors began to use it more and more. Today, a drug called digitalis which is made from foxgloves is used to treat people with a fluttering heart beat. And that's lucky 'cos you'll need to be in good heart for the next chapter. It's foul enough to set your pulse racing.

It really stinks...

FOUL FUNGI

Fungi aren't plants but they're as vile as the most gruesome greenery. In fact the only people who like fungi are gourmets who guzzle them and botanists who study them...

HAVE YOU FINISHED WITH IT YET? I'M STARVING!

So what do you think? Are fungi really that bad? Well, yes, they are. Read on and find out why...

Vicious veg fact file

NAME: Fungi

THE BASIC FACTS: 1 Fungi aren't real plants. They have no stems, no roots and they don't make food by photosynthesis.

2 Unlike plants they don't contain cellulose (that's the stuff in roughage, remember). Instead, they are made up of chitin (kitin). By some weird coincidence this is also the chemical that makes up insects' jaws.

THE VICIOUS DETAILS: Fungi feed by:

🍄 Sticking feeding tubes called hyphae into their food.

🍄 Making an acid that dissolves the food.

🍄 Sucking up the juices.

Sometimes the "food" is a living plant or animal.

Some plants fight back. If they sense the acid, they grow extra-thick roots or leaves so the hyphae can't break in.

Dare you discover ... how to grow your own fungi?

You will need:
A slice of white bread
A little water
A clear polythene bag

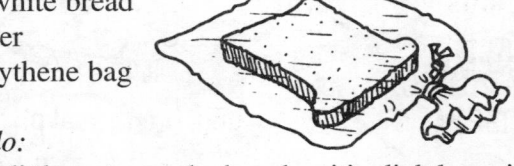

What you do:

1 Sprinkle a little water on the bread so it's slightly moist.

2 Place the bread in the bag and seal it tightly.

3 Leave the bread in a warm place for 2–3 days.

What do you notice?

If you're lucky you should find some grey-green fungi growing on the bread. Where do you think it came from?

a) The bread
b) The bag
c) The air in the bag

EVERYTHING YOU ALWAYS WANTED TO KNOW ABOUT FUNGI BUT WERE AFRAID TO ASK

1 Fungi spread by making spores that are just blobs made of single cells.

2 Many fungi grow the strange objects we call toadstools in order to spread the spores.

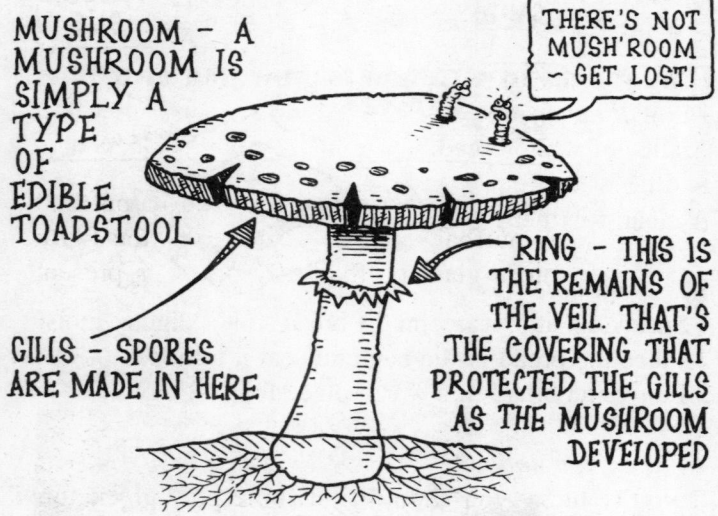

MUSHROOM – A MUSHROOM IS SIMPLY A TYPE OF EDIBLE TOADSTOOL

THERE'S NOT MUSH'ROOM – GET LOST!

GILLS – SPORES ARE MADE IN HERE

RING – THIS IS THE REMAINS OF THE VEIL. THAT'S THE COVERING THAT PROTECTED THE GILLS AS THE MUSHROOM DEVELOPED

3 Spores get everywhere. In fact, for each 0.76 cubic metres of air you're breathing at the moment there are at least 10,000 spores floating around. And they're tough. Just look at what they can survive…

- Boiling water
- Freezing
- Floating in the sea
- Floating in the air as high as a jet airliner

4 Fungi make huge amounts of spores. Some mushrooms produce 10,000,000,000 (ten thousand million) spores in a few days. But that's nothing... The giant puffball fungus can swell to 2.64 metres across. From a distance you could mistake it for a huge dead sheep. It makes 7,000,000,000,000 (seven trillion) spores in less than three months. If you don't believe me, just try counting them.

Scientists reckon that if every spore grew into a puffball and all the new puffballs' spores also grew – the Earth would swell into a giant puffball 800 times its present size! Luckily, in case you hadn't noticed, the Earth isn't like that because most spores don't grow. They end up in the wrong place or get eaten by various tiny creatures.

5 Fungi aren't fussy about what they have for lunch. Quite the opposite – they scoff everything and anything. Different species of fungi can digest:
• Petrol
• Cows droppings*
• Camera lenses
• Plastic
* This foul fungus allows its spores to blow over grass. Cows eat the grass and the spores come out with the droppings. And new fungi feast on the delicious dung.

Wonder if they could manage a school dinner...

6 Some vicious fungi catch and eat living animals. A species of underground fungi makes little hoops.

It also makes a chemical that encourages soil creatures called eel worms to wriggle into the hoop.

The hoop swells, trapping the eel worm. Hypahe grow into the victim's body and suck out the delicious juices.

COULD YOU BE A SCIENTIST?

You're out for a walk in the woods and you notice a fairy ring – that's a circle of toadstools. Can you work out how this circle came to be formed?

Clue – it wasn't planted by fairies.

AND IT WASN'T MADE FOR TOADS TO SIT ON

GOOD TO SEE YOU, BILL

YEAH, IT'S NICE TO HAVE A NATTER, JACK

a) The toadstools were planted by animals. The fact that they form a circle is a complete coincidence.

b) The fairy ring grew outwards as underground hyphae spread out from a single spore.

c) The fairy ring is growing inwards. The fungi can tell where each other are and they're trying to bunch together for protection.

Answer: b) The larger the ring the older the fungus. Bet you never knew the largest living thing on Earth is a fungus. In 2000 scientists found a honey mushroom fungus in Oregon, USA, that covered 890 hectares – that's larger than 824 football pitches! The humungous fungus was the largest lifeform on Earth and the stunned scientists reckoned it was 2,400 years old.

MAKES ME FEEL YOUNG!

Other anti-social fungi include:
- The stinker toadstool. Pongs like coal gas.
- The russula (rus-sel-a) fungus. Reeks of rotting fish.
- A species of boletus (bo-leet-us) fungus. A scientist said that one sickening whiff of this one made him throw up.

NOW WHAT WAS IT I READ...

ABOUT THIS TYPE OF BOLETUS...

AH YES, SPEW! I REMEMBER NOW

VICIOUS VEG EXPRESSIONS

YOU'RE SUFFERING FROM TINEA PEDIS (TIN-EAR PEE-DIS)

Is this fatal?

FOUL FUNGI – THE GOOD, THE BAD AND THE UGLY
THE GOOD

1 The fungus called "lawyer's wig" drips out its spores mixed with a black slime. This is a good source of ink and was once used by country people although it's a bit smelly.

2 Fly agaric toadstools were considered a good fly killer. A bit of skin from the toadstool was left in a saucer of milk. The flies drank the milk and died. But don't touch the fungus yourself because it's a good human-killer too.

3 Forty species of tropical fungi make good night lights. They use chemical reactions to glow after dark with an eerie blue-green light. They do this so that night-clubbing insects will spot them and spread their spores. It's quite a bright idea...

97

THE BAD

These fungi are dressed to kill…

1 The death cap toadstool

Kills 90 per cent of humans stupid enough to eat it. The poisons make the gut all blistered. It's no fun. The victim chucks up all the time until their body dries out, their liver swells up and their heart stops beating. If one of these turns up on your pizza RUN FOR IT!

2 Ergots

These little fungi grow on wet rye. Sound harmless enough, don't they? Er – no. Anyone who eats ergots suffers from a deadly condition called St Anthony's Fire. The effects include madness, throwing up and a burning pain in the bum. Their fingers and toes turn rotten and then drop off. Yep. One dose of that could spoil your whole day.*

* Don't panic – you won't find ergots lurking in your rye crispbread sandwich. Nowadays rye crops are treated with chemicals called fungicides to kill off the ergots.

THE UGLY

No fungus would win a beauty contest. But this lot could win an Oscar in a horror movie.

1 Dead man's foot

A brown lumpy fungus. It starts off below ground and works its way to the surface where it does a weird impression of a rotting human foot. It smells of mushrooms and, surprisingly, it doesn't taste too bad. Anyone fancy a nibble?

2 Dead man's fingers

Grows in the woods of Europe, North America and Asia. Clumps of black bloated objects poking out of the soil. Guess what they remind people of? Scientists reckon this fungus tastes as rotten as it looks. Well, you didn't expect it to be finger-lickin' good, did you?

3 The ox-tongue fungus

Grows on oak and chestnut trees in Europe, North America and Asia. Looks just like a tongue sticking out of a tree trunk. And guess what – if you cut it, red stuff dribbles out. Some brave people have tried the fungus and reported that it has a horrible sharp taste. So, I suppose you could call it a sharp-tongued fungus. Ha ha.

> **Bet you never knew!**
> But there's one fungus that has caused more deaths than the deadliest toadstool. Potato blight Phytophthora (fi-toff thaw-ra) and its favourite food (amazingly enough) is – potatoes. The fungus can turn a whole field of potatoes into a black stinking mess. Unfortunately, in Ireland in 1845 many people lived off potatoes and had little else to eat. So when the blight swept across Ireland around half a million people starved to death.

FOUL EDIBLE FUNGI

Things were so desperate during the Irish famine that the people ate stinging nettles, weeds and seaweed. Of course, there was something else they might have eaten. Fungi. After all, mushrooms are fungi, and some types can be quite a delicacy. Oh yes – it's true…

HORRIBLE HEALTH WARNING!

Don't eat any fungus you find growing in the wild unless:

a) You have a death wish.

b) You are keen to be driven mad – some fungi can have this effect.

c) You actually enjoy violent vomiting.

R.I.P
Here lies Simon, a 'fun guy' poisoned by fungi

FOUL FUNGAL FOODS

1 So you like mushroom soup? Better tuck in before you read this next bit. The term "mushroom" actually has no scientific meaning – it just means a fungus that you can eat. Growing in the dark and feeding on rotting manure is the ideal life for a mushroom.

2 Truffles are smelly underground fungi that look like lumps of coal. So it's strange to think that some people like to eat them. They're a real delicacy in posh restaurants. Truffles can sell for over £1,000 a kilogram. Truffles are traditionally dug up by pigs that eat the fungus and spread the spores in their droppings. But with prices like that the poor old pigs that sniff out truffles for restaurants probably never get to eat any.

3 Of course, some fungi fans will kill for a taste of their favourite fungi. Kill themselves, that is. Take false morel, for example. This is a horrible-looking fungus that looks like a lump of poo and grows in woods in Europe. It's actually poisonous but it can be eaten if it's first very thoroughly boiled to destroy the poisons. Don't try this at home, kids – for one thing, that poo-like lump you find may not actually be a fungus.

4 The plum and custard fungus grow on rotten old pine stumps. Sounds rather delicious, doesn't it? If you like plums and custard. In fact, the name doesn't come from its taste but from its yellow and plum colouring. And although it can be eaten this fungus tastes and smells like rotten old wood.

So you'd have to be as thick as a rotten plank to try it.

FOUR NOT-SO-FOUL FUNGI FACTS

Is your teacher a mycologist?*

* That's a scientist who studies fungi.

If so they might try to persuade you that fungi are really quite friendly and cuddly. And bamboozle you with facts like these:

1 Some fungi kill harmful bacteria. In 1928, Scottish scientist Alexander Fleming (1881–1955) noticed a fungus called penicillium (pe-ni-silli-um) growing on the special lab plates he'd used to grow bacteria on. The scientist had gone on holiday without cleaning the plates properly, and the fungus had killed the bacteria. (Don't get any ideas from this – leaving the washing up for a few weeks won't guarantee a major scientific discovery.)

2 Fleming discovered the fungus that made the germ-killing substance called penicillin. In the Second World War, Australian scientist Howard Florey (1898–1968, German-born Ernst Chain (1906–1979) and Norman Heatley (1911–2004) found out how to make the drug in large amounts. And US drugs companies made the penicillin that saved the lives of thousands of soldiers.

3 Fungi help plants. If fungi didn't eat dead wood the stuff would just pile up and get in the way of growing plants. That's because plants can't scoff wood – well, wooden you just know it! So the fungi take in valuable chemicals from the wood and, when the fungi die and rot, these chemicals can provide food for plants and animals.

4 Friendly fungi also feed plants more directly. About three-quarters of all plants have fungi clinging to their roots. These fungi – called mycorrhizae (my-cor-riz-y) – take in minerals and pass them on to the roots. In return they take some sugars from the roots. So it's fair exchange and everyone wins.

On that happy note let's look at some flowers. This is Horrible Science, of course, so the flowers in the next chapter aren't all pretty and sweet smelling. Some of them are hideously ugly and make such an appalling pong that you might want to throw up. So you'll need a clothes peg on your nose before you begin to read!

FIENDISH FLOWERS

There's something about flowers that make some humans go all gooey and soppy.

Or make up silly poems…

But the vicious truth is that no plant has ever made flowers in order to cheer up humans. The plants are keen to impress insects and other creatures for reasons you're about to find out. And these vicious vegetables are quite capable of using low-down dirty tricks to achieve their aim … pollination.

Vicious veg fact file

NAME: Pollination

THE BASIC FACTS: Pollination is how flowers make seeds. It's a straightforward job.

1 You make pollen in your flowers. See page 107 for the details.

2 You transfer some of your pollen to another plant of your species. OK so far?

3 Then the other plant makes seeds that grow into baby plants. Easy-peasy.

THE VICIOUS DETAILS: All this pollen flying about can give people a stinking dose of hay fever. See page 117 for the grisly details.

HOW'S THE HAY FEVER?

DOT DOO BAD

FLOWERS – THE INSIDE STORY

1 The easiest way for a plant to spread pollen around is to let the wind blow it away. Plants such as grasses and willow trees grow big feathery bits called stigmas to catch the pollen and dangle them out of their flowers.

2 Most flowering plants use animals to take their pollen from one plant to another. But first they need to grab the animal's attention. And for this they need PUBLICITY. Yes, we're talking about razzmatazz – flowers, colours, perfumes – the works!

3 Next they need sticky nectar to feed the animals. I mean, they're not going to shift pollen out of the goodness of their little hearts, are they?

4 Plants employ a surprising range of creatures. There are flies, beetles, hummingbirds, bats – yes, bats. (Some tropical flowers open at night so bats can pollinate them.)

5 To show how it actually works we took this cute little flower…

and hacked it in half…

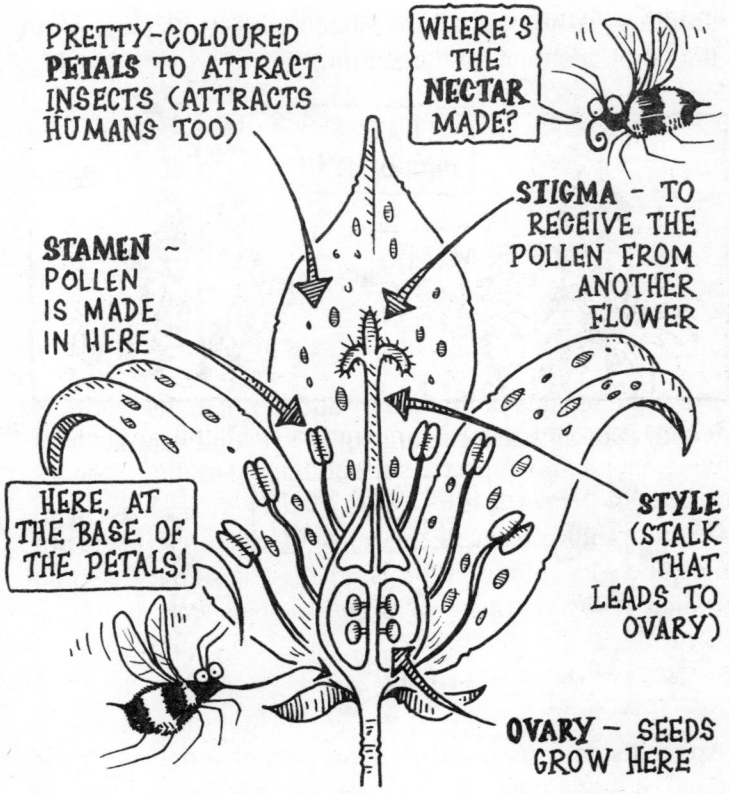

PRETTY-COLOURED **PETALS** TO ATTRACT INSECTS (ATTRACTS HUMANS TOO)

WHERE'S THE **NECTAR** MADE?

STIGMA - TO RECEIVE THE POLLEN FROM ANOTHER FLOWER

STAMEN ~ POLLEN IS MADE IN HERE

HERE, AT THE BASE OF THE PETALS!

STYLE (STALK THAT LEADS TO OVARY)

OVARY ~ SEEDS GROW HERE

But hold on – why do plants go to all this bother?

WHY DON'T PLANTS GO IN FOR DIY POLLINATION?

Yes. Why don't plants just pollinate themselves? In fact, some flowers do and yes, it really is much less fuss. But it's much better to get another plant involved. Here's why...

Pollen and the ovary cells contain chemical codes known as genes that tell the seedlings how to grow and what features to develop. If a plant pollinated itself its seedlings would get all the same codes as its parents, so they'd be identical to the parent.

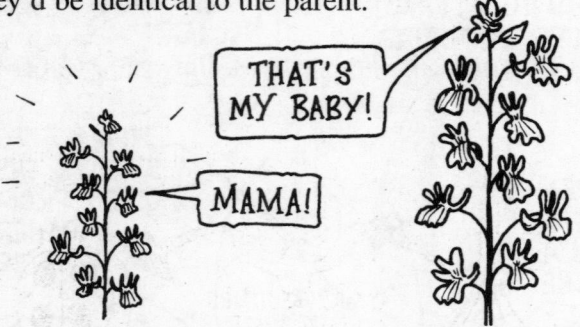

But if the plant is pollinated by another plant its seedlings would take on some features of the second parent.

And in the vicious world of plants a bit of variety is a good thing. It might mean, for example, your seedlings grow up with some vital feature like a few sharp spikes or a deadlier poison to help keep those peckish rabbits at bay.

HOW TO POLLINATE A PLANT IN THREE EASY STAGES

Each species of plant makes pollen grains with a unique code on the outside. The code is made up of a substance called protein. The plant's genes programme their stigmas to sense this code and some plants can even reject their own pollen grains. They only allow pollen grains from another plant of the same species to develop. Now is that clever or what?

Next…

1 A little tube grows from the pollen grain and down into the ovary of the flower.

2 A cell from the pollen grain joins up with a cell from the ovary to make a single extra-large cell.

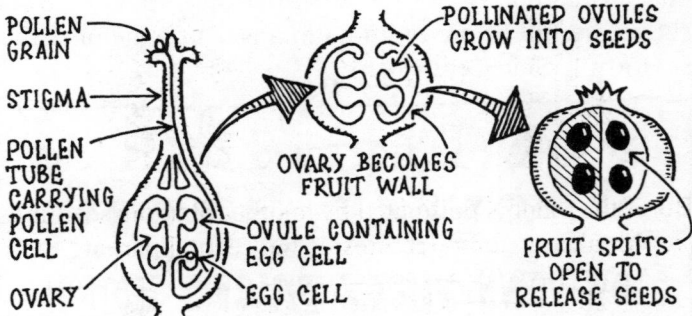

POLLEN GRAIN

STIGMA

POLLEN TUBE CARRYING POLLEN CELL

OVARY

OVULE CONTAINING EGG CELL

EGG CELL

OVARY BECOMES FRUIT WALL

POLLINATED OVULES GROW INTO SEEDS

FRUIT SPLITS OPEN TO RELEASE SEEDS

3 This splits many times to make the seeds of the plant. Clever innit?

Bet you never knew!
1 You can't rely on insects. More often than not those brainless bugs take pollen to another species of flower. In order to make seeds, pollen has to go to a flower belonging to its own species.
2 That's why many species of flowers sign up a type of insect for an exclusive deal. Their flowers are designed so only this particular insect can visit them. That way the plant can be 100 per cent sure its pollen will go to the right kind of flower! For example, one species of orchid from Madagascar has a flower 46 cm deep. And the nectar at the bottom can only be reached by a rare species of hawk moth with an unusually long tongue.

Of course, the moth will then fly on to find another orchid of the same species.

But plants use plenty more vicious tricks to get pollinated. As you're about to find out. Here are a load of flowers that are definitely not to be sniffed at. Normal flower shows are full of pretty little blooms. But remember this is Horrible Science…

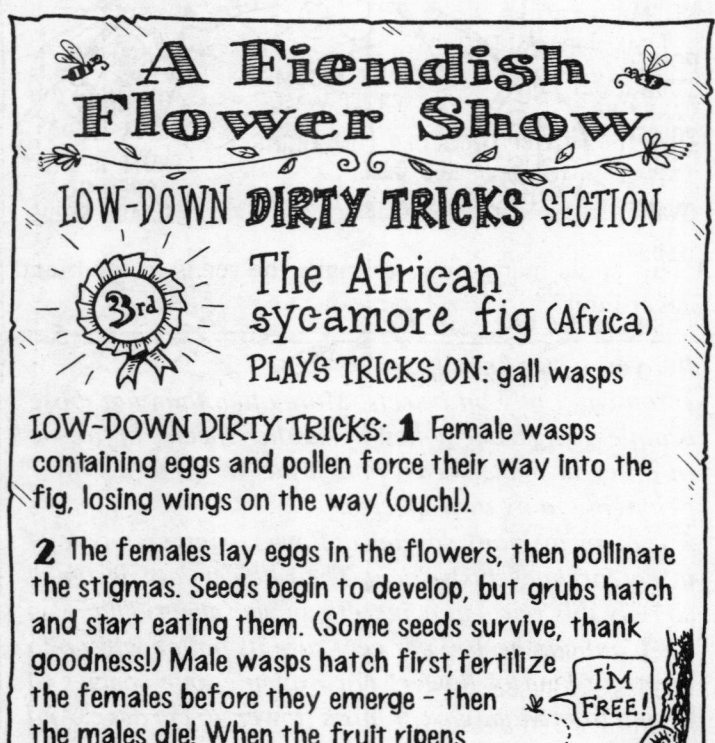

A Fiendish Flower Show

LOW-DOWN DIRTY TRICKS SECTION

3rd

The African sycamore fig (Africa)

PLAYS TRICKS ON: gall wasps

LOW-DOWN DIRTY TRICKS: **1** Female wasps containing eggs and pollen force their way into the fig, losing wings on the way (ouch!).

2 The females lay eggs in the flowers, then pollinate the stigmas. Seeds begin to develop, but grubs hatch and start eating them. (Some seeds survive, thank goodness!) Male wasps hatch first, fertilize the females before they emerge – then the males die! When the fruit ripens the female wasps escape, collecting pollen on the way to take to the next fig flower. Then it all starts again.

I'M FREE!

The mirror orchid
(Western Mediterranean)

PLAYS TRICKS ON:
bees

LOW-DOWN DIRTY TRICKS:

1 The flower fools male bees into thinking it's a female bee. It looks like a female bee and even smells like one.

2 The male bee tries to give the flower a cuddle. The stamens swoop down and whack a blob of pollen on the male bee's head.

3 The bewildered bee flies off in search of another female, and usually ends up taking pollen to another mirror orchid.

111

Dead horse arum
(Mediterranean islands)

PLAYS TRICKS ON: blow flies

LOW-DOWN DIRTY TRICKS:

1 Looks just like rotten meat. Makes a realistic stink so flies think they can lay their eggs inside it. Even provides a hole for them to explore what looks horribly like an empty eye socket.

2 Doesn't lay on food for the fly grubs when they hatch out. So they starve to death.

GET STUCK IN, KIDS

ROTTING MEAT STENCH

3 Traps the female flies in the flower until its stigmas pick up any pollen the flies might be carrying. Many flies die of suffocation inside the fiendish flower. (To be fair the flower does give them some nectar to drink.)

4 Flower only lets the flies out when they've been dusted with pollen. Ready to take to the next dead horse arum.

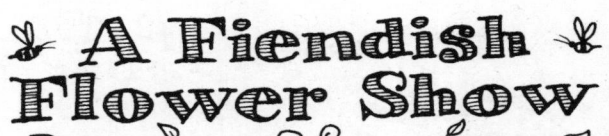

A Fiendish Flower Show

FREAKY FLOWERS SECTION

DON'T LIKE THE COLOUR MUCH

WHY DO I BOTHER?

Puya plant
(Bolivia, South America)

3rd

APPEARANCE: Huge head of flowers – the largest in the world. It can measure up to 10 metres across.

FREAKY FEATURES: Takes 150 years to grow to the stage where it makes flowers. Then it dies. Makes you wonder why the peculiar puya plant bothers.

2nd

Rafflesia (otherwise known as the "stinking corpse lily") (Borneo, Indonesia)

APPEARANCE: Giant orange cabbage-shaped flower up to one metre across. The first European to find it,

Sir Thomas Raffles (1781–1826), called it:

THE LARGEST AND MOST MAGNIFICENT FLOWER IN THE WORLD

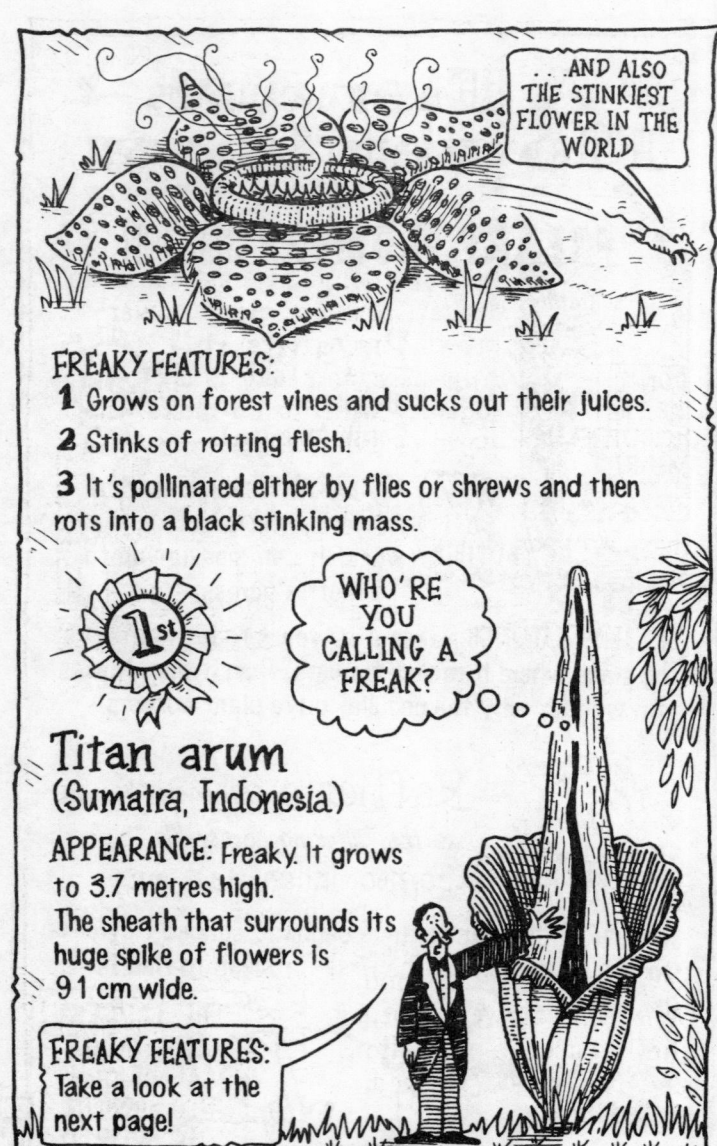

...AND ALSO THE STINKIEST FLOWER IN THE WORLD

FREAKY FEATURES:

1 Grows on forest vines and sucks out their juices.

2 Stinks of rotting flesh.

3 It's pollinated either by flies or shrews and then rots into a black stinking mass.

1st

WHO'RE YOU CALLING A FREAK?

Titan arum
(Sumatra, Indonesia)

APPEARANCE: Freaky. It grows to 3.7 metres high.
The sheath that surrounds its huge spike of flowers is 91 cm wide.

FREAKY FEATURES: Take a look at the next page!

THE TERRIBLE TITAN

BELLISIMO!

In 1878 Italian botanist Odoardo Beccari found a giant flower growing in a forest.

His assistants dug it up together with its 1.5-metre-wide corm or swollen root.

Unfortunately, they dropped the heavy plant. The corm was full of vegetable fat. It splattered everywhere and started to rot.

SPLOOSH!

Eventually Odoardo was able to send some titan arum seeds to Italy and one of the young plants that grew from the seeds ended up at Kew Gardens in London. When the flowers opened they caused a sensation and thousands flocked to see them. . .

SEEDS! WHY DIDN'T I THINK OF THAT SOONER?

THE KEW TIMES
— 22 June 1887 —

What a blooming stink!

Sightseers at Kew to see the titan arum were greeted by a gobsmacking stench from the fiendish flower. Said one visitor, "Phwoar - what a foul stink, worse than a pig farm it was."

Several ladies needed first aid because of the revolting reek. The sickening smell is described as being like rotten fish and burnt sugar mixed together. A

botanist working in the gardens said, "The flowers are pollinated by beetles that eat rotting flesh. The beetles think the smell is heavenly.

I can't say that I agree, in fact I've got to dash. . ."

Artist Matilda Smith (1854–1926) had the unenviable job of painting the flower from close quarters. She nearly passed out from the horrible stench. Still, it could have been worse. She might have had hay fever too.

HORRIBLE HAY FEVER

In the summer pollen gets everywhere. Wind-blown pollen has tiny air bags attached so it can fly really well. Some grains of pollen are blown 4,800 km by the wind and float 5,800 metres into the air. Oh, so you know all about that? Well, if so, chances are you suffer from hay fever. You know the signs. Watery eyes, runny nose, sneezing. It's like having a bad cold all summer long. So, who's to blame?

Well, plants obviously, because they make pollen. But it's your own body that causes the nasty effects of hay fever. When a grain of pollen floats up your nose it often sticks there. S'not fair, is it?

In a hay fever sufferer, the body sends chemicals called histamines (hiss-ta-meens) to fight off the intruder. Unfortunately, they make the area feel horribly sore and that's hay fever.

Mind you, by the end of the summer it's all over. No more smelly flowers and pesky pollen for another year. Hooray! But the plants are still hard at work. You'll have to turn to the next chapter to find out what they're up to.

SPROUTING SEEDS AND ROTTING FRUITS

Did you know the word fruit means "enjoy" in Latin – that's the old Roman language. Yep, the Romans liked a nice bit of fruit.

But you might think fruit tastes rotten and you'd rather wear a cactus in your pants than eat a school dinner fruit salad.

Cheer up, though, because with the help of some of the facts in this chapter, you might be able to argue your way out of ever having to eat another apple again!

Vicious veg fact file

NAME: Fruits and seeds

THE BASIC FACTS: **1** Fruits and seeds are designed with one aim. To make sure the seedlings of a plant grow a distance away from the parent plant. That way they won't be fighting each other for light or water.

2 Seeds come in all shapes and sizes from orchid seeds that weigh 1 millionth of a gram to the 18 kg double coconut, which is also, amazingly, a seed.

THE VICIOUS DETAILS: Unripe fruits taste disgusting. That's the plant's way of making sure animals don't scoff the fruit before they're ripe. Some unripe fruit is even poisonous. Any animal that eats it will end up dead sorry. Well, mostly dead, actually.

> P'RHAPS I'LL LEAVE THEM FOR A FEW MORE DAYS

SEED SECRETS
1 The inside story
A seed is like a space capsule filled with everything a plant needs to survive. Take this harmless little broad bean, for example…

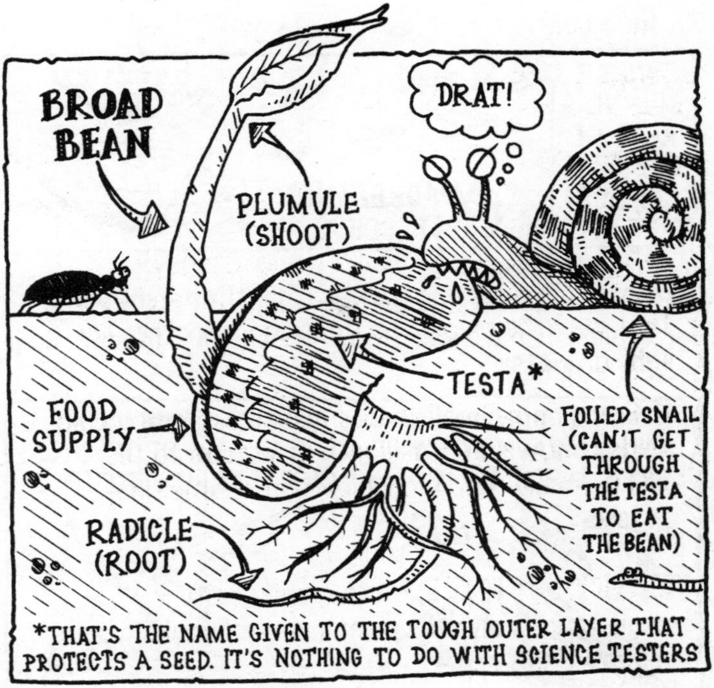

BROAD BEAN

PLUMULE (SHOOT)

DRAT!

FOOD SUPPLY

TESTA*

RADICLE (ROOT)

FOILED SNAIL (CAN'T GET THROUGH THE TESTA TO EAT THE BEAN)

*THAT'S THE NAME GIVEN TO THE TOUGH OUTER LAYER THAT PROTECTS A SEED. IT'S NOTHING TO DO WITH SCIENCE TESTERS

2 Get moving

Plants use loads of viciously ingenious methods to shift seeds. Here are just a few of them:

a) The wind. Some plants give their seeds little parachutes to help them fly. Like dandelion seeds...

BYE MUM!

WHEE!

Or little helicopter wings...

b) Creature comforts

Animals are always on the move and always hungry. So for a plant it makes sense to get animals to shift their seeds for them.

The seeds need a nice thick testa. That'll protect them from acid juices in the animal's guts.

VICIOUS VEG EXPRESSIONS

Did she say germs ate it?

STRANGE SEED STORIES QUIZ

TRUE or FALSE?

1 As the Mediterranean squirting cucumber ripens it makes more and more slimy juice until it explodes. TRUE/FALSE

2 The sharp hooks of the grapple plant seeds stick into an elephant's foot. They only fall off after the hook has been worn out by being walked on for quite a distance. For the elephant this vicious plant is a jumbo-sized problem. TRUE/FALSE

3 But elephants actually help protect acacia tree seeds from beetles by eating the seeds. TRUE/FALSE

4 Deadly nightshade berries kill the animal that eats them and the vicious seedling grows out of the dead animal's body. TRUE/FALSE

5 Australian mistletoe seeds are spread by a bird wiping its bum on a tree. TRUE/FALSE

123

6 The South American hura tree is known as the monkey's dinner bell because of its bell-shaped seeds. Monkeys love to eat them for dinner. TRUE/FALSE

7 Mangrove seeds fall downwards like spears. (That's why it's not a good idea to have a kip under a mangrove tree.) TRUE/FALSE

THEY HANG DOWN... LIKE GREEN SPEARS. I JUST DON'T SEE... THE POINT OF IT – UGH!

Answers:

1 TRUE. It splatters slimy juice and seeds everywhere. Guaranteed to liven up any school dinner.

2 TRUE. Then the seeds germinate and the elephant is left hopping mad.

3 TRUE. Beetles break into the pods and seed capsules and guzzle the seeds. If an elephant eats the pods the seeds survive but the beetles get digested.

4 FALSE.

5 TRUE. Australian mistletoe is a plant that grows on trees. It makes very sticky berries. The mistletoe bird eats the berries and gets rid of the seeds in their poo. But the seeds are also sticky – and they get glued to the bird's bum. So the bird wipes its bum on a tree (no – they don't use toilet paper). The seed sticks to the tree and that's just where the seedling wants to grow. You might like to explain these disgusting details when someone you don't like wants to kiss you under the mistletoe at Christmas.

6 FALSE. The name comes from the popping noise made by the seed cases as they dry up and pop open to scatter the seeds. Which is odd because the sound is like pistol shots and often scares travellers. And it's nothing like a dinner bell.

7 TRUE. Mangrove trees grow on muddy shorelines. The seeds are joined to green spikes and germinate on the tree. Then the spikes fall into the mud below. Roots quickly anchor the spike in the mud and a new tree starts to grow. If the tide is in, the spike floats away like a little boat for an exciting ocean cruise – in search of a new place to grow.

Bet you never knew!
Orchids make tons of seeds. The European spotted orchid, for example, produces 186,000 seeds from a single plant. Naturalist Charles Darwin worked out that if all these seeds germinated, within three generations orchids would cover the Earth.

But most plant seeds fall in the wrong places or get eaten by birds or bugs.

This old rhyme says it all...

Sow four grains in a row
One for the pigeon
One for the crow
One to rot and another to grow

Mind you, seeds are useful to people in unexpected ways...

BETTER STICK TO THE JOB

Swiss inventor George de Mestral had a problem. Ever since the zip on his wife's dress broke just as they were going out he'd been trying to invent a new kind of fastening.

WE'LL USE TAPE TILL I THINK OF SOMETHING BETTER

One day in 1950 George was out for a walk with his dog. He noticed the animal's ears were covered in seeds. They were burdock seeds. They stuck to the dog because they were covered with tiny hooks that clung to the animal's hair. This gave George the seeds of an idea.

YOU'RE A GENIUS, BONZO!

For the next eight years George worked out how to make a fastening based on the burdock. At last, with the help of industrialist Jakob Müller he made a breakthrough.

Together they came up with two strips of nylon. One

strip was coated with tiny hooks and the other with tiny loops. And the name of this new product was Velcro. Today it's used for fastenings on spacesuits and you might even have some on your clothes.

FRIGHTFULLY FRUITFUL FRUITS

People tend to muddle up fruit and veg. Some think all fruit is sweet and veg isn't and that's the way you can tell the difference. But they're wrong. Not all fruits are sweet tasting. Some fruits taste savoury and some are disgustingly sour.

So let's ask a botanist to make things clear...

A FRUIT FORMS FROM THE SWOLLEN OVARY SURROUNDING THE SEEDS.

EH?

Well, the ovary was the bit in the flower that's at the base of the style – take a look at page 107 if you don't remember. After the flower is pollinated the seeds start to form and the ovary swells up around them. Make sense so far? So to be a proper fruit and not just a common or garden vegetable, whatever you're eating had to have started off as the ovary of a flower.

TEST YOUR GREENGROCER*

* If you don't know any greengrocers you could ask your teacher instead.

Which of the following are fruits?

1 CUCUMBER

2 TOMATO

3 GREEN PEPPER

4 PEANUT

6 STRAWBERRY

5 PINEAPPLE

7 RHUBARB

IF YOU EAT IT FOR PUDDING IT'S A FRUIT!

(TEACHER – RED AS A TOMATO)

NOT NECESSARILY

(GREENGROCER – COOL AS A CUCUMBER)

Answers:

Fruits: 1, 2, 3, 4. According to scientists all nuts are fruits. Of course, if you were cruel you might say that some scientists are nuts.

Not fruits: 5 A pineapple forms from several parts of a large number of flowers. This means that scientifically speaking, a pineapple is not a fruit because it doesn't develop from a single ovary.

6 Strawberries also form from several parts of the flower. The fruits are actually the tiny pips on the sides of the strawberry.

7 Rhubarb is the cooked stalk of the rhubarb plant so it's nothing to do with fruits.

VICIOUS VEG EXPRESSIONS

Have all these scientists gone raving mad?

Answers:
Probably not.

1 A pome is a juicy fruit like an apple with a core at the centre containing seeds. Just try biting into one and you'll see it's true.

2 A drupe is a juicy fruit like a peach with a hard seed or stone at the centre.

3 A berry is a fruit with many seeds – examples include grapes and (can you believe it?) tomatoes.

4 Those other words are scientific names for different parts of a fruit.

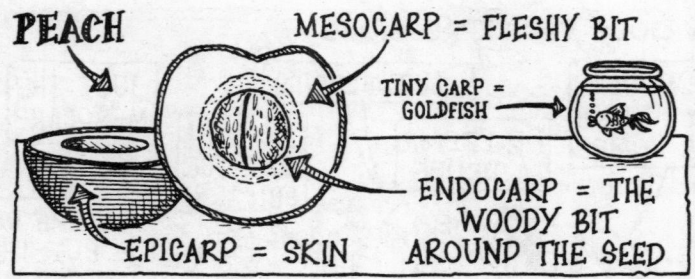

PEACH

MESOCARP = FLESHY BIT

TINY CARP = GOLDFISH

ENDOCARP = THE WOODY BIT AROUND THE SEED

EPICARP = SKIN

Now, you might think that fruits are healthy and harmless. Tasty, even. Surely there's nothing vicious about a banana, is there? But believe it or not, people have fought and even died for fruits. Take the breadfruit for example. The what? No, I didn't make that up. Read on and discover the whole rotten story.

A breadfruit is a green fruit about 20–30 cm across. It has a bland rather boring taste but you can cook it in loads of interesting ways – roasting and frying and boiling it in lots of mouth-watering recipes. And best of all, it's cheap and easy to grow.

Too easy. In the eighteenth century the West Indies was full of slaves who were cruelly forced to grow sugar and tobacco for their wealthy masters. And the masters hatched a vicious plan to save money by feeding their slaves on cheap breadfruit. But first they had to get some plants from Tahiti where they grow.

The slave masters asked for help from Sir Joseph Banks (1744–1820), the boss of Britain's Kew Gardens. Sir Joseph asked the government to provide a ship, HMS *Bounty*, and hired William Bligh (1754–1817) as its captain. Then he hired a young botanist called David Nelson to collect the breadfruit trees. Here's how David Nelson might have described the voyage in his letters to Sir Joseph Banks…

A fruitless journey

The Bounty, off Tasmania, 20 August 1788

Dear Sir Joseph

I hope this letter reaches you safely. The voyage has been BRILLIANT so far. Thank you for sending me and thank you for sending your gardener William Brown to help me. We get on really well. Today we both went ashore and found some new species of plants which I look forward to showing you on my return.

But I'm afraid things aren't going so well between Captain Bligh and his officers. They have spent the whole voyage so far squabbling and bickering. They argue over accounts, supplies - every tiny detail to do with the ship. I don't blame the captain for these rows. Sure Bligh's got a really bad temper and he sometimes yells and curses at his officers. But someone's got to be in command. Anyway, I'm sure everything will be fine when we get to Tahiti.

Squabble! .. Bicker! ..

Yours faithfully
David Nelson

Tahiti ~ 3 April 1789
Dear Sir Joseph
It's been work, work, work
ever since we arrived. I've
been collecting breadfruit
seeds, planting them and
then loading them on the
ship. Thank goodness my
friend Will is there to help. Matter of fact
he's just watering the plants now. It's
back-breaking work and he sometimes has a
good grumble but he's a hard worker and we've
become good friends.

MY CHUM

The crew are having the time of their
lives on Tahiti. The people here are so
friendly it's like one long party.
But I spend all my time looking
after the plants. Anyway, we're setting
sail for home now. See you in about nine months!

Yours faithfully
David Nelson

Somewhere in the Pacific Ocean
26 May 1789
Dear Sir Joseph
Sorry about the shaky writing. I'm
writing this in the corner of a small boat.
The boat is rolling and pitching in the waves.

Four weeks ago I was woken at the crack of dawn by three grim-faced crew members.

"What's going on?" I cried.

"We're taking over the ship," one of them sneered. "We're going back to Tahiti."

"Yeah," agreed another, "and then we'll have some fun like we did before."

They were all laughing as they dragged me up on deck.

On the deck everything was in chaos. Captain Bligh was tied to the mast. He was shouting like crazy – he was so angry. And some of the crew were arguing and swearing.

I saw William Brown.

"Help me, Will!" I cried. He just gave a nasty smile.

W.B.

And that's how I found out. Sir Joseph, I'm sorry to say your gardener, and my so-called friend, William Brown has joined the mutiny. How could he?

I said, "What about the breadfruit, Will?" He stuck his face up close to mine. "I'm sick of those plants," he hissed. "And the crew hate them too 'cos they've been going thirsty. All so there's enough water for your precious breadfruit. Well, now

we're going to chuck them all overboard,"
All my lovely plants. What a waste of
everything – I could have wept.
And that's how I came to be in
this tiny boat. The rebel crew
members forced me, the Captain
and the Captain's friends into the
boat and set us adrift. There are
nineteen of us. We spend all day
bailing water to stop the boat
from sinking.

Food is running short. We
share a morsel of bread each
day. Oh, and there's a tiny slice
of bread fruit for afters.
I will try and write again.
If I live.
Yours faithfully
David Nelson

Somewhere off the coast of Australia
4 June 1789
Dear Sir Joseph
I feel you or someone should know what has
become of us. Of course, I know it's quite
likely that this letter will never reach you.
But I will write it anyway just in case.
We are still in the boat. And I feel sick and

very, very tired. At least my knowledge of plants has come in handy. When we land on deserted islands I search out the plants that are safe to eat. This makes a change from eating that disgusting breadfruit all the time. Then we set off again searching for a settlement with people who can help us.

I can't believe it – Captain Bligh is still quarrelling with the two officers who came with us in the boat. I blame the Captain for this mess. He just can't deal with people. We don't even have a map. All we've got is Captain Bligh's pocket compass. He says he knows which course to steer but the rest of us aren't so sure.

Bligh (the blighter)

I feel awful and fear I won't make it. I'm badly sunburned and I'm terribly weak. My feet and legs are all swollen from being cramped in this boat. Some times I feel like going to sleep and not waking up. Will we all die here in this boat?

I don't want to die.

David

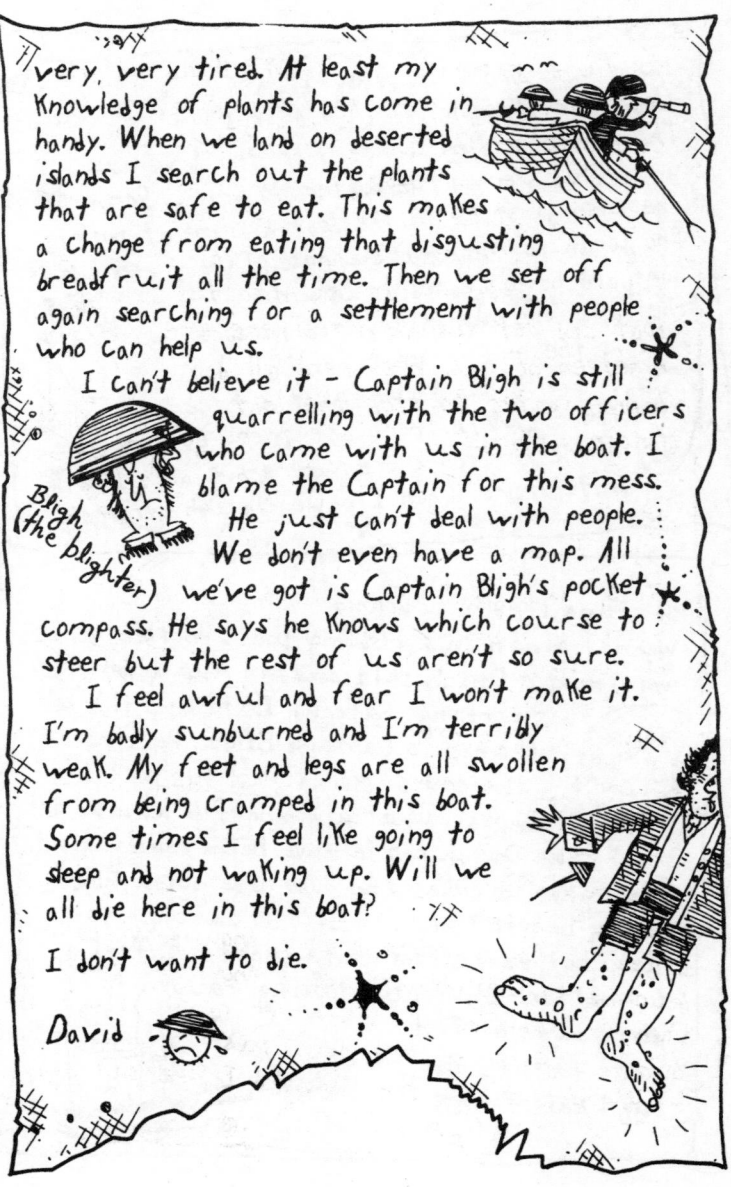

12 June 1789
Dear Sir Joseph
Things are getting worse. For ten days now
we've had very little water to drink. Some of
the men just lie in the boat staring at nothing.
Too weak to move, I suppose. I've given up
hope and have ceased to count
the days. My body is covered in sores.
This is the end.

        Hold on. We've just sighted land!
Yes - LAND! There are trees everywhere.
We're not too sure where we are. I will
write more when I have enough strength.

14 June 1789 ~ Coupang
We met a man in a fishing boat. He told us we
were near a Dutch settlement! And we arrived
this morning. Safe at last! And it's all
thanks to Captain Bligh. He steered
the course using just his pocket
compass. What a wonderful man he is!
Bligh (my hero)
    The Dutch people have been really kind.
They gave us cakes and now I've got a nice
comfy bed to sleep in. It's so amazing to
sleep between clean white sheets. I feel a
lot better. I'm really looking forward to
going home at last.   HOME!
Yours faithfully
David Nelson

136

A PAINFUL POSTSCRIPT

Don't read this bit unless you *like* unhappy endings. Sadly, David wasn't completely better. He went out looking for plants and caught a fever. He died a few days later. William Bligh said:

THE LOSS OF THIS HONEST MAN I VERY MUCH LAMENTED

In 1792 Bligh returned to Tahiti and fetched a new load of breadfruit. Although this time he reached the West Indies his mission was fruitless. The slaves didn't like the fruit and fed it to their pigs. It took years for breadfruit to become as popular a food in the West Indies as it still is in Tahiti today.

Bet you never knew!
The soil is full of seeds. Lurking under every 0.84 square metre of garden lawn there are around 30,000 seeds waiting to burst out of their capsules and grow into adult plants.

Now most seeds grow into weeds but some make useful plants that we can eat or make things from. They are the vital vegetables. Yes, it's time to get your teeth into those greens.

EAT UP IF YOU WANT TO BE BIG AND STRONG LIKE YOUR FATHER

VITAL VEG

We can't live without plants. Without plants there would be no oxygen for us to breathe and nothing to eat. If that wasn't bad enough, life would be much harder in loads of other unexpected ways because plants have strange and unusual uses. Yes, they're even more vital than you might think. And plants pop up all over the place...

Take school dinners for example.

SCHOOL DINNER VEG - THE TERRIBLE TRUTH

You probably don't know it, but the vile vegetables served up in your school dinner have some interesting tales to tell.

1 Odious onions

In the Middle Ages one writer on herbs claimed (wrongly) that eating onions was bad for you:

IT CAUSETH HEADACHE, HURTETH THE EYES AND... DULLETH THE WITS.

Onions make you cry because they contain sulphur-based substances. When you cut an onion, chemical reactions release an irritating gas. The ghastly gas stings your eyes and you cry to wash away the stinging stuff. Afterwards you look more cut up than the onion.

Onions are swollen leaf bases. The onion stores starch to help it grow the following year. In fact, lots of vegetables do this. Examples on your dinner plate include carrots, potatoes and parsnips. Of course, humans regularly spoil the plants' plans by gobbling them up.

2 Crunchy carrots

WILD COLOUR (OK, YOU'LL HAVE TO IMAGINE THIS.)

CRUNCHY SOAP SUDS FLAVOUR

Originally, carrots were a rather tasteful white or purple – that's the colour of wild carrots. Scientists reckon the orange carrots we crunch today were developed in the Netherlands about 500 years ago. From there settlers and explorers took them all over the world.

3 Chewy cabbage

Cabbage probably isn't your favourite veg, but we're lucky today 'cos it used to taste even worse! Wild cabbage is bitter and leathery and grows naturally in Europe. But modern cabbages have been bred to produce juicier and more tender leaves. (Unless they're school dinner cabbages, of course.)

5 Boring baked beans

Yes, baked beans start off as plants. Baked beans are made from American haricot beans, which are actually seeds. The sauce is made from three more plants:

tomatoes, sugar from sugar-cane, and cornflour from ground-up maize. In 1997 scientists were planning to test new kinds of bean that don't make you fart. But so far we haven't heard anything of the results.

6 Revolting rhubarb

Fancy some rhubarb for pudding? Rhubarb grows well when there's lots of manure in the soil. That's why country people used to tip their chamber pots over their rhubarb plants. This *probably* doesn't happen to your school rhubarb. One species of rhubarb *not* usually used in school dinners has a strong laxative effect. That means it makes you poo – three spoonfuls will clean out your insides!

SINISTER SALAD BARS

Out of about 380,000 plants around 80,000 are edible. Humans normally only eat about 3,000 plants. But nowadays people have a taste for unusual plants. They're even served in posh restaurants ... are you ready to order?

The Peculiar Plant Pantry

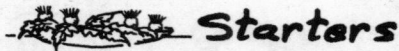 **Starters**

GRATED BETEL NUT MIXED WITH LIME

As chewed in many parts of East Asia.
Delicious flavour helps to wake you up.

IMPORTANT NOTE TO PATRONS

Don't eat too many. Juice makes your breath stink, turns
your teeth black and stains your mouth dark red. You can
spit out your starter in the spittoons provided.

~

DELICIOUS DANDELION AND THISTLE SALAD

A crunchy green salad of dew-fresh dandelion
leaves and boiled thistle shoots. (Don't worry
we've cut all the prickles off – hopefully.)

IMPORTANT NOTE TO PATRONS

Don't eat too many dandelion leaves. They make you pee.
Which explains their charming old name of "wet-a-bed".

~

FRESH STEAMING STINGING NETTLE SOUP

Made with real stinging nettles. Tasty tender
young nettle tops simmered with fried potato
and onion. Full of vitamins and flavour. It's cheap
so it won't sting your pocket either.

Main course
INUIT LICHEN LUNCH

Tender lichens served nice and warm. It's tender
because it's half-digested and cut from a
freshly-killed reindeer's stomach. This is a
traditional delicacy enjoyed by the Inuit people.

IMPORTANT NOTE TO PATRONS
Don't eat too much. It makes you constipated (unable
to produce poo).

Optional side dish
LUXURIOUS LAVER

That's a type of British seaweed that's scraped
off the rocks and boiled with a little vinegar
(optional). Steaming hot and black and slimy –
just make sure you clean your teeth afterwards!

Pudding
DELICIOUS DURIAN FRUIT SALAD

Orangutans love it. Freshly picked in the forests
of Sumatra, Indonesia.

IMPORTANT NOTE TO PATRONS
Don't be put off by the revolting smell of rotten fish and
sewage. Durians are banned in some hotels and on planes
because of their vile smell.

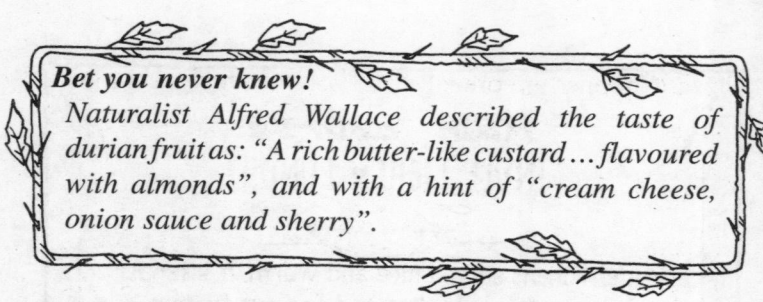
HELPFUL AND HORRIBLE HERBS

What have vanilla ice cream, ginger biscuits and pizza got in common? Yes, I know you'd love to guzzle them all. But they also all include herbs or spices that come from plants.

Ice cream. Vanilla from a dried orchid fruit that grows in America.

Ginger biscuits. Ginger is the roots of a plant from South-East Asia.

144

Pizza. Chopped up oregano and basil leaves. Delicious!

Herbs are pleasant-smelling plants that you can use in cooking or use to make perfumes. Spices are strong-smelling plants used solely in cooking. Here are a few interesting specimens…

1 Tarragon is a herb used to flavour tartar sauce, which is normally eaten with fish. The name means "little dragon" in Latin because people wrongly believed the herb was an antidote for snake bite.

2 The herb saffron is used to flavour rice and give it an interesting yellow colour. It's made from the stigmas of a type of crocus. Saffron has always been expensive because in order to make 1 kg of saffron you've got to pick up to 400,000 flowers.

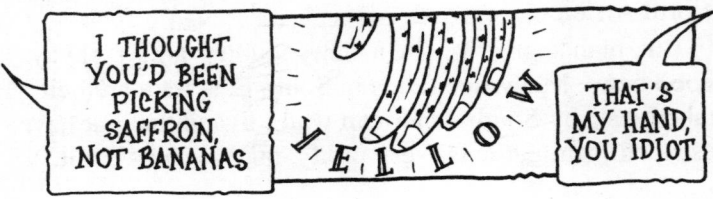

In fifteenth-century Germany two merchants were burned to death for secretly mixing cheaper ingredients with the saffron they sold.

3 Asafoetida (a-sa-fet-tida) is a spice made from the juice of a type of fennel plant from the Middle East. It stinks of rotten garlic but luckily when you cook it the smell disappears and all you're left with is a mild onion-like taste. So that's all right then.

A MOVING STORY...

Humans have changed the plant world for ever. They've moved plants all over the planet to suit their ends. Just think of all that breadfruit sailing off to the West Indies. Many of the vegetables and fruit we eat originally came from many different places around the world.

Scientists reckon cherries first grew in Armenia and peaches first grew in China. Just go into any garden and you might spot fuchsias from South America, wisteria from China, azaleas from the Himalayas and tulips from North Africa.

But plants growing in a new country aren't always good news. Many rice fields in South East Asia are being taken over by South American water hyacinths that have escaped from gardens. Very pretty, but we can't eat it.

TEACHER'S TEA BREAK TEASER

Tap gently on the staffroom door. When it creaks open, smile sweetly and say:

EXCUSE ME, I WAS JUST WONDERING WHERE TEA GREW FIRST?

HUH?

Answers:

Tea plants grew wild in Tibet but it was first grown as a crop in China before 2737 BC. At first tea was grown as medicine until people realized it might make a nice morning cuppa. If you're feeling particularly heartless you could add...

1 That in Tibet people enjoy tea with rancid yaks' milk.

2 According to an old legend, a Buddhist monk cut off his own eyelids in a bid to stay awake as he meditated. The eyelids sprouted into tea bushes. Weird.

But there's more to plants than food and drink. Some plants are special. They're so vital and useful that sometimes whole groups of people have centred their lifestyles around them. Take bamboo, for example. Just imagine you lived in the southern region of ancient China...

My day at school

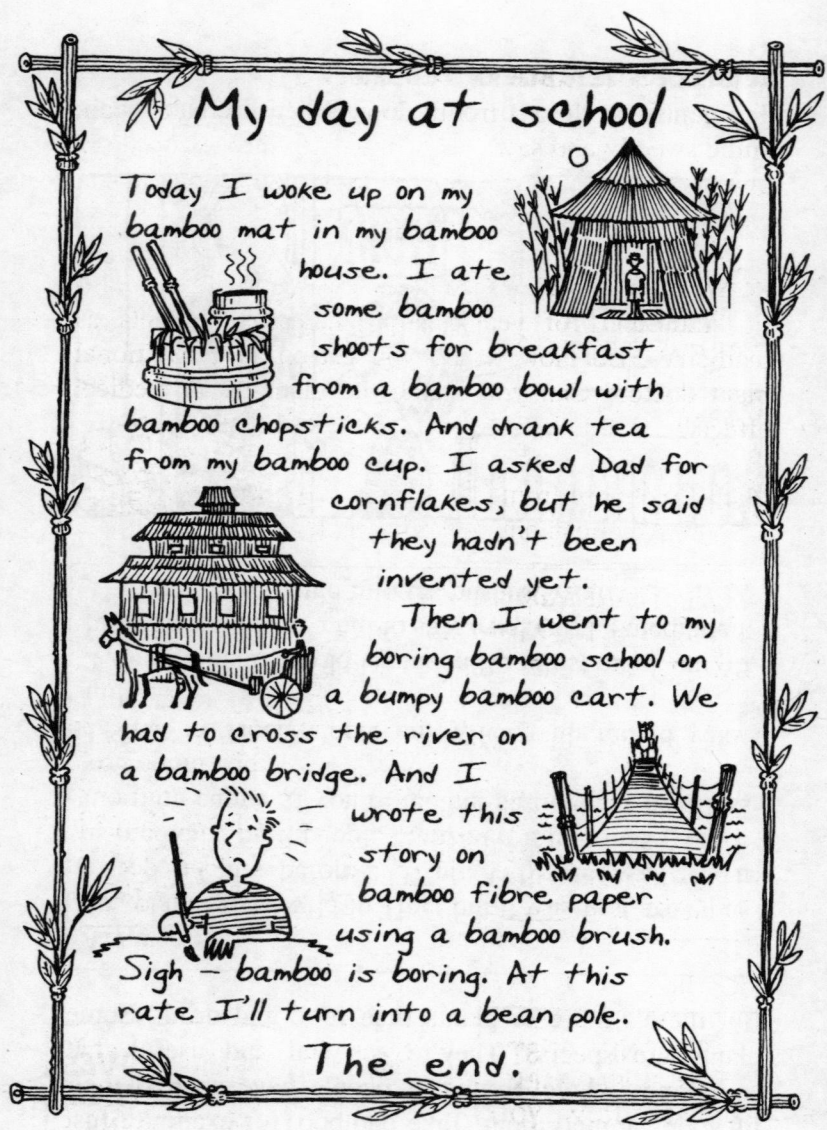

Today I woke up on my bamboo mat in my bamboo house. I ate some bamboo shoots for breakfast from a bamboo bowl with bamboo chopsticks. And drank tea from my bamboo cup. I asked Dad for cornflakes, but he said they hadn't been invented yet.

Then I went to my boring bamboo school on a bumpy bamboo cart. We had to cross the river on a bamboo bridge. And I wrote this story on bamboo fibre paper using a bamboo brush.

Sigh — bamboo is boring. At this rate I'll turn into a bean pole.

The end.

And if the teacher didn't like the story can you guess what his cane was made of?

A VITAL VEGETABLE QUIZ - PART 1

But plants have loads more uses. Here's a two-part quiz you can really get your teeth into. All you have to do is match the following plants with the products they make. Go on – it's easy.

POWERFUL PLANT MEDICINES

For thousands of years people have used plants as medicines. But how would you get on as a traditional plant doctor? Can you match the plant to its medical effects?

Plants to choose from:
1 South American cinchona tree bark

2 Willow bark

3 Garlic

4 Castor oil plant

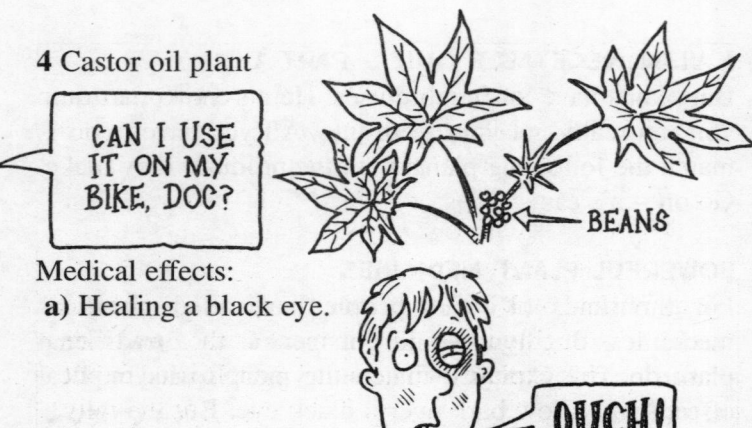

Medical effects:

a) Healing a black eye.

b) Keeps your body healthy. Lowers your blood pressure, kills bacteria and speeds up healing.

c) A laxative that makes you go to the toilet and produce poo.

d) Cures the killer disease malaria.

Answers:

1 d) The bark of the South American cinchona tree contains a drug called quinine. This kills microscopic creatures that cause the deadly disease malaria. Unfortunately, taking the bark kills the tree. But people were so desperate for treatment that in the nineteenth century thousands of trees had to die.

2 a) Willow bark contains a chemical called salicylic acid. It's roughly the same chemical as the painkiller aspirin. This explains why country people used to put strips of willow bark over a black eye. But the wily willow isn't making aspirin for us. Oh no – it's there to kill off hungry beetles. Yes, beetles soon discover that they're barking up the wrong tree. Ha ha.

3 b) Yep – these are official facts. Scientific tests have proved that chewing garlic is good for you. And as long as you've got your health, who needs friends?

4 c) Caster oil is a laxative. It was typically used to torture children. However, castor oil has a sinister secret. It has to be prepared carefully because the castor oil bean contains a poison so deadly that one bean can kill a person.

BEAN HAS BEEN

Bet you never knew!

Another laxative is North American buckthorn tree bark. Its Latin name means "blessed relief". According to one story the priest who invented this name had problems going to the loo. Until he tried this bark and...

ERGHHH!

PLOP!

WHAT A BLESSED RELIEF!

VITAL VEGETABLE QUIZ - PART 2
PRICELESS PLANT PRODUCTS

Can you match the following plants with the products they make?

Plants to choose from:

1 Sugar cane
2 Stinging nettles
3 Seaweed
4 Wheat
5 Lichen
6 The South American bixa tree
7 Cotton
8 Rubber
9 Pine trees

Products to choose from:

a) A pair of very smelly socks
b) Fuel for cars

c) A nice plate of spaghetti

d) Dye

e) A dirty old wellie boot (where's the other one got to?)

f) Forecasting the weather

g) A tablecloth

h) Lovely orange hair

i) This book

Answers:

1 b) In Brazil sugar cane is made into alcohol and this is used as a fuel for cars. People buy it from pumps at garages alongside the more traditional petrol pumps.

2 g) In northern England, in the nineteenth century, people wove stinging nettle stems into tablecloths.

3 f) Laminaria (lam-in-ar-re-a) seaweed feels dry and brittle in dry weather but as rain draws near and the air grows moist, the seaweed takes in water and feels sticky.

4 c) Spaghetti is made out of pasta which is made from semolina. Yes, this is the same paste-like sludge that is served up as a school dinner pudding. And semolina is made from ground-up grains of wheat.

5 d) Lichens were used to make traditional dyes. A typical recipe involved leaving the dye to rot in a mix of stale pee and a chemical called slaked lime. Are you dying to make it?

6 h) Native South Americans use bixa seeds to make groovy orange hair colour. The juice also keeps mosquitoes away.

7 a) The cotton in your socks is made from hairs that help to disperse the seeds of the cotton plants that are inside their seed pods. The hairs are spun using machines to make the cloth.

8 e) Wellington boots are traditionally made from rubber. Rubber is made from the congealed juice, or latex, that oozes from the rubber tree when you cut its bark. Today a lot of rubber is made in factories using artificial chemicals.

9 i) Yes, you probably knew this one. This book is made from trees. That's where paper comes from. The wood is ground into a pulpy mass of tiny bits called fibres and dissolved using chemicals. Further chemical treatment follows including adding glue to stick the fibres together. This disgusting goo is then pressed and dried and cut to size.

THEY'VE GONE TO BE MADE INTO HORRIBLE SCIENCE BOOKS

A TREE-MENDOUS DISCOVERY

The man who first thought of using wood for paper was French scientist René Réamur (1683–1757). One day René found an old wasps' nest in a forest. He took it

154

home and found it was made of … paper. Further study proved that wasps chew up wood and sick it up to make this strange substance.

In 1719 Réamur excitedly told the French Academy that he had proved that paper can be made from plant fibres. (Everyone had forgotten that the Egyptians had been doing this with papyrus thousands of years before.) In Réamur's time, people used mashed-up rags. Although Réamur never made his own paper from wood, his work encouraged other scientists to make paper successfully from seaweed, cabbages, potatoes and old pine cones.

The first effective wood grinding machines for paper-making were developed in Germany in the 1840s.

So there you have it. Where would we be without plants? We eat them, we breathe their gases, and we take them as medicines when we feel sick. And we can make bridges and homes and run cars and make clothes and books and … well, everything.

A BLOOMING MIRACLE

By now you may have realized that vegetables are vicious. Some of them guzzle insects even whilst the poor little creatures are still alive and wriggling. And vegetables are vicious to each other too – strangling their victims, sucking out their juices and stealing light. And that's just for starters…

But what do you expect? Just imagine vegetables were weedy little wallflowers that invited every peckish bug and munching mammal in for a free lunch. These nice scrumptious friendly little vegetables would stand less chance than a bag of chocs on a school bus. Everyone would want a bite. So vegetables have to be vicious just in order to stay alive.

It's a good thing too. Vegetables may be vicious but they're also vital for life. And that's more than you can say for humans. Well, just think about it … humans (and every animal) need plants in order to stay alive. But many vegetables can do very nicely thank you without any of us.

And humans need *every* vegetable – not just the ones we eat or use to make things. Here's why. Every year botanists are finding amazing new plants that we can use for food and medicines. That means even a boring-looking weed could be tomorrow's wonder veg. It could even turn up in your local greengrocer's…

The Wonder Veg Store
just in...

THE BRILLIANT BUFFALO GOURD
(Grows in Mexico and south-western USA)

▶ Huge 3–4 metre tubers.
▶ Weighs 30kg when two years old.
▶ Very tasty and rich in vegetable oils.
▶ Feeds the entire family.

DELIVERY *a lot* EXTRA!

THE WINGED BEAN
(It's a winged wonder)

A bean with wings. Don't like the sound of it? Don't scoff till you try it – you'll be eating your words. Yes, you really can eat the whole plant!

▶ Leaves taste like spinach.
▶ Flowers can be fried.
▶ Seed pods taste like green beans.
▶ Seeds taste like peas.
▶ Tubers cook like potatoes (and they're equally good for you).
▶ All this and it makes the soil full of nitrates thanks to bacteria in its roots. Wow!

THIS PRODUCT IS REALLY TAKING OFF

And on the medicine front scientists are looking at traditional vegetable cures used by native peoples. The aim is to make some of these remedies into drugs that can be used elsewhere in the world. For example, the cryptolepis (crip-toe-leep-is) plant from west Africa has been used to treat the killer disease malaria. It kills germs and may help to fight cancer

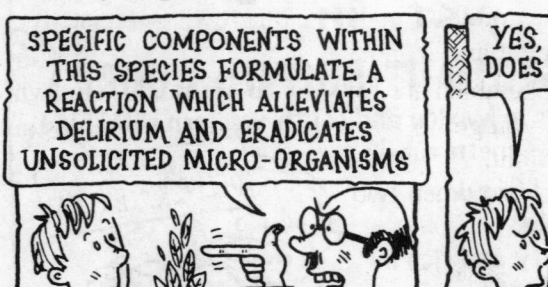

And there's more to botany than finding new foods and drugs. Scientists have found out how to make entirely new kinds of vegetable. It's all done with genes, those little codes in the pollen and ovaries, remember? For example, scientists have taken a gene from bacteria that tells it to make a poison to kill caterpillars. The scientists added the gene to cotton plants. And now the cotton plants grow leaves that bump off caterpillars.

But the most amazing thing to do with vegetables isn't to do with scientists and their discoveries. It's to do with the vegetables themselves. It's the fact that vegetables aren't boring salad ingredients that sit around in gardens. They're incredible living beings. Even a boring little weed contains an awesome living chemical factory that can turn sunlight into food and make a cocktail of vicious poisons. It's enough to make a full-grown botanist weep with excitement and wonder.

OK, so vegetables are bit slow to get going. But who cares? Once you get to know their secrets vegetables are horribly brilliant.

Yes, there's no doubt about it...

GREENS ARE GOOD FOR YOU!

And that's the HORRIBLE truth!

VICIOUS VEG

QUIZ

Now find out if you're a
Vicious Veg expert!

So, you've survived this treacherous trip through the world of vicious veg, but how much have you picked up along the way? Take these quick quizzes and find out...

Baffling botany

You've foraged among the flowers and perused the plants, but are you really a brilliant botanist? Answer these questions and find out.

1 Where do plants get their food?
a) Sunlight, water and carbon dioxide.
b) Sugars in the soil.
c) Sainsbury's.

2 Which of the following substances is *not* made from plants?
a) Rubber
b) Bogeys
c) Sugar

3 How do foul fungi feed?
a) They smother their food with spores and absorb the nutrients.
b) They lure insects with an attractive smell and then eat them alive.
c) They squirt digestive juices over their food and then slurp up the slime.

4 Why do trees shed their leaves in the autumn?
a) The dead leaves help fertilize the ground around their roots.
b) Leaves need too much water, which is hard to suck up in winter.
c) So more sunlight can reach them in the dark winter months.

5 Where are the seeds of coniferous trees found?
a) In a small hole in the trunk
b) In flowers
c) In cones

6 What type of vicious veg is a coconut?
a) A seed
b) A flower
c) A fruit

7 Which of these substances is not found in humus (in soil)?
a) Poo
b) Bacteria
c) Cellulose

8 Where does 70 per cent of the Earth's oxygen come from?
a) Trees in the rainforest.
b) Algae in the sea.
c) A power station in Bognor Regis.

Answers:
1a; 2b; 3c; 4b; 5c; 6a; 7c; 8b

Peculiar plant processes

Veg may be vicious, but it's also curiously clever. Plants can make everything they need to grow and reproduce with just a few basic ingredients. How much do you remember about these amazing survival skills?

1 What gas does plants absorb from the air? (Clue: It's a gruesome greenhouse gas)

2 What stringy substance strengthens the walls of plant cells? (Clue: The answer's in the question – sort of…)

3 What strange structures do fungi grow to spread spores more effectively? (Clue: Froggy furniture?)

4 What gas do plants release as part of photosynthesis? (Clue: Without it, you'd be dead as a dodo)

5 What other energy-giving substance is created during photosynthesis? (Clue: It's a sweet solution)

6 Which part of a plant contains the veins for carrying water? (Clue: The water arrives here, and then…)

7 What important substances do plants absorb from the ground? (Clue: Cunning chemicals)

8 What substance is transferred between flowering plants as part of the reproduction process? (Clue: It might make you sneeze…)

Answers:
1 Carbon dioxide
2 Cellulose
3 Toadstools
4 Oxygen
5 Sugar
6 Leaves
7 Minerals
8 Pollen

Perilous plants

*After reading this book you'll never be fooled by
a flower or tempted to touch a plant again – lots
of them can be disgustingly dangerous. See if you
can identify these grisly veg by their horrible
habits.*

1 I like to crawl up a tree and wrap my beastly
branches around its trunk. I slowly squeeze tighter
and tighter. Then I plant my roots in the ground and
steal all the water, so the tree dies a horrible, thirsty
death, gasping for breath.

2 Unwary insects take a death plunge into my slippery
trumpet-shaped body. While they're taking a swim in
the pool of water inside, I squirt out acid that
dissolves their helpless bodies while they're still alive!

3 I might look innocent on the outside, but my roots
are like a vampire's fangs. Deep underground, they
find other roots and stab into them. Then I can suck
up all the water from the other plants – then watch
them shrivel and die of thirst!

4 If any curious animal is stupid enough to try and eat
me it'll get a shock. The tiny hairs on my leaves will
release poison when touched – enough to give them a
nasty sting.

5 My bright-yellow colour hides a deadly secret. When an ignorant insect lands on me, it gets stuck in the glue that covers my tentacles. Veerrry slowly I close the tentacles around the doomed bug and my digestive juices dissolve it so I can slurp up all the lovely nutrients in its body.

6 I fill my pod-like body with water so that my outer layer bursts open, revealing a slimy, sticky trap for passing bugs. Any that land on me – or even just bump into me – won't get away from the glue-like gunk before I've begun to digest them.

7 If any human is foolish enough to put me on their pizza they're in for a deathly surprise. My poison will make them puke and make them cry, their liver will swell … and then they'll DIE!

8 Foolish flies land on my hairy lips and trigger an electric signal inside my leaves. Then SNAP! The spikes on the edge of the leaves close shut like a pair of jaws, imprisoning the insect, so I can feast on it at my leisure.

a) Sundew plant
b) Shepherd's purse seeds
c) Venus fly-trap
d) Death cap toadstool
e) Strangler fig
f) Christmas tree
g) Nettle
h) Pitcher plant

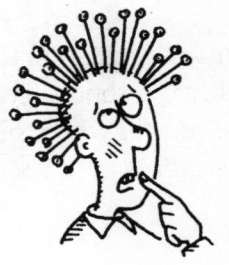

Vicious veg vocabulary

Botanists use some weird and wonderful words to describe different types of plants and their peculiar processes. Can you match the word with the correct meaning?

1 Transpiration
2 Germination
3 Pollination
4 Angiosperm
5 Photosynthesis
6 Chlorophyll
7 Gymnosperm
8 Lignin

a) The process of transferring pollen from one plant to another.
b) A plant with seeds that are open rather than being wrapped in a flower.
c) The process of soaking up water through roots and then losing it through leaves.
d) The green substance used by plants to make food from sunshine.
e) The growth of a baby plant inside a seed.
f) The substance in trees that holds the fibres together.
g) The process of turning sunlight, water and carbon dioxide into oxygen and sugar.
h) A flowering plant.

Answers:
1c; 2e; 3a; 4h; 5g; 6d; 7b; 8f

Frightful flowers

Flowers might look attractive and smell delicious, but there's more to some pretty plants than meets the eye. Dare you discover which of these amazing facts is true and which is false?

1 The mirror orchid fools male bees into carrying its pollen to other flowers by pretending to be a female bee.

2 The rafflesia is the rarest flower in the world.

3 The African sycamore fig repels threatening wasps by its horrible stench.

4 The puya plant is the smallest flower in the world, measuring just 0.1 mm across.

5 Roses stop themselves being eaten alive by bugs by attracting wasps to munch on the hungry insects.

6 A glorious bouquet of *Wolffia globosa* flowers would fit on the head of a pin.

7 The dead horse arum attracts blow flies by giving off a delicious perfumed scent.

8 The eastern skunk cabbage was so-named because of its black-and-white colouring (just like a skunk).

Answers:
1 TRUE. The mirror orchid looks a bit like a girl bee (not enough to fool *you* of course, but boy bees aren't that bright).
2 TRUE. It's also one of the largest and stinkiest flowers in the world. Good thing it's so rare really…
3 FALSE. This foul fig attracts wasps and encourages them to lay eggs inside it!

4 FALSE. The puya plant is the *largest* in the world – measuring up to 10 metres across (and taking 150 years to produce a flower!)

5 TRUE. Roses give off a gas that makes them especially attractive to wasps.

6 TRUE. The *Wolffia* genus produces the smallest flowering plants in the world – an average individual plant is around 0.6 mm long!

7 FALSE. The dead horse arum smells like rotting flesh. Blow flies are still attracted to the putrid pong though...

8 FALSE. If you tear a leaf it makes a revolting stink – but not as bad as a real skunk!

HORRIBLE INDEX

HORRIBLE SCIENCE

FRIGHTENING LIGHT

NICK ARNOLD

illustrated by
TONY DE SAULLES

■SCHOLASTIC

Scholastic Children's Books,
Euston House, 24 Eversholt Street
London NW1 1DB, UK

A division of Scholastic Ltd
London ~ New York ~ Toronto ~ Sydney ~ Auckland
Mexico City ~ New Delhi ~ Hong Kong

First published in the UK by Scholastic Ltd, 1999
This edition published 2009

Text copyright © Nick Arnold, 1999
Illustrations copyright © Tony De Saulles, 1999

ISBN 978 1407 10611 3

18

Printed and bound by CPI Group (UK) Ltd, Croydon, CR0 4YY

The right of Nick Arnold and Tony De Saulles to be identified as the author and
illustrator of this work respectively has been asserted by them in accordance
with the Copyright, Designs and Patents Act, 1988.

CONTENTS

Nick Arnold has been writing stories and books since he was a youngster, but never dreamt he'd find fame writing about frightening light. His research involved tripping up in the dark, staring down the wrong end of telescopes and trying on spectacles and he enjoyed every minute of it.

When he's not delving into Horrible Science, he spends his spare time teaching adults in a college. His hobbies include eating pizza, riding his bike and thinking up corny jokes (though not all at the same time).

Tony De Saulles picked up his crayons when he was still in nappies and has been doodling ever since. He takes Horrible Science very seriously and even agreed to draw an eclipse as it happened. Unfortunately, he couldn't find his crayons in the dark.

When he's not out with his sketchpad, Tony likes to write poetry and play squash, though he hasn't written any poetry about squash yet.

INTRODUCTION

Science is frightening. Frighteningly confusing.

Take the topic of light. You see light every day in sunshine and light bulbs so you might think that the science of light would be light work.

But you'd be wrong. It's hard. Harder to crack than a dried pea from last term's school dinner. And as for the facts – they're harder to untangle than a vat of spaghetti.

See what I mean? Light = instant confusion! It's frightening. And if you ask a scientist to explain about light it's even worse. You're bound to get a long incomprehensible answer with lots of frighteningly complicated scientific words...

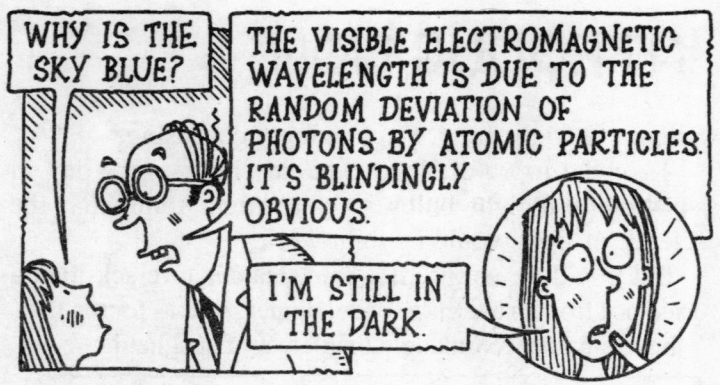

Horrible, isn't it? Yep – it's not surprising that Science can make your flesh creep.

Well, now to look on the bright side – here's a little light relief for you. Simply take this book to a quiet place, sit down and turn the pages. It will shed light on light science, and there are lots of light-hearted facts about eyeballs and laser surgery and ghostly lights and other dark and horrible corners of science. These could really brighten your day – especially when you frighten your teacher with a few tricky questions...

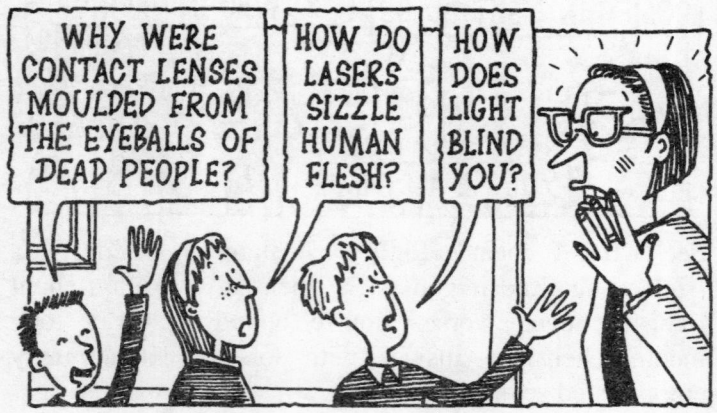

Your new-found knowledge of light science is sure to put your teacher in the shade. And afterwards, who knows? You might even become a leading light in science – then you'll really enjoy the limelight! So now there's only one question...

Are you bright enough to read on?

SEEING THE LIGHT

The sun was sinking behind the Brocken Mountain. The sky was getting darker by the minute and already the climber could scarcely see the narrow twisting goat-path at his feet. The climber was beginning to feel very afraid.

"It's time," he thought. "I'm going to see it any minute," and he peered anxiously at his pocket watch.

"Pull yourself together!" he said to himself. "You're a scientist. There must be a rational explanation. There's no such thing as ghosts."

But he trembled and his mouth felt dry as he wondered for the first time how he would find his way down in the dark. A bead of cold sweat trickled down his neck.

Suddenly his heart started thudding. Tiny hairs prickled on the back of his neck.

Somehow he knew even without a backward glance that he was not alone. There was someone ... or something

8

on the mountain behind him. He tried to turn his head but his neck had locked rigid. At last he forced his whole body to swing round. His jaw dropped open in horror. Behind him, etched on the foggy clouds was a huge dark figure. Rings of ghostly light played around the terrifying outline as it hung in thin air.

The thing seemed to be watching him. Waiting. Waiting to pounce.

For a moment the climber seemed hypnotized. Then he forced himself to react. With trembling hands he pulled out a pocket book and a chewed stub of pencil. And started scribbling unreadable notes. All the time he was mumbling desperately.

"Fascinating phenomenon," he said, over and over again. "Fascinating. I – er – better get moving."

As the climber turned and scurried up the path the giant figure seemed to spring into life. It began climbing silently and effortlessly in the climber's footsteps. And whatever it was, it was coming after him, silently – faster and faster.

And reaching out its long shadowy arms...

DON'T PANIC! As the scientist realized, the figure was only his own shadow. This very real if ghostly effect is called the spectre of the Brocken after the Brocken Mountain in Germany where it's often seen. If you climb a mountain near sunset (not a very safe thing to do – so don't try it on your own) the low sun can cast your shadow on nearby clouds. And you see a huge ghostly figure. But this is just one of many horribly amazing light effects.

Read on for the frightening facts...

Frightening light fact file

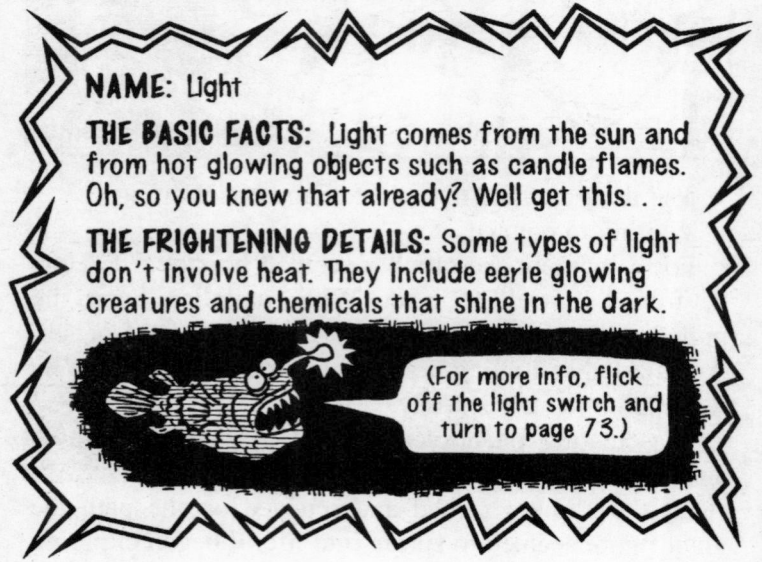

NAME: Light

THE BASIC FACTS: Light comes from the sun and from hot glowing objects such as candle flames. Oh, so you knew that already? Well get this. . .

THE FRIGHTENING DETAILS: Some types of light don't involve heat. They include eerie glowing creatures and chemicals that shine in the dark.

(For more info, flick off the light switch and turn to page 73.)

A GLOOMY THOUGHT

So you really did switch out the lights just then? Well, put them back on and read this.

It's easy to make light appear and disappear, isn't it? Every morning light appears in the sky and you don't even have to get out of bed to make it happen. So maybe that's why people take light for granted. And think it's no big deal.

Well, it is.

Imagine the sun doesn't rise tomorrow. Then imagine that all the light bulbs in the world go *phfutt* at the same instant.

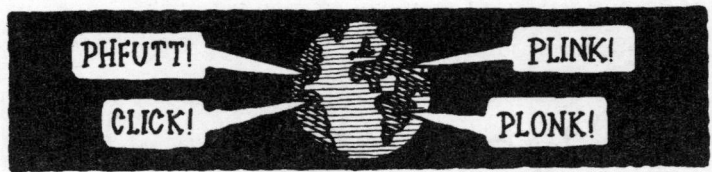

And imagine also that even the distant stars fail to shine. The world would be very cold and very dark. And frightening and dangerous. Without light to see by, people would be bumping into each other and treading on the cat and knocking over priceless ornaments and skidding on banana skins.

And that's not all. Can you work out which other things you need light for?

FRIGHTENING LIGHT QUIZ

Without sunlight you can't see...
1 A rainbow. TRUE/FALSE
2 The moon. TRUE/FALSE

If it's completely dark...
3 Your face wouldn't appear in a mirror. TRUE/FALSE

4 You couldn't take holiday snaps. TRUE/FALSE
5 A poisonous rattlesnake couldn't find where you are hiding. TRUE/FALSE

1 TRUE. A rainbow happens when sunlight shines though droplets of rain. This splits the sunlight into different colours. (Check out pages 28-32 for the colourful details.) You actually get rainbows at night made by moonlight but the colours are too dim for your eyes to make out.

2 TRUE. The moon doesn't make its own light. That pretty silvery moonlight is actually sunlight that's bounced off (or as a scientist might say, reflected from) the moon. The surface of the moon is made of rock and dust but if it was ice it would reflect light really well and the moon would be nearly as bright as the sun.

3 TRUE. A mirror works by reflecting light. There's nothing to stop you looking at the bathroom mirror in the dark. But since there's no light the mirror won't reflect your image. Mind you, according to legend, if you're a vampire the mirror won't show your image anyway.

4 TRUE. Imagine you went pot-holing in a dark cave and left your torch at home. Whoops. You couldn't take any snaps because the chemicals that make a photograph only work if light falls on the film.

5 FALSE. The rattlesnake has a pit on each side of its head full of temperature sensors. These detect heat from your body. It's frightening. And that's why hiding from the snake in a dark cupboard isn't such a clever idea.

13

THE LIGHT FANTASTIC

So light brightens up your life, but take a closer look at light and it becomes even more fantastic... Imagine you could look at a ray of light through an incredibly powerful microscope. It would have to be billions of times more powerful than the world's most powerful microscope. Here's what you might see.

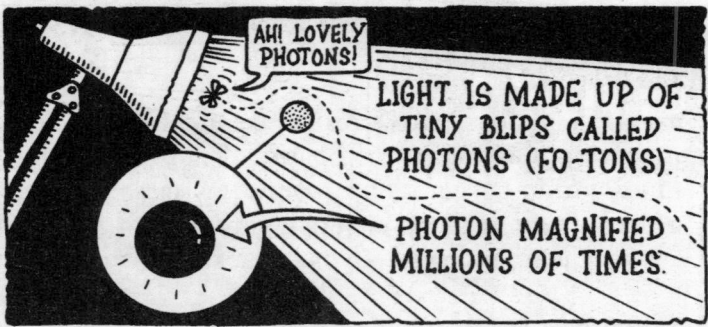

Photons are never still – they whiz along in the form of light waves. And hundreds of light waves could stretch across this full stop.

Photons sound phenomenal, don't they? You can imagine them as tiny little super-heroes flying through the air with awesome powers – so here's a story about one of them. Ooops – before you read it, I ought to tell you that an atom is a tiny ball of matter. Everything in the known universe – including you and me and this book – are made of different combinations of different types of atom.

THE ADVENTURES OF SUPER-PHOTON

IS IT A BIRD? IS IT A PLANE? NO. IT'S SUPER-PHOTON!

The story so far...

HI!

Super-Photon was born deep inside the sun. He leapt fully formed from a super-heated atom.

But he has awesome superhuman energy. He flies in a light wave that wiggles to and fro 600,000,000,000,000 (that's six hundred trillion) times per second to form a light wave. And he never runs out of puff.

Continued overleaf...

ZERO! Super-Photon weighs nothing at all. He's far too small to see, far smaller even than an atom.

Meanwhile on Earth...

ARGH!

NOW I'VE GOT YOU AGENT BRIGHT!

THE EVIL PROFESSOR Z! LOOKS LIKE A JOB FOR SUPER-PHOTON!

WHOOSH!

In a split second Super-Photon leaps clear of the sun and streaks towards the Earth at 300,000 km (186,000 miles) per second.

In just six minutes he flashes past Venus.

HI VENUS – BYE VENUS!

Meanwhile back on Earth...

YOU WON'T GET AWAY WITH THIS, Z!

ANY LAST REQUESTS?

HAS TIME RUN OUT FOR AGENT BRIGHT?

Eight minutes and twenty-five seconds into his mission Super-Photon flashes past the moon. But is he too late?

17

But the most incredible thing about Super-Photon isn't his super-hero powers – it's the fact that he's *nothing special*. You make photons all the times by zapping atoms with energy – for example by heating. That's why the toaster element glowed red when you burnt the toast this morning and that's why bulbs glow when you switch on the light. What happens is the cloud of electrons that whiz around the centre of an atom spit out photons in the form of light waves.

Each light wave is actually made up of a linked electric and a magnetic wave moving in the same direction. And since you can't get one without the other scientists lump them together and say that a light wave is a form of electromagnetic wave.

Bet you never knew!

1 The more energy you blast an atom with the more times the light wave will wiggle per second. And if you want to sound like a scientist you say "I am increasing the frequency of the electromagnetic waves".

2 At lower levels of energy you make radio waves, but turn up the power and you'll make different colours of light (from red going up to violet). Turn it up a bit more and you make ultraviolet light – a kind of high-energy light that you can't see. Keep going to maximum levels and you blast out deadly gamma rays.

3 You might wonder what happens to photons after they hit something. Well, remember a photon is just a blip of energy. It hits an atom and its energy is soaked up. So it's bye-bye photon. But photons do much more than whiz around...

Dare you discover ... what light can do?

To begin with:

Wrap some kitchen foil round the end of a small bright torch.

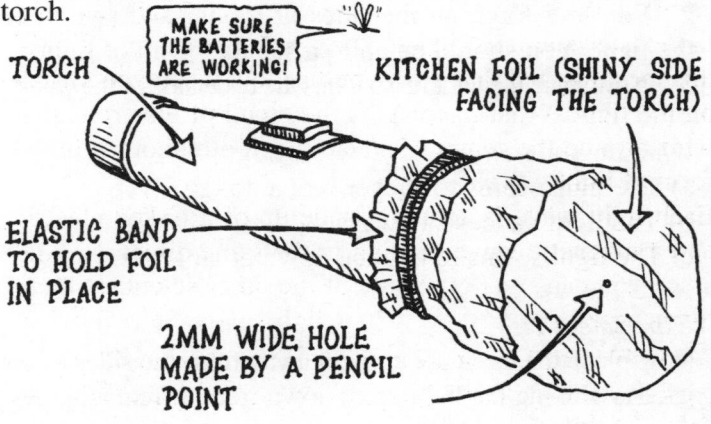

MAKE SURE THE BATTERIES ARE WORKING!

TORCH

KITCHEN FOIL (SHINY SIDE FACING THE TORCH)

ELASTIC BAND TO HOLD FOIL IN PLACE

2MM WIDE HOLE MADE BY A PENCIL POINT

You will need:

ERK! IT'S MILKY AND MURKY!

YOUR TORCH PREPARED AS SHOWN

A SQUARE BOTTLE OR STORAGE JAR WITH 9CM OF WATER. ADD A DROP OF MILK IN WITH THE WATER AND STIR. THE WATER SHOULD BE VERY SLIGHTLY CLOUDY, BUT STILL SEE-THROUGH.

9CM

Experiment 1:

1 Place the jar in front of a dark object. A dark book or some gloomy wallpaper will do.

2 Put your torch up the sides of the jar and switch on the light. You should be able to see the beam of light.

3 Now shine the light up so it hits the underside of the water.

What do you notice?

a) The light seems to flicker like a dodgy TV.

b) The light dances sideways.

c) The light seems to bounce down at an angle.

Experiment 2:

Now place the torch about 5 cm away from the sides of the jar. Try shining the light up or down from different angles.

What do you notice?

a) From some angles the light beam suddenly jumps to one side as it passes through the sides of the jar.

b) The water begins to heat up and bubble as you move the light.

c) No matter how you move the torch the light beam is always a straight line.

Answers:

1 c) The light bounces (reflects) off the underside of the water. The surface of the water is very smooth and the photons of light can all reflect in the same direction.

2 a) Light doesn't always go in a straight line. When light travels from air to water it slows to 224,900 km per second. This is because the photons have to push through lots of atoms in the water – just imagine a crowd of people trying to run.

through another crowd. When a beam of light hits the water at an angle one side of the beam slows before the other. This makes the beam bend

FRIGHTENING EXPRESSIONS

One astronomer says to another...

YOUR REFRACTION IS ALL WRONG!

ERK!

Is this ref action something to do with a football match?

Answer:
No. Scientists call the bending of light refraction (re-frak-tion).

By now you'll have realized...
1 There's more to light than meets the eye.
2 That light is horribly amazing.
But you might also feel puzzled. If photons are so tiny and so fast how come scientists know so much about them? I mean, you can't exactly catch photons in a butterfly net. Well, it took the combined brain power of some frighteningly bright scientists to discover the truth.

TURN THE PAGE AND DISCOVER HOW THEY DID IT. . .

HORRIBLY BRIGHT SCIENTISTS

Much of our knowledge of light is based on the work of two scientific geniuses, Isaac Newton (1642–1727) and Albert Einstein (1879–1955). However, lots of scientists lent a hand. Well, as they say "many hands make LIGHT work", ha ha. Here's a handy spotter's guide to scientists who study light.

Spot the scientist

1. Physicists (Fizzy-cists)

INTERESTED IN: physical forces that shape the world — stuff like heat or electricity. The actual type of physicist featured in this book is an optical physicist. And — you guessed it — they study light.

WHAT THEY DO: set up experiments, make calculations about the speed of light and other exciting topics.

WHERE THEY WORK: university laboratories.

SPOTTER'S NOTE: physicists can be rather scruffy and absent-minded about their clothes. This is because they're too busy thinking about complex experiments to worry about how they look.

THOUGHTS ABOUT COMPLEX EXPERIMENTS

2. Astronomers

INTERESTED IN: stars and planets and other things you find in outer space. Astronomers are interested in light because we can only see space objects because of the light they produce or reflect.

WHAT THEY DO: scan the night sky using telescopes.

WHERE THEY WORK: observatories.

SPOTTER'S NOTE: astronomers are shy creatures that hide away in remote mountain-top observatories – but you can spot them in science conferences

CLOSE-UP OF RARE PHOTO SHOWING ASTRONOMER CREEPING OUT TO HER OBSERVATORY AT NIGHT

3. Ophthalmologists (op-thal-mol-ogists)

INTERESTED IN: eyeballs, their diseases and how they work.

WHAT THEY DO: they're trained doctors who treat patients with eye problems. Some are surgeons who perform operations on the eye.

WHERE THEY WORK: hospital eye departments.

SPOTTER'S NOTE: it's hard to find an ophthalmologist because they're always busy. Loads of people have sight problems, you see?

HAVE YOU SEEN HIM YET?

IF I COULD SEE HIM I WOULDN'T BE HERE

PULLING A FAST ONE

For centuries scientists were keen to measure the speed of light. They knew that this would help them judge the distance of planets and so make more accurate astronomical observations. So loads of scientists had a go. But they had a problem. Light is kind of speedy. All light photons belt along at 299,792,458 metres a second. There's nothing faster in the known universe – not even kids leaving a science class on a Friday afternoon.

Now, you'd think it would be impossible to clock the speed of light. I mean, you'd need amazingly quick reactions and a very good stopwatch to do it – right? So how did scientists manage this impossible feat? First off the mark was Italian scientist Galileo Galilei (1564–1642).

GALLANT GALILEO

One dark night Galileo and a friend went into the mountains. Each man carried a lantern with a shutter.

Galileo climbed a hill. His friend climbed another hill three kilometres away. It was a cold, lonely and dangerous trek and if either man had fallen there was no hope of a quick rescue.

Once he reached the top of his hill Galileo opened the shutter of his lantern and started counting. The plan was for the friend to show his lantern in response to Galileo's signal.

To his relief Galileo saw the light from his friend's lantern and stopped counting.

COULD YOU BE A SCIENTIST?

But great Galileo was wrong – as he found out when he and his long-suffering pal tried climbing hills further apart. Light is so speedy that a few squitty kilometres make no obvious difference to the measurements. Galileo was simply timing how quickly he reacted to the light signals. He realised this and gave up.

LIGHT SPEED CLOCKED

Using complex calculations, astronomers were also trying to clock the speed of light. In 1676 Danish stargazer Ole Roemer (1644–1710) was watching Jupiter's moon Io when he figured out that the further away Earth was from Jupiter, the longer it took light to reach his telescope. Using Roemer's data, scientists reckoned that light travelled at about 225,000 km per second. Not bad – but not right. Then in 1725 British astronomer James Bradley came up with a new figure using brain-blistering sums such as the angle of his telescope and the speed of the Earth. He was just five per cent out.

Meanwhile, back in the hills. In 1849 French physicist Armand Fizeau (1819–1896) shone a bright light from the top of a hill. The light shone through the spokes of a spinning wheel and bounced off a mirror on a hilltop eight km distant before returning through the wheel.

I WORKED OUT THE SPEED OF LIGHT BY MEASURING THE DISTANCE THE WHEEL TRAVELLED, ITS SPEED AND THE DISTANCE LIGHT TRAVELLED

THAT'S 'WHEELY' CLEVER!

His figure of 313,300 km per second was a bit too speedy. But the technique proved to be a bright idea and was used by other scientists.

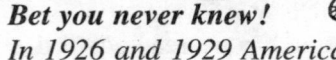

Bet you never knew!
In 1926 and 1929 American Albert Michelson (1852–1931) performed similar tests using a rapidly turning mirror instead of a wheel.

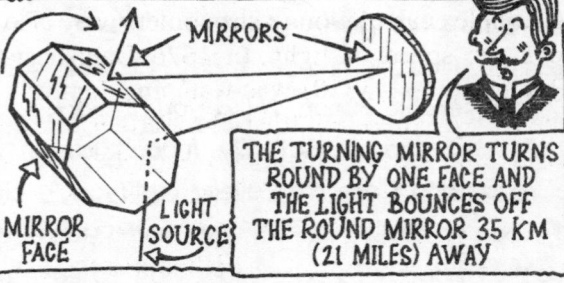

MIRRORS

THE TURNING MIRROR TURNS ROUND BY ONE FACE AND THE LIGHT BOUNCES OFF THE ROUND MIRROR 35 KM (21 MILES) AWAY

MIRROR FACE

LIGHT SOURCE

Michelson's measurements of the distance the light travelled and the speed of his mirror were more accurate than Fizeau's. But Albert's final result was still wrong – too slow by just 18 km a second. Ooops. Modern estimates use a similar approach but more accurate clocks and lasers mean the whole experiment can be controlled more precisely. So you get a more accurate measurement.

IZZY THE INCREDIBLE
One scientist played a key role in bringing the secrets of light to light – he was Isaac Newton. Of course, any old teacher will tell you that Newton is famous for describing the fatal forces that can affect a moving object – forces such as gravity. But do they also know that Newton's pet

dog was named Diamond? Now Diamond wasn't quite as smart as his brainy owner. Here's what his diary might have looked like if he'd learnt to write.

A dog's diary
by Diamond

Cambridge ~ 2 June 1664

My master, Isaac is grumpy today. Oh well, so what — he's a miserable human. Mind you his bark is worse than his bite — ha ha. Actually, Isaac's mum is to blame. Isaac and I are at College but Isaac's skint. Isaac's mum is really rich but she never sends us any pocket money. So poor Isaac has to earn a few pennies by working as a waiter in the College. Then he's allowed to eat the scraps and leftovers. And guess what I get? Isaac's scraps and leftovers.

YUK!

Oh well, it's a dog's life.

31 August

Isaac is barking mad. (Well mad, anyway.) We went to a fair but instead of buying a nice juicy joint of meat for me, Isaac spent his hard-earned pennies on a prism. Well, he calls it a "prism". I call it a stupid triangular lump of glass that you can't even eat. So I whimpered in protest.

Isaac looked down at me in surprise.

"Are you OK?" he asked.

My master often talks to me because he doesn't have too many human friends.

"I'm rough," I replied.

Actually it sounded more like "ruff!" so Isaac ignored me. Well, he's still working and I'm dog-tired. So I'm taking my grumbling belly off to bed.

Woolsthorpe, Lincolnshire ~ 25 December 1665

We're here staying with Isaac's mum. It's all to do with something called "the plague". Well, humans are dropping dead like flies and the College is closed. So we came here. It's a good thing this plague. Now I get fed regularly by Isaac's mum. Yum, yum — Christmas goose bones.

1 January 1666

My master missed supper ... again. As usual, he's up in his room scribbling masses of meaningless numbers and mumbling scientific gibberish about light. He never washes or changes his clothes — phwoar, he's really going to the dogs. Mind you, I'm always ready to help my master. That's why I made sure I was at hand to eat his supper for him. At least it didn't go to waste!

12 January

I sneaked into Isaac's room today. Got a bit of a shock. Isaac has made a small hole in the shutters. (I bet his mum will have a fit when she sees the damage.) A ray of light shone through the hole and made a blob of sunlight on the wall. This proves my theory — Isaac *is* completely bonkers.

13 January

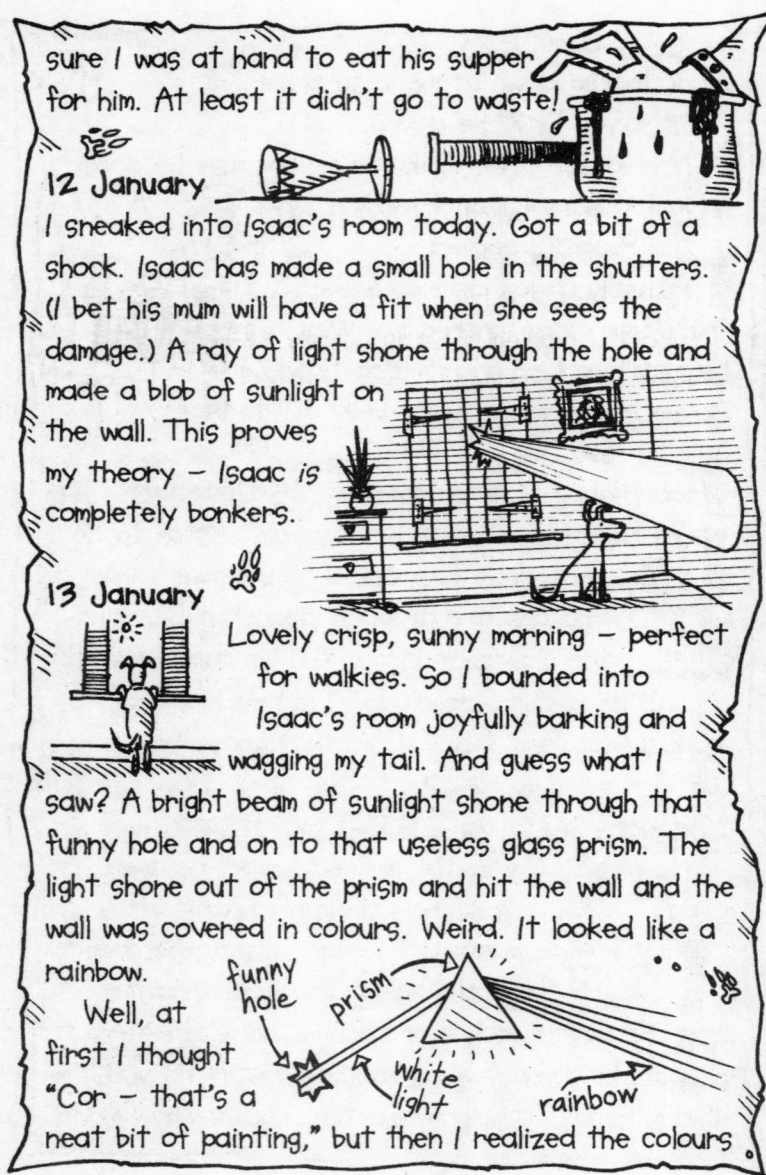

Lovely crisp, sunny morning — perfect for walkies. So I bounded into Isaac's room joyfully barking and wagging my tail. And guess what I saw? A bright beam of sunlight shone through that funny hole and on to that useless glass prism. The light shone out of the prism and hit the wall and the wall was covered in colours. Weird. It looked like a rainbow.

Well, at first I thought "Cor — that's a neat bit of painting," but then I realized the colours

funny hole

prism

white light

rainbow

were made by the light. "Maybe that prism has magical powers," I thought.

Then I saw the broad grin on Isaac's face.

"What do you think of the rainbow, Diamond?" he whispered excitedly, pressing his face up close.

"Woof!" I replied. This is usually the best response when Isaac gets worked up about something.

WOOF!

"Bet you'd like to know how I made it?" asked Isaac.

Well, I was wondering and luckily he went on to explain the trick.

"You see, sunlight is made of different colours."

I wagged my tail and looked interested as Isaac continued in a rather breathless voice.

"When the colours in light hit the prism at an angle they all bend or refract by different amounts. So the colours separate out from the white light and you see a rainbow."

Well, all this Science was a bit over my head and anyway I was bursting for a pee. Luckily Isaac's mum heard me whining and she took me for walkies.

Ah – what a relief!

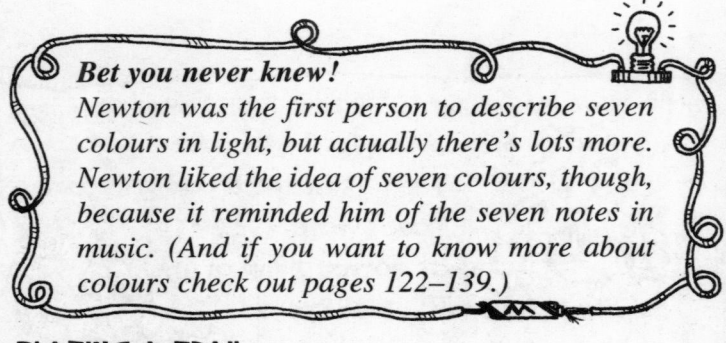

Bet you never knew!
Newton was the first person to describe seven colours in light, but actually there's lots more. Newton liked the idea of seven colours, though, because it reminded him of the seven notes in music. (And if you want to know more about colours check out pages 122–139.)

BLAZING A TRAIL

Although Isaac wasn't the first person to make a rainbow using a prism he was the first to prove colours are part of sunlight and not somehow made by the glass. He did this by shining red light from his "rainbow" through a second prism and finding that it didn't split any further.

RAY OF SUNLIGHT

PRISM 1

LOOK DIAMOND! THE RED LIGHT WON'T SPLIT ANY FURTHER!

NARROW SLIT IN SCREEN ALLOWS ONLY RED BAND OF RAINBOW THROUGH

PRISM 2

Isaac had blazed a trail in Science but his work sparked a blazing row. He sent an account of it to the Royal Society (that's the club for top scientists founded in 1662) but rival scientist Robert Hooke (1635–1703) claimed that Isaac's experiments didn't work properly. In fact, the glass in Hooke's prism probably wasn't as clear as Newton's so he couldn't get the same results. But as a result of the row Newton stopped speaking to Hooke.

Isaac also suffered in another kind of blaze. He returned to Cambridge after the plague but one Sunday he went to church leaving a candle burning in his laboratory. Perhaps Diamond wanted to try a few experiments too. Anyway, he jumped on the table, knocked over the candle and started a fire. According to one report, the blaze destroyed all Isaac's notes on light and all his chemistry equipment. I expect poor Diamond ended up in the dog house.

Isaac rewrote his notes from memory. But he didn't publish any of his work until 1704. By this time Hooke was dead so Isaac got the last word on light. Except, of course, it wasn't the last word. Isaac had reckoned light was made of tiny balls. But there was no way he could see the balls so his idea is a bit of a stab in the dark – ha ha. And within a century a brilliant scientist would see the problem in a different light.

Hall of fame: Thomas Young (1773–1829)
Nationality: British

Young Tom Young was frighteningly clever. He was so brilliant at school that the whole class probably wanted to sit next to him in Science tests. He learnt to read when he was two. By the time he was six he'd read the Bible – twice. By the time he was 14 he was designing telescopes and microscopes with the help of a friendly teacher. By then he could speak four languages besides English and he decided (no doubt as a bit of light relief) to teach himself eight more.

Tom trained as a doctor but in 1797 his uncle died and left him a fortune. This was good news. Well, not for the uncle, but good news for Tom. At last he could afford to do what he really wanted – lots of lovely science experiments.

Unfortunately few people got to hear of Tom's discoveries. His articles were so boring that not many people bothered to read them. Not surprising really – Tom was sacked from a job at the Royal Institution because his lectures were too dull. (Note: this is unlikely to happen to your teacher. So stop daydreaming and get on with this book.)

YOU'RE SACKED FOR DULL TEACHING, MR BROWN! TELL YOUR CLASS TO TAKE THE REST OF THE DAY OFF.

DRONE, WITTER, DRONE

In 1803 Tom proved that light takes the form of light waves. This was quite an achievement because as you know light waves are too small to see – 14,000 light waves could stretch across your thumbnail. In fact, the idea of light waves wasn't totally new. It had been put forward in 1690 by Dutch astronomer Christiaan Huygens (1629-1695) who based his suggestion on complex maths. But it was Thomas Young who dreamt up the experiment that proved light waves really exist.

Here's how he did it...

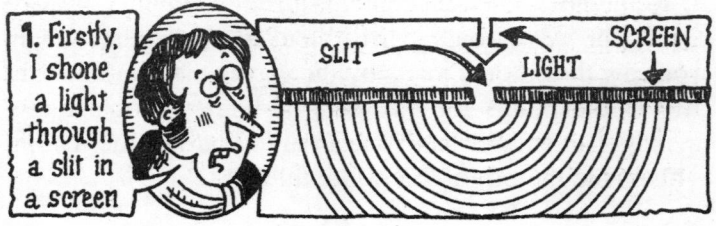

1. Firstly, I shone a light through a slit in a screen

SLIT   LIGHT   SCREEN

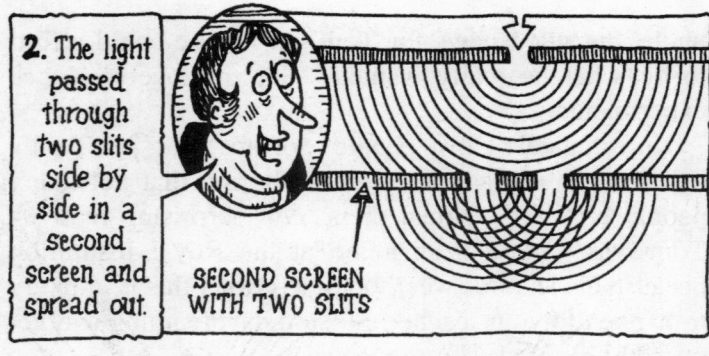

2. The light passed through two slits side by side in a second screen and spread out.

SECOND SCREEN WITH TWO SLITS

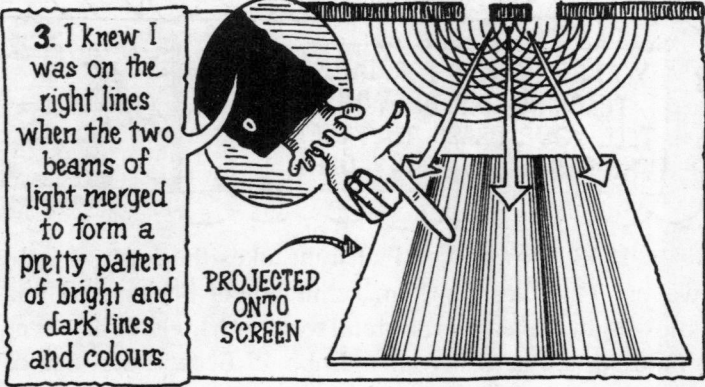

3. I knew I was on the right lines when the two beams of light merged to form a pretty pattern of bright and dark lines and colours.

PROJECTED ONTO SCREEN

4 Tom was able to show how this pattern was made by waves of light spreading out from the two slits. The two sets of waves spread out and passed through each other. Where the waves got in each other's way they made shadows – those were the dark lines.

Remember that light contains different colours? Where two light waves only partly blocked each other's way you saw the colours made by the waves that got through. But at the points the two sets of light waves actually managed to pass through one another you saw them both. This made the bright lines. Got all that?

FRIGHTENING EXPRESSIONS

One physicist says to another...

So who's interfering with the action?

THE FINAL, FINAL WORD?

More evidence built up to show that light took the form of waves and that Huygens and Young were right. For example, in 1818 French physicist Augustin Jean Fresnel (1788-1827) used brilliant maths to show how light waves can produce reflections and refraction. But was light really nothing more than a collection of waves? Was Newton's idea of light just a load of nonsense?

In 1901 German physicist Max Planck (1858-1947), spoilt the party. Planck said light is actually made of blips of energy called "quanta" (kwan-ta). Max's figures explained how the energy of light can be turned into heat inside a black box. But the only way his calculations added up was if light comes in quanta. These quanta are now called photons.

Four years later a scientific mega-genius used maths to prove Planck right. He performed no experiments and used only a pen and notepad for calculations. But he was able to prove that light was made up of photons, but that each blip moves so fast it forms a light wave. This idea was gradually accepted by physicists.

So who was this extraordinary scientist?

EXTRAORDINARY EINSTEIN

Albert Einstein is best known for his theories of relativity which he came up with in 1905 and 1915.

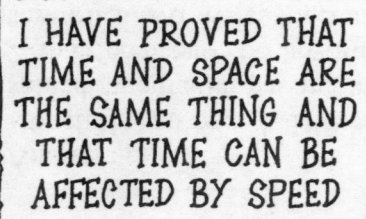

I HAVE PROVED THAT TIME AND SPACE ARE THE SAME THING AND THAT TIME CAN BE AFFECTED BY SPEED

If you haven't a clue what he's talking about, don't worry – you're not alone. There's a good chance that your teacher isn't aware of the finer details either.

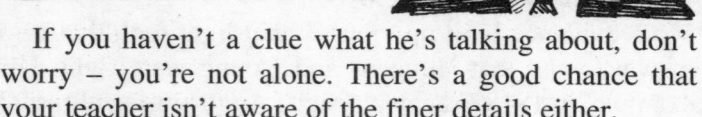

BUT WHAT DOES HE MEAN, MISS?

ER, THAT'S ENOUGH SCIENCE FOR TODAY, ...GET YOUR READING BOOKS OUT

Of course, most well-informed teachers can tell you that Einstein was born in Germany, that he made his 1905 discoveries whilst working in Switzerland, and that from the 1930s he lived in America. But here's five facts they probably don't know about awesome Albert.

1 Einstein got interested in light at the age of 14 when he was daydreaming (no doubt during a particularly boring Science lesson). He imagined he was riding on top of a beam of light.

BEAM ME UP, SCOTTY!

This was dangerous (that's daydreaming, not riding on light – as you know, it's impossible to surf on light). In those days, the punishment for not paying attention was a whack across the knuckles with a cane. History doesn't record whether Albert suffered this punishment but he probably did.

2 Einstein was eventually expelled from school. His teacher couldn't stand the sight of him lolling at the back of the class and smiling and not doing any work. But Einstein was a genius and he was more interested in his own studies. (The chances are you won't get away with this excuse.)

IT'LL TAKE MORE THAN NOT COMBING YOUR HAIR TO MAKE YOU A GENIUS, JENKINS

3 Some people think that Einstein's discoveries about light were actually made by Mileva Einstein – Albert's first wife. Albert once remarked:

EVERYTHING I HAVE CREATED AND ATTAINED I OWE TO MILEVA

However their son, Hans Albert, explained that although Mileva helped with the maths it was Albert who did the scientific thinking. Albert probably meant that having Mileva to look after him gave him the time and confidence to develop his ideas.

4 After Einstein's death, a doctor removed the great man's brain, sliced it into little bits and stored it in a couple of large jars. His aim was to give it away to researchers into genius. At one point the doctor and reporter drove across the USA to present the sliced-up brain to Einstein's grand-daughter. But she didn't want the grily relic.

ALBERT EINSTEIN (GENIUS)

ALBERT SHUTTLEWORTH (DIMWIT)

5 At the same time as his brain was taken, the doctor removed his eyeballs as souvenirs.

Would you want souvenirs like these? Probably not, and if squelching bloodshot eyeballs make you shudder you might want to close your own eyes before you turn the page.

Because the next chapter is *bulging* with them...

BULGING EYEBALLS

Here's a really FRIGHTENING thought. Imagine one morning you opened your eyes and saw nothing – just darkness. As black as the darkest night without even a glimmer of starlight. You'd be in a blind panic, wouldn't you? (Or you might think it actually was night and go back to sleep.)

ARGH! MY EYES AREN'T WORKING!

...OR AM I HAVING A NIGHTMARE ABOUT BEING STUCK IN A GIANT LIQUORICE ALLSORT?

GULP! THIS MUST BE WHAT IT'S LIKE TO HAVE NO EYEBALLS.

Well, thank goodness for eyeballs. If it wasn't for them you wouldn't be able to see any light at all.

BULGING EYEBALLS QUIZ

If you're itching to know more about eyeballs, there's one opposite that's been freshly cut in half. In this quiz each part of the eyeball has a matching fact. All you have to do is match the bits of eyeball to the relevant facts...

EYEBALL BITS AND PIECES

1 Ciliary muscles
2 Iris
3 Optic nerve
4 Retina with rod and cone cells*

5 Cornea
6 Eyelashes
7 Lens
8 Watery bit
9 Sclera (sk-leer-a)
10 Eye muscles

*By the way the "cells" are more than 50 trillion tiny living jelly-like blobs that make up your body. But you probably knew that already.

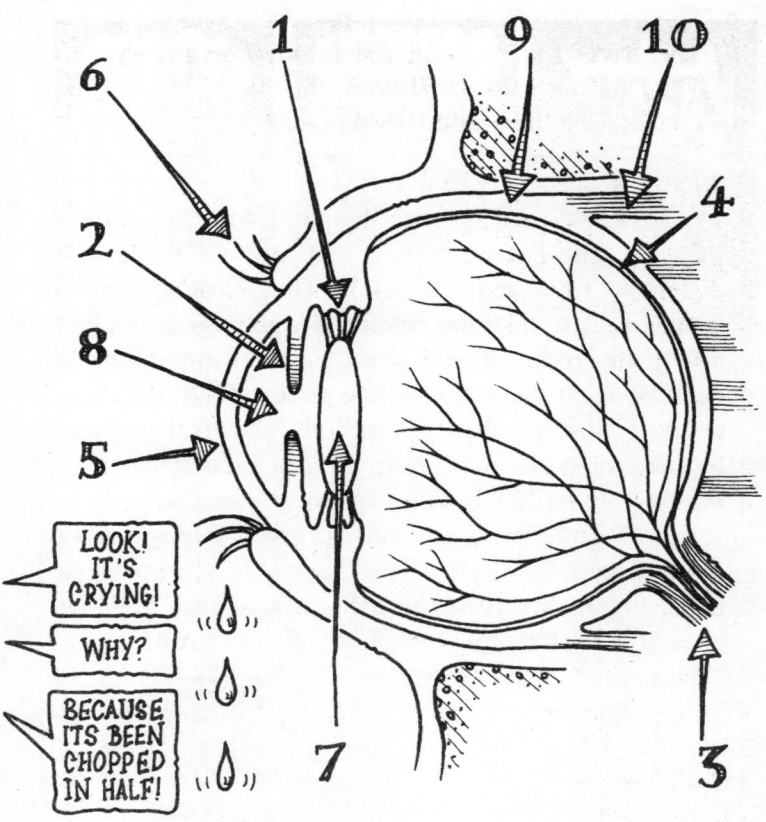

RELEVANT FACTS

a) There are 200 of these.

b) This bit helps to keep the eyeball in shape.

c) They stop your eyeball slopping out of its socket.

d) The colour of this bit stops light getting through and dazzling you.

e) This bit is 6.5 square cm (one square inch). Without it you'd see nothing.

f) This bit changes shape 100,000 times a day.

g) This bit controls the eyeball part mentioned in **f)**.

h) This part sucks in oxygen gas from the air.

i) There are one million fibres in this bit.

j) You can see the blood vessels in this bit.

Answers:

1g) 2d) Light goes through the pupil – the hole in the middle. (The colour of your eye doesn't make any difference to what you see.) **3i)** They're nerve fibres. Their job is to take the pattern of light signals picked up by the retina to the brain in the form of nerve signals. **4e)** It's got 4.5 million cone cells to give you colour vision and about 90 million rod cells that detect light but not colours. (For more info. on colour vision see page 134.) **5h)** The cornea has no blood vessels to supply it with the sugar and oxygen it needs to stay alive. It gets sugars from the gloopy fluid in the eye and oxygen directly from the air. **6a)** They fall out after about three months, but you always grow more.

ERK! MY EYELIDS ARE GOING BALD!

7f) The lens thickens or lengthens so that light from whatever you are looking at is bent (refracted) and so focused on the retina. That's blinking amazing, isn't it? **8b)** Yes, it's true, you're looking at this page through a pool of watery jelly. **9j)** It's the "white" of your eyeball. When the eyeball is injured or has a disease the blood vessels get inflamed and get bigger. And the eyeball looks gungey and bloodshot. **10c)** They also swivel the eyeball round to look at things. Your brain coordinates the muscles on each eyeball so they work together. When this doesn't happen you go cross-eyed.

Bet you never knew!
1 The way your retina lets you see light is horribly complicated. When you look at something, photons of light hit the cells in the retina. These cells contain coloured chemicals called pigments. The photons spark a series of chemical reactions first in the pigments and then in the cells. These create a nerve signal that travels to the brain. And get this – all this confusing chaotic chemistry happens more or less instantly. And all the time.
2 So how good are your eyeballs? Are they sharp as needles or a sight for sore eyes? Why not put them through their paces? Your eyeballs should be good enough to spot a coin in the playground at 65 metres. Better make sure the playground is empty before trying this experiment, though.

Now for another eyeball test.

Dare you discover ... how something horrible appears to happen to your hand?

You will need:

One red piece of A4 paper

One left hand (Go on use your own, it won't hurt ... honest!)

What you do:

1 Roll the paper lengthways into a tube 2.5 cm across.

2 Stand with a window on your right.

3 Put the tube to your right eye. Stare hard with both eyes open.

4 Place your left hand against the left side of the tube with your thumb underneath the tube.

What do you notice?

a) Your hand ... has disappeared.

b) Agggh! A bleeding hole has appeared in your hand.

c) Oh no! You've got two left hands.

Your pupils widen to let in more light in dark conditions. The word "pupil" comes from the Latin word for "little girl". Look at your reflection in a mirror and you'll see a tiny reflection of yourself in your pupil. Sorry boys, the ancient Romans thought this looked like a little girl.

CHEEK!

But talking about dark conditions...

TEACHER'S TEA-BREAK TEASER

This teaser works best in a dark, sinister, gloomy corridor (most schools have a few). You'll need a book with very small print. (Try using a boring science book, not this one, obviously.) Knock on the staffroom door. When the door opens smile sweetly and ask...

CAN YOU READ THIS FOR ME?

Enjoy watching your teacher struggling with the tiny print. Then ask them why people can't read in the dark.

Answer:

This is a particularly fiendish teaser because there are actually two possible answers.

1 Your cone cells can detect light photons but there are not enough to form an image of the text.

2 Your poor old retina does its best. It tries to detect as many light photons as it can – but to do this it has to make use of rod cells covering a wider area than it would normally use to read. And because the retina is responding to light from this wider area it's a hard for you to concentrate on tiny words.

Does your teacher know both answers?

COULD YOU BE A SCIENTIST?

Of course, these vital facts about vision didn't discover themselves. Scientists and doctors had to find them out by careful investigation. The discovery of how the lens in your eye focuses light was made by Thomas Young in 1792 using a real eyeball.

But where did it come from?

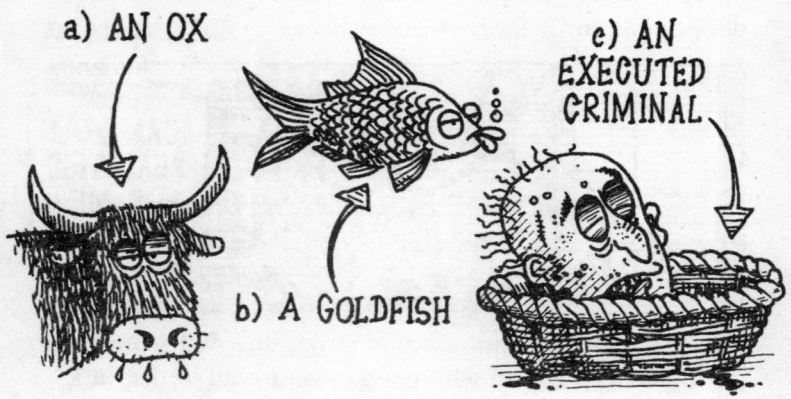

a) AN OX

b) A GOLDFISH

c) AN EXECUTED CRIMINAL

TEST YOUR TEACHER

You can liven up a boring swimming lesson by asking this tricky science question. It's sure to make a big splash.

BLUBBERLUB BERLUB LUBBER LUBBER LUBBER BLUBBERLUB?*

PARDON?

*WHY DOES EVERYTHING APPEAR BLURRED UNDER WATER?

Answer:
Normally light refracts (that's bends, remember) as it passes through the cornea. This bending happens as light passes from the air into the watery cornea. This helps to bend light on to the retina allowing you to see things in focus.

LIGHT BENDS HERE

LOVELY AIR, BUZZ!

When you're underwater the light is already going through water so it doesn't bend into the cornea. As a result the light isn't so well focused on your retina and things appear blurred.

LIGHT DOESN'T BEND

LOVELY WATER, GLUG!

HORRIBLE HEALTH WARNING!

If you can't swim it's very unhealthy to hold your head underwater to check if things appear blurred. It's also very cruel to hold your teacher's head underwater for this purpose.

FRIGHTENING EXPRESSIONS

An ophthalmologist asks...

ARE YOU HAVING ACCOMMODATION PROBLEMS?

Do you say...?

NO, MUM SAYS I CAN STAY AT HOME.

Talking about eye problems, take a very close look at this (if you can).

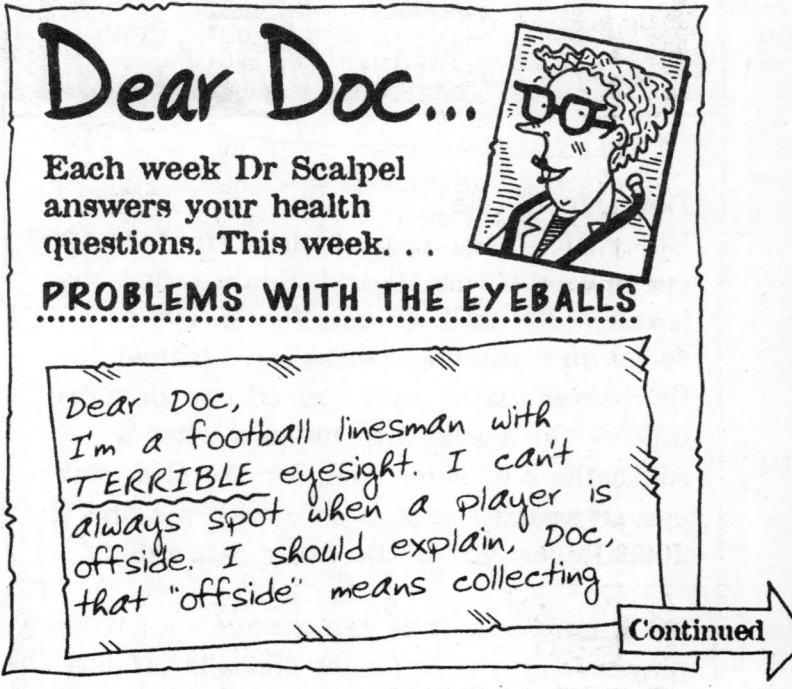

Dear Doc...

Each week Dr Scalpel answers your health questions. This week. . .

PROBLEMS WITH THE EYEBALLS

Dear Doc,
I'm a football linesman with TERRIBLE eyesight. I can't always spot when a player is offside. I should explain, Doc, that "offside" means collecting

Continued

51

a forward pass with no opponents between you and the goal line when the ball is kicked. And it's not allowed. But as I said, I'm not always sure when a player is offside. You see, they move so fast it's very confusing. And when I make the wrong decision the fans call me rude names. It's so hurtful ... I could cry.
Should I retire?

Mr I.B. Worried

Dear Mr Worried

Cheer up – your eyesight is normal. In 1998 eye specialists in Madrid, Spain found that it takes 300 milliseconds for an eye to focus on a moving footballer. Meanwhile the player might have moved two or more metres. So it's hard to be sure when a footballer's offside. Well, Mr Worried, this embarrassing secret is safe with me and the 200,000 readers of the *Daily Searchlight*.

PS Funny how fans can always spot when a player from the opposing team is offside.

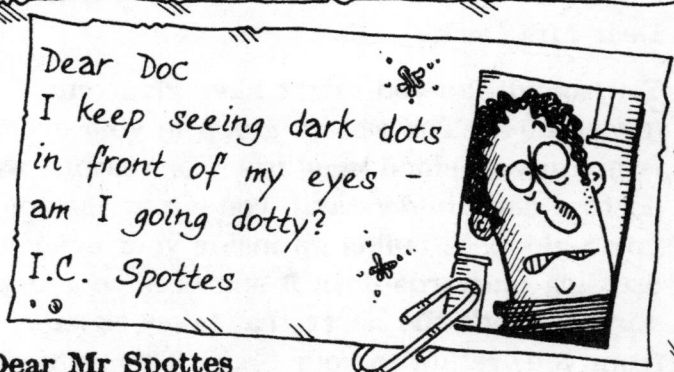

Dear Doc
I keep seeing dark dots in front of my eyes – am I going dotty?
I.C. Spottes

Dear Mr Spottes
The dots you describe are probably caused by blood clots on your retina. A larger dark spot may be caused by damage to your retina. In both cases you should see a doctor. I'm sure they'll spot the problem.

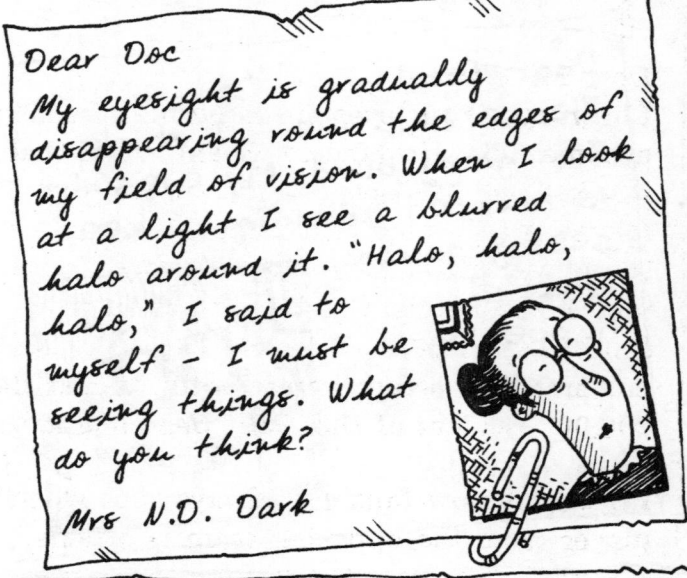

Dear Doc
My eyesight is gradually disappearing round the edges of my field of vision. When I look at a light I see a blurred halo around it. "Halo, halo, halo," I said to myself – I must be seeing things. What do you think?

Mrs N.D. Dark

Dear Mrs Dark

You sound like you might have glaucoma (gly-comb-a). The watery gloop in your eyeball is produced behind your iris. For reasons we doctors don't understand, you can make too much gloop. It builds up inside your eyeball pressing outwards until it squeezes your optic nerve – that's the nerve that takes signals from your retina to your brain. This reduces vision and causes blindness. But don't panic! You can take drops to cut the amount of gloop your eye makes and relieve the pressure on your nerve.

That's a relief – eh?

Dear Doc
Please help me – I think I'm going blind. My eyesight is blurred and dim. I keep seeing double. What's happening to me?

Ms Rabble

Dear Ms Rabble

You could have a cataract. A build up of fluid in the lens leads to chemical changes that cause a cloudy area. Seeing double happens when two cloudy areas refract light from the same object. Fortunately the cataract can be removed in a simple operation.

PS One traditional remedy for cataracts was to plop a warm drop of pee (or urine, as we doctors call it) into the eye. Don't try this – it's useless and may cause infection.

> **DON'T MISS NEXT WEEK.** It 'snot' much fun having problems with your nostrils.
> **Dear Doc** looks into noses...

There's lots of possible causes for cataracts, including damage to the lens after being outside too much under the huge sizzling blinding solar nuclear explosion in the sky.

The what?

The sun, of course.

It's time to put on those shades and turn the page...

SIZZLING SUNSHINE

We're all lucky people. Every day we get hours and hours of free sunshine. Well, OK, that's true for California and it's not quite so true if you're snowed up in Siberia. But even when the weather's grotty – cheer up – the sun's shining up there above the clouds providing warmth and light. And all for free!

But the sun is more than a big light bulb in the sky. The whole future of life on Earth depends on the sun. This fact is so basic even aliens know about it...

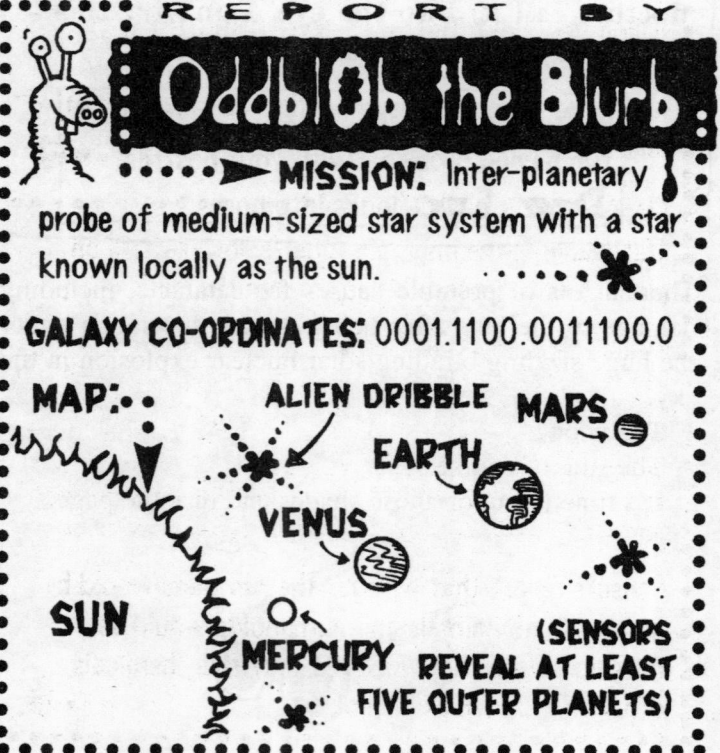

REPORT BY

Oddblob the Blurb

▶ **MISSION:** Inter-planetary probe of medium-sized star system with a star known locally as the sun.

GALAXY CO-ORDINATES: 0001.1100.0011100.0

MAP:

ALIEN DRIBBLE

MARS

EARTH

VENUS

SUN

MERCURY

(SENSORS REVEAL AT LEAST FIVE OUTER PLANETS)

INTELLIGENT LIFE

A species known as humanoids are very abundant on Planet Earth. We have captured a specially trained humanoid known as a "Science teacher" for further research.

Science teacher - emitted squeaky sound like, "ARR-YOR-AN-ALEEE-EN!"

The names given to planets in this report are names used by the humanoid.

STAR STATUS

The sun is in the middle of its life. It is 4.5 billion years old. The centre is 14,000,000° C (27,000,000° F). Light photons are produced by atoms as they are fused together. Just like any other star of this type, really.

PLANET EARTH

This planet is the only one suitable for life. Life on planet Earth depends on light from the sun.

PLANTS - GREEN NON-MOVING LIFE FORMS. PLANTS USE ENERGY FROM SUNLIGHT TO TURN WATER AND CARBON DIOXIDE GAS FROM AIR INTO FOOD.

SUN

ENERGY

HUMANOIDS EAT ANIMALS AND PLANTS.

ANIMALS - MOBILE LIFE FORMS THAT EAT PLANTS OR OTHER ANIMALS.

Sensors report that without the sun there would be no plants, no animals and humanoids would be missing out on their intake of nutritive chemicals otherwise known as lunch.

INVASION POTENTIAL ◄ • • • • • • • • • •

Planet Earth is suitable for invasion – but from our study of the Science teacher we have established that humans spend much of their time communicating boring information. Life on Earth may prove unbearably dull for higher forms of intelligence such as Blurbs. So we have erased the humanoid's memory of our visit and put him back where we found him.

ZONK!...now where was I...ah yes, your science homework, Smith...

AWESOME ECLIPSES

One dramatic effect of the sun is called an eclipse. This is caused by the moon getting in the way of the sun's light so that its shadow falls on the Earth.

SHADOW OF MOON

MOON

EARTH

SUNLIGHT

SUN

ARGH! IT'S UNBEARABLY DULL!

THE HUMANOIDS AGREE WITH US, ODDBLOB!

Oh, so you knew that? Well, in the past many people didn't – so they made up stories and performed rituals to make sense of what was going on.

1 An eclipse can be frightening. If you don't know what's happening, it looks like the moon is swallowing the sun. According to ancient Greek writer Thucydides (460-400 BC) an eclipse halted a battle in Persia in the sixth century BC. The two armies drew back and agreed to go on with the battle after a month, when any bad magical effects had worn off.

2 In ancient China people thought a dragon was eating the sun and banged gongs or pans to scare the monster away.

3 The native peoples of North America fired flaming arrows at the sky in a bid to re-light the sun.

THIS IS AN 'ARROWING EXPERIENCE!

4 The Pampas tribes of South America believed the moon goddess was darkened in an eclipse with her own blood drawn by savage dogs. Of course, they were barking up the wrong tree.

5 Some Tartar tribes in Asia believed the sun and moon were swallowed up by a blood-sucking vampire from a distant star.

6 In many countries people thought (wrongly) that diseases spread during eclipses. The Yukon tribes of Alaska covered their pots and pans during eclipses for this reason. A terrible outbreak of 'flu that claimed thousands of victims in South America in 1918 was blamed by some on an eclipse.

Dare you discover ... how to observe an eclipse?

Eclipses of the sun are fairly rare. There are often less than five a year – so chances are, you won't be able to see one from your own backyard. To see one you might have to travel to far flung places like the North Pole. Well, when you get there, here's a way to watch the eclipse without hurting your eyes.

Note: If there aren't any eclipses coming up you can always use this method to look at the sun safely. You can try it at home in a shaft of bright sunlight.

You will need:
The sun (but of course!)
A large sheet of white paper and something to fix it to the wall with
A small mirror
Ruler
A piece of card
Scissors and sticky tape

What you do:
1 Cut a circle in the card 2.5 cm across.
2 Tape the card over the mirror and stick the paper on the wall in a dark shadowy corner.
3 Hold the mirror so that it reflects the sunlight from the circle onto the white paper. You'll see a nice image of the Sun that's safe to look at.

URGENT HORRIBLE HEALTH WARNING!

Staring at the sun is dangerous. Even a few moments of being blasted by the Sun's high-energy photons kills off cells in your retina and gazing at the Sun too long can cause cataracts and blindness. Any really bright light can be harmful Welders who don't use protective goggles get "arc eye" and go blind for a while – or even for ever. So you'd be blind stupid to risk it.

A SNAP DECISION
If you think the dangers of observing an eclipse sound

rather frightening, spare a thought for Warren de la Rue (1815-1889). In 1860 top astronomer Sir John Herschel (1792-1871) asked this intrepid British photographer to travel to Rivabellosa in Spain to photograph an eclipse and prove a scientific fact.

"So Warren got a nice sun tan and took a few holiday snaps. What's so risky about that?" I hear you ask.

Well, in 1860 cameras were in their infancy and travel was a bit more primitive. So this was quite an undertaking. Here's what Warren's letters home might have looked like...

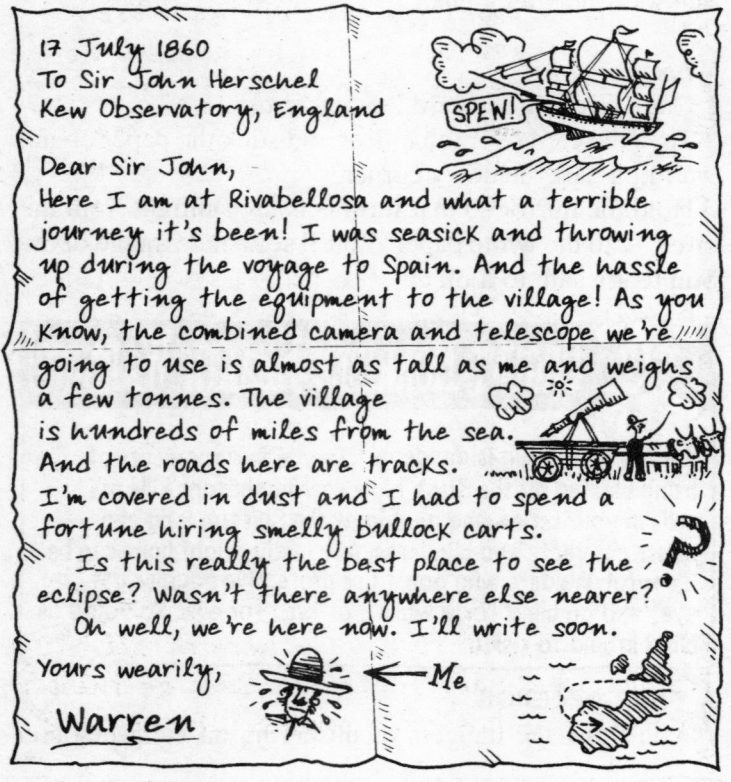

17 July 1860
To Sir John Herschel
Kew Observatory, England

SPEW!

Dear Sir John,
Here I am at Rivabellosa and what a terrible journey it's been! I was seasick and throwing up during the voyage to Spain. And the hassle of getting the equipment to the village! As you know, the combined camera and telescope we're going to use is almost as tall as me and weighs a few tonnes. The village is hundreds of miles from the sea. And the roads here are tracks. I'm covered in dust and I had to spend a fortune hiring smelly bullock carts.

Is this really the best place to see the eclipse? Wasn't there anywhere else nearer?

Oh well, we're here now. I'll write soon.

Yours wearily,

← Me

Warren

18 July 1860 at 2 am
To Sir John Herschel
Kew Observatory
England

Dear Sir John

I may not send this letter. But I can't sleep and I've got to sort out my thoughts. It's just that I'm really scared things won't work out tomorrow. I know you're keen to get pictures of the flares that you see during an eclipse. It would be great to get nice clear pictures and prove the flares come from the sun and not from the moon or the sky as some people think. But no one's ever got a decent photo of an eclipse. What happens if you can't see the flares? And if it's cloudy tomorrow I won't see anything anyway.

I can't stand it. . . . I wish I'd never come to this miserable little village. I want to go home. I don't think I'll send this letter. It might scare you, Sir John, it certainly scares me.

Warren

PS It's all your fault I'm here at all.
PPS The locals are suspicious. Some of them think I've got magical powers. If only.

GOSSIP
MUMBLE
MUTTER

63

Meanwhile some of the people of Rivabellosa must have been wondering what was going on. Here's how events might have appeared to a young boy.

THE ECLIPSE BY PEDRO

Our teacher told us all about the eclipse. But the old people in our village said it would bring sickness and disaster. That's what Grandpa thought. He said the sweaty Englishman had a magic machine to make the sun go dark for as long as he wished.

The day of the eclipse was bright and sunny. I went up the hill with Grandpa to get a good view. Grandpa was still grumbling and saying no good will come of it. There were crowds of people.

The Englishman had his machine set up — I could see the end of it sticking out the top of a shed like a giant gun.

Just before the eclipse, we saw the moon getting close to the sun. Then a horrible dark shadow appeared in the distance. It was the shadow of the moon. The darkness swept over the hills like a thunderstorm. Everything went grey. All the flowers closed up and birds started snoozing in the trees. It was just like evening so I started yawning.

"Bored already?" snapped Grandpa.

Then things got scary.   Grandpa →

Little by little the sun was swallowed up by the moon until all you could see was a black glowing circle. Suddenly my hair stood on end — I was seriously worried. It was dark. The stars had come out.

Maybe Grandpa was right.

Perhaps the sun had gone for ever.

I grabbed hold of his hand.

Meanwhile the Englishman was acting crazy. Shouting at his assistants and disappearing into the shed to work his giant machine. We heard him muttering things to himself.

"He's saying spells," whispered Grandpa.

So Grandpa got down on to his bony knees and started reciting prayers. But there was no sign of the sun.

Where was it?

The minutes dragged by...

Just then a bright bead of light appeared. It looked like a diamond ring around the dark moon. Everyone cheered. I found myself dancing up and down.

"It's a miracle!" cried Grandpa, struggling to his feet.

It began to get light. Soon the sun was shining again in the blue sky. The eclipse was scary but brilliant. No one got ill, nothing terrible happened. I wish we had an eclipse every week. It's much better than listening to Grandpa strumming his guitar and singing awful old songs.

18 July 1860 at 4 pm
To Sir John Herschel
Kew Observatory, England

Dear Sir John
It's over and I'm shattered. Completely drained. Well, I tried. I took 35 shots

including two when the sun was completely covered. But the pictures weren't as good as I'd expected. THEY WERE BETTER! LOADS BETTER! You can see everything. You can see the flares really clearly. It's blindingly obvious the flares are coming from the sun itself!!!

Thank you, Sir John, for sending me to this wonderful little village full of lovely people. Now for a giant party and everyone's invited!!

Love Warren xx
PS Wish you were here!

A scientist writes...

Spanish scientist Father Angelo Secchi (1818–1878) also took a series of photos of the eclipse. Father Secchi was over 400 km to the south-east but the flares in his pictures matched the ones taken by De La Rue. This was the final proof that the flares had definitely come from the sun.

DARK SECRETS

It gets dark during an eclipse because the moon casts its shadow over the Earth. You get a shadow any time a solid object blocks light. (That's how the climber on the Brocken Mountain made the "ghost".) Something that blocks light is described as opaque (o-payk). And you can use an opaque shape to make horrible shadows...

Dare you discover ... what lurks in the shadows?

You will need:
A pencil
A pair of scissors
A piece of black card. You can always paint a white piece of card black.
A piece of wire
Sticky tape
A small, bright torch
A room with light walls.

What you do:
1 Draw and cut out a monster shape.
2 Tape the wire to the bottom of the shape to make a handle.
3 Wait until it gets dark. Draw the curtains and switch on your torch. Place the torch about three metres from the wall.
4 Hold the wire so the shape is between the light and the wall. You can make brilliant sinister shadows. Hold on, sorry to spoil things, but this is a serious scientific experiment, after all. So...

What do you notice?

a) You moved the shape towards the wall and away from the torch. The shadow on the wall got larger.

b) When the shape is closer to the light it blocks more light. This throws a larger shadow on the wall.

c) As you moved the torch the shadow began to move in the opposite direction. Help – it's alive!

Answer:

b) When the shape is closer to the light, it blocks more light. This throws a larger shadow on the wall. The larger shadow has more of a blurred edge than the smaller one. This is because some light from the edges of the torch can still shine past the edges of the shape, but not enough to give a sharp edge to the shadow.

HORRIBLE HEALTH WARNING!

This monster shape is ideal for scaring your little brother or sister. But you know it's wrong – don't you? And you're going to resist the temptation, aren't you? Well ... aren't you?

STRANGE STARLIGHT

Of course, astronomers aren't just interested in sunlight. They're also very excited by the topic of starlight. If you have secret ambitions to be an astronomer you might like to train your telescope on this next bit...

The stars are a long way off. A very long way off. You'll remember that sunlight takes about eight and a half minutes to reach us. But that's a blink of an eye for starlight. Even the light of our next door neighbour star Alpha Centauri takes four years to arrive. But that's nothing. If you live in the northern part of the world the most distant object you'll see is the Andromeda galaxy. The photons from this star cluster set off 2.2 million years before you were born. And you thought waiting for the school bus took for ever.

Astronomers are interested in starlight because without it they wouldn't be able to see stars. And by studying the colour of the light they can work out the surface temperature of the star. For example, a bluish white star is a sizzling 27,760°C and a red star is a nice cool 2,000°C. (OK, that's cool by star standards – the hottest temperatures on Earth include California's Death Valley which reached 49°C in 1917. Any hotter than that here and it would be Death Valley for the human race.)

The brightness of a star can also be used mathematically to work out its distance. This brilliant fact was noted by U.S. astronomer Henrietta Leavitt (1868–1921).

Bet you never knew!
Stars are coloured. It's true! The reason they seem white to us is that most stars are very dim. They only give your eye about 500 photons a second. This means that we can only see them with our dim light detecting rod cells. And the rod cells can't see colours, can they?

COULD YOU BE AN ASTRONOMER?

You've probably heard the rhyme:

Twinkle, twinkle little star
How I wonder what you are!

Next time you gaze at a star consider this puzzle:
Why do stars twinkle?
a) Because their light flashes on and off.
b) Because the starlight is refracted (bent) by gusts of wind.
c) Because fast-moving clouds keep blocking the light.

Answer:
b) As the wind blows, the atoms that make up air may get more crowded together in one area than another. As light passes through this area it refracts (bends) producing a twinkling effect. In fact, moonlight does this too but because the moon appears bigger to us you don't notice it twinkling around the edges.

Bet you never knew!
If you want to spot stars it helps if you live a long way away from the neighbours. In built-up areas the night sky often glows with the light of streetlights and shop signs reflecting off water droplets and dust in the air. This spoils the view of the twinkling stars.

But if lights are bad news for astronomers they're very good news for small frightened kids who are scared of the dark. So if you're reading this at dusk, maybe you'd better turn on the light before you switch to the next chapter.

It will brighten you ... and frighten you.

FRIGHTENING LIGHTING

This is a chapter about things that glow in the dark. And not all of them are light bulbs. Yep – long before anyone flicked a light switch, before even some bright spark invented fire, strange unearthly lights flickered in the darkness.

Intrigued? Let's bring the FRIGHTENING facts to light...

Frightening light fact file

NAME: Bioluminescence (bio-lum-min-nes-ance)

THE BASIC FACTS: 1. Certain living creatures can produce light.

2. Their bodies make a chemical called luciferin (loo-sif-fer-rin) and another called luciferase (loo-sif-fer-raze).

3. Luciferin combines with oxygen from the creature's blood and gives out light. Luciferase speeds up this chemical reaction.

THE FRIGHTENING DETAILS: Some bacteria do this. Some fish (see below) eat the bacteria. The bacteria remain alive and make light in the fish's skin.

'GLO' AWAY, YOU'RE UGLY!

THE GLOW IN THE DARK ZOO

Welcome to the world's first zoo where the animals provide the lighting...

Comb jelly

Jelly-fish-like creature 25-30cm long.

FOUND IN: Pacific and Atlantic Oceans.

LIGHT IS USED FOR: scaring off attackers.

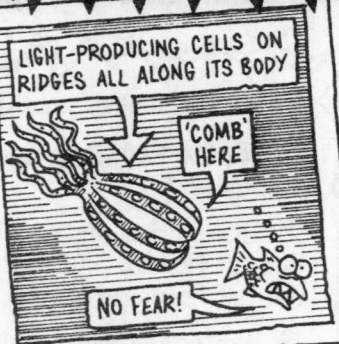

LIGHT-PRODUCING CELLS ON RIDGES ALL ALONG ITS BODY

'COMB' HERE

NO FEAR!

Deep sea angler fish

FOUND IN: deep oceans throughout the world

LIGHT IS USED FOR: catching other fish

WORM-LIKE BLOB (FILLED WITH GLOWING BACTERIA) ON THE END OF A LINE LURES SMALLER FISH TO THEIR DOOM.

HMMM, INTERESTING!

Fire flies and glow-worms

FOUND IN: fire flies live in North America and glow-worms live in Europe. Actually they're both varieties of beetle.

PHWOAR! HE'S NICE!

LIGHT IS USED FOR: signalling for a mate.

HERE I AM, BOYS!

FIRE FLY

Both insects have glowing lights on their bottoms. (Imagine you had one of these – you'd never need a rear bike light.)

GLOW-WORM

Luminous plankton

Tiny creatures often less than 1 mm long called copepods (cope-pods). The plankton also include plants called dinoflagellates (di-no-fladge-gell-ates).

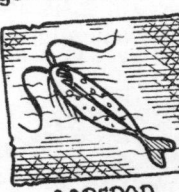

COPEPOD

DINOFLAGELLATE

FOUND IN: every ocean especially where the water is rich in minerals.

LIGHT IS USED FOR: scaring away attackers. Ship toilets are often flushed with seawater – if the plankton are present they make your toilet glow in the dark. (Is this what they call a "flash in the pan"?)

ARGH! WEIRD WEE WEE!

But there are other kinds of light around and these are not made by animals. Not living ones, anyway.

COULD YOU BE A SCIENTIST?

It's 200 years ago. You're walking home and you bravely decide to take a short cut through the graveyard. It's very dark – you're scared ... and suddenly you see an eerie glow. What's causing it?

a) It's a ghost. Yikes I'm out of here.

b) It's a mass of glow-worms feeding off rotting vegetation.

c) It's gases from a rotting body.

Answer:

c) Before new cemeteries were opened up in Victorian times many old churchyards became full up. Dead bodies were buried one on top of the other under a shallow layer of soil. Germs inside the rotting bodies made methane and phosphine (foz-feen) gas. As the gases reached the surface they often caught fire as a result of chemical reactions with oxygen in the air. The result was a pale blue glow that was called a will o' the wisp.

AWFUL ARTIFICIAL LIGHT

We take it for granted that by flicking a switch we can have light whenever we want. It's a part of every day life and without it you wouldn't be able to see this page, or even see to do homework (that would be tragic!). But just imagine you lived a few hundred years before there were light bulbs. Don't worry, you didn't have to use the glowing gas from a dead body. But the alternatives were almost as frightening.

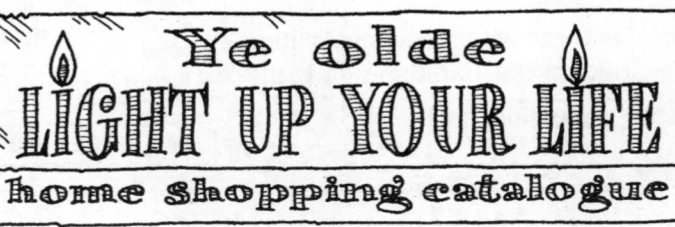

Ye olde LIGHT UP YOUR LIFE
home shopping catalogue

ROMANTIC CANDLES
Why not light your home with a genuine olde worlde candle as used by people since ancient Egyptian times. Wow, what a dazzling choice!

NOW WE HAVE TO WAIT 3500 YEARS FOR SOMEONE TO INVENT MATCHES

CONTINUED...

Traditional tallow candle

▷ Made with boiled up fat from around the kidneys of a dead cow, sheep or horse.

WE'VE RUN OUT OF TALLOW CANDLES, WIFE.

Heat from the flame melts the fat.

▷ Beeswax – the de-luxe alternative. Genuine waxy stuff squirted from the bodies of bees and built up to make chambers for their grubs to live in.

The flame burns the fat

The wick sucks up the fat.

Modern paraffin candle

▷ Made from oil.

▷ Burns with a nice bright flame

SORRY MUM, IT'S MADE A MESS. . .

GRRR, I'LL GIVE YOU WAX!

THE AMAZING ARC-LIGHT

Invented by British scientist Sir Humphrey Davy (1778-1829) in 1808

WELL, CANDLES WENT OUT WITH THE ARK

▷ Electric current jumps across the gap between two carbon rods. (Make sure there's a constant gap between two carbon rods as the light burns otherwise the rods will melt or the light will fizzle out.)

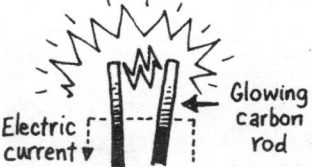

Electric current

Glowing carbon rod

THE SMALL PRINT: This light is a fire hazard. And it could blind you because it's brighter than 4,000 candles. The only practical use anyone ever found for it was in the Dungeness lighthouse. So unless your house happens to be a lighthouse it's probably not such a good idea.

TURN IT OFF!

GASLIGHT

As invented by Scottish inventor William Murdock (1754–1839)

Flame made by burning coal gas

Handy tap to turn the gas on or off

ER – I'M JUST WARMING THE POT, MUM...

GRRR!

after an experiment in 1792 involving heating coal in his mum's teapot.

THE SMALL PRINT: You need pipes all over your house to carry the gas. And the gas is poisonous and can blow up your home. And even when it works the flame is smoky and smelly.

MARVELLOUS MODERN LIGHTS

Nowadays things are looking much brighter. Go into any street and you'll probably see sodium or mercury street lights. These work in roughly the same way.

An electric current passes through the tube. Atoms in the gas take in energy and give out light.

Something else passing through a tube

1 Some atoms are fluorescent (flor-res-sent). That means they soak up high-energy photons and spit out lower-energy photons. For example, fluorescent lights (found in strip lights and long-life light bulbs) zap mercury atoms with electrons to make ultraviolet photons. A substance called phosphor (fos-for) then soaks up the ultraviolet photons and gives out the light we can see.

2 Some scientists think that flickering fluorescent lights make people feel more bad-tempered. Does your classroom have these lights and do they explain your teacher's terrible temper tantrums?

3 Sheepskin flouresces. This means that if you shear sheep and blast it with ultraviolet light it will give off a ghostly glow in the dark.

BRILLIANT BULBS

One invention put the others in the shade. The light bulb. And as every American knows the light bulb was invented by U.S. inventor Thomas A. Edison (1847–1931). And every well-informed Briton knows the light bulb was invented by British inventor Joseph Swan (1828–1914). So what's the truth?

Read on and find out...

Thomas A. Edison's diary

I've got this real smart idea for a new kind of light. All you do is send an electric current through a thin wire. This slows down the flow of electricity. The electric current drags along making the wire heat up and you get light. Simple but brilliant - like most of my inventions...

Hmm - need to pump out the air otherwise the thin wire will catch fire when you heat it up. You can't get fire without air - can you?

THIN WIRE

AIR IS MAKING THIN WIRE CATCH FIRE

ELECTRICITY

THE DAILY SUN

1 September 1878

Let there be light!

Brilliant inventor Thomas Edison is set to light up the world by inventing the light bulb. Already gas lighting company shares are plummeting at the prospect. And Edison hasn't even built a single bulb yet! But whiz-kid Edison is already famous for inventing the phonograph. (That's the new-fangled machine you can use to play music on.)

MR. T. EDISON

And now he's getting on with a bit of light work!

21 January 1879

If only I could make this light work. One day there could be a light bulb in every home. There might even be two in every

81

home. I could become seriously rich. But only if everything goes to plan. I've hurt my eyes staring at the light bulbs... before they burnt out. Work is getting harder.

Those carbon filaments sure can burn. Seems my pumps aren't good enough to get all the air out of the bulbs. So I tried platinum wires instead - but they kept melting. Then I made a switch to cut the power if the platinum gets too hot but the light keeps flickering. Oh well - back to the drawing board. As I like to say, "inventing is 99 per cent perspiration and only 1 per cent inspiration".

1 April 1879

Did I say perspiration? Well, I'm in a cold sweat just now. To be precise, I'm at my wit's end. We've tried thousands of materials - rubber, fishing line, wood and now in desperation we're trying human hair. Two of my assistants volunteered to provide the hair. John Kruesli's got a big bushy beard and J.V. Mackenzie's got wiry sideburns.

J.K.

J.V.M.

My staff are all excited and are even betting which hair will last longest without burning.

A few hours later...

Mackenzie's hair is still producing light! Hold on - looks like the electric current's been turned down and the bulb's too dim to be any use. RATS, I figure someone cheated to win the bets. I can't stand these failures - I should never have allowed the papers to print all that rubbish. Maybe I'll never solve this puzzle and go down in history as a dim failure.

DIM!

DIM!

17 October 1879

I was sitting in the office last night when a bright light bulb seemed to flash in my head. "Oh no - not another light bulb!" I moaned. Then I realized I was having A BRAINWAVE - that's what I mean by INSPIRATION. I thought burnt cotton thread that's turned to carbon might be the answer. Yeah - the magic material has to be carbon. After all, carbon only melts at really high temperatures of about 3500°C (6332°F). And now I've taken delivery of better air pumps the carbon shouldn't burn up. And ... well, I just have a hunch about cotton thread.

BUT WILL IT WORK? ? ? ? ? ? ?

21 October 1879

I could cry. I've been working non-stop for days trying to make a cotton thread filament. Each one takes hours. But they keep breaking at the last moment. They're so thin and fragile. Oh well, here's number three. My heart's in my mouth and I'm switching on the new light bulb. It's burning . . . but for how long?

Keep burning . . . please.

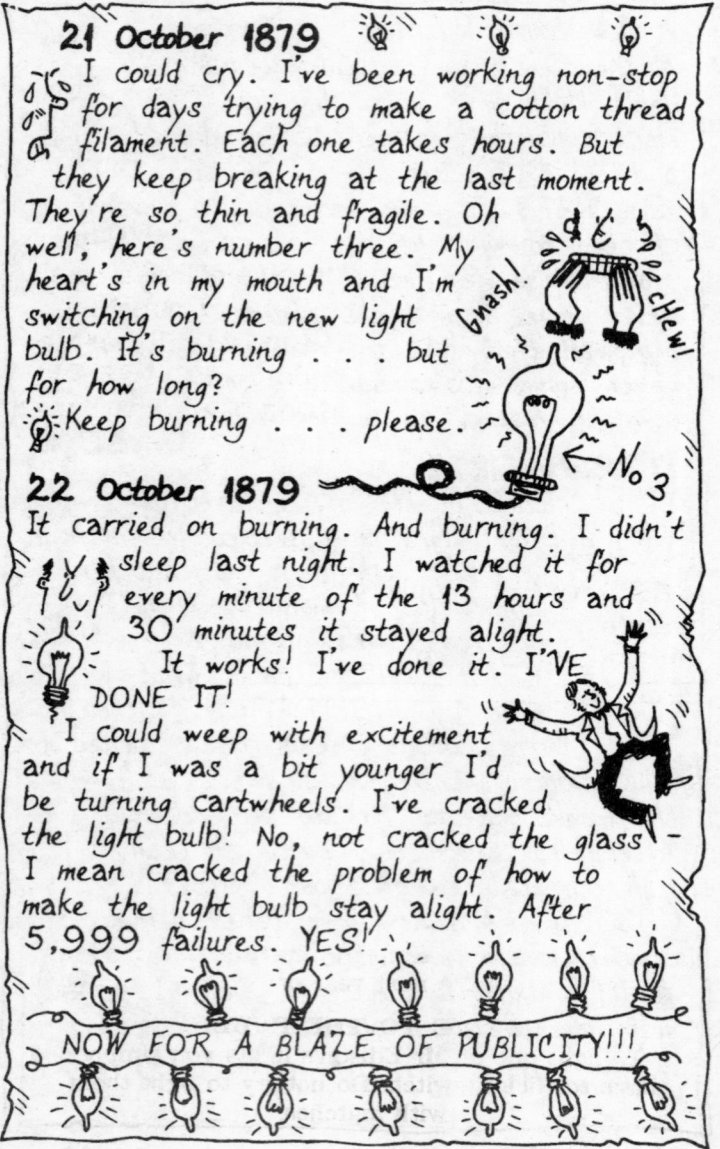

No 3

22 October 1879

It carried on burning. And burning. I didn't sleep last night. I watched it for every minute of the 13 hours and 30 minutes it stayed alight.
It works! I've done it. I'VE DONE IT!
I could weep with excitement and if I was a bit younger I'd be turning cartwheels. I've cracked the light bulb! No, not cracked the glass - I mean cracked the problem of how to make the light bulb stay alight. After 5,999 failures. YES!

NOW FOR A BLAZE OF PUBLICITY!!!

THE DAILY SUN

31 December 1879

Blaze of glory!

Heroic inventor Thomas A. Edison glowed with pride as he showed off his new invention.

Thousands of people watched him light up the whole town with 3,000 newly-invented light bulbs. Each one looks like a globe of sunshine. No more will people huddle in the dark afraid of the shadows. Thomas Edison is a shining example to the whole nation! It's such a pity that 14 of the new light bulbs have already been pinched.

85

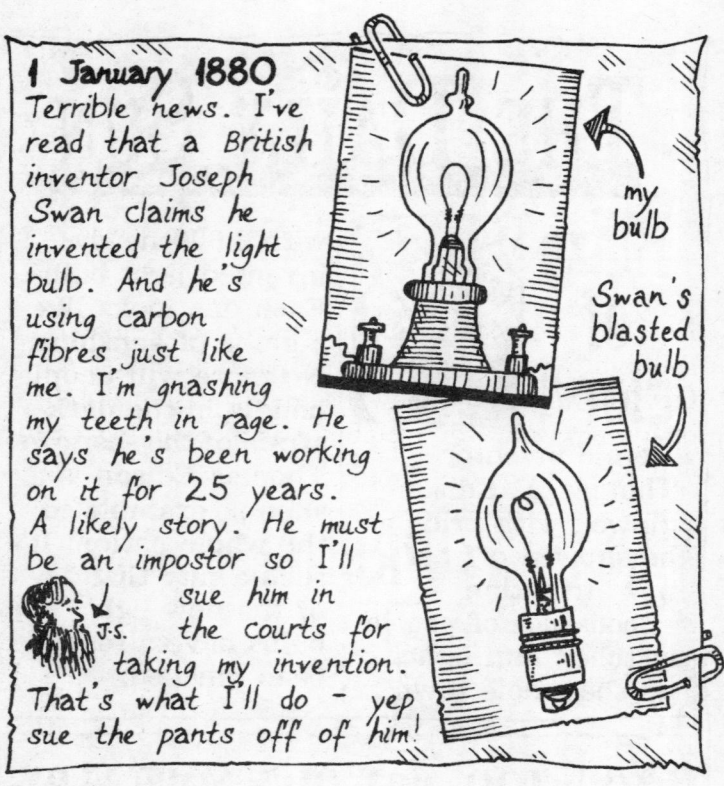

1 January 1880

Terrible news. I've read that a British inventor Joseph Swan claims he invented the light bulb. And he's using carbon fibres, just like me. I'm gnashing my teeth in rage. He says he's been working on it for 25 years. A likely story. He must be an impostor so I'll sue him in the courts for taking my invention. That's what I'll do – yep, sue the pants off of 'him!

J.S.

my bulb

Swan's blasted bulb

But the British courts found that Swan had indeed been making light bulbs before Edison. Swan was a talented chemist whose inventions included artificial silk. He had finally made a successful carbon filament bulb in February 1879. But he didn't patent the invention because he thought people would copy it anyway.

If you were Thomas Edison what would you do next?
a) Pay Swan $1,000,000 to stop making light bulbs.
b) Try to sell cheaper light bulbs than Swan and drive him out of business.
c) Offer to join forces with Swan.

TEST YOUR TEACHER

Here's your chance to put your teacher under the spotlight. Ask them who invented the light bulb. If they know anything they'll say either Thomas Edison or Joseph Swan – or even both. Shake your head sadly and say:

As so often happens in science, the answer gets more complicated the more you find out. Several inventors made carbon filament lights before Swan and Edison. For example, Scottish inventor James Bowman Lindsay made one in 1835. But he didn't tell many people about it. Apparently, he didn't think there would be money in the new invention. And anyway, scientists have continued to improve on Edison's original design. Yes, it really does take quite a few scientists to invent a light bulb...

A BRIGHTER IDEA

A modern light bulb uses a coiled tungsten metal filament surrounded by argon – a harmless gas found in the air.

Modern heat resistant tungsten wires were developed by American William D. Coolidge (1873–1975) (yes, he really did live to 102). The idea of using a gas in the bulb came from another American, Irving Langmuir (1881–1957).

Bet you never knew!
Light bulbs save lives. Nowadays many lighthouses use electric light from powerful bulbs to warn ships away from rocks. Each lighthouse has its own pattern of flashes so that sailors can work out where they are in the dark.

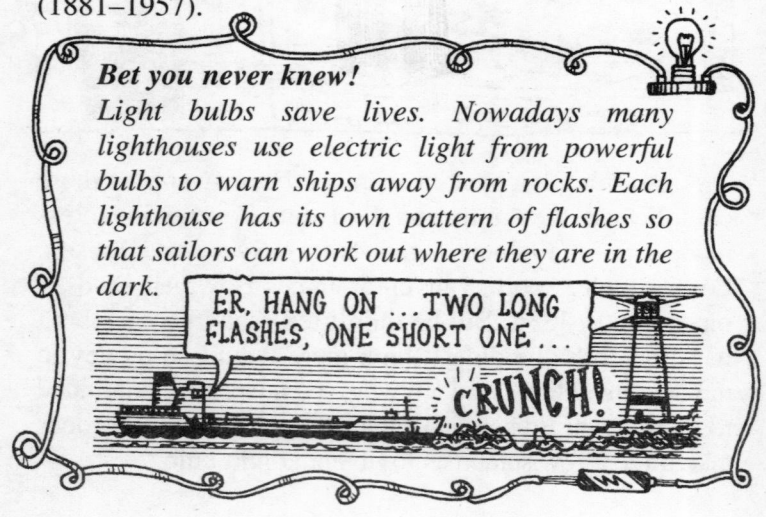

Of course, you'll find bulbs in lots of other places – you might even own a few yourself. Like in your bike lights or your torch.

Take a closer look at any of them and you'll find another amazing light gadget. What is it? A mirror of course, and it's there to reflect the light from the bulb outwards in the direction you want it to go in. And oddly enough, you'll find quite a few mirrors in the next frightening chapter.

FRIGHTENING REFLECTIONS

What's hard, and so shiny you can see your face in it?

No, it's NOT your teacher's bald head.

It's a mirror. When light hits a mirror an amazing thing happens. Light seems to bounce off it to form an image that we call a reflection. Oh, so you knew that already? Well, get this – reflections are unbelievably vital for light science. And they pop up in the most unlikely places.

Why not reflect on this quiz for a moment?

SPOT THE REFLECTION QUIZ

Reflections can help...

1 Road signs glow in the dark. TRUE/FALSE

2 Clouds glow in the sky. TRUE/FALSE

3 A TV set show pictures. TRUE/FALSE

4 A shellfish see. TRUE/FALSE

5 A doctor peer inside your eyeball. TRUE/FALSE

6 A mirage appear. TRUE/FALSE

7 Astronomers detect a black hole in space. TRUE/FALSE

8 The snow blind you. TRUE/FALSE

9 A surgeon peer inside your body without cutting you open. TRUE/FALSE

Answers:

1 TRUE. You can find tiny mirrors in road signs and in road studs. The mirrors reflect car headlights. **2 TRUE.** Clouds reflect sunlight. That's what makes them bright and glowing. Thunderclouds appear dark and gloomy from the ground because they are thicker than ordinary clouds and reflect most of the sunlight upwards. Clouds that glow at night do so because they are high enough in the sky to still catch the sunlight. **3 FALSE.** There are no mirrors inside a TV set. **4 TRUE.** Scallops are a type of shellfish with tiny mirrors in their eyes. Each eye has a shiny layer of crystals that reflect light on to cells inside the eye. A scientist made this discovery whilst looking down a microscope at the shellfish. He saw his own face reflected in the creature's 100 gruesome eyes. **5 TRUE.** A doctor uses an ophthalmoscope (op-thal-mo-scope) to peer inside your eyeball. This instrument shines a light on to a curved mirror that focuses the light beam into your eyeball. The doctor then peers through a hole in the middle of the mirror to inspect your nerves and blood vessels. **6 FALSE.** Mirages are caused by refraction. (Just to remind you, refraction is bended light.) **7 FALSE.** Light can't escape from a black hole (that's why they're black). So you can't spot one with a mirror. **8 TRUE.** Snow reflects light so well that you can be blinded by staring at it for too long in bright sunlight. That's why skiers wear protective goggles. **9 TRUE.** The tube is called an endoscope and it's basically two bundles of optical fibres. One bundle takes light from a light source at one end into the body – just imagine sticking a torch down your throat. The surgeon looks through the other bundle to get a close-up of your innards. And talking about optical fibres...

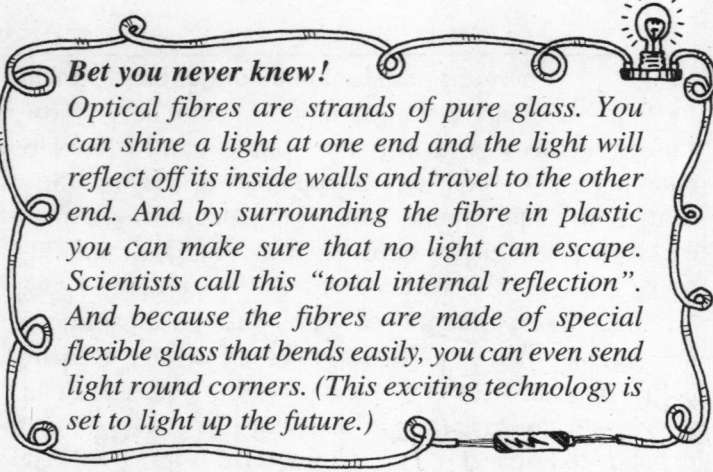

All right, this is what reflections can do. But how do you make reflections to begin with?

Frightening light fact file

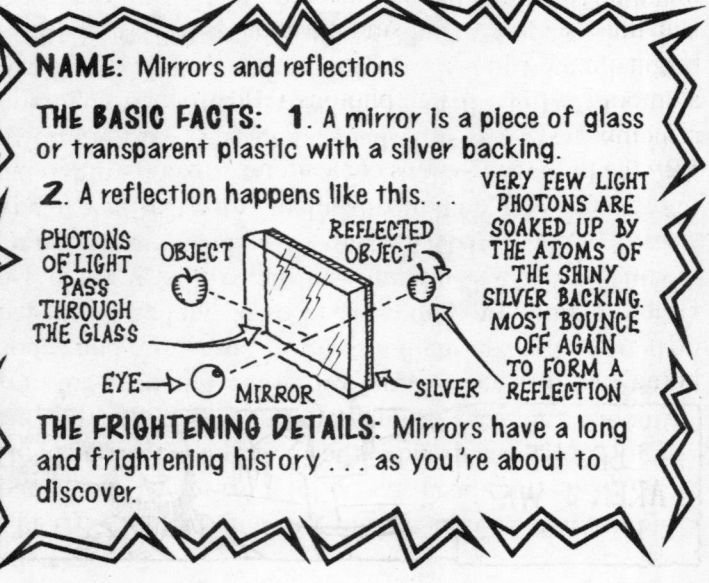

NAME: Mirrors and reflections

THE BASIC FACTS: 1. A mirror is a piece of glass or transparent plastic with a silver backing.

2. A reflection happens like this. . .

PHOTONS OF LIGHT PASS THROUGH THE GLASS

OBJECT

REFLECTED OBJECT

VERY FEW LIGHT PHOTONS ARE SOAKED UP BY THE ATOMS OF THE SHINY SILVER BACKING. MOST BOUNCE OFF AGAIN TO FORM A REFLECTION

EYE → MIRROR SILVER

THE FRIGHTENING DETAILS: Mirrors have a long and frightening history . . . as you're about to discover.

MURDEROUS MIRRORS

• Early people realized that shiny surfaces were great for seeing yourself in. Very handy for helping you brush your hair properly or spot an embarrassing bogie in your nostril.

• In ancient Egypt all sorts of things were used as mirrors including polished metal, wet slates and bowls of water. But none of them was smooth enough to give a clear, bright image. (In order to see your reflection you need a smooth surface so the photons reflect back together – remember?)

• By the time the Romans came along mirrors were much improved. The Romans used glass to make mirrors with a thin backing of tin. Unfortunately, this invention was to cause a few heated moments. According to legend the Greek scientist Archimedes (287–212 BC) used a bank of mirrors to burn Roman ships that were attacking his home city.

BRIGHT, AREN'T WE?

Every mirror reflected sunlight on to a single point on the ship. The wood heated up and burst into flames. This is scientifically possible although there's no proof it happened.

• In the Middle Ages Venice made the finest mirrors in the world. Venetians had learnt to use a mixture of mercury and tin for the backing which was easy to work without heating. This mixture was top secret. A special island was set aside for this work but the mercury was poisonous and many workers died or were driven mad by it. Nevertheless, they were forbidden to pass on the secret on pain of death.

• Somehow by the 1670s the secret had spread to France and then across Europe. In 1840, German chemist, Justus von Liebig (1803–1873) found how to put silver backing on a mirror using heated silver nitrate and other chemicals. And this method is still in use.

• Meanwhile the Chinese had been making excellent mirrors from polished metal for over 2,000 years. Some of these mirrors were called "magic mirrors". Can you solve the riddle of their amazing powers?

COULD YOU BE A SCIENTIST?

You shine a light on a magic mirror. The polished bronze surface reflects back the light on the screen together with a pattern.

But there is no pattern on the surface of the mirror itself. So what causes this strange effect? Only the makers knew the secret. Western and Chinese scientists had been baffled for years. Some Chinese thinkers believed that there was an invisible pattern etched on the front of the mirror that showed up in the reflection.

How would you explain the mirrors?

a) The Chinese thinkers were right. There was a faint pattern on the mirror's surface.

b) The mirrors gave out X-rays that revealed a hidden pattern under the surface.

c) There was a hidden pattern on the back of the mirror that was somehow being reflected from the front.

Answer:

c) The first westerners to find the answer were two British physicists, W.E. Ayrton and J. Perry. In the 1890s they were allowed to visit workshops where the mirrors were made.

1 A PATTERN IS ENGRAVED ON THE BACK OF THE MIRROR

2 THE FRONT SURFACE IS A LAYER OF METAL THAT HAS BEEN SCRAPED UNTIL IT'S VERY THIN

3 LIGHT REFLECTS OFF THE PARTS OF THE SURFACE COVERING THE PATTERN AT A SLIGHTLY DIFFERENT ANGLE TO THE REST OF THE MIRROR

4 THIS CAUSES THE PATTERN TO APPEAR AS DARK LINES ON THE SCREEN

SO WHAT'RE YOU SMILING AT?

The pattern appears as dark lines on the screen.

Bet you never knew!
In the Middle Ages people believed they could see the future by staring at a shiny surface such as a mirror. This practice was known as scrying (sk-ry-ing) – it's the origin of the traditional fortune teller's crystal ball. Other shiny surfaces used were bowls of water or blood.

YOU WILL CROSS THE SEA IN A LARGE BLOOD VESSEL.

And talking about the bad old days...

TEACHER'S TEA-BREAK TEASER

When your grandparents were young, cruel parents and teachers sometimes forced children to shine their shoes until they could see their faces in them. Here's your chance to get a belated revenge. Knock politely on the staffroom door. When it grinds open smile sweetly and enquire...

Note: there's no point in showing your teacher a pair of smelly trainers. Ideally you should be holding a nice pair of shiny shoes for their inspection.

SHINY SHOES   SMELLY TRAINERS

Answer:
Like any non-shiny object, leather is naturally bumpy and reflects light in all directions. That's why you can't see a clear reflection in it. The polish fills in the tiny dips in the leather to make a nice smooth surface that reflects light well and looks jolly smart.

Dare you discover ... what a mirror does to light?

You will need:

A mirror
Two eyebrows and yourself

What you do:

1 Stand in front of the mirror.
2 Raise your left eyebrow. (If you
can't do this just point to your left eyebrow instead.)

What does your reflection do?

a) It raises its left eyebrow.
b) The reflection raises its right eyebrow.
c) The reflection raises its right eyebrow but there's a delay of about half a second.

Answer:

Here's a great teacher teaser: all you have to do is wave a mirror in front of their ugly mug and challenge them to explain why their face appears the wrong way round. In fact the mirror simply reflects the light from a face. So the reflection of your right eyebrow appears on the right side of your reflected image. Normally when you face someone, you see their right eyebrow on the left of their face as you look at it – and that's why a reflected face appears "the wrong way round". If you really want to torture your teacher you can next ask them to explain quantum electrodynamics (QED for short). This is the mathematical theory that explains how atoms swap photons to create a reflection.

One of the first scientists to investigate reflection was born long ago in what is now Iraq. Europeans call him Alhazen but his proper name was Abu al-Hassan ibn al-Haytham. Here's his story...

98

Hall of fame: Ibn al-Haytham (965–1040)
Nationality: Arab

Although he was a great scientist al-Haytham was unlucky enough to serve a mad ruler – Egyptian Caliph al-Hakim (985–1021).

According to an old story, one day the scientist boasted to the Caliph that he could build a dam across the River Nile. Big mistake. The Caliph sent al-Haytham to southern Egypt but there he realized there was no suitable site for the dam. There were too many waterfalls. When al-Haytham returned to admit failure the Caliph was furious. He made the scientist stand on a bench and he had the bench hacked to pieces. The Caliph made it horribly clear that al-Haytham was lucky not to be hacked to pieces himself.

The Caliph gave al-Haytham an obscure government job. But the Caliph was not a man to cross and the scientist decided on a plan to save his life. He pretended to go mad. Al-Haytham was locked up and the Caliph forgot to have him killed. Ironically, a few years later the Caliph went mad himself and was murdered by an unknown hand. Afterwards al-Haytham told everyone that he had just been pretending.

THE BORING TRUTH?

Of course, some boring historians say this is a story that people told after the scientist's death. Al-Haytham never mentioned it in any of his writings. But then why should he? He'd probably have wanted to forget the incident. And why should he risk raking up the past? What do you think?

The scientist got a job teaching at the Azhar mosque and copying ancient Greek manuscripts. And there he became interested in light. So he wrote a book called *The Treasury of Optics* in which he described his brilliant discoveries. (Unfortunately, he didn't describe his experiments in any detail.)

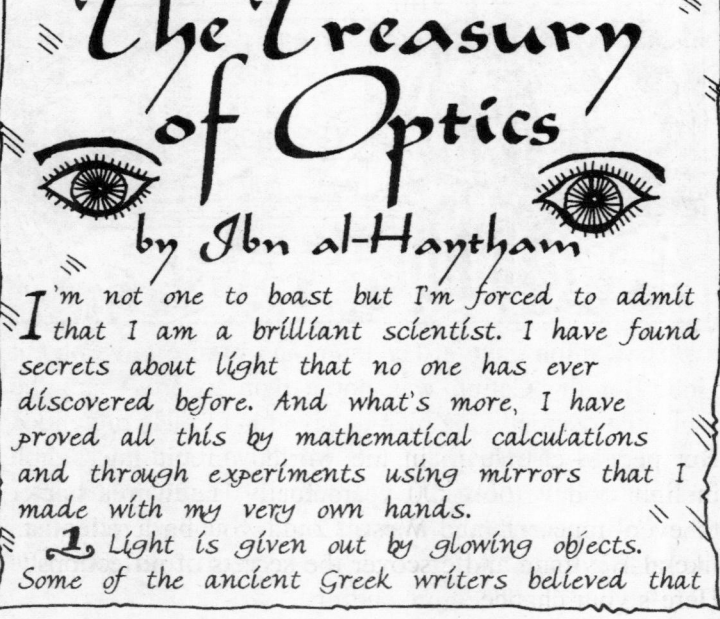

The Treasury of Optics
by Ibn al-Haytham

I'm not one to boast but I'm forced to admit that I am a brilliant scientist. I have found secrets about light that no one has ever discovered before. And what's more, I have proved all this by mathematical calculations and through experiments using mirrors that I made with my very own hands.

1 Light is given out by glowing objects. Some of the ancient Greek writers believed that light came from the eye and it was this that made the object glow. But I, Ibn al-Haytham have proved them all wrong!

2. Light travels in a straight line. Now as I said, I'm not one to blow my own trumpet - but this was one of my most ingenious and clever experiments. I made a hole in my wall so that the shaft of light entered the room. Then I checked the shaft of light and found it was perfectly straight. Brilliant!

3. Light always reflects at a predictable angle. By the most careful and painstaking measurements worthy only of the highest genius I have proved that if light shines from the left of a mirror it will bounce off to the right or vice-versa. And always at the same mathematically predictable angle.

Object

Eye

Mirror

Reflected object

Angle the same but opposite

Although I'm really a very humble, modest person I am sure the name of Ibn al-Haytham will live for ever in history and all the world will want to read of my discoveries!

But people elsewhere in the world weren't interested in light and it took 200 years for al-Haytham's book to even appear in the West. Could you be a scientist like al-Haytham and discover the secrets of reflections? Here's your chance...

Dare you discover ... how mirrors can change your appearance?

You will need:
A shiny tablespoon

What you do:
1 Hold the spoon like a hand mirror.
2 Look in the back of the spoon and then the front.

What do you notice?
a) My face appears upside-down in the back of the spoon and the right way up in the front.
b) My face appears fatter in the back of the spoon and upside-down with a long neck in the front of the spoon.
c) My face appears normal in the back of the spoon. In the front of the spoon I'm the right way up but I have a huge hooter.

Answer:
b) The front of the spoon is concave – that is it curves inwards at the centre. (To remember this word just imagine a cave shaped in the same way.)

Because of this shape, light reflecting from your face reflects downwards from the top of the spoon and upwards from the bottom.

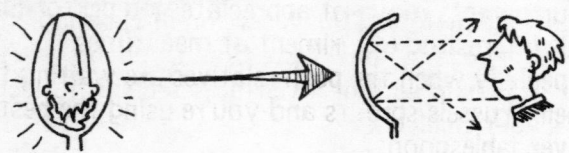

You see the bottom of your face at the top of the spoon and the top at the bottom. And your face appears upside-down. Turn the spoon around and you're faced with a bulging or as scientists say a convex shape.

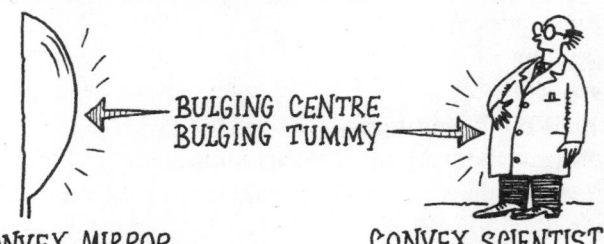

BULGING CENTRE
BULGING TUMMY

CONVEX MIRROR   CONVEX SCIENTIST

The convex shape reflects the light from your face and spreads it slightly outwards. This makes your face appear rounder and fatter (though ths time you're the right way up!).

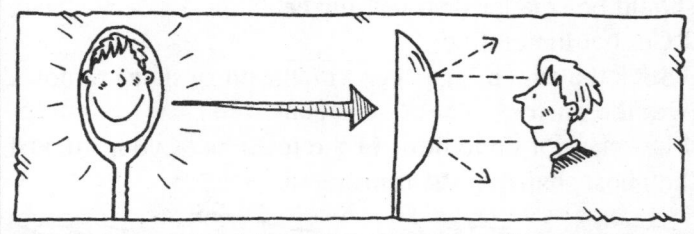

HORRIBLE HEALTH WARNING!

Your parents may not appreciate you performing this interesting experiment at meal times.
Especially when the posh relatives are waiting for their brussels sprouts and you're using the best silver tablespoon.

Dare you discover ... how to make a ghost appear?

(This experiment is so good you'll want to do it again and again. All in the interests of Science, of course.)

You will need:

Sticky tape

Scissors

A small but bright torch

A mirror – about 24 cm x 36 cm is ideal.

A piece of black paper (larger than your mirror).

A pencil

A large black water-based felt-tip marker.

A room with light-coloured walls.

What you do:

1 Draw the outline of your ghost on the black paper. This should be smaller than the mirror.

2 Cut out the outline.

3 Stick the remaining paper with the ghost shape removed over the mirror.

4 Use the felt tip to draw in the features of your ghost in the ghost shape on the mirror.

5 Darken the room. Better still wait until nightfall – after all, that's when ghosts appear.

6 Prop the mirror securely on an arm chair. The mirror should be facing the wall about two metres away. Shine your torch at the mirror. Your ghost appears on the wall.

7 Move the torch so the ghost appears to float in the air.

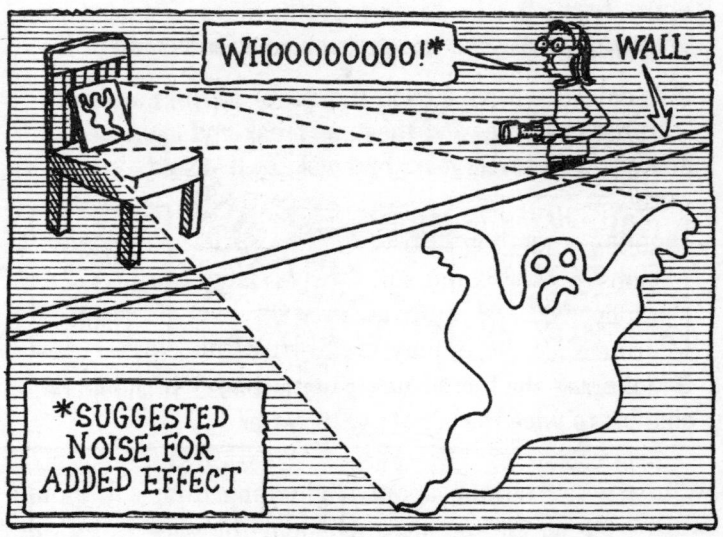

What is the scientific explanation for the ghost?

a) The torch light reflects off the black paper and the felt tip lines.

b) The light reflects off the mirror but not the paper or the lines.

c) The light reflects off everything.

Answer:
b) The lines and the paper are non-reflective. Their atoms soak up the light from the torch. This means there are areas of the mirror's reflection that appear dark and this is what you see.

HORRIBLE HEALTH WARNING!

1 Don't try this experiment until you've checked with your parents it's OK to draw on the mirror. Defacing your granny's priceless antique mirror could prove fatal.

2 Be careful when handling the mirror. Mirrors are glass (surprise, surprise) and they can break and injure people. And give you seven years bad luck, so it's said.

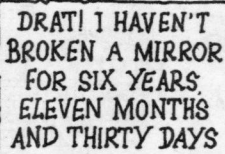

DRAT! I HAVEN'T BROKEN A MIRROR FOR SIX YEARS, ELEVEN MONTHS AND THIRTY DAYS

CRIKEY, THAT'S BAD LUCK, THEN!

3 Make sure the felt-tip pen is water based. It should be possible to wipe the ink off with water.

Whilst we're talking about frightening things, I should warn you about the next chapter. Beware – lurking among the weird facts in the chapter is a sinister-looking spider.

Will it frighten the socks off you? Read on and find out...

FRIGHTENING LIGHT-BENDERS

What have all these things got in common?

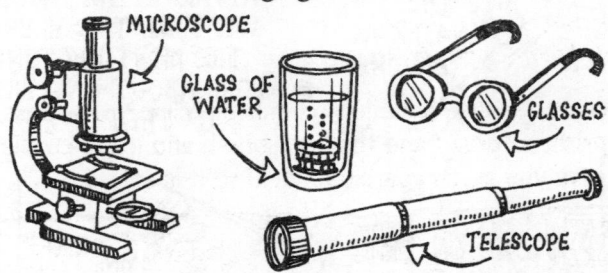

Yes, I know they all contain glass but that *isn't* the only CORRECT answer. Give up? Well, the other answer is that they all bend or refract light. But how do they do it?

Well, bend your eyes to this...

Frightening light fact file

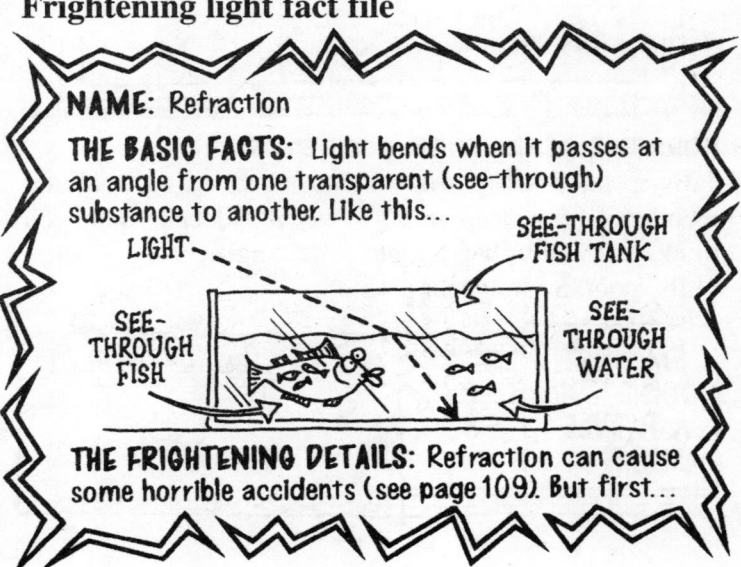

NAME: Refraction

THE BASIC FACTS: Light bends when it passes at an angle from one transparent (see-through) substance to another. Like this...

LIGHT

SEE-THROUGH FISH TANK

SEE-THROUGH FISH

SEE-THROUGH WATER

THE FRIGHTENING DETAILS: Refraction can cause some horrible accidents (see page 109). But first...

Here's a slow-motion replay of refraction as light hits that fish tank.

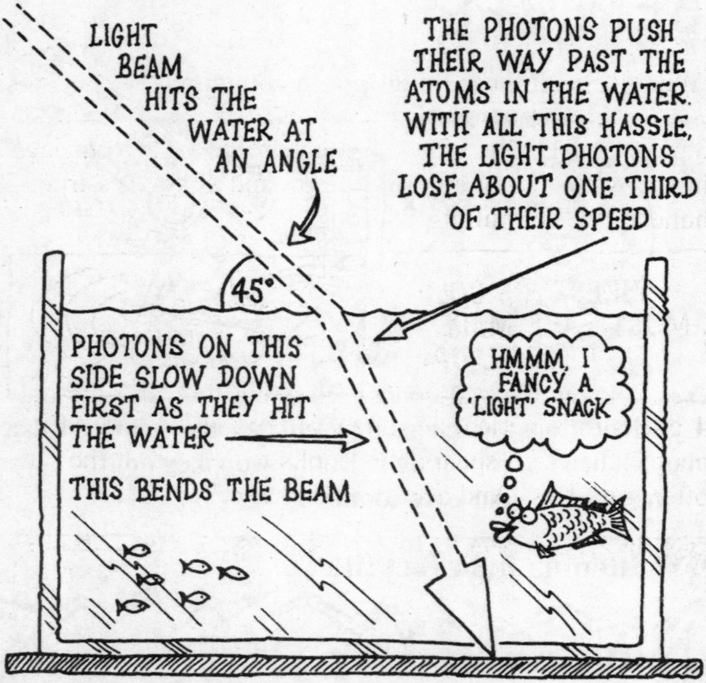

LIGHT
BEAM
HITS THE
WATER AT
AN ANGLE

THE PHOTONS PUSH
THEIR WAY PAST THE
ATOMS IN THE WATER.
WITH ALL THIS HASSLE,
THE LIGHT PHOTONS
LOSE ABOUT ONE THIRD
OF THEIR SPEED

45°

PHOTONS ON THIS
SIDE SLOW DOWN
FIRST AS THEY HIT
THE WATER →

THIS BENDS THE BEAM

HMMM, I
FANCY A
'LIGHT' SNACK

HORRIBLE REFRACTION ACCIDENTS

1 Ever stared straight down into a swimming pool and wondered how deep it is? Well, it's deeper than you think. Refraction bends light reflecting from the bottom of the pool. So it appears closer.

I'M JUST
GOING FOR
A PADDLE,
MUM...

2 Told you...

3 You can see this effect if you stare down at your legs in the water. They appear stumpy and short. It's true – honest, I'm not pulling your leg.

YIKES, THE COLD MUST HAVE MADE MY FEET SWELL UP!

4 In South America, and parts of the Pacific and Africa people fish with spears but thanks to refraction the fish often get away. And accidents do happen...

WATER LOVELY SIGHT!

DISAPPEARING ACTS

But refraction can do even weirder things. Like making objects disappear. Oh, so you don't believe me, well, try this...

Dare you discover ... how to make a coin disappear?

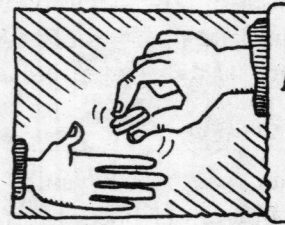

OK, AS LONG AS IT DOESN'T DISAPPEAR DOWN THE SWEETSHOP

You will need:
A £1 coin
A wash basin
A ruler

What you do:
1 Fill the basin with water to a depth of 4 cm.
2 Place the coin in the water.

3 Crouch down so that you can just see the coin over the rim of the wash basin.

4 Lift the plug slightly so the water level in the sink falls slowly.

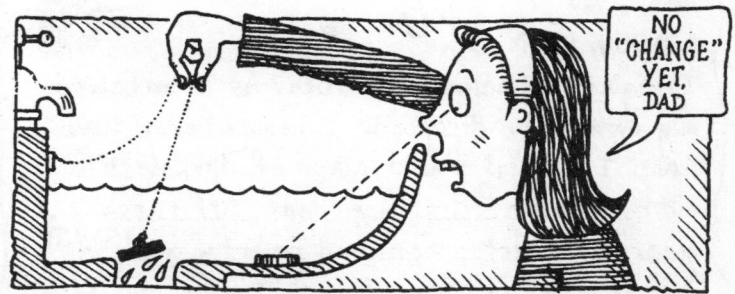

As the water drains down the plug hole the coin gradually disappears. *Why?*

a) Grrrr! My coin has gone down the drain!

b) The water refracted the light reflecting back from the coin so it made the coin look further away than it really was.

c) The light from the coin was refracted so the coin appeared closer.

Answer:

c) The water bent the light towards you so the coin appeared closer. As the water drained away the light refracted less. The coin appeared to move away until it disappeared behind the rim. But actually the coin didn't move.

If refraction can make coins vanish then maybe it can make a larger object disappear. Perhaps even a human being? Here's a story in which this happens – but is it true? What do you think?

Now you see me, now you don't

LONDON, 1897

Tonight I became invisible. As I watched my own body disappear I remembered how hard I worked under cover of darkness so no one could steal my ideas. All those years of frustration and poverty and disappointment. Now, at last I have succeeded.

It was a strange, frightening experience. First I took drugs for several days to remove all the colour pigments from my body. My skin and hair turned snow white. (Even now the side-effects cause me pain.) Then I stood between two electrical power sources. These make the strange invisible rays that I have discovered. Rays that alter the atoms of water in my body so they no longer refract light. In this way, light shines straight through my body as if I were made of air.

As the rays fell on my body I felt I was becoming a ghost. My white face and hair slowly grew dimmer until I could see nothing

112

in the mirror. The skin of my arms and legs looked like glass – I could see the fat and nerves beneath.

And gradually everything faded away until I could stand before the mirror and see nothing but an empty room. . .

Answer:
Great story, isn't it? It's based on *The Invisible Man* by H.G. Wells (1866–1946). But it's only a story because: **1** The rays described don't exist. **2** If the scientist had no pigments then he wouldn't have pigments in his retina to help him see. **3** The lens and cornea of the eye refract light and focus it on to the retina. (Remember that bit from page 45?) But if the scientist's invisible body didn't refract light then these bits of his eye wouldn't refract it either. So he couldn't see the room.

BRILLIANT LENSES

Assuming you're not invisible, lenses are a brilliant way to refract light. They come in two main varieties, convex and concave. (Remember these words?)

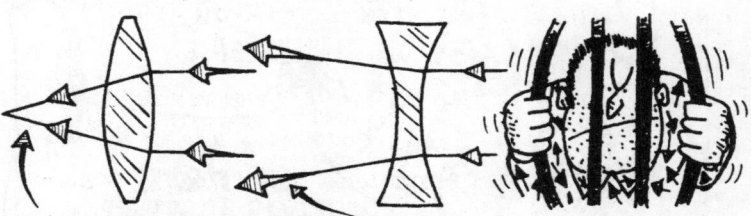

CONVEX LENS LIGHT BENDS INWARDS

CONCAVE LENS LIGHT BENDS OUTWARDS

CONVICT LEN BENDS BARS

OK, let's take a peek through these lenses. And here's a particularly revolting hairy spider to study...

1 Through a convex lens the spider appears bigger. Let's take a look at the spider's head.

2 Light reflects off the spider's ugly little mug.

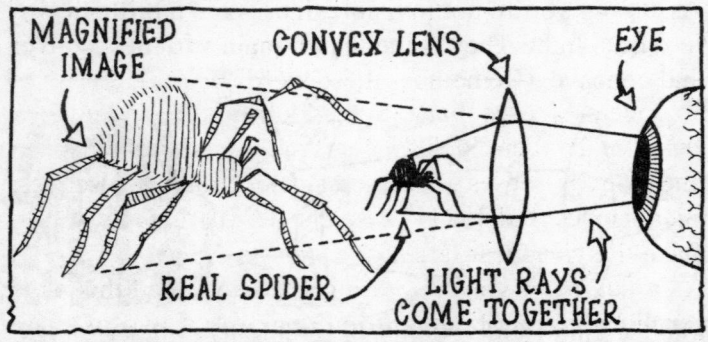

The convex lens bends this light towards a single point.

3 If you put your eye at this point you'll see a close-up view of the spider's head with eight huge beady eyes staring back at you. YIKES!

Let's use a concave lens to take another look at the spider. Yes, it's all in the interests of Science.

1 This lens spreads the light wider.

2 And when you look through the lens the spider appears much smaller. Phew! Not so bad – eh?

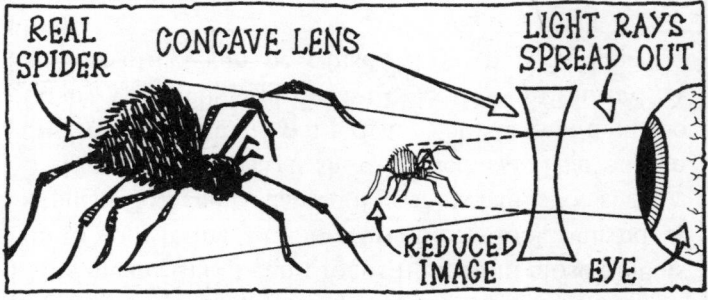

So concave lenses make things look smaller and convex lenses make them look bigger. And not surprisingly you find convex lenses in cameras, binoculars, telescopes, microscopes and loads of scientific instruments which make things appear larger.

Of course, if you're wearing glasses to read this page you'll know all about lenses. You've got two of them perched on the end of your nose. But why wear them?

FRIGHTENING EXPRESSIONS

An ophthalmologist says...

YOU MAY HAVE HYPEROPIA, MYOPIA OR ASTIGMATISM

Are any of these fatal?

Answer:

No, they're eye problems caused by faulty focusing.

1 Hyperopia (hi-per-rop-pia) means that you're long-sighted. The lens of your eye doesn't bend light enough. This means that it can't focus light from close objects on to your retina. So close up objects look blurred. A similar effect can be caused if your eyeball is too short.

2 Myopia (mi-ope-ia) is short-sightedness. That's when the light reflecting from a distant object gets bent too far by your lens and distant objects seem blurred. A similar effect can be caused if your eyeball is too long.

3 Astigmatism (as-stig-ma-tism) is when the cornea is slightly out of shape. This results in part of the image appearing blurred.

If you've got any of these you'll need to wear glasses or contact lenses to correct the problem. Cheer up you'll look dead brainy and they're scientifically fascinating...

SPECTACULAR SPECTACLES

1 The first glasses to be invented had convex lenses. They were probably invented in Italy in the thirteenth century and worn by long-sighted people.

2 As you've just discovered, the long-sighted eye has a lens that doesn't bend the light inwards enough to focus an image on the retina.

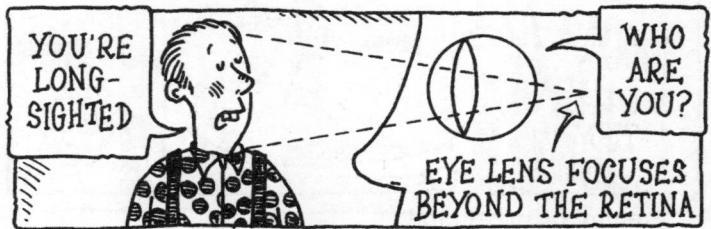

A convex lens bends the light further inwards to focus an image.

3 Concave lenses were first made in around 1451. German churchman Nicholas of Cusa (1401–1464) worked out that this shape could help short-sighted people. What a far-sighted man!

4 A short-sighted eye lens pushes the light inwards too much. So the light focuses before it gets to the retina.

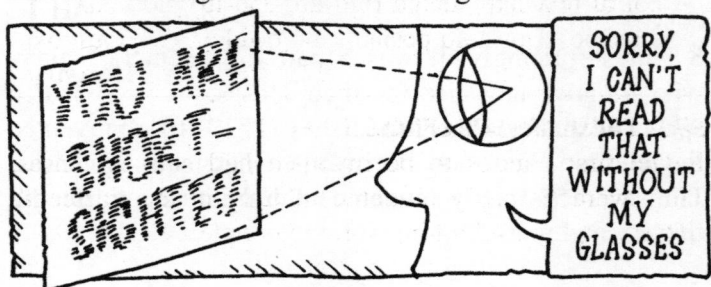

The concave lens spreads the light so it focuses on the retina.

5 Contact lenses do the same job as glasses. Nowadays they're slices of soft watery plastic that fit over the eyeball. But the first lenses invented by German Adolf Fick (1829–1901) in 1888 were made of glass. The glass rubbed against the eyeballs and made them sore. What a sight for sore eyes!

6 And Adolf even managed to make lenses of exactly the right shape to fit over the eyeball and bend light on to the retina. The answer was to shape the lenses in moulds made by using the eyeballs of dead people.

7 DON'T WORRY! Your local optician DOESN'T have a drawer full of eyeballs. Nowadays, they measure the curve of your eyeballs using a keratometer (ker-rato-meter). This instrument directs a beam of light into your eyeball (which reflects it) and records the position of the reflected light. This data is used to calculate its exact curve.

8 Not surprisingly, it was a pair of spectacle makers who found a new use for their lenses. In 1608 Dutch spectacle maker, Hans Lippershey (1570–1618) invented the telescope and soon afterwards his assistant Zacharius Jannsen (1580–1638) invented the microscope. Or did they?

DRAT, IT'S THOSE KIDS. I'D BETTER HIDE THE MONEY.

Anyway, talking about telescopes...

FRIGHTENING EXPRESSIONS...

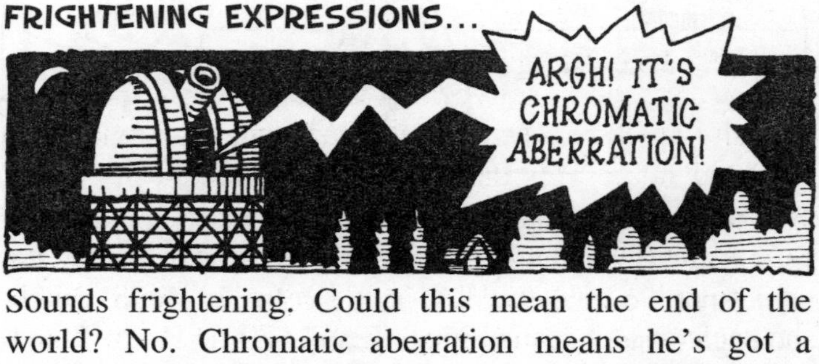

ARGH! IT'S CHROMATIC ABERRATION!

Sounds frightening. Could this mean the end of the world? No. Chromatic aberration means he's got a problem with his telescope. It's caused by different-size light waves being refracted by different amounts.

A traditional telescope has two or more convex lenses.

The lenses focus light from a distant object on to your eyeball.

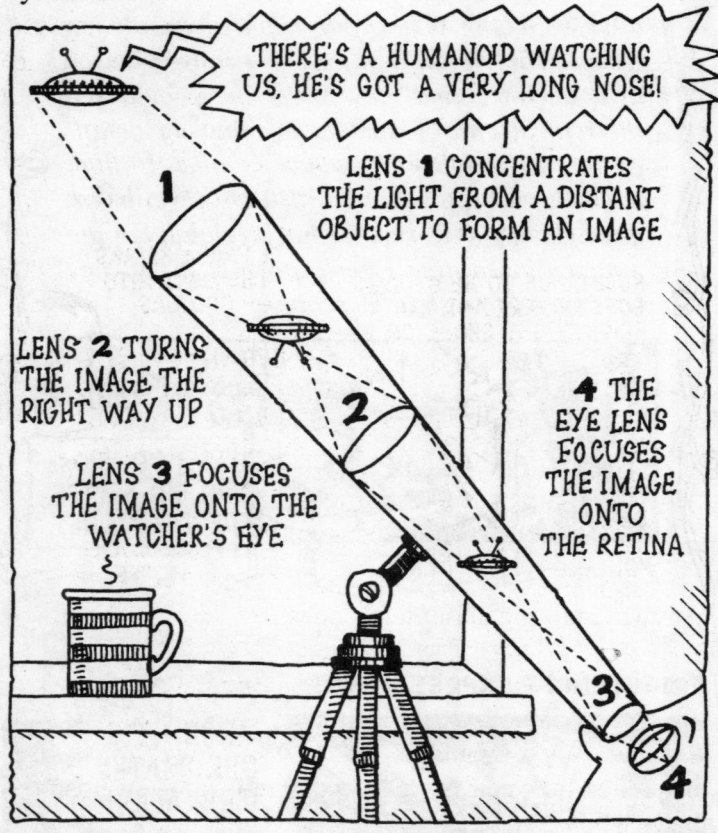

But here's the problem. Because different coloured lights refract at different angles, they don't all focus in exactly the same spot. So images would have a coloured "halo" around the edge – and that's chromatic aberration.

Luckily for astronomers, Isaac Newton solved this problem in 1668. He designed a telescope that used a concave mirror to focus the light instead of a lens.

Because mirrors reflect all wavelengths in the same way, there was no "halo" around the image. And Newton's design is still in use today.

Bet you never knew!
Telescopes aren't just for watching the stars or seeing things in the distance. You'll also find a telescope in a scientific instrument called a spectroscope.

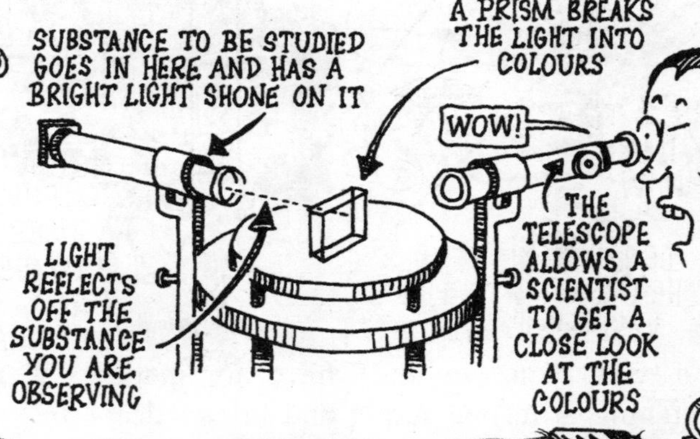

SUBSTANCE TO BE STUDIED GOES IN HERE AND HAS A BRIGHT LIGHT SHONE ON IT

A PRISM BREAKS THE LIGHT INTO COLOURS

WOW!

LIGHT REFLECTS OFF THE SUBSTANCE YOU ARE OBSERVING

THE TELESCOPE ALLOWS A SCIENTIST TO GET A CLOSE LOOK AT THE COLOURS

Talking of colours you'd better read the next chapter. It's full of crucial colourful facts. Yep, colour is CRUCIAL – I mean, where would drivers be if they couldn't tell the difference between a green and a red light? In hospital that's where!

Well, you've got the green light to turn over the page.

READY STEADY TURN!

CRUCIAL COLOUR

Life without colour would be frighteningly boring. Just like an endless awful, old black and white movie. Without colour you'd never get to enjoy the glory of a peacock's tail, a glowing sunset or a garden full of flowers.

Mind you, you wouldn't have to shudder at the frightening crimson, purple and brown decor in your auntie's living room.

A NOTE TO THE READER
We apologize for the loss of colour. Readers will have to imagine the wonderful glowing, vibrant colours described in these pages. And if you do get bored you can always colour them in. **PS** If it's not your book go and buy your own before you pick up your crayons. Anyway, here's how light makes colour appear.

Frightening light fact file

NAME: Colours

THE BASIC FACTS: **1.** White light is a muddled-up mix of all the colours of the rainbow and each colour is made of a light wave with a different frequency (energy level). Remember all that?

2. When light hits an object some of the colours are soaked up and others are reflected. And it's the reflected colours that we see. Got all that?

THE FRIGHTENING DETAILS: When something is black all the colours in light are soaked up so nothing reflects back. This explains the colour of this big black revolting slug.

> YEAH, CHEERS!

Read on for more colourful facts.

THE COLOURFUL FACTS

A green leaf or caterpillar soaks up all the colours in light except green. Green reflects off the leaf (or caterpillar) and that's what you see.

GREEN PLANT

GARDENER'S GREEN FINGERS

GREEN CATERPILLAR

A ripe tomato soaks up all kinds of light except red.

White objects reflect every kind of light. (Don't forget white light is all the colours mixed up.)

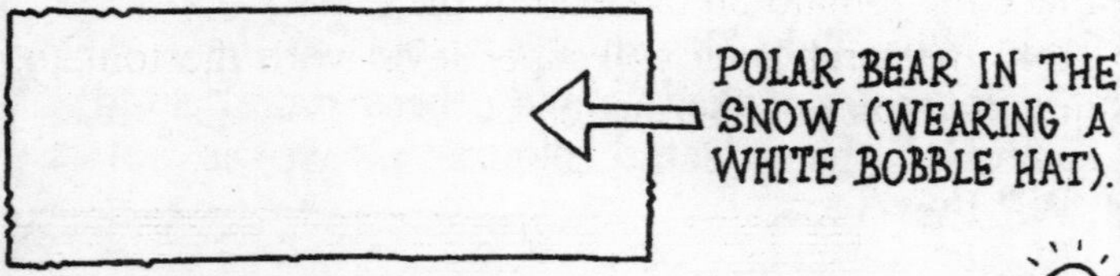

POLAR BEAR IN THE SNOW (WEARING A WHITE BOBBLE HAT).

Bet you never knew!
1 Windows, polythene bags and bottles don't reflect colours. They're see-through or "transparent" as a scientist would say. With a see-through material, such as glass, the atoms form thin layers or are regularly spaced so most light gets through. That's how light manages to shine through your window – it's transparently obvious.
2 Some fish are transparent. For example, the X-ray fish, found in South American rivers has no pigments. This allows it to hide from attackers. The fish is a bit like the Invisible Man on page 112 except you can see its skeleton and guts through the skin.

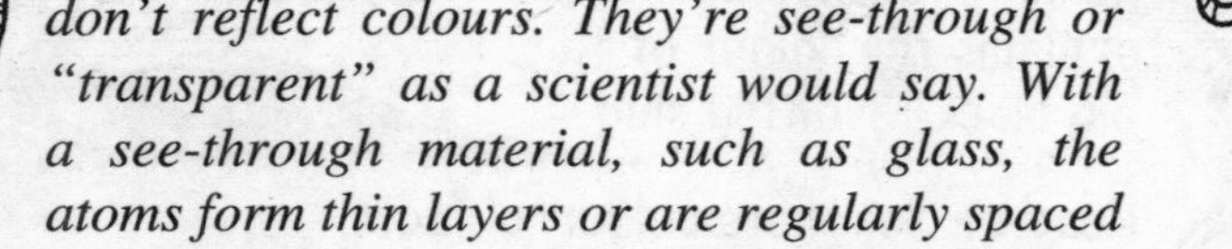

I ADMIRE YOUR GUTS

YOURS LOOK PRETTY COOL, TOO!

Dare you discover ... where colour comes from?

You will need:
A nice juicy red tomato
A piece of white A4 paper
A small but bright torch

What you do:
1 Darken the room or better still wait for nightfall.
2 Place the tomato on one end of the paper.
3 Hold the torch over the paper level with the tomato.
Shine the light on the tomato.

4 Look at the area of shadow under the torch beam. It
should be glowing pink. *Why?*
a) The tomato is reflecting red light on to the paper.
b) It's a trick of my eyes caused by the torch light.
c) The shadow of the tomato is soaking up all the colours
in light except red.

Answer:
a) White paper reflects all the colours of light that fall
on it. The pink glow is due to the red light reflecting
off the tomato and on to the paper. All the other
colours in the light get soaked up by the tomato. The
experiment proves that colours are indeed caused by
the reflection of light.

125

Most objects, though, reflect a mix of different coloured light. Take bananas, for example....

TEACHER'S TEA-BREAK TEASER

You will need a banana and a lot of courage. Rap smartly on the staffroom door. When it squeaks open put on your most innocent expression and enquire...

Answer:
Well, it might appear yellow but it actually reflects red and green light and soaks up blue light. Your eyes see this mix of red and green as yellow. (You can find out how on pages 134-135.)

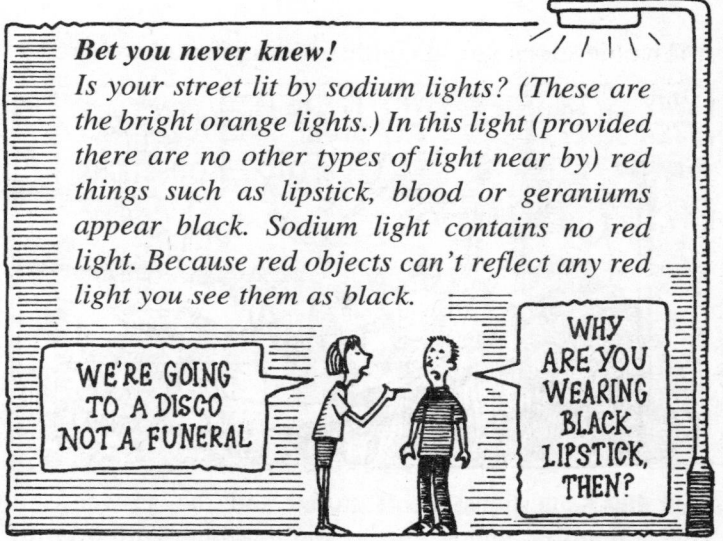

WE'RE GOING TO A DISCO NOT A FUNERAL

WHY ARE YOU WEARING BLACK LIPSTICK, THEN?

Talking about reflecting colours, did you know two scientists spent their holidays reflecting on this very topic? That's sad.

Hall of fame: Chandrasekhara Vankata Raman (1888–1970) Nationality: Indian
John Strutt, Lord Rayleigh (1824–1919) Nationality: British
You couldn't find two more different characters than C.V. Raman and John Strutt.

Raman was a brilliant scientist but he had to work for the Indian civil service as a young man because of a shortage of scientific jobs in India. (In 1917 he became Professor of Physics at Calcutta University.) Strutt was a rich lord with a private laboratory in his mansion and a top university job in England. They worked separately to solve two tricky light questions but by an odd coincidence Raman later became friendly with Strutt's son.

The questions sound childishly simple...

But these questions aren't stupid and the answers are frighteningly complicated ... as you're about to discover.

In 1871 John Strutt went on holiday to Egypt. Cruising through the Mediterranean, he admired the lovely blue sky and sea.

Being a scientist, though, he did more than enjoy what he saw. He used his scientific know-how to explain it. His letter home might have read like this...

To Lord & Lady Rayleigh,
Tering Place, Essex, England.

Dear Mum and Dad,
  Having a great holiday! I've read lots
of science books and there's plenty
of interesting sights to fascinate a
budding scientist like me. Like the
blue sky and sea, for example. I
mean, what makes them so blue? I
suspect atoms in the air reflect
light. I think blue light is
scattered much better than other
lights (I'm not sure why) so we see
more of it. I reckon the sea is blue
because it reflects the sky.
  Oh, I forgot to say, the cruise is OK.
Yours scientifically,
  John

NOTES TO THE READER...

1 John was right. Sunlight contains all the colours of the rainbow, remember? Most colours pass straight through the air. But blue light waves are a similar size to oxygen atoms. They bounce around and reach you from any direction in the sky. The sky appears full of blue light. Who says the blues get you down?

2 But sunsets aren't blue – are they? Well, that proves John right again! You see, when the sun is low its light has a longer path through the air. All the blue light gets

scattered away leaving reddish colours. Grotty dust
scatters the red light and you see a pretty reddish glow. I
bet boffins say "red sky at night scientist's delight."

OK, now back to the story...

In 1921, Raman was sailing to a Science conference
in Britain. Feeling rather bored he decided to test John
Strutt's findings about the sea. By this time the older
scientist was dead so Raman couldn't drop him a postcard.
But he might have written to his pal John Strutt's scientist
son, Robert Strutt, the next Lord Rayleigh (1875–1947).

To Robert Strutt (Lord Rayleigh),
Tering Place, Essex, England.

Dear Bob,
Fab weather! Your old dad was right about
the blue sky. But I don't think the sea
is blue 'cause of the sky. I looked at
the sea using a Nicol prism I had on me.
As you know the atoms of the prism
are arranged so that light from only
one direction can get through. And get
this – although the prism blocked light
reflecting off the sea from the sky, the
sea still glowed blue! The cause of the
glow's got me baffled – but I'm glowing to
find out. Ha ha. Keep you posted.
Your mate, C.V. Raman

So why *was* the sea blue?

Back at his lab in 1922 Raman did a series of experiments that involved shining light through water and found the answer...

Dear Bob,
I've cracked it. I was looking into why the sea is blue – remember? Well, here's what I've found out:
1. Part of the light from the sky is reflected by the surface of the sea. OK – your dad got that bit right. That's why the sea is grey when the sky is dark and cloudy. But lots of photons get into the sea itself...
2. The seawater soaks up most of these photons and only reflects back blue light photons. This is the blue glow I saw.
I'm sure your old dad would have been chuffed.
Your Pal,
C.V. Raman

blue sky

blue photons

light photons

blue glow

For Raman, it must have seemed that the sky (and the sea) was the limit. He went on to find how bonds between atoms in a chemical can affect an atom's wobble and add or remove energy from the reflecting photons. And in 1930 he won the Nobel Prize for this work.

MYSTERIOUS COLOUR MIXING

On their own, colours are fairly straightforward. But try mixing them together and the facts get murky.

Bet you never knew!
Colour photos are made by mixing different light colours.
1 The first colour picture was taken by Scottish physicist James Clerk Maxwell (1831–1879). In 1863 he took three snaps of one of his wife's ribbons. One through a red filter, one blue and one green. Each filter blocked all the colours in light except its particular colour. So the green filter, for example, showed up the green parts of the pattern. He combined the images to make a colour picture.

FASCINATING, CAN I HAVE IT BACK NOW?

2 Nowadays, though, colour films consist of three layers of chemicals. The top layer makes a blue colour from blue light, the second makes green in the same way and the third makes a red colour. Between them the chemicals build up an image. Our brains do the rest of the colour mixing – as you'll discover on pages 134–135.

MUDDY MIXED-UP PAINTS

But just imagine that you tried to make a painting in the same way as a photo. You carefully mixed thin layers of blue, green and red. And produced a muddy black smear.

I CALL THIS, "FLY'S VIEW OF A COWPAT"

Want to know why? Why not ask your art teacher...

TEST YOUR ART TEACHER

If you mix green and red and blue light together you'll get a pale whitish sort of a colour. But if you mix together green and red and blue paints you get black – why?

Answer:
White light is made up of all colours. So the more colours of light you mix the closer you get to white light. But paints and other coloured objects (like tomatoes and bananas) work by soaking up some light colours and reflecting others. So the more paints you add to your mix the closer you get to something that soaks up every colour in light. In other words – black.

YOU'VE ADDED MORE PAINT

YES. NOW IT'S CALLED, "BLACK CAT IN A POWERCUT"

CRUCIAL COLOUR VISION

Whatever colours you manage to mix you'll need a pair of eyes to appreciate them. Humans, birds and apes are lucky in this respect. We view the world in glorious living Technicolor. Unlike for example, a squid, which can only see black and white or your pet cat who sees green and blue and violet but not red. (Scientists aren't quite sure why this is – but when Tiddles finishes off a mouse she sees the blood and gory bits as green.)

HOW YOU SEE IN COLOUR

1 Unlike Tiddles you've actually got three types of cone cells in your retina – one each for green, blue and red light. All the colours you see are made from mixing at least two of these colours. (For more info. on mixing light see page 126.)

2 Your incredible eyes are able to make out up to ten million different colours. It's amazing to think they can do this from just three basic colours. Here's your chance to test this remarkable ability...

Dare you discover ... how you see colours?

You will need:
A piece of black paper
A small piece of yellow paper about 3 cm square.
Your head complete with eyeballs.

What you do:

1 Place the yellow paper on the black paper and stare at it for 30 seconds without moving your head or blinking.

2 You should see a square of blue appearing round the edge of the yellow square.

What do you notice?

a) The cells that fire blue signals take time to work – but now they've detected blue colouring in the black paper.

b) The yellow paper has excited your blue cells so much they've gone into overdrive. And now you're seeing too much blue.

c) The green and red cells that give you yellow are getting tired but the blue cells are still firing.

Answer:

c) Your eye sees yellow by firing green and red cone cells (remember the bananas?). Your brain mixes these sensations to make yellow. But after a while the cells become less sensitive. Meanwhile blue cone cells are still firing in this area of your retina so you see a blue image. You see "after-images" for the same reason. Mind you – it took a few disgusting eyeball experiments before scientists worked this out...

EYEBALL TO EYEBALL

WARNING: DISGUSTING FACTS COMING UP. (Hopefully your breakfast won't be coming up after you read them.)

Isaac Newton reckoned we see colours by changing the shape of our eyeballs. Isaac thought this helped the eye to refract white light into coloured light that then fell on the retina.

135

To test this idea Isaac stuck what might have been a toothpick under his eyeball. A toothpick is a stick for getting bits of food out from between your teeth. Isaac's toothpick was probably encrusted with millions of germs and the stale remains of his supper. YUCK!

Using the toothpick Isaac squeezed his own eyeball to change its shape. He saw a few lights, but not enough to prove his theory.

The germs on the toothpick infected his eyeball. It became so painful that he had to go to bed for two weeks. This proves that even a scientific genius can do very stupid things.

HORRIBLE HEALTH WARNING!

So don't try an experiment like this at home. It has no scientific value. And you don't want an eye infection ... or your eyeball slopping out of its socket, now do you?

MORE COLOURFUL SCIENTISTS...

After Newton, other famous scientists probed colour vision. The story continues with British chemist John Dalton (1766–1844). John Dalton was one of the first people to suggest that there were such things as atoms. But come to think of it, he wasn't too colourful himself.

A fellow scientist said:

HIS STYLE OF WRITING AND CONVERSATION ARE DRY

Nowadays we might call him "boring". Boring John loved to study flowers. Unfortunately, he found that he couldn't see red colours properly...

IT'S BLUE

IT'S RED

NO NEED TO GET ALL BLUE IN THE FACE ABOUT IT

John suffered from colour deficiency – a condition that affects about one in 25 people and he enjoyed giving boring lectures on the subject. According to John colour deficiency was caused by a build up of blue juice in the eyeball. The blue colour soaks up red light.

He made arrangements for his eyeballs to be removed after his death to check for blue juice.

IT WON'T MAKE A BLIND BIT OF DIFFERENCE TO ME IF I'M DEAD

Meanwhile our old pal Thomas Young had been treating patients with colour deficiency. As a result of this work he believed the retina had separate regions that detected red, blue and violet. And Dalton had a problem with his red region.

Unfortunately Young died before Dalton's eyeballs were removed so he never knew the result. In fact, the jelly in Dalton's eyeballs proved to be nice and clear. Dalton would have been dead disappointed if he wasn't already dead.

OH WELL, YOU MIGHT AS WELL POP THEM BACK IN HIS HEAD

EYE EYE, SIR!

THE MYSTERY SOLVED...

The mystery was solved by another famous scientist, James Clerk Maxwell. He spun a disc divided into green and red and blue sections. The colours appeared to merge into white. People who couldn't see the colour red saw white in a spinning disc that had only blue and green sections. This proved...

1 That the cone cells in our eyes can see green, blue and red light.
2 That they make all the other colours from these three. (The white colour was a mix of all the other colours.)
3 In colour deficient people one type of cone cell is missing or not working properly.

Bet you never knew!
As long as your vision's working OK you're bound to enjoy a multi-coloured laser show. By using different chemicals in lasers scientists can change the colour of this light. For example, atoms of ruby produce red light. But you can't enjoy the pretty colours by gazing directly into a laser beam. It's so bright it would probably blind you or heat up your eyeball until it boils.

Dare you take a closer look at lasers? Why not turn to the next frightening chapter?

ER, OK THEN...

BLISTERING LASERS

As you're about to find out, lasers are a huge part of modern life and they're set to brighten up our future too. Like all great inventions, lasers began with a flash of inspiration.

A LASER FLASH OF INSPIRATION

In 1951 US scientist Charles H. Townes was at a scientific conference in Washington.

I'M TRYING TO PRODUCE HIGH-POWERED RADIO WAVES THAT CAN BE USED TO STUDY THE STRUCTURE OF ATOMS

FASCINATING!

That night Townes couldn't sleep. His mind was working overtime on the problem. So very early the next morning before it got light he went for a walk and ended up on a park bench. He was looking for inspiration.

THINK! THINK!

Suddenly he found it. Townes scribbled his ideas on the back of an old envelope. If you could control the speed the atoms wobble and stop the light escaping you could create a powerful beam of light. Since radio waves are made by photons you could do the same things with radio waves.

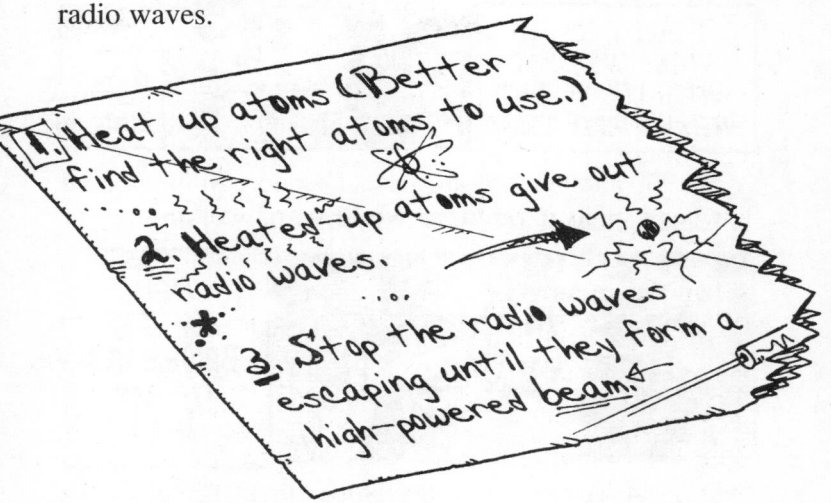

Townes later found out he had been sitting opposite of the house of famous inventor Alexander Graham Bell (1847–1922). And Townes wondered if the dead inventor had provided ghostly assistance.

Later Townes realized that you could use light instead of radio waves. By 1958 working with his brother-in-law, Arthur Schawlow, Townes had worked out how a laser might work. He even coined the name "laser" over lunch. But he had little idea of how useful the laser would become. He later said:

IT WAS BY NO MEANS CLEAR . . . THAT (THE LASER) WOULD SEE SO MANY STRIKING APPLICATIONS.

141

For scientists at the time, building a laser just seemed a fascinating technical challenge.

In 1960 another US physicist, Theodore Maiman used Townes's plans to build the world's first working laser.

In 1964 Townes won the Nobel Prize for his work together with two Russian scientists, Nikolai Basov and Alexander Prokhorov who developed the laser separately but at the same time.

Interesting postscript:
Actually, unknown to Townes, the idea of a laser and perhaps even the name had been dreamt up by another US scientist, Gordon Gould in 1957. Unfortunately, Gould didn't publish his idea and he didn't take out a patent in time so he missed out on the glory.

LASER DEFENCE SYSTEMS

Lasers have loads of uses. One purpose developed by the US military is a laser defence system to shoot down enemy missiles. Sounds exciting? Well, here's how to defend your school from hostile attack with a laser defence system.

 **HORRIBLE HEALTH WARNINGS!**

1 Laser beams can sizzle human flesh. Do not direct your laser beam anywhere near a teacher or any other poor defenceless creatures.

2 This laser is highly destructive. You can only read this section if you promise to use your laser system to PROTECT your school. And NOT to vaporize the buildings before science class on Monday.

HOW TO MAKE YOUR OWN LASER DEFENCE SYSTEM

**TOP SECRET INSTRUCTIONS –
KEEP OUT OF
REACH OF TEACHERS**

Step 1 – assemble your materials.
To build your own laser defence system you will need...
A power supply.
A box lined with mirrors. Leave a partly-silvered mirror in one end for your laser to shine through.
Something to produce light photons (a block of ruby will do).
A bucket of water.
You will also need...
A high-speed jet plane complete with pilot and a

computer controlled high sensitivity heat detecting system. (You may be able to borrow these from your local air force base.)

NO PROBLEM, SON. DROP IT BACK AROUND TEA-TIME

Step 2 – assemble your laser.

1 Place the ruby in the box and link it up to your power supply.

MIRRORS RUBY

POWER SUPPLY

ENEMY AIRCRAFT SPOTTED OVER JUNIOR PLAYING FIELDS... HURRY UP, JENKINS!

2 OK, this is the bit that you've been waiting for. Flick the switch and turn on your power supply.

3 The power surge makes the atoms in the ruby wobble violently. They give out photons of red light. These bump into more atoms which wobble and make more photons.

4 A growing crowd of photons charges up and down the inside of the box reflecting off the mirrors. Eventually the light is so bright the photons actually flash *through* the mirror as a blinding beam of light.

5 All this power makes your ruby very hot. If your machine shows signs of over-heating simply chuck the water over it. (Some lasers have built-in water cooling systems.)

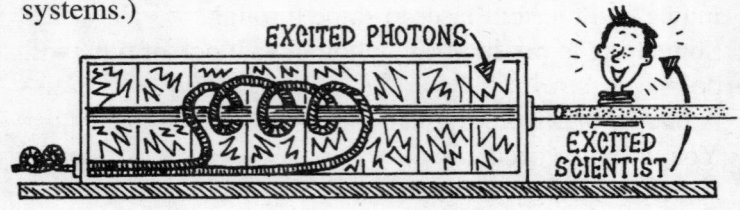

EXCITED PHOTONS

EXCITED SCIENTIST

Step 3 – how to shoot down missiles.

1 Simply get your plane in the air and keep an eye out for incoming missiles. You can use your heat detecting system to track the heat blasting from behind the enemy missile.

2 When you spot a missile aim the laser at its fuel tank. Try to keep the beam steady for a few seconds. The laser's heat will melt the missile's side and set fire to its fuel. The enemy missile will then blow up in mid-air and you'll have saved your school.

MAKING LIGHT WORK

Of course, your laser can do much more than zap enemy missiles. In fact, lasers can make light work of many jobs...

1 A laser beam makes a snappy-snipper! Lasers are used in factories to cut fabric at 15 m a second.

2 Laser beams read bar codes in shops or libraries. Take a look on the back of this book. Can you see a square with a pattern of lines? The pattern is a unique code for *Frightening Light*. If you bought the book you may have seen the shop assistant passing a scanner across the lines. A laser beam in the scanner flickers as it picks up the lines and the flickering beam is read by a computer that recognizes the code from the pattern of flickers. Here's an idea that's really on the right lines.

3 Lasers can be life-savers. They can cut through human flesh and heat seal the edges of a wound so you don't get bleeding. By firing a laser down an endoscope (that's a tube containing optical fibres, remember) you can perform life-saving operations deep within the body. A laser can even weld back a retina that has come adrift from the inside of the eyeball.

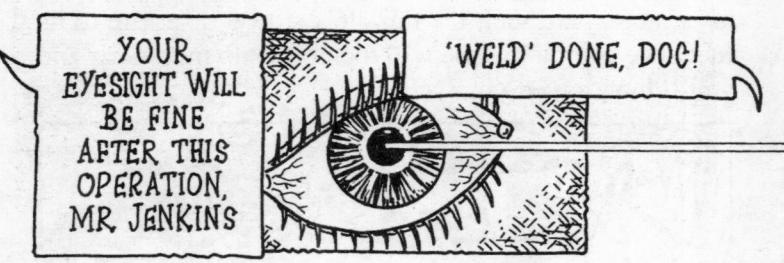

YOUR EYESIGHT WILL BE FINE AFTER THIS OPERATION, MR JENKINS

'WELD' DONE, DOC!

4 A laser beam "reads" a CD by flickering as it reflects off a pattern of pits on its surface. The CD player turns this flickering light signal into electric pulses and then into your fave pop music.

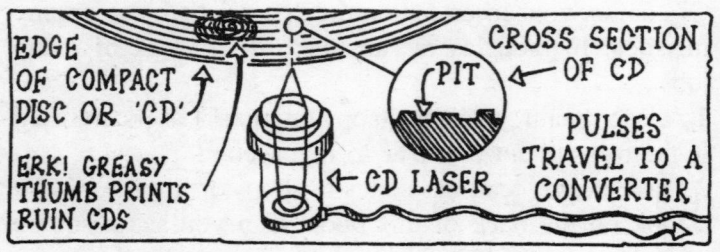

EDGE OF COMPACT DISC OR 'CD'

ERK! GREASY THUMB PRINTS RUIN CDS

PIT

CD LASER

CROSS SECTION OF CD

PULSES TRAVEL TO A CONVERTER

5 Laser beams travel in straight lines so you can use them to build nice straight tunnels. Simply fire a beam from the entrance of the tunnel and get digging along the line of the beam.

6 A laser beam can melt and weld metals. And unlike any other tool a laser beam never gets blunt with use.

7 Laser beams liven up pop concerts. Simply fire the laser into the air and wave it around to make dramatic light patterns. And then who cares if the music's rubbish?

GREAT LASERS!

YEAH, BUT I'M GLAD WE BROUGHT OUR OWN MUSIC!

8 Lasers can measure tiny earthquakes. Lasers on the San Andreas Fault, California are linked up to monitoring equipment. Any wobble in the light beam caused by a tremor in the ground can be instantly detected.

SORRY, THAT TREMOR WAS MY FAULT – WE HAD BAKED BEAN STEW FOR TEA LAST NIGHT

9 Laser printers work by firing an image of the page you're printing on to a light-sensitive drum. This drum has an electrical force which then picks up toner (the black stuff) and prints on to the paper. And laser printers are fast – maybe that's because they keep in toner – ha ha.

But that's just the start of what lasers can do ... they're so useful that scientists have really taken a shine to them, ha, ha.

Bet you never knew!
You can make holograms with lasers. All you have to do is...

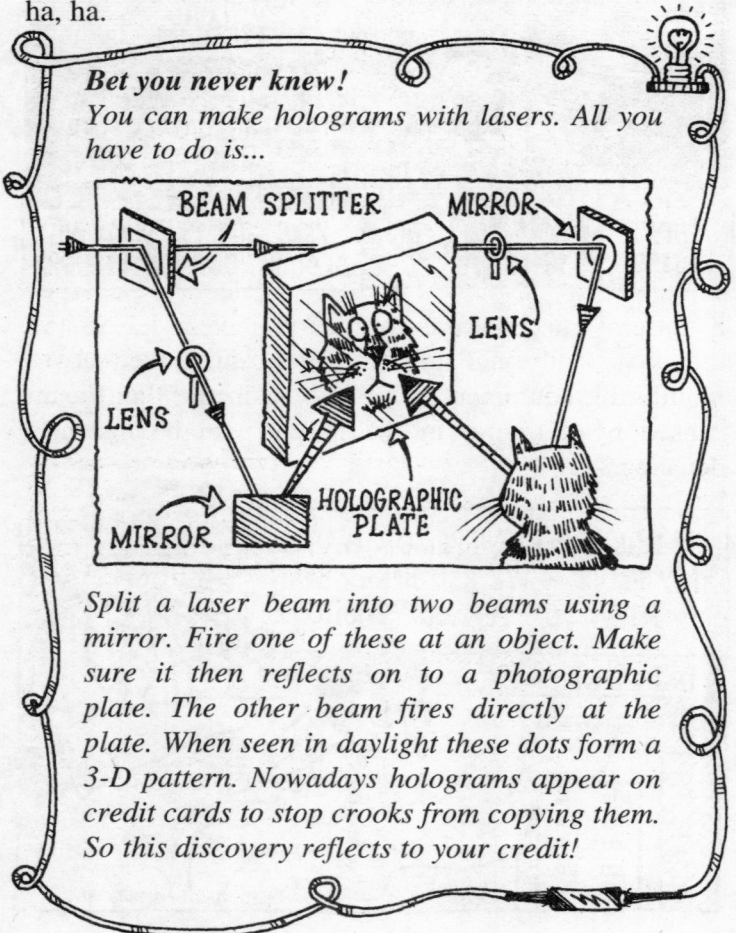

BEAM SPLITTER   MIRROR

LENS

LENS

MIRROR

HOLOGRAPHIC PLATE

Split a laser beam into two beams using a mirror. Fire one of these at an object. Make sure it then reflects on to a photographic plate. The other beam fires directly at the plate. When seen in daylight these dots form a 3-D pattern. Nowadays holograms appear on credit cards to stop crooks from copying them. So this discovery reflects to your credit!

SPEEDY SIGNALS

Don't forget light is *FAST* with a capital F. And so is laser light.

• In 0.14 seconds you can send a laser signal around the world.

• In 2.5 seconds you can send a light signal to the moon *and* back again. (In the 1960s US scientists did this. By timing the signal they were able to calculate the exact distance of the moon.)

• A laser could send a light signal to Mars in just three minutes. (The Martians' reply would take another three minutes.)

But laser signals aren't just for chatting with aliens. You probably use them to natter to your friends. Yes – every time you pick up a phone.

LISTENING LASERS

When you talk into a phone connected to an optical fibre cable the same technology that turns a laser light into sound in a CD works in reverse.

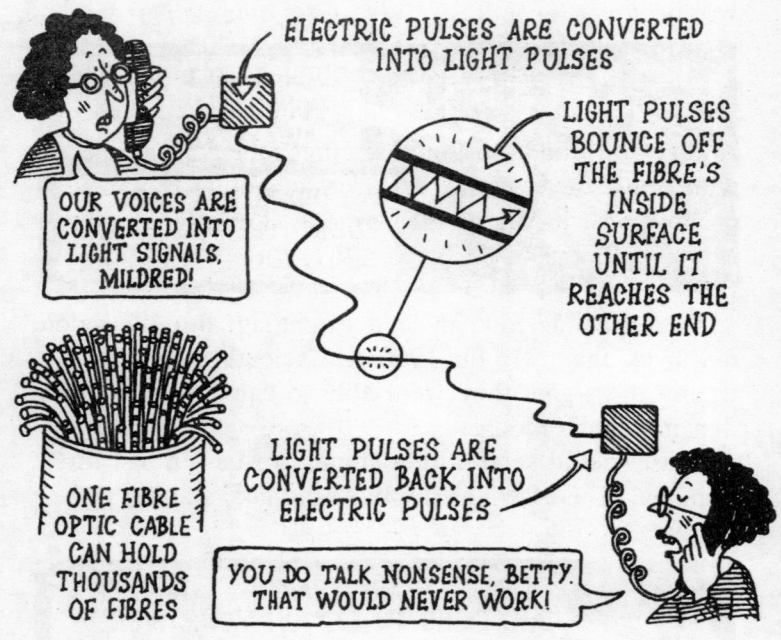

A microphone turns the sound of your voice into electric pulses which are transformed into laser light signals. These whiz down the cable.

At the other end of the line the process is reversed and you hear sounds in your earhole.

And because light moves so fast and a laser can flicker at billions of times a second an optical fibre can carry a conversation down the line in the blink of an eye. And what's more, you can squash thousands of fibres in a single cable.

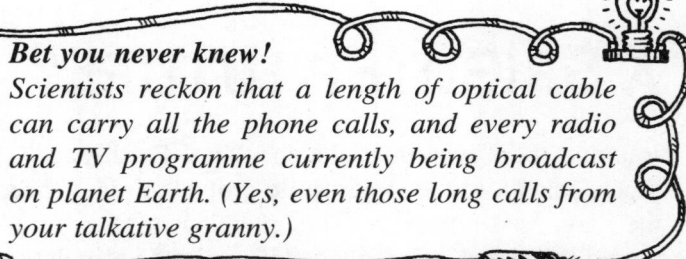

And yet the wonders of optical fibres look pale compared with future developments. But is the future bright with promise or is it dark and frightening? Let's gaze into the crystal ball...

A BRIGHTER FUTURE?

Imagine there was no light on planet Earth except for your pocket torch. People would grope their way through the darkness to marvel at this amazing brightness. They would wonder at its beauty and its ability to turn darkness into colours and shadows.

> WE PRAISE YOU MISTRESS OF THE LIGHT. YOU SHINE YOUR WONDROUS BEAM ON OUR HUMBLE FACES

But light is everywhere. And because we see it every day we don't think too much about it. What a pity.

Light is awesome, unbelievable, fantastic. And although the science of light seems frightening at first – the more you discover the more magical it seems. It's incredible that a humble light bulb makes photons and that these astonishing blips of energy can light up the sky in the day and at night you can see stars because their photons have travelled for millions of years to reach you.

It's even more astonishing to think that it's photons that give colour to a daffodil or power to a laser. And it's gobsmacking to peer in a mirror and know that you can only see yourself because every second billions of photons are bouncing off the mirror to create an image made of light.

But the latest discoveries of physicists are even MORE exciting, even more brain-boggling. And they're about to light up our future in totally unexpected ways. For example...

1 CREATIVE CHEMICAL CHAOS

In the 2000's scientists learnt how to use lasers to trigger chemical reactions. Traditionally, you had to heat things up over a grotty old Bunsen burner like the sort you find in schools.

But by using laser pulses of exactly the right length scientists can break chemicals into smaller groups of atoms to create brand new chemicals. And this could turn every industry that uses chemical reactions upside down.

2 SMALL IS BEAUTIFUL

Nowadays people can make a fibre optic cable thousands of times finer than the eye of a needle. And tiny lasers are possible too. In 1989 IBM made a laser one-tenth the thickness of a human hair. With a bit of careful packing you could fit a *million* of them into this box.

The laser was made from tiny crystals and this technology will make possible micro-holograms and tiny surgical instruments for delicate operations. In fact, miniature versions of any machine that uses a laser.

3 MARVELS IN STORE

By the 2000's, scientists had figured out how to stop and store light. At first this involved cooling atoms to ultra-cold temperature and trapping photons with lasers and magnets. But in 2005 scientists found that a purple substance made by slimy microbes could slow light too.

4 STRANGE LIGHT SIGNALS

By the 2000's scientists were experimenting with a brain-boggling effect called quantum entanglement. If you make a pair of photons, they behave as if they're in contact, even when they're hundreds of kilometres apart. You could even use this pair of freaky photons to send coded signals. And just imagine – you could combine tiny lasers and light storage and secrete photon codes to create something that makes a super computer like something your baby brother plays with...

5 THE ULTIMATE DREAM MACHINE

I'm talking about a computer that does billions of sums at the speed of light using photons to send information. And scientists are dreaming of such a machine – a machine so powerful that it could do all your maths homework for the next ten years in one-millionth of a second. Now that's progress for you!

Sure, light is the fastest moving thing in the universe. But science is beginning to catch up. The future's looking horribly bright – and that's the brilliant truth!

THE END

FRIGHTENING LiGHT

QUIZ

Now find out if you're a
Frightening Light expert!

Light up Your Life!

So, have you been switched on during this lightning journey through light? Are you a bright spark or still in the dark? Take this quick quiz and find out...

1 What are the two main ingredients of a rainbow?
a) Sunlight and a pot of gold
b) Sunlight and rain
c) Sunlight and oxygen

2 What mysteriously occurs when a photon hits an atom?
a) All its energy is absorbed and, exhausted, it disappears
b) It has so much energy that it splits the atom into a million pieces
c) The photon's energy can glue atoms together

3 How long does it take speedy sunlight to reach the Earth?
a) About the time it takes for you to sneeze and wipe the snot on your sleeve during your Science lesson (8.5 seconds)
b) About the time it takes for you to nod off in your Science lesson (8.5 minutes)
c) About the time it takes for you to zoom out of the door at the end of your Science lesson (8.5 milliseconds)

4 How many light waves could stretch across the dot at the bottom of this question mark?
a) Hundreds

b) 4,677 precisely

c) About five

5 Which of the following would make an atom spit out a photon?

a) Asking it nicely

b) Sticking it in the freezer

c) Popping it in the oven

6 What happens to a stream of light when it moves from air into water?

a) It bends, or refracts

b) It bounces back, or reflects

c) It starts doing backstroke

7 Why is the sky blue?

a) Because there are more blue light waves than there are other colours

b) Because more blue light photons are scattered by the air

c) Because light is reflected off the water that covers 70 per cent of the Earth's surface

8 If a plant reflects green light and absorbs all the other colours, what colour light does a banana reflect?

a) Yellow

b) All colours except yellow
c) Red and green

Answers
1b; 2a; 3b; 4a; 5c; 6a; 7b; 8c

Meet the Scientists...

We'd still be living in the dark ages when it comes to light if it wasn't for a few freaky physicists who looked at light in a different way (often nearly blinding themselves in the process!). Can you match the discoveries below with the spectacular scientists responsible?

1 This freaky English physicist used a triangular lump of glass to prove that sunlight was made up of lots of different colours.

2 This German genius suggested that light came in the form of packets that he gave the curious name of 'quanta'.

3 This Dutch daredevil shed light on the mysteries of space by inventing the telescope.

BEAM ME UP, SCOTTY!

4 This mad-haired German-born scientist befuddled everyone by proving that light is both a wave and a particle (eh?!).

5 This ingenious American inventor set the world alight with his light bulb.

6 This famous French physicist found a way of measuring the speed of light using a spinning wheel and a mirror!

7 This amazing Arab scientist discovered that light is given out by glowing objects and that it always reflects at a predictable angle.

8 This energetic Englishman wowed the world with his discovery that light travels in weird waves.

a) Thomas Young
b) Armand Fizeau
c) Thomas Edison
d) Isaac Newton
e) Ibn al-Haytham
f) Hans Lippershay
g) Max Planck
h) Albert Einstein

Answers
1d; 2g; 3f; 4h; 5c; 6b 7e; 8a

What Does It All Mean?

These strange scientists used many weird and wonderful words to describe the ways light behaves and the objects it interacts with. Look at the list of words below – can you remember what on Earth they all mean?

1 Transparent
2 Reflection
3 Frequency
4 Interference
5 Refraction
6 Opaque
7 Diffraction
8 Translucent

a) The bizarre bending of light as it passes from one material to another.
b) The strange spreading out of light waves after they've passed through a small slit.
c) The name for an object that can block light and cast a spooky shadow.

d) The name for a frosty object that isn't so solid no

light can get through ... but isn't completely see-through, either.

e) The bouncing back of light when it hits an object.

f) The name for something that has a thin layer of regularly spaced atoms which means lots of light can pass through.

g) The mysterious meeting of light waves when they make a brighter light or block each other out completely.

h) The number of times a weird wave of light wiggles each second.

Answers
1f; 2e; 3h; 4g; 5a; 6c; 7b; 8d

Light Fantastic

Light is so amazing that you simply won't believe some of the things people say about it. Have a look at these fantastical statements and see if you can figure out which are strange but true and which are just strange...

1 You are only able to see your annoying little brother because light waves are bouncing off him.

2 Light is so brilliant it can even bend around corners.

3 Sunlight is made up of seven colours – red, orange, yellow, green, blue, indigo and violet.

4 Eating carrots helps you to see in the dark.

5 All the light on Earth comes from the sun – without our super star we'd all die in the darkness.

6 Stars seem to twinkle because the light from them is being bent by eerie gusts of wind.

7 People who are colour blind only see things in black and white.

8 Light is faster than anything, anywhere, ever...

Answers

1 TRUE. You'd probably rather be left in the dark...

2 TRUE (AND FALSE). Ha ha! Trick question. Light waves can only travel in straight lines, but amazing scientists have invented things called optical fibres that can carry light round corners.

3 FALSE. Sunlight is made up of these seven colours and everything in between (and others on either side, actually). It's just that we only have specific words to describe seven of them.

4 FALSE. That's just a load of carroty cobblers. If you want to see in the dark, use a torch!

5 FALSE. Light can come from lots of other things – candles, your toaster, even curious creatures like fireflies. But we'd still all die if the sun stopped shining because sunlight is what helps plants grow, which keep us alive (but that's a whole other Horrible Science book...).

6 TRUE. Starlight moves in a straight line, like all other light, but it can be refracted by wild winds.

7 FALSE. People who are colour blind can usually distinguish some colours but not others.

8 TRUE. Nothing in the whole universe can travel faster than light.

Awesome Eyesight

Without your amazing eyes you'd be completely in the dark. These miraculous machines take in light, figure out colours and form an image in your brain. So, let the light waves bounce off the page and use the clues to answer these curious questions about sight.

1 Which bit of your bulging eyeball lets in light? (CLUE: It may be the class swot)

2 What's the matter with you if you have mysterious myopia? (CLUE: You'll have to look closely to answer this one)

3 What happens to an object if you look at it through a concave lens? (CLUE: This is just a tiny clue)

4 What happens to your peculiar pupils when it gets dark? (CLUE: Oh – open your eyes!)

5 Which part of your awesome eye bends the light so you see things in focus? (CLUE: It sounds corny, but it's true)

6 If an object reflects all types of light, what colour do your eyes see it as? (CLUE: You know the answer, all white)

7 Which little bits on your retina allow you to see things in glorious Technicolour? (CLUE: You wouldn't want to put you ice cream in them, though)

8 What kind of lens makes an object look bigger? (CLUE: It's not complex)

Answers
1 The pupil
2 You are short-sighted
3 It looks smaller
4 They get bigger to let in more light
5 The cornea
6 White
7 Cones
8 Convex

GULP!

HORRIBLE INDEX

167

HORRIBLE SCIENCE

**Make sure
you've got
the whole
horrible lot!**

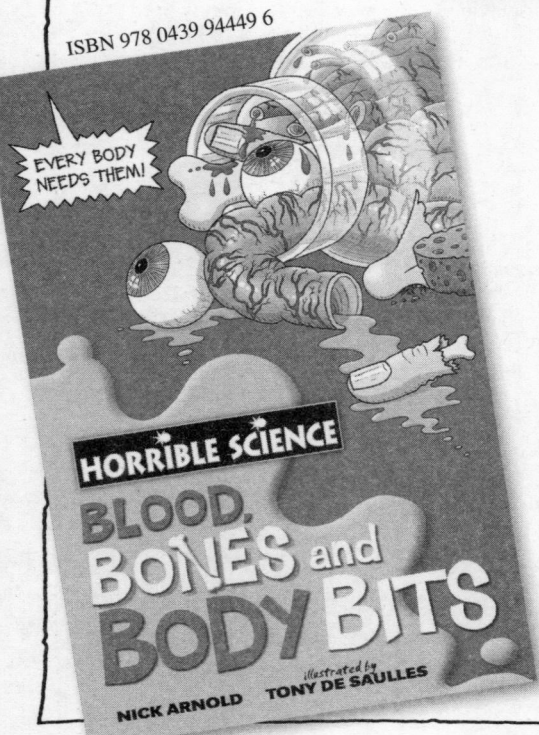

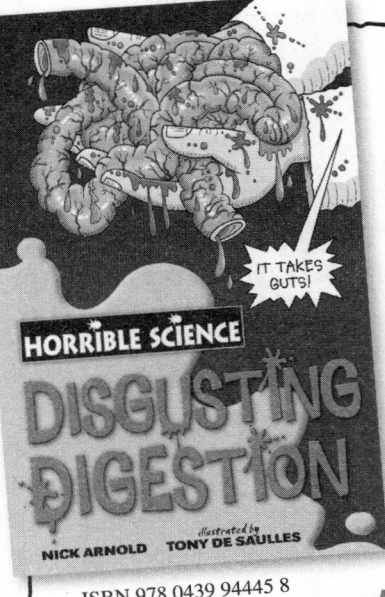

ISBN 978 0439 94445 8

ISBN 978 0439 94450 2

ISBN 978 0439 94451 9

ISBN 978 0439 94452 6

ISBN 978 1407 10359 4

ISBN 978 0439 94408 3

ISBN 978 0439 94407 6

HORRIBLE SCIENCE

NASTY NATURE

NICK ARNOLD

illustrated by
TONY DE SAULLES

■SCHOLASTIC

Visit Nick Arnold at
www.nickarnold-website.com

Scholastic Children's Books,
Euston House, 24 Eversholt Street,
London, NW1 1DB, UK

A division of Scholastic Ltd
London ~ New York ~ Toronto ~ Sydney ~ Auckland
Mexico City ~ New Delhi ~ Hong Kong

First published in the UK by Scholastic Ltd, 1997
This edition published 2008

ISBN 978 0439 94451 9

Printed and bound by CPI Group (UK) Ltd, Croydon, CR0 4YY

26

CONTENTS

Nick Arnold has been writing stories and books since he was a youngster, but never dreamt he'd find fame writing about Nasty Nature. His research involved grappling with lions, talking to dumb animals and cuddling up to snakes and he enjoyed every minute of it.

When he's not delving into Horrible Science, he spends his spare time eating pizza, riding his bike and thinking up corny jokes (though not all at the same time).

Tony De Saulles picked up his crayons when he was still in nappies and has been doodling ever since. He takes Horrible Science very seriously and even agreed to meet some of our beastly beasts before drawing them. Fortunately, he has made a full recovery.

When he's not out with his sketchpad, Tony likes to write poetry and play squash, though he hasn't written any poetry about squash yet.

INTRODUCTION

Brute force. Beastly behaviour. Animal cunning. Whenever humans have anything nasty to say to one another they drag animals into it. And animals bring out the worst in some humans, which can lead to nasty situations...

The science of animals can also provide some nasty surprises (and we're not talking about your brutish, wolfish, slavering teacher here). What, for example, about the odd words scientists use to describe our four-legged friends? They certainly leave a nasty taste in your mouth – when you don't understand them.

*ENGLISH TRANSLATION: COR – WHAT A NICE MOGGIE!

This is rather a pity because it's the nasty side of animals that gives them their horrible fascination. Obviously, we're not talking warm and cuddly here. You might be pleased to wake up and find a fluffy kitten or a playful puppy on your bed. But what about a giant green toad with staring eyes and a warty skin? Or a sociable skunk or even a grinning gila monster with huge claws?

Yep. Some creatures are cold and slimy with gigantic teeth. Others like to suck blood and live in horrible places. In a word – they're NASTY. And oddly enough that's what this book is about. Nasty Nature. The sort of things that 99 per cent of teachers wouldn't dream of teaching in their worst nightmares.

But who knows? After you've read up on reptiles and mugged up on mammals you could persuade your teacher that you're a "natural" scientist. Perhaps you might even discover a new kind of nasty creature. Or feel inspired to keep a new pet...

Don't worry it's not hungry ... yet.

One thing's for sure. Science will never seem the same again!

FREAKY CREATURES

Sometimes it takes a difficult person to crack a really difficult problem. And 300 years ago, scientists had an appallingly difficult problem. Explorers kept discovering freaky new kinds of animals – but how should scientists go about listing this huge variety of new creatures? It was a toughie.

Hall of fame: Carl Linnaeus* (1707–1778)
Nationality: Swedish
(* This was his name in Latin – his real name was Von Linné.)

Carl Linnaeus was a difficult man. It wasn't simply that he was an inspired genius with an incredible memory. The trouble was that he knew he was, and he wanted everyone else to know, too. If anyone criticized him he turned nasty. He sulked like a spoilt child and he never admitted he was wrong – never, ever, ever. Not even when he made big mistakes, like claiming a hippopotamus was a kind of rat!

HIPPOPOTAMUS

BLIMY – MY CAT CAUGHT ONE OF THOSE LAST NIGHT!

To be fair to Carl he'd seen rats before but not hippos.

But when Carl gave lectures, hundreds of students flocked to hear him. Why? Because he also told jokes. (A scientist with a sense of humour – now there's a rarity.)

CARL'S QUEST

Carl Linnaeus had itchy feet – that's to say he never stopped moving around … and working. He travelled 7,499 km across northern Scandinavia and discovered 100 plants that were unknown to science. But his main aim was far more ambitious. This was to sort out all the plants and all the animals in the world into some kind of logical order.

Unfortunately, he liked some animals more than others. He had particularly nasty things to say about amphibia – that's creatures such as frogs and toads that live on land and in water…

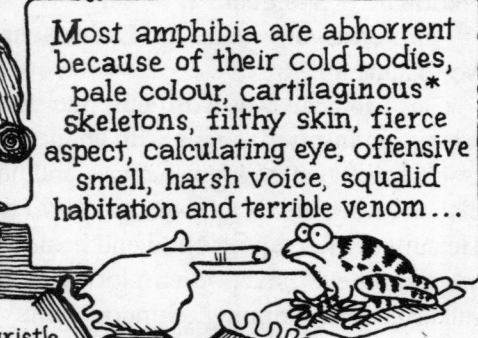

Most amphibia are abhorrent because of their cold bodies, pale colour, cartilaginous* skeletons, filthy skin, fierce aspect, calculating eye, offensive smell, harsh voice, squalid habitation and terrible venom…

*from cartilage = gristle

Carl had his work cut out. There's an enormous variety of animals in the world. And thousands more were being discovered every year in unlikely places.

Bet you never knew!
There are currently about 10,000,000,000,000,000, 000,000,000,000,000,000 (that's 10 billion, trillion, trillion) animals on Earth (give or take a few million) and they come in all shapes and sizes.

NOT A BAD SORT...

So how did Linnaeus sort 'em all out? He said that every type of animal was a species. Take this rather ugly toad.

NO THANKS

But following Linnaeus' plan, scientists call the toad a *Bufo bufo* – *bufo* is the name of the species and *Bufo* is the name of the genus it belongs to. (A genus is a group of similar species.) In fact, Bufo means "toad" in Latin, so the scientific name actually means "Toad toad".

Linnaeus placed each genus into a larger category called a family and grouped the families into classes. (Nothing to do with school you'll be relieved to know!) Our toad belongs to the family *Bufonidae* (Boo-fo-nid-ay) which includes toads and frogs, and the class Amphibia which also includes their slimy relatives, the salamanders and newts.

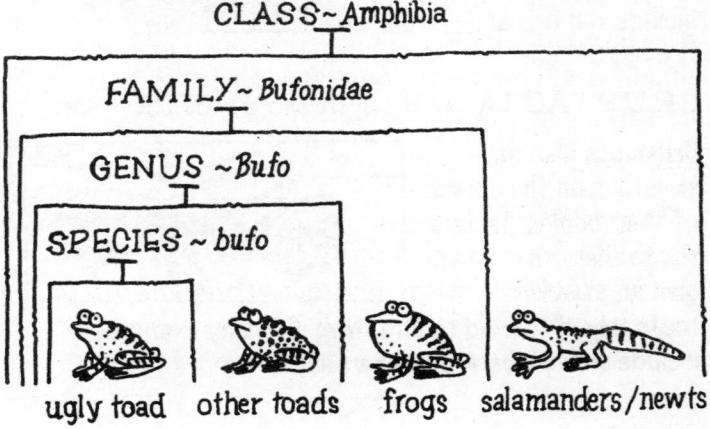

CLASS ~ Amphibia

FAMILY ~ Bufonidae

GENUS ~ Bufo

SPECIES ~ bufo

ugly toad　other toads　frogs　salamanders/newts

9

Gradually scientists throughout the world came to accept Linnaeus' methods of classification and they're still in use today. Here are the main animal classes. Now where do you fit in?

CNIDARIA *(ni-dare-ee-uh)* - 11,000 + species

No, these aren't sci-fi aliens - they just look that way. They live in the sea and their bodies consist of a sort of stomach with tentacles armed with thousands of stinging cells. Nasty examples include jellyfish, sea anemones and corals.

ECHINODERMS *(eck-hi-no-derms)* - 7,000 + species

These freaky creatures also hang out in the sea. They have hard, often spiky skin. Their legs are hollow tubes arranged around a central area. Eerie examples include starfish and sea urchins.

CRUSTACEA *(crus-taysh-she-a)* - 52,000 + species

Crustacea also have skeletons on the outside of their bodies. These are tough shells that would give an attacker toothache if it tried to bite them. Crunchy examples include crabs, lobsters and barnacles.

ARACHNIDS (arack-nids) - 73,000+ species

The bad news: most of this class are spiders. Erk! The worse news: some are scorpions. Arachnids have their head and thorax (the middle bits) of their bodies joined together. Scorpions have a nasty poisonous sting in their  tails but that doesn't stop people in Thailand enjoying roast scorpion. They have 6-12 eyes, eight jointed legs, two pincers and two grasping claws - oh, and I nearly forgot - a nasty poisonous sting in their tails. Some like playing sneaky tricks on humans - like hiding in their shoes!

FISH - 28,000+ species

Most fish have bony skeletons - so when you eat one you can end up with a face full of bones. Other fish such as sharks have gristly skeletons  instead. Fish live in water (surprise, surprise) and take dissolved air from the water through the gills in the side of their heads. Most fish are covered in scales and use fins to swim. Well, they're better than water wings.

AMPHIBIA - 6,000+ species

Amphibia are cold-blooded. That doesn't mean that they're pitiless and ruthless killers, although many are. No, "cold-blooded" means they heat  up and cool down with their surroundings. They have four legs and their skin is thin and slimy. The name amphibia means "double-lives" in Greek. And frogs and toads do live a double-life.

Dr Frog and Mr Tadpole

1 The tadpole hatches from eggs and gobbles up its unlucky brothers and sisters.

2 But in a few weeks it develops into a very different looking but equally repulsive adult.

3 The adult frog doesn't eat its own kind but it does grab flies with its long, sticky tongue.

4 Most amphibia spend the winter buried in mud at the bottom of lakes and ponds.

REPTILES – 8,200+ species

Reptiles are cold-blooded too, and covered in scales. They have small brains for their size and their legs stick out of the sides of their bodies so they have to crawl around. (Unless they're snakes who slither about instead.) Young reptiles are hatched from eggs. (Don't try eating them for breakfast though.)

BIRDS – 10,000+ species

Birds have two legs, a pair of wings and a horny beak. (Bet you bought this book to find that out!) Their bodies are covered with feathers made from keratin – that's the same stuff as your fingernails. Young birds hatch from eggs laid by their mums. That's if the eggs don't get poached and guzzled for breakfast first.

MAMMALS – 5,400 species

Mammals are warm-blooded*
and most of them live on land
and can't fly. Baby mammals
are born alive rather than as
eggs and they are nourished
on milk supplied by their
mums. And guess what – we're
mammals too. Yes, humans
belong to this class.

*This means that their blood is kept warm because their body is
covered with fur or fat to keep the cold out. It's not the same as
being "hot-blooded" – that's when someone keeps losing their temper
and getting into fights.

NASTY HABITATS

Animals are found everywhere you can imagine and a few
places that you wouldn't want to. By the way, scientists
call the place where an animal lives its "habitat". Animal
habitats range from deserts and rainforests to coral reefs
and stinking swamps.

Mountain yaks happily explore the Himalayan mountains
of Tibet at heights above 5,486 metres. And they find the
freezing temperatures of -17°C (1.4°F) well, rather bracing
actually. Red bears are said to climb even higher and that's
how they get mistaken for the legendary yeti.

Animals also lurk in the depths of the oceans. When explorers Dr Jacques Piccard and Lt Don Walsh reached the deepest part of the ocean – 10,911 metres – in 1960, the first thing they saw was ... a fish. As Piccard said later:

The explorers were gob-smacked. They thought the weight of water crushing down on the sea floor would squash any creature.

LITTLE AND LARGE FACTS

The largest animal that has ever lived is the blue whale. This creature can grow to 33 metres long and weigh 80 tonnes. That's 24 times the size of an elephant and even bigger than the biggest dinosaur. Inside the blue whale there are over 8,500 litres of blood protected by a layer of fat 61 cm thick. But here's a nasty thought: since 1900 human hunters have brought at least 378,000 of these stupendous creatures to a horrible end.

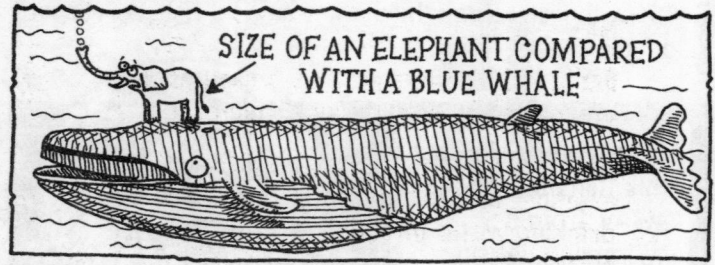

Compare that with … Helena's humming bird. It's only 5.7 cm from bill to tail and weighs a mere 2 grams. This tiny scrap of a creature lives off sweet, sticky nectar from flowers.

The Marshall Islands goby is a tiddler of a fish that lives in the Pacific Ocean. It is only 1.27 cm long.

But there are some creatures that make a goby fish look like a blue whale…

Nasty nature fact file

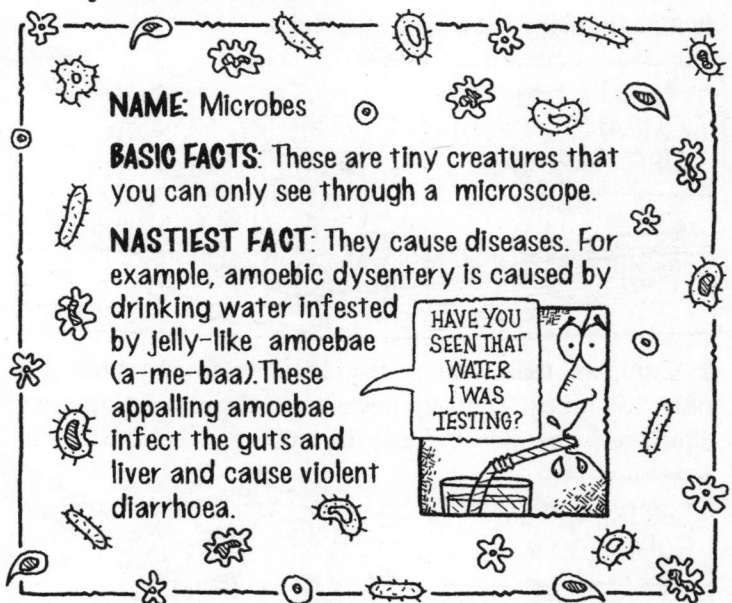

NAME: Microbes

BASIC FACTS: These are tiny creatures that you can only see through a microscope.

NASTIEST FACT: They cause diseases. For example, amoebic dysentery is caused by drinking water infested by jelly-like amoebae (a-me-baa). These appalling amoebae infect the guts and liver and cause violent diarrhoea.

HAVE YOU SEEN THAT WATER I WAS TESTING?

MILLIONS OF MURDEROUS MICROBES

A spoonful of soil can contain:

• 70,000,000,000 (70 billion) bacteria – these are tiny blobs of living matter that cause many diseases.

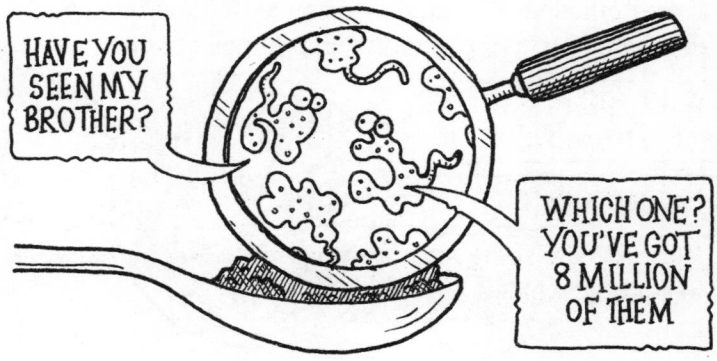

HAVE YOU SEEN MY BROTHER?

WHICH ONE? YOU'VE GOT 8 MILLION OF THEM

- 900,000 flagellata (flad-gell-la-ta) – these are microbes that swim using little whip-like tails.

- 42,000 amoebae – these feed by engulfing bacteria and other microbes. Their bodies are see-through so you can check out what they've had for breakfast.

- 560 ciliates (silly-ates) – these are creatures that use tiny hairs to swim about on damp lumps of soil.

Most of these creatures spend their time happily attacking and eating one another. And when they're not doing that they're pulling themselves in half to make even more murderous microbes. But these creatures aren't completely nasty. By feeding off dead plants and animals they ensure that useful chemicals are returned to the soil where they help make new plants grow. It's all in a good cause.

Bet you never knew!
In 1983 scientists discovered a super microbe lurking in a cavern in Arkansas, USA. It's a blob of jelly made up of millions of amoebae that slither along like a single creature! Its favourite food is bat droppings but it sometimes attacks lumps of fungus. It sends out fighter amoebae to eat the fungus.

If you want to check out some seriously freaky creatures here are some examples. Which of these creatures is too strange to be true?

WEIRD WILDLIFE QUIZ
1 The storsjoodjuret is an ugly looking long-necked reptile that skulks around in Lake Storsjön in Sweden. It's between 10–20 metres long. TRUE/FALSE
2 There's a type of bird with a horn on its head like a unicorn. It's called a "horned screamer". TRUE/FALSE
3 The Jack Dempsey fish is named after a famous American boxer. This small South American freshwater fish got its name because it enjoys ramming into other fish and stealing their eggs. TRUE/FALSE

4 There's a type of snake that can fly short distances.
TRUE/FALSE

5 The Malaysian two-headed bat has a lump on its back that looks just like an extra head. This fools owls that attempt to bite the bat's head off in mid-air. TRUE/FALSE

6 The Indian climbing perch is a fish that climbs trees. TRUE/FALSE

7 The Iberian "singing" goat is an excellent mimic. (That's the posh name for someone who copies voices.) It has been known to imitate the yodelling calls of local mountaineers! TRUE/FALSE

8 There's a creature that hangs out in Australian rivers with a bill like a duck and fur like a beaver. It lays eggs like a bird and has poisonous spines like a lizard. TRUE/FALSE

Answers: 1 Probably FALSE although some people swear they've seen it. Maybe it's a relative of the more famous Loch Ness Monster. The Swedish government has banned attempts to kill or capture the creature just in case it does exist. **2** TRUE. The horn is 15 cm long. The bird itself lives in marshes in tropical South America. You can hear its scream 3 km away. **3** TRUE. **4** TRUE. The golden tree snake can glide 46 metres. The snake launches itself from a high branch and draws its underside in and pushes its body forward as it zooms through the air. **5** FALSE. **6** TRUE. It uses its fins to grab branches. Once in the trees it allows ants to crawl over its body. Then it leaps back in the river. The ants fall off the fish and float around in the water – to be gobbled at leisure! **7** FALSE. **8** TRUE. It's the duck-billed platypus! This strange creature is actually an unusual species of mammal that looks like a mole pretending to be a duck. The puzzling platypus has also got detectors that sense electrical waves given off by small creatures at the bottom of muddy rivers. Classifying this freaky creature could drive a naturalist quackers.

NASTY NATURALISTS

Naturalists are scientists who study the natural world. Some study particular animals and others look at an entire habitat and its wildlife. Mind you, some naturalists have nasty habits. Here's a particularly eccentric example:

Hall of fame: Charles Waterton (1782–1865)

Nationality: British

Charles Waterton enjoyed pretending to be a mad dog and biting his visitors' ankles. A harmless youthful prank you might think, but cranky Chas was still playing this trick at the age of 57! Another curious habit was that he hated sleeping in a bed. He preferred a bare floor with a nice comfy block of wood for a pillow.

He made several trips to South America to find new types of animals – and then shot them. He stuffed their bodies so that he could study them at leisure. (He once captured an alligator alive by wrestling with it.) When at last he returned to his estate in England he spent £10,000 turning it into the world's first nature reserve. Yes, Waterton really liked animals – he even had his stables rebuilt so that the horses could "talk" to one another.

Now you might think Waterton was barking mad – horses don't talk, do they? Animals are not nearly as clever as humans (including naturalists and teachers) or are they? Find out in the next chapter.

DUMB ANIMALS?

So just how brainy are animals? And how good are their senses compared with our own? No one likes the idea that an animal might be brainier than themselves. That's why generations of nasty teachers have sunk to the depths of sarcasm.

YOU HAVE THE BRAIN OF A BIRD WILKINS, WHAT DO YOU SAY TO THAT?

TWEET, TWEET?

But would things seem so bad if your maths teacher had said "You have the brains of a horse"? Decide now as you read the story of...

CLEVER HANS
Berlin, Germany, 1904
The crowd was waiting, expectant. There was a buzz of excited conversation. Tired of standing, old Frau Schmidt turned to her younger friend, Fraulein Stein and whispered, "He's not going to appear!"

" 'Course, he is!" said Fraulein Stein. "Just you wait. He always comes out at this time. And it's true what they say – he counts. That's why they call him 'Clever Hans'."

"How can that be?" asked Frau Schmidt suspiciously. "Horses can't count like humans – not in real-life, I mean."

"This one does – and better. They say that Wilhelm Von Osten – that's its owner, was a school teacher. When he retired he started teaching horses instead of children."

"Go on with you! What would he want to do that for?"

"He reckons horses are just as clever as children and easier to teach too. He even built a special classroom for horses. Mind you, they say Wilhelm used to shout at Hans when he made a mistake. Even used a whip."

Frau Schmidt cackled like an ancient hen. "My old teacher was a bit like that, too."

"Sssh!" snapped the man behind them.

They watched as Hans was led out into the courtyard. People craned their necks for a better look and there were cries of admiration.

"Ooh, isn't he beautiful," whispered Frau Schmidt to her friend. "Who are those people with him?"

"Top level big-wigs. Von Osten wrote to the government asking them to test the horse and prove his powers. So the government set up a committee." The women watched as a man set up something looking suspiciously like a school blackboard.

"Are we ready?" Professor Carl Stumpf asked his committee of experts.

"I still think it's a circus trick," said the circus trainer.

"The horse appears to be healthy enough for the test," said the vet cautiously.

"Hurry up – I'm late for a meeting," said the Very Important Politician looking at his silver pocket watch.

Wilhelm Von Osten was a severe-looking little man with a pointed moustache. But now he looked rather worried. This was the biggest test so far. Would Hans fail?

"Perhaps you'd like to think of a sum for the horse to attempt?" Professor Stumpf asked the politician.

"Humph," said that gentleman pompously. "Well, let me see. What about two times fourteen?"

Von Osten gripped a piece of chalk tightly in his hand and wrote on the blackboard, 2 x 14 = ?

The teacher bowed his head. "Now, Hans," he whispered anxiously, "I've got a nice juicy carrot for you. But you've got to get this sum right."

The courtyard fell silent. Hans gazed steadily at the board. After a few moments he tapped his left hoof twice.

"What's he doing now?" hissed Frau Schmidt.

"He's counting," whispered Fraulein Stein. "Left hoof means tens and right hoof means ones." Hans slowly beat his right hoof on the cobbles. By now everyone was counting the hollow beats. Clop, clop, clop, clop, clop. Hans stopped with his hoof in mid-air. He looked like a wooden horse on a merry-go-round.

"That's only five," announced the politician smugly. "I want it written down – the horse is an imbecile!"

Von Osten gripped the carrot until his knuckles turned white. But Hans hadn't finished.

Clop, clop ... . and then finally . . . clop.

Hans looked at his master and whinnied happily. He knew he was right. The crowd clapped excitedly and a few began to cheer.

The politician's mouth dropped open like a trap door. Von Osten sighed with relief and gave Hans the carrot.

"Is that the right answer?" the circus trainer asked the vet.

"Yes, it is."

"That's incredible," said the trainer, scratching his head. "In all my years under the big top I've never seen anything like it."

"Nor I, in all my years in veterinary medicine."

"I told you so," announced Von Osten proudly.

Professor Stumpf asked the politician for his opinion.

The big, smug man had turned scarlet and was mopping his brow with a huge spotted handkerchief.

"Officially I couldn't possibly comment – but off the record I think I can say that I am … astounded."

He had quite forgotten his meeting.

But was Clever Hans really that clever? What do you think?

a) Von Osten was a ruthless trickster. He trained Hans to tap his hoof even though the horse didn't understand the questions.

b) Hans *was* clever. Since then scientists have proved that horses are better at maths than some humans.

c) Von Osten was giving clues to Hans. It wasn't the teacher's fault. He didn't know he was doing it.

Answer: c) This was proved by a young scientist Oskar Pfungst in 1907. He found that Hans could only answer the questions if he could see the questioner. But if you think about it Hans *was* clever. He had realized that his teacher leant forward to ask him a question and straightened up when he gave the right answer. This is a useful tip for dealing with any teacher's questions.

TEST YOUR TEACHER

So how does your teacher measure up against the best and brightest of the animal world? Can he or she decide how clever these animals really are?

1 In the 1960s Dr Dorothy Megallon of Kentucky, USA ordered a specially designed car for her horse. She then tried to teach the horse to drive. What do you think happened?

28

a) The horse couldn't get started.

b) The horse drove perfectly.

c) The horse crashed soon after getting a ticket for speeding.

2 Gorillas at Frankfurt Zoo, Germany enjoy watching TV. What's their favourite viewing?

a) Soap operas.

b) Wildlife documentaries about other gorillas.

c) Sports programmes including the football results.

THE GIRAFFES SAY "CAN YOU VIDEO IT FOR THEM, PLEASE?"

3 In 1913 a Mrs Moekel of Frankfurt, Germany owned a dog who could solve maths questions by moving beads on an abacus – a type of counting frame. But how smart was the dog?

a) Stupid wasn't the word for him. He only knew his two times table up to 4 x 2 = 9 (or was it 8?).

b) The scientists found that the dog had been trained to do certain sums but had no mathematical understanding.

c) The dog could work out square roots and was smart enough to help Mrs Moekel's children with their maths homework.

4 Keepers at San Diego Zoo, California, USA taught an Indian elephant to paint by holding a brush in her trunk.

How good were these pictures?

a) They were masterpieces as good as some modern art. Copies now hang in the world's major art galleries.

b) They were terrible – just a load of pointless scribble. Mind you, some critics have hailed them as triumphs of "post-modernist expressionism".

c) They were recognizable pictures, but since the keepers were telling the elephant what to do, they didn't count as the elephant's own work.

5 Scientists tested a chimp's intelligence by putting a blob of paint on its face and hanging a mirror in its room. The aim of the test was to see if the chimp realized the paint was on its face. What did the chimp do?

a) Looked in the mirror rather crossly and started rubbing the paint off its face.

b) Made faces at the mirror.

c) Tried to rub paint off the mirror.

6 British scientist Dr John Krebs added harmless amounts of a radioactive chemical to seeds and left them for marsh tits to hide and eat later. Then he used a Geiger counter (a machine that detects radio-activity) to monitor the hidden seeds. What did he discover?

a) Birds are brainy. The marsh tits cleverly hid hundreds of seeds every day. *And what's more, they were able to remember where they all were.*

b) Bird-brained wasn't the word for them. The birds soon forgot where they had hidden the seeds.

c) Nothing. The experiment was called off after the scientist forgot where he'd left his Geiger counter.

7 A scientist decided to teach three octopuses to pull a light lever in their tank in return for a feed of fish. What happened?

a) The octopuses were too stupid to learn the simple trick.

b) The octopuses turned nasty and tried to strangle the scientist with their disgusting long tentacles.

c) They quickly learnt the trick but after a few days they became bored and went on strike.

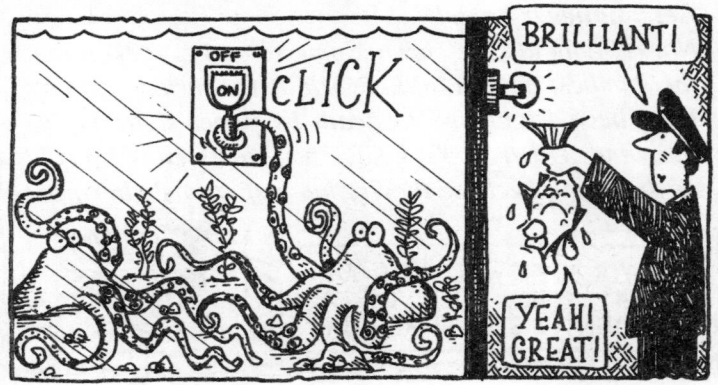

Answers: 1b) The car had levers to control its movement and an accelerator pedal that the horse could step on. The horse operated the steering wheel with its muzzle. Mind you, the horse wasn't allowed out on the open road! 2 c) Obviously they thought that the games were the real monkey business! 3c) Amazing but true. The dog, a three-year-old Airedale terrier named Rolf, was tested by a group of scientists who found that his abilities were real. Could you do with a pet like this? 4c) Elephants also draw "pictures" in the dust with their trunks but these really are meaningless scribbles. 5a) Chimps understand that the image they see in the mirror is their reflection. Monkeys do c) because they're not as smart as a chimp. How do you think your teacher would react first thing on a monday morning? 6a) But this is nothing. The North American nutcracker can hide up to 33,000 seeds – and find them again. 7c) They broke the light lever, squirted water at the scientist, and refused to take part in any more tests.

Bet you never knew!

Not all animals are clever. Some scientists reckon that the dumbest animal in the world is the turkey. Turkeys have been frightened to death by paper fluttering in the wind. Other turkeys have met nasty ends by cold or drowning because they're too stupid to shelter from the weather.

> YES, BUT IF WE GO INTO OUR SHELTER, HOW WILL WE KNOW WHEN IT'S STOPPED RAINING?

FURRY FRIEND'S FEELINGS

For many years scientists believed animals didn't have feelings such as fear, anger and pride. But more recently they have begun to study this intriguing topic and they've come up with some freaky results. For example, baby elephants suffer from nightmares. Babies who have seen their parents killed by hunters wake up in the night crying. When they grow up these elephants sometimes attack humans as if seeking revenge. Is it because they "never forget"?

It's also said that elephants cry. There's a story that a circus elephant burst into tears after being hit by her cruel trainer. But boring old scientists point out that elephant's eyes water a lot anyway. Crocodiles weep too but for them it's a way of getting rid of unwanted salt. That's why we'll say someone's crying "crocodile tears" when they're just pretending to be sad.

NOW ARE YOU SURE THOSE AREN'T JUST CROCODILE TEARS?

Animals can feel happy. Gorillas supposedly sing when they're in a good mood. A singing gorilla sounds like a whining dog so it won't cheer up anyone else. Goats dance around and leap for joy when they're feeling chuffed. Perhaps instead of saying "happy bunny" we should say "happy goat" instead?

So it's official – animals are sensitive. But even if they didn't have feelings, they'd still be sensitive because animals have some pretty incredible senses. Which they need to survive in their favourite habitats. But how do they measure up to humans? Surely they couldn't compete?

STUNNING SENSE STATISTICS

ANIMAL SENSES	HUMAN SENSES

SUPERSNIFFERS When you walk about in bare feet you leave 4 billionths of a gram of sweat in each footprint. To a dog this stinks like a cheesy old pair of socks that haven't been washed for a month.	**DON'T SMELL TOO WELL** A human's sense of smell is one million times weaker than a dog's. EVEN THOUGH HIS NOSE IS TWICE AS BIG
EAGLE EYES A golden eagle can see a rabbit on the ground up to 3.2km away.	**A SIGHT FOR SORE EYES** Some humans trip over rabbits.
A NASTY TASTE IN THE MOUTH Ugly catfish that lurk at the bottom of South American rivers have well over 250,000 taste buds in their tongues. That's how they find food in the murky mud.	**TOTALLY TASTELESS** Humans only have 10,000 taste buds – that's half as many as a pig. (This may explain why pigs don't enjoy school dinners but some humans do.)

HEAR, HERE

1. A dog's ear has at least 18 muscles so it can turn in any direction.

2. The Californian leaf-nosed bat can hear the footsteps of insects.

HARD OF HEARING HUMANS

1. Humans only have nine ear muscles and most people can't even waggle theirs.

2. Can you?

NO!

A TOUCH OF MAGIC

Seals use their ultra-sensitive whiskers to pick up tiny movements in the water caused by another creature.

A TOUCHY SUBJECT

Human whiskers don't even twitch.

IT'S TRUE!

STRANGE SENSES

1. Animals can predict earthquakes. In 2003 Japanese scientists found that mice behave oddly when they detect changes in magnetic forces linked to quakes.

2. The American knife-fish produces an electric signal 300 times every second. This creates a force field around the animal. A disturbance in the field warns the fish there's another creature about.

SENSELESS

1. Weedy humans can't accurately predict earthquakes even using sophisticated scientific instruments.

2. Er . . .

OK, YOU WIN!

Dare you discover … how cats see in the dark?

You will need:

1 torch
1 cat
1 dark room

What you do:

Allow the cat a few minutes to get used to the dark. Shine the torch in the cat's eyes. What do you notice?

a) The cat doesn't notice the light.
b) The cat's eyes reflect back the light.
c) The cat's eyes glow red like a vampire's.

DARK ROOM

SQUELCH! OH YUCK!*

* REMEMBER TO MOVE ANY BOWLS OF CAT FOOD FIRST

Answer: b) The cat has a layer of cells at the back of its eye that act like a mirror. These reflect light inside the eyeball and allow the cat to see better in the dark.

Hall of fame: Karl Von Frisch (1886–1982)

Nationality: Austrian

Karl was the son of a wealthy Austrian professor. He spent his childhood living in an old mill that his father was doing up and making friends with the local wildlife. He grew up to be a famous naturalist who discovered how bees pass on messages by doing little dances. Here's one of his nastiest investigations. Could you solve this problem as easily?

COULD YOU BE A NATURALIST?

Professor Otto Korner of Rostock University cut up fish and found that fish ears didn't work like human ears. So he reckoned fish were deaf. To prove his point he put some fish in a tank and whistled at them. The fish ignored him.

To finally prove his case Otto asked a famous singer to perform a private concert ... for the fish. She bawled out her operatic arias at an ear-splitting pitch. But still the fish took no notice!

Karl Von Frisch took an interest in this research and did his own tests. Imagine you were Karl Von Fish er, sorry, Frisch. What do you think you'd discover?

a) There's no doubt about it – fish are deaf as posts.

b) Don't be daft. It just proves that fish don't like boring old classical music.

c) Fish can hear but they're only interested in sounds to do with important things like food.

Are you sure they can't hear?

Many beasts aren't dumb animals at all. But what would they say to us if they could talk? Well, animals CAN talk … in a manner of speaking.

SNARLS, GROWLS AND HOWLS

Most animals communicate with one another to pass on nasty warnings or to show they're friendly. But creatures such as parrots can talk just like humans. Scientists say they're just copying the sound of the human voice. The animals don't realize what they're saying. Or do they?

CAN ANIMALS REALLY TALK?

Look at these examples and then decide for yourself.

A big-mouthed bird

For 12 years after 1965, the National Cage and Aviary Bird Show award for Best Talking Parrot-like bird was won by an African Grey parrot named Prudle. He knew over 800 words and even made up sentences. This amazed scientists who believed that parrots only copy what humans say.

Who's a pretty boy then?

In 1980, Dr Irene Pepperburg of Purdu University, Indiana, USA, published a report on her research with an African Grey parrot named Alex. This brainy bird could ask for things such as a piece of paper to clean his beak. He knew the names of colours and shapes and even told Dr P that he felt miserable when he moulted (lost his feathers).

A sign of wisdom

In 1966, some American scientists tried to teach chimpanzees sign language for the deaf. One of the first apes to learn this was a female called Washoe.

One day one of the researchers told Washoe that he'd just seen a big black dog with sharp teeth that ate baby chimps. Then he asked Washoe if she'd like to go outside. "NO!" signed Washoe nervously. After that whenever the scientists wanted Washoe to go indoors they told her that they'd seen the dog!

Despite falling for this nasty trick, Washoe proved to be a quick learner. She became so good at sign language she could even make up her own words such as "drink-fruit" (melon) and "water-bird" (swan).

SHE SAYS "YOUR HEAD LOOKS LIKE A MELON".

Washoe gave birth to a baby but sadly the infant fell sick and died at an animal hospital. The scientists came to tell Washoe what had happened.

"Where's baby?" signed the chimp.

"Baby finished," replied one of the researchers.

The poor mother retreated into a corner and wouldn't "talk" to anyone for several days.

In 1979, Washoe adopted a baby chimp and began to teach him sign language. As they say, it's good to talk…

SHE'S TELLING HIM THAT IF HE DOESN'T EAT HIS DINNER, SHE'LL GET THE BIG BLACK DOG

SPEAK FOR YOURSELF

Of course, when animals talk to one another they don't speak in human language. They've got their own forms of communication which can be quite complicated. Could you learn them?

Teach Yourself Language Guides

Liven up your holiday by talking to the wildlife. Now you can learn how to do this in the privacy of your own home. With these handy guides!

WHALE LANGUAGE

Have a "whale" of a time as you learn to sing like a whale for up to 24 hours at a time. Learn to alter your song if you're addressing a female whale. Practise ultra-low noises that can be picked up by whales hundreds of kilometres away! Be careful, though, no one knows what these songs mean so let's hope the whales don't get too excited when you sing to them.

HELP!

KILLER WHALE

DOLPHIN LANGUAGE

Discover how to natter with your flippered friends.

CHIRP – HI BUDDY!
BLOW LITTLE BUBBLES – I'M PLAYING
SCREAM – EXCITED
BLOW MORE BUBBLES – I'M CROSS
SQUAWK – I'M REALLY CROSS

DOLPHIN   SHARK

SQUEAKY WHISTLE, NOW LET ME SEE...

GORILLA LANGUAGE

Ever wanted to gossip with a gorilla?
Here's a few words of gorilla language
to get you going!

WRAAGH! = DANGER!

GRUNT = BEHAVE YOURSELF (USED BY ADULT
GORILLAS TOWARDS THEIR YOUNGSTERS.)

A BARKING HOOTING SOUND = I'M CURIOUS.

HOO, HOO, HOO = KEEP OUT!

BEATING CHEST = I'M BOSS.

SPINY LOBSTER LANGUAGE

You'll need a comb and a finger for this one. Free comb with every
guide, but you'll have to use your own finger. Spiny lobsters rasp
their antennae against a sticking out part of their shells.

SLOW RASP - IT'S SAFE TO FEED.

RAPID RASP - TAKE COVER, THERE'S A SHARK ABOUT!

WHO'S THIS
WEIRDO
TELLING ME
IT'S SAFE TO
FEED?

MANUFACTURERS' WARNING

TO AVOID NASTY SCENES DON'T
PRACTISE YOUR ANIMAL SOUND
EFFECTS AT FAMILY MEAL TIMES.
FARMYARD IMPRESSIONS ARE
ALSO STRICTLY FORBIDDEN!

OINK, OINK!

I WISH HE
WOULDN'T EAT
LIKE A PIG

COULD YOU BE A NATURALIST?

Vervet monkeys in Kenya have different alarm calls for leopards, eagles and snakes. A naturalist played these calls to the monkeys. What do you think they did?

a) Stuck their fingers in their ears and ignored the sounds.

b) The monkeys acted as if these dangerous animals were approaching.

c) The monkeys pelted the tape recorder with rotten fruit.

DON'T LIKE THAT MUCH – GOT ANY MICHAEL JACKSON?

Answer: b) Leopard alarm – monkeys climbed the trees. Eagle alarm – monkeys took cover under trees. Snake alarm – monkeys checked the bushes.

COLOURFUL CHARACTERS

Some animals communicate without saying a word or making a sound. (Certain adults think that children should be able to do this too!)

1 The tilia fish of the Indian Ocean turns dark grey when it wants a scrap. If it loses, the fish turns white – maybe it's scared!

2 When the male tilia fish fancies a female his head turns brown, his jaw turns white and his fins become blood red.

3 Some humans turn an interesting shade of beetroot when they're cross, but did you know that octopuses are similar? A relaxed octopus is a tasteful shade of brown but an angry octopus turns red with rage.

PINK GLOW

DON'T GET CRABBIE WITH ME!

4 Fiddler crabs turn red when they're cross, black when they're scared, and a rather fetching shade of purple when they meet a fiddler crab they fancy.

If you can't change colour, you can always tell people what you think by the look on your face. Birds, reptiles and fish can't make faces, but mammals can. We've all seen the nasty expression on a teacher's face. But did you know monkeys make faces too? Famous naturalist, Charles Darwin, studied these fascinating faces.

Hall of fame: **Charles Darwin** (1809–1882)
Nationality: British
Charles Darwin nearly gave up science at an early age. At school scientific interests were not encouraged and young Charles once got told off for "wasting time" on chemistry experiments. He later wrote:

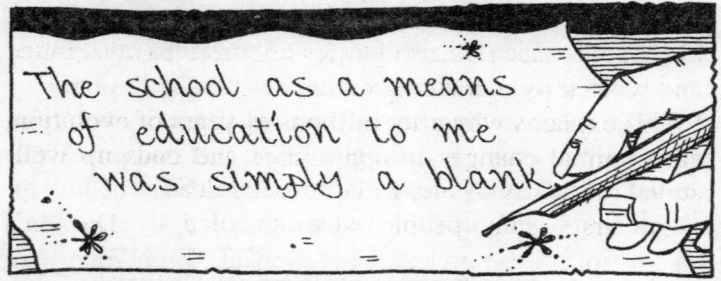

The school as a means of education to me was simply a blank

Try quoting that to your science teacher!

But Charles followed his scientific interests and in 1858 announced his "Theory of Evolution". Studies of fossil bones showed that ancient animals looked different from today's creatures. So the new theory arrived to explain these changes. Darwin suggested:

1 That some animals survive and some get guzzled. (Amazing insight, that.) Naturalists call this grisly business "survival of the fittest". Well, you have to be pretty fit to escape from a hungry tiger.

2 The animals in a species are all slightly different from one another. (You look different to the others in your class, don't you? I mean, even a teacher can tell you apart.)

YES, SIMPKINS, IT IS TRUE THAT YOU LOOK SLIGHTLY DIFFERENT FROM OTHERS IN THE CLASS

3 Some animals in a species have features that give them a better chance of surviving. For example, take a bird like a nightjar. This bird is active at night and by day rests on the ground. Some nightjars are better camouflaged than the others. And you'll be glad to know they pass their crucial colouring on to their offspring.

4 After a while, you get more and more well-camouflaged nightjars because other nightjars are more easily spotted and scoffed by marauding cats.

5 This explains why after millions of years of evolution, each animal changes in appearance and ends up well-suited to its way of life. Either that, or dead.

At first, many people were appalled by Darwin's suggestion that humans had evolved from apes. But nowadays, Darwin's theory is accepted by many scientists as they continue to figure out how evolution operates.

FOR EXAMPLE, THE DODO DID NOT SURVIVE BECAUSE:
1. IT COULDN'T FLY
2. IT WAS EASY TO CATCH
3. PEOPLE ATE IT

MONKEY BUSINESS

London Zoo, 1850

The passers-by stared in horrified disbelief.

"Do you think he ought to be in there?" the young woman asked clutching the arm of the gentleman beside her.

"Assuredly not, my dear," he replied. "Such goings-on should be discouraged by the proper authorities."

An older man now joined them outside the monkey cage. "It's a disgrace," he snorted. "That Darwin should be arrested!"

Inside the cage Charles Darwin, the eminent naturalist, was down on all fours. He was making strange noises in a bid to make friends with a young orangutan. The ape was shrieking and leaping about with excitement.

Darwin tried blowing kisses at the ape. To everyone's amazement, including Darwin's, the orangutan suddenly blew a kiss back. Mr Darwin had made a new friend.

"Aha!" said Darwin to himself, still totally unaware he was being watched. "Very interesting!"

Pausing only to scribble illegible notes in his pocket book, the naturalist showed the ape a mirror. Once again the animal kissed the air with a loud smack of the lips. Then he peered behind the mirror hoping to find another orangutan. "That fooled you," laughed the naturalist.

By now the passers-by had scurried off with backward looks of disgust. But Darwin didn't mind. He'd proved that apes make faces to send messages and, as he was about to find out, we humans aren't so different.

Darwin then turned his attentions to his baby son, William. The naturalist took to creeping up on the infant and shaking a rattle loudly to startle him.

He found that babies don't learn how to smile and frown – they just know. This is called "instinct". So Darwin sent questionnaires to civil servants in other countries and found that people smile and frown all over the world in just the same way. These are natural ways for humans to communicate, whatever their language. This was a major discovery and it all began with a bit of monkey business.

Dare you discover ... how to talk to an ape?

Here are some gestures you might find useful when you meet a monkey. You could practise them in front of a mirror (but not during a science lesson).

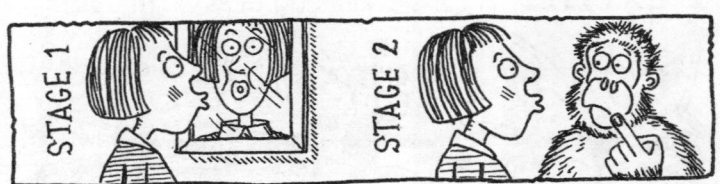

1 Kissing gesture:

Meaning: Help me please, I'm a friend.

Note: If a monkey makes this gesture it's a good idea to copy it. Hopefully you won't actually have to kiss the monkey.

2 Smacking lips:

Meaning: I love you and I want to eat the bits of dead skin and ticks in your hair.

Note: Monkeys do this to their friends. So if you smack lips to a monkey you better be serious about it.

3 Teeth chattering:

Meaning: HELP! I'm scared!

Note: Does anyone else have this effect on you?

Dare you discover … how to "talk" to your pet dog/cat?

If you don't happen to have a pet monkey, you may look out for these expressions on a pet dog or cat.

1 EXCITED EYES Blinking eyes = I'm upset

2 FEARFUL FROWN

Frown. (Eyebrows lowered and eyes half-closed) = There's danger ahead

3 A CROSS CREATURE

Eyebrows down but eyes wide open = I don't like you. Note: It's always extremely rude to stare at a cat or dog. They get upset and if they happen to be much larger than you they might decide to take a chunk out of you.

4 EAGER EARS

Sideways ears = I'm resting

Twitching ears = I'm about to pounce.

Floppy ears =
I surrender!

5 MYSTERIOUS MOUTH

Mouth open but you can't
see teeth = Let's play

Mouth tightly closed =
I'm relaxed

Front teeth exposed =
I'm the boss.

All the teeth exposed =
You're the boss but I don't
like you and I'm going to
get you one day when I'm
feeling really brave.

IMPORTANT NOTE – You'd better "talk" nicely to your pet otherwise it might go wandering. You see, some animals have a nasty urge to drop everything and go on their travels.

TERRIBLE TRAVELS

Just like humans, some animals enjoy travelling, and others prefer to stay put. But animals don't travel for fun or holidays. Oh, no. They're searching for food, for shelter or a mate. And some of their travels are definitely on the nasty side. Luckily some animals aren't too fussy about where they stay.

A NASTY WAY TO GO

Just think of the nastiest, the hottest, the coldest or the WORST journey you've ever made. Now imagine making the same trip but with everything and everyone giant-sized, except you. And somewhere close by, large hungry creatures are waiting to pounce... Scared? That's how it feels to be a small animal on the move.

Yet amazingly, some animals make huge journeys – and can even find their way home from great distances with amazing accuracy. Impossible? How's this for a tall tail – er, tale?

Until 1952 headmaster Stacey Wood lived in California, USA. In that year he retired to a farm in Oklahoma – 3,000 km away. The whole family went except for the cat, Sugar, who was sent to live with neighbours. One year later a cat turned up at the Woods' new home. It was thin and bedraggled as if it had been on a long and desperate journey.

MIAOW!

INCREDIBLE!! I THINK IT'S "SUGAR"

WELL HE CAN WAIT UNTIL MORNING – I'VE JUST GOT INTO BED

Amazingly, against all the odds, the new arrival was Sugar, who had disappeared a few weeks after the family had left California. The cat even had Sugar's bad hip. For an entire year the courageous cat had trekked across the United States to find its family. And to this day no one knows how Sugar did it.

Other animals are also brilliant at finding their way. Take pigeons, for example.

PIGEON POWER

Now you might think a pigeon is a silly-looking bird with a tiny little head and a puny little brain to match. And of course, you'd be right. But when it comes to travelling, pigeons and many other birds are geographical geniuses.

INCREDIBLE EYESIGHT → DIRECTION-FINDING BRAIN

SUPERSONIC HEARING

AMAZING FLYING POWERS

BIG FAT FLUFFY CHEST

1 Pigeons can fly all day at speeds of 48 km per hour (30 mph) and cover 1,120 km and still not get tired.
2 Pigeons' brains contain magnetic crystals sensitive to the Earth's magnetic field. This allows a pigeon to know which direction is north and which direction is home. This was proved in the 1970s when a scientist tied a magnet to a pigeon's head. The magnet confused the pigeon's crystals and the poor pigeon got lost.

3 Like other birds that fly long distances, pigeons can recognize landmarks and use the position of the sun and the stars to work out directions. They can even see rays of sunlight when the sun is behind a cloud.

4 And if all that wasn't enough, pigeons have the ability to hear ultra low-pitched sounds too low for a human ear. For example, a pigeon can hear waves crashing on a beach hundreds of miles away. That's how they know the way to the seaside.

5 With all these amazing abilities you won't be surprised to hear that a homing pigeon that wins races is worth its weight in gold. One such bird, Emerald, was sold in 1988 for £77,000 and even her eggs were worth £2,400 each. Drop a few of those and you could make the world's most expensive omelette.

DOES ANYONE KNOW WHAT HAPPENED TO THE EGGS THAT "EMERALD" LAID YESTERDAY?

But pigeons are just one species of high-flying, long-distance-travelling birds. Lots of birds migrate or travel from one area to another – every year. They do this because they have a powerful urge to fly off in a certain direction to find more food or a suitable nesting site. But scientists don't really understand how and why the birds manage it. Would you enjoy a holiday like this?

WING~IT HOLiDAYS

SWIFT TOURS

Air tours of sunny south-east Africa. Get away from the nasty British winter. Non-stop air flights with in-flight refreshments. Just catch yourself a few crunchy insects on the way. Exclusive washing facilities – just whiz through a thunderstorm. Note to passengers: the trip covers 19,200 km and we won't be landing at all. Not even to visit the toilet.

WANDERING ALBATROSS TOURS

Antarctica is the last unspoilt continent on Earth. Now you can fly around its beautiful coast in search of fish. Enjoy panoramic views and a lovely smooth ride. Your wandering albatross pilot can glide for six days without beating a wing. In-flight meals include mouth-watering raw fish – with that "just caught" taste.

ARCTIC TERN TOURS

A holiday with a difference. Good weather is guaranteed! Yes, you can be sure that every day will "tern" out nice again! Escape the northern winter blues by flying direct to sunny Antarctica where the days are warmest at this time of year. Then back to the Arctic in time for summer. Lovely fish suppers are available all the way too.

THE NASTIEST ANIMAL JOURNEYS

Other animals, besides birds, also migrate. Their journeys are full of difficulties and dangers. Here's some of the nastiest examples. Would *you* want to tag along with this lot?

Ambling amphibia

Every year thousands of fearless frogs and not-so-timid toads return to the ponds where they hatched as tadpoles. They do this to mate and lay eggs. Unfortunately, they often try to hop across roads without looking and end up squashed by cars. Sometimes they get there only to find humans have drained their pond. In other places, however, naturalists have built tunnels under the roads so the wandering wildlife can cross safely.

WE'LL USE THIS PELICAN CROSSING UNTIL THEY BUILD US A TUNNEL

Sociable snakes

Every year 20,000 red garter snakes slither 16 km from their summer homes in the marshes of Manitoba, Canada to their winter hideaways in sheltered rocky pits. After the winter they return to the marshes. Nothing too nasty about that – as long as you don't mind the sight of thousands of snakes. The snakes insist on taking short cuts through people's homes and often inspect their dinner tables.

Loony lemmings

Lemmings are small furry animals that happily scamper about in the Arctic snow. But every 3–4 years things get difficult. A rapid rise in lemming numbers means there isn't enough food to go round. So the lemmings form a huge army and attack anything in their way – including humans. They even do crazy things like trying to swim wide rivers. Where are they going? The lemmings don't know. There's an old story that lemmings leap off cliffs during these migrations – but it's not true. That would be too crazy – even for a lemming!

Terrible turtle treks

Every year green turtles swim to Ascension Island in the Atlantic Ocean to lay their eggs. No one knows why they go there but the island has few large animals that want to eat the turtles. Unfortunately the island is only 13 km by 9 km in size and some turtles have to swim 2,080 km to get there. To make matters worse the tired turtles' top speed is only 3 km (less than 2 miles) an hour.

YOU'VE COME TOO FAR, THIS IS THE PACIFIC

A slippery trip

For 15 years a European eel does nothing very much except squirm around in a muddy river or pond. Every so often it scrunches a passing fish and that's it for excitement. Then one day the eel starts feeling eel – er sorry, ill. It turns from yellow to silver and its eyes bulge.

Its snout gets longer and – eel-longated (ha ha). Then the eel develops an irresistible urge to swim to the sea. So strong is this feeling that an eel will even slither to the nearest river over dry land. The eel swims the length of the river to the sea and wriggles up to 4,000 km to the Sargasso Sea – a vast area of seaweed in the Atlantic Ocean.

When it gets there ... the exhausted eel dies. Bit of a wasted effort you might think – except that just before it dies the eel mates. Its offspring (called elvers), tiny see-through eels, set off for home. Without any help they find their way to the rivers and ponds of Europe.

And guess what? No one knows how eels came to develop this amazing lifestyle or how they find their way on their mysterious migrations.

No matter how far it has to go, every animal's body is suited to getting around. That's why dolphins have flippers, birds have wings and frogs are champion hoppers. Here's your chance to get moving on this topic.

Dare you discover ... how you measure up to a gibbon?

How good are you at brachiation (brach-ee-ay-shun)? If your answer is "my bike brakes are fine", you ought to know that brachiation means leaping from branch-to-branch. It's a dangerous way of getting to school in the morning. But gibbons brachiate all the time. That's not surprising, really – gibbons are apes that live in the trees of south-east Asia.

Here's the secret of their success:

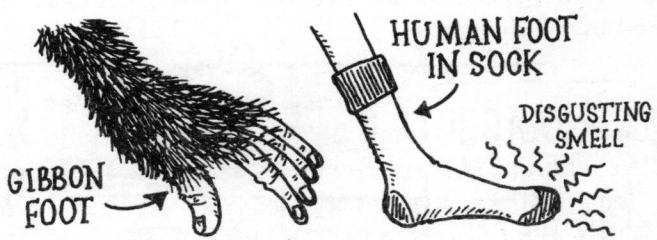

GIBBON FOOT →

HUMAN FOOT IN SOCK

← DISGUSTING SMELL

Take a look at this gibbon's foot. Now compare it to your own right foot. (It helps if you take off your sock.) What do you notice?

a) Nothing. My foot is exactly the same.

b) The gibbon's big toe looks more like my thumb.

c) The gibbon's toes are longer.

> **Answer: b)** Unlike your feet, a gibbon's feet aren't good at walking on the ground. But they're very good at gripping small branches. Can you do this with your big toe? Gibbons have long arms and strong shoulder muscles to hurl themselves from branch to branch.

Eventually, though – just like you at the end of a hard day in the classroom – every animal's thoughts turn to home. But for an animal "home" isn't a place to watch TV or play computer games. It's somewhere to store food, raise young and shelter from larger, fiercer creatures. Bet you wouldn't feel at home in any of these places.

NASTY HOME TRUTHS

1 The Australian white tree frog is a friendly little creature with a big smile on its slimy face. Clearly, this happy hopper is very pleased with its favourite home – a toilet cistern. (Before the invention of the toilet the frogs lived in smelly ponds.)

AAAAGH! THERE'S A FROG IN THE BOG!

2 Snapper turtles in eastern North America are quite at home in smelly stagnant ponds or stinking sewers. It's a bad idea to go paddling in these places (as if you would!). Snapper turtles lurk in the shallows and they'd love nice pink toes for tea.

DON'T WORRY – NOTHING WOULD LIVE IN A SMELLY STAGNANT PLACE LIKE THIS ...

3 An octopus will live in any hollow object lying on the sea bed. They're really not fussy – for a small octopus a human skull makes a cosy little home.

SPOOKY!

4 Eagles and ospreys build large, scruffy twig nests on top of trees. Unfortunately, they also build them on electricity pylons. Sometimes a bird touches a power line and you end up with Kentucky fried eagle.

5 Cave swiftlets are birds related to swifts that live, not surprisingly, in caves. Their nests are made from bits of plants glued together with ... spit. Yes – swiftlet spit sets swift-ly (ha, ha!) to form a strong glue. And this is added to chicken and spices to make traditional Chinese bird's nest soup. Oddly enough, swiftlets eat something similar. They feed their young on balls of insects glued together with tasty all-purpose spit. Yummmeee!

Of course, not all animals build their own homes. It's too much like hard work. Some move into other animals' homes instead. For example, North American black-tailed prairie dogs are squirrel-like creatures that dig a maze of tunnels to live in. Some of these tunnel systems are huge with up to 50 entrances. Soon unwelcome lodgers move in – these include owls, squirrels, salamanders, mice, black-footed ferrets and even the odd rattlesnake.

And that's not the only way that animals take advantage of one another. Some do nasty things like – eating their hosts alive, or slurping their blood. Yikes! Read on if you dare...

THE NEXT CHAPTER'S REALLY GRUESOME!

NICE AND NASTY:
HELPERS AND HANGERS ON

When different animals get together, things happen. Nice things and nasty things. Some animals help one another and some animals are just harmless hangers on ... but others try to help themselves at the expense of other creatures.

ANIMAL AIDERS
The idea of animals doing one another good turns sounds odd – doesn't it? But it shouldn't. After all, we keep pet dogs and cats – or even pet toads and snakes. Pets keep us company, often show us affection and leave little puddles on the carpet. In return, we feed them and provide shelter. And other animals such as horses and sheepdogs work for us in return for more food and shelter. When animals help one another this is known as symbiosis (sim-by-o-sis).

Bet you never knew!

Animals raised by humans sometimes keep pets. One of the apes taught to "speak" using sign language in America, was Koko the gorilla. Now Koko was happy living with researcher Dr "Penny" Patterson. But the gorilla had one wish. More than anything else – she wanted a kitten of her own. So in 1984 kind-hearted Dr Patterson gave her one.

Koko called her new pet "All Ball". She treated All Ball as her baby and even dressed it in cute little hats and scraps of material. Koko often tried to get the kitten to tickle her. (The gorilla enjoyed being tickled by her human friends.) And when the kitten was well-behaved Koko signed that it was a "soft good cat". Altogether now – Ahhhh. But if you like happy endings don't read the bit below.

Soon after, All Ball was run over and killed. Boo hoo! Poor Koko was heart-broken and nothing could cheer her up until Dr Patterson bought her another kitten.

FEATHERED FRIENDS

1 There's one little bird in Africa that's fond of beeswax and the juicy grubs that wriggle around in the sticky honeycomb. But how to get it – that's the problem. The honey is protected by thousands of bad-tempered bees.

So the bird calls to attract a passing honey badger. Then the bird flies towards the bees' nest.

The badger has learnt to follow the bird's signals. The bees can't sting the badger's thick skin as it claws open the nest. Meanwhile, the bird gobbles up any spare honeycomb.

And the name of this bird? The honeyguide bird, of course.

2 Another African bird, the ox pecker, rides on the backs of hippo, zebras and rhinos. The larger animals don't mind. The bird eats the flies that infest their backs. And it even warns of approaching humans.

If the larger animal takes no notice, the bird drums its beak against their head.

HOME HELPERS

Some creatures help each other by providing homes in return for services rendered.

For most fish, getting mixed up in the poisonous tentacles of a Portuguese man-o-war (a jellyfish-like creature) is something they wouldn't live to regret – because they wouldn't live much longer. But for one fish this is home. Nomeus (no-me-us) is a little fish that lives amongst the tentacles, protected from harm by its extra slimy skin. The fish keeps the tentacles nice and clean. When other fish try to catch Nomeus they fall victim to the jellyfish – and Nomeus gets to eat the leftovers.

In a cosy, sandy burrow at the bottom of the sea live a pair of oddly-matched housemates – Luther's goby fish and the blind shrimp. The shrimp dig their burrow and the goby guides his friend on feeding trips. The shrimp keeps his antenna on the fish's tail. If there's danger, goby wags his tail and the two friends run off home.

But helping each other and looking after one another isn't all that animals do. Some even clean one another. And there's a great choice of cleaners – if you don't mind being nibbled.

CREATURE COMFORTS
SERVICES DIRECTORY

HEY FISH – D'YOU FANCY A WASH AND BRUSH UP?

Let your friendly cleaner Wrasse do the job for you. We'll nibble that nasty mould and fungus away and leave your scales as good as new! Speedy personal attention assured.

"Cleaner Wrasse managed to serve a queue of 300 fish in a single session. Highly recommended."

A. Shark (Pacific Ocean)

ALMOST FINISHED

WARNING!

To all customers of Cleaner Wrasse Services: BEWARE OF CHEAP IMITATIONS! Blenny fish try to copy Cleaner Wrasse. They've even copied the stripe on our bodies. But BEWARE! As soon as they get close they'll take a bite out of you and scarper!

GOBIES' GOUPER GOB-GROOMING SERVICES

Are you a gouper fish with bad breath? Special offer – let us clean out your mouth free of charge! We'll eat those nasty bits of rotten food and we won't leave you feeling down in the mouth.

CROCS – ARE LEECHES YOUR PROBLEM?

There's nothing that spoils a good meal more than leeches clinging to your gums and sucking your blood. But spur-winged plovers have the leeches licked. Just open your mouth and we'll eat them for you. Also free danger-warning service. If you hear us chirp – there's a large, fierce animal on the way, so you'd better jump in the river!

COULD YOU BE A NATURALIST?

In coral reefs, fish cleaning is done by shrimps from special areas known as "cleaning stations". A scientist removed all the shrimps from a cleaning station. Can you guess what happened next?

a) The fish started nibbling one another in a vain attempt to keep clean.

WHERE ARE THEY?

DON'T ASK ME, I'M A PRAWN

b) Nothing. The fish weren't bothered whether they were dirty or not.

c) The fish went away in search of another cleaning station.

Answer: c) The fish staged a mass walk-out. Or should that be a swim-out?

PESKY PARASITES

But not all creatures are helpful. Some couldn't be helpful in a month of Sundays. They're known as parasites – animals that don't hunt for food, but steal it in various horrible ways from other creatures. These parasites do their victims no favours at all. Which of these parasites would you least want to meet?

Frigate birds of Central America have an unusual method of getting a free lunch. They wait until another bird has caught a fish then chase their victim and force them to sick up their meal. The foul frigate bird then gulps the sick in mid-air. And if that isn't nasty enough, they also steal eggs and eat other birds' chicks – including baby frigate birds.

European cuckoos lay their eggs in other birds' nests. The cuckoo hatches and chucks the other fledglings out of the nest. The parents feed the cuckoo and don't even notice any difference. Not even when the cuckoo grows up to five times their size. (Would your parents notice if you were replaced by another creature?) As soon as it's fully-grown the cuckoo takes off for a lovely winter holiday in Africa. And guess what? It doesn't even say "thank you".

Sea lampreys have been described as "a yard of garden hosepipe that's been left out all winter". And that's putting it nicely. These foul fish have no mouth or teeth – just suckers and fangs, and they like nothing better than sucking the blood of other fish.

JUST A LITTLE KISS...

Want to know something really scary? There's something that lurks in the South American jungle that makes other parasites seem almost OK. Oh yes, this is much, much worse. D'you want to know what it is? Turn down the lights, close the shutters and draw close to the fire. Here's a tale to make your blood run cold!

WHAT'S EATING YOU?

"I can remember it like it was yesterday." The old man smiled showing the gaps between his yellow teeth. The gaps made him hiss as he spoke. Like a snake.

"But when did it happen, grandpa?" asked the young boy with his eyes like saucers.

"It was in Brazil, back in 1927. We were there to study the wildlife and it was my first time in the jungle. I remember the strange sights and the smells – but do you know what I remember most? The nights. The humming insects and the croaking frogs in the dank, smelly swamps. The wet chill in the air. The big round moon hiding amongst the trees.

"We made camp mostly around nightfall. Well, it gets dark quickly in the jungle and we had to light a fire and put our tents up in good time. Old Dr Beebe's orders. That's William Beebe of the New York Zoological Society – our expedition leader. And Dr B said we should always keep our feet inside the tents."

"Why did he say that, Grandpa?"

"Well, because of the vampires, of course," hissed the old man.

"Vampires? Not real vampires like Count Dracula?" The boy's voice rose higher.

"Dracula wasn't no real vampire, Johnnie. He was a legend. But this is true. As true as I'm sitting here. Real live vampire bats."

The young boy gulped.

"*Bats!* And do they really bite people?" he stammered.

"Sure they do – and animals like cows and horses. Not dogs so much. Dogs can hear 'em coming. The bats flap down from the trees where they live – silent as ghosts.

They've got wings like old leather and huge ears to hear with. They creep along the ground to find your feet. Then they lick your toes to make sure they're nice and soft. And then they *bite* you!"

The boy looked over his shoulder nervously. "Do they really suck blood?"

"No, they lap it up like a cat laps milk. Or at least that's what Dr Beebe told us. He was always going on about bats."

"Well, it was soon after that I got a rude awakening. I was in a deep long sleep. Suddenly, I felt a sharp pain in my big toe like a needle. I shouted and then I was awake. Sweat streamed off me like a waterfall. It was dark but there was a moon and I saw a figure. Someone. Something."

"Wasn't it a bat?"

"No – it looked human. It scared the life out of me, I don't mind telling you. My heart was banging like a drum. I reached for the electric torch. My fingers felt like slippery fish. Somehow I switched on the light and what do you think I saw? Dr Beebe. He was crouching there with a bright sharp pin in his hand. 'Sorry to disturb you,

Jack,' he chuckles. 'Just trying a little test. I wanted to see if a vampire's bite would wake you.'

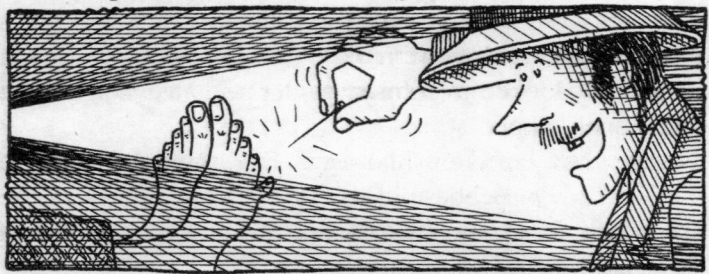

"Well, I was so shocked I just didn't know what to say. So I muttered something like, 'Looks like it just did.' And that was that. I got talking to some of the others the next day and it seems the doctor played the same trick on everyone. 'Practical research' he called it.

"Well, the following night I slept really well. Must have been the rude interruption the night before. When I woke up I felt fine. Until I looked at my feet and saw the blood. Those pesky vampire bats had come by – and I hadn't felt a thing!"

"Now then, Pa," said the woman. "Don't you go filling young Johnnie's head with moonshine. You know it's not true."

"Oh, but it is!" cried the old man sharply. He drew off his scuffed brown shoe and then a worn green sock. His foot was white and sinewy. Little blue veins criss-crossed the parchment-coloured skin. Years after the event his toes were still pitted with white scars. Bite marks.

Mind you – there's one thing worse than being picked on by a blood-sucking bat. And that's having lunch with a horribly hungry hunter. Especially when it's YOU on the menu!

HORRIBLE HUNTERS

When you're hungry you probably pop out to the shops to buy food. It's called "shopping". Animals can't usually do this so, instead, they pop out and nab some unfortunate, small creature for their tea. Here's how they do it.

HORRIBLE HUNTER TYPES

Some hunters, such as lions and tigers eat large animals. For them life is rather relaxing. They spend most of their life sleeping off huge meals. They only hunt when they're really hungry. It helps to keep out of their way at these times. Other hunters such as wild dogs or hyenas will eat anything that comes along and they're always on the look out for a free lunch. Best avoid them at *all* times.

And beware. Hunters play horrible tricks.

HORRIBLE HUNTER TRICKS

1 Sneak up on your victim. If they turn round freeze and pretend to be a twig. The olive green snake of Central America does this. It even sways in the breeze – before it strikes and grabs a poor little baby bird from its nest.

THEY HAVEN'T TWIGGED YET

2 The horned frog sits motionless except for one finger. This twitches until an insect or small creature comes by thinking it's something to eat. Big mistake. It's feeding time all right – feeding time for the frog.

3 There's a type of African mongoose with a bottom that looks like a small flower. The mongoose crouches on a shrub with its bum in the air. When an insect lands on the pretty "flower" the mongoose whips round and snaps it up.

4 White-coated polar bears are almost invisible against the Arctic snow. But the bear's large black nose is embarrassingly obvious when it sneaks up on a seal. So the bears push a lump of ice in front of them to hide their tell-tale noses.

5 Everyone knows that rattlesnakes have a rattle at the end of their tails. Some of their few fans say that the rattle is there to warn people to steer clear. Huh – as if snakes are that thoughtful. In fact, the rattle is there to distract attention away from the head with its fatal fangs.

Could you be as cunning as these horrible hunters? Now's your chance to find out. Imagine you were a lioness living on the plains of Southern Africa. What sort of a hunter would you make?

LION HUNTING TIPS

The lionesses in a pride (group of lions) hunt together. (The lazy males don't take part.)

1 Your pride of lionesses stalk a herd of gazelles (small antelope). From what direction do you approach?
a) With the wind at your back so that the gazelles can smell you. This will scare them so much they won't be able to defend themselves.
b) With the wind blowing in your face so the gazelles can't smell you.
c) From the direction of the sun so that the gazelles are dazzled.

2 Your pride splits into two groups. What do you do next?
a) One group charges the gazelles and chases them towards the second group waiting in ambush.

b) One group goes after the gazelles and the others chase some nearby zebra. This doubles the chance of catching something.

c) One group chases gazelles and the others keep watch for marauding hyenas that might try to steal the meat.

3 You select a gazelle to attack. Which one do you choose?

a) The biggest – more meat for you.

b) The smallest – less likely to put up a fight.

c) The weakest – easier to catch.

4 The males invite themselves to the feast. While you and your sisters have been hunting the males have been lazing about in the sun. Now they're hungry. So who gets the lion's share?

WHAT'S FOR PUDDING, MUM?

a) The lionesses, followed by the cubs. The males are given a few scraps. Serves 'em right for not helping.

b) The males take the best bits. The lionesses and the cubs get what's left. If they're lucky.

c) The cubs. After all they need the food to help them grow.

5 A new male chases away the old males in your pride. He cruelly kills and eats your cubs. What do you do?
a) Run for the hills.
b) Kill him and eat his body.
c) Make friends with him.

6 In the dry season there's little food. What do you eat?
a) Other lions
b) Fish, insects, lizards, mice and the odd tortoise.
c) Bones buried for just such an emergency.

WHAT YOUR SCORE MEANS:
5–6 A roar of approval. You'd make a great hunter.
3–4 You're mane-ly right but you need to lick your skills into shape.
1–2 You'll never be a lion. Best swallow your "pride" and stick to being a human.

COULD YOU BE A NATURALIST?
One fierce hunter from the African plains is the cheetah.

These big cats are the fastest creatures on Earth and reach speeds of 105 km an hour (65 mph) in short bursts. The problem is that a racing cheetah's muscles produce huge amounts of heat. If the cheetah ran at top speed for more than a few seconds it would suffer fatal brain damage. A puffed-out cheetah needs to put its paws up for a few minutes to recover.

In 1937 an animal collector staged races between a cheetah and a greyhound in London. What do you think happened?
a) The greyhound won.
b) The cheetah ate the greyhound.
c) The cheetah won but only sometimes. Most of the time she couldn't be bothered to make the effort.

HE SEEMS TO GO FASTER WHEN HE'S RACING THE CHEETAH

Answer: c) Cheetahs don't like racing. In another race in 1937 a cheetah only completed half the course and then took a breather.

So far all the hunters we've been talking about have been land hunters. But that doesn't mean you'd be safe underwater – especially if you're edible. The seas and rivers swarm with millions of ferocious fish. Which of these fish is too nasty to be true?

FAR-FETCHED FISH FACTS

1 A trumpet fish hitches a ride on a larger but harmless parrot fish. When the trumpet fish spots a small fish to eat it hops off to make a quick killing! TRUE/FALSE

2 Vicious blue fish attack schools of other fish off the Eastern coasts of North America. The brutal blues kill more than ten times the fish they can eat. They guzzle up to 40 at a time and then sick them up so they can go on eating! TRUE/FALSE

3 The halitosis haddock has a deadly and unusual weapon – its disgusting, smelly breath. When a smaller fish comes by, the horrible haddock breathes a cloud of poisonous bubbles to overwhelm its prey. TRUE/FALSE

I DON'T CARE IF WE ARE MARRIED – I'M NOT KISSING YOU!

4 The angler fish has its own fishing rod complete with a small worm-like object that dangles just above its mouth. When another fish comes to investigate the bait the angler fish snaps up its catch. TRUE/FALSE

5 The scissors fish has jaws just like a pair of scissors and it uses these fearsome weapons to slice up its prey. It's even been known to snip through the lines of deep sea anglers. TRUE/FALSE

6 The deep sea viper fish has 1,350 lights inside its mouth. They twinkle in the ocean depths and little fish flock to see the lovely spectacle. Once the fish are inside its mouth the viper fish closes its giant gob. End of show. TRUE/FALSE

> ***Bet you never knew!***
> *One fierce fish that's all too real is the great white shark. Did you know it senses movements in the water up to 1.6 km away? At 400 metres the shark can also sniff blood. It usually sneaks up behind or below its victim. At the last moment, the shark closes its cold black eyes and homes in on its victim's terrified heartbeat. Yes – the heartbeat produces tiny electrical waves and the shark senses these. Then it's GRAB-A-BITE time!*

COULD YOU BE A NATURALIST?

The archer fish of India, Australia and south-east Asia has an unusual secret weapon. A built-in water pistol. This 2-cm-long fish spits water with deadly accuracy at passing insects.

SORRY! I WAS AIMING FOR THE FLY

A public aquarium once kept a school of the fish and splatted 150 g of raw meat on the sides of their tank. The owner wanted to see if the fish could dislodge the food. Could they?

a) These fish are little squirts. So they couldn't budge the meat.

b) The fish kept squirting until all the meat was in the water.

c) Unable to shift the meat by squirting the fish leapt up and grabbed it in their tiny jaws.

> **Answer: b)** Yes – they certainly made a big splash.

One of the fiercest hunters is one that you may have met already. Indeed this ferocious creature may be lurking behind your curtains or even watching your TV! Yes – we're talking about your not-so-cuddly cat. Here's where we let the cat out of the bag. Your pet leads a deadly double-life.

TIDDLES THE TERRIBLE

Tiddles rubs your legs. Just trying to be friendly? No way. She's leaving her scent on you to show you're part of HER family.

THAT'S MY GIRL

Tiddles has her own hunting territory. Normally she won't allow any other cat into this area. The territory is a little larger than your garden.

Tiddles hunts by sneaking up on prey. Sometimes she freezes before moving stealthily forward once more. At the last moment she pounces.

Tiddles enjoys catching insects. They have such a lovely crunchy texture – it's just like you eating crisps.

But she doesn't like catching rabbits or rats. She's scared of rabbits because they're so big. And she thinks that rats taste worse than cheap cat food.

When Tiddles "plays" with mice she's not being cruel. Oh no? She's just a big scaredy-cat. Scared the mouse will fight back (some mice do). So she keeps her distance without losing the mouse.

SAFE DISTANCE

Tiddles eats mice head first. Gulp. Before eating birds she plucks out the feathers with her teeth.

1ST COURSE = MOUSE

2ND COURSE (ALREADY PREPARED) = BIRD

When Tiddles brings you a half-dead mouse or battered bird it's her way of teaching you to hunt. Yes – she wants you to finish it off. Mother cats do this to train their kittens.

ARRRGH!

MUST BE SOME SORT OF BATTLE CRY BEFORE HE JUMPS ON IT

Bet you never knew!
1 The champion hunter of all time was a cat named Towser. By the time she died in 1987 she had caught 28,899 mice at the Glenturret Whisky Distillery, Scotland.
2 A cat's skill in hunting once saved a man's life. The man in question was Sir Henry Wyatt, a 15th-century English knight who was locked in a dungeon and left to starve. But hungry Henry was befriended by a stray cat. The cat brought in birds such as pigeons and kept the knight alive until he was released by friends.

WE'VE COME TO SAVE YOU, MY LORD – YOU MUST BE STARVING

Mind you, if cats have ambitions, it must be every cat's dream to be a really big cat. A really big cat and a really deadly hunter. Something like a tiger, in fact.

TERRIBLE TIGERS

From its nose to the tip of its stripy tail the average tiger is 2.9 metres and weighs 204 kg – that's the weight of three grown men. In the 19th century, Victorian writers gave the tiger a bad press. They saw the tiger as a treacherous enemy that took its victims by surprise. The Hon James Inglis wrote:

...the tiger is...a cunning, sneaking rogue...a cruel, whiskered robber.

19th-century hunters enjoyed "bagging" tigers and they even got paid for their horrible pastime by the Indian government! Many tigers ended up as grisly tiger-skin rugs. But the hunters were far too deadly for the tigers. By 1972 there were only about 1,800 tigers left alive in the whole of India. Hunting was banned in 1971 and thanks to a massive conservation effort, tiger numbers began to increase in some areas. But the naturalists' work raised a nasty dilemma. What should be done when a tiger attacks humans? Was it ever right to kill a tiger?

THE TIGER MUST DIE

India/Nepal border 1978

"The tiger must die. I could have shot it myself!" cried the Forest Park Director thumping his desk.

"You don't understand," said Arjan Singh the tiger expert. He was slightly built and balding and right now his brow was creased with worry.

The Director's mouth set in a hard line. He wiped the sweat off his fleshy face with a damp handkerchief. It was very hot, even though the blinds were drawn and the ceiling fan whirred lazily. "No, Mr Singh, it's you who doesn't understand. Let's review the facts, shall we? On

3 April a man disappeared in the forest. Tiger victim number one. What was left of him after the tiger had finished didn't even fill a shoe box. Three days later another man went missing. I saw the tiger eating his body. I shouted but the monster took no notice. I wish I'd shot the tiger then and there."

His finger curled round an imaginary gun trigger.

"But tigers are protected," said Arjan Singh, "you can't go around shooting them."

"Human beings must be protected too!" roared the Director. "Two men are dead and you're trying to teach me my job!"

"But you don't understand!" repeated Arjan Singh desperately. "Tigers only attack humans because they have to."

"What do you mean they *have to*?!" spluttered the Director wildly, his eyes blazing with fury.

"Tigers don't normally attack humans," said the naturalist. "But humans have wiped out all the tiger's natural prey such as deer and wild pigs. The tiger was starving and there were humans in the forest. The tiger was feeding to stay alive."

"On human flesh," said the Director harshly.

Arjan Singh took a deep breath and tried again.

"Remember, tigers are protected by law. Instead of killing the tiger can't we try another way? Why can't we leave out a few buffalo for it to eat? Then the tiger won't be hungry. And if it's not hungry it won't attack people."

The Director sighed bitterly. "Mr Singh, I'll be frank. If I had my way that tiger of yours would have been dead meat days ago. But my bosses seem to agree with you about not shooting the animal. So I suppose I've got to think your idea over."

But he didn't sound convinced.

A few days passed without a decision from the Director. And meanwhile the tiger struck again. Arjan Singh felt his heart sink as he examined the paw marks.

"Yes, I'm afraid it's the same tiger," he told the wildlife warden who had come with him.

"Well, Mr Singh," said the man grimly. "Looks like the Director will get his way after all. That tiger's a goner now."

A few metres along the path made by the tiger as it dragged its prey, lay a gory human head. It was all that remained of the tiger's latest victim.

Arjan Singh imagined the Park Director's scornful voice. He would say: "I told you so! It's your fault – if I'd had my way that man would still be alive."

The naturalist dreaded the next meeting. Could anything save the tiger now?

WHAT DO YOU THINK HAPPENED NEXT?

a) The Park Director got his way. The tiger was hunted down and shot.

b) Arjan Singh got his way. The Director agreed to put food out for the tiger and it never again attacked people.

c) The tiger was shot with a tranquillizing dart and moved to an area far away from humans.

Answer: b) The Director's bosses still wouldn't allow him to shoot the tiger so he came round to Arjan Singh's idea. The tiger ate the food provided and stopped attacking people. Nowadays many man-eating tigers are moved to areas away from where people live.

TIGER TRACKER'S TIPS

Here are some more tips to avoid being eaten by a man-eating tiger. (Hopefully there aren't too many around where you live.)

1 A tiger tries to creep up on you from downwind. Always keep an eye out for movements from that direction.

2 A tiger is more likely to attack you if you crouch down.

93

It thinks you're a four-legged animal rather than a human. So it's a very bad idea to squat down to go to the toilet in the jungle.

3 Tigers attack from behind you. In 1987 people living in the forests on the borders of India and Bangladesh were issued with plastic face masks to wear over the backs of their heads. Tiger attacks virtually stopped because the tigers thought people were looking at them when their backs were turned. It was the next best thing to eyes in the back of their heads.

4 If a tiger's after you and you've left your mask at home, the best thing to do is to climb a tree. Most tigers can't climb trees.

5 Tigers always attack the neck. For a person bitten by a tiger it's all over. The chances of getting away are one in a hundred. Yikes! Now you might think that tigers or the humans that shoot them are the nastiest hunters. But you'd be wrong. Think of beady little eyes.

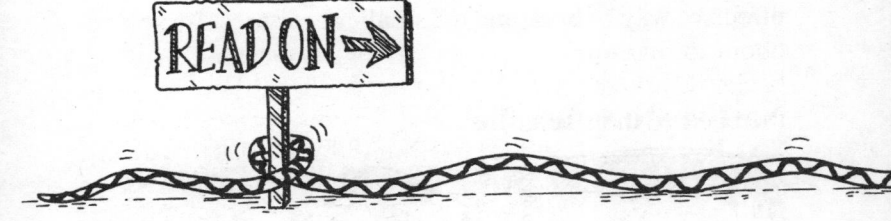

POISONED PREY

Snakes. Ugh! *They're* nasty enough, but there's a whole army of other horrible hunters that also use poison. Why do they do it? Is it to scare us? Well – no, but it's a very effective way of bumping off smaller creatures. As you're about to find out.

Nasty nature fact file

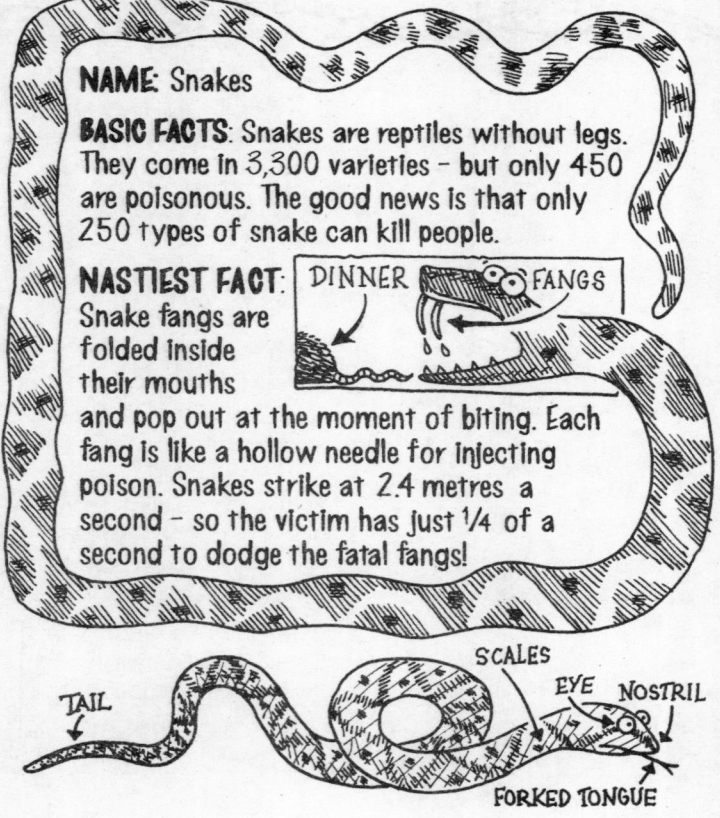

NAME: Snakes

BASIC FACTS: Snakes are reptiles without legs. They come in 3,300 varieties – but only 450 are poisonous. The good news is that only 250 types of snake can kill people.

NASTIEST FACT: Snake fangs are folded inside their mouths and pop out at the moment of biting. Each fang is like a hollow needle for injecting poison. Snakes strike at 2.4 metres a second – so the victim has just 1/4 of a second to dodge the fatal fangs!

DINNER   FANGS

SCALES
TAIL
EYE   NOSTRIL
FORKED TONGUE

SINISTER SNAKES

NAME: King Cobra

DESCRIPTION: Up to 5.5 metres long.

LIVES: India, southern China and south-east Asia.

FIERCE FEATURES: Has a sinister pattern of two eyes and a nose on the hood behind its head. It displays this when it's angry or scared.

HORRIBLE HABITS: Eats other snakes. (Come to think of it this habit could be quite useful.)

THE BAD NEWS: Its poison is strong enough to kill an elephant. So we humans don't stand a chance.

NAME: Okinawa Habu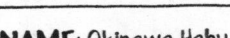

DESCRIPTION: Up to 2 metres. Slender body with blotchy yellow ringed markings.

LIVES: Okinawa and neighbouring islands, Pacific Ocean. (Fortunately it doesn't live anywhere else.)

FIERCE FEATURES: Heat-detectors on its head help it to find warm living flesh.

HORRIBLE HABITS: Enjoys snaking into people's houses through tiny crevices.

THE BAD NEWS: Enjoys biting people.

THE VERY BAD NEWS: It's deadly poisonous.

NAME: Black Mamba

DESCRIPTION: 3-4 metres long. It's the largest poisonous snake in Africa.

LIVES: Africa – south of the Sahara Desert.

FIERCE FEATURES: It can slither as fast as you can run.

HORRIBLE HABITS: It can swallow a whole rat and digest it in 9 hours. Most snakes take more than 24 hours.

Strangely enough, some people like snakes. Indeed, it's an astounding fact that some people even keep snakes as pets! Hopefully, your teacher isn't one of them. Or you might hear facts like these...

FIVE REASONS WHY SNAKES ARE CUDDLY*

* OK, let's just say "not quite so nasty".

1 Snakes are more scared of people than people are of snakes. After all, we're bigger than them.

2 Snakes only bite people if the snake thinks it's being attacked. An Indian tradition says you should stop to chat to a poisonous Russell's viper. That way the snake won't bite you. Talking doesn't help because snakes are deaf (though they can feel sound vibrations passing through the ground). But standing still calms the snake down and could save your life.

3 Snakes are useful. Venom from the Russell's viper is made into a medicine that helps blood clot. Malaysian pit viper poison stops blood from clotting and this could be used to prevent unwanted blood clots inside the body.

4 Many nasty snake stories aren't true. For example, the Malaysian pit viper is nicknamed the "hundred pacer" because that's how far people run after being bitten. Then they die. Not true. Victims get at least ten times that distance.

5 Humans kill far more snakes than snakes kill humans. For example, snake blood is used in traditional Chinese medicines. It's said to be very good for your liver and lungs. But not so good for thousands of wretched snakes.

So, fancy a cuddle? Thought not. But if you really find snakes charming why not become a snake charmer? Here's how to…

CHARM A SNAKE

1 Catch a poisonous snake. A king cobra will do.

2 Remove its venom. Then if things go wrong you won't suffer a fatal bite. This technique is called "milking" the snake. Grasp the snake by the back of its head and make it bite through a piece of paper stuck over a jar. Gently squeeze the poison glands on either side of your snake's head so the lovely poison squirts out. (Don't worry about the snake – it can always make more poison.)

WHAT'S GOING ON?

3 Put the snake in a basket and start playing your flute. After a while the snake will stick its head out to take a look.

4 Keep moving your flute about. The snake can't hear the music but it will follow your movements.

5 Beware – it's deciding when to strike!

6 If you get bitten whilst charming a snake and you forgot step 2 it's a good idea to know some First Aid. So here's some useless advice.

Warning: Almost all these remedies are about as useful as a chocolate hot water bottle.

YE OLDE SNAKE-BITE REMEDIES

1 Drink 4.5 litres of whisky.

2 Cut off your snake-bitten finger with a large knife. Or you could shoot it off with your trusty six-gun. (Traditional cowboy remedy.)

3 Cut the wound open and ask a very good friend to suck out the poison.

4 Soak the bitten hand in paraffin.

5 Wrap chicken meat around the bite. Then burn the meat.

6 Eat a live snake.

7 Squash a toad and squeeze its juices over the wound. (Ancient Roman remedy)

8 Before you get bitten chew some of the snake's poison glands. Or you could make a small wound in your skin and rub in a mixture of spit and poison glands.

Notes

1 This remedy was popular amongst US soldiers in the 1860s. It was even popular with soldiers who hadn't been bitten. In fact, the combined effects of the poison and whisky would probably kill the victim.

THREE MORE PINTS AND YOU'LL BE AS FIT AS A FIDDLE

2 Useless. By the time the cowboy pulled the trigger the poison would have spread to the rest of his body.

3 This is dangerous because the venom could poison your friend too.

4 Useless

5 Utterly useless – especially for the chicken.

6 Useless and cruel. Snakes have feelings too.

7 Equally cruel and useless.

8 Yes – these do work. They're used by the Kung, San and Zulu peoples of Southern Africa. Anyone for a free trial?

SENSIBLE SNAKE ADVICE

By the way, if someone does get bitten (and there's more chance of winning the lottery) they should remember what the snake looked like. Snake bites are treated with a chemical called an anti-venom. This is a chemical produced naturally by the body in a bid to neutralize the poison. Getting extra amounts injected helps the body to recover more quickly. But the doctors need to know which anti-venom to use. The bite victim should keep very still and send someone for help.

OK – so, snake-watching just isn't your favourite pastime. Perhaps a seaside holiday is your idea of fun instead. But just when you thought it was safe to go into the water...

NAUTICAL NASTIES

The most poisonous snakes of all aren't on land. They're in the seas around India and east Asia. Sea-snake poison is amongst the deadliest you can get. That's the bad news. The good news is sea-snakes don't enjoy biting humans. So Indian fishermen often pull the wriggling snakes from their nets using only their bare hands. Is that brave – or what?

Another nautical nasty is the blue-ringed octopus. Yes – the sinister suckers have a poisonous bite. Scientists aren't sure exactly how poisonous the bite is because no one has volunteered to be bitten. Any takers? It's all in the cause of science.

Meanwhile, on land things aren't much better. Besides snakes there's a host of other...

PESKY POISONERS

1 The gila monster has a nasty method of poisoning its prey. This 50-cm-long lizard from the southern USA bites its victim. Then it chews the poison into the wound. Ouch!

2 Hot dry regions of the world are home to scorpions. Yes – they like it tough. A scorpion can live without water for three months and live without food for a year. And if it turns chilly – no problem. A scorpion will come back to life after being frozen for a few hours in a lump of ice. (This could be a problem if you tried to make scorpion-flavoured ice cream.)

3 Scorpions are active at night and hide during the day. Unfortunately, deadly scorpions such as the Trinidad scorpion love to snuggle down in a nice warm shoe. Next morning the shoe's owner gets a nasty surprise. That would really get your day off on the wrong foot.

SPOT THE WOMAN WALKING TO WORK
WITH A SCORPION IN HER SHOE

4 Water shrews are rat-like little beasts. They have poisonous spit that paralyses the frogs and fishes they eat. That way the prey won't try to wriggle free whilst it's being scoffed by the shrew.

5 You've heard of dog eat dog? Well, dog eat toad isn't a very sensible idea either. The toad's warty skin contains glands that make a poison strong enough to kill a dog.

6 Remember the mixed-up duck-billed platypus? Just to confuse you further, the male platypus has poisonous spurs on its ankles. No one knows if the spurs are for fighting off other animals or for stabbing other males in fights over females. I expect they get used on the spur of the moment.

So how do you feel about poisonous creatures now? Worried, anxious, insecure? Join the club. That's what it's like to be a small animal when hungry hunters are on the prowl. Yep – it can be murder out there.

NARROW SQUEAKS

One moment you're nibbling a tasty morsel of smelly cheese. The next, you're running for your life with a hungry monster snapping at your tail. (By the way, the monster's name is Tiddles the cat.) Yes, if you're a mouse, life is full of narrow squeaks.

Yet amazingly, many creatures manage to get away, or even turn the tables on their attackers. Here's how they do it...

Some animals have their very own suits of armour. Could you do with this kind of protection?

NASTY NATURE GUIDE TO SELF DEFENCE

SAFETY FIRST

Stylish armour as worn by the three-banded armadillo of South America. Simply roll in a ball. If you fancy a bit of fun leave a chink in your armour. The attacker will insert a paw into the gap. Then shut the gap like a steel trap. Wham – Crunch – Ouch!

TEACH YOUR ENEMIES A SHARP LESSON

Absolutely foolproof hedgehog and porcupine spiny armour. Choice of defence modes.

Hedgehog: Roll your body in a ball or ram your spines up an attacker's nose. Five thousand spines guaranteed in every hedgehog outfit. *Manufacturer's Warning: Never roll yourself in a ball in front of oncoming lorries. You'll feel a bit flat afterwards.*

Porcupine: Jab your barbed spines into an attacker's body. They won't get them out until their dying day. (That'll be quite soon afterwards.)

FANCY A SWIM?

Don't forget your porcupine fish swimming costume. Just inflate your swimsuit with water and stick your spines out. Gives sharks a real mouthful.

I'M OUT OF HERE!

BE A HERO

With this discreet hero shrew outfit a specially strengthened backbone helps you feel tough inside. Guaranteed – if you're the size of a shrew a fully-grown human can stand on your back and you'll survive.*

NO PROBLEM!

***WARNING**
DON'T DO THIS TO YOUR PET HAMSTER. ONLY HERO SHREWS HAVE THIS PROTECTION. OTHER FURRY ANIMALS GET SQUISHED

NO ARMOUR?

So you can't find a suitable suit of armour? No problem. If an attacker gets too close simply kick up a stink. Take some advice from a skunk. If you want to get rid of an attacker try spraying them with foul juices. See next page for details . . .

Skunk Defence Manual

To be carried by all skunks at all times. You never know when you might need it.

1. Always give your attacker a warning. It's only fair to perform this little dance. Try practising it now.

◀ Stamp your feet and arch your back.

▶ Sway your body backwards and forwards.

◀ Stand on your hands and walk on them towards the attacker until you're about 2.5 metres away.

2. If they don't get the message, they're asking for it. Turn your back on the enemy. Raise your tail in the air. Arch your back. Look over your shoulder and check your aim. Ready, steady, FIRE!

3. You're sending a spray that comes from glands on either side of your bottom. Waggle your behind from side-to-side so your enemy gets a good drenching.

Notes

1 The spray contains a group of chemicals called thiols (thiols) and together they're reckoned to be **the worst smell**

in the world. You can smell skunk juice at least 1.6 km away and it stays smelly for over a year.

2 The stink is so horrible that it damages the inside of the nose.

3 The juices taste so disgusting they make the victim throw up.

4 If the spray gets in the victim's eyes it causes temporary blindness.

5 But it doesn't bother us skunks a bit.

The victim shouldn't complain too loudly either, for at least skunk spray isn't poisonous enough to kill. Some animals have really deadly poisonous defences.

POISONOUS PREY

Sitting on a tin-tack is a mere pin prick. Getting stung by a bee is a sore subject. Jumping in a bed of nettles – that's a little rash. All these things hurt but they're not *really* painful. Nothing like a brush with these creatures...

The stonefish uses its poisonous spines in self-defence. The fish lurks in shallow waters around the Australian coast and looks just like a stone (surprise, surprise) buried in the mud. But its poison causes **the worst pain in the world.** Humans who accidentally tread on the spines writhe in agony. Fortunately there's an antidote that can save the victim's life.

109

Don't spit at a spitting cobra. This 2-metre-long snake is likely to spit back a double jet of fluid from up to 2.5 metres. Just one gram is enough to kill 165 humans or 160,000 mice. As luck would have it the vicious venom won't kill you unless its injected into your blood but if gets in your eyes it can cause blindness. And your eyeballs are the sinister snake's target number one!

In the South American rainforest you'll see happy little frogs hopping about in the trees. "Why are they so brightly coloured?" you wonder. "Perhaps they will want to make friends." No way – they're warning you that they're deadly poisonous. Just 1 gram of the poison produced in their skin is enough to kill 100,000 people. Mind you, that doesn't save some frogs from an even worse torture. Amerindians grill the frogs over a fire and tip their arrows with the frog's deadly sweated juices.

So you don't want a frog in your throat? OK – how about a poisonous fish? People with a taste for danger enjoy eating these fish. Honestly – it's true.

SUSHI RESTAURANT MENU

We serve only the finest sushi - the ultimate Japanese delicacy made from delicious raw fish.

TODAY'S SPECIAL: Fugu

Made from the chopped-up raw flesh of the puffer fish. You'll be dying to try it!

THE SMALL PRINT.

Warning: This dish is hopefully free of any trace of the poisonous liver, guts, blood and eggs of the puffer fish. Our chefs have trained for three years to cut these bits out. But if you should happen to eat any of these bits you'll die. It won't be our fault, OK? I mean - accidents do happen several times a year.

DID HE ENJOY HIS FUGU?

I'M NOT SURE – HE DIED BEFORE I HAD A CHANCE TO ASK

ON THE RUN

If you don't have your own poison, you might try running away. Speedy animals such as antelopes can often out-run a hunter, especially if they've got a head start. The pronghorn – a creature like an antelope from western USA, reaches speeds of 98 km per hour (61 mph); horses and ostriches can gallop at 65 km per hour (40 mph). But how does that compare to us? Well – humans are left gasping. The fastest runners can only run at 36 km per hour (22.5 mph) for short distances. Then they run out of puff.

HURRY UP!

UNDER COVER

If you don't like running, you could stay still and blend in with the scenery. The sloth hangs out in the South American rainforest and moves at a stately 241 metres an hour (0.15 mph). It's so slow-moving that tiny green plants grow on its coat and this colouring makes it hard to spot amongst the trees. The word "sloth" means lazy, and naturalist Charles Waterton objected to the sloth's laid back lifestyle…

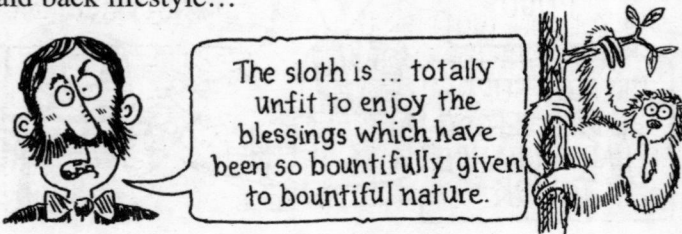

The sloth is … totally unfit to enjoy the blessings which have been so bountifully given to bountiful nature.

So what's wrong with doing no work and hanging around upside down in trees?

Many creatures hide successfully because they're the same colour as their surroundings. This trick is called "camouflage". But the real camouflage experts are creatures that change colour to match their surroundings. Take the flounder, for example – that's a type of flat-fish. A scientist once put a chess board on the bottom of a flounder's tank and within minutes the fish was a tasteful check pattern. Small colour grains in the flounder's skin move together or apart in response to signals from its brain. And this colourful trick leaves an attacker … floundering.

*PLAICE AND FLOUNDERS BELONG TO THE SAME FAMILY

If you can't change colour, you could try being invisible. Amazingly, some creatures such as the glass cat-fish have see-through bodies. They blend into the background because you can see it through their bodies. Yuck – imagine if you could see your school dinner after you'd eaten it.

ANIMAL ACTING AWARDS

If all else fails you could pretend to be another more dangerous creature. Preferably something fierce and poisonous or something you wouldn't want to eat. Yes – animals can be actors too. Welcome to the Animal Oscars.

BEST ACTOR /ACTRESS (Snake Category)

RUNNER-UP

The totally harmless king snake almost won for its superb impression of a poisonous coral snake. The king snake has the same red, yellow and black bands on its body but in a different order. So look carefully!

WINNER

The gopher snake wins for an outstanding performance as a rattlesnake. The gopher snake is harmless but hisses like a rattlesnake and even shakes its tail against dry leaves to rattle an attacker's nerves.

BEST ACTOR /ACTRESS (Plant Impression Category)

RUNNER-UP

The tawny frogmouth bird of Australia gives a terrific performance when it's asleep! It always sleeps on a tree branch and looks just like a rotten old twig.

WINNER

The leafy sea-dragon is a sea-horse. It wins this award because it looks just like a disgusting rubbery bit of seaweed.

MOST DISGUSTING MAKE-UP AWARD

RUNNER-UP
The Budgett's frog from Argentina comes second in this category. It can swell up like a big ball of slime and then scream and grunt if you get too close.

WINNER
Our prize winner is the Ecuador tree frog. It sprawls on a leaf and looks just like a disgusting slimy bird dropping.

STRANGE SURVIVAL STRATEGIES
Animals have plenty more survival tricks and some of them are really strange. Which of these survival strategies is too strange to be true?

1 The horned toad from the western parts of North America squirts blood from its eyes to frighten an attacker. TRUE/FALSE

2 The mimicking macaw of South America warns off attackers with a brilliant impression of an eagle's screech. TRUE/FALSE

3 Pallas's glass snake is actually a legless lizard. (That doesn't mean it's drunk.) When attacked the lizard's 1.5-metre body breaks into wriggling bits. In the confusion the lizard's head end manages to escape. It then grows a new body. TRUE/FALSE

4 *Acanthephyra* (A-can-tha-fi-ra) is a shrimp that lurks in the deep ocean. When attacked it puts on a dazzling display of flashing lights before slipping away into the gloom. TRUE/FALSE

5 The Chilean four-eyed frog has a pair of spots on its thighs that it flashes at would-be attackers. The spots are like a huge pair of eyes and scare most attackers off. TRUE/FALSE

BITING BACK

Some creatures fight back if their friends are around to give them support. This is surprisingly common and the aim is always to frighten a hunter away. Birds, for example, will attack an owl if there's enough of them around. Chimps will gang up on a leopard and ground squirrels kick sand in a snake's face. Would you dare do this to your local bully?

When an animal is cornered without hope of escape it will often fight for its life. Even mice and their babies do this. So if someone says you're as "brave as a mouse" it's quite a compliment.

116

And so you reach the end of the day. A day spent dodging horrible hunters and fighting for your life. You're still alive ... just. Well, congratulations – you must be feeling peckish enough to eat – well, just about anything. I hope so. Now it's time for some gruesome gluttonish guzzling.

GRUESOME GUZZLING

Animals love eating and they always want second helpings. And what's more they don't care about good table manners. Burp! Oh, dear. Look what's coming to dinner...

> ## W A R N I N G
>
> Anyone who is disgusted by guzzling and chomping and slurping should turn to the next chapter. Also, try to avoid reading this chapter aloud at the dinner table. You may find yourself the only person left and then you'll have to scoff everyone's food. Tragic!

INCREDIBLE EATING EQUIPMENT

Every animal has evolved jaws and mouth-parts that are perfectly suited to eating its favourite food. Here are a few examples...

1 Giraffes have tongues 30 cm long. Ideal for grasping leaves and yanking them off tall trees. But that's nothing – the South American anteater uses its sticky 60-cm tongue to lick up ants. It can manage as many as 30,000 a day.

2 The Asian and south-east European hamster has floppy cheek pouches to store seeds. It sometimes stuffs these pouches so full that it can scarcely stagger home. These "cheeky" hamsters store as much as 90 kg of seeds in their burrows.

DINNER → LUNCH

BREAKFAST

3 Crocodiles have huge jaws useful for dragging their prey to a watery grave. A one-tonne crocodile has 13 tonnes worth of crushing power in its jaws. That's 26 times stronger than a human bite.

4 Elephants suck up water with their trunks and then blow it into their mouths. A thirsty jumbo can gulp down 14 litres at a time and drink 200 litres in a day.

5 Snake jaws unhinge to allow them to swallow prey that are bigger than their own heads. The African egg-eating snake uses this trick to swallow eggs without breaking them – and they're not even hard-boiled. Don't try this at home.

GO ON DAD, YOU CAN DO IT!

6 If you're a flamingo you eat by turning your head upside down underwater whilst balancing on your long legs. Tricky. Next you sweep your head from side to side and fill your mouth with water. Then use your tongue and a built-in sieve inside your mouth to suck out little wriggling water creatures. Tasty!

7 Chameleons sit around in trees waiting for insects to drop by. Suddenly a fly buzzes around and the chameleon yawns. Its long sticky tongue shoots out and back before you can see what's happened. The chameleon looks happy – if that's possible – and the fly? It's nowhere to be seen. Frogs and toads feed in the same revolting fashion.

Dare you discover ... how to drink like a cat?

You will need:
Yourself
A bowl of milk or water
A mirror

What you do:

1 Look at your tongue in the mirror. A cat can fold up the sides of its tongue to make a shovel shape. Can you do this?

MUST HAVE RUN OUT OF CLEAN CUPS

2 Try lapping the milk. You then have to flick the milk into the back of your throat with your tongue. How easy is this?

a) No problem at all.

b) It's impossible to get more than a few drops of liquid in your mouth.

c) Totally impossible. Luckily the cat came and drank the milk.

Answer: b) Most humans can't make the right shape with their tongues

TOP TOOL TRICKS

If your eating equipment lets you down you could always use tools to help you eat...

1 Green jays in the USA hold twigs in their beaks to poke under loose bark to dislodge stray insects.
2 Chimpanzees poke twigs into termite nests and lick the fat, wriggling insects off the twig.
3 A sea-otter breaks open mussels on a stone balanced on its chest as it swims backstroke. (Don't try this in your local pool.)
4 Thrushes break open snail shells by banging the molluscs on a stone. You'll find the stones surrounded by broken snail shells.

Apart from the objects they use to help them eat, some animals have...

TERRIBLE TABLE MANNERS

1 A toad or frog uses its eyeballs to help it swallow a huge juicy fly. It blinks as it swallows, pushing the eyeballs backwards into its head forcing the fly down its throat. This makes swallowing easier, even if it looks disgusting. Gulp!

2 The red-billed quela is a small bird that lives in Africa, south of the Sahara desert. Its favourite food is seeds from human crops. Nothing wrong with that, except that the quela likes to fly around in gangs of up to ten million strong. Once that lot have dropped in for dinner there's nothing left for anyone else.

3 Many animals hide spare food. We've all heard of squirrels burying nuts in the autumn, but do you know why dogs bury bones? When they lived in the wild thousands of years ago, dogs buried bones to stop other creatures guzzling the bone marrow. And they're still up to this old trick after all these years. Well – you can't teach an old dog new tricks.

4 The bearded vulture is wild about bone marrow too. The villainous vulture drops bones from a dizzy height of 80 metres on to rocks until they break open. It has been rumoured to do this to unfortunate tortoises as well and even to enjoy dive-bombing mountaineers.

WE'RE RETURNING TO BASE-CAMP. JOHN'S BEEN KNOCKED OUT BY A TORTOISE, OVER...

5 Owls eat small animals whole and then sick up the fur and bones in the form of pellets.

6 Starfish have a stomach-turning method of feeding on rotting fish and other prey. At the vital moment, the starfish squeezes its muscles until its stomach pops out of its mouth. The stomach's digestive juices dissolve the mouldering meal.

7 Many grass-eating animals, such as cows, have a special area of their stomach called the rumen. Here the food is softened for a few hours with stomach juices before being sicked up to the mouth for an extra chew. "Chewing the cud" as it's called, helps to break down the tough plant material so it's easier to digest. Imagine if humans did this. It's certainly something to chew over.

FUNDAMENTAL FOOD FACTS

A food chain is nothing to do with clanking chains or dungeons. It's far more fascinating. "Food chain" is a name used by naturalists to describe the vital links between animals and the unfortunate creatures they guzzle. Most food chains start with plants and a typical food chain goes something like this:

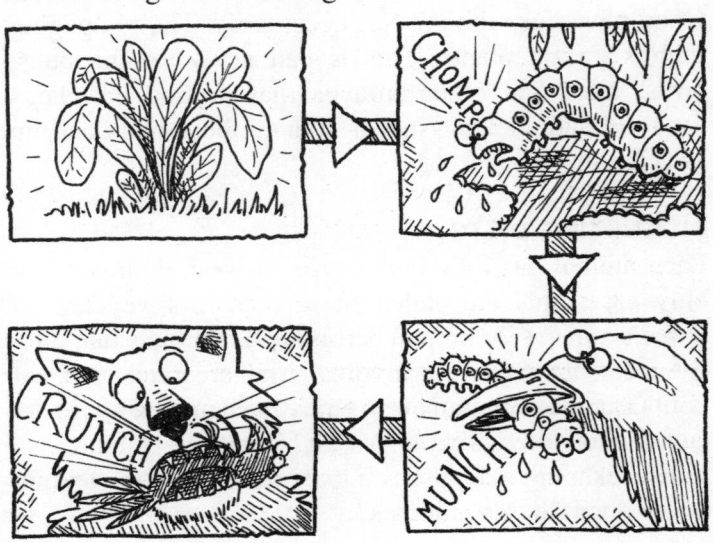

A food web (nothing to do with spiders) links the food chains in a particular habitat. So you might end up with something like this:

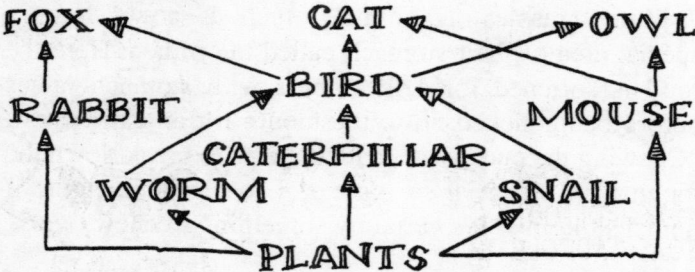

Animals depend on each other and on plants. Take away the plants, and the bugs and rabbits and mice starve. If they disappear the animals that eat them will go hungry too.

Strangely enough if the top animals in the web disappear there can be nasty results too. If the fox died out more rabbits would survive to breed and multiply. Good news for rabbits? Not necessarily. The rampaging rabbits guzzle plants. This is bad news for the bugs, birds, mice and other animals that depend on plants for food and shelter. And of course, the rabbits end up starving too.

DISGUSTING DIETS

Each animal has a favourite type of food. Animals that only eat plants are called herbivores (not vegetarians – that's a name for human herbivores). Animals that only eat meat are called carnivores. And creatures that eat both (including humans who enjoy meat and two veg) are called omnivores. Simple, isn't it? But some animals also scoff sickening side dishes. Could you match the animal to the horrible things it eats?

ANIMALS

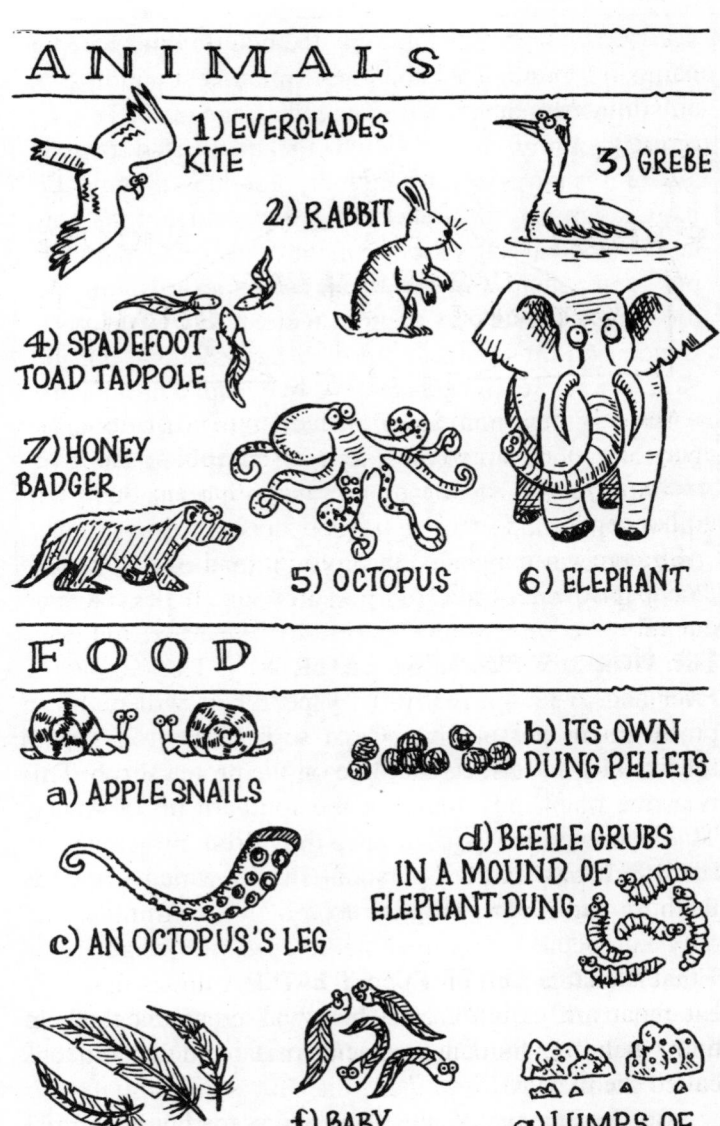

1) EVERGLADES KITE

2) RABBIT

3) GREBE

4) SPADEFOOT TOAD TADPOLE

7) HONEY BADGER

5) OCTOPUS

6) ELEPHANT

FOOD

a) APPLE SNAILS

b) ITS OWN DUNG PELLETS

c) AN OCTOPUS'S LEG

d) BEETLE GRUBS IN A MOUND OF ELEPHANT DUNG

e) FEATHERS

f) BABY TADPOLES

g) LUMPS OF VOLCANIC ROCK

THE WORLD'S FUSSIEST EATER

Ever had to feed a really fussy pet? This will put your problems in perspective. Cape sugarbirds from South Africa only eat insects that live on the protea shrub. This is a rare plant only found at the southern tip of Africa. This feathered fusspot will also only drink protea nectar. Each bird has its own personal shrubs which it guards jealously from other sugarbirds.

THE WORLD'S LEAST FUSSY EATER

Like many other birds, ostriches swallow pebbles to help them grind up food in a special part of their stomachs called the gizzard.

Ostriches normally eat leaves and seeds but according to its owner, one bird ate...

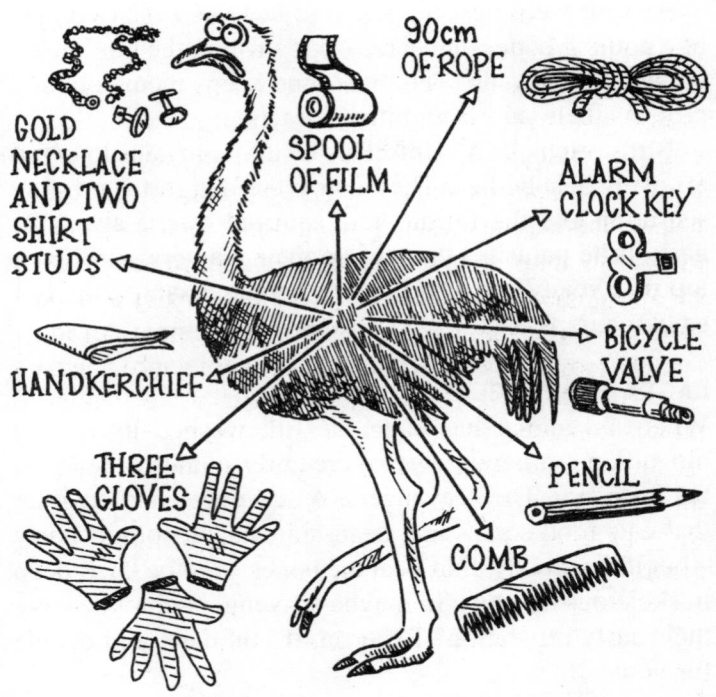

GOLD NECKLACE AND TWO SHIRT STUDS

SPOOL OF FILM

90cm OF ROPE

ALARM CLOCK KEY

HANDKERCHIEF

BICYCLE VALVE

THREE GLOVES

PENCIL

COMB

CLEAN CREATURES

Dirty animals? Filthy beasts? Don't you believe it! Despite their messy eating habits most animals like to get clean afterwards. But your parents might not approve if you copied some of their washing habits...

Cats are supple enough to lick themselves all over. They can even lick their own bottoms – wow! They wash their faces by licking their paws and rubbing their faces. Waste fur sticks to a cat's rough tongue and the front teeth strain out any bits of dirt and dead skin. They sick up any fur they swallow. Like any animal spit, cat spit is good for killing germs in the fur.

African warthogs, hippos, buffaloes and many others like nothing better than a refreshing roll in the mud. It's a sensible thing to do. The thick mud keeps them cool and protects their skin from biting insects.

Birds often clean themselves by allowing ants to crawl all over their bodies. They enjoy the delightful tingling sensation and the formic acid squirted by the ants kills nasty little parasites that get up their feathers. Sitting on top of a really smoky chimney does the same job. The smoke bumps off the pesky parasites.

NASTY SCAVENGERS

When an animal has eaten its fill, washed itself, and moved on – a new crowd of creatures comes to feast on the leftovers. The scavengers. A scavenger is a creature that eats food scraps and dead animals. It sounds nasty – but if somebody didn't eat the bones we'd be knee-deep in skeletons by now. So maybe scavengers don't deserve their nasty reputation? Read on, if you dare, and decide for yourself.

SCARY SCAVENGERS

1 Hagfish (also known as slimefish) look like swimming sausages with no jaws and no bones. They enjoy eating dead fish from the inside out – leaving just the skin and bones.

128

2 Komodo dragons are huge – they're the largest lizards in the world. These 3-metre long creatures skulk on the Indonesian island of Komodo. Despite their fearsome appearance, they mainly sniff out revolting rotting dead deer and pigs for their tea.

3 At Harar in Ethiopia until the late 1960s hyenas were used to keep the streets clean of waste meat from butcher's stalls. Each year the hard-working hyenas were rewarded with a lovely smelly dead cow. The hyenas did a good job but they had an embarrassing habit of digging up dead bodies.

4 While we are on this grisly subject, our old friend the snapper turtle (last seen lurking in the sewers) enjoys scoffing unwanted bodies. So keen is the turtle that the police in Florida, USA use tame snapper turtles to sniff out corpses. Imagine what the turtles might get as a treat! And talking about dead bodies…

Nasty nature fact file

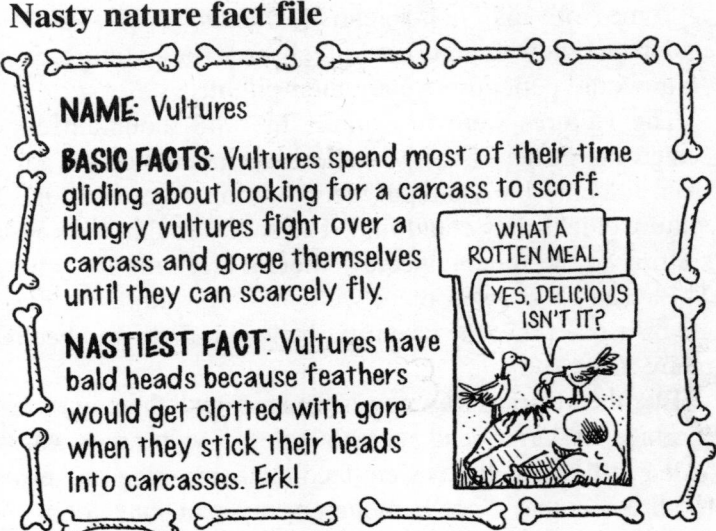

NAME: Vultures

BASIC FACTS: Vultures spend most of their time gliding about looking for a carcass to scoff. Hungry vultures fight over a carcass and gorge themselves until they can scarcely fly.

WHAT A ROTTEN MEAL

YES, DELICIOUS ISN'T IT?

NASTIEST FACT: Vultures have bald heads because feathers would get clotted with gore when they stick their heads into carcasses. Erk!

So would you want to invite a vulture to dinner? Some people would – here's their story.

VULTURE RESTAURANTS

In 1973 John Ledger, director of the Endangered Wildlife Trust in South Africa was a worried man.

"Poor vultures, we must do something to help them," he said to his friends.

Some of his non-scientist friends didn't quite understand how anyone could feel sorry for a vulture. So John would patiently explain their plight.

The vultures were in trouble. In 1948 mountaineers scaled the peaks of the Magaliesberg mountains not far from Johannesburg and put identification rings on all the vulture chicks they could find. The babies fought back by spitting at the mountaineers – there's gratitude for you. The research showed there were 12,000 vultures in the area. At one time, the scientists believed, there had been many more.

But the district was now farmland and there was a shortage of large dead animals for the vultures to eat. Worse still, the vultures were feeding their young on junk food. No – that's not hamburgers but real *junk* food –

such as ring pulls from drink cans. This diet did nasty things to the vulture chick's insides. Small wonder half the chicks were dying every year.

That's where the vulture restaurants came in. The plan was simple, but brilliant. Fence off an area of land and leave a few carcasses lying around. Make sure you remember to break the bones so the vultures can guzzle the tasty bone marrow. So while some people scoffed at the idea, the vultures scoffed some delicious dead animals.

Today there are more than 100 vulture restaurants offering exciting and varied menus of dead racehorses, bulls and the odd elephant.

And once there was even a human on the menu. Devoted vulture-lover Mickey Lindbergh shot himself in 1987 at a vulture restaurant. His last act on Earth was to make sure his beloved vultures got fed. On his own dead body!

But there's one creature that makes vultures look like innocent little doves. A creature that makes the worst teacher seem tame and rather fluffy. The vile, violent, villainous, verminous, vicious, voracious RAT! Just look what this creature can do:

THE ADVENTURES OF SUPER RAT

A rat can fall from a five-storey building and land on its feet – *unharmed*.

It can squeeze through a hole the size of a fifty pence coin.

Fight creatures three times its size ... and win!

A rat can survive being flushed down a toilet. In fact, this could be a new rat water sport.

In 2005 Razza the runway rat escaped from a New Zealand island and swam 400 metres to another one.

Rats will happily eat soap and drink beer. And scoff anything else remotely edible – including school dinners.

But despite its gross eating habits, a rat can taste tiny amounts of poison in its food. Yes – even if the poison is only one *millionth* of the food's weight.

Rats can gnaw through anything including lead pipes, wood, bricks, concrete and live electrical cables.

Rats use smelly pee to mark their way. They pee on each other and even pee near food to show other rats it's nice to eat. You might also like to know that a rat can't vomit or burp even if it doesn't like its dinner.

One fifth of all human food crops are eaten by rats. In India alone the amount of grain eaten by rats would be enough to fill a train 4,800 km (3,000 miles) long.

In return for all this food, rat bites and rat fleas spread deadly diseases such as bubonic plague to humans.

LOVEABLE RATS?

Despite all this some people claim that rats aren't so bad. Do you believe them – or do you smell a rat? Here are some nicer rat facts to rattle around in your brain.

1 All this talk about "dirty rats" is very unfair. Rats spend much of their lives licking themselves clean.

2 Rats don't eat humans – when they're alive. So if you're attacked by a rat you can frighten it off by screaming. Well, you would – wouldn't you? That way the rat knows you're still alive and able to fight back.

3 Rats make more affectionate pets than hamsters and

guinea pigs. Rats enjoy being stroked and cuddled and tickled – but don't try this with wild rats.

4 If you get tired of your pet you could always eat it. Rats taste like rabbit and deep fried rat with coconut oil is a delicious traditional delicacy in the Philippines.

5 One pair of rats can have 70 little rats a year. And if they all produce young, you could end up with 1,500 rats at the end of the year. Despite this, rats really care for their families and only eat their babies when they're *really* hungry.

And compared with some animal lifestyles this really is happy families.

A BIT OF BREEDING

What's your family like? Close, friendly, loving? Or do they row a lot and throw things at one another? Many animals care about their young and look after them as best they can. (Tell that to *your* parents.) But some animal families aren't so happy and they have the nasty habit of eating one another. This gives a totally different meaning to the phrase "family meal-times".

BAFFLING BREEDING

First stage in setting up an animal family is to find a mate – that's a member of the opposite sex to start a family with. Male animals display a range of baffling behaviour to attract a suitable female.

Just as human teenagers dress up to go out in the evening, male birds "dress up" to attract a mate. Many species grow brightly coloured feathers, such as the gorgeous peacock or the bottle-green head of a mallard drake.

Many male birds sing to attract attention and the females choose the loudest singer. But other animals also "sing" to attract a mate. For example, humpback whales' songs can be heard hundreds of kilometres away – just in case there's a suitable mate in some distant corner of the ocean. Even American grasshopper mice get up on their haunches at mating time and sing squeaky little songs.

Another trick used by some male birds is to build the female a nice cosy nest to lay her eggs in. But no bird goes to the baffling lengths of the bower bird of Australia.

Bird-Brain Estate Agents

HELPING YOU TO FIND YOUR IDEAL NEST

FOR SALE
A beautiful bower

IN BRIEF . . .
The accommodation consists of a platform with straight walls made of woven plants.

FANTASTIC FEATURES

The bower comes complete with specially chosen designer contents: an interesting collection of blue coloured shells, feathers, bottle tops, pen tops, pegs, animal bones, bird skulls and bits of dead insects. The present owner has painted the walls a tasteful shade of blue using chewed-up blueberries, spit and a stick held in his bill.

Note: 1. Intending purchasers should bear in mind that the property needs repainting every day in any colour so long as it's blue. Also, the neighbouring bower birds often try to steal things from the nest.*

*** 2.** OK, so you don't like blue. Don't worry. Fawn-breasted bower birds only use pale green objects and Lanterbach's bower bird prefer grey and red. So you've a lovely choice of tasteful colour schemes for your nest.

Another method of finding a mate if you're a male animal is to fight off all the other males. This makes the females fancy you and even if they don't you're the only male around. So they don't have any choice.

Male animals that fight include deer (that's why stags grow antlers), cats and giraffes. The giraffes try to butt each other but it generally turns into a neck and neck contest. Male birds also fight. Like most fights between animals of the same species, it's rare for anyone to get killed. Only horrible humans kill their own kind in any numbers. But why then do robins sometimes meet messy ends?

BLOOD ON THE TRACKS

You probably know robins as cute birds that appear on Christmas cards. But have you heard that jolly little rhyme that sometimes gives young children bad dreams?

"Who killed Cock Robin?
I, said the sparrow,
With my bow and arrow,
I killed Cock Robin."

"What a nasty sparrow," you might say. "How cruel to kill such a cute robin." But was the sparrow's confession genuine? Read on and decide for yourself.

THE CASE NOTES OF CHIEF INSPECTOR BIRD

Monday

Cock Robin was found dead with his legs sticking up in the air at 6 am this morning. The body had been partly plucked. To begin with, I suspected the neighbour's cat. But she was in bed at the time and the post-mortem reveals the victim had been pecked to death. I suspect fowl play. I have offered a reward of 50 dead worms for any information.

PARTLY PLUCKED

ORIGINAL SUSPECT

Tuesday

Cock Robin was last seen fluffing out his red breast and singing loudly in a bid to chase away an intruder. Then there was silence. A sparrow has given himself up and is singing like a canary – but I don't believe his confession. The evidence all points in another direction.

SPARROW CLAIMS HE DID IT

Who do you think really killed cock robin?
a) A female robin.
b) His own son.
c) A passing eagle.

Dare you discover ... how to go to work on an egg?

Some time after mating, female animals give birth. Mammals produce live young but some other groups of animals lay eggs. Dare you discover the secrets hidden inside an egg?

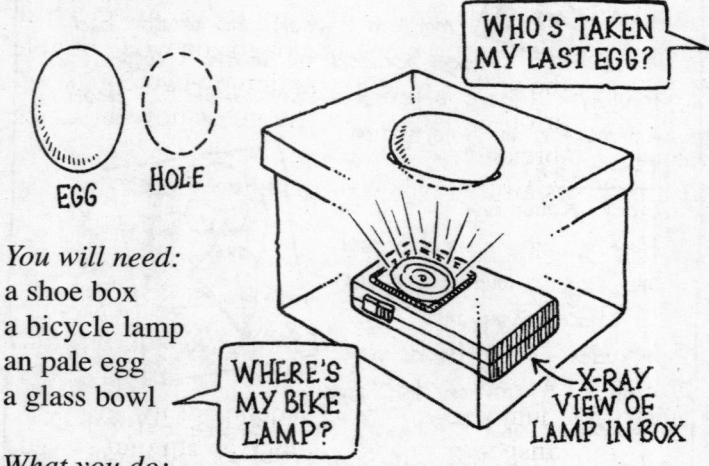

EGG   HOLE

WHO'S TAKEN MY LAST EGG?

You will need:
a shoe box
a bicycle lamp
an pale egg
a glass bowl

WHERE'S MY BIKE LAMP?

X-RAY VIEW OF LAMP IN BOX

What you do:
1 Draw round the egg on the box lid. Cut a hole just large enough for the egg to lie in without falling through.
2 Put the lamp in the box, switch it on and replace the lid. Place the egg in its hole.
3 Darken the room.
4 You should be able to see the yolk inside the egg.

5 Lightly tap the egg on the side of the bowl and allow its contents to slide into the bowl. Note: That's into the *bowl* and not on the floor.

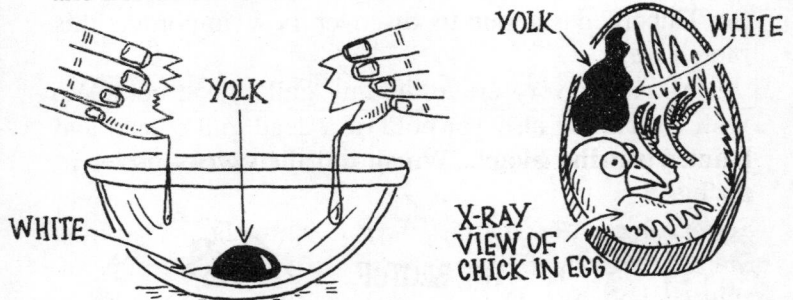

6 The egg's contents consists of the yellow bit or "yolk" and the clear slimy bit or "white", or to use its scientific name – albumen (al-bu-men). Although you won't be able to see this, the yolk is held in position by two cords.

From your observations can you guess how the chick manages to breathe inside the egg?

a) It breathes air that passes through the shell.

b) It doesn't need to breathe before it hatches.

c) There must be an air bubble inside the egg.

Answer: a) The shell lets in air but not water. The air passes into the developing chick's bloodstream. AND c) An air bubble forms in the blunt end of the egg. Half a mark for this answer because the chick only breathes this air for a few days before it hatches.

COULD YOU BE A NATURALIST?

Most birds feed their young by regurgitating their meals down their chicks' throats. Regurgitation – that's the posh word for being sick, chucking up, etc. Lovely.

Dutch naturalist Nikolaas Tinbergen (1903–1988), tried to discover what triggers this. He noticed that herring gull chicks peck at a red blotch on their parents' beaks. So Tinbergen set out to discover how important this blotch was.

He made a very crude dummy gull's head complete with blotch. He also got hold of a dead gull's head and painted out the blotch. Which did the chicks prefer to peck at?

a) The dead gull's head – they thought it was their supper.

b) The dummy head because it had the blotch.

c) Neither – the sight of the dead gull's head upset the chicks so much they forgot to peck at anything.

Answer: b) What did you expect? Would the sight of a human head make you feel hungry? Tinbergen went on to prove that the red colour wasn't important. Any colour was OK as long as the patch was clearly visible.

142

Bet you never knew!

Some babies don't look like their parents and their appearance changes completely as they grow up.

1 Tadpoles don't look like adult frogs or toads. Tadpoles have tails and no legs, for example, and they have breathing gills outside their bodies. Gradually the gills are absorbed and suddenly a leg or two pops through the tadpole's body. For a while a tadpole might have two or three legs. After all four legs appear the tadpole's tail is absorbed into its body. Life for a frog can be horribly confusing.

2 A baby kangaroo looks like a little pink worm the size of a baked bean. It's only one twelve thousandth the size of its mum.

Somehow it crawls through its mum's fur until it finds her pouch and there feeds off her milk.

After seven months the baby kangaroo, or joey, is big enough to hop around outside the pouch. And after eleven months it has to leave the pouch for good.

Almost immediately another baby takes its place.

3 In terms of growing that's nothing. A blue whale begins its life as an egg produced by its mum that weighs only 0.0009922g. The baby blue whale grows to 26 tonnes. That's like you increasing your weight 30,000,000,000 (thirty billion) times.

I HOPE YOU'VE DONE YOUR HOMEWORK, OR THERE'LL BE BIG TROUBLE

GOOD PARENTS AWARDS

Many animal parents feed and lick their babies clean. And here are some especially good parents…

THIRD PRIZE
Ma Croc

Crocodile mums bury their eggs in the sand by rivers. Three months later they hear the babies cheeping from inside their eggs and dig them up again. After the babies hatch, mum carries them in her massive jaws down the river and lets them go. For the next few months she feeds them on choice morsels such as juicy frogs, bits of fish and the occasional crunchy insect.

DON'T FORGET WE'RE IN HERE, MUM!

SECOND PRIZE
Mrs Surinam Toad

She's really ugly – even by toad standards. (Even her friends would agree – if she had any.) She has no eyes, no teeth and no tongue and a huge mouth that eats anything that moves. Yet somehow she loads her tadpoles on to her back and encases them in bubbles under her skin. Then she patiently carries the tadpoles for two months until they emerge as ugly little versions of herself.

FIRST PRIZE
Mr Emperor Penguin
When Mrs Penguin goes down to the sea to hunt fish, Mr Penguin joins thousands of other males standing about in the freezing cold of Antarctica. Each male balances a single large egg on top of his feet to keep it warm. If the egg falls the chick inside will die. And there the male stands for 40 days and nights without food or shelter until his mate returns. Sometimes the temperatures drops to -40°C (-40°F) What a hero!

AWFUL ANIMAL FAMILIES

Of course, not all animal families are as caring as that. Many kinds of fish, reptiles and amphibians simply abandon their eggs and leave the young to survive on their own. If they can.

For fish especially, it doesn't matter if some youngsters get eaten. A single cod can lay six million eggs at a time. If all of them survived the seas would be crammed with cod. And that's what Darwin's idea of natural selection was about. Enough cod will live to breed the next generation.

Not all animals are looked after by both parents. Elephant families, for example, are made up of females under the command of the oldest female. She decides where they go and when they should go for water. The babies are looked after by all the females but when the males grow up they're chased away to live with other males. If you've got an awful brother you might think the elephants have the right idea. If you're a female yourself, that is.

LETHAL LESSONS

If you're a baby animal you need to learn some urgent lessons in survival. And if you're lucky your parents will teach you.

1 Guillemot chicks have to learn how to swim and fly. So their parents chuck them off a cliff. If they fly – good. If not, they'd better learn to swim.

2 Mother swallows take food to their chicks but hover just out of reach. If the chicks want to grab their grub they'd better learn to fly first.

3 Cheetah mums catch a gazelle and then release it for their cubs to chase. If the gazelle escapes the cubs get taught a lesson: they starve.

4 Eventually, when her cubs get too big, a grizzly bear mum chases them up a tree and wanders off. Now begins the biggest lesson of all: how to survive alone.

But every young animal (and human children too) must learn one other lesson. At the end of the day they'll need to go to sleep. But while you're tucked up in your bed some creatures are on the prowl. And they're out to make a killing.

NOCTURNAL NASTIES

Night. A time of mystery and ... danger. It's hard to see in the dark and things appear strange and sinister in the moonlight. There are sudden sounds – a scream or is it just a squawk? Something scuttles through the undergrowth. And in the shadows something dark and menacing is looking for its first meal of the night. Will you live to see the dawn?

Nocturnal (that means active by night) animals are adapted to living at night. Their bodies have evolved to suit their lifestyle in certain ways.

Take an African bushbaby, for example. This cute monkey-like creature lives in trees. It spends the night hunting insects, birds, fruit and anything else it can grab.

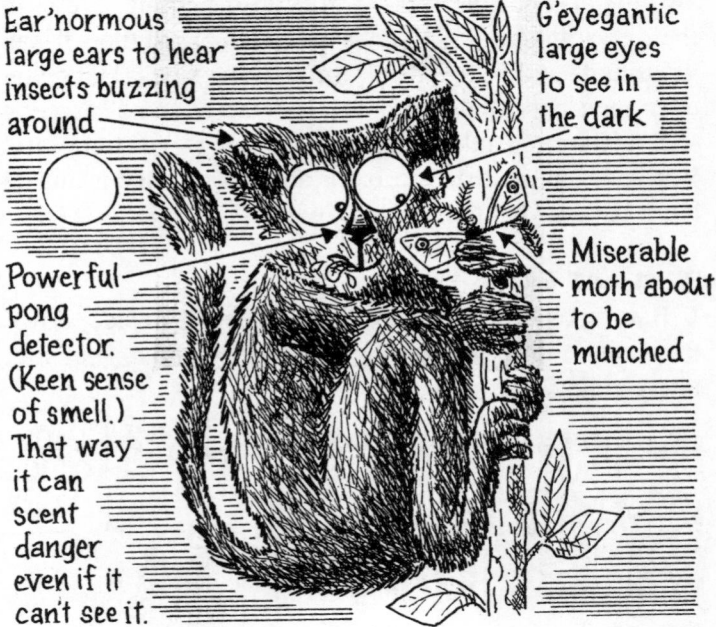

Ear'normous large ears to hear insects buzzing around

G'eyegantic large eyes to see in the dark

Powerful pong detector. (Keen sense of smell.) That way it can scent danger even if it can't see it.

Miserable moth about to be munched

149

You might think that being nocturnal sounds rather tiring. But consider the advantages for a small animal. It's cool and moist at night – which is fine if you live in a hot, dry country. There are lots of shadows to hide in and many of the larger, fiercer creatures are fast asleep.

Unfortunately, there are nocturnal hunters too. Owls swoop out of the darkness to grab unsuspecting shrews in their grasping talons. Hyenas and lions prowl the African grasslands and bats screech through the skies. Have you ever seen bats flapping around in the evening? Creepy – aren't they? And you wouldn't want to get too close. But some naturalists are batty about bats. According to them bats are brilliant. Here's why…

BRILLIANT BATS

1 Bats spend $5/6$ of their lives hanging upside down from the ceiling. According to a bat scientist, that's an interesting way to live.

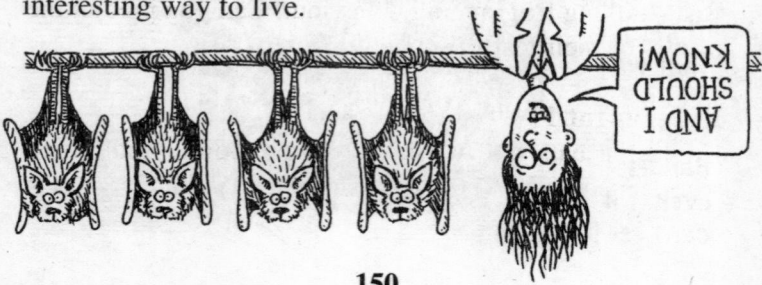

AND I SHOULD KNOW!

150

2 Baby bats are born upside down. Usually their mother catches them before they hit the ground and they cling to their mother's fur with their teeth. Could you imagine a human baby doing this?

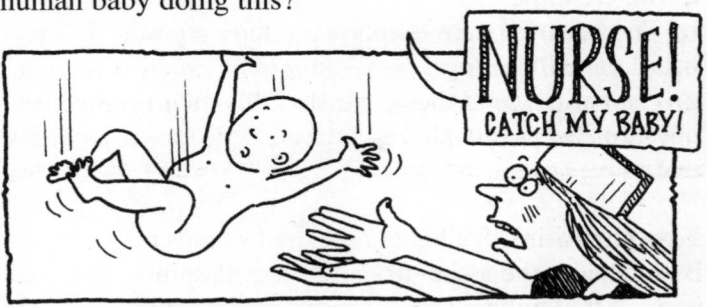

3 You can't say "blind as a bat" because bats aren't actually blind – although they can't see well. But then bats don't need eyes. As they fly, they make high-pitched sounds and listen for echoes bouncing off the body of a flying insect. By homing in on these echoes a bat can gobble up a nice juicy insect in mid-air.

4 A flying bat makes one call a second. The calls get faster and faster as the bat closes in to grab its victim.

COULD YOU BE A NATURALIST?

Naturalist Merlin D Tuttle set up a series of bat experiments in the early 1980s. He wanted to study how bats hunt the frogs that lived in a muddy bug-infested pond in Panama. He was helped by fellow naturalist, Michael Ryan, who was studying frog mating behaviour. Can you predict the results of their tests?

Experiment 1

Could the bats tell which frogs were edible and which were poisonous? The scientists placed a bat in a cage large enough to fly around in. Then they played tapes of edible and poisonous frogs croaking. What happened?

a) The bat attacked the tape recorder whenever it heard a frog croaking.

b) The bat only dive-bombed the tape recorder when it heard the edible frog.

c) The bat attacked the scientists. This didn't answer the question but it did prove that bats will attack anything that moves.

Experiment 2

Next they tested the frogs. Could they see the bats coming to get them? The scientist made a model bat and ran it along a wire above the frogs' pond. What did the frogs do?

a) They couldn't see the model and carried on croaking.

b) They could see the model and croaked even louder to scare the bat away.

c) They went deadly quiet when the model flew over.

Experiment 3

Do bats recognize frogs by their shape or by sound? Tuttle held a silent frog in one hand and rubbed the fingers of his other hand together to make a swishing sound. Did a bat attack the frog or the naturalist's fingers?

a) The fingers and Tuttle got a nasty nip.

b) The frog.

c) Neither, it got tangled in his hair. This proves the bats were bewildered by this sound.

Bet you never knew!
Carlsbad cavern, New Mexico, USA is alive with bats. Up to 20 million Mexican free-tailed bats go there each summer. The babies hanging from its walls are packed together 3,000 to a square metre. But somehow mother bats, returning from a night's hunting, find their own babies using hearing and smell. They recognize the babies in the crowd by their cries and the smell of their bodies. And naturalists have found that the bats are right 80 per cent of the time.

NASTY SLEEPING HABITS

Most animals don't bother to go out at night. They like nothing better than a good night's kip. Many naturalists believe that animals and humans sleep because they've nothing better to do. They can't see in the dark and they've eaten during the day. So why not have a little rest? Mind you, some creatures have nasty sleeping habits.

1 Chimps construct beds from springy branches. But they don't bother to make their beds in the morning.

They simply throw them away together with any dirt and fleas. Don't you wish you could do this?

2 When parrot fish go to sleep they wrap themselves in a ball of slime with a small hole to breathe through. This keeps them safe from marauding eels.

3 Only birds and mammals dream. Fish, amphibia and reptiles don't.

4 The prize for the most uncomfortable sleeping position must go to the blue crowned hanging parrot. This bird sleeps hanging upside down from a branch. Its green back looks like a leaf so there's less chance of being spotted by a hunter.

Some animals find it pays to be asleep most of the time. Take the Australian koala, for example.

A DAY IN THE LIFE OF A KOALA

The night
Clambered about in my tree.

Guzzled 1kg of eucalyptus leaves – this is the life. Yawn. Now for a bit of shut-eye – reckon I've earned it.

5.10am
Found a nice branch to curl up on. Zzzzzz.

7.30am
Some human woke me up! Can't they let a koala have a decent kip? They've slung a rope loop around my neck.

What cheek! Now they're trying to yank me off my tree – better dig my claws in.

NOTES: Koalas are more active at night. The disgusting taste of leathery eucalyptus leaves doesn't bother them at all.

NOTES: The koala's diet of leaves isn't nourishing. In fact, it sends them to sleep!

NOTES: When there are too many koalas in an area it's a good idea to move some before they eat all the eucalyptus leaves and starve. Not all koalas like their new homes, however. Some homesick koalas have made their slow way back to their favourite tree!

7.32am
Araaaagh! They've caught me.
Lucky I've got
sharp claws and
teeth. Grrr!
That will teach
them a lesson.

Notes:
By sleeping in the hottest part of the day the koala avoids over-heating or even getting thirsty. It gets all the moisture it needs from juicy leaves.

10am
I've been moved in a crate. Oh well – this tree looks OK. Back to sleep.
ZZZZ

Notes:
The koala spends over 18 hours a day snoozing its cute little head off. Even when it's awake it usually moves slowly and its lifestyle makes the sloth look like a go-getter in a hurry.

5, 6, 7 pm
Zzzzz

9pm
Yawn. What's for breakfast. Eucalyptus leaves will do just fine.

156

WINTER SLUMBERLAND

Many animals don't stop at sleeping the night away. Some sleep most of the winter and only get really active in the spring. This is called hibernation – but you probably know that already. So here are a few more details to keep you awake.

Hibernation is a good idea because animals need lots of food to keep warm in cold weather. But during the winter there is less food around. By sleeping much of the time an animal can survive without having to find this extra food. Some animals live off stored food in their burrows and others live off their own body fat – built up by guzzling as much as possible in the warmer months.

Animals that hibernate include tortoises, squirrels, dormice, bats and some snakes. During hibernation an animal's breathing and pulse slow down and its body temperature may drop by 50°C (112°F). It's in a very deep sleep and it can appear dead. This has led to early burials for many unfortunate tortoises.

Zzzzz.

NASTY NATURE?

Some animals seem really nasty. They look repulsive and do nasty things to other animals. Some animals have horrible weapons or use nasty cunning tricks to catch their prey. Some eat really foul food. And their eating habits are enough to put you off your dinner.

But so what? You can't expect animals to be polite and kind to one another. These are qualities you might find in humans – if you're lucky. Animals have to be tough to survive in a tough world. For them it's more important to be alive than to be nice. For an animal, every day is a battle for life. Animals don't know when they wake up in the morning whether they'll see the day through, or end up as a tasty snack for a larger creature.

And for all their nasty habits, we humans find animals immensely useful. They provide the raw materials for our food, and horses and dogs work hard for us. Unlike some humans – animals are *never* boring. We laugh at them and enjoy their companionship. Of course, some animals are nasty but they're also beautiful, fascinating and splendid in their dazzling variety.

You can see why naturalists spend their entire lives studying animals in their natural habitats. And how they get horribly excited if they manage to photograph a rare creature from an unusual angle. Yep, there's no doubt – for us humans, animals have a nasty fascination. But that's Horrible Science for you!

NASTY NATURE
QUIZ

Now find out if you're a
Nasty Nature expert!

Amazing animal facts

From awesome amphibians to miraculous mammals, animals have all sorts of amazing attributes. See if you can guess the answers to some of these fascinating facts.

1 Which is the largest land animal that can't jump? (Clue: if it could, it'd be a jumbo jump)

2 Why do flamingos eat with their heads upside down? (Clue: something to wash down your meal, perhaps?)

3 What happens to the octopus when it gets angry? (Clue: it doesn't *see* red, but…)

4 How do you know when a dog is about to pounce? (Clue: did you 'ear the question?)

5 What is the only food eaten by koalas? (Clue: it's a sticky one, this)

6 How can a snake swallow a creature that's bigger than its own head? (Clue: you'd be a bit unhinged if you knew this)

7 How small is an ostrich's brain? (Clue: you'll soon see…)

8 What is beneath a tiger's stripy coat (Clue: tiger tattoo)

Answers:

1 Elephant
2 To strain the water out of their food
3 It turns red
4 It twitches its ears
5 The eucalyptus (gum) tree
6 They can unhinge their jaws
7 It's smaller than its eye!
8 A stripy skin

Horrible hunting habits

It's a dog-eat-dog world out there, but many amazing animals have ways of either catching other creatures or hiding from the hunters. See if you can figure out these tactical tricks...

1 How do polar bears complete their camouflage and disguise their black noses when sneaking up on their prey?
a) They cover it with one of their paws.
b) They walk backwards towards their prey.
c) They push a piece of ice in front of them.

2 What is a rattlesnake's rattle for?
a) To warn its prey that it's coming.
b) To distract its prey from its venomous fangs.
c) To amuse itself as it slithers along.

3 How do big game like lions and tigers hunt?
a) With the wind blowing towards them.
b) With the wind blowing away from them.
c) When there is no wind at all.

4 How does the tropical flounder escape from larger beasts?
a) It changes colour to match its surroundings.
b) It hides behind underwater rocks.
c) It can outswim every other fish in the sea so it doesn't have to worry.

5 What does the smart skunk do to drive away horrible hunters?
a) It squirts a stinky spray from its nose.
b) It squirts a stinky spray from its bottom.
c) It rears up and fights with razor-sharp claws.

6 How do birds like thrushes get to the succulent soft bit of a snail?
a) They stick their beak in the shell and suck.
b) They wait for the snail to come out of its shell.
c) They hold the snail in their beaks and bash it against a stone.

7 How does the deep-sea viper fish attract its prey?
a) It 'sings' and the music echoes through the water.
b) It has lights in its mouth that other fish are drawn to.
c) It has colourful fins that attract other fish.

8 How does the olive green snake fool its food?
a) It disguises itself as a twig.
b) It disguises itself as a cobra.
c) It disguises itself with a false moustache.

Answers:
1c; 2b; 3a; 4a; 5b; 6c; 7b; 8a

Wild survival

Along the way you've met some seriously nutty naturalists who travelled the world, facing many desperate dangers in their search to find out more about nasty nature. But how would you survive in the wild? See if you can separate the true tips from the tall stories listed below.

1 The best way to avoid being bitten by a snake is to run in a zigzag line.

2 If a crocodile gets you in his grip a simple tap on the nose can sometimes make him release you.

3 If you're attacked by a shark you should stay as still as possible.

4 The poison of the king cobra is strong enough to kill an elephant.

5 The best way to escape from a tiger is to climb a tree.

6 If you are attacked by a bear, you should run – they are too slow to catch you.

7 You should treat the bite of a black widow spider by sucking out the poison.

8 Even though a hippo is a herbivore it will still feast on human flesh.

Answers:

1 False – the best way is to stand still, which will hopefully calm the snake down

2 True – crocodiles and alligators sometimes open their mouths when tapped lightly

3 False – fighting back will often scare the shark away

4 True – a human would stand no chance, so avoid making a cobra cross at all costs

5 True – very few tigers will climb trees

6 False – a bear will almost certainly catch you; your best bet is to shout and wave at it to try and face it down

7 False – this doesn't work; it's better to wash the bite with soap and water and raise the affected part of the body to the level of the heart

8 False – but hippos will attack boats and scrunch people to death

Gangs and groups

Clever Carl Linnaeus might have come up with a way of classifying animals by their species, but when groups of the same animal have a get-together they are given another name. The posh name for a group of the same kind of animal is a collective noun. See if you are as cunning as Carl and match the animals with their group names.

1 Kangaroos
2 Lions
3 Bats
4 Crows
5 Leopards

6 Owls
7 Toads
8 Dolphins

a) Colony
b) Leap
c) Knot
d) Pride
e) Mob
f) Pod
g) Parliament
h) Murder

Answers:
1e; 2d; 3a; 4h; 5b; 6g; 7c; 8f

HORRIBLE INDEX

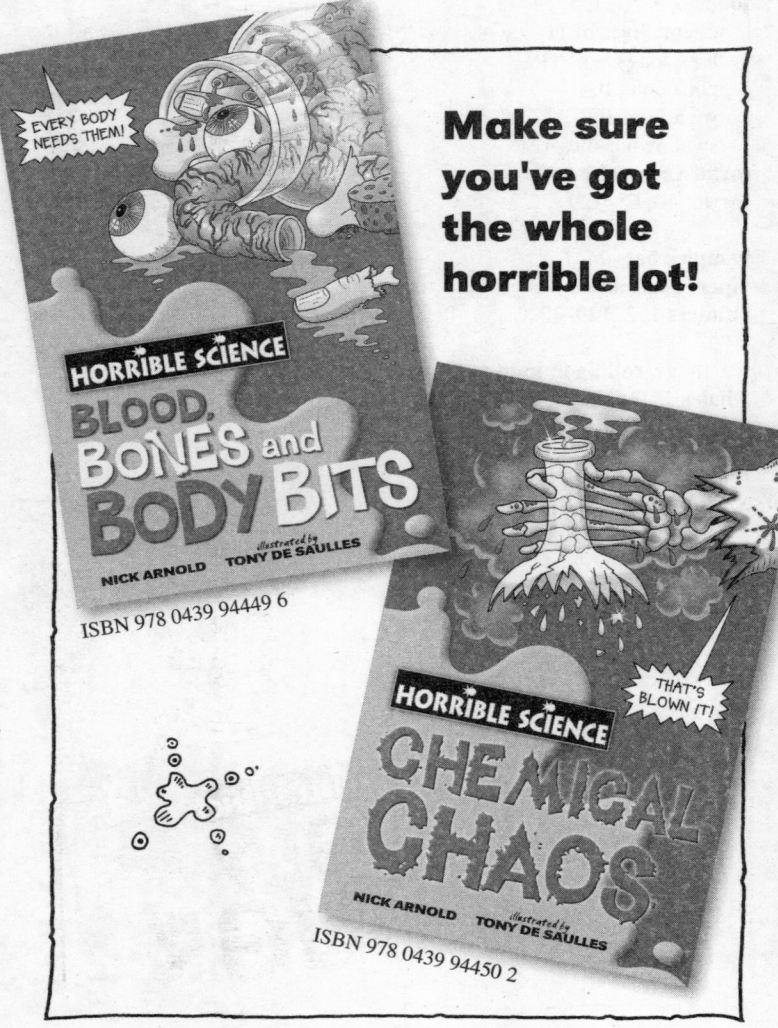

HORRIBLE SCIENCE

DISGUSTING DIGESTION

IT TAKES GUTS!

NICK ARNOLD   *illustrated by* TONY DE SAULLES

ISBN 978 0439 94445 8

HORRIBLE SCIENCE

DEADLY DISEASES

IT'S A GRAVE SITUATION

NICK ARNOLD   *illustrated by* TONY DE SAULLES

ISBN 978 0439 94446 5

HORRIBLE SCIENCE

UGLY BUGS

NOT A PRETTY SIGHT!

NICK ARNOLD   *illustrated by* TONY DE SAULLES

ISBN 978 0439 94452 6